P9-EGB-913

TREATMENTS OF PSYCHIATRIC DISORDERS

VOLUME 3

American Psychiatric Association Task Force on Treatments of Psychiatric Disorders

TREATMENTS OF PSYCHIATRIC DISORDERS

A Task Force Report of the American Psychiatric Association

VOLUME 3

Published by the
American Psychiatric Association
1400 K Street, N.W.
Washington, DC 20005
1989

The findings, opinions, and conclusions of this report do not necessarily represent the views of the officers, trustees, or all members of the Association. Each report, however, does represent the thoughtful judgment and findings of the task force of experts who composed it. These reports are considered a substantive contribution to the ongoing analysis and evaluation of problems, programs, issues, and practices in a given area of concern.

First Edition

The paper used in this publication meets the minimum requirements of the American National Standard for Information Sciences—Permanence of Paper for Printed Library Materials ANSI Z39.48-1984.   ∞

Correspondence regarding copyright permissions should be directed to the Division of Publications and Marketing, American Psychiatric Association, 1400 K Street, N.W., Washington, DC 20005.

The correct citation for this book is:

American Psychiatric Association: Treatments of Psychiatric Disorders: A Task Force Report of the American Psychiatric Association. Washington, DC, American Psychiatric Association, 1989.

Library of Congress Cataloging-in-Publication Data
Treatments of psychiatric disorders.

   "American Psychiatric Association Task Force on Treatments of Psychiatric Disorders" —P. facing t.p.
   Includes bibliographies and indexes.
   1. Psychiatry. 1. American Psychiatric Association. Task Force on Treatments of Psychiatric Disorders. [DNLM: 1. Mental Disorders—therapy. WM 400 T7866]
RC454.T69   1989   616.89'1   89-248
ISBN 0-89042-201-X (set : alk. paper)

ISBN 0-89042-202-8   VOLUME 1
ISBN 0-89042-203-6   VOLUME 2
ISBN 0-89042-204-4   VOLUME 3
ISBN 0-89042-205-2   INDEXES

Contents

VOLUME 1

SECTION 1
Mental Retardation
C. Thomas Gualtieri, M.D., *Chairperson*

Pharmacotherapy

Psychological, Educational, Vocational, and Residential Services

SECTION 2
Pervasive Developmental Disorders

Magda Campbell, M.D., *Co-Chairperson*
Eric Schopler, Ph.D., *Co-Chairperson*

SECTION 3

Specific Developmental Disorders

Theodore Shapiro, M.D., *Chairperson*

Introduction

Clinical Description

Evaluation and Intervention

Treatment of Bulimia Nervosa

SECTION 7
Paraphilias and Gender Identity Disorders
James L. Mathis, M.D., *Chairperson*

VOLUME 2

SECTION 11
Organic Mental Syndromes
Lissy F. Jarvik, M.D., Ph.D., *Chairperson*

SECTION 14
Schizophrenia

Robert Cancro, M.D., *Chairperson*

SECTION 15

Delusional (Paranoid) Disorders

Sir Martin Roth, M.D., F.R.C.P., F.R.C.Psych., *Chairperson*

SECTION 16
Psychotic Disorders Not Elsewhere Classified
Allen J. Frances, M.D., *Chairperson*

VOLUME 3

SECTION 17
Mood Disorders
Gerald L. Klerman, M.D., *Chairperson*

SECTION 18
Anxiety Disorders

Martin T. Orne, M.D., Ph.D., *Co-Chairperson*
Fred H. Frankel, M.B.Ch.B., D.P.M., *Co-Chairperson*

SECTION 23
Sleep Disorders

David J. Kupfer, M.D., *Co-Chairperson*
Charles F. Reynolds III, M.D., *Co-Chairperson*

SECTION 24
Impulse Control Disorders Not Elsewhere Classified

Richard C. Marohn, M.D., *Chairperson*

SECTION 25
Adjustment Disorder

Joseph D. Noshpitz, M.D., *Co-Chairperson*
R. Dean Coddington, M.D., *Co-Chairperson*

SECTION 26
Personality Disorders
John G. Gunderson, M.D., *Chairperson*

Treatment Modalities

INDEXES

List of Consultants

C. Alex Adsett, M.D.
W. Stewart Agras, M.D.
C. Knight Aldrich, M.D.
Arnold Allen, M.D.
Kenneth Z. Altshuler, M.D.
Wayne R. Anable, D.O.
Nancy C. Andreasen, M.D., Ph.D.
Paul A. Andrulonis, M.D.
Laurie Appelbaum, M.D.
Gary K. Arthur, M.D.
Stuart S. Asch, M.D.
Boris M. Astrachan, M.D.

Hrair M. Babikian, M.D.
Thomas H. Babor, Ph.D.
William E. Bakewell, Jr., M.D.
Cornelis B. Bakker, M.D.
Ross J. Baldessarini, M.D.
Gail M. Barton, M.D.
B. Lynn Beattie, M.D., F.R.C.P. (C)
Aaron T. Beck, M.D.
Alan S. Bellack, Ph.D.
Jules Bemporad, M.D.
Elissa P. Benedek, M.D.
R. Scott Benson, M.D.
Norman B. Bernstein, M.D.
Norman R. Bernstein, M.D.
Shashi K. Bhatia, M.D.
Subash C. Bhatia, M.D.
Raman Bhavsar, M.D.
Kay H. Blacker, M.D.
Barry Blackwell, M.D.
Barton J. Blinder, M.D., Ph.D.
Irvin Blose, M.D.
Daniel B. Borenstein, M.D.
Jonathan F. Borus, M.D.
Peter G. Bourne, M.D.
Malcolm B. Bowers, Jr., M.D.
David L. Braff, M.D.
Reed Brockbank, M.D.

Kirk Brower, M.D.
William E. Bunney, Jr., M.D.
Ann W. Burgess, R.N., D.N.Sc.
Ewald W. Busse, M.D.

Dennis P. Cantwell, M.D.
Bernard J. Carroll, M.D., Ph.D.
Stanley Cath, M.D.
Richard D. Chessick, M.D., Ph.D., P.C.
Eve S. Chevron, M.S.
James Claghorn, M.D.
Norman A. Clemens, M.D.
C. Robert Cloninger, M.D.
Raquel E. Cohen, M.D.
Calvin A. Colarusso, M.D.
Bernice E. Coleman, M.D.
Gregory B. Collins, M.D.
Liane Colsky, M.D.
Shirley M. Colthart, M.D.
Arnold M. Cooper, M.D.
Rex W. Cowdry, M.D.
Thomas J. Craig, M.D., M.P.H.
Miles K. Crowder, M.D.
Thomas J. Crowley, M.D.
Homer Curtis, M.D.
Thomas E. Curtis, M.D.

Amin N. Daghestani, M.D.
I. Deborah Dauphinais, M.D.
John M. Davis, M.D.
Jorge G. De La Torre, M.D.
Marian K. DeMyer, Ph.D.
Martha B. Denckla, M.D.
Bharati Desai, M.D.
Daniel A. Deutschman, M.D.
Robert De Vito, M.D.
William G. Dewhurst, M.D.
Leon Diamond, M.D.
Alberto Di Mascio, Ph.D.
David F. Dinges, Ph.D.

C. Wesley Dingman II, M.D.
Susan R. Donaldson, M.D.
John Donnelly, M.D.
Mina K. Dulcan, M.D.
David L. Dunner, M.D.
Jack Durell, M.D.
Maurice Dysken, M.D.

Felton Earls, M.D.
Marshall Edelson, M.D., Ph.D.
Irene Elkin, Ph.D.
Donald E. Engstrom, M.D.
Nathan B. Epstein, M.D.
Jack R. Ewalt, M.D.

Louis F. Fabre, Jr., M.D.
Peter J. Fagan, Ph.D.
Howard Farkas, B.A.
Beverly J. Fauman, M.D.
Ronald R. Fieve, M.D.
Stuart M. Finch, M.D.
Max Fink, M.D.
Paul J. Fink, M.D.
Joseph A. Flaherty, M.D.
Stephen Fleck, M.D.
Don E. Flinn, Jr., M.D.
Marc A. Forman, M.D.
Richard J. Frances, M.D.
Robert O. Friedel, M.D.

Warren J. Gadpaille, M.D.
Pierre N. Gagne, M.D.
Robert S. Garber, M.D.
Max Gardner, M.D.
Russell Gardner, Jr., M.D.
Joseph Gaspari, M.D.
Francine L. Gelfand, M.D.
Robert W. Gibson, M.D.
Stanley Gitlow, M.D.
Rachel Gittelman, Ph.D.
Alexander H. Glassman, M.D.
Ira D. Glick, M.D.
Richard L. Goldberg, M.D.
Charles Goldfarb, M.D.
Stuart J. Goldman, M.D.

Gerald Goldstein, M.D.
Michael J. Goldstein, Ph.D.
Donald Goodwin, M.D.
Tracy Gordy, M.D.
Fred Gottlieb, M.D.
Marvin E. Gottlieb, M.D.
Louis A. Gottschalk, M.D., Ph.D.
Paul Graffagnino, M.D.
Harry Grantham, M.D.
Wayne H. Green, M.D.
Harvey R. Greenberg, M.D.
Lester Grinspoon, M.D.
William N. Grosch, M.D.
Mortimer D. Gross, M.D., S.C.

Seymour Halleck, M.D.
Abraham L. Halpern, M.D.
James A. Hamilton, M.D.
Edward Hanin, M.D.
Richard K. Harding, M.D.
Saul I. Harrison, M.D.
Lawrence Hartmann, M.D.
Irwin N. Hassenfeld, M.D.
Leston Havens, M.D.
David R. Hawkins, M.D.
Robert G. Heath, M.D.
John E. Helzer, M.D.
Hugh C. Hendrie, M.B.Ch.B.
Marvin I. Herz, M.D.
David B. Herzog, M.D.
A. Lewis Hill, M.D.
Douglas P. Hobson, M.D.
James Hodge, M.D.
Charles J. Hodulik, M.D.
Charles C. Hogan, M.D., P.C.
Jimmie C.B. Holland, M.D.
Steven D. Hollon, Ph.D.
Harry C. Holloway, M.D.
Daniel W. Hommer, M.D.
Jeffrey L. Houpt, M.D.

David Israelstam, M.D., Ph.D.

Marc Jacobs, M.D.
Kay R. Jamison, Ph.D.

Michael S. Jellinek, M.D.
Keith H. Johansen, M.D.
Mary Ann Johnson, M.D.
Merlin H. Johnson, M.D.
Charles R. Joy, M.D.
Lewis L. Judd, M.D.
Nalini V. Juthani, M.D.

Nicholas Kanas, M.D.
Sylvia R. Karasu, M.D.
Jack L. Katz, M.D.
Edward Kaufman, M.D.
Jerald Kay, M.D.
David Kaye, M.D.
Alan E. Kazdin, Ph.D.
John F. Kelley, M.D.
Philippe J. Khouri, M.D.
Elizabeth Khuri, M.D.
Chase P. Kimball, M.D.
Donald F. Klein, M.D.
Arthur H. Kleinman, M.D.
Lawrence Y. Kline, M.D.
William Klykylo, M.D.
Peter T. Knoepfler, M.D.
Michael F. Koch, M.D.
Jonathan E. Kolb, M.D.
Lawrence C. Kolb, M.D.
Donald S. Kornfeld, M.D.
Douglas A. Kramer, M.D.
Peter D. Kramer, M.D.
Robert F. Kraus, M.D.
Daniel Kripke, M.D.
Markus Kruesi, M.D.
John W. Kuldau, M.D.

Yves Lamontagne, M.D., F.R.C.P.(C)
Ronald Langevin, Ph.D.
Donald G. Langsley, M.D.
Camille Laurin, M.D.
Ruth L. La Vietes, M.D.
Robert L. Leon, M.D.
Denis Lepage, M.D.
Joseph B. Leroy, M.D.
Stanley Lesse, M.D.
H.J. Leuchter, M.D.

Stephen B. Levine, M.D.
Peritz H. Levinson, M.D.
David J. Lewis, M.D., F.R.C.P.(C)
Robert Paul Liberman, M.D.
Paul Lieberman, M.D.
Rudolf W. Link, M.D.
Margaret W. Linn, Ph.D.
John R. Lion, M.D.
Marvin H. Lipkowitz, M.D.
Zbigniew J. Lipowski, M.D.
Melvin M. Lipsett, M.D.
James W. Lomax, M.D.
Catherine E. Lord, Ph.D.
Maria Lorenz, M.D.
Earl L. Loschen, M.D.
Reginald S. Lourie, M.D.
Eugene L. Lowenkopf, M.D.
Joseph F. Lupo, M.D.

K. Roy MacKenzie, M.D.
John A. MacLeod, M.D.
Leslie F. Major, M.D.
Michael J. Maloney, M.D.
David B. Marcotte, M.D.
John Markowitz, M.D.
Judd Marmor, M.D.
Ronald L. Martin, M.D.
Jules H. Masserman, M.D.
Thomas A. Mathews, M.D.
Kenneth L. Matthews, M.D.
Teresita McCarty, M.D.
Layton McCurdy, M.D.
John J. McGrath, M.D.
F. Patrick McKegney, Jr., M.D.
George N. McNeil, M.D.
Beverly T. Mead, M.D.
Herbert Y. Meltzer, M.D.
James R. Merikangas, M.D.
Harold Merskey, D.M.
Heino F. L. Meyer-Bahlburg, Dr.rer.nat.
Robert Michels, M.D.
Larry Michelson, Ph.D.
Ira Mintz, M.D.
Steven M. Mirin, M.D.
Arnold H. Modell, M.D.

Gordon L. Moore II, M.D.
Robert A. Moore, M.D.
Loren R. Mosher, M.D.
David A. Mrazek, M.D., M.R.C.Psych.
Frances J. Mulvihill, M.D.
Cecil Mushatt, M.D.

Carol C. Nadelson, M.D.
Theodore Nadelson, M.D.
Donald F. Naftulin, M.D.
Carlos Neu, M.D.
Theodore W. Neumann, Jr., M.D.
Robert G. Niven, M.D.
Grayson Norquist, M.D.
John I. Nurenberger, Jr., M.D.

Charles P. O'Brien, M.D., Ph.D.
William C. Offenkrantz, M.D.
Donald Oken, M.D.
Harold S. Orchow, M.D.
Emily Carota Orne, B.A.
Morris G. Oscherwitz, M.D.
Helen J. Ossofsky, M.D.

Lee C. Park, M.D.
Dean X. Parmalee, M.D., F.A.A.C.P.
Robert J. Pary, M.D.
Robert O. Pasnau, M.D.
William Patterson, M.D.
Chester A. Pearlman, Jr., M.D.
William S. Pearson, M.D.
Roger Peele, M.D.
William E. Pelham, Jr., Ph.D.
Irwin N. Perr, M.D.
Helen M. Pettinati, Ph.D.
Betty Pfefferbaum, M.D.
Irving Philips, M.D.
Edward Pinney, M.D.
William Pollin, M.D.
Harrison C. Pope, Jr., M.D.
Robert M. Post, M.D.
Harry Prosen, M.D.
Brigette Prusoff, Ph.D.
Joaquim Puig-Antich, M.D.
H. Paul Putman II, M.D.

Robert Racusin, M.D.
Judith L. Rapoport, M.D.
Allen Raskin, Ph.D.
Robert J. Reichler, M.D.
William H. Reid, M.D., M.P.H.
Karl Rickels, M.D.
Arthur Rifkin, M.D.
Louis Rittelmeyer, M.D.
Lee N. Robins, M.D.
Nicholas L. Rock, M.D.
Paul Rodenhauser, M.D.
Rita R. Rogers, M.D.
John Romano, M.D.
Howard P. Rome, M.D.
Patricia Rosebush, M.D.
Maj-Britt Rosenbaum, M.D.
Milton Rosenbaum, M.D.
Loren H. Roth, M.D.
Bruce Rounsaville, M.D.
Donald K. Routh, Ph.D.
Lester Rudy, M.D.

Benjamin Sadock, M.D.
Virginia Sadock, M.D.
Clifford J. Sager, M.D.
Watt T. Salmon, M.D.
Carl Salzman, M.D.
Alberto Santos, M.D.
Burhan Say, M.D.
Nina R. Schooler, Ph.D.
John Schowalter, M.D.
John J. Schwab, M.D.
Harvey J. Schwartz, M.D.
James H. Scully, M.D.
Peter M. Semkiw, M.D.
Mohammad Shaffii, M.D.
Charles Shagass, M.D.
Brian Shaw, M.D.
Kailie R. Shaw, M.D.
Michael H. Sheard, M.D.
David V. Sheehan, Ph.D.
Edwin Shneidman, Ph.D.
Miles Shore, M.D.
Michael Shostak, M.D.
Lorraine D. Siggins, M.D.

Peter M. Silberfarb, M.D.
Donald J. Silberman, M.D.
Archie A. Silver, M.D.
Joel J. Silverman, M.D.
Everett C. Simmons, M.D.
Bennett Simon, M.D.
George M. Simpson, M.D.
Margaret Singer, M.D.
Phillip R. Slavney, M.D.
William Sledge, M.D.
Gary W. Small, M.D.
Joyce G. Small, M.D.
Erwin R. Smarr, M.D.
Gail Solomon, M.D.
David Spiegel, M.D.
Robert L. Spitzer, M.D.
Daniel J. Sprehe, M.D.
Robert St. John, M.D.
Stephen M. Stahl, M.D., Ph.D.
Monica N. Starkman, M.D.
Dorothy A. Starr, M.D.
Roy Steinhouse, M.D.
Peter E. Stokes, M.D.
John S. Strauss, M.D.
Max Sugar, M.D.
David W. Swanson, M.D.

Zebulin C. Taintor, M.D.
John A. Talbott, M.D.
Allan Tasman, M.D.
Sam D. Taylor, M.D.
Lenore C. Terr, M.D.
Alexander Thomas, M.D.
Gary Tischler, M.D.
Arnold Tobin, M.D.
Garfield Tourney, M.D.
Darold A. Treffert, M.D.
Margaret Owen Tsaltas, M.D.
Gary J. Tucker, M.D.
William M. Tucker, M.D.
Ann R. Turkel, M.D.

Kathleen Bell Unger, M.D.
Yogendra Upadhyay, M.D.

George E. Vaillant, M.D.
Bessel Van der Kolk, M.D.
Christian D. Van der Velde, M.D.
Hugo Van Dooren, M.D.
Herman M. van Praag, M.D., Ph.D.
Ilza Veith, Ph.D., M.D.
Milton Viederman, M.D.

Thomas Wadden, Ph.D.
Raymond Waggoner, M.D.
Richard L. Weddige, M.D.
Walter Weintraub, M.D.
James M.A. Weiss, M.D.
Kenneth J. Weiss, M.D.
Sidney H. Weissman, M.D.
William D. Weitzel, M.D.
Elizabeth B. Weller, M.D.
Charles E. Wells, M.D.
Paul H. Wender, M.D.
Jack C. Westman, M.D.
Kerrin L. White, M.D.
Wayne Whitehouse, Ph.D.
Roy M. Whitman, M.D.
Jan N. Williams, M.D.
C. Philip Wilson, M.D.
G. Terence Wilson, Ph.D.
Ronald Wintrob, M.D.
Michael G. Wise, M.D.
Joseph Wolpe, M.D.
Edward A. Wolpert, M.D., Ph.D.
David R. Wood, M.D.
William M. Wood, M.D.
Sherwin M. Woods, M.D.
Henry H. Work, M.D.
Richard W. Worst, M.D.
Lyman C. Wynne, M.D., Ph.D.

Irvin D. Yalom, M.D.
Alayne Yates, M.D.

Robert G. Zadylak, M.D.
Leonard S. Zegans, M.D.
Norman Zinberg, M.D.
Charlotte M. Zitrin, M.D.
Joel P. Zrull, M.D.

Foreword

T. Byram Karasu and the hundreds of our colleagues who have contributed to this massive effort deserve our highest respect and admiration.

The sheer magnitude of the undertaking would have discouraged most, but the enormous complexity provided the challenge that Dr. Karasu and the APA Task Force on Treatments of Psychiatric Disorders needed to endure this seven-year process. The APA is particularly grateful to Dr. Karasu for his patience, thoughtfulness, and comprehensive intelligence about psychiatric therapies. The result is a work of unprecedented significance. Even though, in its present four volumes, it is by no means a definitive work, this report is a major contribution to the literature and a basis on which much more will be accomplished in the years to come.

Coming to fruition just at the end of my presidency of the American Psychiatric Association, the report advances two of my major interests and concerns. It is the first major attempt to clarify and specify the tools available to psychiatry. As such it will serve as the basis for our continuing effort to describe and define our profession within the world of medicine.

The eradication of stigma has been the theme of my presidency, and it is my hope that *Treatments of Psychiatric Disorders* can help us to demonstrate to the public the positive effective treatments in the psychiatric armamentarium. In its present form it serves to educate the profession, but I hope it will be refined and condensed into material for the general public so that there can be broader understanding of the effectiveness of psychiatric treatment.

Paul J. Fink, M.D.
President, American Psychiatric Association (1988–1989)

Introduction

Science provides only interim knowledge.

Psychiatric treatment, like the rest of medicine, is inherently a flexible and open system which will continuously be influenced by new knowledge. This report represents a description of clinically useful current approaches for the treatment of mental disorders with a balanced perspective. It is important to emphasize that a treatment plan inherently must be an open system. Thus, this report is a working document reflecting a combination of cumulative scientific knowledge and clinical judgment about the treatment of psychiatric patients.

Historical Background

This undertaking began with the establishment of a previous Commission on Psychiatric Therapies in 1977 by Jules Masserman, M.D., then the president of the American Psychiatric Association. The charge was to examine critically the somatic, dyadic, group/family, and social therapies in current use—and to recommend criteria for evaluating therapeutic approaches.

In its attempt to meet this difficult task, the Commission produced two publications, both published by the American Psychiatric Association. The first was a critical review of a large body of evaluation research, entitled *Psychotherapy Research: Methodological and Efficacy Issues* (American Psychiatric Association Commission on Psychiatric Therapies 1982). This work pointed to the complexity of the variables involved in defining both the nature of a psychotherapeutic treatment and its outcome. The second publication, *The Psychiatric Therapies* (American Psychiatric Association Commission on Psychiatric Therapies 1984), was a comprehensive compendium of the many psychosocial and somatic treatment modalities currently in use.

In continuation of the previous Commission, Daniel X. Freedman, M.D., then the president of the APA, established a Task Force on Treatment of Psychiatric Disorders in 1982 to produce a comprehensive document that would describe the state of the art for treatment of psychiatric disorders.

The Process of Development

Because of the multiplicity of psychiatric disorders and their related approaches, the Task Force designated Chairpersons for 26 Panels, each of whom would draw together a working group to review the treatment of a different disorder or group of disorders. Chairpersons and Panel members were chosen from among many well-qualified individuals on the basis of certain criteria: the publication of research or clinical reports concerned with the treatment of a specific category of mental illness; and nomination by peers based on acknowledged eminence in clinical practice, national reputation, past accomplishments, and broad perspective. In order to assist them in their task, each Panel was empowered to retain the specialized services of a wide variety of consultants and representatives of consultant organizations.

The consultants were selected so as to represent a breadth of disciplines and orientations, in appreciation of the diverse patient and treatment variables important in these fields. They encompass expertise in general psychiatry, child psychiatry, psychoanalysis, psychotherapy, pharmacotherapy, and biological and social psychiatry, as well as exposure to treatments in diverse settings. This method of selecting contributors and consultants, and the desire for integration and synthesis of divergent views, led to multiple responses and challenges. We believe this approach has had a salutary effect on the outcome of the report.

Panels were assigned psychiatric diagnostic groups for which they were to provide treatment considerations. They identified distinct categories within the given diagnostic groupings which deserved full narration and discussed the variation of treatment as applied to other categories. The Panels operated on the basis of the clinical model that assumes that, for an individual with specific characteristics who is suffering from a given disorder or combination of disorders, there are one or more preferred treatments and/or combinations as well as acceptable alternative and possibly adjunct treatments.

Once a draft was prepared by the contributors, that document marked the beginning of an elaborate review process, as follows: 1) it was sent to a number of consultants, chosen by the contributor(s) for comments; 2) Draft II was prepared by the contributor(s) on the basis of the consultants' suggestions; 3) the Task Force sent Draft II to five to ten consultants; 4) the comments and critiques of these individuals were sent to the original contributors(s) for preparation of Draft III; and 5) Draft III was then reviewed and finalized by the Task Force. This complex process of consultation and review produced sections that reflect the input and ideas of many experts. Although in some sections a single author, in others a group of authors, and in still others individual chapters are given credits depending upon the level of contribution, the completed product represents the original work of the primary author(s), views of the Chairperson and Consultants of each Panel, and the Members of the Task Force.

Format

As there was no precedent for us to use as a model, and also recognizing that the consideration of treatment for various disorders may require different approaches to their subjects, the Panels were given a relatively free rein as to the format, style, and length of their presentations.

The sections do not deal with the issues of diagnosis, but assume the reader's prior knowledge. Where there was a need for further elaboration of the *Diagnostic and Statistical Manual of Mental Disorders* in its utilization for treatment planning, these issues were discussed. The work progressed during the transitional stage from DSM-III to DSM-III-R. Whenever we were able, we tried to keep the pace.

Naturally, some topics were repeated to varying degrees in different chapters. This also helped to state some of the finer points between them. At times a clinical example was presented to clarify differential diagnostic issues.

In discussion of treatment of a condition from more than one perspective, an attempt was made to integrate multiple points of view within a single section. Wherever this was not feasible, multiple chapters are included from diverse perspectives. A clinician must be able to consider each clinical problem at several conceptual levels in designing the most appropriate treatment program. Often combined applications are included to describe complementary models that are in use. Wherever empirical data were available, they were cited. In newer fields there are detailed discussions of studies instead of conclusions, to allow a proper perspective on the data. Special references were added in the text for readers who may want to study the subject in greater depth.

Use of This Report

This report is a professional document designed to suggest useful treatments for psychiatric disorders as an aid for treatment planning. It is not intended to impose rigid methods. It aims to demonstrate the complexity of the treatment planning process and its application, the true nature of comprehensive diagnosis, and the depth and breadth of knowledge that is required to assess a patient's need for the provision of treatment.

Proper use of this document requires specialized training that provides both a body of knowledge and clinical skills. Furthermore, many specific factors will influence the treatment needs for a particular individual. The chapters in this report do not dictate an exclusive course of treatment or procedures to be followed and should not be construed as excluding other acceptable methods of practice. Therefore, it would be incorrect to assert that any single treatment in this book automatically fits any single patient. Sound use of this book requires a clinician's judgment based on knowledge of a patient and a valid background of training and practice in psychiatry. Ultimately, it is individual practitioners—based upon their clinical judgment, experience, and assessment of the scientific literature—who will determine the usefulness of various therapeutic approaches. Futhermore, the mental disorders discussed in this report do not encompass all of the conditions that a psychiatrist may legitimately treat.

Future Directions

It is also important to note that this report reflects current assessment from an evolving knowledge base. Psychiatry participates in the continual expansion of knowledge that is taking place in all areas of science and medicine. New psychotropic drugs and other somatic approaches are constantly being tested and evaluated. Similarly, new psychotherapeutic and psychosocial techniques are being developed and assessed. In addition, combinations of treatment which hold promise are being evaluated. The continual accrual of new information will need to be integrated into these formulations in an ongoing way.

An important implication of the attempt to systemize our knowledge is that as the Task Force proceeded with its work, both what is known as well as what needs to be known became more evident. In particular, there is a need for increasing refinement of significant variables toward a greater understanding of individual differences in response to different therapeutic approaches. Such refinement will depend upon ongoing research which must take into account specific interventions, specific disorders or patient subgroups of responders and nonresponders, specific dosages, specific durations, and specific combinations and sequences of the treatments—in short, the ultimate establishment of carefully delineated criteria for titrating the nature and timing of various therapies and their combinations to be utilized in a biopsychosocial approach to the treatment of psychiatric disorders (Karasu 1982).

Toksoz Byram Karasu, M.D.

References

American Psychiatric Association Commission on Psychiatric Therapies: Psychotherapy Research: Methodological and Efficacy Issues. Washington, DC, American Psychiatric Association, 1982

American Psychiatric Association Commission on Psychiatric Therapies: The Psychiatric Therapies. Volume 1 (Somatic Therapies) and Volume 2 (Psychosocial Therapies). Washington, DC, American Psychiatric Association, 1984

Karasu TB: Psychotherapy and pharmacotherapy: toward an integrative model. Am J Psychiatry 139:7, 1982

Acknowledgments

This work was accomplished with the generous help of many people. Both the size of this project as well as the spirit of cooperation by which it was undertaken are demonstrated by the large number of clinicians involved and cited as contributors and consultants. I am deeply indebted to all.

I would like to thank the Chairpersons of the Panels and all contributors who not only prepared scholarly documents, but also gracefully allowed their original works to be modified through the consultation process. I would also like to express my gratitude to the consultants for their productive criticism.

I am most thankful for the support of Daniel X. Freedman, M.D., founder President of the Task Force, and Paul J. Fink, M.D., who presided during the crucial stage of the project, as well as to Keith H. Brodie, M.D., George Tarjan, M.D., John A. Talbott, M.D., Carol C. Nadelson, M.D., Robert O. Pasnau, M.D., George H. Pollock, M.D., Herbert Pardes, M.D., who served as Presidents, and also Lawrence Hartmann, M.D., William R. Sorum, M.D., Harvey Bluestone, M.D., Fred Gottlieb, M.D., Roger Peele, M.D., Irvin M. Cohen, M.D., and John S. McIntyre, M.D., who served as Speakers of the Assembly during the lifetime of the Task Force.

My special thanks to Melvin Sabshin, M.D., Medical Director of the American Psychiatric Association, for his unfailing leadership and the wisdom which he provided with great generosity, and to Harold Alan Pincus, M.D., Director, Office of Research, who gave administrative direction to the project and who, jointly with Paul J. Fink, M.D., the chairman of the Joint Ad Hoc Review Committee, weathered the most complicated organizational issues and skillfully brought this project to a successful conclusion.

I want to express my gratitude to Sandy Ferris for her organizational ability; to Philomena Lee, who maintained the highly complicated correspondence with a large number of people and corrected final drafts with exemplary patience, good humor, and dedication; to Betty Meltzer for her elegant editorial assistance; and to Louise Notarangelo, Rita Segarra, and Shirley Kreitman, who assisted them with equal competence and generosity.

My sincere appreciation and gratitude to Ronald E. McMillen, General Manager of the American Psychiatric Press, Inc., Timothy R. Clancy, Editorial Director, and Richard E. Farkas, Production Manager, for their leadership, and to their dedicated staff, Christine Kalbacher, Project Coordinator, Karen E. Sardinas-Wyssling and Lindsay E. Edmunds, Principal Manuscript Editors; to Editorial Experts, Inc., specifically Mary Stoughton and the staff editors, Pat Caudill and the staff proofreaders, and June Morse and the staff indexers, and to Robert Elwood and Nancy Borza at Harper Graphics, Typesetter, and Tom Reed at R. R. Donnelley & Sons Company, Printer, whose expert labors have facilitated the transformation of the raw material into four carefully wrought and handsome volumes.

Toksoz Byram Karasu, M.D.

Cautionary Statement

This report does not represent the official policy of the American Psychiatric Association. It is an APA task force report, signifying that members of the APA have contributed to its development, but it has not been passed through those official channels required to make it an APA policy document.

THIS REPORT IS NOT INTENDED TO BE CONSTRUED AS OR TO SERVE AS A STANDARD FOR PSYCHIATRIC CARE.

SECTION 17

Mood Disorders

Chapter 159

Preface

This section reports on the efforts of the Panel on Depression and Mood Disorders. It is not intended to be a manual like the *Merck Manual* or other similar efforts. The opinion of the panel was that the evidence is not sufficient to allow a definitive prescription of decisions for treatment. Rather, this section summarizes the available evidence for various treatments for mood disorders.

The concept of mood disorders derives from 19th-century thinking about the mind and psychology. Whereas most of medicine during the 19th century organized diseases according to the organs involved (e.g., diseases of the heart, of the kidney, of the brain), no equivalent organ could be developed for psychiatry. Instead, 19th-century psychiatry relied heavily on a faculty psychology. The faculties of the mind include thinking, affect, behavior, etc. The legacy of this mode of thinking in the modern nomenclature are the disorders of thought (schizophrenia and paranoia), disorders of memory and attention (delirium and dementia), and disorders of affect (depression and mania).

To be completely consistent, the category of mood disorders should include more than the affects of depression and elation. Other affects of relevance to human functioning and to clinical work include guilt, anger, anxiety, and pleasure. However, in clinical practice, the term *disorders of affect*, or *diseases of mood*, refers almost exclusively to depression and the related states of elation and mania.

The decision to group these conditions together is purely heuristic. This grouping should not be interpreted as reflecting a single etiology or pathophysiology. The intent is to promote a pluralistic approach. There is no one affective disorder, just as there is no one disease of the heart or one disease of the kidney. There are multiple disorders, each with likely different combinations of etiologic factors (genetics, environment, personality).

The DSM-III and DSM-III-R have taken what has been called an agnostic position with regard to etiology. The criteria for diagnosing the various conditions within the affective disorders do not include etiology but reflect the limited knowledge available as to the etiology of these conditions. Relying heavily on clinical criteria promotes development of homogeneous groups for research. At the same time, it is hoped that these groupings will guide clinicians in decisions as to use in available therapies and promote clinical communication.

Although the contributions in this section are individually authored, it is to be emphasized that this section represents the collective effort of the panel. The effort has been made to integrate a comprehensive approach. This is not intended to be like many multiauthored volumes, which reflect the individual opinions of the separate chapter authors. Rather, this reflects the common view.

Chapter 160

Introduction

Over the past three decades, there have been major advances in our understanding of depression and related mood disorders. In large part, these advances have been stimulated by new treatments introduced since the 1950s.

In a related set of developments, the introduction of these new treatments stimulated marked improvement in the number and quality of controlled clinical studies evaluating the efficacy of treatments for depression, including psychotherapy and psychopharmacology.

The diagnosis and classification of depression, mania, and related mood disorders have long been subjects of interest, research, and controversy within psychiatry. The DSM-III (American Psychiatric Association 1980) was the first official diagnostic system to contain a separate category of "affective disorders." In the DSM-III-R (American Psychiatric Association 1987), this category is changed to "mood disorders."

Purposes of This Chapter

In this chapter, I will summarize the current state of knowledge regarding the treatments of depression and related mood disorders and offer selected recommendations to the APA Task Force.

Three issues will be addressed:

1. Diagnosis and classification: the scope of depression and related mood disorder.
2. Which treatments are used?
3. For specific disorders, which treatments are recommended?

Diagnosis and Classification: The Scope of Depression and Related Mood Disorders

For almost a century, psychiatrists have grouped together depression and manic states as a diagnostic unity. The term used for this complex has varied. Kraepelin used the term *manic depressive insanity*. After World War II, the term *affective disorders* became popular and was incorporated into the DSM-III in 1980.

In common usage, *affect* refers to the minute-to-minute and hour-to-hour fluctuations in emotional state, whereas *mood* refers to the more enduring emotional "tone" that characterizes individuals. Therefore, the term *mood disorders* seems more appropriate than *affective disorders* since the clinical conditions with which we deal are usually enduring over weeks or months. The DSM-III-R and the ICD-10 have adopted the term *mood disorders*.

By clinical convention, mood disorders include the various depressive states as well as manic states. Clinical manic states represent a serious form of states of elation and euphoria. Depression, euphoria, happiness, and joy are part of everyday life, but in clinical condition become states of elation for which *mania* has been the diagnostic term.

Some observers, notably Aubrey Lewis, recommended extending the concept of affective disorders to include anxiety states. Indeed, the overlap between anxiety and depression is considerable, and there is an unresolved scientific issue as to the relative overlap or independence of depressive and anxiety disorders. Nevertheless, I will restrict this chapter to the depressive and elated states included in the DSM-III-R.

The Scope of Depression

The term *depression* is used in psychiatry in a number of ways. Three usages are relevant:

1. Depression as a normal emotion. The capacity to experience depression (sadness, disappointment, "the blues," "being down") is a basic characteristic of the human condition. Vicissitudes of depressive affect and mood are expected components of normal experience.
2. Depression as a symptom. Many individuals coming to primary medical care settings and to mental health professionals will not meet criteria for a DSM-III-R disorder but will have depressive symptoms, emotional distress, and social dysfunctions of varying degrees and durations.

   Depressive symptoms are very prevalent among patients with a wide variety of medical, neurologic, and psychiatric disorders.

   Depressive symptoms also occur as part of the adaptive response of individuals to stressful environmental changes and life events.

   Clinical depressive conditions include a number of dysphoria states and symptoms, including the mood disorders (affective disorders) classified in official diagnostic systems.
3. Depression as psychiatric disorders. The mood disorders (affective disorders) have been recognized for centuries. It is now widely accepted that there is no one mood disease; rather, there are a variety of disorders, acute and chronic, mild and severe.

   The recommended classification of these disorders is that of the American Psychiatric Association. The disorders in the DSM-III that are most relevant in this manual are listed in Table 1.

   In clinical practice, the most prevalent conditions are variants of major depression, dysthymia, and adjustment disorder with depressive mood.

In the DSM-III-R, there is a realignment of the various conditions under affective disorders and also a change in terminology. As noted previously, the change in terminology is to employ the term *mood disorders* for the larger category, instead of the previously used term *affective disorders*.

Within the mood disorders, the basic separation would be into bipolar disorders and into depressive disorders. These changes are outlined in Table 2.

Table 1. Categories of Depression in DSM-III

Name of Disorder	ICD-CM Code Number
Organic affective syndrome	293.83
Bipolar disorders	
Mixed	296.6
Manic	296.4
Depressed	296.5
Major depression	
Single episode	296.2
Recurrent	296.3
Cyclothymic disorder	301.13
Dysthymic disorder	300.40
Atypical anxiety disorder	300.00
Adjustment disorder with depressed mood	309.00
Uncomplicated bereavement	V62.82

Table 2. Categories of Depression and Related Mood Disorders in DSM-III-R

Name of Disorder	ICD-CM Code Number
Organic mood disorder	293.83
Mood disorders (affective disorders)	
Bipolar disorders	
Manic	296.4
Depressed	296.5
Mixed	296.7
Cyclothymic disorder	
Bipolar disorder NOS	
Depressive disorders	
Major depression	
Single episode	296.2
Recurrent	296.3
With psychotic features	
With melancholic features	
Dysthymic disorder	300.4
Depressive disorder NOS	300
Adjustment disorder with depressed mood	309
Uncomplicated bereavement	V62.82

Which Treatments Are Used?

There are currently a number of treatments of mania, depression, and related mood disorders, many of which have demonstrated evidence of their efficacy from controlled clinical trials. These treatments are outlined in Table 3.

The Nature of Evidence for Efficacy

Before discussing the status of the individual treatments, some discussion about the nature of evidence is appropriate. The most convincing evidence for the efficacy of a therapeutic intervention in any field of medicine, including psychiatry, derives

Table 3. Treatments of Depression and Related Mood Disorders

I. Psychotherapies and Psychosocial Treatments
    A. Counseling and psychological management
    B. General psychotherapies
    C. Short-term psychotherapies especially designed for depression
        1) Cognitive-behavior therapy (CBT)
        2) Behavior treatment
        3) Interpersonal psychotherapy (IPT)
        4) Dynamic psychotherapy
        5) Group therapies
    D. Long-term psychotherapies for depression
II. Psychopharmacologic Treatments
    A. Psychomotor stimulants
    B. Neuroleptics
    C. Monoamine oxidase inhibitors (MAOI)
    D. Tricyclic and heterocyclic antidepressants
    E. Lithium and carbamazepine
    F. Benzodiazepines
III. Other Biologic Interventions
    A. Electroconvulsive treatment
    B. Light treatment
    C. Psychosurgery
    D. Sleep deprivation

from the results of controlled clinical trials. Excellent reviews of methodology of controlled clinical trials in depression as well as findings regarding psychopharmacologic treatment and psychotherapy have been published. The level of scholarship in this area is very good and merits careful attention (APA Commission on Psychiatric Therapies, part I and II, 1982; Greist et al. 1982).

The principles of controlled clinical trials for evaluating psychopharmacologic drugs have been described in numerous publications.

As regards research on psychotherapy, the reports of the NIMH expert group summarized by Fiske et al. are highly relevant, as is the report of the APA Task Force on methodology summarized by Karasu (Fiske et al. 1970).

In addition, metaanalysis has been applied to the body of data on depression treatment by a number of reviewers (Smith and Glass 1977; Smith et al. 1980). However, this approach remains controversial.

The Relationship of Research to Clinical Practice

Ideally, in modern scientific medicine, information should flow from research to therapeutic practice. Recent studies of patterns of clinical care of depression indicate a wide gap between the trends in research studies of efficacy and actual clinical practice. Four trends are apparent (Keller et al. 1982):

1. The majority of persons meeting DSM-III diagnostic criteria for mood disorder are not being treated directly for their psychotic condition. This finding has emerged from many epidemiologic studies. The parallel of depression to hypertension is to be noted. At the time when the Public Health Service program for early detection of treatment of hypertension was initiated, only 10 percent of hypertensives were in active treatment.

2. Although the majority of depressed and manic persons are not being treated directly for their mood disorder, a substantial proportion are being cared for in the general health care system. Their psychiatric disorder is often unrecognized or misdiagnosed. Nevertheless, they overuse health services because of bodily complaints.

3. When treatment for the depression or mood disorder is initiated, practitioners tend to use treatments for which there is limited evidence of efficacy. This applies to both pharmacotherapy and psychotherapy. In pharmacologic treatment, the tendency is to prescribe benzodiazepines, particularly by family practitioners, internists, and other primary care nonpsychiatric physicians.

4. With respect to psychopharmacologic practice, when antidepressant drugs are used, the dosage is often lower than that recommended for an inconsistent duration of time.

5. With psychotherapy, there is a tendency to use techniques whose efficacy has not been validated. The brief psychotherapies for which good evidence exists as to efficacy have not been widely diffused into clinical practice.

Given this state of affairs, one of the major challenges to Project D/ART will be to educate health professionals, including nonpsychiatric physicians in primary care and nonpsychiatric mental health professionals, as to the latest research findings on the appropriate use of treatments, both psychotherapeutic and psychopharmacologic.

Psychotherapies and Psychosocial Treatments

The term *psychotherapy* refers to a wide range of techniques used by a designated professional that have as their common feature the attempt to influence the patient's behavior, emotions, thoughts, and attitudes through psychological techniques, most often verbal interchange, in the relationship between the psychotherapist and the patient.

The field of psychotherapy has grown in the types and diversity of treatment, in the number and types of psychotherapeutic practitioners, and in public acceptance as manifested by increased rates of use. There are over 200 "brand names" of psychotherapy (Karasu 1982; Parloff 1982). For the most part, this expansion in the types of psychotherapy has occurred since World War II and has been paralleled by a marked expansion in the type and number of psychotherapists. Psychotherapy is practiced by a number of mental health professionals including psychiatrists, clinical psychologists, counseling and school psychologists, psychiatric social workers, and marriage and family counselors. There are no standards as to designation of psychotherapists and no unified credentialing in process. There are probably about 150,000 professionals in the United States who have some formal training in psychotherapy and who have some professional credentials in psychiatry, social work, psychology, and related fields.

Research on the efficacy of psychotherapy has not been as extensive as research on psychopharmacology. In part this is due to intrinsic difficulties in psychotherapeutic outcome research; in part it is due to the strong power of ideology. There are, however, indications that the situation is changing and that a new wave of psychotherapy research is underway (APA Commission on Psychotherapy 1982; London and Klerman 1982).

Given this general situation in psychotherapy and psychotherapy outcome research, the progress in research on psychotherapy in the treatment of depression has been particularly impressive. In reviewing the literature, Lieberman (1975) noted there were no controlled studies of the efficacy of any form of psychotherapy for depression. Indeed, until the 1960s, very few studies of psychotherapy identified or separated depressed patients but tended to group them together with neurosis and personality disorder. The situation changed in the mid-1970s with the emergence of a number of psychotherapies specifically designed for the treatment of depression: notably Cognitive-Behavioral Therapy (CBT) developed by Beck et al. (1979); Interpersonal Psychotherapy (IPT) developed by Klerman et al. (1984); and various forms of behavior therapy developed by Lewinsohn et al. (1976). Although the quality of research on these treatments has steadily improved (Rush 1982), these treatments have not widely diffused into clinical practice.

Counseling and Clinical Management

Mention needs to be given to various methods of counseling and psychological management. There is no consensus as to the best terminology for these psychological and psychosocial interventions. Sometimes they are called "supportive psychotherapy," sometimes "psychological management," and sometimes "clinical management." The term *psychological management* was coined in discussing the distinction between former psychotherapies and the various techniques of reassurance support and psychoeducational efforts considered part of the "doctor-patient relationship." As part of the NIMH Collaborative Study of the psychotherapy of the outpatient treatment of depression, Epstein and Fawcett, at Rush-Presbyterian-St. Luke's Medical Center in Chicago, developed a manual for clinical management to be used in conjunction with imipramine and placebo. These techniques as developed by Fawcett and Epstein were specifically designed to augment the use of medication.

Similar techniques of psychological counseling are often used in primary care settings. In general, they tend to be brief and are often provided by nonspecialists in psychotherapy, particularly physicians, nurses, and other mental health professionals. In addition, there is the profession of counseling psychologists, who often are involved in nonmedical and nonhealth settings, such as schools, colleges, and universities, as well as in industry and occupational settings. Some form of counseling and psychological management is implicit in most medical transactions, and recent efforts have been made to systematize these interventions of promise, particularly for application in primary care settings.

General Psychotherapies

As noted previously, a large number of psychotherapies are used by psychiatrists and other mental health professionals. For the most part, these have not been designed specifically for depression, and although it is likely that depressed patients are included in many clinical practices of psychotherapists, psychotherapies focused on depression have developed only recently.

Psychodynamic Psychotherapy

In the United States, the most common forms of psychotherapy used by psychiatrists are those derived from psychoanalytic theories. In clinical practice, these psychotherapies are widely applied to patients who would meet diagnostic criteria for depression, although depressive diagnosis may not have been made by the clinician. However, there are no controlled trials of this form of treatment for any mood disorder, and consequently the efficacy of psychodynamic psychotherapy for depression remains to be established.

In the 1970s, a number of brief psychotherapies based on psychodynamic concepts were developed, notably by Mann (1973), Sifneos (1979), and Davenloo (1980). In addition, two forms of short-term psychodynamic psychotherapy have been developed and codified into "manuals." They are Short-Term Dynamic Psychotherapy (STDP) developed by Strupp and associates (1982) at Vanderbilt University, and Supportive and Expressive Treatment developed by Luborsky et al. (1984) in Philadelphia based on experience at the Menninger Foundation. In principle, these brief psychodynamic treatments should be applicable to various forms of depression. However, controlled trials have not been reported.

Short-Term Psychotherapies Especially Designed for Depression

A number of psychotherapies have recently been designed for specific treatment of depression. These have in common brief duration (Rush 1982), and the development of manuals and of explicit training programs (Hirschfeld and Shea 1985).

1. Cognitive-Behavior Therapy (CBT), the most widely used, was developed by Beck et al. (1979). It is based on the premise that "affect states" follow thoughts and cognitions. Cognitive-Behavior Therapy was one of the the two forms of brief psychotherapy included for evaluation in the NIMH Collaborative Study.
2. Interpersonal Psychotherapy (IPT) was developed by Klerman et al. (1984) in a collaboration between their Boston and New Haven research groups. It is based on research evidence linking the onset of depressions to changes in interpersonal relations. It focuses on the "here and now" and relates the patient's depressive condition to a number of areas of interpersonal difficulties: unresolved grief, role transitions, role disputes, and interpersonal deficits.
3. A number of behavior therapies based on the theories of B.F. Skinner have been developed for depression. These include social skills treatments and forms of behavior therapy developed by Peter Lewinsohn et al. (1976). A small number of controlled trials indicate the value of these treatments for ambulatory patients with major depression.
4. Forms of group therapy, marital therapy, and couple therapy have also been applied to depressed patients, but the number of controlled studies remains few.

Long-Term Psychotherapies for Depression

Long-term psychotherapy for severely depressed patients was described by Cohen et al. (1954). However, no systematic exposition of the specific techniques was developed, and no efficacy study was undertaken.

A long-term form of interpersonal psychotherapy for depression has been described (Arieti and Bemporad 1978). However, no systematic study of outcome has been reported.

The NIMH Collaborative Study of the Treatment of Depression

In the mid-1970s, NIMH, under the leadership of Drs. M. Parloff and Irene Elkin, designed and initialed a multicenter controlled study comparing two forms of brief psychotherapy: CBT and IPT. Two-hundred-fifty patients were randomly assigned to four treatment conditions: 1) cognitive therapy, 2) interpersonal psychotherapy, 3) imipramine, and 4) a combination of placebo and clinical management. Each patient was treated for 16 weeks, and extensive efforts were made for the selection and training of psychotherapists. Outcome was assessed by a multidimension battery of scales that assess symptoms, psychological functioning, and cognition.

The preliminary results from the three centers (Oklahoma City, Okla.; Washington, D.C.; and Pittsburgh, Pa.) indicate that the three active treatments were superior to placebo and clinical management and that there was a clinically significant reduction of symptoms over the 16-week treatment period.

The initial entry criterion was a score of at least 14 on the 17-item Hamilton Rating Scale for Depression. Of the 239 patients who entered treatment, 68 percent completed at least 15 weeks and 12 sessions of treatment. The following findings were reported by Elkins at the American Psychiatric Association Annual Meeting, May 3, 1986, in Washington, D.C., and by Elkins et al. at the American Association for the Advancement of Science in Philadelphia, Pa., in June 1986.

1. The overall degree of involvement was highly significant clinically. Over two-thirds of the patients were symptom free at the end of the treatment.
2. More patients in the placebo-clinical management condition dropped out or were withdrawn than did in the three active treatments—twice as many as for interpersonal psychotherapy, which had the lowest attrition rate.
3. At the end of 12 weeks of treatment, the two psychotherapies and imipramine were equivalent in the reduction of depressive symptoms and in patients' overall functioning.
4. The pharmacotherapy, imipramine, had rapid initial onset of action, but by 12 weeks the two psychotherapies had produced equivalent results.
5. Although many of the less severely depressed patients improved with all treatment conditions, including the placebo group, the more severely depressed patients in the placebo position did poorly.
6. For the less severely depressed group there were no differences among the treatments.
7. Forty-four percent of the sample were severely depressed. The criterion of severity used was a score of 20 or more on the Hamilton Rating Scale of Depression. Patients in IPT and in the imipramine groups consistently and significantly had better scores than the placebo group on the Hamilton Rating Scale.
8. Surprisingly, one of the predictors of patient response for IPT was the presence of an endogenous depression symptom picture. This was also true for the imipramine; however, this finding with regard to medication would have been expected. Endogenous depression was measured by the Research Diagnostic Criteria (RDC) following an interview with the Schedule for Affective Disorders-Schizophrenia (SADS).

Combining Drugs and Psychotherapy

In clinical practice and despite theoretical opposition among many schools of psychotherapy, the combination of drug treatment, particularly tricyclic antidepressants, and some form of psychotherapy is widely prescribed and is increasingly supported by research evidence (Beitman et al. 1984; Conte et al. 1986).

The methodological problems in evaluating these treatments are often difficult. Nevertheless, in the field of depression, considerable research supports the value of a combination of drugs and psychotherapy, particularly in ambulatory patients.

Sometimes the two treatments are administered by the same psychiatrists; other times there is a split in the responsibility, with one person, usually a psychiatrist, prescribing the medication and a psychotherapist, or often a psychologist or social worker, providing the psychotherapy (Beitman et al. 1984).

Summary Comments on Psychotherapy

It is of note that all the psychotherapy trials have been conducted on ambulatory patients with nonbipolar and nonpsychotic forms of the disorder. There have been no systematic trials of hospitalized patients or patients with more severe psychotic and bipolar states. There remains considerable controversy as to whether the psychotherapies are effective for subtypes of major depression other than psychotic. Particular controversy centers around the possible interactions with endogenous or melancholic depression. Moreover, the relative efficacy of psychotherapy and tricyclics will be resolved as further results from the NIMH study become available.

Psychopharmacologic Treatments

Historical Background

The modern era of the psychopharmacologic treatments of affective disorder began in Australia in 1949 with the development of lithium therapy by Cade. Only decades later was the significance of Cade's reports diffused and accepted into clinical practice. The phenothiazines, the first of the neuroleptic drugs, were introduced in France in 1952, and initial reports on the phenothiazine treatment of mania and similar excited states heralded the new era of psychopharmacology.

The modern era of psychopharmacologic treatment of depression began in the late 1950s with the almost simultaneous introduction of imipramine, the prototypic tricyclic antidepressant (TCA), and iproniazid, the prototypic monoamine oxidase inhibitor (MAOI). Both discoveries were serendipitous and resulted from astute clinical observations rather than from extrapolations from basic laboratory experiments. Prior to the 1950s, the major somatic treatment for depression was electroconvulsive therapy (ECT), developed in the 1930s and early 1940s. In addition, the amphetamines, first introduced in 1930, were widely used, albeit with limited effectiveness.

Imipramine was developed by Geigy Laboratories in Switzerland as a putative antipsychotic agent because of similarities to chlorpromazine in chemical structure and preclinical screening properties. It proved to be ineffective in treating psychoses but was observed to produce improvement in the affective state of some depressed schizophrenic patients. Subsequent trials showed it to be an effective antidepressant drug.

The story of the introduction of MAOIs is intriguing. Iproniazid, a hydrazine MAOI used to treat tuberculosis, was observed to have mood-elevating side effects in tubercular patients. Crane and Kline, working independently, prescribed the drug to depressives who were not tubercular, with favorable results.

The success of iproniazid and imipramine stimulated considerable interest in the psychopharmacologic treatment of depressive disorders. Interest in antidepressant drugs was further stimulated by the monoamine theories developed in the late 1950s. It was noted that reserpine caused depletion of the central nervous system (CNS) monoamines norepinephrine, serotonin, and dopamine, wheras MAOIs prevented the metabolic breakdown of these amines, thereby increasing the level of the amines in brain centers. However, the clinical efficacy of imipramine provided a dilemma because it influenced neither the synthesis nor the degradation of any CNS amines.

The dilemma was solved by Axelrod, who demonstrated that imipramine blocked the presynaptic re-uptake of norepinephrine. Subsequently, almost all of the compounds introduced in the 1960s and 1970s were tricyclic in structure and had effects on presynaptic re-uptake of either norepinephrine or serotonin. These findings established both the groundwork for the dominant theory of the mode of action of antidepressant drugs and the basis for selection of new compounds for pharmacologic screening and clinical testing.

Amphetamines and Other Psychomotor Stimulants

There is general agreement that the psychomotor stimulants, of which the amphetamines are the prototypes, have only limited clinical effectiveness in the treatment of most of the acute depressions. For some, but not all, depressed persons, the amphetamines and other psychomotor stimulants may temporarily produce increased alertness and a mild-to-moderate elation and euphoria. The euphoric effects, however, are of small magnitude, and in many patients, the adverse effects of the drugs (anxiety, tension, sleep disturbance, irritability, and autonomic-nervous-system stimulation) are discomforting. The amphetamines have demonstrated efficacy in hyperactive children, but this clinical action is beyond the scope of this chapter.

A number of amphetamine-barbiturate combinations have been marketed, and excellent pharmacologic studies on animals and normal human beings indicate that this combination has synergistic effects on selected aspects of behavior. In human beings, the administration of this combination in acute cases is associated with a greater sense of mood elevation and with less of a decrement in psychomotor performance than is produced by either drug separately. In the one double-blind clinical trial available (General Practitioner Research Group 1964), however, the combination was found to be inferior to imipramine and no more effective than placebo.

There are serious adverse effects with the amphetamines. The acute toxic effects are dose related and at times fatal. A chronic psychosis may appear insidiously and may be indistinguishable clinically from chronic paranoid schizophrenic states. The occurrence of this schizophrenic-like psychosis is of considerable theoretical interest; its resemblance to naturally occurring schizophrenia has stimulated the investigation of amphetamine effects on the CNS amine metabolism. Moreover, there is increasing belief that a true withdrawal syndrome, which manifests itself in fatigue, hypersomnia, and increased rapid-eye-movement (REM) sleep, may occur.

Psychic dependence is the main hazard of prolonged use of the amphetamines, but there is also growing evidence for physical dependence. With the development of tolerance, patients often increase their doses. This has consequently generated widespread illicit market traffic.

A number of nonamphetamine psychomotor stimulants have been developed. The most widely used is methylphenidate (Ritalin), which has value as a mood stimulant in mild depressions. In the one controlled study available (Robin and Wiseberg 1958), methylphenidate had only slightly more apparent value than placebo in moderately depressed patients. Methylphenidate has many clinical features in common with the amphetamines, including its usefulness for hyperactive children with learning disorders. Two other psychomotor stimulants merit mention: phenmetrazine (marketed as Preludin), which also produces dependence, addiction, and toxic psychoses; and pipradrol (Meretran), which has not been found to be effective as an antidepressant.

Neuroleptics

Chlorpromazine, the first of the thiazines, was introduced in France in the early 1950s for the treatment of various forms of excited and psychotic states. Many of the early reports included significant numbers of patients with manic psychotic states, and the efficacy of the phenothiazines for manic states was thus widely accepted by the late 1950s.

In the 1950s and 1960s, the neuroleptic drugs were widely prescribed for depressions, particularly those associated with agitation, tension, and insomnia. However, because of the concern with extrapyramidal side effects, particularly tardive dyskinesia, there has been increasing caution over the dangers associated with the neuroleptics in the treatment of depression. The evidence, however, is very good that for psychotic depressions, the combination of a tricyclic and a neuroleptic is better than either compound alone.

The neuroleptics, particularly chlorpromazine and haloperidol, have been well studied for the management of excitement, overactivity, belligerence, and other aspects of behavioral disruption in acutely manic patients. The neuroleptics have a place in the treatment of manic episodes in these patients with bipolar disorders.

Monoamine Oxidase Inhibitors

Although a great many substances inhibit monoamine oxidase (MAO) to some degree, the MAO inhibitors used in psychiatric treatment are usually divided on the basis of their chemical structure into two classes: hydrazines and nonhydrazines. Both chemical types have in common the ability to inhibit the enzyme, monoamine oxidase, which is widely distributed in mammalian tissues, including the CNS, and which plays an important role in the oxidative deamination of monoamines.

Iproniazid, which was originally developed as a rocket fuel, was introduced into clinical medicine in 1950–1951 for the treatment of tuberculosis. Its possible psychiatric usefulness was first suggested from observations of behavioral and affective side effects noted in many of the tuberculosis patients who were treated with this compound. A related compound, isoniazid, introduced at about the same time, was a more effective tuberculostatic agent; but, while it produced neurologic complications, it had no effects on mood, cognition, or behavior. In contrast, iproniazid, although less effective in the treatment of tuberculosis, produced euphoria and weight gain, and increased psychomotor activity and social behavior in many patients. It also induced psychiatric states that resembled hypomanic and schizo-affective psychoses. Between 1953 and 1957, a number of clinicians reported observations of iproniazid's action and explored the possible use of iproniazid in treating depressed and psychomotor-retarded psychiatric patients.

Currently, the definitive place of the MAO inhibitors in clinical practice remains unclear for two reasons. First, although the majority of controlled studies have found that the MAO inhibitors are more effective than placebo, the efficacy of MAOI is usually less than that of electroconvulsive therapy (ECT) or the tricyclic derivatives. Second, patients may experience cardiovascular and autonomic side effects, which may prevent some patients from continuing safely to take the drug and which may even be fatal in rare instances.

Of major significance is the frequent observation of clinicians that some patients respond to MAO inhibitors but not to other antidepressants. Clinical depressions are heterogeneous, and it may be useful, by means of drug response, to develop a "pharmacological dissection" (Klein et al. 1980).

MAO inhibitors seem most useful for patients with various forms of "atypical" depression, particularly those with mood-reactive depressions, intense dysphoric reactions to separation and rejection in interpersonal relations, and depressions with admixtures of anxiety, panic attacks, and phobias.

Nevertheless, even if only a small proportion of depressed patients benefit from the MAO inhibitors, these drugs have had important theoretical implications. Understanding their effect on amine metabolism marks a major early stage in the development of the amine theory of the affective disorders.

Because the MAO inhibitors have potential side effects, they require careful supervision, often using laboratory assays of platelet MAO. For this reason they are best administered by specialists in psychopharmacology and with patients who are knowledgeable and responsible.

Tricyclic Derivatives

Currently there are over a half-dozen tricyclic derivatives approved by the FDA for clinical use in the United States. All of these drugs are clinically efficacious, and during the past 10 years, there has been a gradual but steady increase in their prescription rate. A decreased use of convulsive therapy, a decrease in the hospitalization rate and duration of hospital stay for depression, and an increase in the ambulatory treatment of depression have been associated with this increased use of tricyclics. There is no evidence, however, that the incidence or prevalence of depression has decreased, nor has there been any significant decrease in the suicide rate. Thus, the tricyclic treatments, although better than placebo or control, have contributed to a major change in the pattern of care but still have not contributed to primary prevention of depression.

The introduction of imipramine, the prototypic tricyclic, followed a sequence similar to that of iproniazid. Imipramine was developed by Geigy Laboratories in Switzerland as part of their program for the investigation of the iminodibenzyl derivatives that would have potential sedative and antihistaminic properties. Because of imipramine's structural and pharmacologic similarities to chlorpromazine, the initial clinical trials were made with persons who responded well to chlorpromazine—that is, psychotic patients. These initial trials proved to be unsuccessful, and the compound was shown to have no significant antipsychotic or "tranquilizing" activity. However, Kuhn observed significant antidepressant activity.

Kuhn's persistent observations and the subsequent verifications of his findings (Klerman and Cole 1966; Kuhn 1958) initiated intense clinical and laboratory investigations and introduced tricyclic derivatives, a new class of antidepressant drugs.

Newer Antidepressants

Since 1980, a number of antidepressants structurally different from the TCAs and the MAOIs have been marketed in the United States, and numerous other compounds are in stages of clinical evaluation. These new compounds have been called "second generation antidepressants" or "atypical antidepressants."

These new compounds have led to a reassessment of the biogenic amine hypotheses that were popular in the 1960s and 1970s. The relatively simplistic versions of the noradrenergic and serotonergic hypotheses of antidepressant drug action have been expanded to include findings linking antidepressant effect to binding and sensitivity of pre- and postsynaptic membrane receptors of neurotransmitters at critical brain loci. However, there is still no single theory that satisfactorily explains the mode of action of the wide range of antidepressants in use in the United States and abroad.

The newer tricyclic and heterocyclic antidepressant compounds raise three issues of practical interest for the clinician: 1) do the new compounds expand the range of patients for whom antidepressant drugs are effective? 2) do the newer drugs reduce the risk of cardiotoxicity, anticholinergic effects, and other adverse reactions produced by the traditional antidepressants? and 3) do the newer compounds have a more rapid onset of therapeutic effect than the older drugs?

Recent research has provided answers to the above questions: 1) the new compounds do not expand the range of patients for whom antidepressant drugs are effective; 2) some compounds reduce cardiotoxicity, which in many instances have made their use more accepted by many patients; however, 3) there is little evidence that the new compounds have a more rapid onset of therapeutic effect than the older drugs.

Lithium

Lithium salts were widely used in the 1940s for treatment of cardiac edema. Because of difficulty in regulating dose, a number of fatalities occurred and the use of this compound in general medicine was discontinued. However, an Australian psychiatrist, Cade, had observed "calming" effects on excited manic patients and conducted studies of the value of lithium in treatment of manic excitements. Cade's observations were for the most part forgotten through the 1950s and 1960s because of the great concern in North America and Western Europe with the newly developed phenothiazines and related compounds. However, other investigators replicated Cade's work and slowly the value of lithium diffused. Notable in this development was M. Schou of Aarhus, Denmark, who published papers on the clinical application of lithium to manic-depressive patients through the 1970s.

In the early 1960s, S. Gershon, who had trained in Australia, came to the United States and, along with Yuwiler, published a series of papers on the value of lithium and introduced its use into American psychiatry. During the 1970s, a large number of studies, including a multicenter clinical trial by the VA and NIMH, substantiated the value of lithium in treating acute manic episodes and in preventing the recurrence of both manic and depressive episodes in patients with bipolar illness. The efficacy of lithium for the treatment of mania and for the prevention of relapse contributed to establishing the validity of the concept of bipolar disorder first suggested by Leonhard. This concept has been accepted and is now incorporated into the DSM-III-R and will soon be incorporated into the WHO-ICD-10.

Lithium's value in the treatment of acute manic illness has been well substantiated although, for very excited manic patients, neuroleptics are often more effective in the short run in reducing excitement, overactivity, and socially disruptive behavior. The most important value of lithium is in the prevention of relapse and recurrence, and this clinical action has been substantiated by many systematic studies. Nevertheless, there are serious problems attendant to the safety of lithium. The blood level needs to be monitored carefully since there is acute toxicity associated with excess dosage. Fortunately, blood level determinations are easily available and contribute to careful monitoring and regulation.

Over the long term, problems of lithium toxicity usually involve the thyroid and the kidney. Because of these potential toxicities, attention has gradually shifted to nonlithium agents, most notably carbamazepine.

Carbamazepine

Carbamazepine (Tegretol), interestingly enough, is structurally a tricyclic derivative with demonstrated anticonvulsant properties. It has been widely used in neurology for a number of decades for the treatment of psychomotor epilepsy as well as of tic douloureux.

The application of carbamazepine into the treatment of bipolar illness was facilitated by the theoretical work on "kindling" by Post et al. at the NIMH intramural laboratories. Although the number of controlled studies is few, the evidence is increasing that carbamazepine is a useful substitute for lithium, particularly in long-term treatment aimed at the prevention of relapse. There is an acute toxicity syndrome with carbamazepine, and as with lithium, blood level monitoring is useful. A small percentage of patients develop agranulocytosis, and benign neutropenia may also occur.

Benzodiazepines

The place of the benzodiazepines in the treatment of depression remains controversial. Introduced in the 1960s, these compounds rapidly became the most widely prescribed drugs in the world. A wide variety of benzodiazepines have been synthesized and marketed.

There is a marked discrepancy between the research evidence concerning the limited efficacy of the benzodiazepines in depression and widespread clinical prescription. In clinical practice, benzodiazepines are widely prescribed for depression, particularly in family practice, internal medicine, and general practice. The pharmacodynamics and pharmacokinetics of this compound lend themselves to use in primary medical care. However, controlled studies indicate a limited place for the benzodiazepines in the overall treatment of depression. Effects on sleep, attention, and anxiety are usually short-lived, seldom persisting beyond two to four weeks. The benzodiazepines may be a useful first prescription in a step system similar to that developed in hypertension; in clinical practice they are most effective for acute situational reactions involving anxious mood and when used in depression appear to be of short-term value. There is a tendency toward tolerance and dependence, and an abstinence syndrome involving convulsions has been well documented.

A new benzodiazepine, alprazolam (Xanax), a triazolo-benzodiazepine, has been recently marketed in the United States and approved by the FDA for anxiety associated with depression. There are reports of its therapeutic value equivalent to imipramine and other tricyclics in ambulatory patients; value in hospitalized and severely ill and endogenous patients, however, appears to be less than that of the tricyclics. There are some suggestions that alprazolam has a pharmacodynamic profile, different from standard benzodiazepines, which includes action on beta adrenergic systems. This may provide a pharmacologic basis for the overlapping clinical profile between alprazolam and tricyclics in depression and in panic disorder and agoraphobia. However, these issues remain to be resolved by further laboratory studies and clinical trials.

Other Biologic Treatments

Although most attention has been focused on the new psychopharmacologic agents, it is important to be cognizant of a number of other biologic (or somatic) interventions. For the most part, these require specialized physician teams or are still in the experimental and investigational stage.

Convulsive Therapy

In therapeutic practice, convulsions can be induced by a variety of means: chemicals such as Metrazol; electric current, as with ECT; or gas inhalation, as in Indoklan. Whatever the mode of induction, the passage of sufficient electricity through the brain to produce a grand mal seizure is associated with improvement in severe depressive states.

The first convulsive therapy was introduced by Meduna in Hungary in the 1930s. Meduna believed he had found evidence that there was a negative correlation between schizophrenia and epilepsy, and he reasoned that if this were true, one possible way to treat schizophrenia would be to induce epileptic convulsions. Meduna first used camphor and oil and then Metrazol by injection. Metrazol produced a high percentage of bone fractures as well as intense anxiety bordering on terror. Nevertheless, although its therapeutic value in most forms of schizophrenia proved limited, it did seem to be of value for catatonic schizophrenia and for severe depressive states.

In 1939 Bini and Cerlutti in Italy perfected a technique for safely applying electrical current to the skull, and electric convulsive therapy was widely applied in Western Europe and North America through the 1940s. The technique has been modified through use of short-acting barbiturate anesthesia and curare-like actions, and through instrumentation to control and modify the electrical current. Numerous controlled studies have demonstrated that the essential therapeutic component is the passage of the convulsive dosage of electricity through the frontal-temporal areas of the cortex. Application of the electrodes to the frontal or occipital areas is not of therapeutic value, nor is the application of subconvulsive dose levels. The peripheral manifestations of the convulsion can be blocked by curare-like agents, and in the currently recommended form of treatment, the electrical discharge is monitored by continuous EEG recordings. Several controlled and systematic studies have replicated the value of ECT in severely depressed patients, particularly those with delusions and other psychotic features, severe retardation or severe agitation, intense suicidal drive, and the unusual and uncommon clinical syndrome of "depressive stupor." In depressive stupor, the patient takes to bed, becomes mute and often incontinent, and may appear to be catatonic, lying quietly in the fetal position. Before the advent of ECT, this condition was often fatal due to malnutrition, exhaustion, and intercurrent infections.

The adverse effect most often associated with ECT is memory impairment, which is considered to occur less frequently when unilateral treatment is applied. However, even with unilateral treatment, there are varying degrees of memory impairment, which in many patients can be distressing. No permanent brain damage has been demonstrated. However, it is desirable that the number of treatments give an individual patient over a lifetime should be kept below 50.

ECT was the subject of a recent NIH-NIMH Consensus Development Conference reported by Kupfer (1985).

Light Treatment

Clinical anecdotes and folklore have often referred to seasonal depressions associated with winter and a decrease in sunlight. The validity of this observation has been demonstrated by careful studies, and intervention with light has been the subject of careful studies by Rosenthal and Ware at NIMH and Lowe at Oregon. This treatment is still in the experimental phase, but the preliminary findings are encouraging.

Psychosurgery

Prefrontal lobotomy was widely used in the treatment of hospitalized chronic schizophrenics through the 1940s and 1950s. One consequence of the introduction of the neuroleptic drugs was an almost complete cessation of lobotomy treatments for schizophrenics.

Nevertheless, a very small number of patients receive psychosurgical procedures. It is estimated that this is in the range of 400 to 600 a year. Psychosurgery was among the special topics specified by congressional legislation in the mandate to the National Commission on the Protection of Subjects in Biomedical and Biobehavioral Research. Contrary to expectations, the commission did not recommend a ban on psychosurgery but took note of the uncontrolled but positive evidence from careful follow-up studies, particularly with the cingulotomy. This procedure is recommended for patients with intractable pain, severe excessive compulsive states, and severe depressions with intense emotional anguish, and for those failing to respond to other treatments.

Sleep Deprivation

Another unusual experimental treatment involves the patient staying up all night. Sleep deprivation produces relief of depression and at times a mild euphoria and hypomania in selected subjects. This effect is seldom persistent, and sleep deprivation does not seem to lend itself to routine clinical use.

Treatments for Specific Depressive Conditions

What follows is a review of the current status of research knowledge and treatment practice for the various depressive conditions as described in the DSM-III.

Organic Mood Disorders

The treatment of organic mood disorders requires a careful diagnosis and treatment plan for the preexisting affective disorder such as stroke, thyroid disease, Parkinsonism, etc. Often antidepressant drugs, usually tricyclics, are added when the affective disorder becomes severely symptomatic and/or disruptive of social functioning. The specific treatment plan for individual patients needs to be worked out in consultation with the neurologist or internist treating the organic illness.

Mood Disorders

Bipolar Disorders

Treatment of acute manic episode. Lithium is the major modality for the treatment of acute manic episode. There is fair agreement from research studies that the treatment of severe acute manic episodes involves lithium and/or neuroleptics. Studies have demonstrated that for acutely excited and overactive manic patients hospitalized for severe disturbed behavior, behavioral control is more rapidly achieved with neuroleptics. The best-studied neuroleptics have been chlorpromazine and haloperidol.

Lithium may be used alone for the treatment of the episode, if the patient is not severely disturbed, or in combination with a neuroleptic. The prolonged use of a neuroleptic-lithium combination is not recommended because of potential neurologic toxicity.

Another treatment strategy is to begin with a neuroleptic and then, as the patient's disruptive behavior comes under control, to decrease the neuroleptic as lithium treatment is prescribed and takes effect.

Treatment of acute depressive episode in bipolar disorders.   There are special problems with the treatment of acute depressive episodes because bipolar patients have a tendency to react to tricyclic and MAO inhibitors with a "switch" into manic and/or excited states. Many clinicians, therefore, combine lithium with an antidepressant to treat depressive episodes in individuals with bipolar disorder.

ECT has a role in the treatment of severely depressed bipolar patients, particularly if there are delusional features and also if there is a severe retardation. ECT is also valuable for severely suicidal patients.

Mixed and cycling bipolar patients.   A small minority of bipolar patients will experience frequent changes from depression to mania or will have a mixture of depressive symptoms within a single episode. These patients have a poor outcome and pose particular treatment problems. They often require treatment by a specialist in psychopharmacology.

Cyclothymia.   There is consensus that cyclothymia should best be considered as a variant of bipolar disorder, and treatment with lithium is recommended.

Long-term treatment of bipolar patients.   Among the most significant advances is the demonstrated value of long-term treatment to prevent relapse and recurrence. This has been the subject of the NIMH Consensus Development Conference (Kupfer 1984). This topic has been widely reviewed.

A significant percent of patients often receive a second drug in combination with lithium. This is often a tricyclic, less often a neuroleptic. The value of combined treatment has not been fully established by controlled studies.

Recent research indicates the value of carbamazepine (Tegretol) as an alternative drug for patients who do not respond to lithium or who develop toxicity, particularly thyroid and kidney problems, which may limit their continued use of lithium.

Depressive Disorders

Major depression.   Extensive research has demonstrated the value of considering major depression as heterogeneous.

1. Major Depression with Psychotic Features.   For major depression with psychotic features, the best available evidence indicates the value of combining a phenothiazine neuroleptic with a tricyclic. The most widely studied combination is prophenazine plus amitriptyline. Among the various subtypes of major depression, psychotic depression responds well to ECT. There is no basis from research evidence, at present, to determine whether the combination of tricyclic and neuroleptic drugs or ECT is most effective.
2. Major Depression with Melancholia.   Although the nosologic status of melancholia is still a source of controversy, researchers and clinicians widely agree that patients with the symptom complex that includes neurovegetative science, particularly early morning awakening, dural variation with worsening in the morning,

retardation, guilt, and weight loss respond very well to tricyclic antidepressants. Approximately 60 to 70 percent of such patients will respond in six to eight weeks.
3. Other Forms of Major Depression.   The majority of patients, particularly outpatients, with DSM major depressions do not have psychotic and/or melancholic features. There is no agreement as to how these patients are best characterized or subclassified. Various descriptive terms have been employed, such as "neurotic depression," "atypical depression," hysteroid dysphoria, mood-reactive depression, situational depression, and reactive depression. Various symptom complexes involving neurovegetative signs and loss of pleasure (anhedonia) have been identified and proposed to be especially responsive to MAO inhibitors or other treatments. These treatment recommendations require further verification.

A wide variety of treatments has been shown to be effective with patients with major depression but without psychotic and melancholic features. These treatments include drugs and special forms of brief psychotherapy. At the moment, the best recommendation is that the decision should be offered to the patient and the patient's wishes and preferences should be taken into account. However, if any treatment fails to produce improvement within three to four months, be it psychotherapy or psychopharmacology, the treatment plan should be reviewed and alternative treatments developed.

Dysthymic disorder.   Dysthymic disorder was a diagnostic category included for the first time in the DSM-III (American Psychiatric Association 1980) to include patients previously considered as "psychoneurotic depressive reaction" and also chronic patients sometimes called characterologic depression or depressive personality. Since the diagnostic categories are of relatively recent origin, there have only been a very few controlled clinical trials of drug treatment, notably imipramine.

There are also clinical reports of successful treatment with psychotherapy. It is not possible to make any treatment recommendations for dynamic patients from the available research literature.

Adjustment disorder with depressed mood.   A large number of patients present themselves to primary care settings, outpatient clinics, and mental health centers with symptoms of depression, often mixed with anxiety coming on after significant life events. Although the epidemiology indicates that these conditions are highly prevalent, no systematic studies have been undertaken as to their treatment. In clinical practice the patient receives various combinations of medications, most often benzodiazepines, and psychotherapy, often individual, group, or family counseling. Further research is needed to clarify the most effective treatments for such conditions. Inasmuch as most of these conditions tend to be self-limiting, the purpose of treatment is to reduce subjective distress and to promote social functioning until the period of coping and adaptation has been completed.

Uncomplicated bereavement.   In the DSM-III (American Psychiatric Association 1980) and the DSM-III-R (American Psychiatric Association 1987) uncomplicated bereavements are not considered mental disorders but are rather v codes. In clinical practice, many patients receive brief counseling techniques and supportive psychotherapy. Support programs, particularly widow-to-widow programs, are widely employed. Many patients receive sedative-hypnotic drugs and minor tranquilizers, usually benzodiazepines, for the distressing symptoms of grief and bereavement. Interestingly, there are no systematic studies of tricyclic or MAO inhibitors for patients with bereavement even though the clinical symptomatology resembles many features of major depression. Many psychiatrists believe that bereavement is a normal adaptive process, not reason for intensive treatment, particularly not with psychopharmacologic agents, but rather that the depressive features should be allowed to "run their course" as part of the adaptive process.

Conclusions

Over the past three decades, clinicians have gained experience with a variety of treatments for mood disorder. These new treatments have significantly improved the prognosis for mania and depression, and have significantly improved the prognosis for acute episodes, alleviated symptomatology, and reduced social disability. Although the overall incidence and prevalence of depression have not decreased, there has been a marked shift in the patterns of care. In addition to these therapeutic and public health consequences, the advent of these new treatments has had a major impact on our theoretical understanding. One important observation is that all three classes of antidepressant drugs—the amphetamines and related psychomotor stimulants, and monoamine oxidase inhibitors, and the tricyclic derivatives of imipramine—influence amine metabolism. This understanding has contributed to the realization of the importance of drugs as investigational tools.

Not only are effective new treatments available for the treatment of mood disorders, but also research on these treatments has yielded significantly methodological and theoretical advances. Methodologically, the introduction of the new drugs has provided a major stimulus to the development of experimental methods in clinical research. The double-blind, placebo-controlled clinical trial has gained wide acceptance in drug research, and its success has had significant impact on the quality of all clinical investigations in psychiatry. Control groups, quantitative assessments of behavior, objective techniques for observation, application of advanced statistical techniques, and use of computer technology all have entered clinical psychiatric research during the past two decades, in part as a response to the need for evaluation of the new drugs (Levine et al. 1971). The past decade has also produced a major theory, the amine theory of affective disorders, which was derived from pharmacologic studies.

Similar considerations apply to the place of psychotherapy. The results of the recently reported NIMH Collaborative Study indicate the important role of psychotherapy, particularly for ambulatory patients who are not bipolar or psychotic. However, it is important to emphasize a number of limitations in the possible conclusion regarding the place of psychotherapy in the treatment of depression. All the studies, including those by NIMH, were conducted on ambulatory patients. There are no systematic studies evaluating the efficacy of psychotherapy for hospitalized patients, who are usually more severely disabled and often suicidal.

It is important to recognize that these investigations should not be interpreted as implying that *all* forms of medications in psychotherapy are effective for depression. One significant feature of recent advances in psychotherapy research is the development of psychotherapies specifically designed for depression and of time-limited and brief duration. Just as there are specific forms of medication, there are specific forms of psychotherapy. It would be an error to conclude that all forms of psychotherapy are efficacious for all forms of depression.

These therapeutic investigations on both drugs and psychotherapy indicate that for outpatient ambulatory depression there are a range of effective treatments, including a number of forms of brief psychotherapy as well as various medications, notably MAO inhibitors and tricyclic antidepressants. These therapeutic advances have contributed to our understanding of the complex interplay of psychosocial and biological factors in the etiology and pathogenesis of depression.

Chapter 161

Goals of Treatment

Aside from the maintenance of life, the first obligation of any clinician is to alleviate suffering. All other therapeutic goals become secondary if the pain of the illness so overwhelms the patient that he prefers not to go on living or is so absorbed with his torment that even rudimentary activities are beyond his capacity. Depression is one of those disorders that may in some individuals reduce existence to such a painful state that suicide becomes a reasonable alternative. The depth of despair, complicated by the inability to sleep, to think clearly, or to feel the energy to perform any activity, makes the depressed patient wish to be rid of himself and his misery. Author John Bunyan vividly remembered his own melancholy: "I was both a burden and a terror to myself, nor did I ever so know, as now, what it was to be weary of my life, and yet afraid to die. How gladly would I have been anything but myself" (James 1902, p. 133).

Even when the individual recovers from the acute episode, the memory of the pain may endure, and the fear that he will once again fall ill may cause severe difficulties in his life. In concert with these emotional scars, the individual may make certain decisions during his acute episode that will affect him later on. This is particularly true of manic individuals whose lack of judgment often results in unfortunate consequences, but it may also be seen in delusionally depressed patients.

The immediate goal of therapy is thus to reduce the intensity of the dysphoric state and its concomitant symptoms. The longer-range goal is to prevent future recurrences. While the prognosis for the acute episode of affective illness is usually good, the long-term course of the illness often includes future decompensations or the persistence of milder but chronic mood alterations. To have suffered a major depressive episode is to have been affected at the very core of one's being, and this experience cannot help but influence one's existence after recovery. Similarly, the eruption of a manic episode, with its fearful lack of control and outrageous behavior for which one is later ashamed, together with the prospect of other similar episodes, certainly alters how one faces the future. In those instances in which a clinical episode follows a significant loss or disappointment, the individual may recover from the agony of the acute disorder but must now face life without an important source of gratification or meaning, which leads to a more chronic state of dysphoria and a greater vulnerability to exacerbations. The approach to treatment, therefore, is naturally divided into a consideration of both the current episode and the course of the illness.

Evaluation of the patient during a current episode should include a review of biological, psychological, and social factors. The clinician should first determine what sort of depression he is being asked to treat. Depressive symptoms may occur in a variety of conditions but may so preoccupy the patient that the primary illness is obscured. Depressive and manic syndromes may result from purely physiologic or organic disturbances whose treatment reduces the secondary affective symptomatology. Therefore, a thorough medical as well as psychiatric history is a mandatory part of of any clinical assessment.

However, in those affective disturbances that may result from hidden malignancies or metabolic disorders, there is often a different clinical "feel" to the dysphoria or elation than there is in primary affective disorders. The patient is bewildered by his altered mood; he feels his change in feeling state imposed on him in an ego-alien manner, as if he has been "drugged." Further, he cannot identify any change in his environment or his inner life to account for his change in mood. Finally, his estimation of himself remains stable, and he does not usually describe either the fall in self-regard or the grandiosity seen in a primary affective disorder. His depression appears without content, and he is more disturbed by how his mood interferes with his everyday functioning than by self-depreciating or self-enhancing ideas.

As the patient recounts his story, the narrative is sifted for meaningful connections that may lead to an understanding of what caused this particular individual to fall ill at this particular time. The manner in which the individual relates his history, as well as the values, biases, and judgments that he reveals in the telling, is as pertinent as are the facts in evaluating possible etiologic agents and eventual treatment strategies. This initial goal of treatment is to comprehend the patient's illness through his own view of experience so as to pinpoint those precipitating factors that appear to have resulted in a breakdown of the patient's customary mode of being.

This task is not easily accomplished, and the problems that are really burdening the patient may not be readily apparent. Some depressed patients may be so overwhelmed by their own suffering that they cannot give a reliable history; others may lack sufficient "psychological mindedness" so that they have difficulty looking inward and piecing together their memory of significant events. Finally, some depressives really do not know what caused them to fall ill. In a study of 40 severely depressed individuals admitted to a research ward at NIMH, Leff et al. (1970) found that most could not reconstruct a precipitant until after at least three weeks of intensive contact with a therapist. These authors also found that precipitants had to be understood in terms of the individual patient's worldview so that what might appear to the objective observer as a trivial event could resonate deeply with the threats to the patient's idea of self and cause of profound sense of loss or deprivation.

In piecing together the patient's story, particular attention is given to how a precipitant, when present, combined with the patient's specific personality to culminate in a clinical episode. Studies into the development of depressive episodes report that the clinical entity does not appear immediately but gradually emerges as the individual reacts to a provoking agent over a period of days or weeks. Depression is thus conceptualized as an evaluation of one's psychological situation following a significant deprivation of a source of security or gratification. This painful state would thus arise in most situations that deprive someone of a significant source of meaning or satisfaction. Therefore, dysphoria following the death of a spouse or some other major loss is both understandable and expected.

Gradually, the individual adapts to the deprivation by finding other sources of meaning or by creating other realignments of aspirations and expectations. However, clinically significant episodes of depression demonstrate that, in addition to an external deprivation, the provoking event has caused a transformation in the individual's perception of himself. Sadness or grief may be seen as responses to an impoverished environment while depression is a reaction not only to an external reality that has become intolerable but also to a sense of self that is equally intolerable. In describing a depressive reaction resulting from a narcissistic disappointment, the philosopher Kierkegaard (1899) wrote eloquently of the transformation of the self in depression: "When the ambitious man whose watchword is 'either Caesar or nothing' does not become Caesar, he is in despair thereat. But this signifies something else, namely, that precisely because he did not become Caesar, he cannot endure to be himself" (Kierkegaard 1899, p. 152). His analysis of depression following the loss of a love relationship equally focuses on the sense of self:

> A young girl is in despair over love so she despairs over her lover, because he died, or because he was unfaithful to her. . . . No, she is in despair over herself. This self of hers, if it had become his beloved, she would have been rid of in the most blissful way. . . . This self of hers is now a torment when it has to be a self without "him" (Kierkegaard 1899, p. 153).

Freud (1917) made a similar observation when he noted that in contrast to grief, depression presents with an inner impoverishment, irrational self-reproaches, and a lack of clarity regarding what has been lost in the environment. It may well be this transformation in the sense of self that gives depression its pathologic character and may prevent successful resolution following an external provoking event.

Depression may be seen as pathologic when it does not resolve after a considerable amount of time. For example, Clayton and Darvish (1979) studied depressive symptoms after bereavement in 149 widows and widowers. They found the expected presence of depressive symptoms one month after bereavement in a large percentage of their sample. However, when the group was reevaluated one year later, only 16 percent still exhibited significant depressive symptomatology. In their analysis of these data, Clayton and Darvish found that the only significant differential characteristic between the group that remained depressed and the group in whom the symptoms had abated was a history of psychiatric illness prior to the death of the spouse. It may be speculated that the chronic depressed group could not work through their period of normal mourning because of preexisting personality limitations in dealing with the stress of loss.

Other pathologic reactions to a provoking agent differ in terms of both intensity and the nature of the precipitant. The former describes those instances in which an individual is totally overcome following some frustration or loss, which would indicate an excessive reliance on some external factor for maintenance of psychological equilibrium and a precarious lack of psychological resiliency. The latter pertains to a large percentage of depressive episodes in which the extent of the reaction does not appear commensurate with the acutal deprivation, which may hold an idiosyncratic but highly relevant meaning for the individual in terms of a wished-for sense of self.

In their study of precipitants in depression, for example, Leff et al. (1970) cite the case of a woman who tried to kill herself and began to be severely depressed after her husband, in the course of a heated argument, accused her of being "a whore" like her mother. This particular insult, coming at the time that it did, caused the patient's sense of self as a virtuous, moral person to crumble, and as she doubted her needed identity, she lost an image that supported her fragile narcissism. This loss of an idea of the self initiated her depression.

Brown and Harris (1978) came to similar conclusions based on a study of a large sample of depressed women in England. They found that the precipitants of depressive episodes all involved a loss, if the term *loss* could be widened to include not only that of a person but also that of a role or an idea. As an illustration, they report on a woman who became depressed when she learned that her husband had had an affair some years previously. While there was no material loss, this knowledge affected a loss of her previous conception of her husband, her marriage, and herself.

This digression into the nature of precipitants was prompted by the need to gauge the type and magnitude of these events for the purposes of treatment. Healthy individuals who have experienced a severe personal loss can be expected to develop some depressive symptoms but to readjust in time to their relatively healthy premorbid behavior. Those individuals who show prolonged, excessive, or idiosyncratic reactions to a deprivation will require longer and more intensive treatment if they are to be restored to a higher level of functioning.

The manner in which the depression begins and the relationship of the episode to current and past functioning are helpful in exposing both the immediate precipitating factors and the long-term vulnerability factors that culminated in a depressive episode. Brown and Harris (1978), in the epidemiologic study of 458 working-class women in England cited above, were able to document both provoking agents and vulnerability factors in depressed subjects. Provoking agents could be summarized as threats to a desired idea of oneself in the face of ongoing difficulties such as poor housing or financial problems. While Brown and Harris found that most of the women in their sample had experienced a provoking agent of causal importance within one year of onset, only one out of five women with such negative experiences became clinically depressed. Brown and Harris concluded that these affected women were in some way more susceptible to the provoking agent, and they were able to isolate four characteristics that differentiated the depressed group, suggesting the sources of predisposition. The characteristics, called *vulnerability factors*, were 1) lack of an intimate, confiding relationship with a husband or boyfriend, 2) presence of three or more children under age 14 living at home, 3) lack of employment away from home, and 4) loss of mother before age 11.

One of the relevant findings of this study is that the onset of depression, while frequently following a specific provoking agent, is more likely to affect individuals rendered vulnerable by past events and current hardships. Treatment of affected individuals should follow an evaluation of current stresses in the individual's life since these not only may contribute to the illness but also may alter the ideal response to therapeutic intervention. Similarly, past history regarding not only prior stresses but also previous level of functioning is important in formulating a treatment plan and eventual goals.

The patient's general personality functioning is also of prime importance in determining the response to treatment. Individuals who exhibit a certain resiliency and a willingness to fight off the negative thoughts that accompany a depressive episode will do better than those who seem to collapse in the face of dysphoria and rely extensively on others to make them feel better. Often, individuals who succumb to depression have an inflated narcissistic sense of entitlement and expectations in the demands they put on others or on themselves. Such individuals require a great deal from their environment and feel a sense of moral outrage and victimization when the world does not coincide with their desires. This narcissistic vulnerability complicates their recovery just as it often predisposes them to illness. The lack of a willingness to find or try alternative ways of perceiving oneself and one's possibilities also presents obstacles to effective treatment. Rigidity in beliefs coupled with strong inhibitions may keep the depressive in a life-style that perpetuates feelings of emptiness and discontent and precludes the possibility of gratification.

Other personality traits often seen in depressives include excessive interpersonal dependency, extreme ambitiousness for unrealistic achievements, and the need for a particularly moral view of oneself (Arieti and Bemporad 1980). When these means of maintaining security and self-esteem are challenged by environmental changes, a clinical episode may result, manifesting a painful reestimation of one's self and situation.

Another significant area to be considered in arriving at a workable treatment plan is the amount and quality of social supports in the immediate environment. The availability of close friends or relatives who take genuine interest in the patient's welfare can mitigate the sense of isolation and loneliness that engulfs some depressives. The possibility of productive activity can help the depressive feel worthwhile despite the illness and can divert his attention from his inner pain. The patient's ability to use social supports must also be evaluated. Some depressives have not developed adequate social skills and may not be able to elicit the needed response from environmental figures. Others, out of pride or shame, will hide their dysphoria from friends or family who could be a great comfort. Yet others may drive away potential sources of support by a constant flow of demands and complaints.

The presence of social networks may at times be a mixed blessing for the depressed individuals. Responsibility for the care of young children may force a depressed woman to fight against suicidal wishes or a sense of emptiness, but at the same time it may further her feeling of being trapped in an ungratifying way of life. Similarly, the presence of a caring spouse may ameliorate the feeling of isolation while simultaneously increasing the burden of guilt over causing the other distress or of shame over not living up to marital responsibilities.

A subsequent study of Brown and Harris (Brown et al. 1986) indicates that many individuals who become clinically depressed had been forced to make choices in their past that eventually led to their being locked into ungratifying lives. The authors were intrigued by their earlier finding that early loss of mother was a vulnerability factor in their sample of depressed women. To investigate this variable further, they studied depressed and nondepressed women who had lost their mothers (by death or separation of over one year) prior to age 17.

The depressed group reported life events subsequent to the loss of their mothers that differed markedly from those of the nondepressed controls. Following maternal loss, the future depressed group was placed in foster homes, institutions, or with unwilling relatives, which the authors describe as "lack of care" experiences. These living arrangements were so unfavorable that early marriage and pregnancy often served as a means of escape. However, these hasty marriages did not allow for a careful consideration of one's mate, leading to an unsuitable husband who did not serve as a confidant. Motherhood at an early age also precluded obtaining an education, which would have ensured future employment. Ultimately, these women found themselves in ungratifying marriages, burdened by children, unable to compete for employment, plagued by financial worries, and thus more vulnerable to depression.

The group of women who also lost their mothers but did not become depressed as adults gave a history of different life events. Usually these women were in better financial circumstances at the time of mother loss so that they were kept at home in the family of origin, often with a maternal substitute. They did not seek to escape from these more favorable situations and so were able to finish school and postpone marriage. A few did become pregnant premaritally but did not use this as a means of entering into an inappropriate union. Therefore, the nondepressed group did not report a series of events subsequent to parental loss that culminated in adult lives that offered little meaning or opportunity.

In agreement with the findings in this study, depressed adults seen in clinical practice often reveal a history of having made safe but unrewarding "choices" that end up in a bleak existence that affords little joy or satisfaction. A dead-end career, an unsuitable mate, and overwhelming family responsibilities are often realistic factors that increase vulnerability to and perpetuation of depressed disorders and must be considered in a treatment plan. Significant environmental figures not infrequently sabotage health-promoting behavior and unwittingly attempt to maintain a comfortable relationship with the patient, which promotes relapses or interferes with improvement.

Summary

These are some of the factors that are to be considered, other than diagnosis, in the treatment of depressed patients. Having assessed 1) the relative magnitude of a provoking agent and its meaning to the individual, 2) the premorbid health and level of functioning, 3) the ability of the patient to aid in his own recovery, and 4) the nature of social supports, we suggest two courses of treatment that may be selected. One is to treat only the acute episode; the other is to attempt a more extensive alteration in the patient in order to prevent further difficulties. This choice will obviously depend on a variety of factors. The patient may not require long-term treatment, having exhibited an essentially healthy premorbid level of functioning and, after being subjected to a markedly significant stressor, indicating a good prognosis following recovery (see adjustment disorders). Some patients do not want long-term therapy and only desire relief from the current episode, even when they have suffered from depressive disorders in the past. Other individuals are simply incapable of participating in insight-oriented therapy or may not tolerate maintenance drug management.

The clinician's personal preference for treatment also plays a role in this choice. Depression is seen by some as only a biochemical abnormality, the expression of which is genetically determined. These clinicians may opt for somatic treatment of the episode. Others view depression as entirely the result of a pathologic personality that cannot adapt to the normal vicissitudes of life. These clinicians will perceive anything short of an extensive character change as futile. The majority of clinicians are somewhere in between these two extreme positions but may lean toward one or the other, thus favoring one form of treatment.

Optimal treatment, however, should be based not on personal preferences but on factual data resulting from objective studies. These data are gradually coalescing into a useful basis of clinical knowledge. As we will explore in this manual, the type of treatment chosen rests on particular indications with different treatment modalities appearing more effective in ameliorating different aspects of affective illness. Unfortunately, reality factors beyond the wishes of either patient or clinician may determine the style of treatment received. The availability of clinicians to see patients for frequent sessions over an extended period may be limited in some areas or to economically deprived populations. Limitations on insurance coverage may determine the number of visits allowed to a patient. The high rate of depressive disorders in the face of the paucity of mental health resources has prompted the development of briefer therapies, which aim to go beyond the acute episode to altering basic beliefs or social functions that are thought to foster vulnerability for chronicity or recurrence of depression.

Chapter 162

Diagnostic Considerations in the Treatment of Mood Disorders

Current nosologic conceptualizations of mood disorders embrace a wide range that subsumes many patients who were previously regarded as schizophrenic, personality disordered, neurotic, hypochondriacal, or demented (Akiskal 1983a). This new affective spectrum—which is reflected in the broad concept of mood disorders adopted by DSM-III (American Psychiatric Association 1980) and its revised version—has developed from rigorously conducted studies in the community and among symptomatic volunteers and patient populations. While the emergence of potent therapeutic technologies—both somatic and psychologic—has certainly played some role in broadening the boundaries of mood disorders, this renewed attention to the entire diagnosable range of mood disorders cannot be said to merely reflect therapeutic fashion. Phenomenology, family history, laboratory findings, and course have all been used to support the affective membership of subgroups within this spectrum. Because these new nosologic concepts have important predictive validity for treatment decisions, it would be instructive to devote a chapter to discussing recent clinical research endeavors in the diagnosis, delimitation, and classification of mood disorders. Aspects other than diagnosis relevant to treatment decisions (e.g., early loss, suicidal preoccupations, adequacy of social support, concurrent medical illness) are considered in other chapters.

To facilitate communication with U.S. clinicians, the framework developed by DSM-III-R (American Psychiatric Association 1987) will form the basis of this discussion. Whenever pertinent to treatment decisions, parallels will be drawn to other nosologic systems.

The Impact of New Treatments on the Diagnosis of Mood Disorders

The development of new and powerful techniques to mitigate the suffering of the affectively ill has led to an increased readiness by clinicians to consider affective diagnoses (Akiskal and Cassano 1983). It has also facilitated the ambulatory management of the affectively ill, many of whom are now able to lead socially rewarding lives. The influence of lithium salts in changing diagnostic styles in psychiatry has probably been more far-reaching than that of any other single agent. Unequivocal evidence for lithium's efficacy in manic depressive illness and safe guidelines for its clinical use have helped in redefining as affective much of what was formerly in the realm of schizophrenic psychoses (Pope and Lipinski 1978). Coupled with such developments, artists, politicians, and other prominent citizens have revealed that they have sought treatment for mood disorders, thereby decreasing the stigma attached to this group of mental disorders. Accordingly, a larger number of people with dysphoric and unstable mood are willing to seek assistance from primary care physicians, psychiatrists, and other mental health professionals. This has led to the emergence of mood clinics and other specialized units for mood disorders in many university and private settings; such facilities are devoted to a systematic evaluation of new subtypes of mood disorders or of subtypes inadequately appreciated in the past. Thus, research clinicians are being increasingly exposed to a wide spectrum of mood disorders—from manic psychosis to cyclothymic and related temperaments, from recurrent to dysthymic depressions, and from the classical psychotic melancholia to the mild depressions presenting with somatic complaints; increasing attention is also being paid to mood disorders encountered in medical settings, in children and the elderly, in substance abusers, in eating disorders, and in various other conditions traditionally considered to be "characterologic."

Lifetime Risk for Subtypes of Mood Disorders

The above observations, based on patients presenting for treatment in various clinical settings, have been supplemented by new epidemiologic studies (reviewed in Barrett and Rose, 1986). These studies, unlike their precursors in earlier decades, have utilized interview schedules that tend to elicit syndromal-level disorders rather than depressed or dysphoric mood, which is part of the human condition. According to current U.S. estimates, one out of four individuals will experience some form of affective disturbance during their lifetime. Many of these will be relatively mild and brief experiences for which the sufferer may not even seek help. The importance of these "minor" episodes—which are at least twice as common in women compared with men—lies in the fact that they may constitute a risk factor for subsequent "major" episodes (Akiskal et al. 1978). Major depressive disorders—which could be single episode or recurrent—probably afflict no more than 12 percent of the population (Helgason 1979); the risk is higher in women in a 2:1 ratio. The lifetime risk for bipolar forms is 1.2 percent (somewhat higher than that for schizophrenia), with a sex ratio that is almost even, only slightly favoring women.

If one were to judge from the above epidemiologic figures, roughly one out of 10 clinically depressed individuals would be expected to belong to the bipolar group. However, if one were to focus on primary mood disorders and consider the fact that hypomania is easily overlooked in epidemiologic as well as clinical studies, the unipolar-bipolar ratio may be closer to 4:1 (Akiskal 1983a). There have been recent claims (Akiskal and Mallya 1987; Egeland 1983) that this ratio could be as low as 1:1.

The Nosologic Schema in DSM-III-R

The broad range of mood disorders seen in community and various treatment settings is reflected in DSM-III-R category (Table 1). This approach—subsuming the entire spectrum of mood disorders in private and public, ambulatory and inpatient settings—is one of the innovative features of the new APA classification. Major depressions can be further qualified with respect to seasonality, melancholic or psychotic features, and chronicity; attenuated intermittent expressions are described under the dysthymic rubric. Bipolar disorder can also range from milder cyclothymic mood swings to severe psychotic disorder with mood-incongruent features; seasonal features, when present, should also be specified for bipolar disorders.

In the original version of DSM-III, "atypical" variants were recognized and reserved for patients not meeting the criteria specified for the major and attenuated disorders. To avoid confusion with the British concept of atypical depression (Sargent 1962; West and Dally 1959)—which refers to depressions with various admixtures of anxiety, hypersomnia, hyperphagia, and reverse diurnal variation—DSM-III-R has adopted the "not otherwise specified" (NOS) rubric for mood disorders failing to meet the criteria for the more classical prototypes. There are now two NOS subtypes—a pure depressive one, and a bipolar condition for those cyclic major depressions that, during the elevated periods, do not go beyond hypomania (subsyndromal or mild manic symptoms of shorter duration).

The distinction between major and specific attenuated subtypes depends on syndrome depth and duration. In dysthymic and cyclothymic disorders, a partial affective syndrome—consisting of subdepressive manifestations in the former, and subdepressive and hypomanic manifestations in the latter—is maintained, either intermittently or continuously, for at least two years. Their onset is typically in adolescence or childhood. Major disorders, which are more likely to begin later in life, require the presence of either a full manic or a depressive syndrome—sustained for at least one and two weeks, respectively—and an episodic course, typically permitting recovery or remission from episodes. DSM-III-R now recognizes that 15–20 percent of major depressions fail to achieve full symptomatic recovery for which the qualifying phrases "chronic" residual and "in partial remission" will apply. These will no longer be considered dysthymic, as was the misleading convention in DSM-III.

The distinctions described above are not hard and fast because full-blown bipolar disorder is often superimposed on cyclothymia, which tends to persist after resolution of manic or major depressive epidodes. Likewise, recent evidence indicates that dysthymia may precede depressions by many years (Akiskal 1983b; Kovacs et al. 1984), and dysthymia and major depression often coexist (Keller et al. 1983). Furthermore, many major depressives—in some studies, as many as 30 percent—may subsequently

Table 1.   DSM-III-R Categories of Mood Disorders*

Bipolar Disorders	Depressive Disorders
Bipolar disorder	Major depression
Mixed	Single episode
Manic	Recurrent
Depressed	Dysthymia
Cyclothymia	Depressive disorder not otherwise specified
Bipolar disorder not otherwise specified	

*Summarized from the American Psychiatric Association's *Diagnostic and Statistical Manual of Mental Disorders* (1987)

develop manic episodes and are reclassified as bipolar (Akiskal et al. 1983b; Rao 1977; Strober and Carlson 1982). Finally, unexpected "crossing" from dysthymia to bipolar episodes has also been described, suggesting that some forms of dysthymia are sub-affective or milder precursors of bipolar disorder (Akiskal 1983b).

The clinical significance of the above observations lies in the fact that many of the DSM-III-R subtypes of mood disorders are not "pure" entities and that considerable overlap and switches in polarity take place. These considerations provide some explanation, for instance, as to why lithium may be effective in some apparently "unipolar" depressions (Kuper et al. 1975; Mendels 1976), whether major or dysthymic. There are also emerging data to suggest that bipolars whose premorbid and interepisodic adjustment is cyclothymic—especially when predominantly hyperthymic in temperament—are at risk for tricyclic-induced rapid-cycling—that is, rapid succession (at least four per year) of major episodes (Akiskal and Mallya 1987; Kukopulos et al. 1983).

The Concept of Major Depressive Disorder

The DSM-III-R diagnosis of major depression requires 1) dysphoric mood or decreased interest in usual activities and 2) at least four additional classic depressive signs and symptoms, 3) which must be sustained for at least two weeks, and 4) which cannot be explained by a process known to cause depressive symptoms, such as normative bereavement or certain medical conditions commonly associated with depression.

This definition raises several questions. The first is conceptual. Should the rubric of major depression be limited to depressions of unknown etiology (e.g., without documented medical causes)? The DSM-III-R approach has basically taken the posture that, whenever etiology is known, the condition should be diagnosed as an organic mood disorder. The problem with this approach lies in the fact that many common medical factors associated with depression—for example, reserpine—do not seem to be causative in the etiologic sense but as triggering agents in otherwise predisposed individuals (Akiskal and McKinney 1973; Goodwin and Bunney 1971). This is analogous to the situation with life events, which are no longer used in making distinctions between subtypes of depression; these events are now believed to precipitate depression in vulnerable individuals and do not seem to be limited to so-called reactive and neurotic depressions. To be consistent, future revisions of DSM should consider coding medical precipitants on Axis III—already reserved for concurrent medical conditions having a bearing on treatment—just as psychosocial precipitants are coded on Axis IV.

The second problem with the DSM-III-R definition of major depression is in its requirement of dysphoric mood or anhedonia as a prerequisite for diagnosing a major depressive disorder. This may disqualify a large universe of the affectively ill seen in private care medical settings from the depressive rubric. Many of these patients present with somatic complaints; deny subjective change in mood, anhedonia, and many other psychological symptoms of depression; and have low scores on depression rating scales, yet they exhibit validating criteria for primary mood disorder (Akiskal 1983a; Kielholz et al. 1982). They have phasic course and family histories loaded with affective disorder; clinical experience suggests that they would respond well to thymoleptic agents and, when inadequately treated, that they might engage in serious suicidal behavior during prospective observation.

The third problem with the DSM-III-R definition of major depression has to do with the question of setting the threshold at which a constellation of depressive manifestations can be said to constitute a condition distinct from the ordinary "blues." In the current definition, it is sufficient for an individual to experience—in response to a setback, for example—lowering of the spirits, self-doubt, difficulty in sleep and concentration, and decreased sexual interest for 14 days to qualify for a major depressive diagnosis of mild severity. Some authorities would consider such a condition to represent more of a minor depression, probably no more than an adjustment disorder. It would appear that criteria other than signs and symptoms and duration would be necessary to differentiate clinical depression from adjustment reactions to life situations. The following considerations—adopted only in part by DSM-III-R—can serve as guidelines to make such a differentiation.

1. The clinical disorder is usually incapacitating. Hitherto, much attention has been paid to interpersonal consequences. Recent evidence indicates that measurable deficits in work performance are often early manifestations (DeLisio et al. 1986). Afflicted individuals are also unable to benefit from leisure—hence, the well-known futility of "prescribing" vacations.
2. Depressive illness is usually perceived as a break from one's usual or premorbid self. This may be so striking that sufferers may feel they are losing their minds. This feature may prove particularly useful in differentiating clinical depression from uncomplicated grief (Clayton et al. 1974).
3. Marked psychomotor retardation (which is almost never observed in normative reactions to loss) (Clayton et al. 1974; Widlocher 1983) can be considered a sturdy clinical marker for clinical depression.
4. Recurrence—especially periodicity (seasonality or regular recurrence)—is characteristic of mood disorder (Akiskal and Mallya 1987; Zis and Goodwin 1979). While one should be aware of so-called anniversary reactions, recent data (Clayton et al. 1974) suggest that severe anniversary reactions do not occur in uncomplicated bereavement.
5. Consecutive-generation family histories for mood disorder—especially when "loaded"—are characteristic of affective illness. For instance, in a University of Tennessee study (Akiskal 1983a) where "minor" or "neurotic" depressives were prospectively followed, it was found that such pedigrees predicted the development of major episodes.

The Partial Deletion of the Neurotic-Endogenous Dichotomy

Although DSM-III deleted the category of "neurotic depression"—now reclassified under both dysthymic and major depressive disorders—the endogenous subtype was retained as a qualifying phrase for major depressions, except that it is now evoked under the classical concept of melancholia. What is the basis of these far-reaching decisions that have received much criticism in North America and especially in Europe?

Two independent studies (Akiskal et al. 1978; Klerman et al. 1979) have shown that neurotic depression, defined as a "reactive" (i.e., precipitated), nonpsychotic depression of mild to moderate severity with predominant anxiety and characterologic pathology, does not constitute a distinct nosologic entity. While such a presentation is common in clinical practice, the prospective follow-up course of these patients is extremely heterogeneous. For instance, in the Akiskal et al. study (1978), the most common outcomes were as follows: 8 percent evolved into panic disorder and 8 percent into somatization disorder, while 18 percent developed manic, 24 percent psychotic depressive, and 36 percent melancholic episodes. Characterologic patholgy did not distinguish between these groups, suggesting that this was an orthogonal dimension distinct from mood disorder (and thus suggesting the value of a separate axis to code character disorder). The progression of a precipitated, relatively mild depression (reactive illness) to a severe psychotic depression with melancholic autonomy during prospective observation suggested that melancholic illnesses may have their onset in milder depressions, that neurotic and psychotic depressions do not refer to distinct illnesses but to disorders differing in severity, and that the presence of precipitating stress carries little diagnostic weight in differentiating subtypes of depression (although the absence of such stress might be used to support a melancholic level of major depression).

The current thinking is that what counts in the characterization of melancholic states is not only their autonomy from stresses that may have precipitated them, but also their unresponsiveness to other environmental input. This is embodied in Klein's concept of "endogenomorphic depression" (1974), which could be precipitated and mild while exhibiting disturbances of hedonic mechanisms refractory to current interpersonal contexts. These are not merely theoretical adumberations but considerations of practical import. Many authorities believe that autonomy dictates the need to use somatic approaches to reverse the maladaptive autonomy and restore response to interpersonal feedback; that is, psychotherapeutic approaches are deemed largely ineffective until the autonomy is somatically lysed.

Melancholia, then, appears to be a clinical common pathway, developing in the setting of major depressions (Akiskal 1983a). However, on occasion it may also arise from minor depressions. It may acquire psychotic depth in about 15 percent of patients, for reasons that are not fully understood at this time. These psychotic depressions, especially when early in onset, often represent initial episodes of bipolar disorder (Akiskal et al. 1983; Strober and Carlson 1982). When psychotic depression develops for the first time after age 40, it represents the most severe expression of major depressive illness. Unlike its bipolar counterparts, which typically last a few months, these more "involutional" depressions tend to linger on for several years. Despite attempts to suggest a neurochemical uniqueness—based on the need for neuroleptic treatment in the acute phase of many of these patients—familial and other external validators have failed to support psychotic depression as a separate entity (Winokur et al. 1986), hence the decision of DSM-III and its revised version to use "psychosis" merely as a qualifier for major depression.

Chronic and Dysthymic Depressions

DSM-III and its revised version recognize the existence of chronic depressions that are typically of subsyndromal severity and intermittent in course. Current estimates are that 15–20 percent of depressions pursue such a chronic course. Residual symptomatic, interpersonal, and vocational disturbances have been reported in the interepisodic phase of many depressives (Cassano et al. 1983). Findings from the NIMH Collaborative Study on Depressive Disorders (Keller et al. 1983) have revealed that nearly a third of major depressions seen in university hospital or clinic settings have an underlying low-grade depressive pattern; this condition, dubbed as "double-depression," rather than being a nosologic category, should be viewed as a descriptive term for major depression arising from the substrate of a low-grade and often lifelong depression. It is important to recognize the affective basis of these low-grade, residual interepisodic depressive manifestations because some—including "characterologic" disturbances—may show favorable response to competent pharmacotherapy (Akiskal 1983b; Kocsis et al. 1985).

Studies conducted at the University of Tennessee (reviewed in Akiskal 1983b) have revealed that about a third of chronic depressions represent residual symptomatic phases of primary major unipolar episodes typically occurring after the age of 40 years; in another third, clinically characterized as "characterologic depressions," they conform to the double-depression pattern and are usually early in age of onset; and in a final third they are secondary to nonaffective disorders such as incapacitating anxiety disorders, somatization disorder, and certain chronically disabling medical-neurologic conditions of childhood or adolescent onset. In many of these chronic depressive groups, hostile dependence and a pessimistic outlook and attitude are woven into the personality structure.

Clearly, then, chronic depressions are quite heterogeneous. Unlike DSM-III, which had subsumed all these conditions under "dysthymic disorder," DSM-III-R formally distinguishes between major depressive disorder, chronic or residual type, and dysthymic disorder. In the latter category, further subdivision along early or late and primary versus secondary subtypes is suggested. While much more research lies ahead of us in this complex area, such distinctions underlie the belief that differential therapeutic responsiveness can be demonstrated for some of these subtypes. As an example of such potential predictive validity for specific dysthymic subtypes, Table 2 summarizes proposed criteria for thymoleptic responsive early-onset primary dysthymic disorder that have emerged from University of Tennessee research.

The Classification of Bipolar Disorders

Kraepelin (1921) had subsumed the majority of the affectively ill requiring hospitalization under the manic-depressive rubric. This included even those who had never experienced distinct elevated periods. Leonhard challenged this "unitary" concept by separating the group of monopolar depressives (no excited periods) from the bipolars (those with history for excited periods). Leonhard's position was partially supported in the 1960s by three independent investigators working in different coun-

---

Table 2.　Clinical Characterization of Dysthymia as a Subaffective Disorder*

Phenomenologic features

- Low-grade subsyndromal depression
- Early onset (<21 years)
- Intermittent fluctuating course
- Habitually anhedonic and hypersomnolent
- Psychomotor inertia
- Above signs and symptoms worse in morning

Schneiderian criteria for depressive personality

- Gloomy, pessimistic, humorless, or incapable of fun
- Quiet, passive, and indecisive
- Skeptical, hypercritical, or complaining
- Brooding and given to worry
- Conscientious or self-disciplining
- Self-critical, self-reproaching, and self-derogatory
- Preoccupied with inadequacy, failure, and negative events to the point of morbid enjoyment of one's failures

*Adapted from Akiskal (1983b)

tries (Angst 1966; Perris 1966; Winokur et al. 1969). The dichotomy had a dominant influence on research in mood disorders, and many differences between the two types of illness were described (Goodwin and Bunney 1973). For instance, bipolars were reported to have equal sex ratios, earlier age of onset, and shorter but more frequent episodes, usually with retarded-hypersomnic pattern. Biologically, bipolars were more likely to be "augmenters" on the average evoked-potential technique, to have lower platelet monoamine oxidase (MAO) activity, to develop hypomanic responses during tricyclic treatment, and to benefit from lithium salts even when depressed. More recent findings suggest that the differences between bipolar and unipolar disorders are not that sharp (Akiskal 1983c).

For instance, the existence of "soft" bipolars, who symptomatically occupy an intermediate position between "typical" bipolars (with mania) and those with major recurrent depressions (but not elevated periods), is now well documented (Akiskal and Mallya 1987; Cassano et al. 1988). The family histories of unipolars and bipolars in more recent studies have not been shown to differ as much as they did in the older studies (see, for instance, Gershon et al. 1982).

Some of the former suggestions regarding the unipolar-bipolar dichotomy may have resulted from the pratice of subsuming all nonbipolar depressions under the unipolar rubic. Recent data (Bland et al. 1986) suggest that recurrent and nonrecurrent major depressives are different in familial background. It would appear that bipolar and at least some recurrent depressions are on a nosologic continuum (Akiskal 1983c; Klerman 1981). Clearcut mania, which at its height is of psychotic intensity, defines the bipolar I subtype (Fieve and Dunner 1975); depressive episodes—though present sometimes during the course of this disorder—are not necessary for this definition, which approximates the DSM-III-R concept of bipolar disorder. All other bipolar conditions—with less unequivocal evidence for excited periods with hypomanic coloring—are subsumed under cyclothymic, atypical bipolar (DSM-III) or under bipolar disorder not otherwise specified (DSM-III-R); in these subtypes of bipolar disorders, hypomania can be spontaneous (bipolar II) or pharmacologically occasioned (bipolar III). Bipolar III is also often used synonymously with recurrent major depressions with bipolar family history. The importance of this last subtype lies in its possible predictive validity in terms of lithium response.

The distinction between cyclothymic disorder and the unspecified bipolar conditions is more a question of degree than of quality. Bipolar disorder NOS is characterized by major depressions and hypomanic periods; cyclothymic disorder by subdepressive (subsyndromal) and hypomanic periods. Special variants of cyclothymia include those with predominantly hypomanic swings (hyperthymic disorder) or dysthymics with bipolar family history and propensity to hypomania upon pharmacologic challenge with tricyclic drugs (subaffective dysthymia). As shown in Figure 1, together they appear to form a "soft" bipolar spectrum, defined by hypomania (spontaneous or pharmacologic) with various admixtures of depression (major or minor). Recent systematic clinical observations (Akiskal and Mallya 1987; Kukopulos et al. 1983; Wehr and Goodwin 1979) have led to the suggestion that these patients are at risk for rapid cycling, especially when overexposed to heterocyclic antidepressants.

Cyclothymia, previously considered to be a personality disorder, is now classified with the mood disorders; the mini-episodes of retarded depression and hypomania are often masked with interpersonal and vocational complaints imposed by cyclical moods, beginning in adolescence—or earlier—and typically pursuing a lifelong course. Bipolar NOS, like cyclothymics, often receive additional diagnoses such as Axis II "histrionic" or "borderline" personalities. The tempestuous life-style associated with unstable moods is the principal factor in these ancillary diagnoses. Table 3 summarizes

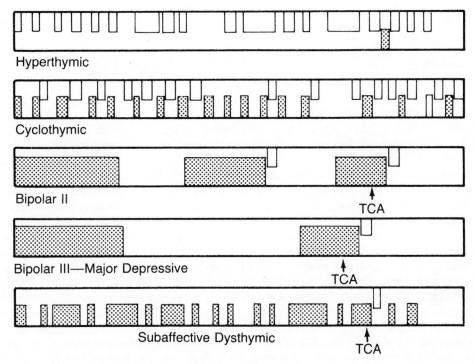

Figure 1. The "soft" spectrum of bipolar disorders. Reproduced from Akiskal and Mallya (1987)

Table 3. Clinical Presentations of Cyclothymia and Bipolar Disorder NOS*

1. Repeated romantic and marital separation or failure, often associated with promiscuity.
2. Academic and vocational dilettantism: beginning a given activity with great enthusiasm and even promise, yet soon despairing in their ability to carry it through.
3. Geographic instability: history of repeated moves from one locale to another.
4. Tendency to join various eschatologic cults, often followed by disillusionment in a short period of time.
5. An episodic pattern of substance abuse that tends to alternate between "downers" and "uppers."

*Summarized from Akiskal et al. (1977)

the clinical presentations in cyclothymic and atypical bipolar patients studied at the University of Tennessee (Akiskal et al. 1977). In these patients interpersonal and social instability were found to be correlated with unstable moods. It is not a conceptual leap from such observations to suggest the possibility that a proportion of antisocial offenders might be suffering from unrecognized bipolar disorders. Indeed, recent clinical experience indicates that bipolar disorder is not uncommon in a "criminal" population. Lithium has been shown effective in certain types of violent antisocial individuals (Sheard 1975). While lithium may possess independent antiaggressive effects, the possibility of a cryptic bipolar disorder may explain some of these findings. The exact percentage of those with antisocial conduct and alcohol and substance abuse who have an underlying bipolar disorder is a question for future studies.

Likewise, future research should develop criteria by which individuals with alcohol or other substance abuse—as a result of bipolar disorder—can be distinguished from those without such a diathesis.

Diagnosis of Depressive, Manic, and Mixed Phases of Bipolar Disorder

The Pittsburgh group (Detre et al. 1972; Kupfer et al. 1975) has convincingly argued that the uncomplicated depressive phase of bipolar illness is typically manifested by hypersomnia and psychomotor retardation. When mixed states supervene, either spontaneously or in the context of sedative and alcohol abuse, agitation and insomnia often replace them (Himmelhoch et al. 1976). Although bipolar depressions do not always acquire full-blown melancholic features, autonomy of episodes is a fundamental characteristic. Psychotic features, including occasional Schneiderian symptoms, have also been described in the depressive phase. But they are not as common as during the manic phase. Stupor, on the other hand, is not an uncommon mode of psychotic presentation of bipolar illness. This is especially true in adolescents and young adults, where the mistaken diagnosis of catatonic stupor is often made (Akiskal et al. 1983). Pseudodemented "organic" presentations have been described in the elderly (Cowdry and Goodwin 1981). Other common expressions of bipolar depression are periodic anergia, hypersomnolence, and weight gain. This is particularly true of seasonal depressions that begin in the fall and winter; hypomania may supervene in the spring. Bipolar depressives will not ordinarily complain of hypomanic mood disturbances because they are experienced either as rebound relief from depression or as pleasant, short-lived, ego-syntonic moods (Jamison et al. 1980). Skillful questioning is often required in the diagnosis of these conditions; collateral information from family members is often crucial. When in doubt, direct clinical observation of hypomania (not uncommonly elicited by tricyclic pharmacotherapy) will provide definitive evidence for the bipolar nature of the disorder. However, in some cases, depressive and hypomanic periods are not easily discerned because of superimposed caffeinism (Neil et al. 1978).

Momentary tearfulness, depressed mood, and even suicidal ideation are not uncommon at the height of mania or during transition from mania to retarded depression (Kotin and Goodwin 1972). Another common mixed feature is racing thoughts in the context of a retarded depression. These labile and transient mixed periods, which occur in at least two-thirds of bipolar patients, must be contrasted with totally mixed attacks. These less common mixed bipolar episodes are characterized by dysphorically elevated moods, severe insomnia, psychomotor agitation, racing thoughts, suicidal ideation, grandiosity, and hypersexuality, as well as by persecutory delusions and auditory hallucinations (Himmelhoch et al. 1976). Mixed states are often misdiagnosed as unipolar depression and, worse, as atypical or neurotic depression, while severely psychotic forms of the illness are misdiagnosed as paranoid schizophrenia. Correct diagnosis is mandatory for proper management because both tricyclics and MAO inhibitors, when used singly, may further contribute to the mixed pathology of these patients, and neuroleptics may prove ineffective or may even aggravate the depressive component. Clinical experience suggests that lithium carbonate alone or in combination with antidepressants is usually required for producing satisfactory remissions in the nonpsychotic group, while electroconvulsive therapy (ECT) may be required in the psychotic group.

Cross-sectional diagnosis of mania, especially in its psychotic form, is customarily considered unreliable since it shows considerable overlap with such conditions as schizophrenia and drug-induced psychoses. However, currently used operational definitions (Feighner et al. 1972; Helzer et al. 1977; Spitzer et al. 1978) have produced good to excellent interrater reliabilities, ranging from 0.82 to 0.93. These definitions are now incorporated into the DSM-III concept of mania. DSM-III-R requires 1) a distinct period that represents a break from premorbid functioning, 2) a duration of at least one week, 3) an elevated or irritable mood, 4) at least three to four classic manic signs and symptoms, and 5) absence of any toxic factors that could account for the clinical picture. Extreme psychotic manifestations, including mood-incongruent delusions and hallucinations, are permissible so long as they occur in the midst of the full affective syndromes. This definition acknowledges three features of mania that until recently were not widely accepted. First, it recognizes that mania as a syndrome is sometimes secondary to medical or toxic factors and that these factors need to be excluded when diagnosing the more commonly occurring manic states as part of bipolar disorder. Second, while elation is common in mania, DSM-III recognizes that a broader range of affects also occurs, including dysphoria, irritability, and hostility. Third, DSM-III acknowledges that severe psychotic disorganization is not incompatible with the diagnosis of mania, provided it occurs in the setting of the manic syndrome. In addition to elation, euphoria, and ecstacy, the manic patient experiences labile mood, chracterized by alteration of euphoria with irritability and depression and sometimes with irritable and angry periods that, in the extreme, may explode into destructive rage. The labile mood, especially in its irritable-angry coloration, reflects manic and depressive admixtures characteristic of a mixed state and is a common presentation of mania (Himmelhoch et al. 1976). Manics, not paranoid schizophrenics, are the most hostile patients encountered in psychiatric practice. Thus, the mood in mania, far from being invariably pleasant, is frequently dysphoric. This is one reason why family and friends are often alienated from the patient. Recent studies have also shown that mood-incongruent psychotic experiences (Schneiderian) are not uncommon in mania (Berner 1980; Carlson and Goodwin 1973; Clayton 1982). There is now convincing evidence that Schneider's first-rank symptoms are not pathognomonic for schizophrenia and may occur in as many as one-fourth of all manicdepressives. Furthermore, Andreasen's systematic work (1979) has documented that most types of formal thought disorder are common to both schizophrenic and affective psychoses. Only poverty of speech content (vagueness) emerges as significantly more common in schizophrenia. Finally, even certain catatonic features such as posturing and negativism have been shown to occur in mania (Abrams and Taylor 1976). Although not specifically mentioned in the DSM-III-R definition, confusion, even pseudodemented presentations, can occur in mania (Clayton 1981).

Mania is most commonly expressed as a phase of circular bipolar disorder, which has strong genetic determinants (Mendlewicz and Rainer 1977). Available evidence does not permit separating unipolar mania as a distinct nosologic entity from these circular forms. Some preliminary findings (Winokur 1981) do suggest that postpartum mania without depression is distinct from familial bipolar disorder, in which both depressive and manic episodes can occur in the postpartum period; this evidence for a distinct puerperal manic disorder is not compelling at this time. However, a recent review (Krauthammer and Klerman 1978) has suggested that phenocopies of mania occur in the context of medical disorders such as influenza, thyrotoxicosis, systemic lupus erythematosus or its treatment with steroids, rheumatic chorea, multiple sclerosis, diencephalic and third ventricular tumors, and stroke. Family history is reportedly low in these cases, suggesting a relatively low genetic predisposition and hence a lowered risk for recurrences. Less well defined phenocopies of mania are the so-called reactive manias or maniacal grief reactions (Racamier and Blanchard 1957). Personal loss and bereavement are hypothesized to be triggering factors (Ambelas

1979), and the reaction is essentially conceptualized in psychodynamic terms as a denial of loss. While such explanations may be plausible in individual cases, no systematic data are available to suggest that these patients differ in family history from other manics. This also applies to the elevated periods of depressed patients who switch to hypomania or mania subsequent to abuse of amphetamine-type stimulants or treatment with antidepressant drugs or sleep deprivation (Bunney 1978). With these patients, a bipolar diathesis is usually manifest, either in family history for mania or in spontaneous hypomanic periods during prospective observation. Although the concept for pharmacologically occasioned switches has been contested (see, for instance, Lewis and Winokur 1982), clinical experience suggests that bipolar switches commonly occur during the first few weeks of antidepressant treatment, especially in those at the "softer" end of the bipolar spectrum.

Mania, like depression, appears to be a syndrome rather than a disease entity. It is the final common pathway of many etiologic factors, both biologic and psychological. At this time, biologic factors, especially familial-genetic predisposition, are the most established causes. But while genetic predisposition is a necessary substrate, it needs to be activated by environmental precipitants. These environmental causes are not always obvious, which then gives the appearance of endogenous mood swings. Moreover, environmental factors alone (including interpersonal factors) rarely account for manic states, with the possible exception of medically induced secondary mania.

To summarize, bipolar illness appears to express itself in a spectrum of phenotypes ranging from subaffective temperamental deviations (such as cyclothymia) to recurrent depressions with infrequent hypomanias, to full-blown bipolar psychosis (Akiskal 1983c). Many patients do not make the transition from one form to another, but transitional forms occur frequently enough to suggest a psychopathologic process that is common to the entire spectrum, as originally hypothesized by Kraepelin (1921).

Affective Psychosis versus Schizoaffective Disorder

DSM-III-R, like its precursor DSM-III, recognizes that major affective episodes—whether manic, mixed, or depressive—can be of extremely psychotic proportions, including the presence of mood-incongruent delusional and hallucinatory experiences (Pope and Lipinski 1978). The family histories of patients manifesting such features are essentially similar to those of nonpsychotic affectively ill individuals; if anything, the morbidity risk for affective disorder is higher in the first-degree relatives of "mood-incongruent" probands when compared with those of "mood-congruent" ones (Gershon et al. 1982). Furthermore, many of these patients, formerly classified under the schizoaffective rubric, have positive dexamethasone suppression (Carroll 1982) and REM latency tests (Kupfer et al. 1979) indistinguishable from those of individuals with primary mood disorder. This is particularly true for bipolar schizoaffectives (i.e., those with history of mania); unipolar schizoaffectives appear to be more heterogeneous, some being related to primary mood disorder, others to schizophrenia (Clayton 1982).

Whether a "third psychosis" (schizoaffective or cycloid) exists is a much-debated issue. Some believe that complex partial seizures of temporal lobe origin account for some of these unclassified psychoses (Blumer 1984). Schizoaffective illness should not be confused with the relatively common secondary depressions occurring in the setting of well-established schizophrenic disorders; the nature of these depressions is contested in that some consider them to be inherrent to schizophrenia or conceptualize them as demoralization or existential suffering in young schizophrenics, and still others regard them as neuroleptic induced. DSM-III had reserved the schizoaffective rubric to those psychotic patients with syndromal affective episodes that were beyond the boundaries of episode-limited, mood-incongruent features and that could not be classified as schizophrenic; no operational criteria were provided. DSM-III-R has rectified this omission though the selectivity of the new criteria remains to be tested.

The advent of lithium carbonate and carbamazepine has provided a compelling reason to identify correctly the psychotic forms of bipolar disorders; furthermore, the unnecessary risk for tardive dyskinesia resulting from inappropriate long-term treatment with neuroleptics is unacceptable here. Because clinical differential diagnosis between mood and other psychiatric disorders with prominent psychotic features is of such paramount importance, phenomenologic aspects of manic and depressive psychoses should be carefully evaluated (Akiskal and Puzantian 1979).

Mood Disorders in Children and Adolescents

The delineation of mood disorders in children and adolescents is a new development. Many of these children were formerly classified as conduct disorders. The possibility is now recognized that some forms of conduct disorders may represent early manifestations of bipolar disorder. Another problem in evaluating mood disorder in younger individuals—especially children—arises from the inability of many of these children to express subjective depression in words. Pozanski (1982) has suggested that subjective dysphoria is often unexpressed in children but that the morbid affect can be directly and reliably observed by the clinician. (There is much to recommend this approach for use in adults with somatic presentations of affective illness, as it relies on clinical observation, a long-sanctioned method of medical science.)

There has been an upsurge of recent interest in affective illness in children and adolescents (Akiskal and Weller, in press; Cantwell and Carlson 1979; Puig-Antich 1980; Varnaka et al. 1987). These studies have revealed that 1) depression is not uncommon in children and becomes even more common in adolescence; 2) it is often of low-grade chronicity (dysthymic); 3) as in the adult counterpart, family history for mood disorder is often positive; 4) hypomania and mania, though more common in adolescence, may, in selected instances, appear before puberty; and 5) the last decade has witnessed an alarming increase in suicide rates in adolescents and young adults, which in part can be ascribed to unrecognized or inadequately treated mood disorders.

However, not all the children of the affectively ill can be considered to be experiencing a genetically transmitted disorder. In some cases, the "depressive" condition of the child may simply reflect the adverse sequelae of being raised by a psychiatrically ill parent—if not two ill parents (in view of the frequency of assortative mating, which may involve mood disorder, alcoholism, or personality disorder). While it will take more research to delineate the full-scale relationship of child and adult depressions, it would appear from recent evidence that the roots of bipolar disorders are buried in mid- or early adolescence and often extend to early childhood. It is therefore likely that some—perhaps one-third to one-half—of depressed children and adolescents may grow up to be bipolar adults. This conclusion is supported by a recent prospective study conducted at the University of Tennessee (Akiskal et al. 1985) on the offspring of bipolar probands, which demonstrated that the most common form of onset of bipolar illness is depressive (major depression and dysthymia combined). Although the recognition of bona fide mood disorders in childhood and adolescence is of major public health significance in terms of preventing the educational, interpersonal, and characterologic complications of these disorders, systematic pharmacotherapeutic research has not been undertaken yet on large populations.

Such research is vital in preventing the adverse social and characterologic sequelae of early-onset mood disorders and may have special relevance in preventing suicide in young individuals.

Mood Disorders in the Elderly

While depressive symptoms are common in the elderly, mood disorders occurring for the first time after the age of 65 are relatively uncommon. The median age of onset of bipolar conditions is in the twenties; for unipolars, in the thirties. Most elderly subjects with depressive or manic conditions severe enough to require hospitalization are experiencing a *recurrence* of an illness that had first shown signs of onset many decdes ago. Depression beginning for the first time in old age has often been described as a psychotic illness. Late-onset manic conditions without prior bipolar history, while uncommon, have also been described (Shulman and Post 1980). While old age per se does not seem to be associated with chronicity, there is a tendency for cycle length to shorten in recurrent depressions, and in previously established bipolar disorder, depressive episodes tend to predominate over mania (Angst et al. 1979). Furthermore, compared with younger depressives, the ratio of completed-to-attempted suicide is higher in the elderly, especially elderly men, though the two rates have come closer in the last decade.

In an elderly individual without past history for affective episodes, a depressive presentation should prompt appropriate physical evaluation to rule out occult abdominal malignancies, cerebral tumors, side effects from antihypertensive drugs, etc. As discussed earlier, Krauthammer and Klerman (1978) have also drawn attention to the existence of "secondary manias" occurring in the setting of medical conditions or their pharmacologic treatment.

Perhaps the most important advance in this area has been the increasing realization that severe but reversible cognitive deficits mimicking dementia occur in old-age depressions (Roth 1976; Wells 1979). These pseudodemented depressions deserve tricyclic antidepressants or ECT. Pharmacologic treatment of the depression, even when secondary or concurrent to a dementing illness, will often make the dementia clinicaly more manageable.

Finally, it would be appropriate to remind the reader that the first onset of a neurotic illness (generalized anxiety, panic, phobic, obsessive-compulsive, and somatization disorders) is so rare after age 45 that such neurotic symptoms in elderly individuals—as well as in middle-aged patients—with unremarkable premorbid adjustment should raise the suspicion of melancholia (Akiskal 1983a). Watts (1966), writing from the vantage of a primary care physician, has shown in an open, systematic study a gratifying response to thymoleptic drugs or ECT in "anxiety" states with first onset in middle-aged and elderly patients.

Concluding Remarks

The physician now has a broad array of thymoleptic agents to mitigate the suffering of many patients previously considered to have dementia, schizophrenia, neurotic and personality disorder, or undiagnosed medical disease. It is the gratifying response of these patients to these new agents—particularly to lithium carbonate—that has forced the widening of the nosologic boundaries of mood disorders reflected in the official American classification (Akiskal and Cassano 1983).

The most important implication of this nosologic revision is the awareness of the enormous phenomenologic heterogeneity in mood disorders. The emerging picture of mood disorders is one that embraces somatic, cognitive, neurotic, characterologic, and behavioral as well as mood disturbances (Akiskal 1983a). Depending on the clinical setting, one set of manifestations may dominate over others. Therefore, studies conducted in one setting may not necessarily generalize to others. Long-term treatment of mood disorders has also shown that these conditions are often chronic. The conventional clinical belief that they are episodic illnesses is based on observations emphasizing major or psychotic episodes. We now know that the interepisodic phase of mood disorders is often characterized by mild symptoms, neurotic adjustment, or characterologic and temperamental deviations. The social and vocational consequences of these disorders can so impair day-to-day functioning that interpersonal friction and suffering become habitual existential modes. These manifestations are not fully controlled with medication and may require considerable psychotherapeutic attention. Several innovative brands of practical psychotherapeutic techniques have emerged in the past two decades to address the interepisodic maladjustments of the affectively ill. More systematic data are needed to clarify the usefulness of these psychotherapies to the various subtypes of mood disorders. Despite assertions for efficacy in major depressions by psychotherapeutically oriented clinicians, the general sentiment among biologically oriented clinicians is that the efficacy of these psychotherapies is limited at best to the milder nonmelancholic depressions with anxiety disorder or characterologic substrates.

The natural course and prognosis of mood disorders may have changed as a result of the new somatic treatments. Affective manifestations tend to be less severe, vegetative signs may be muted or absent, and "atypical" relapses with predominantly "psychologic" symptoms prevail. Finally, patients with primary mood disorders who, in the older epidemiologic literature, were most likely to commit suicide may escape this fate with modern energetic treatments (Khuri and Akiskal 1983; Martin et al. 1985). Now depressions secondary to personality disorders, substance and alcohol abuse, and schizophrenic disorders—which do not respond well to thymoleptic drugs— appear overrepresented in more recent suicide statistics, especially those based on clinical samples.

Whereas data demonstrating that more than half of the mood disorders pursuing an intermittent or episodic lifelong course are widely accepted, it is uncertain how long these disorders should be treated with medication. This is an important question in view of the possibility that long-term use of heterocyclic antidepressants may induce rapid-cycling, especially in those with "soft" indicators of bipolarity. It is unlikely that lithium induces *de novo* depressive episodes; yet many lithium-treated bipolar patients complain of a *relative* depression, presumably because their cyclothymic oscillations have been evened out. Such factors probably contribute to the noncompliance so characteristic of recurrent mood disorders.

The minimal threshold of five affective symptoms over two weeks may well be inadequate to distinguish social misery from clinical depression. Likewise, such a threshold, while relevant for patients and those who have been cases previously, may be inappropriate for research in nonclinical settings. Although some symptomatic volunteers appear to have levels of illness comparable to those seen in a clinical population, depressive symptoms in untreated populations may reflect nonspecific dysphoric symptoms unrelated to primary mood disorders. These considerations suggest that the psychosocial findings revealed in such community studies as those of Brown and Harris (1978) in lower-class women may not generalize to all clinical depressives. The same type of reservation may apply to psychosocial treatments in depressed volunteers who have not previously been clinical cases—even if they were to meet the criteria for major depression. The foregoing considerations underlie the belief of some authorities to the effect that operational definitions of mood disorder (e.g., those in DSM-III-R) should include the additional requirement that an experienced clinician finds affective manifestations to be part of a coherent clinical syndrome that cannot be explained by another psychiatric illness.

To summarize, the ability of potent pharmacologic agents to reverse psychotic affective pathologies, abort the minor variants, or alleviate the chronic forms has broadened the diagnosable spectrum of mood disorders to bring the benefits of these treatments to millions of sufferers. The emergence of this new affective spectrum does not merely reflect therapeutic fashion but has been supported by validating criteria external to the clinical picture. These include familial-genetic background and prospective course. The development of potent thymoleptic drugs has once again made psychiatric diagnosis respectable and has stimulated sophisticated research methods in psychiatric classification. We have also learned the limits of somatic treatments and the need for psychosocial modalities that address residual interpersonal and characterologic difficulties. Certain innovative brands of psychotherapy have been designed to address specific cognitive, dynamic, and interpersonal aspects of depression. The need to tailor treatments to rigorously defined groups has made precise diagnosis a prerequisite for clinical practice. These findings and related data reviewed in this chapter illustrate the close link between diagnosis and treatment in psychiatry.

Chapter 163

The Choice of Treatment Setting

Who we treat, as well as where and how we do it, is in part determined by society's constantly changing views and values (Spencer and Mattson 1979; Appendix). Other chapters delineate the current expanded universes of both the who and the how. There has been remarkably little attention, however, given to the where, except to note the impact of changing ideologies. With the push toward deinstitutionalization, development of partial hospitalization, and expansion of outpatient capacity, more patients in general, and more patients with depression in particular, are receiving treatment, and a higher percentage of patients are treated in a variety of outpatient settings, clinics, therapists' offices, emergency rooms, or day programs. Our current bias, supported in some instances by carefully collected data, is to keep people out of the hospital. In contrast to patients with uncertain or mixed diagnosis or patients with schizophrenia, there are almost no studies of the relationship between treatment setting and outcome in depression. There are, therefore, no data other than clinical impressions (the folklore of medicine) to guide us in directing individual patients to particular programs or facilities. It is important to remember that depression is often recurrent and sometimes persistent or chronic. This means that treatment planning should include attention to the long-term course of the illness, as well as to the acute episode.

Paykel et al. (1970) demonstrated a complex sorting process that at least in some communities determines the site of treatment of depressed patients. Depressed inpatients were significantly different from outpatients on 21 of 46 variables examined. Hospitalized patients were older (despite age limits of 21–65 for the study), more likely to have a history of previous depressions and hospitalizations, and more severely ill. Day hospital and emergency treatment patients were intermediate in severity and chronicity. In addition, it appeared that "the day hospital represents a secondary treatment resource for depressed patients who have had previous trials of outpatient treatment, particularly with medication, but have only had a partial response such that their illness is not so severe as to require full hospitalization, but not so mild that they can sustain themselves on outpatient treatment alone." Emergency treatment unit patients were especially characterized by previous suicide attempts.

Another study (Pilowsky and Spence 1978) compared 20 general practice outpatients treated with tricyclic antidepressants (TCAs) with 20 patients admitted to a hospital for depressive illness. They reported clear differences between the samples and stressed "the importance of the conceptual distinction between depressive severity and depressive classification." Many of the outpatients reported feeling depressed but did not fit a typical depressive syndrome. The data do not indicate whether these different treatment settings have any effect on the outcome of treatment.

Inpatient treatment has traditionally been used for patients with severe, life-threatening, or treatment-refractory depressions. The hospital provides support, structure, and safety; it is a place to reestablish mechanisms of coping or to learn and test new adaptive behaviors. It can help both patient and family accept depression as an illness and perhaps improve compliance with medications and psychotherapy. It is also a place to clarify the diagnosis; to distinguish dementia from depression; and to investigate the possibilities of causative, contributing, or complicating medical or neurologic disease.

Perhaps those most likely to be hospitalized are patients judged to be seriously suicidal. There are no clear rules for estimating risk; denial of suicidal thoughts, plans, or intention cannot be taken at face value. The impulsion to die, severity of the depression, guilt, and hopelessness, along with sufficient energy to act, bode ill. Being older, alone, unmarried or friendless, unemployed, physically ill, recently bereaved, a drinker, and male, and having made previous attempts, are additional risk factors. Other suicides in the family also increase risk, although family and religious ties and a supportive network are somewhat protective. Nonsuicidal severe depression—for example, depressive stupor—can also be life threatening as a result of dehydration, malnutrition, secondary infections, and other complicating medical illness. Despite the absence of data, it is agreed that such patients require inpatient care.

Patients with severe depression, particularly accompanied by suicidal risk or delusions, or patients who do not respond to antidepressants are candidates for electroconvulsive therapy (ECT). Older patients, particularly those with cardiovascular or neurologic disease, may be at high medical risk. Particularly for such patients, it may be advisable that ECT be done in an inpatient setting with available medical services.

The outpatient who fails to respond to usual regimens of treatment is often referred for inpatient care. In the hospital, such patients can be monitored more easily for medication compliance, and blood levels can be regularly obtained. In addition, closer observation may raise other diagnostic possibilities, and the milieu—including separation from home and work, from family and friends, and the move from the pressures of life to the "asylum" of the hospital—may also be helpful in alleviating stress and promoting reintegration and adaptive behaviors. However, hospitalization may stigmatize and result in a further lowering of self-esteem and an increase in self-denigration. The impact of separation of parents from children or of increasing the likelihood of job loss must also be considered, along with the danger of inducing hospital dependency.

Most would agree that patients with mild, uncomplicated depressions are best treated as outpatients. This is particularly true if there is a family that can provide loving support and permit illness behavior temporarily, and if other aspects of the environment are not too stressful. This evaluation of home and work or school is important in deciding treatment setting. These milieus must be considered from the point of view not only of their impact on the patient, but also of the patient's impact on his human environment. For example, even a mild depression may be damaging to an already compromised parent-child relationship.

Partial hospitalization has been reported (Beigel and Feder 1970) to be as effective overall in the treatment of depressives as it is in the treatment of schizophrenics. However, the basis of treatment assignment and the specifics of diagnosis are not clearly stated. An early study (Craft 1958) comparing day hospital and hospital ward treatment found no differences in outcome. As indicated above, Paykel et al. (1970) suggest that day hospitals are more likely to be used for patients with a subacute duration, previous unsuccessful treatment, and anxiety.

The decision about the setting for treatment is also influenced by the stage of the patient's illness and by the clinician's prior acquaintance with the patient. The more we know about a particular patient's episode course of illness and the clearer our understanding of the patient's life history and psychodynamics, the more informed our decision and the less likely an unnecessary hospitalization. For many patients, the changing course of their illness will require a variety of settings—now inpatient, now out—and at times of slow recovery or work impairment, day programs.

Closely related to the issue of treatment setting is the issue of time in treatment within a setting. Often because of fiscal constraints, this is most discussed in relation to inpatient stay. The development of prospective reimbursement is likely to increase pressure to shorten these hospitalizations. Unfortunately, few data are available to help guide us. In a controlled study of models of short (21–28 days) versus long (90–120 days) hospitalization, Glick et al. (1977) were able to follow the outcome in 18 patients with affective disease, reporting that "the long-term subjects seemed to be functioning better at both one year and two years." The small size of the sample makes it difficult to rely on these findings. However, "there was some anecdotal suggestion that short-term hospitalization may not have allowed for proper diagnosis and treatment for some members of that [affective] group." Certainly, for those patients who legitimately require inpatient care, the known rate of response to treatment and the need for patient and family education may require more than the now common very brief stay if the patient is to achieve optimal response. For example, the patient requiring evaluation for and then administration of ECT followed by recovery from the transient induced organic brain syndrome may need to stay in the hospital longer. Similarly, a patient who requires a second antidepressant or ECT following failure on a drug of first choice may also require an extended stay. No specific criteria for length of treatment have been detailed for either outpatient or partial hospitalization.

In summary, depression is a complex, often recurrent or chronic illness for which the treatment parameters of time and setting have not been well studied. It is clear that Axis I diagnosis of depression alone does not sensibly determine either setting or time. Other Axis I diagnoses (e.g., an impulse disorder) and the other axes, personality, medical illness, external stress, and functional abilities (particularly at the time of evaluation) may be more important contributors to these decisions. A series of controlled studies are indicated. Until the data are available, we must use our best judgment and clinical wisdom within the limits of current restraints.

Appendix

The American Psychiatric Association Manual of Psychiatric Peer Review, 2nd ed., includes model screening criteria for adult inpatient treatment for several depressive diagnoses.

Approaches to the problem of peer review have also been made from the point of view of the patient's functional capacities. An example is the criteria for psychiatry developed by the New York County Health Services Review Organization.

(APA Manual of Psychiatric Peer Review, 2nd Edition)

Depressive neurosis
DSM-II 300.4
Major depression with melancholia
Dysthymic disorder
Adjustment disorder with depressed mood
DSM-III 296.22
.32
300.40
309.00

I. Admission Review

   A. *Reasons for Admission*

      1. Potential danger to self, others, or property, *or*
      2. Need for continuous skilled observation, high dose medication, or therapeutic milieu, *and*
      3. Impaired social, familial, or occupational functioning
      4. Legally mandated admission

   B. *Initial Length of Stay Assignment*

   Locally established based on statistical norms

II. Continued Stay Review

   A. *Reasons for Extending the Initial Length of Stay*

      1. Continuation of danger to self, others, or property
      2. Need for stabilization of medication or continuation of therapeutic milieu

3. Complications of medication

III. Validation of

    A. *Diagnosis*

        1. Depression
        2. Psychomotor retardation or agitation
        3. Depressive thought content (ruminations, hopelessness, inadequacy, or guilt)

    B. *Reasons for Admission*

        1. Documentation of potential danger to self, others, or property (I-A1)
        2. Documentation of failure or unavailability of appropriate outpatient management (I-A2, 3)

IV. Critical Diagnostic and Therapeutic Services

    A. Treatment plan to include problem formulation, treatment goals, and therapeutic modality (e.g., psychotherapy, pharmacotherapy, social therapies, behavior modification)   100%
    B. More than two psychotropic medications at any given time   0%
    C. Change of psychotropic medication more than twice during any seven-day period   0%
    D. ECT   0%

V. Discharge Status

    A. Achievement of inpatient treatment goals (as outlined in IV-A)
    B. Specific follow-up treatment plan established

VI. Complications

    A. *Primary Disease and Treatment—Specific Complications*

        1. Suicide or attempt
        2. Development of psychotic symptomatology (e.g., hallucinations, delusions, paranoia, or unrealistic feelings of guilt or worthlessness)
        3. Complications of medication
        4. Lack of improvement in admitting symptomatology after seven days

    B. *Nonspecific Indicators*

        1. Elopement or discharge against medical advice
        2. Hypnotic medication after 14 days
        3. IM psychotropic medication beyond seven days
        4. Readmission within 30 days of discharge

Depressive psychosis
DSM-II 296.00
        .2
        .34
    298.00
Depression with psychotic features
DSM-III 296.x4

I. Admission Review

   A. *Reasons for Admission*

      1. Potential danger to self, others, or property, *or*
      2. Impaired reality testing accompanied by disordered behavior, *or*
      3. Need for continuous skilled observation, ECT, high dose medication, or therapeutic milieu, *and*
      4. Impaired social, familial, and occupational functioning
      5. Legally mandated admission

   B. *Initial Length of Stay Assignment*

      Locally established based on statistical norms

II. Continued Stay Review

   A. *Reasons for Extending the Initial Length of Stay*

      1. Continuation of potential danger to self, others, or property, or of impaired reality testing accompanied by disordered behavior
      2. Continued need for ECT, stabilization of medication, or therapeutic milieu
      3. Complications of medication or ECT

III. Validation of

   A. *Diagnosis*

      1. Mental status examination documenting:

         a. Depression, *and*
         b. Psychomotor retardation or agitation, *and*
         c. Impaired reality testing (e.g., hallucinations, delusions, paranoia, or unrealistic feelings of guilt or worthlessness)

   B. *Reasons for Admission*

      1. Documentation of potential danger to self, others, or property (I-A1)
      2. Documentation of impaired reality testing (as defined above) and disordered behavior (psychomotor retardation or agitation) (I-A2)
      3. Documentation of failure or unavailability of appropriate outpatient management (I-A3,4)

IV. Critical Diagnostic and Therapeutic Services

   A. Major tranquilizer, antidepressant medication, or ECT   100%
   B. Treatment plan to include problem formulation, treatment goals, and therapeutic modalities (e.g., psychotherapy, pharmacotherapy, social therapies, behavior modification)   100%
   C. More than three psychotropic medications at any one time   0%
   D. Change of psychotropic medication more than twice during any seven-day period   0%

V. Discharge Status

    A. Achievement of inpatient treatment goals (as outlined in IV-B)
    B. Specific follow-up treatment plan established

VI. Complications

    A. *Primary Disease and Treatment—Specific Complications*

       1. Suicide or attempted suicide
       2. Complications of medication or ECT
       3. Lack of improvement in admitting symptomatology after 14 days

    B. *Nonspecific Indicators*

       1. Elopement or discharge against medical advice
       2. Hypnotic medication after 14th day
       3. Readmission within 30 days of discharge

New York County Health Services Review Organization
Criteria For Psychiatry

Guidelines and Standards

Admission and Continued Stay Criteria

A. Presence of a mental disorder as defined in DSM-III and at least one of the following that is related to the mental disorder:

B. The patient should not remain outside the hospital or be discharged because

    1. The patient has need of a specific form of psychiatric treatment, which can be provided in or by remaining in the hospital and cannot be provided outside the hospital.

       a. Structured environment of this hospital.
       b. Specific observations for evaluation and disposition.
       c. Specific observations for conducting treatment.
       d. Control of behavior necessary for effective somatic or psychotherapy.

    2. The patient is unable to care for self, and others are unable to care for him.

    3. The patient is experiencing symptoms and/or exhibiting deviant behavior, the magnitude of which is not tolerable to him or to society.

4. The patient's behavior is a serious threat to his adaptation to life, and hospitalization is necessary at this time to control it.

5. The patient has a condition other than mental disorder that requires in-hospital care, but psychological components cannot be handled as well on other units.

6. There is an immediate physical danger to self or others.

7. Ambulatory treatment has been unsuccessful in halting or reversing the course of the mental illness, and inpatient treatment at this level of care is needed.

Chapter 164

Antidepressants: Pharmacology and Clinical Use

Faced with the growing array of antidepressants and the knowledge that the efficacy of all these antidepressants for treating depression is similar, the clinician can rely on a firm base of pharmacologic data for choosing the appropriate drug for his or her patient. Uppermost in a clinician's choice of a particular drug is the desirability of avoiding certain side effects and drug-drug interactions when the antidepressant drug is prescribed for a particular patient. The purpose of this chapter is to review some of the basic and clinical pharmacology of antidepressants and to explain how data from in vitro studies can be used to anticipate side effects as well as drug-drug interactions. Types of antidepressants and their pharmacologic actions and pharmacokinetics are reviewed, and the clinical implications of all this information are discussed.

Types of Antidepressants

Not too long ago, antidepressants approved for use in the United States could be classified into two groups: tricyclic antidepressants and monoamine oxidase inhibitors. This classification mixes structural (tricyclic) and functional (inhibition of monoamine oxidase) criteria. Ideally, a classification based on either structure or activity would be best. However, for the new chemical entities that have entered the marketplace within the last several years—amoxapine, maprotiline, trazodone, and fluoxetine—and for those being developed for marketing in the next few years—for example, bupropion—it is difficult to arrive at a satisfying classification based on either of these criteria. For the time being, the best, albeit unsatisfying, way to classify antidepressants is by the number of rings in their structure (Table 1). However, there is a great deal of confusion in the literature about the use of the terms *bicyclic*, *tricyclic*, and *tetracyclic*. These terms apply only to structures that have *fused* rings number two, three, and four, respectively. Thus, for example, the antidepressant trazodone contains four rings but it is not a tetracyclic because all these rings are not fused. In addition, the term *heterocyclic* cannot be applied usefully to a structural classification of antidepressants since this term describes any ringed structure that contains within a ring an atom different from carbon. By this definition, then, doxepin is heterocyclic but amitriptyline is not.

Basic Pharmacology

The Synapse: An Important Site of Action of Antidepressants

The locus of the pharmacodynamic effects of antidepressants that appears to be especially relevant clinically is the synapse. In various ways antidepressants alter the effects of neurotransmitters at this site. Neurotransmitters are the chemicals that neurons use to communicate with one another and with other cell types (e.g., acetylcholine at neuromuscular junctions). These small molecules, usually amino acids or their derivatives, are released from the nerve ending to interact with specific receptors on the outside surface of cells. Receptors are highly specialized proteins that are very selective in their ability to bind neurotransmitters. When the chemical messenger stimulates its receptor, the receiving neuron is changed electrically and biochemically as a result of the coupling of the complex of neurotransmitter and receptor to other components of the membrane in which the receptor resides. Neurons can also regulate their own activity by feedback mechanisms involving receptors on

Table 1. Antidepressants in Use in the United States Classified According to the Number of Rings in Their Structure

Number of Rings			
1	2	3	4
Phenelzine (Nardil)[a]	Isocarboxazid[a] (Marplan)	Amitriptyline (Elavil, Endep)	Amoxapine (Asendin)
Bupropion (Wellbutrin)	Tranylcypromine[a] (Parnate)	Doxepin (Adapin, Sinequan)	Maprotiline (Ludiomil)
	Fluoxetine (Prozac)	Imipramine (Tofranil, SK-Pramine)	Trazodone (Desyrel)
		Trimipramine (Surmontil)	
		Desipramine (Norpramin, Pertofrane)	
		Nortriptyline (Pamelor)	
		Protriptyline (Vivactil)	

[a]Classified functionally as monoamine oxidase inhibitor.

the nerve ending (autoreceptors). An example of an autoreceptor is the α_2-adrenergic receptor on noradrenergic nerve endings, which modulate release of norepinephrine. When stimulated, this presynaptic receptor inhibits further release of norepinephrine.

For some biogenic amine neurotransmitters (e.g., norepinephrine, serotonin, and dopamine), it has been established that after release they are taken back into the nerve ending (a process called uptake or re-uptake). Re-uptake is a mechanism that prevents overstimulation of receptors in the synapse. Neurotransmission can be enhanced acutely by blocking this uptake with a drug. But blockade of uptake can ultimately diminish neurotransmission as the receptor undergoes a compensatory change and becomes less sensitive (desensitized) to the neurotransmitter (Richelson and El-Fakahany 1982). Antidepressants of many types probably acting by different mechanisms can desensitize receptors for catecholamines, and this effect is the basis for one hypothesis of their mechanism of action (Sulser 1983).

By blocking the postsynaptic receptor with an antagonist, neurotransmitter effects can be selectively and acutely abolished. Very often with chronic blockade, the receptor undergoes another type of compensatory change and becomes more sensitive (supersensitized) to the neurotransmitter. Supersensitivity may be the mechanism of adaptation to some receptor-related side effects of certain drugs, and may be related to the development of tardive dyskinesia following chronic treatment with neuroleptics, which block dopamine receptors.

Antidepressants can block uptake of biogenic amine neurotransmitters and antagonize certain receptors. In addition, some antidepressants inhibit the activity of monoamine oxidase, a ubiquitous enzyme that is important in the degradation of catecholamines, serotonin, and other biogenic amines. Since this enzyme is present in mitochondria, which are found in most cells and in the nerve endings, its inhibition results in an elevation in the concentration of neurotransmitters available for release at the synapse.

Blockade of Neurotransmitter Uptake by Antidepressants

One of the earliest discovered pharmacologic effects of tricyclic antidepressants was the blockade of uptake of both norepinephrine and serotonin at the presynaptic nerve ending (Dengler et al. 1961; Glowinski and Axelrod 1964). These activities were found soon after the discovery of their usefulness in treating depression, and together they form one of the cornerstones of the so-called biogenic amine hypothesis of affective illness. In simplest terms, this hypothesis states that a deficiency of certain biogenic amines at functionally important synapses causes depression and that an excess produces mania (Maas 1975).

Early data on the relationship between structure of tricyclic antidepressants and their activity at inhibiting uptake of norepinephrine and serotonin appeared to indicate that the tertiary amine compounds (e.g., amitriptyline) were more potent at blocking uptake of serotonin than of norepinephrine and that the reverse was true for the secondary amine compounds (e.g., desipramine). On the basis of this information, the concepts of serotonin- and norepinephrine-deficient depressions have evolved.

More recent data, however, do not support these earlier results (Richelson and Pfenning 1984). Thus, most of the antidepressants listed in Table 2 are more selective at blocking uptake of norepinephrine than of serotonin. This selectivity ranges from 470- fold for maprotiline to 2.8-fold for amitriptyline (Table 2). Two drugs, trazodone and fluoxetine, are more than 20-fold more potent at blocking re-uptake of serotonin

Table 2. Antidepressant Potencies[a] for Blocking Re-Uptake of Norepinephrine and Serotonin and Affinities[b] for Some Neurotransmitter Receptors

Drug (generic and trade names)	Re-uptake blockade[a,c]			Receptor blockade[b,d]						
						α-Adrenergic				
	NE	5-HT	Ratio NE/5-HT	Histamine H$_1$	Muscarinic	α$_1$	α$_2$	Dopamine D$_2$	Serotonin S$_2$	
Tricyclic: tertiary amines										
Amitriptyline (Elavil, Endep)	4.2	1.5	2.8	91	5.5	3.7	0.11	0.10	3.4	
Doxepin (Adapin, Sinequan)	5.3	0.36	15	420	1.2	4.2	0.091	0.042	4.0	
Imipramine (Tofranil, SK-Pramine)	7.7	2.4	3.2	9.1	1.1	1.1	0.031	0.050	1.2	
Trimipramine (Surmontil)	0.20	0.040	5.0	370	1.7	4.2	0.15	0.56	3.1	
Tricyclic: secondary amines										
Desipramine (Norpramin, Pertofrane)	110	0.29	380	0.91	0.50	0.77	0.014	0.030	0.36	
Nortriptyline (Pamelor)	25	0.38	66	10	0.67	1.7	0.040	0.83	2.3	
Protriptyline (Vivactil)	100	0.36	280	4.0	4.0	0.77	0.015	0.43	1.4	
Dibenzoxazepine										
Amoxapine (Asendin)	23	0.21	110	4.0	0.10	2.0	0.038	0.625	170	
Tetracyclic										
Maprotiline (Ludiomil)	14	0.030	470	50	0.18	1.1	0.011	0.28	0.83	
Triazolopyridine										
Trazodone (Desyrel)	0.020	0.53	0.038	0.29	0.00031	2.8	0.20	0.026	14	
Benzenepropanamine										
Fluoxetine (Prozac)	0.36	8.3	0.043	0.016	0.050	0.017	0.0077	0.36	0.48	
Propiophenone										
Bupropion (Wellbutrin)	0.043	0.0064	6.7	0.015	0.0021	0.022	0.0012	0.00048	0.0011	
Reference Compounds										
d-Amphetamine (Dexedrine)	2.0									
diphenhydramine (Benadryl)				7.1						
atropine					42					
phentolamine (Regitine)						6.7	2.3			
haloperidol (Haldol)								25		
methysergide (Sansert)									15	

[a]$10^7 \times 1/K_i$, where K_i = inhibitor constant in molarity
[b]$10^7 \times 1/K_d$, where K_d = equilibrium dissociation constant in molarity
[c]Data from Richelson and Pfenning (1984)
[d]Data for human brain from Richelson and Nelson (1984) and Wander et al. (1986)

over norepinephrine. Most antidepressants are relatively weak at blocking re-uptake of dopamine (Richelson and Pfenning 1984).

Selectivity should not be equated with potency since selectivity is derived from a ratio of potencies. For example, although maprotiline is more selective at blocking uptake of norepinephrine than is desipramine, it is much less potent than desipramine at this blockade (Table 2). Similarly, although fluoxetine is slightly less selective than trazodone at blocking uptake of serotonin, it is about 16 times more potent than trazodone at this blockade (Table 2).

The important message from all these data is that there is no strict dichotomy between tertiary amine tricyclic antidepressants and secondary amine compounds in terms of their selectivity for blockade of uptake. All tertiary amine tricyclic compounds except trimipramine are reasonably potent at blocking uptake of norepinephrine, and some secondary amine compounds are more potent than tertiary amine compounds at blocking uptake of serotonin (Table 2). In addition, trimipramine is quite weak at blocking uptake of either norepinephrine or serotonin, so this property is not essential for antidepressant efficacy. Thus, from these data, a conclusion about the type of depression (serotonin-deficient verses norepinephrine-deficient) a patient has, based on the response to a particular tricyclic antidepressant, is unwarranted. On the other hand, research aimed at testing a hypothesis relating to a deficiency of serotonin or norepinephrine in depression (Maas 1975) could utilize the serotonin-selective re-uptake blocker fluoxetine or the norepinephrine-selective re-uptake blocker maprotiline, respectively.

Although uptake blockade of neurotransmitters may not be necessary for antidepressant effects, this property likely relates to certain adverse effects of antidepressants and to some of their drug-drug interactions (table 3). For example, blockade of norepinephrine uptake possibly is the cause of tachycardia and tremor in some patients.

In addition, erectile and ejaculatory dysfunction, which are side effects associated with antidepressant therapy, may be related to this blockade. Although the physiology of erection and ejaculation is not well understood, it appears that a proper balance between acetylcholine and catecholamines at their respective receptor sites is essential for these phenomena to occur. Disturbing this balance—for example, by blocking uptake of norepinephrine and thereby increasing the amount of this catecholamine at synapses—may cause problems. This idea received some support from a case report showing that a cholinergic agonist reverses the dysfunction induced by antidepressant drugs and an anorectic agent, which potently block uptake of norepinephrine (Yager 1986). Thus, norepinephrine uptake blockade may be responsible for sexual dysfunction in patients.

In addition, norepinephrine uptake blockade by antidepressants likely explains their blockade of the antihypertensive effects of guanethidine (Ismelin and Esimil) (Mitchell et al. 1967) and is predictive of a similar interaction with guanadrel (Hylorel). For these antihypertensive drugs to work, they need to be taken into the nerve ending by the same pump that takes up norepinephrine. Blockade of norepinephrine uptake will also potentiate the pressor effects of sympathomimetic amines, which are inactivated in part by being transported into the noradrenergic nerve ending. Antidepressants with higher potencies for norepinephrine uptake blockade (table 2) are more likely to cause these problems than the drugs with lower potency.

Aside from the possibility that inhibition of serotonin uptake is involved with the alleviation of depression, the possible clinical relevance of this property is uncertain. However, it may be a mechanism causing the gastrointestinal disturbances (i.e., anorexia, nausea) and anxiety seen in some patients taking the potent and selective serotonin uptake blockers (e.g., fluoxetine).

Table 3. Pharmacologic Properties of Antidepressants and Their Possible Clinical Consequences

Property	Possible clinical consequences
Blockade of norepinephrine uptake at nerve endings	• Alleviation of depression • Tremors • Tachycardia • Erectile and ejaculatory dysfunction • Blockade of the antihypertensive effects of guanethidine (Ismelin and Esimil) and guanadrel (Hylorel) • Augmentation of pressor effects of sympathomimetic amines
Blockade of serotonin uptake at nerve endings	• Alleviation of depression • Gastrointestinal disturbances • Anxiety
Blockade of histamine H_1 receptors	• Potentiation of central depressant drugs • Sedation drowsiness • Weight gain • Hypotension
Blockade of muscarinic receptors	• Blurred vision • Dry mouth • Sinus tachycardia • Constipation • Urinary retention • Memory dysfunction
Blockade of α_1-adrenergic receptors	• Potentiation of the antihypertensive effect of prazosin (Minipress) • Postural hypotension, dizziness • Reflex tachycardia
Blockade of α_2-adrenergic receptors	• Blockade of the antihypertensive effects of clonidine (Catapres), guanabenz (Wytensin), and α-methyldopa (Aldomet) • Priapism
Blockade of dopamine D_2 receptors	• Extrapyramidal movement disorders • Endocrine changes (prolactin elevation)
Blockade of serotonin S_2 receptors	• Ejaculatory dysfunction • Hypotension • Alleviation of migraine headaches

Blockade of Neurotransmitter Receptors by Antidepressants

The blockade of certain neurotransmitter receptors by antidepressants (Table 2) is responsible for numerous side effects of treatment and drug-drug interactions (Table 3). Monoamine oxidase inhibitors have very weak direct effects on these receptors and are practically devoid of activity (Lin and Richelson, unpublished data). The antidepressants that have been available and in standard use for some time in the United States are similar in their α_2-adrenergic receptor affinities but have a wide range of histamine H_1, muscarinic, α_1-adrenergic (El-Fakahany and Richelson 1983; Richelson and Nelson 1984), and serotonergic S_2 (Wander et al. 1986) affinities. Antidepressants are generally weak at blocking histamine H_2 receptors (Kanba and Richelson 1983) and have weak or no direct effects on many other receptors such as β-adrenergic, GABA, opioid, and benzodiazepine receptors (Hall and Ögren 1981). The side effects of the greatest importance for drug selection in a medical situation are the anticholinergic (more precisely, antimuscarinic), antihistaminic H_1, and α_1-adrenergic effects (Branconnier et al. 1985). In general, the tertiary amine tricyclic antidepressants are associated with major antihistaminic and anticholinergic side effects, and the secondary amines, particularly desipramine, cause less severe antihistaminic and anticholinergic side effects. Trazodone, fluoxetine, and bupropion are remarkable primarily for their practical absence of anticholinergic side effects (Richelson and Nelson 1984). Their efficacy and tolerability with regard to associated cardiac (Aronson and Hafez 1986; Cassem 1982; Irwin and Spar 1983; Janowsky et al. 1983; Rausch et al. 1984) and central nervous system (Gammon and Hansen 1984; Goldberg and Spector 1982; Jabbari et al. 1985; Kim 1982; Koval et al. 1982; Price and Mukherjee 1982; Ramirez 1983; Schwartz and Swaminathan 1982; Trimble 1980) side effects are still not clearly established. In addition, trazodone appears to be unique among antidepressants in causing priapism (Kogeorgos and de Alwis, 1986; Scher et al. 1983), possibly the result of relatively potent α_2-adrenoceptor blockade in combination with low muscarinic blocking potency (Table 2).

Antidepressants competitively antagonize the dopamine D_2 receptor but most are weak at doing so (Table 2). There is ample evidence to show that this interaction is of clinical importance for the most potent drug on the list, amoxapine, which is a metabolite of the neuroleptic loxapine (Loxitane), and can cause extrapyramidal and endocrine side effects. However, for the other drugs listed, there is little evidence to suggest that this effect in vitro is important clinically except perhaps when patients are taking conjugated estrogens (Krishnan et al. 1984).

Clinical Pharmacology

Pharmacokinetic studies indicate wide interindividual variation in the absorption, distribution, and excretion of the antidepressants (Sjöqvist et al. 1971). In addition, drug clearance generally declines with aging (Dawling et al. 1980; Nies et al. 1977). Table 4 outlines the usual daily doses for projected optimal therapeutic plasma ranges of tricyclic and other antidepressants. It should be noted that the American Psychiatric Association Task Force on the Use of Laboratory Tests in Psychiatry (1985) has concluded on the basis of available data that the plasma level measurements are clinically useful in certain situations for only three tricyclic antidepressants: imipramine, desipramine, and nortriptyline. Thus, because of insufficient data and contradictory results, the Task Force concluded that optimal therapeutic ranges for other antidepressants have yet to be established. Nonetheless, the projected ranges presented in Table 4 can be used as a guide in clinical practice.

Of particular note is the substantiated 10- to 30-fold variation in individual metabolism (Table 4), which necessitates specific attention to individualization of drug dosage and emphasizes the need to monitor drug plasma levels to achieve an appropriate therapeutic response, particularly in the elderly patient. The concept of a therapeutic window (i.e., a blood level range below and above which the drug is ineffective) has been thoroughly evaluated only for nortriptyline (APA Task Force 1985). Protriptyline and nortriptyline, in comparison with other tricyclic antidepressants, demonstrate increased potency (table 4); therefore, a smaller mean daily dose of these drugs should be prescribed. The longer elimination half-life ($T_{1/2}$) for protriptyline may in part explain the requirement for a lower dosage.

The mean elimination half-lives of most of the tricyclic antidepressants in table 4 are in the 15- to 30-hour range. The half-lives of maprotiline, protriptyline, and

Table 4. Pharmacokinetics, Daily doses, and Projected Therapeutic Plasma Ranges of Tricyclic and Other Antidepressants[a]

Drug (generic and trade names)	Individual variation in metabolism	Elimination half-life, $T_{1/2}$ (h) Mean	Range	Starting dosage[b] (mg/day)	Usual daily dose for adults (mg)	Usual dosage range (mg/day)	Projected[c] optimal therapeutic plasma range (ng/ml)
Tricyclic: tertiary amines							
Amitriptyline (Elavil, Endep)	10-fold	21	13-36	50	150-200	50-300	80-250[d]
Doxepin (Adapin, Sinequan)	10- to 15-fold	17	8-24	50	75-150	50-300	150-250[e]
Imipramine (SK-Pramine, Tofranil)	30-fold	28	18-34	50	75-150	50-300	150-250[f]
Trimipramine (Surmontil)	...	13	...	50	100-200	50-300	150-250
Tricyclic: secondary amines							
Desipramine (Norpramin, Pertofrane)	10-fold	21	12-30	50	100-200	50-300	125-300
Nortriptyline (Pamelor)	30-fold	36	14-79	20	75-100	30-125	50-150
Protriptyline (Vivactil)	10- to 15-fold	78	55-127	10	15-40	10-60	70-260
Dibenzoxazepine							
Amoxapine (Asendin)	...	8	8-30[g]	50	200-300	50-400	200-600[h]
Tetracyclic							
Maprotiline (Ludiomil)	...	43	...	50	100-150	50-225	200-600
Triazolopyridine							
Trazodone (Desyrel)	...	7	3-16	50	150-400	50-600	800-1600
Benzenepropanamine							
Fluoxetine (Prozac)	...	87	26-220	20	20-80	20-80	...
Propiophenone							
Bupropion (Wellbutrin)	...	9.8	3.9-23.1	200[i]	300[j]	100-450[k]	...
Monoamine Oxidase Inhibitors							
Isocarboxazid (Marplan)	...	...	...	30	10-30	10-30[l]	...
Phenelzine (Nardil)	...	2.8	1.5-4	15	45-60	45-90[m]	...
Tranylcypromine (Parnate)	4-fold	2.4	1.5-3	10	30-40	30-60	...

[a]References used for this table include Abernethy et al. 1984; Aronoff et al. 1984; Bayer et al. 1983; Caccia et al. 1982; Dawling et al. 1980; Kobayashi et al. 1985; Mallinger et al. 1986; Orsulak 1986; Richardson and Richelson 1984; Robinson et al. 1985; Schulz et al. 1985; Winstead et al. 1984.
[b]Dosage should be divided initially for all listed drugs, and elderly persons should be treated with about half of the usual dosage for adults.
[c]Only amitriptyline, imipramine, nortriptyline, and desipramine have been significantly studied for blood level versus clinical response (Task Force on the Use of Laboratory Tests in Psychiatry 1985).
[d]Amitriptyline + nortriptyline.
[e]Doxepin + desmethyldoxepin.
[f]Imipramine + desipramine.
[g]Amoxapine, eight hours; 8-hydroxyamoxapine, 30 hours.
[h]Amoxapine + 8-hydroxyamoxapine; of total drug measured, amoxapine–20 percent; 7-hydroxyamoxapine–15 percent; and 8-hydroxyamoxapine–65 percent.
[i]Dose should be divided, 100 mg b.i.d.
[j]Divided dose by 4th day of treatment.
[k]Maximum recommended divided dose achieved if no response after 3 weeks at the lower dosage.
[l]Dose should be reduced to a maintenance level of 10–20 mg daily (or less) once response begins because of the drug's cumulative effects.
[m]1 mg/kg (Robinson et al. 1978).

fluoxetine, however, are much longer; consequently, use of these drugs results in not only the requirement of a longer time to achieve a steady state after initiation of treatment but also the need for a longer period of observation of complications after ingestion of an overdose. Based upon pharmacokinetic considerations (Gibaldi and Levy 1976), a rational dosing interval for an antidepressant drug is equal to its elimination half-life (table 4). In practice, a single daily dose is appropriate for those drugs with half-lives of around 15 hours or greater (Weise et al. 1980); and it is reasonable to consider prescribing the very long half-life compounds—protriptyline, fluoxetine, and maprotiline—less frequently, especially in the elderly patients.

Other pharmacokinetic information of clinical importance is that these agents are highly lipid soluble and therefore have a high volume of distribution. They are also strongly bound to plasma proteins. Changes in body fat and plasma proteins with aging, therefore, can have effects on the clearance of a drug and its potency (Richelson 1984).

Published reports have also described rare hematologic (agranulocytosis) (Ebert and Shader 1970) effects, drug interactions (Gualtieri and Power 1978), and possible teratogenicity (Rachelefsky et al. 1972), which should be a consideration in prescription and clinical management.

Clinical Applications

Much of the aforementioned information is derived from in vitro studies, and individual patient variability is considerable in terms of side effects and symptom response. Nevertheless, a general set of guidelines for choosing a drug in various clinical situations can be constructed on the basis of all the pharmacologic information. All of the antidepressants mentioned appear to have equivalent clinical efficacy; however, some of them have been available and in clinical use for a long time and therefore have a longer established efficacy. In general, these older drugs are also considerably less expensive. A patient will usually tolerate the side effects if they are carefully explained and monitored through the initial period of treatment. The initial dose is approximately one-fourth of the maximal usual daily dose for adults (Table 4). The dose is then adjusted incrementally every second or third day, as tolerated, until this maximal dose is reached. Because individual metabolism varies extensively, particularly in elderly patients, achievement of adequate, nontoxic dosages may necessitate checking the blood level of the drug after a steady state has been reached (usually after a time equal to four times the elimination half-life). For most patients, however, careful clinical supervision and monitoring are adequate.

If antimuscarinic side effects (Table 3) become intolerable, use of one of the more expensive, but generally better tolerated, newer antidepressants (fluoxetine, trazodone, or bupropion) may be helpful.

Knowledge of the pharmacologic features of the antidepressants facilitates the development of a rationale for improved selection of antidepressants in certain clinical situations in which depression coexists with a major medical disorder. Table 5 summarizes the preferred antidepressants in those situations.

Cardiovascular

At therapeutic blood levels, amitriptyline and imipramine appear to produce more tachycardia and postural hypotension than does nortriptyline (Georgotas et al. 1987; Roose et al. 1987). Maprotiline, a tetracyclic compound, may have fewer arrhyth-

Table 5.   Preferred Antidepressants When Specific Medical Disorders Coexist with Depression

I.   Cardiovascular
    A. Congestive heart failure or coronary artery disease—nortriptyline
    B. Conduction defect—maprotiline
    C. Hypertension treated with guanethidine or guanadrel—trazodone, bupropion, trimipramine, fluoxetine
    D. Hypertension treated with prazosin—fluoxetine, bupropion, desipramine, protriptyline
    E. Hypertension treated with clonidine, guanabenz or α-methyldopa—bupropion, fluoxetine, maprotiline
    F. Untreated mild hypertension—imipramine, monoamine oxidase inhibitor
    G. Postural hypotension—bupropion, fluoxetine, maprotiline (avoid imipramine and amitriptyline).
II. Neurologic
    A. Seizure disorder—monoamine oxidase inhibitor best, secondary amine (desipramine) better than tertiary amine (e.g., imipramine). Avoid maprotiline, amoxapine, trimipramine, bupropion.
    B. Organic brain syndrome—trazodone, bupropion, fluoxetine, amoxapine, maprotiline, desipramine
    C. Chronic pain syndrome—amitriptyline, doxepin
    D. Migraine headaches—trazodone, doxepin, trimipramine, amitriptyline
    E. Psychosis—antidepressant plus neuroleptic, amoxapine
    F. Parkinsonism—amitriptyline, protriptyline, trimipramine, doxepin, imipramine. Avoid amoxapine.
    G. Tardive dyskinesia—trazodone, desipramine, doxepin, imipramine. Avoid amoxapine.
III. Allergic—doxepin, amitriptyline, trimipramine, imipramine, nortriptyline
IV. Gastrointestinal
    A. Chronic diarrhea—doxepin, trimipramine, amitriptyline, imipramine, protriptyline
    B. Chronic constipation—trazodone, bupropion, fluoxetine, amoxapine, maprotiline, desipramine
    C. Peptic ulcer disease—doxepin, trimipramine, amitriptyline, imipramine
V.   Urologic
    A. Neurogenic bladder—trazodone, bupropion, fluoxetine, amoxapine, maprotiline, desipramine
    B. Organic impotence—trazodone, bupropion, fluoxetine, amoxapine, maprotiline, desipramine
VI. Ophthalmologic (angle-closure glaucoma)—trazodone, bupropion, fluoxetine, amoxapine, maprotiline, desipramine

mogenic effects than do tricyclic antidepressants (Brorson and Wennerblom 1982). Therefore, in patients with congestive heart disease or ischemic heart disease, nortriptyline is preferred; and in patients with conduction defect, maprotiline. Although initially thought to be free of myocardial effects, trazodone has recently been reported to have some effects on cardiac rhythm (Aronson and Hafez 1986; Irwin and Spar 1983; Janowsky et al. 1983; Rausch et al. 1984). In studies of patients with heart disease, therapeutic doses of tricyclic antidepressants (nortriptyline, imipramine, and doxepin) produce no appreciable effect on left ventricular ejection fraction or left ventricular wall motion (Glassman et al. 1983; Roose et al. 1986; Taylor and Braithwaite 1978; Veith et al. 1982).

Only one study has been published on the use of an antidepressant drug in the period immediately after myocardial infarction (Selvini et al. 1976), and none has been published on antidepressant use in the period immediately after coronary artery bypass. Selvini et al. (1976), using a low dose of maprotiline (25 mg bid) on patients who were in the early stages of acute myocardial infarction, found this drug to be well tolerated and efficacious. Imipramine has been used with efficacy and safety in patients with depression four months after severe cardiac injury (Raskind et al. 1982). However, postural hypotension is a problem with this drug.

Trazodone, trimipramine, and fluoxetine inhibit norepinephrine uptake the least and, therefore, are appropriate choices in treating a depressed patient who requires guanethidine (Mitchell et al. 1967). Desipramine and protriptyline have the least affinity for α_1-adrenergic receptors and should produce the least potentiation of the antihypertensive effects of prazosin, an antihypertensive drug with potent α_1-adrenoceptor blocking activity. In general, the antidepressant compounds are relatively weak α_2-adrenergic receptor antagonists (maprotiline, desipramine, and protriptyline are the weakest) but in some cases can interfere with antihypertensive treatment with clonidine or α-methyldopa (Briant et al. 1973; Van Spanning and Van Zwieten 1973; Van Spanning and Van Zwieten 1975). Imipramine produces orthostatic hypotension more often than does nortriptyline (Roose et al. 1987). In some patients, use of monoamine oxidase inhibitors obviates other antihypertensive treatment.

Neurologic

Maprotiline, amoxapine, trimipramine, and imipramine lower the seizure threshold more than desipramine or a monoamine oxidase inhibitor does; thus, these last two drugs are preferred in depressed patients with seizure disorders (Itil and Soldatos 1980; Jabbari et al. 1985; Kim 1982; Koval et al. 1982; Price and Mukherjee 1982; Ramirez 1983; Schwartz and Swaminathan 1982; Trible 1980). For bupropion, the observed rate of seizures was 0.4 in a prospective study of 3,331 depressed patients over eight weeks. The cumulative rate of all patients meeting criteria of being on a minimum dose of 90% of 300 mg and greater (2,708 patients) in the eight-week study was 0.36 (Johnston 1989).

Because anticholinergic effects can increase confusion in patients with organic brain syndrome, trazodone, fluoxetine, maprotiline, amoxapine, and desipramine are preferred if such patients require antidepressant treatment. The same rationale applies to patients with neurogenic bladder, prostatism, or erectile dysfunction. Patients with organic psychosis and depression are usually treated with a combination of a neuroleptic agent and an antidepressant, although amoxapine (a neuroleptic metabolite with some dopamine-blocking activity [Richelson and Nelson 1984]) may be of some benefit in these patients. (There is a risk of tardive dyskinesia and other extrapyramidal side effects with use of this agent.) Amoxapine also has the advantage of low risk for anticholinergic exacerbation of confusion.

Migraine headaches may benefit the most from the choice of an antidepressant with a relatively high affinity for serotonin receptors such as trazodone and amoxapine, compounds that are equal to and at least 10-fold more potent, respectively, than methysergide at blocking the serotonin S_2 receptor (table 2). Although drugs such as trazodone, amitriptyline, and doxepin block serotonin re-uptake at the nerve ending, they more potently block the serotonin S_2 receptor so that the likely net effect is receptor blockade rather than receptor activation (Wander et al. 1986). More potent blockade of serotonin S_2 receptors could explain the usefulness of amitriptyline in the prophylaxis of migraine headaches (Couch and Hassanein 1979). Antidepressants such as amitriptyline (Carasso et al. 1979; Edelbroek et al. 1986) and doxepin (Hameroff et al. 1984) are also used to treat chronic pain, but the evidence for their efficacy in treating this problem is very limited (Walsh 1983).

Patients with parkinsonism and depression may benefit from the anticholinergic effects of amitriptyline, protriptyline, doxepin, or imipramine. Amoxapine should be avoided because it blocks dopamine receptors, an effect that can aggravate parkinsonism or bring about this problem as well as other extrapyramidal difficulties (Gammon and Hansen 1984; Lapierre and Anderson 1983; Ross et al. 1983; Thornton and Stahl 1984).

Allergic Diseases

In patients with depression and severe allergic disorders, including dermatologic allergies and idiopathic pruritus, doxepin (Goldsobel et al. 1986; Greene et al. 1985; Sullivan 1982), trimipramine, amitriptyline, and maprotiline, with their antihistaminic side effects (Richelson 1979, 1983), are the preferred drugs.

Gastrointestinal

Patients with severe chronic diarrhea and depression may benefit from the antimuscarinic side effects of doxepin, amitriptyline, trimipramine, protriptyline, or imipramine. Conversely, in a depressed patient with chronic constipation, trazodone, fluoxetine, amoxapine, maprotiline, and desipramine are preferred. In patients with peptic ulcer disease and severe depression, trimipramine and doxepin, with their anticholinergic and histamine H_2-antagonist effects, would be preferred although clinical evidence is as yet inconclusive (Richelson 1982b, 1983; Ries et al. 1984).

Ophthalmologic

In general, the anticholinergic side effects of antidepressants should be avoided in patients with angle-closure glaucoma; thus, trazodone, fluoxetine, amoxapine, maprotiline and desipramine are the preferred drugs (Schwartz 1978).

General Clinical Guidelines

In addition to consideration of the medical disorder, type of depression, and antidepressant side effects for determining the appropriate choice of drug in any particular clinical situation, certain clinical guidelines exist for drug choice, dosage, duration, maintenance, termination, and alternatives to treatment with antidepressants. Table 6 outlines these guidelines.

The first step is the appropriate choice of drug. In general, choose a tertiary amine tricyclic or a more sedating drug for patients with episodes of agitated depression, and a secondary amine tricyclic or a less sedating drug for those patients with retarded depressive episodes. History of a previous response of the patient or a family member to a particular antidepressant drug can sometimes be helpful in selecting a drug for a patient.

The second important guideline is the appropriate dose of medication. Most patients tolerate treatment best if the beginning dose is one-fourth of the maximal, usual daily dose for adults (table 4). The dose should be divided initially and increased in a stepwise fashion every two to three days until the maximal, usual daily dose has been achieved, if tolerated. For example, for desipramine the target dose is 200 mg per day (Table 4). A patient could be started on desipramine 25 mg bid for two days;

Table 6. Clinical Guidelines for Use of Antidepressants

1. Appropriate choice: select on the basis of the profile of side effects, particularly sedative effects in agitated patients, or on the basis of previous response or family history of a response to a particular antidepressant
2. Adequate dose: check blood level if toxicity ensues or if response is inadequate
3. Adequate duration: administer for a minimum of four months after recovery
4. Adequate termination or maintenance: for first depressions, four to five months after recovery, taper dose gradually for two to four months, and then discontinue therapy. For recurrent unipolar depression, maintain therapy with antidepressant
5. Adequate therapy: for almost all types of depression, a combination of psychotherapy (usually, brief supportive) and antidepressants may be slightly more effective than antidepressants alone
6. Adequate alternative: change drug, add lithium carbonate, add thyroid hormone, use monoamine oxidase inhibitor in combination with a tricyclic antidepressant (avoiding imipramine), or use electroshock therapy

then 25 mg tid for two days; then 50 mg bid for two days; then 50 mg tid for two days; and finally, if no very troublesome adverse effects are present, 100 mg bid. After about one to two weeks at this target dosage, patients may take antidepressants with the longer elimination half-lives (around 15 hour or greater, table 4) one a day at bedtime. Elderly patients may benefit from being continued on the divided dosage schedule so that high blood levels (possibly leading to adverse effects) do not occur during the night when the patient may arise to eliminate.

Use of monoamine oxidase inhibitors requires special considerations. These are very efficacious drugs for treating depression, are well tolerated by the elderly (Georgotas et al. 1986), and should be used when a patient fails to respond to antidepressants of other classes (Roose et al. 1986) or when specific conditions prevail, as noted in table 5. However, these drugs are not for all cases because of the need for the patient on a monoamine oxidase inhibitor to avoid certain foodstuffs, especially those containing tyramine, and certain drugs, especially over-the-counter cold remedies containing sympathomimetics. The clinician must make the patient aware of these important precautions when prescribing a monoamine oxidase inhibitor, and a convenient way to ensure that the patient has all the information in hand is to give him a copy of the American Medical Association Patient Medication Instruction Sheet (PMI) "MAO Inhibitor Antidepressants" (PMI 076). When a patient is not willing or able to comply with these precautions, another type of antidepressant should be prescribed.

If the patient is taking a tricyclic antidepressant or another monoamine oxidase inhibitor, this drug should be discontinued for 10 days before starting another monoamine oxidase inhibitor. To be underscored in the list of drugs that should be avoided in patients on monoamine oxidase inhibitors are meperidine, imipramine and fluoxetine. However, it is possible to combine safely a monoamine oxidase inhibitor with a tricyclic antidepressant other than imipramine in special circumstances, as discussed further below.

Of the three different monoamine oxidase inhibitors currently in use in the United States (Table 4), phenelzine has probably been studied the most. From this research it is known that around two weeks are needed to achieve maximal inhibition of platelet monoamine oxidase when depressed patients are given phenelzine (Murphy et al. 1977; Robinson et al. 1978) and about the same length of time is necessary to recover activity after the drug is discontinued. Patients with 80 percent or greater inhibition of this platelet enzyme have a better antidepressant response than do those with less inhibition of their enzyme (Robinson et al. 1978). Although laboratories are making available the measurement of platelet monoamine oxidase, a clinically useful rule of thumb is to target a dosage of 1 mg/kg body weight per day for the patient (Robinson et al. 1978) to achieve this desired level of inhibition.

As with other antidepressants, monoamine oxidase inhibitors may be started slowly. For example, when starting a patient on phenelzine, the clinician may prescribe 15 mg the first day, 15 mg bid the second day, 15 mg tid the third day, and so forth until the target dosage is achieved.

A treatment period of two to four weeks is usually necessary before the onset of therapeutic effects of any type of antidepressant. During the initial period of treatment, the patient may need a thorough explanation of the side effects to be expected and encouragement to persist with treatment until a clinical response ensues. If the clinical response is inadequate in three to four weeks and the adverse effects are minimal, increase the dose a step further. Underdosing is a common error in therapeutics with these drugs. As in the example above with desipramine, increase the dosage another 25 to 50 mg per day; with phenelzine, increase the dosage another 15 mg per day. However, if poor response persists after two more weeks at the higher dosage or if toxicity supervenes, plasma levels of the drug, provided that it is not a monoamine oxidase inhibitor, should be ascertained. Although therapeutic plasma concentrations have been firmly established for only imipramine, nortriptyline, and desipramine (APA Task Force 1985), enough data are available for other antidepressants (other than monoamine oxidase inhibitors) to determine for problem patients or elderly patients whether a dosage of a drug appears to be adequate. The projected optimal therapeutic plasma range presented in Table 4 for the other antidepressants is to be used only as a rough guide.

Elderly patients are likely to require about half of the usual daily dose that is recommended for a younger adult and may require a slower escalation of the dosage to the maximal level because of their increased sensitivity to the adverse effects of antidepressants. However, underdosing can again be a mistake in treating elderly patients, and plasma levels should be utilized more often with this group. Achievement of a steady state in these patients may take longer as well (Salzman 1982).

Third, adequate duration of treatment is important. After a complete clinical response has been achieved, therapy should be continued for at least four to five months (Prien and Kupfer 1986).

The fourth important clinical guideline involves termination of antidepressant therapy or maintenance therapy for patients with recurrent illness. Four to five months after complete recovery, the drug dose should be tapered gradually over two to four months (this length of time is suggested on the basis of clinical experience, since there is a lack of research on this topic to guide us) and then discontinued; this is because abrupt withdrawal of medication may predispose the patient to relapse of depressive symptoms or to uncomfortable symptoms—for example, dysesthesias and severe sleep disturbance (Dilsaver et al. 1983; Gelenberg and Klerman 1978; Kramer et al. 1961; Santos and McCurdy 1980; Stern and Mendels 1980; Tyrer 1984). Maintenance therapy with the same antidepressant (at a lower dosage of drug, if possible) should be used for those patients with recurrent unipolar depression (Prien et al. 1984).

The fifth clinical guideline is that adequate therapy for almost all types of depression should include some form of psychotherapeutic alliance between the patient and doctor at least to ensure compliance with the pharmacotherapy. This may be achieved through brief (10- to 20-minute) supportive visits with the primary physician or, in some cases, more extensive psychotherapy. However, a combination of antidepressants and psychotherapy may be only slightly more effective than antidepressants alone (Conte et al. 1986).

Finally, adequate knowledge of alternative or adjunctive treatments for depression is important. A change in primary antidepressant drug to an antidepressant of a different chemical class; the addition of lithium carbonate (De Montigny et al. 1981) in a dosage to achieve a blood level in the range of 0.8 to 1.2 mEq/l; the addition of thyroid hormone (1-triiodothyronine 25 to 50 micrograms per day) (Goodwin et al. 1982); or, more controversial, the combination of a tricyclic antidepressant with a monoamine oxidase inhibitor (Razani et al. 1983; Spiker and Pugh 1976; White and Simpson 1981) may be beneficial. If this latter approach is elected, the safest course is to withdraw the patient from the antidepressant for 10 days and begin both types of medications at low doses together. Combination of the tertiary amine tricyclic antidepressant imipramine and a monoamine oxidase inhibitor must be avoided. In addition, combination of fluoxentine and a monoamine oxidase inhibitor may cause significant adverse effects. Electroconvulsive therapy is still the most effective for refractory depression and may be the treatment of choice in certain medical situations that contraindicate the use of antidepressant medication (American Psychiatric Association Task Force Report 1978; Avery and Winokur 1977; Davidson et al. 1978; Fink 1978), in conditions of extremely high suicidal risk, or in depression with psychotic features (Lykouras et al. 1986). In this latter case, the combination of an antidepressant with a neuroleptic may be superior to either drug alone (Kaskey et al. 1980). Psychostimulants may also be useful to treat depression in certain medical and surgical patients (Woods et al. 1986), while their efficacy in more general cases of depression is not established (Chiarello and Cole 1987; Mattes 1985).

Chapter 165

Drug Treatment of Resistant Depression

The "treatment-resistant" patient is, by definition, one who has failed to respond to therapeutic intervention. Discussion of treatment options for nonresponders, however, must first consider the adequacy of prior treatment before describing the patient as "resistant." Suboptimal improvement occurs commonly in depressed patients. In many dozens of antidepressant clinical trials over the last three decades, 20–40 percent of subjects consistently failed to respond to treatment (Baldessarini 1985; Davis 1985). Further, for these studies, "responders" were generally those who "improved," rather than those who were restored to euthymia. The number of "nonresponders" would have been yet higher if all patients suffering residual symptoms had been considered in addition to those initial responders who lost benefit (Cohen and Baldessarini 1985). In clinical practice, the goal of treatment is to seek complete remission of the patient's depressive syndrome; whereas a residual Hamilton Depression Scale score of 10–12 in a treatment study may reflect a drug effect, this outcome might fall short of a patient's premorbid baseline. Thus, if the goal of treatment is remission, substantial numbers of patients achieve an inadequate result.

An initial threshold for the label of treatment resistance would be for a patient to fail to respond to one attempt at *adequate* antidepressant treatment, as with a tricyclic antidepressant (TCA) at a dose of 150 mg (in imipramine equivalents) or more for a period of four to six weeks. Such a regimen might be considered a minimum adequate intervention. Below this level of treatment are patients who appear resistant but who have failed to respond to *inadequate* treatment. Inadequate treatment is not a trivial clinical issue and may well be the most common level of intervention (Keller et al. 1982; Keller et al. 1986). Data from the NIMH Collaborative Study on the Psycho-biology of Depression indicate that a minority of patients with major depressions are treated with any antidepressant and that a very small number receive the equivalent of 150 mgm or greater. (These data were derived from patients in or seeking treatment, not from epidemiologic samples.) Subtherapeutic prescribing may reflect prescriber unfamiliarity with antidepressants or concern about possible risks associated with antidepressants; an additional major contribution to the high rate of inadequate treatment, however, is the difficulty some patients have in tolerating adequate dosing as a consequence of side effects (Pollack and Rosenbaum 1987). Excessive side effects, in turn, are at times an indicator of prescriber unfamiliarity with titrating dosing and managing treatment-emergent adverse effects. Thus, before reviewing treatment strategies for the resistant patient, factors associated with inadequate treatment should be considered.

First Considerations

Before introducing novel pharmacologic strategies or drug changes, the essential clinical task in evaluating the nonresponder is a careful assessment of the adequacy of treatment to date. Systematic scrutiny must be first directed toward the following:

1. whether the current medication *dose* and that of prior medication trials were adequate;
2. whether these agents were administered for adequate *duration*; and
3. whether the patient had understood medication instructions and had *complied* with the prescription.

With respect to dose, one author (JR) estimates that a substantial number (more than half) of depressed patients referred to one psychopharmacology unit for "treatment resistance" respond after following a recommendation to increase medication dose. This observation reflects two factors: 1) the range of medication dosing traditionally believed adequate for antidepressant treatment (e.g., a target dose of 150 mgm of imipramine or its equivalent) is, for many, too low (Quitkin 1985); 2) some clinicians, while willing to prescribe an antidepressant, are nonetheless uneasy about potential adverse effects and consequently are reluctant to prescribe more than relatively low doses. Accumulating evidence points to higher rates of treatment response in clinical trials that permit dosing beyond the 150 mgm standard (Quitkin 1985). For example, Stewart et al. (1980) report an 85 percent response rate in depressed patients (both inpatients and outpatients) when the mean maximum dose of desipramine prescribed was over 280 mgm.

Ambulatory patients with milder and chronic forms of depression are particularly likely to receive suboptimal levels of treatment. The notion that milder forms of depression require less vigorous dosing exposes patients to the risks of drug treatment with diminished likelihood of response. Available evidence suggests that patients with milder and chronic forms of depression may eventually respond to standard agents when dosage is raised to adequate levels (Kocsis et al. 1985). It is possible, furthermore, that mild and residual forms of depression may be relatively more resistant and may require higher dosing; Keller et al. (1983), for example, have reported that patients with double depression—those who develop acute major depression on a background of dysthymia or a milder chronic depression—readily recover to their dysthymic or mildly depressed baseline. It appears that residual symptoms (the last 10–15 points on the Hamilton Depression Scale) may be particularly difficult to achieve and thus may require more vigorous intervention.

In some cases, as with nortriptyline and possibly with other secondary amine tricyclics such as desipramine, nonresponse may reflect a need for dosing *decrease* (APA Task Force 1985). The "therapeutic window" evident in clinical trials of nortriptyline suggests that optimal patient response occurs above a certain plasma level threshold (usually 50 micrograms per liter) and below an upper level (usually 150 micrograms per liter). These numbers, however, reflect means from groups of patient studied, and the window for individual patients may vary and be determined by a number of unmeasured factors, such as the amount of free and protein-bound drug, and other idiosyncratic differences.

Another critical source of treatment failure is inadequate duration of antidepressant administration (Quitkin et al. 1986). Just as 150 mgm proves to be a suboptimal dose for many patients, a two- to four-weeks' latency to antidepressant response is also frequently inadequate. While some patients do respond early, clinical research and experience suggest that a significant number of patients require additional weeks before the expected antidepressant response appears. Quitkin et al. (1984) compared the rate of antidepressant response to a TCA in clinical trials at week four versus week six; more than a third of patients who were ultimately responders at week six had failed to show improvement by week four. Thus, impatience on the part of the prescriber or the patient may lead to frequent changes of apparently ineffective medications, which, with more time, may have yielded a treatment response. Further, if six weeks were required for some to respond, *more* than six weeks may yield response for others (Quitkin et al. 1986). Thus, a patient describing treatment failure on a number of agents may have been subjected to a series of trials of suboptimal duration. Evaluation of the treatment-resistant patient, therefore, must include an attempt to detail not only dosing but also duration of each trial undertaken. Further, there is an important relation between dose and duration; that is, neither adequate dose nor adequate duration alone may be sufficient to allow for response. The patient must take an adequate dose for an adequate length of time.

With respect to treatment compliance, failure to ingest the tablet is the first obstacle to bioavailability. Unless considerable time is allowed to prepare the patient for antidepressant treatment, to explain the rationale for the administration of medication, and to describe the critical nature of dose and time, some patients may have unrealistic expectations for the medication (e.g., they may be looking for therapeutic effects with each dose), leading to frustration and premature abandonment of treatment. In addition to dose and duration of treatment, patients must be made aware of likely treatment-emergent adverse effects and their management (Pollack and Rosenbaum 1987). Preparation of the patient for the antidepressant treatment is as critical as the "prep" of the patient for any other medical procedure. Failure to allow adequate time for this task will create obstacles for optimal response. For example, a patient uninformed about the possibility of postural hypotension and experiencing light-headedness or dizziness in the early days of treatment may well abandon treatment; on the other hand, if this side effect is anticipated and explained, the patient will know to inform the physician and be more likely to form an alliance to seek strategies to overcome or eliminate the effect.

Predicting Response

Certain features of a patient's clinical history and presentation reassure the clinician that the pursuit of alternative pharmacotherapeutic strategies is indicated and that it is reasonable to expect a therapeutic benefit from biological treatment. For example, history of response to antidepressant treatment for the patient (or a family member) is considered a predictor of drug responsiveness. Few data, however, support this common assertion. Similarly, first choice of agent typically includes drugs that the patient has responded to in the past or that have been helpful for a family member. On the other hand, the patient may at one point in time fail to respond to a formerly successful treatment or may at a later time respond to a regime that had previously proven unsuccessful. Thus, due to idiosyncratic variations in patient responsiveness to treatment, prior treatment response history is an uncertain guideline.

One reassuring piece of clinical history is a patient report of prior periods in life of well-being. The history of depression-free times gives the clinician and patient a therapeutic target and suggests that the patient's psychopathology and neurobiology are capable of euthymia. Nonetheless, chronicity does not preclude response.

Determinations of those depressive symptoms or clusters of symptoms most predictive of a positive response to drug treatment describe the "RDC endogenous subtype" of depression, or DSM III (American Psychiatric Association 1980) melancholia, as being the diagnosis most associated with response to antidepressant treatment. Certain specific symptoms—psychomotor retardation, anhedonia (loss of interest and pleasure), and emotional withdrawal—have also been associated with higher rates of antidepressant response (Bielski and Friedel 1976; Friedel 1983; Nelson and Charney 1981). Nelson et al. (1984) determined 10 symptoms associated with favorable response to desipramine in patients with nondelusional melancholia: depressed mood, hopelessness, guilt, worthlessness, early morning awakening, decreased interest in work and activities, decreased appetite, loss of energy, anhedonia, and somatic anxiety.

One of the most challenging differential diagnostic assessments in psychiatry is to distinguish a dysphoric state that reflects "characterological" problems from one that is due to a pharmacologically reversible chronic depression or dysthymia (Akiskal 1982, 1983; Akiskal et al. 1980). The diagnosis of characterological depression implies refractoriness to drug treatment and possible response to psychotherapy. Unfortunately, the patient with chronic depression who fails to respond to initial pharmacologic treatment may be prematurely assigned a characterological diagnosis and denied further vigorous antidepressant treatment. The characterological depressive diagnosis, therefore, may signal physician frustration at treatment failure.

The relationship between personality, life events, and mood state is a complicated one, and most depressive syndromes are best understood as a consequence of an interaction among intrapsychic structures, environmental stressors, and a dysregulated central nervous system (CNS). Nevertheless, there are individuals who are not "depressed" in the syndromic sense but who suffer primarily from object relations pathology, feeling empty, alone, bored, and easily fragmented by life stress into a state of intense dysphoria. Their problem is often best understood in terms of internal objects and interpersonal relations, but their complaint may be expressed as depression and anxiety. Complicating the differential diagnosis, however, is the fact that character pathology and syndromic depressions are not exclusive disorders; indeed, the former may predispose to the latter, and optimal treatment will require both intensive psychotherapy and antidepressant pharmacotherapy.

In the past, selection of a treatment modality for depression relied heavily on the identification of an antecedent or precipitant of depression to distinguish a "reactive" from an "endogenous" condition. The latter was presumed to be drug responsive while the former was presumed to require psychotherapy. Nonetheless, emotional reactivity to life events appears not to be a consistent predictor of a negative response to drug. In fact, marked interpersonal reactivity of mood, for example, is associated with a positive response to monoamine oxidase (MAO) inhibitors in particular (Liebowitz et al. 1984). Further, major depressive syndromes with a greater number of antecedent life events were particularly likely in one report to have a favorable course (Monroe et al. 1985); that is, reactive depressions appear more likely to respond to drug or other treatment, possibly indicating enhanced reversibility of a syndrome where the underlying diathesis required external stress for its manifestation.

Just as certain life events, such as separations and losses, are more frequently implicated as provocative of depression in those predisposed, chronic or recurrent exposure to these triggers (as with persistent marital conflict) may be the source of chronicity of depressive suffering. Thus, an optimal intervention must address the "depressogenic" environment and the intrapsychic and interpersonal patterns that sustain it. In the consulting room, a psychological-biologic dichotomy poorly serves most patients.

Considerable data indicate that psychotherapy and pharmacotherapy are effectively co-administered (Conte et al. 1986; Rounsaville et al. 1981) and, therefore, that psychological management is an integral part of the treatment of all patients with depression where possible. Every clinician must be alert to syndromic as well as intrapsychic and interpersonal issues.

Biologic Causes of Refractoriness

Several biologic or medical factors should be reviewed in the history of a patient who has failed to respond to adequate treatment:

1. Despite seemingly appropriate dosages, plasma antidepressant levels may be suboptimal (APA Task Force 1985; Lydiard 1985) or, in some cases as noted above, too high.
2. Interactions with or effects of nonantidepressant medication may interfere with an antidepressant outcome (Cassem 1987). The clinician should suspect *any* agent in regular use by a refractory patient, especially antihypertensives. Medications

may impede antidepressant efficacy by altering absorption or metabolism or by interfering with CNS mechanisms of action. A patient on beta blockers may be nonresponsive to treatment, only to respond adequately when the antihypertensive medication is changed, for example, to an angiotensin-converting enzyme inhibiter.

3. Not only may excessive alcohol intake or other drug overuse lead to increased metabolism of psychotropic drugs, but depression may be secondary to chronic alcohol overuse, with remission of the depressive syndrome following detoxification and sustained sobriety.

4. The clinician should consider a variety of medical illnesses that may be either a source of treatment resistance or the underlying cause of the depressive syndrome (Cassem 1987). Examples include endocrine dysfunction (e.g., hypothyroidism and hypoadrenalism), infectious diseases (e.g., hepatitis, mononucleosis, and other viral or postviral syndromes), CNS diseases (e.g., Parkinson's, Huntington's, and Alzheimer's), or neoplastic disease. A positive response to antidepressant treatment, on the other hand, does not rule out these disorders. A recent concern is the possibility that the first manifestation of AIDS may be a psychiatric disorder.

5. Age may be considered a biologic cause of refractoriness (Brown et al. 1983); older patients may have more resistant depressive syndromes. Platelet MAO levels increase with age, suggesting that MAO inhibitors (MAOIs) may be particularly useful for some older patients (Jenike 1984, 1985) and for treatment-resistant geriatric depressed patients, in particular (Georgotas 1983).

6. Treatment resistance for many, and particularly for the aged, derives from the inability to tolerate treatment-emergent adverse effects of antidepressants. As mentioned earlier, this may be a source of relative resistance, and the clinician should be aware of the side-effect profiles of available antidepressants. Most side effects of a given class of drug can be managed or minimized by a selection of agents with the most favorable profile (Pollack and Rosenbaum 1987).

Treatment Options for the Resistant Depressed Patient

The array of possible antidepressant treatments, including combinations and adjuncts (Akiskal 1985; Brotman et al. 1987; Gerner 1983; Paykel and Van Woerkom 1987; Zetin et al. 1986), is daunting, and no clear algorithm has emerged to guide the clinician as to the correct sequence of treatment selection. When planning treatment for a patient who has been refractory to standard inventions, it is valuable to have familiarity with all the potential therapeutic strategies (see Table 1).

After a TCA

Given adequate dose and duration of treatment with a TCA, for example, there are few systematically gathered data to guide subsequent choices (e.g., to pursue the same agent for more time at higher doses, to change to another TCA, to select from another class of non-MAOI, or to change to an MAOI). The use of "adjuncts" has been gaining appeal, given the expendiency of adding a second agent to potentiate a first. Adjuncts or adjuvants such as lithium carbonate and thyroid hormones allow the clinician to avoid discontinuation of one medication before instituting a new treatment. The patient, therefore, need not endure withdrawal of one agent, followed by titration of a new drug to therapeutic levels and additional latency before response.

Table 1. Biologic Treatment Options

Tricyclic antidepressants • Lithium • T_3 • Stimulant • Neuroleptic • Reserpine • MAOI • "Precursor" Monoamine Oxidase Inhibitors • Lithium • T_3 • Stimulant • Neuroleptic • "Precursor" "Newer" antidepressants	Other treatments or adjuvants • Carbamazepine • Stimulants • L-tryptophan and other precursors • Estrogen and testosterone Nonpharmacologic therapies • Partial sleep deprivation • Advancing sleep phase • High-intensity light Electroconvulsive therapy

A traditional initial approach has been to change to a different agent of the same class—a patient of imipramine, for example, changing to amitriptyline or nortriptyline. With a lack of data on this strategy, one TCA would appear to have the same spectrum of efficiacy as another. Although clinical experience suggests that some patients respond to one TCA when they have failed on another, it is also apparent that these agents are more alike than different. Thus, the use of an adjunct with a TCA, in addition to the advantages of continuing an ongoing treatment and possibly accelerating its benefits, represents a more distinct treatment change than switching to another TCA.

The Lithium "Boost"

An important development in antidepressant pharmacotherapy was the observation that an addition of relatively low doses of lithium to standard antidepressant therapies resulted in dramatic improvement in a number of patients whose initial response had been suboptimal. Beginning with a report by de Montigny et al. (1981), the strategy of adding "low-dose lithium" to standard antidepressant treatment has been increasingly employed. The earliest report (de Montigny et al. 1981) suggested that patients who had failed to respond to standard doses of imipramine (e.g., 150 mgm for four weeks) would experience dramatic remissions of depression in a period as brief as 48 to 72 hours on doses as low as 600 mgm a day. While subsequent reports (Heninger et al. 1983; Price et al. 1986; Zusky et al. 1988) have been less optimistic about very rapid responses in all nonresponders, the strategy has taken its place in the antidepressant pharmacopoeia. Later reports (de Montigny et al. 1983; Heninger et al. 1983; Price et al. 1986; Zusky et al. 1988) indicate three possible outcomes of adding lithium to antidepressant treatment. First, some nonresponders—more than 50 percent in one large series (Cohen et al. 1988)—at low doses do experience a dramatic "switch" to euthymia within a few days of lithium addition. Others do not respond so rapidly or dramatically to low doses of lithium but do manifest a more gradual onset of benefit at more standard lithium doses (e.g., 900–1200 µg a day) with a longer latency, such as three weeks. A third group of patients fail to benefit from the strategy.

It is unknown whether low-dose lithium is more effective with one antidepressant than with another; the strategy has been observed to be effective for patients on a variety of agents, however, including both TCAs and MAOIs (Price et al. 1985). The use of low-dose or standard-dose lithium as an addition to TCA treatment does not result in increased antidepressant side effects or plasma levels and has also been reported to be effective for patients with either nonpsychotic or psychotic depression. In the latter case, nonresponders to combined TCA and neuroleptic experienced remissions similar to those reported for nonpsychotic depressions with the addition of lithium (Nelson and Mazure 1986).

Lithium may convert nonresponders or partial responders to responders or may merely accelerate the time to response for eventual responders. The question of whether the patient would have eventually responded without lithium can be addressed clinically. If the patient recovers, lithium adjunctive therapy can be withdrawn; should the patient relapse, treatment can be reinstituted. If the patient does not relapse, the treatment continues with the antidepressants alone.

De Montigny et al. (1983) had based their rationale for adding lithium on the observed neuropharmacologic effects of lithium as a rapid 5-HT augmentor. Recognizing that intact noradrenergic and serotonergic inputs are required to down-regulate postsynaptic beta adrenergic receptors (a common effect of antidepressant agents), a boost to 5-HT transmission was thought to facilitate this adaptation once the system was primed with noradrenergic firing but lacked adequate serotonergic input. Whether or not explained by this hypothesis, low-dose lithium is a fine adjuvant when successful, yielding a rapid benefit without significant side effects, or drug washouts.

Strategies for implementing low-dose lithium vary. One approach is to begin with 300 mgm bid; if there is no response in the first week, the dose is increased to 900 mgm a day with more standard monitoring of levels and an additional two weeks' wait. Thereafter, a more standard lithium level is sought—0.4–0.8 mEq/l, for example. If no response occurs at these levels over two to three weeks, discontinuation in favor of another strategy is in order. Choosing standard-dose lithium addition, with its greater side effect potential as opposed to low-dose lithium addition as a therapuetic alternative prior to considering other treatments is a more difficult clinical decision.

Adjunctive Thyroid Hormone

The usefulness of augmenting antidepressant response with thyroid hormone has been mainly registered in small series or uncontrolled reports (Coppen et al. 1972; Earle 1981; Goodwin et al. 1982; Prange et al. 1969). Similar to the response to adjunctive lithium, the addition of thyroid hormone, in particular T_3, has been touted as an expedient strategy for the antidepressant nonresponder, purportedly decreasing the latency time to response as well as converting nonresponders to responders. The latency to response for some is claimed to be a few days while as many as 50 percent of resistant patients, but particularly women, have been said to benefit. As with lithium, no apparent changes in TCA levels occur, and thus, one would expect minimal increases in antidepressant treatment-emergent adverse effects.

The usual strategy is to initiate treatment with 10–25 mcg of liothyronine a day, with increases in dose every few days to a maximum of 50–75 mcg a day. Patients who have not responded at 50 mcg a day tend not to do well with further increases. As with low-dose lithium, some patients subsequently discontinue thyroid hormone and maintain their response while others relapse when T_3 is withdrawn. The presumed mechanism of thyroid hormone is the ability to enhance the sensitivity of central catecholamine receptors to catecholamines (Whybrow and Prange 1981).

While adjunctive thyroid hormone has been recommended in particular for those with subnormal thyroid function or with evidence of subclinical dysfunction, as with blunted TSH response to TRH testing (Targum et al. 1984), abnormal thyroid function is, nonetheless, not a condition for response to this treatment (Schwarcz et al. 1984). Depressed women, particularly those suffering from fatigue and anergia, are deemed more likely to benefit. Certain side effects—including flushing, tachycardia, increased blood pressure, and anxiety—may limit the usefulness of T_3 for some patients. Elderly people may be more sensitive to adverse effects, particularly cardiac.

While T_3, in the form of liothyronine, is the usual choice of a thyroid hormonal adjuvant, T_4 has also been a successful adjuvant (Targum et al. 1984). Either form of thyroid hormone may be effective, but T_3 appears to have a faster onset of action and more stimulant-like activity. Further, if one possible explanation for the efficacy of this strategy is the inability of some patients to convert T_4 to T_3 at the cellular level effectively, more specificity of benefit would be expected with T_3.

Reserpine

Recent studies (Amsterdam and Berwish 1987; Price et al. 1987) failed to demonstrate the previously claimed efficacy of acute administration of reserpine (e.g., 5 mg I.M. bid) as an antidepressant or a tricyclic potentiator.

Over time, reserpine is a catecholamine depletor associated with the emergence of depression, but acutely, it generates presynaptic release of monoamines, including norepinephrine, serotonin, and dopamine. By this mechanism of acute monoamine release, reserpine may potentiate antidepressant response although its efficacy now appears in doubt. While some may respond acutely, the issue of maintaining benefit is also not addressed by this strategy.

TCA Plus Neuroleptic

Patients with delusional or psychotic depressions are probably a heterogeneous group (Glassman and Roose 1981) suffering particularly severe symptomatology, who may at times respond to vigorous treatment with a TCA alone with adequate dose and duration (Quitkin et al. 1978). Other than electroconvulsive therapy (ECT), however, the treatment of choice for delusional depression is the combined use of a TCA and a neuroleptic, a combination superior to either drug individually (Spiker et al. 1985) but offering both increased anticholinergic effects and increased TCA plasma levels. Whether the neuroleptic addition is useful only for treating depressive psychosis or potentiates an antidepressant effect in general is a question. To date, there is minimal evidence of a neuroleptic role in the acute treatment of nonpsychotic depression. Lithium augmentation has also been reported to convert nonresponding psychotic depressive patients to responders (Nelson and Mazure 1986) when added to the TCA and neuroleptic combination; thus, low-dose lithium may be a useful adjunct for treatment-resistant delusional depressives who have not responded to a TCA plus neuroleptic.

Addition of Sexual Hormones

Although lacking support from systematic trials, the addition of conjugated estrogen in the dose range of .125 to .375 mgm a day has been associated with onset of antidepressant response in post- or perimenopausal female patients (Prange 1972; Zohar et al. 1987). The addition of estrogen may "potentiate CNS adrenergic functioning" (Klaiber et al. 1979). High-dose estrogen therapy alone has also been reported to benefit severely depressed women (Klaiber et al. 1979) although the safety of this strategy over time is not established. Similarly, the synthetic androgen, mesterolone, may have antidepressant potential for men (Vogel et al. 1985). Before either of these strategies is put to use, the patient's clinical situation should be one that justifies adverse effects of hormonal therapy; medical and/or gynecological consultation should be considered before introducing hormones for the affective illness alone.

TCA Plus MAOI

Prescribing a TCA and an MAOI together is daunting, given the fear of triggering a major adverse reaction such as malignant hyperthermia, delirium, convulsions, coma, and death; combining an MAOI and a TCA, however, appears safe if both treatments are initiated in low doses simultaneously and gradually increased together (White and Simpson 1981). While the addition of an MAOI to ongoing TCA treatment is usually safely accomplished, conservative practice would be to prescribe a one- to two-week washout of the TCA and, possibly, to avoid imipramine (the TCA most often implicated in major adverse affects with this combination). Adding a TCA to an MAOI, on the other hand, is potentially lethal and thus to be avoided without a two-week or greater washout period of the MAOI. A patient on combined therapy mainly risks additive side effects such as hypotension; the risk of hypertensive crises from dietary tyramine, however, may be decreased for this regimen as amitriptyline appears to block the uptake of tyramine as it does norepinephrine (Kline et al. 1982). Despite the apparent safety of the TCA and MAOI combination if properly administered and despite clinical reports of patients who benefit uniquely from the combination (but not from either drug alone), there is little evidence to suggest this approach is, in general, more effective than either of the components (Davidson et al. 1978; White et al. 1980; Young et al. 1979). Bearing in mind the difficulty in researching this question in clinical trials of treatment-resistant patients, it is possible that an occasional patient has some unique response to the combination.

Monoamine Oxidase Inhibitors

Monoamine oxidase inhibitors (MAOIs) have reemerged as major players in the antidepressant pharmacopoeia (Zisook 1985). While concerns about hypertensive crises and dietary proscriptions have restricted general use for many years, considerable recent data indicate that the MAOIs have a special role in treating depression. Although deemed most useful in patients with "nonendogenous neurotic" depressive syndromes, when prescribed in adequate doses (usually 1 mgm/kg or more of phenelzine), MAOIs appear as effective as TCAs for the treatment of patients with major depression and melancholia (Robinson et al. 1985). With adequate dosing, as reflected in platelet MAO inhibition of 80 percent or more, for example, most patients with depression respond. Moreover, there are additional special indications for an MAOI where these agents appear to be particularly effective compared with a TCA.

Certain features of a depressive syndrome are associated with enhanced responsiveness to MAOIs. One such feature is the presence of panic attacks (Liebowitz et al. 1984), which, when coexisting with depressive symptoms, is a possible marker of increased efficacy with an MAOI. One cluster of patient characteristics reported to predict enhanced response to MAOIs is the so-called hysteroid dysphoria profile (Liebowitz et al. 1984), consisting of interpersonal reactivity of mood, rejection sensitivity, leaden "paralysis" or anergia, and dramatic, hysteroid personality features.

"Atypical" depressions in general, including those with interpersonal reactivity of mood as well as those with "reversed endogenous" symptoms of hypersomnia and hyperphagia (McGrath et al. 1987), are found to be more responsive to treatment with MAOIs; patients who overeat and oversleep may be preferential responders to MAOIs. Indeed, this work indicates that MAOIs frequently are effective in this population when a TCA has failed; for instance a majority of nonresponders to a TCA will respond to an MAOI while only a minority of nonresponders to an MAOI will respond to a TCA. Thus, MAOIs not only are effective for major depression but also offer increased benefit for depressions with mood reactivity, panic attacks, hysteroid dysphoric features, and possibly reversed endogenous symptoms. Further, it would appear that failure on a TCA still leaves open the likelihood of response to an MAOI.

Adequate dose and duration of treatment are also important variables in considering treatment adequacy with an MAOI. Unfortunately, except for measures of platelet MAO activity, no routinely available measures assure the clinician of having achieved an adequate dose. Some patients who have failed on standard dosing (e.g., phenelzine 30–75 mg a day) have gone on to respond to higher doses. With MAOIs, the main difficulty in administering adequate or optimal treatment is side effects, not so much in the initiation of treatment as with TCAs, but often after days or weeks of treatment with treatment-emergent side effects that occur. These include an array of difficult-to-manage side effects such as insomnia, edema, weight gain, and hypotension, and neurologic-like side effects such as paresthesias, nocturnal myoclonus, and headache (Rabkin et al. 1984). Nonetheless, awareness and anticipation of these side effects, with appropriate management strategies (Pollack and Rosenbaum 1987; Rabkin et al. 1985), frequently allow for treatment to continue. Some patients do remain daunted, however, by the need to be vigilant about drug and dietary interactions.

Clinical experience indicates that the failure to do well on one type of MAOI, such as a hydrazine-type (e.g., phenelzine), does not necessarily predict poor response to a nonhydrazine-type MAOI (e.g., tranylcypromine). For example, an occasional patient who poorly tolerates phenelzine, as with increased weight gain or postural hypotension, will be free of these difficulties on tranylcypromine. Thus, change from one MAOI to another may be a strategy to manage side effects or to pursue alternative trials for a treatment-resistant patient. Based on a few case reports (Gelenberg 1987), it is considered good practice to discontinue phenelzine for 10 to 14 days before initiating treatment with tranylcypromine.

As with the TCAs, lithium (Price et al. 1985) and thyroid hormone (Hullett and Bidder 1983) may serve as adjuvants for a patient who has failed to respond to a trial of MAOI. Also, for delusional depression, a neuroleptic may be added to an MAOI.

"New" Antidepressants

While change from a non-MAOI to an MAOI for a treatment-resistant patient is most likely to yield response, the advantages are less clear in the change from one non-MAOI to another. Given prescriber and patient discomfort with the risks associated with an MAOI, it is common for treatment-resistant patients to have multiple trials of non-MAOIs before a trial of an MAOI. While some do respond to one non-MAOI after failing on another, the rate of conversion to response for drugs that are more alike than different is unknown. To maximize benefit, clinicians usually choose a second agent that is deemed dissimilar from the first. Thus, there is always interest in the availability of "new" antidepressants that might offer a different spectrum of efficacy or have a more favorable side effect profile than standard agents. More recently introduced non-MAOIs have included amoxapine, trazodone, maprotiline, alprazolam, bupropion, nomifensine, and fluoxetine. With introduction of each new antidepressant, there is hope of improved safety and toxicity profiles and increased efficacy, particularly for patients who have not responded to available agents. In general, however, the so-called second generation has been a disappointment in this regard.

Without reviewing the considerable clinical literature on the second-generation antidepressants, it is apparent that no currently available agent at the time of this writing either offers enhanced efficacy or is free of toxicity limitations (Gelenberg 1984). For example, amoxapine's claim of rapidity of response is exaggerated, and the drug is particularly dangerous in overdose, with a high rate of seizures and renal failure (Gelenberg 1984). Further, its 7-OH metabolite has neuroleptic properties, subjecting the patient to neuroleptic side effects and risks.

Trazodone, the nation's most frequently prescribed branded antidepressant, owes its success in large measure to the absence of anticholinergic and quinidine-like effects. However, the agent is quite sedating, can cause postural hypotension, and is associated with gastrointestinal side effects (Gelenberg 1984). Reports of increased rates of ventricular irritability also diminish the claims of cardiac safety based on the absence of intracardiac conduction delay; its tendency, compared with other antidepressants, to cause priapism (Kogeorgos and De Alwis 1986) in men has also been of concern. Further, determinations of dosage adequacy are not easily made for this agent, where 50–100 mgm may at times be excessively sedating and yet 400–600 mgm may be necessary for an adequate response. Plasma levels are not yet a guide to dosing.

With a low degree of anticholinergic effects, maprotiline resembles desipramine but appears to be limited by a high rate of skin reactions and propensity to cause seizures in doses over 225 mg. Alprazolam, a triazolo-benzodiazepine with clinical trial reports of efficacy as an antidepressant (Feighner et al. 1983; Rickels et al. 1985) but with a side effect and response profile similar to that of other benzodiazepines, has been controversial. One study found alprazolam is equal to imipramine and superior to diazepam and placebo for treatment of depression (Rickels et al. 1987); yet some clinicians remain skeptical of a "true" antidepressant effect of this drug. Occasional reports of manic switch and a considerable body of industry-sponsored research claiming antidepressant effects suggest the agent is worth considering in the antidepressant pharmacopoeia when other, less controversial treatments have been unavailing. As with any short-acting benzodiazepine, drug discontinuation syndromes (rebound, withdrawal) are a concern.

Bupropion, at the time of this writing, is "on hold" in light of reports indicating a high rate of seizures, particularly in one cohort of bulimic women. While bupropion is free of anticholinergic effects and has a somewhat more stimulating, nonsedating profile with presumed usefulness in older patients, other unusual effects such as nightmares and hallucinations have also emerged. Nomifensine has been withdrawn from the market because of immunologic side effects.

Recently introduced is fluoxetine, the first of a next generation of serotonergic antidepressants. Whether this agent's spectrum of efficacy will be more favorable than that of other antidepressants remains to be observed. It is, however, not anticholinergic, it appears free of cardiovascular toxicity, and it does not cause weight gain; there is, in fact, some indication that the drug can cause weight loss, with an initial stimulatory effect and possibility of decreasing appetite. It may prove a favorable option for atypical depressives with reversed endogenous features. Nausea and increased anxiety attend initiation of treatment for some patients.

Fluoxetine, the first of a new generation of more selective serotonergic antidepressants, has achieved wide clinical acceptance in its first year after introduction. Whether this agent's overall spectrum of clinical efficacy is more favorable than other antidepressants remains to be observed. It is, however, not anticholinergic, appears free of cardiovascular toxicity, and does not cause weight gain; the drug can occasionally cause weight loss, decreased appetite and may prove particularly favorable for atypical depressed patients with reversed endogenous features. Nausea and increased anxiety limit initiation of treatment for some patients. When combined with tricyclic antidepressants, fluoxetine may elevate tricyclic plasma levels; therefore, tricyclic doses need to be decreased prior to the introduction of fluoxetine. Some clinicians have observed enhanced or synergistic effects in antidepressant nonresponders by combining fluoxetine with certain non-MAOI antidepressants such as the tricyclic desipramine, and the nontricyclic trazodone. The latter agent may serve to treat fluoxetine induced insomnia while possibly offering enhanced clinical efficacy. Whether combinations of fluoxetine and other non-MAOI antidepressants prove more successful than either drug alone requires more definitive study. Lithium augmentation has also improved response for patients on fluoxetine. In general, for most depressed patients 20 mg or 40 mg is an adequate dose, but the necessary duration of treatment may be somewhat longer than for standard antidepressants, with increasing response noted in some cases beyond six to eight weeks of treatment.

Stimulants

There has been a rekindling of interest in the use of stimulant drugs in psychiatry. Because of concerns about tachyphylaxis and abuse and because of heightened control by government authorities, prescribers have been reluctant to use stimulants such as dextro-amphetamine or methylphenidate in the treatment of depression. Nonetheless, a growing body of literature suggests a potentially important role for stimulants (Chiarello and Cole 1987). In particular, lacking the latency to response and the toxicity of standard agents, stimulants have found a place in the rapid treatment of depression in the medical setting, particularly for older patients (Woods et al. 1986). For example, a depressed patient with chronic respiratory disease, unable to wean from a respirator, may be effectively and rapidly treated with stimulants to improve mood and motivation. Tachyphylaxis has not been observed in medically ill patients maintained on stimulants.

Stimulants may also be employed as adjuvants, potentiating antidepressant treatment for patients with inadequate initial response (Wharton et al. 1971). Addition of stimulants is not only reported for TCAs but also is claimed safe for patients on MAOIs when the dose is initiated and titrated with small (e.g., 2.5 mgm) increments (Feighner et al. 1985). One particular advantage in using combined stimulant and antidepressant treatment is the possibility of diminishing antidepressant-induced hypotensive effects as well as enhancing antidepressant response.

Stimulants have been proposed as predictors of specific antidepressant response (Goff 1986), with reports suggesting that patients who benefit acutely from initial doses of a stimulant such as methylphenidate or dextro-amphetamine are more likely to respond to a noradrenergic tricyclic such as desipramine.

Carbamazepine

Carbamazepine has become a drug to consider for "treatment-resistant anything." While its efficacy for the treatment of mania and the maintenance treatment of bipolar patients is better studied, clinicians have come to use carbamazepine additionally as an alternative for depressed patients who have not responded to standard treatment. There is suggestion that unipolar depressive patients with EEG or BEAM abnormalities may be most likely to benefit (Schatzberg et al. 1984).

L-Tryptophan and Other Precursors

The possibility that amino acids, precursors to the synthesis of central mono-amines, might have pharmacologic effects has considerable appeal. First, as "natural" agents, presumably without toxicity or risk, they find favor with those vigilant about toxicity or the use of "chemicals." The catecholamine hypothesis had postulated that affective psychopathology reflected relative deficiencies of such neurotransmitters as serotonin and norepinephrine; since the rate-limiting step for the synthesis of these monoamines is the availability of amino acid precursors, agents such as L-tryptophan and tyrosine have been considered as potential antidepressant treatment adjuvants.

The greatest degree of scrutiny has been devoted to L-tryptophan and L-5-hydroxytryptophan, precursors to serotonin (5-HT) (van Praag 1981), with the L-tryptophan relatively available over-the-counter at pharmacies or at health food stores. To summarize an extensive literature, the efficacy of L-tryptophan alone as an anti-depressant treatment is mostly unsupported (D'Elia et al. 1978). While large-scale, rigorous, systematic trials in resistant depressives are lacking, clinical reports are difficult to assess as well, given uncertainties about dose and method of administration. Dose ranges of L-tryptophan have varied from 2 g to 10 g or more a day, variably co-administered with vitamin B3, vitamin C, vitamin B6, allopurinol, and a sweet to enhance absorption. Since the optimal regimen for administering L-tryptophan is unclear, the agent could have relatively greater efficacy with one method over another.

The use of L-tryptophan as an *adjunct* to antidepressants, but particularly MAOIs, has support from case series (Coppen et al. 1963; Glassman and Platman 1969; Walinder et al. 1976). That the addition of this amino acid has a pharmacologic effect is apparent from a series of reports indicating the emergence of a cluster of side effects presumed to derive from rapid serotonergic augmentation. Patients on MAOIs who have supplemented treatment acutely with 2 gm or more of L-tryptophan have suffered the onset of tremulousness, ocular oscillations, moderately elevated vital signs, and myoclonic jerks (Brotman and Rosenbaum 1984). Similarities between these effects and the so-called serotonin syndrome in animals (Insel et al. 1982) support the assertion that L-tryptophan as a precursor may have a pharmacologic effect on serotonergic transmission. The serotonin syndrome may be avoided by a more gradual introduction of L-tryptophan addition. While there is not a body of convincing data to allow an assertion of L-tryptophan's efficacy as an adjuvant, its relative safety and ease of administration support its place as a therapeutic option.

Some support has been mustered for other amino acid precursors such as L-phenylalanine as a precursor to phenylethylamine synthesis. Sabelli and Mosnaim (1974) and Sabelli et al. (1983) have suggested that patients with low levels of urinary secretion of acetic acid (PAA) are those who might benefit from supplemental L-phenylalanine (Sabelli et al. 1986), also available through health food stores or pharmacies; the use of this agent either alone or as an adjunct has not been widespread. Again, methods for optimal administration and a wide range of potential dosing (2-14 mgm/day) reflect residual uncertainties about the usefulness of this strategy, which has not found its way into general practice.

Tyrosine, an amino acid precursor of norepinephrine, has also shown some promise in initial reports (Gelenberg 1982) but has generally failed to live up to its promise when subjected to rigorous therapeutic trials (Gelenberg, unpublished data).

With all the amino acid precursors, while there may be particular patients or depressive subtypes predictive of good response, or while there may be a role for these agents when used adjunctively with standard antidepressants, questions remain as to their place in the treatment algorithm for resistant patients.

Electroconvulsive Therapy

There is no question of the efficacy of ECT in the treatment of depression. Nonetheless, it is often unclear where to put ECT in the treatment algorithm for resistant patients. While ECT is frequently the most rapidly and dramatically effective antidepressant intervention, its usefulness is often limited by administrative obstacles or patient acceptance. In general, ECT is most attractive as a strategy when a depression is particularly severe or of life-threatening proportions due to either suicidality or cachexia, or when pharmacologic treatments are unable to be effectively administered.

Other Treatments

While this discussion is intended to focus on pharmacologic strategies, there are innovative nonpharmacologic strategies that deserve mention in this context, partly because of the possibility of effective combination with drug treatments. One such strategy is partial sleep deprivation. When a depressed patient is sleep deprived for one or two nights, usually by awakening at or shortly after midnight and remaining awake through the night, rapid and dramatic improvements in depression are seen. Unfortunately, relapse also rapidly follows recovery sleep. There has been some effort to use sleep deprivation to accelerate antidepressant response (Elsenga and van den Hoofdakker 1983) and, conversely, a drug treatment (lithium) to extend the response initially achieved by partial sleep deprivation (Baxter et al. 1986).

Similarly, advancing sleep phase by having patients go to sleep 3 to 6 hours later on each subsequent night until they have "reset" their circadian rhythms has been proposed as a treatment for depression (Souetre et al. 1987). Whether this approach can be synergistic with drug treatment has not been well studied.

For patients with seasonal affective disorder (SAD), spending upwards of two hours a day in front of high-intensity, full spectrum lights often yields dramatically positive results (Lewy et al. 1987). While adjunctive "phototherapy" is now being used as an adjunct to pharmacotherapy for resistant depressives (G. Sachs, personal communication), there is little data to define its role and, in particular, to determine whether it will serve only resistant depressives with a seasonal, cycling component.

As mentioned earlier, psychotherapies are, in general, synergistic with drug therapy, and comprehensive clinical care requires attending to a patient's psyche as well as soma. Nonetheless, recent interest in cognitive therapies in particular has revived interest in the relative role of drug and talking therapies. While cognitive therapy appears to have an antidepressant capability comparable to the use of a single antidepressant agent (Murphy et al. 1984), the role of cognitive-behavioral approaches as adjuncts for the resistant or residually depressed patient requires study. In one small series (Fennell and Teasdale 1982), cognitive therapy alone was minimally effective in drug-refractory depressed patients. Patients with chronically low self-esteem and partial response to antidepressants may improve in overall function when cognitive behavioral approaches are "added" to a standard antidepressant.

Summary

In conclusion, there is an extensive list of potential antidepressant strategies and combinations for patients with depressive syndromes. While large systematic studies of patients with treatment resistance are lacking, the clinical impression is that when this array of approaches is made available to patients with depression, higher rates of response can be achieved. Indeed, the number of treatments available makes the designation of "treatment resistance" a complicated one. Now that a number of possibly useful adjuncts has been described, it is apparent that these, themselves, may be combined (Coppen et al. 1972; Hale et al. 1987) in the effort to augment treatment response, as with a TCA plus lithium, thyroid, and L-tryptophan, for example. Who is truly treatment resistant and who simply had inadequate trials? Further, there is little to guide the clinician in moving from one treatment approach to another. One possible treatment algorithm is offered (Figure 1).

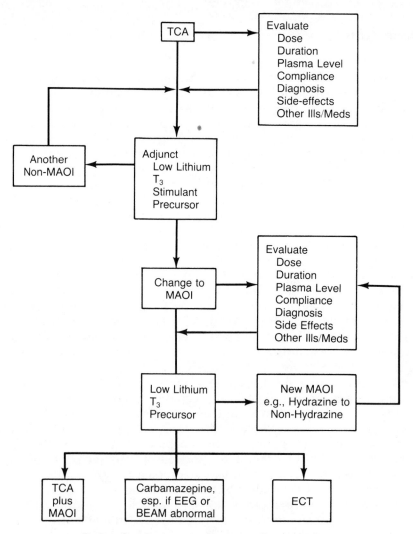

Figure 1. Treatment-Resistant Depression

Chapter 166

Electroconvulsive Therapy

Intentional induction of generalized seizures was first introduced as a psychiatric therapy in 1934, using chemical agents that lowered the seizure threshold (Fink 1984). Although the treatment had dramatic efficacy in certain psychotic and depressive disorders, chemical induction proved technically difficult, and in 1938 electrical induction was introduced by Cerletti and Bini (Fink 1979). Because of its greater safety and ease of administration, initiation of seizure activity with an electrical impulse soon became the standard treatment technique. Electroconvulsive therapy (ECT) was then tried in many types of psychiatric disorders but was soon found to be most effective in severe depression. During the 1950s and 1960s, the treatment was extensively used and perhaps overprescribed, but subsequently its use declined and indications became more specific. Although no recent survey of use has been taken, there has been an increase in research interest, education, and the introduction of new ECT instruments in this decade.

For many drug-resistant or drug-intolerant depressed patients, ECT remains the only effective treatment (American Psychiatric Association Task Force Report 1978, pp. 13–30). Consequently, the recent evolution of this therapy has been toward improving efficacy and reducing adverse effects and risks, rather than toward eliminating the treatment altogether.

Indications

The principal indication for ECT is major depression with melancholia. The symptoms that predict a good response to ECT are anorexia, weight loss, early morning awakening, impaired concentration, pessimistic mood, motor restlessness, speech latency, constipation, and somatic or self-deprecatory delusions, all occurring as part of an acute illness (Carney et al. 1965). The acute loss of interest in activities that formerly gave pleasure is the central feature of the illness. These are exactly the same symptoms that predict a good response to antidepressant drugs (Bielski and Friedel 1979).

The effectiveness of ECT in the treatment of depressive illness has been extensively studied. In two large prospective trials in the 1960s, ECT was compared with tricyclics and monoamine oxidase (MAO) inhibitors. One study performed in the United States found marked improvement in 76 percent of patients receiving ECT, in 49 percent of patients receiving imipramine, and in 50 percent of patients receiving phenelzine (Greenblatt et al. 1964). In a similar British study, response rates for ECT, imipramine, and phenelzine were 71 percent, 52 percent, and 30 percent, respectively (Medical Research Council Clinical Psychiatry Committee 1965). In a large retrospective study, Avery and Winokur (1977) reported a marked improvement in 90 percent of patients treated with ECT, while those receiving adequate treatment with imipramine or equivalent showed a 74 percent rate of marked improvement.

ECT has also been compared with sham ECT, administering anesthesia without the seizure, in 11 studies. In all but one of these, ECT was found superior to the sham treatment. The one study that failed to show significant differences employed a type of ultrabrief stimulus that had previously been shown to be less effective than a conventional stimulus (Lambourn and Gill 1978).

Finally, the efficacy of ECT in patients unresponsive to antidepressant drugs has also been assessed. DeCarolis et al. (1964) treated 282 depressed patients with therapeutic doses of imipramine, with 61 percent response rate. The drug-resistant 39 percent were given ECT, with an 85 percent response to the treatment. When delusional depressives were separately considered, they showed only a 40 percent response rate to imipramine, but 83 percent of those nonresponders treated with ECT showed significant improvement. In a more recent study of drug-resistant patients, Paul et al. (1981) reported a response rate of 90 percent in a drug-resistant patient cohort.

Although ECT has consistently been reported to yield a higher response rate and prompter remission than antidepressants, the present convention is to treat depressive illness initially with drugs, reserving ECT for the drug-resistant patient (American Psychiatric Association Task Force Report 1978). The definition of drug resistance varies from patient to patient, since younger individuals may appropriately receive four or five aggressive regimens of drug treatment while elderly or infirm patients may be at serious risk with even one drug trial at moderate dosage.

The use of ECT without prior trials of medication may be justified in the following six groups, although these are not all-inclusive.

1. Those patients who have not responded to adequate trials of antidepressants during prior depressive episodes may be unlikely to respond to further drug trials.
2. Patients with depression marked by delusions (usually paranoid, somatic, or self-deprecatory) have a response rate to antidepressants significantly lower than patients without delusions. While a tricyclic-neuroleptic combination is more effective in delusional depression than a tricyclic alone (Spiker et al. 1985), the anticholinergic and hypotensive side effects associated with this combination make it suitable only for the majority of patients. ECT remains the most effective treatment for delusional depression, with a reported overall response rate in excess of 80 percent (Kroessler 1985).
3. Patients with preexisting cardiac illness are often more safely treated with ECT than with antidepressants.
4. Patients who have remained in an untreated depressive illness and are severely dehydrated, malnourished, and exhausted are medically at high risk and require the most prompt and effective treatment available.
5. Approximately two-thirds of the cases of catatonia found in general hospitals are most appropriately classified as suffering from mood disorder (Abrams and Taylor 1976). Although data on response rates are lacking, it appears that catatonia of this type is exquisitely sensitive to ECT (Mann et al. 1986). Because of the severity of complications of catatonia, including pneumonia, dehydration, irreversible muscular contractures, and pulmonary emboli, prompt treatment with ECT is indicated.
6. Although the etiology of neuroleptic malignant syndrome is unknown, a growing body of uncontrolled case reports indicates that ECT may be associated with improvement in up to 50 percent of cases (Addonizio and Susman 1987). However, this use of ECT is associated with increased risk of severe cardiac complications, and there is a consensus in the literature that discontinuation of the neuroleptic,

supportive medical care and administration of dantrolene and bromocriptine remain the essential elements of treatment (Levenson 1985).

In addition to its use in the disorders just described, ECT also continues to play an important adjunctive role in the treatment of schizophrenia and mania. Although schizophrenia was once widely treated with ECT, this use of the treatment has declined, and the most recent survey indicated that only 17 percent of the treatments done in the United States were for schizophrenia (Report of the Task Force on Electroconvulsive Therapy of the American Psychiatric Association 1978). Among most schizophrenic patients with a history of chronicity, ECT offers no advantage over treatment with neuroleptics (Small 1985a). On the other hand, there are two subgroups in whom the treatment appears to be effective. In acute cases without a history of chronicity, studies of the efficacy of ECT report a remission or a marked improvement in 40–80 percent of cases (Salymar 1980). And retrospective studies report a good or moderate response to ECT in a significant proportion of patients following nonresponse to neuroleptics (Ries et at. 1981; Wells 1973). Those patients most likely to benefit from the treatment had an acute course, schizoaffective symptoms, or catatonic presentation. A recent uncontrolled trial, using ECT combined with thiothixene in the treatment of schizophrenia refractory to drugs alone, reported remission in eight of nine patients (Friedel 1986); a second similar trial of ECT and neuroleptics reported improvement in seven of eight patients (Gujavarty et al. 1987). Although these results are extremely encouraging, they must be viewed with caution until controlled trials are performed. It appears clear, then, that for selected patients with symptoms of schizophrenia, ECT is still a reasonable and indicated therapy even though overall response rates are generally not as high as for major depression.

ECT was widely used in the treatment of mania prior to the introduction of lithium, and the available evidence indicates that ECT is as effective as lithium in the short-term treatment of mania (Small 1985b). Because of the encouraging response rates reported in most studies, ECT should be considered in manic patients who are refractory to drug treatment. The most recent ECT trials in manic patients report a clear superiority of bilateral over unilateral treatment (Milstein et al. 1987).

Risks

There are no absolute contraindications to ECT, but there are a number of important risk factors that must be balanced against the danger of remaining in an untreated depression. Depressed patients who do not receive effective treatment have a reported mortality rate of 36 percent at 31 months, and the mortality rate is probably much higher in the elderly (Avery and Winokur 1976). Consequently, rather than dismiss ECT outright in the high-risk patient, it is more appropriate to first explore every possible means of risk reduction through good medical management and specific modification of anesthetic technique.

The most important physiologic stress is to the heart (Jones and Knight 1981). Immediately after the electrical stimulus, there is a 5–10 second period of bradycardia and, occasionally, asystole. Then tachycardia and hypertension develop in most patients, and cardiac work may increase several-fold during the seizure. At the end of the seizure, there is sometimes an abrupt shift to bradycardia, presumably due to ictal vagal discharge. Because of these stresses, patients with recent myocardial infarction (MI), congestive heart failure, conduction abnormalities, coronary artery disease, hypertension, and impaired pulmonary function may require specific modifications in anesthetic technique in order to be safely treated (Gaines and Rees 1986).

Although studies of patients with coronary artery disease do not report increased ECT-associated morbidity (Moore 1947) these patients probably do carry increased risk, and consultation with a cardiologist prior to treatment is advisable to assure the maximum possible compensation of cardiac function. Postponing treatment in the face of a recent MI does not improve mortality until at least six months after the event (Rao et al. 1983) and consequently, in life-threatening depression, it is reasonable to proceed with caution as soon as the heart is electrically stable, doing everything possible to reduce cardiac work. Digitalis toxicity is an important cardiac risk factor with the potential for profound bradycardia or even arrest following the cessation of seizure activity, and the blood level should be checked prior to ECT in all digitalized patients. Modern cardiac pacemakers contain an electrical shield, and patients with these devices may be safely treated with ECT (Abiuso et al. 1979). Synchronous atrioventricular pacemakers may raise their firing rate in response to the stimulus, but demand pacemakers are unaffected by it.

Increased intracranial pressure is often mentioned as a contraindication for ECT. During the seizure the rise in cerebral blood flow is approximately 100 percent (Lovett-Doust et al. 1974), and one study of ictal cerebrospinal fluid (CSF) pressures reported a mean rise of 55 cm H_2O (White et al. 1961). The rise in intracranial pressure during the seizure itself could theoretically induce herniation of the brain stem, but there is a paucity of evidence that this actually occurs in the clinical setting. When ECT is clearly indicated, the preferable course may be to proceed with it after taking appropriate measures to lower intracranial pressure before and during the treatment.

Brain tumor, in particular, has erroneously been elevated to the status of absolute contraindication in the psychiatric literature, in the absence of supporting evidence. Indeed, there is growing evidence that patients with brain tumor, when appropriately managed, can safely undergo ECT (Dressler and Folk 1975; Maltbie et al. 1980). Other intracranial lesions such as artero-venous (AV) malformation, arterial aneurysm, infarction, and hemorrhagic stroke all present specific challenges in risk reduction through appropriate medical management, but none of these is an absolute contraindication to treatment when treatment is indicated.

There is a small but reassuring series of case reports regarding the use of ECT during pregnancy (Fink 1979). In cases using modern technique, ECT did not precipitate labor, and there were no discernible long-term adverse effects to mother or fetus. Since there is some question regarding the teratogenicity of tricyclic antidepressants, phenothiazines, and lithium, ECT may offer less risk for the severely depressed pregnant mother. However, fetal monitoring is advisable during the treatment itself (Remick and Maurice 1978).

Consent

Most informed patients consent willingly to have ECT, just as with any effective medical procedure. The patient and family should be given a full explanation of risks, side effects, and potential benefits. For some patients, a videotape presentation of the treatment may help to demystify it (Remick and Maurice 1978), and written information about ECT is useful for the patient to keep on hand for reference (Report of the Task Force on Electroconvulsive Therapy of the American Psychiatric Association 1978, pp. 174–178). A signed consent form should be part of the permanent medical record.

A significant number of patients either are too inert to carry out meaningful consent or oppose treatment because of negativistic or paranoid ideation that is part of their depressive illness. In these cases it is incumbent upon the physician, and in the patient's best interest, to seek substituted judgment regarding treatment. Legal requirements vary according to state, but there has been a trend toward requiring court review of individual cases prior to involuntary treatment (Winslade et al. 1984). Although this often involves lengthy delay of treatment while complex medical decisions are made by individuals untrained in medicine, the physician is obliged to defer treatment until appropriate legal steps are taken. Whether consent is voluntary or substituted, it is not permanent and may be withdrawn at any time by the consenting party.

Treatment Technique

Because of the seizure, major physiologic changes occur during ECT that are not ordinarily seen in other procedures performed under brief anesthesia. Although ECT is often considered an innocuous or even trivial exercise in management, quite the contrary is true, and both the psychiatrist and anesthesiologist should have specific training and expertise in the complexities of the treatment (Gaines and Rees 1986; Glenn and Weiner 1985). The staff performing the treatment should be accustomed to working with each other and in concert about the strategies for administering anesthesia and managing medical complications.

The workup prior to ECT includes a medical history, physical examination, and any pre-anesthetic lab work that the clinician considers indicated. In addition, thyroid function tests may be helpful if they have not been performed recently, and serum albumin and total protein may be useful to assess nutritional status.

An EEG and cranial CT scan are indicated whenever there is a question of structural central nervous system (CNS) lesion. This may be a difficult decision since many depressed patients present with signs of dementia in the absence of localizing neurologic signs (McAllister 1983). Careful neuropsychological testing reveals that this "pseudodementia of depression" has two characteristics: diffuse deficits in attention and performance that mimic nonspecific organic brain syndrome, and specific deficits in sequencing and abstraction that suggest localization to frontal lobes (Henderson 1983; Weingartner et al. 1981). Since the distinction between depression and other causes of dementia can usually not be made with confidence on the basis of clinical signs, a neurologic workup is often necessary to make a diagnosis of exclusion.

Severely malnourished elderly patients present a special management problem. While their depressive illness itself is life threatening, they are also at risk for treatment and should first undergo a period of careful rehydration and nutrition, with feeding tube if necessary. During the rehydration phase, these patients require meticulous attention to sudden shifts in fluid, electrolyte, and osmotic status, and they may require several days of such care before they stabilize. Stress ulcer is common in chronic untreated depression in the elderly, and stools must always be checked for hemoglobin. Many elderly patients present with massive fecal impaction, and this must also be routinely assessed in every depressed patient on admission.

The clinician must review all medications prior to ECT. As mentioned above, digitalized patients should have their levels checked. Patients with baseline hypertension tend to have a pronounced rise in blood pressure during the treatment, and they should be adequately treated with oral antihypertensives prior to starting ECT (Jones 1983). Reserpine is probably contraindicated since it has been associated with death during treatment in one case report (Bracha and Hes 1956). Concurrent use of tricyclics or MAO inhibitors during a course of ECT has not been shown to increase efficacy, and in most patients the operative risk is reduced by discontinuing these medications prior to treatment. While traditionally a 10-day washout period has been recommended for MAO inhibitors, there is a paucity of data to support this practice (El-Ganzouri et al. 1985), and medically stable patients may be treated, with caution, immediately after discontinuation of an MAO inhibitor (Freese 1985). Although several uncontrolled case reports have described confusional states following treatment with lithium and ECT (Ayd 1981) there is no solid evidence that lithium does in fact increase the cognitive side effects of ECT. There is likewise no evidence that lithium increases the efficacy of ECT, but it may reduce the chances of inducing mania in some bipolar patients, and its concurrent use in this situation is reasonable.

All medications that raise the seizure threshold, such as benzodiazepines, should be discontinued prior to treatment since they inhibit both the induction and the generalization of the seizure and may therefore reduce efficacy of the treatment (Stromgren et al. 1980). Patients who are already on anticonvulsants for an ictal disorder may be kept on their usual regimen for safety, although this requires a more intense stimulus at the time of treatment to override the anticonvulsant drugs.

ECT should be performed in a treatment room equipped with oxygen, suction equipment, a cardiac monitor, and appropriate intravenous medications to manage complications of treatment. There should be adequate reception and recovery areas staffed by personnel familiar with the mental and physiologic problems common to these patients. Most patients receive ECT on an inpatient basis, but outpatient treatment offers advantages for the younger, stable patient who is not prone to intentional or accidental self-injury. Although driving is prohibited during a course of treatment, these patients may pursue safe activities at home without the expense and disruption of a lengthy hospitalization. It is most convenient to keep patients fasting after midnight, treat them early in the morning, and leave the rest of the day free for whatever activities are indicated.

When the patient enters the treatment room, fasting status is ascertained and blood pressure and pulse are taken in the supine position. While a cardiac monitor is not mandatory, some centers now use it routinely (Standards of Practice-Minimal Monitoring 1985). A pulse oxygen analyzer is also useful to monitor percent saturation of aterial blood. Venous access may be obtained with a butterfly although in any medically unstable patient, a large bore indwelling venous catheter is preferable.

Anticholinergic treatment prior to ECT is optional. The rationale for its use is to reduce oral secretions and, by vagal blockade, to inhibit bradyarrhythmias (Miller et al. 1987). Objective study of secretions shows no difference between treated and untreated patients (Wyant and Macdonald 1980). Some investigators report a reduction in the incidence of poststimulus asystole and postictal bradycardia in treated patients (McKenna et al. 1970) while others do not (Wyant and Macdonald 1980). Anticholinergics do have the undesirable effect of increasing cardiac work by increasing heart rate, and they may be contraindicated in the face of coronary insufficiency.

While many clinicians routinely pretreat with anticholinergic agents, it is also reasonable to reserve the use of these agents for those patients who develop bradyarrhythmias. Atropine 0.4 mg is usually administered, either intramuscularly one-half hour prior to treatment or intravenously immediately before the anesthetic. Glycopyrrolate 0.2 mg in lieu of atropine has the advantage of being less likely than atropine to cause tachycardia (Greenan et al. 1983; Kramer et al. 1986).

Methohexital is the most commonly used barbiturate (Gaines and Rees 1986) at a starting dose of .75 to 1.0 mg/kg, which may be adjusted up or down in subsequent treatments depending on response. Since methohexital is also an anticonvulsant, the dose should be only high enough to maintain unconsciousness during the period of muscular paralysis. It is given as a bolus, followed immediately by succinylcholine at .75 to 1.0 mg/kg (Gaines and Rees 1986). It is generally best not to wait for sleep prior to injecting succinylcholine, since this delays the return of muscular function relative to the period of unconsciousness and increases the likelihood of the patient waking up in a paralyzed state.

Since patients are fully paralyzed, positive pressure ventilation is necessary, but for most patients laryngeal intubation is inadvisable and may cause injury. Ordinarily, an ambu bag with 5–10 liters per minute of oxygen flow is sufficient. Most ambu bags deliver a maximum of only 40–60 percent oxygen, and for medically complicated cases in which higher concentrations are desirable, an anesthesia machine is necessary. The anesthetist must bear in mind that hyperventilation is indicated. First, it lengthens seizure duration, increasing the chances of a sustained, fully generalized seizure (Bergsholm et al. 1984). Second, and perhaps more important, both the heart (Jones and Knight 1981) and brain (Plum et al. 1974) undergo a burst of markedly increased metabolic activity during treatment. It is not sufficient to simply ventilate the patient well enough to avoid cyanosis since even noncyanotic patients may show marked ischemic changes on the EKG during treatment. Color of the patient is not an appropriate guide and does not accurately reflect oxygenation of heart and brain tissue during and after the seizure.

Once fasciculations have been observed in the lower extremities and the patient is areflexic, the stimulus may be given. Electrode sites should be briefly scrubbed with normal saline or alcohol to remove skin oil and keratin since these significantly increase electrical resistance. Generous amounts of electrode gel should be applied to treatment electrodes to avoid skin burns from point contact. A rubber or gauze bite block inserted at this point reduces the chance of dental injury during the forceful contraction of the masseters caused by the electrical impulse itself. While there are various types of bite blocks available, it is essential that the load be placed on the molars rather than on the incisors, and any bite block that bears on the incisors should be avoided.

ECT instruments presently in use deliver either sine wave or brief pulse current. Sine wave stimulus was the most commonly used modality following the introduction of ECT, but recently there has been a trend toward the use of brief pulse wave form (Raskin 1986). For reasons that are presently unclear, generalized seizure activity may be induced with brief pulse stimulus using less than one-third the total energy required with sine wave stimulus (Weaver et al. 1977). Studies comparing the two wave forms indicate that they are equally effective therapeutically, but that brief pulse is associated with less posttreatment confusion and memory disturbance (Weiner et al. 1986). Whichever wave form is used, stimulus intensity should be set high enough to induce generalized seizure activity of 30–60 seconds in duration if possible.

The clinician may elect either bilateral or unilateral nondominant electrode placement. In spite of over 40 comparative trials, it remains unclear whether unilateral placement is as effective therapeutically as bilateral placement (Abrams 1986; Sackeim and Mukherjee 1986; Weiner and Coffey 1986). Most reports of lower efficacy with unilateral placement are associated with very low stimulus intensity (Malitz et al. 1986), small distance between unilateral treatment electrodes (Abrams et al. 1983), manic symptomatology (Small et al. 1986) or older patient age (Pettinati et al. 1986). In practice, some clinicians give only bilateral treatment while others routinely use unilateral, reserving bilateral for those patients who do not respond to six to 12 unilateral treatments.

Of the various unilateral nondominant placements, the d'Elia placement has become standard. One electrode is placed at the temple and the other electrode at the vertex, 3 cm lateral to the midline. This placement has been found to have lower energy requirements and fewer side effects than other unilateral placements (Erman et al. 1979) and it has been the technique used in recent trials that have found unilateral ECT equivalent in efficacy to bilateral (Horne et al. 1985; Welch et al. 1982).

Following the electrical stimulus, the EEG shows about 5–10 seconds of low-voltage, high-frequency activity (tonic phase), which then shifts into three cycles per second spike and wave pattern (clonic phase). The length of the seizure tends to be related to stimulus intensity, with higher intensity producing longer seizures. Seizures of less than 20 seconds in duration are thought to be less effective (Ottosson 1962), although some elderly patients sustain seizure activity no longer than 5–10 seconds per treatment and still have a good therapeutic result. Seizures of over 60 seconds in duration are redundant, producing increased cognitive effects without increased efficacy. Very rarely the seizure may persist longer than three minutes, and at this point it should be promptly terminated with an intravenous barbiturate or benzodiazepine.

Since the seizure is the effective component of the treatment, it is essential that some form of monitoring be used to ascertain its occurrence and generalization. In anesthetized patients, motor activity is often entirely absent, and piloerection, tachycardia, and mydriasis occur variably (Fink and Johnson 1982). The most reliable way to observe the occurrence of the seizure is by inflating a blood pressure cuff above systolic pressure on the arm prior to injection of succinylcholine. The convulsion can then be observed unmodified in that hand. In unilateral treatment, the cuff is placed on the arm ipsilateral to the stimulus, indicating that the seizure has crossed the diencephalon if convulsive activity is observed. Most modern ECT instruments include either a paper or an auditory single-channel EEG monitor, and this represents a significant advance in technique. Unfortunately, the single-channel EEG does not distinguish reliably between fully generalized seizures and partial or unilateral seizures, which are known to be ineffective (Ulett et al. 1954). Consequently, the cuff should be used to ascertain generalization while the EEG is a more accurate measure of seizure duration.

There are several cardiovascular disturbances that commonly require intervention. Severe hypertension (systolic over 240 or diastolic over 140) during the treatment may be blunted with an infusion of nitroglycerine (Abrams and Roberts 1983) or, in more refractory cases, nitroprusside (Ciraulo et al. 1978). Application of cutaneous nitroglycerine paste prior to treatment has also been shown to blunt the hypertensive response (Lee et al. 1985). Trimethaphan and labetolol are also available for intravenous use but may be more difficult to titrate. Once intravenous antihypertensive treatment is initiated, the greatest risk is overshoot, particularly as one enters the posttreatment period of bradycardia and hypotension (Liu et al. 1984). The need for intravenous therapy can often be eliminated by starting aggressive oral antihypertensive treatment prior to the next ECT (Jones 1983). Elderly or hypovolemic patients occasionally become hypotensive postictally and may require intravenous pressors, which should be readily available at all times.

The reported incidence of arrhythmia during ECT varies considerably from 8 percent in well patients (Pitts et al. 1965) to 75 percent in high-risk patients (Richardson et al. 1959). Since these disturbances are the result of both vagal and sympathetic stimulation, they cover a wide range of conduction disturbances. While they rarely require treatment, the use of intravenous antiarrhythmics is occasionally necessary (Usubiaga et al. 1967). However, the use of intravenous lidocaine has been associated with difficulty in seizure induction, and it may prevent a successful seizure (Hood and Mecca 1983). Bradycardia immediately following the stimulus or in the postictal period may be treated immediately with a bolus of atropine or glycopyrrolate, repeating incrementally as needed. The incidence of enduring EKG changes following ECT is extremely low (Dec et al. 1985).

Following the seizure, the patient should be vigorously ventilated until spontaneous respiration resumes and then rolled to one side to reduce the chance of aspiration. Vital signs should be taken immediately after the seizure, then at five-minute intervals for 30 minutes.

While mild posttreatment restlessness is common, agitation occasionally presents a risk to the patient or others. This degree of agitation may be effectively treated with diazepam 5–10 mg or haloperidol 2–5 mg, given as a bolus intravenously. Several doses may be necessary in prompt succession before adequate sedation is achieved. Patients so treated require close and sometimes prolonged observation of vital signs during the recovery period.

Patients commonly experience headache after treatment and, in the absence of localizing signs, may be treated with aspirin. The most effective antidote for nausea is droperiodol 1.25–2.5 mg given intravenously immediately after the seizure.

Adverse Effects

A mortality rate of 4.5 deaths per 100,000 treatments was reported in 1973 in the largest recent study of this issue (Reshe and Roeder 1976). It is not significantly different from the mortality rate in brief anesthesia alone. In the largest reported series of deaths, the leading cause was cardiovascular complication, which was responsible for 55 percent of deaths (Maclay 1953).

Posttreatment confusion varies widely from patient to patient, and may range from complete lucidity at the time of awakening to disorientation lasting several hours. Factors associated with more severe confusion are bilateral electrode placement, high-energy sine wave stimulus, prolonged seizure activity, large number of previous treatments, and closely spaced treatments (Glenn and Weiner 1985).

Study of memory impairment associated with ECT is confounded by the fact that patients with depression score lower on memory assessment tests than do normal controls (Abrams and Taylor 1987; Steif et al. 1986). It is clear, however, that both retrograde and anterograde amnesia commonly occur following ECT. The most consistent finding regarding retrograde amnesia is that it is most severe for events most proximate in time to the treatment. Testing conducted seven months after treatment reveals that memory for events during and immediately before a course of ECT contains numerous gaps while memory for events that occurred two years before ECT is largely intact (Squire et al. 1981).

Most patients experience difficulty retaining new information during the course of ECT and up to several months after the last treatment, following which memory usually returns to normal (Squire 1986). Careful memory testing at six months after ECT finds no measured difference in performance between ECT patients and untreated controls (Squire and Chace 1975). However, some patients continue to complain of a subjective sense of impaired memory up to three years after a course of ECT, and it is unclear why there is a difference between measured and subjective assessment.

Bilateral ECT has a more pronounced effect on cognition than does unilateral nondominant ECT (Price 1982). This is true for both retrograde and anterograde amnesia and for both subjectively reported and objectively measured memory deficit. When verbal recall is separately measured following ECT, bilateral electrode placement is associated with much greater deficit than unilateral nondominant. Some studies also report greater deficit of nonverbal recall with bilateral technique, but this finding is not as clear-cut (Portnoy 1986). Overall memory deficit is lowest with unilateral brief pulse stimulus, following which treated patients are not statistically different from untreated controls on comprehensive memory testing (Weiner et al. 1986).

Nonmemory cognitive effects of ECT, including orientation, psychomotor function, discrimination, synthesis, and abstraction, have also been extensively studied (Price 1982). The effect of ECT on these functions appears to be transient, resolving within two months, but it may be marked. Disturbances of all nonmemory functions are more severe with bilateral than with unilateral technique, but the difference is most striking with regard to posttreatment confusion, which may result in acute organic brain syndrome in up to 40 percent of bilateral patients (Summers et al. 1979).

Following a course of ECT, EEG slowing is common at 10 days but most EEGs return to normal within a month, and residual slowing or spiking thereafter probably occurs in less than 10–15 percent of patients (Weiner 1980). The reports of spontaneous seizures subsequent to a course of ECT are confined to the era prior to modern anesthetic technique, and contemporary patients with a history of ECT have no higher incidence of spontaneous seizures than does the general population (Blackwood et al. 1980).

A persistent concern is whether ECT causes neuronal degeneration or loss. This question was carefully addressed in Weiner's encyclopedic 1984 review of the adverse effects of ECT (Weiner 1984). Human postmortem neuropathologic studies yield unreliable data because of other concurrent disease processes at the time of death. A large number of animal studies have been performed to assess this question, measuring neuronal damage caused both by the seizure itself and by the passage of electrical current. Pathologic changes do not appear in animals until after at least an hour of continuous seizure activity without oxygenation and paralysis, or after three hours of continuous seizure activity with oxygenation and paralysis. It appears that pathologic changes due to the passage of current do not occur until at least 1,600 joules are applied, which is many times the intensity of the typical ECT stimulus. It appears, then, that structural neuronal changes occur only with seizure activity and current doses far in excess of what is used in clinical practice, and ECT as presently used is not associated with such changes.

Mechanism of Action

The mechanism of action of ECT is poorly understood. It is clear that the seizure is the therapeutic component and that it must be fully generalized (Ottosson 1960). Indirect evidence suggests the importance of diencephalic, and particularly hypothalamic, involvement in the seizure process (Fink and Ottosson 1980). In animal studies, consistent changes in receptor activity occur following electrical-induced seizures, with a down-regulation of beta (Pandey et al. 1979) and alpha 2 receptors (Cross et al. 1979) and up-regulation of serotonin (Deakin et al. 1981) and dopamine (Costain et al. 1982) receptors, but it is unclear whether these changes are linked to therapeutic effect. In humans, ECT responders tend to show increases in seizure threshold during a course of treatment while nonresponders do not, suggesting that induction of GABA-mediated stabilizing systems may also play a role in the mechanism of action

(Sackeim et al. 1986). It is clear, however, that ECT not only normalizes specific physical symptoms of depression such as anorexia and early morning awakening, but also corrects disregulation of the hypothalamic-pituitary-adrenal axis (Albala et al. 1980).

Continuation Therapy

Following a successful course of ECT, there is over a 50 percent chance of relapse during the next 12 months if the patient is not on a continuation antidepressant (Zis et al 1980). Follow-up studies with imipramine (Seager and Bird 1962), amitriptyline (Kay et al. 1970), phenelzine (Imlah et al. 1965), and lithium (Perry and Tsuang 1979) indicate that all of these medications reduce the one-year relapse rate to 10–20 percent. There is no statistical advantage of any specific drug, and the choice should be made according to the individual patient, considering underlying diagnosis, prior drug response, and individual tolerance of side effects. Maintenance ECT, the administration of one treatment per month for the indefinite future, has been widely practiced but is usually unnecessary if contemporary strategies for antidepressant medication are used.

Conclusion

While ECT is a highly charged political and emotional issue, it also remains the most effective and, for some patients, the safest treatment for major depression. In spite of advances in the use of antidepressant drugs, ECT remains a life-saving treatment for thousands of patients who otherwise would not recover from depressive illness. In recent years the technology of ECT has become increasingly sophisticated, and the administration of the treatment is now a relatively complex procedure that requires special training and expertise on the part of both the anesthesiologist and the psychiatrist. While the mechanism of therapeutic action remains unknown, the prospects for its elucidation in the near future are good, and with this will come greater understanding of the pathophysiology of mood disorders.

Chapter 167

Psychotherapy in the Treatment of Depression: New Technologies and Efficacy

When the past decade of progress in understanding the efficacy of psychotherapy in relationship to pharmacotherapy was reviewed in 1976 for the ACNP *Review of a Generation of Progress*, the task was simple (Weissman 1978). Empirical evidence was meager and only a few studies were available. While there had been a movement from ideologically dominated reports about the value of psychotherapy in the preceding decade, there was a lack of empirical studies. However, there was considerable promise for the next decade because several important clinical trials were under way.

That ACNP review came only two years after Lieberman's (1975) scholarly report of the 1967–1974 literature on the psychotherapy of depression, which reached pessimistic conclusions about the quality of the research. It was also one year after Parloff and Dies (1975) reviewed group psychotherapy outcome research and reached equally pessimistic conclusions about the quality of efficacy studies for depressive disorders. Among the more than 200 articles that Lieberman reviewed, he found no completed controlled trials of psychotherapy that included homogeneous samples of depressed patients, that used minimum scientific standards for clinical trials, and that had more than 10 patients per treatment cell.

The reviews by Lieberman (1975) and Parloff and Dies (1975) had been preceded by the independent reviews of Cristol (1972) and Luborsky et al. (1975), which had noted the methodological flaws in studies of psychotherapy. The pessimism of Lieberman, Parloff, and Dies was not about the benefits that might be achieved by the use of psychotherapy for depression but about the lack of well-designed studies. In 1974, there were no data that met reasonable scientific standards on the efficacy of psychotherapy specifically among depressed patients. Even though numerous studies had been conducted, all included diagnostically heterogeneous, inadequately defined populations and inadequately described procedures for selection and allocation to treatment. By 1976, the design and execution of clinical trials to evaluate the efficacy of psychotherapy had improved. Though structured diagnostic interviews and specified criteria had not yet been published, several studies had begun to focus on homogeneous samples of depressed patients. There were several clinical trials examining the efficacy of psychotherapy alone, in comparison or in combination with a controlled condition (see Weissman 1978, 1979 for reviews). These were primarily pilot studies testing behavioral or cognitive approaches in small samples of depressed patients. In general, they demonstrated efficacy of the active treatment over various control groups.

The Past Decade

Since 1976, the situation has changed dramatically. There are now at least 18 clinical trials of psychotherapy in comparison or in combination with pharmacotherapy for major depression. There are many others comparing psychotherapy with a control group (Weissman et al. 1987). Moreover, the groundwork for improving the scientific conduct of these studies has taken place. Some of the developments include the following:

A Catalog of Outcome Measures

In 1975, Waskow and Parloff published a catalog of outcome measures suitable for measuring change in psychotherapy outcome studies. They emphasized the importance of using multiple outcome measures and noted that psychotherapy might influence several domains, including social functioning. The main effects of their catalog were to encourage greater uniformity in the use of change measures and to facilitate comparisons between studies.

Impact of the Therapist's Characteristics

In 1978, Parloff et al. reviewed studies on therapist variables, such as experience, personality, and empathy, that could affect a patient's progress and outcome in psychotherapy and should therefore be an important consideration when planning outcome. This review followed the many observations by clinicians that some therapists consistently did better than others. However, Parloff et al. (1978) found only a few therapist characteristics that were promising predictors of patient progress and/or outcome in psychotherapy. According to Luborsky et al. (1975), there was moderate support for the value of psychological similarities between patient and therapist and for the therapist's psychological health-sickness ratings, with healthier therapists providing a more positive experience for the patients.

Improved Patient Specification

Between 1974 and 1979, Spitzer et al. (1978) developed and published the Research Diagnostic Criteria (RDC), which made available operationally defined diagnostic criteria, and in 1980 the DSM-III (American Psychiatric Association 1980) was accepted as the official diagnostic criteria by the American Psychiatric Association. As the positive results from the psychopharmacologic trials began to focus attention on the importance of studying diagnostically homogeneous groups (Morris and Beck 1974), more reliable methods of defining diagnoses became available and were incorporated into efficacy studies of psychotherapy.

Improved Treatment Characterization

The last decade has witnessed the use of manuals of psychotherapy in efficacy studies. These manuals specify the main procedures of the particular psychotherapy to be tested and enhance consistency among the therapists engaged in the treatment. Treatment manuals began to appear in the late 1970s. They were designed to specify the identifying characteristics of the psychotherapy, including therapeutic strategies and tactics as well as the sequence and indications for particular tactics. The tactics were operationalized by definition and illustrated by case examples. In some instances, videotape examples were provided.

The behavior therapists were the first to design manuals. The behaviorists' ability to specify interventions (e.g., implosion, desensitization, etc.) with precision (although used with disorders other than depression) gave impetus to the field by providing a model to follow. The first manual was developed for cognitive therapy (CT) in 1973. The first nonbehaviorally oriented treatment manuals (supportive-expressive and psychoanalytically oriented psychotherapies) were developed by Luborsky in 1976, 1977, and 1984.

The development of treatment manuals for outcome studies is now a burgeoning field. Several psychotherapies, both for depression (Beck 1976; Klerman et al. 1984) and for other disorders (Strupp and Binder 1982), have been developed and specified in manuals. In fact, treatment manuals are not just applicable to psychotherapy. Fawcett and Epstein at Rush Presbyterian Medical School, Chicago, have developed a comparable manual (unpublished) for the administration of antidepressant medication, which is being used in the NIMH Treatment of Depression Collaborative Research Program (Elkin et al. 1985). There are many psychotherapies that are amenable both to specification and testing but for which manuals are not yet available. In the 1980s, manuals have become an essential feature of clinical trials as they enhance the procedural consistency and reliability of the treatments under study.

Improved Therapist Training

Another important development in empirical studies of psychotherapy has been the use of standardized training programs, which are based on psychotherapy manuals. The training programs developed for psychotherapy outcome studies were not designed to teach the inexperienced person how to become a therapist, nor were they designed to teach fundamental therapeutic skills such as empathy, handling of transference, and timing. Instead, these training programs were designed to align the practices of the fully trained, experienced, and competent psychotherapists with those procedures specified in the manual (Rounsaville et al. 1984; Rush 1983; Weissman et al. 1982). The development of a shared language and of specified procedures in an agreed-upon sequence was a major focus (Elkin et al. 1984).

Certification criteria for the psychotherapists were developed and utilized in these training programs, based on the goals and tasks outlined in the treatment manual. Through the viewing of videotapes of the trainees' psychotherapy sessions, several independent evaluators could determine whether the therapists had met competence criteria and could be certified to participate in the clinical trials (Chevron and Rounsaville 1983; Chevron et al. 1983; Shaw 1984).

The First NIMH Collaborative Study of Psychotherapy

These technological advances in the study of psychotherapy efficacy, many of them developed by members of the National Institute of Mental Health (NIMH) staff, together with the promising data on the efficacy of psychotherapy, led NIMH in 1978 to begin planning and piloting the first multisite collaborative study of the treatment of depression that would include psychotherapy. Based on the models used to test the efficacy of the new psychotropic drugs in the 1960s, this study was designed to test two psychotherapies: interpersonal psychotherapy (IPT) and cognitive therapy

(CT). Depressed patients were studied in three university centers simultaneously, and clinicians underwent standardized training for both psychotherapies and for the reference pharmacotherapy (imipramine) condition (Elkin et al. 1984). Preliminary results were reported in May 1986 at the American Psychiatric Association Meeting in Washington, D.C., and the full results of this study will be available soon.

Summary of the Evidence for Major Depression

Status and Number of Studies

There have been at least 18 studies, 15 completed and three in progress, that have examined the efficacy of psychotherapy in comparison or combination with pharmacotherapy for the treatment of major depression; these were controlled clinical trials and included homogeneous samples of depressed patients (Weissman et al. 1987). There are many other studies not described that have tested the efficacy of psychotherapy but have not included a pharmacotherapy treatment cell.

Type of Treatment Studied

The most commonly studied approaches have been CT, IPT, and behavioral (39 percent, 28 percent, and 22 percent of the trials, respectively) (Table 1). There has been an increase in CT and IPT trials over the past decade, but the major change has been in behavioral treatments. Before 1976 there were no behavioral studies that included a pharmacotherapy cell; now there are at least four. There has not been a continuation of marital and family studies; only one such study has been published in the past decade. The use of combination pharmacotherapy and psychotherapy as a treatment condition has continued, and over three-quarters of the studies now include that combination. However, there has been a decrease in the use of low-contact or waiting list control groups in psychotherapy, and there has also been a shift downward in the use of placebo controls in pharmacotherapy; only 36 percent of the studies in the last decade, in contrast with 75 percent of the studies prior to 1976, included placebo controls. This change may reflect the accumulated data from numerous placebo-controlled clinical trials on the efficacy of pharmacotherapy for the

Table 1.   Type of Treatment Studied in Clinical Trials for Major Depression (Only Studies Including a Pharmacotherapy Condition Included)

Type of Treatment Studied[a]	N	%
CT (Individual or Group)	7	39
IPT	5	28
Behavioral	4	22
Marital or family	2	11
Group	1	6
Drug and psychotherapy combination	14	77
Low-contact control for psychotherapy	7	39
Placebo control for drugs	8	44
Other psychotherapy control[b]	5	28
Total	18	

[a]Treatments are not mutually exclusive.
[b]Control treatments include insight (N=2), relaxation (N=1), counseling (N=1), group (N=1).

treatment of major depression. However, one might question the wisdom of this shift in view of the usefulness of the placebo-control condition to determine whether the treatments are active. It is interesting to note that insight psychodynamic therapy has been used as a comparison for behavioral or cognitive studies in only two trials despite the fact that insight psychotherapy, however defined, is the major psychological treatment in clinical practice. Data on the efficacy of insight psychodynamic therapy are still sparse. The previous trials of IPT and CT, with few exceptions, were conducted by the investigators who developed the manuals for these treatments. For the past decade, both the CT and IPT trials have been conducted at sites other than the place of their origin. These trials have been most important for determining the effectiveness and the transmissibility of the respective treatments to other centers.

Duration of Treatment

Most of the studies have been short term, only one study goes beyond 36 weeks, and the Kupfer and Frank study is still in progress. Duration of 12–16 weeks is the most frequent treatment period, representing over 60 percent of the studies (Table 2), and this proportion has not changed since the previous decade. Thus, there are still sparse data on the efficacy of long-term psychotherapy for major depression. Also, there is a paucity of data on the relationship between duration of treatment and outcome, and on the need for "booster sessions" for the prevention or recurrence of relapse.

Psychotherapy versus Pharmacotherapy

Four studies have data that suggest that psychotherapy may be better than pharmacotherapy for the treatment of some major depressions, and two studies have suggested equivalent efficacy. The treatments represented in these studies are behavior therapy, CT, and IPT, though there is only partial evidence for CT and IPT.

Rush et al. (1977)—in a study that included 41 acutely ill, unipolar depressed outpatients randomly assigned to twice-a-week cognitive behavioral therapy, compared with a group treated with imipramine up to 250 mg/day for a maximum of 12 weeks—found statistically significant decreases in depressive symptomatology for both treatments. Cognitive therapy resulted in significantly greater improvement than did pharmacotherapy on both self-report and clinician-completed measures of depressive symptomatology. Moreover, 79 percent of the patients in cognitive therapy,

Table 2.   Duration of Treatment Phase in Studies Testing Efficacy of Psychotherapy in Comparison or Combination with Pharmacotherapy for Major Depression

Duration of trial (in weeks)	N	%
8	1	6
10	1	6
12	8	44
16	4	22
28	1	6
32	1	6
36	1	6
176	1	6
Total	18	

as compared with 23 percent of the pharmacotherapy patients, showed marked improvement or complete remission of symptoms. The dropout rate was substantially lower in cognitive therapy.

McLean and Hakstian (1979), in a sample of patients with primary major depression, found that behavior therapy was better than amitriptyline, which was equal to relaxation therapy and better than insight. However, the drug dose was fixed at 150 mg/day of amitriptyline, and clinical assessments were by self-report only.

Blackburn et al. (1981) and Blackburn and Bishop (1983) found evidence for the efficacy of CT over pharmacotherapy but only for patients attending the general practitioner. These patients are likely to be less chronic and less likely to have received prior treatment of any kind.

Sloane et al. (1985) found partial evidence for the efficacy of IPT over nortriptyline in an elderly sample at six weeks, primarily because the elderly did not tolerate the medications well.

On the other hand, Weissman et al. (1979), in a study of the treatment of acute depression, showed that IPT was equal to pharmacotherapy on symptom reduction, and the preliminary results from the recent NIMH Collaborative Study showed that CT and IPT were similar to imipramine in symptom reduction. All active treatments were better than placebo, and the onset of effect was earlier in pharmacotherapy.

Combined Treatment versus Either Treatment Alone

Seven studies have partial evidence suggesting the efficacy of combined treatment versus either pharmacotherapy or psychotherapy alone. Three independent maintenance trials that used both pharmacotherapy and psychotherapy in the treatment of depression have been conducted:

1. The New Haven-Boston Collaborative Study, which examined eight months of maintenance treatment on amitriptyline, placebo, or no pill, with or without individual interpersonal psychotherapy, in 150 partially recovered depressed women (Klerman et al. 1974; Weissman et al. 1979).
2. The Baltimore study, which compared 16 months of maintenance treatment on imipramine, diazepam, or placebo, with or without four months of group therapy, in 149 partially recovered depressed women (Covi et al. 1974).
3. The Philadelphia study, which compared three months of treatment on amitriptyline or placebo, with or without marital therapy, in 196 married depressed men and women (Freidman, 1975). This study was considered a maintenance trial since patients were followed through to their recovery.

There was remarkable similarity in findings. All three studies showed an effect for tricyclic antidepressants. Maintenance antidepressants, compared with placebo or psychotherapy, were most efficacious in preventing relapse or the return of symptoms. But although some recovery of social performance occurred as a result of the reduction of symptoms, medication alone had only a limited impact on problems in living and psychosocial functioning.

All three studies showed a positive effect for psychotherapy in areas related to problems in living, particularly in interpersonal relationships, when compared with low contact or with medication alone. The psychosocial intervention was not as effective as medication, however, in reducing symptoms of the depressive syndrome or in preventing symptomatic relapse.

Preliminary results of the Hollon study (S.D. Hollon, personal communication

January 8, 1986) indicated that a combination of pharmacotherapy and CT was superior to pharmacotherapy alone and evidenced a nonsignificant trend relative to CT at the end of 12 weeks.

For acute treatment, Weissman et al. (1979) found that combined treatment (IPT and amitriptyline) was additive in effect and resulted in less symptomatic failure and greater reduction of symptoms than either treatment alone. Blackburn et al. (1981) found that CT plus drug was better than either treatment alone for depressed psychiatric outpatients. In the Murphy et al. (1984) study, there was a trend for the efficacy of combined treatment as compared with pharmacotherapy on dropout. Dropout was highest in the pharmacotherapy alone group. Covi et al. (in press) noted a trend for the clinical evaluators to find CT plus imipramine to be the most efficacious treatment although this finding was not evident in the psychiatrists' or the patients' reports.

It is of particular note that no studies of CT in combination with pharmacotherapy have found the combination better than cognitive therapy alone. Beck et al. (1985) found a trend for patients receiving CT plus amitriptyline to be doing better one year after treatment, although this same trend was not shown at 12 weeks (which was the end of acute treatment). Roth et al. (1982) found that desipramine plus self-control therapy was better than self-control alone in speeding symptom reduction and improvement.

Two studies showed that psychotherapy plus pharmacotherapy was equal to either psychotherapy or pharmacotherapy alone. Hersen et al. (1984) found that all treatments, whether combined or individual, whether pharmacotherapy or social skills, were of equal efficacy. Wilson (1982) also showed that behavioral techniques of various kinds plus amitriptyline were the same as behavioral techniques without pharmacotherapy at the end of eight weeks. Patients on amitriptyline had more rapid symptom improvement initially. There was some suggestion that relaxation therapy was better than minimal therapy.

No published studies have found that psychotherapy plus pharmacotherapy produced results worse than psychotherapy alone. Three studies have shown that psychotherapy plus pharmacotherapy was equal to psychotherapy alone. The Beck et al. (1985) study showed that CT plus pharmacotherapy equaled CT alone at the end of 12 weeks. Covi et al. (in press) showed similar results on patient and doctor ratings but not on the independent evaluators' ratings, where there was a trend for the combined treatment to be better. Murphy et al. (1984) found that CT and nortriptyline together were equal to either treatment alone.

One study by Waring and Patton et al. (1984, unpublished manuscript) found that family CT plus pharmacotherapy was worse than pharmacotherapy alone. They concluded that the addition of family therapy for depression during the acute phase of illness was not useful.

A review of 11 controlled studies of psychotherapy plus pharmacotherapy in the treatment of outpatients with unipolar depression, using a new statistical technique based on metanalysis, found that the combined active treatments were appreciably more effective than placebo or minimal contact conditions and slightly but consistently superior to psychotherapy alone, pharmacotherapy alone, or either of these treatments in combination with placebo (Conte et al. 1986).

Differential Outcome by Patient Type

Information emerging from the studies conducted over the past decade will begin to answer the question about the specificity of the treatments for particular patients. Prusoff et al. (1980) found that endogenous, nonsituational depressed patients responded best to the combination of drugs and psychotherapy (IPT) and worse to IPT alone. The situationally depressed patients did equally well with drugs, IPT, or the combination, and better with any of these treatments than with a nonscheduled control treatment.

Blackburn et al. (1981) did not find a treatment difference between endogenous and nonendogenous patients but found that psychiatric clinic patients (i.e., the more chronic or refractory patients), as compared with patients coming for treatment to a general practitioner, did best on the combination of cognitive therapy and pharmacotherapy. As noted earlier, Blackburn et al. (1981) found CT alone or in combination with drugs to be slightly better than drugs alone among general-practice patients.

Kovacs (1980) did not find a correlation between endogenous depression and poor response to cognitive therapy. The Blackburn et al. (1981) and Kovacs (1980) studies did not separate out endogenous patients who were also diagnosed as having situational depression from the patients who were diagnosed as having only endogenous depression, and neither study used RDC or DSM-III criteria for the endogenous or melancholic subtypes.

Differential Effects of Drugs and Psychotherapy

DiMascio et al. (1979) found a differential effect of drugs and IPT psychotherapy. IPT had its effect on depressed mood and on the patient's involvement in work and in other interests, whereas amitriptyline had its effect on the vegetative symptoms of depression. The effects of psychotherapy on direct measures of social functioning were found at one-year follow-up.

Rush et al. (1982) found that CT had a more pervasive and significant impact on self-concept and produced a greater reduction in hopelessness than did imipramine. They also found that cognitive symptoms remitted before the vegetative symptoms with CT but not with imipramine.

Specificity of the Psychotherapies

Zeiss et al. (1979) studied three behavioral approaches and found no differential outcome among them. Similar findings were also reported by Jarvik et al. (1982) studying cognitive group therapy versus psychodynamic group therapy in elderly depressed patients. However, in the studies by Bellack et al. (1981) and Hersen et al. (1984) comparing behavioral approaches with insight psychotherapy, the behavioral approaches were found to be somewhat more efficacious.

A partial answer to the question of specificity of treatments awaits the results of the NIMH Treatment of Depression Collaborative Research Program, in which two different psychotherapies, CT and IPT, are being compared (Elkin et al. 1985). The most important features of the NIMH study are that the treatments were not developed in the centers conducting the trials, there is no ideological commitment to either form of treatment, and the therapists have been well trained and monitored in both treatments.

Can the Psychotherapies Be Differentiated?

DeRubeis et al. (1982) undertook a study to determine whether it was possible to identify distinct and theoretically meaningful differences between two forms of therapy, CT and IPT, used in the treatment of depression. Blind ratings of videotapes enabled 12 raters to distinguish the treatments consistently in the direction of experts' predictions. Similar findings for different treatments were reported by Luborsky et al. (1982), who found that independent judges were also able to distinguish three different forms of psychotherapy—cognitive-behavioral, supportive-expressive psychoanalytically oriented psychotherapy, and drug counseling. A new system for rating psychotherapies for depression to determine if they can be differentiated has been developed by Hollon and Beck (1979) and has been used in the NIMH Treatment of Depression Collaborative Research Program.

Are Psychotherapy Effects Sustained?

Two separate studies (Kovacs et al. 1981; Weissman et al. 1981) found that acutely depressed patients who had received psychotherapy alone and in combination with pharmacotherapy were doing better one year after treatment than those who had received only pharmacotherapy. The effects of IPT were on social functioning and were only evidenced after 16 weeks of treatment (Weissman et al. 1981). Beck (1985) reported follow-up results from two CT studies (Blackburn et al. 1985; Simons et al. 1986). In both studies, CT compared with pharmacotherapy showed greater long-term effects, as well as prophylactic effects, over the two-year period.

The Blackburn et al. (in press) study, a two-year follow-up, included depressed patients who responded to either CT or pharmacotherapy, or the combination, and found significantly more relapses at six months in the pharmacotherapy as compared to CT alone or the combination treatment groups. The number of patients who relapsed at some point over two years was also significantly higher in pharmacotherapy than in either of the treatment groups with CT. While the findings are promising, they are still too few to draw definite conclusions about the sustained effects of psychotherapy.

In summary, over the last decade a number of well-designed clinical trials of the efficacy of psychotherapy have been initiated, and the pace of this research has been sustained. There has been increasing interest in understanding the elements of the therapeutic relationship or alliance between the patient and therapist, which facilitates the application of therapeutic techniques and constructive patient change (Rush et al. 1981). There has also been increased interest in the feasibility, methodology, and policy implications of psychotherapy outcome studies (American Psychiatric Association 1982; Greenspan and Sharfstein 1981; Hersen et al. 1984; Karasu 1980, 1982; Klerman 1986; London and Klerman 1982; Parloff 1980).

The precision of the available studies—particularly the efforts to specify treatments, patients, and therapists—has shown vast improvement over the past decade. There continues to be considerable interest in the efficacy of psychotherapy (particularly CT) in comparison with drugs. Research efforts to determine the specificity of which treatment for which patient are beginning to yield findings, some of which will be published in the NIMH Treatment of Depression Collaborative Research Study. Definitive conclusions must await these results.

To summarize the most recent efficacy data, there is some suggestion that psychotherapies and pharmacotherapies are approximately equivalent for the milder depressions and that the psychotherapies may even be superior. The evidence for the efficacy of the combination of pharmacotherapy and psychotherapy over either treatment alone still persists although these findings are strongest in the earlier maintenance trials. There is no evidence for a negative effect of combined treatment. There is some evidence from one- and two-year follow-up studies for the long-term effects of psychotherapy.

Future Directions for Research

While selected psychotherapies appear to reduce depressive symptoms, it is now important to identify under what conditions that effect is found or can be maximized. Especially important are studies to evaluate the comparative efficacy and indications for combined drug and psychotherapy. Studies to identify which depressed patients are most likely to respond are needed. Studies that modify the "standard" treatment are indicated to determine whether different packages are called for in different personalities or by differing histories of illness (e.g., are chronic depressions to be treated with a modified package?).

Conditions that influence treatment can be divided into two broad categories. The first category includes the relationship between the types of treatment selected and the patients' presenting cluster of problems, symptoms, and characteristics. In studying treatment-patient interactions, it may become clearer which patients respond or fail when exposed to which treatments, or to which set(s) of treatments in what sequence(s).

The second category includes the variables that influence the administration or provision of treatment. In pharmacotherapy, this category equals the dose-finding studies. In psychotherapy, it includes such technical questions as format of therapy presentation (individual or group, patient alone or couple), duration and frequency of treatment (biweekly versus weekly, booster sessions versus no booster sessions), and therapist training (criterion-demonstrated competency versus continued evaluation with feedback).

In beginning to examine the conditions that maximize the therapeutic effect of drugs, specific psychotherapies, or their combinations, the "effect" desired must be specified. It is likely that some treatments are more efficacious for improving acute depressive symptoms and some may be better than others in improving social withdrawal, interpersonal problems, or cognitive distortions found in many depressed persons.

By studying the conditions that influence therapeutic effects, investigators will be confronted with the conditions associated with the treatment failures and thus can begin to study modifications of existing interventions or can design new interventions that increase the probability of a positive treatment response with maintenance across subsets of depressed patients, varied symptoms, and time.

Available data suggest that a prophylactic effect may occur. However, these data are sparse. Long-term follow-up studies are required to fully evaluate whether, when, and for whom prophylaxis is obtained with each form of psychotherapy.

Finally, it should be emphasized that all of the studies that have been described here deal with major depression and make no claims for the use of psychotherapy with psychotic depression or bipolar disorder, or for all psychotherapies, or for long-term treatment.

A considerable gap still remains between clinical practice and research studies. Most depressed patients, if they receive any treatment at all and if that treatment is psychotherapy, are more likely to receive a psychodynamic psychotherapy than cognitive, behavioral, or interpersonal treatments. To close the gap between research and clinical practice, the next wave of clinical trials should include psychodynamic psychotherapeutic treatments. However, the studies should also include the technological advances in the specification of treatments and training procedures. Another method of bridging the gap between research and practice is to foster continuing education opportunities for practitioners to learn psychotherapeutic approaches whose efficacy are currently supported by empirical data from clinical trials.

Chapter 168

Intensive Psychotherapy and Psychoanalysis

Psychoanalytic psychotherapy, as a therapeutic modality, was not developed for the specific treatment of mood disorders. Psychoanalysis grew out of the efforts to treat hysterical disorders, and it was only after pioneer psychoanalysts had investigated phobias, obsessions and compulsions, and paranoia, as well as a wealth of normal psychological phenomena, that they turned their attention to melancholia and manic-depressive states (Abraham 1960a). Even then, the methods of psychoanalytic psychotherapy were not altered to accommodate mood disorders, but these psychopathologic states were investigated and treated according to the general principles of psychoanalysis prevalent at that time. Over the course of almost a century, these principles and their therapeutic derivations have evolved and are continuing to be modified and refined, for psychoanalytic psychotherapy is but one facet of a more universal theory of psychological functioning with ramifications encompassing ideas of culture, normal development, and, basically, the human condition. Therefore, in attempting to describe the treatment of mood disorders by this method, it might be best to start with a very brief description of the process of psychoanalytic psychotherapy, what it hopes to accomplish and how, and then to consider how it may be applicable to the treatment of mood disorders.

Psychoanalytic Psychotherapy

As stated above, this therapeutic method has been and continues to be in a state of constant evolution. Since Breuer and Freud launched the discipline of psychoanalysis in 1893 with the publication of "On the Psychical Mechanisms of Hysterical Phenomena," innumerable contributions on psychoanalysis have appeared and constant schisms within the field have occurred, resulting in conflicting views as to the nature of psychoanalysis. It is thus difficult to find a simple definition of psychoanalytic therapy that would meet with unanimous approval from practitioners. In searching for a unifying theme among the variety of psychoanalytic therapies, one that stands out is that this form of therapy achieves its results by increasing the patient's conscious knowledge of crucial aspects of his psychological functioning, of which he was previously unaware or only dimly aware. It is assumed that these aspects of the personality can be traced back to significant childhood experiences that shaped the individual's evolving personality structure. It is also assumed that these aspects were pushed out of awareness because their conscious apprehension was painful to the individual. Finally, it is assumed that although out of awareness, these aspects continue to affect psychological functioning and that their discovery will free the individual to live his life in a more satisfying and constructive manner. As Offenkrantz and Tobin (1974) have summarized, there are two phases in the analytic task. The first is to "make the 'here and now' experience between patient and analyst come alive with feeling in order to discover the ways in which the past is still active in the patient's current perceptions and behavior"; the second is "to help the patient grasp the way in which the present is different from the past" (Offenkrantz and Tobin 1974, p. 594).

While psychoanalysts would agree that atavistic parts of the self are inappropriately carried forward into present functioning, there is disagreement as to how to conceive of these remnants of the past. Originally, it was believed that painful memories of actual events were at the core of psychopathology. Later, forbidden instinctual representations in the form of fantasies or desires made up the content of repressed parts of the self. Both of these views still hold some currency today, although, in recent decades, a growing body of work (Arieti and Bemporad 1978; Beck 1976; Bowlby 1980; Peterfreund and Schwartz 1971) has suggested that what remains from childhood are erroneous beliefs or assumptions, based on either valid or distorted perceptions. The individual continues to live out his life according to these dictates (or programs) although they are never clearly articulated in his consciousness.

The salient processes through which the therapist aids the patient in bringing these aspects of himself into awareness are the overcoming of resistance and the analysis of transference. In a famous passage in *The History of the Psychoanalytic Movement* (1914, p. 16), Freud identifies these two features of treatment as essential:

> It may thus be said that the theory of psychoanalysis is an attempt to account for two striking and unexpected facts of observation which emerge whenever an attempt is made to trace the symptoms of a neurotic back to their sources in his past life: the facts of transference and of resistance. Any line of investigation which recognizes the two facts and takes them as the starting point of its work may call itself psychoanalysis, though it arrives at results other than my own.

In the many decades since these words were written, transference and resistance have remained the essential concepts defining psychoanalytic psychotherapy (Greenson 1967). Resistance is the individual's largely unconscious method of impeding the conscious awareness of his intrapsychic world. Transference represents the unconscious misrepresentation of people in current life to conform to characteristics of individuals who were significant in the past. The patient is unaware of this inappropriate distortion but is affected greatly by the vicissitudes of his relationships with individuals who have become the objects of his transference reactions. While some practitioners would analyze transference reactions only when they themselves have become their object, others would include distortions of individuals other than the therapist as suitable for investigation and interpretation.

In the context of a close and trusting relationship, the patient gradually reveals the hidden pathogenic aspects of himself, which in turn the therapist identifies, interprets according to a meaningful system, and, hopefully, transforms into more appropriate appraisals of reality. Since much of what is hidden is linked to painful memories and realizations, there is a constant effort to resist awareness and change. Obviously, the relinquishing of atavistic modes of assessing oneself and others takes a long time, with only gradual and, at times, unpredictable progress.

Applicability to Mood Disorders

While it is hoped that the restructuring of the personality accomplished as a result of psychoanalytic psychotherapy will protect the individual against future episodes of illness or at least ameliorate preexisting chronic discomfort, these effects are to be expected only after therapy has progressed to a certain degree. Therefore, immediate symptom relief at the start of therapy is not anticipated. An initial improvement may be observed based on the patient's optimism because he has embarked on a mode of treatment or because he has made emotional contact with a sympathetic listener; however, this assuaging of symptoms can be seen in most forms of interpersonal therapy and cannot be ascribed to the particular techniques of psychoanalytic psychotherapy.

This form of treatment does not attack depressive symptoms directly but strives to make the individual less vulnerable to severe mood disturbances in the future. Symptoms are treated indirectly by increasing the individual's ability to cope with situations that, in the past, would have precipitated the recurrence of psychopathology.

Since pharmacologic agents with demonstrated efficacy in the treatment of acute depressive episodes have been developed, these may be used concurrently with the initiation of psychoanalytic psychotherapy. At one time it was argued that a reduction in symptoms would lessen the individual's resolve to face the unpleasant discoveries inherent in the therapeutic process. While some psychological discomfort may be necessary to motivate the patient to endure the rigors of therapy (see Greenson 1967), there is little point in depriving any human being of relief from the extreme torment of a severe mood disorder. Furthermore, remission of a severe depression—and, in particular, of the melancholic symptoms that are so unbearable—will reduce the patient's obsession with his misery and make him more available for productive therapeutic work. Experienced analysts, such as Jacobson (1971) or Arieti (1976), who successfully used psychoanalytic psychotherapy with severely depressed individuals for many decades strongly recommend the use of antidepressants and report no impedence to the process of therapy.

While medication has made some severe depressions amenable to psychoanalytic treatment and enlarged the scope of this form of therapy, there are still some mood disorders for which it remains contraindicated. Psychoanalytic psychotherapy inherently arouses strong affects and requires a relative lessening of control over usual rational thought processes. Some individuals cannot tolerate these stresses and may respond with an exacerbation of illness. Bipolar patients, even when maintained on medication, may not be able to withstand the extremes of emotion engendered in the therapeutic process. Patients who have experienced psychotic episodes also may not be able to regain appropriate reality testing and may continue to act out gross transference distortions outside of the office setting. For such patients, modified therapy, in which defenses or resistances are left intact and transference is discouraged, may be beneficial.

In contrast to these individuals who may be too ill to withstand psychoanalytic psychotherapy, this treatment may be inappropriate for some who are too healthy. Depression is a ubiquitous experience, and even people who have led satisfying and productive lives may succumb to depressive episodes following a massive loss or frustration. It may be argued that such an extensive, costly, and lengthy treatment is not required since these types of "adjustment disorders" will clear with time and support. But as in the case of very ill patients, modified psychotherapy can be very useful for such individuals in helping them to get through the period of crisis and to prevent the experience of depression from adversely affecting their future functioning.

Psychoanalytic psychotherapy is most indicated for so-called characterological depressions, in which psychopathology is an inherent part of the individual's mode of processing everyday experience and permeates his values, relationships, and self-assessment. Such individuals present with chronic depression since early life and so limit their existence that they themselves perpetuate their symptomatology. Others harbor powerful atavistic patterns of thinking, feeling, and behaving that result in frequent episodes of depression following trivial frustrations or deprivations. Still others have been able to fend off clinical depression by aberrant life-styles, only to fall ill when these are no longer possible or adaptive. All these individuals present histories of long-standing maladaptive patterns and of inappropriate modes of evaluating self-worth. It is toward changing these underlying processes that psychoanalytic psychotherapy is directed, with the eventual result of decreasing vulnerability to clinical illness in the face of life's vicissitudes.

Psychoanalytic Formulations of Depression

The earliest attempts to encompass depression from a psychodynamic point of view appear to have been direct applications of the then prevailing psychoanalytic theory. In this manner, Abraham (1960a) first considered depression as a blockage of libido and later (1960b) as a regression to preoedipal modes of gratification and object relations.

It was not until the publication of "Mourning and Melancholia" in 1917 that Freud turned his attention to depressive states and formulated an original interpretation that was specific to these disorders. As is well known, this work explained depression as resulting from anger directed inward toward the lost love object, which, by incorporation, had become part of the ego.

A decade later, Rado (1927) modified this basic formulation according to the general changes that had been introduced by the structural theory. In Rado's revision, the superego becomes the punishing agent, and the preoedipal introjection is conceived of as a dual process with the good aspects of the object becoming part of the superego and the bad aspects part of the ego. These works represent the classic period of psychoanalytic thought, during which basic mental structures were proposed and then used to account for various clinical phenomena. During this formative and creative period of psychoanalytic thought, great emphasis was given to intrapsychic structures, processes, and conflicts, with theory becoming more complex and more removed from presenting clinical data.

Depression as a Basic Affect

A radically new way of conceptualizing depression arose in the 1950s and 1960s, showing the influence of ego psychology but also reflecting a disenchantment with complicated and unprovable metapsychological theories and the wish to propose simpler models that were conceptually closer to observable manifestations. This newer view was initiated by Bibring (1953), who postulated that depression be considered as a basic state of the ego, which cannot be reduced further and which arises automatically when the individual finds himself in a situation that forces him to give up strongly held narcissistic aspirations. Since different frustrations or deprivations may cause different people to feel powerless to attain needed narcissistic goals, depression cannot be the universal manifestation of an oral fixation or of retroflected anger following object loss. Rather, the feeling of depression is seen as the emotional expression of the ego's helplessness in maintaining a desired sense of self. Bibring's innovative interpretations shifted the focus of study from the internal intersystemic conflicts that were thought to produce depression intrapsychically to those situations that precipitated a sense of ego helplessness. Taking the experience of depression as a given, he also speculated on the type of person who would have difficulty overcoming or defending against lowered self-esteem following narcissistic frustration.

A decade following Bibring's presentation, Sandler and Joffee (1965) furthered this line of reasoning by suggesting that depression be considered a negative emotion, much like anxiety. Depression was said to arise whenever the individual experienced the loss of a former state of well-being. In the case of depression following the loss of a loved one, these authors postulated that it was not the loss of the object per se that provoked the dysphoria but rather the loss of the state of well-being that the object had supplied.

Another significant contribution was Sandler and Joffee's delineation of two stages in the depressive sequence. The first type of depression immmediately follows the loss of a state of well-being. This stage of depression is called a "psychobiological reaction" and was believed to be a ubiquitous, if not a normal, response. Most individuals can overcome this initial dysphoria by finding new ways to obtain a state of well-being, and so their depressions are self-limited and, perhaps, even beneficial. However, some individuals cannot mobilize themselves to alter this condition of deprivation, and they go on to experience the second form of depression: the clinical episode. The predisposition to clinical depression, therefore, resides in the particular individual's inability to find sources of well-being after a loss or frustration. This two-stage sequence also proposes that depression be viewed as a process that culminates over time as the individual faces a future bereft of needed gratification. In this sense, clinical depression is more than a reactive dysphoria that passes with time as the individual readjusts his narcissistic equilibrium. It entails an alteration in one's sense of self and has definite clinical and psychodynamic features that go beyond the transient unhappiness secondary to the usual vicissitudes of life. Clinical depression may be seen both as a way of organizing experience and as the reemergence of childhood modes of thinking and relating to oneself and others that are no longer appropriate to adult life.

In severe or chronic depressions, it is postulated that external events reverberate with dimly conscious and threatening views of the self and others, confirming a negativistic worldview that now appears unalterable. These dreaded assumptions, believed to be based on childhood experiences, usually consist of the acceptance that one will never be loved or does not deserve to be loved by needed others, that one can never be a worthwhile human being, or that one will always suffer at the mercy of a world he cannot control. When reality appears to prove, either in actuality or in distorted fantasy, the veracity of these assumptions, the individual automatically experiences a depressive affect appropriate to their content.

Bowlby (1980) has enumerated these underlying beliefs and the childhood experiences from which they are thought to derive. These experiences are not single events but long-term patterns of familial interaction, which may occur singly or in combination. One is the child's "bitter experience of never having attained a stable or secure relationship with the parents despite having made repeated efforts to do so, including having done his utmost to fulfill their demands and perhaps also unrealistic expectations they may have had of him" (Bowlby 1980, p. 247). Another relates to the child having been "told repeatedly how unlovable, and/or how inadequate, and/or how incompetent he is" (Bowlby 1980, p. 247). Last is the possibility that the child was "more likely than others to have experienced actual loss of a parent . . . with consequences to himself that, however disagreeable they might have been, he was impotent to change" (Bowlby 1980).

Most individuals construct defenses to protect themselves against the realization of these ideas. Some insist on constant displays of affection to prove they are loved, others strive to become wealthy or powerful to feel adequate, while others may become overconscientious workers to ensure the admiration of surrogate parental figures. When these props are shattered by a stressor, the ideas come to the surface, together with a sense of despair and depression.

Psychoanalytic psychotherapy also aims at the removal of these defenses so that the underlying ideas may be altered. However, this goal is achieved in a gradual and supportive manner, allowing the individual to relinquish the defenses on his own. As Badel (1962) wrote in his report of the psychoanalytic treatment of a severely depressed patient; "The reasons for the cyclical nature of the attacks seemed to be that there was a chronic internal state of severe dissatisfaction, creating a sensitive balance which could be disturbed by slight traumata. It is to this chronic internal state that we direct our attention, but only after a long analysis of defenses could it be reached."

Process of Therapy

Depressives usually seek out treatment when they are in the midst of an acute clinical episode, and whatever they may verbalize at this point of their illness, there is an underlying wish for magical relief from psychic pain. The affected individual feels debilitated, helpless, and at times isolated. He may thus look upon the therapist as his only hope for cure and overly idealize him. The patient may ingratiate the therapist with narcissistically gratifying remarks or attempt to elicit inappropriate nurturance by proclamations of misery.

Jacobson (1971, 1975) has written specifically about problems in transference during the early sessions with depressives. She describes how these patients become overinvolved with their therapists and experience an initial improvement because they have formed illusory expectations of nurturance. They express devotion to the therapist but eventually will demand equal devotion in return and, when this is not received, will leave treatment, become angry, or experience an intensification of their depressive symptoms. Kolb (1956) has also noted that the beginning of treatment with depressives is stressful to the therapist because of the guilt-provoking dependency of the patient. He writes: "The depressed patient demands to be gratified. He attempts to extract or force the gratification from the therapist by his pleas for help, by his exposure of his misery, and by suggesting that the therapist is responsible for leaving him in his unfortunate condition."

The therapist should be warm and encouraging but consistently make clear that the burden of therapy and cure rests on the patient's shoulders. New topics can be introduced to break the repetitive cycle of complaints and misery. Idealization should be detected early and transference distortions corrected as these arise. In this regard, the therapist must be honest about his own shortcomings and the limitations of psychotherapy to produce miraculous and rapid cures. This openness, which has been recommended by Kolb (1956), is very important since the depressive has all too often been raised in an atmosphere of deceit, manipulation, and secret obligations, and he must be shown that it is possible to be honest and forthright without being criticized or abandoned.

Once therapy has begun on the proper course, the patient should be encouraged to look inward toward the causes of his dysphoria. This search involves the patient relating the precipitating factor for the clinical episode to his particular personality organization. The environmental loss, frustration, or rejection that provokes a severe depression has a deeper meaning for the individual, which threatens his needed sense of self and his sources of narcissism. Therefore, what appears to the casual observer as a trivial event may reverberate with a deep-seated fear and shame in the vulnerable individual.

An illustration of the profundity of the effect of a precipitant is the case of a middle-aged man who suffered a severe exacerbation of depression after he lost a substantial sum of money in the stock market, although his loss did not affect his day-to-day way of life. He became sullen, self-denigrating, and more dependent on others, and he exhibited vegetative signs. This severe reaction was more understandable when he explained not only that he was reacting to the loss of funds but also that he had hoped he could earn a sufficient income from his investments so he could quit his job, which he despised. Therefore, the loss dashed his dreams for a better future.

However, this deeper meaning still did not account for his drastic alteration in his estimation of himself and for his depressive decompensation. The extent of his reaction became clearer as he recalled his childhood experience, during which he had been forced to achieve and excel and yet was never able to satisfy his parents' demands. Despite his outstanding academic record, he was repeatedly told he would never amount to anything and should strive for a secure, if limited and unsatisfying, position in life. He accepted his family's judgment and took up a lucrative but, to him, boring vocation. Throughout his life he had dreamed of making a financial killing that would prove to his family that he was worthy of their admiration and would quell his own recurrent feelings of inadequacy. The failure of his financial venture represented his total failure as a person. His family had been correct in their estimation. He was inferior and not deserving of their love. He subjected himself to the same ruthless criticism and humiliation that he would have received at their hands.

The setting of the proper course of therapy in terms of dependency and transference, the realization that the clinical episode is the resultant of premorbid personality organization, and the connecting of the precipitating events with particular maladaptive modes of gaining and maintaining a sense of worth comprise the major objectives of the first stage of therapy.

The patient's realization that his basic beliefs are irrational or that his everyday reactions are self-defeating does not automatically ensure that his self-conceptions or previous activities will change automatically. Characterological psychopathology is not easily relinquished, for these older, ingrained patterns have offered security, predictability, structure, and occasional gratification. The patient would gladly relinquish his symptoms but resists changes in a personality that forms the basis of those very dreaded symptoms. The overcoming of these resistances and the gradual process of change comprise the middle stage of therapy.

This is the time of "working through," which is the real battleground of therapy with frequent advances, regressions, and stalemates. The fundamental struggle involves the depressive giving up his excessive reliance on external props for self-esteem and his risking to venture into new modes of deriving pleasure and meaning. The resistances that are usually encountered are a fear that one's life will be totally empty without the familiar, if stifling, structure that the former beliefs and adaptations had provided, and a crippling anxiety that one will be abandoned or ridiculed if one dares to break the childhood taboos. The inappropriate extent that the depressive relies on the judgment of others reveals the irrationality that lies behind this clinical disorder.

For example, a highly skilled physician who managed a large practice and was a respected teacher and researcher truly believed that if she angered her father and lost his favor she would become impoverished, be unable to complete any task, and lose her professional talents. She believed she owed all her accomplishments to his tutelage so that she was merely a reflection of his ability. The value of her activities depended on how the father responded to them. When she spoke to her father, he always took the opportunity to remind her that he would die soon and to demand to know what she had done to make his last days on earth more tolerable. This woman dreaded weekends unless she could fill her free time with work. She mentally structured her activities so she could give an accounting of herself and not be judged as lazy or indulgent, and she could not bring herself to spend money except for absolute necessities. As she realized the irrationality of her behavior through therapy and attempted to do minor, enjoyable things such as going to a movie or a play, she began to experience terrifying dreams of being abandoned and left painfully vulnerable. She would awake from these dreams in a state of panic and would believe that her parents were dead and that she was left all alone. Eventually, these dreams were traced to an actual event that occurred when she was five or six years old. She was traveling with her parents and made some demand for candy or ice cream, insisting after her parents had told her not to bother them. Her father pulled the car to the side of the road, yanked her out, and drove off, leaving her screaming in terror. After what must have seemed an eternity, her parents returned to pick her up and proceeded to lecture her on her selfishness and lack of consideration for them. This remembrance, terrible as it is, was probably a screen memory that crystallized the many prior threats and acts of abandonment that followed her normal attempts at satisfying childhood needs. Throughout her childhood and adolescence, this woman was inculcated with the belief that she was put on earth only to please her parents and that she was basically an evil and wanton being whom no one else would tolerate, much less love. A further memory that reveals this psychological seduction is one of her father telling her that she would never be accepted to graduate school without his "behind-the-scenes" manipulations. Despite her having obtained an almost perfect academic record and having excelled in extracurricular activities, she believed his outrageous view of her prospects.

This patient's irrational mode of evaluating herself and others also manifested itself in the therapeutic relationship. In the initial stages of therapy, she behaved as she believed a model patient would in order to gain the approval and avoid the criticism of the therapist: she was inordinately considerate and polite, apologized for presenting "boring" material, and regretted taking up the therapist's time with her complaints. As she felt more confident in therapy and less afraid of alienating the therapist, she confided her dread of her father and her simultaneous need for his constant reassurance. She also experienced the therapist as two distinct individuals: a sympathetic and helping person, and a punitive and depriving critic. She believed the therapist was only pretending to be encouraging while secretly disapproving of her. She feared that her admitting desires would be seen as a sign of betrayal by the therapist, who would then terminate treatment to punish her. She reported dreams in which the therapist treated her shabbily, as her father had in her childhood. Eventually, she reported a terrifying dream in which the therapist turned into her father, blatantly demonstrating her transferential distortions.

As her transference was explored, the patient realized that as much as she feared her father's criticism and stifling demands, she could not conceive of existing without a paternal figure to structure her existence and give meaning to her efforts by promising praise. She recounted having sought out repeated relationships with older men whose support defended against her basic feelings of worthlessness and unlovability. If she could please these men through hard work and self-sacrifice, she could resist the terrible self-evaluations that were accepted in childhood. It became clear to her that it was just the failure to please one of these transferential father figures that had brought about her most recent episode of depression. Through her experience and analysis of transference in therapy, this woman was able to comprehend her need to distort others to fend off the dreaded ideas about herself. She had to reconstruct her childhood situation and force this reconstruction to reassure her sense of worth. In the therapy, the archaic beliefs underlying the distortion were made conscious and their irrationality appreciated with subsequent changes in her sense of herself. In turn, this newer and more realistic estimate of herself was revealed in her feelings, behavior, and resistance to illness.

At times she protested that she felt worse than ever, that she wanted to stop treatment, and that if she lost her magical relationship to her father she would go insane. However, at the same time, she was able to initiate a number of satisfying relationships and find time to pursue enjoyable if "unproductive" activities.

Each individual presents personally idiosyncratic distortions, fears, and resistances that relate to the different past history he has experienced. However, the basic theme is that of assertion and gratification versus inhibition and guilt or fear. As the old inhibitions are challenged and the usual manipulative ways of obtaining esteem are discarded, more appropriate sources of worth and pleasure arise automatically. As the patient begins to experience new freedoms and realizes he will not be abandoned or humiliated, he finds the courage to venture further along new paths. And as these new ventures solidify, they form the nucleus for a new system of estimating the self and others that will protect the individual from future episodes of clinical illness.

Within the therapy sessions, careful attention is given to the dreaded view of self that had been so threatening in the past. This view is accepted without shame by a now more tolerant personality. However, this dreaded sense of self is also understood as a personification that was imposed upon the patient as a child and is no longer applicable to the real potentialities available to the patient as an adult. Once the patient understands that with maturity comes a degree of autonomy and freedom from the control of significant others, he is well along the path toward change.

The last stage of treatment concerns external barriers more than internal ones. As patients alter their behavior as a result of therapy, they often find that others in their immediate environment resent these changes. Significant others will react negatively to the new and, for them, alarming or irritating sense of self that emerges in the therapeutic process. This resistance to change may be found in parents, colleagues, or employers of depressives but is most strongly manifested in the spouses of older patients. These marital partners truly want the patient to be cured and certainly do not wish him to suffer the terrible episodes of clinical depression. At the same time, they do not want to give up the type of relationship that fostered recurrent episodes of melancholia.

If therapy has proceeded well to this point, the depressive will exhibit a new integrity in his relationships, he will show his feelings of anger as well as spontaneous enjoyment openly, and he will no longer resort to devious manipulations that typified so many of his previous interpersonal transactions. Other characteristics that are indicative of more profound change include a sense of spontaneity and humor in behavior, as well as a more philosophic attitude toward the failures and rejections that are inevitable in everyday life. Another positive sign is the relinquishing of a hypermoral view of all events so that everything that occurs has to be someone's fault. Most significant is the evolving ability to achieve genuine empathy with others and to cease viewing other people transferentially as bestowers of praise or rewards or dispensers of criticism or rejection.

Finally, there should be a coming to terms with the ghosts of the past. Just as the patient begins to perceive others in his current life as necessarily imperfect beings who are struggling against their own difficulties to find a satisfactory mode of life, he should also understand that the significant others in his past had to deal with their own problems and shortcomings. Too often there is a rapid reversal from idealization of parents or teachers to bitter recriminations and unproductive anger. The psychological significance of the past is for those events and forces that helped shape the patient's personality to be understood and not to serve as ammunition to cast at the important personages of childhood. Hopefully, this understanding will correct past distortions and prevent the individual from having to repeat errors in living that ultimately result in clinically significant illness.

Effectiveness of Psychodynamic Psychotherapy

There are no large follow-up studies of depressed patients treated with psychoanalytic psychotherapy reported in the literature, nor are there controlled studies comparing this form of therapy with other types of treatment. Most psychoanalytic therapists, by the very nature of their work, can see only a few patients at one time and so do not compile a sizable treatment sample. Also, these clinicians are not inclined to perform research studies. Finally, some believe that while depression presents specific core problems, each patient engaged in psychodynamic therapy is unique with his own particular constellation of defenses, memories, fantasies, and life situation, so that comparison between individuals would not be valid. Others may doubt that the true efficacy of therapy resulting in a different appreciation of one's inner self or the freeing of neurotic inhibitions could be measured accurately by objective methods.

Nevertheless, two senior psychoanalysts with decades of experience in the therapy of severe depressives have reported their results. Jacobson (1971) reported follow-up status of severely depressed patients in an anecdotal manner without giving the size or selection of her sample. She found that severely depressed patients often did well for 20 or more years after analysis. They continued to experience episodes of dysphoria secondary to life stresses, but these instances were much milder than those before treatment. She remarks that almost all showed marked improvement in their social functioning and were able to initiate satisfying relationships, raise families, and perform rewarding and productive work. Some returned for more treatment after a major change in their lives, which she described as helpful and successful. The two types of depressives who did not do as well were those with chronic rather than episodic severe depression and those who experienced depression with suicidal ideation in childhood.

Arieti (1977) reported a three-year (or more) follow-up of his psychodynamic therapy of 12 severely depressed patients treated on an ambulatory basis. Of these patients, nine were female and three male; 10 had suicidal ideation. Arieti found that seven showed full recovery with no relapses, four showed marked improvement, and one was classified as a treatment failure.

While these two reports are neither sufficiently large nor scientific, they do suggest that psychoanalytic psychotherapy can be an effective treatment modality.

Chapter 169

Cognitive-Behavioral Psychotherapy for Depression

Psychosocial treatments have been developed specifically for depression, and these treatments have been empirically investigated within the past decade. Lieberman (1975), Hollon and Beck (1979), Rehm and Kornblith (1979), Whitehead (1979), Weissman (1979), Blaney (1981), Hollon (1981), Jarrett and Rush (1986) and Weissman et al. (1987) have carefully reviewed the literature on psychotherapies for depression.

In this chapter I will describe the cognitive-behavioral approach of Aaron T. Beck et al. (1979) in the treatment of depressed patients. This short-term approach is aimed at symptom reduction and prophylaxis. I will also review the theoretical underpinnings, typical course of therapy, and comparative efficacy data based on this therapy. Investigations of efficacy were selected if 1) a well-documented, moderately to severely depressed sample was used; 2) reliable, dependent measures were used; and 3) methodological quality was apparent.

Cognitive Theory of Depression

Cognitions or automatic thoughts are what people think about themselves in a particular situation. The cognitive model, which hypothesizes that cognitions or automatic thoughts (images and thoughts) affect emotional and behavioral patterns, is grounded in phenomenological psychology, which assumes that behavior is influenced by an individuals' perception of themselves and the world. The model suggests that a central feature of depression is distorted, negatively biased thinking. Other symptoms typical of depression (e.g., motivational deficits, suicidal impulses, and sadness) are amplified by these distorted thinking patterns. The cognitive model indicates that automatic thoughts importantly affect feelings and behaviors that occur in particular situations. These negative thoughts are automatic, involuntary, plausible, and persistent, and often contain a theme of loss (Beck 1963). Beck has distinguished between objective descriptions and private meanings of particular events. He emphasizes that private interpretations of events are critical to emotional responses. The emphasis on private meanings derives from this model's roots in phenomenological psychology. The disparity between private and public meanings of events leads to a discrimination between distorted and realistic automatic thoughts.

Beck (1967, 1972, 1976) has identified three essential elements to the psychopathology of depression: 1) the cognitive triad, 2) silent assumptions, and 3) logical errors.

The cognitive triad refers to negative views held by depressives about themselves, their immediate interpersonal world, and their future (e.g., "I'm no good," "My life is disappointing," and "Things will never improve"). Depressed patients assume that they, their world, and their future lack some feature(s) that is essential for happiness. For instance, depressed individuals may view themselves as unworthy, inadequate, or incompetent; their environment as continually demanding and unsupporting; and their future as hopeless. They may predict that these inadequacies and this current pain will continue indefinitely. These negative views (the cognitive triad) exacerbate or contribute to other symptoms commonly found in depression. That is, thinking "Everything I do turns out badly" may lead patients to refrain from initiating new behaviors as they assume this notion is valid. These negative views are evident in the context of automatic thoughts, which can be identified by depressed individuals in specific situations.

Silent assumptions, the second element, are unarticulated rules that influence emotional, behavioral, and thinking patterns (e.g., "If someone's angry, it's probably my fault," "If others don't like me, I can't be happy," or "If I get close to others, they'll hurt me"). As silent assumptions are psychological constructs, they are not easily reported by patients. It is as if patients base their emotional, cognitive, and behavioral responses on these assumptions. For example, an individual may repeatedly perceive social disapproval even when objective evidence for this idea is lacking or weak. These perceptions may increase feelings of sadness. It is as if the person believes, "If I am not loved by everyone, I'm unworthy." These assumptions are conceptualized as stable beliefs that have developed from early experience and continue to shape responses to current situations, providing, according to the model, a basis for negative automatic thoughts. Such assumptions are usually "if-then" premises that can be inferred from patterns of automatic thoughts and behavioral responses that occur across various situations.

To illustrate how these assumptions are inferred from themes found in negative automatic thoughts, consider a depressed person who reported sadness when her spouse failed to compliment her on her appearance. She reported thinking, "He is not attracted to me any more because I am ugly." She also reported feeling dysphoric when a friend talked to her for only five minutes in the grocery store. "She would want to spend more time with me if I weren't so dull." Through a dialogue, therapist and patient may infer the silent assumption, "If others don't attend to me, it is disturbing, and it is due to a deficit I have." The cognitive model posits that during depression these dysfunctional assumptions are activated more frequently than more adaptive alternative assumptions, and that as depression becomes more severe, an individual's thinking becomes less and less related to the objective evidence.

The cognitive model suggests that negative automatic thoughts contain various systematic errors, which can be identified by examining the logical relationship between the actual event and the associated negative automatic thinking. Logical errors include arbitrary inference, selective attention, overgeneralization, magnification or minimization, and personalization. Arbitrary inference occurs when conclusions are derived that do not inhere in the environmental event itself. Selective attention refers to emphasizing certain details while ignoring others. Overgeneralization is drawing general conclusions about one's ability or worth based on a single incident. Magnification or minimization refers to exaggerating or diminishing the importance of an event. Personalization involves associating events with oneself when logic or data do not support such inferences (Beck et al. 1979).

Beck's (1976) model hypothesizes that dysfunctional silent assumptions increase one's vulnerability to depressive relapse. These assumptions develop through interactions with significant others and are often learned in the context of unfavorable life situations (e.g., the loss of a parent or chronic rejection by peers). Later in life, when individuals are exposed to situations analogous to the original unfavorable life situations, they employ the previously learned assumptions. Once activated, these assumptions are applied to a wider and wider range of stimulus situations and thereby lead to ever-increasing negative automatic thinking. Persons overly concerned with approval from others may, for instance, personalize normal day-to-day interpersonal interactions as if it meant that they were not liked by anyone (e.g., a stewardess on the airplane who does not smile means "No one likes me.").

This negative automatic thinking serves to maintain or exacerbate typical emotional, motivational, and behavioral depressive symptoms (e.g., hopelessness, apathy, suicidal ideation, or guilt). As depressive symptoms worsen, distorted thinking increases. The relationship between depressive symptoms and negative thoughts forms a vicious cycle, leading to the downward spiral of depression.

The Course of Cognitive Therapy

Establishing a Therapeutic Alliance and Rationale

A critical first step in cognitive therapy requires the development of a rapport with the patient, establishing the therapeutic alliance (Rush 1985). The therapist functions as a guide to the patient. Each session begins with therapist and patient listing and prioritizing agenda items to be covered. The competent cognitive therapist must have solid general psychotherapeutic skills (e.g., he or she must be warm, genuine, empathic, and able to understand and reflect the patient's thinking) and be able to remain objective and logical about the patient's thinking and emotional responses. The therapist usually employs questions as opposed to statements to help the patient clarify his or her thoughts. The therapist avoids attempting to "persuade" the patient that these thoughts are dysfunctional. Rather, the therapist encourages the patient to test the objectivity or validity of specific thoughts by examining their inherent logic and/or by seeking supportive or disconfirming data from the patient's daily life. This relationship has been called "collaborative empiricism" (Beck et al. 1979).

The therapeutic alliance is critical in work with depressed patients, who typically overpersonalize and are likely to respond negatively to neutral or even positive interpersonal interactions. When problems within the therapeutic relationship occur, they are conceptualized from a cognitive perspective. Thoughts and emotions surrounding the alliance are identified, and problem-solving strategies are implemented. For instance, a depressed patient may report missing a therapy session after thinking, "I've been depressed before and received therapy. Since I am depressed again, this treatment will not work, either." The report of these thoughts provides an opportunity for the therapist and patient to review 1) how the past and current therapies (are/are not) alike, 2) evidence to support (or refute) the idea that cognitive therapy will not work, 3) the gains of cognitive therapy to date, and 4) modifications that may need to be made in therapy.

The therapeutic alliance is further strengthened by providing an introductory rationale for treatment and for the steps within therapy (e.g., homework assignments). This introductory rationale is supplemented by asking patients to read a pamphlet, *Coping with Depression* (Beck and Greenberg 1974), which is used to socialize patients to treatment. Strategies to manage the therapeutic alliance have been discussed elsewhere (Rush 1985).

Self-Monitoring

Self-monitoring helps patients to identify thoughts that accompany uncomfortable emotions and difficult situations. By completing the Daily Record of Dsyfunctional Thoughts (Beck et al. 1979) and through dialogue, patients learn to discern the relationship between events, emotions, thoughts, and behavior. For example, the patient may note that 1) when a co-worker did not say "Good Morning" (situation), 2) she felt sad (emotion) and 3) thought, "Nobody likes me here enough to say hello" (automatic thought). By identifying the covariation between situation, emotion, and thought, the patient can now see how she logically avoids office coffee breaks.

After patients have learned to self-monitor, they can then begin to identify themes (ideas that recur across situations—e.g., fearing rejection, seeking approval) by reviewing past records and sessions. These pervasive themes provide a basis for inferring general rules or silent assumptions.

Testing Automatic Thoughts and Silent Assumptions

Following self-monitoring, patients learn to evaluate the extent to which their automatic thoughts and silent assumptions correspond to more objective appraisals of their situations. When thoughts or assumptions do not match the evidence, patients are taught to consider alternative conceptualizations that are more accurate and to carry out responses consistent with these alternative views.

The validity of automatic thoughts or silent assumptions is evaluated by various techniques (e.g., activity scheduling, mastery and pleasure ratings, reattribution techniques, and homework to test both old and new assumptions). The basic goal is for patients to recognize that thoughts and beliefs are inferences about the world, rather than facts. When patients conceptualize thoughts as hypotheses rather than facts, they develop some distance from the emotions associated with these thoughts. Hence, they learn to scrutinize their thoughts by asking questions such as 1) what part of my situation is a fact and what part is my belief? 2) what evidence supports or refutes my thoughts? 3) what are alternative explanations for this situation? 4) how might a nondepressed person view this situation? 5) even if my thoughts match the facts, are the consequences as bad as they seem? and 6) what strategies can be used to deal with the situation (once objectively defined)? Such questions help patients gain a perspective on their problems and initiate realistic problem solving.

In addition to logically evaluating their thinking, patients learn to test these hypotheses empirically. They learn to 1) state their automatic thoughts in a testable form (i.e., make a prediction), 2) define and implement a test of the prediction, 3) record the results, 4) compare the results with the prediction, and 5) query whether additional experiments are necessary to test the validity of the thought. For example, a depressed lawyer reported, "I'm so disorganized and distracted, I'll never complete my work." Such a prediction is especially suited to the technique called "graded task assignment," which required this patient to operationalize her "work" (e.g., a legal report) and to break it down into small, specific, realistic tasks to be completed over time. Within the experiment, the lawyer predicted that she could not complete even the first step (e.g., gathering the related legal books and removing all other distracting materials from her desk). Negative thinking that interfered with task completion (e.g., "I'm too incompetent to complete the first step") was identified, with the therapist emphasizing partial successes. Each step in the completion of the legal report was specified, and accomplishing each step was viewed as an experiment, during which the lawyer recorded her progress and compared these results to her initial prediction.

By the end of the experiment, she concluded that she was, in fact, able to make some progress on her legal report and had made overly pessimistic predictions that interfered with her work.

Homework

Cognitive therapy relies heavily on homework assignments that are completed between therapy sessions. Homework is designed to address the automatic thoughts, silent assumptions, or particular symptom targets chosen by patient and therapist. Each session begins with a review of the homework. Noncompliance with homework is dealt with from a cognitive perspective (e.g., "What thoughts or feelings occurred when you had difficulty beginning the homework?").

Frequency, Length, and Modality of Treatment

Few studies have evaluated the relationship between the frequency or length of treatment and response to cognitive therapy. In one preliminary study with moderately to severely depressed outpatients, fewer dropouts and greater symptom reduction was found with twice weekly rather than with once weekly treatment, though treatment assignment was not randomized in this study (Beck et al. 1979). Cognitive therapy is typically provided twice weekly for the first four weeks and then weekly for a total of 20 sessions. Experienced cognitive therapists recommend that session frequency be guided by the severity of the depressive symptoms (greater symptomatology requires more frequent treatment).

In practice, patients sometimes participate in maintenance or "booster" sessions (once or twice a month) for six to 12 months after a course of cognitive therapy. However, no studies have yet examined the effect of booster sessions on therapeutic response. Typically, cognitive therapy is provided in individual sessions. Rush and Watkins (1981) compared cognitive therapy in individual versus group formats and found a slight advantage for individual sessions. This finding was replicated in the treatment of depressed alcoholics with cognitive-behavioral therapy (Turner and Wehl 1984). Clinical experience (Rush et al. 1980) suggests that cognitive therapy can be used in a couples format as well.

The Efficacy of Cognitive Therapy

Table 1 summarizes the outcome studies designed to evaluate the efficacy of cognitive therapy in clinically depressed patients. Control comparison conditions have included other psychotherapies, antidepressant medications, and combinations of cognitive therapy plus antidepressants. Cognitive therapy reduced depressive symptoms more than did wait-list comparisons in seven studies (Carrington 1979; Comas-Díaz 1981; Magers 1978; Morris 1975; Shaw 1977; Thompson and Gallagher 1984; Wilson et al. 1983). In two studies (Besyner 1979; Muñoz 1977), the effects of "cognitive modification" equaled those of the wait list. However, both Muñoz and Besyner employed only a few techniques from Beck's cognitive therapy package. These studies strongly indicate that symptom reduction attributed to the cognitive therapy package exceeds that found in the symptomatic fluctuations of the disorder.

In comparisons with other psychotherapeutic approaches, cognitive therapy has generally equaled or exceeded these other treatments. Only McDonald (1978) found that cognitive modification plus day care did not reduce depression more than day care alone. Thompson and Gallagher (1984) found that behavior therapy, Beck's cognitive therapy, and short-term dynamic therapy were all equal in symptom reduction in a geriatric population with major depression. In another geriatric sample (Steuer et al. 1984), Beck's cognitive therapy exceeded psychodynamic group therapy in reducing Beck Depression Inventory (BDI) (Beck et al. 1961) scores. Covi and Lipman (1987) found that group cognitive therapy was more effective than traditional group therapy (based on interpersonal psychodynamic theory and techniques) in outpatients with major depression. Cognitive therapy exceeded the effects of a nondirective treatment (Shaw 1977) as well as of insight-oriented therapy (Carrington 1979; Morris 1975).

In general, cognitive therapy compares equally with behavior therapy (Taylor and Marshall 1977; Thompson and Gallagher 1984; Wilson et al. 1983). Comas-Díaz (1981), who worked with a sample of depressed Puerto Rican women, found no difference between the two approaches and found a slight (statistically significant) advantage for behavioral therapy during a five-week follow-up. Besyner (1979) found an advantage for behavioral therapy. Conversely, Shaw (1977) found cognitive therapy more effective than a Lewinsohn-type of behavioral approach, which itself did not exceed the effects of an attention/comparison group. That most studies have found no difference between cognitive and behavior therapies may follow from the fact that much of the technology used is shared by both approaches (i.e., Beck's cognitive therapy employs "behavioral techniques" as well as those aimed directly at cognitive change). Indeed, Taylor and Marshall (1977) found that the combination of cognitive change and behavioral strategies exceeded those of either strategy alone.

Pharmacotherapy is a well-established treatment for unipolar depression. Therefore, antidepressant medications have been used as a standard for comparison with cognitive therapy in several studies. The first such study (Rush et al. 1977) found that cognitive therapy reduced depression more than imipramine, and cognitive therapy was associated with fewer dropouts. Likewise, in a sample of general practice patients, Blackburn et al. (1981) also found that cognitive therapy exceeded antidepressant medication in symptom reduction.

Recently, Murphy et al. (1984) attempted to replicate the Rush et al. (1977) findings by comparing Beck's cognitive therapy, nortriptyline, cognitive therapy plus nortriptyline, and cognitive therapy plus active placebo in carefully diagnosed outpatients with nonpsychotic, major depression. All treatments reduced depression equally. The highest dropout rate occurred in the drug alone condition. Likewise, Teasdale et al. (1984) found that cognitive therapy plus "treatment as usual" (typically antidepressant medication) was more effective than "treatment as usual" alone. These findings are similar to the Blackburn et al. (1981) findings in hospital clinic patients with major depression—that the combination of Beck's cognitive therapy plus drug was more effective than drug or cognitive therapy alone. Conversely, in general practice patients, Blackburn et al. (1981) reported no such advantage for the combined approach (cognitive therapy plus antidepressants). Other studies (Beck et al. 1985; Covi and Lipman 1987; Rush and Watkins 1981) have found that the combination of antidepressant medication and Beck's cognitive therapy did not *lead* to greater symptom reduction than cognitive therapy alone. Taken together, these studies suggest that the combination treatment is not always optimal for depressed patients but that certain patient groups—perhaps the more chronic—would benefit more with the combination than with either treatment alone.

Table 1. Efficacy of Cognitive Therapy

Study	Sample	Treatment	Weeks	Results
Morris (1975)	51 nonbipolar depressives	1) cognitive-behavioral (Beck) 2) insight-oriented therapy 3) wait list	3 or 6	—cognitive-behavioral > all groups
Muñoz (1977)	Not available	1) cognitive modification 2) wait list 3) normal control 4) nondepressed control	4	—cognitive modification = wait list —did not use Beck's treatment
Rush et al. (1977)	41 nonbipolar major depressives	1) cognitive therapy (Beck) 2) imipramine	12	—cognitive > imipramine —78.9% cognitive therapy completely remitted —22.7% imipramine therapy completely remitted
Shaw (1977)	32 nonbipolar depressives	1) cognitive therapy (Beck) 2) behavioral therapy 3) attention/assessment control 4) wait list/assessment control	4	—cognitive > behavioral = attention assessment —all treatments > wait list
Taylor and Marshall (1977)	28 depressed volunteers	1) cognitive + behavioral 2) cognitive modification 3) behavioral therapy 4) wait list	6 sessions	—combination > all groups —cognitive = behavioral —all treatments > wait list
Magers (1978)	18 clinic patients	1) cognitive-behavioral (Beck) 2) wait list	6	—cognitive-behavioral > wait list
McDonald (1978)	28 depressed clinic patients	1) cognitive modification + day care 2) day care	12	—both treatments were equal
Besyner (1979)	41 symptomatic community volunteers	1) cognitive modification 2) behavior therapy 3) nonspecific therapy 4) wait list	4	—behavior therapy < cognitive modification (not Beck's) —cognitive = wait list —all > nonspecific
Carrington (1979)	30 nonbipolar symptomatic volunteers	1) cognitive 2) analytic 3) wait list	12	—cognitive > analytic —analytic > wait list on BDI and VAS
Blackburn et al. (1981)	64 major depressives	1) cognitive therapy (Beck) 2) cognitive + drug 3) drug	12	—General practice patients: cognitive = cognitive + drug > drug alone —Psychiatric outpatients: cognitive + drug > cognitive = drug

Study	Sample	Treatment	Weeks	Results
Comas-Díaz (1981)	26 nonbipolar depressed women	1) cognitive group therapy (Beck) 2) behavioral group therapy (Lewinsohn) 3) wait list/assessment	4	—cognitive = behavioral > wait list
Rush and Watkins (1981)	39 nonbipolar depressives	1) group cognitive (Beck) 2) individual cognitive 3) individual cognitive + medication	10–12	—individual cognitive = cognitive + medication —individual cognitive > group cognitive
Wilson et al. (1983)	25 depressed volunteers	1) behavioral therapy (Lewinsohn) 2) cognitive therapy (Beck) 3) no treatment	8	—behavioral = cognitive > no treatment —maintained at 5 month follow-up
Murphy et al. (1984)	70 nonbipolar depressives	1) cognitive therapy (Beck) 2) nortriptyline 3) cognitive therapy + nortriptyline 4) cognitive therapy + placebo	12	—all treatments were equal —gains maintained at 1-month follow-up —higher dropout rate in drug alone
Teasdale et al. (1984)	34 depressed general practice patients	1) treatment as usual (typically anti-depressants) 2) treatment as usual + cognitive therapy (Beck)	15(?)	—combination > treatment as usual —no difference at 3-month follow-up (attributed to improvement by treatment as usual group)
Thompson and Gallagher (1984)	37 elderly with major depression	1) behavioral 2) cognitive (Beck) 3) short-term dynamic 4) delayed treatment control	12	—all active treatment > control —all active treatments were equal —9 percent behavioral or cognitive relapsed in one year; 56 percent dynamic relapsed —pilot data suggest nonendogenous more likely to respond and respond quicker
Steuer et al. (1984)	20 nonbipolar depressed geriatric patients	1) cognitive-behavioral therapy 2) psychodynamic group therapy	36	—both groups associated with pre to post changes —cognitive-behavioral > psychodynamic on BDI
Beck et al. (1985)	33 major depressives	1) cognitive therapy (Beck) 2) cognitive therapy + amitriptyline	12	—both treatments were equal
Covi and Lipman (1987)	70 major depressive volunteers	1) traditional group therapy 2) cognitive group therapy 3) cognitive group therapy + imipramine	12	—cognitive group therapy equalled cognitive group therapy + imipramine > traditional group therapy —results maintained at 9-month follow-up

Note.   BDI—Beck Depression Inventory (Beck et al. 1961); VAS—Visual Analog Scale (Aitken 1969).

Prophylactic Effects

Table 2 summarizes studies relevant to the prophylactic effects of cognitive therapy. Kovacs et al. (1981) conducted a follow-up one year after the Rush et al. (1977) clinical trial. Cognitive therapy patients had lower BDI scores than patients who received imipramine at one-year posttreatment. Further, the relapse risk was twice as great for drug-treated compared with cognitive therapy cases though this failed to attain statistical significance, perhaps due to sample size.

Similarly, Simons et al. (1986) conducted a follow-up one year after the Murphy et al. (1984) clinical trial. No differences were found between Beck's cognitive therapy, nortriptyline, cognitive therapy plus nortriptyline, and cognitive therapy plus placebo. However, when the groups treated with cognitive therapy were combined, they were significantly less likely to relapse than were those treated with drug alone. Higher levels of dysfunctional thoughts and poorer social adjustment were associated with relapse, independent of initial treatment provided.

Specific Effects

With regard to specific effects (Table 3), Rush et al. (1981) found that with Beck's cognitive therapy, both mood and patients' views of themselves and their futures changed *before* the vegetative symptoms changed. With imipramine, the pattern of response was inconsistent. Rush et al. (1982) also reported that cognitive therapy resulted in a greater reduction of hopelessness than imipramine during the first five weeks of treatment. By the end of treatment, cognitive therapy improved self-concept to a greater extent than did medication treatment.

Blackburn and Bishop (1983) found cognitive therapy (in combination with drugs

Table 2. Prophylactic Effects of Cognitive Therapy

Study	Sample	Treatment	Weeks	Results
Kovacs et al. (1981)	35 nonbipolar depressives	1) cognitive therapy (Beck) 2) imipramine	One-year follow-up to Rush et al. (1977)	—cognitive therapy > imipramine on BDI
Simons et al. (1986)	70 nonbipolar depressives	1) cognitive therapy (Beck) 2) nortriptyline 3) cognitive therapy + nortriptyline 4) cognitive therapy + placebo	One-year follow-up	—no significant difference between four treatments —36 percent relapse rate in responders —patients who received cognitive therapy (alone or with drugs) least likely to relapse —dysfunctional attitudes and social adjustment best predicted relapse

Table 3. Specific Effects of Cognitive Therapy

Study	Sample	Treatment	Weeks	Results
Rush et al. (1981)	35 major depressives	1) cognitive therapy (Beck) 2) imipramine	12	—with cognitive therapy, mood and views of self/future changed before vegetative and motivational systems —with imipramine, pattern was inconsistent
Rush et al. (1982)	35 major depressives	1) cognitive therapy (Beck) 2) imipramine	12	—cognitive therapy > imipramine in improving self-concept and hopelessness —no difference at 3-month follow-up
Blackburn and Bishop (1983)	64 major depressives	1) cognitive therapy (Beck) 2) cognitive + drug 3) drug	12	—measures of self, world, and future showed: —General practice patients: cognitive = cognitive + drugs > drug alone —Psychiatric outpatients: cognitive + drugs > cognitive > drugs
Simons et al. (1984a)	28 major depressives	1) cognitive therapy (Beck) 2) nortriptyline	12	—positive changes in mood and cognitions associated with both treatments

or alone) improved views of the self, the world, and the future more than did drugs alone. On the other hand, Simons et al. (1984a) found that both cognitive therapy and drug therapy were associated with equivalent improvements in dysfunctional attitudes and negative thinking, which suggests that cognitive disturbances are state dependent and improve independent of the type of treatment employed.

Active Ingredients

Only a few studies of the therapeutic ingredients involved in cognitive therapy are available (Table 4). Teasdale and Fennell (1982) examined the differential effects of the therapist gathering information about dysfunctional thoughts versus imple-

Table 4. Active Ingredients of Cognitive Therapy

Study	Sample	Treatment	Weeks	Results
Teasdale and Fennell (1982)	5 chronic, moderately to severely depressed patients	—within subject design phases within standard cognitive —thought exploration —thought change	Not applicable	—thought change > thought exploration in improving mood and changing belief in thought
Zettle and Hayes (1985)	18 depressed female volunteers	with and without homework: 1) rational restructuring 2) distancing + rational restructuring 3) comprehensive distancing		—comprehensive distancing > other components (1 and 2) —distancing + rational restructuring > rational restructuring
Jarrett and Nelson (1987)	37 depressed volunteers	—cognitive-behavioral therapy components compared within two sequences (ABC vs. ACB) —A = self-monitoring —B = logical analysis —C = hypothesis testing	6	—logical analysis = hypothesis testing > self-monitoring on BDI, MMPI-D, frequency of dysfunctional thoughts, and pleasant events —some analyses suggested logical analysis > hypothesis testing in: reducing belief in dysfunctional thoughts; improving interpersonal relationships

Note. BDI–Beck Depression Inventory (Beck et al. 1961); MMPI-D–Minnesota Multiphasic Personality Inventory–Depression Scale (Hathaway and McKinley 1942).

menting strategies to change the thoughts. The latter improved mood and changed beliefs more than the former. Similarly, Jarrett and Nelson (1987) divided cognitive therapy into three components: self-monitoring dysfunctional cognitions, self-monitoring dysfunctional cognitions plus logical analysis, and self-monitoring dysfunctional cognitions plus hypothesis testing. The latter two were equally effective in improving mood, reducing the frequency of dysfunctional thoughts, and increasing pleasant events. However, a slight advantage for self-monitoring plus logical analysis in reducing belief in dysfunctional thoughts and in improving interpersonal relationships was noted in some analyses. Zettle and Hayes (1985) conducted a process analysis of Beck's cognitive therapy for depression and concluded that the treatment components within cognitive therapy are additive rather than interactive. The order of effectiveness of their therapeutic components was comprehensive distancing, distancing plus rational restructuring, and rational restructuring.

Indications

Roughly 55–70 percent of outpatients with nonpsychotic, nonbipolar, major depression respond well to cognitive therapy (see Table 5). Simons et al. (1985) found that patients with high scores on the Self-Control Scale (SCS) (Rosenbaum 1980) did better in cognitive therapy than those with low scores. Conversely, those with low SCS scores faired better with nortriptyline than those with high scores.

The endogenous/nonendogenous dichotomy was *not* predictive of a preferential response to cognitive therapy (Blackburn et al. 1981; Kovacs et al. 1981; Spitzer et al. 1978) although neither study employed Research Diagnostic Criteria (RDC) for this differential diagnosis.

Conclusion

The preceding outcome data suggest that Beck's cognitive therapy is more effective than no treatment and is *at least* as effective as antidepressant medication in the treatment of nonpsychotic, nonbipolar depressed outpatients. While some patients preferentially benefit from a combination of medication plus cognitive therapy, this combination is not always more effective than cognitive therapy alone. Several studies show cognitive modification (n = 2) plus Beck's cognitive therapy (n = 4) equals or exceeds the effect of behavioral therapy. Several other studies suggest that cognitive therapy is associated with fewer dropouts than pharmacotherapy (possibly because there are fewer side effects). The prophylactic effect of cognitive therapy appears promising but requires further investigation. Given the established efficacy of pharmacotherapy in endogenous depression, this approach should presently be considered a standard for this subgroup. Whether cognitive therapy is preferred over tricyclics with nonendogenous depression remains to be investigated.

Shaw (1984) has refined procedures for training and evaluating cognitive therapists, which should aid in determining how competently cognitive therapy was employed in a particular study.

The National Institute of Mental Health Depression Collaborative Study (Elkin et al. 1985) has compared interpersonal psychotherapy, cognitive therapy, imipramine plus clinical management, and placebo plus clinical management. These data are yet

Table 5. Indications for Cognitive Therapy

Study	Sample	Treatment	Weeks	Results
Simons et al. (1985)	35 major depressives	1) cognitive therapy 2) nortriptyline	12	—no difference in treatments —pretreatment scores on SCS predicted response: highs > lows with cognitive therapy; lows > highs with nortriptyline

Note. SCS–Self-Control Scale (Rosenbaum 1980).

unpublished but are likely to provide further insight, especially into the relationship between competency and outcome and into predictors of response.

Additional questions requiring study include 1) which psychosocial interventions are best suited to which depressed patients and under what conditions? 2) when is the combination of cognitive therapy and pharmacotherapy the treatment of choice? 3) are "booster sessions" needed to maintain gains within a subset of depressed patients? 4) how, if at all, does the modality of administering treatment (e.g., group versus individual) influence response to treatment? 5) how can one determine when patients have developed skills necessary for prophylaxis? 6) what factors affect whether the patient will use the learned skills? and finally 7) by what mechanism does cognitive therapy achieve its effects?

Chapter 170

Behavioral Approaches to the Treatment of Unipolar Depression

The past 15 years have witnessed a veritable explosion in the development and study of behavioral treatments for unipolar depression. As recently as 1975, Lieberman concluded that there was little scientific evidence to the efficacy of verbal psychotherapy, including behavioral interventions, in treating depressive disorders. Similarly, Becker (1974) observed that behavioral theorists had relatively little to say about depression. As we have noted elsewhere (Lewinsohn and Hoberman 1982b), behavioral researchers were particularly late in attempting to study and treat depression, relative to other psychiatric disorders. Consequently, it is especially striking that, at present, there are a variety of behaviorally oriented treatment packages for depressive disorders and well over 50 outcome studies of behavioral approaches for ameliorating depression. In a short time, both the quantity and the sophistication of behavioral treatments for depression have increased dramatically. Additionally, a number of thoughtful and comprehensive reviews of this literature have appeared (e.g., Blaney 1981; Craighead 1981; DeRubeis and Hollon 1981; Hersen and Bellack 1982; Lewinsohn and Hoberman 1982a; Rehm and Kornblith 1979; Rush and Beck 1978). Stimulated by the increasing evidence that a variety of structured behavioral therapies are effective in treating depression, this prolific activity has resulted in an increased acceptance of such approaches among clinicians. Indeed, the problem facing the practitioner in this area is one of shifting and choosing from a range of promising therapeutic formulations and approaches.

Beyond the cumulative support for their efficacy, behavioral approaches are worth considering for several more specific reasons (Rush and Beck 1978). First, such therapies offer patients new behavior skills and/or new ways of thinking about themselves. Another advantage of behavioral therapies, when applied in a patient's social system, is that they may modify predisposing or etiologically critical interactions by restructuring the content of these problematic interactions. Additionally, behavioral methods may significantly decrease the dropout rate for outpatient treatment. Relatedly, in conjunction with chemotherapy, specific behavior techniques may be utilized to increase compliance with medical prescriptions and to decrease premature termination from biologic treatments. Finally, depressed persons who either refuse or cannot take antidepressant medication, or who do not respond to adequate trials of chemotherapy, may respond to behavior therapies.

The purposes of this chapter are twofold. First, we aim to provide the reader with a general understanding of the therapeutic strategies that are the basis of behavioral approaches to the treatment of unipolar depression. Second, we will review the available research literature as to both the efficacy and the clinical parameters of these interventions. In particular, we shall focus on two treatment packages for unipolar depression developed at the Depression Research Unit of the University of Oregon: an individual therapy approach and a psychoeducational group intervention. For contrast, we will then describe other behavioral treatment approaches. Last, we will present a brief review of current research programs investigating aspects of behavioral treatments for depression.

Conceptual and Historical Perspectives

The development of behavioral approaches to the treatment of psychological disorders had its basis in two initially distinct but sequential movements within psychology: attempts to explain human behavior in terms of experimental studies of learning, and dissatisfaction with intrapsychic conceptions of abnormal behavior and related treatment approaches. Currently, behavior therapy can best be understood as a scientific approach to the understanding and treatment of problematic behavior, rather than as a specific theoretical basis or set of techniques. Thus, writers like Kazdin (1982) have suggested that behavior therapy can be characterized by a number of principles: a reliance on findings or techniques derived from general psychology; a focus on the current rather than historical determinants of behavior; a direct focus on the maladaptive behavior for which an individual seeks treatment; a specification of treatment in objective and operational terms; and an emphasis on the ongoing interaction between assessment and the process of treatment.

Early behavioral theories of depression conceptualized depression as a reduction of behavior due to environmental changes (e.g., Skinner 1953; Ferster 1966). Costello (1972) argued that depression results from the loss of reinforcer effectiveness. Lewinsohn (e.g., Lewinsohn and Shaw 1969) contended that a low rate of response-contingent positive reinforcement constituted a sufficient explanation for aspects of the depressive syndrome such as dysphoria and the low rate of behavior; he also emphasized deficiencies in social skills as an important antecedent to a low rate of positive reinforcement and secondary gain as important in the maintenance of depression.

An Integrative Behavioral Theory of Depression

Perhaps the most important role a theory of depression plays, at least from a clinical perspective, is to provide a useful guide for treatment efforts. In specifying the functional relationships between certain antecedent events and the occurrence of depression, a theory represents a statement or explanation about the likely reasons for an individual's depressive episode. Thus, the theory indicates the goals for therapy such that their accomplishment should lead to a change in the level of depression.

Lewinsohn and his colleagues (e.g., Lewinsohn et al. 1976, 1979) have consistently called attention to the relationship between depression and reinforcement. Dysphoria and a lowered rate of behavior (e.g., depression) are viewed as a function of a decrease in the quality of one's interactions with the environment (e.g., response-contingent reinforcement); such a change comes from a lack or reduction in positive reinforcement or an increase in aversive experiences. Changes in the quality of experiences are viewed as a function of their availability, of an individual's personal skills to act on the environment, or of a change in potency of types of events.

Recently, Lewinsohn et al. (1985) have proposed a new theoretical model of the etiology and maintenance of depression. This model represents an attempt to integrate the findings of our epidemiologic (e.g., Lewinsohn et al. 1987) and treatment outcome studies (e.g., Zeiss et al. 1979) with an increasing body of work in social psychology of the phenomenon of self-awareness (e.g., Carver and Scheier 1982).

As we see it, the depressogenic process begins with the occurrence of antecedents of "evoking events." Such stressors initiate the path to a depressive episode to the extent that they disrupt substantial, important, and relatively automatic ("scripted") behavior patterns of individuals. The disruption of these scripted patterns, which constitute typical but crucial aspects of a person's interactions with the environment, produces an initial, immediate negative emotional response (e.g., dysphoria). As a result, the balance of the quality of a person's interactions with the environment (reinforcement) is shifted in a negative direction.

A continuing inability to reverse the change in reinforcement is hypothesized to lead to a heightened state of self-awareness. Such a state has been demonstrated to lead to an increase in self-evaluation, self-criticism, self-attribution of negative outcomes, intensification of negative affect, and behavioral withdrawal. The elicitation of a state of self-awareness breaks through an individual's self-protective, self-enhancing cognitive schema (e.g., Alloy and Abramson 1979; Lewinsohn et al. 1980b) and heightens the individual's awareness of having failed to live up to his or her expected standards of coping. This in turn is seen as engendering a state of further self-denigration and behavior withdrawal. Finally, the increasing dysphoria is assumed to lead to many of the behavioral, cognitive, emotional, and interpersonal changes that have previously been shown to be associated with depression. These changes are presumed to "lock" the heightened state of self-awareness and heightened dysphoria into a "vicious cycle," which serves to maintain the depressive state.

The proposed integrative model of depression allows for a great variety of individual and environmental differences to increase ("vulnerabilities") and decrease ("immunities") the risk of a depressive episode at a number of points in the depressogenic process. The use of this model for the clinician is twofold: it takes into account much of what has been learned through studies of depression, and it provides direction to the practitioner for the development and application of efficacious treatment programs.

Behavioral Strategies for Treating Depression

A theory, however, is only a set of abstract statements suggesting general treatment goals for depressed persons (or, at least, for certain kinds of depressives). A comprehensive treatment approach must also have a strategy. A treatment strategy translates the theory into a set of specific operations and procedures that can be used to formulate treatment goals for the depressed person and to direct the parameters of the treatment process. Research studies to investigate the behavioral theory of depression as well as clinical experience in applying the theory during treatment have generated a set of procedures useful for work with depressed patients. The guiding assumption in the treatment of depressed patients is that the restoration of an adequate schedule of positive experiences is essential to the reduction of dysphoria, and thus depression. Alterations in the frequency, quality, and range of the patient's activities and social interactions are the most common foci for achieving such a change in a schedule of reinforcement. What follows is a description of a number of assessment and treatment strategies that in the experience of behavior therapists, have proven useful in ameliorating depression.

Diagnostic and Functional Assessment

When an individual presents him- or herself to a clinic with apparent symptoms of depression, two important assessment goals must be met: differential diagnosis and a functional analysis of depressive behavior. First, an assessment for differential diagnosis must occur to determine whether depression is *the*, or at least *a*, problem for the individual. Individuals who are experiencing an episode of depression may manifest a heterogeneity of symptoms; additionally, symptoms of depression, and depression itself, occur in a large number of patients suffering from medical and other psychiatric disorders. Consequently, if depression is a presenting problem, an adequate medical and psychiatric history must be obtained to determine whether the depression is secondary to physical illness or a medical regime, or is subsequent to a manic or hypomanic episode. In all these cases, it would be important to recommend an individual for specific additional assessment and treatment for the primary condition (e.g., lithium for a bipolar patient) before proceeding with behavioral treatment for the depression.

Existing assessment instruments allow a clinician to describe a patient in regard to depression severity, to delineate the specific constellation of symptoms shown by that patient, and to evaluate the absence or presence of other psychiatric symptoms and conditions. In this regard, we have used the Schedule for Affective Disorders and Schizophrenia (SADS) (Endicott and Spitzer 1978) and the Research Diagnostic Criteria (RDC) (Spitzer et al. 1978), by means of which it is possible to assign patients to diagnostic categories with considerable reliability. In addition, we recommend the use of one of the many convenient, short, and easy-to-use self-report measures of depression level, such as the Beck Depression Inventory (BDI) (Beck et al. 1961), the Zung Self-Rating Depression Scale (SDS) (Zung 1965), and the Center for Epidemiologic Studies-Depression Scale (CES-D) (Radloff 1977). These instruments are particularly useful both for measuring the severity of depression and for assessing the outcome of treatment.

While differential diagnosis may be common to behavioral as well as to other treatment approaches, the second stage of assessment is relatively specific to behavioral interventions. A functional diagnosis or analysis of depressive behavior involves pinpointing specific person-environment interactions and events related to a particular patient's depression. This part of the diagnostic process is needed to guide the formulation of a treatment plan designed to change the events contributing to that patient's depression. The prototypical means of identifying behavioral events and activities functionally related to depression involves the use of the Pleasant Events Schedule (PES) (MacPhillamy and Lewinsohn 1971) and the Unpleasant Events Schedule (UES) (Lewinsohn 1975c). Both of these tests have been described in greater detail elsewhere, and test manuals providing normative data are available (Lewinsohn 1975a, 1975c; MacPhillamy and Lewinsohn 1982). Briefly, each schedule consists of 320 items assumed to represent an exhaustive sample of interactions with the environment that many people find pleasant or unpleasant. The client first rates the frequency of each event's occurrence during the past month and then rates the subjective impact of the events. The frequency ratings are assumed to reflect the rate of occurrence of the events during the past month. The subjective impact ratings are assumed to indicate the individual's potential for positive reinforcement and for punishment. Cross-product scores of the frequency and impact ratings are assumed to reflect the total amount of positive reinforcement and of aversiveness experienced during the past month.

Normative data on both schedules allow evaluation of the client's scores relative to others of the same sex and age. PES scores below the norms and UES scores above the norms on various subscales suggest the kinds of reinforcing and punishing events potentially related to the client's depression. Patterns among scores are often important. For example, a client may have a low score for pleasant sexual events but a high score for marital distress events. This immediately suggests potential reasons for this client's depression and even some potential treatment tactics. In addition, the analysis of PES and UES scores also provides individualized lists of specific events that are potentially pleasant or unpleasant for a patient. We share these working hypotheses with the patient and use them to formulate some intermediate treatment goals.

Conceptualization of Presenting Problems

Another important strategy essential to behavior therapy for depression involves the development of a shared conceptualization of a patient's presenting problems between the therapist and the patient. Patients usually enter therapy with their own view of their problems. As McLean (1981) has written, depressed patients often see themselves as victims of their moods or of environmental forces. Rarely do patients see their own behaviors and/or interpretations of their behaviors and/or the behaviors of others as causes for the depression. To complicate things further, many members of the professional community are convinced that there are only biogenic causes of all depression. This is often meant to imply the insignificance of psychological and environmental variables as causal factors. Thus, depressed patients often initially assume a passive stance; that is, they believe that something analogous to a physical disease has happened to them and that there is nothing they can do to alter their condition. Although they may emphasize specific behavioral problems (e.g., sleeplessness, lack of social involvement, obsessive thoughts), typically the focus is on "depression." Thus, it usually takes a considerable amount of work to move patients from a construct usage of the term *depression* to a recognition of the importance of specific problematic behavioral events that may be related to their dysphoria.

One goal of the initial phase of treatment is for therapist and patient to redefine the patient's problems in terms that will give the patient a sense of control and a feeling of hope, and especially in terms that will lead to specific behavioral interventions. Thus, the therapist tries to understand the patient's description and definition of the problem but does not uncritically accept the patient's view of the problem.

Instead, therapist and patient attempt to redefine the problem in terms that are acceptable to both of them. Information obtained through the functional assessment of depressive behavior may be especially useful in developing a shared understanding of the genesis and maintenance of the patient's depression. It is the reformulation or conceptualization phase, then, that sets the stage for behavioral change. We see it as essential for successful treatment that the patient and the therapist evolve a common conceptualization with common expectations; such a conceptualization should lead naturally to specific behavioral changes that will benefit the patient in real-life situations.

Monitoring of Mood and Activities

As noted earlier in this chapter, an essential element of behavior therapy in general is the continual feedback between ongoing assessment and treatment interventions. This characteristic is especially true of behavioral treatments for depression. From the first day of therapy, the depressed patients are typically asked to monitor and rate their moods on a daily basis for the duration of treatment. These ratings can be made on a simple nine-point visual analog scale (where "one" indicates very happy and "nine" indicates very depressed) or on the Depressive Adjective Checklist (DACL). In rating their moods on a daily basis, depressed individuals are provided the opportunity to note the degrees of variation in their mood. Daily mood ratings also permit the therapist to note particular days when a patient is more or less depressed and to explore the specific circumstances and/or repeated patterns that influence fluctuations in the patient's mood.

Similarly, patients are asked to monitor the occurrences of pleasant and aversive events on a daily basis. Generic activity schedules can be used for this purpose although behavior therapists typically prefer to generate an individualized list of events and activities for the individual to monitor (e.g., through the computer analysis of the PES and UES). The main purpose of monitoring activities and mood daily is to enable the patient and the therapist to become aware of the covariance that typically exists between mood and the rates of occurrences of pleasant and unpleasant events and activities. This covariance permits evaluation of the functional diagnosis and further specification of the person-environment interactions influencing the patient's mood. Inspection of a graph of the daily mood and event scores provides an easy means of estimating concomitant changes in the levels of each of these variables. The graphing and its interpretation provide patients with a framework for understanding the relationship between the rate and nature of their activities and their dysphoria; it also suggests specific tactics to deal with their depression.

Progressive Goal Attainment and Behavioral Productivity

An increase in goal-defined behavior is essential to all behavioral treatments for depression. McLean (1981) has described a number of issues concerning goals common to depressed patients. He notes that many depressives are often problem or crisis focused and are unable to identify goals they wish to pursue. Typically, when depressed persons are able to formulate personal goals, their goals are often unrealistic and their criteria for achievement are expressed in an "all-or-none" manner. Depressed individuals, thus, are frequently characterized by frustration in attempting goals that have a low probability of attainment or, in those cases in which goals are absent or undefined, by an aimless reactivity to the environment. In both cases, the general result of these deficiencies in goal setting is likely to be a decrease in purposeful behavior, particularly behavior that might have antidepressive consequences.

Given these deficits in goal setting and goal-related behavior, a major behavioral treatment strategy involves educating depressed individuals with regard to goals and goal-directed behavior. Depressives are taught to routinely set, plan, and review their goals. Each goal that is defined must be clearly relevant to the patient's needs. As Biglan and Dow (1981) note, patients are encouraged to decide on their own priorities among goals since this is likely to enhance their involvement in therapy. Additionally, patients are encouraged to take global goals (e.g., happiness, success) and break them down into smaller and more attainable goals. After defining realistic objectives (e.g., aspects of the person or environment that can be changed), performance tasks are graduated "into as small units as are necessary in order to reduce the task demands to the point that successful performance is relatively guaranteed" (McLean 1976, p. 80). Throughout treatment, an ongoing effort is made to keep intermediate treatment goals mutually meaningful and specific.

Although the reciprocal interaction among thoughts, feelings, and behavior is acknowledged, the emphasis in behavior therapy for depression is that thoughts and feelings can be most effectively influenced by behavior change. Consequently, a graduated goal-oriented behavioral focus is established early in treatment, and the utility of this position is identified throughout the course of therapy. The focus on behavioral productivity is accomplished through the use of regular homework assignments that emphasize gradual behavior change designed to ensure a high probability of successful performance on the part of the depressive.

Contracting and Self-Reinforcement

A central element of behavioral treatments for depression involves the "activation" of the depressed individual's motivation via an increase in that individual's behavioral output. Both the assessment and the treatment of a depressed patient require effort on the patient's part. For example, the patient may be asked to fill out the PES, to keep track of mood variations, to monitor activities on a daily basis, and so on throughout the course of treatment. Moreover, the patient may be asked to take steps that involve substantial changes in daily activities. A variety of response-induction procedures can be used to mobilize initial behavior, which can then be shaped into distinct performance steps. It has been found useful to take advantage of various contingencies that may motivate patients to engage in treatment-relevant activities. In particular, we advise patients to make specific agreements with themselves to give themselves rewards, but only if they perform the specifics of the agreements. The purpose of the contract is to arrange in advance the specific positive consequence (reinforcement) to follow the achievement of a goal. For example, a contract might state that the patient will have dinner at a favorite restaurant if and only if mood monitoring is faithfully carried out for one week. We recommend the inclusion of contracting because it has been our experience that it makes the accomplishment of goals easier for many patients.

Reinforcers may take many forms: 1) material rewards that are available in the patient's environment (e.g., favorite meals, magazines, books, clothes, records, and other objects requiring money), and 2) time (e.g., to do things the patient likes to do but rarely has time for, such as taking a relaxing bath, sleeping late, sunbathing, talking on the phone, or just "wasting time"). A patient's responses on the PES also suggest appropriate reinforcers.

Another important means of cultivating motivation in depressed patients involves developing their ability and inclination to self-reinforce. The relative importance of a performance task and the criteria for acknowledging its achievement are determined at the time of goal setting. If and when the goal is accomplished, the behavior therapist provides appropriate social reinforcement for this success. More importantly, the patient is encouraged (and reinforced) to use any of a number of self-reinforcing practices e.g., self-praise for a completed task, thinking about one's own good points and accomplishments, or mental "treats" (e.g., daydreaming about pleasurable things, meditating, listening to music).

Other motivational tactics we have used include making the next appointment contingent on the completion of certain tasks and reducing patient fees for keeping appointments and for completing assignments. Frequently, at the beginning of treatment, a depressed patient is asked to generate a "reward menu" consisting of five or 10 potentially pleasurable rewards. The reward menu consists of events the patient would like to do and is capable of doing. The patient then specifies the degree of goal satisfaction needed to earn each reward and then bestows the self-rewards when he or she has engaged in and completed treatment-relevant activities.

In summary, we use contingency contracts and self-reinforcement schedules in ways that are consistent with the overall goal of treatment, which is to increase the amount of response-contingent positive experiences. Contingency contracts can also serve to clarify progress toward the accomplishment of goals.

Specific Skills—Remediation and Therapeutic Decision Making

Behavioral theories of depression place considerable weight, etiologically speaking, on a decrease in response-contingent pleasurable activities, particularly as a result of specific performance and skill deficits. As a review of the empirical literature on depression has demonstrated, depressed individuals as a group show marked deficiencies in the areas of social skills, coping with stressors, cognitive and affective self-regulation, among others (Lewinsohn and Hoberman 1982b). Hence, a significant aspect of all behavioral treatment programs for depression involve the systematic remediation of the performance and skill deficits presented by depressed patients. Treatment approaches thus focus on teaching depressed patients the skills they can use to change detrimental patterns of interaction with their environment, as well as the skills they need to maintain these changes after the termination of therapy. Specific interventions in skills training will vary from case to case, ranging from highly structured standardized programs to individually designed ad hoc procedures. Training typically involves the following processes: didactic introduction to the skills involved, modeling and coaching by the therapist, role playing and rehearsal, practice by the patient during and after treatment sessions, and application of the skills in the real world. A wide variety of specific skills are available to a therapist to employ in treating depressed individuals. Among those that may be included in behavioral treatment programs for depression are self-change skills; contingency-management skills; social skills, such as those of assertiveness and communication; relaxation and stress-management skills; skills in identifying and increasing rewarding activities; and a number of cognitive and self-control skills. Consequently, this is the aspect of therapy on which behavioral treatment programs differ the most from each other, in that different programs (and different therapists) often emphasize the application of different skills to reach similar strategic goals.

While depressives as a group show a number of performance and skill deficits, it must be remembered that, as individuals, depressed persons are remarkably heterogeneous with regard to symptoms, presenting problems, and functional difficulties. This fact points to the importance of therapeutic decision making in the behavior therapy of depressed individuals. Treatment decision making must necessarily be a dynamic process involving the nature of a patient's performance deficits, the nature of a patient's personal and social environmental resources, and ongoing treatment response (McLean 1976).

Structural Parameters of Therapy

Behavioral treatment approaches are typically designed to be applied within a prespecified number of moderately well-structured sessions. A time limit for treatment is always part of the initial contract. Time limits have ranged from four weeks to three months, typically involving 12 treatment sessions, and they should be determined for each patient on the basis of the period of time that likely will be required to achieve the treatment goals. The existence of a time limit makes it essential for both the therapist and the patient to define and accept treatment goals they can reasonably expect to be accomplished during the allotted time. Of course, when deemed necessary by the patient or the therapist, treatment goals and time limits can be and are renegotiated.

Outcome Evaluation

A paramount concern of behavior therapy is the accountability of the therapist to the patient. While this is true on a general level of treatment so that the therapist employs procedures that have been previously demonstrated to be efficacious, it is also true on the level of individual patient needs. This means that the selection and continuation of specific treatment techniques must be justified on the basis of the ongoing evaluation of the patient's progress. Evaluation involves periodic assessment not only of changes in depression level but also of concomitant changes in the events presumed to be related to the patient's depression. This two-pronged approach to assessment allows the therapist to evaluate the effectiveness of treatment and to change the targeted behavior patterns and then determine whether these are accompanied by changes in depression level. Typically, at the end of therapy and at some point after the end of treatment (e.g., one month later), patients are asked to repeat the various intake questionnaires—for example, the Pleasant Events and Unpleasant Events schedules—as well as some measure of depression level (e.g., the Beck Depression Inventory). Comparison of the patient's pre- and postscores allows assessment of the direction and amount of change in person-environment interactions and depression level.

Practical Concerns in Implementing Behavioral Treatments

Patient compliance with the procedures suggested by behavioral strategies for treating depression is the critical element in the actualization of behavior change. The behavioral approach requires considerable effort on the part of the patient and is dependent on the patient's keeping accurate records, being willing to learn how to chart the daily monitoring data, and agreeing to carry out other assignments from time to time. While reservations regarding the ability of depressed individuals to carry out such assignments are frequently expressed, this is generally found not to be a problem. Patients typically are quite cooperative as long as they are convinced that the procedures suggested are an integral part of a treatment program designed to benefit them. Thus, the crucial factor in eliciting a patient's cooperation is the therapist's ability to present a convincing rationale for the procedures. The therapist must be able to convince the patient that the self-monitoring and other assignments will help him or her pinpoint specific goals, learn self-management of depression techniques, and evaluate progress.

McLean (1981) has pointed to a number of high-frequency "complications" that interfere with rationale acceptance and compliance on the part of patients in behavioral treatment programs. He notes that depressives are prone to become preoccupied with attempts to understand the causes of their depression. In particular, critical analysis of one's life history (as well as any number of other hypotheses regarding depression onset offered in the popular media) may exacerbate existing self-preoccupation and self-devaluation. Further, depressed patients, like many people, generally do not understand the relationships between personal behavior and social interaction, thought content, and mood. Consequently, as we discussed earlier, it is essential in the beginning of treatment for the therapist to thoroughly discuss and illustrate the elements of the behavioral rationale for the onset, maintenance, and improvement of depressed mood.

Behavioral Tactics for Treating Depression

The final major component of a comprehensive approach to the treatment of depression is a set of tactics with which to accomplish the goals that have been pinpointed during the diagnostic process. Tactics are the specific interventions used to accomplish the strategic goals of therapy. Useful tactics are those that dependably produce clinically desired changes in the events related to the depression. In general terms, behavioral treatment tactics are aimed at increasing the person's pleasant interactions with the environment and decreasing the unpleasant ones. Tactics thus fall into three general categories: 1) those that focus on implementing changes in the actual environment of a patient (e.g., having someone move from an isolated home into a more populated area); 2) those that focus on teaching depressed individuals skills that they can use to change problematic patterns of interaction with the environment (e.g., assertiveness training); and 3) those that focus on enhancing the pleasantness and decreasing the aversiveness of person-environment interactions (e.g., relaxation training). Some combination of these types of tactics constitutes the different behavioral treatment programs for depression.

To best illustrate how behavioral theories of depression and strategies for treating the disorder inform the actual choice of tactics, we will describe several behavioral treatments for unipolar depression. The first two programs we will describe were developed at the Depression Research Unit at the University of Oregon. Following this, we will review other behavioral treatment programs for depression. For each therapy program discussed, we will also describe the outcome literature to document the efficacy of these approaches.

Decreasing Unpleasant Events and Increasing Pleasant Events: An Individualized Approach to Depression

Lewinsohn et al. (1980a, 1982) have described a behavioral program that aims to change both the quality and the quantity of the depressed patient's interactions with the environment in the direction of increasing positive and decreasing negative events. The treatment is time limited (12 sessions) and highly structured, and a therapist manual is available to assist in the implementation of specific tactics.

During the diagnostic phase preceding treatment, extensive use is made of the PES and UES to begin to pinpoint specific person-environment interactions related to the patient's depression. An activity schedule (Lewinsohn 1976) consisting of 80 items rated by the patient as most pleasant and most frequent and 80 items rated by the patient as most unpleasant and most infrequent is developed. Patients begin daily monitoring of the occurrence of pleasant and unpleasant activities and their mood; this continues throughout treatment. Self-monitoring allows for the pinpointing of specific person-environment interactions that influence a patient's dysphoria. From a functional perspective, patients learn to diagnose their own depression—to recognize the particular unpleasant events in their daily lives and, of equal importance, to become aware of the range of pleasant experiences potentially accessible to them.

Treatment typically proceeds in two phases. In the first phase, treatment is aimed at assisting the patient in decreasing both the frequency and the subjective aversiveness of unpleasant events in his or her life; in the second phase, the focus is on increasing pleasant events.

A typical treatment plan begins with some type of relaxation training. In our experience, relaxation training is a multipurpose tactic. It reduces feelings of anxiety, which tend to magnify the aversiveness of unpleasant events and reduce the enjoyment of pleasant events; anxiety also impairs the depressive's thinking and may be central to sleep disturbances. From the perspective of the process of therapy, relaxation training is a procedure that is easy to master and that enhances nonspecific, positive components of treatment. Relaxation procedures used include the deep muscle relaxation of Jacobson (1929) and techniques suggested by Benson (1975) and Rosen (1977).

The therapy next moves to teaching patients to manage specific aversive events. First, patients are taught to practice a variety of tension-reducing relaxation techniques in specific situations in which they feel tense. Second, a small number of negative interactions or situations that trigger a patient's dysphoria are targeted. The therapist then selects from a range of tactics to remediate these situations. Typically, interventions fall into three categories. First, stress-management skills are taught based on procedures described by Meichenbaum and Turk (1976) and by Novaco (1975). In addition, patients are taught both general and specific problem-solving skills. Second, interventions are aimed at changing unpleasant social interactions. Two areas of the patient's behavior are targeted: their assertiveness and their interpersonal style of expressive behavior. Patients are asked to read *Your Perfect Right* (Alberti and Emmons 1974). Additionally, covert modeling based upon Kazdin's work (1974, 1976) and social skills training (involving instruction, modeling, rehearsal, and feedback) are employed to address specific problematic social situations and elements of interpersonal style. Finally, therapy is directed at teaching patients to become aware of and change the way they think about situations that disturb them. A variety of cognitive interventions can be used, including the scheduling of "worrying time," exaggeration of potentially negative consequences (the "blowup technique"), Meichenbaum's "self-talk" (1977) procedures, and rational-emotive techniques for disputing irrational thoughts (Ellis and Harper 1961; Kranzler 1974).

A bridge between the two phases of intervention involves helping patients learn time-management using a book by Lakein (1974). Depressed individuals learn to plan, anticipate, and arrange a better balance between activities they want to do and those they feel they "have" to do. Weekly and daily planning also lays the groundwork for patients to increase pleasant events, which become the focus of the remainder of treatment. Using their self-monitoring of mood and activity schedules, patients identify events they enjoy. They are taught to establish systematic, specific goals to increase the number of pleasant events, particularly those that show a strong relationship to their positive mood. Patients are especially encouraged to attempt experiences that make them feel more competent and to increase their pleasant social activities. These efforts are spread out over a number of sessions, and goals are gradually increased.

For those interested, a more detailed description of this individualized treatment approach and case illustrations are presented by Lewinsohn et al. (1980a,b).

Clear evidence exists that mood becomes more positive as a function of increasing the number of pleasant events engaged in (Lewinsohn 1975b; Rehm 1978) or even simply as a consequence of self-monitoring activity (Harmon et al. 1980). With regard to the efficacy of the program of "Decreasing Unpleasant Events and Increasing Pleasant Events," Lewinsohn et al. (1979) examined the relationship between reinforcement and depression across four samples of depressives. As predicted, the rate of negative experiences decreased and of positive experiences increased as clinical depression diminished; these changes were greater for patients who showed the most improvement. Lewinsohn et al. (1980a,b) showed that a program that decreased unpleasant events and increased pleasant events and one that simply increased pleasant events both demonstrated significant amounts of clinical improvement.

The Coping With Depression Course

The Coping with Depression (CWD) course is a multimodal, psychoeducational group treatment for unipolar depression. The major vehicle for treatment is an explicit educational experience designed to teach people techniques and strategies for coping with the problems that are assumed to be related to their depression. Thus, the course emphasizes the attainment of knowledge and skills over an intensive relationship with a therapist. The CWD course consists of 12 two-hour sessions conducted over eight weeks. Sessions are held twice a week during the first four weeks of treatment, and once a week for the final four weeks. One-month and six-month follow-up sessions, called "class reunions," are held to encourage maintenance of treatment gains.

The first two sessions of the CWD course are devoted to the definition of course ground rules, the presentation of the social learning view of depression, and instruction in basic self-help skills.

The course is a highly structured, time-limited, skill-training program that makes use of a text, *Control Your Depression* (Lewinsohn et al. 1978), from which reading assignments are made; a participant workbook (Brown and Lewinsohn 1984), which was developed to supplement the text; and an Instructor's Manual (Steinmetz et al. 1979) to ensure comparability of treatment across instructors.

The participant workbook contains goal statements, assignments for each session, and monitoring forms for recording specific behaviors, thoughts, and feelings relevant to the class assignments. Group time is divided among lectures, review of the assignments, discussions, role play, and structured exercises. The instructor's main goals are to deliver the course information accurately, to promote the effective application of the information, to help participants solve problems related to the material, and to facilitate a supportive group interaction.

An important feature of the CWD course is that participants are able to meet effectively in groups to assist each other in overcoming their depression. With relatively few exceptions (Barrera 1979; Fuchs and Rehm 1977; Lewinsohn et al. 1970), previous cognitive behavioral treatments have been offered exclusively in an individual therapy mode. This is not surprising since most authorities in the area of group therapy (e.g., Yalom 1975) advise against homogeneous groups of depressed patients. Our results indicate that within the structure presented by the course depressives work together very effectively. Another feature of the course is that it presents a cost-effective, community-oriented outreach approach to impact on the great majority of depressives who never avail themselves of the services of clinics and mental health professionals. The educational focus reduces the stigma involved in seeking "psychiatric" or "psychological" treatment, which is especially important to the poor, elderly, and rural depressed.

Three treatment outcome studies on the CWD course have been completed (Brown and Lewinsohn 1979; Steinmetz et al. 1983; Teri and Lewinsohn 1981), and two are currently in progress (Saenz et al. 1985; Hoberman et al. 1985). In each of these studies, course participants were carefully assessed on a wide range of variables at four points in time: pretreatment, posttreatment, one month, and six months following treatment.

The CWD course was compared to individual tutoring based on the CWD manual, a minimal phone contact procedure (Brown and Lewinsohn 1979), and individual behavior therapy (Teri and Lewinsohn 1981). The results indicated that the differences between all the active treatment conditions were small. In each study, depressed individuals participating in the CWD course showed substantial improvement at posttreatment and maintained improvement at both one-month and six-month follow-ups. This was true with regard to both self-report and clinical diagnoses. Improvement from the CWD course has been comparable in magnitude to that shown by subjects in individual therapy in studies of cognitive-behavioral therapy for depression. Antonuccio et al. (1982) evaluated the relationship between a number of group leader variables and clinical outcome; despite differences among leaders, there was no differential impact on outcome.

Social Interaction Therapy

The social interaction theory of depression postulated by McLean (1976, 1981) considers the depressed person's interaction with his or her social environment to be crucial for the development and reversal of depression. As McLean views it, depression results when individuals lose the ability to control their interpersonal environment. When ineffective coping techniques are utilized to remedy situational life problems, the consequence may be a decrease in positive events and thus depression. Social interaction therapy aims to maximize the patient's competence in specific coping skills, particularly those important to effective interpersonal relationships.

Social interaction therapy incorporates behavioral and cognitive techniques and places a marked emphasis on therapeutic decision making regarding appropriate intervention components. It is distinguished by its incorporation of procedures for including relevant social network members (e.g., spouse) as integral components of treatment; evaluation and intervention may include the patient's living arrangements, marital status, and satisfaction.

Six specific therapeutic components are suggested by McLean: communication training, behavioral productivity, social interaction training, assertiveness training, decision-making and problem-solving training, and cognitive self-control. While the first three components are used in the treatment of all depressed patients, the latter three are optional, depending upon assessment of a patient's particular deficiencies in the problem areas. Perhaps the most distinctive component of social interaction therapy involves a structured form of communication training between the patient and his or her spouse or significant other to counteract both aversive marital interactions and a constricted quantity in range of interactions. Communication exercises aim to provide opportunities for positive feedback, to enhance self-esteem, and to facilitate other forms of social interaction. Additionally, the inclusion of a relevant social network member is important in the promotion of social interaction and in maintaining treatment effects. At the end of treatment, patients are assisted to prepare for future episodes of depression, and contingency plans are established and rehearsed.

McLean et al. (1973) developed a therapeutic program based on the aforementioned components and found it to produce significant changes in problematic behaviors and in verbal communication styles.

Self-Control Therapy

A treatment based on a self-control theory of depression (Rehm 1977) has been described by Fuchs and Rehm (1977). The treatment consists of six sessions (over a six-week period) with two sessions devoted to each of three self-control processes: self-monitoring, self-evaluation, and self-reinforcement. Rehm and Kornblith (1978) presented a revised self-control therapy protocol, which expanded treatment from six to 12 sessions. The therapy program begins with a didactic presentation of self-control deficits in relation to depression; early sessions are devoted to reviewing the process and consequences of self-monitoring mood and activities and to increasing activities. Later sessions emphasize developing realistic criteria for setting goals (e.g., for activities) and for modifying self-attributions for success and failure. Finally, emphasis is placed on patients developing "reward menus," which they self-administer as they complete specific, goal-related positive activities.

Comparing a group version of the initial six-session self-control therapy program to a nonspecific group therapy condition and waiting list control group, Fuchs and Rehm (1977) found that a self-control group showed significantly more improvement than the other conditions at termination and at the six-month follow-up. Rehm et al. (1979) compared two treatment conditions: self-control therapy and a social skills treatment. Results indicated that each treatment was efficacious through a six-week follow-up and that each treatment produced greater improvement in its target area (e.g., self-control or social skills). Most recently, Roth et al. (1982) compared self-control therapy both alone and in conjunction with antidepressant medication. Both treatments produced a similar reduction in depressive symptomatology although the combined treatment group evidenced a more rapid improvement in symptoms.

Social Skills Training for Depression

Bellack et al. (1981a) have theorized that the depressed patient has either lost socially skillful responses as the result of anxiety, the course of a psychiatric illness or hospitalization, or that the patient has never possessed social skills in his/her repertoire. Social skills treatment was conceived of as a reeducation or education for depressed patients.

Typically, treatment takes place over 12 weekly therapy sessions, followed by 6–8 booster sessions spread over a six-month period. Therapy begins with a careful behavioral analysis of social skills deficits. Three social skills are emphasized in treatment: positive assertion, negative assertion, and conversational skills. Training is provided across four social contexts: with strangers, with friends, with family or in heterosocial interactions, and at work or school. Social skills training employs careful instruction in a skill, followed by rehearsal, feedback modeling and coaching, social reinforcement, and graded homework assignments. Patients are also educated regarding social cues and mores, relevant aspects of the social context, and predicting interpersonal consequences.

Two pilot studies of social skills training (Hersen et al. 1980; Wells 1979) demonstrated that this intervention resulted in improvement in specific social skills as well as on self-report and psychiatric rating scales.

An Operant Reinforcement Approach

Azrin and Besalel (1981) describe an innovative program combining both behavioral and cognitive tactics to produce an increase of reinforcement to facilitate the amelioration of depression. Initially, patients are asked to specify four changes they desire in behavioral terms. They are also asked to rate their degree of happiness in eight life areas (e.g., care of children, sex, finances, social activities, and so on). At this point, a variety of potential treatment tactics are discussed with the patient and a contract is signed.

At the beginning of treatment, the emphasis is on increasing enjoyable experiences for the depressed patient. Using several instruments indicating positive attitudes and experiences, patients develop their own lists of "happiness reminders," "nice qualities about themselves," and probable pleasant activities. Daily and weekly schedules are agreed to for engaging in pleasant activities. On a cognitive level, patients are taught to engage in compensatory, positive statements whenever a depressive state or response occurs; to review a list of severe traumatic events (e.g., "My house burned down") to induce contrast; or to look for benefits from the occurrence of stressors. Each of these procedures is designed to refocus the patient's cognitive and affective experience. Next, patients receive training in social skills to produce more satisfactory relationships. Finally, individuals with specific marital, vocational, employment, or other problems are assisted in translating amorphous complaints into specific behavioral objectives. Patients are then given condensed interventions for their particular concerns. In contrast to other behavioral interventions, there is no attempt to have the patient master one procedure before proceeding to the next one.

Azrin and Besalel (1981) also reported on the results of an outcome study of their operant reinforcement approach to treating depression. The study employed a waiting-list, within-subjects design, in which a two-week waiting period was scheduled after an intake session. A total of 29 subjects were treated. While little or no change occurred after the waiting period, significant and substantial changes from pre- to posttreatment were demonstrated on traditional depression measures. Additionally, patients indicated a decrease in the percentage of time spent feeling unhappy and reported that they attained, on an average, 75 percent of their specified individual treatment goals. In an absolute sense, 62 percent of the subjects had very favorable outcome measures on all assessment measures. Treatment gains were shown to persist at a seven-week follow-up, and there was no significant difference in improvement for persons with more or less severe depression. The average number of sessions was seven (range: 4–10), and the reduction in depression was most pronounced after the second session of treatment.

Comments on Behavioral Treatment Programs

As we noted at the beginning of this chapter, a number of well-defined behavioral treatment programs for unipolar depression presently exist. All of these programs share a conceptualization of the etiology of depression that emphasizes changes in the quality of an individual's interactions with the environment. Behavioral theories assume that the depressed patient has acquired maladaptive reaction patterns, which can be unlearned. Symptoms are seen as important in their own right rather than as manifestations of underlying conflicts, and treatments are aimed at the modification of relatively specific behaviors and cognitions rather than at a general reorganization of the patient's personality. All behavioral treatments are structured and time limited.

For each specific behavioral treatment program, empirical support for its therapeutic efficacy has been demonstrated. Each program appears to produce significant decreases in depression level and depressive symptomatology, although relatively little difference in outcome measures has been observed between treatment programs.

The question can be raised as to how all the different behavioral treatment programs can be similarly effective. Several possibilities might account for these findings. Clearly, there is great commonality across the behavioral approaches with regard to specific tactics employed to reduce depression level. However, even when specific behavioral techniques are used and assessed, there appears to be no selective impact on target behaviors. Zeiss et al. (1979) compared brief behavioral interventions based on increasing pleasant activities, improving social skills, or reducing negative cognitions and found that participants receiving different treatments all improved equally in their activity, social skills, and cognitions. Similar results were reported by Rehm et al. (1982). Given the results, it may be argued that behavioral treatment packages as currently implemented may include some common "core" of strategies or tactics. For example, Rosenbaum and Merbaum (1984) have suggested that self-control procedures may account for the therapeutic success of behavioral treatments of depression and anxiety. Similarly, in a study attempting to disassemble a behavioral treatment program, Rehm et al. (1981) found that self-monitoring procedures alone produced a treatment effect similar to the complete self-control treatment package. Thus, there seems to be some empirical support for the importance of self-monitoring as a critical element in behavioral treatment programs.

The authors of two treatment outcome studies for behavioral treatments of depression have offered their hypotheses as to the critical components for successful short-term behavioral treatments for depression. Zeiss et al. (1979) concluded that efficacious behavioral treatments should include the following characteristics:

1. Therapy should begin with an elaborated, well-planned rationale.
2. Therapy should provide training in skills that the patient can use to feel more effective in handling his or her daily life.
3. Therapy should emphasize independent use of these skills by the patient outside of the therapy context and thus provide enough structure so that the attainment of independent skills is possible for the patient.
4. Therapy should encourage the patient's attribution that improvement in mood is caused by the patient's increased skillfulness and not by the therapist's skillfulness.

Similarly, McLean and Hakstian (1979) noted that high structure, a social learning rationale, a goal-attainment focus, and an increase in social interaction were significant elements in the behavioral treatment of depression.

Current and Future Directions in Behavioral Treatments for Depression

Buoyed by initial progress in developing a variety of behavior therapy programs for treating depression and in demonstrating their efficacy, researchers are continuing to systematically expand their studies of aspects of the treatment of depressed individuals. At present, efforts are being made in a number of different directions, including refining the strategies and tactics of behavioral treatments, identifying those depressives most and least likely to benefit from behavioral treatments, and modifying existing treatment programs to ameliorate depression in groups other than the typical middle-aged depressive.

Several studies have attempted to evaluate the contribution of individual components of behavioral treatment programs (e.g., self-monitoring or increasing activities) (Rehm et al. 1981; Turner et al. 1979). These investigations indicate that both self-monitoring and increasing activities are critical to the success of behavioral treatments.

Other reports have examined the value of matching treatment components to patient characteristics (e.g., deficits) to provide a problem-specific approach to treating depression as advocated by Biglan and Dow (1981) and McLean (1981). Both Heiby (1986) and McKnight et al. (1983) showed that matched treatment did produce enhanced treatment effects; thus, social skills training and cognitive interventions were most effective with patients having difficulties in those respective areas.

Several studies have examined the amount of therapist contact needed to produce clinical improvement. Brown and Lewinsohn (1984) and Schmidt and Miller (1983) demonstrated that minimal phone contact and bibliotherapy, respectively, produced equivalent improvement to group and individual treatment. Selmi et al. (1982) reported on their endeavors to develop a computer-assisted, cognitive-behavior therapy program for depression.

Predictors of treatment response, nonresponse, and recurrence have also been studied. Four studies have examined predictors of improvement for depressives participating in the Coping with Depression course (Brown and Lewinsohn 1984; Hoberman et al. 1985; Steinmetz et al. 1983; Teri and Lewinsohn 1981). Five variables have tended to consistently emerge as such predictors: expectations of improvement, greater life satisfaction, lack of concurrent psychotherapy or medication, higher levels of perceived family social support, and younger age. Similarly, Steinmetz et al. (1982) showed that the combination of perceived control over symptoms and expected improvement together identified patients likely to improve. Both Rabin et al. (1985) and Zeiss and Jones (1982) investigated characteristics of treatment failures while Gonzales et al. (1985) and Monroe et al. (1983) looked at characteristics of individuals who experienced reoccurrences of depression after treatment.

Several investigators have in recent years attempted to examine the efficacy of behavioral treatments with a number of special groups. Thompson et al. (1983) modified the CWD course to make it better suited for elderly adults. This intervention, also described by Steinmetz et al. (1984), was shown by Hedlund and Thompson (1980) to be efficacious with clinically depressed elderly. Similarly, Antonuccio et al. (1983) conducted a pilot study, which indicated that inpatients with "drug refractory" depression responded favorably to a modified version of the CWD program. Turner et al. (1980) showed that a behavior therapy program was successful in treating depressed inpatient alcoholics. Finally, Clarke and Lewinsohn are at present conducting an outcome study for depressed adolescents based on the CWD program. In short, behavioral treatments for depression are increasingly being demonstrated as having efficacy with a variety of depressed persons, suggesting a widespread applicability of behavior therapy approaches for treating depression.

In conclusion, the last 10 years have been a period of exciting progress in the development and study of behavioral treatments for unipolar depression. Treatment strategies and tactics have been hypothesized and tested, with a now considerable number of studies demonstrating the efficacy of behavioral programs for ameliorating depression. Presently, these approaches are being refined, outcome studies are endeavoring to become more precise in identifying those most likely to improve from behavioral treatments, and behavioral programs are being generalized across special populations of depressives. Given the rapid strides made to date, the field of behavior therapy for depression can likely look forward to increasing advances in the future.

Chapter 171

Interpersonal Psychotherapy

Interpersonal psychotherapy (IPT) is based on the evidence that most clinical depressions—regardless of symptom patterns, severity, presumed biologic vulnerability, or personality traits—occur in an interpersonal context. Understanding and renegotiating the interpersonal context associated with the depression is important to the depressed person's recovery and to the prevention of possible further episodes. IPT is a brief (usually 12–16 weeks) weekly psychotherapeutic treatment developed for the ambulatory, nonbipolar, nonpsychotic depressed patient and focused on improving the quality of the depressed patient's current interpersonal functioning. It is suitable for use, following appropriate training, by experienced psychiatrists, psychologists, or social workers. It can be used alone or in conjunction with pharmacologic approaches.

IPT has evolved from the New Haven–Boston Collaborative Depression Project over 15 years of treating and researching ambulatory depressed patients. It has been tested alone as well as in comparison and in combination with tricyclics in two clinical trials with depressed patients—one of maintenance (Klerman et al. 1974; Weissman et al. 1974) and one of acute treatment (DiMascio et al. 1979; Weissman et al. 1979). Three additional clinical trials with depressed patients are currently underway (Weissman 1984).

The concept, techniques, and methods of IPT have been operationally described. To standardized the treatment so that clinical trials could be undertaken (Klerman et al. 1984), a training program for experienced psychotherapists of different disciplines providing the treatment for these clinical trials has been developed.

It is our experience that a variety of treatments may be suitable for depression and that the depressed patient's interests are best served by the availability and scientific testing of different psychological as well as pharmacologic treatments, to be used alone or in combination. Ultimately, clinical testing and experience will determine which is the best treatment for the particular patient.

In this chapter, I will describe the theoretical and empirical basis for IPT, summarize the procedures for conducting IPT, and present data demonstrating its efficacy in comparison and in combination with tricyclics with ambulatory depressed patients.

Theoretical Framework for IPT

IPT is derived from a number of theoretical sources. The earliest is Adolph Meyer, whose psychobiologic approach to understanding psychiatric disorders placed great emphasis on the patient's current psychosocial and interpersonal experiences (Meyer 1957). In contrast to Kraepelin and the concept of psychiatric illness derived from continental European psychiatry, Meyer saw psychiatric disorders as part of the patient's attempt to adapt to the environment, usually the psychosocial environment.

Meyer viewed the patient's response to environmental changes as determined by early developmental experiences, especially in the family, and by the patient's membership in various social groups. He attempted to apply the Darwinian concept of adaptation to understanding psychiatric illness.

Among Meyer's associates, Harry Stack Sullivan stands out for his theory on interpersonal relations and also for his writings linking clinical psychiatry to anthropology, sociology, and social psychology (Sullivan 1953a, 1953b). The theoretical foundation of IPT was best summarized by Sullivan, who noted that psychiatry is the scientific study of people and the processes that involve or go on between people, as distinct from the exclusive study of the mind, society, or the brain.

The IPT emphasis on interpersonal and social factors in the understanding and treatment of depressive disorders draws upon the work of many others, especially Cohen et al. (1954) and more recently Arieti and Bemporard (1978). Among others, Becker (1974) and Chodoff (1970) have also emphasized the social roots of depression and the need to attend to the interpersonal aspects of the disorder. An interpersonal conceptualization has been applied to psychotherapy in the writings of Frank (1974), who stressed mastery of current interpersonal situations as an important component in psychotherapy.

The Empirical Basis for Understanding Depression in an Interpersonal Context

The empirical basis for understanding and treating depression in an interpersonal context derives from several divergent sources, including development research on ethological work with animals, the study of children, and clinical and epidemiologic studies of adults. This review of empirical studies is not meant to be exhaustive.

Attachment Bonds and Depression

Attachment theory has emphasized that the most intense human emotions are associated with the formation, disruption, and renewal of affectional attachment bonds. The way in which the individual forms affectional bonds is learned largely by experience within the family—especially, but not exclusively, during early childhood. The studies of Bowlby, based on earlier investigations of the animal ethologists and later applied to studying the mother-child relationship, have demonstrated the importance of attachment and social bonds to human functioning; the vulnerability of individuals to impaired interpersonal relations if strong attachment bonds do not develop early; and the vulnerability of individuals to depression or despair during disruption of attachment bonds (Bowlby 1969). Many types of psychiatric disorders result in a person's inability to make and keep affectional bonds.

Based on these observations, Bowlby (1977) proposed a rationale for psychotherapy: to assist the patient in examining current interpersonal relationships in order to understand how they may be construed on the basis of the patient's experiences with attachment figures in childhood, adolescence, and adulthood.

The work of Bowlby has been extended by Rutter (1972) to show that relationships other than that of the mother and child have an impact on the formation of attachment bonds. Closely derived from these effects has been the work of Henderson et al. (1978). In a series of studies, this group has found that deficiency in social bonds in the current environment is associated with neurotic distress. However, it is unclear whether there is a real deficiency in bonds or whether the deficiency is a reflection of the depressed person's negative cognition.

Intimacy as a Protection Against Depression

The most sophisticated empirical work defining an aspect of attachment bonding (i.e., intimacy and a confiding relationship) and examining its relationship to the development of depression has been completed by Brown et al. (1977). In a community survey of women living in the Camberwell section of London, this group found that the presence of an intimate, confiding relationship with a man, usually the spouse, was the most important protection against developing a depression in the face of life stress.

In a similar work with medical patients, Miller and Ingham (1976) found that women who reported to general physicians the lack of an intimate confidant had more severe psychological symptoms.

Recent Social Stress and the Onset of Depression

Stemming from the demonstration by Holmes et al. (1950) that the rate of upper respiratory illness increases with the number of life events, a considerable body of research demonstrating the relationship between "stress" (defined as recent life events) and the onset of psychiatric illness, particularly depression, has emerged.

The studies of Paykel et al. (1969) are most relevant to the study of stressful life events and depression. This group studied depressed patients and found that exits of persons from the social field occurred more frequently with depressed patients than with normals in the six months prior to the onset of depression. This group also found that marital friction was the most common event reported by depressed patients prior to the onset of depression.

Similar observations were made by Ilfeld (1977) in a survey of about 3,000 adults in Chicago. Depressive symptoms were closely related to stress, particularly to stresses in marriage but less frequently to those of parenting. In a closer look at the data, Pearlin and Lieberman (1979) found that chronically persisting problems within intact marriages were as likely to produce distress and depressive symptoms as was the total disruption of the marriage by divorce or separation.

Bloom et al. (1978), in a critical analysis of several studies related to the consequences of marital disputes and divorce, linked these events (marital disruption) with a wide variety of emotional disorders, including depression.

Impairment of Interpersonal Relations Associated with Clinical Depression

The impairment in close interpersonal relations of depressed women has been studied in considerable detail by Weissman and Paykel (1974). In a comparison study of depressed women and their normal neighbors, they found that the depressed women were considerably more impaired in all aspects of social functioning: as workers, wives, mothers, family members, and friends. This impairment was greatest with close family, particularly spouses and children, with whom considerable hostility, disaffection, and poor communication were evident. With symptomatic recovery, most, but not all, of the social impairments diminished. Marital relationships often remained chronically unhappy and explosive. There has been some debate as to whether the marital difficulties associated with depression are the cause or the consequence of the disorder (Briscoe and Smith 1973; Kreitman et al. 1970). Studying the interactions of depressed patients and normal subjects, Coyne (1976) demonstrated that depressives elicit characteristic, unhelpful responses from others.

This brief review is meant to summarize some of the key empirical findings that provide a rationale for understanding depression in an interpersonal context and for developing a psychotherapy for depression based on interpersonal concepts. In general, studies show the importance of close and satisfactory attachments to others in the prevention of depression, and alternately, the role of disruption of attachments in the development of depression.

The Nature of IPT

Depression is viewed as having three component processes:

1. Symptom formation, which involves the development of depressive affect and the vegetative signs and symptoms and which may derive from psychobiologic and/or psychodynamic mechanisms.
2. Social and interpersonal relations, which involve interactions in social roles with other persons and which derive from learning based on childhood experiences, concurrent social reinforcement, and/or personal mastery and competence.
3. Personality, which involves the enduring traits such as inhibited expression of anger, guilt, poor communication, and/or difficulty with self-esteem. These traits determine the person's unique reactions to interpersonal experience. Personality patterns may provide part of the person's predisposition to episodes of illness and intervene in the first two processes—symptom formation and social and interpersonal relations. Because of the relatively brief duration of the treatment and the low level of psychotherapeutic intensity, there are few claims that this treatment will have impact on enduring aspects of personality structure.

IPT facilitates recovery by relieving the depressive symptoms and by helping the patient develop more productive strategies for dealing with current social and interpersonal problems associated with the onset of symptoms.

The first goal is achieved by educating the patient about the depression: the patient is told that the vague and uncomfortable symptoms of depression are part of a known syndrome that is well described, well understood, and relatively common; that it responds to a variety of treatments; and that it has a good prognosis. Psychopharmacologic approaches to alleviate symptoms may be used in conjunction with IPT.

The second goal is achieved by helping the patient understand the interpersonal context of the depression—for example, determining with the patient which of four common problems associated with the onset of depression (grief, role disputes, role transitions, and interpersonal deficits) is related to the patient's depression—and by focusing the psychotherapy around the patient's coping more effectively with the particular problem.

In achieving these goals, reliance is on techniques such as reassurance, clarification of internal emotional states, improvement of interpersonal communication, and reality testing of perceptions and performance. These techniques conventionally are grouped under the rubric of "supportive" psychotherapy. However, in our view, the term supportive psychotherapy is a misnomer since most of what is called supportive psychotherapy attempts to assist the patient to modify his or her interpersonal relations, to change perceptions and cognitions, and to reward behavior contingencies.

IPT differs from other psychotherapies in that it is time limited and focuses primarily on both the patient's current symptoms of depression and the interpersonal context associated with the depression. It has been developed for the treatment of a single disorder—depression and is an acknowledged amalgam of many therapeutic techniques. The main efforts during IPT are on current issues at the conscious and preconscious levels: current problems, conflicts, frustrations, anxieties and wishes defined in an interpersonal context. The influence of early childhood experience is recognized as significant to the presenting problems, but this component is not emphasized in therapy. Rather, an effort is made to define problems in "here-and-now" terms. It includes a systematic analysis of relations with significant others in the patient's current situation. The brevity of the therapy (usually 12–16 sessions) precludes major reconstruction of personality, and no assumptions are made about unique personality styles among persons who become depressed.

The Conduct of IPT

The following material gives a brief outline of IPT.

Goals

1. Reduction of depressive symptoms with restoration of morale and improved self-esteem.
2. Improvement in the quality of the patient's interpersonal relationships and social adjustment by helping him or her develop more effective strategies for dealing with current interpersonal problems.

Methods of Dealing with the Depressive Symptoms

1. Review symptoms and make a diagnosis.
2. Give symptoms a name.
3. Describe depression, its epidemiology, course, prognosis, and treatment.
4. Evaluate the need for medication.
5. Give the patient the "sick role" temporarily.
6. Determine the interpersonal problem areas to be worked on in psychotherapy.

Interpersonal Problems Commonly Associated with Acute Depression

1. Abnormal grief reaction: refers to depression (not normal bereavement) associated with the death of a significant other. The goals of treatment are
   - to facilitate the delayed mourning process; and
   - to help the patient reestablish interests and relationships that can substitute for those that have been lost.
2. Interpersonal role disputes: refers to a situation in which the patient and at least one significant other have nonreciprocal expectations about their relationship. The goals of treatment are
   - to help the patient identify the issue(s) in the dispute;
   - to guide the patient in making choices about a plan of action; and

- to encourage the patient to modify maladaptive communication patterns and/ or to reassess expectations to bring about a satisfactory resolution to the interpersonal dispute.
3. Role transitions: refers to depression associated with a patient's unsuccessful attempt to cope with life changes. The goals of treatment are
    - to enable the patient to regard the new role(s) in a more positive, less restricted manner—perhaps as an opportunity for growth; and
    - to restore self-esteem by developing in the patient a sense of mastery vis-à-vis demands of the new role.
4. Interpersonal deficits: refers to depression associated with a history of social impoverishment, including inadequate or unsustaining interpersonal relationships and poor social skills. Depressed patients who present with a history of severe social isolation tend to be more severely disturbed than those with other presenting problems. The goals are
    - to help the patient identify any past positive relationships and experiences to use as a model; and
    - to find new situations and persons in which to develop more satisfactory relationships.

Efficacy Data on IPT for Depression

Two controlled clinical trials of IPT for depression—one of acute and one of maintenance outpatient treatment—have been completed, and four are under way.

Diagnosis

IPT has been designed for ambulatory patients who meet the criteria of major depression as currently defined by DSM-III (American Psychiatric Association 1980) or Research Diagnostic Criteria (RDC).

Current efficacy data on IPT in depressed patients are for ambulatory, nonpsychotic, and nonbipolar patients of either sex and of various racial groups and educational levels. While the earlier trial of IPT was conducted prior to the availability of RDC or DSM-III diagnostic criteria on rediagnosis, the patients included would meet these criteria. Mentally retarded and chronic alcoholic patients have been excluded from these studies; persons with personality disorders as defined by the DSM-III or the RDC have not.

There has been one trial among opiate addicts in which IPT added to the standard drug abuse program was compared with the drug abuse program alone (Rounsaville et al. 1983). The results indicated that IPT did not offer any advantage over the standard program in opiate-addicted populations. Thus, the value of IPT or its required modification (if any) with certain personality disorders or other diagnoses requires testing.

IPT as Acute Treatment

The study of the acute treatment of ambulatory depressed men and women compared using IPT alone, amitriptyline alone, and the two in combination against a nonscheduled treatment group for 16 weeks (Weissman et al. 1979). IPT was administered weekly by experienced psychiatrists. A total of 81 depressed patients entered the randomized treatment study (DiMascio et al. 1979; Weissman et al. 1979).

In nonscheduled treatment control group, no active treatment was scheduled but patients were assigned a psychiatrist whom they were told to telephone whenever they felt a need for treatment. If a patient's needs were of sufficient intensity, a 50-minute session (maximum of one per month) was scheduled. A patient who required further treatment—and who was still symptomatic after eight weeks or whose clinical condition had worsened sufficiently to require other treatment—was considered a failure of this treatment and was withdrawn from the study. This procedure served as an ethically feasible control for psychotherapy in that it allowed a patient to receive periodic supportive help "on demand." Assessments of the patient's clinical condition were made by a clinician who was blind to the treatment the patient was on and did not participate in the clinical phase of the study (the independent clinical evaluator).

IPT as Compared with Nonscheduled Treatment for Acute Treatment

The probability of symptomatic failure over 16 weeks was significantly lower in IPT than in nonscheduled treatment. These results were upheld by a variety of symptom measures made by the independent clinical evaluator, the patient self-report, and the treating psychiatrist. These effects on the patient's social and interpersonal functioning took six to eight months to fully develop. At the one-year follow-up, patients who had received IPT, with or without tricyclics, were functioning at a less impaired level in social activities with their spouse, children, and other relatives.

IPT as Compared with Tricyclics for Acute Treatment

Overall, the rate of symptomatic improvement was similar for patients receiving IPT alone as compared with those receiving tricyclics alone, and both treatments were better than nonscheduled treatment. However, there was a differential effect of the treatments on symptoms (DiMascio et al. 1979). IPT had its impact on improving mood, work performance, interest, suicidal ideation, and guilt. The effects became statistically apparent after four to eight weeks of treatment, and they were sustained. Amitriptyline had its impact mainly on vegetative signs and symptoms of depression—namely, sleep and appetite disturbance and somatic complaints. The effect on sleep was early, within the first week of treatment.

IPT in Combination with Tricyclics

Because of the differential effects of IPT and tricyclics on the type of symptoms and because patients have a range of symptoms, patients receiving combination treatment as compared with either treatment alone had greater overall improvement in symptoms, lower attrition, and a lower chance of symptomatic failure (Weissman et al. 1979). Patients receiving combination treatment were less likely to refuse it initially and less likely to drop out before the 16 weeks when the study treatment ended. Combination treatment was both more acceptable and better tolerated (Herceg-Baron et al. 1979). The effects were additive (Rounsaville et al. 1981). There were no negative interactions between drugs and psychotherapy.

Predictors of Response to Active Treatment

Patients who had an endogenous, nonsituational depression responded best to combined IPT and drugs and less well to IPT alone, just as had the nonscheduled treatment group. The group of patients who received drug alone achieved a response somewhere between those receiving IPT alone and those receiving the combination treatment. Alternately, patients who had situational, nonendogenous depression did equally well on drug alone, IPT alone, or the combination, and better than those on nonscheduled treatment (Cohen et al. 1954; Prusoff et al. 1980).

The patient's personality type, as measured by a variety of inventories or by the presence of a depressive personality diagnosis according to RDC, did not affect response to any of the short-term treatments (Zuckerman et al. 1980). This finding suggested that the presence of a personality disorder in addition to major depression does not preclude the use of drugs or IPT for the acute episode.

Follow-up After Acute Treatment

Patients were followed up one year after treatment had ended. As noted before, patients who had received IPT either alone or in combination were functioning better in social activities, both as parents in the family and overall (Weissman et al. 1981).

IPT as Maintenance Treatment

IPT as maintenance treatment was tested in an eight-month trial for 150 women recovering from an acute depressive episode who were treated for six to eight weeks with amitriptyline.

This study tested the efficacy of IPT (administered weekly by an experienced psychiatric social worker) as compared with a low-contact control (brief monthly visits for assessments) with either amitriptyline, placebo, or no pill. Treatment was by random assignment (Klerman et al. 1974).

Maintenance IPT as Compared with Low Contact

The findings showed that maintenance IPT as compared with low contact significantly enhanced social and interpersonal functioning for patients who did not relapse. The effects of IPT on social functioning took six to eight months to become statistically apparent (Weissman et al. 1974). Patients receiving IPT as compared with low contact were significantly less socially impaired, particularly in work, their extended families, and marriage. Overall improvement in social adjustment was significantly greater in IPT than in low contact.

Maintenance IPT as Compared with Tricyclic

Maintenance IPT as compared with amitriptyline was less efficacious in the prevention of symptomatic relapse. Patients on amitriptyline only, as compared with IPT alone, showed less evidence of depressive symptoms during maintenance treatment (Paykel et al. 1976).

Maintenance IPT in Combination with Tricyclic

Because of the differential impact of IPT and of tricyclics on relapse and on social functioning, the combination treatment was the most efficacious overall. Patients who received the combination drug and IPT had a lower risk of relapse and greater improvement in social functioning. Moreover, as was shown for acute treatment, the effects were additive. There were no negative interactions between drugs and psychotherapy.

Follow-Up After Maintenance Treatment

All patients were followed up at both one and four years after the end of the eight-month maintenance treatment. At one year, 30 percent were completely without symptoms, 60 percent had had mild return of symptoms over the year and 10 percent were chronically depressed (Weissman et al. 1978; Weissman and Klerman 1977). While the presence of personality problems did not interfere with the short-term acute treatment, the long-term outcome patients who scored high on the neurotic personality scale and who did not receive maintenance treatment of either drugs or IPT were doing less well (Weissman et al. 1978).

Clinical Trials of IPT in Progress

There are currently three studies in progress testing out the efficacy of IPT in ambulatory depressed patients (Weissman 1984). Some preliminary information is available from two of these studies. The first study is a multisite NIMH-sponsored collaborative study on the treatment of depression, testing the efficacy of IPT, cognitive therapy, imipramine and clinical management, and placebo and clinical management for 16 weeks in 250 ambulatory, depressed patients at three sites (George Washington University, University of Pittsburgh, University of Oklahoma) (Elkin et al. 1986). Overall, the preliminary findings showed that all active treatments were superior to placebo in the reduction of symptoms over a 16-week period. Over two-thirds of the patients were symptom free at the end of treatment.

More patients in the placebo-clinical management condition dropped out or were withdrawn—twice as many as for interpersonal psychotherapy, which had the lowest attrition rate. At the end of 12 weeks of treatment, the two psychotherapies and imipramine were equivalent in the reduction of depressive symptoms and in overall functioning. The pharmacotherapy, imipramine, had rapid initial onset of action, but by 12 weeks, the two psychotherapies had produced equivalent results. Although many of the less severely depressed patients improved with all treatment conditions, including the placebo group, the more severely depressed patients in the placebo condition did poorly. For the less severely depressed group, there were no differences among the treatments.

Forty-four percent of the sample were severely depressed. Patients in IPT and in the imipramine groups had significantly fewer symptoms than the placebo group on the Hamilton Depression Scale. Only imipramine plus IPT was significantly superior to placebo for the severely depressed group.

A second study, under way at the University of Southern California, is testing the efficacy of nortriptyline placebo/IPT in 60 to 90 ambulatory depressed elderly patients over 16 weeks. Preliminary results found partial evidence for the efficacy of IPT over nortriptyline in the elderly sample at six weeks, primarily because the elderly did not tolerate the medications well (Sloane et al. 1985).

Because of the enduring nature of marital problems in depressed patients (Foley et al. 1987; Rounsaville et al. 1979) and the tendency for patients with marital problems to have chronic depressive symptoms, Rounsaville, Weissman, and Klerman have focused their research on the treatment of marital disputes in depressed patients. Following the development and pilot testing of a manual for conjoint IPT for marital disputes and the training of therapists, the efficacy of individual versus conjoint marital IPT for depressed patients with marital problems was tested in a pilot study.

The results in a small sample suggested some minor benefit in marital functioning for conjoint versus individual IPT (Foley et al. 1987).

Conclusion

IPT is a short-term, interpersonal psychotherapy designed specifically for depressed patients, decodified in procedural manuals, and tested in several clinical trials. A training program for experienced therapists interested in undertaking research in its use has been developed.

In two clinical trials with ambulatory nonbipolar major depressives, we have demonstrated that for acute treatment, IPT as compared with nonscheduled treatment was more efficacious for symptom reduction and later for enhancing social functioning, and was about equal to tricyclics for symptom reduction. For maintenance treatment, IPT compared with low contact in recovering patients was more efficacious for enhancing social and interpersonal functioning. However, IPT was not as good as tricyclics for the prevention of relapse. The effects on social functioning take at least six to eight months to become apparent. In both the acute and the maintenance studies, the combination of IPT and tricyclic was better than either treatment alone. For the endogenous-nonsituational depressive, IPT alone did not offer anything above nonscheduled treatment. There was some suggestion that IPT had some enduring effect on social functioning one year after treatment ended and that the presence of personality problems did not affect short-term outcome. The results of the three studies currently under way in centers that did not develop IPT will provide more definitive information on its efficacy.

It should be emphasized that all the studies thus far have only included ambulatory nonbipolar depressed patients. While these patients represent the majority coming for treatment, these results on the efficacy of interpersonal psychotherapy cannot be generalized to depressed patients who are hospitalized, psychotic, or bipolar.

Chapter 172

Short-Term Dynamic Therapies for Depression

Progress in psychotherapy has been predicated on the "specificity principle," a formulation that links relatively specific therapeutic interventions to a relatively specific "problem" or "condition" in need of modification or remediation. Once a reasonable alignment of these two basic conditions has been achieved, it may become possible to examine the effectiveness of a particular treatment. Conversely, in the absence of such an articulation, assessments of treatment outcomes must necessarily remain indeterminate. The evaluation of treatment outcomes in all forms of psychotherapy, including those dealing with depression, has been greatly hampered by vaguely defined patient populations and clinical problems, insufficient descriptions of treatment methods, and lack of rigorous outcome criteria. The complexities of these issues have become increasingly appreciated, and steps are gradually being taken to address them. However, it should also be emphasized that most patients do not neatly fit DSM-III (American Psychiatric Association 1980) categories and that "depression" is a concomitant of many psychiatric disorders.

The "specificity principle," as might be expected, is not especially congenial to the psychodynamic tradition. Thus, it is hardly surprising that no *specific* psychodynamic treatment for depression has emerged despite the resurgence of theoretical and clinical interest in this disorder. Because of its diffuse, complicated, and multifaceted character, depression may well illustrate the fact that patients' problems do not come in "neat" packages. It may also serve as a telling illustration of the enormous difficulties besetting the seemingly simple goal of developing specific forms of treatment for specific conditions.

Without attempting to retrace the evolution of psychodynamic conceptions of depression, I shall summarize salient conclusions (for a more extensive discussion, see Arieti and Bemporad 1978, chapter 2):

1. Depression is basically a problem of disturbed interpersonal relations. It highlights the close association between maintenance of self-esteem (an intrapsychic emphasis) and maintenance of a close, intimate relationship (an emphasis on "behavior" or "performance"). Concomitantly, depression is frequently seen in terms of systems theory, which stresses the interactive character of the problem, in terms of both the person's past and present-day relationships with significant others.
2. The predisposition and origin of depressive disorders are found in early childhood—notably in disappointments with significant others, which lead to pervasive ambivalence in all relationships (Arieti and Bemporad 1978, pp. 23–24). These early experiences exert a lasting influence on the patient's life and typically are reinforced and exacerbated by current relationships with significant others.
3. Under the influence of developments in structural theory and ego psychology, depression is increasingly seen as a problem in adaptive functioning. More specifically, it relates to the regulation of self-esteem (Fenichel 1945) and reflects a disparity between the actual state of self and a desired ego ideal (Arieti and Bemporad 1978, p. 29). According to Bibring (1953), the person suffering from depression has experienced a severe blow to his or her self-esteem (e.g., disappointment or loss). This results in a conflict between actual or imaginary helplessness (an activation of a potent childhood state) and extremely high aspirations (e.g., for perfection, control, love), which the person feels unable to fulfill. The problem is complicated by the fact that the original experience of deprivation or loss sets in motion an overwhelming rage, which because of the child's dependency could not be directed outward and which is instead internalized (repressed) and directed against the self.

The preceding considerations have critical implications for psychotherapy. In accordance with psychodynamic conceptualizations, the so-called sadness (which may be contrasted with all other conditions in which biochemical and genetic factors may play a more important part) are not a disease, syndrome, or specific disorder; instead, they are particular manifestations of "problems in living" with which all psychotherapists in the psychodynamic camp have been concerned. By the same token, depressives employ basically the same neurotic tactics and maneuvers as other patients. Thus, the psychodynamic therapist endeavors to strengthen the patient's adaptive capacities (i.e., to come to the aid of the patient's "beleaguered ego"). The goal of treatment is to produce a more satisfactory alignment of the conflicting strivings that the patient has learned to handle in a maladaptive manner.

There are many ways in which a therapist can strengthen the patient's adaptive capacities (e.g., by reassurance, guidance, counsel, promotion of greater self-understanding through insight). However, in all instances there must be a human relationship in which an understanding, accepting, and empathic therapist partially gratifies the patient's wishes for dependency and succor.

From a psychodynamic perspective, psychotherapy is ideally aimed at a lasting reorganization of the patient's personality, thereby serving a prophylactic function. The short-term approaches to be described here hold out considerable promise for helping depressed patients in the short run and appear to be at least as effective as other available methods. It remains an open question whether any intervention technique can prevent recurrences of depressive episodes.

Modus Operandi of Short-Term Dynamic Psychotherapy

While brief dynamic psychotherapy is often promoted as an innovative therapeutic approach, its treatment methods are firmly grounded in classical psychoanalytic principles. Historically, in an attempt to offset the "stagnation" of the analytic treatment process (circa 1920), early theorists such as Ferenczi and Rank (1925), and later Alexander and French (1946), began to explore means whereby psychoanalytic principles could be preserved and applied more efficiently. Despite the significance of these theoretical contributions, they gained little acceptance within the traditional analytic community. Efforts to provide more expedient treatment alternatives, therefore, were largely dominated by the conservative, or crisis intervention, school of psychoanalytic therapy (e.g., Bellak and Small 1965; Wolberg 1965). This relatively atheoretical approach postulates that limited goals (i.e., the restoration of homeostasis) could be achieved in a very few sessions with primarily supportive measures such as reassurance and advice giving.

Renewed interest in short-term analytic treatment methods has been prompted by a desire to study the analytic process within a manageable time frame and by the increased realization of the need for broadening the scope of service delivery. David Malar and Peter Sifneos, working independently in England and Boston, arrived nearly simultaneously at what has been termed the "radical" formulation of short-term dynamic principles: long-standing neurotic patterns of behavior could be reversed through a time-limited psychotherapy employing all the essential types of interpretation found in psychoanalysis. Other theorists, most notably Balint et al. (1972), Davanloo (1978), Horowitz (1976), and Mann (1973), have reported similar results through the use of comparable procedures.

Despite certain quantitative differences between classical psychoanalysis and time-limited approaches based on dynamic principles, the underlying assumptions are basically identical:

1. The patient always seeks to achieve gratification by strategies learned in the past, some of which are maladaptive and interfere with productive adult living.
2. Since these learned strategies and behavior patterns are rooted in early significant relationships and their vicissitudes (e.g., deprivation, trauma, etc.), they can only be resolved within an interpersonal framework that in some ways resembles the earlier one but that, in important respects, is different from it. To the extent that the present-day relationship is experienced by the patient as similar to (reminiscent of) the earlier one, it will evoke the conflictual patterns of relatedness; conversely, to the extent that it is experienced by the patient as different, it can serve a therapeutic function (Alexander's concept of the "corrective emotional experience").

Fundamentally, the technique for bringing about the necessary corrections has two major components:

a. The therapist facilitates and encourages development of a viable interpersonal relationship between the patient and himself or herself.
b. The therapist seeks to identify and correct maladaptive patterns of relatedness by helping the patient to understand their futility.

In general, short-term therapists seek to accomplish their aims both through refined technical operations and special modifications of procedures and through improved methods for selecting patients who will be amenable to these interventions. The common elements that appear integral to all time-limited approaches will be briefly summarized:

Technical Operations

1. Time is ultimately the variable that distinguishes the modern short-term dynamic approaches from traditional psychoanalytic practice. Nevertheless, the notion of time-limited treatment has loose boundaries as consensus has yet to be reached regarding the length of therapy that would sharply differentiate the short- and long-term therapies. Thus far, the term *brief* psychotherapy has been applied to interventions ranging from crisis intervention to 40 sessions. The brevity of the treatment process is considered by some to be an inverse function of the severity of the individual patient's pathology and the relative ambitiousness of the particular therapist's goals.
2. While short-term therapeutic approaches assign to the therapist a more active role than is typical in dynamically oriented therapy, it still remains important to enlist the patient's active participation in the therapeutic process. Failure to do so transforms the therapist into a "magical helper" and defeats the major strength of dynamic psychotherapy, that of fostering the patient's autonomy and sense of mastery.
3. Central to the technique of short-term dynamic psychotherapy is the active and vigorous interpretation of the transference. The ultimate goal, as in all psychoanalytic procedures, remains the achievement of insight. This goal is approximated by the search for meaningful connections between the patient's historical past, current interpersonal relationships, and the transference relationship with the therapist. While some therapists (e.g., Alexander and French 1946; Castelnuove-Tedesco 1975) have advised against the interpretation of negative transference in the time-limited setting, more recent theorists such as Davanloo (1978), Sifneos (1979), and the Vanderbilt group (Strupp and Binder 1984) see the early interpretation of

negative transference reactions (often within the first interview) to be an essential step, particularly with hostile, resistant patients.

Selection of a Suitable Patient Population

Perhaps the central variable accounting for the success of these time-limited approaches may be seen as the rigorous, systematic application of selection criteria: procedures designed to ensure that the resulting treatment population possesses the substantial personality resources (as well as the will) to withstand the frequently painful, and always concentrated, nature of the therapeutic interventions. In practice, this means that short-term therapists have tended to exclude the more "difficult" patients (e.g., those suffering from personality disorders), and in doing so they have employed standards so stringent as to closely resemble those used to select candidates for psychoanalysis (cf. extensive literature on "analyzability," Bachrach and Leaff 1978). Short-term therapy patients nevertheless represent a relatively broad range of presenting pathology, with little attention given to the identification or restriction of persons according to formal diagnostic categories. Considerable agreement exists with regard to the most important of these selection criteria:

1. *Motivation for change* is perhaps the prime selection factor; only patients strongly committed to resolving their difficulties through insight (and who are willing to alter basic adaptational styles) are judged as able to withstand the stress of this anxiety-provoking procedure and to derive eventual therapeutic benefit.
2. A demonstrated ability to become involved in a *mutual, mature relationship* (which Sifneos [1979] defines as a history of at least one significant "give and take" relationship) implies an ability for basic trust and a willingness to undergo the risks inherent in a therapeutic involvement.
3. Evidence of *ego strength* and adaptive capacities is considered critical; patients should be of at least average intelligence and have demonstrated adequate adjustment in work, social, and educational realms.
4. *Psychological-mindedness*, a concept that loosely refers to the individual's capacity for introspection and ability to conceptualize problems within an intrapsychic framework, signifies the degree to which the patient can accept and utilize insights into the factors underlying his or her maladaptive cognitions, feelings, and behaviors.
5. The potential of short-term therapy candidates to ultimately appreciate the significance of their life circumstances is thought to be intimately related to their *affective involvement*, or capacity to express relevant emotions directly.
6. In classical analysis, it is frequently necessary to expend considerable time and effort to bring a conflict into focus, whereas for best results the patient coming into brief therapy should experience a *focal conflict*. In the absence of such a conflict—usually characterized by pronounced anxiety, distress, and suffering—brief dynamic therapy may have little chance of success.

The following thumbnail sketches of contemporary forms of brief psychotherapy based on psychodynamic principles are intended to provide a concise overview. The list is selective rather than comprehensive.

Short-Term Anxiety-Provoking Psychotherapy (STAPP)

Sifneos (1972, 1979) set out to determine whether psychoanalytically oriented methods could be adapted to a time-limited form of psychotherapy to help patients with significant neurotic problems. In keeping with psychoanalytic teachings, it had previously been assumed that short-term therapy (12–20 sessions) could produce symptom relief in patients suffering from acute distress but that no enduring characterological changes were to be expected. Challenging this tradition, Sifneos developed an approach whose principal features include an emphasis on patient selection and specialized technical management.

With respect to patient selection, Sifneos carefully selects patients who, despite their neurotic disturbances, manifest notable ego strength. Components of the latter include psychological-mindedness, honesty, introspectiveness, curiosity, readiness to collaborate actively with the therapist, willingness to experiment with more adaptive behavior, and realistic expectations of therapy. These criteria are subsumed under the concept of motivation for change (or, alternately, minimal defensiveness). Sifneos also stipulates that conflicts be limited to certain circumscribed areas of functioning (usually heterosexual relationships) and that they be susceptible to formulation in oedipal terms (a triangular relationship conflict). This condition allows the therapist to define a narrow target area of work: the oedipal focus.

Selection is made contingent on a detailed history (to determine the presence of oedipal issues), as well as on an informal mental status examination, aimed at an evaluation of relevant personality characteristics. On the basis of this assessment, a focus for therapy is established and presented to the patient. This takes the form of an intellectual explanation of the patient's maladaptive behavior, with stress on the enduring influence of relationship patterns originating in family conflicts.

Sifneos wished to demonstrate that the foremost technique of psychoanalysis, genetic transference interpretations, could also be the technical foundation of short-term dynamic psychotherapy. Thus, having selected patients who demonstrate the highest qualifications for any form of analytic therapy, he focuses the therapeutic work on interpretations of the transference and on genetic reconstructions. Correspondingly, there is less emphasis on what occurs in the therapeutic relationship although the existence of a good working alliance is taken for granted and considered a prerequisite for the patient's ability and willingness to become immersed in therapeutic work. The curative effects of Sifneos's anxiety-provoking psychotherapy are attributed largely to correct interpretations of oedipal constellations.

Therapy usually lasts 12 to 15 sessions, and no time limits are set in advance. Sifneos reports that his patients frequently take the initiative in bringing up the issue of termination. He believes that the stringency of his selection criteria precludes the acceptance of patients who are prone to form dependent attachments. The therapist's active stance is undoubtedly another factor in decreasing the chances of this eventuality.

Time-limited Psychotherapy: James Mann

Boston psychoanalyst James Mann (Mann 1973; Mann and Goldman 1982) has developed a form of time-limited psychotherapy that places the experience and meaning of time at the center of attention. His approach has two unique features: a rigid adherence to 12 sessions, conducted on a weekly basis; and use of the issue of time limits to understand the entire process and progress of treatment. Underlying this approach is the assumption that all emotional conflicts treatable by Mann's therapy ultimately have their affective roots in the patient's struggle between unconscious wishes for endless nurturance and love versus the conscious awareness of the finiteness of time, reflecting limitations on the degree to which one's wishes can be gratified.

This form of time-limited therapy is considered suitable for a broad spectrum of psychopathology, and the central issue can range across oedipal and preoedipal conflicts. Furthermore, Mann's selection criteria do not include a broad survey of ego functions. Thus, he views his criteria as more flexible than those of Sifneos or Malan. Mann believes that serious psychopathology may be treated if the patient's overall ego strengths are adequate. In a departure from the other exponents represented here, he states that if diagnostic errors are made, the treatment plan can be changed accordingly, without harm to the patient. However, the two ego functions that Mann does assess—the capacity for rapid affective involvement and the capacity for rapid affective disengagement (the capacity to tolerate loss)—may be seen as rather stringent. In fact, Mann's patients evidently demonstrate a remarkable capacity to respond positively to the kind of therapy and relationship he offers.

A therapeutic focus, close to the patient's subjective experience, is defined. In the first one to four interviews, Mann attempts to articulate the patient's "chronically endured pain," which reflects a rigidly fixed negative self-image. The treatment process rides a dual track: it consists of an examination of the central issue, followed later in the treatment by a thorough exploration of the patient's feelings about termination. The latter, Mann believes, inevitably combines the patient's unique problems with a negative self-image and the universal reactions to separation and loss.

Careful patient selection and a strong therapeutic alliance carry the treatment even through periods of intense disappointment and ambivalence. Accordingly, Mann is not confronted with conflicts in the therapeutic relationship created by the patient's chronic problems with trust and intimacy. He is thus free to devote his attention to elaborating the self-defeating interpersonal consequences of the patient's distortion of the meaning of termination in terms of his or her negative self-image. Countertransference is viewed as a problem primarily in terms of the therapist's discomfort (or neurotic conflicts) about the rigid termination deadline.

The Tavistock Group: David Malan

In the 1950s, a group of psychoanalytically oriented therapists working in London under the leadership of Michael Balint (Balint et al. 1972) began to develop a form of time-limited psychotherapy based on psychoanalytic principles. Balint's seminal ideas were developed further by David Malan (1976), who after Balint's death emerged as the most eloquent and influential spokesperson for this group. Malan also recognized the great importance of undergirding his clinical observations with systematic research of process and outcome, which he has pursued with great diligence over the years.

The Tavistock group initially subscribed to the then prevailing notion that short-term psychotherapy might reduce symptoms of acute neurotic conflicts in generally well-functioning individuals but that such efforts were a second-best substitute for long-term, intensive therapeutic efforts. The work, however, took a different direction when it was found that few such patients could be located among the typical applicants to the Tavistock Clinic. Instead, patients frequently manifested chronic problems and greater disturbances than seemed theoretically optimal for time-limited therapy. Bowing to this reality, the Tavistock workers chose to be flexible in their selection procedures, particularly if one of the collaborating therapists expressed a strong desire to accept a particular person for treatment. This flexibility resulted in the unexpected finding that patients showing marked deficiencies in ego strength and other criteria considered necessary for time-limited therapy could still be helped. Indeed, in numerous instances the results were quite impressive even though time-limited therapy in some cases lasted up to 40 hours.

Typically, a calendar date marks the planned termination. Malan states that this procedure avoids the problem of deciding whether to make up sessions missed by the patient. A crucial quality characterizing these patients (also stressed by Sifneos) is a positive response to interpretations in the area of the focal conflict. Malan calls this quality a "dynamic interaction." By this he means that the patient must be appropriately responsive to the form of therapy and the kind of relationship offered by the therapist. Promising patients are those able to quickly develop trust in the therapist, as evidenced by open communication of feelings, which in turn allows the therapist to arrive at a better understanding of the patient's problems and to communicate that understanding.

Diagnostic assessment plays an important part in Malan's approach. In addition to assessing the patient's background and current functioning along fairly traditional lines, the diagnostic assessments serve the twofold goal of establishing a focal conflict theme and forecasting what will happen when therapy gets under way. The forecasting then serves two additional purposes: to gauge the patient's vulnerability to severe disruptions in day-to-day functioning and to predict the manner in which the focal theme will manifest itself during the course of therapy. Although Malan acknowledges the importance of balancing attention between formal history taking and fostering a therapeutic alliance, the balance seems to be skewed in the direction of diagnostic operations.

Malan believes that the patient's responsiveness to the particular therapeutic techniques proposed in the Tavistock approach is a crucial predictor of outcome. Thus he recommends the use of trial interpretations in order to gauge the patient's willingness and ability to work in psychoanalytic therapy. One form of trial interpretation consists of interpreting the patient's resistances as soon as they are noticed. If the patient does not readily relinquish these resistances, particularly those occurring around the focal conflict, Malan considers his approach contraindicated.

In this form of therapy, the emotional conflicts potentially included in the therapeutic focus are not limited to oedipal issues but may take other forms as long as a circumscribed area of work can be demarcated. Furthermore, it is theoretically possible to work on several foci, provided they are clearly related. With regard to identifying a focus, Malan speaks of an "interpretive theme that gradually crystallizes over a few sessions."

Like Sifneos, the Tavistock workers assert that with appropriate patients, genetic transference interpretations can be successfully employed in time-limited dynamic psychotherapy. Thus, transference-parent links (T/P links)—interpretations connecting transference experiences with family constellations in childhood—are considered the essential therapeutic ingredient. Furthermore, all interpretive work is targeted within the circumscribed area of conflict.

Malan focuses major attention on technical problems surrounding interpretations of the transference. Correspondingly, there is less emphasis on the dyadic character of the patient-therapist relationship and on the therapist's personal reactions to the patient's behavior in therapy. Patients who evoke strong (negative) reactions from the therapist are presumably judged unsuitable for Malan's approach.

The Montreal Group: Habib Davanloo

Another approach to the time-limited psychotherapy is exemplified by the work of Habib Davanloo (1978), an analyst who spearheaded short-term therapy at Montreal General Hospital. Distinguishing features include an emphasis on selection of certain types of resistant patients and an active and persistent confrontation of the patient's resistances from the beginning of therapy, which typically lasts 15–30 sessions and is carried out in weekly interviews (45–50 minutes).

Davanloo's diagnostic assessments are essentially similar to those of Malan. He gathers extensive background information to assess the patient's ego functions, and he attempts to identify a focus for therapeutic work. However, unlike Malan, he actively confronts the patient's resistances even after initial trial interventions have failed to produce an impact. The immediate goal is to undercut the patient's difficulties in establishing a productive working alliance with the therapist.

Whereas Sifneos, Mann, and (to a lesser extent) Malan consider marked resistances emerging in the initial encounter as contraindications to time-limited dynamic psychotherapy, Davanloo prefers to work with patients who, while clearly possessing significant adaptive resources, manifest massive (typically intellectualizing) defenses (character armor). In Davanloo's view, these defensive operations must be identified, challenged, and defused as rapidly as possible. The therapist therefore becomes what Davanloo calls a "relentless healer" who seeks to break through the patient's barriers against human relatedness. If the effort succeeds, the patient is well on the way to forming a productive working alliance, and the outcome of therapy may be successful; conversely, the patient's struggle may become intensified, conceivably leading to anger and hostility directed at the therapist and/or to premature termination. According to Davanloo, the latter rarely happens, but this may be a function of his having selected patients who respond positively to the therapist's challenges. At any rate, strong resistances become the principal target of trial interpretations, which determine whether the patient can work within the framework of Davanloo's confrontational approach. It may also be seen that the therapist, from the beginning, creates for himself a position of dominance, which the patient must accept.

Davanloo subscribes to the traditional psychoanalytic view of transference as the arena in which unconscious conflicts are being enacted. Like Malan, he endeavors to interpret transference manifestations by linking them to childhood experiences (the T/P link). The therapeutic effort, therefore, is largely encompassed by interpretations aimed at eroding the patient's resistances as they manifest themselves in relation to the therapist and at clarifying the nature of the patient's conflict with reference to past family constellations.

Since the kinds of patients selected by Davanloo—often individuals with entrenched obsessional trends—vigorously oppose intimacy in any form (even dominance-submission) by fighting off a therapist whose object is to penetrate their characterological defenses, countertransference reactions are more likely to occur here than in any of the other approaches mentioned. Predictably, such reactions will interfere with the therapist's optimal functioning. Davanloo warns that they may result in an appropriate exclusion of a patient from short-term therapy; conversely, if the patient is accepted, the therapist's countertransference may become a "major vehicle in the development of misalliances with the patient" (Davanloo 1978). Aside from this warning, Davanloo does not systematically pursue the patient's impact on the therapist's personal reactions. Instead, he takes the position that the patient's persistent failure to respond positively to the therapist's confrontations is a contraindication for this form of therapy. Although Davanloo presses the patient harder for a commitment than does Sifneos, Mann, or Malan, the judgment of suitability depends markedly on the patient's receptivity to the therapist's unique approach and the role it assigns to the patient. Consequently, patients who cannot work productively within the therapist's framework either are rejected or may withdraw on their own initiative because they find the therapy too threatening.

Davanloo does not set a termination date at the beginning of treatment. Instead, he tells the patient that therapy will last "only as long as necessary to resolve the main conflicts." He tries to select patients who do not appear to have noticeable problems with dependency or separation, and his active approach is designed to counteract the patient's wishes for dependency. On the other hand, this may force the patient to adopt a submissive stance vis-à-vis the therapist's authority. Davanloo's therapies tend to last 15 to 30 sessions although the length may be extended, if necessary.

The Vanderbilt Group: Time-limited Dynamic Psychotherapy (TLDP)

Although the Vanderbilt form of time-limited dynamic psychotherapy (TLDP) shares a number of elements with other systems having similar objectives, there are also conceptual and practical differences (Strupp and Binder 1984). The similarities include the following points:

Patient selection. A patient is assessed for the ability to engage in time-limited therapy in terms of features of personality organization that are considered relevant to the task required by the treatment. That is, the nature of the patient's psycho-pathology (symptoms, diagnostic categorization) is secondary to evidence of his or her potential to form a collaborative relationship with a psychotherapist. The primary source of this evidence is the patient's handling of trial interventions made in the first few interviews.

Definition and pursuit of a dynamic focus or cyclical maladaptive pattern (CMP). Along with other workers in the area, it is considered essential to formulate an area of work defined in terms that are specific and meaningful to therapist and patient. The TLDP formulation of a CMP, however, diverges from that of other formulations in terms of its interpersonal emphasis.

Transference and countertransference analysis as major areas of work. The enactment in the therapeutic relationship of the patient's emotional conflicts is con-sidered the major goal for interpretive work. TLDP is unique, however, in consistently viewing all therapeutic transactions within a dyadic, interpersonal framework. This view also assigns a critically important role to the therapist's personal reactions to the patient's enactments. Thus, instead of relegating these countertransferences to a class of phenomena seen as impeding the therapeutic process, the Vanderbilt workers regard the therapist's reactions as potentially valuable data about the patient's CMP, which, if sensitively handled, can be an extremely valuable aid in advancing the achievement of therapeutic goals.

Time limits. Although fairly liberal (25 to 30 hours), time limits are set at the outset, and issues surrounding termination are continually addressed throughout treatment.

In summary, TLDP is an approach to individual psychotherapy that integrates clinical concepts from a variety of psychodynamic perspectives and that is aimed at the achievement of circumscribed objectives in 25 to 30 sessions. It is intended for patients whose difficulties in living manifest themselves through anxiety, depression, and conflicts in interpersonal relations (inhibitions, social withdrawal, inability to achieve intimacy). Furthermore, it is considered particularly appropriate for those patients whose conflicts are enacted in the therapeutic relationship in a way that poses significant obstacles to the establishment and maintenance of a working relationship. Current interpersonal difficulties, in this view, are typically the product of chronic maladaptations. Accordingly, TLDP does not focus on presenting symptoms—although improvements in the patient's feeling-state are obviously expected—but rather aims at a more lasting modification of the patient's character structure.

Major emphasis is placed on the contemporary transactions between patient and therapist, and on the patient's increased understanding and appreciation of their role and function in his or her current life. The therapeutic relationship thus comes to serve both as a laboratory for studying in vivo the patient's difficulties in living and as a means for correcting them.

The therapist's principal tools are empathic listening; understanding of the psychodynamics of the patient's current difficulties as much as possible in terms of the patient's history; and clarification of their self-defeating character, particularly as they occur in the immediacy of contemporary patient-therapist transactions. The goal is to mediate a constructive experience in living that results in improvements in the patient's self-concept and the quality of his or her interpersonal relations.

Finally, the emphasis is on integration of theoretical and technical aspects of the therapist's work. Thus, the goal is to make psychotherapy more realistic by linking the approach to systematic investigations designed to define more stringently the limits of what therapy can accomplish with particular persons and with specified investments of therapeutic time and effort.

Supportive-Expressive (SE) Psychoanalytically Oriented Psychotherapy

This approach is designed to standardize principles of psychoanalytically oriented psychotherapy. Developed by Luborsky (1984), it is based on his psychoanalytic training and work at the Menninger Foundation as well as on his subsequent research on the therapeutic alliance (Luborsky 1976; Luborsky et al. 1984) and the core conflictual relationship theme (Luborsky 1977). The treatment extends from 6 to 25 sessions but may also be open-ended. More recently, the treatment has been adapted for work with drug-dependent patients (Luborsky et al. 1985).

SE psychotherapy is based on the premise that any successful psychotherapy involves supportive and expressive aspects, and the combination of these is determined by the goals, resources, and pathology of the patient. Tolerance of anxiety, capacity for self-reflection, and ego strength are necessary for emphasis on the expressive aspects. Luborsky recommends an initial diagnostic assessment of the patient's presenting problem, interpersonal history, and resources. This is followed by a socialization interview (preferably by someone other than the therapist) to explain the nature of the treatment and to develop appropriate expectations. Time limits are discussed and set early in treatment, and they appear to be a matter of convenience and preference for therapist and patient. If, at the end of the time limit, old goals are not attained or new goals have emerged, an extension of therapy may be arranged. With this flexibility, Luborsky asserts that SE psychotherapy is appropriate for a wide range of patients with problems ranging from mild adjustment reactions to borderline psychotic disorders.

The supportive aspects facilitate the patient's experience of being supported by the therapist and are not aimed at increasing understanding. Supportive techniques include acceptance, liking, encouragement, a realistically hopeful attitude, recognition of progress made, and support of adaptive defenses and activities. The critical consideration is that the patient perceives and experiences the therapist's actions as supportive. The initial assessment can indicate in what areas and when the patient will need support. The supportive techniques are intended to provide the patient with a sense of security within the therapeutic relationship and are considered necessary for the rigors of the expressive work. They also serve to enhance self-esteem and to reduce anxiety. The greater the pathology, the greater must be the supportive aspect of therapy.

The expressive techniques are methods for facilitating the patient's experience, understanding, and working through of conflicts underlying his or her symptoms. These are described as standard psychoanalytic techniques, including interpretation of the transference. As mentioned, ego strength, tolerance of anxiety, and capacity for self-reflection determine suitability for this facet of therapy.

The focus of time-limited SE psychotherapy is the main relationship theme (or some aspect of it) associated with the presenting symptoms. Through the core conflictual relationship theme (CCRT), Luborsky has provided a method for identification of a patient's conflict between wishes or between a wish and its expected (usually negative) consequences. Within the first few sessions, the therapist seeks to identify this relationship theme by attending to relationship problems accompanying the main problems and to redundancies in information about current and past relationships with significant others. The therapist is alert to the reenactment of the CCRT in the therapeutic relationship, where it can then be worked with directly. As termination approaches, reappearance of the original symptoms or issues around separation may provide valuable therapeutic material for working through the CCRT. Luborsky's research indicates that with successful treatment, the CCRT can still be identified but the patient has a greater sense of mastery and more positive expectations.

The SE treatment manual was written to facilitate training and research, and it contains rating scales for evaluation of adherence to SE psychotherapy as well as further delineation of the CCRT method.

Treatment Effectiveness

All of the prominent short-term dynamic theorists have reported success in treating depressed patients (e.g., Davanloo 1978; Malan 1976; Sifneos 1972). These reports, however, consist mainly of individual case studies, and the effectiveness of these brief, analytic procedures has not been examined in a controlled or comparative empirical manner. Despite their different technical emphases, the views of the short-term theorists are remarkably congruent with respect to the factors accounting for the success of their approaches. The achievement of therapeutic gain within this restricted time interval is generally credited to the careful assessment of potential patients and the use of highly focused technical interventions. The existence of depression is not regarded by these authors as a contraindication to a patient's treatment, nor has depressive symptomatology been reported to be of significant prognostic value in predicting treatment outcome. (For a detailed critical review, see Suh et al. 1986.)

Conceptual and Methodological Considerations

Although brief dynamic psychotherapy has been found to be effective in reducing depressive symptomatology, no definitive statement can be made regarding the unique effectiveness of short-term dynamic treatment approaches for the amelioration of depression. (For a more detailed discussion, see Strupp et al. 1982.) In fact, most of the research on short-term dynamic approaches has not addressed this specific issue.

Rather, the techniques have been applied to persons experiencing acute stress reactions (Gottschalk et al. 1967; Gottschalk et al. 1973; Green et al. 1975; Horowitz 1976; Horowitz et al. 1984), individuals exhibiting a global distress syndrome (Sloane et al. 1975; Strupp and Hadley 1979), and patients selected on the basis of their appropriateness for short-term techniques (Davanloo 1978; Malan 1976; Sifneos 1972; Stewart 1972). Although most patients manifested depressive symptomatology, none were selected on the basis of their depression, nor were changes in depressive symptomatology isolated in many studies.

The majority of available studies failed to include more than a cursory description of the nature of the therapeutic approach, making it difficult to determine exactly what was being practiced under the rubric of "brief dynamic therapy" and to evaluate accurately the results of these efforts. Thus, it is likely that many of these therapies were dynamically oriented and brief although specialized techniques were not employed. Analyses of patient-therapist interactions in the Vanderbilt Project (Strupp 1980a, 1980b, 1980c) revealed that the psychodynamic therapists adhered to the psychoanalytic model of long-term intensive therapy (i.e., by assuming a passive-expectant stance, allowing the patient freedom to choose topics for discussion) rather than adapting their techniques to the abbreviated treatment period. Similarly, the description of the psychodynamic therapy employed in the Temple study (Sloane et al. 1975) does not indicate that short-term techniques were systematically employed.

Several other methodological inadequacies lessen the informational value of existing investigations. Notably, many researchers have failed to include appropriate control or comparison groups in the design of their investigations whereas others used treatment groups that did not allow conclusions to be drawn.

The question of the therapist's level of experience and other qualities becomes crucial when viewed in the context of treating a depressed patient population (cf. Luborsky et al. 1985). With these patients, extreme care and clinical sensitivity must be employed, particularly when the therapy is intense and "anxiety-provoking" (e.g., Sifneos 1979). As Lambert et al. (1977) have noted, negative effects are more likely to occur when therapy is conducted by inexperienced therapists and the therapeutic process has not been closely planned.

The brief therapy literature (with the exception of Malan and Davanloo) has not been optimistic regarding the likelihood of radically changing deep-seated characterological problems. However, the impediments supposedly created by pervasive maladaptive patterns of behavior have not been systematically examined in the context of brief therapy. Generally, the focus of treatment and assessments of outcome in this literature have been directed toward behavior, symptomatology, and day-to-day functioning rather than toward broader personality or characterological traits. This emphasis may be appropriate for short-term crisis intervention procedures, which have as their goal the relief of situationally determined anxiety and depression. To achieve a better understanding of the potential for change with the more radical short-term dynamic techniques, systematic comparisons and comprehensive assessments of diagnostic and outcome indices are indicated. Furthermore, long-term follow-up measures should be included since these brief therapeutic interventions are frequently referred to as the "jumping-off point" from which more enduring and pervasive change may ensue. These issues are currently being addressed in a major process and outcome study by the Vanderbilt Group.

Chapter 173

Couples and Family Therapy

Recent research suggests that the most effective intervention for acute and recurrent depression is a combination of drug treatment and psychotherapy (Beitman et al. 1984; Conte et al. 1986). The rationale for psychotherapy is based, in part, on the finding that interpersonal problems, often in the form of marital disputes, are associated with (or result from) depressive symptomatology or character structure (Briscoe and Smith 1973; Brown et al. 1977; Coleman and Miller 1975). Therefore, either individual treatment that focuses at least in part on the marital or family problems (Rounsaville et al. 1979) or marital/family treatment may be particularly beneficial for depressed individuals. In this chapter we will focus on models of family context and depression, and on the indications and efficacy of marital/family therapy for depressive disorders.

Models of Family Interaction and Depression

Models that include psychosocial variables in the etiology and course of depression (e.g., Billings and Moos 1985; Brown and Harris 1978a, 1978b; Klerman and Weissman 1986) emphasize variables that are temporarily associated with the occurrence of depression: extraordinary life events and stressors; less dramatic but still stressful occurrences of everyday life—that is, daily hassles; environmental support, usually seen as interpersonal support emanating from family, friends, community, etc.; and personal attributes of the individual, such as personality, social skills, coping style, and biologic and genetic predispositions to affective illness.

Many studies explicate each of the complicated variables in the models of depression noted above. (This has been reviewed elsewhere, see Haas and Clarkin 1988; Haas et al. 1985.) However, we will summarize briefly the points made by these studies in an attempt to demonstrate the clinical logic for the use of family and marital treatment when one or more family members are depressed.

1. It appears that marital and family functioning is particularly influenced by depressive episode(s) in a member. Over half of a sample of depressed women reported marital difficulties (Rounsaville et al. 1979). Depressed women are most impaired in their roles as wives and mothers (Weissman and Paykel 1974). Interpersonal friction, poor communication, dependency, and diminished sexual satisfaction characterize these marriages, and many women continue to experience such interpersonal difficulties after the alleviation of the depression. Relationships between depressed women and their children are characterized by a lack of involvement and affection (Weissman and Paykel 1974), and as many as 50 percent of these children have a diagnosable disorder (Cytryn et al. 1982). Also, there is less problem-solving behavior and less self-disclosure in couples with a depressed member (Biglan et al., in press).

2. There is an empirical relationship between relatively high levels of stress and low social support in individuals who experience depression. Families low in cohesion and expressiveness and high in interpersonal conflict report more depressive symptoms (Billings and Moos 1982; Billings et al. 1983). While depressed individuals residing in the community report seeking more social support than do nondepressed people, they also perceive themselves as receiving less support (Coyne et al. 1981; Schaefer et al. 1981).
3. The coping styles of depressed individuals are not as effective as those of nondepressed controls. Depressives are more likely to seek emotional or informational support, engage in wishful thinking (Coyne et al. 1981), and involve themselves in negative self-preoccupations, which interfere with efficiency and decisiveness in coping strategies. Depressives also use an inordinate amount of confrontation, self-control, and escape-avoidance (Folkman and Lazarus 1986).
4. Those individuals who experience episodes of depression are also likely to have personality disorders that affect their interpersonal relationships prior to, during, and after the depressive episodes. Depression and interpersonal difficulties bode poorly for treatment outcome (Weissman et al. 1978), and certain chronic forms of personality disorder and social maladjustment appear to develop over the course of repeated depressive episodes (Akiskal et al. 1978; Cassano et al. 1983).
5. There may be a relationship between the type of depression and the interpersonal context. Endogenous depression tends to occur within the context of an intact relationship while episodes of neurotic depression are frequently precipitated by the breakup of a conjugal relationship (Matussek and Feil 1983).

Controlled Studies of Family Treatment

Despite the many studies done on efficacy of marital/family therapy (Gurman et al. 1986), there are only two controlled studies (and one partially controlled study) in which the identified patient suffers from affective disorder.

Friedman (1975) used a random-assignment, placebo-controlled, 12-week clinical trial to assess the relative effectiveness of amitriptyline and marital therapy, administered separately and in combination. Subjects were 196 patients with a primary diagnosis of depression (including 172 neurotic or reactive depression types, 15 with psychotic depressions, and nine with either manic-depressive psychosis or involutional psychotic reactions). Outcome was assessed in the areas of symptom severity, global improvement, family and marital relations, and attitudes toward medication. Results indicated that both drug and marital therapies had beneficial effects compared with their respective control treatments (placebo drug and minimal contact, individual therapy). Of particular interest, however, was evidence of some differential effects of these two major modes of treatment. Whereas drug therapy was associated with significant early improvement in clinical symptoms, marital therapy was associated with significant positive changes in patient self-report measures of family role behavior and marital relations.

McLean et al. (1973) used behavioral techniques to record and intervene in verbal interactions between couples, one member of which was clinically depressed. With a total n of 20, half of the couples were given feedback boxes designed to signal positive and negative feedback during ongoing conversation. Not only did the feedback procedure significantly reduce remarks considered negative, but couples in this intervention group showed significantly reduced negative interchanges while comparison group couples did not. The total behavioral treatment package—including the feedback procedure, training in the use of behavioral contracting, and social learning principles—produced significant improvement on target complaints for the experimental treatment group as compared with the nontreatment comparison group.

Glick et al. (1985) have assessed the incremental efficacy of hospitalization with inpatient family intervention (IFI) versus hospitalization without family intervention for patients diagnosed as having major affective disorder. Inpatient family intervention, of at least a six-session duration, is designed to 1) modify maladaptive family patterns associated with the problems of the identified patient, 2) facilitate family communication, and 3) promote more adaptive family role functioning and attitudes toward the identified patient.

Results at hospital discharge indicated that affective disorder patients treated with IFI were significantly better than control patients on measures of global outcome and symptomatology (Haas et al. 1988). This result was mostly attributable to the positive effect of IFI on the female affective disorder patients and their families. Results at six- and 18-month follow-ups (Clarkin et al., unpublished manuscript) indicated that IFI was differentially effective depending on the subdiagnosis of affective disorder. IFI was effective in producing changes (in symptomatology and role functioning) in bipolar patients and their families in comparison with control patients, while unipolar depressed patients and their families were better off with the control treatment.

There are several ongoing controlled studies of marital and family therapies for treatment of depression. Weissman and her group (at Yale) are in the process of assessing the relative efficacy of individual marital therapy as compared with conjoint marital therapy for women (outpatients) who present with depression and marital disputes. Jacobson (1987) is in the process of assessing the effectiveness of cognitive-behavioral marital treatment when one spouse is depressed. His preliminary data suggest that cognitive techniques as used in marital therapy are superior to individual therapy for depression when there is concurrent marital discord.

Treatment Planning

Linkages to Environment

There are a number of possible linkages between affective symptoms in the individual and the psychosocial environment (Haas et al. 1985). These can be summarized in terms of four primary linkage models:

1. Marital/family stressors may elicit or precipitate the onset of depressive symptoms in a biologically predisposed individual.
2. Marital/family stress or the lack of an intimate relationship may potentiate the effects of other environmental stressors, leading to a depressive episode in a biologically vulnerable individual.
3. Depressive symptoms in one family member may trigger negative response from other family members, thus acting to elicit marital/family conflict.
4. Subclinical depressive or characterological traits, behavior patterns, etc., in one or more family members may potentiate marital/family discord, which in turn triggers the onset of a depressive episode.

These four linkages, while different, could all lead to the conclusion that one should introduce family or marital treatment as a major or minor element in a treatment regimen, the timing of which would depend on the mediating goals of treatment. Linkage 1 would call for drug treatment concomitant with or followed by marital treatment. Linkage 3 would call for drug treatment followed by brief family intervention leading to equilibrium.

Indications for Family Intervention

The survey of the various linkages of affective disorder to the marital/family environment persuade us of the need for systematic assessment of affective symptoms/behaviors within the family context, specification of indications for family intervention, and formulation of mediating goals of family/marital therapy.

Indications for family/marital intervention with affective disorder follow the guidelines for family intervention in general (Frances et al. 1984; Glick et al. 1987): when a family member (child, adolescent, or adult) shows affective symptoms, a family evaluation should be done. However, when symptoms of affective disorder are present in one or more family members, the assessment process needs to be more specific. The focus of the interpersonal evaluation should be on assessment of the linkages (as described above) between the affective symptoms/behavior and the interpersonal context.

In many cases of depression, marital or family conflict is reported as the primary precipitant to the episode. In such cases, marital or family therapy may be used to reduce aversive communication, induce more frequent and optimal mutual support, and modify distorted cognitive and perceptual responses to the behavior of the partner. Antidepressant medication should be combined with this psychosocial intervention without compromising the effectiveness of either modality. In fact, they probably enhance each other.

In cases of endogenous depression, the stress of intimate relations with the depressed patient and the negative impact of the patient's symptoms on other members of the family (Targum et al. 1981) suggest the need for a biphasic treatment program. During the beginning phase of treatment, drug treatment is begun and short-term supportive marital or family therapy is used to ameliorate the family's negative reactions to the depressive symptoms and to educate the patient and family about the nature of the disorder. After the florid symptoms have cleared and the patient and family have reached a plateau or stable stage of adjustment, a second phase of family therapy can begin to modify maladaptive communication patterns.

There are cases in which marital or family conflict appears not to be a contributing factor in the depressive episode, and marital and family life goes back to normal following the episode. In such cases, the identified patient should be treated with appropriate medication and then reevaluated for psychotherapy. Short-term supportive marital and/or family therapy may be useful in helping to engage the patient in the recommended medication regimen.

Focus and Strategies of Family Intervention

The focus and strategies of the family/marital intervention when one individual has an affective disorder will depend on the specifics of the patient and the family environment. The review of the literature suggests several key areas for intervention with the marital/family system when affective disorder is involved:

Severity and Nature of the Affective Episodes

The severity of the affective disorder (indicated by the number and length of episodes, the psychotic versus nonpsychotic nature of symptoms, associated character pathology, and level of functioning between episodes) will be an important factor that determines the need for pharmacotherapy and the setting and timing of treatment. When affective symptoms appear as part of a well-circumscribed episode that begins and ends with dramatic changes in functioning (e.g., a clear bipolar manic episode), one might use psychoeducational approaches for patient and family.

Cognitive Factors

The specific cognitions and cognitive style of the depressed individual may be key in determining the focus of intervention. Assessment of the cognitive/attributional style of the spouse and intimate others can also yield important information regarding the interpersonal context of the affective disorder and functional characteristics of the patient's interpersonal world, which need be utilized or addressed in treatment.

Poor Social Skills

The inability to engage effectively in supportive social interaction and the failure to secure positive social reinforcements may be the central targets of intervention and skill building (e.g., behavioral marital therapy).

Hostile Interaction

The interactions of depressed individuals with their spouses are characterized by hostility and perceived criticism. Therapeutic strategies and techniques focused on reducing such behavior and increasing more supportive interchange have been recommended.

Lack of Intimacy

Research indicates that an intimate relationship is a strong buffer against depression. Moreover, the marriages of depressed individuals may be lacking in support, comfort, and other aspects of intimacy. Therapeutic techniques that assist in developing such intimacy are highly relevant to the alleviation of depression and the prevention of future episodes.

Stress and the Coping Process

The problem-solving skills and coping behavior of the depressive-prone individual might be an appropriate and necessary focus of intervention. In addition, the way in which the well spouse perceives and copes with the disorder needs to be assessed and addressed in treatment. More specifically, there must be some attention given to how the individuals in the family cope with the depressive and manic behaviors of the patient. For example, inpatient family intervention (IFI) for affective disorders focuses directly on educating and training the family and patient in coping with the symptoms.

Parenting Skills

Depression and bipolar disorder typically interfere with parenting functions. This can contribute to increased risk of psychiatric illness among the children of parent(s) with affective disorder. Family intervention can, in such cases, help the children cope with the effects of depressed "parenting time," which they might otherwise perceive as rejection.

Conclusion

In summary, we have reviewed models of family interaction and depression, controlled studies of family treatment, treatment planning, and indications for family intervention. We believe the available evidence is not definitive but strongly suggests that the treatment of choice for most forms of depression associated with interpersonal distress is a *combination* of drug treatment and marital/family therapy. How these treatments are sequenced and combined and for which diagnostic subtypes await further research.

Chapter 174

Light Therapy

Although it is only in the past five years that light treatment (phototherapy) for depression has attracted widespread interest, the concept of light as a therapeutic agent is by no means a new one. Even before the development of the drugs that are the mainstay of biologic treatments of depression and other psychiatric ailments, the quality of environmental light was considered to be important for an individual's welfare, along with proper nutrition, fresh air, and sufficient rest. The use of light baths was commonplace in Europe in the early decades of this century, and books were devoted to the subject (Humphris 1924; Kovacs 1932). However, there are important distinctions between these light baths and the phototherapy that has been the focus of recent therapeutic attention. First, descriptions of these earlier light baths indicate that the body was bathed in light while the face was shielded from it; second, ultraviolet light was regarded as an important therapeutic ingredient; and finally, the proponents of this treatment claimed it was helpful for many different conditions. In contrast, phototherapy, as it has been used in the past few years, has involved exposing the eyes to light containing very little ultraviolet light in patients suffering from specific conditions.

Most of the reseach in phototherapy has been confined to patients suffering from seasonal affective disorder (SAD), a condition characterized by recurrent fall and winter depressions alternating with nondepressed periods in spring and summer (Rosenthal et al. 1984). There have also been a few reports on phototherapy in non-seasonal depression (Kripke 1985, 1988; Kripke et al. 1986; Yerevanian et al. 1986), and some papers have suggested that light may also be beneficial in treating jet lag and other abnormalities of circadian rhythms (Daan and Lewy 1984; Eastman 1988; Joseph-Vanderpool et al. 1988; Lewy et al. 1983, 1984). By way of giving due historical credit, it should be noted that Esquirol, one of the earliest clinicians to describe a patient with a syndrome resembling SAD, effectively treated the patient by recommending that he winter in sunny Italy instead of Belgium (Esquirol 1845). Later in the 19th century, an insightful ship's doctor observed that his crew became lethargic in the dark days of an arctic winter, and he treated their languor with bright artificial light (Jefferson 1986).

Lewy et al. (1980) made an important observation that ushered in the modern use of phototherapy—namely, that nocturnal human melatonin secretion could be suppressed by exposing subjects to bright artificial light but not to light of ordinary indoor intensity. It has been shown that melatonin in animals is secreted nocturnally by the pineal gland in a circadian rhythm generated by the suprachiasmatic nuclei of the hypothalamus. Light rays impinging on the retina are converted into nerve impulses, which influence the secretion of melatonin by connections between the retina and the hypothalamus (Tamarkin et al. 1985). This demonstration that one physiologic effect of light in humans, transmitted presumably via the hypothalamus, has a threshold intensity far higher than that required for vision, suggested that there might be other effects of light on the brain that require high-intensity light.

The Syndrome of Seasonal Affective Disorder (SAD)

The cardinal criteria for SAD, as outlined by Rosenthal et al. (1984), are 1) a history of at least one episode of major depression, as defined by the Research Diagnostic Criteria (Spitzer et al. 1978); 2) recurrent fall–winter depressions, at least two of which occurred during successive years, separated by nondepressed periods in spring and summer; and 3) no other DSM-III (American Psychiatric Association 1980) Axis I psychopathology. These criteria have been modified and included in DSM-III-R (American Psychiatric Association 1987) as "seasonal pattern," a descriptor that may qualify any recurrent mood disorder.

Defined by the above criteria, most patients with SAD have been women with an onset of the condition in the early twenties. Besides showing the usual affective and cognitive features of depression, their winters are also generally characterized by atypical vegetative symptoms: overeating, oversleeping, carbohydrate craving, and weight gain; fatigue and social withdrawal are also prominent features. Since these symptoms are not suitably represented by the Hamilton Depression Scale (Hamilton 1967), it has been suggested that supplementary items be added to this scale to measure adequately the extent of the symptoms in this condition (Rosenthal and Heffernan 1985). Some researchers have found that most SAD patients report a history of hypomania during spring and summer (Rosenthal et al. 1984) whereas others have observed a recurrent unipolar pattern, with euthymia in spring and summer (Yerevanian et al. 1986).

Many patients with SAD report a marked responsiveness to changes in climate, latitude, and lighting conditions. Thus, many have noted improvement in depressive symptoms following moves to warmer, sunnier climates and latitudes closer to the equator. Similarly, patients may respond favorably to an improvement in the weather or to being moved from a windowless office to one with a window. Conversely, deterioration in mood and energy levels is often observed when the amount of environmental light is reduced.

Although the above description is typical for SAD, many variations are seen. For example, the symptom pattern may more closely resemble that seen in endogenous depression. A variant of SAD has been reported to occur in children and adolescents; this variant appears to respond to phototherapy (Rosenthal et al. 1986). A milder version of SAD with prominent atypical vegetative features but without the affective cognitive or affective symptoms has also been observed. This has been called atypical SAD (Rosenthal et al. 1985), seasonal energy syndrome (Mueller and Davies 1986), or subsyndromal SAD (Kasper et al., in press), and it also appears to respond to light (Kasper et al., in press; Rosenthal et al. 1985). A winter condition of disrupted sleep without affective symptoms has been reported to occur in Norway, where it has been termed *midwinter insomnia* and has been shown to improve after treatment with bright light in the morning (Lingjaerde et al. 1986).

Seasonal depressions may occur on a regular basis at other times of the year. For example, regularly occurring summer depression has been described by Wehr et al. (1987) and by Boyce and Parker (1988). There have not as yet been any tests of the efficacy of phototherapy in such summer depression.

The Efficacy of Phototherapy in SAD

Following effective bright light treatment of a single patient with recurrent winter depressions (Lewy et al. 1982), several research groups have undertaken controlled treatment studies of phototherapy in patients with SAD. Researchers have sought both to establish the efficacy of the treatment and to find out which parameters are important for obtaining a treatment response. Most researchers have used crossover designs in which each patient has been exposed both to the treatment condition presumed to be active and to an alternate (control) treatment condition in a random-ordered fashion. Using such a design, phototherapy has been found to be effective in six studies by the NIMH group (Jacobsen et al. 1986; James et al. 1985; Rosenthal et al. 1984, 1985; Wehr et al. 1986a, 1986b), two studies by Lewy et al. in Oregon (1987a, 1987b), two studies by Wirz-Justice et al. in Switzerland (1986), and studies by Hellekson et al. in Alaska (1986), Terman et al. in New York City (1987), and Isaacs et al. (1988) and Checkley et al. (1986), both in London.

Since so many groups have by now replicated the basic finding that bright artificial light has antidepressant effects in SAD and there have not to date been any studies to the contrary, it has now been generally accepted that phototherapy is a viable treatment for the condition. However, those properties of phototherapy that are necessary or optimal for achieving an antidepressant effect continue to be a focus of interest and research (Rosenthal et al., in press). There is a consensus that intensity of light is important and that bright light (2,500 lux) has been found to be superior to dimmer light (400 lux or less) in several studies (Checkley et al. 1986; Isaacs et al. 1988; Lewy et al. 1982, 1987b; Rosenthal et al. 1984, 1986). Terman et al. (1987) have suggested that even brighter light (10,000 lux) may be superior to the conventional 2,500 lux (Terman, in press), but the use of such bright light remains experimental at this time.

Optimal timing of light treatment has been somewhat more controversial. It appears as though two hours of light treatment in the morning may be more effective than two hours in the evening (Lewy et al. 1987a, in press; Rosenthal et al. in press; Terman et al. 1987; Terman et al., in press). However, other studies have shown that light treatment may be quite effective if administered only in the evening (Hellekson et al. 1986; James et al. 1985; Rosenthal et al., in press; Wehr et al., in press) or even during the day (Isaacs et al. 1988; Jacobsen et al. in press; Wehr et al. 1986a). A cross-center analysis supports the findings that morning light treatments are superior to evening treatments though certain individuals respond to the latter (Terman, in press). Although early studies used five to six hours of light per day, more recent studies suggest that two hours of treatment per day may be effective (Lewy et al. 1987b; Terman et al. 1987; Wirz-Justice et al. 1986). In some cases, as little as 30 minutes of light in the morning have been reported to be effective (Lewy et al. 1987b). However, there does seem to be some relationship between duration and efficacy, with greater effects occurring as duration is increased (Terman et al. 1987; Wirz-Justice et al. 1986).

Although most studies have used full-spectrum light, it is unclear exactly what spectral properties are necessary to achieve an antidepressant effect and whether full-spectrum lighting provides any advantages. Only one study has thus far addressed the necessary route of administration of effective light therapy, which appears to be the eye rather than the skin (Wehr et al. 1986b).

Practical Considerations in Phototherapy

We have not yet been using phototherapy for long enough to outline definitively the best way of administering it. The method outlined below represents the combined experience of several different centers.

The light source most frequently used has been full-spectrum fluorescent light (Vitalite®). However, other, less expensive full-spectrum fluorescent lamps are available. Six Powertwist® or eight regular 40-watt tubes are inserted into a rectangular metal fixture, approximately two by four feet, with a reflecting surface behind them and a plastic diffusing screen in front. Smaller, more convenient fixtures are currently being marketed, but studies comparing the efficacy of different fixtures are lacking. Patients are asked to place the box at eye level, either horizontally on a desk or table or vertically on the floor, and to sit approximately three feet away from it in such a way as to expose their eyes to the lights. The intensity resulting from this setup is 2,500 lux, the amount of light to which one would be exposed by looking out of a window on a spring day in the northeastern United States. This is five to 10 times brighter than ordinary room lighting. We do not know whether it is necessary for patients to glance directly at the lights intermittently, as they have usually been asked to do, since we do not know where the relevant photoreceptors are in the retina. Indeed, only recently has it been shown that the effects of phototherapy are probably mediated by the eye and not the skin in most cases (Wehr et al. 1986b). If the relevant photoreceptors are the rods on the periphery of the retina, it may be unnecessary for patients to glance at the lights directly at all. It is certainly unnecessary, and probably inadvisable, for patients to stare continuously at the lights.

In treating a patient with SAD, the initial suggestion for timing and duration of treatment is a matter of clinical judgment; since it does not appear that timing is crucial for obtaining an effect in many patients, some clinicians initially recommend times that are convenient for the patient. An alternative approach would be to begin with light treatments in the morning, which produces optimal effects in many patients. An initial dose of two to four hours per day seems reasonable. In fact, there is some evidence that an extra two hours of treatment in the evening does not enhance the response of two-hour treatment sessions in the morning. The clinician should feel free to titrate the dosage up or down, depending on the patient's response after one week of treatment. When a response occurs, it is almost always apparent within the first four days (Rosenthal et al. 1985). If no response occurs within the first week, one can either increase the duration or alter the timing. It is critical at this point to check that the patient is complying with all aspects of treatment. Treatment may be given in conjunction with antidepressant medications, an approach that may enable the patient to be treated with a lower dosage of medication or may convert a partial light responder into a complete responder.

The technology of phototherapy is in its infancy. Although most researchers have used light fixtures similar to that described above, Yerevanian et al. (1986) have described clinical success in nine SAD patients treated with indirect incandescent light exposure. As noted above, Terman et al. (in press) have reported superior results with fixtures delivering higher lighting intensities. Other lighting delivery systems are currently being developed in an attempt to make treatment more effective and convenient.

Side Effects of Phototherapy

Although side effects are uncommon, patients sometimes complain of irritability (of the kind seen in hypomania), eyestrain, headaches, or insomnia. The latter is most likely to occur when patients use lights late at night. Side effects can generally be reversed easily by decreasing the duration of treatments or suggesting that patients sit further from the light source. In a few cases, however, treatment may have to be discontinued altogether because of severe eye irritation. Although hypomanic responses have been observed in several cases, very few cases of florid mania following phototherapy in any typical SAD patients have been noted to date. Thus far, there have been no reports of any long-term adverse effects of phototherapy when properly administered.

Mechanism of Action of Phototherapy in SAD

The mechanism of action of the antidepressant effects of SAD is not known. Rosenthal et al. (1986) suggested that bright light might exert its antidepressant effects by the suppression of melatonin secretion. However, they went on to show in a series of studies that this mechanism is probably not of central importance in most cases. Lewy et al. (1987a) have suggested that light exerts its antidepressant effects by means of its circadian phase-shifting properties, a theory that continues to be actively explored. It appears as though certain individuals have a neurochemical vulnerability (perhaps genetically determined), which, in the absence of adequate environmental light exposure, produces the behavioral changes seen in SAD. Bright light, probably acting via the eye and presumably via retino-hypothalamic projections, appears capable of reversing this biochemical abnormality if the light is of high enough intensity and is used regularly and for sufficient duration.

It should be noted that bright light has been shown to be capable of producing changes in the P300 component of the visual event-related potential (Duncan et al., unpublished manuscript), in the increase in plasma norepinephrine seen when a patient stands up (Skwerer et al. 1987), and in peripheral lymphocyte function, as measured by in vitro exposure of patients' lymphocytes to a variety of mitogens (Skwerer et al. 1987). Whether these observed biologic changes have any relationship to the antidepressant effects of light remains to be seen.

Treatment of Nonseasonal Affective Disorder

Studies on the effects of phototherapy in nonseasonal depressives have been conducted by Kripke (1985, 1988), Kripke et al. (1986), and Yerevanian et al. (1986). Although recent data by Kripke et al. (1986) appear encouraging, the efficacy of phototherapy in this group is far less clear than it is in patients with SAD, and further studies are required before bright light can be recommended clinically for nonseasonal depressives.

Therapeutic Use of the Phase-shifting Effects of Light

The timing of environmental light and dark is well known to be an important circadian time cue (zeitgeber) in many animal species (Rusak and Boulos 1981). Wever and Aschoff, however, in their pioneering studies of humans in environmentally isolated conditions, concluded that light cues are weak zeitgebers in humans (Wever 1979). Czeisler et al. (1981) subsequently showed that light and dark cycles were sufficient to entrain environmentally isolated humans, and Lewy et al. (1984) suggested that bright artificial light might indeed be a more powerful zeitgeber than the light of lower intensity used by Wever in his earlier studies. Wever later used bright artificial light in free-running human subjects and found that it was indeed a far more powerful zeitgeber than his earlier studies had led him to believe (Wever 1979). Since then, Czeisler et al. (1986) have shown bright artificial light capable of shifting circadian rhythms in a single subject. Lewy et al. (1987a) have shown that bright light is capable of shifting the timing of circadian rhythms, as measured by 24-hour temperature minima and the timing of onset of melatonin secretion when subjects are kept in dim light. They have suggested that this shifting function may be therapeutically beneficial in depression and disorders of circadian timekeeping (Lewy et al. 1984). In a study of one patient with a temporary disorganization of circadian functioning, namely jet lag, Lewy and Daan (1984) showed that judiciously timed bright light exposure appeared to ameliorate the jet-lag symptoms.

In animals, light stimuli are capable of shifting the timing of circadian rhythms either earlier or later to different degrees, depending on when the light stimulus occurs in the course of the animal's daily rhythms. The relationship between the timing of the light stimulus and the resulting direction and extent of shift of circadian rhythms is known as the animal's phase response curve to light (Pittendrigh 1981). This characteristic biologic functioning has been observed in many different species and appears to conform to certain rules. In general, light stimuli occurring late in the animal's subjective night (its inactive period) tend to shift the animal's rhythms earlier. Conversely, light stimuli occurring early in the animal's subjective night tend to shift its rhythms later. These basic principles would need to be borne in mind in evaluating the effects of bright light on human circadian rhythms.

Preliminary results from a study of patients with delayed sleep phase syndrome suggest that bright light in the morning, combined with dim light in the evening, may be beneficial in normalizing the sleep-wake schedule of these chronic "night-owls" (Joseph-Vanderpool et al. 1988). Similarly, Eastman (1988) has suggested that bright light, timed appropriately, may be helpful to those suffering the adverse effects of shift-work.

Conclusion

In summary, phototherapy (treatment by means of bright artificial light) has been shown to be effective in SAD, where it is a viable clinical treatment and, in many cases, the treatment of choice. The efficacy of phototherapy has not as yet been established in nonseasonal depression, and further research is required before it can be generally recommended for this condition. It seems probable that bright artificial light is capable of shifting the timing of circadian rhythms in humans, which may be helpful in conditions of abnormal circadian rhythms, be they acute, as in jet lag and shift-workers, or chronic, as in delayed sleep phase syndrome.

Chapter 175

Psychosurgery

It has been estimated that 40,000 prefrontal lobotomies were done in the United States from the late 1930s through the 1950s. The number of procedures performed dropped precipitously with reports of undesirable side effects and the introduction of psychoactive drugs. Unfortunately, most of these procedures were done during what might be thought of as the prescientific era in psychiatry. Although there are case reports and even series reports, there was little systematic collection and analysis of outcome data. Interest in psychosurgery was aroused again in the early 1970s, in part by the possible political implications of such procedures, which resulted in a report and recommendations concerning the use of psychosurgery by the National Commission for the Protection of Human Subjects of Biomedical and Behavioral Research (1977).

The commission contracted for a retrospective evaluation of psychosurgical patients, as well as for acceleration and expansion of an independent study that was, at least in part, prospective with the patients seen preoperatively as well as postoperatively.

The retrospective evaluation studied 27 people who received surgery and a group of eight unoperated controls with similar psychiatric illness. "The primary symptoms of the majority of patients included depression or affective illness, obsessive-compulsive behaviors, phobias, acute anxiety, and chronic pain. These symptoms were usually presented in varying combinations and were accompanied in some cases by a diagnosis of schizophrenia. The patients . . . had had their symptoms on the average of 17 to 20 years and had received a large variety of other psychiatric therapies (usually with little or no lasting benefit) before undergoing surgery." (National Commission for the Protection of Human Subjects of Biomedical and Behavioral Research pp. II-41 and -42) Evaluation by a team, including psychiatrists, psychologists and neurologists, on the basis of a report by patient and other informant, and supported by the results of independent psychiatric and sociologic evaluations, led the authors to conclude: Fourteen of the cases were judged to have had a very favorable outcome unaccompanied by detectable neurological deficit. The remaining 13 had less favorable outcomes, but again without significant evidence of neurological deficit attributable to the operation. "The results suggested that the symptom of depression was especially amenable to psychosurgery in these patients, and that the greatest change in those with very favorable outcomes was with that symptom." "Furthermore, there was no evidence of over-all cognitive and intellectual deficit attributable to the psychosurgery, although this is difficult to assess considering the distressed state of the patients prior to surgery."

The other study examined 34 cases treated with cingulotomy. Eighteen of these cases were seen both before and after surgical intervention. Of the subgroup of seven patients who complained primarily of depression, five gave convincing reports of either full or partial relief whereas two cases with long-standing unipolar depression thought they had not been helped. "In at least 3 cases circumstances point at (p. III-5) the strong possibility that the patients would have succeeded in commiting suicide without a therapeutic intervention." "All 7 cases had been consistently refractory to ECT and heavy medication with a great variety of agents had not produced enough relief." In all, the operations were elected as a measure of last resort.

The commission's recommendations stated that psychosurgery should continue to be performed within a variety of constraints in order to ensure appropriate ethical review, informed consent, technical ability of the surgeon, and reasonable expectation of benefit. A statement in the *British Journal of Psychiatry* (Bartlett et al. 1981) also suggests that modern, more limited stereotactic surgery is appropriate for depression of the endogenous type, chronic or persistently recurrent with a limited or absent response to routine therapies. They further state, however, that patients with pronounced hysterical or antisocial personalities do not do well even if the presenting symptoms are appropriate.

Chapter 176

Secondary Depressions

The Development of the Concept of Secondary Depression

Secondary depressions are generally defined by their sequential relationship to other significant psychiatric or medical disorders. The idea of depressions consequent to other illness is not new. Bleuler (1950), for example, states: "The melancholic symptom triad of depressive affect, inhibition of thinking, and of action, is one of the most frequent acute disturbances in schizophrenia. . . . The schizophrenic depression has all the various characteristics which we have come to know in other diseases: simple, painful feelings and emotions independent of events; anxiety mounting to panic; more rarely crying, but often loud screaming and desperate lamentations; and finally, depressive inhibition up to complete immobility." During the 1950s and 1960s, the distinction between primary and secondary depressive illness was reinforced in the attempt by investigators to separate homogeneous groups for study. In what is usually considered the first published specific reference, Munro (1966) writes: "Only patients suffering from primary depressive illness (i.e., with no previous history of psychiatric disorder apart from affective illness or cyclothymic personality) were investigated, so as to reduce extraneous psychopathologic factors to a minimum." Even earlier, the group centered at Washington University were thinking, talking, and teaching the distinction between primary and secondary depression, with secondary depression defined in temporal terms as a depression following other psychiatric illness: alcohol or substance abuse, schizophrenia, and various neuroses (Clayton 1981).

Depression related to other medical illness, and sometimes to prescribed medication, had also been described. Yaskin (1931) had already noted in 1931 that in some instances depression was the earliest manifestation of carcinoma of the pancreas. In the 1950s, the role of rauwolfia compounds in the onset of depression was widely discussed (Muller et al. 1955), and in the years since, the term *secondary depression* has been expanded to include these medical and iatrogenic linkages.

The Purpose of Discriminating Secondary from Primary Depression

Studies of a wide variety of secondary depressions have demonstrated that the symptom patterns of both primary and secondary depressions are often similar, if not identical (Akiskal et al. 1979; Andreasen and Winokur 1979; Weissman et al. 1977). The original distinction between primary and secondary depression was temporal, derived from the sequence of onset. The goal was to isolate a group of depressive illnesses that were "purer" and, therefore, more suitable for some kinds of research and more likely to provide answers in treatment outcome studies. It was psychiatry's equivalent to distinguishing pneumococcal from tuberculous pneumonias for the evaluation of penicillin. It is clear that what have been labeled secondary depressions are necessarily the remaining heterogeneous group, representing a panoply of diagnostic and treatment issues.

Etiologic Relationships Between Primary Disorders and Secondary Depression

We cannot assume a causal link between the primary illness and the secondary depression in the absence of specific data. Some secondary depressions may indeed be causally linked to the primary illness. This linkage may be either biologic or psychological. It is reasonable to assume that at least some illnesses and medications affect neurotransmitters in ways parallel to whatever the biologic processes are that may exist in primary depression. A particular illness may also have particular psychological significance for an individual and understandably precipitate a depressive response.

It is important to recognize that most of the evidence for secondary depression is based on symptom lists rather than on full syndromal descriptions. There may be widely differing origins for many symptoms. For example, fatigue and lassitude may be the direct result of debilitating disease, yet they may be mistakenly experienced as or attributed to depression. This may more appropriately be called "pseudo-depression." Conversely, there are times when people have more than one disease, and the heuristic advantages of isolating secondary depression may at times obscure individual instances when a secondary depression is in no way different from primary depression. At least on occasion, secondary depression is merely the occurrence of a depression in somebody with another preexistent disease. Additionally, a review by Kathol and Petty (1981) of the relationship of depression to medical illness indicates that diseases in the medical specialties of endocrinology, neurology, cardiology, and gastroenterology appear to be increased in patients with depression, with a suggestion of a causal relationship of uncertain etiology.

Secondary depression appears to be a common phenomenon, occurring in perhaps 25 percent of medical inpatients and similar numbers of schizophrenics. Nevertheless, there have been remarkably few studies of the treatment of secondary depressions. Those studies that have been reported are often preliminary in nature, with small sample sizes and uncontrolled variables that could potentially influence outcome. A program of well-designed research on the efficacy of antidepressants and other approaches to the treatment of secondary depression is clearly indicated. For purposes of this chapter, the data available will be separated into the treatment of depression secondary to medical illness and medication, followed by the treatment of depression secondary to psychiatric illness.

Depression Secondary to Medical Illness: An Overview of Diagnostic and Treatment Issues

Diagnosis and treatment of secondary depression in the medically ill patient present a unique challenge to clinicians and researchers because the symptoms of depression and medical illness often are similar and overlapping. For example, the standard vegetative symptoms of depression, insomnia, anorexia with weight loss, retardation, and lethargy have diminished diagnostic potency in the medically ill patient whose medical illness or somatic therapy may produce these same symptoms. Conversely, chronic pain and other somatic complaints without organic etiology may be manifestations of a "masked" depression but inaccurately attributed to a medical illness. In addition, depression may result from medical illness or its treatment. Correction of the depressogenic medical disorder or medication may not resolve the depression, which then merits psychiatric intervention. Treatment of depression in the medically ill may be complicated by medical contraindications to somatic therapies, drug interaction effects, altered pharmacokinetics, or the necessary treatment of a medical illness with depressogenic agents.

Estimates of the prevalence of depressive symptoms in a medically ill population range from 11 percent to 50 percent, depending on the diagnostic criteria used and the type of medical disorder studied (Bukberg et al. 1984; Cassem and Hackett 1977; Cavanaugh 1983; Derogatis et al. 1983; Maguire et al. 1974; Moffic and Paykel 1975; Nielsen and Williams 1980; Salkind 1969; Schwab et al. 1967; Stern et al. 1977; Stewart et al. 1965). A follow-up study of depressed medical patients reported that 72 percent were still depressed at the time of discharge (Moffic and Paykel 1975), and more than 70 percent of a postmyocardial infarction sample were depressed at follow-up one year later (Stern et al. 1977).

Depression in the medically ill patient has the same implications for increased morbidity and mortality as it does for the medically healthy patient (Farberow et al. 1971), with some researchers reporting that the presence of medical illness in the depressed patient increases the risk of suicide (Abram et al. 1971; Dorpat et al. 1968). In addition, there may be the more subtle self-destructive complications of noncompliance with or refusal of medical treatment (Rodin et al. 1981) and other behavior and attitudes that affect the patient's ability to participate in his own recovery. Therefore, accurate diagnosis and efficacious treatment of depression in the medically ill patient is of critical importance but is complicated by a lack of effective diagnostic criteria and established treatment guidelines.

Methodological issues in studies involving the diagnosis and treatment of depression in medically ill patients are summarized by Rodin and Voshart (1986). These include 1) the absence of assessment measures that have been standardized on medically ill patients; 2) the variability within a medical diagnostic group, including the organ systems affected, metabolic abnormalities present, dose and nature of medication, and degree of disability; 3) the absence of appropriate control groups; 4) the unwillingness of some patients to report symptoms of depression; 5) the nonspecific diagnostic significance of depressive symptoms that may be transient or that do not reflect a depressive syndrome; and 6) false negative diagnoses that occur when pain or somatization are the chief manifestations of the depression but are incorrectly attributed to a physical illness.

Physically ill depressed patients may meet the DSM-III-R (American Psychiatric Association 1987) criteria for the various mood disorders, schizoaffective disorder, adjustment disorder with depressed mood, or organic mood syndrome, including the psychoactive substance mood disorder. Cognitive affective symptoms have generally been found more discriminatory for depression than vegetative symptoms in a medically ill population (Bukberg et al. 1984; Cavanaugh 1983; Cavanaugh et al. 1983; Clark et al. 1983); this is particularly true of a sad or dysphoric mood and anhedonia that do not respond to treatment of the underlying medical conditions. Elements of the depressed mood may include suicidal ideation, a sense of failure, a feeling of being punished, diminished social interest, crying, indecision, and dissatisfaction (Clark et al. 1983). Somatic symptoms such as anorexia, weight loss, sleep disturbance, retardation, and fatigue may be used to support a diagnosis of depression if they are severe, unresponsive to medical treatment, out of proportion to the medical illness, and temporally related to the affective-cognitive symptoms. Additional symptoms may include pain and hypochondriacal complaints, irritability, noncompliance with or refusal of treatment by patients who have previously been compliant, and impaired cognitive functions, such as concentration and memory.

Family history of affective disorders, the past psychiatric history of the patient, and information about predisposing personality pathology may also prove diagnostically valuable—for example, a patient with narcissistic personality disorder may be less able to tolerate loss of appearance or functioning. Similarly, a patient with compulsive personality disorder may have trouble accommodating the changes and loss of control a medical illness may impose. Loss, broadly interpreted, is frequently linked to the onset of depression, and it may therefore be important to establish what the physical illness represents to the patient and whether a sense of loss is present. An assessment of the presence or absence of psychosocial stressors and social supports and of the level of the patient's premorbid coping resources may lend support to a diagnosis of depression, and may also identify areas for intervention once a diagnosis is established.

Depression has been reported in conjunction with most medical conditions (Hall 1980; Klerman, in press). Illnesses that involve endocrine and metabolic disturbances, infections, central nervous system (CNS) lesions, cancer, or drug toxicity may have a causal relationship to the depression, which may or may not clear when the underlying condition is adequately treated. Other medical conditions may not have a biologic depressogenic effect but may precipitate a depression due to an impaired sense of body integrity, social constraints, professional liabilities, etc.

Treatment of depressed medical patients has been underresearched because of the routine exclusion of patients with significant medical illness from antidepressant efficacy trials. Researchers working within the domain of a specific illness have begun to generate data describing treatment of depression in patients with that specific medical illness. Sample sizes are often small and intervening variables poorly controlled due to the difficulty of collecting data from a sufficient number of depressed subjects with the specific illness. Diagnostic and treatment considerations relevant to a specific illness—for example, the cardiotoxicity of tricyclics when treating cardiac patients—make it important to study patients with specific medical disorders. One solution may be a multicenter collaborative study, based on an NIMH model, that combines subjects from a number of sites into a data pool of sufficient size to conduct well-controlled research into the treatment of depression for patients with specific medical disorders. In the interim, a clinical rationale for using one antidepressant rather than another when a specific physical disorder or drug treatment is present has been developed by Fava and Sonino (1987). A summary of medical conditions frequently associated with high risk for affective disorder is presented in Table 1.

In the following sections, I will review reports of treatment of depression in medically ill patients, and I will group these studies into the categories of depression secondary to chronic pain, cancer, AIDS, cardiac disease, endocrine disorders, neurologic disorders, and prescribed medications. A related section on depression secondary to psychiatric disorders, including eating disorders, alcoholism, drug addiction, and schizophrenia, will follow.

Chronic Pain

Nearly 30 years ago, George Engel identified the pain-prone patient as suffering from chronic pain in the absence of a significant related somatic disorder and described the etiology as primarily psychological (Engel 1959). The DSM-III-R includes the category of somatoform pain disorder to describe severe and prolonged pain in the absence of plausible organic pathology. Despite the recognition of the syndrome, chronic pain remains underdiagnosed, and effective treatment strategies are still evolving. A federal study estimates that chronic pain accounts for 700 million lost work days annually in the United States and costs $65 billion for treatment, com-

Table 1. Medical Conditions Frequently Associated with Higher Risk for Affective Disorder

1. Endocrine causes
   a. Acromegaly
   b. Hyperadrenalism
   c. Hypoadrenalism
   d. Hyperinsulinism secondary to insulinoma
   e. Hyperparathyroidism
   f. Hypoparathyroidism
   g. Hypopituitarism
   h. Hyperthyroidism
   i. Hypothyroidism
   j. Inappropriate antidiuretic hormone (ADH) secretion

2. Vitamin and mineral disorders
   a. Beri-beri (Vitamin B_1 deficiency)
   b. Hypervitaminosis A
   c. Hypomagnesemia
   d. Pellagra (nicotinic acid deficiency)
   e. Pernicious anemia (Vitamin B_{12} deficiency)
   f. Wernicke encephalopathy

3. Infections
   a. Encephalitis
   b. Hepatitis
   c. Influenza
   d. Malaria
   e. Mononucleosis
   f. Pneumonia
   g. Syphilis
   h. Tuberculosis

4. Neurologic disorders
   a. Multiple sclerosis
   b. Tuberous sclerosis
   c. Wilson disease

5. Collagen disorders
   a. Systemic lupus erythematosus
   b. Polyarteritis nodosa

6. Cardiovascular disease
   a. Cardiomyopathy
   b. Cerebral ischemia
      i. Hypotension of cardiac origin
      ii. Cerebral arteriosclerosis
      iii. Cerebral embolization
   c. Congestive heart failure
   d. Myocardial infarction

7. Malignancy
   a. Carcinoid malignancy
   b. Pancreatic carcinoma
   c. Pheochromocytoma

8. Metabolic disorders
   a. Porphyria

Note. From *Antidepressant Treatment* by J. Griest and T. Griest. 1979. Baltimore: Williams & Wilkins. Reprinted by permission.

pensation, and litigation (Bonica 1981). Many patients who meet criteria for somatoform pain disorder elude diagnosis because they are unwilling to accept that their chronic pain is primarily psychological in origin and are therefore likely to seek out doctors with a somatic focus. The result is often unnecessary surgery, abuse of or addiction to prescribed medications, continued suffering, diminished personal and occupational functioning, and reinforcement of the sick role.

Many contemporary workers in the field of chronic pain emphasize the relationship of depression to the chronic pain syndrome. Swanson (1984) describes both depression and nonprogressive chronic pain as states of anguish without appropriate external cause that have neurochemical correlates, similar treatments, similar effects of chronicity, and an overlap in their clinical manifestations. Conversely, some investigators, using standardized instruments and DSM III (American Psychiatric Association 1980) criteria to diagnose depression in patients with chronic pain, caution against routinely equating chronic pain with depression (France et al. 1984; Keefe et al. 1984; Reich et al. 1983). However, the validity of using standardized depression rating scales and diagnostic instruments not normed for a population often associated with alexithymia has yet to be established.

Blumer and his group (Blumer 1982; Blumer and Heilbronn 1984; Winokur et al. 1978) studied over 1,000 patients with chronic pain who had no significant related somatic disorder. Blumer views chronic pain as a specific psychobiologic variant of depressive disease and calls it the pain prone disorder, in keeping with Engel's original description of the syndrome. Most of the patients studied had been in constant pain that began at midlife and lasted an average of 6.5 years. The disorder was more prevalent in females and blue-collar workers although all socioeconomic levels were represented. The patients were somatically preoccupied despite recurrent negative examinations, and many desired a surgical solution. They denied conflicts, idealized their role at work and in the family, and tended to be alexithymic. Their premorbid history of excessive work performance reversed dramatically following the onset of pain, and anhedonia, anergia, insomnia, helplessness, and decreased libido became prevalent. Their suffering was experienced physically more than mentally, and one-third of Blumer's patients strongly denied a depressed mood although many would admit despair in relation to the pain. The family histories of these patients had a high incidence of unipolar depression and alcoholism as well as pain prone disorder, suggesting that pain prone disorder may be a depressive spectrum disorder (Winokur et al. 1978).

Additional support for the view of pain prone disorder as a variant of depressive disease comes from biologic marker studies of samples of Blumer's patients. Nonsuppression on the dexamethasone suppression test (DST) occurred in 40 percent of the sample studied, and 40 percent had an abnormally short REM latency. Postdexamethasone cortisol levels correlated significantly with REM latency, and both predicted response to tricyclic antidepressants. Atkinson et al. (1983) replicated the findings of a positive family history of affective disorder, alcoholism, and chronic pain in a small sample of chronic pain patients, and also obtained high levels of nonsuppression on the DST and high concentrations of plasma B-endorphin/B-lipotropin-like immune reactivity.

Potential support of Blumer's view of pain prone disorder as a variant of depressive disease comes from the finding that 89 percent of 391 of the patients in his study who were available for follow-up responded to treatment with tricyclic antidepressants with a significant improvement of pain and depressive symptoms for a minimum duration of three months (Blumer 1982; Blumer and Heilbronn 1984; Blumer et al. 1984). Nonresponders tended to be less compliant and complained of more side effects. Blumer reports a 65 pecent dropout rate that was independent of response status, and he interprets this as documentation of the bias pain prone disorder patients have against psychiatric treatment, even when their pain returns.

Blumer et al. (1984) recommend a sedative-type antidepressant, such as amitriptyline (AMI), doxepin, or maprotiline for patients with insomnia and imipramine or desipramine for patients without sleep disorders. Blumer finds monoamine oxidase (MAO) inhibitors to be ineffective. Daily doses of antidepressant begin at 25 mg twice daily and increase daily in 25 mg increments to 50 mg three times per day, with doses reduced by one-third in patients over 60. Further increases are only prescribed if necessary, after three to four weeks of therapy and in stepwise increments to a maximum of 300 mg daily. If the maximum dose of antidepressant is determined to be ineffective, combination therapy is implemented, using one-half or less of the maximum antidepressant dose and either lithium carbonate brought to a therapeutic level or low doses of a neuroleptic—for example, 30 mg amitriptyline to 1 mg trifluoperazine, up to 150 mg amitriptyline to 5 mg trifluoperazine. Blumer recommends that the lithium be prescribed in two or three daily doses and the antidepressant medication be taken at bedtime, although anxious patients may also benefit from divided doses of the latter. Blumer describes the necessity of educating the patient and significant others about the side effects and time course of response to antidepressants, and of preparing the patient to continue treatment for many months. The pain must be deemphasized while activity is encouraged, with the goal being the resumption of a life-style not centered around the pain. Once the pain has subsided and the patient has found a more meaningful role in life, the medication may be phased out although some patients may require maintenance treatment.

Walsh (1983) and Blackwell et al. (1984) emphasize the importance of using antidepressants that act selectively on serotonin metabolism (e.g., amitriptyline or trazodone) since serotonin pathways appear important in pain mediation. Blackwell points out that the patient is better able to engage in rehabilitation when sleep is restored and fatigue is diminished, and that the increased activity and sense of accomplishment are also likely to enhance mood.

Blumer (1982) and Blackwell et al. (1984) note that analgesics and antianxiety drugs are contraindicated because they provide no sustained relief, are habituating, and tend to exacerbate the depression and pain. Cohen (1984) observes that as many as one-half of chronic pain patients are dependent on a narcotic or sedative and require detoxification. There may also be drug interaction effects because a number of doctors may be treating the patient simultaneously. Patients often report feeling better or mentally clearer following detoxification than when overmedicated. Cohen (1984) recommends hydroxyzine and the sedative antihistamines if a supplement to tricyclics is needed for nocturnal sedation, and tegretol and dilantin for antinociceptive effects, when a central pain component is present.

The personality and social factors that facilitated development of a somatoform pain disorder must also be considered in treatment planning. Brena (1984) describes the experience of pain as a continuous interplay between physical sensations and their emotional and cognitive interpretation. He suggests that by operationally defining pain in terms of somatic, personality, and social factors as well as degree of depression and anxiety, researchers may identify strategies for management that may predictably lead to successful outcome. A psychoeducational approach for the patient, his primary care provider, and his significant others may help direct reinforcement away from pain-related behaviors. Assertiveness and social skills training, vocational counseling, and resolution of compensation issues may be relevant in helping the patient avoid depressogenic situations and continue pain management in his natural environment. Brief relapses should be anticipated and their management planned for.

Cancer

The relationship of depression to cancer is complex. Some investigators (Whitlock and Siskind 1979) report a high number of cancer deaths in males previously treated for depression, and they propose a predisposing relationship between malignant neoplasm and affective disorder. Other studies are less convincing although it has been well documented that pancreatic carcinoma is often first manifested as a severe depression (Fras et al. 1967; Martin 1983; Perlas and Faillace 1964). This cancer occurs most often in men between the ages of 50 and 70, and the features of the depression commonly include feelings of imminent doom, a relative absence of guilt, presence of weight loss and weakness, and no previous psychiatric history, in the context of abdominal pain radiating to the back.

Estimates of the prevalence of depression in patients diagnosed with cancer vary as a function of both the type of cancer and the method by which the depression is identified—for example, self-report (Craig and Abeloff 1974), DSM-III criteria (Derogatis et al. 1983), clinician's judgment (Levine et al. 1978), or standardized rating scales (Plumb and Holland 1977). Bukberg et al. (in press) propose reliance on psychological symptoms when diagnosing depression in cancer patients because the neurovegetative signs of fatigue, anorexia, and diminished libido that are usually indicative of depression are not distinguishable from the symptoms of advanced cancer. Similarly, diminished concentration may be due to organic involvement. However, an additional diagnostic complication is that cancer patients frequently use denial of affect as a coping mechanism.

Plumb and Holland (1977) report that 23 percent of 97 hospitalized patients with advanced cancer characterized themselves as moderately to severely depressed on the Beck Depression Inventory, yet in studies of psychiatric consultations, less than 3 percent of cancer patients were referred for consultation and found to be depressed (Massie and Holland 1984). These data, combined with Plumb and Holland's (1977) prevalence data, suggest that a large number of depressions in cancer patients go unrecognized and untreated. Conversely, Levine et al. (1978) report that 26 percent of hospitalized cancer patients with organic brain syndrome were misdiagnosed as depressed by the referring physician. This group emphasizes utilization of the mental status exam to discriminate between organic brain syndrome and depression in cancer patients.

A review of the cancer literature by Greer and Silverfarb (1982) suggests that distress is likely to be high when patients are dealing with the emotional impact of the diagnosis "cancer," when treatment side effects occur, when the cancer is progressing or has reoccurred, and when there is a loss of cerebral functioning associated with the cancer. The clinician may be alerted to an increased possibility of depressive episodes at these points in the course of the illness. Inquiry as to suicidal thoughts or plans may be especially relevant at these times.

Evans et al. (1986) investigated the usefulness of the dexamethasone suppression test (DST) and the thyrotropin-releasing hormone (TRH) stimulation test to determine the prevalence of major depression in cancer patients. Approximately one-quarter of patients screened had to be excluded due to medical factors known to invalidate the results of these measures, and positive findings were often related to the combined influence of weight loss and tumor load. These results suggest that further study is indicated before these or other biologic markers can be applied to a cancer population, and that careful clinical evaluation remains the most effective diagnostic tool for identifying depression in cancer patients.

Guidelines for evaluating and resolving factors that may contribute to the cancer patient's depression have been comprehensively described by Goldberg (1981) and are summarized briefly here. Goldberg notes that identification and correction of depressogenic medical factors may resolve depressive symptoms, rendering further intervention unnecessary. If symptoms then fail to resolve, or if no contributing medical factors are found, an assessment of potential psychosocial contributors to depression should be instituted. Such contributors may include feelings of a loss of social acceptability, or isolation and a sense of abandonment, brought on by the withdrawal of friends, family members, and co-workers. Such withdrawal may be prompted by fears of contagion or of not knowing what to talk about with the patient during a visit, or feelings of guilt or anger toward the patient. The strain of new responsibilities and emotional demands and the loss of physical intimacy may prompt a spouse to be less available. Goldberg (1981) suggests meeting with the patient and significant others whenever possible to observe their interaction and facilitate sharing and communication. He also notes the tendency of many physicians to withdraw from the advanced cancer patient due to a sense of failure or a belief that there is little left to do, and the tendency of the patient to interpret this behavior as abandonment. He points out that it is therefore important for the physician to maintain regular contact and communication and to remain available and supportive. The sense of loss of control associated with their diagnosis and the related experience of learned helplessness may prompt depression, as well as anger, noncompliance, and other antitherapeutic behaviors, in the cancer patient. Physicians can help by giving patients choices and opportunities to exercise control over their therapy and environment—for example, learning relaxation techniques, keeping a journal of medication doses, or teaching other oncology patients how to overcome side effects, etc. A sense of intellectual mastery may be facilitated by providing the patient with information about his diagnosis, the course of his disease, and its treatments. The loss of bodily integrity or of a body part has a personal meaning for each patient that needs to be shared and understood. Problems with mobility, self-care, or role function may prompt a depressive reaction, particularly if adequate rehabilitation therapy is not instituted.

Massie and Holland (1984) recommend psychiatric consultation when the cancer patient's acute symptoms of distress last longer than a week, when they worsen rather than improve, or when they interfere with the patient's ability to cooperate with the planned treatment. Massie and Holland find that four to six sessions of supportive psychotherapy, focused on adaptation to diagnosis and treatment, are usually sufficient to reduce symptoms to a manageable level. They note that cancer patients in a poorer physical state, with inadequately controlled pain and with advanced stages of illness, particularly pancreatic cancer, are at higher risk for depression. They suggest that tricyclic antidepressants are indicated for the depressed cancer patient who has symptoms severe enough to interfere with function.

Massie and Holland (1984) have developed guidelines for pharmacologic treatment of the depressed cancer patient that are reviewed briefly here. They observed that cancer patients respond to antidepressants quickly and at relatively low doses, possibly because tumors alter the activity of the hepatic enzymes involved in the metabolism of antidepressants. They suggest starting treatment at a low dose—for example, 10 mg of amitriptyline twice a day—and increasing it as tolerated up to 75 to 150 mg per day. Amitriptyline combines analgesic, sedative, and antidepressant actions and is particularly useful for management of pain and insomnia. Amitriptyline and imipramine may be given parenterally for a more rapid effect or for those patients who cannot take medication by mouth. Nortriptyline is available in liquid form for those patients who cannot take a tablet. Tricyclics are contraindicated with procarbazine (Matulane), a chemotherapeutic agent that is an MAO inhibitor. Antidepressants with weak anticholinergic effects (e.g., doxepin, trazodone, or maprotiline) are indicated for patients who have gastrointestinal or genitourinary cancer, who have had gastrointestinal surgery, or who have stomatitis secondary to chemotherapy or radiation. Delirium is another anticholinergic side effect that may be more likely to occur in older patients or in those receiving other anticholinergic drugs such as atropine, scopolamine, or antipsychotics. Tricyclics should also be used cautiously with neutropenic patients because agranulocytosis can occur as a side effect of tricyclics. Massie and Holland (1984) note that patients who have been receiving lithium or MAO inhibitors prior to their cancer illness should continue to be maintained on them. They caution that patients on lithium should be monitored closely during pre- and postoperative periods when fluids and salts may be restricted, as should patients receiving cis-platinum (cisplatin, DDP), since both lithium and cis-platinum are potentially nephrotoxic. MAO inhibitors are rarely prescribed for oncology patients because of the presence of other extensive dietary restrictions. The psychostimulant, dextroamphetamine, may improve appetite and promote an increased sense of well-being, starting at 2.5 mg twice a day and increasing as tolerance develops. Amphetamines can also be used to potentiate the analgesic effects of opiates. Finally, Massie and Holland (1984) note that cancer patients rarely abuse psychotropic or narcotic medications and, in fact, often reduce or discontinue them as their perceived need diminishes, thus requiring encouragement to take enough.

Cardiac Disease

Rates of depression occurring in the year following myocardial infarction have been estimated at between 12 percent (Stern et al. 1976) and 22 percent (Singh et al. 1970). Longitudinal study of a sample of 29 psychiatric inpatients with a history of myocardial infarction revealed depression to be the most frequently occurring (90 percent) psychiatric diagnosis (Stern et al. 1976). In this sample, 72 percent were characterized by a symptom shift from depression to myocardial infarction, with periodic alterations between the two, and in 28 percent the depression followed the myocardial infarction. On the basis of this chronology, the authors suggest that depressive etiology may vary among patients and may involve the following: 1) an endogenous tendency toward depression, 2) emotional upset caused by the myocardial infarction, or 3) injury to the cerebrovascular system through cardiac insufficiency caused by myocardial infarction, bringing about metabolic disturbances in the brain. The appearance of myocardial infarction in some patients when depression appears to improve, and further dramatic improvement of depression after myocardial infarction, lead the authors to suggest that myocardial infarction may be a somatic equivalent of depression. The authors also propose that a synergistic action of depression and infarction increases suicidal tendencies, with 55.2 percent of patients studied making actual suicide attempts either pre- or postmyocardial infarction.

The elevated rates of depression and suicide in patients with heart disease underscore the need for accurate diagnosis and efficacious treatment of depression in this population. Rabkin et al. (1983) demonstrated that standard DSM-III criteria can be used to make a diagnosis of depression in a sample of hypertensives. Reports of treatment of depression in a cardiac population primarily involve tricyclic antidepressants (TCAs), with caveats regarding safety due to reports of cardiac arrhythmias and conduction disturbances following overdose (Spiker et al. 1975), and an association with sudden death in acutely ill hospitalized cardiac patients (Coull et al. 1970).

Glassman et al. (1983) examined the effect of imipramine hydrochloride on left ventricular performance (LVP) in a group of 15 patients with notable preexisting left ventricular dysfunction. They report that although no further impairment in resting LVP occurred, the drug had to be discontinued in seven of the patients due to severe orthostatic hypotension. The authors conclude that patients with impaired LVP should be observed closely for orthostatic changes when being treated with imipramine. However, the average plasma concentrations of imipramine and its desmethyl metabolite in this sample were 388 ng/ml, approximately twice the stardard level. The relationship of drug concentration to blood pressure changes may be relevant in understanding the high incidence of orthostatic changes and therefore important to monitor closely in patients with impaired LVP.

In a recent prospective study, Roose et al. (1987) compared the risk of cardiac complication in TCA-treated depressed patients with normal electrocardiograms and in those with either prolonged PR interval and/or brundle branch block. The prevalence of second-degree atrioventricular block was significantly greater in patients with preexisting bundle branch block (9 percent) than in patients with normal electrocardiograms (0.7 percent). In addition, orthostatic hypotension occurred significantly more frequently with imipramine than with nortriptyline and in patients with heart disease. The authors conclude that if a TCA is necessary for depressed patients with bundle branch block, measures of cardiac conduction (ECGs, 24-hour continuous ECG recordings), blood pressure recordings, and TCA plasma concentrations should be monitored to ensure safety as well as efficacy. Cases of severe depression in the presence of conduction disease may alternatively be treated with electroconvulsive therapy (ECT). Pomeranz et al. (1968) report the successful electroconvulsive treatment of depression in a patient with a surgically corrected aortic aneurysm and in another patient with a large aneurysm of the abdominal aorta. They note that ECT is a generally safe and efficacious treatment of depression in medically ill patients, provided that subclinical heart failure, pulmonary insufficiency, uncontrolled diabetes mellitus, hypertension, and other diseases are either ruled out or corrected.

Rabkin et al. (1983) report that in a sample of 452 psychiatric outpatients, DSM-III diagnoses of major depression were three times more common among subjects with hypertensive disease than among those without hypertension. Age, sex, psychosocial stress, chronic medical illness, and current antihypertensive medication were not related to the presence of depression in this sample. Witton (1966) studied blood pressure patterns in the population of a 600-bed mental hospital and found that 8.5 percent were hypertensive, 18.9 percent were hypotensive, 15.2 percent were labile or borderline patterns, and only 57.4 percent were in the normal range. He reports the successful treatment of a case of circulatory lability (hypertension and orthostatic hypotension) with a depressive reaction, using amitriptyline, 25 mg twice daily, and a medical regime to stabilize the blood pressure pattern. Witton emphasizes that if circulatory lability is not recognized, psychiatric treatment may be unsuccessful.

Raskind et al. (1982) studied 12 men with ischemic heart disease and depression secondary to myocardial infarction or coronary artery bypass-graft surgery, who were treated with imipramine for four weeks. The myocardial infarctions were well healed, surgery was at least four months prior, and all patients were free of clinically significant conduction defects, unstable cardiac arrhythmia, or poorly controlled congestive heart failure. Depression improved significantly by clinician and self-report, and there was a significant reduction in mean premature ventricular contractions per hour at week four and a significant increase in heart rate at all treatment weeks compared with baseline. Clinically significant disturbances in cardiac conduction did not develop, but orthostatic hypotension developed in one patient after three days of treatment, which resulted in discontinuing the drug. Doses started at 50 mg/day at bedtime and were increased by 25 mg every three days until substantial adverse effects occurred or a daily dose of 175 mg was reached.

In summary, the careful use of tricyclic antidepressants in patients with stable cardiac disease and major depressive disorder appears beneficial and indicated, although these conclusions are based on a very limited number of studies, all of which had very small sample sizes. Significant orthostatic hypotension occurred with imipramine treatment, indicating the importance of careful monitoring of blood pressure changes during antidepressant therapy. Additionally, antidepressant plasma levels varied widely at modest doses, suggesting the importance of monitoring drug plasma levels in the cardiac patient. The presence of significant heart disease always indicates the necessity of careful ECG monitoring during antidepressant therapy. Electroconvulsive therapy may offer a safe and efficacious treatment of severe depression in patients for whom TCAs are medically contraindicated. The safety of nontricyclic antidepressants in patients with serious heart disease has yet to be tested.

Endocrine Disorders

In a review of organic diseases masquerading as psychiatric disorders, Martin (1983) identifies endocrine dysfunctions as among the most common physical causes for what appears to be a primary psychiatric disorder. Hypoactivity or hyperactivity of the endocrine glands (thyroid, parathyroid, adrenal cortex, and pancreas) is known to affect internal homeostatic cycles that in turn affect mood and cognitions. For example, cases of both depression (Haskett 1985; Kelly et al. 1983) and mania (Haskett 1985; Kane and Keeler 1962) have been commonly reported in patients with hyperadrenalism, or Cushing's syndrome. However, a depressive disorder may be mistaken for Cushing's syndrome, especially in overweight and hirsute patients. Conversely, early Cushing's syndrome may be mistaken for depression, in that excessive amounts of cortisol are produced in both depression and Cushing's syndrome and both disorders commonly involve sleep disturbance and decreased libido and appetite (Kolata 1986). Correct diagnosis is imperative since treatment of Cushing's syndrome may involve removal of adrenals or pituitaries and treatment of depression may involve antidepressant medication or other therapies. In addition, diagnosis of neuroendocrine pathology may also be obscured or delayed by response of the manifest depressive symptoms to psychiatric treatment, despite their organic etiology. For example, Mandel (1960) reports on a case of recurrent depression in a 67-year-old housewife that a serum calcium assay revealed to be due to an adenoma of the parathyroid gland, despite a history of at least partial response to a number of trials of ECT. The importance of excluding neuroendocrine factors in recurrent depressions is again emphasized.

In Kolata (1986), Gold and Chorusos report on a biochemical test to aid in discriminating between Cushing's disease and depression. To summarize this work, if patients with depressive symptoms respond normally to administration of corticotropin-releasing hormone (CRH), they are depressed. If they overproduce adrenocorticotropic hormone (ACTH) in response, they have Cushing's disease. Kelly et al. (1983) report that correction of the hyperadrenalism alleviated depressive systems in a sample of 26 patients with active Cushing's syndrome, whereas Haskett (1985) found that depressive symptoms lingered months or years from the time of correction of the hypercortisolemia in a sample of 30 patients studied longitudinally. The differences in outcome between these two studies underscore that a depressogenic medical illness may be resolved, but the depression may have taken on a life of its own or the emotional impact of being diagnosed as having a serious but controlled medical disorder may have prompted a depressive reaction for which psychiatric intervention is warranted. There may also be an interaction effect between the depression and neuroendocrine illness. For example, Crammer and Gillies (1981) report a case of depression secondary to diabetes mellitus, in which the insulin requirement rose during depression despite good control of diet.

To summarize, neuroendocrine disorders and depressive disorders may be clinically indistinguishable. Biologic marker studies and assays such as serum calcium concentrations may be helpful in diagnosing neuroendocrine disease. However, treatment of the medical disorder may reveal a depression that has become independent and requires treatment in its own right. The treatment of such a depression—whether with antidepressant medication, ECT, or psychotherapy—is indicated since an untreated depression may have a negative impact on both the psychological and medical health of the patient.

Neurologic Disorders

Many neurologic disorders may be misdiagnosed as a primary affective disorder because affective symptoms are the chief complaint, or sometimes the only complaint, during the prodromal phase of the disease. These symptoms may include fatigue, listlessness, irritability, vague somatic complaints, anorexia, tearfulness, and impaired concentration. Additionally, a progressive loss of brain function may prompt a secondary depression that is diagnosed before the underlying neurologic disorder is detected.

The following neurologic disorders often manifest symptoms that mimic those of affective disorders: myasthenia gravis, Alzheimer's disease, multiple sclerosis, chronic subdural hematoma, brain tumors, lead intoxication, aseptic meningoencephalitis, and meningal cryptococcosis (Doghranji and Dubin 1985; Harris 1965; Martin 1983; Schottenfeld and Cullen 1984; Thienhaus and Kholsa 1984). Differential diagnosis is further complicated in the elderly by atypical symptoms and a tendency to attribute behavioral or cognitive abnormalities to the aging process. In addition, organic affective syndrome may temporarily respond to somatic treatments of depression such as lithium, ECT, or antidepressants, further delaying correct diagnosis.

Personality changes and psychiatric symptoms in patients with no prior psychiatric history, serial slowing on repeat EEGs compared with baseline, a history of exposure to environmental toxins at home or in the workplace, peripheral neuropathies, lightheadedness and dizzy spells, parathesias, irregularities in gait or vision or speech, incontinence, memory difficulties, headaches, vomiting, seizures, abnormal lab values, and confusion in response to antidepressant medication, especially if the confusion continues when the type of antidepressant is changed, may be clues to an underlying organic process in a predominantly affective symptom presentation.

The dexamethasone suppression test (DST) has been demonstrated to be a useful tool in diagnosing depression in some patients already identified as having an organic syndrome and in predicting response to treatment (Evans and Nemeroff 1984). For example, Evans and Nemeroff (1984) report that four of six patients who met DSM-III criteria for organic affective syndrome failed to suppress on the DST, a rate similar to that observed in major depression. Three of these nonsuppressors were retested after treatment response and had normal DSTs. The DST may be a particularly useful diagnostic aid for patients in whom brain damage distorts the clinical picture.

Epidemiologic studies offer information about organic disorders that secondary depression is likely to accompany. Such information can help ensure that the depression is not overlooked in an at-risk population. Schiffer and Babigian (1984) examined prevalence rates of depression in patients with multiple sclerosis as compared with control diseases of temporal lobe epilepsy, a disease with a chronic and fluctuating course, and amyotrophic lateral sclerosis, a disease with a particularly poor prognosis. A significantly higher rate of depression (61.97 percent) was found in patients with multiple sclerosis than in patients with the other diseases. The fact that the two control diseases had comparatively low rates of depression makes it difficult to dismiss the findings as reactive depression. The authors speculate that patients with multiple sclerosis may have a particular vulnerability to depression due to the structural involvement of limbic regions by demyelination, shared genetic vulnerabilities to both depression and multiple sclerosis, and selective alterations of monoamine metabolism within the central nervous system. In support of a localization hypothesis, Schiffer et al. (1983) report that multiple sclerosis patients with predominantly cerebral involvement of their demyelinating disease were significantly more likely to have major depression than those with predominantly spinal cord and cerebellar involvement. Thus, whereas multiple sclerosis patients in general may be at greater risk for depression, those with predominantly cerebral involvement should be viewed as a subpopulation at particular risk for depressive illness.

Additional neuropathic processes commonly associated with depression include idiopathic Parkinson's disease (Schiffer and Babigian 1984) and stroke (Lipsey et al.

1983; Robinson and Benson 1981; Robinson et al. 1984a, 1984b). A longitudinal study (Robinson et al. 1984b) of mood disorders in 50 poststroke patients revealed that depression present during the acute period following infarction is likely to endure for at least six months, and that the prevalence of major depression increases steadily for the first half year after a cerebral hemorrhage or ischemic lesion. Considerable work has been done in relating poststroke mood disorders to the locus of the brain injury (Lipsey et al. 1983; Parikh et al. 1987; Robinson 1987; Robinson and Benson 1981; Robinson et al. 1984a). Robinson (1987), Robinson et al. (1984b, 1985), and Parikh et al. (1987) found depression to be significantly more prevalent in patients with left frontal hemisphere infarcts (60 percent) than with lesions in any other brain area, and the severity of depression correlated strongly with the proximity of the lesion to the frontal pole. Robinson and Benson (1981) demonstrated that patients with non-fluent aphasia following brain injury were more depressed than patients with global or fluent aphasias (more posterior lesion location), despite equivalence of physical and cognitive impairment. The authors note that nonfluent aphasics had anteriorly localized lesions while fluent aphasics had more posterior lesions. They speculate that the anterior lesions of the nonfluent aphasics may disrupt more catacholamine pathways than the posterior lesions and consequently produce more depression. Robinson (1987) reports successful treatment of depressed stroke patients with nor-triptyline, with onset of effect and required blood levels similar to those found in functional (nonbrain injured) major depression. The importance of recognizing and treating depression in stroke patients is underscored by the finding of Parikh et al. (1987). This group reports that acute stroke patients who were the most depressed in the hospital and were untreated for depression were likely to be the most physically impaired two years after stroke. A conclusion drawn from this study is that depression has a significant impact on the course of poststroke recovery.

Treatment of depression secondary to neurologic disorders may include reha-bilitation programs to help patients decrease feelings of helplessness and hopelessness by developing compensatory strategies if areas of functioning are compromised by the disorder. Intensive psychotherapy may serve to place the disorder in the context of the patient's life course and character style, help the patient adjust goals and responsibilities to decrease feelings of alienation, diminish somatic preoccupations, and reduce self-destructive or impulsive acts. Perry and Markowitz (1986) point out that many depressed patients with a fatal illness view suicide as a reasonable option. They recommend telling a patient that suicidal ideation is a common symptom of depression and that the option of suicide can be evaluated rationally only after the depression has been treated. Yudofsky (1985) suggests that ECT be implemented when the risk of suicide is high in patients with multiple sclerosis and notes that such patients require fewer treatments (three to five) to achieve a therapeutic result than patients without multiple sclerosis. Weaver and Remick (1982) report the successful resolution of depressive symptoms following a course of 13 ECTs in a 67-year-old woman with nontabetic parenchymatous neurosyphilis. The patient had presented with sleep and appetite disturbance and symptoms of disorientation and mental confusion that diminished under sodium amytal interview, leading the authors to conclude that her mental state reflected pseudodementia associated with depression. They emphasize the importance of not trying to treat organic problems to the exclusion of depression.

Response to antidepressant medication has been reported for patients with depression secondary to a broad range of neurologic disorders. However, despite generally encouraging reports, there are patients for whom the use of antidepressants is problematic or contraindicated. For example, Fullerten et al. (1981) report that tricyclics had to be stopped within six days due to circulatory side effects, including automatic dysreflexia, in two depressed patients with spinal cord injuries. Alternatively, Kaufman et al. (1984) report five medically ill patients with neurologic disease and major depression, who either had serious adverse effects or failed to respond to antidepressant medication and who were successfully treated with psychostimulants (e.g., methylphenidate or dexedrine). Response to small doses was quick, there were few toxic side effects, and there was no recurrence of depressive symptoms at six-months' follow-up. These preliminary results suggest a possible alternative treatment for neurologic patients with secondary depression who fail to respond to standard antidepressants or who experience serious adverse effects. Similarly, Shulka et al. (1987) report a low (13 percent) response rate to lithium, with a high (51 percent) rate of significant neurologic side effects, in a sample of 39 patients with organic mania. The relapse rate was significantly lower in the patients treated with other medication combinations, such as carbamazepine or neuroleptics, than in those treated with lithium alone.

Acquired Immune Deficiency Syndrome (AIDS)

Holland and Tross (1985) suggest that distinguishing the symptoms of reactive depression from central nervous system complications of AIDS is best accomplished with psychological testing and EEG recordings, and they recommend antidepressants for control of depressive symptoms, especially insomnia, in AIDS patients. Perry and Markowitz (1986) suggest that the choice of antidepressant and dosage be determined by the neurovegetative symptoms and underlying physical illness in this patient population. For example, if a patient is lethargic and has a pulmonary infection, they recommend a more activating drug such as imipramine or desipramine to increase alertness and respiratory movements. For an agitated patient with gastroenteritis, a more anticholinergic drug such as amitriptyline may increase sedation and diminish diarrhea.

Prescribed and Over-the-Counter Medications

Depressive symptoms may appear while patients are taking any of a broad range of commonly used drugs (Abramowicz and Aaron 1984), and they usually disappear when the drug is stopped. Drugs that have been associated with such depressive symptoms include anticonvulsants (Tollefson 1980), especially in high doses or plasma concentrations (ethosuximide–Zarontin; phenytoin–Dilantin, others; primidone–Mysoline); asparaginase (Carbone et al. 1970; Elspan); baclofen (Skausig and Korsgaard 1977; Lioresal); barbiturates (Abramowicz and Aaron 1984); cimetidine (Jefferson 1979; Tagamet); oral contraceptives (Abramowicz and Aaron 1984); corticosteroids (Judd et al. 1983; prednisone, cortisone, ACTH; others), particularly in higher doses; cycloserine (Abramowicz and Aaron 1984; Seromycin); diazepam (Hall and Joffe 1972; Valium); disopyramide (Ahmad et al. 1979; Norpace); disulfiram (Quail and Karalese 1980; Antabuse); ethionamide (Lees 1965; Trecator); halothane (Davison et al. 1975; Fluothane); isoniazid (Abramowicz and Aaron 1984; INH; others); levodopa (Presthus and Holmsen 1974; Dopar; others); methyldopa (Johnson et al. 1966; Aldomet); metrizamide (Penn and Mackenzie 1983; Amipaque); nalidixic acid (Abramowicz and Aaron 1984; NegGram); naproxen (Goodwin and Regan 1982; Naprosyn); pentazocine (Kane and Pokorny 1975; Talwin); phenylephrine (Snow et al. 1980; Neo-Synephrine); propranolol (Shader and Greenblatt 1983; Inderal) especially after dosage increase; rauwolfia alkaloids (Freis 1975; resperpine–Serpasil; others); thyroid hormones (Josephson and Mackensie 1980); timolol (Nolan 1982; Timoptic); and vinblastine (Abramowicz and Aaron 1984; Velban). The above listing is limited to single drugs associated with depressive reactions. Drug interactions may also have depressogenic effects.

Sometimes depressive symptoms first appear when a drug is stopped. This may represent a withdrawal phenomenon and has been associated with discontinuation of amphetamines (Abramowicz and Aaron 1984) and similar anorexic agents; baclofen (Skausig and Korsgaard 1977; Lioresal), particularly after sudden withdrawal; barbiturates (Abramowicz and Aaron 1984); corticosteroids (Judd et al. 1983; prednisone, cortisone, ACTH; others); and diazepam (Hall and Joffe 1972; Valium). A summary of the administration or termination of medications associated with depressive reactions is presented in Table 2.

Discriminating between depression as an adverse drug effect and depression as an autonomous clinical entity is often trickier than it first appears. For example, withdrawal reactions from long-acting drugs may not occur until shortly before hospital discharge and may be incorrectly diagnosed as a depressive response to leaving the hospital or to surgery, etc. Similarly, depressive symptoms are known to occur in the presence of both a given disease and the drug used to treat it, leading to a dilemma as to whether to increase or decrease the dosage of the drug. When depression due to drugs does not respond to withdrawing the causative agent, or when the drug must be continued to control the disease, active treatment of the depression should be considered.

Few reports exist of treatment of depression that is secondary to medication. Bant (1978) studied 89 hypertensive patients who were predominantly treated with either reserpine, methyldopa, or adrenergic blockers. He found similar rates of depression in each treatment group and concluded that it was doubtful that such a variety

Table 2. Prescribed Drugs That May Cause Psychiatric Symptoms During Treatment or Following Termination of the Drug

Depressive Reactions Associated with Administration of:

Anticonvulsants: ethosuximide (Zarontin), phenytoin (Dilantin and others), primidone (Mysoline)	Ethionamide (Trecator)
	Halothane (Fluothane)
	Isoniazid: INH, others
Asparaginase (Elspan)	Levodopa: (Dopar), others
Baclofen (Lioresal)	Methyldopa (Aldomet)
Barbiturates	Nalidixic Acid (Neggam)
Cimetidine (Tagamet)	Naproxen (Naprosyn)
Contraceptives, Oral	Pentazocine (Talwin)
Corticosteroids: prednisone, cortisone, ACTH, others	Phenylephrine (Neo-Synephrine)
	Propranolol (Inderal)
Cycloserine (Seromycin)	Rauwolfia alkaloids: reserpine (Serpasil), others
Diazepam (Valium)	
Disopyramide (Norpace)	Thyroid hormones
Disulfiram (Antabuse)	Timolol (Timoptic)
	Vinblastine (Velban)

Depressive Reactions Associated with Termination of:

Amphetamines	Corticosteroids: prednisone, cortisone, ACTH, others
Baclofen (Lioresal)	
Barbiturates	Diazepam (Valium)

of drugs with different pharmacologic actions would cause patients to have more severe depressions. Bant offers the alternative hypothesis that difficulty adjusting to an illness that can only be controlled and not cured may predispose the patient to a reactive depression. He suggests that an "illness effect" depression is unlikely to respond to antidepressant medication, and he notes that antidepressants are relatively or absolutely contraindicated in the cases of some epileptics and in patients on adrenergic blockers and clonidine.

Croog et al. (1985) compared the quality of life of 620 men one month before and six months after beginning antihypertensive therapy on either captopril, methyldopa, or propranolol. Significantly fewer patients treated with captopril quit therapy due to adverse effects, and most actually improved from their untreated state on measures of functioning frequently disturbed by depression. Conversely, in addition to having higher dropout rates, patients treated with methyldopa and propranolol grew significantly worse on measures of functioning related to depression. This finding challenges Bant's (1978) attribution of depression subsequent to treatment with reserpine, methyldopa, or adrenergic blockers to illness effects. It also emphasizes the need for physicians treating patients with antihypertensive therapy to monitor social, emotional, and professional functioning and to adjust therapy accordingly to avoid noncompliance with a treatment that the patient may experience as more debilitating than the disease.

The fatigue-asthenia symptoms resulting from human leukocyte interferon alpha therapy were studied in 10 patients with metastatic renal cell carcinoma by Adams et al. (1984). Moderately severe changes in behavior and slight to moderate changes in cognition, affect, and personality were observed. The temporal association between the symptoms and the onset of therapy, as well as their reversible nature, lead the authors to conclude that the symptoms were drug and not disease related. The authors stress the importance of recognizing this clinical syndrome and reassuring patients and their significant others that the behavioral symptoms are biochemically mediated and not the result of giving up, self-pity, or laziness. This intervention strategy may be meaningfully applied to all patients treated with drugs known to cause depressive symptoms.

A recent review of the influence of steroids on mood (Barnes 1986) indicates that some steroids depress nerve cell activity in the brain and others enhance it. Fluctuations in steroid production, as a result of disease or stress, may contribute to fluctuations in mood, ranging from euphoria to depression. Mania as well as depression may likewise occur secondary to pharmacologic antecedents. Krauthammer and Klerman (1978), in a review of cases of secondary mania, observe that depression is the most common psychiatric sequela of abnormal endogenous steroid production (Cushing's and Addison's diseases), and that euphoria and mania are common side effects of exogenous steroids used primarily in the treatment of collagen disorders. These authors also review cases of mania secondary to the prescription of isoniazid, procarbazine, levodopa, and bromide. Mania remitted in most cases with dose cessation or reduction. Cases that lasted well beyond termination of the pharmacologic cause were variously treated with electroconvulsive therapy, injections of vitamin B concentrate, or chlorpromazine. Additional cases of mania secondary to use of decongestants, bronchodilators, procyclidine, phencyclidine, metaclopramide, tolmetin, and possibly cannabis were reported by Stasiek and Zetin (1985). These authors also review a case of mania secondary to abrupt cessation of reserpine therapy and a case secondary to hypocalcemia. Bunney's review (1978) of 80 studies of antidepressant therapy revealed a 9.5 percent incidence of mania or hypomania in patients with no prior manic episodes. However, these cases would not meet criteria for secondary mania due to a preexisting affective disorder.

Krauthammer and Klerman (1978) suggest that secondary mania be suspected in cases of late onset and negative family history, and that the psychiatric workup include toxic screening and a review of drug ingestion and medications. If resolution of the pharmacologic cause is impossible or unsuccessful, the authors suggest that a trial of lithium carbonate or neuroleptic medication may be indicated. Prophylactic lithium maintenance therapy would seem unnecessary unless a patient requires another trial of medication known to have produced a manic syndrome in the past. In that case, a short trial of lithium therapy may be helpful in preventing recurrence.

In summary, affective symptoms, both manic and depressive, have been found to occur in response to a broad range of medication. It is important to establish whether a history of affective disorders exists in the patient, or in his immediate family members, when a trial of medication is being considered that is known to have affective side effects. This determination may help to identify patients at risk so that an alternative medication may be chosen or the patient may be followed closely to identify a developing affective disturbance. Patients may either develop an affective illness or become noncompliant with a medication that induces depressive symptoms. Similarly, a patient's family members may become concerned if they believe the patient is developing a demoralization syndrome or a depressive syndrome that is, in fact, a drug effect.

A careful history, combined with toxic screening, can help discriminate primary affective disorder from affective disorder secondary to medication effects. Most cases of the latter resolve with dose adjustment or termination. Cases of depression that continue beyond cessation of depressogenic medication, or beyond the transient symptoms associated with withdrawal from specific drugs, may require antidepressant medication, ECT, psychotherapy, or some combinations of the above. Cases of mania that fail to resolve with reduction or cessation of the pharmacologic cause may require treatment with lithium or a neuroleptic. The choice of treatment will require consideration of medical contraindications to a specific treatment and interaction effects with medications needed to manage a medical illness. Close consultation with the primary care provider is indicated in these cases.

Depression Secondary to Psychiatric Illness

The evidence for the efficacy of the tricyclic antidepressants in the treatment of depression secondary to alcoholism, opiate addiction, and schizophrenia has been summarized by Weissman (1983). Her review includes clinical treatment trials that 1) included homogeneous samples of specific types of secondary depression, 2) tested the efficacy of a tricyclic antidepressant, 3) used random assignment of treatment with control groups or placebo, and 4) had quantitative outcome measures. The studies included in this section on depressions secondary to psychiatric illness adhere to similar criteria wherever possible.

Eating Disorders

Ongoing debate in the field of eating disorders centers on whether the frequent association of depression represents a primary disorder, a secondary disorder, or a concurrent condition. Swiff et al. (1986) report that their anorexic patients rarely express worthlessness or self-reproach and are not preoccupied with thoughts of death and suicide as are depressed patients. This group and others point out that many symptoms of depression, including dysphoric mood, irritability, weight loss, sleep disturbance, decreased libido, social withdrawal, and inability to concentrate may be more concisely explained by a semistarvation syndrome. This explanation, while relevant for anorexics, does not apply to bulimics because the majority of these patients are at or above normal body weight. Bulimics also tend to be more depressed than anorexics and tend to have a more favorable response to antidepressants. Therefore, to understand the relationship of depression to the eating disorders and consequent treatment implications, the data from anorexics (food restrictors) will be reviewed separately from that of bulimics (bingers).

Anorexia.   Using a variety of assessment instruments, investigators have found a wide range of severity of depression in samples of anorexics (Eckert et al. 1981; Hendren 1983; Katz et al. 1984). Eckert et al. (1981) observed that depressed mood correlated with more severe anorexic symptoms and that subsequent weight gain correlated with a decrease in depression. However, Hendren (1983) failed to find a correlation between severity of depression and weight loss, and suggested that the depression seen in anorexia may be a function of factors other than semistarvation.

Families of anorexics have been studied in order to understand any genetic link between anorexia and affective disorder. Biederman et al. (1985) found higher rates of depression in first-degree relatives of anorexics with major depression than in those of anorexics without current depression or in those of normal control subjects. Winokur et al. (1980) likewise found a higher incidence of primary affective disorder in the relatives of anorexics than in those of normal control subjects. However, although Gershon et al. (1984) and Strober (1984) found a higher prevalence of affective disorder in the relatives of eating disorder patients, they failed to find a higher prevalence of eating disorders in first-degree relatives of patients with affective disorders. Such a discrepancy fails to support the hypothesis that anorexia is a manifestation of the tendency to affective disorders. In addition, Strober found increased rates of various eating disorders in the relatives of anorexic probands and suggests that the various eating disorders may represent various expressions of a common underlying psychopathology.

Biologic studies tend to lend support to the hypothesis that anorexia nervosa and affective disorders are independent syndromes. In a preliminary study of CSF parameters, Gerner et al. (unpublished) found that depressed subjects had low GABA but anorexics did not. Conversely, anorexics had decreased HVA, 5H1AA, and tyrosine, but depressed subjects did not. Although the anorexic findings could be secondary to weight loss, none of the CSF variables correlated with percent of ideal weight. Gerner and Gwirtaman (1981) report that anorexics at less than 80 percent of their ideal body weight had abnormally high postdexamethasone cortisol levels and low MHPG levels, regardless of mood. The authors propose that both anorexia and depression may be related to dysfunction of norepinephrine regulation although it is not yet clear why the dysfunction may be associated with primary affective disorder in one patient and with anorexia in another. In a thorough review of the neuroendocrine literature, Halmi (1985) concludes that there are more differences than similarities in both the biologic and psychological features of depression and anorexia. Walsh (1982) arrives at a similar conclusion in his review of endocrine data. He notes that increased physical activity is a prominent feature of anorexia, which may lead to altered production of endorphins or other neuromodulators that have some beneficial effect on mood. In this manner, anorexia may be an attempt to cope both biologically and psychologically (through dietary control) with a disturbance of mood. Moore (1977) also views eating disorders as a reciprocal interplay of biologic, psychological, familial, and sociocultural variables that comprise a heterogeneous disorder that does not possess a single pathogenesis. They underscore the importance of identifying subgroups of patients with eating disorders (e.g., depressed and non-depressed) for both treatment and research applications.

A small number of studies have been reported that involve antidepressant medication, lithium, or ECT for the treatment of anorexia nervosa (Eckert et al. 1981; Halmi 1985; Jampola 1985; Moore 1977), with mixed results. Antidepressants that prevent reuptake of 5-HT and decrease its turnover in the brain (e.g., chlorimipramine and amitriptyline) appear the most promising in treating anorexia (Halmi 1985). However, as Halmi (1985) points out, there are many pharmacologic actions associated with these drugs, and the mechanism by which they can induce weight and behavioral changes in anorexics has yet to be ascertained.

Bulimia. Subgroups of bulimic patients, and of anorexic patients with bulimia, that are similar to patients with primary affective disorder have been identified in studies involving family history of affective disorder (Hudson et al. 1982; Piran et al. 1985), assessment of presence and severity of depressive symptoms (Halmi 1985; Wold 1983), and nonsuppression on the dexamethasone suppression test (Halmi 1985; Hudson et al. 1982, 1983a; Musisi and Garfinkel 1984) in the absence of significant weight loss. In addition, Herzog and Copeland (1985) reviewed animal and treatment outcome literature to formulate a hypothesis of abnormal norepinephrine metabolism and decreased serotonin turnover in bulimia.

Bulimics have been found to have a significant response to imipramine (Hudson et al. 1983b; Pope and Hudson 1982), desipramine (Hughes et al. 1986), trazodone (Pope et al. 1983a), tranylpromine, and phenelzine (Pope et al. 1983a; Walsh et al. 1982). The generalized response to antidepressants, the time to respond, and rate of response are similar for bulimics and major depressives. These findings, in conjunction with the positive correlations between a decrease in depression and a decrease in bingeing, have led Pope et al. (1983b) to suggest that bulimia may represent a form of affective disorder. Walsh et al. (1982) also found a positive correlation between depressive and bulimic symptoms but caution that not all patients with atypical depression develop bulimia, and it has not been established that all bulimics experience significant mood disturbance. Nevertheless, the responsiveness of bulimic symptoms to antidepressants, particularly MAOIs (Pope et al. 1983a), suggests that antidepressants are an indicated treatment for this disorder.

Pope et al. (1983a) have outlined treatment guidelines for patients with bulimia. They stress the importance of assessing each patient's medical condition and suicidality, and they recommend hospitalizing those seriously at risk for suicide and prescribing small quantities of antidepressants for outpatients to guard against overdose. Suicidal patients on MAOIs may also deliberately overeat tyramine-rich foods. Bulimics may require more education and reassurance than is common with regard to apprehension about antidepressants' mind-altering or addictive qualities, side effects, promotion of weight gain, or incompatibility with psychotherapy. Bulimics are cautioned to avoid vomiting or abusing laxatives during a two- to three-hour period after taking the drug, and plasma levels must be checked, particularly in nonresponders, to ascertain whether an adequate level of drug is circulating.

In terms of choice of medication, imipramine, desipramine, and nortriptyline have established therapeutic plasma levels and milder sedative and anticholinergic side effects than amitriptyline. Trazodone may be of comparable therapeutic efficacy to the above antidepressants but does not have the advantage of easily interpretable plasma levels. MAOIs are probably the most clinically efficacious choice for bulimics, and platelet MAO determinations can be used to identify patients who may be on an inadequate dose or who may be losing some of the drug through purging. However, the possibility of highly impulsive patients bingeing on tyramine-rich foods may justify prescribing an MAOI after failure on a trial of a tricyclic or trazodone. Pope et al. (1983a) report that up to three adequate therapeutic trials of a tricyclic, MAOI, and/or trazodone may be necessary to obtain satisfactory clinical results, although a certain number of patients will not respond satisfactorily to persistent pharmacologic treatment.

Alcoholism

When depression exists concurrently with alcoholism, impairment in function and risk of suicide increases (Berglund 1984; Hamm et al. 1979; Pottenger et al. 1978). Consequently, depression in association with alcoholism has received considerable clinical attention and study. Schuckit (1983a, 1983b, 1985) has written extensively on the importance of distinguishing between primary alcoholism and alcoholism secondary to other psychiatric disorders. He defines primary alcoholics as patients who met DSM-III criteria for alcoholism prior to the onset of any other major psychiatric disorder. This discrimination between primary and secondary alcoholism is important both clinically and in terms of interpreting treatment outcome research, because Schuckit has found that alcoholics with a primary diagnosis of antisocial personality disorder or substance abuse disorder have a generally poorer treatment outcome than do patients with primary alcoholism. Similarly, differing treatment strategies may be indicated for patients with primary depression and secondary alcoholism than for patients with primary alcoholism and secondary depression (Schuckit 1985).

Determining the chronology of depression and alcoholism or opiate addiction is somewhat problematic because it is often difficult to disentangle the symptoms of depression from withdrawal symptoms. Schuckit (1983b) has found that affective symptoms usually clear within several days to two weeks of abstinence and concludes that these depressive symptoms are probably a result of alcoholism rather than its cause. Schuckit's findings underscore the importance of waiting for acute withdrawal symptoms to clear before assigning primary and secondary psychiatric diagnoses.

The rates of depression concomitant with alcoholism reported in the literature have been inconsistent, varying from 3 percent to 98 percent. This variability may be a function, in part, of the time that has elapsed since the last drink, as discussed above. Additionally, Weissman and Myers (1980) have shown that the rates depend on whether the depression is assessed by diagnostic interview or by symptom scale, with the symptom scales yielding considerably higher rates. Using epidemiologic survey techniques, they have shown that approximately 15 percent of subjects who were currently alcoholic had coexisting major depression. About 40 percent of those who had coexisting alcoholism and major depression could clearly be termed secondary depressives. That the depression may indeed be secondary is supported by the findings of McClellan et al. (1979), who had the opportunity to follow cohorts of substance abusers prospectively over time. They showed that, following years of exposure, sedative and alcohol abusers were diagnosed in significant numbers as suffering from clinical depression and organic mental syndromes although they were not so diagnosed six years earlier.

The presence of depressive symptomatology in conjunction with alcoholism must always be taken seriously, and the need for treatment of the depression must be carefully assessed. In a study that used the Hamilton and Raskin rating scales as diagnostic instruments, Pottenger et al. (1978) report that 59 percent of 61 alcoholics studied were clinically depressed but that only 3 percent received antidepressant medication. Depressive symptoms noted at admission were present at follow-up one year later, and a significant relationship was found between depression at follow-up and continued drinking. Other studies have also reported higher rates of depression in relapsed than in abstinent alcoholics (Hatsukami and Pickens 1982; Hatsukami et al. 1981).

Lithium has been investigated as a treatment modality for maintaining abstinence both because of its effectiveness in treating affective disorders and because of a demonstrated reduction in volitional consumption of alcohol by rats treated with lithium (Ho and Tsai 1976). Outcome studies of lithium treatment of chronic alcoholics have reported contradictory findings (Fawcett et al. 1984; Kline et al. 1974; Merry et al. 1976; Pond et al. 1981; Young and Keeler 1981).

Recently, in a double-blind placebo-controlled study of 84 alcoholics, Fawcett et al. (1984) reported a significant relationship between abstinence at six months and therapeutic serum levels of lithium when noncompliant subjects were eliminated from the comparison. This study demonstrated that compliance with a treatment program is an important component of abstinence and that adequate blood levels of lithium may be effective in maintaining sobriety for some subjects. However, the link between drinking and depression was again underscored in this study, with lithium not effecting a positive change in depressive symptomatology as measured by the Beck Depression Inventory (BDI) and with higher BDI scores being related to relapse. Given these findings and the possible serious adverse effects of lithium therapy (Muniz et al. 1981), tricyclic antidepressant (TCA) medication may be a viable alternative treatment to alcoholism. With TCAs, depressive symptomatology might be better treated or prevented.

Several studies have examined the efficacy of TCAs or other pharmacologic treatments during either withdrawal or detoxification to determine their value in reducing drinking and enhancing social function. The rationale for this approach is based on the observation that many alcoholics are depressed and anxious. However, none of these studies included a specifically selected sample of alcoholics with secondary depression. No published study of antidepressant therapy with alcoholics exists in which drug plasma levels have been measured to demonstrate that patients have complied and that standard clinical levels of drug are circulating. This is important because evidence exists that alcoholics metabolize TCAs abnormally and may require higher doses to reach a standard range (Ciraulo et al. 1982, 1986; Sandoz et al. 1983). In their review of studies of alcoholism treated with TCAs, Ciraulo and Jaffe (1981) concluded that most studies failed 1) to differentiate subtypes of depression, 2) to measure plasma levels to ensure adequate dosage and compliance, and 3) to measure changes in both depression and drinking in response to treatment.

Kissin and Gross (1968) and Kissin et al. (1968) looked at amitriptyline (AMI) and imipramine (IMI) as treatments for large samples of alcoholics with abstinence as the outcome measure. The dose ranges were well below what Ciraulo et al. (1982) and Sandoz et al. (1983) found therapeutic for alcoholics, and no meaningful drug effect was obtained. In a one-year study of chronic alcoholics, Kissin et al. (1968) made the methodological contribution that evaluation of sobriety after a minimum of six months is almost as meaningful and stable as that after 12 months.

Studies that used dosages of TCAs that approached the usual range employed in the treatment of depression demonstrated more promising drug effects in terms of depression, but these studies did not include sobriety as an outcome measure and were briefer than six-months' duration. In a three-week study, Butterworth (1971) obtained a difference in depression scores between IMI- (dose: 75–200 mg) and placebo-treated alcoholics that approached significance at the .06 level. Shaw et al. (1975) found a significant decrease in the Zung Self-Rating Depression Scale but no difference on the BDI or MMPI for subjects treated for 30 days with IMI 150 mg plus chlordiazepoxide 40 mg versus placebo. Shaw attributed this differential effect to the Zung having more items that describe the physiologic symptoms of depression known to respond to TCAs. Conversely, in a three-week comparison of 75 mg of doxepin versus 15 mg of diazepam, Butterworth and Watts (1971) obtained significantly greater improvement in the Brief Psychiatric Rating Scale than in the Zung for the doxepin group. This dose of doxepin may have been too low to affect the physiologic symptoms of depression measured by the Zung. Wilson et al. (1970) obtained a significant decrease in depression, with physiologic symptoms showing the greatest difference, in a six-week study of IMI 150 mg versus placebo. In a three-week trial, Overall et al. (1973) found chlordiazepoxide 30 mg less effective than mesoridazine 75 mg or AMI 75 mg in reducing depression and anxiety. Here again, the dose of AMI may have been too low. Gallant et al. (1969) compared doxepin 150 mg versus doxepin 75 mg versus diazepam 15 mg versus placebo in a three-week trial and found no drug effect, although doxepin 150 mg relieved symptoms more rapidly than diazepam.

To summarize, TCAs may offer a safer and more effective treatment of depression in recovering alcoholics than lithium. Evaluation of depression should be performed after at least a week of sobriety to avoid confusing symptoms of detoxification with those of depression. Monitoring of TCA plasma levels is indicated to establish both compliance and the circulation of a standard therapeutic level of drug, due to evidence that alcoholics metabolize TCAs abnormally and may require higher doses. Recovering alcoholics should be warned that TCAs can potentiate the effect of alcohol should they resume drinking.

Substance Abuse

Depression has been identified as the most frequently occurring psychiatric disorder among opiate addicts seeking treatment, occurring even more commonly than sociopathy (Khantzian and Treece 1985; Rounsaville et al. 1982, 1983; Woody et al. 1983). Data from the New Haven methadone/psychotherapy study (Rounsaville et al. 1983) indicate that initially high levels of depression abate for many subjects after six weeks in the methadone program. However, Khantzian and Treece (1985) report that 48 percent of 133 narcotic addicts met DSM-III criteria for affective disorder after being drug free for at least one month, and they found a lifetime disorder of 67 percent for this sample. Similarly, Rounsaville and Kleber (1985) report a lifetime prevalence of affective disorder of 73 percent for opiate users seeking treatment and of 56 percent for an untreated community sample. Depression has also been reported secondary to the abuse of cocaine and crack (Abramowicz and Aaron 1984; Gawin and Kleber 1984, 1986; Kleber 1987; Kosten et al. 1987a; Small and Purcell 1985; Tennent and Sagherian 1987).

Diagnostically, it is difficult to differentiate the symptoms of depression in opiate and cocaine addicts from withdrawal symptoms or from the side effects of opiates. Withdrawal from opiates can produce disturbed sexual functioning as well as appetite and sleep disorders. Similarly, withdrawal from cocaine may include anorexia, fatigue, sad mood, impaired concentration, irritability, and insomnia (Tennent and Sagherian 1987). The presence of depression in the drug-abusing population is of particular concern because of its confounding effect on treatment response. Batki et al. (1986) report that opiate addicts with a history of major depressive disorder have more intense withdrawal symptoms and are less likely to complete detoxification treatment than are addicts to other drugs. Kosten et al. (1987b) found depression to be a significant risk factor for escalating cocaine abuse in both methadone and drug-free treated subjects. Hence, pharmacologic and psychotherapeutic interventions to reduce depressive symptoms may be of particular benefit to substance abusers. Furthermore, diagnosing the presence of secondary psychiatric disorders such as depression may serve to identify subtypes of drug abusers with differing courses and indications for ancillary treatments (Perkins et al. 1986). Dackis et al. (1984) report a sensitivity of 80 percent and a specificity of 93 percent using the dexamethasone suppression test (DST) to diagnose major depression in opiate addicts. This group suggests that the DST in combination with a structured clinical interview may enhance the reliability of diagnoses of true affective disorder in this patient population.

Woody et al. (1983) compared treatment outcomes of opiate addicts treated with either supportive-expressive or cognitive-behavioral psychotherapy in conjunction with drug counseling with outcomes of addicts receiving drug counseling alone. All treatments were manual guided, with therapists who were experienced in the use of their techniques and were supervised throughout the project. A comprehensive battery of outcome measures was administered at intake and at termination; within-treatment measures were also recorded. These measures demonstrated an overall improvement in outcome when psychotherapy was added to drug counseling. Further, although depressed patients were not specifically chosen, data were analyzed to see if psychiatric diagnosis was an additional predictor of outcome. The largest therapy effect was observed in those patients with depression. These findings support the idea that psychotherapy is helpful for depression secondary to opiate use. Rounsaville et al. (1983) observed that both depression and opiate addiction are associated with disturbances in interpersonal functioning, and they hypothesized that Interpersonal Psychotherapy (IPT) would prove a valuable ancillary treatment for methadone-maintained addicts. Methodological difficulties apparently contributed to a lack of significant outcome differences between IPT and a low-contact control group in this study.

Efficacy studies of antidepressant medication in addicts have also yielded contradictory findings. Woody et al. (1975) and Woody (1981) obtained greater reduction of depressive symptoms in methadone-maintained opiate addicts with doxepin compared with placebo. Similarly, in a five-week double-blind study, Titievsky et al. (1982) examined the effectiveness of doxepin as an adjunctive treatment in comparison with placebo in 46 depressed, anxious patients attending a methadone maintenance program. Patients with other diagnosable psychiatric illnesses were excluded. Doxepin was superior to placebo on clinical global impression and several depression rating scales. No clinically significant potentiation of side effects was observed with the combined administration of doxepin and methadone. Conversely, Kleber et al. (1983) failed to obtain outcome differences for imipramine versus placebo treatment of methadone-maintained addicts engaged in a full-service methadone maintenance program. Given the response of both treatment groups to the full-service methadone-maintenance program, they recommend reserving antidepressants for addicts with depressions that last longer than four to six weeks. One way to explain this variability in antidepressant efficacy is to hypothesize that addicts, who are often known to have high levels of anxiety in conjunction with depression, may respond better to a more sedating antidepressant such as doxepin than to those with comparatively low sedative properties, such as imipramine and desipramine.

Antidepressants have also been found to be effective in reducing the craving associated with cocaine withdrawal (Gawin and Kleber 1984; Kleber 1987; Small and Purcell 1985; Tennent and Sagherian 1987) that often prompts relapse. Due to the delayed onset of antidepressant therapeutic effect, Kleber (1987), Tennent and Sagherian (1987), and Kosten et al. (1987a) suggest the initial use of amantadine to mitigate the severity of cocaine withdrawal. Kosten et al. (1987a) and Kleber (1987) stress the importance of monitoring antidepressant plasma levels in this population. Kleber (1987) reports a desipramine blood level of 100–200 ng/ml, maintained over a two- to three-month period, to be an effective treatment course for cocaine withdrawal.

Schizophrenia

The occurrence of depression in patients during and emerging from schizophrenic psychotic episodes has been carefully described, and its frequency in various studies ranges from 12 percent to 50 percent, with the average estimated roughly at 25 percent (Weissman et al. 1977). Prusoff et al. (1979) specifically tested the efficacy of perphenazine and amitriptyline versus perphenazine and placebo in 35 chronic schizophrenic outpatients who also met the criteria for secondary depression. All patients were maintained on perphenazine for at least one month prior to inclusion in the study, and perphenazine was adjusted to achieve optimum control of psychotic symptoms. In addition, patients were randomly assigned in a double-blind manner to a flexible dose of 100–200 mg amitriptyline or matching placebo. Patients were followed for four months. Results showed that the addition of amitriptyline to perphenazine when compared with perphenazine alone was more effective in reducing the symptoms of depression after four months of treatment. However, there was a slight worsening of thought disorder in the amitriptyline group at the end of one month and at the end of the study. At the end of four months, patients in the amitriptyline group showed significantly reduced symptoms of depression and an overall improvement in social well-being. The benefits of amitriptyline were due to a general improvement of many patients rather than to a considerable change in only a few. However, the results are not straightforward since the addition of amitriptyline may require additional perphenazine for adequate management of psychotic symptoms.

It has been suggested (Van Putten and May 1978) that what appears to be depression may, in some schizophrenics, be subclinical or undiagnosed phenothiazine side effects, the syndrome of neuroleptic-induced akinesia. Johnson (1981) studied 40 Schneiderian or Feighner positive chronic schizophrenic patients on depot neuroleptics who scored a minimum of 15 on the Beck Depression Inventory in the absence of overt morbidity from extrapyramidal symptoms. Patients were rated on the Hamilton Rating Scale for depression at the end of the first, fifth, and ninth weeks. They then received either orphenedrine 50 mg twice daily or placebo in identical tablets. At the end of four weeks, the placebo and active drug were discontinued. There was a small, nonsignificant improvement in depression among patients on orphenedrine. These patients had experienced significantly more muscle weakness and stiffness and may have had neuroleptic-induced akinesia rather than depression. However, the sample was carefully chosen to exclude patients with morbidity from extrapyramidal symptoms, and it may be that orphenedrine has either a true antidepressant effect or a mood-elevating action of its own. The author, however, considers it most likely that the drug has another effect and reversed a more subtle and less easily detected syndrome, which the patient described as depression. The author also notes a high placebo response and concludes that his data do not justify routine use of antiparkinsonian drugs.

The same author reports a double-blind trial of nortriptyline in 50 schizophrenic patients maintained in remission who developed an acute episode of depression. Patients met criteria similar to those of his other study. They noted the same strong placebo response as in the orphenedrine trial, with 40 percent showing at least some improvement. This made it unlikely that a level of statistical difference could be reached in a sample of only 50. However, more patients in the nortriptyline group were free of depression at the completion of the trial. If this trend had continued, a level of significance might well have been achieved. However, even so, only a minority of the total of depressed patients would have responded, and the author concludes that his findings do not support the common practice of prescribing antidepressants to depressed schizophrenics and continuing such medication for lengthy periods in the absence of an early clinical response.

Van Kammen et al. (1980) recently reported that six of 11 drug-free schizophrenic patients who were depressed following remission of their illness showed a significant decrease in their depressive symptomatology during a double-blind placebo-substitution lithium trial. Except for one patient who received a diagnosis of paranoid schizophrenia, all were diagnosed as schizoaffective disorder depressed. All patients were off neuroleptic drugs for at least two weeks prior to the study. Lithium carbonate was given for three weeks with a starting dose of 1,800 mg/day; the dose then changed according to blood levels, which during the study ranged from 0.7 to 1.3 mEq/l. Identical placebo capsules were given at least two weeks before, during, and for two weeks after the lithium trials, with patients receiving a constant number of capsules throughout the procedure. Patients were rated daily for global depression and psychosis using the 15-point Bunney-Hamburg Rating Scale. As noted, six of the 11 patients experienced a significant decrease in depressive symptomatology, with two becoming almost symptom free. However, the antidepressant response was only moderate, and three weeks are inadequate to show a sustained effect. The authors conclude that "lithium should be evaluated further as an adjunct in the clinical management of schizophrenia."

Siris (1985) and Siris et al. (1978, 1982, 1983, 1986, in press a, in press b) have contributed a body of research aimed at an understanding of the relationship of depression to schizophrenia and at the development of appropriate treatment strategies. This group studied 15 cases of postpsychotic depression prospectively over three weeks (Siris et al. 1986), with eight cases remaining unchanged, five remitting spontaneously, and two decompensating into psychosis. The authors suggest that implementation of antidepressant treatment of a postpsychotic depression is best delayed for a week or two since depression may remit spontaneously or progress to psychosis. Consequently, studies in which therapy was implemented at the onset of depression may yield misleading conclusions both about antidepressant efficacy as compared with placebo and with regard to the triggering of psychotic decompensation. These authors also emphasize the importance of discriminating between the akinetic extrapyramidal side effects of neuroleptic medication and depression because extrapyramidal side effects are not known to respond to antidepressants. Siris suggests adjusting neuroleptic dosage and antiparkinsonian dosage (e.g., a one-week trial of oral benzotropine mesylate 2 mg tid) to facilitate an alleviation of extrapyramidal depression-like symptoms (Siris 1985; Siris et al. 1978). For those patients whose depression remains unchanged, Siris has found imipramine in doses of 100 mg/day to be beneficial, with no psychotic exacerbation in patients whose psychosis was controlled by fluphenazine (Siris et al. 1982, 1983, in press a, in press b). The symptoms most likely to respond include dysphoria, insomnia, poor appetite, anergia, poor concentration, and self-reproach. Siris advises that drug plasma levels be obtained because tricyclic antidepressant concentrations may be increased above expected levels when neuroleptics are administered at the same time, thus increasing the potential for toxicity. There may also be an overlap between negative symptoms and postpsychotic depression, in which case a trial of antidepressant medication is probably indicated.

Conclusions

In all primary psychiatric disorders studied, the prevalence of secondary depression is high and presents both diagnostic and treatment problems. Diagnostic difficulties include establishing the chronology of the depression and other psychiatric disorders, and differentiating the depression from the other psychiatric disorders. In addition, a secondary diagnosis of depression is often obscured by an overlap of the symptoms of depression with treatment side effects or withdrawal.

Treatment of a primary psychiatric disorder may be undermined if a secondary depression is untreated. The efficacy data for treatment of secondary depression are scanty in large part because the numbers of depressed patients who are alcoholics, addicts, or schizophrenics or who suffer from other significant psychiatric illness have been excluded from most treatment efficacy trials involving depressed patients. No data are available, therefore, unless a study has been specifically designed to examine these groups.

Well-controlled studies of the efficacy of treatments of secondary depression are needed. These studies should ideally include 1) differential diagnoses of both the primary and secondary disorder, using standardized diagnostic criteria; 2) inclusion of unequivocal cases of secondary depression; 3) testing of an appropriate treatment for the secondary depression against a control treatment in a randomly assigned, double-blind design; 4) use of appropriate treatment for the primary disorder, if one is indicated; 5) control of potential confounding variables such as age, chronicity, etc.; 6) methods to determine compliance with and adequacy of drug dosage—for example, drug plasma levels; 7) adequate treatment duration; and 8) clear differentiation of outcome using standardized instruments that address whether the treatment helps the secondary depression, the primary disorder, or both.

Chapter 177

Bipolar Disorders

Recent advances in the epidemiology, psychobiology, and pharmacotherapy of manic-depressive conditions have led to a greater recognition of this illness in all of its varieties. The lifetime risk for bipolar conditions is at least 1.2 percent, making them slightly more common than schizophrenic disorders. A higher percentage of acute psychiatric hospital admissions is now being assigned to the category of manic depression, and recognition of clinically attenuated outpatient forms of the illness is increasing.

Reasons for the current focus on the entire diagnosable range of bipolar conditions are several. Predominant among these is the tendency of diagnostic practice to follow the availability of effective treatment modalities (Lehmann 1970). After the discovery of chlorpromazine, North American psychiatrists were tacitly encouraged to elicit subtle degrees of formal thought disorder from their patients so as to bring them the benefits of this new class of drugs. By the early 1970s, schizophrenia had become more or less synonymous with psychosis (exclusive of organic brain syndrome). With the advent of lithium carbonate treatment—and its well-documented efficacy for bipolar disorders—this trend became reversed in favor of bipolar disorders. In the DSM-III (American Psychiatric Association 1980), the concept of schizophrenia is largely restricted to a core group of deteriorating psychotic disorders while mood disorders have been broadened to include even those with mood-incongruent psychotic features that coincide with affective episodes. This diagnostic approach reflects more than just therapeutic fashion; it is supported by familial aggregation, course, and outcome. Available evidence indicates that mood disorders are often recurrent and, especially in bipolar conditions, can lead to considerable impairment in developmental, conjugal, and social spheres. Suicide is a common outcome, seen in at least 15 percent of those who receive inadequate or no treatment, and must be considered a preventable complication (Khuri and Akiskal 1983). Finally, medicolegal considerations dictate avoiding the unnecessary and unacceptable risk of tardive dyskinesia in misdiagnosed bipolar patients.

At the other end of the spectrum, milder degrees of bipolar disorder—subsumed under the rubrics of cyclothymic disorder and bipolar disorder not otherwise specified—are now categorized as mood disorders rather than being grouped with neurotic or personality disorders. Although these milder and "atypical" variants may not be easily distinguishable from nonaffective personality disorders, the clinician is advised to err on the side of affective diagnosis because of the availability of specific treatments. However, a positive response to lithium in a therapeutic trial would not necessarily support an affective diagnosis. External validating strategies—such as family history, course, and interepisodic temperamental features—are often necessary to confirm the diagnosis of these affective variants (Cassano et al. 1988).

The past decade has witnessed an increased diagnostic rigor concomitant with the introduction of new and effective treatments for mood disorders. These developments have also led to the establishment of mood clinics where patients with bipolar and recurrent mood disorders are studied and treated. Medical sophistication is one of the hallmarks of such clinics.

Lithium Workup and Pharmacokinetic Considerations

More than any other development, the introduction of lithium has emphasized the role of physicianship in psychiatry. The scientific literature and clinical wisdom on the therapeutic aspects of this salt have been well summarized in a monograph by Jefferson et al. (1983). The success of lithium treatment is dependent on the thoroughness of the initial workup, on dosage titration procedures, and on appropriate monitoring throughout therapy.

The type of workup depends on the age of the patient and concurrent medical conditions (Table 1). In young (less than 40 years), physically healthy subjects, preparation for lithium therapy should include medical history (especially focused on neurologic, renal, cardiac, gastrointestinal, endocrine, and cutaneous systems), physical examination, and laboratory evaluation focusing on electrolytes and thyroid. In older patients or those with a history of cardiac disease, a baseline electrocardiogram (EKG) should be obtained and an electroencephalogram (EEG) performed if brain disease is suspected; if there is a history of renal disease, thorough evaluation of baseline kidney function is mandatory. Given rigorous indications for lithium, major medical illness and abnormalities in laboratory indices do not necessarily contraindicate its use; they do dictate, however, greater medical vigilance, including frequent determination of blood levels and use of lower doses.

A short-term lithium trial in the controlled environment of a hospital is relatively easy to administer and is recommended for acutely manic, medically ill, or elderly subjects. In outpatient practice, the physician must make sure that the patient and significant others understand the importance of compliance with periodic laboratory procedures and monitoring of side effects.

Lithium is rapidly and completely absorbed from the gastrointestinal tract and peaks in the serum in about 1.5 to 2.0 (standard forms) or 4.0 to 4.5 hours (slow-release forms), depending on age. Its half-life varies from 24 to 36 hours; steady state is reached in about four days. Lithium is not protein-bound and is excreted unchanged almost entirely through the kidneys. It can be safely combined with most classes of drugs except diuretics and nonsteroidal anti-inflammatory agents (other than aspirin), which tend to increase the serum lithium level.

Acutely manic—and possibly bipolar depressive—patients have a high tolerance for lithium and preferentially retain it during the first 10 days while excreting sodium;

Table 1. Recommended Laboratory Workup of Patients Considered for Lithium Therapy

Healthy < 40 years	All others
● Weight	● EKG
● CBC	● EEG
● T_4/TSH	● TRH test
● FBS/serum electrolytes	● 24-hr urine volume
● Urinalysis	● Urine concentration test
● BUN/creatinine	● Creatinine clearance

a regular diet is recommended. Postpubertal bipolar patients, who typically have excellent glomerular function, require higher doses to achieve the same level of equilibrium in the serum. The reverse is true in the geriatric age group (Vestegaard and Schou 1984). Elderly subjects with adequate glomerular function have been shown to benefit considerably from lithium salts in two open studies (Schaffer and Garvey 1984; Shulman and Post 1980). However, greater medical vigilance is required for this group; initial doses should be low (150–300 mg/d), with frequent clinical and laboratory monitoring to maintain blood levels in the lower range (0.3–0.8 mEq/L). Special attention must be paid to signs of sinus node dysfunction (bradycardia) or neurotoxicity; the latter is particularly likely in patients with concurrent neurologic disease or sedative and alcohol abuse (Himmelhoch et al. 1980).

In healthy subjects who achieve good episode prevention, quarterly serum levels (12 hours after the last dose) and serum creatinine are generally sufficient; thyroid indices must be obtained at least once a year. For elderly or medically compromised patients, laboratory tests should be repeated as dictated by the medical condition, with frequent serum lithium levels; the dosage should be kept at the lowest possible level compatible with prophylaxis.

Pharmacotherapy of Bipolar Disorder

Depressive Phase

Despite clinical opinion to the contrary, lithium has been found effective in acute depressives in 10 of 13 controlled comparisons with either placebo or tricyclic antidepressants (TCAs) (reviewed by Fieve and Peselow 1983). The greatest response rate was seen in bipolar depressives, but even "unipolars" responded to this salt, albeit in lower percentages. This is due to the heterogeneity of unipolar depressions, some of which are related to bipolar disorder. Onset of antidepressant effect may require two to three weeks and is generally thought to require a serum lithium level more than 0.6 mEq/L.

The antidepressant effect may be augmented when lithium is given in combination with a heterocyclic antidepressant (HCA) or a monoamine oxidase inhibitor (MAOI). Again, in many instances positive responses may not occur before a latency of two to three weeks; it is best to opt for suboptimal doses of the antidepressant and gradually raise it when no response occurs within this time frame. Although the efficacy of lithium-TCA combinations is better documented (de Montigny et al. 1981; Heninger et al. 1983), clinical opinion tends to favor lithium-MAOI combinations (Himmelhoch and Neil 1980). Part of the reason for this discrepancy is due to the fact that lithium augmentation of HCAs was not specifically tested in bipolar depressives. As discussed later in this chapter, some authorities believe that antidepressants contribute to the risk for rapid-cycling; therefore, it is advisable to discontinue the HCA as soon as an antidepressant effect is achieved in bipolar patients.

Positive responses to lithium augmentation were also reported in an open trial of psychotic depressives (Nelson and Mazure 1986); these patients, who had established prior bipolar course and who were previously unresponsive to a TCA-neuroleptic regimen, did benefit significantly from the addition of lithium to that regimen. Bipolar depressions that are unresponsive to pharmacotherapy, especially when the patient is psychotic or stuporous, often remit quickly with electroconvulsive therapy (ECT) (Fink 1979). Lithium should be discontinued two to three days before initiating ECT because of the potential for neurotoxicity with coadministration (Ayd 1981).

Manic and Mixed Phases

Manic psychosis typically presents as a social emergency and is best managed on an inpatient ward. Since Cade's (1949) open trial in Australia, numerous controlled studies have documented the antimanic efficacy of lithium salts (reviewed in Kocsis 1980). However, in the presence of extreme manic psychosis, neuroleptics have an edge over lithium in terms of rapid control (Garfinkel et al. 1980; Goodwin and Zis 1979; Tyrer 1985). In patients with mania of moderate severity or milder hypomanic states, lithium is preferred in view of its hypothesized specificity for the underlying biologic substrates of bipolar disorder.

After a proper lithium workup, lithium carbonate is generally started at 300 mg orally bid, with the dosage increased over a seven- to 10-day period until a serum level of 0.8 to 1.2 mEq/L is reached. Although some patients require serum levels as high as 1.5 mEq/L before a response is seen, lower levels are preferable to avoid toxicity. Because of the four- to 15-day latency before the onset of action, it may be necessary to coadminister an intramuscular neuroleptic such as trifluoperazine, thiothixene, or haloperidol (5 to 10 mg bid to tid) until the manic psychosis is under control. Antiparkinsonian drugs are sometimes needed to control acute extrapyramidal reactions during this phase.

A neuroleptic-lithium combination is almost routinely required in the management of manic patients with mixed features. Those unresponsive to the combination often benefit from six to 10 treatments with ECT (Black et al. 1987; Kukopulos and Réginaldi 1980). Postpartum mania, which often takes the form of a mixed state, responds particularly well to ECT (Katona 1982). In extremely hyperactive and uncooperative patients, who often have suboptimal and precarious food and fluid intake, it is advisable to lyse the psychosis with vigorous neuroleptic treatment (e.g., haloperidol, 30–60 mg/day) before initiating lithium (Rifkin and Siris 1983). Delirious mania (characterized by unremitting frenzied physical activity) constitutes a rare medical emergency and requires almost daily sessions of bilateral ECT for five to seven days (Small et al. 1986). The evidence for the efficacy of ECT in mania is derived from systematic clinical studies; double-blind placebo-controlled—for example, ECT versus sham ECT-controlled—studies would be ethically objectionable in view of the severity of the psychosis.

In all combination therapies, the neuroleptic should be discontinued as soon as symptomatic control is achieved. Although the risk of neurotoxicity in neuroleptic-lithium combination has been exaggerated (Gelenberg 1983), it is desirable to limit the patient's exposure to high doses of two potent psychoactive drugs. Careful monitoring of vital signs and mental status indicators of neurotoxicity is essential, especially during the first two weeks of combined therapy.

Lithium therapy for an isolated manic episode should be continued for about six months. This also applies to manias secondary to drugs (e.g., exogenous steroids) or to medical disorders (e.g., systemic lupus erythematosus). Vigorous treatment of the underlying medical condition is also recommended in these organic mood disorders, although it is not always successful without adjunctive lithium therapy. Most commonly, however, a manic episode is part of a recurrent bipolar disorder, and indefinite maintenance with lithium carbonate is indicated except for those rare cases with infrequent episodes.

Maintenance Phase

The prophylactic effects of lithium carbonate against recurrent episodes of mania and depression represent one of the best-documented treatments in all of medicine (Davis 1976; Prien 1983; Schou 1968).

The course of illness prior to the index episode is a good predictor of future course and aids the decision as to when to use maintenance lithium (Angst et al. 1979a,b). Generally, a patient who has experienced two or more major episodes within five years should be considered for long-term lithium maintenance. In adolescence, when affective episodes can disrupt crucial developmental tasks, maintenance lithium should probably be considered with the first manic episode and continued until graduation from high school; the need for further maintenance can be reassessed after a closely monitored lithium holiday. The clinician should also give consideration to administering prophylactic lithium to adolescent psychotic depressives in their first episodes—in view of their high risk for development of mania—until major developmental tasks are accomplished (Akiskal et al. 1983; Strober and Carlson 1982).

Maintenance serum levels are generally held within the range of 0.4 to 1.0 mEq/L, usually achieved with three to five 300-mg pills per day. It often takes as long as two years to determine the optimal blood level for a given patient—that is, one that provides sufficient protection against major episodes without intolerable side effects. Patients should be advised of the possibility of relapses until stabilization is achieved.

Depressive Relapses

Minor depressive relapses are best treated with supportive psychotherapy. It is desirable to limit the use of TCAs in bipolar patients to major depressive relapses and to opt for short-term modest doses because of indications from systematic clinical studies that use of these agents, even in conjunction with adequate lithium levels, can accelerate the cyclicity of the disorder (Akiskal and Mallya 1987; Kukopulos et al. 1980; Wehr and Goodwin 1979). Since MAOIs appear somewhat less likely to produce this effect, it is recommended that the physician consider their use (e.g., tranylcypromine 10–40 mg/day) in the management of retarded depressive relapses on lithium (Quitkin et al. 1981). When borderline and rarely frank hypothyroid indices (Extein and Gold 1986) account for these depressive relapses under lithium carbonate, T_3 supplementation, 25–50 mcg/day, is recommended, though it is not always effective.

Hypomanic and Manic Relapses

Since most patients welcome hypomanic swings, minor elevations of mood should generally not be treated. For more serious relapses in a manic or mixed direction, the clinician may attempt, for a duration of two to three weeks, either an upward adjustment of the lithium dose or the addition of a neuroleptic (thioridazine, 50–400 mg/day, or another suitable agent, preferably given at bedtime).

In the noncompliant aggressive manic, a depot phenothiazine such as fluphenazine decanoate, 12.5 to 50.0 mg IM every three to six weeks, is often necessary. Because of the risk of tardive dyskinesia, lithium should be substituted as soon as possible. Intermittent courses of such neuroleptics may also be necessary in bipolar patients with mood-incongruent psychotic features that are beyond the usual boundaries of a "pure" mood disorder; as discussed later in this chapter, evidence is accumulating about the efficacy of carbamazepine for such patients.

Side Effects and Toxicity

The most common benign side effects of lithium are tremor, nausea, diarrhea, polyuria, edema, and weight gain (partly attributed to increased intake of high-calorie beverages). These are usually transient and may respond to a slight downward adjustment of the lithium dosage and to the use of slow-release preparations. Tremor is usually more severe with concurrent TCA or neuroleptic medication; thus, one option is to either lower the dosage of such medication or change to a class less likely to be tremorogenic (e.g., tranylcypromine or thioridazine). Some clinicians advocate short courses of atenolol, 25 mg orally tid or qid, for incapacitating tremor; however, caution must be exercised in elderly patients because of the likelihood that beta blockers will increase the risk of lithium-induced bradycardia; other contraindications in this age group—such as heart failure—should also be kept in mind.

Weight gain is one of the most troublesome side effects of lithium, especially in weight-conscious women. Periodic lithium holidays can be planned, with caution, in stabilized patients who gain excessive weight on a maintenance regimen. Diet and exercise programs can sometimes be more successfully instituted during such holidays and, it is hoped, carried through the next phase of maintenance. As with all drug holidays, the physician must first make sure that the patient is reliable and motivated and will report the earliest signs of relapse.

Other side effects seen during lithium maintenance include mild leukocytosis of no functional significance; hypothyroidism, which can be successfully managed with thyroid supplementation; exacerbation or precipitation of psoriasis, which may not respond well to conventional treatments; and acneiform eruptions, which generally respond well to standard treatment. In the latter situation, it is best to monitor the lithium level closely because, while antibiotics used for acne have not been shown definitely to raise this level, clinical vigilance is necessary before such a drug interaction is conclusively ruled out. Nephrogenic diabetes insipidus, which is an uncommon complication, may respond to reduction of, a single daily dosage of, or a two- to three-week interruption of lithium therapy, or, paradoxically, to a thiazide diuretic (Himmelhoch et al. 1977).

In all patients suspected of kidney disease, serial serum creatinine or creatinine clearance should be performed and consultation with a nephrologist obtained. Grof's review (1983) summarizes the emerging clinical wisdom in this area. Paradoxically, giving the entire amount of lithium in a single dose (standard-release preparations) may protect the kidney, but it creates problems in interpreting the 12-hour serum lithium level. Patients with preexisting parenchymal kidney disease are at risk for structural damage to the distal tubules; therefore, serum lithium levels should generally be maintained at the lowest level compatible with freedom from incapacitating mood swings. Lithium nonresponders may be at a greater risk than responders for developing kidney damage (as assessed by greater 24-hour urine volume), a fact that underscores the importance of limiting maintenance lithium therapy to compliant patients who have shown definitive evidence of response. Promising alternatives to lithium are fortunately becoming available for patients whose physical health does not permit its safe use.

Lithium toxicity is initially manifested by gross tremor, ataxia, persistent headache, slurred speech, vomiting, and mental confusion, which may progress to incontinence, stupor, seizures, and cardiac arrhythmias. Apart from overdoses, such toxicity is more likely in patients who have renal disease with decreased creatinine clearance or excessive sodium loss from profuse sweating, severe vomiting, or diarrhea, or who are concurrently using thiazide and potassium-sparing diuretics. Acute lithium toxicity (Schou 1980) is a medical emergency and is typically seen with serum levels greater than 2 mEq/L (although toxicity can sometimes occur with "therapeutic" blood levels). In cases of overdose, all psychoactive medication must be withheld, and gastric lavage is often necessary. Infusing 1,500 to 3,000 mEq of sodium chloride over six hours to force lithium diuresis can be attempted for mild to moderate intoxication; hemodialysis may be indicated, in more severe intoxication or when these measures fail.

Special Considerations in Pregnancy

In women who desire to have a child, it is best to wait for at least two years of episode-free maintenance on lithium before prescribing a lithium holiday (which should come prior to discontinuation of contraception). Conception during such a holiday would avert the risk for cardiovascular malformations such as Ebstein's anomaly, known to occur in the first trimester of lithium use (Schou and Weinstein 1980). Also, although it is uncertain whether HCAs are teratogenic, they should also be avoided in the first trimester. If there is a serious relapse soon after conception, ECT may be a safer alternative than medication. If necessary (e.g., in a patient who has had previous postpartum episodes or who shows signs of relapse), lithium or an appropriate HCA can be reinstituted during the second trimester but must be stopped two weeks before delivery and resumed immediately postpartum. These mothers should not nurse because lithium and HCAs are secreted into milk. The psychiatrist must enlist the support of the patient's spouse or significant others and work closely with the patient's obstetrician and a neonatologist.

Alternatives to Lithium

The efficacy of carbamazepine (CBZ) has been upheld in randomized double-blind trials against chlorpromazine (Okuma 1983) and against lithium (Lerer et al. 1987; Placidi et al. 1986), and in a double-blind crossover study in rapid-cyclers (Ballenger and Post 1980). Therefore, a CBZ trial is worthwhile in patients who are unable to tolerate lithium or are resistant to it (Lerer 1985; Post 1985). Although not yet FDA-approved for uses other than epilepsy and trigeminal neuralgia, CBZ is emerging as an alternative drug for manic and bipolar depressive patients who fail to respond to lithium—especially rapid-cycling patients and those with mood-incongruent psychotic features. Judging from dropout rates during the acute phase of the Placidi et al. (1986) double-blind comparison of CBZ versus lithium, mood-incongruent affective and schizophreniform patients respond preferentially to CBZ (figure 1). EEG findings or other evidence of seizure disorders are not related to responsiveness of affective disorders to CBZ (Okuma 1983). Indeed, Italian experience (Placidi et al. 1986) indicates that CBZ is effective in a broad range of mood disorders, ranging from high-episode frequency recurrent and major depressive to bipolar and mood-incongruent categories. In brief, the effectiveness of CBZ does not appear restricted to rapid-cycling, atypical, mood-incongruent, or lithium-resistant patients.

Although the above systematic trials have provided documentation for efficacy, psychiatric experience with CBZ is relatively new and the total number of patients treated is still limited. Dosage should be increased gradually, starting at 400 mg/day given with meals in two divided doses (upper limit = 1,600 mg/per day). Blood levels, although not entirely reliable as an indicator of clinical response, should generally be maintained between 7 and 12 μg/ml; plasma levels of the metabolite carbamazepine-10,11-epoxide appear to correlate better with response (Post and Ballenger 1983). CBZ

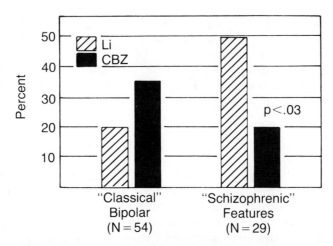

Figure 1. Dropouts during acute phase of pharmacotherapy in lithium (Li) and carbamazepine (CBZ) treated patients compared by diagnostic class. Reproduced from Placidi et al. (1986).

has been safely combined with lithium and other thymoleptic drugs. In such combinations, it is prudent to avoid maximal therapeutic doses of either drug. Also, it must be kept in mind that MAOIs raise CBZ blood levels.

The acute side effect profile of CBZ, consisting of nausea, drowsiness, ataxia, and slurred speech at high doses, can be minimized by a slow build-up to the therapeutic dose. Hematologic toxicity is considered to be the major drawback of this drug. Conservatively, the clinician may monitor the CBC weekly during the first months of treatment and then monthly for six to nine months; the drug is discontinued if white blood count (WBC) falls below 3,000 per mm^3, hematocrit is below 32.0 percent, and platelets are less than 0.3 percent. Clinical monitoring for early signs of agranulocytosis (e.g., sore throat or unexplained fever) is probably a more efficient method of detecting hematologic toxicity. Because CBZ slows atrioventricular (A-V) conduction, EKG monitoring is indicated in patients with heart block. Monitoring of liver and kidney function is necessary for patients with preexisting disease in these organs.

Other drugs under experimental consideration for refractory mania include the benzodiazepines clonazepam (Chouinard et al. 1983) and lorazepam (Lenox et al. 1986), the anticonvulsant sodium valproate (Puzynski and Klosiewicz 1984), and the calcium channel blocker verapamil (Dubovsky and Franks 1983). Although these drugs are promising in selected cases—even during the depressive phase in some instances—extensive experience about their safety and differential indications is lacking at this point.

It may also be feasible to limit pharmacotherapy for some patients with periodic or seasonal episodes to the months of greatest risk, thereby giving them a few months of lithium holidays per year (Akiskal 1985).

Increasing home lighting by using bright white light (2,500 lux) for an extra four to six hours per day over a one- to two-week period is a new experimental approach for bipolar depressives, especially those with seasonal occurrence (Rosenthal et al. 1985). This treatment is difficult to evaluate on a double-blind basis. The effectiveness of phototherapy has been demonstrated in controlled trials (i.e., bright versus dim light) in at least four different centers. Another nonpharmacologic approach to bipolar depressives is total sleep deprivation two or three times per week. This treatment, which also cannot be easily evaluated on a double-blind basis, has been shown to be modestly effective in several European and U.S. studies (reviewed by King 1977); sleep deprivation has the potential to activate hypomania and even mania, and is believed to work via eliminating REM sleep (Vogel et al. 1980).

Pharmacotherapy of Bipolar Variants

The premorbid and interepisodic phases of bipolar disorder can be "normal" or "supernormal," or they may be characterized by temperamental and characterological instability. In perhaps one-third to one-half of all bipolar patients—especially those encountered in ambulatory settings—syndromal (major affective) and subsyndromal (cyclothymic) cycles are so closely interwoven that the illness takes an essentially intermittent or chronic form. These conditions present a considerable diagnostic and therapeutic challenge.

The pharmacologic approaches discussed below are not specifically FDA approved for these special forms of bipolar disorder. The clinician must judge how closely these conditions approximate the "classic" forms of bipolar disorder (which assume at least one documented period of mania), for which lithium carbonate is presently the treatment of choice. If one adheres too closely to a "narrow" definition of bipolar disorder, a large number of patients who might otherwise benefit from lithium would be left without specific treatment. Of course, any decision to use lithium should carefully weigh the risk-benefit ratio for these atypical patients.

Cyclothymic Disorder

The advent of lithium treatment rekindled interest in cyclothymia. The psychiatric presentation of these young adults is almost entirely of a characterologic nature, including repeated conjugal and romantic failure, impulsive promiscuity, uneven school and occupational record, dilettantism, and geographic instability (Akiskal et al. 1979). Indeed, many patients simultaneously meet criteria for such Axis II labels as "histrionic," "antisocial," or "borderline." The affective basis of their condition may not be apparent, but it could be prospectively supported by biphasic manifestations on a lower plane of severity, bipolar familial background, and hypomanic responses to TCAs.

In its most typical form, cyclothymia is characterized by cyclic alteration of subdepressive and hypomanic swings. Subdepressive periods dominate in some patients and hypomanic periods dominate in others; irritable periods—subdepressive and hypomanic admixtures occurring simultaneously—are also observed in many cyclothymics. Those with predominantly subdepressive and irritable swings are more likely to present for clinical advice.

Patients with predominantly hypomanic swings are unlikely to seek help unless full-blown mania develops. In the absence of manic decompensation, many hypomanic individuals function exceedingly well and are often leaders in industry, business, professions, and public office. When they develop major depressions, the premorbid hypomanic adjustment may unfortunately be overlooked—or mislabeled "compulsive." These considerations are of important clinical significance because premorbid hypomanic adjustment is a risk factor for rapid-cycling (Kukopulos et al. 1983).

The decision to initiate a lithium trial in cyclothymia depends on the degree to which the patient's life is disrupted by unstable moods. Successful prophylaxis with lithium carbonate has been reported in an open study (Akiskal et al. 1979) and a controlled trial (Peselow et al. 1982). It may take three to four months before a significant attentuation of mood swings can be demonstrated in cyclothymia, and as long as one year for optimal results. Although it is uncertain how long lithium maintenance should be continued, patients should probably be given the option of lithium holidays after two years of satisfactory stabilization, with subsequent reassessment of any further treatment needs.

Bipolar Disorder Not Otherwise Specified

This condition is characterized by recurrent hypersomnic-retarded major depressive episodes and occasional brief periods of mild elevation that fall short of the symptomatic threshold for full-blown mania. These brief hypomanic periods, which typically precede or follow the depressive episodes, are often pleasant, adaptive, and ego-syntonic, and are therefore rarely reported to the physician. As a result, the bipolar nature of the illness is typically missed.

When given TCAs, these patients either fail to respond, rapidly cycle out of a depression, or develop brief hypomanic excursions (Akiskal et al. 1979). A hypomanic shift may be mislabeled "flight into health" or a "transference cure" (Akiskal 1985). Long-term exposure to HCAs may shift the course of these patients in the direction of rapid cycling (Kukopulos et al. 1983). Furthermore, repeated episodes of uncontrolled depression lead to interpersonal havoc. Although combined treatment (TCA + lithium) is commonly employed in practice, therapy with lithium carbonate alone is preferable and has proven effective in two controlled studies (Dunner et al. 1982; Kane et al. 1982). Should an antidepressant be absolutely necessary, clinical wisdom would favor the addition of an MAOI over a period of a few weeks (Himmelhoch and Neil 1980).

Rapid-Cycling Forms

Although the contribution of HCAs to rapid-cycling is not established in randomized prospective studies, the available systematic clinical literature (e.g., Wehr et al. 1988; and others cited below) can be used as a guide for preventive and therapeutic efforts in this difficult group of patients.

Rapid-cycling may complicate the course of a previously "typical" bipolar disorder, or it may begin de novo and continue relentlessly over many years (Dunner 1979). The incidence of rapid-cycling may be as high as 10 percent among bipolar patients; the phenomenon is more common in women, especially those with low thyroid indices and those who have been exposed to long-term TCAs (Kukopulos et al. 1980). The controversy over whether TCAs and the larger class of HCAs induce cycling is possibly due to the fact that those who oppose the idea (e.g., Lewis and Winokur 1982) have studied samples—largely inpatient—that exclude bipolars at highest risk.

Some patients may simply respond to discontinuance of TCAs (while maintaining lithium), others may respond to thyroid supplementation of lithium. Related recommendations are to supplement lithium with either a low dose of one of the traditional MAOIs (or the experimental MAOI clorgyline) or carbamazepine. Finally, the clinician should give consideration to clonazepam, valproic acid, or verapamil. This list is itself evidence of the generally unsatisfactory nature of available therapies for rapid-cycling bipolar patients and emphasizes the need for prevention by withholding TCAs from those at risk (Table 2).

Clinical appreciation of the phenomenon of cycling in recurrent mood disorders is of recent origin (Akiskal et al. 1979; Bunney 1978; Kukopulos et al. 1980, 1983; Wehr and Goodwin 1979, 1987). It is submitted that the entire cyclothymic-bipolar II spectrum—what has been termed the "soft bipolar spectrum" (Akiskal and Mallya 1987)—is at risk for rapid-cycling when overexposed to HCAs. Soft bipolars, whose bipolarity is hidden from cross-sectional clinical (or even research) evaluations, are often mislabeled "unipolar" and may be overexposed to HCAs without the benefit of protection by lithium, thereby putting them at risk for modifications in the inherent cyclicity of their illness. In view of the gross underdiagnosis of the soft bipolar spectrum—resulting in overzealous treatment with HCAs—research clinicians have encountered several "natural experiments" among the large number of patients referred to specialized mood clinics.

In one such naturalistic study, Akiskal and Mallya (1987) observed a predominantly fall and winter distribution of nearly all bipolar II depressives presenting to the University of Tennessee Mood Clinic; the single case with hypomania came in the spring. The distribution was particularly striking for patients presenting with depression and previously untreated with medication. Those who had received TCAs developed episodes that, by history, altered their natrural course, thereby forcing a redistribution in the fall–winter occurrence of their depressions, which now appeared in the spring. Such data point to the potency of TCAs in effecting changes in the underlying infradian mechanisms of the illness.

In another study involving 68 juvenile offspring or siblings of strictly defined bipolars, Akiskal et al. (1985a,b) observed that manic and mixed onsets accounted for 16 percent, cyclothymic for 15 percent, polysubstance abuse for 16 percent, dysthymic for 18 percent, and major depressive for 35 percent. This meant that at least 53 percent of onsets were depressive (major or dysthymic). During prospective follow-up, an additional 11 percent switched, half under TCA challenge. In a subsequent reanalysis of these data, Akiskal and Mallya (1987) compared the pattern of recurrence over three years in depressive onsets (treated primarily with TCAs) with that of cyclic or manic and mixed onsets (treated primarily with lithium); all patients receiving medication were postpubertal. TCA-treated depressives, as compared with lithium-treated cyclic cases, had unexpectedly higher rates of recurrence (80 percent versus 54 percent, $p < .01$, two-tailed). Although posttreatment rapid-cycling per se (i.e., more than four episodes per year) occurred in only a few patients, it was limited to the TCA group. These data underscore the risks involved in the prescription of TCAs to unipolar patients with bipolar familial background and suggest the wisdom of lithium prophylaxis in such patients.

Rigorous guidelines as to how one should treat prepubertal bipolar disorder are unavailable at this time. Rapid-cycling and mixed bipolar forms with severe conduct disorder, though relatively uncommon in these age groups, are overrepresented in institutional settings; they often coexist with mental retardation (Carlson 1979). Cyclothymic, bipolar II, and chronic hypomanic forms have been described in prepu-

Table 2. Hypothesized Risk Factors for Rapid-Cycling in Bipolar Patients

• Female gender	• Premorbid cyclothymia or hyperthymia
• Borderline or frank hypothyroid indices	• Bipolar II subtype
• Menopause	• Extensive exposure to TCAs

bertal outpatients without concurrent nonaffective psychopathology (Akiskal et al. 1985a,b). Uncontrolled clinical experience (Campbell et al. 1984; DeLong and Nieman 1983; Youngerman and Canino 1978) suggests that lithium carbonate may benefit many of these patients and—in view of the considerations on rapid-cycling reviewed above—would be preferable to TCAs.

Chronic Depression in Bipolar Illness

Chronicity of depression lasting over one year is an uncommon occurrence in bipolar disorder. These patients typically have mixed features such as irritability, racing thoughts, agitation, confusion, intense suffering, insomnia, and hopelessness. Systematic data on the management of these difficult patients is unavailable. Clinical experience (Akiskal 1985a,b) would suggest the value of continued lithium maintenance, avoidance of HCAs, and possible synergism with sleep deprivation, low-dose MAOIs, T_3 or carbamazepine; ECT could also break such chronic cycles.

Chronic Mania

Continuously excited forms of mania constitute less than 5 percent of the bipolar spectrum (Akiskal 1986). They usually arise from the substrate of recurrent mania. Chronic alcohol use and concurrent cerebral pathology have been cited as possible contributing factors. Delusional grandiosity (e.g., of inventive genius or aristocratic ancestry), coupled with social deterioration, often leads to the misdiagnosis of paranoid schizophrenia. From a therapeutic point of view, this may be of minimal consequence; because chronic excitement is so personally reinforcing, subjective distress so minimal, and insight so lacking, such patients have no motivation to adhere to maintenance lithium therapy. Thus, the physician may have little choice but to resort to intermittent courses of depot neuroleptics.

Figure 2, adapted from Janicak and Boshes (1987), provides a decision tree to help the clinician approach different degrees of resistance to lithium as a function of the atypicality of the bipolar disorder. It must be kept in mind that when mood-incongruent psychosis occurs outside affective episodes and when rapid-cycling occurs irregularly on an hourly or daily basis, schizoaffective and organic mood disorder with an Axis III diagnosis of complex partial seizures, respectively, may better characterize these patients (Blumer 1984). The psychopathologic manifestations in these patients are typically pleomorphic and involve not only shifts in mood but also symptoms observed in neurotic, schizophreniform, and organic deliria.

Psychosocial Aspects and Psychotherapeutic Considerations

Formal psychotherapies alone—whether behavioral, cognitive, or psychodynamic—are not of proven efficacy in modifying the acute phase and long-term course of bipolar disorders. However, psychotherapy may be a valuable adjunct in combination with competent pharmacotherapy. Psychotherapeutic approaches represent a mixture of education, support, and more formal therapies. We shall focus on three areas that deserve special attention in bipolar disorders and its variants.

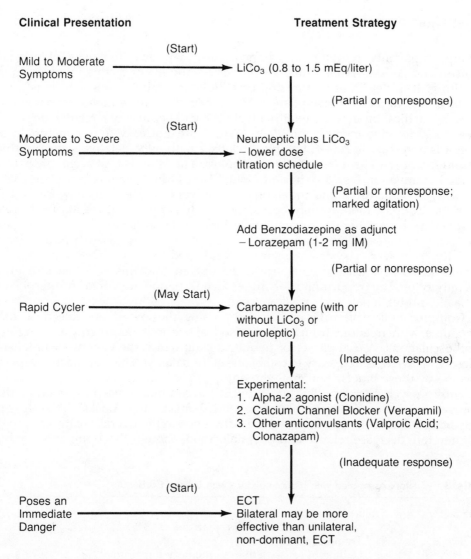

Figure 2. Strategies for the Pharmacotherapy of Manic and Related Excited Psychoses. Reproduced from Janicak and Boshes (1987).

Genetic Counseling

Although considerable evidence favors a genetic etiology, no genetic markers have been validated yet. The risk for offspring is 25 percent with bipolar parents and 35 percent with schizoaffective parents (Gershon and Goodnick 1981); the risk for offspring may be as high as 75 percent when both parents have an affective illness. Such information should be preferably discussed in couples sessions so that spouses or prospective mates can plan conception accordingly.

In monozygotic co-twins discordant for frank mood disorders, the risk for the discordant twin is about 70 percent (Bertlesen et al. 1977). The normal twin should probably be placed on lithium prophylaxis with the first disruptive affective episode.

Compliance

Bipolar patients are notoriously noncompliant with maintenance oral medication (Jamison and Akiskal 1983). Table 3 summarizes the major factors involved in drug defaulting. It is clear that minimizing or eliminating lithium side effects is a major goal in efforts to increase compliance. Many patients whose mood swings are controlled by medication may complain of feeling "flat" because of a relative depression; others may describe memory problems, which are not easy to document. In such cases, it is necessary to rule out atypical relapses without vegetative signs or lithium-induced hypothyroidism (especially in women). The latter is best accomplished with the TRH stimulation test (Extein and Gold 1986). Other patients complain that the loss of hypomanic drive and indefatigability adversely affects their work and relationships. Couples therapy may be indicated when treatment results in decreased assertiveness in a patient who previously took an aggressive, active role in sexual and social activities. Other patients may complain of decreased productivity and creativity. However, a systematic survey conducted by Schou (1981) among artists showed actual decreases in creativity to be uncommon; this is so because lithium generally offers the opportunity for more "even" periods devoted to interpersonal, scholastic, professional, and artistic pursuits.

Compliance can often be enhanced by using the lowest possible dose that is compatible with freedom from major episodes, without necessarily preventing all mood oscillations. A trial-and-error period, during which the patient's mental status is closely followed, is necessary to establish such a balance. This approach is especially welcome by those bipolar patients who enjoy hypomanic moods.

Group psychotherapy ("lithium groups") is commonly used in mood clinics to improve compliance (Gitlin and Jamison 1984; Jamison and Akiskal 1983). It is generally believed such groups improve the adherence to the overall treatment program and therefore decrease relapse and hospitalization, though this opinion is not based

Table 3.　Factors Associated with Noncompliance with Lithium Carbonate*

Drug factors	Side effects: 　Nausea, gastric irritation, diarrhea 　Tremor, incoordination 　Dulling of sense, lethargy, memory impairment Nuisance of blood levels Daily intake reminding patient of lifelong nature of illness Unusual reinforcement schedules, e.g., cessation is paired with positive reinforcement (hypomania) and compliance is paired with postmanic depression
Illness factors	Atypical depressive relapse (without vegetative signs) Lack of insight
Patient factors	Missing "highs," feeling "flat" Removal of hypomanic indefatigability "Reduced creativity" Sense of being less outgoing and confident
Physician factors	Ambivalence about lithium "Overselling" of lithium to patient Failure to educate patient and family

*Summarized from Jamison and Akiskal (1983).

on controlled randomized comparisons with routine clinic treatment (Shakir et al. 1979). It should be emphasized that bipolar patients are generally too disruptive in heterogeneous therapy groups.

Characterological Pathology

Recommendations regarding psychotherapeutic efforts in treating this aspect of bipolar disorder are also largely based on clinical considerations rather than on systematic outcome studies.

Many bipolar patients have considerable psychological assets, such as personal charm, affective warmth, creative bent, and a high drive to fight for or advance various causes. These assets can often be capitalized in attempts to reconstruct lives that have been shattered because of impulsiveness and poor social judgment. In general, depth interpretations are unlikely to change these impulsive excesses, and voluntary control of such behavior is desirable—for example, turning over the checkbook to the spouse (Akiskal et al. 1979; Stone 1979).

Characterological aspects are particularly relevant in the treatment of the cyclothymic-bipolar II spectrum. Because these conditions begin at an early age and pursue a periodic lifelong course, they may be mistaken for primary characterological disorders. These soft bipolar conditions are distinguished from the classical (or so-called major) mood disorders in that their baseline manifestations are subsyndromal, intermittent, and typically lifelong. That is, in the patient's *habitual* condition, the affective psychopathology does not typically crystallize into discrete episodes. However, clearcut and unmistakable syndromal episodes are not uncommonly superimposed on the lifelong course of these temperaments. It is this very intermittence that creates their resemblance to personality disorders. This is further reinforced by lifelong maladjustment in scholastic, occupational, and conjugal areas, secondary to chronically unstable and unpredictable moods. Finally, the mood change is often quite subtle, with behavioral and personal disturbances dominating the clinical presentation. For instance, in the University of Tennessee study of cyclothymic patients (Akiskal et al. 1979), affective manifestations were masked by interpersonal crises. Repeated marital failure or romantic breakups, episodic promiscuous behavior, alcohol and drug abuse, uneven work and school record, geographic instability, and dilettantism were the cardinal reasons for which these patients had come to clinical attention.

Unpredictability of moods is a major source of distress for cyclothymic individuals, who can't predict from one day to the next how they will feel. This undermines their sense of self and gives rise to apprehension, even during euthymic periods (Akiskal et al. 1979). Indeed, this temperamental propensity to change from one affective state to another with very little ego control over the change is one of the principal reasons why psychodynamically oriented clinicians may consider cyclothymic and bipolar II disorders as an expression of borderline characterological psychopathology. Recent evidence (Akiskal et al. 1985b) suggests that in many cases the direction of causality is in the opposite direction—that is, that borderline features arise from the affective instability. Mixed states of short duration with extreme irritability occur in all subtypes of cyclothymia and are often associated with sedative-hypnotic and alcohol abuse. Borderline characterological psychopathology is usually most severe in cases in which such irritable periods predominate. These irritable cyclothymics (Akiskal and Mallya 1987) are habitually moody—irritable and choleric—with infrequent euthymia; they tend to brood; are hypercritical, complaining, and obtrusive; and typically evidence dysphoric restlessness and impulsivity.

In view of their propensity to affective recurrences, cyclothymia and bipolar disorder NOS are at high risk for having stormy object relations, which often give rise to serious interpersonal disturbances. While these disturbances warrant considerable psychotherapeutic attention, such attention may prove futile in the absence of competent pharmacotherapy of the affective instability.

Chapter 178

Dysthymic Disorder

Dysthymic disorder (DD) is a term introduced by the authors of DSM-III (American Psychiatric Association 1980) to refer to chronic, mild, or "subsyndromal " states of depression, usually beginning insidiously in childhood or early adulthood and often associated with a personality disorder. Specific criteria for the diagnosis are listed in Table 1 and include a duration of at least two years of depressed or dysphoric mood (one year for children and adolescents); persistent symptoms with no more than a few months of remission at a time; presence of at least three from a list of 13 signs and symptoms of depression; absence of psychotic features; and, when superimposed on a preexisting mental disorder, a clear differentiation of the depression from the individual's usual mood.

Aside from co-morbidity with personality disorders, DSM-III suggests that dysthymic disorders might coexist with other affective or nonaffective psychiatric disorders, chronic medical illness, or chronic psychosocial stressors. It also suggests that a second subgroup of chronic depressive disorders might begin later in life, often following an episode of major depressive disorder. This subgroup is considered further in the chapter "Major Depression: Chronic," and the present discussion will be restricted to chronic depression with early age of onset of "lifelong" depression.

Dysthymic disorder has been a controversial category because it represents quite a radical departure from previous nosological convention. In DSM-II (American Psychiatric Association 1968), chronic states of depression are subsumed under cyclothymic personality or depressive neurosis and are classified with the personality disorders and neuroses. DSM-III relabels chronic depressions with the new designation DD and classifies them within the affective disorders section. These changes are in the spirit of recent trends in American psychiatry to broaden the inclusiveness of the affective disorders categorization, and they reflect the notion that mild, chronic forms of depression are on spectrum with the more florid and acute variants of affective disorder. The creation of the DD category and the choice of its specific diagnostic criteria were based on very limited empirical evidence. However, the new system has the virtue of attempting to distinguish chronic subsyndromal from acute

Table 1.　DSM III Criteria for Dysthymic Disorder

A.　During the past two years (or one year for children and adolescents), the individual has been bothered most or all of the time by symptoms characteristic of the depressive syndrome that are not of sufficient severity and duration to meet the criteria for a major depressive episode.

B.　The manifestations of the depressive syndrome may be relatively persistent or separated by periods of normal mood lasting a few days to a few weeks, but no more than a few months at a time.

C.　During the depressive periods there is either prominent depressed mood (e.g., sad, blue, down in the dumps, low) or marked loss of interest or pleasure in all, or almost all, usual activities and pastimes.

D.　During the depressive periods, at least three of the following symptoms are present:
1.　insomnia or hypersomnia
2.　low energy level or chronic tiredness
3.　feelings of inadequacy, loss of self-esteem, or self-deprecation
4.　decreased effectiveness or productivity at school, work, or home
5.　decreased attention, concentration, or ability to think clearly
6.　social withdrawal
7.　loss of interest in or enjoyment of pleasurable activities
8.　irritability or excessive anger (in children, expressed toward parents or caretakers)
9.　inability to respond with apparent pleasure to praise or rewards
10.　less active or talkative than usual, or feels slowed down or restless
11.　pessimistic attitude toward the future, brooding about past events, or feeling sorry for self
12.　tearfulness or crying
13.　recurrent thoughts of death or suicide

E.　There are no psychotic features such as delusions, hallucinations, or incoherence.

F.　If the disturbance is superimposed on another mental disorder or on a preexisting mental disorder such as obsessive compulsive disorder or alcohol dependence, the depressed mood, by virtue of its intensity or effect on functioning, can be clearly distinguished from the individual's usual mood.

major depression and has stimulated research to determine descriptive characteristics and treatment response of chronic depression.

An innovative and important proposal for subtyping DDs was put forth by Akiskal in 1983. The author divided early onset DDs into three groups. Subaffective dysthymic disorder referred to DDs that were thymoleptic responsive, showed reduced latencies for REM sleep, sometimes developed brief pharmacologic hypomania, and had higher than expected family prevalences of both unipolar and bipolar affective illness. Akiskal revived the Kraepelinian notion that such disorders represent attentuated variants of manic-depressive illness, a conceptualization that heavily influenced the inclusion of DD in the affective disorders section of DSM-III (Frances 1980). A second group, character spectrum disorders, referred to patients having prominent "unstable" character pathology, high rates of substance abuse, and poor response to antidepressant medications. The third group, secondary dysphorias, included patients whose chronic depression was superimposed on long-standing nonaffective psychiatric or incapacitating medical disorders. Some validating evidence for these subtypes has been given by Akiskal et al. (1980, 1981). However, the empirical basis for subcategorizing early onset chronic depression is sparse and remains an area of active investigation. There is accumulating evidence that chronic depressions are commonly encountered in both clinical and community samples (Keller and Shapiro 1982; Robins et al. 1984; Rounsaville et al. 1980; Weissman and Klerman 1977; Weissman and Myers 1978) and that they deserve increased diagnostic recognition and research attention. In this chapter treatment strategies for proposed subgroups of DD will be outlined and discussed.

Pharmacotherapy of Dysthymic Disorder

Several reports have appeared that have suggested the efficacy of various antidepressant medications in some patients with chronic depression. Ward et al. (1979) treated 15 patients who met Research Diagnostic Criteria (RDC) (Spitzer et al. 1978) for major depressive disorder with doxepin (up to 300 mg) on an open basis for four weeks. All subjects had been depressed for at least one year although 11 had durations of longer than two years and three of longer than 10 years. Eighty percent of the sample experienced marked or moderate improvement on the Clinical Global Impression Scale during this study. As a part of a double-blind comparison of amitriptyline, perphenazine, and a combination of the two for treatment of outpatients with RDC major depressive disorder, the study of Rounsaville et al. (1980) included 23 patients who also had a diagnosis of intermittent depressive disorder. Improvement in the Hamilton Depression Scale (HAM-D) total score after four weeks of treatment was significant, and it was equivalent in the groups having major plus intermittent depression and major depression alone. Results were not divided by treatment group, and no placebo control group was included. Akiskal et al. (1980) treated 50 "characterologic depressives" described as outpatients with chronic, mild, insidious onset depressions—with a variety of antidepressant medications on an open basis at variable doses. After at least six months of treatment, patients were categorized as responders or nonresponders by "global clinical criteria." Forty percent were found to be responsive under these conditions. Paykel et al. (1982) randomly assigned 131 outpatients with mild-moderate depression to six weeks of double-blind treatment with phenelzine (up to 75 mg), amitriptyline (up to 187.5 mg) or placebo. Fifty-six subjects (43 percent) met criteria of Klein and Davis (1969) for "neurotic dysphoria," which was described as "a pattern of long-standing or recurrent depression, without clear differentiation of episodes from personality and with evidence suggesting depressive personality." In this subgroup no significant differences occurred for outcome measures between the amitriptyline- and placebo-treated groups, both of which improved considerably. Phenelzine-treated patients experienced significantly worse outcomes than the other two groups on most measures. Harrison et al. (1986) recently presented results of a study in which 12 patients who met DSM-III criteria for dysthymic disorder were randomly assigned to a continuation trial of phenelzine or placebo for six months, following an initial favorable response to phenelzine. All seven patients randomized to placebo and only one of the five phenelzine-maintained patients experienced relapse.

Preliminary results of an ongoing, double-blind, placebo-controlled trial of imipramine (up to 300 mg) conducted by Kocsis et al. (1985, 1986) have recently been published. Subjects met DSM-III criteria for DD and were included if they had coexisting major depressive disorder (i.e., "double-depression" [Keller and Shapiro 1982]) or personality disorder, but they were excluded if they had major nonaffective psychiatric or serious medical disorders. All subjects included in this study reported an insidious onset of their depression, usually at an early age, and 95 percent met

DSM-III criteria for both DD and major depressive disorder at the time of treatment. Forty-seven percent were diagnosed as having a DSM-III personality disorder, with the most common subtypes being dependent (23 percent) and avoidant (10 percent). Seventy-six percent of these patients had previously participated in intensive psychotherapy without relief of depression while only 18 percent had ever received an adequate trial of antidepressant medication. Seven of 13 (54 percent) imipramine-treated patients and two of 14 (14 percent) placebo patients were rated as responders following six weeks of treatment. HAM-D and Global Assessment Scale scores showed significantly greater improvement in the imipramine-treated group.

The studies described above have varied considerably in terms of diagnostic criteria for inclusion, types of medication treatment, and method for evaluation of outcome. The results suggest efficacy for various antidepressant medications in some proportion of patients with DDs. Predictors of favorable response might include current symptom exacerbation (superimposed major depression) and family history of affective illness. Future research will be needed to confirm the effectiveness of tricyclic antidepressants (TCAs) and to investigate the role of monoamine oxidase inhibitors. Implications of variations in the course of illness (e.g., "double-depression"), symptom pattern (e.g., "atypical depression"), and presence of various types of personality disorder for response to pharmacotherapy need further exploration.

Psychotherapy of Dysthymic Disorder

Although states of chronic depression have been demonstrated to be common in clinical psychiatric settings, little systematic investigation has been conducted on the effectiveness of various forms of psychotherapy for their treatment. In the process of recruiting outpatients with DD for a controlled trial of imipramine treatment, Kocsis et al. (1986) found that 76 percent of subjects had received at least six months of psychotherapy given at a frequency of once weekly or greater. Although the types of psychotherapy delivered were not specified, the geographical location (NYC) and nature of referral sources suggested that long-term, psychodynamically oriented psychotherapy may be commonly applied in this setting. Anecdotally, it has been noted by the investigators conducting this study that DD patients who have received long-term dynamic therapy have often reported increased self-awareness but lack of relief of dysphoria and associated depressive symptoms. The sample of patients was obviously biased because they were seeking a second consultation and treatment. However, when pharmacotherapy was effective in reducing depression, the patients frequently reported a sudden increase in the ability to "make use of" the insights they had gained in therapy, possibly related to increased energy, motivation, and optimism. Such anecdotes suggest a hypothesis that pharmacotherapy and psychotherapy might have synergistic effects in chronic depression, and that successful pharmacotherapy may facilitate "operationalization" of insights gained in psychotherapy. Such speculations remain goals for testing in future research.

One controlled study in the literature has addressed the issue of the effectiveness a short-term behavioral intervention—cognitive-behavioral therapy (CBT), in chronic depression. Gonzales et al (1985) presented results of a one-year follow-up of depressed outpatients who had been treated with 12 sessions of CBT in a two-month period. They were able to perform one-year evaluations on 113 of an original sample of 167 patients with the following diagnoses according to RDC on admission: major depressive disorder (MDD) = 59, intermittent depressive disorder (IDD) = 28, and MDD plus IDD (double depression) = 26. Recovery was defined as the absence of symptoms of depression for at least eight weeks, and it was achieved by 70 percent of MDD, 43 percent of IDD and 27 percent of double depression subjects within the first year, a significant difference. This result suggests the relative ineffectiveness (no placebo control was employed) of CBT for more chronic forms of depression in comparison with its established effectiveness for acute MDDs. Furthermore, these findings support the importance of distinguishing acute MDDs from double depression—that is, MDDs occurring in the context of a preexisting chronic depression—in research on treatment of depression.

Klerman has reviewed the psychoanalytic literature concerning psychodynamic psychotherapeutic approaches to chronic depressive or dysthymic patients (1980). Important modifications of classic psychoanalytic theory and techniques for treatment of depression have been developed by the "interpersonal school," which includes Meyer, Sullivan, Cohen, and Bonime. The basic thesis is that adult personality features predisposing to dysthymic disorders develop from family psychopathology. Bonime (1976) postulated that the dysthymic patient develops maladaptive interpersonal maneuvers to manipulate key figures in the social environment based on transferred anger secondary to childhood deprivation; an unwillingness to assume adult responsibility; and lack of capacity for mutuality, commitment, and collaboration. He advocated an active, "interpersonal" form of long-term dynamic psychotherapy for these problems. But as Klerman (1980, p. 1335) has pointed out, "Intriguing as those formulations are, . . . they have unfortunately not been subjected to systematic clinical trials."

Based upon premises developed by the interpersonal school, Klerman et al. (1984) have developed a brief form of psychotherapy for depression, Interpersonal Psychotherapy (IPT), which has been demonstrated in controlled trials to be effective for acute, nonbipolar, nonpsychotic MDDs in outpatients. On theoretical grounds this would seem an interesting approach for treatment of chronic depression, either as a sole treatment or in combination with pharmacotherapy. However, such studies have not yet been attempted.

Another brief psychotherapeutic modality, social skills therapy (SST), is currently under investigation as a treatment for DD. SST and SST plus nortriptyline are being compared with placebo and "crisis supportive psychotherapy" (a psychotherapy placebo) in a controlled trial by Becker and Heimberg (1985). Results of this study are as yet unavailable.

This brief review of psychotherapeutic approaches to DD supports the following conclusions:

1. No psychotherapeutic modality has yet been reported as effective for DD based on results from a controlled clinical trial.
2. Psychoanalytic and behavioral theories and treatment approaches with potential relevance to chronic depression have been proposed, and anecdotal case reports suggest possible effectiveness; however, no systematic outcome data have been published.
3. A single published follow-up of outpatients treated with CBT included a chronically depressed sample. CBT was found to be less effective for the chronically depressed groups than for the acute MDD group. No placebo control group was included in this study, so efficacy of CBT versus placebo for chronic depression could not be assessed.
4. Anecdotal evidence suggests that antidepressant medication may enhance response to long-term, dynamically oriented psychotherapy in cases resistant to that form of psychotherapy.

5. Future research on the application of psychotherapy to chronic depression is merited. Chronic states of depression (i.e., duration greater than two years) should be studied separately from acute forms of depression. Psychotherapeutic modalities with potential importance include long- and short-term psychodynamic therapy, IPT, CBT, and SST. Combined treatment with antidepressant medication also deserves investigation.

Summary and Conclusions

Dysthymic disorders and related states of chronic depression have been demonstrated to be common in the community and in psychiatric settings. The inclusion of a separate category within the affective disorders section of DSM-III, with operational criteria for diagnosis, has facilitated early clinical investigations of the psychopathology and treatment of these disorders.

Akiskal (1983) has proposed an interesting subclassification of DDs, which deserves further study and which has potential relevance for differential treatment selection for these disorders. Several reports have now appeared supporting the effectiveness of antidepressant medications for chronic depressive patients; however, much work remains to establish the efficacy of pharmacotherapy and to refine the clinical indications for this form of treatment. Psychoanalysts and behaviorists have proposed theories of chronic depression based on clinical experience. These have led to a number of psychotherapeutic approaches with potential relevance to the dysthymic patient. Some of the brief psychotherapies (CBT, IPT) have been demonstrated to be effective for acute depression in controlled clinical trials and would be especially interesting treatments for future investigations in chronic depressions. Theoretical considerations as well as some anecdotal evidence also support the possibility of benefit from combined medication and psychotherapy in dysthymic disorders, and this also deserves investigation.

While validation of DD subtypes has scientific and theoretical importance, clinicians may proceed with, and patients may benefit from, treatment utilizing guidelines based on available knowledge. A plausible approach might be to subdivide early onset chronic depressions into "pure" or "affective" types, which might be expected to benefit from a trial of antidepressant medications; characterological types, which might be more suitable for a psychotherapeutic intervention, at least initially; "secondary" types—that is, accompanying substance abuse, anxiety disorder, schizophrenia, etc., in which prognosis and treatment can be viewed as closely linked to an underlying disorder; and "demoralization" types, in which dysphoria can be related to the presence of chronic medical illness or severe psychosocial stressors, and treatment might be best directed toward adaptation to or resolution of these associated problems. Such guidelines must be viewed as tentative at best because our ability to distinguish such subtypes is primitive and few of the treatments have been subjected to controlled clinical trials in patients selected for chronic depression. Sequential and/ or combined trials of psychotherapy and medication may also prove to be of value.

Chapter 179

Adjustment Disorder with Depressed Mood

The DSM-III (American Psychiatric Association 1980) criteria for the general category of adjustment disorder are listed as follows:

A. There is a maladaptive reaction to an identifiable psychosocial stressor that occurs within three months of the onset of the stressor.
B. The maladaptive nature of the reaction is indicated by either of the following:
   1) impairment in social or occupational functioning
   2) symptoms that are in excess of a normal and expectable reaction to the stressor.
C. The disturbance is not merely one instance of a pattern of overreaction to stress or an exacerbation of one of the mental disorders previously described.
D. It is assumed that the disturbance will eventually remit after the stressor ceases or, if the stressor persists, when a new level of adaptation is achieved.
E. The disturbance does not meet the criteria for any of the specific disorders listed previously or for uncomplicated bereavement.

The more specific criteria for adjustment disorder with depressed mood are that "this category should be used when prominent manifestation involves such symptoms as depressed mood, tearfulness, and hopelessness." A further qualification is that this disorder needs to be differentiated particularly from major depression and uncomplicated bereavement.

This definition essentially describes an individual who, following a major environmental stressor, exhibits a depressive reaction that is without marked vegetative symptoms and that is not severe enough to qualify for a diagnosis of major depression yet is not so normal or expected a reaction as to be classified under a V code category, which precludes a mental disorder. Furthermore, the individual should present with a history free from any chronic psychopathology that could produce the reaction as an acute exacerbation. Therefore, information regarding features not necessarily connected with the Axis I diagnosis becomes important in assessing adjustment disorders. Axis II, which defines prior personality patterns or disorders, Axis IV, which indicates the presence and severity of psychosocial stressors, and Axis V, which notes the highest level of adaptive functioning in the past year, contribute valuable data in the diagnostic process.

While attempting to define objective criteria for the diagnosis of adjustment disorder, which are quite helpful to the practitioner, ultimately the DSM-III leaves the decision as to what constitutes symptoms that "are in excess of a normal and expectable reaction" or significant "improvement in social or occupational functioning" to clinical judgment.

One way to conceptualize depressive adjustment disorders from a theoretical framework is to adopt the sequence of the depressive process as outlined by Sandler and Joffee (1965). These authors propose that there are two temporal and clinical forms of depression. The first is a basic psychobiologic response to the deprivation of a former state of well-being, and it may be seen in all individuals who have suffered a significant loss of an important source of narcissism or security. Most people eventually find ways of eliminating this initial dysphoria by actively finding new ways to substitute other sources of well-being. Some, however, cannot deal with the initial dysphoria and, because of either a lack of personal resources or external factors, progress to the second phase in the depressive process, which is the clinical episode. Arieti (1978) also proposed a continuum between normal sadness, which is the expectable dysphoria after a loss of a meaningful relationship, role, or self-image, and severe depression, which is an excessive reaction and demonstrates the predisposed individual's incapacity to master the period of sadness in an adequate manner.

Adjustment disorders appear midway in this spectrum. They are not commensurate with the stressor, so the reaction seems unjustifiable; and they do interfere with the individual's functioning. At the same time, such disorders do not present with massive incapacitation, nor do they impair the individual for a prolonged period of time. The individual with a depressive adjustment disorder may be conceptualized as a basically healthy individual who has experienced a particular stress that resonates with specific problem areas of the personality.

A clinical example of this type of reaction in an adult was seen in a 24-year-old woman who moved back to her hometown when her husband began a medical internship. Two months after the relocation she found herself feeling sad, losing interest in her activities, and having difficulty sleeping. She also felt lonely because her husband worked long hours and she missed her old friends, whom she frequently saw in the city from which she recently moved. A further stressor was her having to care for her young infant, which prevented her from working or leaving her small apartment. She described feeling trapped, alone, and without pleasure in her life. She felt she could not complain because of how hard her husband worked and how tired he seemed, while she had "nothing to do" all day.

This woman underwent a series of changes in her life-style that precluded her usual manner of obtaining meaning and gratification from her daily activities. She needed to maintain a concept of herself as a good wife and homemaker, so she did not express her anger at her unsatisfying situation. At the same time, her healthy resiliency and adaptability were evidenced by her obtaining employment three afternoons a week, which allowed her to get out of the house, return to a more acceptable role for herself, and earn enough to hire a "mother's helper" to aid in the care of her child and in doing household chores. She had also begun making some new friends, and she was able to start socializing.

She was aware that these progressive steps would ease her predicament and that her ungratifying situation was temporary—that in a few months her husband would be more available, that her child's demands would ease as he matured, and that she would eventually be able to work—yet she still felt that she had reverted to being like a bad child who could do nothing correctly and had no rights in the world of adults. This alteration of her sense of self and in her feelings of self-worth became more understandable when she related that since her moving back to her hometown she had had increasing contact with her mother, who criticized everything she did and managed to make her feel guilty and inadequate most of the time. She described this mode of relating as typical for most of her life with her mother, but in the past she had been able to either stay out of close contact or build up her sense of self through other relationships. Now she was realistically dependent on her mother, who would help her care for her child and have her over for dinner frequently when her husband was on call at the hospital. She found herself trapped in a relationship that subtly sabotaged her view of herself as a capable adult and made her feel like a burdensome child. Her father refused to interfere in his wife's behavior and essentially offered little help to the patient.

This young woman was actually unaware of how debilitating her renewed contact with her mother was until she started discussing this relationship in therapy. The mother had a disguised way of debasing her that could neither be openly responded to nor easily avoided. For example, the mother invited the patient to a dinner party for her own birthday. The patient jumped at an opportunity to put on a feminine dress and makeup and temporarily discard her usual uniform of jeans and sweatshirts. She arrived at the party thinking she looked particularly attractive. Her mother greeted her with an annoyed look, commenting, "Why do you have to get *so* dressed up?" The patient immediately felt overdressed, out of place, and as if she had "goofed again."

This woman responded well to brief psychotherapy. She was able to affect changes in her life that shored up a satisfying view of herself and could defend against her mother's continuing deflating remarks. She also accepted her mother as an unhappy and competitive person who was critical of most women and not just the patient.

There is good reason to predict that this woman would have done well eventually, even without therapy. She had been able to resolve her problems with her mother in the past, and she was independently making arrangements to ease the other stresses that provoked her dysphoria. Her history indicated that she was able to find inner resources to master disappointments and losses. However, psychotherapy speeded her recovery and relieved her depressive symptoms by allowing her to ventilate her feelings freely and to analyze carefully the events that led to her brief disorder. The move back to her hometown robbed her of many activities and relationships that had allowed her to feel good about herself and brought satisfaction and meaning to her life. The temporary loss of her husband's companionship, of her friends and her career, coupled with the restraints of child care, made her vulnerable to doubts about the possibility of gratification and her own social role. This vulnerability made her more susceptible to her mother's criticism and to her disapproval of her own dependency.

Therapy did not attack her defenses nor aim for characterological change. Symptom removal was effected by allowing the patient to gain some objectivity on her situation, by encouraging effective action toward modifying her situation, by sanctioning the expression of her feelings, and by engendering an acceptance of some undesirable traits such as her excessive reactivity to the mother's disapproval. Therefore, therapy aimed at helping the patient get through a period of stress, utilizing the patient's inherent healthy coping skills to remove the stressor, as much as possible, and to regain a satisfactory sense of self.

While depressive adjustment disorders secondary to bereavement, economic reversals, and career disappointments are not uncommon in adults, such disorders appear more frequently in adolescents and young adults who are experiencing more rapid changes (and thus stressors) in their daily lives and are more apt to react with brief but excessive episodes of dysphoria. At this stage of development, youngsters may lack a perspective on the long-term effect of negative events and may erroneously generalize from one unfortunate experience. The sense of self is also not well crystallized so that the individual is overly vulnerable to the reactions and opinions of others. These factors contribute to an exaggerated reaction to stressors with often flagrant symptoms that remit fairly quickly and do not carry the same dire prognosis as they would in an adult. However, although the symptoms may abate, there is danger that permanent scars remain in terms of limitation of functioning or deviation of the normal progression of development.

Such adjustment disorders are frequently seen when youngsters move away from home for the first time or when they encounter a new social environment. For example, a 14-year-old boy became withdrawn, anorexic, and tearful after starting high school. A few days later he refused to go to school, stayed in his room all day, and made vague but obvious references to suicide. In therapy, he eventually explained that in middle school he had been one of the leaders of his class academically and athletically and was very popular with his peers. In contrast, he felt lost and insignificant in the large high school and believed he would lose his hard-earned superior status. He felt himself inferior and believed others would ridicule him or perceive him as a failure. Therapy focused on the reasons for his ability to feel comfortable only if he were superior to others, an inquiry that included his parents as well as himself, and the burden that this need must be to him. He was encouraged to return to school, where he found that no one humiliated him and that older students proved helpful. His dysphoria rapidly disappeared. His competitiveness took longer to work through but did not require extensive therapy.

Other youngsters may experience transient depressive reactions following social rejections, scholastic setbacks, or clashes with parental dictates. The common causal factor in all of these episodes appears to be a threat to a needed sense of self and the belief that the loss of pride or the humiliating experience will never be rectified. This attack on one's view of what one wants to be gives these reactions their particular depressive cast and makes them exceed what would be a normal and acceptable response. However, the real magnitude of the stressor, the past healthy resiliency of the individual, and the absence of malignant symptoms preclude the diagnosis of a more permanent or protracted disorder.

Anthony (1975) described the difference between these transient disorders of adolescence and the more severe forms of affective illness as follows:

> The normative variety is recognizable as an unstable interlude in an otherwise emotionally stable individual, whose future, like his past, is ordained to take a normative course. Moreover, it has a reactive quality to it, whereas clinical depression, in addition to the "stage" upheavals during childhood development, has on the whole less meaningful connection to the current experience except as a resonant or sensitized response to minimal provocation.

Treatment of adjustment disorders aims at diminishing stress-induced symptoms and encouraging the individual's inherently healthy modes of coping. Medication may be used to reduce symptoms and enhance or hasten recovery. For example, the patient may have trouble sleeping or may feel a good deal of anxiety along with his dysphoria. In prescribing medication, it should be kept in mind that the goal is to ameliorate stress-induced symptoms and that a major underlying disorder is absent. Therefore, the use of antidepressants is questionable for these conditions.

Chapter 180

Affective Disorders in Children and Adolescents

Depressive states in children and adolescents have become one of the most popular areas of study in psychiatry. Over the past decade, an increasing number of articles, books, and symposia on this topic have appeared. This current surge of interest markedly contrasts with the almost uniform neglect of childhood depression by clinicians and researchers alike before the mid-1960s. The few times that prepubertal depression had been mentioned in the literature was to indicate that such a disorder did not exist.

The reasons for the present acceptance of childhood affective illness appear to be 1) a revision in psychoanalytic formulations of depression so that this disorder is no longer conceptualized as necessitating intrapyschic stuctures that were thought to be beyond the immature psychic status of children; 2) the development of biochemical theories of depression, based on the action of certain antidepressants and other findings which have been generalized from studies of adults to those involving children; and 3) the initiation of large epidemiologic studies using standardized criteria for the assessment of psychopathology in populations of normal and disturbed children. Along with this great flurry of activity, there has also been a certain amount of contradiction and controversy regarding the manifestation of depression at different stages of development and the utility and validity of diagnostic scales based on the symptoms of adults for the appropriate assessment of children. The status of depressive equivalents as a diagnostic entity has proven to be a particularly polarizing issue. For years, clinicians (Sperling 1962; Toolan 1962) proposed that children exhibited depression by nondepressive symptoms such as somatic complaints (headache or gastrointestinal upsets), behavioral difficulties (delinquency, encopresis), or loss of adequate functioning (academic failure, social withdrawal). So established was the belief that these symptoms were childhood expressions of affective illness that depressive equivalents were included into diagnostic classifications. (Cytryn and McKnew 1972; Malimquist 1971). At the same time, the validity of this entity was being questioned on the basis that there was no logical connection between the proposed equivalent symptom and an underlying depression and that any possible pathologic deviation from the norm could be said to be a manifestation of depression at the whim of the clinician (Rie 1966). Eventually, this diagnosis fell into disrepute as large-scale studies showed that a depressive core could be discovered in all depressed children if in-depth interviews or projective tests were performed (Carson and Cantwell 1980; Cytryn et al. 1980).

Some authors believe that while children do become depressed and manifest this symptom directly rather than through postulated equivalents, the lack of cognitive and physiologic maturation results in a different symptom picture than is found in adults. This same hesitation to apply adult criteria to childhood problems has led some to doubt whether biochemical indices of adult illness are meaningful in child patients. Despite these objections, numerous studies have reported finding in children and adolescents some biologic abnormalities similar to those seen in adults. The highlights of this extensive and burgeoning literature will be reviewed briefly here. A number of good surveys of this literature have been published (Puig-Antich 1982, 1986) for the reader desiring a more detailed exposition.

Lowered urinary MHPG in depressed children has been reported by McKnew and Cytryn (1979). Puig-Antich (1982) found cortisol hypersecretion in two of four depressed children, simulating the disturbed circadian rhythm of adult depressives. Poznanski et al. (1982) also found higher plasma cortisol levels in depressed children, as well as nonsuppression on the dexamethasone suppression test (DST) in eight of nine children with an endogenous type of depression. Puig-Antich et al. (1984) reported that a decreased growth hormone response to insulin-induced hypoglycemia, which is found in depressed adults, was also found in endogenously depressed children. However, studies of sleep architecture have not shown similar disturbances—particularly shortened REM latency—in child and adult depressives (Puig-Antich 1982). Although these studies await replication on larger samples, they suggest that some depressed children show similar biochemical alterations to those found in the depressive episodes of some adults. Difficulties remain, however, in the small number of children used; the extremely severe impairment of the children, suggesting the possibility of other diagnoses, such as schizophrenia, or of massive environmental stress, such as significant abuse; and thus in the generalizability of these findings to the usual depressed child seen in common clinical practice.

A related controversy is over the criteria for diagnosis, particularly when research rating scales based on adult symptoms are used (Achenback 1980; Rie 1966). The DSM-III (American Psychiatric Association 1980) does not contain a special diagnostic category or description for depression in childhood and proposes that adult criteria may be used for children with minor modification. However, when structured diagnostic instruments based on adult criteria were used to assess the incidence of depression in various groups of children by different investigators, widely divergent results were found. Weinberg et al. (1973) evaluated 72 prepubertal children referred to an educational diagnostic center and found that 58 percent met criteria for depression. Albert and Beck (1975) assessed 63 children attending a parochial school and found that 33 percent could be diagnosed as moderately to severely depressed. Kashani and Simmonds (1979) found that, in a general population, only 1.9 percent of children seen meet adult criteria for depression although 17.4 percent of their sample displayed sadness as a symptom. The great diversity in incidence obviously raises questions as to the ability of such measures to accurately assess depression in children. Phillips and Friedlander (1982), in a thoughtful review, suggest that rating scales may identify depressive symptoms but that more is required to confer a diagnosis of depression, which they believe necessitates a comprehensive clinical interview. They further argue that use of these instruments may lead to false positives by diagnosing depression on the basis of selected symptoms and to false negatives by not picking up depression when manifested by symptoms not included in the particular scale. Phillips and Friedlander (1982) correctly conclude that the real problem lies in whether one accepts the adult model of depression as appropriate to all age groups or one views depression as being greatly modified by the psychological immaturity of childhood.

Whether one ascribes to a genetic, biochemical, or psychosocial model of depression, it would be difficult to ignore developmental differences in the manifestation and underlying mechanisms of disease. Examples from general medicine, where symptoms and etiology are known much more precisely, amply demonstrate this point. Endocrine and nutritional disorders affect children in different ways than they do adults. Similar symptoms, such as hypertension or seizures, are usually caused by different pathogenic processes in children and carry different prognoses in each age group. Yet the physiologic differences between child and adult are relatively insignificant when compared with the tremendous contrast seen in cognitive and emotional abilities. Therefore, it would appear warranted to view depression as being characterized by the relative psychological limitations and abilities of each developmental stage of ontogenesis. Anthony (1975), Bemporad (1982) and Phillips (1979) have independently advocated such an approach, stressing that the experience and expression of depression develops commensurate with the overall development of the child.

Therefore, in considering childhood depression, we are dealing with a variable entity that differs with the cognitive and social abilities of the child as he proceeds through the various levels of ontogenesis. The treatment of depression thus depends on the age of the child, his cognitive and social sophistication, and the amount of internalization of views of the self and others that has occurred. Each stage of development presents a particular set of circumstances in terms of the precipitants of dysphoria and the specific psychodynamics that are active, and the developmental limitations and capabilities of the child, so that intervention must be stage-appropriate. Toward this end, a review of the depression-like states that are seen at various developmental stages is warranted with particular emphasis toward treatment. Throughout the following discussion, it should be kept in mind that we are not asking whether depression occurs in childhood but rather how the particular abilities and liabilities of each stage stamp their specific mark on the experience of this emotional state.

Depression and Development

Some of the earliest clinical reports of childhood depression specifically referred to infants. Spitz's (1946) classic papers on hospitalism and anaclitic depression described the infant's turning away from his environment and becoming listless and apathetic following separation from his mother. Follow-up showed these maternally deprived children to be developmentally retarded and prone to infection. Other researchers found that, as adults, maternally deprived infants were predisposed to psychopathic personality organization. Bowlby (1960) has augmented Spitz's pioneer studies with his work on the stages of the separation process in infants. Bowlby has delineated the three-stage sequence of protest, despair, and detachment in children deprived of the maternal figure. The stages of despair and detachment have been taken as analogous to adult depressive states. Finally, Engel and Reichman (1956) have documented the "conservation-withdrawal" response in an infant who suffered emotional deprivation. This turning away from others was seen as an innate protective mechanism, possibly predisposing to later depressive illness.

There is little doubt about the validity of these observations, but there may be questions regarding their interpretation as depressive states. We shall probably never know what the infant who has been separated from his mother actually experiences, but it is doubtful that his feeling is of the same range of emotion that is available to the adult. It may be that the infant is responding to the sudden loss of emotional and cognitive stimulation, if these two parameters can even be separated at this early stage of life. The dissimilarity between these infant states and adult-type depression becomes more apparent when one considers that lack of stimulation and even malnutrition can produce the same listless state in the child. Conversely, it has been found that the older infant may not go through the Bowlby separation sequence if a lively, warm environment is provided during the child's time away from his mother.

This is not to suggest that the mother is unimportant to the infant; she is his most important source of stimulation and well-being. Her loss, if not appropriately substituted, may well result in a decrease of well-being. However, this loss of well-being may be compensated partially by an appropriate environment. Finally, the state of the infant may be seen as one of pure deprivation of an important factor necessary for further growth rather than a depressive state.

In contrast to infants, children of preschool age are rarely reported as manifesting depressive-like states. Poznanski and Zrull (1970) reviewed the charts of 1,788 children seen at the Children's Psychiatric Hospital at the University of Michigan for the years 1964 through 1968 and could find only one child under the age of five who possibly might fit clinical criteria for depression. (Even then, the authors were hesitant to make this diagnosis without a follow-up evaluation when the child was five years of age.)

The lack of depressive symptomatology seen in this age group may be explained partially by our knowledge of normal development. The toddler is innately an exuberant, curious, active creature who has been characterized as having a love affair with the world. He delights in doing and exploring and seems impervious to the repeated falls and hurts that he encounters daily. At the same time, he deals with frustration by active, physical protest or by distraction to more pleasant situations. The toddler does not dwell on his thoughts or experiences; rather, he searches unceasingly for new stimulation and experiences, and if he does express a negative reaction to a situation, it is by action rather than cogitation. These developmental characteristics obviously make it difficult for the young child to become depressed. Instead, what may be seen in children at this age is a sabctaging of the normal individuation process and/or a thwarting of the innate curiosity that is the hallmark of this ontogenic epoch. When this occurs, the child is not depressed but rather is overly inhibited, clinging and whiney. Mahler (1961) has described these children as having poor relationships with their mother and yet being reluctant to separate from her and grieving excessively over her departure. Sometimes these children are overly mature and lack the rebellious oppositionalism that represents the budding of the child's sense of willfulness. However, these children usually resume the normal enthusiastic behavior typical of their developmental stage if they are placed in a less punitive or restrictive setting, such as a nursery school or kindergarten.

Treatment of these children involves altering their environment so as to allow for the normal tasks of development to proceed without distortion. Work with the parents, or with the parents and child together, in the attempt to demonstrate how the parent is inhibiting normal growth is the optimal modality when possible. At times, family therapy has to be augmented with the placement of the child in a therapeutic nursery school for part of the day while work with the parents is progressing. In extreme cases, where the parental pathology is excessive, foster care or residential treatment should be considered. This is particularly true in those instances when the parent is so profoundly depressed that the home environment is barren and the child lacks the appropriate responses to his gleeful exploration of the world. It is also needed in those cases where the child is abused and neglected so that his existence is continuously painful and stifled. It must be stressed again that, at this stage, the child cannot be said to be depressed in an adult sense. Treatment is aimed at preventing the internalization and solidification of a view of self and others that may predispose to depression in later life.

As the child reaches school age, there is a gradual transformation in cognitive and social capabilities. Moods become more sustained and less stimulus bound, exploration via locomotion fades into problem solving through cognitive means, and expression through direct action is replaced by symbolic play and language. Children at this stage have been reported as exhibiting periods of sadness, particularly in reaction to frustration or loss. McConville et al (1973) report that a group of dysphoric children between the ages of six and eight showed an almost pure sense of sadness without any accompanying cognitive content. This observation fits Piaget's description of this developmental period as being "intuitive," meaning that the child does not give reasons for his experiences or judgments. These simply "occur" and are accepted on an intuitive basis by the child. Therefore, the young latency-age child may feel sad or unhappy without a concomitant low self-esteem. He may even have difficulty verbally describing his feelings or the events that have led to his sense of sadness. However, he can communicate important details of his inner life through doll play and other projective techniques with a sensitive therapist after a trusting relationship has developed. This information can then be used to make changes in the life of the child so as to decrease the instances that lead to recurrent feelings of dejection or sadness. It is rare to see children of this age with persistent moods of sadness unless they are in almost constantly frustrating circumstances, such as coping with chronic illness, living in abusive families, or suffering important losses that have not been compensated. Most children of this age normally fend off feelings of sadness through denial, distraction, or fantasy. Therapy is still indicated to discover the causes of dysphoria through symbolic play and to give the child a safe haven where he will be appreciated and attended to in an ego-strengthening manner. For a child of this age, therapy is taken as part of life and is not seen as an artificial relationship. It is hoped that the benevolent relationship with the therapist will cause a solidification of a good sense of self that in later years will maintain self-esteem.

These defensive mechanisms are not as readily utilized by children as they approach puberty. By this time, children do not react directly to their environment but react instead to subjective, yet reasoned, judgments they make on an inferential basis as a result of their experiences. The older child will search out reasons for his own feelings as well as for the behavior of others. In Piagetian terms, cognition becomes "operational," meaning that the older child turns to thought rather that to perception in interpreting his environment, and he seeks relationships underlying the occurrence of events.

At this stage, the child is no longer simply sad or unhappy but seeks a cause, albeit often a mistaken one, for his plight. Therefore, a child may blame himself if his parents separate and divorce, or he may believe himself to be the cause of his parents' unhappiness. The pain of depression at this stage is no longer a response to the environment but is generated from within as a result of the child's self-evaluations.

Thus, McConville et al. (1973) found that depressed children between the ages of eight and ten expressed ideas of negative self-esteem, which had been absent in younger children. Similarly, Poznanski and Zrull (1970) report that as children mature, they react less to unpleasantness in the environment and more to feelings of disappointment with themselves. The depression manifested at this age is quite similar to that seen in adults for it involves an estimation of the self, a judgment about one's environment, and the ability to perpetuate the dysphoria long beyond the frustrating experiences. In view of these cognitive and social advances in development, individual psychotherapy is usually the treatment of choice. Parental counseling is still important in reinforcing changes that occur within therapy, but an alteration in parental behavior alone usually does not lead to lasting improvement because the distorted views that perpetuate the depression have been internalized and are part of the child's mode of dealing with others and viewing himself. The therapy sessions at this age rely more on talking and less on symbolic play, with appropriate interpretations given in the context of the therapeutic relationship. The goal of therapy is to modify those frames of reference and attitudes that initiate and perpetuate feelings of depression. This may be achieved in the age-appropriate therapeutic techniques of actively doing things together with the therapist, such as playing board games, building models, or making drawings or telling stories that serve as concrete vehicles for the therapist to comment on the child's attitudes and behaviors. It is often difficult for a child of this age to simply sit and talk for an entire session, so tangible props may be used to focus the conversation on specific topics. The child's sense of himself and others becomes manifest through these activities and in turn can be altered by the therapist's behavior and interpretations. Special attention should be paid to the depressed child's propensity for giving up on a project, for blaming himself for a less than perfect performance, and for an overly cautious attitude toward new experiences.

The older child displays the distortions of thinking, the negative self-esteem, and pathologic defenses that are characteristic of adult depression. However, there is one important element of adult melancholia that is still missing from these dysphoric states; the apprehension of the future. The older child does not truly relate his present state of dysphoria on a continuum with his future experiences. Rie (1966), in his review of childhood depression, made this distinction a cardinal difference between the depressive states of children and adults. The latter contain a sense of hopelessness and despair that results from a mature perspective of time, which is beyond the understanding of the child. Children do not complain that they are unable to face their future or that they will remain depressed eternally. They do not defend against the prospect of an unbearable future; they simply do not think of it.

This sense of the future is not seen until the depression of adolescence, when it appears to overshadow all other considerations. The concept of time and the relation of the future to the present plays a large role in the thought of the adolescent, which, in addition, is not tempered by the greater life experience of the adult that teaches that most things, in time, will pass. This time-centered obsession gives the depressions of adolescence a characteristic urgency, which, together with the lack of moderation found in this development stage, often leads to the tragic consequence of suicidal acts. The adolescent fears that nothing will ever change, that he is doomed forever to perpetual torment. Thus, a social rebuff means that one will forever be alienated from peers, a disappointment on a date means one will never by able to form a satisfying relationship, or a bad grade on an exam means that one is doomed to academic failure.

These characteristics help describe the distinctive form of adolescent depression but not the causes of this disorder. While there are multiple reasons for a youngster succumbing to depression, perhaps the most frequently observed is the inability of the individual to successfully obtain satisfaction from his experience because of continued adherence to inappropriate parental values or because of self-inhibitions that were concretized during earlier years. In our culture, adolescence is a time when the individual is forced to obtain his esteem and meaning from activities and relationships that are outside of the family orbit. The transition from family to society is not always a smooth one, and disappointments, frustrations, and losses are the rule. Beneath most of the surface manifestations of depression in adolescence may be discerned the belief that one is not "making it" in the real world. The depressed youngster feels guilty because he is not fulfilling parental expectations, or lost because he is deprived of the reassuring security of an accepting home environment, or desperate because he cannot successfully relate to the people around him.

Therapy with these individuals is, in a word, difficult. The extremes of behavior and the propensity for suicide require the therapist to schedule unexpected sessions and be available by telephone at all hours. The narcissistic vulnerability of these youngsters limits the usefulness of interpretations that may be taken as criticism or further proof of inferiority. Some adolescents generalize or externalize their problems to include entire philosophical or social systems in true sophomoric fashion. For example, one bright 14-year-old, who was depressed over not fitting in after starting in high school, delivered a polemic against capitalism and the free enterprise system that allowed for large suburban schools.

In these situations, the therapist should try to be a nonjudgmental adult who will eventually become a bridge and a guide between the home environment and the outside social world. The adolescent should see the therapist as an adult who is markedly different from his recollections of adults from the past. Repeated transference interpretations may be needed as the adolescent unconsciously tries to fit the therapist into the form of past figures that were either too nuturing or too demanding. Yet interpretations are never as important as the engendering of a sense of trust and openness in which the adolescent feels free to air his own aspirations and values rather than those that may have been, or are still being, imposed upon him from significant others.

Adolescence is a time of a harsh clash of values for individuals. The older familial standards and expectations may differ markedly from those of new significant adults and again from those of peers. The depressed adolescent often has a history of slavishing adhering to the dictates of others and of inhibiting his true needs in return for the secure rewards and acceptance by others. He will feel lost and desperate when suddenly confronted by conflicting demands and the unexpected freedom to choose his own behavior. This urgent need for structure may result in his joining a cult or group whereby he substitutes the rule of a charismatic leader for the older strictures of the parent. The therapist must be careful not to assume this dominant position in the adolescent's psychic life. Rather, he should gently encourage autonomy and independence. Here again the therapist has to resist the transferential role that the adolescent wishes him to fulfill.

Throughout therapy, the developmental tasks of this stage of life should be kept in mind. The youngster should gradually find his place in society outside the home; he should replace parental figures with new models, begin to venture into heterosexual and emotional relationships, and start deciding the kind of adult he would like to become within the reality of his limitations and abilities. Obviously, aspects of our current society conspire against the easy resolution of these tasks. All too often the adolescent is expected to perform perfectly in school or in work, he is expected to be popular and sought after, and he is told that he can become anything he wishes, if only he tries hard enough. Depression may easily ensue when the individual believes he has to do more than is humanly possible and then blames himself for what he perceives as his own failure, or when the individual has not been prepared adequately for the stresses of new expectations and is overcome by feelings of bewilderment, shame, and inferiority.

Juvenile Bipolar Affective Illness

While numerous works have appeared regarding childhood depression, very few contributors have focused on bipolar illness before adolescence. Kraepelin (1921) noted that a few of his adult manic-depressive patients could date the onset of their illness to the age of 10, one as early as age five. The validity of these retrospective accounts is problematic in view of the extreme rarity of observed manic attacks before puberty. A variety of behaviors have been labeled as childhood mania, but this diagnosis has not withstood the test of appropriate clinical criteria. Anthony and Scott (1960) reviewed 28 such case reports in the literature, using a list of 10 accepted criteria for diagnosis. They found that only three reported children met over five of their criteria and that none scored over seven. These three children, all of whom were 11 years old, did show alternating depression and mania. The other reports could be contested as misdiagnosis, according to Anthony and Scott. These authors did report a case of their own, who presented at age 12 with symptoms of acute mania and, in the ensuing 10 years, demonstrated episodes of mania and depression, necessitating four hospitalizations.

Clinicians have reported the onset of bipolar illness in adolescents, calling attention to the difficulty in differentiating these episodes from schizophrenia because of the flagrant symptoms presented in this age group. However, recent reports of manic illness in younger children are quite scarce, and these few reports are open to the same criticism as those reviewed by Anthony and Scott (1960). The difficulty in accurate diagnosis is that many children are naturally moody and overly active, and they utilize denial and grandiosity, so that characteristics of mania are to be expected in normal children under certain circumstances. The finding of increased activity, emotional lability, and distractability in children with attentional deficit disorder (ADD) has suggested that this childhood illness is a juvenile expression of adult mania and that some reports of "manic children" may be descriptions of hyperactive children. The two disorders are actually quite different. Bipolar illness responds to lithium while ADD responds to stimulants. ADD has associated neuropsychologic difficulties not found in mania, and children with ADD do not experience bipolar illness as adults to any greater degree than does the general population. Finally, bipolar illness has an episodic course while ADD is a chronic illness with some modifications seen only after the physiologic changes of puberty.

In conclusion, juvenile bipolar illness may have its onset in adolescence but is rarely seen in childhood. Even when the latter occurs, the affected children are close to pubertal age. Care must be taken in making the diagnosis since in younger children the condition may be confused with ADD and in adolescents, with schizophrenia.

Pharmacotherapy

The role of medication in the treatment of depression in childhood is controversial. In a critical review of psychopharmacology in children, Klein et al. (1980) concluded that there is as yet insufficient evidence for the routine use of antidepressants in children despite the large number of articles on drug treatment for depression in the pediatric population. This hesitancy may have been prompted by methodological limitations of many research studies including nonsystematic diagnosis of the treatment group, nonrandom selection, lack of control group, lack of a double-blind procedure, variable dosage and length of therapeutic trial, and lack of controls for other possible beneficial factors. The most vigorous studies are by Puigh-Antich et al. (1985), in which prepubertal depressed children were studied in a five-week double-blind, placebo-controlled study using imipramine in doses up to 5.0 mg/kg/day. Both groups were found to have a 60 percent response rate, indicating no superiority for the medicated group. However, when the plasma levels of imipramine were examined for the treated group, it was found that those children with a plasma level above 155 ng/ml showed 100 percent response while the low plasma subgroup showed only 33 percent response. Puig-Antich concludes that drug plasma levels rather than dosage may be the key to predicting improvement. Puig-Antich et al. (1985) also found that antidepressant medication ameliorates the symptoms of major depression but has more limited effects on the psychosocial functioning of the child. These results are similar to those found in studies of differential effects of antidepressants in adults (Klerman and Schecter 1982) and suggest that medication may be most effective in those depressions in which vegetative symptoms are a predominant part of the syndrome. Since this endogenous or "melancholic" form of depression appears quite rare before adolescence, the generalizability of these findings for the average child with depression must be carefully considered. The children used in these studies were severely impaired, some with mood-congruent delusions and other stigmata of profound illness. The fact that even such severely ill children showed a 60 percent improvement rather rapidly on placebo should make the decision to use a tricyclic antidepressant, with its possible cardiovascular side effects, one to be made with some caution.

Conclusion

In summary, depressive states in childhood are now largely accepted as valid diagnostic entities. Since this acceptance has been achieved only in the past decade, it is no surprise that discordant views are being expressed regarding the exact symptom picture, the continuity with adult affective illness, the role of biochemical markers, the validity of structured rating scales, and the mose effective form of treatment. This particular field of research into affective illness is an exciting and rapidly expanding area for study, which is still in its infancy but shows great promise for clarifying the nature of depression in all of its diverse manifestations, the role of childhood dysphoria in later adult illness, the discovery of possible genetic or biochemical markers for affective illness, and the role of the developmental process on the expression of psychopathology.

References

Section 17
Mood Disorders

Abernethy DR, Greenblatt DJ, Shader RI: Plasma levels of trazodone: methodology and applications. Pharmacology 28:42–46, 1984

Abiuso P, Dunkelman R, Proper M: Electroconvulsive therapy in patients with pacemakers. JAMA 240:2459–2460, 1979

Abraham K: Notes on the psychoanalytic treatment of manic depressive insanity and allied conditions (1911), in Selected Papers on Psychoanalysis. New York, Basic Books, 1960a

Abraham K: The first pregenital stage of libido (1916), in Selected Papers on Psychoanalysis. New York, Basic Books, 1960b

Abram HS, Moore GL, Westervelt FB Jr: Suicidal behavior in chronic dialysis patients. Am J Psychiatry 127:1199–1204, 1971

Abramowicz M, Aaron H (eds): The medical letter on drugs and therapeutics. The Medical Letter, Inc 26:75–78, 1984

Abrams J, Roberts R: First North American conference on nitroglycerine therapy. Am J Med 74:1–66, 1983

Abrams R: A hypothesis to explain divergent findings among studies comparing the efficacy of unilateral and bilateral ECT in depression. Convulsive Therapy 2:253–257, 1986

Abrams R, Taylor MA: Catatonia: a prospective clinical study. Arch Gen Psychiatry 33:579–581, 1976

Abrams R, Taylor MA: Cognitive dysfunction in melancholia. Psychol Med 17:359–362, 1987

Abrams R, Taylor MA, Faber R, et al: Bilateral versus unilateral electroconvulsive therapy: efficacy in melancholia. Am J Psychiatry 140:463–465, 1983

Achenback TM: DSM-III in light of empirical research on the classification of childhood psychopathology. J Am Acad Child Adolesc Psychiatry 19:395–412, 1980

Adams F, Quesada JR, Gutterman JV: Neuropsychiatric manifestations of human leukocyte interferon therapy in patients with cancer. JAMA 252:938–941, 1984

Addonizio G, Susman V: ECT as a treatment alternative for patients with symptoms of neuroleptic malignant syndrome. J Clin Psychiatry 48:102–105, 1987

Ahmad S, Sheik AI, Meeran MK: Disopyramide-induced acute psychosis. Chest 76:712, 1979

Aitken RCB: Measurement of feelings using visual analogue scales. R Soc Med 62:989–993, 1969

Akiskal HS: Factors associated with incomplete recovery in primary depressive illness. J Clin Psychiatry 43:266–271, 1982

Akiskal HS: Diagnosis and classification of affective disorders: new insights from clinical and laboratory approaches. Psychiatr Dev 1:123–160, 1983a

Akiskal HS: Dysthymic disorder: psychopathology of proposed chronic depressive subtypes. Am J Psychiatry 140:11–20, 1983b

Akiskal HS: The bipolar spectrum: new concepts in classification and diagnosis, in Psychiatry Update: The American Psychiatric Association Annual Review, vol 2. Edited by Grinspoon L. Washington, DC, American Psychiatric Association, 1983c

Akiskal HS: A proposed clinical approach to chronic and "resistant" depressions: evaluation and treatment. J Clin Psychiatry 46:32–36, 1985a

Akiskal HS: The clinical management of affective disorders, in Psychiatry. Edited by Michels R, Cavenar JO, et al. Philadelphia, JB Lippincott Company, 1985b

Akiskal HS, Cassano GB: The impact of therapeutic advances in widening the nosologic boundaries of affective disorders. Pharmacopsychiatr 16:111–118, 1983

Akiskal HS, Mallya G: Criteria for the "soft" bipolar spectrum: treatment implications. Psychopharmacol Bull 23:68–73, 1987

Akiskal HS, McKinney WT: Depressive disorders: towards a unified hypothesis. Science 182:20–28, 1973

Akiskal HS, Puzantian VR: Psychotic forms of depression and mania. Psychiatr Clin North Am 2:419–439, 1979

Akiskal HS, Weller E: Mood disorders and suicide in children and adolescents, in Comprehensive Textbook of Psychiatry, 5th ed. Edited by Kaplan HI, Sadock BJ. Baltimore, Williams and Wilkins (in press)

Akiskal HS, Djenderedjian AH, Rosenthal RH, et al: Cyclothymic disorder: validating criteria for inclusion in the bipolar affective group. Am J Psychiatry 134:1227–1233, 1977

Akiskal HS, Bitar AH, Puzantian VR, et al: The nosological status of neurotic depressions: a prospective three- to four-year follow-up examination in the light of the primary-secondary and the unipolar-bipolar dichotomies. Arch Gen Psychiatry 35:756–766, 1978

Akiskal HS, Rosenthal RH, Rosenthal TL, et al: Differentiation of primary affective illness from situational, symptomatic, and secondary depressions. Arch Gen Psychiatry 6:635–643, 1979a

Akiskal HS, Khani MK, Scott-Strauss A: Cyclothymic temperamental disorders. Psychiatr Clin North Am 2:527–553, 1979b

Akiskal HS, Rosenthal TL, Haykal RF, et al: Characterologic depressions: clinical and sleep EEG findings separating "subaffective dysthymias" from "character spectrum disorders." Arch Gen Psychiatry 37:777–783, 1980

Akiskal HS, King D, Rosenthal TL, et al: Chronic depressions, I; clinical and familial characteristics in 137 probands. J Affective Disord 3:297–318, 1981

Akiskal HS, Walker PW, Puzantian VR, et al: Bipolar outcome in the course of depressive illness: phenomenologic, familial, and pharmacologic predictors. J Affective Disord 5:115–128, 1983

Akiskal HS, Downs J, Jordan P, et al: Affective disorders in the referred children and younger siblings of manic-depressives: mode of onset and prospective course. Arch Gen Psychiatry 42:996–1003, 1985a

Akiskal HS, Chen SE, Davis GC, et al: Borderline: an adjective in search of a noun. J Clin Psychiatry 46:41–48, 1985b

Albala AA, Gredon JF, Tavika J, et al: Changes in serial dexamethasone suppression tests among unipolar depressives receiving electroconvulsive treatment. Biol Psychiatry 16:551–560, 1980

Albert N, Beck AT: Incidence of depression in early adolescence: a preliminary study. J Youth Adol 4:301–307, 1975

Alberti RE, Emmons ML: Your Perfect Right. San Luis Obispo, Calif, Impact Pubs, 1974

Alexander F, French TM: Psychoanalytic Therapy. New York, Ronald Press, 1946

Alloy LB, Abramson LY: Judgment of contingency in depressed and nondepressed students: sadder but wiser? J Exp Psychol Gen 108:441–485, 1979

Ambelas A: Psychologically stressful events in the precipitation of mania episodes. Br J Psychiatry 135:15–21, 1979

American Psychiatric Association: Diagnostic and Statistical Manual of Mental Disorders, 2nd ed. Washington, DC, American Psychiatric Association, 1968

American Psychiatric Association: Diagnostic and Statistical Manual of Mental Disorders, 3rd ed. Washington, DC, American Psychiatric Association, 1980

American Psychiatric Association: Diagnostic and Statistical Manual of Mental Disorders, 3rd ed, revised. Washington, DC, American Psychiatric Association, 1987

American Psychiatric Association: Manual of Psychiatric Peer Review, 2nd ed. Washington, DC, American Psychiatric Association, 1981

American Psychiatric Association: Report of the Task Force on Electroconvulsive Therapy of the American Psychiatric Association, no. 14. Washington, DC, 1978

American Psychiatric Association, Commission on Psychotherapies: Psychological Research, Methodological and Efficacy Issues. Washington, DC, American Psychiatric Association, 1982b

American Psychiatric Association, Commission on Psychotherapies: Psychotherapy Research: Methodological and Efficacy Issues. Washington, DC, American Psychiatric Association, 1982a

American Psychiatric Association: Task force on the use of laboratory tests in psychiatry. Am J Psychiatry 142:155–162, 1985a

American Psychiatric Association, Task Force Report: Tricyclic antidepressants: blood level measurements and clinical outcome. Am J Psychiatry 142:155–182, 1985b

Amsterdam JD, Berwish N: Treatment of refractory depression with combination reserpine and tricyclic antidepressant therapy. J Clin Psychopharmacol 7:238–242, 1987

Andreasen NC: Thought, language, and communication disorders, II: diagnostic significance. Arch Gen Psychiatry 36:1325–1330, 1979

Andreasen NC, Winokur G: Secondary depression: familial, clinical, and research perspectives. Am J Psychiatr 136:62–66, 1979

Angst J: Zur Atiologie und Noslogie endogener depressiver Pschosen. Berlin, Springer-Verlag, 1966

Angst J, Grof P, Karasek M, et al: Patient selection for long-term lithium treatment in clinical practice. Arch Gen Psychiatry 36:894–897, 1979a

Angst J, Felder W, Frey R: The course of unipolar and bipolar affective disorders, in Origin, Prevention and Treatment of Affective Disorders. Edited by Schou M, Stromgren E. New York, Academic Press, 1979b

Anthony EJ: Two contrasting types of adolescent depression and their treatment, in Depression and Human Existence. Edited by Anthony EJ, Benedek T. Boston, Little Brown, 1975a

Anthony EJ: Childhood depression, in Depression and Human Existence. Edited by Anthony EJ, Benedek T. Boston, Little Brown, 1975b, p. 446

Anthony EJ, Scott P: Manic depressive psychosis in childhood. Child Psychol Psychiat 1:53–72, 1960

Antonuccio DO, Lewinsohn PM, Steinmetz JL: Identification of therapist differences in a group treatment for depression. J Consult Clin Psychol 50:433–435, 1982

Arieti S: Psychoanalysis of severe depression: theory and therapy. J Am Acad Psychoanal 4:327–345, 1976

Arieti S: Psychotherapy of severe depression. Am J Psychiatry 134:864–868, 1977

Arieti S: The psychology of sadness, in Severe and Mild Depression: The Psychotherapeutic Approach. Edited by Arieti S, Bemporad JR. New York, Basic Books, 1978

Arieti S, Bemporad J: Severe and Mild Depression: The Psychotherapeutic Approach. New York, Basic Books, 1978

Arieti S, Bemporad JR: The psychological organization of depression. Am J Psychiatry 137:1360–1365, 1980

Aronoff GR, Bergstrom RF, Pottratz ST, et al: Fluoxetine kinetics and protein binding in normal and impaired renal function. Clin Pharmacol Ther 36:138–144, 1984

Aronson MD, Hafez H: A case of trazodone-induced ventricular tachycardia. J Clin Psychiatry 47:388–389, 1986

Atkinson JH, Kremer EF, Risch SC, et al: Plasma measures of beta-endorphin/beta-lipotropin-like immunoreactivity in chronic pain syndrome and psychiatric subjects. Psychiatry Res 9:319–327, 1983

Avery D, Winokur G: Mortality in depressed patients treated with electroconvulsive therapy and antidepressants. Arch Gen Psychiatry 33:1029–1037, 1976

Avery D, Winokur G: The efficacy of electroconvulsive therapy and antidepressants in depression. Biol Psychiatry 12: 507–523, 1977

Ayd FJ: Lithium-ECT induced cerebral toxicity. International Drug Therapy Newsletter 16:21–23, 1981

Azrin, NH, Besalel VA: An operant reinforcement method of treating depression. J Behav Ther Exp Psychiatry 12:145–151, 1981

Bachrach HM, Leaff LA: Analyzability: a systematic review of the clinical and qualitative literature. J Am Psychoanal Assoc 26:881–920, 1978

Badel DW: The repetitive cycle in depression. Int J Psychoanal 43:113, 133–141, 1962

Baldessarini RJ: Chemotherapy in psychiatry, principles and practice. Boston, Harvard University Press, 1985, pp 162–163

Balint M, Ornstein PH, Balint E: Focal Psychotherapy. London, Tavistock Publications, 1972

Ballenger JC, Post RM: Carbamazepine in manic-depressive illness: a new treatment. Am J Psychiatry 137:782–790, 1980

Bant WP: Antihypertensive drugs and depression: a reappraisal. Psychol Med 8:275–283, 1978

Barerra M: An evaluation of a brief group therapy for depression. J Consult Clin Psychol 47:413–415, 1979

Barnes DM: Steroids may influence changes in mood. Science 232:1344–1345, 1986

Barrett JE, Rose RM (eds): Mental Disorders in the Community—Findings from Psychiatric Epidemiology. New York, Guilford Press, 1986

Bartlett J, Bridges P, Kelly D: Contemporary indications for psychosurgery. Br J Psychiatry 138:507–511, 1981

Batki SL, Rowbotham M, Sorenson JL, et al: Depressed opiate addicts: diagnosis and treatment. New Research Abstract 75, American Psychiatric Association Annual Meeting, 1986

Baxter LR Jr, Liston EH, Schwartz JM, et al: Prolongation of the antidepressant response to partial sleep deprivation by lithium. Psychiatry Res 19:17–23, 1986

Bayer AJ, Pathy MSJ, Ankier SI: Pharmacokinetic and pharmacodynamic characteristics of trazodone in the elderly. Br J Clin Pharmacol 16:371–376, 1983

Beck AT: Thinking and depression, I: idiosyncratic content and cognitive distortion. Arch Gen Psychiatry 9:324–333, 1963

Beck AT: Depression: Clinical, Experimental and Theoretical Aspects. New York, Harper and Row, 1967

Beck AT: Depression: Cause and Treatment. Philadelphia, University of Pennsylvania Press, 1972

Beck AT: Cognitive Therapy and the Emotional Disorders. New York, International Universities Press, 1976

Beck AT: The Behavior Therapist, in press.

Beck AT, Greenberg R: Coping with Depression. Philadelphia, Center for Cognitive Therapy, 1974.

Beck AT, Ward GH, Mendelson M, et al. An inventory for measuring depression. Arch Gen Psychiatry 4:561–571, 1961

Beck AT, et al: Cognitive Theory of Depression. New York, Guilford Press, 1979

Beck AT, Hollon SD, Young JE, et al: Treatment of depression with cognitive therapy and amitriptyline. Arch Gen Psychiatry 42:142–148, 1985b

Becker J: Depression: Theory and Research. New York, Holt, Rinehart and Winston, 1974

Becker RE, Heimberg RG: Social skills training approaches, in Handbook of Clinical Behavior Therapy with Adults. Edited by Hersen M, Bellach AS. New York, Plenum Press, 1985

Beigel A, Feder SL: Patterns of utilization in partial hospitalization. Am J Psychiatry 126:1267–1274, 1970

Beitman BD, Carlin AS, Chiles JC: Pharmacotherapy-psychotherapy triangle: a physician, a non-medical psychotherapist and a patient. J Clin Psychiatry 45:458–459, 1984

Bellack AS, Hersen M, Himmelhoch J: Social skills training for depression: a treatment manual. Journal Supplement Abstract Service Catalog of Selected Documents 11:36, 1981

Bellak L, Small L: Emergency Psychotherapy and Brief Psychotherapy. New York, Grune & Stratton, 1965

Bemporad JR: Childhood depression from a developmental perspective, in American Psychiatric Association Annual Review, vol 1. Edited by Grinspoon L. Washington, DC, American Psychiatric Association, 1982

Benson H: The Relaxation Response. New York, William Morrow, 1975

Berglund M: Suicide in alcoholism. Arch Gen Psychiatry 41:888–894, 1984

Bergsholm P, Gran L, Bleie H: The effect of hypocapnia induced by hyperventilation and the effect of ventilation with oxygen. Acta Psychiatr Scand 69:121–128, 1984

Berner P: Modification in the psychopathologic definition of schizophrenia: alterations during the last two decades—expectations for the future. Compr Psychiatry 21:475–482, 1980

Bertlessen A, Harvald B, Hauge M: A Danish study of manic-depressive disorders. Br J Psychiatry 130:338–351, 1977

Besyner JK: The comparative efficacy of cognitive and behavioral treatments of depression: a multiassessment approach, in Dissertation Abstracts International 39:4568-B (University Microfilm no. 79-04956) 1979

Bibring E: The mechanism of depression, in Affective Disorders. Edited by Greenacre P. New York, International Universities Press, 1953

Biederman J, Rivinus T, Kemper K, et al: Depressive disorders in relatives of anorexia nervosa patients with and without a current episode of nonbipolar major depression. Am J Psychiatry 142:1495–1497, 1985

Bielski RJ, Friedel RO: Prediction of tricyclic antidepressant response. Arch Gen Psychiatry 33:1479–1489, 1979

Biglan A, Dow MG: Toward a "second generation" model of depression treatment: a problem specific approach, in Behavior Therapy for Depression: Present Status and Future Directions. Edited by Rehm LP. New York, Academic Press, 1981

Biglan A, Hops H, Sherman L, et al: Problem-solving interactions of depressed women and their spouses. Behav Res Ther (in press)

Billings AG, Moos RH: Social support and functioning among community and clinical groups: a panel model. J Behav Med 5:295–311, 1982

Billings AG, Moos RH: Psychosocial stressors, coping, and depression, in Handbook of Depression: Treatment, Assessment and Research. Edited by Beckham EE, Leber WR. Homewood, Ill, Dorsey Press, 1985

Billings AG, Cronkite RC, Moos RH: Social-environmental factors in unipolar depression: comparisons of depressed patients and nondepressed controls. J Abnorm Psychol 92:119–133, 1983

Black DW, Winokur G, Nasrallah A: Treatment of mania: a naturalistic study of electroconvulsive therapy versus lithium in 438 patients. J Clin Psychiatry 48:132–139, 1987

Blackburn IM, Bishop S: Changes in cognition with pharmacotherapy and cognitive therapy. Br J Psychiatry 143:609–617, 1983

Blackburn IM, Bishop S, Glen AIM, et al: The efficacy of cognitive therapy in depression: a treatment trial using cognitive therapy and pharmacotherapy, each alone and in combination. Br J Psychiatry 139:181–189, 1981

Blackburn IM, Eunson KM, Bishop S: Br J Psychiatry, in press

Blackwell B, Galbraith JR, Dahl DS: Chronic pain management. Hosp Community Psychiatry 35:999–1008, 1984

Blackwood DHR, Cull RE, Freeman CPL, et al: A study of the incidence of epilepsy following ECT. J Neurol Neurosurg Psychiatry 43:1098–1102, 1980

Bland RC, Newman SC, Orn H: Recurrent and nonrecurrent depression: a family study. Arch Gen Psychiatry 43:1085–1089, 1986

Blaney PH: The effectiveness of cognitive and behavioral therapies, in Behavior Therapy for Depression: Present Status and Future Directions. Edited by Rehm LP. New York, Academic Press, 1981

Bleuler E: Dementia Praecox; or, the Group of Schizophrenias. Translated by Zinkin J. New York, International Universities Press, 1950, p 208

Bloom BL, Asher SJ, White SW: Marital disruption as a stressor: a review and analysis. Psychol Bull 85:867–894, 1978

Blumer DB: Chronic pain as a psychobiologic phenomena: the pain prone disorder, in Psychiatric Aspects of Neurologic Disease, vol 2. Edited by Benson DF, Blumer D. New York, Grune & Stratton, 1982

Blumer DB (ed): Psychiatric Aspects of Epilepsy. Washington, DC, American Psychiatric Press, 1984

Blumer DB, Heilbronn M: Antidepressant treatment for chronic pain: treatment outcome of 1,000 patients treated with the pain-prone disorder. Psychiatric Annals 14:796–807, 1984

Blumer DB, Heilbronn M, Rosenbaum AH: Antidepressant treatment of the pain-prone disorder. Psychopharmacol Bull 20:531–535, 1984

Bonica JJ: Preface, in New Approaches to the Treatment of Chronic Pain. Edited by Ng LKY. Rockville, Md, Alcohol, Drug Abuse, and Mental Health Administration, 1981

Bonime W: The psychodynamics of neurotic depression. J. Am Acad Psychoanal 4:301–311, 1976

Bowlby J: Grief and mourning in infancy and early childhood: Psychoanal Study Child 15:9–52, 1960

Bowlby J: Attachment and Loss. London, Hogarth, 1969

Bowlby J: The making and breaking of affectional bonds, II: some principles of psychotherapy. Br J Psychiatry 130:421–431, 1977

Bowlby J: Loss, Sadness and Depression. New York, Basic Books, 1980, p 247–248

Boyce P, Parker G: Seasonal affective disorder in the southern hemisphere. Am J Psychiatry 145:97–99, 1988

Bracha S, Hes JP: Death occurring during combined reserpine-electroshock treatment. Am J Psychiatry 113:257, 1956

Branconnier RJ, Harto NE, McNiff ME, et al: The adverse reaction potential of antidepressant drugs: prediction from multivariate models of in vitro uptake inhibition and receptor affinity for neurotransmitters. Am Coll Neuropsychopharmacol Abs, 1985, p 118

Brena SF: Chronic pain states: a model for classification. Psychiatric Annals 14:778–782, 1984

Breuer J, Freud S: On the psychical mechanisms of hysterical phenomena (1893). Standard Edition, 2, 1893

Briant RH, Reid JL, Dollery CT: Interaction between clonidine and desipramine in man. Br Med J 1:522–523, 1982

Briscoe CW, Smith JB: Depression and marital turmoil. Arch Gen Psychiatry 29:811–817, 1973

Brorson L, Wennerblom B: Effect of the tetracyclic antidepressant drug maprotiline on cardiac electrophysiology in human volunteers. J Cardiovasc Pharmacol 4:531–535, 1982

Brotman AW, Rosenbaum JF: MAOs plus tryptophan: a cause of the serotonin syndrome? Biological Therapies in Psychiatry 7:45–46, 1984

Brotman AW, Falk WE, Gelenberg AJ: Pharmacological treatment of acute depressive subtypes, in Psychopharmacology: The Third Generation of Progress. Edited by Meltzer HY. New York, Raven Press, 1987

Brown GW, Harris TO: Social origins of depression: a study of psychiatric disorder in women. London, Tavistock Publications, 1978a

Brown GW, Harris TO: Social origins of depression: a reply. Psychol Med 8:577–588, 1978b

Brown GW, Harris TO, Copeland JR: Depression and loss. Br J Psychiatry 130:1–18, 1977

Brown GW, Harris TO, Bifulco A: Long-term effects of early loss of parent, in Depression in Young People. Edited by Rutter M, Igard CE, Read PB. New York, Guilford Press, 1986

Brown R, Lewinsohn PM: A psychoeducational approach to the treatment of depression: comparison of group, individual, and minimal contact procedures. J Consult Clin Psychol 52:774–783, 1984

Brown RP, Sweeney J, Frances A, et al: Age as a predictor of treatment response in endogenous depression. J Clin Psychopharmacol 3:176–178, 1983

Bukberg J, Penman D, Holland JC: Depression in hospitalized cancer patients. Psychosom Med 46:199–212, 1984

Bunney WE Jr: Psychopharmacology of the switch process in affective illness, in Psychopharmacology: A Generation of Progress. Edited by Lipton MA, Di Mascio A, Killam KF. New York, Raven Press, 1978

Butterworth A: Depression associated with alcohol withdrawal. Q J Study Alcohol 32:343–348, 1971

Butterworth A, Watts RD: Treatment of hospitalized alcoholics with doxepin and diazepam. Q J Study Alcohol 32:78–81, 1971

Caccia S, Fond MH, Garattini S, et al: Plasma concentrations of trazodone and 1-(3-chlorophenyl) piperazine in man after a single oral dose of trazodone. J Pharm Pharmacol 4:605–606, 1982

Cade JFJ: Lithium salts in the treatment of psychotic excitement. Med J Aust 2:349–352, 1949

Caine D, Shoulson I: Psychiatric syndromes in Huntington's disease. Am J Psychiatry 140:728–733, 1983

Calyton PJ, Collins EL: The significance of secondary depression. J Affective Disord 3:25–35, 1981

Campbell M, Small AM, Green WH, et al: Behavioral efficacy of haloperidol and lithium carbonate: a comparison in hospitalized aggressive children with conduct disorder. Arch Gen Psychiatry 41:650–656, 1984

Cantwell DR, Carlson G: Problems and prospects in the study of childhood depression. J Nerv Ment Dis 167:522–529, 1979

Carasso RL, Yehuda S, Streifler M: Clomipramine and amitriptyline in the treatment of severe pain. Int J Neurosci 9:191–194, 1979

Carbone PP, Haskell CM, Levanthal BG, et al: Clinical experience with L-asparaginase. Recent Results Cancer Res 33:236–243, 1970

Carlson GA: Affective psychoses in mental retardates. Psychiatr Clin North Am 2:499–510, 1979

Carlson GA, Cantwell DP: Unmasking masked depression in children and adolescents. Am J Psychiatry 137:445–449, 1980

Carlson GA, Goodwin F: The stages of mania. Arch Gen Psychiatry 28:221–288, 1973

Carney MWP, Roth M, Garside RF: The diagnosis of depressive syndromes and the prediction of ECT responses. Br J Psychiatry 3:659–674, 1965

Carrington CH: A comparison of cognitive and analytically oriented brief treatment approaches to depression in black women, in Dissertation Abstracts International, 40 (University Microfilm no 79-26513). College Park, Md, University of Maryland, 1979

Carroll BJ: The dexamethasone suppression test for melancholia. Br J Psychiatry 140:292–304, 1982

Carver CS, Scheier MF: Control theory: a useful conceptual framework for personality, social, clinical, and health psychology. Psychol Bull 92:111–135, 1982

Cassano GB, Maggini C, Akiskal HS: Short-term subchronic and chronic sequelae of affective disorders. Psychiatr Clin North Am 6:55–67, 1983

Cassano GB, Musetti L, Perugi G, et al: A new approach to the clinical subclassification of depressive illness. Pharmacopsychiatry 21(suppl):19–23, 1988

Cassem NH: Cardiovascular effects of antidepressants. J Clin Psychiatry 43(sec 2):22–28, 1982

Cassem NH: Depression, in Massachusetts General Hospital Handbook of General Hospital Psychiatry, 2nd ed. Edited by Hackett TP, Cassem NH. Littleton, Mass, PSG Publishing Company, 1987, pp 227–260

Cassem NH, Hackett TP: Psychological aspects of myocardial infarction. Med Clin North Am 61:711–721, 1977

Castelnuovo-Tedesco P: Brief psychotherapy, in American Handbook of Psychiatry, 2nd ed, vol. 5. Edited by Arieti S. New York, Basic Books, 1975

Cavanaugh SV: The prevalence of emotional and cognitive dysfunction in a general medical population using the MMSE, GHQ and BDI. Gen Hosp Psychiatry 5:15–24, 1983

Cavanaugh SV, Clark DC, Gibbons RD: Diagnosing depression in the hospitalized medically ill. Psychosomatics 24:809–815, 1983

Checkley S, Winton F, Franey C, et al: Antidepressant effects of light in seasonal affective disorder. Presented at the Royal College of Psychiatry, Southampton, England, June 1986

Chevron E, Rounsaville BJ: Evaluating the clinical skills of psychotherapists. A comparison of techniques. Arch Gen Psychiatry 40:1129–1132, 1983

Chevron E, Rounsaville BJ, Rothblum E, et al: Selecting psychotherapists to participate in psychotherapy outcome studies. Relationship between psychotherapist characteristics and assessment of clinical skills. J Nerv Ment Dis 171:348–353, 1983

Chiarello RJ, Cole JO: The use of psychostimulants in general psychiatry: a reconsideration. Arch Gen Psychiatry 44:286–295, 1987

Chodoff P: The core problem in depression, in Science and Psychoanalysis. Edited by Masserman J. New York, Grune & Stratton, 1970

Chouinard G, Young SN, Annable L: Antimanic effect of clonazepam. Biol Psychiatry 18:451–466, 1983

Ciraulo DA, Jaffe JH: Tricyclic antidepressants in the treatment of depression associated with alcoholism. J Clin Psychopharmacol 1:146–150, 1981

Ciraulo DA, Lind L, Salzman C: Sodium nitroprusside treatment of ECT-induced blood pressure elevations. Am J Psychiatry 135:1105–1106, 1978

Ciraulo DA, Alderson IM, Chapran DJ, et al: Imipramine disposition in alcoholics. J Clin Psychopharmacol 2:2–7, 1982

Ciraulo DA, et al: Antidepressant pharmacokinetics in alcoholics. New Research Abstracts, American Psychiatric Annual Meeting, Washington, DC, May 13, 1986

Clark DC, Cavanaugh SV, Gibbons RD: The core symptoms of depression in medical and psychiatric patients. J Nerv Ment Dis 171:705–713, 1983

Clarke G, Lewinsohn PM: A psychoeducational approach to treating depression in high school adolescents (manuscript in preparation). Eugene, University of Oregon

Clarkin JF, Glick ID, Haas G, et al: Inpatient family intervention: a controlled study, V: follow-up results for affective disordered patients. (Unpublished manuscript)

Clarkin JF, Haas G, Glick ID (eds): Affective Disorder and Family Intervention (Chap 1). New York, Guilford Press (in press)

Clayton PJ: The epidemiology of bipolar affective disorder. Compr Psychiatry 22:31–43, 1981

Clayton PJ: Schizoaffective disorders. J Nerv Ment Dis 170:646–650, 1982

Clayton PJ, Darvish HS: Course of depressive symptoms following the stress of bereavement, in Stress and Mental Disorders. Edited by Barret JE. New York, Raven Press, 1979

Clayton PJ, Herjanic M, Murphy GE, et al: Mourning and depression: their similarities and differences. Can J Psychiatry 19:309–312, 1974

Cohen LS, Rosenbaum JF, Hirshfeld DR: Adjunctive lithium carbonate in treatment resistant depression. Presented at the 141st Annual Meeting of the American Psychiatric Association, Montreal, 1988

Cohen MB, Baldessarini RJ: Tolerance to therapeutic effects of antidepressants. Am J Psychiatry 142:489–490, 1985

Cohen MB, Baker G, Cohen RA, et al: An intensive study of twelve cases of manic-depressive psychoses. Psychiatry 17:103–137, 1954

Cohen S: The chronic intractable benign pain syndrome. Drug Abuse & Alcoholism Newsletter, vol 13, no 4, 1984

Coleman RE, Miller AG: The relationship between depression and marital maladjustment in a clinical population: a multitrait-multimethod study. J Consult Clin Psychol 43:647–651, 1975

Comas-Diaz, L: Effects of cognitive and behavioral group treatment on the depressive symptomatology of Puerto Rican women. J Consult Clin Psychol 49:627–632, 1981

Conte HR, Plutchik R, Wild KV, et al: Combined psychotherapy and pharmacotherapy for depression: a systematic analysis of the evidence. Arch Gen Psychiatry 43:471–479, 1986

Conte HR, Plutchik R, Karasu TB, et al: Arch Gen Psychiatry, in press

Coppen A, Shaw DM, Farrell JP: Potentiation of antidepressant effect of a monoamine oxidase inhibitor by tryptophan. Lancet 1:79–80, 1963

Coppen A, Whybrow PC, Noguera R, et al: The comparative antidepressant value of L-tryptophan and imipramine with and without attempted potentiation by liothyronine. Arch Gen Psychiatry 26:234–241, 1972

Costain DW, Cowen PJ, Gelder MG, et al: Electroconvulsive therapy and the brain: evidence for increased dopamine-mediated responses. Lancet 2:400–404, 1982

Costello CG: Depression: loss of reinforcers or loss of reinforcer effectiveness? Behavior Res Therapy 3:240–247, 1972

Couch JR, Hassanein RS: Amitriptyline in migraine prophylaxis. Arch Neurol 36:695–699, 1979

Coull DC, Crooks J, Dingwall-Fordyce I, et al: A method of monitoring drugs for adverse reactions, II: amitriptyline and cardiac disease. Eur J Clin Pharmacol 3:51–55, 1970

Covi L, Lipman RS, Derogatis LR, et al: Am J Psychiatry 131:191–198, 1974

Covi L, Lipman RS: Cognitive behavioral group psychotherapy combined with imipramine in major depression: a pilot study. Psychopharmacol Bull 23:173–176, 1987

Covi L, Lipman RS, Roth D, et al: Am J Psychiatry in press

Cowdry RW, Goodwin FK: Dementia of bipolar illness: diagnosis and response to lithium. Am J Psychiatry 138:1118–1119, 1981

Coyne JC: Depression and the response of others. J Abnorm Psychol 85:186–193, 1976

Coyne JC, Aldwin C, Lazarus RS: Depression and coping in stressful episodes. J Abnorm Psychol 90:439–447, 1981

Craft M: An evaluation of treatment of depressive illness in a day hospital. Lancet 149–151, 1958

Craig TJ, Abeloff MD: Psychiatric symptomatology among hospitalized cancer patients. Am J Psychiatry 131:1323–1327, 1974

Craighead WE: Behavior therapy for depression: issues resulting from treatment studies, in Behavior Therapy for Depression: Present Status and Future Directions. Edited by Rehm LP. New York, Academic Press, 1981

Crammer J, Gillies C: Psychiatric aspects of diabetes mellitus: diabetes and depression. Br J Psychiatry 139:171–172, 1981

Cristol AH: Compr Psychiatry 13:189–200, 1972

Croog SH, Williams GH, Sudilovsky A: The effects of antihypertensive therapy on the quality of life. N Engl J Med 314:1657–1664, 1985

Cross AJ, Deakin JFW, Lofthouse R, et al: On the mechanism of action of electroconvulsive therapy: some behavioral and biochemical consequences of repeated electrically induced seizures in rats. Br J Pharmacol 66:111, 1979

Cytryn L, McKnew DH Jr: Proposed classifications of childhood depression. Am J Psychiatry 129:149–154, 1972

Cytryn L, McKnew DH, Bunney WE: Diagnosis of depression in children: a reassessment. Am J Psychiatry 177:22–25, 1980

Cytryn L, McKnew DH, Bartko JJ, et al: Offspring of patients with affective disorders, II: J Am Acad Child Adolesc Psychiatry 21:389–391, 1982

Czeisler CA, Richardson GS, Coleman RM, et al: Entrainment of human circadian rhythms by light-dark cycles: a reassessment. Photochem Photobiol 34:239–247, 1981

Czeisler CA, Allan JS, Strogatz SH, et al: Bright light resets the human circadian pacemaker independent of the timing of the sleep-wake cycle. Science 233:667–671, 1986

Daan S, Lewy AJ: Scheduled exposure to daylight: a potential strategy to reduce "jet lag" following transmeridian flight. Psychopharmacol Bull 20:566–568, 1984

Dackis CA, Pottash ALC, Gold MS, et al: The dexamethasone depression test for major depression among opiate addicts. Am J Psychiatry 141:810–811, 1984

Davenloo H: Basic Principles and Techniques in Short-Term Dynamic Psychotherapy. New York, Spectrum Publications, 1978

Davenloo H: Short-Term Dynamic Psychotherapy. New York, Jason Aronson, 1980

Davidson J, McLeod M, Law-Yone B, et al: Comparison of electroconvulsive therapy and combined phenelzine-amitriptyline in refractory depression. Arch Gen Psychiatry 35:639–642, 1978

Davis JM: Overview: maintenance therapy in psychiatry, II: affective disorders. Am J Psychiatry 133:1–13, 1976

Davis JM: Antidepressant drugs, in Comprehensive Textbook of Psychiatry, vol 4, 4th ed. Edited by Kaplan HI, Sadock BJ. Baltimore, Williams and Wilkins, 1985

Davison LA, Steinhelber JC, Eger EI, et al: Psychological effects of halothane and isoflurane anesthesia. Anesthesiology 43:313–324, 1975

Dawling S, Crome P, Braithwaite R: Pharmacokinetics of single oral doses of nortriptyline in depressed elderly hospital patients and young healthy volunteers. Clin Pharmacokinet 5:394–401, 1980

Deakin JF, Owen F, Cross AJ, et al: Studies on possible mechanisms of action of electroconvulsive therapy: effects of repeated electrically induced seizures on rat brain receptors for monoamines and other neurotransmitters. Psychopharmacology 73:345–349, 1981

Dec GW, Stern TA, Welch C: The effects of electroconvulsive therapy on serial electrocardiograms and serum cardiac enzyme values. JAMA 253:2525–2529, 1985

DeCarolis V, Gibertz F, Roccatagliata G, et al: Imipramine and electroshock in the treatment of depression. Sistema Nervoso 16:29–42, 1964

D'Elia G, Hanson L, Raotma H: L-tryptophan and 5-hydroxytryptophan in the treatment of depression: a review. Acta Psychiatr Scand 27:238–252, 1978

DeLisio G, Maremmani I, Perugi G, et al: Impairment of work and leisure in depressed outpatients. J Affective Disord 10:79–84, 1986

DeLong GR, Nieman GW: Lithium-induced behavior changes in children with symptoms suggesting manic-depressive illness. Psychopharmacol Bull 19:258–265, 1983

DeMontigny C, Grunberg F, Mayer A, et al: Lithium induces rapid relief of depression in tricyclic antidepressant drug non-responders. Br J Psychiatry 138:252–256, 1981

DeMontigny C, Cournoyer G, Morissette R, et al: Lithium carbonate addition in trycyclic antidepressant-resistant unipolar depression. Arch Gen Psychiatry 40:1327–1334, 1983

Dengler HG, Spiegel HE, Titus ZO: Effect of drugs on uptake of isotopic norepinephrine by cat tissues. Nature 191:816–817, 1961

Derogatis LR, Morrow GR, Fetting J, et al: The prevalence of psychiatric disorders among cancer patients. JAMA 249:751–757, 1983

DeRubeis RJ, Hollon SD: Behavioral treatment of affective disorders, in Future Perspectives in Behavior Therapy. Edited by Michelson L, Hersen M, Turner S. New York, Plenum Press, 1981, pp 103–129

DeRubeis RJ, Hollon SD, Evans MO, et al: J Consult Clin Psychol 50:744–756, 1982

Detre T, Himmelhoch J, Swartzburg M, et al: Hypersomnia and manic-depressive disease. Am J Psychiatry 128:1303–1305, 1972

Dilsaver SC, Feinberg M, Greden JF: Antidepressant withdrawal symptoms treated with anticholinergic agents. Am J Psychiatry 140:249–251, 1983

DiMascio A, Weissman MM, Prusoff BA, et al: Differential symptom reduction by drugs and psychotherapy in acute depression. Arch Gen Psychiatry 36:1450–1456, 1979

Doghramji K, Dubin WR: Meningoencephalitis presenting as depression. Hosp Community Psychiatry 36:884–885, 1985

Dorpat TL, Anderson WF, Ripley HS: The relationship of physical illness to suicide, in Suicidal Behaviours: Diagnosis and Management. Edited by Resnik HL. Boston, Little Brown and Company, 1968

Dressler DM, Folk J: The treatment of depresson with ECT in the presence of brain tumor. Am J Psychiatry 132(12):1320–1321, 1975

Dubovsky SL, Franks RD: Intracellular calcium ions in affective disorders: a review and an hypothesis. Biol Psychiatry 18:781–797, 1983

Duncan CC, Deldin PJ, Skwerer RG, et al: Phototherapy enhances visual brain potentials in patients with seasonal affective disorder. (unpublished manuscript)

Dunner DL: Rapid cycling bipolar manic depressive illness. Psychiatr Clin North Am 2:461–467, 1979

Dunner DL, Stallone F, Fieve RR: Prophylaxis with lithium carbonate: an update. Arch Gen Psychiatry 39:1344–1345, 1982

Earle BV: Thyroid hormone and tricyclic antidepressants in resistant depression. Am J Psychiatry 138:252–256, 1981

Eastman CI: Bright light in work-sleep schedules for shift worker: application of circadian rhythm principles, in Temporal Disorder in Human Oscillatory Systems. Edited by Rensing L, Van der Heiden V, Mackey M. Berlin, Springer-Verlag, 1988

Ebert MH, Shader RI: Hematological effects, in Psychotropic Drug Side Effects: Clinical and Theoretical Perspectives. Edited by Shader RI, DiMascio A. Baltimore, Williams and Wilkins, 1970, pp 164–174

Eckert EE, Goldberg SC, Halmi K, et al: Depression in anorexia nervosa. Psychol Med 11:1–8, 1981

Edelbroek PM, Linssen ACG, Zitman FG, et al: Analgesic and antidepressive effects of low dose amitriptyline in relation to its metabolism in patients with chronic pain. Clin Pharmacol Ther 39:156–162, 1986

Egeland JA: Bipolarity: the iceberg of affective disorders? Compr Psychiatry 24:337–344, 1983

El-Fakahany E, Richelson E: Antagonisms by antidepressants of muscarinic acetylcholine receptors of human brain. Br J Pharmacol 78:97–102, 1983

El-Ganzouri AR, Ivankovich AD, Braverman B: Monoamine oxidase inhibitors: should they be discontinued preoperatively? Anesth Analg 64:592–596, 1985

Elkin I: Psychotherapy Research: Where Are We and Where Should We Go? Edited by Williams JBW, Spitzer RL. New York, Guilford Press, 1984, pp 150–159

Elkin I, Parloff MB, Hadley SW, et al: NIMH treatment of depression collaborative research program: background and research plan. Arch Gen Psychiatry 42:305–316, 1985

Elkin I, Shea T, Watkins J, et al: Comparative treatment outcome findings. Presentation of NIMH Treatment of Depression Collaborative Research Program. Annual Meeting of the American Psychiatric Association, Washington, DC, 1986

Ellis A, Harper RA: A Guide to Rational Living. Hollywood, Calif, Wilshire Book, 1961

Elsenga S, van den Hoofdakker RH: Clinical effects of sleep deprivation and clomipramine in endogenous depression. J Psychiatr Res 17:361, 1983

Endicott J, Spitzer RL: A diagnostic interview: the Schedule for Affective Disorders and Schizophrenia. Arch Gen Psychiatry 35:837–844, 1978

Engel G: Psychogenic pain and the pain prone patient. Am J Med 26:899–918, 1959

Engel G, Reichman F: Spontaneous and experimentally induced depression in an infant with gastric fistula. J Am Psychoanal Assoc 4:428–456, 1956

Erman MK, Welch CA, Mandel MR: A comparison of two unilateral ECT electrode placements: efficacy and electrical energy considerations. Am J Psychiatry 136:1317–1319, 1979

Esquirol E: Mental Maladies: Treatise on Insanity. Edited by Hunt EK. Philadelphia, Lea and Blanchard, 1845, pp 275–315

Evans LE, McCartney CF, Nemeroff CB, et al: Depression in women treated for gynecological cancer: clinical and neuroendocrine assessment. Am J Psychiatry 143:447–451, 1986

Evans LE, Nemeroff CB: The dexamethasone suppression test in organic affective syndrome. Am J Psychiatry 141:1465–1466, 1984

Extein I, Gold MS: Psychiatric applications of thyroid tests. J Clin Psychiatry 47(suppl 1):13–16, 1986

Farberow N, Ganzler S, Cutter F, et al: An eight-year survey of hospital suicides. Life Threatening Behaviour 1:184–202, 1971

Fava GA, Sonino N: The use of antidepressant drugs in the medically ill. Psychiatric Annals 17:42–44, 1987

Fawcett J, Clark DC, Gibbons RD, et al: Evaluation of lithium therapy for alcoholism. J Clin Psychiatry 45:494–499, 1984

Feighner JP, Robins E, Guze SB, et al: Diagnostic criteria for use in psychiatric research. Arch Gen Psychiatry 26:57–63, 1972

Feighner JP, Aden GC, Fabre LF, et al: Comparison of alprazolam, imipramine, and placebo in the treatment of depression. JAMA 249:3057–3064, 1983

Feighner JP, Herbstein J, Damlouji N: Combined MAOI, TCA, and direct stimulant therapy of treatment-resistant depression. J Clin Psychiatry 46:206–209, 1985

Fenichel O: The Psychoanalytic Theory of Neurosis. New York, Norton and Company, 1945

Fennell MJV, Teasdale JD: Cognitive therapy with chronic, drug-refractory depressed patients: a note of caution. Cognitive Ther Res 6:455–460, 1982

Ferenczi S, Rank O: Development of Psychoanalysis. Translated by Newton C. New York, Nervous and Mental Disease Publishing Company, 1925

Ferster CB: Animal behavior and mental illness. Psychological Record 16:345–356, 1966

Fieve RR, Dunner DL: Unipolar and bipolar affective states, in The Nature and Treatment of Depression. Edited by Flach F, Draghi S. New York, John Wiley and Sons, 1975

Fieve RR, Peselow ED: Lithium: clinical applications, in Drugs in Psychiatry, vol. 1, Antidepressants. Edited by Burrows GD, Norman TR, Davies B. Amsterdam, Elsevier, 1983

Fink M: Efficacy and safety of induced seizures (EST) in man. Compr Psychiatry 19:1–18, 1978

Fink M: Convulsive Therapy: Theory and Practice. New York, Raven Press, 1979

Fink M: Meduna and the origins of convulsive therapy. Am J Psychiatry 141:1034–1041, 1984

Fink M, Johnson L: Monitoring duration of electroconvulsive therapy seizures. Arch Gen Psychiatry 39:1189–1191, 1982

Fink M, Ottosson JO: A theory of convulsive therapy in endogenous depression: significance of hypothalamic functions. Psychiatry Res 2:49–61, 1980

Fiske DW, Hunt HF, Luborsky L, et al: Planning of research on affectiveness of psychotherapy. Arch Gen Psychiatry 22:22–32, 1970

Foley SH, Rounsaville BJ, Weissman MM, et al: Individual versus conjoint interpersonal psychotherapy for depressed patients with marital disputes. Presented at the Annual Meeting of the American Psychiatric Association, Chicago, Ill, May 1987

Folkman S, Lazarus RS: Stress processes and depressive symptomatology. J Abnorm Psychol 95:107–113, 1986

France RD, Houpt J, Skott A, et al: The phenomenology of depression in chronic pain. Abstract 91A, American Psychiatric Association, 1984

Frances AJ: The DSM-III personality disorders section. Am J Psychiatry 137:1050–1055, 1980

Frances AJ, Clarkin JF, Perry S: Differential Therapeutics: A Guide to the Art and Science of Treatment Planning in Psychiatry. New York, Brunner/Mazel, 1984

Frank JD: Psychotherapy: the restoration of morale. Am J Psychiatry 131:271–274, 1974

Fras I, Litin EM, Pearson JS: Comparison of psychiatric symptoms in carcinoma of the pancreas with those in some other intra-abdominal neoplasms. Am J Psychiatry 123:1553–1562, 1967

Freese KJ: Can patients safely undergo electroconvulsive therapy while receiving monoamine oxidase inhibitors? Convulsive Therapy 1:190–194, 1985

Freis ED: Reserpine in hypertension: present status. Am Fam Physician 11:120–122, 1975

Freud S: The History of the Psychoanalytic Movement (1914). Standard Edition, vol 14, 1985

Freud S: Mourning and melancholia (1917), in Complete Psychological Works Standard Edition 14:151–169

Friedel RO: Clinical predictors of treatment response: an update, in The Affective Disorders. Edited by Davis JM, Maas JW. Washington, DC, American Psychiatric Association, 1983

Friedel RO: The combined use of neuroleptics and ECT in drug-resistant schizophrenic patients. Psychopharmacol Bull 22:928–930, 1986

Friedman AS: Interaction of drug therapy with marital therapy in depressive patients. Arch Gen Psychiatry 32:619–637, 1975

Fuchs CZ, Rehm OP: A self-control behavior therapy program for depression. J Consult Clin Psychol 45:206–215, 1977

Fullerten DT, Harvey RF, Klein MH, et al: Psychiatric disorders in patients with spinal cord injuries. Arch Gen Psychiatry 8:1369–1371, 1981

Gaines GY, Rees I: Electroconvulsive therapy and anesthetic considerations. Anesth Analg 65:1345–1356, 1986

Gallant DM, Biship MP, Guerro-Figueroa R, et al: Doxepin versus diazepam: a controlled evaluation in 100 chronic alcoholic patients. J Clin Pharmacol 9:57–65, 1969

Gammon GD, Hansen C: A case of akinesia induced by amoxapine. Am J Psychiatry 141:283–284, 1984

Garfinkel PE, Stancer HC, Persad E: A comparison of haloperidol, lithium carbonate and their combination in the treatment of mania. J Affective Disord 2:279–288, 1980

Gawin FH, Kleber HD: Cocaine abuse treatment. Arch Gen Pscyhiatry 41:903, 1984

Gawin FH, Kleber HD: Abstinence symptomatology and psychiatric diagnosis in cocaine abuses. Arch Gen Psychiatry 43:107–113, 1986

Gelenberg AJ: Tyrosine for depression. J Psychiatr Res 17:175–180, 1983a

Gelenberg AJ: Lithium, neuroleptics, and neurotoxicity. Biological Therapies in Psychiatry 6:24, 1983b

Gelenberg AJ: New antidepressant drugs: a clinical perspective. Psychopharmacol Bull 20:291–294, 1984

Gelenberg AJ: Switching MAOIs, III. Biological Therapies in Psychiatry 10:7, 1987

Georgotas A, Friedman E, McCarthy M, et al: Resistant geriatric depressions and therapeutic response to monoamine oxidase inhibitors. Biol Psychiatry 18:195–205, 1983

Georgotas A, McCue RE, Hapworth W, et al: Comparative efficacy and safety of MAOIs versus TCAs in treating depression in the elderly. Biol Psychiatry 21:1155–1166, 1986

Georgotas A, McCue RE, Friedman E, et al: Electrocardiographic effects of nortriptyline, phenelzine, and placebo under optimal treatment conditions. Am J Psychiatry 144:798–801, 1987

Gerner RH: Systematic treatment approach to depression and treatment resistant depression. Psych Annals 13:37–49, 1983

Gerner RH, Gwirtaman HE: Abnormalities of dexamethasone suppression test and urinary MHPG in anorexia nervosa. Am J Psychiatry 138:650–653, 1981

Gerner RH, Cohen DJ, Fairbanks L, et al: CSF in anorexia nervosa compared to normal and depressed women (unpublished manuscript)

Gershon ES, Goodnick PJ: Lithium use in affective disorders. Psychiatric Annals 11:38–57, 1981

Gershon ES, Hamovit J, Guroff JJ, et al: A family study of schizoaffective, bipolar I, bipolar II, unipolar, and normal control probands. Arch Gen Psychiatry 39:1157–1167, 1982

Gershon ES, Schreiber JL, Hamovit JR: Clinical findings in patients with anorexia nervosa and affective illness in their relatives. Am J Psychiatry 141:1419–1422, 1984

Gibaldi M, Levy G: Pharmacokinetics in clinical practice, II: applications. JAMA 235:1987–1992, 1976

Gitlin MJ, Jamison KR: Lithium clinics: theory and practice. Hosp Community Psychiatry 35:363–368, 1984

Glassman AH, Platman SR: Potentiation of a monoamine oxidase inhibitor by tryptophan. J Psychiatry Res 7:83–88, 1969

Glassman AH, Roose SP: Delusional depression: a distinct clinical entity? Arch Gen Psychiatry 38:424–427, 1981

Glassman AH, Johnson LL, Giardina EV, et al: The use of imipramine in depressed patients with congestive heart failure. JAMA 250:1997–2001, 1983

Glenn MD, Weiner RD: Electroconvulsive Therapy: A Programmed Text. Washington, DC, American Psychiatric Association, 1985

Glick ID, Hargreaves WA, Drues J, et al: Short versus long hospitalization: a prospective controlled study. Arch Gen Psychiatry 34:314–317, 1977

Glick ID, Clarkin JF, Spencer JH, et al: Inpatient family intervention: a controlled evaluation of practice—preliminary results of the six-months follow up. Arch Gen Psychiatry 42:882–886, 1985

Glick ID, Clarkin JF, Kessler D: Marital and Family Therapy, 3rd ed. New York, Grune & Stratton, 1987

Glowinski J, Axelrod J: Inhibition of uptake of tritiated noradrenaline in the intact rat brain by imipramine and structurally related compounds. Nature 204:1318–1319, 1964

Goff DC: The stimulant challenge test in depression. J Clin Psychiatry 47:538–543, 1986

Goldberg RJ: Management of depression in the patient with advanced cancer. JAMA 246:373–376, 1981

Goldberg MJ, Spector R: Amoxapine overdose: report of two patients with severe neurologic damage. Ann Intern Med 96:463–464, 1982

Goldsobel AB, Rohr AS, Siegel SC, et al: Efficacy of doxepin in the treatment of chronic idiopathic urticaria. J Allergy Clin Immunol 78:867–873, 1986

Gonzales LR, Lewinsohn PM, Clarke G: Longitudinal follow up of unipolar depressives: an investigation of predictors of relapse. J Consult Clin Psychol 53:461–469, 1985

Goodwin FK, Bunney WE: Depressions following reserpine: a reevaluation. Semin Psychiatry 3:435–448, 1971

Goodwin FK, Bunney WE: A psychological approach to affective illness. Psychiatric Annals 3:19–53, 1973

Goodwin FK, Zis AP: Lithium in the treatment of mania: comparisons with neuroleptics. Arch Gen Psychiatry 36:840–844, 1979

Goodwin FK, Prange AJ Jr, Post RM, et al: Potentiation of antidepressant effects by L-triiodothyronine in tricyclic nonresponders. Am J Psychiatry 139:34–38, 1982

Goodwin JS, Regan M: Cognitive dysfunction associated with naproxen and ibuprofin in the elderly. Arthritis Rheum 25:1013–1015, 1982

Gottschalk LA, Mayerson P, Gottlieb AA: Prediction and evaluation of outcome in an emergency brief psychotherapy clinic. J Nerv Ment Dis 144:77–96, 1967

Gottschalk LA, Fox RA, Bates DE: A study of prediction and outcome in a mental health crisis clinic. Am J Psychiatry 130:1107–1111, 1973

Green BL, Gleser GC, Stone WN, et al: Relationships among diverse measures of psychotherapy outcome. J Consult Clin Psychol 43:689–699, 1975

Greenan J, Dewar M, Jones CJ: Intravenous glycopyrrolate and atropine at induction of anesthesia: a comparison. J R Soc Med 76:369–371, 1983

Greenblatt M, Grosser GH, Wechsler H: Differential response of hospitalized depressed patients to somatic therapy. Am J Psychiatry 120:935, 1964

Greene SL, Reed CE, Schroeter AL: Double-blind crossover study comparing doxepin with diphenhydramine for the treatment of chronic urticaria. J Am Acad Dermatol 12:669–675, 1985

Greenson R: The Technique and Practice of Psychoanalysis. New York, International Universities Press, 1967

Greenspan SL, Sharfstein SS: Arch Gen Psychiatry 36:1213–1219, 1981

Greer S, Silverfarb PM: Psychological concomitants of cancer: current state of research. Psychol Med 12:563–573, 1982

Greist JH, Jefferson JW, Spitzer RL (eds): Treatment of Mental Disorders. New York, Oxford University Press, 1982

Grof P: Lithium update: selected issues, in Affective Disorders Reassessed: 1983. Edited by Ayd FJ, Taylor IJ, Taylor BT. Baltimore, Waverly Press, 1983

Gualtieri CT, Powell SF: Psychoactive drug interactions. J Clin Psychiatry 39:720–729, 1978

Gujavarty K, Greenberg LB, Fink M: Electroconvulsive therapy and neuroleptic medication in therapy-resistant positive-symptom psychosis. Compulsive Therapy 3:185–195, 1987

Gurman AS, Kniskern DP, Pinsof WM: Research on the process and outcome of marital and family therapies, in Handbook of Psychotherapy and Behavior Change. Edited by Garfield SL, Bergin AE. New York, John Wiley and Sons, 1986

Haas GL, Clarkin JF: Affective disorders and the family context, in Affective Disorders and the Family. Edited by Clarkin JF, Haas GL, Glick ID. New York, Guilford Press, 1988, pp 3–28

Haas GL, Clarkin JF, Glick ID: Marital and family treatment of depression, in Handbook of Depression: Treatment, Assessment and Research. Edited by Beckham EE, Leber WR. Homewood, Ill, Dorsey Press, 1985

Haas GL, Glick ID, Clarkin JF, et al: Inpatient family intervention: a randomized clinical trial. Arch Gen Psychiatry 45:217–224, 1988

Hale AS, Procter AW, Bridges PK: Clomipramine, tryptophan and lithium in combination for resistant endogenous depression: seven case studies. Br J Psychiatry 151:213–217, 1987

Hall H, Ögren SO: Effects of antidepressant drugs on different receptors in the brain. Eur J Pharmacol 70:393–407, 1981

Hall RCW: Depression, in Psychiatric Presentations of Medical Illness: Somatopsychic Disorders. Edited by Hall RCW. New York, SP Medical and Scientific Books, 1980

Hall RCW, Joffe JR: Aberrant response to diazepam: a new syndrome. Am J Psychiatry 129:114–118, 1972

Halmi KA: Relationship of the eating disorders to depression: biological similarities and differences. International J of Eating Dis 4:667–680, 1985

Hameroff SR, Weiss JL, Lerman JC, et al: Doxepin's effects on chronic pain: a controlled study. J Clin Psychiatry 45 (3)(sec 2):47–53, 1984

Hamilton M: Development of a rating scale for primary depressive illness. Br J Soc Clin Psychol 6:278–296, 1967

Hamm JE, Major LF, Brown GL: The quantitative measurement of depression and anxiety in male alcoholics. Am J Psychiatry 136:580–582, 1979

Harmon TM, Nelson RO, Hayes SC: Self-monitoring of mood versus activity by depressed clients. J Consult Clin Psychol 48:30–38, 1980

Harris J: Depression and hysteria as symptoms of brain tumor. Henry Ford Hosp Med J 13:457–459, 1965

Harrision W, Rabkin J, Stewart JW, et al: Phenelzine for chronic depression: a study of continuation treatment. J Clin Psychiatry 47:346–349, 1986

Haskett RF: Diagnostic categorization of psychiatric disturbance in Cushing's syndrome. Am J Psychiatry 142:911–916, 1985

Hathaway SR, McKinley JC: Minnesota Multiphasic Personality Inventory (MMPI). University of Minnesota Press, 1942

Hatsukami D, Pickens RW: Post-treatment depression in an alcohol and drug abuse population. Am J Psychiatry 139:1563–1566, 1982

Hatsukami D, Pickens RW, Svikis D: Post-treatment depressive symptoms and relapse to drug use in different age groups of an alcohol and other drug abuse population. Drug Alcohol Depend 8:271–277, 1981

Hedlund B, Thompson LW: Teaching the elderly to control depression using an educational format. Presented at the Meeting of the American Psychological Association. Montreal, 1980

Heiby EM: Social versus self-control skills deficits in four cases of depression. Behavior Res Therapy 17:158–169, 1986

Helgason T: Epidemiological investigations concerning affective disorders, in Origin, Prevention, and Treatment of Affective Disorders. Edited by Schou M, Stromgren E. New York, Academic Press, 1979

Hellekson CJ, Kline JA, Rosenthal NE: Phototherapy for seasonal affective disorder in Alaska. Am J Psychiatry 143:1035–1037, 1986

Helzer JE, Clayton PJ, Pambakian R, et al: Reliability of psychiatric diagnosis, II: the test/retest reliability of diagnostic classification. Arch Gen Psychiatry 34:136–141, 1977

Henderson M: Frontal Lobe Functions in Depressed Patients Before and After ECT. Doctoral dissertation. Boston, Boston University, 1983

Henderson S, Bryne DG, Duncan-Jones P, et al: Social bonds in the epidemiology of neurosis. Br J Psychiatry 132:463–466, 1978

Hendren RL: Depression in anorexia nervosa. J Am Acad Child Psychiatry 22:59–62, 1983

Heninger GR, Charney DS, Sternberg DE: Lithium carbonate augmentation of antidepressant treatment: an effective prescription for treatment-refractory depression. Arch Gen Psychiatry 40:1335–1342, 1983

Herceg-Baron RL, Prusoff BA, Weissman MM, et al: Pharmacotherapy and psychotherapy in acutely depressed patients: a study of attrition patterns in a clinical trial. Compr Psychiatry 20:315–325, 1979

Hersen M, Bellack AS: Perspectives in the behavioral treatment of depression. Behav Modif 6:95–106, 1982

Hersen M, Bellack AS, Himmelhoch JM: Treatment of unipolar depression with social skills training. Behav Modif 4:547–556, 1980

Hersen M, Bellack AS, Himmelhoch JM, et al: Behav Ther 15:21–40, 1984

Herzog DB, Copeland PM: Eating disorders. N Engl J Med 295–303, 1985

Heshe J, Roeder E: Electroconvulsive therapy in Denmark. Br J Psychiatry 128:241–245, 1976

Himmelhoch JM, Neil JF: Lithium therapy in combination with other forms of treatment, in Handbook of Lithium Therapy. Edited by Johnson FN. Lancaster, England, MTP Press, 1980

Himmelhoch JM, Mulla D, Neil JF, et al: Incidence and significance of mixed affective states in a bipolar population. Arch Gen Psychiatry 33:1062–1066, 1976

Himmelhoch JM, Forrest J, Neil JF, et al: Thiazide-lithium synergy in refractory mood swings. Am J Psychiatry 134:149–152, 1977

Himmelhoch JM, Neil JF, May SJ, et al: Age, dementia, dyskinesias, and lithium response. Am J Psychiatry 137:941–945, 1980

Hirschfeld RMA, Shea T: Affective disorders: psychosocial treatment, in Comprehensive Textbook of Psychiatry, 4th sec, vol. 1, chap 18.6. Edited by Kaplan HI, Sadak BJ. Baltimore, Md, Williams and Wilkins, 1985

Ho AD, Tsai CS: Effects of lithium on alcohol preference and withdrawal. Ann NY Acad Sci 273:371–374, 1976

Hoberman H, Lewinsohn PM, Tilson M: Predictors of Treatment Response in the Coping with Depression Course (manuscript in preparation). Eugene, Ore, University of Oregon

Holland JC, Tross S: The psychosocial and neuropsychiatric sequelae of the acquired immunodeficiency syndrome and related disorders. Ann Intern Med 103:760–764, 1985

Hollon SD: Comparisons and combinations with alternative approaches, in Behavior Therapy for Depression: Present Status and Future Directions. Edited by Rehm LP. New York, Academic Press, 1981

Hollon SD, Beck AT: Cognitive therapy for depression, in Cognitive-Behavioral Interventions: Theory, Research, and Procedures. Edited by Kendall PC, Hollon SD. New York, Academic Press, 1979

Hollon SD, Evans M, Waskow IE, et al: Presented at the Annual Meeting of the American Psychiatric Association, Los Angeles, 1984

Holmes TH, Goodell H, Wolf S: The Nose: An Experimental Study of Reactions Within the Nose in Human Subjects During Varying Life Experiences. Springfield, Ill, Charles Thomas Publishers, 1950

Hood DD, Mecca RS: Failure to initiate electroconvulsive seizures in a patient pretreated with lidocaine. Anesthesiology 58:379–381, 1983

Horne RL, Pettinati HM, Sugarman AA: Comparing bilateral to unilateral electroconvulsive therapy in a randomized trial with EEG monitoring. Arch Gen Psychiatry 42:1087–1092, 1985

Horowitz MJ: Stress response syndromes: character style and dynamic psychotherapy. Arch Gen Psychiatry 31:768–781, 1976

Horowitz MJ: Brief psychotherapy of bereavement reactions: the relationship of process to outcome. Arch Gen Psychiatry 41:438–448, 1984

Hudson JI, Laffer PS, Pope HG: Bulimia related to affective disorder by family history and response to the dexamethasone suppression test. Am J Psychiatry 139:685–687,1982

Hudson JI, Pope HG, Jonas JM, et al: Hypothalamic-pituitary-adrenal axis hyperactivity in bulemia. Psychiatry Res 8:111–117, 1983a

Hudson JI, Pope HG, Jonas JM: Treatment of bulimia with antidepressants: theoretical considerations and clinical findings. Psychiatric Annals 13:965–969, 1983b

Hughes PL, Wells LA, Cunningham CJ, et al: Treating bulimia with desipramine: a double-blind, placebo-controlled study. Arch Gen Psychiatry 43:182–186, 1986

Hullett FJ, Bidder TG: Phenelzine plus triiodothyronine combination in a case of refractory depression. J Nerv Ment Dis 171:318–321, 1983

Humphris FH: Artificial Sunlight and its Therapeutic Uses. London, Humphrey Milford Oxford Press, 1924

Ilfeld FW: Current social stressors and symptoms of depression. Am J Psychiatry 134:161–166, 1977

Imlah NW, Ryan E, Harrington JA: The influence of antidepressant drugs in the response to electroconvulsive therapy and subsequent relapse states. Journal of Neuropsychopharmacology 4:439–442, 1965

Insel TR, Roy BF, Cohen RM, et al: Possible development of the serotonin syndrome in man. Am J Psychiatry 139:954–955, 1982

Irwin M, Spar JE: Reversible cardiac conduction abnormality associated with trazodone administration. Am J Psychiatry 140:945–946, 1983

Isaacs G, Stainer DS, Sensky TE, et al: Phototherapy and its mechanisms of action in seasonal affective disorder. J Affective Disord 14:13–19, 1988

Itil TM, Soldatos C: Epileptogenic side effects of psychotropic drugs: practical recommendations. JAMA 244:1460–1463, 1980

Jabbari B, Bryan GE, Marsh EE, et al. Incidence of seizures with tricyclic and tetracyclic antidepressants. Arch Neurol 42:480–481, 1985

Jacobsen FM, Wehr TA, Skewerer RA, et al: Morning versus midday phototherapy of seasonal affective disorder. Am J Psychiatry, in press

Jacobson E: Progressive Relaxation. Chicago, University of Chicago Press, 1929.

Jacobson E: Depression. New York, International Universities Press, 1971

Jacobson E: The psychoanalytic treatment of depressed patients, in Depression and Human Existence. Edited by Anthony EJ, Benedek T. Boston, Little Brown and Company, 1975

Jacobson N: Presentation at the 140th Annual American Psychiatric Association Meeting, Chicago, Ill, May 1987

James SP, Wehr TA, Sack DA, et al: Treatment of seasonal affective disorder with light in the evening. Br J Psychiatry 147:424–428, 1985

James W: Varieties of Religious Experience (1902). New York, Mentor Edition, 1958

Jamison KR, Akiskal HS: Medication compliance in patients with bipolar disorder. Psychiatr Clin North Am 6:175–192, 1983

Jamison KR, Gerner RH, Hammen C, et al: Clouds and silver linings: positive experiences associated with primary affective disorders. Am J Psychiatry 137:198–202, 1980

Jampola VC: Anorexia nervosa: a variant form of affective disorder? Psychiatric Annals 15:698–704, 1985

Janicak PG, Boshes GA: Advances in the treatment of mania and other acute psychotic disorders. Psychiatric Annals 17:145–149, 1987

Janowsky D, Curtis G, Zisook S, et al: Ventricular arrhythmias possibly aggravated by trazodone. Am J Psychiatry 140:796–797, 1983

Jarrett RB, Nelson RO: Mechanisms of change in cognitive-behavioral therapy of depression. Behav Res Ther 18:227–241, 1987

Jarrett RB, Rush AJ: Psychotherapeutic approaches to depression, in Psychiatry, vol. 1, chap 65. Edited by Cavenar JO. Philadelphia, JB Lippincott Company, and New York, Basic Books, 1986

Jarvik LF, Mintz J, Steuer J: Treating geriatric depression: a 26-week interim analysis. J Am Geriatr Soc 30:713–717, 1982

Jefferson JW: Central nervous system toxicity of cimetidine: a case of depression. Am J Psychiatry 136:346, 1979

Jefferson JW: An early study of seasonal depression. Am J Psychiatry 143:261–262, 1986

Jefferson JW, Greist JH, Ackerman DL, et al: Lithium Encyclopedia for Clinical Practice. Washington, DC, American Psychiatric Association, 1983

Jenike MA: The use of monoamine oxidase inhibitors in the treatment of elderly, depressed patients. J Am Geriatr Soc 32:571–575, 1984

Jenike MA: Monoamine oxidase inhibitors as treatment for depressed patients with primary degenerative dementia (Alzheimer's disease). Am J Psychiatry 142:763–764, 1985

Johnson DAW: Studies of depressive symptoms in schizophrenia. Br J Psychology 139:89–101, 1981

Johnson P, Kitchin AH, Lowther CP, et al: Treatment of hypertension with methyldopa. Br Med J 1:133–137, 1966

Johnston A: Personal communication, Burroughs Wellcome. January, 1989

Jones RM: ECT for patients with hypertensive heart disease. Am J Psychiatry 140:139, 1983

Jones RM, Knight PR: Cardiovascular and hormonal responses to electroconvulsive therapy. Anesthesiology 36:795–799, 1981

Joseph-Vanderpool JR, Souetre E, Kelly KA, et al: Delayed sleep phase syndrome: preliminary effects of phototherapy. Presented at the 141st Annual Meeting of the American Psychiatric Association. Montreal, 1988

Josephson AM, Mackensie TB: Thyroid-induced mania in hypothyroid patients. Br J Psychiatry 137:222–228, 1980

Judd FK, Burrows GD, Norman TR: Psychosis after withdrawal of steroid therapy. Med J Aust 2:350, 1983

Kanba S, Richelson E: Antidepressants are weak competitive antagonists of histamine H_2 receptors in dissociated tissue from the guinea pig hippocampus. Eur J Pharmacol 94:313–318, 1983

Kane FJ Jr, Keeler MH: Mania seen with undiagnosed Cushing's syndrome. Am J Psychiatry 119:267, 1962

Kane FJ Jr, Pokorny A: Mental and emotional disturbance with pentazocine (Talwin) use. South Med J 68:808–811, 1975

Kane JM, Quitkin FM, Rifkin A, et al: Lithium carbonate and imipramine in the prophylaxis of unipolar and bipolar II illness: a prospective, placebo-controlled comparison. Arch Gen Psychiatry 39:1065–1069, 1982

Karasu TB: Am J Psychiatry 137:1502–1512, 1980

Karasu TB: Psychotherapy and pharmacotherapy: toward an integrative model. Am J Psychiatry 139:1102–1113, 1982

Kashani J, Simmonds J: Incidence of depression in children. Am J Psychiatry 136:1203–1205, 1979

Kaskey GB, Nasr S, Meltzer HY: Drug treatment of delusional depression. Psychiatry Res 2:267–277, 1980

Kasper S, Rogers S, Yancey A, et al: Seasonal Affective Disorders and Phototherapy. Edited by Rosenthal NE, Blehar M. New York, Guilford Press (in press)

Kathol RG, Petty F: Relationship of depression to medical illness. J Affective Disord 3:111–121, 1981

Katona CLE: Puerperal mental illness: comparisons with non-puerperal controls. Br J Psychiatry 141:447–452, 1982

Katz JL, Kuperberg A, Pollack CP, et al: Is there a relationship between eating disorders and affective disorders? New evidence from sleep recordings. Am J Psychiatry 141:753–759, 1984

Kaufman MW, Cassem NH, Murray GB, et al: Use of psychostimulants in medically ill patients with neurological disease and major depression. Can J Psychiatry 29–49, 1984

Kay D, Fahy T, Garside R: A seven month double blind trial of amitriptyline and diazepam in ECT treated depressive patients. Br J Psychiatry 116:667–671, 1970

Kazdin AE: Effects of covert modeling and model reinforcement on assertive behavior. J Abnorm Psychol 83:240–252, 1974

Kazdin AE: Effects of covert modeling, multiple models, and model reinforcement on assertive behavior. Behavior Therapy 7:211–222, 1976

Kazdin AE: History of behavior modification, in International Handbook of Behavior

Modification and Therapy. Edited by Bellack AS, Hersen M, Kazdin AE. New York, Plenum Press, 1982

Keefe JF, France RD, Urban BJ: Relationships between pain behavior and depression. Abstract 91E, American Psychiatric Association, 1984

Keller MB, Shapiro RW: "Double depression": superimposition of acute depressive episodes on chronic depressive disorders. Am J Psychiatry 139:438–442, 1982

Keller MB, Klerman GL, et al: Treatment received by depressed patients. JAMA 248:1848–1855, 1982

Keller MB, Lavori PW, Endicott J, et al: "Double-depression": two-year follow up. Am J Psychiatry 140:689–694, 1983

Keller MB, Lavori PW, Klerman GL, et al: Low levels and lack of predictors of somatotherapy and psychotherapy received by depressed patients. Arch Gen Psychiatry 43:458–466, 1986

Kelly D: Leucotomy, in Handbook of Affective Disorders. Edited by Paykel ES. New York, Guilford Press, 1982, pp 286–293

Kelly WF, Checkley SA, Bender DA, et al: Cushing's syndrome and depression: a prospective study of 26 patients. Br J Psychiatry 142:16–19, 1983

Khantzian EJ, Treece C: DSM III psychiatric diagnosis of narcotic addicts. Arch Gen Psychiatry 42:1067–1071, 1985

Khuri R, Akiskal HS: Suicide prevention: the necessity of treating contributory psychiatric disorders. Psychiatr Clin North Am 6:193–207, 1983

Kielholz P, Poldinger W, Adams C: Masked Depression. Koln-Lovenich, West Germany, Deutscher Arzte-Verlag, 1982

Kierkegaard S: The Sickness Unto Death (1899). New York, H Doubleday, 1954

Kim WY: Seizures associated with maprotiline (letter). Am J Psychiatry 139:845–846, 1982

King D: Pathological and therapeutic consequences of sleep loss: a review. Dis Nerv Syst 38:873–879, 1977

Kissin B, Gross MM: Drug therapy in alcoholism. Am J Psychiatry 125:31–41, 1968

Kissin B, Charnoff SM, Rosenblatt SM: Drug and placebo responses in chronic alcoholics. Psychiatry Res 24:44–60, 1968

Klaiber EL, Broverman DM, Vogel W, et al: Estrogen therapy for severe persistent depressions in women. Arch Gen Psychiatry 36:550–554, 1979

Kleber H: New approaches to the treatment of cocaine abuse. Presented at the Joint Meeting of the Research Society for Alcoholism and the Committee on Drug Dependence, Philadelphia, 1987

Kleber HD, Weissman MM, Rounsaville BJ: Imipramine as treatment for depression in addicts. Arch Gen Psychiatry 40:647–653, 1983

Klein D, Davis JM: Diagnosis and Drug Treatment of Psychiatric Disorders. Baltimore, Williams and Wilkins, 1969

Klein D: Endogenomorphic depression: a conceptual and terminologic revision. Arch Gen Psychiatry 31:324–331, 1980

Klein D, Gittleman R, Quitkin F, et al: Diagnosis and Drug Treatment of Psychiatric Disorders. Baltimore, Williams and Wilkins, 1980

Klerman GL: Other specific affective disorders, in Comprehensive Textbook of Psychiatry III. Edited by Kaplan HI, Freedman AM, Sadock BJ. Baltimore, Williams and Wilkins, 1980, p 1335

Klerman GL: The spectrum of mania. Compr Psychiatry 22:11–20, 1981

Klerman GL: The efficacy of psychotherapy as the basis for public policy. Am Psychol 38:929–934, 1983a

Klerman GL: The scope of depression, in The Origins of Depression: Current Concepts and Approaches. Edited by Angst J. Berlin, Springer-Verlag, 1983b

Klerman GL: Handbook of Psychotherapy and Behavior Change, 3rd ed. Edited by Garfield S, Bergin AS. New York, John Wiley and Sons, 1986

Klerman GL: Depression associated with medical and neurological diseases, drugs, and alcohol, in Measurement of Depression. Edited by Marsella, Hirschfeld, Katz. New York, Guilford Press (in press)

Klerman GL, Cole JO: Clinical pharmacology of imipramine and related antidepressant compounds. Pharmacol Rev 17:101–141, 1966

Klerman GL, London P: Evaluating psychotherapy. Am J Psychiatry 139:709–717, 1982

Klerman G, Schecter G: Drugs and psychotherapy, in Handbook of Affective Disorders. Edited by Paykel ES. New York, Guilford Press, 1982

Klerman GL, Weissman MM: The interpersonal approach to understanding depression, in Contemporary Directions in Psychopathology: Toward the DSM-IV. Edited by Millon T, Klerman GL. New York, Guilford Press, 1986

Klerman GL, DiMascio A, Weissman MM, et al. Treatment of depression by drugs and psychotherapy. Am J Psychiatry 131:186–191, 1974

Klerman GL, Endicott J, Spitzer R, et al: Neurotic depressions: a systematic analysis of multiple criteria and meanings. Am J Psychiatry 136:57–61, 1979

Klerman GL, Weissman MM, Rounsaville BR, et al: Interpersonal Psychotherapy of Depression. New York, Basic Books, 1984

Kline NS, Wren JC, Cooper TB, et al: Evaluation of lithium therapy in chronic and periodic alcoholism. Am J Med Sci 268:15–20, 1974

Kline NS, Pare M, Hallstrom C, et al: Amitriptyline protects patients on MAOIs from tyramine reactions. J Clin Psychopharmacol 2:434–435, 1982

Kobayashi A, Sugita S, Nakazawa K: Determination of amoxapine and its metabolites in human serum by high-performance liquid chromatography. Neuropharmacology 24:1253–1256, 1985

Kocsis JH: Lithium in the acute treatment of mania, in Handbook of Lithium Therapy. Edited by Johnson FN. Lancaster, England, MTP Press, 1980

Kocsis JH, Frances AJ, Mann JJ, et al: Imipramine for the treatment of chronic depression. Psychopoharmacol Bull 21:698–700, 1985

Kocsis JH, Voss C, Mann JJ, et al: Chronic depression: demographic and clinical characteristics. Psychopharmacol Bull 22:192–195, 1986

Kogeorgos J, De Alwis C: Priapism and psychotropic medications. Br J Psychiatry 149:241–243, 1986

Kolata G: Depression, anorexia, Cushing's link revealed. Science 232:1197–1198, 1986

Kolb LC: Psychotherapeutic evolution and its implications. Psychiatric Q 30:1–19, 1956

Kosten TR, Gawin F, Schumann B, et al: A pilot study using desipramine for cocaine abusing methadone maintenance patients. Presented at the Joint Meeting of the Research Society for Alcoholism and the Committee on Drug Dependence, Philadelphia, 1987a

Kosten TR, Rounsaville BJ, Kleber HD: A 2½ year follow-up of cocaine use among treated opioid addicts. Arch Gen Psychiatry 44:281–284, 1987b

Kotin J, Goodwin FK: Depression during mania: clinical observations and theoretical implications. Am J Psychiatry 129:679–686, 1972

Kovacs M: The efficacy of cognitive and behavior therapies for depression. Am J Psychiatry 137:1495–1501, 1980

Kovacs M, Rush AJ, Beck AT, et al: Depressed outpatients treated with cognitive therapy or pharmacotherapy: a one-year follow up. Arch Gen Psychiatry 38:33–39, 1981

Kovacs M, Feinberg TL, Crose-Novak M, et al: Depressive disorders in childhood,

II: a longitudinal study of the risk for subsequent major depression. Arch Gen Psychiatry 41:643–649, 1984

Kovacs R: Electrotherapy and the Elements of Light Therapy. Philadelphia, Lea and Febiger, 1932

Koval G, Van Nuis C, Davis TD: Seizures associated with amoxapine (letter). Am J Psychiatry 139:845, 1982

Kraepelin E: Manic-Depressive Insanity and Paranoia. Edinburgh, E and S Livingstone, 1921

Kramer BA, Allen RE, Friedman B: Atropine and glycopyrrolate as ECT preanesthesia. J Clin Psychiatry 47:199–200, 1986

Kramer JC, Klein DF, Fink M: Withdrawal symptoms following discontinuation of imipramine therapy. Am J Psychiatry 118:549–550, 1961

Kranzler G: You Can Change How You Feel. Eugene, Ore, 1974

Krauthammer L, Klerman GL: Secondary mania: manic syndromes associated with antecedent physical illness or drugs. Arch Gen Psychiatry 5:1333–1339, 1978

Kreitman N, Collins J, Nelson B, et al: Neurosis and marital interaction, I: personality and symptoms. Br J Psychiatry 117:33–46, 1970

Kripke DF: Therapeutic effects of bright light in depression, in The Medical and Biological Effects of Light. Edited by Wurtman RJ, Baum MJ, Potts JT. Ann NY Acad Sci, 453:270–281, 1985

Kripke DF: Chronobiologic models for light treatment of depression. Presented at First Meeting Society for Research on Biological Rhythms, Charleston, SC, May 1988

Kripke DF, Mullaney DJ, Gillin JC, et al: Phototherapy of non-seasonal depression, in Biological Psychiatry. Edited by Shagass C, et al. Elsevier, 1985

Krishnan R, France KR, Ellinwood EH Jr: Tricyclic-induced akathisia in patients taking conjugated estrogens. Am J Psychiatry 141:696–697, 1984

Kroessler D: Relative efficacy rates for therapies of delusional depression. Convulsive Therapy 1:173–182, 1985

Kukopulos A, Reginaldi D: Recurrence of manic-depressive episodes during lithium treatment, in Handbook of Lithium Therapy. Edited by Johnson FN. Lancaster, England, MTP Press, 1980

Kukopulos A, Reginaldi D, Laddomada P, et al: Course of the manic-depressive cycle and changes caused by treatments. Pharmakopsychiatr-Neuropsychopharmakol 13:156–167, 1980

Kukopulos A, Caliari B, Tundo A, et al: Rapid cyclers, temperament, and antidepressants. Compr Psychiatry 24:249–258, 1983

Kupfer DJ: Long-term treatment by NIMH consensus conference, 1985

Kupfer DJ, Pickard D, Himmelhoch JM, et al: Are there two types of unipolar depression? Arch Gen Psychiatry 32:866–871, 1975

Kupfer DJ, Broudy D, Spiker DG, et al: EEG sleep and affective psychoses, I: schizoaffective disorders. Psychiatry Res 1:173–178, 1979

Lakein A: How to Get Control of Your Time and Your Life. New York, New American Library, 1974

Lambert MJ, Bergin EA, Collins JL: Therapist-induced deterioration in psychotherapy, in Effective Psychotherapy. Edited by Gurman AS, Razin AM. New York, Pergamon Press, 1977

Lambourn J, Gill D: A controlled comparison of simulated and real ECT. Br J Psychiatry 133:514–519, 1978

Lapierre YD, Anderson K: Dyskinesia associated with amoxapine antidepressant therapy: a case report. Am J Psychiatry 140:493–494, 1983

Lee JT, Erbguth PH, Stevens WC, et al: Modification of electroconvulsive therapy induced hypertension with nitroglycerine ointment. Anesthesiology 62:793–796, 1985

Lees AW: Ethionamide 1,000 mg and isoniazid 400 mg in previously untreated cases of pulmonary tuberculosis. Br J Dis Chest 59:228, 1965

Leff ML, Roatch JF, Bunney WE: Environmental factors preceding the onset of severe depression, Psychiatry 33:293–311, 1970

Lehmann H: The impact of the therapeutic revolution on nosology, in The Schizophrenic Syndrome, vol 1. Edited by Cancro R. New York, Brunner/Mazel, 1970

Lenox RH, Modell JG, Weiner S: Acute treatment of manic agitation with lorazepam. Psychosomatics 27:28–32, 1986

Lerer B: Alternative therapies for bipolar disorder. J Clin Psychiatry 46:309–316, 1985

Lerer B, Moore N, Meyendorff E, et al: Carbamazepine versus lithium in mania: a double-blind study. J Clin Psychiatry 48:89–93, 1987

Levenson JL: Neuroleptic malignant syndrome. Am J Psychiatry 142:1137–1145, 1985

Levine PM, Silberfarb PM, Lipowski ZJ: Mental disorders in cancer patients. Cancer 42:1385–1391, 1978

Lewinsohn PM: The behavioral study and treatment of depression, in Progress in Behavior Modification, vol. 1. Edited by Hersen M, Eisler RM, Miller PM. New York, Academic Press, 1975a

Lewinsohn PM: Engagement in pleasant activities and depression level. J Abnorm Psychol 84:729–731, 1975b

Lewinsohn PM: Activity schedules in the treatment of depression, in Counseling Methods. Edited by Thoreson CE, Kromholtz JD. New York, Holt, Rinehart, and Winston, 1976

Lewinsohn PM: The unpleasant events schedule. Eugene, Oregon, University of Oregon (unpublished manuscript)

Lewinsohn PM, Hoberman HM: Behavioral and cognitive approaches to treatment, in Handbook of Affective Disorders. Edited by Paykel ES. Edinburgh, Churchill-Livingston, 1982a

Lewinsohn PM, Hoberman HM: Depression, in International Handbook of Behavior Modification and Therapy. Edited by Bellack AS, Hersen M, Kazdin AE. New York, Plenum Press, 1982b, pp 397–429

Lewinsohn PM, Shaw D: Feedback about interpersonal behavior as an agent of behavioral change: a case study in the treatment of depression. Psychother Psychosom 17:82–88, 1969

Lewinsohn PM, Weinstein M, Alper T: A behavioral approach to the group treatment of depressed persons: a methodological contribution. J Clin Psychol 26:525–532, 1970

Lewinsohn PM, Biglan T, Zeiss A: Behavioral treatment of depression, in Behavioral Management of Anxiety, Depression, and Pain. Edited by Davidson P. New York, Brunner/Mazel, 1976, pp 91–146

Lewinsohn PM, Munoz RF, Youngren MA, et al: Control Your Depression. Englewood Cliffs, NJ, Prentice-Hall, 1978

Lewinsohn PM, Youngren MA, Grosscup SJ: Reinforcement and depression, in The Psychobiology of Depressive Disorders: Implications for the Effects of Stress. Edited by Dupue RA. New York, Academic Press, 1979

Lewinsohn PM, Sullivan JM, Grosscup SJ: Changing reinforcing events: an approach to the treatment of depression. Psychotherapy: Theory, Research, and Practice 47:322–334, 1980a

Lewinsohn PM, Mischel W, Chaplin W, et al: Social competence, and depression: the role of illusory self-perceptions. J Abnorm Psychol 89:203–212, 1980b

Lewinsohn PM, Sullivan JM, Grosscup SJ: Behavior therapy: clinical applications, in

Short-term Psychotherapies for the Depressed Patient. Edited by Rush AJ. New York, Guilford Press, 1982

Lewinsohn PM, Antonuccio DO, Steinmetz JL, et al: The Coping with Depression Course: A Psychoeducational Intervention for Unipolar Depression. Eugene, Ore, Castalia Publishing, 1984

Lewinsohn PM, Hoberman HM, Teri L, et al: An integrative theory of depression, in Theoretical Issues in Behavior Therapy. Edited by Reiss S, Bootzin R. New York, Academic Press, 1985

Lewinsohn PM, Hoberman HM, Rosenbaum M: Risk factors for unipolar depression. J Abnorm Psychol (in press)

Lewis JL, Winokur G: The induction of mania: a natural history study with controls. Arch Gen Psychiatry 39:303–306, 1982

Lewy AJ, Wehr TA, Goodwin FK, et al: Light suppresses melatonin secretion in humans. Science 210:1267–1269, 1980

Lewy AJ, Kern HA, Rosenthal NE, et al: Bright artificial light treatment of a manic-depressive patient with a seasonal mood cycle. Am J Psychiatry 139:1496–1498, 1982

Lewy AJ, Sack RL, Fredrickson RH, et al: Neuropsychobiology of circadian and seasonal rhythms: light as a "drug"? Psychopharmacol Bull 19:523–525, 1983

Lewy AJ, Sack RL, Singer CL: Assessment and treatment of chronobiologic disorders using plasma melatonin levels and bright light exposure: the clock-gate model and the phase response curve. Psychopharmacol Bull 20:561–565, 1984

Lewy AJ, Sack RL, Miller S, et al: Antidepressant and circadian phase-shifting effects of light. Science 235:352–354, 1987a

Lewy AJ, Sack RL, Singer CM, et al: The phase shift hypothesis for bright light's therapeutic mechanism of action: theoretical considerations and experimental evidence. Psychopharmacol Bull 23:349–353, 1987b

Lewy AJ, Sack RL, Singer CM, et al: Winter depression and the phase shift hypothesis for bright lights therapeutic effects: history, theory and experimental evidence. J Biol Rhythms (in press)

Lieberman M: Survey and Evaluation of the Literature on Verbal Psychotherapy of Depressive Disorders (report). Clinical Research Branch, National Institute of Mental Health, Bethesda, Md, 1975

Liebowitz MR, Quitkin FM, Stewart JW, et al: Phenelzine versus imipramine in a typical depression. Arch Gen Psychiatry 41:669–677, 1984

Lingjaerde, Bradlid T, Hansen T, et al: Seasonal affective disorder and midwinter insomnia in the far north: studies on two related chronobiological disorders in Norway, in Clinical Neuropharmacology, vol 9, suppl 4. New York, Raven Press, 1986, pp 187–189

Lipsey JR, et al: Mood change following bilateral hemisphere brain injury. Br J Psychiatry 143:266, 1983

Liu WS, Petty WC, Jeppsen A, et al: Attenuation of hemodynamic and hormonal responses to ECT with propranolol, xylocaine, sodium nitroprusside, or clonidine. Anesth Analg 63:244, 1984

London P, Klerman GL: Evaluating Psychotherapy. Am J Psychiatry 139:709–717, 1982

Lovett-Doust JW, Barchha A, Lee RYS, et al: Acute effects of ECT on the cerebral circulation in man. Eur Neurol 12:47–62, 1974

Luborsky L: Helping alliances in psychotherapy, in Successful Psychotherapy. Edited by Claghorn JL. New York, Brunner/Mazel, 1976a, pp 92–111

Luborsky L: A General Manual for Supportive-Expressive Psychoanalytically Oriented Psychotherapy (unpublished manual). Hospital of the University of Pennsylvania, Philadelphia, Pa, 1976b

Luborsky L: Individual Treatment Manual for Supportive-Expressive Psychoanalytically Oriented Psychotherapy: Special Adaptation for Treatment of Drug Abuse. Hospital of the University of Pennsylvania, Philadelphia, 1977a

Luborsky L: Measuring a pervasive psychic structure: the core conflictual relationship theme, in Communicative Structures and Psychic Structures. Edited by Freedman N, Grand S. New York, Plenum Press, 1977b, pp 367–395

Luborsky L: Principles of Psychoanalytic Psychotherapy: A Manual for Supportive-Expressive Treatment. New York, Basic Books, 1984

Luborsky L, Singer B, Luborsky L: Comparative studies of psychotherapies. Is it true that everyone has one and all must have prizes? Arch Gen Psychiatry 32:995–1008, 1975

Luborsky L, Woody G, McLeelan AT, et al: Can independent judges recognize different psychotherapies? An experience with manual-guided therapies. J Consult Clin Psychol, 50:49–62, 1982

Luborsky L, Crits-Christoph P, Alexander L, et al: Two helping alliance methods for predicting outcomes of psychotherapy: a counting signs versus a global rating method. J Nerv Ment Dis 171:480–491, 1983

Luborsky L, et al: Principles of Psychoanalytic Psychotherapy: A Manual for Supportive-Expressive Treatment. New York, Basic Books, 1984

Luborsky L, McLellan AT, Woody GE, et al: Therapist success and its determinants. Arch Gen Psychiatry 42:602–611, 1985

Lydiard RB: Tricyclic-resistant depression: treatment resistance or inadequate treatment? J Clin Psychiatry 46:412–417, 1985

Lykouras E, Malliaras D, Christodoulou GN, et al: Delusional depression: phenomenology and response to treatment. A prospective study. Acta Psychiatr Scand 73:324–329, 1986

Maas JW: Biogenic amines and depression. Arch Gen Psychiatry 32:1357–1361, 1975

Maclay WS: Death in treatment. Proc R Soc Lon 46:13–20, 1953

MacPhillamy DJ, Lewinsohn PM: The pleasant events schedule (unpublished technical paper). Eugene, Ore, University of Oregon, 1971

MacPhillamy DJ, Lewinsohn PM: The pleasant events schedule: studies on reliability, validity, and scale intercorrelations. J Consult Clin Psychol 50:363–380, 1982

Magers BD: Cognitive-behavioral short-term group therapy with depressed women, in Dissertation Abstracts International, 38:4468–B (University Microfilm no 78-01687) California School of Professional Psychology, 1978

Maguire GP, Julier DL, Hawton KE, et al: Psychiatric morbidity and referral on two general medical wards. Br Med J 1:268–270, 1974

Mahler M: Sadness and grief in childhood. Psychoanal Study Child 16:332–351, 1961

Malan DH: The Frontier of Brief Psychotherapy. New York, Plenum Press, 1976

Malimquist C: Depression in childhood and adolescence. N Engl J Med 284:887–893, 955–961, 1971

Malitz S, Sackeim HA, Decina P, et al: The efficacy of electroconvulsive therapy: dose-response interactions with modality. Ann NY Acad Sci 462:56–64, 1986

Mallinger AG, Edwards DJ, Himmelhoch JM, et al: Pharmacokinetics of tranylcypromine in patients who are depressed: relationship to cardiovascular effects. Clin Pharmacol Ther 40:440–450, 1986

Maltbie AA, Wingfield RS, Volow MR, et al: Electroconvulsive therapy in the presence of a brain tumor. J Nerv Ment Dis 168:400–405, 1980

Mandel M: Recurrent psychotic depression associated with hypercalcemia and parathyroid adenoma. Am J Psychiatry 117:234, 1960

Mann J: Time-Limited Psychotherapy. Cambridge, Mass, Harvard University Press, 1973

Mann J, Goldman R: A Casebook in Time-Limited Psychotherapy. New York, McGraw Hill, 1982

Mann SC, Caroff SN, Bleier HR, et al: Lethal catatonia. Am J Psychiatry 143:1374–1381, 1986

Martin MJ: A brief review of organic diseases masquerading as functional illness. Hosp Community Psychiatry 34:328–332, 1983

Martin RL, Cloninger CR, Clayton PJ: Mortality in a follow-up of 500 psychiatric outpatients. Arch Gen Psychiatry 42:58–66, 1985

Massie MJ, Holland JC: Psychiatry and oncology, in Psychiatry Update, vol 3. Edited by Grinspoon L. Washington, DC, American Psychiatric Association, 1984

Mattes JA: Methylphenidate in mild depression: a double-blind controlled trial. J Clin Psychiatry 46:525–527, 1985

Matussek P, Feil WB: Personality attributes of depressive patients: results of group comparisons. Arch Gen Psychiatry 40:783–790, 1983

McAllister TW: Overview: pseudodementia. Am J Psychiatry 140:528–533, 1983

McConnville B, Boag L, Purohit A: Three types of childhood depression. Can J Psychiatry 18:133–138, 1973

McDonald AC: A cognitive/behavioral treatment for depression with veterans administration outpatients (doctoral dissertation), in Dissertation Abstracts International, 39:2944-B (University Microfilm no. 78-22829) Salt Lake City, University of Utah, 1978

McGrath PJ, Stewart JW, Harrison W, et al: Treatment of tricyclic refractory depression with a monoamine oxidase inhibitor antidepressant. Psychopharmacol Bull 23:169–172, 1987

McKenna G, Engle RP, Brooks H, et al: Cardiac arrhythmias during electroshock therapy: significance, prevention and treatment. Am J Psychiatry 127:530–533, 1970

McKnew DH, Cytryn L: Urinary metabolites in chronically depressed children. J Am Acad Child Adolesc Psychiatry 18:608–615, 1979

McKnight DL, Nelson RO, Hayes SC, et al: Importance of treating individually assessed response classes in the amelioration of depression (unpublished manuscript). Greensboro, NC, University of North Carolina

McLean P: Therapeutic decision-making in the behavioral treatment of depression, in Behavioral Management of Anxiety, Depression, and Pain. Edited by Davidson P. New York, Brunner/Mazel, 1976, pp 54–89

McLean P: Remediation of skills and performance deficits in depression: clinical steps and research findings, in Depression: Behavioral and Directive Strategies. Edited by Clarkin J, Glazer H. New York, Garland Publishing, 1981, pp 172–204

McLean PD, Hakstian AR: Clinical depression: comparative efficacy of outpatient treatments. J Clin Consult Psychol 47:818–836, 1979

McLean PD, Ogston K, Grauer L: A behavioral approach to the treatment of depression. J Behav Ther Exp Psychiatry 4:323–330, 1973

McLellan AT, Woody GE, O'Brien CP: Development of psychiatric illness in drug abuse: possible role of drug preference. N Engl J Med 301:1310–1314, 1979

Medical Research Council Clinical Psychiatry Committee: Clinical trial of the treatment of depressive illness. Br Med J 1:881–886, 1965

Meichenbaum D: Cognitive Behavior Modification. New York, Plenum Press, 1977

Meichenbaum D, Turk D: The Cognitive-Behavioral Management of Anxiety, Depression and Pain. New York, Brunner/Mazel, 1976

Mendels J: Lithium in the treatment of depression. Am J Psychiatry 133:373–378, 1976

Mendlewicz J, Rainer JD: Adoption study supporting genetic transmission in manic-depressive illness. Nature 268:327–329, 1977

Merry J, Reynolds CM, Bailey J, et al: Prophylactic treatment of alcoholism by lithium carbonate. Lancet 481–482, 1976

Meyer A: Psychobiology: A Science of Man. Springfield, Ill, Charles C Thomas Publishers, 1957

Miller ME, Gabriel A, Herman G, et al: Atropine sulphate premedication and cardiac arrhythmia in electroconvulsive therapy. Convulsive Therapy 3:10–19, 1987

Miller P, Ingham JG: Friends, confidants, and symptoms. Soc Psychiatry 11:51–58, 1976

Milstein V, Small JG, Klapper MH, et al: Uni- versus bilateral ECT in the treatment of mania. Convulsive Therapy 3:1–9, 1987

Mitchell JR, Avias L, Oates JA: Antagonism of the antihypertensive action of guanethidine sulfate by desipramine hydrochloride. JAMA 202:149–152, 1967

Moffic HS, Paykel ES: Depression in medical inpatients. Br J Psychiatry 126:346–353, 1975

Monroe SM, Bellack AS, Hersen M, et al: Life events, symptom course, and treatment outcome in depressed women. J Consult Clin Psychol 51:604–615, 1983

Monroe SM, Thase ME, Hersen M, et al: Life events and the endogenous-nonendogenous distinction in the treatment and post-treatment course of depression. Compr Psychiatry 26:175–186, 1985

Moore DC: Amitriptyline therapy in anorexia nervosa. Am J Psychiatry 134:1303–1304, 1977

Moore MT: Electrocerebral shock therapy: a reconsideration of former contraindications. Arch Neurol 57:693–711, 1947

Morris JB, Beck AT: Arch Gen Psychiatry 30:667–674, 1974

Morris NE: A Group Self-instruction Method for the Treatment of Depressed Outpatients. Canadian Thesis Division, No 35272, National Library of Canada, 1975

Mueller PS, Davies RK: Seasonal affective disorders: seasonal energy syndrome? Arch Gen Psychiatry 43:188–189, 1986

Muller JC, Pryor WW, Gibbons JE, et al: Depression and anxiety occurring during rauwoltia therapy. JAMA 199:836–839, 1955

Muniz CE, Perillo LJ, Troiano AG, et al: Lithium: overview of practical considerations. J Fla Med Assoc 68:819–822, 1981

Munoz RF: A Cognitive Approach to the Assessment and Treatment of Depression. Doctoral dissertation. Eugene, Ore, University of Oregon, 1977

Munro: Some familial and social factors in depressive illness. Br J Psychiatry 12:429, 1966

Murphy DL, Brand E, Goldman T, et al: Platelet and plasma amine oxidase inhibition and urinary amine excretion changes during phenelzine treatment. J Nerv Ment Dis 164:129–134, 1977

Murphy GE, Simmons AD, Wetzel RD, et al: Cognitive therapy and pharmacotherapy, singly and together in the treatment of depression. Arch Gen Psychiatry 41:33–41, 1984

Murphy GE, Simons AD, Wetzel RD, et al: Arch Gen Psychiatry 41:33–41, 1984

Musisi SM, Garfinkel PE: The DST in bulimia, depression, and normal controls. Abstract 129, American Psychiatric Association, 1984

National Commission for the Protection of Human Subjects of Biomedical and Behavioral Research: Psychosurgery: Report and Recommendations. DHEW Publication no. (OS) 77-0001. March 14, 1977. Superintendent of Documents, U.S. Government Printing Office, Washington, D.C. 20402

National Commission for the Protection of Human Subjects of Biomedical and Behavioral Research: Psychosurgery: Appendix. DHEW Publication no (OS) 77-0002. Washington, DC, US Department of Health, Education, and Welfare, 1977

Neil JF, Himmelhoch JM, Mallinger AG, et al: Caffeinism complicating hypersomnic depressive episodes. Compr Psychiatry 19:377–385, 1978

Nelson JC, Charney DS: The symptoms of major depressive illness. Am J Psychiatry 138:112, 1981

Nelson JC, Mazure CM: Lithium augmentation in psychotic depression refractory to combined drug treatment. Am J Psychiatry 143:363–366, 1986

Nelson JC, Mazure C, Quinlan DM, et al: Drug-responsive symptoms in melancholia. Arch Gen Psychiatry 41:663–668, 1984

Nielsen AC, Williams TA: Depression in ambulatory medical patients: prevalence by self-report questionnaire and recognition by nonpsychiatric physicians. Arch Gen Psychiatry 37:999–1004, 1980

Nies A, Robinson DS, Friedman MJ, et al: Relationship between age and tricyclic antidepressant plasma levels. Am J Psychiatry 134:790–793, 1977

New York County Health Services Review Organization: Clinical Psychiatry Screening Criteria for Inpatient Units of General Hospitals, New York, 1976

Nolan BT: Acute suicidal depression associated with use of timolol. JAMA 247:1567, 1982

Novaco RW: Anger Control. Lexington, Mass, D.C. Heath, 1975

Offenkrantz W, Tobin A: Psychoanalytic psychotherapy. Arch Gen Psychiatry 30:593–606, 1974

Okuma T: Therapeutic and prophylactic effects of carbamazepine in bipolar disorder. Psychiatr Clin North Am 6:157–174, 1983

Orsulak PJ: Therapeutic monitoring of antidepressant drugs: current methods and applications. J Clin Psychiatry 47(10, suppl):39–50, 1986

Ottosson JO: Experimental studies on the mode of action of electroconvulsive therapy. Acta Psychiatr Scand (Suppl 145) 35:1–141, 1960

Ottosson JO: Seizure characteristics and therapeutic efficiency in electroconvulsive therapy: an analysis of the antidepressant efficiency of grand-mal and lidocaine-modified seizures. J Nerv Ment Dis 135:239–251, 1962

Overall JE, Brown D, Williams JD, et al: Drug treatment of anxiety and depression in detoxified alcoholic patients. Arch Gen Psychiatry 29:218–221, 1973

Pandey GH, Heinze W, Brown B, et al: Electroconvulsive shock treatment decreases beta adrenergic receptor sensitivity in rat brain. Nature 280:234–235, 1979

Parikh RM, Robinson RG, Lipsey JR, et al: Poststroke mood disorders: prognosis of one- and two-year outcome. Abstract No 40, American Psychiatric Association, 1987

Parloff MB: Psychotherapy and research: an anaclitic depression. The twenty-third Annual Frieda Fromm-Reichmann Memorial Lecture. Psychiatry 43:279–293, 1980

Parloff MB: Psychotherapy research evidence and reimbursement decisions: Bambi meets Godzilla. Am J Psychiatry 139:718–727, 1982

Parloff MB, Dies RR: The naracissism of small differences—and some big ones. Int J Group Psychother 27:281–319, 1975

Parloff MB, Waskow IE, Wolfe BE: Handbook of Psychotherapy and Behavior Change, 2nd ed. Edited by Garfield SL, Bergin AE. New York, John Wiley and Sons, 1978, p 233

Paul SM, Extein I, Calil HM, et al: Use of ECT with treatment-resistant depressed patients at the NIMH. Am J Psychiatry 138:486–489, 1981

Paykel ES, Van Woerkom AE: Pharmacologic treatment of resistant depression. Psychiatric Annals 17:May 5, 1987

Paykel ES, Myers JK, Dienelt MN, et al: Life events and depression: a controlled study. Arch Gen Psychiatry 21:753–760, 1969

Paykel ES, Klerman GL, Prusoff BA: Treatment setting and clinical depression. Arch Gen Psychiatry 22:11–21, 1970

Paykel ES, DiMascio A, Klerman GL, et al: Maintenance therapy of depression. Pharmakopsychiatrie Neuro-Psychopharmakologie 9:127–136, 1976

Paykel ES, Rowan PR, Parker RR, et al: Response to phenelzine and amitriptyline in subtypes of depressed outpatients. Arch Gen Psychiatry 39:1041–1049, 1982

Pearlin LI, Lieberman MA: Social sources of emotional distress, in Research in Community and Mental Health. Edited by Simmons R. Greenwich, Conn, JAI, 1979

Penn JR, Mackenzie TB: Organic mental disorder associated with metrizamide. Psychosomatics 24:849–853, 1983

Perkins KA, Simpson JC, Tsuang MT: Ten-year follow up of drug abusers with acute or chronic psychosis. Hosp Community Psychiatry 37:481–484, 1986

Perlas AP, Faillace LA: Psychiatric manifestations of carcinoma of the pancreas. Am J Psychiatry 121:182, 1964

Perris C: A study of bipolar (manic-depressive) and unipolar recurrent depressive psychoses. Acta Psychiatr Scand 31:7–18, 1966

Perry A, Tsuang M: Treatment of unipolar depression following electroconvulsive therapy. J Affective Disord 1:123–129, 1979

Perry SW, Markowitz J: Psychiatric interventions for AIDS-spectrum disorders. Hosp Community Psychiatry 37:1001–1006, 1986

Peselow ED, Dunner DL, Fieve RR, et al: Lithium prophylaxis of depression in unipolar, bipolar II, and cyclothymic patients. Am J Psychiatry 139:747–752, 1982

Peterfreund E, Schwartz JT: Information Systems and Psychoanalysis. New York, International Universities Press, 1971

Pettinati HM, Mathisen KS, Rosenberg J, et al: Meta-analytical approach to reconciling discrepancies in efficacy between bilateral and unilateral electroconvulsive therapy. Convulsive Therapy 2:7–17, 1986

Phillips I: Childhood depression. Am J Psychiatry 136:511–515, 1979

Phillips I, Friedlander S: Conceptual problems in the study of depression in childhood, in American Psychiatric Association Annual Review, vol 1. Edited by Grinspoon L. Washington, DC, American Psychiatric Association, 1982

Pilowsky I, Spence ND: Depression: inside and outside the hospital setting. Br J Psychiatry 132:265–268, 1978

Piran N, Kennedy S, Garfinkel PE, Owens M: Affective disturbance in eating disorders. J Nerv Ment Dis 173:395–400, 1985

Pittendrigh CS: Circadian systems: entrainment, in Handbook of Behavioral Neurobiology, vol 4, Biological Rhythms. Edited by Aschoff J. New York, Plenum Press, 1981, pp 95–124

Pitts FN, Desmarais GM, Stewart W, et al: Induction of anesthetic with methohexital and thiopental in electroconvulsive therapy. N Engl J Med 273:353–360, 1965

Placidi GF, Alessandro L, Lazzerini F, et al: The comparative efficacy and safety of carbamazepine versus lithium: a randomized, double-blind 3-year trial in 83 patients. J Clin Psychiatry 47:490–494, 1986

Plum F, Howse DC, Duffy TE: Metabolic effects of seizures. Assoc Res Nerv Mental Dis 53:141–157, 1974

Plumb MM, Holland J: Comparative studies of psychological functions in patients with advanced cancer, I: self-reported depressive symptoms. Psychosom Med 39:264–276, 1977

Pollack MH, Rosenbaum JF: Management of antidepressant-induced side effects: a practical guide for the clinician. J Clin Psychiatry 48:3–8, 1987

Pomeranze J, Karliner W, Triebel WA, et al: Electroshock therapy in the presence of serious organic disease. Geriatrics 122–124, 1968

Pond SM, Becker CE, Vandervoort R, et al: An evaluation of the effects of lithium in the treatment of chronic alcoholism. I. Clinical results. Alcoholism Clin Exp Res 5:247–251, 1981

Pope HG, Hudson JI: Treatment of bulimia with antidepressants. Psychopharmacology 78:176–179, 1982

Pope HG, Lipinski JF: Diagnosis in schizophrenia and manic depressive illness. Arch Gen Psychiatry 35:811–828, 1978

Pope HG, Hudson JI, Jonas JM: Antidepressant treatment of bulemia: preliminary experience and practical recommendations. J Clin Psychopharmacol 3:274–281, 1983a

Pope HG, Hudson JI, Jonas JM, et al: Bulimia treated with imipramine: a placebo-controlled, double blind study. Am J Psychiatry, 140:554–558, 1983b

Portnoy S: The cognitive side-effects of electroconvulsive therapy. Ann NY Acad Sci 462:353–356, 1986

Post RM, Ballenger JC: Carbamazepine (Tegretol) and affective illness. Curr Affect Illness 2:7–9, 1983

Post RM, Uhde TW: Carbamazepine in bipolar illness. Psychopharmacol Bull 21:10–17, 1985

Pottenger M, McKernan J, Patrie LE, et al: The frequency and persistence of depressive symptoms in the alcohol abuser. J Nerv Ment Dis 166:562–570, 1978

Poznanski EO: The clinical characteristics of childhood depression, in Psychiatry 1982: The American Psychiatric Association Annual Review. Edited by Grinspoon L. Washington, DC, American Psychiatric Association, 1982

Poznanski EO, Zrull P: Childhood depression. Arch Gen Psychiatry 239:8–15, 1970

Poznanski ED, Carroll BJ, et al: The dexamethasone suppression test in prepubertal depressed children. Am J Psychiatry 139:321–324, 1982

Prange AJ Jr: Estrogen may well affect response to antidepressant. JAMA 219:143–144, 1972

Prange AJ Jr, Wilson IC, Rabon AM, et al: Enhancement of imipramine antidepressant activity by thyroid hormone. Am J Psychiatry 126:39–51, 1969

Presthus J, Holmsen R: Appraisal of long-term levodopa treatment of parkinsonism with special reference to therapy limiting factors. Acta Neurol Scand 50:774–790, 1974

Price LH, Charney DS, Heninger GR: Efficacy of lithium-tranylcypromine treatment in refractory depression. Am J Psychiatry 142(5):619–623, 1985

Price LH, Charney DS, Heninger GR: Variability of response to lithium augmentation in refractory depression. Am J Psychiatry 143:1387–1392, 1986

Price LH, Charney DS, Heninger GR: Reserpine augmentation of desipramine in refractory depression: clinical and neurobiological effects. Psychopharmacology 92:431–437, 1987

Price SL, Mukherjee S: More on maprotiline-induced seizures. Am J Psychiatry 139:1080–1081, 1982

Price TRP: Short- and long-term cognitive effects of ECT, I: effects on memory. Psychopharmacol Bull 18:81–91, 1982a

Price TRP: Short- and long-term cognitive effects of ECT, II: effects on nonmemory associated cognitive functions. Psychopharmacol Bull 18:91–101, 1982b

Prien RF: Long-term maintenance therapy in affective disorders, in Schizophrenia and Affective Disorders: Biology and Drug Treatments. Edited by Rifkin A. Boston, John Wright, 1983

Prien RF, Kupfer DJ: Continuation drug therapy for major depressive episodes: how long should it be maintained? Am J Psychiatry 141:18–23, 1986

Prien RF, Kupfer DJ, Mansky PA, et al: Drug therapy in the prevention of recurrences in unipolar and bipolar affective disorders. Arch Gen Psychiatry 41:1096–1104, 1984

Prusoff BA, Williams DH, Weissman MM, et al: Treatment of secondary depression in schizophrenia. Arch Gen Psychiatry 36:569–575, 1979

Prusoff BA, Weissman MM, Klerman GL, et al: Research diagnostic criteria subtypes of depression: their role as predictors of differential response to psychotherapy and drug treatment. Arch Gen Psychiatry 37:796–803, 1980

Puig-Antich, J: Affective disorders in childhood. Psychiatr Clin North Am 3:403–424, 1980

Puig-Antich J: Psychobiological correlates of major depressive disorder in children and adolescents, in American Psychiatric Association Annual Review, vol 1. Edited by Grinspoon L. Washington, DC, American Psychiatric Association, 1982

Puig-Antich J: Psychobiological markers: effects of age and puberty, in Depression in Young People. Edited by Rutter M, Izard CE, Read PB. New York, Guilford Press, 1986

Puig-Antich J, Novacenko H, Davies M, et al: Growth hormone secretion in prepubertal children with major depression. Arch Gen Psychiatry 41:443–460, 1984

Puig-Antich J, Lukens E, Davies M, et al: Psychosocial functioning in prepubertal major depressive disorders. Arch Gen Psychiatry 42:511–517, 1985

Puzynski S, Klosiewicz L: Valproic acid amide as a prophylactic agent in affective and schizoaffective disorders. Psychopharmacol Bull 20:151–159, 1984

Quail M, Karalese RH: Disulfiram psychosis. S Afr Med J 57:551–553, 1980

Quitkin FM: The importance of dosage in prescribing antidepressants. Br J Psychiatry 147:593–597, 1985

Quitkin FM, Rifkin A, Klein DF: Imipramine response in deluded depressive patients. Am J Psychiatry 135:806–811, 1978

Quitkin FM, McGrath P, Liebowitz MR, et al: Monoamine oxidase inhibitors in bipolar endogenous depressives. J Clin Psychopharmacol 1:70–74, 1981

Quitkin FM, Rabkin JG, Ross D, et al: Duration of antidepressant drug treatment. Arch Gen Psychiatry 41:238–245, 1984

Quitkin FM, Rabkin JG, Stewart JW, et al: Study duration in antidepressant research: advantages of a 12-week trial. J Psychiatry Res 20(3):221–216, 1986

Rabin AS, Kaslow NJ, Rehm LP: Factors influencing continuation in a behavioral therapy. Behav Res Ther 23:695–698, 1985

Rabkin JG, Charles E, Kass F: Hypertension and DSM III depression in psychiatric outpatients. Am J Psychiatry 140:1072–1074, 1983

Rabkin JG, Quitkin FM, Harrison W, et al: Adverse reactions to monoamine oxidase inhibitors, I: a comparative study. J Clin Psychopharmacol 4:270–278, 1985a

Rabkin JG, Quitkin FM, McGrath P, et al: Adverse reactions to monoamine oxidase inhibitors, II: treatment correlates and clinical management. J Clin Psychopharmacol 5:2–9, 1985b

Racamier PC, Blanchard M: De l'angoise a la manie. L'Evolution Psychiatrique 3:558–587, 1957

Rachelefsky GS, Flynt JW Jr, Ebbin AJ, et al: Possible teratogenicity of tricyclic antidepressants (letter). Lancet 1:838, 1972

Radloff LS: The CES-D scale: a self-report depression scale for research in the general population. Applied Psychological Measurement 1:358–401, 1977

Rado S: The problem of melancholia (1927), in Collected Papers, vol 1. New York, Grune & Stratton, 1956

Ramirez AL: Seizures associated with maprotiline. Am J Psychiatry 140:509–510, 1983

Rao AV, Nammalvar J: The course and outcome in depressive illness: a follow-up study of 122 cases in Madurai, India. Br J Psychiatry 130:981–992, 1977

Rao TLK, Jacobs KH, El-Etr AA: Reinfarction following anesthesia in patients with myocardial infarction. Anesthesiology 59:499–505, 1983

Raskin D: A survey of electroconvulsive therapy: use and training in university hospitals in 1984. Convulsive Therapy 2:293–299, 1986

Raskind M, Veith R, Barnes R, et al: Cardiovascular and antidepressant effects of imipramine in the treatment of secondary depression in patients with ischemic heart disease. Am J Psychiatry 139:1114–1117, 1982

Rausch JL, Pavlinac DM, Newman PE: Complete heart block following a single dose of trazodone. Am J Psychiatry 141:1472–1473, 1984

Rehm LP: A self-control model of depression. Behavior Res Therapy 8:787–804, 1977

Rehm LP: Mood, pleasant events, and unpleasant events: two pilot studies. J Consult Clin Psychol 46:854–859, 1978

Rehm LP, Kornblith SJ: Self-control therapy manual, 1-2 session manual (unpublished mimeo), Pittsburgh, University of Pittsburgh, 1978

Rehm LP, Kornblith SJ: Behavior therapy for depression: a review of recent developments, in Progress In Behavior Modification, vol. 7. Edited by Hersen M, Eisler RM, Miller PM. New York, Academic Press, 1979

Rehm LP, Fuchs CZ, Roth DM, et al: A comparison of self-control and social skills treatments of depression. Behavior Res Therapy 10:429–442, 1979

Rehm LP, Kornblith SJ, O'Hara MW, et al: An evaluation of major components in a self-control therapy program for depression. Behav Modif 5:459–490, 1981

Rehm LP, Rabin AS, Kaslow NY, et al: Cognitive and behavioral targets in a self-control therapy program for depression. Presented at the Annual Meeting of the Association for the Advancement of Behavior Therapy, Los Angeles, Calif, 1982

Reich J, Tupin JP, Abramowitz SI: Psychiatric diagnosis of chronic pain patients. Am J Psychiatry 140:1495–1498, 1983

Remick RA, Maurice WL: ECT in pregnancy. Am J Psychiatry 135:761–762, 1978

Richardson JW, Richelson E: Antidepressants: a clinical update for medical practitioners. Mayo Clin Proc 59:330–337, 1984

Richardson JW, Lewis WH, Gahagan LH, et al: Etiology and treatment of cardiac arrhythmias under anesthetic for electroconvulsive therapy. NY State J Med 57:881–886, 1959

Richelson E: Tricyclic antidepressants and histamine H_1 receptors. Mayo Clin Proc 54:669–674, 1979

Richelson E: The use of tricyclic antidepressants in chronic gastrointestinal pain. J Clin Psychiatry 43(sec 2):50–55, 1982

Richelson E: Novel uses for tricyclic antidepressants. Modern Medicine 51:74–86, 1983

Richelson E: Psychotropics and the elderly: interactions to watch for. Geriatrics 39:30–42, 1984

Richelson E, El-Fakahany E: Receptor sensitivity changes and the actions of some psychotherapeutic drugs. Mayo Clin Proc 57:576–582, 1982

Richelson E, Nelson A: Antagonism by antidepressants of neurotransmitter receptors of normal human brain in vitro. J Pharmacol Exp Ther 230:94–102, 1984

Richelson E, Pfenning M: Blockade by antidepressants and related compounds of biogenic amine uptake into rat brain synaptosomes: most antidepressants selectively block norepinephrine uptake. Eur J Pharmacol 104:277–286, 1984

Rickels K, Feighner JP, Smith WT: Alprazolam, amitriptyline, doxepin, and placebo in the treatment of depression. Arch Gen Psychiatry 42:134–141, 1985

Rickels K, Chung HR, Csanalosi IB, et al: Alprazolam, diazepam, imipramine, and placebo in out-patients with major depression. Arch Gen Psychiatry 44:862–866, 1987

Rie H: Depression in childhood: a survey of some pertinent contributions. J Am Acad Child Adolesc Psychiatry 5:653–685, 1966

Ries RK, Wilson L, Bokan JA, et al: ECT in medication resistant schizoaffective disorder. Compr Psychiatry 22:167–173, 1981

Ries RK, Gilbert DA, Katon W: Tricyclic antidepressant therapy for peptic ulcer disease. Arch Intern Med 144:566–569, 1984

Rifkin A, Siris SG: Drug treatment of mania, in Schizophrenia and Affective Disorders. Edited by Rifkin A. Boston, John Wright, 1983

Robin AA, Wiseberg S: A controlled trial of methyl phenidate (ritalin) in the treatment of depressive states. J Neurol Neurosurg Psychiatry 21:55–57, 1958

Robins LN, Helzer JE, Weissman MM, et al: Lifetime prevalence of specific psychiatric disorders in three sites. Arch Gen Psychiatry 41:949–958, 1984

Robinson DS, Kayser A, Corcella J, et al: Panic attacks in out-patients with depression: response to antidepressant treatment. Psychopharmacol Bull 21:562–567, 1985a

Robinson DS, Cooper TB, Jindal SP, et al: Metabolism and pharmacokinetics of phenelzine: lack of evidence for acetylation pathway in humans. J Clin Psychopharmacol 5:333–337, 1985b

Robinson DS, Nies A, Ravaris L, et al: Clinical pharmacology of phenelzine. Arch Gen Psychiatry 35:629–635, 1978

Robinson RG: New findings on poststroke depression. Abstract No 21E, American Psychiatric Association, 1987

Robinson RG, Benson DF: Depression in aphasic patients: frequency, severity, and clinical-pathological correlations. Brain Lang 14:282–291, 1981

Robinson RG, Starr LB, Lipsey JR, et al: Course and prognosis in poststroke depression. Presented at the Annual Meeting of the American Psychiatric Association, 1984a

Robinson RG, Starr LB, Price TR: A two-year longitudinal study of mood disorders following stroke. Br J Psychiatry 144:256–262, 1984b

Robinson RG, Lipsey JR, Bolla-Wilson K, et al: Mood disorders in left-handed stroke patients. Am J Psychiatry 142:1424–1429, 1985

Rodin GM, Voshart K: Depression in the medically ill. Am J Psychiatry 143:696–705, 1986

Rodin GM, Chmara J, Ennis J, et al: Stopping life-sustaining medical treatment: psychiatric considerations in the termination of renal dialysis. Can J Psychiatry 26:540–544, 1981

Roose SP, Glassman AH, Walsh BT, et al: Tricyclic nonresponders: phenomenology and treatment. Am J Psychiatry 143:345–348, 1986a

Roose SP, Glassman AH, Giardina EGV, et al: Nortriptyline in depressed patients with left ventricular impairment. JAMA 256:3253–3257, 1986b

Roose SP, Glassman AH, Giardina EGV, et al: Tricyclic antidepressants in depressed patients with cardiac conduction disease. Arch Gen Psychiatry 44:273–275, 1987

Rosen GM: The Relaxation Book. Englewood-Cliffs, NJ, Prentice-Hall, 1977

Rosenbaum M: A schedule for assessing self-control behaviors: preliminary findings. Behav Ther 11:109–121, 1980

Rosenbaum M, Merbaum M: Self-control of anxiety and depression: an evaluative review of treatments, in New Developments in Behavior Therapy: From Research to Clinical Application. Edited by Franks CM. New York, Haworth, 1984, pp 105–155

Rosenthal NE, Heffernan MM: Bulimia, carbohydrate craving, and depression: a central connection? in Nutrition and the Brain, vol 7. Edited by Wurtman RJ, Wurtman JJ. New York, Raven Press, 1985, pp 139–166

Rosenthal NE, Sack DA, Gillin JC, et al: Seasonal affective disorder: a description of the syndrome and preliminary findings with light therapy. Arch Gen Psychiatry 41:72–80, 1984

Rosenthal NE, Sack DA, Carpenter CJ, et al: Antidepressant effects of light on seasonal affective disorders. Am J Psychiatry 142:163–170, 1985a

Rosenthal NE, Sack DA, James SP, et al: Seasonal affective disorder and phototherapy, in The Medical and Biological Effects of Light. Edited by Wurtman RJ, Baum MJ, Potts JT. Ann NY Acad Sci 453:260–269, 1985b

Rosenthal NE, Sack DA, Jacobsen FM, et al: Melatonin in seasonal affective disorder and phototherapy. J Neural Transm (Suppl) 21:257–267, 1986a

Rosenthal NE, Carpenter CJ, James SP, et al: Seasonal affective disorder in children and adolescents. Am J Psychiatry 143(3):356–358, 1986b

Rosenthal NE, Sack DA, Skwerer RG, et al: Phototherapy of seasonal affective disorder. J Biol Rhythms (in press)

Ross DR, Walker JI, Peterson J: Akathisia induced by amoxapine. Am J Psychiatry 140:115–116, 1983

Roth D, Bielski R, Jones M, et al: A comparison of self-control therapy and combined self-control therapy and antidepressant medication in the treatment of depression. Behavior Res Therapy 13:133–144, 1982

Roth M: The psychiatric disorders of later life. Psychiatric Annals 6:417–444, 1976

Rounsaville BJ, Kleber HD: Untreated opiate addicts. Arch Gen Psychiatry 42:1072–1077, 1985

Rounsaville BJ, Weissman MM, Prusoff BA, et al: Marital disputes and treatment outcome in depressed women. Compr Psychiatry 20:483–490, 1979

Rounsaville BJ, Sholomskas D, Prusoff BA: Chronic mood disorders in depressed outpatients. J Affective Disord 2:73–88, 1980

Rounsaville BJ, Klerman GL, Weissman M: Do psychotherapy and pharmacotherapy for depression conflict? Evidence from a clinical trial. Arch Gen Psychiatry 38:24–29, 1981

Rounsaville BJ, Weissman MM, Wilber CH, et al: The heterogeneity of psychiatric diagnosis in treated opiate addicts. Arch Gen Psychiatry 39:161–166, 1982

Rounsaville BJ, Glazer W, Weissman MM, et al: Short-term interpersonal psychotherapy in methadone maintained opiate addicts. Arch Gen Psychiatry 40:629–636, 1983

Rounsaville BJ, Chevron ES, Weissman MM: Psychotherapy Research: Where Are We and Where Should We Go? Edited by Williams JBW, Spitzer RL. New York, Guilford Press, 1984, pp 160–172

Rusak B, Boulos Z: Pathways for photic entrainment of mammalian circadian rhythms. Photochem Photobiol 34:267–273, 1981

Rush AJ (ed): Short-Term Psychotherapies for Depression. New York, Guilford Press, 1982

Rush AJ: Cognitive therapy of depression: rationale, techiques, and efficacy. Psychiatr Clin North Am 6:105–128, 1983

Rush AJ: The therapeutic alliance in short-term directive therapies, in Psychiatry Update, vol 4. Edited by Francis AJ, Hales RE. Washington DC, American Psychiatric Association, 1985, pp 562–572

Rush AJ, Beck AT: Behavior therapy in adults with affective disorders, in Behavior Therapy in the Psychiatric Setting. Edited by Hersen M, Bellack AS. Baltimore, Williams and Wilkins, 1978

Rush AJ, Watkins JT: Group versus individual cognitive therapy: a pilot study. Cognitive Therapy Res 5:95–103, 1981

Rush AJ, Beck AT, Kovacs M, et al: Comparative efficacy of cognitive therapy and pharmacotherapy in the treatment of depressed outpatients. Cognitive Therapy Res 1:17–37, 1977

Rush AJ, Shaw BF, Khatami M: Cognitive therapy of depression: utilizing the couples system. Cognitive Therapy Res 4:103–113, 1980

Rush AJ, Kovacs M, Beck AT, et al: Differential effects of cognitive therapy and pharmacotherapy on depressive symptoms. J Affective Disord 3:221–229, 1981

Rush AJ, Beck AT, Kovacs M, et al: Comparison of the effects of cognitive therapy and pharmacotherapy on hopelessness and self-concept. Am J Psychiatry 139:862–866, 1982

Rutter M: Maternal Deprivation Reassessed. London, Penguin, 1972

Sabelli HC, Mosnaim AD: Phenylethylamine hypothesis of affective behavior. Am J Psychiatry 131:695–699, 1974

Sabelli HC, Fawcett J, Gusovsky F, et al: Urinary phenylacetate: a diagnostic test for depression? Science 220:1187–1188, 1983

Sabelli HC, Fawcett J, Gusovsky F, et al: Clinical studies on the phenylethylamine hypothesis of affective disorder: urine and blood phenylacetic acid and phenylalanine dietary supplements. J Clin Psychiatry 47:66–70, 1986

Sackeim HA, Mukherjee S: Neurophysiological variability in the effects of the ECT stimulus. Convulsive Therapy 2:267–276, 1986

Sackeim HA, Decina P, Prohovnik I, et al: Dosage, seizure threshold, and the antidepressant efficacy of electroconvulsive therapy. Ann NY Acad Sci 462:398–410, 1986

Salkind MR: Beck Depression Inventory in general practice. J R Coll Gen Pract 18:267–271, 1969

Salzman C: The use of ECT in the treatment of schizophrenia. Am J Psychiatry 137:1032–1041, 1980

Salzman C: A primer on geriatric psychopharmacology. Am J Psychiatry 139:67–74, 1982

Sandler J, Joffee WG: Notes on childhood depression. Int J Psychoanal 46:80–96, 1965

Sandoz M, Vandel S, Vandel B, et al: Biotransformation of amitriptyline in alcoholic depressive patients. J Clin Pharmacol 24:615–621, 1983

Santos AB Jr, McCurdy L: Delirium after abrupt withdrawal from doxepin: case report. Am J Psychiatry 137:239–240, 1980

Sargent W: The treatment of anxiety states and atypical depressions by the monoamine oxidase inhibitor drugs. J Neuropsychiatr 3:96–103, 1962

Schaefer C, Coyne JC, Lazarus RS: The health-related functions of social support. J Behav Med 4:381–406, 1981

Schaffer CB, Garvey MJ: Use of lithium in acutely manic elderly patients. Clinical Gerontologist 3:58–60, 1984

Schatzberg AF, Elliott GR, Duffy FH, et al: Studies in atypical and refractory depression. Presented at the 137th Annual Meeting, American Psychiatric Association, May 1984, p 68

Scher M, Krieger JN, Juergens S: Trazodone and priapism. Am J Psychiatry 140:1362–1363, 1983

Schiffer RB, Babigian HM: Behavioral disorders in multiple sclerosis, temporal lobe epilepsy, and amyotrophic lateral sclerosis. Arch Neurol 41:1067–1069, 1984

Schiffer RB, Caine ED, Bamford KA, et al: Depressive episodes in patients with multiple sclerosis. Am J Psychiatry 140:1498–1500, 1983

Schmidt M, Miller WR: Amount of therapist contact and outcome in a multidimensional depression treatment program. Acta Psychiatr Scand 67:319–332, 1983

Schottenfeld RS, Cullen MR: Organic affective illness associated with lead intoxication. Am J Psychiatry 141:1423–1426, 1984

Schou M: Lithium in psychiatric therapy and prophylaxis. J Psychiatr Res 6:67–95, 1968

Schou M: The recognition and management of lithium intoxication, in Handbook of Lithium Therapy. Edited by Johnson FN. Lancaster, England, MTP Press, 1980

Schou M: Problems of lithium prophylaxis: efficacy, serum lithium, selection of patients. Bibl Psychiatr 160:30–37, 1981

Schou M, Weinstein MR: Problems of lithium maintenance treatment during pregnancy, delivery, and lactation. Agressologie 21:7–10, 1980

Schuckit MA: Alcoholic patients with secondary depression. Am J Psychiatry 140:711–714, 1983a

Schuckit MA: Alcoholism and other psychiatric disorders. Hosp Community Psychiatry 34:1022–1027, 1983b

Schuckit MA: The clinical implications of primary diagnostic groups among alcoholics. Arch Gen Psychiatry 42:1043–1049, 1985

Schulz P, Dick P, Blaschke TF, et al: Discrepancies between pharmacokinetic studies of amitriptyline. Clin Pharmacokinet 10:257–268, 1985

Schwab JJ, Bialow MK, Brown JMK, et al: Diagnosing depression in medical inpatients. Ann Intern Med 67:695–707, 1967

Schwarcz G, Halaris A, Baxter L, et al: Normal thyroid function in desipramine nonresponders converted to responders by the addition of L-triiodothyronine. Am J Psychiatry 141:1614–1616, 1984

Schwartz B: The glaucomas. N Engl J Med 299:182–184, 1978

Schwartz L, Swaminathan S: Maprotiline hydrochloride and convulsions: a case report. Am J Psychiatry 139:244–245, 1982

Seager CR, Bird RL: Imipramine with electrical treatment in depression: a controlled trial. Journal of Mental Science 108:704–707, 1962

Selmi PM, Klein MH, Greist JH, et al: An investigation of computer-assisted cognitive-behavior therapy in the treatment of depression. Behavior Research Methods and Instrumentation 14:181–185, 1982

Shader RI, Greenblatt DJ: Propranolol's psychiatric side effects. J Clin Psychopharmacol 3:65, 1983

Shakir SA, Volkmar FR, Bacon S, et al: Group psychotherapy as an adjunct to lithium maintenance. Am J Psychiatry 136:455–456, 1979

Shaw BF: Comparison of cognitive therapy and behavior therapy in the treatment of depression. J Consult Clin Psychol 45:543–551, 1977

Shaw BF: Specification of the training and evaluation of cognitive therapists for outcome studies, in Psychotherapy Research: Where Are We and Where Should We Go? Edited by Williams J, Spitzer R. New York, Guilford Press, 1984, pp 173–189

Shaw JA, Donley P, Morgan DW, et al: Treatment of depression in alcoholics. Am J Psychiatry 143:641–644, 1975

Sheard MH: Lithium in the treatment of aggression. J Nerv Ment Dis 160:108–118, 1975

Shulka S, Hoff A, Aronson T, et al: Treatment outcome in organic mania. New Research Abstract 134, American Psychiatric Association, 1987

Shulman K, Post F: Bipolar affective disorders in old age. Br J Psychiatry 136:26–32, 1980

Sifneos P: Short-Term Psychotherapy and Emotional Crisis. Cambridge, Mass, Harvard University Press, 1972

Sifneos P: Short-Term Psychotherapy: Evaluation and Technique. New York, Plenum Press, 1979

Simons AD, Garfield SL, Murphy GE: The process of change in cognitive therapy and pharmacotherapy for depression. Arch Gen Psychiatry 41:45–51, 1984a

Simons AD, Levine JL, Lustman PJ, et al: Patient attrition in a comparative outcome study of depression: a follow-up report. J Affective Disord 6:163–173, 1984b

Simons AD, Lustman PJ, Wetzel RD, et al: Predicting response to cognitive therapy of depression: the role of learned resourcefulness. Cognitive Therapy Res 9:79–89, 1985

Simons AD, Murphy GE, Levine JL, et al: Cognitive therapy and pharmacotherapy for depression: sustained improvement over one year. Arch Gen Psychiatry 43:43–48, 1986

Singh J, Singh S, Singh S, et al: Sex life and psychiatric problems after myocardial infarction. J Assoc Physicians India 18:503–507, 1970

Siris SG: "Depression" in schizophrenia: a distinct syndrome. The Bulletin. Area II Council, American Psychiatric Association, 27:3–6, 1985

Siris SG, Van Kammen DP, Docherty JP: Use of antidepressant drugs in schizophrenia. Arch Gen Psychiatry 35:1368–1377, 1978

Siris SG, Rifkin A, Reardon GT: Response of post-psychotic depression to adjunctive imipramine or amitriptyline. J Clin Psychiatry 43:485–486, 1982

Siris SG, Rifkin A, Reardon GT, et al: Comparative side effects of imipramine, benztropine, or their combination in patients receiving fluphenazine decanoate. Am J Psychiatry 140:1069–1071, 1983

Siris SG, Rifkin A, Reardon GT, et al: Stability of the post-psychotic depression syndrome. J Clin Psychiatry 47:86–88, 1986

Siris SG, Morgan V, Fagerstrom R, et al: Adjunctive imipramine in the treatment of post-psychotic depression: a controlled trial. Arch Gen Psychiatry (in press[a])

Siris SG, Federico A, Cohen M, et al: Targeted treatment of depression-like symptoms in schizophrenia. Psychopharmacol Bull (in press[b])

Sjöqvist F, Alexanderson B, Åsberg M, et al: Pharmacokinetics and biological effects of nortriptyline in man. Acta Pharmacol Toxicol 3:255–280, 1971

Skausig OB, Korsgaard S: Hallucinations and baclofen. Lancet 1:1258, 1977

Skinner BF: Science and Human Behavior. New York, Free Press, 1953

Skwerer RG, Jacobsen FM, Duncan CC, et al: The neurobiology of seasonal affective disorder and phototherapy. J Biol Rhythms (in press)

Sloane RB, Staples FR, Cristol AH, et al: Psychotherapy Versus Behavior Therapy. Cambridge, Mass, Harvard University Press, 1975

Sloane RB, Staple FR, Schneider LS: Clinical and Pharmacological Studies in Psychiatric Disorders: Biological Psychiatry—New Prospects. Edited by Burrows GD, Norman TR, Dennerstein L. London, J Libby and Company, 1985

Small GW, Purcell JJ: Trazodone and cocaine abuse. Arch Gen Psychiatry 42:524, 1985

Small JG: Efficacy of electroconvulsive therapy in schizophrenia, mania and other disorders, I: schizophrenia. Convulsive Therapy 1:263–270, 1985a

Small JG: Efficacy of electroconvulsive therapy in schizophrenia, mania and other disorders, II: mania and other disorders. Convulsive Therapy 1:271–276, 1985b

Small JG, Milstein V, Klapper MH, et al: Electroconvulsive therapy. J Clin Psychiatry 47:366–367, 1986a

Small JG, Milstein V, Klapper MH, et al: Electroconvulsive therapy in the treatment of manic episodes. Ann NY Acad Sci 462:37–49, 1986b

Smith ML, Glass GV: Meta-analysis of psychotherapy outcome studies. Am Psychol 32:752–760, 1977

Smith ML, Glass GV, Miller TI: The Benefits of Psychotherapy. Baltimore, Md, Johns Hopkins University Press, 1980

Snow SS, Logan TP, Hollender MH: Nasal spray 'addiction' and psychosis: a case report. Br J Psychiatry 136:297–299, 1980

Souetre E, Salvati E, Pringuey D, et al: Antidepressant effects of the sleep/wake cycle phase advance: preliminary report. J Affective Disord 2:41–46, 1987

Spencer JH, Mattson MR: Utilization review and resident education. Hosp Community Psychiatry, 30:269–272, 1979

Sperling M: Equivalents of depression in children. Journal of Hillside Hospital 8:138–148, 1962

Spiker DG, Pugh DD: Combining tricyclic and monoamine oxidase inhibitor antidepressants. Arch Gen Psychiatry 33:828–830, 1976

Spiker DG, Weiss AN, Chang SS, et al: Tricyclic antidepressant overdose: clinical presentations and plasma levels. Clin Pharmacol Ther 18:539–546, 1975

Spiker DG, Weiss JC, Dealy RS, et al: The pharmacological treatment of delusional depression. Am J Psychiatry 142:430–436, 1985

Spitz R: Anaclitic depression. Psychoanal Study Child 5:113–117, 1946

Spitzer RL, Endicott J, Robins E: Research Diagnostic Criteria for a Selected Group of Functional Disorders, 3rd ed. New York, Psychiatric Institute Biometrics Research Division, 1978a

Spitzer RL, Endicott J, Robins E: Research Diagnostic Criteria: rationale and reliability. Arch Gen Psychiatry 35:773–782, 1978b

Squire LR: Memory functions as affected by electroconvulsive therapy. Ann NY Acad Sci 462:307–314, 1986

Squire LR, Chace PM: Memory functions six to nine months after electroconvulsive therapy. Arch Gen Psychiatry 32:1557–1564, 1975

Squire LR, Slater PC, Miller PL: Retrograde amnesia following ECT: long-term follow up. Arch Gen Psychiatry 38:89–95, 1981

Standards of Practice: Minimal Monitoring. Harvard Medical School, Department of Anesthesia, Cambridge, Mass, July 3, 1985

Stasiek C, Zetin M: Organic manic disorders. Psychosomatics 26:394–402, 1985

Steif B, Sackeim HA, Portnoy S, et al: Effects of depression and ECT on anterograde memory. Biol Psychiatry 21:921–930, 1986

Steinmetz JL, Breckenridge JN, Thompson LW, et al: The role of client expectations in predicting treatment outcome for elderly depressives. Presented at the Annual Meeting of the Gerontological Society of America, Boston, Mass, 1982

Steinmetz JL, Lewinsohn PM, Antonuccio DO: Prediction of individual outcome in a group intervention for depression. J Consult Clin Psychol 51:331–337, 1983

Steinmetz JL, Zeiss AN, Thompson LW: The life satisfaction course: an intervention for the elderly, in Handbook of Behavioral Group Therapy. Edited by Upper D, Ross SM. New York, Plenum Press, 1984

Steinmetz JL, Antonuccio DO, Bond M, et al: Instructor's Manual for Coping with Depression Course (unpublished mimeo). Eugene, Ore, University of Oregon

Stern MJ, Pascale L, McLeone JB: Psychosocial adaption following an acute myocardial infarction. J Chronic Dis 29:513–526, 1976

Stern MJ, Pascale L, Ackerman A: Life adjustment postmyocardial infarction: determining predictive variables. Arch Intern Med 137:1680–1685, 1977

Stern SL, Mendels J: Withdrawal symptoms during the course of imipramine therapy. J Clin Psychiatry 41:66–67, 1980

Steuer JL, Mintz J, Hammen CL, et al: Cognitive-behavioral and psychodynamic group psychotherapy in treatment of geriatric depression. J Consult Clin Psychol 52:180–189, 1984

Stewart H: Six-months, fixed-term, once-weekly psychotherapy: a report on 20 cases with follow ups. Br J Psychiatry 121:425–435, 1972

Stewart JW, Quitkin F, Fyer A, et al: Efficacy of desipramine in endogenomorphically depressed patients. J Affective Disord 2:165–176, 1980

Stewart MA, Drake F, Winokur G: Depression among medically ill patients. Dis Nerv Syst 26:479–485, 1965

Stone MH: A psychoanalytic approach to abnormalities of temperament. Am J Psychother 33:263–280, 1979

Strober M: A family study of anorexia nervosa. Presented at the International Conference on Anorexia Nervosa and Related Disorders, Swansea, Wales, 1984

Strober M, Carlson G: Bipolar illness in adolescents with major depression: clinical, genetic and psychopharmacologic predictors in a three- to four-year prospective follow-up investigation. Arch Gen Psychiatry 39:549–555, 1982

Stromgren LS, Dahl J, Fieldborg N: Factors affecting seizure duration and number of seizures applied in unilateral electroconvulsive therapy: anesthetics and benzodiazepines. Acta Psychiat Scand 62:158–165, 1980

Strupp HH: Success and failure in time-limited psychotherapy: a systematic comparison of two cases. Arch Gen Psychiatry 37:595–603, 1980a

Strupp HH: Success and failure in time-limited psychotherapy: a systematic comparison of two cases (comparison 2). Arch Gen Psychiatry 37:708–716, 1980b

Strupp HH: Success and failure in time-limited psychotherapy: further evidence (comparison 4). Arch Gen Psychiatry 37:831–841, 1980c

Strupp HH: Time Limited Dynamic Psychotherapy (TLDP). New York, Basic Books, 1982.

Strupp HH, Binder JL: Time Limited Dynamic Psychotherapy (TLDP): A treatment manual. Nashville, Tenn, Center for Psychotherapy Research, 1982

Strupp HH, Binder JL: Psychotherapy in a New Key: A Guide to Time-Limited Dynamic Psychotherapy. New York, Basic Books, 1984

Strupp HH, Hadley SW: Specific versus nonspecific factors in psychotherapy: a controlled study of outcome. Arch Gen Psychiatry 36:1125–1136, 1979

Strupp HH, Sandell JA, Waterhouse SJ, et al: Short-term therapies for depression: theory and research, in Short-Term Psychotherapies for the Depressed Patient. Edited by Rush AJ. New York, Guilford Press, 1982

Suh CS, O'Malley SS, Strupp HH: The Vanderbilt Psychotherapy Process Scale (VPPS) and the Negative Indicators Scale (VNIS). Edited by Greenberg LS, Pinsof WM. 1986

Sullivan HS: Conceptions of Modern Psychiatry. New York, Norton and Company, 1953a

Sullivan HS: The Interpersonal Theory of Psychiatry. New York, Norton and Company, 1953b

Sullivan TJ: Pharmacologic modulation of the whealing response to histamine in human skin: identification of doxepin as a potent in vivo inhibitor. J Allergy Clin Immunol 69:260–267, 1982

Sulser FJ: Mode of action of antidepressant drugs. J Clin Psychiatry 44 (sec 2):14–20, 1983

Summers WK, Robins E, Reich T: The natural history of acute organic mental syndrome after bilateral electroconvulsive therapy. Biol Psychiatry 14:905–912, 1979

Swanson DW: Chronic pain as a third pathologic emotion. Am J Psychiatry, 141:210–214, 1984

Swiff WJ, Andrews D, Barklage NE: The relationship between affective disorder and eating disorders: a review of the literature. Am J Psychiatry 143:290–299, 1986

Tamarkin L, Baird CJ, Almeida OFX: Melatonin: a coordinating signal for mammalian reproduction? Science 227: 714–720, 1985

Targum SD, Dibble ED, Davenport YB, et al: The family attitudes questionnaire: patients' and spouses' reviews of bipolar illness. Arch Gen Psychiatry 38:562–568, 1981

Targum SD, Greenberg RD, Harmon RL, et al: The TRH test and thyroid hormone in refractory depression. Am J Psychiatry 141:463, 1984

Taylor DGE, Braithwaite RA: Cardiac effects of tricyclic antidepressant medication: a preliminary study of nortriptyline. Br Heart J 40:1005–1009, 1978

Taylor FG, Marshall WL: Experimental analysis of a cognitive-behavioral therapy for depression. Cognitive Therapy Res 1:59–72, 1977

Teasdale JD, Fennell MJV: Immediate effects on depression of cognitive therapy interventions. Cognitive Therapy Resource 6:343–351, 1982

Teasdale JD, Fennell MJV, Hibbert GA, et al: Cognitive therapy for major depressive disorder in primary care. Br J Psychiatry 144:400–406, 1984

Tennent FS, Sagherian AA: Double-blind comparison of amantadine and bromacriptine for ambulatory withdrawal from cocaine dependence. Arch Intern Med 147:109–112, 1987

Teri L, Lewinsohn PM: Comparative efficacy of group versus individual treatment of unipolar depression. Presented at the meeting of the Association for the Advancement of Behavior Therapy, San Francisco, Calif, 1981

Terman J: On the question of mechanism in phototherapy: considerations of clinical efficacy and epidemiology. J Biol Rhythms (in press)

Terman M, Quitkin FM, Terman JS, et al: The timing of phototherapy: effects on clinical response and the melatonin cycle. Psychopharmacol Bull 23:354–357, 1987

Thienhaus OJ, Kholsa N: Meningeal cryptococcis misdiagnosed as a manic episode. Am J Psychiatry 141:1459–1460, 1984

Thompson LW, Gallagher D: Efficacy of psychotherapy in the treatment of late-life depression. Adv Behav Res Ther 6:127–139, 1984

Thompson LW, Gallagher D, Nies G, et al: Evaluation of the effectiveness of professionals and nonprofessionals as instructors of Coping with Depression classes for elders. Gerontologist 23:390–396, 1983

Thornton JE, Stahl SM: Case report of tardive dyskinesia and parkinsonism associated with amoxapine therapy. Am J Psychiatry 141:704–705, 1984

Titievsky J, Seco G, Barranco M, et al: Doxepin as adjunctive therapy for depressed methadone maintenance patients: a double-blind study. J Clin Psychiatry 43:454–456, 1982

Tollefson G: Psychiatric implications of anticonvulsant drugs. J Clin Psychiatry 41:295–302, 1980

Toolan J: Depression in children and adolescents. Am J Orthopsychiatry 32:404–415, 1962

Trimble MR: New antidepressant drugs and the seizure threshold. Neuropharmacology 19:1227–1228, 1980

Turner RW, Wehl CK: Treatment of unipolar depression in problem drinkers. Adv Behav Res Ther 6:45, 1984

Turner RW, Ward MF, Turner DJ: Behavioral treatment for depression: an evaluation of therapeutic components. J Clin Psychol 35:166–175, 1979

Turner RW, Wehl CK, Cannon DS, et al: Individual treatment for depression in alcoholics: A comparison of behavioral, cognitive, and nonspecific therapy (unpublished manuscript). Salt Lake City, Utah, VA Medical Center

Tyrer SP: Clinical effects of abrupt withdrawal from tri-cyclic antidepressants and monoamine oxidase inhibitors after long-term treatment. J Affective Disord 6:1–7, 1984

Tyrer SP: Lithium in treatment of mania. J Affective Disord 8:251–257, 1985

Ulett GA, Gleser GC, Caldwell BW, et al: The use of matched groups in the evaluation of convulsive and subconvulsive photoshock. Bull Menninger Clin 18:138–146, 1954

Usubiaga JE, Gustafson W, Moya F, et al: The effect of intravenous lidocaine on cardiac arrhythmias during electroconvulsive therapy. Br J Anaesth 39:867–875, 1967

Van Kammen DP, Alexander PE, Bunney WE Jr: Lithium treatment in post-psychotic depression. Br J Psychiatry 136:479–485, 1980

van Praag HM: Management of depression with serotonin precursors. Biol Psychiatry 16:291–310, 1981

Van Putten T, May PRA: Akinetic depression in schizophrenia. Arch Gen Psychiatry 35:1101–1107, 1978

Van Spanning HW, Van Zwieten PA: The interference of tricyclic antidepressants with the central hypotensive effect of clonidine. Eur J Pharmacol 24:402–404, 1973

Van Spanning HW, Van Zwieten PA: The interaction between alpha-methyldopa and tricyclic antidepressants. Int J Clin Pharmacol Res 11:65–67, 1975

Varnaka TM, Weller EB, Weller RA, et al: Treating manic children with psychotic features. Presented at the 140th Annual Meeting of the American Psychiatric Association, Chicago, Ill, May 1987

Veith RC, Raskind MA, Caldwell JH, et al: Cardiovascular effects of tricyclic antidepressants in depressed patients with chronic heart disease. N Engl J Med 306:954–959, 1982

Vestergaard P, Schou M: The effect of age on lithium dosage requirements. Pharmacopsychiatry 17:199–201, 1984

Vogel GW, Vogel F, McAbee RS, et al: Improvement of depression by REM sleep deprivation. Arch Gen Psychiatry 37:247–253, 1980

Vogel GW, Klaiber EL, Broverman DM: A comparison of the antidepressant effects of a synthetic androgen (mesterolone) and amitriptyline in depressed men. J Clin Psychiatry 46(1):6–8, 1985

Walinder J, Skott A, Carlsson A, et al: Potentiation of the antidepressant action of clomipramine by tryptophan. Arch Gen Psychiatry 33:1384–1389, 1976

Walsh BT: Endocrine disturbances in anorexia nervosa and depression. Psychosom Med 44:85–91, 1982

Walsh BT, Stewart JW, Wright L: Treatment of bulimia with monoamine oxidase inhibitors. Am J Psychiatry 139:1629–1630, 1982

Walsh TC: Antidepressants in chronic pain. Clinical Neuropharmacol 6:271–295, 1983

Wander TJ, Nelson A, Okazaki H, et al: Antagonism by antidepressants of serotonin S_1 and S_2 receptors of normal human brain in vitro. Eur J Pharmacol 132:115–121, 1986

Ward NG, Bloom VL, Friedel RO: The effectiveness of tricyclic antidepressants in chronic depression. J Clin Psychiatry 40:49–52, 1979

Waring EM, Patton D: Marital intimacy and depression. Br J Psychiatry 145:641–644, 1984

Waring EM, Frelick L, Keil WE, et al: The effectiveness of combined antidepressant medication and marital therapy in unipolar major depression in married families (unpublished manuscript)

Waskow IE, Parloff MB (eds): Psychotherapy Change Measures (report) Clinical Research Branch. Washington, DC, National Institute of Mental Health, 1975

Watts CAH: Depressive Disorders in the Community. Bristol, John Wright and Sons, 1966.

Weaver G, Remick R: Treatment of depression should not be secondary. J Clin Psychiatry 1982

Weaver LA, Ives JO, Williams R, et al: A comparison of standard alternating current and low-energy brief pulse electrotherapy. Biol Psychiatry 12:525–543, 1977

Wehr TA, Goodwin FK: Rapid cycling in manic-depressives induced by tricyclic antidepressants. Arch Gen Psychiatry 36:555–565, 1979

Wehr TA, Goodwin FK: Can antidepressants cause mania and worsen the course of affective illness? Am J Psychiatry 144:1403–1411, 1987

Wehr TA, Jacobsen FM, Sack DA, et al: Phototherapy in seasonal affective disorder: time of day and suppression of melatonin are not critical for antidepressant effects. Arch Gen Psychiatry 43:870–875, 1986a

Wehr TA, Skwerer RG, Jacobsen FM, et al: Eye- versus skin-phototherapy of seasonal affective disorder. Am J Psychiatry, 1986b

Wehr TA, Sack DA, Rosenthal NE: Reverse seasonal affective disorder with spring-summer depression and fall-winter hypomania: possible relationship to environmental temperature. Am J Psychiatry 144:1602–1603, 1987

Wehr TA, Sack DA, Rosenthal NE, et al: Rapid cycling affective disorders: contributing factors and treatment responses in 51 patients. Am J Psychiatry 145:179–184, 1988

Weinberg WA, Rutman J, Sullivan L, et al: Depression in children referred to an educational diagnostic center: diagnosis and treatment. J Pediatr 83:1065–1072, 1973

Weiner RD: Persistence of ECT-induced EEG changes. J Nerv Ment Dis 168:224–228, 1980

Weiner RD: Does electroconvulsive therapy cause brain damage? The Behavioral and Brain Sciences 7:1–53, 1984

Weiner RD, Coffey CE: Minimizing therapeutic differences between bilateral and unilateral nondominant ECT. Convulsive Therapy 2:261–265, 1986

Weiner RD, Rogers HJ, Davidson JRT, et al: Effects of stimulus parameters on cognitive side-effects. Ann NY Acad Sci 462:315–325, 1986

Weingartner H, Cohen R, et al: Cognitive processes in depression. Arch Gen Psychiatry 38:42–47, 1981

Weise CC, Stein MK, Pereira-Ogan J, et al: Amitriptyline once daily versus three times daily in depressed outpatients. Arch Gen Psychiatry 37:555–560, 1980

Weissman MM: Psychopharmacology: A Generation of Progress. Edited by Lipton MA, DiMascio A, Killam KF. New York, Raven Press, 1978, pp 1313–1321

Weissman MM: The psychological treatment of depression: evidence for the efficacy of psychotherapy alone, and in comparison with, and in combination with pharmacotherapy. Arch Gen Psychiatry 36:1261–1269, 1979

Weissman MM: The treatment of depression secondary to alcoholism, opiate addiction, or schizophrenia: evidence for the efficacy of the tricyclic antidepressants, in Treatment of Depression: Old Controversies and New Approaches. Edited by Clayton PS, Barrett JE. New York, Raven Press, 1983

Weissman, MM: Psychotherapy Research: Where Are We and Where Should We Go? Edited by Williams JBW, Spitzer RL. Guilford Press, New York, pp 89–105 1984

Weissman MM, Klerman GL: The chronic depressive in the community: unrecognized and poorly treated. Compr Psychiatry 18:523–532, 1977

Weissman MM, Myers JK: Affective disorders in a US urban community. Arch Gen Psychiatry 35:1304–1311, 1978

Weissman MM, Myers JK: Clinical depression in alcoholism. Am J Psychiatry 137:372–379, 1980

Weissman MM, Paykel ES: The Depressed Women: A Study of Social Relationships. Chicago, University of Chicago Press, 1974

Weissman MM, Klerman GL, Paykel ES, et al: Treatment effects on the social adjustment of depressed patients. Arch Gen Psychiatry 30:771–778, 1974

Weissman MM, Pottenger M, Kleber H, et al: Symptom patterns in primary and secondary depression. Arch Gen Psychiatry 34:854–862, 1977

Weissman MM, Prusoff BA, Klerman GL: Personality and the prediction of long-term outcome of depression. Am J Psychiatry 135:797–800, 1978

Weissman MM, Prusoff BA, DiMascio A, et al: The efficacy of drugs and psychotherapy in the treatment of acute depressive episodes. Am J Psychiatry 136:555–558, 1979

Weissman MM, Klerman GL, Prusoff BA, et al: Depressed outpatients: results one year after treatment with drugs and/or interpersonal psychotherapy. Arch Gen Psychiatry 38:51–55, 1981

Weissman MM, Rounsaville BJ, Chevron E: Training psychotherapists to participate in psychotherapy outcome studies. Am J Psychiatry 139:1442–1446, 1982

Weissman MM, Jarrett RB, Rush AJ: Psychotherapy and its relevance to the pharmacotherapy of major depression: a decade later (1976–1985), in Psychopharmacology: The Third Generation of Progress. Edited by Meltzer HY. New York, Raven Press, 1987, pp 1059–1069

Welch CA, Weiner RD, Weir D, et al: Efficacy of ECT in the treatment of depression:

wave form and electrode placement considerations. Psychopharmacol Bull 18:31–34, 1982

Wells CE: Pseudodementia. Am J Psychiatry 136:895–900, 1979

Wells DA: ECT for schizophrenia: a ten-year survey in a university hospital psychiatry department. Compr Psychiatry 14:291–298, 1973

West ED, Dally PJ: Effects of iproniazid in depressive syndromes. Br Med J 1:1491–1494, 1959

Wever RA: The Circadian System of Man. New York, Springer-Verlag, 1979

Wharton RN, Perle JM, Dayton PG, et al: A potential clinical use for methylphenidate with tricyclic antidepressants. Am J Psychiatry 127:55–61, 1971

White K, Simpson G: Combined MAOI-tricyclic antidepressant treatment: a reevaluation. J Clin Psychopharmacol 1:264–282, 1981

White K, Pistole T, Boyd JL: Combined monoamine oxidase inhibitor-tricyclic antidepressant treatment: a pilot study. Am J Psychiatry 137:1422–1425, 1980

White PT, Grant P, Mosier J, et al: Changes in cerebral dynamics associated with seizures. Neurology 11:354–357, 1961

Whitehead A: Psychological treatment of depression: a review. Behav Res Ther 17:495, 1979

Whitlock FA, Siskind M: Depression and cancer: a follow-up study. Psychol Med 9:747–752, 1979

Whybrow P, Prange AJ: A hypothesis of thyroid-catecholamine receptor interaction. Arch Gen Psychiatry 38:106–113, 1981

Widlocher DJ: Psychomotor retardation: clinical, theoretical, and psychometric aspects. Psychiatr Clin North Am 6:27–40, 1983

Wilson LC, Alltop LB, Riley L: Tofranil in the treatment of post-alcoholic depressions. Psychosomatics 11:488–493, 1970

Wilson PH: Combined pharmacological and behavioural treatment of depression. Behav Res Ther 20:173–184, 1982

Wilson PH, Goldin JC, Charbonneau-Powis M: Comparative effects of behavioral and cognitive treatments of depression. Cog Ther Res 7:111–124, 1983

Winokur G: Depression: The Facts. London, Oxford University Press, 1981

Winokur G, Clayton P, Reich T: Manic-Depressive Illness. St. Louis, CV Mosby, 1969

Winokur G, Behan D, Van Valkenburg MD, et al: Is a familial definition of depression both feasible and valid? J Nerv Ment Dis 166:764–768, 1978

Winokur G, March V, Mendels J: Primary affective disorder in relatives of patients with anorexia nervosa. Am J Psychiatry 137:695–698, 1980

Winokur G, Dennert J, Angst J: Independent familial transmissions of psychotic symptomatology in the affective disorders, or does delusional depression breed true? Psychiatrica Fennica 9–16, 1986

Winslade WJ, Liston EH, Ross JW, et al: Medical, judicial, and statutory regulation of ECT in the United States. Am J Psychiatry 141:1349–1355, 1984

Winstead DK, Schwartz BD, Pardue LH, et al: Amoxapine serum levels and clinical response. Curr Therap Res 35:211–219, 1984

Wirz-Justice A, Buchelli C, Graw P, et al: Light treatment of seasonal affective disorder in Switzerland. Acta Psychiatr Scand 74:193–204, 1986

Witton K: Circulatory lability and depression. J Am Geriatr Soc 14:1081–1084, 1966

Wolberg L: Short-Term Psychotherapy. New York, Grune & Stratton, 1965

Wold PN: Anorexic syndromes and affective disorder. Psychiatr J Univ Ottawa 8:116–119, 1983

Woods SW, Tesar GE, Murray GB, et al: Psychostimulant treatment of depressive disorder secondary to medical illness. J Clin Psychiatry 47:12–15, 1986

Woody GE: Use of antidepressants along with methodone in maintenance patients.

Presented at the Conference on Opioids in Mental Illness, New York, October 29, 1981

Woody GE, O'Brien BP, Rickels K: Depression and anxiety in heroin addicts: a placebo controlled study of doxepin in combination with methadone. Am J Psychiatry 132:447–450, 1975

Woody GE, Luborsky L, McLellan AT: Psychotherapy for opiate addicts: does it help? Arch Gen Psychiatry 40:639–645, 1983

Wyant GM, Macdonald WB: The role of atropine in electroconvulsive therapy. Anaesth Intens Care 8:445–450, 1980

Yager J: Bethanechol chloride can reverse erectile and ejaculatory dysfunction induced by tricyclic antidepressants and mazindol: a case report. J Clin Psychiatry 47:210–211, 1986

Yaskin JC: Nervous symptoms as earliest manifestations of carcinoma of the pancreas. JAMA 96:1164–1168, 1931

Yerevanian BI, Anderson JL, Grota LJ, et al: Effects of bright incandescent light on seasonal and non-seasonal major depressive disorder. Psychiatry Res 18:355–364, 1986

Young JPR, Lader MH, Hughes WC: Controlled trial of trimipramine, monoamine oxidase inhibitors, and combined treatment in depressed patients. Br Med J 4:1315–1317, 1979

Young LD, Keeler MH: Effect of lithium carbonate on alcoholism in 20 male patients with concurrent affective disorder, in Currents in Alcoholism, vol 8. Edited by Glanter M. New York, Grune & Stratton, 1981, pp 175–181

Youngerman J, Canino IA: Lithium carbonate use in children and adolescents. Arch Gen Psychiatry 35:216–224, 1978

Yudofsky SC: Prior cognitive problems as the key to treating a patient with resistant depression. Hosp Community Psychiatry 36:11–12, 21, 1985

Zeiss AM, Jones SL: Behavioral treatment of depression: examining treatment failures, in Failures in Behavior Therapy. Edited by Foa EB, Emmelkamp MG. New York, John Wiley and Sons, 1982

Zeiss AM, Lewinsohn PM, Munoz RF: Nonspecific improvement effects in depression using interpersonal, cognitive, and pleasant events focused treatments. J Consult Clin Psychol 47:427–439, 1979

Zetin M, Warren S, Pangan EA, et al: Refractory depression. Stress Medicine 2:153–167, 1986

Zettle RD, Hayes SC: Cognitive therapy of depression: behavioral analysis of component and process issues. Affective Disorders Network Bulletin 2:March 1985

Zis AP, Goodwin FK: Major affective disorder as a recurrent illness. Arch Gen Psychiatry 36:835–839, 1979

Zis AP, Grof P, Webster MA, et al: Prediction of relapse in recurrent affective disorder. Psychopharmacol Bull 16:47–49, 1980

Zisook S: A clinical overview of monoamine oxidase inhibitors. Psychosomatics 26:240–251, 1985

Zohar J, Shapira B, Oppenheim G, et al: Addition of estrogen to imipramine in female-resistant depressives. Psychopharmacol Bull 21:705–706, 1987

Zuckerman DM, Prusoff BA, Weissman MM, et al: Personality as a predictor of psychotherapy and pharamcotherapy outcome for depressed outpatients. J Consult Clin Psychol 48:730–735, 1980

Zung WWK: A self-rating depression scale. Arch Gen Psychiatry 123:62–70, 1965

Zusky PM, Biederman J, Rosenbaum JF, et al: Adjunct low-dose lithium carbonate in treatment resistant depression: a placebo-controlled study and review. J Clin Psychopharmacol 8:120–124, 1988

SECTION 18

Anxiety Disorders

Chapter 181

Introduction

The presumed incidence of anxiety disorders is controversial. It has been estimated "that from 2% to 4% of the general population has at some time had a disorder that . . . would classify as an Anxiety Disorder" (American Psychiatric Association 1980, p. 225). However, a major epidemiological study found that the lifetime prevalence of anxiety or somatoform disorders in three different sites ranged from 10 to 25 percent of the population (Robins et al. 1984).

In outpatient populations, anxiety disorders appear to account for over a third of the presenting symptoms. Apparently this proportion has been stable for some time. For example, a study found that 37 percent of psychotherapy patients presented with anxiety complaints in 1938, a percentage that was virtually unchanged at 36 percent in 1978, whereas the incidence of other symptoms changed considerably over this 40-year period (Gill 1985).

Anxiety disorders, like depression, touch virtually every area within psychiatry. Therefore neither is it feasible to cover all the important issues in a comprehensive, systematic fashion, nor is it possible to discuss every therapeutic approach for which success has been reported. Instead, the strategy taken here focuses on the use of three major clinical paradigms (psychoanalytic psychotherapy, behavior therapy, and pharmacotherapy) in the treatment of anxiety disorders, as well as on the use of adjunctive techniques (relaxation, hypnosis, and biofeedback). A final chapter gives special consideration to posttraumatic stress disorder (PTSD).

There were a number of reasons for focusing on psychoanalytic psychotherapy, behavior therapy, and pharmacotherapy. Foremost among these was the fact that although the psychosocial, behavioral, and biologic treatment approaches have addressed all of the major psychiatric disorders, each of these therapeutic paradigms has claimed to have had a particular effectiveness in the treatment of generalized anxiety, phobias, panic disorders, and PTSD. In the domain of anxiety disorders, dynamic psychotherapy was first developed, behavior therapy staked out its initial claims, and, more recently, psychopharmacology has been effectively applied. These three therapeutic paradigms continue to dominate in the treatment of anxiety disorders, although to varying degrees adjunctive techniques for symptom control have been integrated into each of the approaches.

Although initially we sought to develop a report that fully integrated each therapeutic approach, it became clear that the treatment of anxiety disorders and the empirical work needed to understand the processes germane to efficacy had not progressed far enough to make this goal possible. As an alternative strategy, each contributor was asked to provide a review of a given therapeutic modality that focused on the therapeutic advantages of the particular treatment of anxiety disorders and also emphasized the limitations of the approach.

Each of the chapters attempts to distill the perspective of a clinical approach to anxiety disorders in a way that permits an understanding of how the therapeutic modality may be most useful. To clarify how special adjunctive procedures such as hypnosis, self-hypnosis, and biofeedback may be useful, a chapter illustrating the utilization of these techniques in the context of different therapeutic orientations was added. Finally, a chapter on the treatment of PTSD was included because of the increasing recognition of this syndrome in civilian as well as military life and the close relation it has to generalized anxiety disorder.

In considering each chapter, it is important to appreciate the often wide disparity that exists between the theory underlying a particular therapeutic approach and its implementation in actual practice. Although this gap permits many practitioners to eclectically integrate features of each treatment paradigm into clinical practice, the theoretical models underlying the treatment approaches often preclude integration.

Disparity Between Theory and Practice

Some of what appears to be the essential distinctiveness of the major therapeutic approaches is due to the tendency of clinicians to discuss their treatments in abstract terms. The nitty gritty of technique was generally taught by the system of preceptorship. Training in theory typically preceded practice. Although the high-level theoretical constructs rarely provided an adequate guide for therapeutic intervention, they apparently facilitated communication among colleagues of similar theoretical persuasions.

For example, psychodynamic theory may indicate that a particular problem area would require interpretation or confrontation to facilitate a resolution. The timing of the confrontation, however, depended on the strength of the therapeutic alliance, the stage of the patient's transference, and other factors that determined when the therapeutic intervention would be useful. Unfortunately, to use even these relatively low-level theory derived statements is a long way from providing guidance about what the therapist ought to do in a particular situation.

The behavior therapy literature may indicate that theory does indeed predict what should be done. The relationship between theory and practice, however, is more complex than is realized. In treating phobic symptoms, for example, different procedures that are theoretically contradictory have been shown to be effective (see Chapter 183). As London (1972) pointed out, behavior therapy is no more able than psychotherapy to show a close link between what is predicted by theory and what works in actual practice.

Psychopharmacology, having developed with little guidance from a comprehensive theory, has somewhat less difficulty in this regard. Other aspects of biologic psychiatry, however, share the difficulty in linking practice to theory.

Not only is theory not an adequate guide for much of the therapist's behavior in treatment, but at least equally problematic is that theory specifies what the observer should attend to as important factors in treatment. For the psychodynamically oriented therapist, intrapsychic conflicts are the central data of therapy. For the behavior therapist, the environmental contingencies are crucial. For the psychopharmacologist, response to the psychotropic agent is paramount. Fortunately, this is largely a caricature, because clinicians, regardless of the paradigm to which they are committed, come to recognize the importance of each of these therapeutic interventions.

Moving Toward Common Language and Integration

It is imperative that we continue to strive to develop an intellectual understanding of why a particular treatment is effective. Medicine is characterized by the attempt to understand how and why a therapy works. Although medicine has traditionally taken advantage of the curative powers of drugs before their mechanism of action has been elucidated, it has always sought to find a rational comprehensive explanation of how the treatment works.

It is increasingly clear that many of the practical maneuvers that are effective in a therapeutic context are given different names and different rationales in different therapeutic systems. One of the reasons why psychodynamic views have played such a crucial role in the development of modern psychiatry is that they provided a language to talk about many of the phenomena seen in treatment. This common language was shared by most psychiatrists and many psychologists and, as such, was useful above and beyond the theoretical framework from whence it came. Eventually one would hope that theory in psychiatry, at least as far as behavioral and psychodynamic approaches are concerned, will find a common language that is perhaps more theoretically neutral.

It would seem that the development of cognitive therapy (e.g., Beck et al. 1985) reflects a coming together of some aspects of behavioral and psychodynamic views. Thus, it allows for subjective experience to be phrased in terms that are acceptable to many behavior therapists and makes it possible for psychodynamic concepts to be translated into terms that are more adapted to modern research approaches. For a discussion of the similarities between psychodynamic and behavioral concepts, see Wachtel (1977) and Orne (1975). Perhaps it is too soon to expect a unified theory of psychiatry, but it is certainly not too soon to build bridges among the various paradigms.

Ultimately, psychiatry will need to go beyond the comparison of two or more overlapping treatment packages in outcome research. It is essential that we specify those factors a theory defines as effective therapeutic components and those that are considered to be unimportant and that we empirically document the distinctions. Only when these distinctions are accomplished will it be possible to develop meaningful outcome studies that can test the effectiveness of two or more truly different therapeutic approaches.

While these are goals for the future, at present we hope that the modest attempt at integration within this task force report will be useful to colleagues seeking to develop an effective therapeutic approach to anxiety disorders and willing to adopt a variety of metaphors in their psychiatric thinking.

Chapter 182

Psychoanalytic Psychotherapy

This chapter is organized on the following principles:

1. All anxiety states have a relevant psychodynamic context.
2. This context should be understood regardless of whether the patient is being treated with psychotherapy or other modalities.
3. The difficulty with ignoring the dynamic context is not the risk of symptom substitution but, rather, the danger of overlooking significant impairments in the patient's ego functions, especially his capacity to relate. These may be as much at the root of the patient's distress as the manifest anxiety symptoms.
4. Psychotherapy does have an important role in the treatment of the larger context of the disorder and can usefully be combined with other modalities directed specifically at the manifest symptoms.

These principles will be demonstrated through summaries of the relevant literature and through the use of clinical examples. The topical discussions will follow various DSM-III-R (American Psychiatric Association 1987) diagnostic categories. These will be taken up in a sequence that differs from that used in the manual in order to make the presentation of certain psychodynamic concepts more coherent. An overview will precede the topic headings in order to present a general summary of the psychoanalytic theory of anxiety.

Overview of the Psychoanalytic Theory of Anxiety[1]

Modern biological psychiatrists have unwittingly recapitulated an early trek of Freud's. In his first researches into the subject of anxiety, Freud (1894) was impressed with its physiology. Diarrhea, nausea, dizziness, agoraphobia, and panic are so frequently part of the anxious patient's presentation that the somatic elements seemed to outweigh the psychological ones. He deemed these anxiety illnesses actual neuroses to distinguish them from the disorders due to mental complexes, the psychoneuroses. The cause of the actual anxiety was believed to be the buildup of the end products of bodily, especially sexual, tensions. For various reasons these tensions did not result in mental activity but instead were transformed into bodily effects. This so-called transformation theory reigned for a long while.[2] Eventually its central idea was applied by Freud (1905) to the psychoneuroses as well:

> One of the most important results of psychoanalytic research is the discovery that neurotic anxiety arises out of the libido, that it is the product of a transformation of it, and that it is thus related to it in the same way as vinegar is to wine. (p. 224)

The transformation theory gave expression to a major trend in Freud's thoughts concerning affects. This trend held that anxiety should be likened to a primitive process, like one belonging to id. After all, it derived directly from libido and tended to overwhelm the individual and to evoke opposition to itself from conscious, rational aspects of the personality. However, Freud (1926) also expressed a very opposite trend in his thoughts, namely, that anxiety seemed to serve the purposes of conscious rationality via a guarding function. To be anxious was to be forewarned. This idea was expanded into the signal theory of anxiety. In this view, anxiety anticipated prototypic dangers, like castration, that might have to be faced if certain instinctual trends, like rivalry toward the father, were consciously expressed.

The signal theory did not replace but actually incorporated the transformation hypothesis as its basis. The primal danger upon which all other dangers were founded was the state of being overrun by instinctual needs.[3] This first danger was accompanied by automatic anxiety, a quality virtually identical to the anxiety of the transformation theory. In a word, this type of anxiety passively rose as an overflow product and occurred whenever the individual was overrun with instinctual needs. Any situation producing automatic anxiety was designated a traumatic state. The purpose of signal anxiety was to inform the ego in order to prevent this situation from happening. Birth was considered an example of the traumatic state because the infant was overwhelmed with needs that automatically generated anxiety. However, once the infant could associate mother with the alleviation of need, he could utilize her absence as the signal of an impending traumatic state. In a word, the signal of earliest need was given an essential connection to the dynamics of the tie between the mother and child.

Psychoanalysis since Freud has gradually expanded its interest in the interpersonal or "object relations" perspective. Ego psychology, object relations theory proper, and self psychology have all contributed to the building of a "two-person" psychology. This theoretical development has been accompanied or spurred by the work of developmental researchers, like Benjamin (1961, 1963), Bowlby (1960, 1973), Brazelton (1974), and Spitz (1950). In the process, they have also refined the understanding of anxiety.

The following is a summary of their views. They regard the very earliest manifestations of infant distress, like mass reflex responses, as protoanxiety because the infant probably experiences little mental content other than a quality of unpleasantness. These researchers generally agree that anxiety proper is a more complex psychobiologic state. For many, (cf. Bowlby 1960), it implies that early learning has occurred. In other words, the infant is remembering and anticipating the consequences of an environmental change, like the potential absence of mother. However, maternal comings and goings are the most clearly identifiable in a series of increasingly ambiguous variables that determine the quality of this first attachment. For instance, this quality partly comprises a mutual mother-child attunement that is illustrated in this description by Stern (1977) of a routine feeding:

> Until this point a normal feeding, not a social interaction was underway. Then a change began. While talking and looking at me the mother turned her head and gazed at the infant's face. He was gazing at the ceiling but out of the corner of his eye he saw her head turn toward him and turned to gaze back at her. This had happened before, but now he broke the rhythm and stopped sucking. He let go of the nipple and the suction around it broke as he eased into the faintest suggestion of a smile. The mother abruptly stopped talking and, as she watched his face begin to transform, her eyes opened a little wider and her eyebrows raised a bit. His eyes locked on to hers, and together they held

motionless for an instant. The infant did not return to sucking and his mother suddenly shattered it by saying, "Hey!" and simultaneously, the baby's eyes widened. His head tilted up and as his smile broadened, the nipple fell out of his mouth . . ."

Many concepts have been utilized in the attempt to clearly describe the qualitative aspects of early relatedness. These can be further categorized, first, as those that pertain to the description of the provisions needed from the mother by the infant, and second, as those that pertain to the description of how these parental provisions are utilized by the infant in the service of growth.[4]

From the category of parental provisions, two important concepts are holding and affirmation. Holding is a term coined by Winnicott (1956) to evoke the larger meanings of the image of an infant being comforted in its mother's arms. It implies the containment of distress provided by the devoted parent in her general dealings with her child. She effects a "holding environment." Defective holding leaves the child with an anxious vulnerability to feeling unprotected and empty. Affirmation (or mirroring) was addressed by Arieti (1978), Balint (1968), Winnicott (1956, 1974), and others, but has become most central to the work of Kohut (1971).[5] It refers to the reflection of approval by a parent that is necessary for the attainment of a cohesive sense of self. The lack of critical affirmation will leave an individual vulnerable to experiencing anxiety of self-fragmentation.

Three concepts that describe how the child utilizes what the parent provides are maturation, conflict resolution, and internalization. These are processes within the infant that "metabolize" parental holding and affirmation. The psychoanalytic idea of maturation (Hartmann 1950) is identical to that in other literatures. It refers to the unique ripening of genetically based potential by adequate environmental support. For example, adequate mirroring allows native talents to flourish.

Conflict resolution takes a different form with each of the two major modes of conflict. The first of these, conflicts of defense, are those most identified with psychoanalysis. For instance, primitive rage and the severe anxiety that attends its expression can both be avoided by a phobic defense. However, conflicts of ambivalence (Kris 1984) are not based on avoidance. These are the either-or (Kris 1977) crises that accompany developmental bridgeheads. For example, both toddler and adolescent must waver between their equally strong yearnings both for merged attachment and for separateness. Throughout life, their form and prominence may change, but both orders of desire will continue to be significant sources of satisfaction. Conflict exists not because one or the other order must be defended against, but rather because each in its very essence precludes the other.

Internalization refers to a series of processes (Hartmann 1950; Loewald 1980; Mahler 1967, 1975; Shopper 1978) by which the child gradually takes in the functions of holding and affirmation so that he can provide them for himself.

The relevance of these concepts for treatment will be illustrated in the section on the generalized anxiety disorder. They will then be referred to in subsequent discussions and clinical examples in the other sections.

Generalized Anxiety Disorder

The endpoint that is most frequently used to mark the point in time when the child is capable of providing himself with holding and affirmation is the attainment of a solid inner comfort or relative freedom from anxiety. This has been termed libidinal object constancy (Fraiberg 1969; Mahler 1967). A critical measure of this capacity is the child's ability to feel sustained as though by his mother's loving presence even when she is gone. One necessary precondition is the maturation of the child's "evocative memory" (cf. Adler 1985; Adler and Buie 1979). This is the cognitive ability to call up representations of absent objects. However, to have libidinal constancy, the child must in addition be able to evoke not only the mother's image but also her love. Lastly, the child must be able to hold onto this loving presence even in the face of feeling deprived and enraged (cf. Kernberg 1975; Winnicott 1954).

Two consequences follow from unsatisfactory relations to parents in earliest life. First, the child lacks a real-life template from which to form an inner loving presence. In addition, chronic deprivation makes him feel enraged at his parents. When he invokes their already compromised images in times of need, he feels impulses to destroy them. As a result of this dilemma, the child is left with chronic emptiness and anxiety bordering on dread. The child splits his inner views of self and others into good and bad; he keeps the two categories of experience completely separate from each other so that rage-contaminated images will not obliterate the small pocket of good ones. This is the unconscious, defensive process labelled "splitting" (Adler 1985; Isenstadt 1980; Kernberg 1975).

The literature of child psychoanalysis has provided many case reports of deficient object constancy and its treatment. For instance, Bornstein (1949) reported her work with Frankie, a 5½-year-old boy. Although the presenting symptom was his school phobia, he suffered from pronounced chronic anxiety for several years prior to its occurrence. In her childhood, Frankie's mother had felt unloved by her mother who she felt showed preference for her brother. The arrival of Frankie made manifest how mother had identified with her inner image of the unloving grandmother. She unwittingly treated Frankie much like she felt the grandmother had treated her. Things worsened greatly with the birth of Frankie's sister:

> Upon the mother's return from the hospital he displayed marked anxiety. He grew more ill tempered toward his mother . . . he accepted neither medicine nor food from her. Nevertheless he insisted tyrannically on her presence at all times and had outbursts of wild aggression if she did not adhere meticulously to his demands.

Thus, the normative trauma, the birth of sister Mary, added its inevitable potential for insult to the injury of a deficient sense of mother's love.

Fleming (1975) compiled a series of cases involving deficient object constancy in adults. Many of these patients had experienced the death of a parent. Much of the literature on the treatment of borderline personality disorder (Adler 1985; Isenstadt 1980) also deals with this issue. The following clinical example will convey a sense of the technique appropriate to treating chronic anxiety due to deficient object constancy.

> Ms. P, a 35-year-old counselor for the homeless, was hospitalized for suicidal feelings at the beginning of a second marriage. Her first husband had died when her children were quite young. Evaluation revealed that in addition to depressive symptoms, the patient suffered chronic anxiety that would now be classified as a generalized anxiety disorder. She was restless and startled easily. She complained of sweaty palms, lightheadedness, and frequent stomach aches. She always felt on edge.
>
> Her childhood had been very unhappy. She had been adopted at birth by a mother she experienced as quite cold and aloof. A repeated memory was of being angrily confronted by her mother and responding by visually "fading" her image from view. During the treatment, the patient would experience this visual dissociation (a temporal lobe epilepsy workup had been negative) whenever she was severely disappointed in or enraged at her therapist.

The therapeutic work involved a gradual approach to the root of her difficulties. First among these was her core sense of being unloved. Second was the attendant feeling that her rage was cause and not effect of her abiding sense of being abandoned by others. Interpretation was only minimally useful at the very beginning of the treatment. Concrete signs of the therapist's reliable interest were the major instruments of change. Benzodiazepines administered during crises were one of these. Their utility as transitional objects may have equaled their effectiveness as medications (Group for the Advancement of Psychiatry 1975). The emphasis here is not on the importance of specific interventions, but rather on the centrality of deficient object constancy as the source of symptoms and the target of psychotherapy.

The capacity to bear anxiety is in itself a major developmental achievement that both parallels and overlaps the achievement of object constancy. Failure to acquire this ability is another risk factor for generalized anxiety. Zetzel (1949) studied traumatic neuroses in World War II. She noted that the most severe reactions occurred in individuals who had had difficulty bearing anxiety in their earlier years. They literally avoided the experience of being afraid because they intuited in themselves an inability to contain anxiety once it got started. They tended to experience automatic rather than signal anxiety. Schur (1958, 1971) noted that the tolerance for anxiety involved 1) desomatization, i.e., being limited in its tendency to produce a radiation of bodily symptoms, and 2) the achievement of the dominance of secondary over primary process thinking. The latter factor refers to the intrinsic tendency of primary process, the mode of wish, fantasy, and dream elaboration, to represent potential consequences of inner drives as imminent and inevitable. Secondary, or rational, process introduces reality testing that removes the sense of inevitability. Yorke and Wiseberg (1976) offer a similar view. Other authors note that the critical role early object relations play in acquiring these processes affect tolerance functions. Tolpin (1971), for instance, elaborates on the way in which a young child and its mother mutually regulate the buildup and dissipation of anxiety. If this interaction is favorable, the child attains the ability to use anxiety as a signal.

With an analogous outlook, Isenstadt (1980) elegantly presented his work concerning a 7½-year-old boy with deficient anxiety tolerance. The boy had been diagnosed as hyperactive as a child. Whatever the organic contribution may have been, interactional factors also played an important part in the child's condition. The mother felt that the child was too much for her and withdrew from helping him in his recurrent frenzies. The treatment revealed that all feeling and fantasy was experienced in a primary process mode and overwhelmed him with anxiety. For example, consider this description of the play that dominated many early sessions:

> Billy would be in his boat and would be unsuspecting and helpless as he sailed toward some unforeseen catastrophe: an onrushing typhoon, an approaching waterfall, a surfacing whale. At home port I would either give a warning signal so that Billy could avoid danger, or if Billy was unable to make his own way safely back to port, I would send out a rescue boat to save him.

As Isenstadt (1980) reliably intervened with a variety of maneuvers all directed toward preventing Billy from becoming overwhelmed, Billy gradually formed a protective identification.

Here is a similar presentation in an adult:

> Mr. N. was a 40-year-old lawyer who complained of severe, chronic anxiety. He was constantly jittery, experienced muscle cramps, and had daily gastrointestinal upsets. He was preoccupied with fears of intruders at home. He had to maintain a constant vigilance.

He was also very sensitive to slights. Comments from partners about his written reports, even when intended as mild and constructive, were experienced as crushing blows. Early in the treatment he revealed his marked preoccupation with retaliating for the innumerable slights he experienced in everyday life. However the moment he entertained an angry fantasy, he was convinced that the object of his anger would strike first. This conviction overrode his otherwise sound sense of reality.

In childhood, the patient had experienced his mother as a devastating presence. She had attacked him whenever he had jeopardized her own fragile sense of self. The chief injury he had afflicted on her was growing up and leaving instead of remaining in the tightly confined orbit she needed him to occupy for maintenance of her self esteem.

The patient presented material that amply corroborated Tolpin's (1971) views. He felt that his anger was met by his mother with terrifying enactments. She had threatened and beaten him. The result was a partial arrest of his ability to internalize self-holding, to utilize secondary process, and to contain and tolerate anxiety. The interventions that proved helpful resembled those utilized in treatment of deficient object constancy. First, the therapist demonstrated a consistent willingness and ability to help the patient before his anxiety reached unbearable proportions. At times all that was required was mentioning that the therapist understood how flooded and pained the patient was. These frequent exchanges gradually convinced the patient that the angry and provocative feelings he experienced would not only not be met in kind but also could be tempered by the therapist's understanding. Eventually, the patient was able to modulate his anxiety so that he could elaborate on his fantasies without becoming flooded. He was able to work through a variety of conflicts at the basis of his impoverished sense of self.

Agoraphobia With or Without Panic Attacks

In the general literature, a distinction is made between panic and agoraphobia. Klein (1981), Sheehan (1982), and others regard panic attacks as a primary, biologically determined illness. Agoraphobia is viewed as a name given to the expectable consequences of experiencing paroxysms of overwhelming anxiety. First, the sufferer begins to feel anticipatory anxiety in all situations that even remotely relate to those in which the original panic episodes occurred. Then, he learns to avoid situations to curb both the anticipatory anxiety and the panic. The psychoanalytic literature does not hold to these sharp distinctions. Various dynamic theories have regarded both phases of the illness as having primary relevance.

In the classical psychoanalytic viewpoint (Abraham 1913; Fenichel 1945), the agoraphobia was an integral feature of the illness. The underlying defense conflict was usually depicted as a clash between a desire for and prohibition of unfettered sexuality. The compromise formation became physical confinement. The panic, then, represented an ego state close to automatic anxiety. It was engendered by ignoring of the prohibition and the resultant breaking through of repressed impulses. Deutsch (1965) added some speculations concerning the phobic companion who is so often the mother or a substitute for her. Deutsch felt that uncommonly hostile relations existed between mother and daughter prior to the onset of the illness. Oedipal rivalry further augmented rage that had accumulated in the preoedipal years. As a result, the daughter morbidly feared being out because to feel sexual was inevitably to feel unbearably murderous toward her major rival. Staying close to the mother reactively defended against both the sexual and aggressive wishes.

The classical theory appreciated the content of the symptoms but did not adequately address the reasons for their form. As noted in the overview, ego psychology, object relations theory, and self psychology have suggested plausible reasons. Most contemporary analytic studies of panic and agoraphobia center not just on the symptom complex but on the ways in which that complex adumbrates a serious difficulty in the patient's pattern of relationships.[6] The issue then becomes what the most helpful clinical definition of the illness is for a given patient. Even when a history of compromised object relations exists, many panic-susceptible patients will deny its significance and accept only symptomatic treatment. In these instances, medication and symptom-directed behavioral paradigms are the treatment of choice. However, in the current psychiatric climate, the physician must cautiously avoid conspiring with the patient to limit the exploration and treatment to medical modalities alone.[7] It is often a unique feature of the anxiety-prone patient's character that he will feel legitimized to complain only of the manifest symptoms. Careful interviewing can help the patient make the more serious depth of his problem clearer, especially after the panic episodes have been satisfactorily controlled with medications. The following case will illustrate the discussion:

> Mr. G. was a 26-year-old troubleshooter for an engineering firm when he presented to the psychiatrist with the symptoms of severe panic attacks and agoraphobia. The first had occurred after smoking pot in college. The patient had always been heavily into drugs. However, following the incident, he avoided them completely out of dread of re-experiencing the panic. Not until many years later, when he had met the woman he eventually lived with, did he experience another panic episode. At this point he followed a familiar progression from more frequent attacks to severe anticipatory anxiety. He began to avoid many places, but especially movies, restaurants, and planes.
>
> In eliciting the history, the therapist noted that in addition to the severe symptoms, the patient demonstrated a more generalized pattern of "darting" to and from relationships with women. He showed a striking inability to describe what made him either stay or go. He also avoided many opportunities for career advancement, largely out of a very deficient belief in his self worth.

The first episode was probably related to the pharmacologic effects of the marijuana. However, his tie to a woman was also a contributing precipitant. The second occurrence was more clearly related in its timing to the meeting of another woman with whom he eventually lived. Although the precipitants of any one episode could not be clearly determined, the history revealed a greater context to his distress, namely, difficulties with intimacy.

In the case of Mr. G., long-standing difficulties in achieving stable intimacy were noted by both patient and therapist. The following early history was pertinent:

> Mr. G. had been born into a family with enduring money troubles. The major focus of the patient's meager descriptions of his life was his mother. She was a nervous, over-sensitive person. She was volatile in her moods. In her frequent rages, she hurled abusive criticism at the patient which bordered on the irrational. She also had obsessional concerns about cleanliness that at times lapsed into paranoid suspicions of being contaminated.
>
> The most serious consequence of this early experience was that, although he presented himself to the world with humor and confidence, he had a deeper, often unconscious sense of himself as never able to do anything right. For most of the early sessions of his treatment, he could not trace his abiding self representation to its origins. It was as though it were too painful to emotionally confirm for himself or his therapist the destructive impact that mother had had on him. However, the message was effectively delivered by indirect means. He faithfully brought in the voluminous one way correspondence his mother addressed to him. Every letter was a bitter invective that decried

his worth, his loyalty, his emotional stability, and his chances of ever succeeding in the world.

Mr. G.'s damaged self-representation was discovered to be very relevant to his panic episodes. As mentioned earlier, they occurred in the context of a developing relationship. Therapeutic exploration uncovered the sense of jeopardy Mr. G. felt whenever he had to function dependably in the presence of his girl friend. His self-esteem was on the line. He needed to constantly appear all powerful in her eyes in order to prevent any faltering in her admiration of him. Whenever his actions fell short of his omnipotent ideals, he experienced a loss of self that bordered on fragmentation. The visible result was panic. The complementary determinant of this fragmentation was a latent dependency. The quest for an absolute autonomy was in part a defense against a much more repressed longing for the woman's unquestioning love and the rage that ensued when this longing was not met. He believed that this kind of love alone could heal the damage done to his core self during childhood.

The vignette illustrates the gist of most contemporary analytic reports of panic anxiety. Frequent reference has been given to the etiologic importance of vulnerability to self-fragmentation caused by failures of early holding and affirmation.[8] Weiss (1964), Rhead (1969), and Frances and Dunn (1975) all alluded to this vulnerability even though they postulated varying explanations of its causes. Diamond (1985) directly cites self-fragmentation as the central pathology in panic, as do Stolorow and Lachmann (1980). These latter authors have described a case of a woman whose mother was "invasive, sadistically controlling and binding." The patient suffered agoraphobic symptoms. In her analysis, she related her symptoms to fears of being "trapped in the spotlight." These fears in turn were

traced to repeated early traumata in which her independent grandiose-exhibitionistic strivings and her actual accomplishments were consistently met with complete unresponsiveness, undermining belittlement, or relentless criticism, thereby discouraging intrapsychic separation and strengthening the masochistic, symbiotic like bond (p. 133).

In summary, this emphasis on developmental trauma in the areas of self-cohesion and object constancy should inform therapeutic technique, regardless of what combination of interventions is ultimately selected (e.g., medication, behavior therapy, hypnosis, or psychotherapy). The therapist should pursue an evaluation of the enduring personality weaknesses, such as emptiness and impoverished self-esteem, that underlie the symptoms. The therapist must also realize that these deficits are complemented by equally fixed patterns of relating. The patient will demonstrate character traits that latently express dependency on others for variable combinations of affirmation, protection, love, and guidance.

The therapist faces major obstacles in trying to see into the underlying deficits. The panic patient (like the phobic patient) is unusually resistant to open-ended exploration of his emotions. This resistance serves to block any arousal of latent, dependent transferences. In a word, the transferences to affirming or protecting others would threaten a traumatic state if they were to surface. For example, Mr. G. adamantly avoided any awareness of his need of and vulnerability to women because of the repeated devastation he had experienced from his mother. He, like all other panic patients, feared most an even greater fear, to be in a self-fragmenting terror. The major cost of his vigilance against this danger was a skittish manner of relating. He could not bear to receive any serious feedback from his girl friend whether it was delivered in words or manner. For this reason, initially, he could not report the content of any arguments in his sessions. He would jokingly offer the refrain: "Women!"

The presence of these resistances explains what is most syntonic for the patient, namely, the need to be cohesive and self-reliant under any circumstances. Even when an outsider observes that the patient is enmeshed with the parents, the patient himself will be consciously aware only of the intense struggle to be independent of their influence. This conscious counterdependence is responsible for a constant feature of panic patients, their dread that an attack will occur in public.[9] They cannot bear the shame that would result. In dynamic terms, this shame is a projection of their own humiliating regard for their latent neediness and rage.

Because of the patient's conscious, defensive investments, the therapist will fare poorly if he attempts to interpret the central need for reparative objects prematurely. A better approach is to empathize with the patient's intense self-reliance and his self-critical regard of dependency. If enough of this resistance can be worked through, the patient can confront his central vulnerability.

A number of particular measures may ease the way. Several of these can be illustrated from Mr. G.'s treatment. First, the therapist's use of medications (and other symptom-directed measures) conveyed the therapist's readiness to uncritically accept and assist the patient in his state of helplessness. Second, the therapist worked with Mr. G.'s denial of his mother's effect on him. The therapist asked to keep all letters sent by the mother to counter the patient's tendency to rip them up without reading them. When he felt the patient was in better control of himself, he began to take them out of his drawer and read them aloud. The patient was able to admit the annihilating effect the words tended to have on his self-esteem. The therapist helped the patient to postulate reasons the mother might react like she did in order to help him understand her criticism and not personalize it. Third, the therapist linked current experiences to childhood ones in order to develop the patient's awareness of his latent needs. Mr. G. began to understand that behind his bemused deprecation of his girl-friend lay a fear of her potential motherliness that, if invested in, could either validate or destroy his sense of self.

Fourth, careful attention was paid to the transference. From the very beginnings of any psychotherapy, the patient is keenly aware of the therapist's responses to him. Even benign suggestions that the patient confront his symptoms may augment the patient's shame and therefore mistrust of the therapist. Similarly, a forced supportive interest will upset the patient's investment in his self-reliance and may paradoxically increase his resistance. This occurred with Mr. G., who was initially quite threatened by too much attention on his distress. Eventually, the "core" conflict may be approached in the transference. Mr. G., for instance, became most dependent on the therapist's responses for his sense of self. The medium of this mirroring was not the therapist's actual personal responses to the patient. Instead, the economy of exchange was a combination of explanation, interpretation, and a general attitude of helpfulness. Consider the following vignette from the case of Mr. G:

> In the height of his transference vulnerability, Mr. G. was dating another woman. He angrily refused to attend a recreational event with her and her father. The therapist first clarified the fact that behind Mr. G.'s annoyance at her "ridiculous" demands for his participation lay the fear of how well he would meet them. He also feared her father's opinion of him. This anxiety represented a displacement of his intense concerns for his therapist's regard of him at this time. Part of the working through was achieved by means of the therapist helping Mr. G. to raise all of the potential blunders he could make during the outing. He more realistically was able to try them on for size. He was then able to understand further how impossible were the demands he placed on himself in order to fend off any possibility of being criticized by the therapist.

The discussion has so far focused on the etiologic importance of developmental arrests in this class of anxious patients. However, it should be made clear that the classical view, namely, the theory of neurosis based on drive conflict, is also quite essential to appreciating how the vulnerability to loss of cohesion in the self-organization may arise (cf. Horowitz and Zilberg 1983). The following example illustrates this.

> Ms. L., a 22-year-old student, experienced the onset of panic attacks several months after moving away from home to an apartment with a female roommate. She casually mentioned that the roommate was more socially active than she. The patient had attended parochial school. Her mother had a major investment in religion and had always been exceptionally close to her daughter. Although the parents' marriage seemed superficially sound, the patient felt that the mother bore more allegiance to her than to her husband. Mother had sustained major disappointments from her own father. As a result, the patient had never heard overt warnings about men but was aware that the mother was unusually preoccupied with the possibility of strange men abusing her. Her overprotection had a damaging effect on the patient's ability to feel comfortable as an adolescent. She excused herself from most of the normal activities of her peer group. College followed a similar pattern. Casual dates with men seldom led to further contact. The patient could openly admit her fear and confusion regarding what she would do if things became sexual.

For Ms. L., a number of factors conspired to foster her enmeshment with her mother. First, the mother's own mother had deprecated the maternal grandfather. Mother had been coopted into this devaluing stance toward him. She in turn subtly enjoined the patient to side with her against her husband. Thus, for at least two generations the women of this family had attained faulty oedipal resolutions that separated them from men and bound them to women. Ms. L.'s move to the apartment represented a genuine wish to be free of the enmeshment but confronted her with the dread of doing so. Years of incorporating the mother's view of men led to a primary distrust and inhibition of her sexuality. The cost of repression was not just the development of neurotic conflict but also an arrest in her individuation and attainment of separateness. To be sexual was to be not just murderous toward mother but dangerously apart from her. Moreover, she feared that no sexual tie to a man could adequately replace the "symbiotic" mother she still needed.

Medication was successfully used to ameliorate entry into panic states. However, even without the symptoms, the patient returned to her constricted mode of living and her considerable unhappiness with her life was barely veiled. She seemed to shun any exploration of her larger difficulties for reasons similar to those of Mr. G. With pride, she invested in the notion that she was not tied to mother in any inordinate way, i.e., that she was not prone to helplessness. Acknowledgement on the therapist's part of this invested self-reliance helped the patient to admit to the severe distress the was in. The therapist could then broach and clarify the several conflicts at issue.

Simple Phobia

Although DSM-III separates panic spectrum from simple phobia, the analytic literature does not. Both types of anxiety disorders often involve similar underlying conflicts and personality deformations. If a phobic symptom can be treated in isolation by hypnotherapy and behavioral techniques, it should be. The following discussion will briefly review phobia as a discrete symptom and will then illustrate instances in which phobia signals a broad personality disturbance requiring psychotherapy in addition to or instead of symptom-oriented treatment.

The classical psychoanalytic view of simple phobia is outlined in the case of little Hans (Freud 1909). At age 4¾, he began to fear being bitten by a horse. At that time, Hans was noted to have been in the midst of oedipal conflict. Freud suggested that the presenting symptom represented the displacement of a castration threat from father onto horse. Other conflicts were also represented by the fear. For instance, the biting was also a projection of Hans' passive homosexual wishes.[10] The Wolf-Man's (Freud 1918) symptoms rested on similar dynamics. Authors since Freud have offered case reports of phobias whose manifest fears have been of Santa Claus (Settlage 1971), dogs (Schnurmann 1949), spiders (Sperling 1982), bamboo (Renik 1978), and many other objects (Spitzer 1981). The underlying conflicts have been noted to involve, in addition to oedipal contents, symbiotic closeness (Lewin 1952; Sperling 1982), sexual differences (Sperling 1982), and rage (Harley 1971).

While one aspect of the literature has dealt with the content of phobias, another aspect has addressed the question of why phobia rather than another form of symptom comes to represent a given conflict (Arieti 1978; Khan 1974; Wangh 1967). Consider the following case:

> Ms. C. was a 29 year old vertebrate zoologist whose counterphobic style belied her chronic fearfulness and vulnerability to phobias. Her need to project herself as dauntless led her to attempt research projects which had a high likelihood of provoking her fears. On one occasion, the experiments called for decapitation of a sample of mice. She felt compelled to volunteer for the task. As soon as she began it, she felt nauseous and faint.
>
> The patient's mother was a very nervous, overprotective woman who saw potential danger everywhere. The patient dreaded any contamination by mother's world view because of its paralyzing effects on everyday functioning. Despite the patient's efforts to separate herself from mother, both women eventually shared certain phobias, like the dread of bodily injury. However, in recounting the lab incident, Ms. C. denied that the mice had elicited her own concerns for bodily intactness and instead emphasized her humiliation at having become overwhelmed. She nodded with relief when her therapist said that her greatest fear was of being overtaken by fear.

First, the patient with simple phobia shared with the panic patient a dread of being overwhelmed. The example again emphasizes how the building of a therapeutic alliance depends on several factors. The patient learns that the therapist accepts and understands this basic dread. In addition, the therapist conveys to the patient that her expectations of becoming totally anxiety free must be modified.

Second, the fear of fear derives from a problematic identification with a troubled parent. In the case of Ms. C., it was noted that her mother caused her to feel that little was safe or possible. She warded off this early identification with a later one that mirrored her father. His style involved throwing caution to the wind. Therefore, as has been generally observed in phobic patients (Schur 1971), Ms. C. suffered from a conflict of identifications (a species of ambivalence conflict). This implies that the phobia is linked not simply to instinctually derived content, like anger or bodily injury, but also to a clash of personality modes with which to deal with these instinctual concerns.

Another case example will help to clarify this concept and its usefulness for treatment.

> Ms. B., a 45 year old systems analyst, had a number of phobias among which was a fear of elevators. She had a difficult early background. Most problematic was her relation to her mother. She was a depressed woman who had been abandoned in her own childhood

by the grandmother. Mother's suffering from this injury manifested itself in her habit of frequently leaving Ms. B. in the lurch. For example, Ms. B. would be left precipitously in charge of a younger sibling when she herself was much too young to cope. At another time, the mother was out of the house when the patient was knocked down by a car. The only sense of protection and safety she ever experienced was with her father. He was a very successful but egotistical businessman who demonstrated his love by showing off his power. At the same time he was unable to tolerate any real closeness to her. In adulthood, the patient began to notice that intimacy with friends or lovers always provoked her fears and that being alone confronted her with painful emptiness. The beginning of therapy occasioned an outbreak of the elevator phobia. Using free association, in connection with the symptom, she began to feel empty and then immediately experienced a compulsion to jump down the shaft. The therapist commented that the current precipitant of the phobia was her doubt as to whether he would care enough to protect her from being overwhelmed in her life. She became tearful, but quickly 'sealed over.' In subsequent sessions, she began to show her more public self. This part of her identity exuded unshakeable confidence which could be harnessed to aggressive pursuit of her corporation's goals.

In sum, the phobia represented a repetition in the transference of the exposure to overpowering and abusive childhood situations because of the mother's helpless indifference. The panic, emptiness, and suicidal thoughts were not only a reaction to, but an identification with, this mother. The vulnerability that accompanied this identification was almost unbearable. She could feel intact only insofar as the therapist-parent could effectively respond to her. To defend against this state of liability, she embraced a counterphobic identification with father, whom she idealized as being omnipotent. She was caught with a choice between extremes.

The third point to be made is that the resolution of this conflict of identifications hinges on the capacity to bear affect. Although the phobias highlight anxiety as the central problem, it is the by-product of a more fundamental difficulty, namely, intolerance of affects relevant to earliest attachments (cf. Russell, to be published). For example, Ms. B. at first could not get close to men because even normal expectations, like getting together on weekends, could become linked to dangerous unconscious desire, such as a wish for their absolute presence in order to feel safe. The signal of her getting too near these desires was an outbreak of phobic symptoms. The resolution involved fleeing into a denial of need by means of her counterdependent identification. The therapist often mistakes this as evidence that the patient is withholding feelings. This pattern was confronted repeatedly. The goal was not simply insight. More vital at this stage was the patient's gradual ability to acknowledge and experience her needs. The following vignette provides an illustration of how this is achieved in treatment.

Ms. B. reacted to news of her therapist's vacation by missing the next two appointments. Her phobias worsened. She did not consciously connect these events. Instead, she was preoccupied with a profound sense of guilt over her own absences. She felt she had been 'bad' and irresponsible. The therapist pointed out to her that the recriminations had been turned against herself for two reasons. First, she wanted to avoid her rage at yet another parent who left her in the lurch. Second, and even more importantly, she wanted to deny what that rage implied, namely her intense need of the therapist's consistency in order to experience feeling safe and loved (i.e., to establish object constancy). She began to realize that she mistook feeling entitled to knowing what she wanted as being entitled in the more perjorative sense. As Kris (1976) has noted, in fearing that she wanted too much, she inevitably settled for too little. In this instance she was finally able to ask the therapist to write her once during the vacation so that she would not feel so vulnerable.

Fourth, all patients in these categories suffer a tendency to perceive danger, stemming from within and without, as imminent. As stated earlier, this sense of imminence is connected to the primary process mode of thinking in which the phobic patient is fixed. They need to develop a means to contain anxiety by regarding most consequences as possible but unlikely.

Lastly, as was stressed in the discussion on panic disorder, there is a definite role for behaviorally oriented techniques even when the symptom is not being treated in isolation. The patient will undoubtedly feel even more satisfied if in addition to improvements in underlying personality, he achieves a resolution of the phobic symptoms. There is a considerable literature on combined approaches (Cohen 1980; Friedman 1972; Goismian 1983; Klein and Rabkin 1981; Marks 1966; Rhodes 1974).

Social Phobia

A paradigmatic social phobia is illustrated in the *DSM-III Case Book* (Spitzer et al. 1981). The patient, "the silent student" (p. 258), is unable to participate in her law school class discussions. She is afraid that anything she says will be viewed as "dumb." Several dynamic hypotheses could be generated to explain this difficulty. However, as an isolated symptom, her fear could be most expediently treated by behavior therapy, hypnosis, or medication (cf. other contributions of this manual).

The psychoanalytic literature does not deal with social phobia in isolation (Salzman 1968). It is usually listed as part of a constellation of presenting features that point to a particular character assessment. The meaning of the phobia derives from the nature of the assessment. Two case examples will be provided to demonstrate instances in which social phobia is best regarded as part of a larger disorder requiring psychotherapy. The two examples will illustrate opposite ends of the developmental spectrum.

Mr. E. was a 32 year old single advertising professional who sought consultation for work difficulties. He was ambivalent about entering psychotherapy but was afraid to ignore the advice of his employer who doubted he could continue to hold the job unless he sought help. He said that his employer complained of his lack of social sensitivity. For instance, after being on the job for only several weeks, he took a lamp from a conference room in order to furnish his office. He did not see what was wrong with that. His own complaints revolved around his extreme anxiety. He felt paralyzed in group settings and greatly feared appearing inept or unmanly. As a result he was either inordinately quiet or brashly intrusive.

The patient described a painful early life. His mother and her sisters had been devaluing and critical of the patient. His father was a barely successful man who covered his frequently shaken pride with bravado. The father was also prone to taking ethical shortcuts in his business dealings. The patient sensed that the father was not so much dishonest as overly hungry for a success which would finally alleviate his shame at not having achieved more. The patient identified with this hunger and noted that he himself was often being accused of being slippery. He noted that two previous therapists had gotten angry at him for not paying the bill and he argued for one reason or another that he did not have to.

The therapist regarded the social phobia as part of broader evidence indicating a fairly severe narcissistic character disturbance. The central underlying issue was the patient's need for special recognition. The inhibition in groups was based upon a latent wish to exhibit himself in a grandiose way in order to capture all the attention in the room. All that was conscious was the defensively elaborated fear of appearing inadequate. The taking of the lamp was an unconscious retaliation aimed at a supervisor who had wounded Mr. E. by criticizing him. The action "said" that he had a right to seize what was not freely given, namely the kind of esteem he needed.

The key to the working through of the social phobia was the understanding of a dream in the first year of the therapy. It featured Mr. E.'s coming late to a screen test and thus being disqualified. The inhibition in the dream paralleled his reluctance in group settings. Associations led directly to a fantasy of not only wishing but also expecting to be recognized as a great star.

Like Mr. G., Mr. E. also defended against the embarrassing recognition of his needs from others. However, the emphasis for Mr. E. was more on the content of his wishes. In other words, he did not want to find himself in situations where his grandiose desires could condition his falling into empty despair if they were not met. For Mr. G., there was more investment in an intermediate defensive measure. The exposure of just the idea that he was helpless in the face of his need for others, regardless of the content of that need, would inevitably occasion the helplessness and injury. This differentiation between the ego states of the panic-prone and the social-phobia-prone patient has general validity.

Furthermore, this case example points to the reason why psychodynamic assessment is a critical part of the initial evaluation in social phobia. In this instance, the presenting complaint was not a symptom that could be taken in isolation like that of the silent student. Instead, it was the sign of a diffuse personality disturbance. The core issue was the patient's difficulty experiencing adequate self-valuation in everyday life. Psychotherapy in this instance proved to be of considerable benefit by helping the patient to recognize his basic lack of confidence, his need for exaggerated reparative responses from others, and his poorly contained vengeance when these responses were not forthcoming. Simple behavioral paradigms could not encompass the relevant center of the difficulty.[11]

The second case illustrates a social phobia based on neurotic conflict:

> Mr. Z. was a 19 year old college student who avoided parties and mixers. He was not afraid to talk to a girl, but he did dread the possibility of her making any kind of overture to him. Over the course of several sessions he expanded the picture of the most dreaded outcome. If he were to be put in a sexual situation, he would instantly have an erection. He had always been well accepted in peer groups and was not naive about sex. Actually, he was subliminally aware of his attractiveness and the fact that he was sought after by campus women. The problem found its source in his early history. The patient was the youngest child and only son of his family. His father had died when he was very young and he became the adored object of his mother and sisters.

Thus the phobia embodied two major conflicts. The first, a conflict of defense, was oedipally based. Unconsciously, as evidenced in dreams and fantasies, he was invested in his manliness and envisioned his erect state as devastatingly superior to that of all his friends who by displacement were "the father." The embarrassment hid his hubris. Second, a conflict of ambivalence existed because the early loss had led to a fear of manhood and its vulnerability and had increased his investment in being mother's protected "baby." This liability made it difficult for him to resolve a major adolescent ambivalence: did he want to be a boy or a man (cf. Kris 1984)? The therapy was helpful in removing obstacles to his development and his symptoms gave way to a phase of freer exploration of his sexuality.

Summary

The role of psychoanalytic psychotherapy in treatment of the anxiety disorders has been outlined. The major points have been as follows:

1. The DSM-III views anxiety states as symptom disorders. However, they occur in a relevant psychodynamic context. Case illustrations have emphasized the point that the anxious patient often suffers from concomitant personality difficulties.
2. Disturbances in interpersonal relations are both cause and effect of the more serious anxiety states. In these instances, symptomatic treatment may successfully eliminate panic or phobia, but leave untouched a compromised capacity for intimacy.
3. The key to treating the larger context of anxiety states is an understanding of how certain parental provisions, like holding and affirmation, are essential for the basic maturation and integration of a child's ability to feel loved, protected, and soothed.
4. The later capacity to bear and resolve the anxiety of neurotic conflict is shaped by these earlier experiences.
5. The formulations that have been given are those most likely to help the clinician generate helpful, integrated interventions.

Notes

[1] For a more complete theoretical survey, cf. Compton (1972a, 1972b, 1980) and Nemiah (1981, 1984).

[2] Much psychoanalytic debate has been conducted over the validity of the concept of actual neurosis (Blau 1952; Brenner 1953; Gediman 1984; Rangell 1955).

[3] In the classical theory, there is a developmental hierarchy of dangers that are heralded by signal anxiety. The mentioned implosion of instincts is first and is followed by loss of the object (e.g., mother), loss of the object's love, castration, and disapproval by the superego.

[4] For the sake of clarity, the present discussion has been limited to a sketch of a very complicated mass of ideas. A certain amount of injustice is done to important subtleties. The citations of Balint, Flemming, Fraiberg, Kahn, Kohut, Russell, and Winnicott included in the bibliography contain fuller explanations.

[5] For conciseness, the separate mirroring and idealizing functions described by Kohut are both being referred to with the one term, affirmation.

[6] The behavioral literature (Thorpe and Burns 1983a) also acknowledges this larger view of the panic spectrum.

[7] Cf. Cooper's (1985) effort to describe a balanced orientation.

[8] Subtle and important differences exist in the orientation of all the authors quoted here. They represent viewpoints as far from each other as classical theory is to self psychology. However, consideration of these distinctions would serve to diffuse the present discussion.

[9] This feature of the syndrome has eluded explanation by any of the behavioral or medical paradigms.

[10] Unconscious fantasies determine the following equations: to be bitten = to be eaten = to be loved.

[11] Modern behaviorism and psychoanalysis may fruitfully converge in the area of

cognitive learning. This latter branch of behaviorism could well offer a hypothesis of underlying trait, e.g., notions of self-deficit, that might proscribe a more comprehensive treatment plan. Research comparing more structured dynamic to cognitive approaches would greatly refine our ability to prescribe treatment.

Chapter 183

Behavior Therapy

It was in the late 1950s that behavior therapy emerged as a major approach to the assessment and treatment of a broad spectrum of clinical disorders. In its early stages of development, behavior therapy was defined as the application of modern learning theory to the treatment of clinical problems. The phrase "modern learning theory" then referred to the principles and procedures of classical and operant conditioning. Behavior therapy was seen as the logical extension of behaviorism to complex forms of human activities. In little more than the two decades since its inception, behavior therapy has undergone significant changes in both nature and scope. This rapid change and growth is one of the striking features of behavior therapy, which has been responsive to advances in experimental psychology and innovations in clinical practice. It has grown increasingly more complex and sophisticated. As a result, behavior therapy can no longer be simply defined as the clinical application of classical and operant conditioning theory.

Taking a broad view, the various approaches in contemporary behavior therapy include 1) applied behavior analysis, 2) a neobehavioristic mediational stimulus-response model, and 3) cognitive social learning theory. Basically, these approaches differ in the degrees to which they use cognitive concepts and procedures. At one end of this continuum is applied behavior analysis, which focuses exclusively on observable behavior and rejects all cognitive mediating processes. At the other end is a social learning approach that relies heavily on cognitive theories (Bandura 1986; O'Leary and Wilson 1987).

There is no more active area of theorizing, research, and clinical application in behavior therapy than the investigation and treatment of the anxiety disorders. Progress in the conceptualization and treatment of anxiety disorders ranks as one of behavior therapy's most notable accomplishments (Barlow and Wolfe 1981). Among the anxiety disorders, phobias have been the most intensively researched.

Phobic Disorders

There is a huge literature on the behavioral treatment of phobic disorders, with several comprehensive reviews of treatment outcome (Barlow 1988; Mathews et al. 1981; Taylor and Arnow 1988).

Simple Phobias

Several behavioral methods have proved effective in treating simple phobias. In systematic desensitization (Wolpe 1958), after isolating specific events that trigger unrealistic anxiety, the therapist constructs a stimulus hierarchy in which different situations that the patient fears are ordered along a continuum from mildly stressful to very threatening. The patient is instructed to conjure up a clear and vivid image of each item while he or she is relaxed. In the event that any item produces much anxiety, the patient is instructed to cease visualizing the particular item and to restore feelings of relaxation. The item is then repeated, or the hierarchy adjusted, until the patient can visualize the scene without experiencing anxiety. Only then does the therapist present the next item of the hierarchy.

Clinical and experimental studies strongly attest to the efficacy of systematic desensitization. Methodologically sophisticated studies, utilizing some of the most stringent controls ever employed in the treatment outcome research, have consistently shown that the success of systematic desensitization cannot be attributed solely to so-called nonspecific effects, such as placebo influences or expectations of therapeutic improvement (Rachman and Wilson 1980). The effects of this and related behavioral techniques are maintained after treatment is terminated, and no evidence of symptom substitution has been uncovered. The effective ingredient in systematic desensitization is repeated exposure to anxiety-eliciting cues; relaxation might facilitate this process but it is not essential to treatment success.

As an example of this evidence, Gelder et al. (1973) compared systematic desensitization and another behavioral technique, flooding, to a credible attention-placebo control method in the treatment of phobic disorders. In the placebo condition, the therapist presented phobic images to initiate each patient's free association, but made no attempt to control the content of subsequent imagery or verbal responses. The patients were told that this exploration of their feelings would enhance self-understanding and decrease their anxiety. All treatments were carried out by experienced therapists explicitly trained in the administration of the different methods. An attempt was made to induce a high expectancy of success in half of the subjects by describing the treatment and therapist chosen in very favorable terms and showing them a videotape of a patient who had benefitted from the treatment they were to receive. Treatment effects were evaluated in terms of measures of behavioral avoidance, blind psychiatric ratings, patient self-ratings, physiological responsiveness, and standardized psychological tests. The adequacy of the control group in eliciting expectancies of treatment success, in comparison with those evoked by the two behavioral methods, was assessed directly, and the effects were shown to be comparable across all three treatments. Patients were assigned to treatments and therapists in a factorial design that permitted an analysis of the possible interactions among treatment effects, therapist differences, type of phobia, and levels of expectancy. Treatments were administered in 15 weekly sessions. In all, the study was sufficiently well designed and well executed to answer the question, "What treatment method has what specific effect on what problem in whom?"

Both behavioral treatments produced greater improvement than the control condition on the behavioral avoidance tests, physiological arousal measures, psychiatric ratings of the main phobia, and patients' self-ratings of improvement. Simply put, both systematic desensitization and flooding were twice as effective as the convincing pseudotherapy control treatment was. The more disturbed the patients were, the greater was the difference between specific behavioral methods and suitable pseudotherapy control.

Imaginal flooding involves prolonged exposure to high-intensity anxiety-eliciting images. The evidence, as illustrated by the Gelder et al. (1973) study, has shown that imaginal flooding is at least as effective as systematic desensitization (Marks 1981).

Several types of modeling procedures have been shown to reliably eliminate simple phobias (Rosenthal and Bandura 1978). In symbolic modeling, the patient observes a live or filmed model systematically engaging in progressively more threatening interactions with the phobic object (e.g., a small animal). Covert modeling is a method in which the patient does not observe a live or filmed model, but imagines a model engaging in phobic behavior. The following factors enhance treatment outcome: imagination of multiple models; reinforcement of models for overcoming their problem; and imaging of a coping model who gradually overcomes initial fear, as opposed to a mastery model who performs fearlessly from the outset. There appears to be little differential effectiveness among symbolic and covert modeling and systematic desensitization.

The most effective behavioral treatment is that in which the patient is systematically exposed (typically in a graduated manner) to the actual phobic situation in vivo in contrast to imaginal or vicarious exposure (Bandura 1986; Mathews et al. 1981). Details of this procedure are covered in the section on agoraphobia. Suffice it to note here that in vivo exposure, or performance-based treatment, is generally more efficient and effective than symbolic modeling, imagery-based techniques such as systematic desensitization, or covert modeling.

Klein et al. (1983) reported that supportive psychotherapy was as effective as behavior therapy (systematic desensitization) in the treatment of agoraphobia, mixed phobia, and simple phobia. They conclude that the results of their study are consistent with the therapy outcome literature in showing that there are no significant differences among psychological treatments. For phobic patients, they all achieve their effect by instigating "corrective activity" between therapy sessions in the form of in vivo exposure. If there are differences among treatments, they reduce to the theoretically uninteresting matter of rapidity of change. Undoubtedly, Klein et al. are right in observing that many forms of nonbehavioral therapies serve the instigating function they describe. But there are both practical and theoretical limitations to this analysis.

The first point that must be made is that not all psychological therapies, either deliberately or unwittingly, encourage or instigate some form of in vivo exposure.

A second point that can be made in connection with Klein et al.'s analysis raises a more fundamental issue. Because it is agreed that some form of corrective activity (in vivo exposure) is central to overcoming phobic disorders, it makes sense to use the most efficient methods for accomplishing this task. These methods would ideally be those that follow logically from a theoretically sound conceptualization of the effective ingredients in exposure treatment. Klein et al. correctly reject an explanation of exposure in terms of reciprocal inhibition. But current conceptualizations of fear reduction processes and exposure treatment are quite different. These newer analyses emphasize both conditioning and cognitive concepts (Bandura 1986; O'Leary and Wilson 1987; Rachman 1983).

As an example, social learning theory recognizes that there is no isomorphic relationship between behavioral accomplishments, as during in vivo exposure practice, and the cognitive processing of these events. In terms of this framework, behavioral performance provides a source of information that either raises or lowers patients' sense of self-efficacy, namely, the subjective estimate that one can cope with a threatening situation. Increased self-efficacy results in reduction in phobic avoidance and fear arousal (Bandura 1986). According to this theory, all psychological treatment methods, including those that rely upon verbal and imaginal operations, are effective to the extent that they increase the patient's sense of personal efficacy. Behavioral performance, or in vivo exposure, is a most powerful means of altering self-efficacy.

Given this view, it follows that it is not the amount of exposure to the feared situation that is critical to treatment success, but the impact that exposure has on self-efficacy that will determine anxiety reduction. Clients with anxiety disorders may show distortions in the way in which they process personally relevant events (Mathews and McLeod 1985). These cognitive distortions might undermine the therapeutic effects of exposure. Explicit therapeutic attention to patients' subjective interpretations of success and failure experiences during in vivo exposure practice is often necessary in sustaining motivation and preventing relapse following treatment (Hand and Wittchen 1986; Mathews et al. 1981).

Finally, self-efficacy theory does not require that exposure be a necessary condition of phobic anxiety reduction. Although exposure treatments have been shown to be the most effective methods, anxiety reduction can occur in the absence of exposure (de Silva and Rachman 1981).

Social Phobias

Less attention has been given to the treatment of social phobias. The evidence from studies that included social phobics, together with simple phobics and agoraphobics (e.g., the Gelder et al. 1973 investigation), indicate that social phobias can be treated as effectively as simple phobias by either systematic desensitization or flooding (Emmelkamp 1982; Marks 1981). Additional support for this conclusion comes from a 4-year follow-up of different phobic patients who had originally been treated with systematic desensitization (Marks 1971). Over 20 percent of these 65 patients suffered from social phobias. No differences were observed between these patients and their counterparts with simple phobias or agoraphobia, either at posttreatment or during the long-term follow-up.

Butler et al. (1984) compared two behavioral methods to a waiting-list control group in the treatment of social phobics. One method was in vivo exposure (EX) plus anxiety management (AM) training. AM consisted of progressive relaxation training, distraction, and rational self-talk. The latter was a form of cognitive restructuring in which patients identified negative or self-defeating thoughts and then rehearsed more constructive alternative thoughts. EX focused exclusively on encouraging patients to participate in situations they had been avoiding. No instructions about coping with anxiety were given. Both treatment groups improved significantly more than the waiting-list control group, which showed no improvement on most measures. Treatment effects were maintained, or increased, at a six-month follow-up, with the EX/AM treatment producing broader therapeutic effects on cognitive as well as behavioral measures and across different situations.

Social skills training, in which patients are helped to become more assertive and effective in coping with interpersonal issues, has also shown promise. Social skills training may be especially useful with social phobics whose primary problem is behavioral (interpersonal) impairment rather than unnerving physiological arousal (Ost et al. 1984).

Agoraphobia

Agoraphobia is generally regarded as the most complex and most difficult to treat of the phobic disorders. Also, clinicians are more often called upon to treat agoraphobics than other phobic patients. For these reasons, it is instructive to provide more detail on the behavioral treatment of agoraphobia with and without panic attacks.

Clinical experience and experimental research have shown that the most effective procedures are those that rely on systematic in vivo exposure to the feared situations (Barlow 1988; Mathews et al. 1981). Two major forms of in vivo exposure treatment have been used to treat agoraphobic patients: 1) flooding in vivo, which is designed to elicit maximum anxiety by confronting the patient with his or her most intense anxiety-eliciting cues as soon as possible; and 2) graduated in vivo exposure, which is conducted on a graduated or hierarchical basis so as to confront the patient with his or her feared situations but without evoking intense anxiety. Controlled clinical research, much of it conducted in the United Kingdom, has significantly furthered our understanding of the clinical practice and effects of in vivo exposure methods. This information may be summarized as follows:

1. Both flooding and graduate exposure in vivo are more efficient and effective than their imaginal counterparts, as in the case of simple phobias. It is noteworthy that in demonstrations of the efficacy of flooding in the treatment of agoraphobic patients, such as the Gelder et al. (1973) study, imaginal exposure was followed in each session by in vivo exposure to the feared situation.
2. The longer the exposure to the feared situation is, the more effective flooding is likely to be. For instance, Stern and Marks (1973) found that two hours of continuous exposure in vivo was significantly more effective than four separate half-hours in one afternoon in the treatment of agoraphobics. Too short a duration of exposure may, in certain circumstances, actually result in a temporary increase in phobic arousal.
3. It is unnecessary to elicit intense expression of anxiety during in vivo exposure. Patients' anxiety levels during flooding do not correlate with subsequent outcome. Graduated exposure is as effective as flooding, and the most widely used method today.
4. Flooding and graduated in vivo exposure conducted within a group setting seem to be as effective as individual treatments.
5. In vivo exposure treatment in which the exposure is patient controlled may be as effective as therapist-controlled exposure, and it is more cost-effective (Ghosh and Marks 1987).
6. With appropriate patients, home-based treatment, making use of a treatment manual, and active spouse involvement, produce improvement comparable to that achieved with more intensive therapist-administered treatment in the clinic (Jannoun et al. 1980). Home-based, spouse-assisted treatment is not only cost-effective but might also result in superior maintenance of treatment-produced change (Munby and Johnston 1980).

7. In vivo exposure treatment conducted by nursing personnel under the supervision of a professional behavior therapist may, in some instances, be comparable to treatment carried out by clinical psychologists. This increases the cost-benefit ratio for efficient delivery of treatment services (Marks et al. 1977). Yet it would be well to note that a therapist effect was evident in two major studies, despite the highly standardized treatment format (Jannoun et al. 1980; Mathews et al. 1976).

8. Exposure treatment is not a uniform procedure that is directly comparable from one study to the next (Hand and Wittchen 1986). Although exposure treatment is a straightforward method, its effective use frequently depends on success in dealing with clinical issues, such as increasing motivation, facilitating compliance, coping with anticipated anxiety attacks during exposure sessions, and overcoming cognitive distortions. The effective use of exposure cannot be encompassed by simply describing it as an extinction technique aimed at producing habituation of fear. In addition to prescribing the basic behavioral tasks of gradually approaching phobic situations, the clinical practice of exposure treatment occurs in a context of strategies for coping with thoughts and feelings that would otherwise undermine therapeutic progress.

   Detailed consideration of these clinical strategies is beyond the scope of this chapter, but consider as an example the following excerpt from the Mathews et al. (1981) demonstrably effective treatment program. With reference to the maintenance of treatment-produced change, they instruct their patients as follows: "Hardly anyone recovers from agoraphobia without having at least one 'setback.' Feelings vary, sometimes from day to day, and what you did successfully yesterday may seem impossible today. Even then, you could make real progress. What counts is how you cope with whatever feelings you experience. So, a little done on a bad day can be worth more than a lot done on a good day" (p. 184). Here and elsewhere in their program, Mathews et al. (1981) help patients to interpret (others might say reframe) critical events in constructive, rather than negative, self-defeating ways. By anticipating the possibility of a setback at some point in the future, they explicitly attempt to defuse the otherwise detrimental effects of an unexpected anxiety attack just when patients feel they are improved. In the field of addictive disorders, this strategy is known as the cognitive-behavioral technique of relapse prevention training (Marlatt and Gordon 1985). Mathews et al. (1981, p. 183) provide patients with a short set of summary rules about what to do if a panic strikes. These include the following: "1. The feelings are normal bodily reactions; 2. They are not harmful; 3. Do not add frightening thoughts; . . . 9. Plan what to do next . . ." The parallel to relapse prevention training (in which patients are provided very similar rules that bear on attributional processes) and coping strategies is striking. Similarly, Hand and Wittchen (1986, p. 107) emphasize that they "never raise the expectation that treatment will completely eliminate episodes of anxiety or depression. Instead, we want to provide the real-life experience that the consequences of giving in to those feelings on a motor-behavior level probably create to a large extent the illness of chronic agoraphobia. If disconnected from phobic anticipatory cognition, the occurrence of further anxiety attacks and depressive episodes will, for the majority of patients, be rare and usually manageable events."

9. Agoraphobics with good marriages at the onset of exposure treatment maintain the reductions they make on phobic anxiety and avoidance better than their counterparts with poor marriages (Bland and Hallam 1981). Including husbands in their agoraphobic wives' exposure treatment program (couples training) may achieve results superior to those from treating wives alone. Couples training may be par-

ticularly useful in treating patients whose marriages are poor to begin with (Barlow et al. 1983).

Long-Term Efficacy of Treatment

The effects of exposure treatments have been maintained at lengthy follow-ups. In England, Munby and Johnston (1980) conducted a long-term follow-up of the agoraphobic patients of three major clinical studies, including the Gelder et al. (1973) investigation. Of the 66 patients who had been treated in these three studies, 95 percent were interviewed by a psychiatric research worker five to nine years later. Follow-up measures, repeating those used in the original studies, were compared with those obtained prior to treatment and six months after treatment ended. On most measures of agoraphobia, the patients were much better at follow-up than they had been before treatment. The assessor's ratings suggested that there had been little change in the patients' agoraphobia since six months after treatment. Some of the patients' self-ratings showed evidence of a slight improvement over this period. No evidence of any symptom substitution was found. The patients who showed the greatest reductions in agoraphobia were, at follow-up, among the least anxious and depressed. However, interpretation of these findings must be tempered by the report that a sizeable number of these former patients had received additional treatment over the follow-up period. Excluding these subjects from the analysis of the data did little to change the outcome, however. Another result that suggests caution in evaluating these data is that at the end of follow-up, over 50 percent of these patients had received psychotropic medication. Twenty-one patients reported that they had experienced "a period of severe relapse, lasting at least a month."

Four other long-term follow-ups provide further support for the durable effects of in vivo exposure treatments of agoraphobic patients. Holland et al. (1979) followed up 70 outpatient agoraphobics, derived from a sample of 81 patients who had received exposure treatment four years previously. All information was obtained from questionnaires that were mailed to patients. Improvements in phobic fear and avoidance obtained during treatment were maintained, and on some of the measures further improvement occurred; there was also a reduction in depression in the follow-up period, and no new neurotic disturbances developed. In Scotland, McPherson et al. (1980), using a postal follow-up of 56 agoraphobics who had shown improvement when treated with in vivo exposure, similarly found that treatment gains were maintained four years later. Finally, in England, Marks (1971) and Burns et al. (1986b) reported satisfactory maintenance of treatment effects in agoraphobics at four- and eight-year follow-ups, respectively.

Clinical Outcome of Exposure Treatment

The preceding summary of the behavioral treatment of agoraphobics has been based on reports of statistically significant differences between treatments and control conditions. These criteria leave unanswered the question of clinical significance—namely, precisely what is meant by treatment success? What is the likelihood that an individual agoraphobic seeking therapy will be helped, and, specifically, what can that person expect if therapy is successful?

Although it can be concluded that systematic exposure methods are usually superior to alternative forms of psychological treatment, their limitations must be noted. Barlow et al. (1983) estimate that roughly 25 percent of agoraphobics fail to benefit from exposure treatment. Of the remaining 75 percent, many make only limited improvements and few ever reach that stage where they are completely free of at least periodic anxiety symptoms. This latter point is made clear by long-term follow-ups, as indicated previously. Moreover, this estimate of outcome must be interpreted in the light of an attrition rate from exposure treatment of roughly 10 to 20 percent, depending on the particular study.

Estimates of this sort are naturally somewhat arbitrary, and a host of moderating factors, some of which are discussed in the following paragraphs, could affect the treatment outcome across different settings. Nonetheless, given these outcome statistics, what is the extent of improvement that is achieved? The primary dependent measure in a majority of studies has been independent clinical ratings of treatment outcome (Marks 1981). Although these ratings are very reliable, they do not provide an adequate picture of clinical change. Fortunately, some studies have measured changes in behavioral avoidance directly, showing substantial improvement in functioning in this domain (e.g., Mathews et al. 1981).

Exposure treatment not only reduces phobic anxiety and avoidance, but also panic (Mavissakalian et al. 1983; Telch et al. 1985). In addition, exposure treatment is usually associated with significant decreases in depression. Marital satisfaction, although not directly treated, has also been shown to improve following exposure therapy (Barlow et al. 1983; Marks 1981; O'Leary and Wilson 1987). No evidence of symptom substitution or therapy-induced negative effects has been found. As Zitrin (1981) concluded about the effects of behavior therapy, based on the Klein et al. (1983) study, "We found a significant improvement in the quality of their lives; better functioning at home and at work, increased social life, expanded interests and activities, and improved interpersonal relationships. In general, there was a greater richness in the fabric of their lives" (p. 169).

The Clinical Practice of Behavior Therapy

The foregoing conclusions are based primarily on research studies that evaluated the effects of a specific therapeutic technique—namely, some form of exposure. The requirements of controlled research militated against individual assessment of each patient's problems, as would be standard clinical practice. Such individual assessment, a cardinal feature of clinical behavior therapy, would in all likelihood have led to multifaceted interventions in many cases. In vivo exposure would have been supplemented with such diverse strategies as assertion training, behavior rehearsal, behavioral marital therapy, and self-regulatory procedures where appropriate. In short, it can be argued that the therapeutic results obtained in the controlled research described represent a conservative index of the outcome that might be achieved with clinical practice (e.g., Chambless and Goldstein 1982).

An illustration of how exposure treatment may be usefully complemented by additional behavioral strategies is shown in a controlled study by Arnow et al. (1985). Agoraphobic patients are frequently lacking in assertiveness and too dependent in their personal relationships. Accordingly, these investigators supplemented exposure treatment with a focus on interpersonal issues, namely, training in communication skills. The expanded behavioral treatment significantly enhanced therapeutic outcome.

Panic attacks are reduced by exposure treatment in many cases, but in others, particularly where there is no clear pattern of avoidance behavior, additional intervention is required. Specific techniques are described in the later section on panic disorder.

Comparative Efficacy of Behavior Therapy and Alternative Treatments

Few comparative outcome studies of different psychological approaches to the treatment of agoraphobia have been completed, and those that are available have their methodological limitations (Kazdin and Wilson 1978; Rachman and Wilson 1980). The Klein et al. (1983) study indicating no difference between imaginal desensitization and a supportive psychotherapy with all phobic disorders, has been discussed. Gillan and Rachman (1974) found that systematic desensitization was significantly superior to psychotherapy, although the psychotherapy used in this study cannot be readily generalized to psychotherapy in general. Gelder et al. (1967) showed that systematic desensitization was more efficient, and on some measures more effective, than individual or group psychotherapy.

Behavioral Versus Pharmacological (Antidepressant) Treatments

Several controlled studies have compared exposure therapy to imipramine treatment. Collectively, this clinical research has shown that behavioral treatment either is as effective as the use of imipramine, or significantly enhances the therapeutic effects of drug treatment.

It is particularly important to evaluate the effects of antidepressant drugs independent of concomitant exposure to feared situations. Telch et al. (1985) randomly assigned agoraphobics to the following conditions: 1) imipramine alone, 2) imipramine plus in vivo exposure, and 3) placebo plus in vivo exposure. To control for the effects of exposure, subjects in the imipramine alone condition were given counter-practice instructions that emphasized the importance of refraining from entering phobic situations for the first eight weeks so that the medication would have time to take effect. The in vivo exposure treatment consisted of a total of nine hours of therapist-assisted group exposure spread over three consecutive days followed by a partner-assisted home-based exposure method described by Mathews et al. (1981).

Two other studies evaluated behavioral treatment together with imipramine. In one, Mavissakalian et al. (1983) compared imipramine to imipramine combined with exposure treatment. The combined treatment was more effective, leading these investigators to endorse "the clinical argument that agoraphobics treated with imipramine require additional behavioral treatment for phobic avoidance and anxiety" (p. 352). In the other, Zitrin et al. (1983) paired imaginal desensitization with either imipramine or a placebo. Agoraphobic patients treated with desensitization and imipramine improved significantly more than patients who received desensitization and the placebo.

The rationale for using an antidepressant drug is that it has specific antiphobic properties. As such, it is said to reduce the primary problem in agoraphobia, namely, spontaneous panic attacks (Zitrin et al. 1983). Phobic anxiety and avoidance are allegedly secondary reactions that may then be treated with behavioral methods.

In terms of clinical practice, these comparative outcome data must be evaluated with the following practical clinical considerations in mind. First, as Telch et al. (1983) point out, many agoraphobics dislike—and avoid—pharmacotherapy. For example, Telch et al. (1985) found that almost 20 percent of all agoraphobics who contacted the clinic expressed an unwillingness to take medication and thus were not accepted into the study.

Second, adverse physical side effects of drug treatment must be taken into account. These side effects are undoubtedly a cause of the relatively high rates of attrition associated with drug treatment. According to Telch et al. (1983), "drop-out rates from the antidepressant trials published to date consistently average between 35 and 40%, well above the mean of 10% for drug-free behavioral treatment." (Marks et al. 1983 report an attrition rate of 36 percent; the comparable figure for behavioral treatment studies conducted by this group is 16 percent.) This phenomenon, together with the refusal of many agoraphobics to enter into pharmacotherapy in the first place, means that a nontrivial number of agoraphobics must necessarily be treated with psychological methods.

Nonphobic Anxiety

Behavior therapy methods for nonphobic anxiety states are largely untested. An indication of the value of behavior therapy can be gleaned from the Sloane et al. (1975) study, in which 57 of the 94 patients were diagnosed as anxiety reactions using the DSM-II (American Psychiatric Association [1969]) classification. The findings of this study showed that in terms of the target symptoms, 48 percent of the control group and 80 percent of the behavior therapy and psychotherapy groups were considered improved or recovered. Behavior therapy was significantly superior to the other groups on the global rating of improvement. At the one-year follow-up, there was no overall difference among the three groups on any of the dependent measures. Behavior therapy in this study included a range of methods such as imaginal desensitization, assertion training, direct advice, and relaxation training.

In DSM-III (American Psychiatric Association 1980), anxiety states were divided into generalized anxiety disorder (GAD) and panic disorder (PD). Behavior therapy for these nonphobic anxiety disorders has focused primarily on modifying their physiologic (somatic) and cognitive dimensions. Exposure treatment is typically unsuitable because patients with these disorders do not avoid particular situations; in a sense they are continually exposed to anxiety cues.

Generalized Anxiety Disorder

Treatments focusing on the somatic component of GAD have consisted mainly of biofeedback and relaxation procedures (Rice and Blanchard 1982). As in other areas of application, biofeedback (specifically, EMG feedback) is not reliably superior to progressive relaxation training. Moreover, clinical improvement has not been linked to reductions in muscle tension, as required by the logic of EMG biofeedback indicating that other factors account for therapeutic change. Overall, treatment of GAD with biofeedback and relaxation procedures has yielded distinctly modest results. For example, Raskin et al. (1980) suggest that an improvement rate of no more than 40 percent can be expected.

Treatments featuring a combination of relaxation training and some form of cognitive restructuring have shown some positive effects. Woodward and Jones (1980) compared the following four conditions in the treatment of outpatients diagnosed as suffering from anxiety states: 1) cognitive restructuring, consisting of elements of both rational-emotive therapy and Meichenbaum's (1977) self-instructional training; 2) modified systematic desensitization, emphasizing coping rather than mastery imagery; 3) a combination of 1) and 2); and 4) a waiting-list control. The combined treatment proved to be significantly superior to all others in reducing anxiety. Cognitive restructuring alone had little therapeutic effect. Jannoun et al. (1982) reported significant success in treating patients with generalized anxiety and panic attacks with a combination of relaxation and self-instructional training. Aside from improvements in anxiety ratings, treatment produced a 60 percent reduction in anxiolytic drugs patients took. Improvement was maintained at a three-months' follow-up.

Panic Disorder

Based on a cognitive model of panic disorder, Clark et al. (1985) developed a respiratory control method that promises to be an effective treatment. This cognitive model posits that panic attacks are catastrophic misinterpretations of bodily sensations such as those produced by hyperventilation. The model is consistent with evidence indicating that panic patients often report that they first detect unpleasant bodily sensations followed by negative cognitions (Hibbert 1984). Margraf et al. (1986) reported an experimental test of a key tenet of the model by directly manipulating panic patients' perceptions of somatic changes using false heart rate feedback. Both panic patients and controls accepted the false heart rate as accurate and showed increased self-reported anxiety. However, only the patients showed increased actual physiologic arousal in response to the false feedback. Margraf et al. concluded that these data indicated that "perceived cardiovascular arousal may act as an internal cue that, together with other factors, triggers or exacerbates panic attacks" (p. 36).

The respiratory control technique consists of (a) brief, voluntary hyperventilation, which is intended to induce a mild panic attack; (b) explanation of the effects of overbreathing and reattribution of the cause of a patient's attacks to hyperventilation; and (c) training in slow breathing incompatible with hyperventilation. Using this method, Clark et al. (1985) obtained substantial reductions in frequency of panic attacks within two weeks despite the documented absence of exposure to feared situations. A behavioral as opposed to a cognitive view of this treatment emphasizes the importance of repeated exposure to internal (physiological) cues that trigger panic attacks.

Other behavior therapy programs that have proved successful in treating panic attacks have used combinations of controlled breathing, relaxation training, and cognitive anxiety management (e.g., Barlow 1988; Gitlin et al. 1985). Barlow et al. (1984) treated GAD and PD patients with a procedure that combined EMG biofeedback, relaxation training, and cognitive restructuring. Compared to a waiting-list control group, treated patients improved significantly in clinicians' ratings, psychophysiologic measures, and patients' daily self-monitoring of background anxiety and panic. This improvement was maintained at a three-month follow-up. The waiting-list controls did not improve. Although the PD patients showed greater somatic reactions on self-report and physiologic measures prior to therapy, both groups of patients responded equally well to the treatment.

Limitations and Prospects

Historically, behavior therapy has been most extensively applied in the treatment of relatively specific or focused problems. Within the anxiety disorders, this means that the phobic disorders and compulsive rituals have been the most intensively studied. Most of the existing behavioral research has concentrated on simple phobias, agoraphobia, and compulsions, and it is with these particular disorders that behavior therapy has been most effective. Far less attention has been devoted to more diffuse, nonphobic anxiety problems such as GAD, PD, and "existential" anxieties. Currently, the relative lack of controlled clinical research precludes any firm conclusion about the efficacy of behavior therapy with these nonphobic anxiety disorders.

Contemporary behavior therapy is characterized by a much greater emphasis on cognitive processes and strategies than was originally the case (O'Leary and Wilson 1987). The preceding discussion of Bandura's self-efficacy, and its implications for clinical practice, illustrate this trend. The realities of clinical practice with the full range of anxiety disorders have been a major impetus for this move towards a more sophisticated, more cognitive approach. This clinical push also has dovetailed with the ascendance, within the discipline of experimental psychology that nourishes the theory of behavior therapy, of information processing models of human behavior, attribution theory, and social learning theory. The roles of self-schemas, attributional bias, and nonconscious processes are increasingly taken into account in behavior therapy (Goldfried and Robins 1983; Wilson 1986). This broader cognitive-behavioral-conceptual framework has led to the study and treatment of nonphobic anxieties such as GAD and PD. It is no coincidence that current treatment methods for the latter two disorders rely heavily on cognitive concepts, as noted (Beck and Emery 1985; Clark et al. 1985).

Inevitably, as behavior therapy has broadened its nature and scope, the degree of overlap with other shorter term directive psychotherapies has increased. Some clear similarities with other approaches can be identified. Nevertheless, critical differences, both in theory and practice, remain.

Chapter 184

Treatment with Antianxiety Agents

Anxiety, a universal human condition, exists along a continuum ranging from normal, mild apprehension to disabling emotional disorder. When not severe, the experience of anxiety can be helpful in the development of planning and coping behavior. In its more extreme form, anxiety preoccupies and sometimes overwhelms and impairs adequate coping behavior. At this degree of severity, medical relief from symptoms is usually sought. In this chapter, I will describe the use of psychotropic drugs for the treatment of anxiety that is of sufficient severity to interfere with normal daily functioning. Rather than serve as an exhaustive review of clinical and research studies of antianxiety agents, I will trace the clinical use of antianxiety agents and then focus on the clinical use, abuse, and potential hazards of these medications. The basic theme that will underlie the clinical information that is presented will emphasize the use of lowest therapeutic doses of antianxiety drugs for the shortest period of time.

History of Early Pharmacologic Treatments

Chemical agents used to decrease anxiety and provide relaxation have been known to man since the start of recorded history. Many of these agents were effective and enjoyed widespread acceptability. However, each treatment was also associated with side effects and overdosage fatalities that tended to limit their usefulness. In addition, tolerance to the antianxiety effect often developed, so that progressively larger doses were required. As doses increased, dependence and addiction often developed, and continued use became necessary to prevent withdrawal symptoms. As dependence and tolerance progressed, dosage increases were inevitable and the cycle of addiction, tolerance, and further dose increase was maintained. This pattern was especially characteristic of four commonly used antianxiety substances—alcohol, barbiturates, bromides, and propanediol drugs.

Alcohol

Alcohol is the oldest of the antianxiety agents and still the most commonly used. Two properties of alcohol make it a widely used antianxiety agent. First, the onset of its antianxiety effect is rapid. Second, most people with a little bit of practice learn to titrate the dose of alcohol necessary to produce adequate antianxiety effect without producing overdose, i.e., drunkenness. The antianxiety effect, at least for a brief period of time, is remarkably effective, as alcohol use in social gatherings and at airports demonstrates; alcohol also has the advantage of being relatively cheap, and very readily available. Unfortunately, alcohol has many properties that limit its usefulness as a therapeutic antianxiety substance. It is rapidly metabolized so that its antianxiety effect is very brief. It has a very low therapeutic-to-toxic ratio—that is, the dose that produces toxicity (drunkenness) is very close to the dose that produces antianxiety effect. The side effects of alcohol overdose are particularly unpleasant, and in severe cases may lead to coma, seizures, and death. More commonly, however, if alcohol is used to self-medicate anxiety, repeated dosing is necessary because of its brief effect. Tolerance to the antianxiety effect of alcohol develops rapidly, so that progressively increasing doses are required, leading to the problem of physiologic addiction and psychological dependence. These factors, combined with the social usefulness of alcohol as an antianxiety agent and its ready availability, lead to a very great potential for abuse.

Side effects of alcohol often accompany its antianxiety effects and further limit its usefulness. Modest overdoses commonly produce sedation, disinhibition, and intoxication. With prolonged use, hepatic enzyme induction (activating hepatic enzymes so that the metabolism of alcohol or other antianxiety agent is accelerated and blood levels and therapeutic effect diminished), amnestic syndrome, hallucinations, abstinence and withdrawal syndrome, seizures, and death may occur. Alcohol also interacts with all central nervous system sedatives to depress central nervous system arousal levels. For these reasons, alcohol is not acceptable as a treatment for anxiety.

Barbiturates

In the 1930s, the development of barbituric acid derivatives provided a new alternative to alcohol as an antianxiety substance. Barbiturates were found to be very effective antianxiety agents, considerably better than placebo, and were inexpensive to use. Although the onset of their therapeutic activity was slower than that of alcohol, and their sedating side effects somewhat limiting, barbiturates gained wide use as antianxiety agents alone or were often combined with other drugs to provide relief from anxiety associated with other medical illnesses. Some physicians may still prefer to prescribe low doses of phenobarbital for anxiety, especially because it is inexpensive.

Many factors, however, interfere with the therapeutic usefulness of barbiturates. The drugs, like alcohol, have a low therapeutic-to-toxic ratio, so that therapeutic antianxiety doses may become sedating, disinhibiting, and intoxicating. There is rapid metabolism of some barbiturates; others have a very long duration of action with accumulation of drug in the blood system and long-lasting clinical and toxic effects. Barbiturates induce hepatic metabolism of themselves so that pharmacokinetic tolerance develops rapidly; receptor-site tolerance develops as well so that with prolonged use, increasing doses of barbiturates are often necessary to maintain clinical antianxiety effect. Like alcohol, therefore, barbiturate tolerance leads to a cycle of recurrent addiction and dependence with recurring withdrawal symptoms. Barbiturates, like alcohol, also interact with all other central nervous system sedating drugs to produce further sedation, disinhibition, potential intoxication, seizures, and death.

Bromides

Bromides were first used to alter central nervous system functioning in epileptic patients in 1857 and quickly became extremely popular antianxiety substances. In the late 19th and early 20th centuries, bromides were a central part of a variety of patent medicines, nerve tonics, and headache remedies. Bromides are widely distributed throughout the body, including the brain and cerebrospinal fluid, and at therapeutic concentrations they are mild sedatives and may induce drowsiness and relaxation. However, bromides have a very long elimination time (elimination half-life of 12 days) and accumulate in the bloodstream, leading to toxicity. Toxicity is characterized by lethargy, irritability, delirium, delusions, hallucinations, neurologic disturbances, dermatitis, and gastrointestinal irritation. With the development of newer antianxiety agents, bromides have virtually disappeared from use.

Propanediols

In the 1950s, a new family of compounds was developed in an attempt to replace barbiturates and bromides with less acutely and chronically toxic substances. These new drugs, the propanediols, became very popular in the mid-1950s. The most common of these, meprobamate, was so widely used for antianxiety effect and muscle relaxant properties that it became the object of contemporary humor of the time (i.e., S. J. Perelman's book: *The Road to Miltown* or *Under the Spreading Atrophy*).

Meprobamate was comparable in effectiveness to barbiturates and substantially more effective than placebo. It was prescribed in doses of 400 to 800 mg, one to four times per day. However, as experience with meprobamate grew, it was soon realized that it possessed all the same problems as the barbiturates, bromides, and alcohol. Tolerance developed at high doses with recurring use, and increasing doses were necessary to maintain therapeutic effect. Sedation and disinhibition were common side effects. Side effects associated with chronic use or high doses included an abuse potential, seizures upon withdrawal, and coma or death. Thus, it became apparent that these drugs offered little advantage over the barbiturates. However, they continued in widespread use until the early 1960s when chlordiazepoxide (Librium), the first of the soon-to-be overwhelmingly popular benzodiazepine antianxiety agents was developed. Meprobamate is still in limited use, and some patients claim that the therapeutic effect of the drug is not equaled by these newer antianxiety agents, the benzodiazepines.

Benzodiazepines

The development of the benzodiazepine antianxiety agents heralded a new era in the pharmacological treatment of anxiety. These compounds were more potent antianxiety agents (on a per milligram basis) than meprobamate, and were safer and more effective than alcohol, barbiturates, bromides, or meprobamate. The first of these drugs, chlordiazepoxide (Librium), was released for clinical use in the early 1960s. A number of studies (see Klein and Davis 1969, p. 346) attested to its therapeutic superiority as compared to placebo, and the popularity of this drug rapidly increased.

Chlordiazepoxide was soon supplanted by diazepam (Valium), a related benzodiazepine compound that was approximately two to five times more potent. Diazepam, in addition to its antianxiety effect, was also reported to have muscle relaxant properties and began to be used widely for musculoskeletal spasms and presurgical relaxation, as well as for its antianxiety effect.

Several years after the introduction of diazepam, oxazepam and lorazepam were synthesized for clinical use and became the first of the so-called short half-life benzodiazepines. Unlike chlordiazepoxide and diazepam, oxazepam and lorazepam do not undergo further metabolic transformation to other active metabolites and are eliminated from the blood more rapidly. Alprazolam, the benzodiazepine most recently released for clinical use in the United States, has an intermediate half-life. Thus, benzodiazepine compounds that are available for clinical use today may be divided into long half-life, intermediate half-life, and short half-life benzodiazepines, as illustrated in Table 1.

Regardless of their individual pharmacokinetic properties, benzodiazepines have substantial advantages as antianxiety agents compared with all substances used previously. In most cases, tolerance to the clinical effect does not occur, so that doses do not need to be increased. There is a substantially lower incidence of dependence when these drugs are used in therapeutic doses and virtually none when they are used intermittently for short periods of time. Withdrawal reactions from benzodiazepines are less severe than from other antianxiety agents and usually do not constitute a significant clinical problem except at high doses. There are very few drug interactions other than benzodiazepine enhancement of sedation of other central nervous system sedatives. Hepatic enzyme metabolism is not induced by benzodiazepines so that other drug effects are not compromised. Clinically, the drugs are safe for use. Lethal overdoses of benzodiazepines alone are rare, although as already

Table 1. Pharmacologic Properties of Benzodiazepines

Drug	Trade Names	Rate of Oral Absorption	Rate of Metabolism	Active Metabolites	Elimination 1/2-life (hrs)	Therapeutic Dose Range (mg/day)*
Chlordiazepoxide	Librium	Intermediate	Long	Yes	5–30	10–40
Diazepam	Valium	Fast	Long	Yes	20–50	2–20
Clorazepate	Tranxene	Fast	Long	Yes	36–200	7.5–30
Prazepam	Centrax	Slow	Long	Yes	36–200	20–60
Halazepam	Paxipam	Intermediate	Long	Yes	50–100	20–100
Alprazolam	Xanax	Intermediate	Intermediate	Yes	12–15	0.25–4
Lorazepam	Ativan	Intermediate	Short	No	10–14	0.5–6
Oxazepam	Serax	Slow	Short	No	5–10	15–60

*Approximate range: some patients may require higher or lower dosages.

mentioned, when mixed with other central nervous system sedatives, particularly alcohol, considerable sedation and disinhibition may result.

Because of these many advantages, benzodiazepines have become widely prescribed. Diazepam is one of the most widely prescribed drugs used throughout the world. Recent reports in the lay press, as well as in novels and movies, have suggested, without scientific foundation, that there is an epidemic of benzodiazepine overuse in the United States and perhaps even in Europe. Americans are portrayed as being dependent upon these drugs for daily activities, and women are pictured as especially needy.

Surveys of drug use throughout the world prior to 1978 suggest that antianxiety agents were occasionally taken by 8 to 15 percent of the population and that at least 80 percent of this use was accounted for by benzodiazepines (Marks 1978). A recent, careful survey of drug use conducted in the United States in 1979 revealed that 11 percent of the population has used antianxiety drugs one or more times in the 12 months preceding the survey (Mellinger et al. 1984). Of these, only 15 percent used the drug on a regular daily basis for more than a year, and this group accounted for a rate of use of only 1.6 percent of the total population between the ages of 18 and 79. Eighty-nine percent used the drugs for fewer than 30 days a year. Most significantly, those people who used antianxiety drugs for a long period of time had two to four chronic health problems, most commonly cardiovascular or musculoskeletal. These people suffered from true physical illness and the emotional consequences; 18 percent also used antidepressants. These data point to a rather consistent finding—most benzodiazepines are used for legitimate medical and psychiatric purposes, are used at therapeutic doses for short periods of time, and are neither overprescribed nor inappropriately used (Woods et al. 1987).

On the basis of these surveys, it seems reasonable to conclude that although benzodiazepines may be abused by some people and overprescribed by some physicians, benzodiazepine usage is clinically appropriate and necessary. Most benzodiazepines are prescribed by family practitioners, general practitioners, and internists. The drugs are prescribed primarily for those with chronic physical illness, often for people with several chronic illnesses. Those who take the drugs on an extended, regular basis are under considerable emotional stress, and find the drugs therapeutic.

Pharmacology of Benzodiazepines

The clinical effect of benzodiazepines depends on adequate concentration of the drug and its active metabolites at specific receptor sites in the brain. These receptor sites are part of the gamma-aminobutyric acid (GABA) benzodiazepine complex. A cascade of events occurs when benzodiazepines bind to their receptor sites leading to the activation of GABA receptors. Activation of inhibitory GABA neurotransmission is thought to lessen anxiety.

Adequate concentration of benzodiazepines at the receptor sites depends on both the pharmacokinetics (the absorption, distribution, binding, and metabolism of the drug) and the pharmacodynamics (the penetration of the drugs through the blood-brain barrier and binding at the receptor site). All benzodiazepines are lipid soluble and therefore penetrate the blood-brain barrier. However, recent information has suggested that there is differential penetration of these drugs, diazepam (being the most lipid soluble) penetrating the fastest, accounting for its rapid effect.

The benzodiazepines differ markedly from one another in pharmacokinetic parameters. Long half-life benzodiazepines such as diazepam and chlordiazepoxide, as well as prodrugs (clorazepate and prazepam) for diazepam, have complicated metabolic pathways and prolonged time for elimination. Each has an active metabolite that also has a prolonged elimination half-life. Consequently, after abrupt cessation of these drugs, there is a gradual tapering effect over approximately a five- to eight-day period. During this time blood levels of the prescribed drug and its active metabolite decrease by half, approximately every 24 to 30 hours in young adults. (In the elderly, this period is greatly extended.) Short or intermediate half-life benzodiazepines such as oxazepam, lorazepam, and alprazolam undergo more rapid metabolic transformation, and are eliminated much more quickly. After abrupt cessation, oxazepam blood levels are reduced by half after approximately 8 to 10 hours, lorazepam after 10 to 12 hours, and alprazolam after 14 to 14 hours. (These elimination periods are not affected by the aging process.) These pharmacokinetics are summarized in Table 1. In the treatment of the anxious patient, the clinician need be aware only of the fact that benzodiazepines may be subdivided into these two classes—the long half-life and the short half-life. These differences are significant only with repeated and constant dosage given for at least one week. For occasional use or one-time dosage, the pharmacokinetic differences have little clinical relevance.

Because benzodiazepines tend to be prescribed repeatedly, especially for patients with chronic and recurrent physical and emotional symptomatology, pharmacokinetic differences become significant. Long half-life benzodiazepines take longer to build up in the blood, so that they must be given on a regular basis for about five days until so-called steady-state plasma concentrations of the drug are reached. At this point, the long half-life benzodiazepines may need to be given only once or twice a day. For older patients, once a day is all that is necessary because these drugs are slowly eliminated from the body. Once-a-day or twice-a-day dosing is a significant advantage in many cases, because the chronically ill patient may be taking a variety of other medications, each with its own dosage scheduling. The necessity of following the fewest number of different dosage schedules is, quite obviously, a significant advantage for the patient. Long half-life benzodiazepines also have a more gradual tapering effect when discontinued. Because of the slow elimination time of the drug and its active metabolites, withdrawal symptoms tend to be milder and spread out over a longer period of time.

Short half-life benzodiazepines do not have active metabolites, build up more quickly in the blood stream, and are eliminated more quickly when terminated. Because of their pharmacokinetics, short half-life benzodiazepines must be prescribed three or four times a day on a regular basis. This offers the advantage of more flexibility should dosages require adjustment. Should toxicity occur, or should it be necessary to stop the benzodiazepines, these drugs are eliminated from the body more rapidly. This swiftness is often a particular advantage for older patients who may become overly toxic with any central nervous system sedative, including the benzodiazepines. However, withdrawal reactions tend to be more severe upon abrupt cessation of short half-life benzodiazepines, and as a general principle these drugs should be tapered rather than abruptly discontinued.

Advanced age may also influence other pharmacokinetic parameters of the benzodiazepines. These drugs tend to be more widely distributed throughout the body as people get older because they are lipid soluble and the amount of body fat tends to increase with age. Benzodiazepines are also extensively bound to plasma proteins. These proteins tend to diminish slightly with age but may also diminish with disease and malnutrition. The clinical consequences of decreased protein binding may be an increase in side effects. With advanced age, the benzodiazepine receptor site may also be more sensitive to benzodiazepines so that smaller amounts of drug are needed to produce adequate therapeutic effect. Thus, for both pharmacodynamic and pharmacokinetic reasons, dosages of benzodiazepines should be reduced in older patients.

It has been assumed that tolerance to benzodiazepines does not occur for the therapeutic antianxiety effects. With repeated doses, the antianxiety effect continues, and dosages do not need to be increased for maintenance of the clinical effect. Most patients who take long-term benzodiazepine therapy therefore do not increase their doses but remain on constant amounts of benzodiazepines. Recent data, however, suggest that tolerance to the anxiolytic effect of benzodiazepines may, in fact, occasionally develop (Boning 1985).

Tolerance to the sedative effects of benzodiazepines, however, is well documented. Clinically, this is manifested as drowsiness or sedation the first three days to a week of treatment (sometimes longer in the elderly). These sedative effects then disappear and do not return unless there is an increase in dosage.

Dependence on Benzodiazepines

Although survey data do not support "epidemic" uses of benzodiazepines, it is clear that a substantial number of people are dependent on benzodiazepines. Dependence on benzodiazepines is traditionally considered to take two forms: physiologic and psychological. The question of the frequency and severity of true psychological dependence, as well as of the physiologic dependence, continues to be of clinical importance.

The presence of symptoms of withdrawal and abstinence following discontinuation of any drug suggest a physiologic need for that agent. Benzodiazepines, like other sedative-hypnotics, produce a predictable discontinuance syndrome. Discontinuance, usually following abrupt cessation of benzodiazepines, consists of three categories of symptoms. The first is termed "recurrence," and consists of a return of the original symptoms for which the benzodiazepine was originally prescribed. These recurrent symptoms are of the same severity as the original symptoms, and tend to persist for extended periods after drug cessation. The second category of discontinuance symptoms is termed "rebound," and consists of symptoms that are more severe than the original symptoms. Rebound symptoms often are the first to appear following drug cessation, and are usually short lived, lasting only hours or days. The third category of discontinuance symptoms is termed "withdrawal," and consists of new symptoms that were not present when the drug was originally prescribed. These new symptoms are sometimes called an abstinence syndrome and indicate the presence of a true state of physiologic drug dependence.

In general, discontinuance symptoms are more severe when benzodiazepines have been taken in high doses and for long periods of time. Discontinuance symptoms have been noted to occur in 43 percent of patients treated for more than eight months, whereas only 5 percent of patients treated for less than eight months experienced such symptoms (Rickels et al. 1983).

The complete discontinuance syndrome includes severe sleep disturbance, irritability, increased tension, anxiety, panic attacks, hand tremor, profuse sweating, decreased concentration, retching, nausea, weight loss, palpitations, muscular pains, stiffness, seizures, and psychosis (Lader 1983; Lader and Petursson 1983). Less severe reactions, however, are more common. These include increased anxiety, dry mouth, a choking feeling, hot and cold feelings, "legs like jelly," and irritability. Hand tremor, sweating, decreased appetite, nausea, occasional morning vomiting, and mild but short-duration depression also occur. There may be insomnia for several days following abrupt discontinuance of the drug with a return to normal sleep eight to ten days after discontinuation. The sleep disturbance (rebound insomnia) is noted more typically after discontinuation of short half-life benzodiazepines. There is a comparable rebound anxiety with symptoms that may be virtually indistinguishable from the original anxiety symptoms present when the drugs were first prescribed. In some cases, the anxiety following benzodiazepine discontinuance is a recurrence of the original anxiety that was suppressed by the benzodiazepines (Greenblatt and Shader 1983) rather than a manifestation of withdrawal and abstinence. Recurrence and rebound, as well as true withdrawal, commonly occur together (Haskell 1984; Rickels 1980).

The time of onset and the severity of discontinuance symptoms depend on pharmacokinetic differences among the benzodiazepines. Because of a gradual elimination time, the natural tapering effect of blood levels of long half-life benzodiazepines tends to produce less severe withdrawal reactions, if any. The onset of symptoms often occurs three to four days after the period of discontinuation. Short half-life benzodiazepines, on the other hand, are eliminated more rapidly from the body. Thus, the tapering effect is absent, and symptoms of withdrawal and abstinence begin rather abruptly and tend to be more severe (Owen and Tyrer 1983). The aging process has little effect on tapering or severity of withdrawal symptoms of short half-life benzodiazepines (Salzman 1984).

Although the presence of a predictable abstinence syndrome suggests that true physiologic dependence to benzodiazepines is possible, the nature and extent of such addiction in humans is unknown. True physiologic dependence to benzodiazepines has been observed in patients who received therapeutic doses of benzodiazepines as well as those receiving higher doses. Dependence also occurs in individuals with an addiction-prone personality who may ingest very large doses and who also tend to be polydrug abusers. It is clear, however, that true dependence also occurs in non-addiction-prone users (Maletsky and Klotter 1976).

In addition to true physiologic dependence, psychological dependence may develop. Psychological dependence, also termed habituation, is a craving for the drug and may be associated with subjective feelings of distress in its absence. Physiologic and psychological dependence may or may not coexist. Undoubtedly, there are also people who keep benzodiazepines in medicine chests at home or in medicine kits when traveling but take them only occasionally, in circumstances of extreme stress. Self-medication of this sort is likely to be low-dose, extremely short-lived, and unconnected with dependence or addiction to other drugs. Some people also occasionally take benzodiazepines to assist in sleep and, if successful, do not need to continue to take medication on a nightly basis. Simply knowing that the medication is available if necessary may also provide sufficient antianxiety effect to produce sleep. These people do not fall within the usual definition of psychological dependence but are *reliant* on the availability of medication when needed. There are no data to suggest that reliance on the availability of benzodiazepines or occasional intermittent use leads to dependence or withdrawal reactions.

In summary, the data on physiologic dependence, discontinuance reactions, and psychological dependence suggest that benzodiazepines, in therapeutic doses over long periods of time, as well as in high doses, may cause both psychological and physiologic dependence. The severity of this dependence is quite mild in most cases and the discontinuance symptoms, although uncomfortable, are usually mild and short lived. It is not possible to say, however, whether or not everyone or anyone who takes benzodiazepines for a lengthy time in therapeutic doses is liable to addiction and withdrawal reactions. Because it is now clear that dependence and discontinuance reactions, albeit mild, may develop even in some patients taking therapeutic doses, it is prudent to treat anxiety with the lowest possible doses of benzodiazepine for the shortest period of time. Prolonged treatment should be avoided whenever possible, and benzodiazepines should never be abruptly discontinued.

Treatment of the Anxious Patient

The decision to use benzodiazepines as part of the treatment of anxiety rests on several factors. When anxiety results from acute stress, the physician may wish to use benzodiazepines for a brief period of time and then discontinue them. In these circumstances, the benzodiazepines are primarily used to augment coping strategies rather than as an ongoing part of a therapeutic program. In the treatment of medical illness with associated anxiety, benzodiazepines contribute to the reduction of a state of hyperarousal that is either part of the illness or a reaction to it and that contributes to damage that may be done by the illness. For example, patients suffering from musculoskeletal or cardiovascular diseases (the two most common medical illnesses associated with benzodiazepine use) may suffer harm from the presence of anxiety. In these conditions, as in many other physical illnesses, the reduction of anxiety through benzodiazepine use may also bring about some amelioration of physical symptoms. In states of chronic anxiety that are not associated with medical illness but that interfere with normal day-to-day functioning and productivity, judicious use of benzodiazepines may allow the patient to function more adequately. This is the most typical psychiatric indication for benzodiazepine use. Lastly, high levels of anxiety may interfere with psychotherapeutic work. Judicious use of benzodiazepines under these circumstances may actually allow psychotherapy, behavioral therapy, or psychoanalytic work to proceed more efficiently and productively with the ultimate goal of further reduction in anxiety without drugs.

Once the decision to use benzodiazepines has been made, the physician is faced with the choice of a number of different agents, of long half-life, intermediate half-life, or short half-life. All benzodiazepines are equivalent in terms of their antianxiety properties if milligram dosages are equalized for a therapeutic effect. Thus, there is no particular therapeutic reason to choose a long over a short half-life drug or any long half-life benzodiazepine over another, or any one short half-life benzodiazepine over any other. Long half-line benzodiazepines are preferred for younger patients and for those who are reliable, do not take other sedatives or hypnotics, or drink excessively. Short half-life benzodiazepines are preferred for elderly patients, patients who take other sedating or central nervous system depressing drugs, and patients who do not reliably follow dosage schedules. A few of the benzodiazepines may be given by injection, although in most cases the treatment of anxiety only requires oral dosing.

Regardless of whether benzodiazepines are used for short-term or long-term treatment of anxiety and regardless of which benzodiazepine is selected, certain basic principles of use should be remembered:

1. Symptoms of anxiety must be carefully differentiated from physical states that may produce similar symptoms. Apprehension, fear, and anxiety must be differentiated from normal worry and concerns of everyday life. Day-to-day concerns should not be medicated with benzodiazepines or other drugs.
2. As a general principle, physicians should maintain close contact with patients receiving benzodiazepines and try to minimize the use of benzodiazepines and repeated prescriptions.
3. In many patients, the use of benzodiazepines is meant primarily as adjunctive or supportive treatment. The use of benzodiazepines should be discussed with the patient at the beginning of the prescription period. Patients should be informed of potential risks of dependence and discontinuance reactions.
4. Patients should be carefully cautioned about interactions between benzodiazepines and other drugs, particularly central nervous system sedatives and alcohol.
5. Physicians should continue to make frequent assessments of the severity of the patient's anxiety and decrease or discontinue benzodiazepines whenever possible.
6. Brief benzodiazepine use may be indicated in general hospital settings to reduce anxiety during the period of hospitalization. This is appropriate use of benzodiazepines but certain precautions must be exercised:

- Patients in hospitals or who are acutely ill may be too upset to fully comprehend the long-term risks of benzodiazepine use. Physicians must take it upon themselves, therefore, to ensure that benzodiazepine use is not continued beyond the period necessary for the treatment of anxiety and agitation.
- Whenever possible, benzodiazepines should be discontinued when the patient leaves the hospital or shortly thereafter. All too commonly, prescriptions are renewed when not entirely necessary.
- Physicians must be aware of the possibility of polypharmacy and drug interactions. A survey of psychotropic drug use in a general hospital found that benzodiazepines flurazepam and diazepam were among the most commonly prescribed drugs in general hospital settings (Salzman 1981) and are often combined with other sedating drugs so that patients may be oversedated. At times this may be a necessary part of the therapeutic program, but all too often oversedation is not necessary and leads to confusion, disorientation, and fear on the part of the patient. This is particularly true for elderly patients who may become quite confused from benzodiazepines as well as from oversedation. Physicians must also be aware of pharmacokinetic interactions; cimetidine, for example, inhibits benzodiazepine metabolism, increasing benzodiazepine blood levels and causing benzodiazepine toxicity.

Concern for potential benzodiazepine dependence has led to the development of an alternative benzodiazepine-prescribing practice known as the "repeated single-dose regimen" or "benzodiazepines on demand" (McCurdy 1980). Using this regimen, benzodiazepines are prescribed only when symptoms of anxiety develop, analogous to the use of aspirin for muscle pain or fever. Patients are asked to maintain a daily record of the frequency, severity, and etiology of their anxiety attacks. If medication is required, this is noted in the daily log. Initially, patients are seen once or twice a week by the physician so that dosage requirements and maximum daily dosage can be agreed upon between patient and physician. The patient is also instructed at the beginning of treatment that the need for medication will be evaluated after four weeks of treatment. The use of a diary, initial instructions, and limitation upon long-term prescription help to allow the patient to develop a sense of control over anxiety. Allowing the patient to control dosage and dosage intervals similarly enhances a sense of self-confidence. In both clinical practice and research settings, this form of on-demand or symptomatic prescribing has not led to overuse of benzodiazepines or the development of dependence. This form of treatment is particularly well suited to patients with intermittent anxiety following identifiable cause. It is less well suited to anxiety with no clear-cut source or to chronic free-floating anxiety states.

Other Antianxiety Agents

Pharmacologic treatment of anxiety has been extended beyond the use of benzodiazepines to include other psychotropic drugs such as the antidepressants and antipsychotic drugs, as well as the use of medical drugs that are not ordinarily used by psychiatrists such as the beta blockers and antihistamines. In addition, a new antianxiety drug, buspirone, has become available for clinical use in the United States.

Propranolol

Propranolol, a beta-receptor blocking agent used for cardiovascular disorders, is sometimes prescribed for the treatment of mild situational anxiety states characterized by peripheral autonomic symptoms such as sweating, tachycardia, sighing, and tremor (Pitts and Allen 1982). Whether or not propranolol has a central nervous system antianxiety effect is unknown. There are no data comparing propranolol with benzodiazepine agents as an antianxiety drug for more chronic or generalized anxiety states. There are also no data comparing propranolol with other beta-blocking drugs for the treatment of anxiety.

Potential side effects of propranolol include hypotension, congestive heart failure, interference with cardiac conduction, and exacerbation of asthma. Other side effects are increased susceptibility to hypoglycemia in diabetic patients and rebound angina or hypertension when propranolol is suddenly withdrawn. Some patients who take propranolol experience depression.

Despite these side effects and uncertainties in the mechanism of action, propranolol is sometimes used for specific anxiety settings such as stage fright. In such circumstances, low doses of propranolol, such as 10 or 20 mg shortly before the anxiety-inducing circumstance, are reported to be beneficial. Longer term use of propranolol for ongoing anxiety symptoms is not advisable at this time.

Antipsychotic Drugs

Antipsychotic drugs are rarely useful for the treatment of anxiety. For certain patients, however, in a prepsychotic state due to a weakening of ego defense mechanisms, the threat of emerging psychosis produces states of intermittent terror and anxiety. These states are often not responsive to benzodiazepines except at very high dosages. Such patients may respond to low doses of neuroleptic drugs.

The selection of neuroleptic drug depends on whether or not sedation is desired. Sedating neuroleptics such as chlorpromazine may be prescribed in doses of 10 to 75 mg (occasionally more) for short-term relief of such prepsychotic anxiety. Neuroleptics such as haloperidol or trifluoperazine are often used with great advantage because sedation is less common with these drugs.

Neuroleptics should be used for a short period of time for these forms of anxiety. If prepsychotic anxiety persists, it is likely that a true psychotic process is beginning and more traditional neuroleptic treatment should be undertaken. Otherwise, these drugs should be discontinued by slowly tapering as soon as possible. In addition, one must consider the risks of tardive dyskinesia when prescribing antipsychotic agents.

Antihistamines

Antihistamines are sometimes used to treat anxious patients, particularly those in general hospitals or with physical illness. Hydroxyzine is the antihistamine drug most commonly prescribed. It possesses anti-emetic and antihistamine properties as well as sedative antianxiety effects and is often used, therefore, in the treatment of allergic skin reactions and motion sickness, and as a preanesthetic.

Hydroxyzine and other antihistamines decrease the seizure threshold and should be used carefully in patients with a prior history of seizures.

Imipramine

Recent data from a double-blind, carefully controlled study suggests that imipramine may have an antianxiety effect equal to, or superior to, chlordiazepoxide in anxious outpatients (Kahn et al. 1986). The clinical implications of this finding are not clear; most clinicians do not routinely use imipramine for other cyclic antidepressants to treat anxiety that is not associated with depression.

Buspirone

Buspirone is a new antianxiety agent with a chemical structure that differs from the benzodiazepine class of compounds. It has demonstrated an antianxiety effect equivalent to diazepam. The two drugs are equally potent on a per-milligram basis, so that 5 mg of buspirone is therapeutically equivalent to 5 mg of diazepam (Rickels et al. 1982). Buspirone is less sedating than antianxiety agents and has less potential for abuse (Cole et al. 1982). The long-term effectiveness of buspirone is still unknown, and its general usefulness in the average clinical setting compared with benzodiazepines is equally unknown. It may be the antianxiety of choice for patients with a history of substance abuse. Buspirone is not effective as a substitute for benzodiazepines for the prevention or treatment of benzodiazepine withdrawal. Buspirone is also not useful for the rapid treatment of acute anxiety because it takes between one to two weeks at therapeutic doses for the antianxiety effect to appear.

Drug Treatment of Phobias and Panic Anxiety

Until recently, pharmacologic treatment of severe phobic states and accompanying anxiety was limited to the use of sedative compounds. Similarly, pharmacologic treatment of overwhelming states of panic that produced phobic avoidance as a secondary defense response was also limited to the use of sedative drugs such as barbiturates and propanediols. However, very high doses were often necessary to reduce the anxiety of these states. Although symptom reduction could sometimes be achieved through sufficient sedation, patients rarely had any reduction in the actual phobic avoidance or panic anxiety symptoms. From a pharmacologic perspective, the use of available benzodiazepines, even in high doses, or even the use of neuroleptic drugs did not alter phobic avoidance behavior, fear, or panic anxiety symptoms.

Initial empirical evidence demonstrated that low doses of imipramine, a drug used in the treatment of depression, was successful in ameliorating school phobic behavior in children without producing central nervous system sedation. Imipramine was then tried in adult states of agoraphobic avoidance and panic anxiety with re- markably positive results (see Klein et al. 1980, pp. 548–552). Soon, several reports noted that monoamine oxidase inhibitors were also useful in treating patients whose depressive symptoms also included large amounts of phobic anxiety symptoms. It soon became apparent that for panic anxiety and agoraphobia, traditional benzodi- azepine treatment was inferior to antidepressants.

Cyclic antidepressants and monoamine oxidase inhibitors are essentially equiv- alent in the treatment of panic with and without agoraphobia. Of the cyclic antide- pressants, imipramine has been used most frequently, whereas phenelzine has been the monoamine oxidase inhibitor most commonly used in therapeutic trials and in double-research studies. Alprazolam, an intermediate half-life benzodiazepine, is also widely used to treat panic and agoraphobia. In the clinical situation, the selection of these drugs for the treatment of the patient with panic anxiety and phobic avoidance behavior depends primarily on four factors: 1) physical health of the patient; 2) pres- ence or absence of other medications; 3) drug-taking compliance of the patient; and 4) differences in frequency and severity of side effects of each of the drugs.

Cyclic Antidepressants: Imipramine

The use of imipramine for the treatment of phobic and panic anxiety states resembles its use for patients with major depressive disorder. After a careful diagnostic evaluation, patients should have a physical examination and work-up; the elements of this work-up are listed in Table 2. Patients are started on 50 or 75 mg of imipramine daily after an initial test dose to rule out drug allergy. Dosage increments of 25 mg may be made every two to three days following assessment of pulse and seated and standing blood pressures. Doses of imipramine below 150 mg per day may not be effective although some patients with these disorders seem to be exquisitely sensitive to cyclic antidepressants and develop side effects at low doses. It may be necessary, therefore, to increase the dosage slowly.

Side effects from imipramine treatment of phobic and panic anxiety disorders are

Table 2.   Pretreatment Evaluation

- Physical examination
- Review of current medications
- Assessment of cardiovascular status (EKG for patients over 40 or who have cardiac dysfunction)
- Blood pressure (seated and standing)
- Baseline weight
- Assessment of sexual function and responsiveness

similar to those side effects seen during the treatment of major depressive disorders. Initial sedation or stimulation is often noticed with rapid tolerance developing to these side effects. Dizziness and orthostatic hypotension is common, as well as tachycardia and occasional cardiac arrhythmias. Anticholinergic symptoms, particularly dry mouth and constipation, are also common. Weight gain and diminution in sexual responsiveness sometimes occur in patients taking imipramine.

Monoamine Oxidase Inhibitors: Phenelzine

Treatment of panic anxiety and phobic avoidance states with phenelzine resembles the use of phenelzine for the treatment of depressive disorders. After an accurate diagnostic assessment is made, patients should receive a thorough physical evaluation as listed in Table 2. Patients must be instructed about dietary restrictions and medication interactions that may occur with the use of phenelzine or other monoamine oxidase inhibitors. These restrictions are listed in Tables 3 and 4.

After an initial trial of a single 15-mg dose of phenelzine to rule out drug allergy, patients may be started on 30 or 45 mg of phenelzine in divided doses. If there is no response to 45 mg of phenelzine sulfate after one week, the dose may be increased to 60 mg; many patients with severe panic anxiety and phobic disorders will not show any clinical response until at least 60 mg of phenelzine. Doses may be increased by 15 mg every three or four days up to 90 mg per day. If there has been no response at this point, platelet monoamine oxidase inhibitor levels should be reassessed.

Although clinical response has not been correlated with degree of inhibition of platelet monoamine oxidase, the measurement of the degree of inhibition of this enzyme may provide a guideline for further increase in dosage. Doses above 90 or 105 mg per day on an outpatient basis should be undertaken with extreme caution and only by experienced psychiatrists. Although some patients demonstrate an almost immediate reduction in panic anxiety symptoms following onset of phenelzine treatment, it may take four weeks at higher dosage ranges before the clinical effect is apparent.

Side effects that are commonly seen with phenelzine treatment include orthostatic hypotension, weight gain, and diminution of sexual responsiveness (anorgasmia). Patients who have had a therapeutic response to phenelzine are often scrupulously

Table 3.   Dietary Restrictions for Use with Monoamine Oxidase Inhibitors

Foods that must be avoided

- Cheese (particularly hard, aged, aromatic); cream, cottage, and American are acceptable
- Smoked fish and meats
- Chicken liver
- Chianti wine
- Monosodium glutamate

Foods that must be limited

- Fava (broad) beans
- Yeast products (Bovril, Marmite)
- Pickles, sauerkraut
- Chocolate
- Coffee
- Soy sauce
- Avocado
- Sour cream

Table 4.　Medications to Be Avoided When Taking Monoamine Oxidase Inhibitors

1. Stimulants: Amphetamine (Benzedrine)
　　　　　　　Dextroamphetamine
　　　　　　　Methamphetamine (Desoxyn)
　　　　　　　Methylphenidate (Ritalin)
　　　　　　　Epinephrine (Adrenalin)
　　　　　　　Dopamine (Intropin)

2. Cold, allergy,
　asthma preparations: Ephedrine (Tedral)
　　　　　　　　　　　Pseudoephedrine (Actifed, Sudafed)
　　　　　　　　　　　Phenylpropanolamine (Dimetane, Coricidin, others)

3. Narcotics: Meperidine (Demerol)

4. Antihypertensives: Reserpine (Serpasil)
　　　　　　　　　　Methyldopa (Aldomet)

5. Cyclic antidepressants

6. Other monoamine oxidase inhibitors

careful in both their diets and use of other medications so that hypertensive crises, when they occur, are usually accidental or inadvertent. Some clinicians instruct their patients to carry one tablet of chlorpromazine (50 mg) to be taken in the event of severe headache or suggest that they carry a note in their wallet or pocketbook stating they are taking monoamine oxidase inhibitors. Elevated blood pressure is treated with phentolamine (Regetine).

Alprazolam

Recent data have suggested that alprazolam is efficacious in the treatment of patients with panic anxiety as well as agoraphobia (Ballenger et al. 1988; Noyes et al. 1988; Pecknold et al. 1988). Alprazolam has demonstrated antipanic effects in doses of 4 to 10 mg per day (Sheehan et al. 1984). Patients are usually started on 0.5 mg three times daily with meals, and dosage increments of 0.5 to 1.0 mg every one to two days are usually well tolerated. There may be dosage plateaus during the initial weeks of treatment until a stable antipanic dose is reached (Sheehan 1985; Sheehan et al. 1984). The antipanic properties of alprazolam may be especially therapeutic in patients whose panic is mild to moderate. In patients with very severe panic disorder, alprazolam often reduces or attenuates the panic episodes, but does not eliminate them entirely. Alprazolam may also be very effective as an adjunct to imipramine or phenelzine for panic attacks, should the patient experience only partial therapeutic response at full therapeutic doses of these drugs. The typical side effects of alprazolam include sedation, unsteadiness, and slurring of speech. Occasional forgetfulness, irritability, and impairment of motivation have been noted (Sheehan 1985). Patients may become dependent on alprazolam and have difficulty discontinuing this drug.

Duration of Treatment

Although imipramine, phenelzine, and alprazolam may produce dramatic diminution in the frequency and intensity of panic anxiety attacks and phobic avoidance behavior, they may not completely eliminate all symptoms. However, patients often find the quality of their lives so dramatically improved by these drug treatments that they are able to adjust to the remaining symptoms and learn to restructure their lives to accommodate the remaining anxiety.

Unfortunately, although these drugs produce marked diminution in symptoms, the underlying basis for the symptoms rarely is ameliorated. Many patients experience a return of symptoms when these drugs are discontinued. This is most discouraging for those patients who, during treatment, feel that they have been virtually cured. The return of symptoms following drug discontinuation is sometimes taken as a personal failure or evidence of underlying pathologic constitution, and physicians must be prepared to help patients with this disappointment.

Because of relapse and recurrence of symptoms in a high proportion of patients, many who have had a therapeutic response choose to remain on medication for long periods of time. It is suggested that drugs not be discontinued until a patient has experienced 6 to 12 months during which symptoms are absent or significantly reduced.

Conclusion

Given the efficacy of all three drug approaches, the clinician must select among these options on the basis of a number of other factors such as severity of panic symptoms; cardiovascular status; potential sensitivity to anticholinergic, orthostatic hypotensive, and cardiac side effects; as well as use of concomitant medication. Thus, cyclic antidepressants should not be prescribed to patients with panic disorder or agoraphobia who also are taking quinidine-type drugs. Monoamine oxidase inhibitors should not be prescribed to patients who cannot comply with the dietary restrictions, or who may be taking concomitant contraindicated medication. Alprazolam should not be prescribed to patients with the severest form of panic anxiety, who are taking other central nervous system sedatives, who are unable to restrict their alcohol intake, or who have a history of substance abuse or dependence.

Using these constraints as prescribing guidelines, the following differential therapeutic suggestions can be made (Salzman and Green 1987). For the least severely impaired panic disorder patient, alprazolam is a reasonable first therapeutic choice. If no therapeutic response occurs at doses of 4 to 6 mg, or if sedation or other side effects compromise daily functioning, then the patient should be switched to either imipramine or phenelzine. For patients with the most severe crippling panic disorder, phenelzine probably produces a more rapid and slightly more thorough blockade of panic symptoms than the other drugs. A pretreatment platelet monoamine oxidase level should be obtained. Most patients will show a response to a dose of 45 to 75 mg of phenelzine daily. In responsive patients who develop marked weight gain or anorgasmia, a switch to tranylcypromine may be helpful (Klein 1985). In nonresponding patients, the dose should be increased until pretreatment platelet monoamine oxidase levels have been suppressed to at least 80 percent, unless side effects become too intense.

Imipramine is the best overall treatment for moderately severe panic symptoms as well as for those patients who have not responded to alprazolam or phenelzine, who are intolerant of the side effect, or who are unreliable for diet restriction. For patients who show a partial but incomplete response to either phenelzine or imipramine, alprazolam may be added as an adjunct.

Regardless of which antidepressant is chosen, patients should be treated for at least 6 to 12 symptom-free months before dose tapering or drug discontinuance is considered. Relapse figures are variable and are, at best, estimates. Typically, however, many patients who discontinue drugs may experience a return of panic or phobic symptoms even after continuous drug treatment of two or more years (Klein 1985). Drug withdrawal from alprazolam is often more difficult than discontinuing tricyclics or monoamine oxidase inhibitors because like other benzodiazepines, withdrawal produces heightened anxiety and insomnia.

Chapter 185

Strategies of Relaxation, Self-Control, and Fear-Mastery

Several therapeutic techniques other than those already reviewed in this task force report appear to be useful adjuncts in the treatment of anxiety and panic disorders.[1] These techniques include relaxation, meditation, hypnosis, self-hypnosis, autogenic training, and biofeedback (Benson and Klipper 1976; Brown 1977; Kroger 1977; Luthe 1969; Townsend et al. 1975). Such procedures are considered adjunctive because they are used in an overall therapeutic program and are rarely, if ever, appropriate for the treatment of anxiety or panic disorders outside of such a larger context.

Although the techniques vary considerably, they can all be characterized as facilitating relaxation and calm, both in psychological and physiologic terms, while simultaneously conveying therapeutic suggestions, implied or explicit. Generally, the achievement of physiologic resting levels is associated with a sense of ease, and vice versa. The techniques for the most part depend on cognitive and behavioral procedures that are intended to provide the patient with coping strategies that he or she may draw upon in future life situations outside the therapeutic context. In addition to the relaxation that results, patients gain reassurance and not infrequently a sense of mastery and control over symptoms and fears that previously were disruptive and threatening.

The techniques typically encourage patients to narrow the focus of their attention. An important consequence of biofeedback, meditation, or hypnosis seems to be a shift of one's appreciation of reality, of who and where one is, to the periphery of awareness and to disconnect it from the major focus of the moment (Shor 1959).

Biofeedback involves providing an external signal of internal events that makes it easier for the patient to become aware of physiological events, typically by means of electronic sensors and visual or auditory displays. In the treatment of anxiety disorders, frontalis muscle feedback using electromyographic (EMG) signals has been employed most often. From feedback of muscle tension, the patient can learn to decrease it and presumably thereby decrease the level of anxiety.

In meditation, attention is directed toward a specific thought, object, or physical activity. The meditator is required to maintain his or her focus and to ignore both irrelevant internal and external stimuli, one consequence of which is the decrease of anxiety.

In hypnosis, the generalized reality orientation and critical judgment are partially suspended, facilitating dissociation (Hilgard 1977). With suggestibility increased, patients can become responsive to suggestions to experience altered perceptions, memory, and mood (Orne 1977). Hypnosis may also facilitate the patients' bringing forth affect-laden associations and memories. The whole sequence is generally initiated in a relaxed context and occurs to varying degrees, depending on the aptitude of the patient for such voluntary dissociation.

It is often useful for the patient, especially early in therapy, to have available specific procedures to use at home and to use them in anxiety-inducing situations outside the therapeutic context. For example, self-hypnosis as taught by a therapist after or during the administration of an induction of heterohypnosis is used widely in clinical practice (Fromm et al. 1981). Among patients who are taught self-hypnosis and who are directed to practice it at home to control anxiety between therapy sessions, many appear to achieve some symptom relief on their own (Soskis 1986).

Autogenic training is a variant of self-hypnosis that involves a series of graded mental exercises that the patient is required to practice between office visits. Over time, the patient becomes able to master the more difficult procedures that permit him or her to control the level of tension and anxiety (see Luthe 1969).

Progressive relaxation is a related technique based on the premise that it is not possible to be anxious if one is physically relaxed. Described by Jacobson in 1938, the procedure involves much feedback based on observations concerning when the patient relaxes, where areas of bodily tension persist, and the like. It also uses the technique of asking patients to tense muscle groups to become aware of the difference between relaxation and tension.

Treating Generalized Anxiety

Many clinical reports attest to the effectiveness of each of these techniques in the treatment of anxiety. (For the most part these patients would now be classified as having general anxiety disorder.) There are few systematic studies available; however, in virtually all case reports and studies of groups, significant improvement occurs in patients following any of these interventions when patients are compared before and after treatment. The area where the most systematic outcome studies have been carried out involves EMG biofeedback. Typically, improvement is evaluated both in terms of the patient's success in decreasing muscle tension as indexed by the frontalis EMG and some kind of self-report anxiety change score.

Probably because biofeedback was initially conceptualized as a form of conditioning by some investigators, there was considerable interest in and controversy about whether or not conditioning could explain the therapeutic effects of EMG feedback.

In a number of studies, frontalis EMG biofeedback was compared with other techniques. For example, one study compared chronically anxious patients treated either with EMG biofeedback or group psychotherapy. Significant decreases in EMG levels and in subjectively rated anxiety were observed in the biofeedback group, with no such changes seen in the psychotherapy group (Townsend et al. 1975).

In another study, 28 anxiety neurotics, half of which received EMG biofeedback and the other half Jacobson's relaxation training, were compared. Both groups reported significant improvement. However, 12 of those treated with biofeedback as opposed to only seven of those with relaxation training reported improvement. Even greater outcome differences were noted in therapists' reports. Most interesting, investigators found the level of the EMG decrease was significantly correlated with reported improvement (Canter et al. 1975).

In contrast to the findings of these two clinical studies, which suggest that EMG biofeedback is the specific agent responsible for improvement, are the findings of a number of other studies. For example, 40 students with severe test anxiety were given one of the following four treatments: EMG feedback, relaxation, attention-placebo relaxation, and a no-treatment control. Compared to the no-treatment control, all three groups showed improvement, *but* there were no differences between these groups (Beiman et al. 1978).

Another study compared EMG feedback with progressive relaxation and self-relaxation for dental phobic patients. EMG feedback and progressive relaxation both were more effective in relieving dental state anxiety than self-relaxation, but there was no difference between them (Miller et al. 1978).

Similar results were obtained in comparing three groups of anxiety disorder patients. The first group received EMG feedback, the second muscle relaxation training, and the third transcendental meditation. Forty percent of the patients demonstrated significant decreases in anxiety, but there were no differences between the three groups in terms of effectiveness (Raskin et al. 1980).

One study that directly addressed the question of mechanism involved 12 students who reported anxiety and difficulty in managing everyday stress. Half of these received EMG biofeedback and the other half (yoked controls) received feedback *not* contingent upon changes in muscle tension. The group receiving true EMG feedback showed significant reduction in muscle tension during a stress task when compared to individuals who did not receive contingent feedback. Nonetheless, analogous to observations reported in other studies, there were no differences between the groups on measures of subjective anxiety (Gatchel et al. 1978).

Though it is clear that EMG biofeedback has been therapeutically useful, the theoretical rationale upon which it was based—that is, that anxiety will be reduced by teaching patients to decrease the tonic level of frontalis muscle tension—has not been justified by subsequent research. Thus, in later studies there was generally no relationship found between anxiety relief and the ability to learn relaxation as indexed by the frontalis EMG. Similarly, the relief of tension headaches, for which one would expect frontalis EMG to be a specific factor, is also unrelated to an individual's ability to learn frontalis muscle relaxation—though the procedure itself is quite effective in providing symptomatic relief (Orne 1980). In summarizing work in this area, Gatchel (1982) states ". . . that this procedure may be clinically effective with patients suffering primarily from anxiety. However . . . methods such as progressive relaxation training are at least equally effective" (pp. 392–393).

Regarding the other techniques discussed in this section, the question of whether they are *specific* therapeutic agents has not been addressed as cogently as in the biofeedback literature. It should be clear, however, that the failure to find differences between muscle relaxation training and EMG biofeedback challenges the specificity of relaxation training as much as that of EMG training. Indeed, both of these procedures are challenged by the fact that curarized individuals are by no means without anxiety. Again the fact that studies have shown no differences between EMG feedback, relaxation training, and meditation raises questions about the specific effect of each of these procedures. The failure to document differences in outcome between meditation and self-hypnosis in the treatment of anxiety does not help support the view that either have specific therapeutic effects (Benson et al 1978).

The insights offered by Frank (1961) seem particularly relevant. He points to a number of characteristics common to all treatments. Thus, the therapist is a culturally sanctioned expert, with relevant special training. Both the patient and the healer need to have faith in the curative power of the treatment. It is carried out in a place designated for this purpose. All treatments have some rationale that makes sense within the culture—but are not necessarily correct from our current scientific perspective.

Whatever the intervention, it must make it possible for the patient to attribute his improvement to the treatment. The relationship between therapist and the patient is of considerable importance, and the person of the therapist and his or her attributes greatly affect the outcome. Finally, if the procedure requires much of the patient— hard work, discomfort, great cost, dramatic affects—the likelihood of cure is enhanced.

These nonspecific factors, which in psychopharmacology are in part subsumed under placebo effects, are remarkably powerful. They are therefore often difficult to disentangle from specific effects that may be swamped by the placebo components of a dramatic treatment. Conversely, a specific drug effect may be negated in the absence of the necessary nonspecific components of treatment (see Rickels 1968).

The importance of the interpersonal relationship in the biofeedback situation is, for example, illustrated by Beiman et al. (1978) who found that live relaxation was superior to taped progressive relaxation and self-relaxation. Similarly, among those patients who are helped by these techniques, the meditators, for example, report far more success at least initially when meditating with their teacher than by themselves. Similarly, the majority of patients practicing self-hypnosis report that the experience is not as rich as when hypnotized during their therapy hour. This does not appear to be a matter of the patient's ability to respond, but rather it is likely to reflect the central importance of the relationship between the patient and the therapist. It would seem that motivation or talent is of itself likely to be insufficient unless allowed to function within the context of a therapeutic relationship and its many levels of meaning.

Treating Phobias, Panic, and PTSD

While the techniques aimed at relaxation often work quite well in the alleviation of generalized anxiety, they offer limited help in the treatment of obsessive-compulsive rituals. When used to treat phobias, panic, and posttraumatic stress disorders, they become effective only when they are specifically adapted to the particular patient's needs.

The literature contains many examples of the adjunctive use of hypnosis in the treatment of phobic symptoms (McGuiness 1984). It may well be relevant that individuals who suffer from simple and social phobias tend to be more highly hypnotizable than other patients (Frankel and Orne 1976).[2] Such patients can be helped to overcome simple and social phobias either by the encouragement of ego-strengthening techniques (Hartland 1982), by uncovering emotionally traumatic material (Frankel 1976), or by blending behavior modification methods such as imaginal desensitization or implosion with the hypnosis (Kroger and Fezler 1976).

Although there is an extensive history and literature on the use of each of these techniques in the treatment of anxiety, neither the clinical reports nor the available studies are adequate to determine what is specific to the success of the treatment.

This lack is perhaps less problematic than it might seem, because, as we have discussed, these procedures are primarily adjunctive components in the treatment of anxiety and panic disorders. Neither biofeedback, hypnosis, meditation, nor relaxation procedures are seen here as treatments in their own right. They are techniques that are useful when woven into the fabric of a treatment plan; they facilitate and enrich the therapy by adding dimensions to it that would otherwise be wanting. For these reasons, it may be most useful to illustrate how these procedures can be applied as adjunctive techniques within the broader therapeutic context. The ultimate purpose here is to show how they can contribute to the therapeutically desired change in the patient's experience of anxiety or panic.

Case Histories

In the following case vignettes, we will try to determine the predominant therapeutic themes elicited or purposefully shaped by the use of the adjunctive techniques.

Case 1[3]

A 29-year-old bachelor engineer presented with marked insomnia and general tension. His treatment plan consisted of individual and group psychotherapy as well as relaxation training with electromyograph feedback.

He was described in the initial interviews as if carved of wood. His movements were restricted and he showed little or no affect. Of note in his family history are psychotic parents, a father functioning as a therapist, and a mother confined to an institution for the mentally ill.

He responded in part well to two months of biofeedback training, learning to relax his muscles. However, his anxiety and insomnia increased to a point at which the biofeedback was discontinued, and the thrust of the treatment concentrated on the psychotherapy. It was here that he was able to focus on his watchfulness at night, which kept him from sleeping, and his anxiety. Recognizing that he could now relax his body and was yet unable to relax his mind, he was led to a memory of a bizarre sexualized threat made repeatedly by his father as he was growing up: "Some day you and I are going to tangle backsides." He had repressed a memory that reappeared now in a flood of fearful affect and an awareness of the need to remain vigilant throughout the night. This was followed by an improvement in the insomnia and the anxiety.

Over a period of seven months, he became more emotionally expressive and found new freedom socially and elsewhere. Later in the therapy he recalled a long repressed memory that his father had indeed raped him at the age of nine years. Within two weeks of the recall and the start of working through the feelings associated with this memory, the patient had his first successful sexual experience with a woman.

Case 2

A 45-year-old man sought assistance for impotence of recent onset. He had been in the throes of a crumbling marriage over the previous six months, with a final decision by his wife that she wanted a divorce. At the time of his first visit, they were negotiating the settlement in an atmosphere of anger and counter-accusation.

It was during this period that he met a woman roughly his age similarly struggling with the breakup of her marriage. They dated a few times, felt a great fondness for each other, and after a few weeks of increasing mutual interest moved toward intercourse.

Although he had been greatly aroused during the courting, he found he could not sustain an erection after penetration. The repeated failure on three subsequent occasions prompted him to seek help. His partner had been constantly supportive and encouraging throughout.

He was the youngest of four siblings in an upwardly mobile family, encountering few problems as he grew up other than the pressure to succeed at least as well as his older siblings. His college education prepared him for business administration, and he had achieved some success in low-key middle management, earning a modest income. He had married at 24 to a woman three years his junior and had two teenage daughters. His marriage had been marred by his wife's limited interest in sex with him and her fairly constant criticism of his achievements and his style. She disparaged him by describing him as too soft and saintly.

Although acquiescing periodically to his sexual interests, she participated very little in the encounters and had told him several times of late that she loved him but was not in love with him. His sexual history for many years had included prostitutes and masturbation with occasional uninspired relationships at home. He could not remember having had difficulty with erections prior to the impotence experienced by him in the weeks preceding his request for treatment.

He had come to believe but was unable to prove that his wife's choice of divorce had to do with her recent involvement with an assertive and successful physician who had been part of their social circle. The course of events over the following six months were to prove him correct.

Clinical course. In describing his sexual difficulties, he made it clear that he was now troubled by his feelings of tension and long-unexpressed anger at his wife's fairly constant denigration of him. He was encouraged to elaborate on this in the sessions, and to refrain in the immediate future from sexual intercourse and attempts to prove his sexual competence. After three sessions in which he talked openly for the first time ever about his dissatisfactions with his marriage, he felt relieved but still anxious about his adequacy to complete the sexual act with his new partner. It was at this point that the topic of hypnosis was introduced as a means of assisting him to relax and regain his confidence. He rapidly agreed to the idea.

In the fourth visit, he responded in a limited way to a hypnotic induction, experiencing good relaxation and a tingling feeling in his forearm when altered perceptions were suggested. There was, however, no response to the suggestion that the hand and forearm would involuntarily float upwards, and little to suggest a marked alteration in his state of awareness. He nevertheless was able to achieve considerable calm and comfort, and in this state was able to visualize himself in a successful sexual encounter. He was confident that he could practice the self-hypnosis and relaxation exercise at home, and also rehearse sexual success in his mind's eye while doing so.

He returned for the fifth visit, having accomplished the act on more than one occasion to his and his partner's total satisfaction. He claimed that the exercise had boosted his confidence to such an extent that he had known with certainty that he would succeed, so he went ahead.

He reported a year later that all was well and that he and his new partner were planning on marriage.

Formulation: Cases 1 and 2

In both cases 1 and 2, progress became apparent when the individuals succeeded in mastering the physical accompaniments of the anxiety, in case 1 through EMG feedback and in case 2 through hypnosis and self-hypnosis. In case 1, this paved the way to the uncovering of repressed memories and insight, and in case 2 it led to a surge of justifiable confidence.

In case 1, the group plus individual therapy could well have been primarily responsible for the progress in treatment. Similarly, in case 2 the relaxation and successful imagery in hypnosis could have contributed to the patient's success, but the three previous psychotherapy sessions had been very supportive and had freed him from a considerable affective burden he had not been able to share with others before then.

To both patients, success was attributable largely to the adjunctive methods that were added to the treatment plan—a difficult position to argue with because it might be partially accurate. However, the addition of a noticeably different therapeutic procedure in which patient participation was emphasized might well have provided opportunities for enhancing self-esteem. Both patients believed that gaining control of some aspect of their dysfunction enabled them to work more effectively toward resolving the whole problem.

Case 3

A 50-year-old business executive had been prevented from flying for 18 years by an intense fear of flying. He had been a flight engineer in World War II and had then flown for five or six years as a passenger. Experiencing increasing anxiety, he finally found himself backing away from a planned business flight at the last moment and had not flown since. He talked of a sense of increasing anxiety when he thought of flying and his concern that he would make a fool of himself on the plane if the anxiety got out of control. He believed his knowledge of engineering added to his problems, and the introduction of the large jet carriers reaffirmed his belief that flying was dangerous.

He sought assistance through hypnosis on the recommendation of an associate who had successfully overcome his fear through hypnotically aided therapy, because business interests were at stake. Having to delegate the long-distance trips to his subordinates was affecting the level of his business success.

His past and personal histories appeared to be noncontributory, other than his report of a fear of riding in elevators that had arisen about the time of the flight phobia and that had improved but not completely disappeared after a few years. He was the youngest of four siblings who flew frequently as had his parents (now deceased). His wife and three teenage sons took air trips; his wife, however, was generally concerned about flying and fully sympathetic. He was surprised and embarrassed at his complacency when driving his family to the airport to board their flights, which he viewed as completely safe provided he was not a fellow passenger.

He was a warm person who related well, with a sense of humor when discussing his problems. He was clear in his intent that he was less interested in understanding the origins of his fears and keen only to resolve them. He was matter-of-fact in discussing his feelings about the issues under consideration, with a very practical approach that shunned any psychological interpretations. He had studied business methods after graduating from high school and was very much attuned to that style. He had no exposure to hypnosis and knew only what his associate had told him about his own experience. He scored nine out of a possible 12 on the Harvard Group Scale of Hypnotic Susceptibility (Shor and Orne 1962), which placed him in the high category of hypnotizability.

After some deliberation, he agreed to follow a course of hypnotically aided imaginal desensitization, meeting on a weekly basis for about an hour.

Clinical course.   After the second treatment session in which he had experienced hypnosis and learned to induce it himself at home, he reported that he had been more relaxed and had been able to sleep restfully at night and to curb his occasional intolerance of the excesses and noise created by his teenage children.

Having successfully dealt in hypnosis with the total of 15 items on the hierarchy by the end of the next three sessions, he continued to practice self-hypnosis at home and to discuss his progress and his plans in each subsequent session. Thereafter, about 15 to 20 minutes at the end of each visit were devoted to a hypnosis exercise in which his skills were reaffirmed and positive suggestions were added. He planned first to focus on flights in small aircraft. He got close to taking short local flights on a few occasions but changed his mind when he found he was unable to carry out the self-hypnosis exercises on the day before the scheduled trip. Encouragement was constant throughout the interviews, and he was repeatedly reminded of the value of the hypnotic methods by the subjectively real trance phenomena he was able to achieve in the hypnosis exercises. Without any intimation from the therapist, he feared that the treatment would be discontinued were he to delay for too long his plans to fly. He requested repeatedly during this period that the treatments continue, claiming that even if he did not succeed in flying, the treatment was helpful to him in many other ways.

At the 13th session, eight sessions after mastering the last item on the hierarchy, which involved the imagined rehearsal of sitting in a plane as it took off from the runway, he announced that he had flown. He had attended the funeral of a close relative in a city 2,000 miles away, an event that could not have been accomplished in the limited time available by any other means. This marked the initiation of increasingly ambitious flights involving transAtlantic trips within the next six months. During this time his therapy visits were spaced at two- to four-weekly intervals. He was proud of his achievement and claimed that his flights were already of benefit to his business interests.

Roughly a year after his first request for treatment he began to experience back pain. His medical advisors recommended bed rest and relaxation, and he returned for an appointment to determine whether he could use hypnosis to alleviate the pain. During the trance, in addition to suggestions for comfortable relaxed feelings in his back, he was advised to imagine a very restful scene in which he could feel totally relaxed and at peace. He disclosed, with some amusement, after the hypnosis exercise that the scene he found most helpful was the memory of a flight he had taken over the Swiss Alps.

A follow-up six years later revealed a story of continued success with few if any concerns about flying.

Case 4

A 34-year-old banker sought help for his fear of heights. This soft-spoken and very pleasant man had fallen from a tree at the age of seven, after which time he had experienced mild anxiety whenever he was obliged to climb trees or scale heights with his friends.

At the age of 20, after he had already left home, his parents moved to a 16th-floor apartment. It was here that he became aware of the more severe nature of his problem. He found himself avoiding the balcony, and experiencing discomfort when even thinking of stepping on to it. He would stand well back from the edge. For a few years prior to his request for treatment, he had become aware of an increasingly panic-like experience whenever he made his way on to the balcony or thought of doing so. Rather than subsiding with time, the problem appeared to be worsening, extending to involve other situations. Traveling on elevated highways and bridges had become threatening, and for some time before his first visit he had become aware of a fear that he might jump off or drive over the edge unless he exercised considerable control. Furthermore, he began to recognize in these situations that he experienced physical distress with palpitations, cold sweats, muscle tension, and shortness of breath. The panic lasted the full length of the exposure to the feared situation.

His strong tendency for several months had been to avoid the challenges and to remain indoors when he visited his parents' home. He found that when he was closed in, there seemed to be less reality to the height, and he therefore learned to protect himself as often as possible by escaping the visual impact of the fearsome scene. This avoidance seemed eventually to aggravate the problem, according to him, and he was irked by his growing concern. The factor most responsible for his request now for treatment was his recent reluctance to drive on a convenient route near his home because it entailed traveling over a bridge. He was struck by the fact that as he recounted his history in the interview, he found himself recreating the phobic fear and panic response as he spoke. This was his first attempt to get help for the problem.

Personal history.   He was the oldest of three siblings in a comfortable middle class family with little in the way of obvious or unusual problems. He claimed uneventful and reassuring relationships with his parents and his siblings. He had attended a fine undergraduate school, and then went on to acquire a degree in business administration and a very satisfactory post in a bank. His marriage at 23 to a woman of the same age was described as happy, as were his relationships with his four children, the oldest of whom had become vaguely aware of his problem.

Clinical course.   He was keen on obtaining relief as rapidly as possible, and came asking whether he could be treated in a program that involved hypnosis, which he had learned about as an undergraduate. He proved to be highly responsive, achieving a score of 10 out of a possible 12 on the Harvard Group Scale (Shor and Orne 1962).

In the subsequent two sessions, he readily mastered a seven-item hierarchy of increasingly fearsome situations. This accelerated program, modeled on the imaginal desensitization procedure of Wolpe (1958), was administered while the patient was in hypnosis. He was ultimately able to rehearse successfully, in his mind's eye, an encounter with the most threatening of bridges, and a view through the window of a 13th story apartment. During his practice sessions in self-hypnosis at home, he then modified the item by adding a balcony to the situation. He was enthusiastic throughout the procedure and strongly encouraged by his discovery of the evidence that it was his frame of mind rather than the external situation that influenced the level of his anxiety.

The evaluation, hypnotizability rating, and treatment program were thus accomplished in a total of four sessions. Two months later, he sent a postcard with the following message: "Thanks for allowing me to increase my enjoyment of my vacation. I've enjoyed the sheer cliffs of the Oregon coast and now the depths of the Grand Canyon."

Formulation: Cases 3 and 4

These case histories demonstrate how the hypnotic experience can be shaped to augment imaginal desensitization and the mastery of phobic fear. It is well known that in some instances a single session involving hypnosis and instruction in self-hypnosis can enable fearful individuals to board a plane and sit through the journey in a sort of self-induced trance state. Patients benefit both from a sense of calm and a sense of mastery over a situation that had previously seemed beyond their control.

The treatment plan is predicated on the idea that the intense fearful states (in which phobic patients keep suggesting to themselves that doom or panic is close at hand) are akin to spontaneous dissociative or hypnosis-like events. These can occur in hypnotizable persons as a defense against intense affects. The experience in self-hypnosis then informs the individual patient that he can initiate a trance state voluntarily, and end it at will. The similarity between the self-induced trance state and the spontaneous dissociative phobic state becomes apparent.

Case 5

A 25-year-old musician, raped two years earlier, was referred by her current therapist to determine whether hypnosis would help her resolve her problems. Although engaged in psychotherapy for much of the period since the rape, she continued to experience occasional flashbacks, disturbing dreams, and a high level of anxiety. She dwelt for lengthy periods of time on questions regarding her role in the rape and whether she could have escaped or done otherwise to prevent it. She was especially concerned that her passivity and compliant style had been seen by her assailant as encouragement. She requested hypnosis hoping that it would enable her to recall the event in greater detail and establish for her what the facts had indeed been.

The rape took place in a remote building on a college campus, where she worked alone. After returning to her floor from a visit to the restroom downstairs, she came upon her assailant, masked and armed, crouching at the door to her office. He spotted her as she entered the corridor, moved rapidly toward her, and getting behind her placed his right hand over her mouth as he placed the gun in his left hand against her neck. She felt paralyzed and rooted to the spot as he walked her into the office, demanding the keys to the safe and the money. As he forced her to search through desks and her own pocketbook, all the while standing close up against her, threatening and abusive in a hoarse whisper, she realized he had an erection. With the gun at her neck she felt forced to undress at his command and was subjected to sexual assault.

She felt frozen throughout the event and shattered by it. With the act completed he left with the money, leaving her to telephone her husband to come to pick her up and begin the arduous course of trying to put her life together again with a visit to the nearest emergency ward.

Despite what she described as useful therapy for almost two years, she continued to wonder whether she had indeed had the time to flee from the hallway when she first spotted him at the door of her office, and whether her subservience had not led him to shift his intentions from robbery only, to include rape as well.

Her own tendency to passivity had been a problem for her since adolescence, a problem initiated by her struggle to come to terms with her verbally abusive father. She had sought therapy during her late teens and had developed a fair understanding of her ambivalent feelings toward him. Having been his favorite until she reached puberty, she now recognized that the shift in his attitude was related in some way to her physical maturity. She knew from her discussions in therapy since the rape that she had seen similarities between her father's style and the demands of the rapist.

In other respects her personal history revealed sympathy for her mother, whom she saw as browbeaten, and a long-standing ambivalence toward authority figures. She was a college graduate with keen intellectual interest and had married at 21 to a geologist six years her senior.

Clinical course.   She was intent on revisiting the traumatic episode in hypnosis, to determine whether she could recall it or describe it under those circumstances, in a manner that would help her resolve her major question: namely, had she in some way caused the event to happen and could she have escaped it? Despite her commitment to the procedure, she recognized that she was likely to interpret hypnosis as another version of a rape, with herself passive and under the control of someone else. To obviate this, the second and third sessions were devoted by the therapist to discussing hypnosis and modeling it. When, in the fourth session, an induction procedure was introduced, she was invited to keep her eyes open or open them whenever she chose as she became accustomed to the events that were to lead to relaxation and recall. In the subsequent six sessions, constant and firm but gentle emphasis was placed on the fact that she was entitled to feel relaxed, and that, although in hypnosis, she was nonetheless at liberty to recall only as much as she chose to. Furthermore, she was invited to share with the therapist only that which she felt comfortable sharing. She acknowledged that she was deeply embarrassed at the thought of describing the details of the assault, and was encouraged to report only that which she felt she could.

In the fifth visit with the aid of hypnosis she recounted the events of the rape with considerable affect. She described how she had loathed doing what he demanded of her and argued back and forth about how much she could or could not have resisted the muzzle of the gun at her neck. She pleaded for patience and assistance in the therapy while coming to terms with the event. In subsequent hypnotic sessions much of the same ground was covered, with her repeating some of the same details but able to do so with less distress. She required constant reassurance and reminders of the fact that whatever had taken place during the rape had occurred under duress.

In discussions before the hypnosis in each session, and then during hypnosis, time was spent dealing with her resentment at having to accept the rape as part of her experience. She discussed at length how her previous two therapists had encouraged her to accept the rape as a part of herself and her history and to attempt to integrate it. Her desire was to keep it outside of herself, attached to her body or limbs perhaps, but because of its evil nature she preferred it to remain outside of her body rather than be part of her. In discussion she tried to think of it as a corn or a callus, extraneous, somewhat bothersome, but not capable of influencing or shaping the whole of her self-image and her future.

By the 12th session, she described feeling considerably easier about the problem although not yet totally at peace about it. The turning point had come after the sixth session when she experienced a dream in which she found herself reporting that she had aborted the rape. This was interpreted by her to mean that she would be able to accept as much of the rape as she had to and yet be able to survive.

She described the most valuable part of the procedure as being her ability to view the hypnotic event as a protected situation. Behind this protective screen, once she had gone through the induction procedure, she felt she could examine the history of the details closely, gain familiarity with them, and then emerge from the protective environment of the trance with as much of the rape as she chose to carry out with her. She appreciated the permission not to have to say everything that came into her mind, and that in some way she could own the feelings she felt before having to describe them. This all provided a means for her to exert some mastery over the memories and over the event that had seemed until then to be totally beyond her control.

Formulation

In the process of coming to terms with the painful affect associated with the original trauma, she found the trance state useful in allowing her to titrate just how much turbulence she would tolerate at any one time. By degrees, she permitted herself to experience increasing amounts of discomfort, confident that she could retreat behind the hypnotic screen should she prefer to do so. This helped to allow her to see the rape as aborted, as not part of her intimate self, and merely an external attachment denigrated to the role of a corn or a callus.

It is difficult to deny the importance of the altered state of awareness in the hypnosis in allowing her to feel protected and in control to this extent. However, in evaluating the role of hypnosis in this case, one must also weigh the use of therapeutic techniques that have little to do with hypnosis, and that are useful to any form of therapy dependent on compassionate understanding. She was introduced in stages to the new procedure; she was supported and encouraged in remembering only that which she felt prepared for; she was given permission to share only that information which she chose to; and she was free to interpret the technique in a way that was meaningful to her. All of these criteria contribute to a trusting relationship and in many instances to an effective therapy, regardless of the particular type.

Discussion

The clinical vignettes may help to illustrate how procedures like hypnosis, self-hypnosis, and biofeedback can be integrated into either the dynamic or the behavioral approach. The use of this group of procedures in the manner illustrated is congenial at least to the present authors and appears clinically useful. Certainly, therapists with other perspectives report having used these techniques in a different therapeutic context, following other rationales more congenial to their own theoretical views.

We have tried to emphasize that the procedures discussed here are used in an overall therapeutic context. Although both the patient and the therapist may view a technique such as hypnosis as *the* treatment, it may not be so. Inevitably complex treatment packages are involved, and it is rarely possible to identify the active component. This problem is clearly demonstrated in outcome studies using hypnosis. Because individuals differ greatly in their ability to respond to hypnosis, one would expect that those individuals who are able to enter hypnosis to a profound degree should obtain significantly more help from the technique than those who are not so responsive if the therapeutic effect depends upon the presence of hypnosis. Such a relationship has not been demonstrated in the use of hypnosis to help individuals stop smoking (Wadden and Anderton 1982). On the other hand, there is a very clear and reliable correlation between hypnotizability and the extent to which hypnosis can help the individual block the experience of acute pain (Hilgard and LeBaron 1984).

Few data are available about the relationship of hypnotizability to the amount of relief that is provided to patients with anxiety symptoms. One study does indicate that more hypnotizable individuals obtain more relief from anxiety with hypnosis than less hypnotizable patients. Meditation training was equally effective; moreover, the therapeutic effectiveness of meditation also correlated positively with hypnotizability assessed independently (Benson et al. 1978). These findings would indicate that the ability to respond to hypnotic suggestion is related to the effectiveness of hypnosis in the treatment of generalized anxiety disorders. Furthermore, the fact that hypnotizability also predicts the therapeutic response to meditation implies that these two procedures may belong in the same domain.

In our present state of knowledge, it seems reasonable to assume that if the positive therapeutic effects of muscle biofeedback are frequently not correlated with a decrease in muscle tension, then the active therapeutic agent is not the specific biofeedback treatment (American Psychiatric Association 1980 and Gatchel 1982). Similarly, in those circumstances where hypnotizability is unrelated to the likelihood of therapeutic success with hypnosis, it is also unlikely that it involves a specific hypnotic process. In each instance, nonspecific factors are likely to play a major role. This observation should not, however, obscure the fact that both of these procedures are effective in helping a great many patients.

Of considerable clinical importance is a phenomenon described by Borkovec and his associates (Borkovec et al. 1978; Heide and Borkovec 1983) that is called "relaxation-induced anxiety" (RIA). They point to the fact that while patients generally find relaxation exercise calming and reassuring, some find that it exacerbates the anxiety. In a recent study, Heide and Borkovec (1983) reported that 31 percent of subjects gave clinical evidence of increased anxiety while using progressive relaxation and 54 percent showed increased anxiety while using a meditative technique of relaxation. Case 1 described earlier is an excellent example of this phenomenon, demonstrating RIA in response to EMG feedback training.

Not only is RIA of considerable importance for the clinical use of relaxation technique, but it also speaks to the likelihood that there are some specific consequences of relaxation-inducing procedures, and it underscores the importance of establishing a meaningful therapeutic relationship even when using those techniques that superficially seem to involve simple relaxation.

As we have pointed out, there are important similarities between relaxation training, hypnosis, self-hypnosis, biofeedback, and meditative disciplines. Each seeks to use an ability of the person to master anxiety, panic, or other forms of stress. The goal of these therapies is to have the patient learn how to treat himself so that he can not only tolerate the discomfort but prevent its occurrence. They all involve the focusing of attention on mental processes, an induction of hypoarousal, and a purposive ignoring of extraneous bodily sensations. Each of the techniques involves an element of learning, though there are considerable individual differences in the ability to practice these skills. Each method creates strong expectations that undoubtedly produce powerful placebo effects.

To the extent that one is able to quantify an individual's responsivity as, for example, with hypnosis, it becomes possible to do systematic research. It is likely that criteria will eventually be developed to identify the extent of an individual's skill for each of these processes. For instance, Zen meditators are able to identify those who are virtuosos (masters) and those who are not, even though they may have meditated for the same number of years. The question to what extent the mental processes involved overlap in these procedures is a question that future research will need to answer.

Meanwhile, it is worth considering integrating those methods that are congenial to the therapist into his treatment of anxiety, phobia, and panic. The fact that there may be no overall differences in results from biofeedback as opposed to relaxation training should not obscure the equally important fact that some patients respond far better to one technique than to another. Unfortunately, until these processes are better understood, we can only illustrate their use with clinical vignettes and point to the possible differences and similarities among them.

Notes

[1] We wish to express our appreciation to our fellow task force members who commented on this manuscript and to our colleagues David Dinges, Emily Carota Orne, and Thomas Wadden, who made valuable comments and suggestions. The substantive research upon which the theoretical outlook presented in this chapter is based was supported in part by grant MH-19156 from the National Institute of Mental Health and in part by a grant from the Institute for Experimental Psychiatry.

[2] Although one study (Frischholz et al. 1982) has thus far not confirmed this finding, others have (Foenander et al. 1980; Gerschman et al. 1979; John et al. 1983).

[3] Acknowledgments to C. N. Legalos (1973), who first reported Case 1.

Chapter 186

Posttraumatic Stress Disorder

A traumatic experience is a major life event that occurs in a sudden or forceful way. It is recognized as highly relevant to the self and does not fit well with the self's usual view of the world and personal response capabilities. The result is an association of the event with alarm emotions, ideas of harm, altered states of mind, and special memory encoding. These psychological stress responses have biologic implications as well; catecholamine, corticosteroids, and other neurotransmitters and hormonal systems are aroused. Because there is a possibility for individual response, a variety of stress response syndromes can be diagnosed.

Diagnosis

The diagnosis of posttraumatic stress disorder (PTSD) is based on a combination of external events and internal psychological responses to these events. It is the particular combination of the nature of the life event and the psychological responses that form the basis of this nosological category. Both features must be clearly assessed and described as part of a clinical diagnostic series of interviews.

Although no life event occurs in isolation, the situational feature of the PTSD diagnosis requires a major external episode. This stressor event will usually set in motion a cascading series of other life events, as when a flood wrecks a house and then leads to years of economic difficulty and separations from important neighbors. To qualify as a precipitant of PTSD, a life event should be somewhat unusual for the person and outside the ordinary range of everyday, reasonably protected human life events. Some examples of major events that are frequent precipitants of PTSD are episodes of violence that constitute a serious threat to one's physical or psychological integrity, witnessing another person's being mutilated or killed, and destruction of community by natural disaster. Sexual abuse, extremely painful and frightening medical procedures, mugging, burglary, automobile accidents, environmental upheavals, and severe bereavements, even of a pet, may sometimes precipitate PTSD. Combat, torture, and kidnapping may also be precipitating events.

In terms of the response characteristics, the information contained in traumatic events tends to emerge in both intrusive and denial phases of response. These are reflected in the symptomatic criterion diagnosis as summarized in Table 1. The tendencies of these phases occur in sequence, and the fuller designation of signs and symptoms of each phase are shown in Tables 1-4 (Horowitz et al. 1980).

In DSM-III-R (American Psychiatric Association 1987), there is a stated requirement that the person must have at least five of the symptoms shown in Table 1. Three of these must fall into the intrusion signs and symptoms, and two into the avoidance or denial signs and symptoms. In its definitions, DSM-III-R does not require that these symptoms occur at the same time, but that they occur at one time or another within a six-month period. This DSM-III (American Psychiatric Association 1980) decision rule may be necessary in order to have systematic usage across a large number of cases. The accurate diagnosis of an individual, however, could probably be made if a person had a single major symptom, such as a recurrent and intrusive distressing recollection of the stress event that is very disorganizing at work and in social life, that is clearly related to a major traumatic event such as being raped or assaulted, and that is not on a course of spontaneous resolution.

Experiences such as the signs and symptoms listed in Tables 1 through 4 are a matter of *form* as well as *thematic content*. That is, they deal with unusual qualities of conscious experience derived from processes that are not part of conscious thought. These qualities are extremes—intrusions and unusual omissions that differ from the person's usual range of thought experience before the occurrence of the traumatic event. Inquiring about intrusion and omission usually involves direct questioning because the average person does not commonly have language for describing these qualities of inner subjective experience. The fear of suggesting symptoms to the patient has been overemphasized, and direct questioning about signs and symptoms is in order with persons who might have this syndrome. Patients are often better at de-

Table 1. Signs and Symptoms of PTSD According to DSM-III-R

Intrusion Signs and Symptoms
1. recurrent and intrusive distressing recollections of the event without any awareness of environmental stimuli that trigger the reaction
2. recurrent distressing dreams of the event
3. sudden acting or feeling as if the traumatic event were recurring (includes a sense of reliving the experience, illusions, hallucinations, and dissociative (flashback) episodes, even those that occur upon awakening or when intoxicated)
4. physiologic reactivity or intense psychological distress at exposure to events that symbolize or resemble an aspect of the traumatic event (e.g., a woman who was raped in an elevator breaks into a sweat when entering any elevator)
5. difficulty falling or staying asleep
6. irritability or outbursts of anger
7. difficulty concentrating
8. hypervigilance
9. exaggerated startle response

Denial-Avoidance-Numbing Signs and Symptoms
1. deliberate efforts to avoid thoughts or feelings associated with the trauma
2. deliberate efforts to avoid activities or situations that arouse recollections of the trauma
3. inability to recall an important aspect of the trauma (psychogenic amnesia)
4. markedly diminished interest in significant activities
5. feeling of detachment or estrangement from others
6. restricted range of affect, e.g., "numbing," unable to have loving feelings

Table 2. Stress Response and Pathologic Intensification

Normal	Pathological
→ Event	
→ Outcry	→ Panic, paralysis, exhaustion
→ Denial	→ Maladaptive avoidances: social withdrawal, suicide, drug or alcohol excesses, counterphobic impulsivity
→ Intrusive	→ Flooded, pressured, confused, distraught, or impulsive states, physiological disruptions
→ Working through—Blocked	→ Anxiety and depressive states, hibernative frozen states, psychosomatic changes
→ Completion—Not reached	→ Inability to work, create, or love

Note. Reproduced with permission from Horowitz (1986).

scribing the common thematic contents of PTSD such as preoccupations with fear of repetition of the traumatic event, terror at sharing the fate of deceased or mutilated victims, rage at perpetrators of the event, guilty anger at those spared from the stress, shame over helplessness, remorse over bad thoughts or actions during the traumatic episode, and survivor guilt.

Table 3.   Common Symptoms or Signs During Denial States

1. *Perception and attention*
   - Daze
   - Selective inattention
   - Inability to appreciate significance of stimuli
   - Sleep disturbances (e.g., too little or too much)

2. *Consciousness of ideas and feelings related to the event*
   - Amnesia (complete or partial)
   - Nonexperience of themes implied as consequences of the event

3. *Conceptual attributes*
   - Disavowal of meanings of current stimuli in some way associated to event
   - Loss of a realistic sense of appropriate connection with ongoing world
   - Constriction of range of thought
   - Inflexibility of purpose
   - Major use of fantasies to counteract real conditions

4. *Emotional attributes*
   - Numbness

5. *Somatic attributes*
   - Tension-inhibition responses of the autonomic nervous system, with felt sensations such as bowel symptoms, fatigue, headache, muscle pain

6. *Action patterns*
   - Frantic overactivity
   - Withdrawal
   - Failure to decide how to respond to consequences of event

Note.   Reproduced with permission from Horowitz (1986).

Table 4.   Common Symptoms or Signs During Intrusive States

1. *Perception and attention*
   - Hypervigilance, startle reactions
   - Sleep and dream disturbances

2. *Consciousness of ideas and feelings related to the event*
   - Intrusive-repetitive thoughts, emotions, and behaviors (illusions, pseudohallucinations, nightmares, unbidden images, and ruminations)
   - Feeling pressured, confused, or disorganized when thinking about event related themes

3. *Conceptual attributes*
   - Overgeneralization of stimuli so that they seem as if related to event
   - Preoccupation with event related themes with inability to concentrate on other topics

4. *Emotional attributes*
   - Emotional "attacks" or "pangs" of affect related to event

5. *Somatic attributes*
   - Sensations or symptoms of flight or fight-readiness (or of exhaustion from chronic arousal), including tremor, diarrhea, sweating (adrenergic, noradrenergic, or histaminic arousals) with felt sensations such as pounding heart, nausea, lump in throat, weak legs

6. *Action patterns*
   - Compulsive repetitions of actions associated with the event or of search for lost persons or situations

Note.   Reproduced with permission from Horowitz (1986).

Differential Diagnosis

Every individual will at some time or another experience very stressful life events. These stressors may lead to alterations in states of mind including entry into extremely emotional states such as being very sad, frightened, angry, guilty, or ashamed. Such highly emotional states after a serious life change are neither surprising nor pathologic. PTSD and other pathologic stress response syndromes are intensifications of normal stress response tendencies and are pathologic deflections from the quality of normal responses. This general concept is contained in Table 2. The clinician appraising the person after a stressor event must evaluate the nature of the external news, the degree of stress experienced immediately, and the quality of the change in the patient's states of mind over time after the initial stressor event, in relation to the cascading series of stressor events that may follow the sharpest shock.

In the past, neuropathologic changes were invoked as the explanation of syndromes that might follow such traumatic life events as being in a train wreck (reviewed in Horowitz 1986). Now we know that the psychological signs and symptoms may occur alone or may interact with neurobiologic signs and symptoms. Any event that involves a sharp impact (as in a car accident) or prolonged diversion from usual physiological status (as in being lost without food or water) can lead to prolonged neurobiologic changes. The presence of these changes may mean that a complex diagnosis both of PTSD and organic brain syndrome might be indicated.

A latency period of months or even years may follow the event, and the earlier statement in DSM-III about "onset within six months of the stress event" is no longer justified, nor is it contained in DSM-III-R. Furthermore, persons trying to avoid reexperience of stress-related ideas and feelings may abuse alcohol, sedatives, narcotics, food, tobacco, or sex. This may lead to syndromes that require a variety of other diagnoses. These should be made in addition to, rather than instead of, the PTSD diagnosis.

The most frequent diagnostic distinctions will be between normal or pathologic bereavement and PTSD, between PTSD and adjustment disorders, between PTSD and brief reactive psychosis, and between any of these syndromes and malingering. The adjustment disorders do not contain the degree of intrusion and avoidance signs and symptoms that exemplify PTSD, and the events that have required adjustment are not as sharp in terms of shock affect on the individual. They are more likely to include difficulties with child rearing, illness or disabilities, economic troubles, a new form of work, graduation from college, moving from one house to another, social separations, or cultural upheaval and migration. In contrast, PTSD is most likely to have events related to accidents, injuries, violence, and sudden loss.

The brief reactive psychoses have a sudden onset, usually occurring within a few hours or as much as two weeks after the stressor event. The clinical picture includes the kind of intrusion and emotional turmoil found in PTSD, but has in addition the presence of at least one gross psychotic symptom such as an expressed delusion or a major evidence of thought disorder such as an inability to assemble rational communicative sequences. Because hallucinations and pseudohallucinations may occur during an intrusive phase of PTSD, without prolonged psychosis, one should use careful clinical judgment before making a brief reactive psychosis diagnosis on the grounds of such vivid uncontrolled internal imagery alone.

Many traumatic events such as natural and civil disasters involve the death of loved ones and other losses. One should not confuse normal mourning processes with PTSD. The loss of a loved one leads to a period of at least one year of disturbance in most persons, and three years of disturbance is not uncommon. Bereavement reactions include states of mind of shame, guilt, personal fear of dying, and sadness. In normal grief, anger at the person who is deceased, at the self, and also at persons who are exempted from the tragedy are not uncommon. The person passes through such states of mind with a sense of progressing along a mourning process. However, in pathological grief, the person may become frozen in one or more of these states, without progress over weeks and even months. There may be additional signs of inertia, hypochondriasis, numbness, unaccountable irritability, feelings of gross worthlessness, and apathy. In some instances, the combination of intrusive symptoms, avoidances, and the nature of the death experience itself warrants a diagnosis of PTSD as a special form of pathologic grief reaction. (For the actual distribution of such cases in a diagnostic series see Horowitz et al. 1984b, and for case expositions see Horowitz et al. 1984a.)

The traumatic event may activate latent neurotic conflicts or exacerbate existing problems in living. Not only do life events occur in a matrix of other life events; they are always interpreted according to the meaning structure of the individual who experiences them. The vast range of the population has existing neurotic conflicts, and these may be intensified by the experience of a shocking event. The fact that this is so does not exempt them from the diagnosis of PTSD.

Studies, as reviewed elsewhere (Horowitz 1986), indicate that the more an individual is exposed to shocking events resulting from a general disaster in the population, the more likely that individual will have signs and symptoms of PTSD (see also Shore 1986). In addition, many persons prone to anxiety or depressive disorders, may have stressor life events as one factor in the exacerbation of a cyclic illness pattern or in the first episodic occurrence of these disorders. Also, the incipient stage of the development of some disorders may lead some persons to expose themselves to increased risks and hazards. Therefore careful case formulation should encompass an understanding of the preevent history and life problems of the patient.

Etiology

Biologic Response Systems

From Selye's (1936) classical exposition of general physiologic stress responses to modern (e.g., Levine 1983) concerns for the effects of stress on immunity, there has been considerable discussion of the mind-body interaction after serious life events disrupt homeostasis. Although the processes remain to be worked out, stressor life events may be followed by changes in how neurotransmitters and hormones are formed, released, metabolized, and dissipated. In addition to heightened excretion of corticosteroids, catecholamines also seem to change in times of stress.

Catecholamines regulate blood pressure, heart rate, fat breakdown, sugar metabolism, and other functions. Because of diffuse distribution of these chemicals and their receptors throughout nerve cells, they act as both hormones and neurotransmitters in the brain and throughout the body. Neurons high in catecholamine content are found in networks that connect the limbic, cortical, cerebellar, and hypothalamic structures. Disturbances in these regions sometimes lead to increased disturbances in arousal level, regulation of emotional response (as in rage attacks), reward or gratification-seeking behavior, and motor functions. It is conceivable that these are one route into the turbulent shifts in states of mind that characterize PTSD.

Epinephrine is the principal catecholamine synthesized in the adrenal medulla.

Activation of epinephrine production is a function of the sympathethic nervous system extending down the spinal cord from the brain. There is now the hypothesis that the most prominent catecholamines in a physiologic reaction to stress are dopamine and norepinephrine. As neurotransmitters, they seem to be highly concentrated in the locus ceruleus and other neural clusters that may be involved in alarm reactions (Redmond 1984). It is speculated that a series of alarms, traumas, or even chronic cascades of stressor life events may alter synaptic transmission of these alerting and arousing systems and cause repeated false alarms (anxiety) or depressions of function, at least in animal models of anxiety (Kandel 1983).

Recent measurements of urinary norepinephrine metabolites in Vietnam veterans with PTSD have shown that there appears to be a chronic elevation in noradrenergic activity, compared with controls having other psychiatric diagnoses (Kosten et al. 1985). Kolb has shown that clonidine, an alpha-2-adrenergic antagonist that diminishes release of norepinephrine presynaptically and that also diminishes postsynaptic noradrenergic activity, has been effective in reducing the hyperreactivity of PTSD (Kolb et al. 1984). These data support the role of the noradrenergic system in the development of the hyperreactive symptoms of PTSD, but such treatments are still very much in the experimental, investigative stage.

Psychological Response Systems

A traumatic life event is by definition enormously serious, in terms of its implications to self-organization, attachments, and meaning structures. Such events must eventually change the victim's inner schematic models of how the self articulates with the world. The processing of information that leads to such change in meaning structures of the mind is slow; therefore, extended time to review the implications of news inherent in stressful life events is essential. Evolution seems to have provided for this time by special memory endurance for traumatic perceptions. This may be why they tend to return as intrusive images (Horowitz 1986).

To repeat, a traumatic event is coded as memories. These can be gradually integrated with mental schematizations. The memories and their gradual permutations are stored in what I choose to call "active memory," because they tend toward repeated mental representation or behavioral expression. This phenomenon and assumption are what Freud (1920) called the compulsion to repeat.

Each repeated representation once again sets in motion information processing of the kind that may eventually revise inner schematizations of meanings about self and the self-surrounding world. As new schematic meaning structures are established, the news about revised circumstances becomes a part of long-term memory, and the codifications decay in active memory.

The processing of the news of a traumatic event entails a rapid appraisal of how best to cope with it (Lazarus and Folkman 1984). A low level of inhibitory regulation leads to excitation of emotional systems, to physiologic alarm reactions, and to the behaviors associated with emotional outcry, as shown in Table 2. The amount of information requiring changes in schemas is usually so great that complete processing and integration are impossible in a short time and emotional implications too overwhelming.

Inhibiting regulatory efforts are initiated so that the stressful information can be gradually assimilated, dose by dose. Excessively high inhibitory controls may interrupt the assimilation and accommodation process. A high level of control in relation to the tendency of active memory toward repeated representation leads to denial and numbing phases of stress response syndromes. Failures of control lead either to a continuation of outcry, as in prolonged panic stricken states, or other intrusive states. Optimally adaptive controls keep ideational and emotional processing within tolerable levels, providing the dose-by-dose assimilation of implications that characterizes the working-through phase shown in Table 2.

Therapeutic efforts are often aimed at reducing excessive controls or replacing deficient ones. By improving self-regulation, the therapist aids the patient's own natural stress response of seeking optimal adaptive levels of coping and defense. These efforts bolster the sense of self-competency and allow the patient to take advantage of readily available social support systems.

The self-organization stands at the boundary of psychological and biologic levels of stress response and at the boundary of psychological and social or interpersonal levels of response. Because each person is individually capable of more than one type of self-view, the nature of the self-view used in organizing assessments of the implications of the stressor event is crucial to what coping and defensive strategies are selected and to what states of mind will ensue. If latent, weak, damaged, defective, or bad self-concepts are activated by association with meanings of the traumatic event, then the person is more likely to be thrown into conflict, fear, and despair than if resilient, competent, strong, or good self-concepts serve as dominant organizers of the current sense of identity.

This psychodynamic view, reported in more detail elsewhere (Horowitz 1987, 1988; Horowitz et al. 1984a) is in keeping with modern views in cognitive-behavioral theory (Bandura 1982; Beck et al. 1985; Wilson 1984) and represents an important convergence. Moreover, activation of the more competent self schemata in an individual repertoire is likely to lead to stress response tactics that emphasize personal action, mobility, and assertiveness, whereas activation of less competent self schemata is more likely to lead to selection of hiding, energy-conserving, and self as subordinate to responses. As suggested by Henry (1980), the former response could lead to increased catecholamine and testosterone release and increased amygdala activity, the latter response to corticosteroid release, lowered testosterone, and arousal of the hippocampal septum. Such variances in aroused biologic substrates, speculatively mentioned here, could have a feedback to emotional tone and sense of vigor in terms of perceived state of mind.

We are on less inferential and speculative ground when we move to the interface of intrapsychic self organization and the interpersonal or social milieu during the time of trauma and posttraumatic response to stress. Human support is a vital force in creating a resilient personal response to traumas; withdrawal of support, or recognition of evil intentions in others is an important ingredient in causing PTSD.

Social Response Systems

Conditions in a community may either foster resiliency among community members or increase the likelihood of PTSD after a disaster. Good leadership, high group affiliation, and strong, unambivalent ideologies seem to increase endurance (Hamburg and Adams 1967; Pearlin and Schooler 1978). Cultures that provide support only after a threshold of illness is crossed will increase the likelihood that such illness will occur. The most important social ingredient after a disaster is extended care giving as modulated by shared values. Failures in social coherence will increase the rate of non-resolution of stress responses. Something of this sort occurred after the war in Vietnam. Returning American servicemen were sometimes socially ignored or treated as if they were responsible for the war (Lifton 1973). The diagnosis of PTSD in these men was predicted, but at first underrepresented in military and Veteran's Administration psychiatry (Horowitz and Solomon 1975). It then became a major political issue (Figley 1978), with a delayed socially restorative process and treatment outreach.

Treatment

A multimodel treatment approach is recommended; one which emphasizes psycho-social elements such as interpersonal relationship and social supports and facilitation of healthy working through of the implications of the serious life events and their subsequent modification of the person's life. The priorities in such treatment are shown in Table 5.

Description and explanation of signs and symptoms are the essential steps to optimal treatment of PTSD, as in any disorder. For PTSD, these steps mean understanding the phase of response and issues of acute- and chronic-episodic responsiveness. In very chronic cases, one may be dealing with posttraumatic character disorder rather than PTSD.

During a pathologically overwhelmed outcry period, the first step is to provide protection and consolation to the victim of a traumatic event. In crisis work of this kind, relationship support is the most powerful method of reducing alarms and distress. It should be used as the first form of intervention before resorting to antianxiety agents for sedation if human support is insufficient. When insomnia does produce fatigue and lowered coping capacity, companionship (even of an animal)

Table 5. Priorities of Treatment

Patient's Current State	Treatment Goal
Under continuing impact of external stress event.	• Terminate external event or remove patient from contiguity with it. • Provide temporary relationship. • Help with decisions, plans, or working-through.
Swings to intolerable levels: • Ideational-emotional attacks. • Paralyzing denial and numbness.	• Reduce amplitude of oscillations to swings of tolerable intensity of ideation and emotion. • Continue emotional and ideational support.
Frozen in overcontrol state of denial and numbness with or without intrusive repetitions.	• Help patient "dose" reexperience of event and implications that help remember for a time, put out of mind for a time, remember for a time, and so on. • During periods of recollection, help patient organize and express experience. Increase sense of safety in therapeutic relationship so patient can resume processing the event.
Able to experience and tolerate episodes of ideation and waves of emotion.	• Help patient work through associations: the conceptual, emotional, object relations, and self-image implications of the stress event. • Help patient relate this stress event to earlier threats, relationship models, self-concepts, and future plans.
Able to work through ideas and emotions on one's own.	• Work through loss of therapeutic relationship. • Terminate treatment.

Note. Reproduced with permission from Horowitz (1986).

may help. If not feasible or successful, sedation with one of the antianxiety agents may be used on a single-dose or night-by-night basis. Smaller doses of the same agent may be prescribed, again on a dose-by-dose basis, during the day, if the person has distraught, flooded, or panic states. If substance abuse is not a danger, small doses of alcoholic beverages might have a similar effect. However, the patient and persons close to the patient should be cautioned against the use of multiple mood control agents, and especially cautioned against combining alcohol with prescribed medications. Antidepressive agents usually need not be prescribed to relieve immediate anxiety, sadness, and despondency responses to loss.

During the early phase of response, even when not on medication, the patient should be advised to avoid driving, operating dangerous machinery, or engaging in tasks where alertness is essential for safety. Accidents are more likely to result with persons recently exposed to traumatic events because they commonly suffer lapses of attention, concentration, and sequential planning and can have startle reactions that may disrupt their motor control.

For the average case of PTSD, the search for help will begin weeks or even months after the traumatic event. One reason for this is that people expect to be quite upset right after the event and call up reserves of resiliency and healthy denial of some implications of the stressor event. Later, those who develop the disorder often realize they are not processing the response to the event in an optimal manner and quite correctly seek out professional help. For the average case, brief psychotherapy without medication may suffice. Sometimes a brief period of antianxiety medication may help control overwhelming states of resurgent fear. The long-term use of these agents is, at present, regarded as inadvisable.

Psychotherapy will be discussed shortly. Before turning to that topic, the use of medications in protracted, complicated, severe, and recurrent cases of PTSD will be considered. In such instances, the concomitant psychotherapy should be time unlimited rather than brief, and careful assessment for depression should be included.

Several published case reports as well as open, comparative drug trials have suggested the possible therapeutic efficacy of a number of different antidepressant medications (see Table 6). Both tricyclics and monoamine oxidase inhibitors have been associated with a decrease in intensity and frequency of protracted nightmares, flashbacks, panic attacks, and episodes of anxiety as well as improvement in mood and the ability to modulate anger. The lack of control for a placebo response makes the interpretation of any drug study difficult. An important question raised but not answered by the case reports is whether antidepressant medication has any effect that is specific to the syndrome of posttraumatic stress or whether the observed therapeutic responses are secondary to the treatment of concurrent diagnoses such as depression and panic disorder.

In many of the reports summarized in Table 6, improved sleep and alleviation of nightmares or night terrors are noted, suggesting that antidepressants work by affecting sleep architecture. Both tricyclics and monoamine oxidase inhibitors are powerful REM suppressors (Marshall 1975). Tricyclics appear to lengthen sleep and reduce spontaneous awakenings (Thompson 1977). The exact sleep stage location of disturbing dreams is not always clear. It is likely that they can arise from all stages of sleep, especially stage 4 and REM sleep. The effectiveness of antidepressant medication has been understood in different ways depending upon whether the nightmares are considered to be arousal phenomenon, stage 4, or REM disturbances.

It has been suggested that antidepressant medication may work by "enhancing abreaction" (Hogben and Cornfield 1981) through unclear mechanisms. Alternatively, it has been proposed that the drugs work by treating overwhelming symptoms, thereby increasing self-control and making psychotherapy possible (Levenson et al. 1982). At any rate, drugs should not be prescribed for these disorders in isolation, but should be part of a multimodal approach that includes psychotherapeutic efforts at working through the personal implications of traumatic memories.

In addition to treatment of PTSD with antidepressants, a variety of other psychotropic drugs have been used to reduce the symptoms, with varying success. Benzodiazepines have been effective in modulating entry into explosive states of mind characterized by uncontrolled emotional pangs and expressive actions, as well as decreasing nightmares. Propranolol in doses up to 640 mg/day has been reported to reduce the autonomic activation that accompanies fear and startle responses in these disorders by Van der Kolk (1983), who has also reported the effectiveness of lithium in 8 of 14 Vietnam veterans who had had frequent nightmares and startle reactions: autonomic hyperarousal markedly decreased, and alcohol use diminished. Antipsychotic drugs have not been useful in treating the chronic symptoms of posttraumatic stress, but have been helpful during acute entry into psychotic states of mind with extreme hyperarousal and severely disordered thinking. As soon as the psychotic state decreases in intensity, such agents should be discontinued to avoid the hazardous, long-range potential side effects.

Psychotherapy

Psychotherapy of PTSD begins with telling the story of the events before, during, and after the major episode of injury, threat, or loss. It is very important to integrate this story with self-organization by 1) recognizing the reality of the violent events rather than leaving them in a depersonalized form of memory experience based on what was felt at the time of the occurrence, 2) recognizing the events in relation to an intact self concept rather than leaving the memories related to an overwhelmed, weak self concept that was felt at the time of occurrence (Horowitz 1988), and 3) differentiating realistic properties of the occurrence from fantasy attributions associated with it during and after the episode. How this is done is quite an individual matter, best illustrated with extensive case examples, such as provided elsewhere (Horowitz 1986, 1987; Horowitz et al. 1984a).

The denial phase need not be addressed unless it has maladaptive components, such as failure to come out of it over time or avoidance of necessary life tasks such as making decisions about needed surgery. It is during the intrusive phase that the patient will usually seek help. When a person seeks help, the therapist establishes a working alliance that allows him to assist the patient in working through his reactions. In addition, he may seek to modify preexisting conflicts, developmental difficulties, and defensive styles that rendered the person unusually vulnerable to traumatization by this experience.

Therapy begins with the establishment of a safe relationship. This, together with specific interventions, alters the status of the patient's controls. The patient can then begin to reappraise what felt overwhelming and make the necessary revisions of his inner models of himself and the world. As this reappraisal and revision takes place, the person is able to make new decisions and to engage in adaptive actions. He can practice desired behavioral patterns until they gradually become automatic.

As the person achieves new levels of awareness, this process is repeated and deepened. That is, as the patient's trust of the therapist increases, he is able to modify controls further and assimilate more warded-off thoughts about the traumatic event.

Table 6. Studies of Pharmacotherapy for PTSD

Author	Nature of Study	N	Drug	Previous Treatment
Marshall (1975)	Case reports	3	Imipramine (75–300 mg) No levels	No previous treatment with anti-depressants
Thompson (1977)	Open trial Alternate assignment to either drug or weekly psycho-therapy	50	Perphenazine (4 mg) and amitriptiline (125 mg)	Yes-nature not specified
Hogben and Cornfield (1981)	Case reports	5	Phenelzine 45–75 mg No MAO inhibition test 1 patient given LiCO3 1200 mg as well	Various other antidepressants used previously in most
Levenson (1982)	Case report	1	Phenelzine 75 mg	Benzodiazepines. Psychotherapy
Burstein (1983)	Case report	1	Imipramine 250–350 mg No levels	No
Shen and Park (1983)	Case report	1	Phenelzine 105 mg followed by Tranylcypromine 40 mg	Neuroleptics Tricyclics
White (1983)	Open trial	18	Doxepin 25–100 mg Occasional use of benzodiazepines (Psychotherapy)	Not clear
Burstein (1984)	Open Trial	10	Imipram. 250 mg (mean)	Benzodiazepines used in 5 pts.
Falcon et al. (1985)	Open trial for 6–8 weeks	17	Amit. = 10 Imip. = 1 Desip. = 4 Doxep. = 1	Not stated

Note. Courtesy of Dr. Carl Salzman and his colleagues, Patricia Rosebush, M.D., and Bessel Van der Kolk, M.D.

Concurrent Diagnoses	Outcome Measures	Results	Length of Follow-up
Depression	Night terrors (frequency & intensity) No rating scales used	Complete cessation in 1 patient Decreased intensity & frequency in 1 patient	Several months
Not clear All patients involved in disability litigation	Panic, Anxiety Nightmares Phobias Rating scale not referenced or elaborated upon by author	Drug therapy superior to weekly psycho-therapy for all symptoms	1 year
Panic attacks in all 5	Nightmares (intensity and frequency) Panic attacks Flashbacks Chronic anxiety Rating scales not used	Cessation of nightmares day 5–30 Cessation of panic attacks day 1–7 Decreased flashbacks day 7–18 Decreased anxiety day 7–21	6 months 3 patients discontinued drug without sequelae after 3–6 months
"Very depressed" and suicidal	Symptoms of DSM-III PTSD Depression Rating scales not used	More sociable & calm within one week Cessation of nightmares	2 months
Not clear	Flashbacks No rating scales	Ceased at 350 mgm/day, 3 wks after starting medication	2 months
Alcohol abuse	Nightmares Flashbacks Violent outbursts	Cessation of nightmares and flashbacks Both MAOIs effective but associated with erectile dysfunction at dosages necessary to Rx. PTSD symptoms.	1 year
Not clear	Symptoms of DSM-III PTSD No rating scales used	"Dramatic response," particularly sleep disturbance Few details	Not stated
Not clear	Impact of Event Scale (Horowitz) includes intrusive & avoidance items Completed before and after trial	Significant change in IES for intrusive items but not for avoidance items Greatest change in sleep and nightmares.	2–3 weeks
Pts. with major affective disorder excluded Anxiety disorder = 2 Substance abuse (not active) = 5	Clinical Global Impression Scale at beginning and at point of "maximum" improvement. Initial ratings made retrospectively in some cases	14 (82%) much improved by CGI scale Patients with history of substance abuse seemed to do less well	3 months–3 years

Finally, he will need to work through his reactions to the approaching loss of the therapist and the therapy.

Introduction of a plan for the termination of therapy (several sessions before the final one) leads to a reexperience of loss, often with a return of symptoms. This time, however, the loss can be faced gradually rather than suddenly, actively rather than passively, and in the context of a communicative and helping relationship. Specific interpretations of the link between the termination experience and the stress event should be made, and the final hours of therapy may be centered on this theme. The 12-session brief dynamic approach to PTSD, as used at the University of California, San Francisco Center for the Study of Neuroses, is summarized in Table 7. A brief vignette illustrates some of the features of such brief treatments of PTSD. Outcomes have been reported as satisfactory (Horowitz et al. 1984b; Horowitz et al. 1986).

A 25-year-old man had served as a lifeguard of a neighborhood pool for some years. On one busy summer day, the pool accommodated a large crowd of children from another neighborhood. There were many people in the pool and also various unruly episodes on the deck. The young man was quite busy and realized that he was so overloaded with demands for his attention that he could not be sure that everyone was safe. He blew his whistle and ordered the pool cleared. To his horror there was an inert body at the bottom of the pool. He dove in at once and brought the small figure to the deck, attempting cardiopulmonary resuscitation. This failed to revive the small boy, who was dead.

Overcome with remorse, the young man nonetheless went to the funeral of the deceased child. Although not directly accosted by the relatives, he was greeted with many angry scowls and was upset by the grief-stricken faces of the child's mother and father.

He suffered an initial outcry period and was sustained by close support from his friends and relatives. He went through turbulent periods of remorse, insomnia, attacks of anxiety, guilt, shame, and dread of dying himself. He took on another line of work, but had difficulty concentrating, and had phobic avoidances of any reminders of pools, children, or the neighborhood where this event occurred.

Six months after the event, he began having frightening nightmares in which there were visual images derived from perceptions at the time of the traumatic event. This included the underwater appearance of the blurred face of the child, the face of the child while resuscitation was about to be undertaken, and the angry faces of the child's relatives at the funeral ceremony. Such images and preoccupations with his own feelings of remorse disrupted his concentration at his work. He had outbursts of anger with companions, including people who were friendly toward him.

These intrusions occurred despite his efforts to avoid such thoughts and feelings, and his intellectual pronouncement to his family that he was finished with the event, having done whatever he could to expiate his own contributions to it. Nonetheless he could not sustain interest in his career or recreational activities. Everything in his world was cloaked with a kind of greyness, and he felt a pervasive lack of pleasure. This was quite different from his amiable demeanor and enthusiastic character traits before the drowning.

The beginning phase of psychotherapy was marked by his apathetic and distant response to the psychotherapist. This was ameliorated as the psychotherapist indicated an empathic recognition of the various experiences that the young man reported. The therapist's ability to link his experiences to responses of other persons who had traumatic events also seemed to encourage an increase in cooperation.

In the middle phase of therapy, an important and repetitive activity was to attempt to disentangle the realistic aspects of his responsibility as a lifeguard for the

Table 7. A General Layout of a Time-Limited Twelve-Session Therapy for Posttraumatic Stress Disorders

Session	Therapeutic Alliance	Patient Activity	Therapist Activity
1	Initial positive feeling for helper.	Patient tells story of traumatic event.	Preliminary focus discussed as relation of traumatic event to "the self."
2	Lull as sense of pressure is reduced.	Traumatic event related to life context of patient at the time it occurred.	Takes psychiatric history, makes diagnoses and early formulations.
3	Patient tests therapist to see if fears of what may happen are justified, e.g., fear of precipitation into emotional overload.	Patient adds associations expanding meaning to self of the trauma and its sequelae.	Realignment of focus to more specific issues; interpretation of resistances with empathic recognition of transferences.
4	Therapeutic alliance deepened.	Patient often begins to bring up warded off themes here.	Further interpretation of defenses and warded off contents. Clear, reconstructive linking of warded off emotions and ideas to traumatic event.
5	Transference reactions often emerge here.	Work on what has been avoided.	Linking of observed major transference reactions to meaning of traumatic event in relation to preexisting maladaptive interpersonal behavior problems.
6	Transference reactions often emerge here.	Work on what has been avoided.	Time of termination discussed, asks patient to reflect on relationship with therapist.
7–11	Meaning of termination in relation to therapeutic alliance may lead to further clarification of transference projections.	Continued working through of central conflicts and issues of termination as related to the trauma. Giving up the therapist as restorer of what was lost.	Clarification and interpretation related to central preexisting conflicts and how these relate to traumatic events and the pending termination; clarification of unfinished issues.
12	Saying goodbye.	Realization of work to be continued on own.	Acknowledgment of real gains and real future work. Additional recommendation as needed. Set follow-up time.

Note. Reproduced with permission from Horowitz (1986).

safety of everyone in the pool and his fantasy elaborations of reasons why he was terribly guilty. In order to do this, it was necessary to get beyond his surface statements that he had already worked through this issue, that it was the fault of others that there were too many people at the pool, and that he had acted in the best possible way under the circumstances and now was no longer remorseful. Part of this activity, after patiently going over all the events and associations, was to ask how much remorse he had to have and to separate the issue of making up to others in whatever way he could for what had happened, from the need to be self punitive, as in seeking to fail in his current career efforts.

This working through process led to turbulent feelings in which there was rage at the pool managers for putting him in an overly demanding situation, as well as rage at himself for not having acted sooner. During the same period of therapy, the patient was encouraged to confront the neighborhood, the pool, and even the gravesite in a gradual manner, taking on whatever task he felt he could, and going there with companions. This led to some reaction towards the therapist, including rage that the therapist was expecting too much of him, and a warded-off but gradually emergent feeling that "recovery was too good for him." It was also important to work through memories of how he had piled toys onto his unwanted younger brother in an effort to get rid of him when the patient was only four years old himself.

As termination approached, the patient became very frightened that his improvement would prove to be dependent on being with the therapist and that he would quickly relapse after the treatment ended. Nonetheless, by the next-to-last session, he himself felt that he could stop at the appointed time, provided he could return for follow-up visits if needed. Brief therapy is not indicated for all cases of PTSD. Persons with narcissistic personality disorder, borderline personality disorder, and dependent personality disorder may require support and interventions throughout the mourning and reacting process and may require treatment for a year or more. In addition, persons who have had a previous traumatic experience may have had a change in character as a consequence of a long-standing unresolved stress response syndrome, exacerbated by a recent stressor event. In such instances, a longer term therapy may be required.

Beginning a therapy without a time limit is possible, but there should be an agreement to focus on the meanings of the traumatic event to the self, and an aim to obtain a restoration to the status of personal functioning before the disastrous life events. This may be reexamined by therapist and patient along the way, as the intersecting personality features become apparent to both of them. They can then decide to retain the focus on working through the events or to enlarge aims to include efforts at personality change.

The goal of restoration to the status of functioning before the traumatic life event is an ideal, not an achievable goal. Instead, the person is changed by the experience. There may be gains as well as losses in personal adaptive capacity, and the goal of treatment is to make this outcome as adaptive as possible. Because periods of denial and intrusion may fluctuate even after working through some themes of response, follow-up visits are often advisable.

A psychodynamic understanding as described by Fishman (1989) can be used as the "container" of decisions about which cognitive, behavioral, and chemotherapeutic approaches to use, as well as the effects on remembering, transference, and defensive positions against working through warded-off aspects of the trauma. Of the cognitive and behavioral techniques, in vivo exposure is probably the one most likely to be helpful to combat irrational avoidance behaviors in PTSD. Such avoidances are often based on fear of repetition of the traumatic events, and the conscious and unconscious associations of certain situational conditions to the experience of extreme fright during the traumatic events. This may take the form of phobias about objects and places that are reminiscent of the situation, or of trigger sensations such as smells or sounds that may excite emotions similar to those that reached overwhelming intensity during the trauma. These phobias may take the form of progressive generalizations, leading to agoraphobic conditions. Although not of phobic proportions, the person may nonetheless have pathologic avoidances of certain work or social conditions. In such instances, direct exposure to the feared situations, in a condition of as much safety as possible, is a useful technique.

Such in vivo exposure of persons who have phobic avoidances, either spontaneously or as a product of traumatic life events, has been systematically reviewed by Marks (1981) and can be regarded as a well-documented and effective technique when the avoidant conditions prevail. In the situation of major disasters such as airplane crashes, floods, or combat, there has been an attempt to use visual image flooding as a different way of recontacting the stressful event. The success of this technique, which was begun by Stampfl and Lewis (1967), has not been documented in clinical trials for PTSD, but case reports have been published. In the cases reported, these techniques have been worthwhile in terms of reducing the out-of-control intensity of emotions that accompany the theme of memories of the traumatic event (Fairbank and Keane 1982; Keane and Kaloupek 1982; Saigh, in press).

Because traumatic events usually involve strong perceptual memories that return often as sensory, intrusive image experiences, the use in therapy of image modes of representation and expression, as well as lexical communications, should be considered, as alluded to here and discussed in more detail elsewhere (Horowitz 1983). The person may learn to increase a sense of control over the memories of identification with the therapist's belief that such mastery is possible. The unrecollectable and the unforgettable may thus become part of the courageously accepted tragedies but realities of life, matters that can be deliberately contemplated and also deliberately put out of awareness. At that point, the individual may have recovered from PTSD.

Prevention

Although systematic studies of the routes to preventing PTSD need to be undertaken, some clinical pointers may help those who have an opportunity to aid disaster victims. Socialization about the impact of the disastrous events is very important, and it is valuable to communicate with others who shared the experience, or at least persons who can be supportive and understanding. If at all possible, this review of the situation and its meaning should take place before sleep, so that the socialization is part of the same-day experience as the frightening and unreal-appearing events. For example, even a single individual involved in an automobile accident might find it helpful to go over that situation with an empathic person before sleep and dreaming.

Group sessions that allow sharing of views and experiences may be valuable and should be instituted as soon as possible, although they may be valuable even if instituted years after the disaster. It probably is best to have these led by an experienced professional, ideally one who has had the type of experience that has impacted on the group members. Members, at least, should have had similar experiences, although their individual responses may vary.

Social rituals are also important, such as the systematic stages of the mourning process instituted in some cultures at specified times, including at the one-year anniversary. Such rituals say, in effect, when it is good to share intense feelings, and when it is time to resume normal life functions. They relieve some doubt as to how to respond to events that are known culturally but are novel to the individual who confronts them for the first time. This applies as well to soldiers who return from combat experiences. Rituals of reuniting with the civilian population and resuming their usual roles will help to clarify passages that are otherwise depersonalizing.

The psychological suffering of PTSD, and of stress-response syndromes in general, is sometimes caught up in issues of litigation. Most clinicians favor rapid and decisive settlement of claims with treatment continued after this has occurred.

In closing, it should be kept in mind that every trauma contains real or threatened damage to the self concept. When there is damage to the self concept later in life, as with illness, accidents, or incapacity due to aging, a recapitulation of symptoms of an earlier traumatic response may occur. Memories of traumatic events seem to be unconsciously preserved for decades in such a way that, when reawakened, they can return with nightmarish vividness. When this happens, it is important to once again help the patient differentiate reality from fantasy associations about both the earlier traumatic events and the recent stressor experiences. This may usefully include pointing out the similarity in emotional states of mind and threatening ideas between the recent and remote experiences.

References

Section 18
Anxiety Disorders

Abraham K: A constitutional basis of locomotor anxiety, in Selected Papers on Psycho-Analysis. New York, Brunner/Mazel, 1913

Adler G: Borderline Psychopathology and Its Treatment. New York, Jason Aronson, 1985

Adler G, Buie DH: Aloneness and borderline psychopathology: the possible relevance of child development issues. Int J Psychoanal 60:83–96, 1979

American Psychiatric Association: Diagnostic and Statistical Manual of Mental Disorders, 2nd ed. Washington, DC, American Psychiatric Association, 1969

American Psychiatric Association: Diagnostic and Statistical Manual of Mental Disorders, 3rd ed. Washington, DC, American Psychiatric Association, 1980

American Psychiatric Association: Diagnostic and Statistical Manual of Mental Disorders, 3rd ed, revised. Washington, DC, American Psychiatric Association, 1987

American Psychiatric Association: Task Force Report 19: Biofeedback. Washington, DC, American Psychiatric Association, 1980

Arieti S: On Schizophrenia, Phobias, Depression, Psychotherapy and the Further Shores of Psychiatry. New York, Brunner/Mazel, 1978

Arnow B, Taylor CB, Agras WS, et al: Enhancing agoraphobia treatment outcome by changing couple communication patterns. Behav Res Ther 16:452–467, 1985

Balint M: The Basic Fault: Therapeutic Aspects of Regression. London, Tavistock Publications, 1968

Ballenger JC, Burrows GD, DuPont IM, et al: Alprazolam in panic disorder and agoraphobia: results from a multicenter trial, I: efficacy in short-term treatment. Arch Gen Psychiatry 45:413–422, 1988

Bandura A: Self-efficacy mechanisms in human agency. Am Psychol 37:122–147, 1982

Bandura A: Social Foundations of Thought and Action: A Social Cognitive Theory. Englewood Cliffs, Prentice Hall, 1986

Barlow DH: Anxiety and Its Disorders. New York, Guilford Press, 1988

Barlow DH, Wolfe B: Behavioral approaches to anxiety disorders: a report on the NIMH-SUNY, Albany Research Conference. J Consult Clin Psychol 49:448–454, 1981

Barlow DH, O'Brien GT, Last CG, et al: Couples treatment of agoraphobia: initial outcome, in Advances in Clinical Behavior Therapy. Edited by Craig KD, McMahon RJ. New York, Brunner/Mazel, 1983

Barlow DH, Cohen AS, Waddell M, et al: Panic and generalized anxiety disorders: nature and treatment. Behav Res Ther 15:431–449, 1984

Beck AT, Emery G: Anxiety Disorders and Phobias. New York, Basic Books, 1985

Beck AT, Emery G, Greenberg RL: Anxiety Disorders and Phobias: A Cognitive Perspective. New York, Basic Books, 1985

Beiman I, Israel E, Johnson SA: During-training and posttraining effects of live and taped extended progressive relaxation, self-relaxation, and electromyogram biofeedback. J. Consult Clin Psychol 46:314–321, 1978

Benjamin JD: Some developmental observations relating to the theory of anxiety. J Am Psychoanal Assoc 9:652–668, 1961

Benjamin JD: Further comments on some developmental aspects of anxiety, in Counterpoint: Libidinal Object and Subject. Edited by Gaskill HS. New York, International Universities Press, 1963, pp. 121–153

Benson H, Klipper MZ: The Relaxation Response. New York, William Morrow and Co, 1976

Benson H, Frankel FH, Apfel R, et al: Treatment of anxiety: a comparison of the usefulness of self-hypnosis and a meditational relaxation technique—an overview. Psychother Psychosom 30:229–242, 1978

Bland K, Hallam R: Relationship between response to graded exposure and marital satisfaction in agoraphobics. Behav Res Ther 19:335–338, 1981

Boning J: Benzodiazepine dependence: clinical and neurobiological aspects, in Chronic Treatments in Neuropsychiatry. Edited by Kemali D, Ragagni G. New York, Raven Press, 1985

Borkovec TD, Grayson JB, Cooper KM: Treatment of general tension: subjective and physiological effects of progressive relaxation. J. Consult Clin Psychol 46:518–528, 1978

Bornstein B: The analysis of a phobic child: Some problems of theory: and technique in child analysis. Psychoanal Study Child 3/4:181–226, 1949

Bowlby J: Separation anxiety. Int. J. Psychoanal 41:7–12, 1960

Bowlby J: Separation, anxiety and anger, in Attachment and Loss, vol II. New York, Basic Books Inc, 1973

Brazelton TB, Koslowski B, Main M: The origins of reciprocity: the early mother-infant interaction, in The Effect of the Infant on Its Caregiver. Edited by Lewis M, Rosenblum LA. New York, John Wiley & Sons, 1974

Brown BB: Stress and the Art of Biofeedback. New York, Harper and Row, 1977

Budzynski TH, Stoyva JM, Adler CS, et al: EMG biofeedback and tension headache: a controlled-outcome study. Psychosom Med 35:484–496, 1973

Burns D, Thorpe GL, Cavallaro LA: Agoraphobia 8 years after behavioral treatment: a follow-up study with interview, self-report, and behavioral data. Behavior Therapy 17:580–591, 1987

Burstein A: Treatment of flashbacks by imipramine. Am J Psychiatry 140:509, 1983

Burstein A: Treatment of posttraumatic stress disorder with imipramine. Psychosomatics 25:681–682, 1984

Butler G, Cullington A, Munby M, et al: Exposure and anxiety management in the treatment of social phobia. J Consult Clin Psychol 52:642–649, 1984

Canter A, Kondy CY, Knott JR: A comparison of EMG feedback and progressive muscle relaxation training in anxiety neurosis. Br J Psychiatry 127:470–477, 1975

Chambless D, Goldstein A (eds.): Agoraphobia. New York, Wiley, 1982

Clark DM, Salkovskis PM, Chalkley AJ: Respiratory control as a treatment for panic attacks. J Behav Ther Exp Psychiatry 16:23–30, 1985

Cohen IH, Pope B: Concurrent use of insight and desensitization therapy. Psychiatry 43:146–154, 1980

Cole JO, Orack MH, Beake B, et al: Assessment of the abuse liability of buspirone in recreational sedative users. J Clin Psychiatry 43:69–74, 1982

Compton A: A study of the psychoanalytic theory of anxiety, I: the developments of Freud's theory of anxiety. J Am Psychoanal Assoc 20:3–44, 1972a

Compton A: A study of the psychoanalytic theory of anxiety, II: developments in the theory of anxiety since 1926. J Am Psychoanal Assoc 20:341–394, 1972b

Compton A: A study of the psychoanalytic theory of anxiety, III: preliminary formulation of the anxiety response. J Am Psychoanal Assoc 28:739–773, 1980

Cooper A: Will neurobiology influence psychoanalysis? Am J Psychiatry 12:1395–1402, 1985

De Silva P, Rachman S: Is exposure a necessary condition for fear-reduction? Behav Res Ther 19:227–232, 1981

Deutsch H: Agoraphobia, in Neuroses and Character Types. New York, International Universities Press, 1965, pp 97–116

Diamond DB: Panic attacks, hypochondriasis and agoraphobia: a case report with a self psychology formulation. Am J Psychother 39:114–125, 1985

Emmelkamp PMG: Phobic and Obsessive-Compulsive Disorders. New York, Plenum, 1982

Emmelkamp PMG, Kuipers ACM: Agoraphobia: a follow-up study four years after treatment. Br J Psychiatry 134: 352–355, 1979

Falcon S, Ryan C, Chamberlain K, et al: Tricyclics: possible treatment for post-traumatic stress disorder. J Clin Psychiatry 46, 9:385–388, 1985

Fenichel O: The Psychoanalytic Theory of Neurosis. New York, WW Norrow, 1945

Figley C (ed): Stress Disorders Among Vietnam Veterans. New York, Brunner Mazel, 1978

Fishman G: Psychoanalytic psychotherapy, in Treatments of Psychiatric Disorders vol. 2. Washington, DC, American Psychiatric Association, 1989

Fleming J: Some observations on object constancy in the psychoanalysis of adults. J Am Psychoanal Assoc 23:743–760, 1975

Foenander G, Burrows GD, Gerschman JA, et al: Phobic behaviour and hypnotic susceptibility. Aust J Clin Exp Hyp 8:41–46, 1980

Fraiberg S: Object constancy and mental representation. Psychoanal Study Child 24:9–47, 1969

Frances A, Dunn P: The attachment-autonomy conflict in agoraphobia. Int J Psychoanal 56:435–439, 1975

Frank JD: Persuasion and Healing: A Comparative Study of Psychotherapy. Baltimore, Johns Hopkins Press, 1961

Frankel FH: Trance as a Coping Mechanism. New York, Plenum Medical Book Co, 1976

Frankel FH, Orne MT: Hypnotizability and phobic behavior. Arch Gen Psychiatry, 33:1259–1261, 1976

Freud S: The justification for detaching from neurasthenia a particular syndrome: the anxiety-neurosis. Collected Papers 1:76–127, 1894

Freud S: Three essays on the theory of sexuality. Standard Edition, 7:125–243, 1905

Freud S: Analysis of a phobia in a five-year-old-boy. Standard Edition, 10:3–149, 1909

Freud S: From the History of an Infantile Neurosis. Collected Papers 3:390–585, 1918

Freud S: Inhibitions, symptoms, and anxiety. Standard Edition, 20:7–174, 1926

Freud S: Beyond the Pleasure Principle (1920). (Standard Edition 18). London, Hogarth Press, 1959

Friedman DE: A synthetic approach to anxiety. Psychiatry 35:336–344, 1972

Frischholz EJ, Spiegel D, Spiegel H, et al: Differential hypnotic responsivity of smokers, phobics, and chronic pain control patients: a failure to confirm. J Abnorm Psychol, 91:269–272, 1982

Fromm E, Brown DP, Hurt SW, et al: The phenomena and characteristics of self-hypnosis. Int J Clin Exp Hyp 26:189–246, 1981

Gatchel RJ: EMG biofeedback in anxiety reduction, in Clinical Biofeedback: Efficacy and Mechanisms. Edited by White L, Tujrsky B. New York, Guilford Press, 1982

Gatchel RJ, Korman M, Weis CB, et al: A multiple-response evaluation of EMG biofeedback performance during training and stress-induction conditions. Psychophysiology 15:153–258, 1978

Gediman HK: Actual neurosis and psychoneurosis. Int J Psychoanal 65:191–202, 1984

Gelder MG, Marks IM, Wolff HH: Desensitization and psychotherapy in the treatment of phobic states: a controlled inquiry. Br J Psychiatry 113: 53–73, 1967

Gelder MG, Bancroft JHJ, Gath D, et al: Specific and non-specific factors in behaviour therapy. Br J Psychiatry 123:445–462, 1973

Gerschman J, Burrows GD, Reade P, et al: Hypnotizability and the treatment of dental phobic behavior, in Hypnosis 1979. Edited by Burrows GD, Collison DR, Dennerstein L. New York, Elsevier/North Holland, 1979

Ghosh A, Marks IM: Self-treatment of agoraphobia by exposure. Behav Res Ther 18:3–16, 1987

Gill H: Complaints of patients presenting for psychotherapy in 1938 vs 1978. Br J Med Psychol 58:55–56, 1985

Gillan P, Rachman S: An experimental investigation of desensitization in phobic patients. Br J Psychiatry 124:392–401, 1974

Gitlin B, Martin J, Shear MK, et al: Behavior therapy for panic disorder. J Nerv Ment Dis 173:742–743, 1985

Goismian R: Therapeutic approaches to phobia: a comparison. Am J Psychother 37:227–234, 1983

Goldfried MR, Robins C: Self-schemas, cognitive bias, and the processing of therapeutic experiences, in Advances in Cognitive-Behavioral Research and Therapy, vol 2. Edited by Kendall PC. New York, Academic Press, 1983

Greenblatt DJ, Shader RI: Dependence, tolerance, and addiction to benzodiazepines: clinical and pharmacokinetic considerations. Drug Metab Rev 8(1):13–28, 1978

Greenblatt DJ, Shader RI: Current status of benzodiazepines II. N Engl J Med 309(7):410–416, 1983

Group for the Advancement of Psychiatry (GAP) Committee on Research, Pharmacotherapy, and Psychotherapy: Paradoxes, Problems, and Progress, vol. IX, report 93, 1975, pp. 95–117

Hamburg D, Adams J: A perspective on coping behavior, seeking, and utilizing information in major transitions. Arch Gen Psychiatry 17:277–284, 1967

Hand I, Wittchen H: Panic and Phobias. New York, Springer-Verlag, 1986

Harley M: The current status of transference neurosis in children. J Am Psychoanal Assoc 19:26–40, 1971

Hartland J: Medical and Dental Hypnosis and Its Clinical Applications, 2nd ed. London, Bailliere Tindall, 1982

Hartmann H: Comments on the psychoanalytic theory of the ego, in Essays on Ego Psychology. New York, International Universities Press, 1950, pp 113–141

Haskell D: Letter to the editor. N Engl J Med 310:465, 1984

Heide FJ, Borkovec TD: Relaxation-induced anxiety: Paradoxical anxiety enhancement due to relaxation training. J. Consult Clin Psychol 5:171–182, 1983

Henry J: Present concepts of stress theory, in Catecholamines and Stress: Recent Advances. Edited by Usdin E, Kvetnansky R, Kopin I. New York, Elsevier Press, 1980

Hibbert GA: Ideational components of anxiety. Br J Psychiatry 144:618–624, 1984

Hilgard ER: Divided Consciousness: Multiple Controls in Human Thought and Action. New York, Wiley, 1977

Hilgard JR, LeBaron S: Hypnotherapy of Pain In Children with Cancer. Los Altos, Calif, William Kaufmann Inc, 1984

Hogben GL, Cornfield RB: Treatment of traumatic war neurosis with phenelzine. Arch Gen Psychiatry 38:440–445, 1981

Hollister LE: Benzodiazepines—an overview. Br J Clin Pharmacol 11:1175–1195, 1981

Horowitz M: Image Formation and Psychotherapy. New York, Aronson, 1983

Horowitz M: Stress Response Syndromes, 2nd ed. New York, Aronson, 1986

Horowitz M: States of Mind, 2nd ed. New York, Plenum, 1987

Horowitz M. Introduction to Psychodynamics. New York, Basic Books, 1988

Horowitz M, Solomon G: A prediction of delayed stress response symptoms in Vietnam veterans. J Soc Issues 31:67–80, 1975

Horowitz M, Zilbert N: Regressive alterations of the self concept. Am J Psychiatry 140:284–289, 1983

Horowitz M, Wilner N, Kaltreider N, et al: Signs and symptoms of posttraumatic stress disorder. Arch Gen Psychiatry 37:85–92, 1980

Horowitz M, Marmar C, Krupnick J, et al: Personality Styles and Brief Psychotherapy. New York, Basic Books, 1984a

Horowitz M, Marmer C, Weiss D, et al: Brief psychotherapy of bereavement reactions: the relationship of process to outcome. Arch Gen Psychiatry 41:438–448, 1984b

Horowitz M, Marmar C, Weiss D, et al: Comprehensive analysis of change after brief dynamic psychotherapy. Am J Psychiatry 143:582–589, 1986

Hutchings DF, Reinking RH: Tension headaches: what form of therapy is most effective? Biofeedback Self-Regul 1:183–190, 1976

Isenstadt L: From panic to signal anxiety: the acquisition of signal structure in a hyperactive boy. Int Rev Psychoanal 7:469–482, 1980

Jannoun L, Munby M, Catalan J, et al: A home-based treatment program for agoraphobia: replication and controlled evaluation. Behav Res Ther 11:294–305, 1980

Jannoun L, Oppenheimer C, Gelder M: A self-help treatment program for anxiety state patients. Behav Res Ther 13:103–111, 1982

John R, Hollander B, Perry C: Hypnotizability and phobic behavior: further supporting data. J Abnorm Psychol 92:390–392, 1983

Kahn RJ, McNair DM, Lipman RS, et al: Imipramine and chlordiazepoxide in depressive anxious disorders. Arch Gen Psychiatry 43:79–85, 1986

Kandell E: From metapsychology to molecular biology: explorations into the nature of anxiety. Am J Psychiatry 140:1277–1293, 1983

Kazdin AE, Wilson GT: Evaluation of Behavior Therapy: Issues, Evidence and Research Strategies. Cambridge, Ballinger, 1978

Keane TM, Kaloupek DG: Imaginal flooding in the treatment of posttraumatic stress disorder. J Consult Clin Psychol 50:138–140, 1982

Kernberg O: Borderline Conditions and Pathological Narcissism. New York, Jason Aronson Inc, 1975

Khan M: Role of phobic and counterphobic mechanisms and separation anxiety in schizoid character formation, in Privacy of the Self. New York, International Universities Press, 1974, pp 69–81

Klein DF: An update on panic disorder. Currents 4:5–10, 1985

Klein DF, Davis JM: Diagnosis and Drug Treatment of Psychiatric Disorders. Baltimore, Williams and Wilkins, 1969

Klein DF, Rabkin JG (eds): Anxiety: New Research and Changing Concepts. New York, Raven Press, 1981

Klein DF, Gittelman R, Quitkin F, et al: Diagnosis and Drug Treatment of Psychiatric Disorders: Adults and Children. Baltimore, Williams and Wilkins, 1980

Klein DF, Zitrin CM, Woerner MG, et al: Treatment of phobias. Arch Gen Psychiatry 40:139–145, 1983

Kohut H: Analysis of the Self. New York, International Universities Press, 1971

Kohut H: Restoration of the Self. New York, International Universities Press, 1977

Kolb LC, Burris BC, Griffiths S: Propranolol and clonidine in the treatment of posttraumatic stress disorders of war, in Post Traumatic Stress Disorder: Psychological and Biological Sequelae. Edited by Van der Kolk BA. Washington, DC, American Psychiatric Press, 1984

Kosten TR, Mason JW, Giller EL, et al: Sustained urinary norepinephrine and epinephrine elevation in posttraumatic stress disorder. Presented at the APA meeting, New Research Sector. Dallas, May 1985

Kris AO: On wanting too much. The exceptions revisited. Int J Psychoanal 57:85–95, 1976

Kris AO: Either-or dilemmas. Psychoanal Study Child 32:91–117, 1977

Kris AO: The conflicts of ambivalence. Psychoanal Study Child 39:213–234, 1984

Kroger WS: Clinical and Experimental Hypnosis. Philadelphia, J B Lippincott Co, 1977

Kroger W, Fezler WD: Hypnosis and Behavior Modification: Imagery Conditioning. Philadelphia, JB Lippincott Co, 1976

Krupnick JL, Horowitz MJ: Victims of violence. Services for Survivors, 1980

Lader M: Dependence on benzodiazepines. J Clin Psychiatry 44:121–127, 1983

Lader M, Petursson H: Abuse ability of anxiolytics, in Anxiolytics: Neurochemical, Behavioral and Clinical Perspectives. Edited by Malick JB, Enna SJ, Yamamura HI. New York, Raven, 1983

Lazarus RS, Folkman SK: Psychological Stress Appraisal and Coping. New York, Springer, 1984

Legalos CN: Biofeedback and psychotherapy, in Biofeedback: Behavioral Medicine. Edited by Birk L. New York, Grune & Stratton, 1973

Lehrer PM: Effects of progressive relaxation in anxiety neurotic patients and of progressive relaxation and alpha feedback in non-patients. J Consult Clin Psychol 45:389–404, 1978

Levenson H, Lanman R, Rankin M: Traumatic war neurosis and phenelzine. Arch Gen Psychiatry 39:1345, 1982

Levine S: A psychological approach to the ontogeny of coping, in Stress, Coping, and Development in Children. Edited by Garmezy N, Rutter M. New York, McGraw-Hill, 1983

Lewin BD: Phobic symptoms and dream interpretation. Psychoanal Q 21:295–372, 1952

Lifton R: Home From the War. New York, Simon & Schuster, 1973

Loewald HW: On Motivation and Instinct Theory, in Papers on Psychoanalysis. New Haven, Yale, 1980, pp 91–128

London P: The end of ideology in behavior modification. Am Psychol 27:913–931, 1972

Luthe W (ed): Autogenic Therapy, vols 1–6. New York, Grune & Stratton, 1969

Mahler MS: On human symbiosis and vicissitudes of individuation. J Am Psychoanal Assoc 15: 740–763, 1967

Mahler MS, Pine F, Begman A: The Psychological Birth of the Human Infant: Symbiosis and Individuation. New York, Basic Books, 1975

Maletsky BM, Klotter J: Addiction to diazepam. Int J Addict 11:95–115, 1976

Margraf J, Ehlers A, Roth WT: Panic attacks: theoretical models and empirical evidence, in Panic and Phobias. Edited by Hand I, Wittchen H. New York, Springer-Verlag, 1986

Marks IM: Phobic disorders four years after treatment: a prospective follow-up. Br J Psychiatry 18:683–688, 1971

Marks IM: Cure and care of the neuroses. New York, John Wiley & Sons, 1981

Marks IM, Gelder MG: The common ground between behavior therapy and psychodynamic methods. Br J Med Psychol 39:11, 1966

Marks IM, Hallam RS, Connolly J, et al: Nursing in Behavioural Therapy. London, The Royal College of Nursing of the United Kingdom, 1977

Marks IM, Gray S, Cohen D, et al: Imipramine and brief therapist-aided exposure in agoraphobics having self-exposure homework. Arch Gen Psychiatry 40:153–162, 1983

Marks J: The Benzodiazepines: Overuse, Misuse, Abuse. Lancaster, MTP Press, 1978

Marlatt GA, Gordon J: Relapse prevention. New York, Guilford Press, 1985

Marshall R: The treatment of night terrors associated with posttraumatic syndrome. Am J Psychiatry 132–133, 1975

Mathews AM, McLeod C: Selective processing of threat cues in anxiety states. Behav Res Ther 23:563–570 1985

Mathews AM, Johnston DW, Lancashire M, et al: Imaginal flooding and exposure to real phobic situations: treatment outcome with agoraphobic patients. Br J Psychiatry 129:362–371, 1976

Mathews AM, Gelder MG, Johnston DW: Agoraphobia: Nature and Treatment. New York, Guilford Press, 1981

Mavissakalian M, Michelson L: Self-directed in vivo exposure practice in behavioral and pharmacological treatments of agoraphobia. Behav Res Ther 14:506–519, 1983

Mavissakalian M, Perel J: Imipramine in the treatment of agoraphobia: dose response relationships. Am J Psychiatry 142:1032–1036, 1985

Mavissakalian M, Michelson L, Dealy RS: Pharmacological treatment of agoraphobia: imipramine versus imipramine with programmed practice. Br J Psychiatry 143:348–355, 1983

McCurdy L: The short-term use of benzodiazepines. Arzneimittel-Forschung: Drug Research 30:895–897, 1980

McGuiness TP: Hypnosis in the treatment of phobias: a review of the literature. Am J Clin Hypn 26:261–272, 1984

McPherson FM, Brougham L, McLaren L: Maintenance of improvement in agoraphobic patients treated by behavioural methods in a four year follow-up. Behav Res Ther 18: 150–152, 1980

Meichenbaum D: Cognitive Behavior Modification. New York, Plenum Press, 1977

Mellinger GD, Balter MB, Uhlenhuth EH: Prevalence and correlates of the long-term regular use of anxiolytics. JAMA 251:375–379, 1984

Miller MP, Murphy PJ, Miller TP: Comparison of electromyographic feedback and progressive relaxation training in treating circumscribed anxiety stress reactions. J Consult Clin Psychol 45:1291–1298, 1978

Munby M, Johnston DW: Agoraphobia: the long-term follow-up of behavioural treatment. Br J Psychiatry 137:418–427, 1980

Nemiah JC: The psychoanalytic view of anxiety. Anxiety: New Research and Changing Concepts. Edited by Klein DF, Rabkin J. New York, Raven Press, 1981

Nemiah JC: The Psychodynamic View of Anxiety, in Diagnosis and Treatment of Anxiety Disorder. Edited by Pasnau R. Washington, DC, American Psychiatric Press, 1984

Norton GR, Allen GE, Hilton J: The social validity of treatments for agoraphobia. Behav Res Ther 21:393–399, 1983

Noyes R, Dupont RL, Pecknold JC, et al: Alprazolam in panic disorder and agoraphobia: results from a multicenter trial, II: patient acceptance, side effects, and safety. Arch Gen Psychiatry 45:423–428, 1988

O'Learly KD, Wilson GT: Behavior therapy: application and outcome, 2nd ed. Englewood Cliffs, Prentice Hall, (in press)

Orne MT: Psychotherapy in contemporary America: its development and context, in American Handbook of Psychiatry, 2nd ed, vol 5. Treatment. Edited by Freedman DX, Dyrud JE. New York, Basic Books Inc, 1975

Orne MT: The construct of hypnosis: implications of the definition for research and practice. Ann NY Acad Sci 296:14–33, 1977

Orne MT: Assessment of biofeedback therapy: specific vs. nonspecific effects, in American Psychiatric Association: Task Force Report 19: Biofeedback. Washington, DC, American Psychiatric Association, 1980

Ost L, Jerremalm A, Johansson J: Individual response patterns and the effects of different behavioral methods in the treatment of social phobia. Behav Res Ther 22:697–708, 1984

Owen RT, Tyrer P: Benzodiazepine dependence: a review of the literature. Drugs 25:385–398, 1983

Pearlin L, Schooler C: The structure of coping. J Health Soc Behav 19:2–21, 1978

Pecknold JC, Swinson RP, Kuch K, et al: Alprazolam in panic disorder and agoraphobia: results from a multicenter trial, III: discontinuation effects. Arch Gen Psychiatry 45:5:429–436, 1988

Rachman S: The modification of agoraphobic avoidance behaviour: some fresh possibilities. Behav Res Ther 21:567–574, 1983

Rachman S, Wilson GT: The Effects of Psychological Therapy. Oxford, Pergamon Press, 1980

Ramsay R: Bereavement: A behavioral treatment of pathological grief, in Trends in Behavior Therapy. Edited by Sjoden PO, Bates S, Dockens WS. New York, Academic Press, 1979

Rangell L: On the psychoanalytic theory of anxiety: a statement of a unitary theory. J Am Psychoanal Assoc 3:389–414, 1955

Raskin M, Bali LR, Peeke HV: Muscle relaxation and transcendental meditation: a controlled evaluation of efficacy in the treatment of chronic anxiety. Arch Gen Psychiatry 37:93–97, 1980

Redmond DE Jr: Neurochemical basis for anxiety and anxiety disorders: evidence from drugs which decrease human fear or anxiety, in Anxiety and the Anxiety Disorders. Edited by Tuma AH, Maser JD. Hillsdale, NJ, Erlbaum, 1984

Renik O, et al: Bamboo phobia in an eighteen month old boy. J Am Psychoanal Assoc 26:255–330, 1978

Rhead C: The role of pregenital fixations of agoraphobics. J Am Psychoanal Assoc 17:848–861, 1969

Rhodes JM, Feather BW: The application of psychodynamics to behavior therapy. Am J Psychiatry 131:17–20, 1974

Rice KM, Blanchard EB: Biofeedback in the treatment of anxiety disorders. Clin Psychol Rev 2:557–577, 1982

Rickels K (ed): Nonspecific Factors in Drug Therapy. Springfield, Ill, Charles C Thomas, 1968

Rickels K: Clinical comparisons. Psychosomatics 21(10 Suppl):15–20, 1980

Rickels K, Weisman K, Norstead N, et al: Buspirone and diazepam in anxiety: a controlled study. J Clin Psychiatry 43:81–86, 1982

Rickels K, Case WG, Downing RW, et al: Long-term diazepam therapy and clinical outcome. JAMA 250:676–771, 1983

Rickles WH, Onoda L, Doyle CC: Biofeedfback as an adjunct to psychotherapy. Biofeedback Self Regul 7:1–33, 1982

Robins LN, Helzer JE, Weissman MM, et al: Lifetime prevalence of specific psychiatric disorders in three sites. Arch Gen Psychiatry 41:949–958, 1984

Rosenthal T, Bandura A: Psychological modeling: theory and practice, in Handbook of Psychotherapy and Behavior Change. Edited by Garfield SL, Bergin AE. New York, John Wiley and Sons, 1978

Russell PL: Emotional growth and crises of attachment (in press)

Saigh PA: Childhood PTSD. Prof School Psychol (in press)

Salzman C: Psychotropic drug use and polypharmacy in a general hospital. Gen Hosp Psychiatry 3:1–9, 1981

Salzman C: Treatment of anxiety, in Clinical Geriatric Psychopharmacology. Edited by Salzman C. New York, McGraw-Hill, 1984

Salzman C, Green AI: Differential therapeutics: Psychopharmacology, in American Psychiatric Association Annual Review, Vol. 6. Edited by Hales RE, Frances AJ. Washington, DC, American Psychiatric Press, 1987, pp. 415–427

Salzman C, et al: American Psychiatric Association Task Force on Benzodiazepine Dependence and Withdrawal (in press)

Salzman L: Obsessions and phobias. Int J Psych 6:451–468, 1968

Schnurmann A: Observation of a phobia. Psychoanal Study Child 3/4: 253–270, 1949

Schur M: The ego and the id in anxiety. Psychoanal Study Child 13:190–222, 1958

Schur M: Metapsychological aspects of phobias, in The Unconscious Today: Essays in Honor of Max Schur. Edited by Kanzer M. New York, International Universities Press, 1971

Selye H: A syndrome produced by diverse noxious agents. Nature 138:32, 1936

Settlage CF: On the libidinal aspect of early psychic development and the genesis of infantile neurosis, in Separation-Individuation: Essays in Honor of Margaret S. Mahler. Edited by McDevitt J, Settlage CF. New York, International Universities Press, 1971, pp 131–156

Sheehan DV: Current concepts in psychiatry: panic attacks and phobias. N Engl J Med 307:156–158, 1982

Sheehan DV: Monoamine oxidase inhibitors and alprazolam in the treatment of panic disorder and agoraphobia. Psychiatr Clin North Am 8:49–62, 1985

Sheehan DV, Coleman JH, Greenblatt DJ, et al: Some biochemical correlates of panic attacks with agoraphobia and their response to a new treatment. J Clin Psychopharmacol 4:66–75, 1984

Shen WW, Park S: The use of monoamine oxidase inhibitors in the treatment of traumatic war neurosis: case report. Milit Med 148:430–431, 1983

Shopper M: The role of audition in early psychic development with special reference to the use of the pull-toy in the separation individuation phase. J Am Psychoanal Assoc 26:283–310, 1978

Shor RE: Hypnosis and the concept of the generalized reality orientation. Am J Psychother 13:582–602, 1959

Shor RE, Orne EC: The Harvard Group Scale of Hypnotic Susceptibility: Form A. Palo Alto, Calif, Consulting Psychologists Press, 1962

Shore J: Disaster Stress Studies: New Methods and Findings. Washington, DC, American Psychiatric Press, 1986

Sloane RB, Staples FR, Cristol AH, et al: Psychotherapy versus Behavior Therapy. Cambridge, Harvard University Press, 1975

Soskis DA: Teaching Self-Hypnosis: An Introductory Guide for Clinicians. New York, W.W. Norton, 1986

Sperling M: The Major Neuroses and Behavior Disorders in Children. New York, Jason Aronson, 1982

Spitz R: Anxiety in infancy: a study of its manifestations in the first year of life. Int J Psychoanal 31:138–143, 1950

Spitzer RL, Skodol AE, Gibbon M, et al: DSM-III Casebook. Washington, DC, American Psychiatric Association, 1981

Stampfl TG, Lewis DJ: Essentials of implosive therapy: a learning theory based on psychodynamic behavioral therapy. J Abnorm Psychol 72:496, 1967

Stern D: The First Relationship: Infant and Mother. Cambridge, Harvard University Press, 1977

Stern R, Marks I: Brief and prolonged flooding. Arch Gen Psychiatry 28:270–276, 1973

Stolorow RD, Lachmann FM: Psychoanalysis of Developmental Arrests. New York, International Universities Press, 1980, pp. 119–143

Telch MJ, Leaman BH, Taylor CB: Antidepressant medication in the treatment of agoraphobia: a critical review. Behav Res Ther 21:505–518, 1983

Telch MJ, Agras WS, Taylor CB, et al: Combined pharmacological and behavioral treatment for agoraphobia. Behav Res Ther 23:325–336, 1985

Thompson GN: Post traumatic psychoneurosis: evaluation of drug therapy. Dis Nerv Syst 38:617–619, 1977

Thorpe GL, Burns LE: The Agoraphobic Syndrome. New York, John Wiley and Sons, 1983a

Thorpe G, Burns LE: The Nature and Treatment of Agoraphobia. London, Wiley, 1983b

Tolpin M: On the beginnings of a cohesive self: an application of the concept of transmuting internalization to the study of the transitional object and signal anxiety. Psychoanal Study Child 26:316–352

Townsend RE, House JF, Addario DA: A comparison of EMG feedback and progressive muscle relaxation training in anxiety neuroses. Am J Psychiatry 132:598–601, 1975

Van der Kolk BA: Psychopharmacologic issues in posttraumatic stress disorder. Hosp Community Psychiatry 34:683–691, 1983

Wachtel PL: Psychoanalysis and Behavior Therapy: Toward an Integration. New York, Basic Books Inc, 1977

Wadden TA, Anderton CH: The clinical use of hypnosis. Psych Bull 91:215–243, 1982

Wangh M: Psychoanalytic thought on phobia: its evolution and its relevance for therapy. Am J Psych 123:1075–1080, 1967

Weiss E: Agoraphobia in the Light of Ego Psychology. New York, Grune & Stration, 1964

Wilson GT: Clinical issues and strategies in the practice of behavior therapy, in Annual Review of Behavior Therapy, vol. 9. Edited by Wilson G, Franks C, Brownell K, et al. New York, Guilford, 1984

Wilson GT: Social psychological processes in behavior therapy, in Social Cognition and Behavior Therapy. Edited by Eelen P. New York, Erlbaum, 1986

Winnicott DW: The depressive position in normal emotional development, in Through Paediatrics to Psycho-Analysis. New York, Basic Books, 1954

Winnicott DW: Primary Maternal Preoccupation, in Through Paediatrics to Psycho-Analysis. New York, Basic Books, 1956

Winnicott DW: The Theory of the Parent-Infant Relationship in the Maturational Processes and the Facilitating Environment. New York, International Universities Press, 1974

Wolpe J: Psychotherapy by reciprocal inhibition. Stanford, Calif, Stanford University Press, 1958

Woods JH, Katz JL, Winger G: Abuse liability of benzodiazepines. Reviews 39:251–419, Dec 1987

Woodward R, Jones RB: Cognitive restructuring treatment: a controlled trial with anxious patients. Behav Res Ther 18:401–407, 1980

Yorke C, Wiseberg S: A developmental view of anxiety. Psychoanal Study Child 31:107–135, 1976

Zetzel E: Anxiety and the capacity to bear it. Int J Psychoanal 30, 1949

Zitrin CM: Combined pharmacological and psychotherapeutic treatment of phobias, in Phobia: Psychological and Pharmacological Treatment. Edited by Mavissakalian M, Barlow D. New York. Guilford, 1981

Zitrin CM, Klein DE, Woerner MG, et al: Treatment of phobias. Arch Gen Psychiatry 40:125–138, 1983

Obsessive Compulsive Disorders

Chapter 187

Behavior Therapy and Pharmacotherapy

The outlook for treatment of patients with obsessive compulsive disorder (OCD) was not very promising until recently. Indeed, Salzman and Thaler (1981), in their review of the treatment literature prior to 1978, noted that for drugs, surgery, and other experimental and physiological therapies in OCD patients "there is neither convincing nor suggestive evidence that more can be accomplished than the relief of some anxiety—at a cost that often outweighs the potential benefits" (p. 295). This pessimistic conclusion reflected a tradition that considered OCD as a rare, treatment refractory syndrome (Woodruff and Pitts 1969). In the last decade, however, two new insights about OCD have emerged. First, epidemiological studies have revealed that OCD is not as rare as has been believed. And second, specific behavioral and pharmacologic treatments have been developed which offer considerable promise for these patients.

In this chapter, after a brief summary of diagnostic and epidemiologic issues in OCD, we will review those behavioral and pharmacologic treatments which, when tailored to the specific symptoms of the OCD patient, are likely to yield significant clinical improvement.

Clinical Features

Obsessive-compulsive disorder (OCD) involves the persistent intrusion of intense, unwanted, senseless thoughts (obsessions) often accompanied by repetitive, ritualistic behaviors (compulsions) which the patient feels driven to perform in order to reduce the obsessional distress. Four of the most common symptom clusters in OCD are summarized below.

Washers. About 50 percent of most OCD samples (Rachman and Hodgson 1980) are obsessed with dirt, contamination, germs, or bugs. These patients may spend several hours each day washing their hands or showering. Typically, they try to avoid sources of "contamination," like public restrooms and door knobs. Although the patient states, "I know I am not really going to transmit a fatal disease if I don't wash," he or she may find a stubborn refusal to shake hands or to touch public phones. Occasionally, washers are not even certain why they are washing, expressing a vague presentiment that "something terrible will happen if I don't."

Checkers.   A second common feature of OCD involves pathologic doubt accompanied by compulsive checking. Some patients have an incessant need for symmetry with hours spent checking that the papers on the desk are lined up "just right." However, typically the checker is concerned about the possibility that someone will be harmed if he fails to check carefully. For patients with OCD, checking, which is enough to resolve "normal" uncertainty, often only contributes to the obsessional's doubt. For instance, a housewife with a persistent doubt that the stove had been turned off, returned home several times each day to check the burners. Ultimately, by some inscrutable means, the patient resolves a particular doubt only to have it replaced by a new obsessional preoccupation. Resistance, which in this case is the attempt to refrain from checking, leads to difficulty concentrating and exhaustion from the never-ending assault of nagging uncertainties.

Pure obsessions.   A third clinical picture is that of the pure obsessional. Approximately 25 percent of OCD patients are in this category according to Akhtar et al. (1975). Repetitive, intrusive thoughts, often sexual or aggressive, and always reprehensible, may be associated with impulses (which have been called horrific temptations) or fearful images. When the obsession is an aggressive impulse, it is most often directed at the one person most loved by the patient. Cognitive rituals (e.g., counting or counter-thoughts) rather than behavioral rituals, are common. A patient who was afraid that he would decapitate his younger brother struggled with this impulse by avoiding sharp objects, then avoiding his family, and ultimately avoiding letters of the alphabet in his brother's name. In addition, each time he would encounter the word "ax" or his brother's initials, he went through an extensive internal "counter-ritual" to undo the image of decapitation.

Primary obsessional slowness.   Finally, there is the rare and disabling syndrome of primary obsessional slowness (Rachman 1974). Although slowness results from most rituals, occasionally it becomes the predominant symptom. These patients feel that everything needs to be "just right" and so it may take them an hour or more to brush their teeth or prepare breakfast.

In many cases, washing and checking coexist. In addition, one may see adult patients with pure obsessional complaints who give a history of compulsive hand-washing or compulsive checking during young adulthood (Insel 1984). Thus, within individuals, these different symptom clusters may overlap or may develop sequentially. However, for therapeutic intervention, it is crucial to identify these symptom clusters. For instance, a patient with pure obsessions might be less amenable to behavior therapy than to a pharmacologic approach. On the other hand, a patient with considerable avoidance (i.e., washers) might be most directly helped by behavioral techniques. Obsessional slowness, which includes several complex symptoms, usually requires a combination of behavioral, pharmacologic, and psychosocial interventions.

Diagnostic Issues

Although both obsessions and compulsions are found in a variety of psychiatric disorders as well as in normal mental life, OCD is distinguished by two cardinal features. First, the symptoms are ego dystonic—the individual attempts to ignore or suppress the obsessions or the compulsions and recognizes that these preoccupations are excessive or unreasonable. Second, the obsessions and the compulsions cause marked distress, are time consuming (should take more than one hour each day according to DSM-III-R [American Psychiatric Association 1987]), and lead to significant interference in functioning.

In DSM-III-R, in contrast to DSM-III, another Axis I disorder may be present. However, the content of the obsession should be unrelated to it; that is, guilty thoughts in the presence of major depressive disorder or thoughts about food in the presence of eating disorder should not be considered as symptoms of OCD.

Other behaviors which are engaged in excessively and with a sense of compulsion, such as pathologic gambling, overeating, alcohol or drug abuse, and sexuality, are also distinguished from true compulsions since to some degree they are experienced as pleasurable, while compulsions are not inherently pleasurable.

OCD, variously referred to as obsessional neurosis, compulsion neurosis, or obsessional disorder, is frequently confused with compulsive personality disorder. Compulsive personality disorder refers to individuals afflicted with perfectionism, orderliness, and rigidity, often with an inability to grasp "the big picture." For an individual with compulsive personality disorder, these traits are *ego syntonic* (i.e., the individual does not attempt to ignore or suppress them, and the traits are not usually associated with a sense of compulsion). Moreover, epidemiologic evidence reveals that a substantial number of patients with OCD do not exhibit premorbid compulsive traits (Rasmussen and Tsuang 1984). These two disorders are not necessarily on a single continuum and thus, if an individual meets the criteria for both disorders, both diagnoses should be recorded.

Another source of diagnostic difficulty might arise in very severe OCD patients who may briefly relinquish the struggle against their symptoms. At such times the obsessions or compulsions may appear to shift from an ego dystonic intrusion to a psychotic delusion. Since follow-up data reveal that such psychotic-like decompensations may occur in patients with OCD who never go on to develop schizophrenia, Insel and Akiskal (1986) suggested that these patients should be considered as having "obsessive-compulsive psychosis," analogous to the association between psychotic depression and depression.

Prevalence

The lifetime prevalence of OCD in the general population has been reported to be more than 2.0 percent in an NIMH-sponsored Epidemiologic Catchment Area (ECA) Survey (Robins et al. 1984). This surprisingly high prevalence is more than 40 times greater than the traditional estimate of 0.05 percent from clinical studies (Woodruff and Pitts 1969). Another study, which involved direct interviews of children in the general population, found a prevalence of 0.5 percent (Flament et al. 1988). Only one-third of adult cases of OCD report onset in childhood, and since OCD is a chronic disorder (Insel 1984), this finding would project a prevalence of 1.5 percent in the general population, roughly in agreement with the ECA results.

If the lifetime prevalence of OCD in the general population is more than 1 percent, why is it that we do not see these patients more often? Perhaps the stigma attached to the disclosure of bizarre and irrational thoughts or behaviors coupled with the lack of public awareness leads patients to be very secretive about their obsessive-compulsive symptoms. Many of them do not seek help unless they develop complications (the most common being depression) (Goodwin et al. 1969), and the diagnostic workup of the complication may not reveal the presence of OCD. For instance, many patients with skin irritation from excessive washing seek treatment from dermatologists and are never referred for psychiatric evaluation (Rasmussen 1985). Hence, it might be important to include direct, specific questions about obsessions and compulsions in a screening interview since many times, unless specifically asked, patients with OCD will not reveal their symptoms.

Treatment

Obsessive-compulsive disorders have long been considered among the most intractable of the neurotic disorders. Breitner (1960) noted that "most of us are agreed that the treatment of obsessional states is one of the most difficult tasks confronting the psychiatrist and many of us consider it hopeless" (p. 32). Traditional psychotherapy has not proven effective in ameliorating obsessive-compulsive symptomatology (Black 1974). In a sample of 90 inpatients, Kringlen (1965) found that only 20 percent had improved at a 13- to 20-year follow-up. Somewhat more favorable results were reported by Grimshaw (1965): 40 percent of an outpatient sample was improved at a 1- to 14-year follow-up.

Behavioral Treatments

Some improvement in the prognostic picture emerged with the application of treatments derived from learning theories. These methods can be divided into two classes: 1) exposure procedures aimed at reducing the anxiety and discomfort associated with obsessions, and 2) blocking or punishing techniques directed at decreasing the frequency of either obsessive thoughts or ritualistic behaviors.

The most commonly employed exposure treatment was systematic desensitization. Despite initial claims for its efficacy with obsessive-compulsive disorders, a review of the literature indicated that systematic desensitization affected improvement in only 30 to 40 percent of the cases reported (Beech and Vaughn 1978; Cooper et al. 1965). Treatment procedures utilizing prolonged exposure to feared cues (e.g., paradoxical intention, imaginal flooding, satiation, and aversion relief) have also been employed with this population. These procedures, which have been examined largely through case reports, do not appear to significantly benefit a majority of OCD patients.

The second set of treatment methods, blocking or punishing procedures includes thought-stopping, aversion therapy, and covert sensitization. Thought-stopping has proven largely ineffective in several case studies. The value of aversion therapy using electric shock, the snapping of a rubber band on the wrist, or covert sensitization remains unclear. As with the exposure procedures discussed above, our knowledge of the efficacy of blocking techniques is based largely on case reports which tend to be biased toward positive outcomes.

If obsessive-compulsive symptoms are composed of obsessions which evoke anxiety and compulsions which reduce it, then treatment should consist of techniques that are directed at decreasing anxiety and procedures that suppress compulsions. It follows that the simultaneous use of interventions directed at both obsessions and compulsions would be expected to yield superior results to treatment directed at only one set of symptoms.

Exposure and Response Prevention

In 1966, Victor Meyer developed a therapeutic program, later labeled "apotreptic therapy" (Meyer et al. 1974), which consisted of two basic components: 1) in vivo exposure to discomfort-evoking stimuli: placing the patient in the "real life" feared situation (e.g., a washer avoiding "bathroom germs" would sit on the floor of a public restroom for two hours each day), and 2) response prevention: blocking the compulsive behaviors (e.g., not allowing the patient to wash). The results were impressive: of the 15 patients treated with this program, 10 were rated as much improved or symptom-free, and five were rated as improved. Only two patients relapsed during the follow-up period. At the same time, Stampfl and Levis (1967) formulated a therapeutic procedure consisting of prolonged imaginal exposure to fear-evoking scenes. Called "implosive" therapy, this method was applied primarily to phobics. A few reports with single patients suggested that this therapy might reduce obsessive-compulsive symptoms.

Variants of in vivo exposure and response prevention have been investigated in numerous studies. In contrast to the relatively poor prognosis for obsessive-compulsives with traditional psychotherapy, the overall success rates with these two behavioral procedures were quite high; about 75 percent of patients improve markedly with these treatments (e.g., Emmelkamp and Kraanen 1975; Marks et al. 1975). Slightly better results have been noted with a combination of imaginal and in vivo exposure (Foa and Goldstein 1978). [Extensive reviews have been done by Foa et al. (1985) and Rachman and Hodgson (1980).] At present, exposure in vivo and response prevention, sometimes with the addition of imaginal exposure, have been adopted as the treatment of choice for obsessive-compulsive ritualizers. Is it necessary, however, to apply all three procedures? Several studies have examined the role of each of the three treatments in an attempt to answer this question.

Differential effects of exposure in vivo and response prevention.   It has now become clear that prolonged exposure to an obsessional stimulus is associated with a decrease in the anxiety evoked by the stimulus (Foa and Chambless 1978; Grayson et al. 1982; Nunes and Marks 1975). If rituals are maintained only because of their ability to reduce obsessional anxiety, then prolonged exposure alone should be sufficient to reduce ritualizing and response prevention should be unnecessry. In some cases, however, prolonged exposure eliminates anxiety yet compulsive behavior persists (Marks et al. 1969; Walton and Mather 1963). Perhaps, then, exposure and response prevention operate through separate mechanisms, both of which are required to successfully reduce obsessive-compulsive symptoms.

In studies comparing exposure, response prevention, and the two procedures together, they appear to have somewhat different effects (Foa et al. 1984). Immediately after treatment, deliberate exposure decreased anxiety more than did response prevention. Ritualistic behavior, in turn, was ameliorated more by response prevention than by exposure. The group who received both treatments benefited most on measures of anxiety associated with contaminants and time spent washing. At a nine-month follow-up, the superiority of the combined group was retained on measures of obsessional anxiety. With regard to compulsions, at follow-up the three groups did not differ on time spent washing; however, on other measures of compulsions (i.e., urges to ritualize and severity of main ritual), the combined group improved the most.

Exposure in vivo versus exposure in imagination.   As stated earlier, imaginal exposure has been employed in the treatment of obsessive-compulsives. Some authors reported success with this procedure (Frankl 1960; Stampfl and Levis 1967); others have found it ineffective (Marks et al. 1969; Rachman et al. 1970). The literature suggests that actual confrontation with feared situations is superior to exposure in fantasy with simple phobics (e.g., Marks 1978; Mathews 1978). It is reasonable to assume, therefore, that when obsessive fear is evoked primarily by tangible cues (e.g., urine, dirt), exposure in vivo will fare better than imaginal exposure.

For many patients, however, anxiety is generated by both tangible cues from their environment and by anticipation of harm that might ensue from confrontation with these cues; the latter (e.g., death, disease, house burning down) can be presented only in fantasy. For example, the patient who is afraid of running over someone, and therefore constantly rechecks his path, can be exposed in vivo to his fears by requiring him to drive without checking. Obviously, the exposure session will not include the actual hitting of a pedestrian and leaving him behind to die because of failure to check carefully. Exposure to such a "disaster" can be accomplished only in imagination.

If it is important to match the content of the exposure situation to a patient's internal fear model (Lang 1977), then those who fear disastrous consequences (which cannot be produced in reality) should improve more with the addition of imaginal exposure. Indeed, results from one study which addressed this directly (Steketee et al. 1982) suggest that the addition of imaginal exposure to in vivo exposure does not affect short-term treatment gains but does improve the maintenance of such gains. In this study, only 19 percent of patients who received 90 minutes of imaginal exposure followed by 30 minutes of in vivo exposure lost gains over time, in contrast to the 40 percent relapse rate among those who received exposure in vivo only. It appears, then, that when feared disasters are not directly addressed, the reduction of discomfort to environmental (concrete) situations tends to be temporary, perhaps because the core of the fear, that is, concern with future catastrophes, has not changed. It is important to note that not all patients in the nonimaginal exposure group lost gains at follow-up. Perhaps patients who can generate their entire internal fear model (including fears of disasters), when presented with concrete cues, do not require the addition of imaginal exposure.

In summary, the results of the studies discussed above argue for the use of deliberate in vivo exposure in combination with response prevention. They also suggest that imaginal exposure be added for OCD patients who manifest fears of future catastrophes.

Shortcomings of Behavioral Therapy

Innovations in behavioral treatment, particularly exposure and response prevention, have profoundly improved the prognostic picture for many OCD patients. However, some patients, particularly those with secondary depression and those with overvalued ideas (i.e., strong belief that their obsessional fears are realistic) may be unable or unwilling to comply with the demands of behavioral treatment. Furthermore, those patients who enter a course of treatment rarely find themselves entirely symptom free at the completion of this regimen. Maintenance of gains is problematic for about 20 percent of patients (Foa et al. 1983) with relapse most common among those patients who are only partially improved at the end of treatment. The use of medication with behavioral treatment or the use of repeated brief behavioral interventions may prove helpful in some of these cases.

Pharmacologic Treatment

Clomipramine

A wide variety of medications have been given to OCD patients. The most promising developments, however, have been with the tricyclic antidepressant clomipramine (Anafranil, Ciba-Geigy) (Zohar and Insel 1987a,b). This drug, which has been widely used for treatment of depression in Europe and Canada for over 20 years, is not marketed in the United States but may become available in the near future.

Since 1980, eight carefully controlled double-blind studies using clomipramine have been published (Ananth et al. 1981; Flament et al. 1985; Insel et al. 1983; Marks et al. 1980; Montgomery 1980; Thoren et al. 1980; Volavka et al. 1985; Zohar and Insel 1987a). In all eight of these studies, clomipramine appears more effective than placebo or a comparison drug for reducing OCD symptoms. Perhaps the most important practical implication from these studies is that several other excellent antidepressants studied, including nortriptyline (Thoren et al. 1980), desipramine (Zohar and Insel 1987a), and clorgyline (Insel et al. 1983), do not appear better than placebo, and in this disorder, placebo treatment is consistently without beneficial effects (Montgomery 1980). A second finding that deserves special attention is that patients with rituals, as well as those with pure obsessions, appear to respond equally well to clomipramine. Combining the data from all of these studies, of 116 OCD patients treated with clomipramine, approximately two-thirds improved significantly as measured by blind clinical ratings of their obsessive-compulsive symptoms. However, most of the patients who responded to clomipramine were not entirely free of their obsessions; instead, they reported that it was easier for them to resist the obsessive-compulsive symptoms, and consequently they would spend significantly less time being engaged in OCD symptoms.

It is noteworthy that these studies generally describe a longer period for treatment response than might be expected for antidepressant effects. In several studies, maximum therapeutic effects were not evident until 10 or 12 weeks of treatment. Hence, clomipramine at a full dose should be given for at least six weeks before a trial is abandoned.

Would clomipramine be effective in nondepressed patients with OCD as well?   Data from nine different studies that examine this question (Ananth et al. 1981; Flament et al. 1985; Insel et al. 1982a, 1983; Mavissakalian et al. 1985; Montgomery 1980; Thoren et al. 1980; Volavka et al. 1985; Zohar and Insel 1987a) indicate that clomipramine maintains its antiobsessive and anticompulsive effects in nondepressed OCD patients. It seems, therefore, that depression is not a prerequisite for an antiobsessional response to clomipramine. In this regard, OCD resembles other nonaffective disorders, such as panic disorder, anxiety disorder, bulimia, eneuresis, migraine, and chronic pain syndrome, in which tricyclics are found to be effective also in the absence of initial (either primary or secondary) depression (Murphy et al. 1985).

Dosage.   Clomipramine is therapeutically effective in the same dose ranges as that of other tricyclics (i.e., 100–300 mg for an adult and 5 mg/kg for a child). While prescribing clomipramine, it is usually advisable to start at a dosage of either 25 or 50 mg per day administered in a single dose at bedtime. The dose then can be increased by 25–50 mg every other day. The desirable daily dosage is 200–300 mg per day, but if the patient cannot tolerate a dose in this range, lower dosage still might be beneficial. As with other tricyclic antidepressants, clomipramine can be administered in a single dose at bedtime because of its long half-life.

Side effects.   The side effects of clomipramine, like the side effects observed with other tricyclic antidepressants, are mainly due to their anticholinergic effects and include dry mouth, constipation, urinary retention, and excessive sweating. Patients treated with clomipramine may also experience weight gain, tremor, malaise, delayed ejaculation, and anorgasmia. The last two appear to be fairly frequent complaints with clomipramine and should be asked about if the patient does not volunteer this information. Lowering the dose for a short time often circumvents some of these side effects while maintaining the therapeutic effects.

Plasma levels. Clomipramine is metabolized to desmethylclomipramine (DCMI), which is present at about twice the concentration of clomipramine in human plasma (Thoren et al. 1980). There are conflicting reports about the relationship between plasma level of clomipramine and DCMI and treatment effects. Stern et al. (1980) and Insel et al. (1983) found that the plasma level of clomipramine (which selectively blocks serotonin reuptake) but not the plasma level of DCMI (which blocks both serotonin and norepinephrine reuptake) correlates significantly with a reduction in OCD symptoms. Flament et al. (1985) did not find such a correlation and Thoren et al. (1980) found a significant negative relationship between the plasma level of clomipramine and the reduction in OCD symptoms. Unfortunately, all of these correlations are based on relatively small sample sizes and differences in methodology preclude pooling the data across studies.

Mean plasma levels of clomipramine measured about 12 hours after ingesting the last dose in studies with OCD patients have been in the range of 81 ng/ml (Flament et al. 1985) to 136 ng/ml (Insel et al. 1983), a range that is considered therapeutic for depression (Traskman 1979).

Because there is considerable variance between individuals in the plasma concentration following a given dose of clomipramine, measuring clomipramine plasma concentration might be useful, especially for treatment-resistant patients on high doses or patients with marked side effects at low doses. In such cases, plasma levels may serve as a guide for adjusting the dose into a therapeutic range. Measuring plasma levels might also help to assess compliance and may aid in the diagnosis of suspected intoxication.

How long should the patient with OCD be maintained on clomipramine? There is only one study which addressed this question specifically (Pato et al. in press). In this study, clomipramine was discontinued in double-blind, placebo-controlled conditions after four to eight months, eight to 12 months, or over 12 months of clomipramine treatment. All but two of 18 patients studied relapsed within seven weeks after discontinuation of clomipramine. However, all the patients regained the therapeutic effects when clomipramine was readministered.

It seems, therefore, that, unlike patients with major depressive disorder, most patients with OCD should be maintained on clomipramine for at least 18 months before attempting to discontinue treatment. Future studies may find that an even longer period of time will be required before withdrawing a patient with OCD from clomipramine.

Fluvoxamine and fluoxetine

What sets clomipramine apart from other tricyclics is its potency as a serotonin reuptake blocker (Zohar and Insel 1987a). Other nontricyclic selective serotonin reuptake blockers, such as fluvoxamine and fluoxetine, also have been reported in pilot studies to be effective in OCD treatment (Price et al. 1987; Turner et al. 1985). Pending further studies, these medications might be an alternative to clomipramine in the treatment of OCD.

Other tricyclics

The antiobsessional effects of clomipramine have been compared to nortriptyline (Thoren et al. 1980), amitriptyline (Ananth et al. 1981), imipramine (Volavka et al. 1985), and desipramine (Zohar and Insel 1987) in controlled studies that were carried out in order to evaluate other antidepressants for antiobsessional effects. Clomipramine was found to be clearly more effective than desipramine in a crossover double-blind placebo-controlled study in a nondepressed cohort of 10 OCD patients (Zohar and Insel 1987b). Thoren et al. (1980) reported that the effects of nortriptyline were intermediate between placebo and clomipramine and not significantly different from either. Volavka et al. (1985) reported clomipramine to be more effective than imipramine in its antiobsessional properties at 12, but probably not at six, weeks of treatment. Taken together, the current state of the literature would suggest that, in contrast to the treatment of depression, clomipramine appears specifically more effective than other tricyclic drugs in the treatment of OCD.

Lithium augmentation

Rasmussen (1984) reported a patient who did not respond to clomipramine, 225 mg per day for six weeks, but who had dramatic improvement after adding lithium (lithium blood level was 0.9 meq per liter). The response peaked after a month yet was noticeable as early as five days after lithium addition. Others (Eisenberg and Asnis 1985; Stern and Jenike 1983) have also reported lithium addition converts a partial response of OCD patients to imipramine to a full response after three weeks of combined treatment.

Although lithium appears to increase certain side effects of clomipramine, particularly weight gain, it still might be worthwhile to try lithium augmentation in clomipramine nonresponders.

MAO inhibitors

Although the findings with clorgyline have been pessimistic (Insel et al. 1983), there have been several reports documenting positive responses to other, non MAO-inhibitors. A selective MAO inhibitors like tranylcypromine or phenelzine (Annesley 1969; Jain et al. 1970; Jenike 1981) that have stimulant effects and that structurally resemble amphetamines. It seems, therefore, that for a patient who does not respond or cannot tolerate treatment with potent serotonin reuptake blockers, such as clomipramine fluoxetine or fluvoxamine, an MAO inhibitor might be a reasonable alternative, and perhaps even more so if the patient has a history of panic attacks (Jenike et al. 1983).

Note that caution should be taken in starting clomipramine after an MAOI as this particular combination has been associated with a neurotoxic syndrome (myoclonus, ataxia, dysarthria) even four weeks after discontinuing the MAOI (Insel et al. 1982b).

Anxiolytics

OCD is considered an anxiety disorder in DSM-III-R; therefore, one might expect patients with this disorder to respond to anxiolytics. As anxiolytics have not been adequately investigated in OCD, one must rely on case reports based on a few patients (Tesar and Jenike 1984; Tollefson 1985). However, conclusions drawn from such a small number of patients must be treated with caution. Our experiences have not been promising with alprazolam or other benzodiazepines for OCD patients. Moreover, as OCD is a chronic disorder, there is substantial concern about the dependency produced by these compounds while taken over long periods of time.

Neuroleptics

Very little is known about the efficacy of neuroleptics in OCD. Ananth (1984) has suggested that neuroleptics might be useful during acute exacerbations of OCD. O'Regan (1970) reported on two cases of OCD who had a beneficial response to haloperidol, but others (Hussain and Ahad 1970) could not replicate this. Since currently there are insufficient data on the efficacy of neuroleptics in OCD, it seems that neuroleptics, with their possible adverse long-term side effects, should be used only in cases of obsessive-compulsive psychosis or in the treatment-resistant OCD patient.

Other treatments

There are reports documenting response to lithium alone (Stern and Jenike 1983), trazodone (Prasad 1984), clonidine (Knesevich 1982), and L-tryptophan alone or in combination with clomipramine (Yaryura-Tobias and Bhagavan 1977). The practical therapeutic value of each of these treatments is limited and awaits further studies.

Electroconvulsive treatment

Most textbooks (Kalinowsky and Hippins 1969; Roth 1965; Sargant and Slater 1950; Sternberg 1974) have advocated against the use of ECT in OCD patients; however, there are several case reports that indicate that ECT might be useful. Mellman and Gorman (1984) reported an excellent response to ECT in a nondepressed 60-year-old male. Loucas and Stafford-Clark (1965) described a 16-year-old OCD patient who recovered after bilateral sinewave treatments. In a recent review of eight patients with OCD who received ECT, only one had a good antiobsessional response that was sustained (L Guttmacher, J Zohart, TR Insel, unpublished observation).

Psychosurgery

With the increasing effectiveness of pharmacologic treatments, the use of psychosurgery has fallen out of fashion in the past two decades. Earlier, cingulectomy or cingulotomy—the bilateral transection of the cingulate cortex—was recognized as an effective treatment for OCD. Indeed, Lewin (1961) in describing cingulectomy noted that ". . . it is the obsessional disorder which seems to respond best of all to this particular operation." A second procedure, anterior capsulotomy, a variant of the original frontal lobotomy, also has been reported to decrease the symptoms of OCD (Post et al. 1968; Smith et al. 1976; Strom-Olsen and Carlisle 1971; Tippin and Henn 1982). Mitchell-Heggs et al. (1976) reported on 44 OCD patients who received both stereotactic cingulotomy and anterior capsulotomy. Improvement occurred in 89 percent of the patients with 19 percent rated as "cured" at the 16-month follow-up interview. It appears that improvement evolves slowly with relatively few adverse effects. Indeed, extensive assessment of cognitive, neuropsychologic, and psychosocial functioning in these patients revealed postoperative improvement rather than deficits on most measures (Kelly 1980).

The assessment of psychosurgery is complex as control procedures (e.g., sham surgery) are not done. Nevertheless, the generally low rate of placebo response in OCD and the inclusion of only chronic, intractable cases in these studies highlight the reported beneficial effects of psychosurgery. In addition, a report of abnormal local cerebral glucose use provides the beginning of the data needed for a neuroanatomic model of OCD, a model for which specific psychosurgical interventions can provide therapeutic evidence (Baxter et al. 1987). Whatever the mechanism, the existing data on psychosurgery recommend stereotactic leucotomy with cingulotomy only for patients unresponsive to all other treatments.

Conclusion

A specific form of behavior therapy, exposure coupled with response prevention, has been shown to be an effective treatment for OCD especially for patients with rituals and avoidant behavior. The tricyclic clomipramine and other bicyclic and unicyclic serotonin reuptake blockers, also appear to be useful as a treatment, even for patients without depression. Other tricyclics do not appear to be consistently effective in this disorder. However, it should be noted that the availability of effective behavioral and pharmacologic treatments are essential but not sufficient for the comprehensive treatment of OCD. The context in which the symptoms of OCD have persisted needs careful evaluation and attention. Providing a therapeutic role for the family and encouraging the patients to take risks and to push themselves into work or school may be critical to the ultimate outcome.

Chapter 188

Psychodynamic Psychotherapy

Psychotherapy for Obsessive-Compulsive Disorder

The essential task in psychotherapy for obsessive-compulsive disorder is that of conveying insight and initiating learning and change without getting caught in the "obsessional tug-of-war," a term that describes obsessional behavior which results in hostile and antagonistic exchanges with others.

As with all neurotic difficulties, the work lies in the identification, clarification, and, finally, in the alteration of the defensive patterns which maintain the neurosis.

Progress becomes possible when the patient's self-esteem or ego strength becomes sufficiently strengthened to withstand the major assaults against his defenses. While the problems that brought about the obsessional defenses are comparatively easy to uncover, the defensive structure which develops around these issues are most difficult to unravel. At times, the particular issues of the patient are obvious and plainly stated in obsessional ruminations or compulsive rituals. For example, a ritualistic avoidance of knives may be a clear statement within the awareness of the patient that there is some uneasiness about losing control of hostile impulses. Thus the identification of the problem—which is the fear of loss of control of hostile impulses—is simple enough. However, it is soon evident that it is not only a fear of injuring someone else that is involved but rather an uneasiness and uncertainty about the possibility of losing control in general, or of being unable to control oneself at all times.

It is paradoxical that in the attempts to clarify an obsessional's life, the issues become more complicated and confused. Ordinarily, increasing one's knowledge of a particular problem helps to focus on the relevant components. The obsessional's tendency to qualify all data to be totally accurate often appears as though the patient is deliberately confusing the situation with new issues when there is a danger to clarifying something. Actually, the patient is trying to be precise and to avoid making errors. The additional factors are generally raised as the patient gets close to seeing his responsibility or failure in some activity. Before the patient is ready to accept an observation about some matter in which he played a responsible role, he tries to involve every possibility outside himself. Therefore, it looks as if he does this purposefully as these new factors often lead the investigation into a cul-de-sac from which no fruitful return is possible.

In therapy it is imperative that such communication entanglements be worked through so that the patient can see exactly what he does and how he defeats attempts at understanding. He must recognize that while he may not do this deliberately, it nevertheless occurs frequently and regularly. The therapist should retrace the conversation and point out every new digression the patient develops. The therapist must resist all temptations to follow every lead and every rationalization and distraction. Recording sessions can be very useful in this regard, but the compulsiveness of the therapist (which would be required to record all the sessions) may outweigh the advantages gained by the patient, who can hear just how he frustrates clarity even while he is searching for clarification.

It is inevitable that the therapist will occasionally get caught in the "fly paper" of the obsessional's way of life and must recognize it as quickly as possible and limit the patient's sense of power at succeeding in sidetracking the therapist.

The patient must have at least a minimum of trust in the therapist and a willingness to accept the role of patient for the process to begin. The readiness to admit the need for help does not mean a total acceptance of another's ability to provide such help. While there are many formal requirements for the doctor-patient relationship, such as keeping appointments, paying the fees, saying whatever comes to mind—all of which can be agreed upon in advance—there are some requirements which cannot be met so easily in view of the nature of obsessional dynamics. The obsessional patient will try to follow the formal requirements scrupulously. However, the more pervasive tendencies of omniscience and omnipotence, the characteristic doubts, the grandiose contempt, and the tendencies to distract will play havoc with the therapeutic process unless these matters are always kept in the forefront of the therapist's attention in spite of the apparent cooperativeness of the patient.

The obsessional does not deliberately sabotage the therapy; he is simply behaving like an obsessional. His behavior is not resistance nor is it a need to defeat either the therapist or the therapy; it is merely another manifestation of obsessional behavior. It would be naive to expect that a neurotic who has difficulty in coming to grips with an issue or who procrastinates and is given to indecisiveness will be able to commit himself quickly to a process that demands total commitment and involvement.

It will be a long time before the obsessional will be able to verbalize his doubts about himself, the therapist, and the process. It is essential that he hold himself aloof and free of entanglement and commitment so that he can avoid being hurt and humiliated. He will need to know his therapist and experience a number of incidents with him before the more subtle safeguards can be dropped and trust can begin. It is inevitable that a person who must know everything and never be deficient or fallible will view treatment as a challenge or a threat. To learn one must be receptive as well as motivated, which means to be free of the obstacles which interfere with learning. One must be able to listen with an open mind without immediate denial or derogation of the material presented. Therapy is a learning process which requires the active interest and participation of the patient; this is true whether one views the dynamics of cure as the result of insight, genetic reconstruction, resolution of transference neurosis, reconditioning, corrective emotional experience, or simple relearning. Therefore, it is necessary to motivate the patient to explore his way of living to discover the inappropriate patterns of behavior and their sources. It is also necessary to interest and encourage him to take steps to change his way of life. The patient must acquire sufficient trust, self-esteem, and readiness to take some risks and face the possibility of failure.

This process poses particular difficulties for the obsessional. In addition to learning problems, there are often insurmountable obstacles in attempting to try out new ways of functioning. Since most of the obsessional patterns of behavior arise from feelings of powerlessness and uncertainty, the patient finds it particularly threatening to try out new solutions unless he can have some guarantees and expectations of success. In spite of their unsatisfactory results, the old patterns are more familiar. There must be strong incentives to attempt new solutions.

The obsessional's need to control may be counter to his dependent needs, and, therefore, the therapeutic relationship should not be of an authoritarian type if it is to succeed. However, the very structure of the psychotherapeutic situation tends to encourage a development in which the therapist is the teacher, and the patient is the pupil. The pupil is dependent on the teacher, who is viewed as a magician. Such an atmosphere may tend to produce an outwardly compliant attitude with an inwardly resistive and negativistic defense. The obsessional ordinarily proceeds only by being forced, either by circumstances or strong pressure, to overcome indecisive ruminations. While he needs pushing, he nevertheless resents it and insists that he be allowed to act on his own, free from compulsion. Therefore, the therapist may be caught in a double bind if he takes a strong hand to forestall the controlling tendencies of the patient while allowing opportunities for the patient to make decisions. The prevailing atmosphere must be one of freedom—with an absence of compulsion and authority, a minimum of rules and rituals, and a maximum of exchange—in which the rights and limits of both parties are clearly understood. For the patient to perceive clearly his patterns of operation, the therapeutic atmosphere must not parallel the life experience of the obsessional. In every respect, the treatment behavior of the obsessional must be understood in its contradictory aspects in order to maintain the cooperation and participation of the patient.

The ultimate goal in therapy is to effect a change in the patient's living, not merely to induce insight. Insight is only the prelude to change; it provides the tools for the alteration in one's patterns of living. But the therapist must also assist the patient in implementing these new understandings. This demands an approach which is less rigid and less tied to traditional methodology. The therapist must feel free to be of active assistance in the process. Obsessional patterns which are so heavily involved with ritualistic forms of behavior cannot be resolved by therapeutic measures which are just as overloaded with ritual. The therapist must be flexible enough to try novel approaches and techniques.

The process of therapy, therefore, while described in general terms, must leave room for considerable variation and flexibility. Broad tendencies and characteristic maneuvers of both patient and therapist can be discussed, but detailed exchanges and specific interventions will vary with each patient and therapist.

Not every obsessional patient will present all the typical characteristics. Some elements will be more obvious and may play an important role in one patient yet be of secondary importance in another. It is the therapist's job to recognize the main themes as well as the subsidiary themes in each case. Therapeutic emphasis must be placed on the major issues while acknowledging the patient's concerns with substitute devices.

Problems in Obsessional Patient Therapy

In the psychotherapy of obsessional patients, the issue of discouraging defenses against change is especially relevant since the essence of the obsessional's defenses is to militate against the exposure of the patient's deficits. Obsessionals often steadfastly reject any new awareness which would require admissions that there are matters about which they are unaware. Thus, the therapist may need to make an observation or an interpretation many times before it is acknowledged.

For the obsessional, an overriding need to control one's inner and outer world requires orderly, manageable, and guaranteed living. Adaptive devices such as the ritual, maintenance of doubts, and unwillingness to commit oneself, along with attempts at omniscience, omnipotence, and striving for perfection and superhuman performance—all these are attempts to control oneself and one's universe to provide an illusory feeling of being safe, secure, and in control. Being in control means maintaining an absolutely secure stance, which prevents one from developing enough trust to take the risks necessary for human relationships to develop. The therapist must persistently make this observation, as it is the focal issue in maintaining obsessional defenses.

Obsessionals spend endless time in distracting avoidances and contentious disagreements, although they are intellectually astute and cognitively capable of clearer analysis. Affectively, they are totally unengaged until well into therapy. This is in contrast to the hysteric, whose volubility, labile emotionality, and histrionic readiness to become involved facilitates the beginning of therapy. The deceptive quality of this facile commitment is, of course, subject to later examination and interpretation. For the obsessional, the process of developing trust may occupy a large part of the therapeutic program. It may never be overcome, regardless of ostensibly cooperative behavior and willingness to be a patient in an extended program.

The need for perfection hampers the therapeutic process and must be dealt with in the patient's living as well as in the transference. To be absolutely safe and certain about oneself, it becomes necessary to know everything in order to predict the future and prepare for every eventuality. Patients emphasize intellectual attainments above all else. To maintain the fiction of perfection they must never make an error or admit any deficiency. Thus they will not risk making a definite decision or committing themselves to a point of view or course of action in case it turns out to be the wrong one. This avoidance of definitive actions is intimately related to the tendency to doubt as a way of guaranteeing one's omniscience. The patient must recognize how his actions all serve the purpose of maintaining the illusion of an individual secure and safe because he is in control.

Pervasive doubt produces some of the bizarre obsessional symptoms, such as trying a door dozens of times to make certain it is indeed locked. Doubting also produces the yes-no continuum. Obsessionals feel they must entertain both feelings or support both sides of every issue in order to be correct and in control of the situation. Thus doubts are maintained and positive feelings and attitudes avoided. The absence of affect and expression of feelings, both positive and negative, which characterize the obsessional, should be identified and the expressing of feelings encouraged.

For the obsessional, word magic is tied to magical thinking and the omnipotence of thought. Thoughts or words are presumed to have control over the behavior of others. Words can magically undo unacceptable behavior or produce untold malevolence for which obsessionals assume guilt. Moreover, since obsessionals want to be precise and clear, they introduce more and more qualifications into their presentation to be certain the matter is presented in its fullest and most complete form. Instead of clarifying, this tends to obfuscate the issues. The therapist may even mistakenly assume that patients are deliberately trying to be confusing.

Therapeutic Techniques

Activity on the part of the therapist is absolutely essential from the beginning of therapy to the end. An understanding of the dynamics of the obsessional states require the therapist to avoid techniques which defeat communication to continue for too long. Yet, the therapist's activities must never be so intense as to overwhelm patients or make them feel as if they are being controlled. The endless, detailed communication designed to prevent omission or error must be interrupted and the patient admonished to see what he is doing to defeat understanding. The therapist must also select areas for further elaboration that are relevant to the patient's tendencies toward total control.

In treating the obsessional whose recollections are pervaded with doubts that limit conviction, interpretations of past events are subject to endless bickering, qualifying, and uncertainty. The analysis of the current situation is most suited to developing insight into functioning since it is the current situation that has the greatest clarity and conviction and is also least open to doubting. The investigation of recent events also permits the patient to look more clearly at his feelings in a particular situation and avoid the obsessional's capacity to distort, displace, or otherwise avoid awareness. While past feelings can be described and experienced calmly, judiciously, and intellectually, present hostilities and frustrations, especially as they involve ongoing relationships, are more difficult to acknowledge, as they may be viewed as failures or deficiencies.

Sharing feelings of distrust, dislike, or liking for the therapist is difficult. The overriding tendency toward control blankets both tender and hostile feelings; consequently, obsessionals appear to be calm and controlled. However, their hostile feelings are more available to them and are invariably expressed in subtle but unmistakable ways, such as derogating, sniping, and pettiness.

Tender impulses and affectionate reactions are securely bound and rarely exposed. These are felt to be threatening and dangerous. Control over tender feelings, which constitutes a part of the obsessional defense, often causes retaliatory behavior from others, to which the obsessional reacts with wrath and hostile rejoinders. Release of consequent stored-up hostilities is critical. Obsessionals must learn to identify their feelings and express them.

To deal with feelings of powerlessness and assumption of omnipotence, obsessionals often develop condescending attitudes toward others as well as toward the therapist. Patients remain distant but proper in fulfilling their role. Secretly, they feel superior and contemptuous of the therapist and feel they are "on to" all that is going on. They catalog all the therapist's deficiencies, storing them up for use at a proper time. The therapist, therefore, cannot take for granted that patients, even though they appear to be pursuing the therapeutic process, are in fact doing so. They may simply be doing the right thing. It is a long time before such patients can experience and express doubts and concerns about the process. They resist interpretations which require them to admit ignorance, especially about their interpersonal relationships.

The process of therapy involves time-consuming examination and exposure of those patterns of behavior which patients compulsively maintain and reluctantly alter. The therapist's task is to strengthen patients' awareness of those patterns and assist in overcoming them. Before any moves can be made to change behavior, individuals must have a strong conviction about the need to change and a trust in the understanding derived from collaboration with the therapist. They must be encouraged to see how they will be benefitted, instead of visualizing the disasters that will confront them when they feel helpless and out of total control.

The nature of the compulsive symptom is such that it is repeated with no alteration or deviation in spite of knowledge of its lack of validity and its destructive potential. Consequently, a large part of the therapeutic process is concerned with a review and reexamination of issues already dealt with. The therapeutic skill lies in the therapist's ability to see the same issues in a new light, adding an additional piece of insight and reviving an additional recollection to strengthen and fortify the patient's conviction about the understanding so that it is as if discovered by the patient alone. The working-through process is thus crucial to the resolution of an obsessional disorder.

Not every obsessional patient presents all the obsessional characteristics. Some are more prominent than others. Some deal with the need to be in total control by bringing lists or agendas to the session. Others will have severe rituals or phobias that occupy the forefront of the communication process. Some are hampered by their grandiosity and contempt for others, and still others are overwhelmed by their need for guarantees and certainties that prevent them from taking risks or accepting new interpretations. The particular elements which are most prominent in the patient being treated determine the general principles that need to be applied in each instance. Where intellectual discussions seem to be preeminent, the therapist must be somewhat spontaneous in expressing some personal feelings and weaknesses. The patient is thus allowed to recognize that human fallibility is not a cause for total rejection by others. In this connection it is important for the therapist to be aware of how he or she is being controlled or manipulated by the obsessional's tactics. The therapist may become caught in the sticky mesh of obsessional communication. A review of such entrapments can be illuminating. In general, each occasion in the development of the interaction with the therapist needs to be seen in the light of the obsessional mechanisms and the therapist's fallibility. This allows the process of therapy to be one which is not autocratically determined by the expert and a helpless patient, but by two people attempting to explore an issue together.

Goals of Treatment

The goals of treatment require:

1. Discovery and elucidation of the basis for excessive feelings of insecurity which require absolutes to guarantee one's existence before any action is attempted. This requires the examination of each symptom and obsessional tactic to show how it ties into the overriding need to control. Rituals, phobias, and personality traits are explored in terms of their role in giving the patient the illusory feelings of absolute control;
2. Demonstration by repeated interpretation and encouragement to action that such guarantees are not necessary and instead interfere with living. This involves motivating the individual to attempt novel and unfamiliar patterns of behavior through active assistance in stimulating new adventures. It can help patients to attempt counterphobic activity and overcome conditioned avoidance reactions to unexplored areas of functioning; and
3. Recognition that the foregoing is possible only when patients can accept some anxiety as part of living. They must acknowledge the universality of anxiety as a companion to all human endeavors. This means abandoning attempts at perfection and accepting limited goals utilizing the most creative resources available. Patients must learn to accept their human limitations.

In this process the anxiety may be so severe that pharmacologic agents should be used to enable patients to attempt changes in their lives (see Pharmacotherapy chapter). The therapist must maintain the anxiety at a level that will facilitate learning rather than impede it. The therapeutic focus must be on feelings rather than cognitive exchanges, facilitated by a confronting, here-and-now approach to the role of defenses. Before patients can relinquish their extensive defense system, they must allow themselves to experience and accept failure, some loss of false pride and prestige, and possible humiliation.

References

Section 19
Obsessive-Compulsive Disorders

Akhtar S, Wig NH, Verma VK et al: A phenomenological analysis of symptoms in obsessive-compulsive neuroses. Br J Psychiatry 127:342–348, 1975

American Psychiatric Association: Diagnostic and Statistical Manual of Mental Disorders, 3rd ed, revised. Washington, DC, American Psychiatric Association, 1987

Ananth J: Treatment of obsessive-compulsive neurosis: pharmacological approach. Psychosomatics 17:180–184, 1976

Ananth J: Pharmacotherapy of obsessive-compulsive disorder, in Obsessive-Compulsive Disorder. Edited by Turner SM, Michelson L. New York, Plenum Press, 1985

Ananth J, Pecknold JC, van der Steen N, et al: Double blind comparative study of clomipramine and amitriptyline in obsessive neurosis. Prog Neuropsychopharmacol Biol Psychiat 5:257–264, 1981

Annesley PT: Nardil response in a chronic obsessive compulsive. Br J Psychiatry 115:748, 1969

Baxter LR, Phelps ME, Mazziotta JC, et al: Local cerebral glucose metabolic rates in obsessive-compulsive disorder. Arch Gen Psychiatry 44:211–218, 1987

Beech HR, Vaughn M: Behavioural Treatment of Obsessional States. New York, John Wiley and Sons, 1978

Black A: The natural history of obsessional neurosis, in Obsessional States. Edited by Beech HR. London, Methuen, 1974

Breitner C: Drug therapy in obsessional states and other psychiatric problems. Diseases of the Nervous System 31:354, 1960

Cooper JE, Gelder MG, Marks IM: Results of behavior therapy in 77 psychiatric patients. Br Med J 1:1222–1225, 1965

Eisenberg J, Asnis G: Lithium as an adjunct treatment in obsessive-compulsive disorder (letter). Am J Psychiatry 142:663, 1985

Emmelkamp PMG, Kraanen J: Therapist-controlled exposure in vivo: a comparison with obsessive-compulsive patients. Behav Res Ther 15:491–495, 1975

Flament MF, Rapoport JL, Berg CJ, et al: Clomipramine treatment of childhood obsessive-compulsive disorder: a double-blind controlled study. Arch Gen Psychiatry 42:977–983, 1985

Flament M, Whitaker A, Rapoport JL, et al: Obsessive-compulsive disorder in adolescents: An epidemiological study. J Am Acad Child Adolesc Psychiatry 27:764–771, 1988

Foa EB, Chambless DL: Habituation of subjective anxiety during flooding in imagery. Behav Res Ther 16:392–399, 1978

Foa EB, Goldstein A: Continuous exposure and complete response prevention in the treatment of obsessive-compulsive neurosis. Behav Res Ther 9:821–829, 1978

Foa EB, Steketee G, Grayson JB, et al: Treatment of obsessive-compulsives: when do we fail? in Failures in Behavior Therapy. Edited by Foa EB, Emmelkamp PMG. New York, John Wiley and Sons, 1983

Foa EB, Steketee G, Grayson JB, et al: Deliberate exposure and blocking of obsessive-compulsive rituals: immediate and long-term effects. Behav Res Ther 15:450–472, 1984

Foa EB, Steketee GS, Ozarow BJ: Behavior therapy with obsessive-compulsives from theory to treatment, in Obsessive-Compulsive Disorder: Psychological and Pharmacological Treatment. Edited by Mavissakalian M. New York, Plenum Press, 1985

Frankl VE: Parodoxical intention: a logotherapeutic technique. Am J Psychother 14:520–525, 1960

Goodwin D, Guze S, Robins E: Follow-up studies in obsessional neurosis. Arch Gen Psychiatry 20:182–187, 1969

Grayson JB, Foa EB, Steketee G: Habituation during exposure treatment: distraction versus attention focusing. Behav Res Ther 20:323–328, 1982

Grimshaw L: The outcome of obsessional disorder, a follow-up study of 100 cases. Br J Psychiatry 111:1051–1065, 1965

Hussain MZ, Ahad A: Treatment of obsessive-compulsive neurosis. Can Med Assoc J 103:648–649, 1970

Insel TR: Obsessive-compulsive disorder: the clinical picture, in New Findings in Obsessive-Compulsive Disorder. Edited by Insel TR. Washington, DC, American Psychiatric Press, 1984

Insel TR, Akiskal HS: Obsessive-compulsive disorder with psychotic features: a phenomenologic analysis. Am J Psychiatry 143:1527–1533, 1986

Insel TR, Alterman I, Murphy DL: Anti-obsessional and antidepressant effects with clomipramine. Psychopharmacol Bull 18:315–319, 1982a

Insel TR, Roy BF, Cohen RM, et al: Possible development of the serotonin syndrome in man. Am J Psychiatry 139:954–955, 1982b

Insel TR, Murphy DL, Cohen RM, et al: Obsessive-compulsive disorder—a double-blind trial of clomipramine and/or clorgyline. Arch Gen Psychiatry 40:605–612, 1983

Jain VK, Swinson RP, Thomas JE: Phenelzine in obsessional neurosis. Br J Psychiatry 127:237–238, 1970

Jenike MA: Rapid response of severe obsessive-compulsive disorder to tranylcypromine. Am J Psychiatry 138:1249–1250, 1981

Jenike MA, Surman OS, Cassem NH, et al: Monoamine oxidase inhibitor in obsessive-compulsive disorder. J Clin Psychiatry 4:131–132, 1983

Kalinowsky LB, Hippius H: Pharmacological, Convulsive, and Other Somatic Treatments in Psychiatry. New York, Grune & Stratton, 1969

Kelly D: Anxiety and Emotions: Physiological Basis and Treatment. Springfield, Ill, Charles C. Thomas Publishers, 1980

Knesevich JW: Successful treatment of obsessive-compulsive disorder with clonidine hydrochloride. Am J Psychiatry 139:364–365, 1982

Kringlen E: Obsessional neurotics, a long-term follow up. Br J Psychiatry 111:709–722, 1965

Lang PJ: Imagery in therapy: an information processing analysis of fear. Behav Res Ther 8:862–886, 1977

Lewin W: Observations on selective leucotomy. J Neurol Neurosurg Psychiatry 24:37, 1961

Loucas KP, Stafford-Clark D: Electronarcosis at Guy's. Guy's Hospital Reports 114:223–237, 1965

Marks IM: Behavioral psychotherapy of adult neurosis, in Handbook of Psychotherapy and Behavior Change. Edited by Garfield S, Bergin A. New York, John Wiley and Sons, 1978

Marks IM, Crowe E, Drewe E, et al: Obsessive-compulsive neurosis in identical twins. Br J Psychiatry 15:991–998, 1969

Marks IM, Hodgson R, Rachman S: Treatment of chronic obsessive-compulsive neurosis by in vivo exposure, a two-year follow-up and issues in treatment. Br J Psychiatry 127:349–364, 1975

Marks IM, Stern R, Mawson D, et al: Clomipramine and exposure for obsessive compulsive rituals. Br J Psychiatry 136:1–25, 1980

Mathews AM: Fear-reduction research and clinical phobias. Psychol Bull 85:390–404, 1978

Mavissakalian M, Turner S, Michelson L, et al: Tricyclic antidepressants in obsessive-compulsive disorder: anti-obsessional or antidepressant agents, II. Am J Psychiatry 142:572–576, 1985

Mellman LA, Gorman JM: Successful treatment of obsessive-compulsive disorder with ECT. Am J Psychiatry 141:596–597, 1984

Meyer V, Levy R, Schnurer A: A behavioural treatment of obsessive-compulsive disorders, in Obsessional States. Edited by Beech HR. London, Methuen, 1974

Mitchell-Heggs N, Kelly D, Richardson A: Stereotactic limbic leucotomy—a follow-up at 16 months. Br J Psychiatry 128:226–240, 1976

Montgomery SA: Clomipramine in obsessional neurosis: a placebo controlled trial. Pharmacol Med 1:189–192, 1980

Murphy DL, Siever LJ, Insel TR: Therapeutic responses to tricyclic antidepressants and related drugs in non-affective disorder patient populations. Prog Neuro-psychopharmacol Biol Psychiatry 9:3–13, 1985

Nunes JS, Marks IM: Feedback of true heart rate during exposure in vivo. Arch Gen Psychiatry 32:933–936, 1975

O'Regan JB: Treatment of obsessive-compulsive neurosis with haloperidol. Can Med Assoc J 103:167–168, 1970

Pato MT, Zohar-Kadouch R, Zohar J, et al: Return of symptoms after discontinuation of clorimipramine in patients with obsessive-compulsive disorder. Am J Psychiatry 145:1521–1525, 1988

Post F, Rees WL, Schurr PH: An evaluation of bimedial leucotomy. Br J Psychiatry 114:1223–1246, 1968

Prasad A: Obsessive-compulsive disorder and trazodone (letter). Am J Psychiatry 141:612–613, 1984

Price LH, Goodman WK, Charney DS, et al: Treatment of severe obsessive-compulsive disorder with fluvoxamine. Am J Psychiatry 144:1059–1061, 1987

Rachman SJ: Primary obsessional slowness. Behav Res Ther 11:463–471, 1974

Rachman SJ, Hodgson RJ: Obsessions and Compulsions. Englewood Cliffs, NJ, Prentice-Hall, 1980

Rachman S, Hodgson R, Marzillier J: Treatment of an obsessional-compulsive disorder by modelling. Behav Res Ther 8:383–392, 1970

Rasmussen SA: Lithium and tryptophan augmentation in clomipramine-resistant obsessive-compulsive disorder. Am J Psychiatry 141:1283–1285, 1984

Rasmussen SA: Obsessive-compulsive disorder in dermatologic practice. J Am Acad Dermatol 13:965–967, 1985

Rasmussen SA, Tsuang MT: The epidemiology of obsessive-compulsive disorder. J Clin Psychiatry 45:450–457, 1984

Robins LN, Helzer YE, Weissman MM, et al: Lifetime prevalence of psychiatric disorders in three communities. Arch Gen Psychiatry 41:949–967, 1984

Roth M: Physical methods of treatment in mental disease. Practitioner 194:613–620, 1965

Salzman L, Thaler FH: Obsessive-compulsive disorders, review of literature. Am J Psychiatry 138:286–296, 1981

Sargant W, Slater E: Proceedings of the Royal Society of Medicine 43:1007–1010, 1950

Smith JS, Kilom LG, Cochrane N: A prospective evaluation of open pre-frontal leucotomy. Med J Aust 1:731–735, 1976

Stampfl TG, Levis DJ: Essentials of implosive therapy: a learning-theory-based psychodynamic behavioral therapy. J Abnorm Psychol 72:496–503, 1967

Steketee GS, Foa EB, Grayson JB: Recent advances in the behavioral treatment of obsessive-compulsives. Arch Gen Psychiatry 39:1365–1371, 1982

Stern RS, Marks IM, Wright J, et al: Clomipramine: plasma levels, side effects, and outcome in obsessive-compulsive neurosis. Postgrad Med J 56:134–139, 1980

Stern TA, Jenike MA: Treatment of obsessive-compulsive disorder with lithium carbonate. Psychosomatics 24:673–674, 1983

Sternberg M: Physical treatments in obsessional disorders, in Obsessional States. Edited by Beech HR. London, Butler and Tanner, Ltd, 1974

Strom-Olson R, Carlisle S: Bi-frontal stereotactic tractotomy: a follow-up study of its effects on 210 patients. Br J Psychiatry 118:141–154, 1971

Tesar GE, Jenike MA: Alprazolam as treatment for a case of obsessive-compulsive disorder. Am J Psychiatry 141:689–690, 1984

Thoren P, Asberg M, Cronholm B, et al: Clomipramine treatment of obsessive-compulsive disorder, I: a controlled clinical trial. Arch Gen Psychiatry 37: 1281–1285, 1980

Tippin J, Henn FA: Modified leucotomy in the treatment of intractable obsessional neurosis. Am J Psychiatry 139:1601–1603, 1982

Tollefson G: Alprazolam in the treatment of obsessive symptoms. J Clin Psychopharmacol 5:39–42, 1985

Traskman L, Asberg MN, Bertilsson L, et al: Plasma levels of clomipramine and its desmethyl metabolite during treatment of depression. Clin Pharmacol Therap 26:600–609, 1979

Turner SN, Jacob RG, Beidel DC, et al: Fluoxetine treatment of obsessive-compulsive disorder. J Clin Psychopharmacol 5:207–212, 1985

Volavka J, Neziroglu F, Yaryura-Tobias JA: Clomipramine and imipramine in obsessive-compulsive disorder. Psychiatry Res 14:83–91, 1985

Walton D, Mather MD: The application of learning principles to the treatment of obsessive-compulsive states in the acute and chronic phases of illness. Behav Res Ther 1:163–174, 1963

Woodruff R, Pitts F: Monozygotic twins with obsessional illness. Am J Psychiatry 120:1075–1080, 1969

Yaryura-Tobias JA, Bhagavan HN: L-Tryptophan in obsessive-compulsive disorders. Am J Psychiatry 234:1298–1299, 1977

Zohar J, Insel TR: Obsessive-compulsive disorder: psychobiological approaches to diagnosis, treatment, and pathophysiology. Biol Psychiatry 22:667–687, 1987a

Zohar J, Insel TR: Drug treatment of obsessive-compulsive disorder. J Affective Disord 13:193–202, 1987b

Somatoform and Factitious Disorders

Chapter 189

Introduction

There are no adequate outcome studies on which definite recommendations for the treatment of somatoform disorders can be based. In this chapter we have tried to provide guidelines for each of the somatoform disorders as classified in the DSM-III-R (American Psychiatric Association 1987). This division is arbitrary in some places; for example, the treatments recommended for somatization disorder probably apply equally to a severe or chronic undifferentiated somatoform disorder. Moreover, symptoms of several DSM-III-R disorders may occur in the same patient; for instance, patients with somatoform pain disorder may have hypochondriacal concerns. Thus more than one of the treatment strategies outlined in the various sections may apply to any one patient, and the reader should turn also to the other pertinent sections.

The proposed treatment guidelines are intended for psychiatrists; however, often a psychiatrist will not treat the patient himself but will advise the patient's general physician or other medical staff, a procedure which is economical as well as effective (Smith et al. 1986). Cooperation with the primary physician is emphasized in the various sections that follow; details of the techniques of consultation have been described in several previous publications, and they are beyond the scope of this chapter.

The present chapter and the studies quoted were written before the DSM-III-R was published. Since then, all terms have been changed to those of the DSM-III-R, and the differences between the categories of the DSM-III-R and those of the previous edition are listed in Table 1. These changes in diagnostic categories have no bearing on the recommendations for treatment; a knowledge of the older terms, however, is relevant for parts of the discussion.

Table 1. A Comparative Listing of DSM-III and DSM-III-R Terms and Categories

DSM-III	DSM-III-R
SOMATOFORM DISORDERS	SOMATOFORM DISORDERS
Somatization disorder	**Somatization disorder**
The symptom list was revised so that the number of symptoms required for the disorder is the same for males and females. Seven of the symptoms are highlighted to serve as a screening list since the presence of any two of them suggests a high likelihood of the disorder.	
Conversion disorder	**Conversion disorder** **Specify: single episode or recurrent**
Culturally sanctioned response patterns have been excluded. The criterion excluding a diagnosis of somatization disorder or schizophrenia has been eliminated.	

(continued)

Table 1. A Comparative Listing of DSM-III and DSM-III-R Terms and Categories   (continued)

DSM-III	DSM-III-R
Psychogenic pain disorder	**Somatoform pain disorder**

The new term and revised criteria acknowledge that the disorder frequently appears in the absence of clear evidence of the etiologic role of psychological factors.

Hypochondriasis	**Hypochondriasis**

A required duration of six months has been added to exclude transient reactions.

	Body dysmorphic disorder

In DSM-III dysmorphophobia is an example of an atypical somatoform disorder. This often-described condition, which is not a true "phobia," is renamed and included in DSM-III-R as a specific category.

	Undifferentiated somatoform disorder

This category recognizes that whereas cases meeting the full critera for somatization disorder are relatively rare, there are many more cases of chronic multiple physical complaints that are apparently of psychological origin and do not meet the criteria for any other somatoform disorder.

Atypical somatoform disorder	**Somatoform disorder NOS**
FACTITIOUS DISORDERS	FACTITIOUS DISORDERS

The symptoms of factitious disorder are not truly "voluntary," hence the revised criteria more accurately refer to them as "intentionally produced or feigned."

Factitious disorder with psychological symptoms	**Factitious disorder with psychological symptoms**
Factitious disorder with physical symptoms	**Factitious disorder with physical symptoms**
Atypical factitious disorder with physical symptoms	**Chronic factitious disorder NOS**

Chapter 190

Somatoform Pain Disorders

Accurate diagnosis, a clear understanding of etiology, and the ability to predict the effect of a specific intervention tend to be difficult and occasionally elusive in this disorder.

Its diagnosis can be and frequently is confusing; its etiology may include a combination of biologic, psychological, and social factors, and its treatment includes diverse methods frequently used simultaneously. Therefore, the effect individual treatment methods have on the outcome may be difficult to assess. Treatment strategies must include those considerations.

Brief discussions about diagnosis and etiology precede recommendations for treatment. The description of management is focused on therapeutic principles as much as on individual treatment methods and is followed by consideration of difficulties in outcome evaluation.

Diagnosis

The DSM-III-R (American Psychiatric Association 1987) category that deals with chronic pain has been changed from psychogenic pain disorder to somatoform pain disorder. Both terms have shortcomings. The word psychogenic was originally introduced to deal with hysteria and was broadened to cover the psychological contribution to virtually all types of neurosis and functional psychosis. Lewis (1972) reviewed the widespread misuse of this term in the German and English literature and recommended that it be dropped. It is often used to imply that pain is less real or different from pain that is organic in origin. (Merskey 1984).

The category is also unsatisfactory because it overlaps to a considerable extent with other DSM-III-R categories. Reich et al. (1983) reported on the DSM-III diagnosis of 43 consecutive patients with chronic pain evaluated during a one-year period at a university pain clinic. Although psychogenic pain disorder (somatoform pain disorder) was the most frequent Axis I diagnosis (32 percent), substance abuse disorder (28 percent) and affective disorder (29 percent) were almost equally common. More than one Axis I diagnosis was sometimes assigned. Another survey (Tyrer 1985) found that only about half of chronic pain patients have a psychiatric diagnosis and two-thirds of these had depression. Other evidence in the literature (Romano and Turner 1985) suggests that about one-third of patients attending pain clinics of various sorts have depression. Another study (Katon et al. 1985) found that more than half the patients with chronic pain had a prior history of affective disorder and a third had a family member with affective illness. Over 40 percent of patients with chronic pain who fulfilled the DSM-III (American Psychiatric Association 1980) criteria for major depression had an abnormal dexamethazone suppression test (France et al. 1984). If a diagnosis of major affective disorder or dysthymic disorder can be provided for these patients it may be questioned whether it is always necessary to also place them in the category of somatoform pain disorder, although the presence of pain deserves emphasis in the diagnosis.

The next reason for doubt concerning the category of somatoform pain disorder is that the criteria are imprecise and allow cases to be diagnosed too readily when there might be an alternative explanation. Most patients being referred for psychiatric help with a chronic pain diagnosis typically have more than one Axis I diagnosis as well as an organic disorder. In others a physical disease is the principal factor in their complaints. If the organic disorder is overlooked (Jamieson and Merskey 1984), it is quite easy to suppose that the patients fit the category of somatoform pain disorder so that this category may serve as a covert way of making a diagnosis of conversion disorder for which several of the DSM-III-R criteria overlap.

In effect, a discussion of somatoform pain disorder and its treatment must therefore focus on pain, which is not accounted for by other psychiatric diagnoses and which might otherwise be thought of as conversion (hysterical) pain, or what some clinicians call operant pain. With these reservations in mind, it remains important to understand the nature of chronic pain and the clinical features with which it may be associated.

The Nature of Chronic Pain

Unlike acute pain, chronic pain continues past the usual time for the particular disorder or lesion to heal and then may persist for long periods (often defined as over six months) reaching a plateau of discomfort which fluctuates but seldom progresses. Chronic pain usually lacks evidence of autonomic reactivity although concurrent stress and autonomic arousal may worsen the pain. Chronic pain is also frequently designated "intractable" since patients in pain clinics or referred to psychiatrists tend not to respond to single interventions, whether they be medical, surgical, or psychological. While there are patients with chronic pain in pain clinics who do not have psychiatric disturbance (Merskey et al 1986; Tyrer 1985), a process of selective referral results in those patients with psychological problems and chronic pain being found there. Those without psychological problems but with chronic pain may exist in the community without troubling the medical profession. It is well established that the personality characteristics of patients with protracted nonfatal conditions in both hospital and general practice are liable to be distorted as a result of referral and selection factors (Banks et al. 1975; Pond and Bidwell 1959).

Features Associated with Chronic Pain

As pointed out in one text on treatment of mental disorders (Getto and Ochitill 1982), the DSM-III category of psychogenic pain disorder (or somatoform pain disorder) is incompletely defined. A much broader characterization has been developed by Pinsky (1978) which overlaps with the features of chronic abnormal illness behavior (Wooley et al. 1978) suggesting that while pain is the most common symptom in medical practice, other somatic symptoms may be similarly elaborated to become the focus of a patient's distress.

The Committee on Taxonomy of the International Association for the Study of Pain has avoided defining a specific chronic pain syndrome (IASP 1986). It emphasized the recognition of individual diagnoses—whether they relate to organic or psychological disorder. For that reason, the present discussion avoids the term "syndrome" but describes features that are often observed to be present in individuals who suffer from chronic pain.

These features are important because they match the principles of management. They are as follows:

1. Pain complaints and disability disproportionate to detectable somatic lesion or to known pathophysiologic mechanisms.
2. A continuing search for an organic diagnosis or relief based on relatively fixed beliefs about physical causes for pain, associated with a fear and distrust of psychiatry and psychotherapy.
3. Exposure to most if not all standard medical and surgical techniques for symptom control without sustained success but often with resultant drug dependency.
4. An implicit appeal to the physician to take responsibility for a cure rather than making personal attempts at coping.

5. Behavior that obtains attention and sustains the sick role but which eventually leads to alienation and rejection.
6. Avoidance of healthy roles, due to lack of skills, excessive expectations, or fear of failure.
7. Adoption of the sick role due to environmental rewards from family, friends, physicians, or social entitlement programs.

It must be emphasized that many of the features listed may also arise on the basis of pain caused by physical disease, and a number of them might represent appropriate efforts to adjust to an unsatisfactory situation or to resolve it. Secondary depression, anger with others, a pursuit of better diagnosis, reliance upon compensation payments, and acceptance of help from members of the family all follow reasonably if an individual has a painful chronic physical disease. The frequency with which all or most of the features apply to individuals or to groups of patients who satisfy other criteria of somatoform pain disorder has not been established by research.

Etiology

Chronic pain has numerous causes which may be biologic, psychological, social, or environmental, and often more than one of these factors plays a part (Blackwell et al. 1984; Merskey 1984). In somatoform pain disorder, some medical or surgical event has invariably contributed to the initiation of chronic pain, and these disturbances may continue to interact and account for behavioral changes to a variable degree. The condition may develop from acute trauma or disease, such as back injury or myocardial infarction, or it can occur in association with intermittent or chronic conditions such as migraine, angina, sickle cell disease or rheumatoid arthritis. In many cases, physical and psychological factors coexist and interact, but their relative contribution varies from one person to another. The most prevalent sources of chronic pain seen in pain clinics (but not necessarily in psychiatric practice) are back pain, neurologic diseases producing deafferentation disorder (nerve tract damage and altered sensory innervation), and various types of headache.

The importance which patients attach to pain and the behavior that they demonstrate in relation to it are determined partly by their existing personalities and prior experience. The attention given to pain may also be conditioned by the function which the symptom serves in relieving an unconscious difficulty (primary gain), in avoiding a consciously recognizable difficulty (avoidance learning), and by the rewards of the sick role (secondary gain).

Woodforde and Merskey (1972) found that male patients with organic lesions and pain had higher scores for phobias and obsessionality on the Middlesex Hospital Questionnaire than patients with pain and no lesion. This suggest that some of the emotional characteristics of patients with chronic pain may be consequences rather than their cause. The therapist needs to bear in mind that a patient with chronic pain suffers regardless of its etiology; chronic pain deprives a person of pleasure and is demoralizing, so that many features of the patient's behavior are consequences of severe and interminable disease.

The validity or generalizability of anecdotal or stereotypical descriptions of patients with chronic pain which infer their psychodynamic or behavioral evolution should be viewed with the utmost caution given a heterogeneity of chronic pain populations and the kaleidoscopic manner in which multiple variables often act on an individual patient.

Management

The degree to which an individual psychiatrist can effectively manage patients with chronic pain varies with the resources available and the patient's willingness, or lack of it, to cooperate. The individual psychiatrist is in a position to do a great deal, if interested. Working as a consultant or therapist without being part of an organized clinic, a psychiatrist can make a substantial contribution by maintaining a working relationship with other specialists. This can include support, family and individual therapy when indicated, prescription of appropriate psychotropic medication, and collaboration in social and rehabilitative arrangements. Alternatively, psychiatrists may work as part of a team which provides assessment and initiation of treatment and continuing care in a formal chronic pain management program, of which there are now several hundred in the United States and Canada. The role of the psychiatrist working in British pain clinics has recently been described (Tyrer 1985), and the psychotherapeutic measures which may be implemented by an individual psychiatrist have also been outlined (Merskey 1984).

There is no single model of a chronic pain clinic. Specific details may vary with the patient population, disciplines of the sponsoring departments, and the technology available. For instance, clinics that specialize in post-therapeutic pain and are located in departments of anaesthesia may rely heavily on nerve blocks, while clinics supervised by a psychiatrist may select patients with marked depressive features and make use of psychotropic medication. With a few exceptions to be discussed there is no proof at the present time that one or another approach is to be preferred, and psychiatrists who work in pain clinics seem to contribute by the provision of their specific skills as much as by their membership of the team as a whole (Large 1980). The view is nevertheless widespread that many chronic pain patients benefit from the general and comprehensive multidisciplinary approach found in an increasing number of pain clinics (Ng 1981).

The features of somatoform chronic pain described are matched by management principles, each of which is implemented by a number of strategies and individual treatment methods. The sequence probably contributes to success. After a thorough assessment, the therapist needs to indicate that he understands the patient's ordeal. Only after a trusting relationship has been established can the patient's problem be reframed in a rehabilitative manner. Treatment is then directed to ways of enhancing skills that facilitate healthy behavior and finally to the redeployment of environmental rewards that support and maintain this behavior. The reason for this sequence is that it places primary emphasis on alleviating the patient's pain or suffering and is designed to give the patient new skills and coping strategies before any attempt is made to tamper with whatever rewards of the sick role may exist. If this sequence is reversed, it is likely to produce anxiety and distrust of the therapist, who is perceived as uncaring. There may even be an escalation of pain complaints in an attempt to make the therapist understand the seriousness of the patient's ordeal.

Thorough Biopsychosocial Assessment

The patient's conviction of a serious undiscovered disease, the complexity of the etiology of chronic pain, and the large number of previous investigations or treatments make a thorough assessment mandatory. This provides a safe basis for a rehabilitative approach since it establishes trust in the patient and confidence among nonphysician team members who may later be required to minimize pain complaints or maladaptive behavior. Anything less thorough allows the patient to suppose that some cause for pain may have been overlooked or to assume that a perfunctory evaluation amounts to an accusation of malingering.

A traditional medical history, a review of symptoms, and a physical examination are essential. The information obtained should also include assessment of current work status, compensation, and pending litigation issues. An interview with a spouse or relative provides essential information about interpersonal pain behavior and potential social reward systems.

Additional investigation may include psychological testings, such as the MMPI profile, to assess psychopathology; but the psychiatrist should be aware of erroneous conditions from the test scores. The presence of pain will inevitably produce elevations both on the hypochondriasis scale and on the hysteria scale, which employs half of the same questions as the hypochondriasis scale. Insomnia due to pain will cause an increase in the depression scale as will other physical symptoms. This weakness of the MMPI was stated by its originators but is frequently neglected in practice.

A psychophysiologic appraisal of muscle tension and stress responses may be useful. Individual clinics select or have developed additional test instruments of their own to further assess key social or psychological factors. These include the Beck Depression Inventory, the Hamilton Rating Scale for Depression, the Zung Self-Rating Depression Scale, the Irritability/Depression and Anxiety Scale of Snaith et al., the Eysenck Personality Inventory, the Crown-Crisp Experiential Inventory, the Hospital Anxiety and Depression Scale of Zigmond and Snaith, the Levine-Pilowsky Depression Questionnaire, the Pilowsky Illness Behavior Questionnaire as well as more generalized probes in social and psychological areas, such as the Millon Behavioral Health Inventory and the Wisconsin Psychosocial Pain Inventory. In some centers the Holmes and Rahe Life Events Scale is used also, although its value and validity in pain research has not been established. The assessment of any psychological test result in the presence of physical disease and severe pain requires special caution. The results appear to represent predominantly the effects of the patients' current suffering, rather than measuring premorbid personality traits (Kellner 1986).

Methods that measure the effects of chronic pain are the Sickness Impact Profile (Follick et al. 1985; Gilson et al. 1975) the Psychosocial Factor Evaluation (Heaton et al. 1982) and the Westhaven-Yale Multidimensional Pain Inventory (WHYMPI) (Kerns et al. 1985).

Another useful way of collecting pertinent data, including information on drug-taking and its relationship to pain or environmental events, is to have the patient keep a daily behavioral diary. The diary may provide clues to motivation.

Reframing the Pain Problem

Considerable skill is required when it becomes necessary to redefine the patient's pain complaints in a manner that ends investigation without challenging their reality. Explanations are more likely to be acceptable if the results of the assessment can be presented in a manner consistent with the patient's own attitudes or beliefs. Patients with chronic pain are highly sensitive to suggestions that their symptoms are imaginary or manufactured in some way. It helps to discuss pain as the source rather than the product of stress since even the premature discussion of the role of stress in pain may provoke angry rejection of a treatment plan. It is, then, productive to have patients define what the pain prevents them from doing and to develop strategies that help patients accomplish specific goals while learning to tolerate pain. This process is facilitated by discussing the possible neurochemical and neurophysiological substrates of painful experience.

Once an adequate review has been made of the physical status and emotional situation, and this has been discussed with the patient, it is important to arrive at closure without ordering still additional tests or investigations that foster the patient's doubt and uncertainty. If the patient's beliefs persist that a disease exists which the physician has failed to diagnose, the strategies described in the chapter on hypochondriasis should be considered.

Methods of Symptom Control

Distress reactions and requests for analgesic relief are likely to occur until alternative methods of symptom control have been obtained or learned. Multiple or simultaneous interventions may be necessary. The choice from among the available strategies discussed later may be empirical or based on parsimony—selecting the safest, least complex, expensive, or time-consuming intervention first with response in a selected target symptom followed by generalization to other areas.

Although insurance companies are increasingly reluctant to pay for six to eight weeks of treatment for inpatient management, at least in some patients it is ultimately less expensive. Relative indications include serious drug dependency, multiple somatic complaints requiring further investigation, severe physical disability, and overpowering environmental contingencies, such as an extremely solicitous spouse incapable of setting limits. By contrast, patients with single or localized pain (such as headache), less severe limitations, and cooperative relatives can usually be managed as outpatients or in a day hospital setting.

Traditional psychotherapy

Contemporary articles and reviews of pain management often make only cursory mention of psychotherapy. At best they are cautious about its benefits and more often are pessimistic. This is particularly true of individual psychodynamically oriented therapy, which has been largely displaced by an emphasis either on more cognitive-behavioral approaches or by group forms of psychotherapy (Merskey 1984). At least three factors have contributed to this neglect.

First, as elsewhere in the psychotherapy literature on pain, there is a dearth of outcome research. The only controlled study to date (Bassett and Pilowsky 1985) compared 26 patients assigned to either 12 sessions of psychodynamic psychotherapy or six sessions of cognitively oriented supportive psychotherapy. The study was marred by the selective nature of the patient sample, the high number of dropouts and inequalities in the two patient populations, and in the amounts of treatment given to them. Nevertheless, there were trends in favor of psychodynamic therapy, and one measure (activity level at 12 months follow-up) was significantly superior.

Second, the bulk of writing and research emanates from contemporary chronic pain programs which may serve a skewed population of patients who have the most severe or intractable symptoms. In the milder cases, pain plays a less central role or perhaps even has an adaptive function and is more amenable to psychotherapeutic intervention (Engel 1959; Kolb 1982).

Finally, the pain patient's innate resistance to psychological explanations makes successful referral for psychotherapy unlikely and therapy difficult. Both Engel (1959) and Pilowsky (1985) have noted that Freud's earlier writings contained a wealth of case material concerning pain while he practiced as a neurologist but, later on, as Freud's technique became increasingly psychological, pain rarely received any mention.

Despite all of these factors, the older literature does contain a solid core of descriptive material concerning the psychodynamic understanding of pain, and there is a modest resurgence of interest in how to apply these principles in contemporary pain management even though there is no research evidence to suggest that psychodynamic psychotherapy is of advantage over other methods. However, the psychiatrist who wishes to treat patients with chronic pain within a psychodynamic frame of reference may find the following principles and strategies of interest.

Chronic pain has both symbolic and functional significance in the patient's life. It is postulated that the symbolic significance may be to represent sublimated aggression, expiation of guilt, atonement of sin, or incorporation of a lost love object (Engel 1959). Functionally, pain may serve to help in avoiding repressed conflict (primary gain) or to obtain the fulfillment of dependency needs (secondary gain). To identify and understand these complex factors requires a detailed anamnesis that links the experiences of pain to historical, developmental, and contemporary life events. Information may have to come from multiple sources, including spouse or family members. The therapist must be skilled and flexible enough to obtain this information and use it (if necessary in couples or family sessions) while preserving trust and confidentiality with the patient in individual therapy.

Chronic pain is almost always intertwined within a matrix of organic disease and suffering. In describing therapy for psychosomatic patients, Alexander (1950) emphasized that a basic requirement was a "general knowledge of pathology—both psychological and somatic," and he went on to note that "psychotherapy conducted in such cases without the cooperation of the medical specialist must be considered wild therapy." Psychological setbacks in therapy or in the patient's life will be reflected in worsening of bodily symptoms and complaints that may require medical explanation or management. It is no accident that the pioneers in psychological management of chronic pain were individuals with a strong background in medicine who made the seminal contribution to explaining pain's psychological components and went on to propose a systems-oriented biopsychosocial model of medical understanding. The fact that today's psychiatrists are again becoming more medically sophisticated will be a valuable asset for their involvement in chronic pain management. Rutrick and Aronoff (1983) have described in detail how this may be accomplished in tandem with the medical team. They offer examples of the different approaches and collaborative strategies used by an individual psychotherapist and the medical director working together in a chronic pain program.

Patients with chronic pain have particular psychological characteristics and defensive styles that may limit or dictate the type of individual therapy. Some say that the frequent presence of alexithymia, a harsh superego, and predominant defense mechanisms of denial, rationalization, suppression, or projection makes many patients unwilling to accept referral or difficult to engage in therapy. Walters (1961), who treated a large series of patients with "psychogenic regional pain," recommended that the patients be treated "no different than other psychiatric disorders" and that the "background of their emotional troubles is the center of attack." Pilowsky (1985) has described how these characteristics may disrupt the six basic but nonspecific components which Frank (1972) believes to be the common features of all successful psychotherapy. These obstacles can be overcome in some instances, and there are several useful discussions of how psychodynamic methods may contribute to this

(Aronoff and Rutrick 1985; Pilowsky 1985). Principles derived from Freudian, Kleinian, and object relations theory can be incorporated within relatively short-term and eclectic psychotherapy (Pinsky and Malyon 1979).

There are two basic tenets which are generally agreed upon in the conduct of individual therapy with chronic pain patients. The first is the need to develop a strong empathic bond by acknowledgment of the severity of the patient's suffering and avoidance of any challenge to its reality. The second is that some of the traditional techniques of psychodynamic therapy are unhelpful. For example, some therapists believe painful interpretations, evocation of fantasies, free association, and dream analysis are harmful.

New methods of symptom control

Managing pain complaints.   In some centers both staff and patients are trained to minimize complaints of pain since sensation is reinforced by attention. The well-known fact that pain feels worse when talked about is used to form the basis of an agreement not to do so. Instead, staff and patients learn to focus on the achievement and accomplishment of defined treatment goals. When patients have a new complaint or wish to discuss existing pain, they do so at a set time and place, usually daily physician rounds. If time to talk about pain is restricted in this way, the rationale must be explained and cooperation obtained lest the patient conclude that the physician does not take the pain seriously. It is important to be willing to discuss with patients the extent to which their actual subjective distress is being alleviated. Such an approach can avoid the confrontation which is inherent in the doctrinaire attempt to describe pain only in terms of external behavior. If the patients' pain is discussed as a normal part of their concern, but it is also indicated that for a while it may be worse or that treatment should be pursued despite the pain, patients can cooperate to reduce their consumption of narcotics and to increase their level of activity.

Drug detoxification and reducing dependence.   Since requests for analgesics are the most common source of attention to pain, they must be dealt with early in treatment. Among pain patients approximately equal numbers use no addicting medications, are dependent on narcotics alone, or are addicted to both narcotics and sedatives (Turner et al. 1982). When there is clear evidence of physiologic dependence on narcotic analgesics, the patient may be tapered off medication over 10 to 14 days using blind substitution of active ingredients in a liquid base (Fordyce 1976) provided the patient fully understands the procedure and agrees to it. Of course, it is not always necessary for the substitution to be blind, and it is possible to negotiate a staged reduction of narcotic analgesics or sedatives openly, perhaps covering the withdrawal and insomnia which frequently result with the help of sedative antidepressants, such as amitriptyline, and if necessary also, phenothiazines, which are believed to have analgesic properties. When there is evidence of habituation or psychological dependency (especially with benzodiazepines or narcotic analgesics), such a system of self-regulated reduction should be negotiated with the patient, who is asked to set weekly goals for a progressive decrease in daily intake and to keep records of progress; the patient is then rewarded with praise (Wooley et al. 1978).

If antidepressants or phenothiazines are not used, the strategies to reduce dependence upon other medication are unlikely to succeed until the patient has been provided with alternative methods of coping with pain.

Use of psychotropic medications.   Psychotropic medication for pain appears to work in three main ways apart from any placebo effects. First, there are a few patients in whom the reduction of anxiety will effectively lead to a reduction of pain. Presumably these are patients in whom a muscle contraction mechanism is prominent and whose treatment will come under other headings in the present volume. However, traditional methods for the relief of anxiety are generally of very little use in patients with chronic pain, and unless there are definite indications, such as a coexisting anxiety disorder, continuous prescribing of benzodiazepines should be avoided. Antidepressants have been found to be effective in a substantial population of patients with anxiety (Kahn et al. 1986) and are the treatments of choice.

The second way in which psychotropic medication may be useful in the management of chronic pain is by the relief of depression in those patients in whom the pain appears to be a consequence of depression.

The relationship between chronic pain and depression and the potential use of antidepressants has been the subject of a review by Romano and Turner (1985). The review documents 20 studies on the prevalence of depression in chronic pain populations. Methodological shortcomings and variability between studies limit the conclusions to the obvious fact that the two conditions commonly coexist and that at least two equally common subgroups occur, one in which pain and depression commence simultaneously, and the other in which depression follows pain. Efforts to explain the common occurrence of the two conditions include psychodynamic, behavioral, and neurochemical speculations.

The pharmacologic literature on the use of antidepressants for pain is as complicated as the descriptive work (Blumer and Heilbronn 1984; Rosenblatt et al. 1984; Walsh 1983). Based on experimental and animal research on pain pathways, it has been suggested that tricyclic antidepressants with selective actions on serotonin pathways are more effective. However, two of the most serotonergic drugs, clomipramine and zimeldine, have not been shown to be particularly useful in the management of chronic pain. Monoamine oxidase inhibitors have also been claimed as specific remedies (Davidson 1985) but on equivocal evidence.

A review of 18 studies (Rosenblatt et al. 1984), including six different tricyclic compounds in dosages of up to 100 mg daily, found that all reported pain relief ranging from 50 to 100 percent. Only seven studies were double-blind, but four showed substantial relief for up to six months. A consensus derived by the authors of this review was that low-dosage tricyclic antidepressants are effective for the majority and frequently produce a substantial benefit that occurs earlier than a customary antidepressant action. An attempt to use higher dosages of amitriptyline (150 mg daily) in a crossover design with placebo (Pilowsky et al. 1982) produced some reduction in pain but also a high drop-out rate possibly contributed to by poor compliance and side effects (to which somatizing patients are sensitive). This point is emphasized by Blumer and Heilbronn's (1984) finding that 65 percent of 1,000 chronic pain patients treated with antidepressents failed to complete treatment.

It has been shown clearly (Watson et al. 1982) that in post-herpetic neuralgia, amitriptyline in median doses of 75 mg daily relieved pain and depression where the two were present together and also relieved pain where the patients were not depressed, at least as measured by the Beck Depression Inventory. This study was undertaken double-blind with placebo control and with estimation of plasma antidepressant levels. It supports the long-held view that some antidepressants such as amitriptyline are analgesic independent of their antidepressant effect. A detailed review of the effects of psychotropic medication on pain which examines these findings is presented by Monks and Merskey (1984). The possibility of other, more specific, pharmacologic effects on particular types of pain also cannot be overlooked. For example, antagonism of histamine-2 receptors of some tricyclic antidepressants may contribute to chronic pain relief and ulcer healing in patients with peptic ulcer (Richelson 1982), and anticonvulsants may benefit individuals with chronic but paroxysmal lancinating pain (Swerdlow 1984). Carbamazepine is recommended on the basis of its effectiveness in trigeminal neuralgia.

On the basis of our experience and review of the literature, antidepressants contribute most to chronic pain management when the following conditions are observed:

1. Tricyclic compounds are used in relatively low dosages (below 100 mg), amitriptyline being so far the only substance which is definitely known to be analgesic as well as antidepressant. There is reason to believe from examination of the literature that doxepin (Okasha et al. 1973) and imipramine (Gingras 1976) may have similar actions, and there is a current opinion, which has not yet been proven, that trazodone is useful.
2. The more sedative compounds are given in a single dose two hours before bedtime to reduce daytime side effects, secure sound sleep (frequently disturbed in pain patients), and enhance compliance.
3. The medication is presented as part of a total rehabilitative program and as an adjunct to secure sleep, improve coping, and help minimize pain rather than as a specific cure.
4. Side effects are anticipated and explained but minimized before they appear.
5. The rationale for prescribing is explained to the patient as the correction of an abnormal pain perception rather than as a drug to treat depression.
6. The patients are given all relevant information to participate in the choice of medication and titration of dosage. They need to be told that accurate predictions are impossible and that there are differences between individuals in response. This emphasizes that the patient is expected to contribute to decisions about treatment.

Physical rehabilitation.   Chronic pain is thought to be perpetuated by a vicious cycle of muscular atrophy, disuse, fatigue, and lack of stamina that discourages activity and worsens pain when effort is made. A progressive stepwise plan of physical retraining under skilled medical supervision is a keystone to most effective programs. The patient is told that aggravation of the pain by exercise does not mean that the pain will be made permanently worse but that this may be a necessary step to long-term recovery. Specific goals or "quotas" are set to the activity level required to restore the individual's independence at work or in the home. The usefulness of exercise quotas for chronic pain patients has been demonstrated in a controlled study (Doleys et al. 1982), although the results showed a lack of generalization to other physical activities suggesting that reinforcement from staff was more powerful than any internalized sense of accomplishment. This finding emphasizes the fact that if prolonged recovery is to occur, attention must also be paid to facilitating patient responsibility and building networks of environmental encouragement for physical activity (discussed under environmental rewards).

Cognitive therapy.   If patients are asked to ignore pain they must be provided with methods to facilitate doing so. The various cognitive therapies are therefore a logical approach which have been shown by Khatami and Rush (1982) to work for specific individuals in pain at specific points in their care. Extensive reviews have been provided by Tan (1982) and also by Turner and Chapman (1982b), Spence (1984), and Trifiletti (1984). Detailed methods of treatment can be found in the book by Turk et al. (1984).

While cognitive therapy entails systematic tasks and procedures, perhaps its essential feature in the treatment of pain is to make systematic what we all think of doing empirically. This includes distancing oneself from pain and saying, "It isn't really me that is suffering," or favoring distraction techniques which emphasize pleasant experiences (thinking about some nice experience which may help to reduce the impact of current pain).

Tan (1982) mentions the provision of anticipatory coping skills. These skills comprise strategies like imaginative inattention (think of a pleasant day at the beach), imaginative transformation of the pain (those sensations are really contractions, not pain), imaginative transformation of the context (that hurts but it's like being the hero in a James Bond film), diversion of attention (counting ceiling tiles, doing mental arithmetic), and focusing on the part in pain but analyzing the experience (as if for a biology report).

Relaxation, deep-breathing exercises, and the provision of external distractions (e.g., tasks which preoccupy the individual) all form part of the complex of strategies which may be called cognitive therapy. Some workers (Turk et al. 1984) have developed "stress inoculation procedures" in which the individual is exposed to painful or noxious stimuli, usually in the laboratory, as part of a process of becoming accustomed to the painful situation and adapting to it with the various cognitive techniques recommended. There is evidence that such procedures can have beneficial effects in acute pain such as that experienced during dental work, but at present there is no evidence that they are helpful in chronic pain.

On the whole, the precise benefit of cognitive therapy is still speculative and well-designed outcome studies are scanty (Spence 1984). There is reason to think that it may work best in pain of mild or moderate severity (Melzack et al. 1963). However, since all the gains with cognitive therapy are obtained at little or no risk, they deserve always to be considered and sometimes at least attempted. In practice, many patients with chronic pain have already tried such methods in a partial fashion themselves.

Relaxation training and biofeedback. Teaching the patient to relax may facilitate the cognitive and distraction procedures described but may also have a more direct and specific action on physiological parameters believed to cause or aggravate pain such as muscle contraction or vascular dilatation. These goals are accomplished either by progressive muscular relaxation techniques or a variety of biofeedback procedures that have included the EEG, skin temperature, vascular pulsation, or electromyographic (EMG) feedback. Biofeedback has also been used as a tool to secure generalized muscular relaxation.

A critical review of 10 controlled studies on relaxation training and over 40 studies on biofeedback (Turner and Chapman 1982a) confirmed the conclusions of earlier reviews (Blanchard et al. 1978; Jessup et al. 1979; Nuechterlein and Holroyd, 1980; Turk et al. 1979) that generalized relaxation training was simpler, less expensive, and as effective as biofeedback in tension and migraine headaches. In other chronic pain neither treatment was likely to succeed in the absence of a comprehensive approach.

Hypnosis. Hypnosis and post-hypnotic suggestions are means by which the patient can learn to employ dissociative strategies or evoke images and metaphors that distract from or reinterpret pain sensations. There is some evidence from controlled studies that hypnosis can be effective in a few highly amenable individuals with such conditions as disseminated breast cancer (Spiegel and Bloom 1983) and low back pain (Crasilneck 1979). Reviews on the use of hypnosis in chronic pain (Covino and Warfield 1985; Savitz 1983), while anecdotal, also emphasize that hypnosis alone is seldom effective in relieving chronic pain but can be useful as part of a comprehensive approach when developed to encourage the patient from a passive to an active role and to modify attitudes to the painful experience.

Sensory stimulation.   The alteration of sensory input has been a traditional folk remedy to alleviate pain over the centuries. It includes massage, heat, cold, vibration, mustard plasters, acupuncture, and various forms of electrical stimulation. Many of these methods were considered to be elaborate placebos until the Melzack-Wall Gate control theory gave them credibility in 1965. This theory proposed that noxious stimuli were modulated by descending inhibitory nerve pathways of both suprasegmental and segmental origin. Attempts to invoke this mechanism have traversed the nervous system, including cingulotomy, stereotactic implantation of electrodes in periventricular gray matter, internal capsule, or lateral thalamus (Richardson 1983), implantation of electrodes into the spinal cord (Demirel et al. 1984), and more mundane and less intrusive methods of peripheral stimulation. The latter include the transcutaneous nerve stimulations (TNS) which are lightweight, portable instruments that deliver electrical stimulation through electrodes to the skin in varying voltages, frequencies, wave forms, and pulse widths.

TNS units appear to offer relief in excess of placebo and are most effective when there is skin sensitivity or nerve damage as in causalgia (Melzack and Wall 1984). The interpretation of results with TNS is complicated by the use of high frequency (10 to 100 Hz) or low frequency (1 to 4 Hz) stimulation and by difficulty in devising appropriate placebo controls. Low frequency stimulation is postulated to invoke endorphin mediated (naloxone sensitive) pathways and high frequency to involve serotonin pathways. Such elegant hypothesizing is somewhat invalidated by results that showed equally good pain relief to both methods of stimulation and an elaborate placebo in chronic pain due to rheumatoid arthritis (Langley et al. 1984). A comparison of vibratory stimulation with high and low frequency TNS (Lundberg 1983) found that four out of five patients experienced relief of chronic pain with any modality, and two-thirds also responded to placebo vibration. Administration of naloxone did not modify pain relief. Because they are simple to use and free of side effects, except for occasional skin irritation, TNS units are often an initial treatment for chronic pain.

Acupuncture is now regarded as a form of low frequency stimulation which produces some relief in approximately 60 percent of chronic pain patients particularly in musculoskeletal conditions (Lewith 1984) and headaches (Hansen and Hansen 1981). A review of seven randomized controlled trials (Lewith and Machin 1983) found that acupuncture was more effective than sham procedures and random needling. A report that symptom relief with acupuncture was correlated with an increase in plasma metenkephalin (Kiser et al. 1983) was not supported by the failure of naloxone to modify pain relief in a double-blind controlled study (Kenyon et al. 1983). Furthermore, its benefit may be short-lived in chronic pain patients compared to TNS units which are easily obtained and can be continuously or repeatedly applied.

Nerve blocks.   Nerve blocks are widely used, especially in programs where neurologists or anesthesiologists are active, for both diagnosis and treatment. Differential spinal blockade using placebo and various strengths of local anesthetic injected into the epidural space is used to distinguish central effects and reflex sympathetic dystrophy from peripheral causes of pain. When the latter are identified, this may lead to permanent chemical or surgical ablation (Pawl 1979).

Sometimes when nerve blocks are used they are part of a multimodal approach and specific benefit is difficult to ascribe (Catchlove and Braha 1984). However, there are some very specific indications for nerve blocks, such as reflex sympathetic dystrophy, where they are the treatment of choice. A trial of epidural injections for low back pain is also a recognized practice in most patients with chronic low back pain due to mechanical causes.

Surgical procedures.   Invasive surgical procedures are certainly treatments of last choice, and the results are not always dependent on surgery alone. Only six out of 33 patients, showed long-term benefits (over two years) after spinal cord stimulation, but patients were not even evaluated psychologically (Demirel et al. 1984). On the other hand, brain implantation of electrodes produced long-term relief in two-thirds of 90 patients operated on in a 10-year period (Richardson 1983). But these patients were all extensively evaluated in a multidisciplinary pain unit and treated concurrently with stress management techniques and for depression. The National Commission on Protection of Human Subjects in Biomedical and Behavioral Research reviewed the entire recent literature on psychosurgery since 1951 on cingulotomy and found that nine out of 11 patients with chronic pain had benefited surprisingly well. The literature on leucotomy of various sorts indicates that some patients with pain improve, sometimes strikingly. However, it has never been shown that improvement was obtained unless either the patients had significant depressive illness or the operation caused an extensive effect upon the personality. Hence, leucotomy for somatoform pain disorder could be considered for patients who had severe intractable depression with pain not responding to other appropriate measures.

Electroconvulsive therapy.   Given the intractable nature of chronic pain and its frequent association with severe depression, it is not surprising that there is an older literature on the effects of ECT. Good results are reported in several uncontrolled studies (Boyd 1956; Hohman and Wilkinson 1953; Mendels 1965; Von Hagen 1957; Weiss et al. 1958), but a poor result was also reported (Weinstein et al. 1959). It cannot be recommended in the absence of the usual criteria of affective disorder.

Experimental techniques.   The frequency and intractable nature of chronic pain and lack of any simple treatment will continue to invite innovative strategies to treat it. For example, low-power laser irradiation was shown in a double-blind study to produce benefit in 19 out of 26 chronic pain patients, and the benefit was sustained for six months in 15 individuals (Walker 1983). The mechanism is presumably similar to TNS. Another (uncontrolled) study (Larbig et al. 1984) concerned the intravenous administration of a delta sleep-inducing neuropeptide (DSLP), which alleviated both pain and depression in six out of seven chronic pain patients after five days of administration. Only double-blind controlled prospective studies will show if such effects are specific or differ from those due to conventional antidepressants.

The Shift to a Rehabilitative Approach

In explaining the shift from finding a cure to helping the patients cope with their disability and symptoms, it is helpful to first review the information that has led to a conclusion that the cause of the pain is not progressive, malignant, or fatal. This leads naturally to a discussion of the areas in which the pain is interfering with the patient's life, and the ways in which the sufferer can be helped in learning to cope with disability and to lead a more satisfying life despite it. The goal is to obtain a subtle but profound shift in the locus of control from physician to patient and a change in expectations from cure to coping. Approximately a third of patients may reject this offer of rehabilitative help and insist on continuing the search for a definitive biomedical answer elsewhere, often at famous or well-known clinics. This is especially likely if the spouse or parent shares a false conviction about etiology, often with "folie a deux" firmness of belief. It is most helpful at this stage to avoid the kind of confrontation which in the past often led to discharge against medical advice. It is more fruitful to encourage the patient to return for rehabilitative help and to request a copy of the next clinic's (almost inevitably confirmatory) findings.

Alteration of Pain Behavior

In the diagnostic process, early in rehabilitation and later at times of partial relapse, patients will frequently display the reactions that accompany the sick role. In diagnostic shorthand these are often characterized as dependent, histrionic, or passive-aggressive behavior. Complaints, demands, threats, and hostility cause the provider to feel guilty and try harder; helplessness and passive compliance invoke caretaking. The amount of staff attention may also be increased by splitting or playing off one health professional against another.

In order to sustain the rehabilitative approach, the treatment team must be skilled in both recognizing and responding to these reactions. This requires the simultaneous avoidance of excessive caretaking or overdirection with the promotion of autonomy by firm and consistent placement of responsibility on the patient for effort, persistence, and progress toward the goals which have been defined. This must be accomplished in a manner that recognizes and respects the subjective reality of the patient's suffering.

Enhancement of Healthy Behavior

Sometimes the clinician becomes convinced that the patient remains trapped in the sick role and suffers chronic pain because there is some impairment of the ability to function in a healthy manner. Irreconcilable conflicts, unreasonable expectations, lack of skills, or fear of failure may all contribute to avoidance of healthy behavior and adoption of the sick role.

These difficulties may be in occupational, marital, or sexual roles and may remain hidden for a variety of reasons including the patient's conviction that they are unsolvable and shameful. The patient may also lack trust in the therapist or have difficulties negotiating within an emotional framework.

A number of strategies exist to enhance healthy behavior.

Skills training

Patients with chronic pain often lack the ability to get needs met in a healthy, assertive manner. Instead, they learn to control or avoid situations by pain complaints or by being sick and will selectively solicit and reward caretaking from others (Wooley et al. 1978). Assertiveness training and role playing can help patients to express their needs in a more direct fashion. Other specific skills training in interpersonal behaviors, communication, sexual, or vocational areas may also be helpful but have not been systematically evaluated in chronic pain patients.

Individual psychotherapy

Psychodynamic psychotherapy was originally fostered by Hart (1947) and by Engel (1959) in their approach to the pain-prone patient. As discussed earlier (see section on symptom control), individual psychotherapy may play a useful role in chronic pain management, not only in the resolution of underlying conflicts and removal of symptoms but also in assisting the patient to improve interpersonal behaviors and adjustment to the problems of coping with residual chronic pain.

Reentry planning

As discharge from a program approaches, pain patients often become concerned about their ability to apply newly acquired skills in everyday life. Often there is a brief renewal of pain complaints. This underlines the need to practice pain management in the natural environment and to plan realistically for reentry into occupational and social life. Brief relapses can be anticipated and their management discussed in a relapse-prevention framework (Marlatt and Gordon 1980). Employers and unions vary in their willingness to facilitate a phased return to work. Little has been done to systematically study this as part of pain rehabilitation, but there is no doubt that work conditions contribute considerably to industrial accidents and reluctance to return to work (Brodsky 1975).

Redeployment of Environmental Rewards

For short-term change in pain behavior to occur and for long-term maintenance of healthy behavior, it is helpful to modify environmental responses to the patient. The techniques involve the use of social rewards to encourage and praise desired change. Some have conceptualized this approach in terms of operant conditioning and external contingency management. Others prefer to see it as part of the social adaptation of patients and the assistance of the physician in achieving it.

Despite the widespread use of operant techniques, particularly among inpatient programs, there is scant research of a conclusive nature (Latimer 1982; Trifiletti 1984). Turner and Chapman (1982b) reviewed 14 studies and found some evidence of sustained improvement in two instances, but they point to the highly selected sample of patients studied. In attempting to alter the environment in which the patient functions, attention should be given to specific situations and strategies.

Couples or family therapy

A role of the spouse and family in rewarding pain behavior has been reported by Shanfield et al. (1979) and Block (1981).

The relatives are often ready to learn new ways to encourage the patient's attempts to master pain and develop new skills. They may also be prepared to alter some of their own behavior which may be contributing to the patient's distress. Several uncontrolled studies suggest beneficial short- and long-term impact of couples or family therapy on chronic pain (Hudgens 1979; Painter et al. 1980).

Primary physicians

Primary physicians carry the major brunt of managing chronic pain in the community, and communication with them is essential for successful long-term management (Carron 1979). Both the patient and the primary physicians should have the same perspective on what the response to physical complaints and requests for medications will be; doctor shopping among subspecialists should be discouraged.

Pain clinics have adopted a variety of mechanisms, such as a simple jargon-free discharge letter, for informing primary physicians of the treatment plan and for involving them in it. Some units have patients share in the preparation of discharge letters and provide them with a copy. Since patients may wear out their primary sources of medical care, willingness to accept the patient back should be assessed, preferably at the time of the initial referral.

Peer support

The sustained support and encouragement of a peer group has obvious potential in the long-term maintenance of behavior change. Group therapy appears to be beneficial in uncontrolled studies (Catchlove and Cohen 1982; Pinsky et al. 1979), and some inpatient programs incorporate aspects of a therapeutic community in group meetings and mutual problem solving. The assessment of the advantages of group therapy over other forms of treatment, except for lower cost, await controlled studies with follow-up.

Compensation and disability payments

Financial rewards for disability incurred at work or elsewhere are obvious incentives to adopt the sick role, especially within an adversarial legal system based on contingency fee payments (Carron 1982). The older term, "compensation neurosis" carried with it the implication that money might be the major determinant of disability which would resolve following financial settlement. This is not the case (Mendelson 1984; Merskey 1984).

One study of patients with low back pain (White et al. 1980) concluded that family factors were more common and more potent reinforcers than financial incentives. Compensation is simply one aspect of chronic pain to which attention must be paid.

Outcome Evaluation

The art of chronic pain management has outstripped its science. The evolution of pain clinics during the last decade came on the heels of an expanded view of etiology and management derived from a biopsychosocial model of disease in general and the gate control theory of chronic pain in particular. These multivariate models and the multimodal treatments they demand are too complex for evaluative techniques developed earlier this century to solve simpler questions (Feinstein 1983).

Short-term outcome is reported to be excellent in most centers (Ng 1981), but referral and selection biases are seldom stipulated and an unspecified number of individuals with chronic pain avoid or decline a rehabilitative approach. For example, one pain clinic (Sturgis et al. 1984) found that out of over 100 patients referred, 65 attended for evaluation, 23 completed the program, and 14 were available for long-term follow-up.

Long-term follow-up studies report mixed success. In one study of 200 patients (Swanson et al. 1979), 65 percent of the successfully treated remained well one year later, but this represented only 25 percent of those originally referred. In one of the most careful and optimistic studies (Roberts and Reinhardt 1980), 77 percent of patients were leading normal lives one to eight years after treatment.

Pain is seldom eliminated and results are usually reported in terms of improved functioning. A 12-month follow-up (Cinciripini and Floreen 1982) found that 55 percent of patients were free from analgesic use and 61 percent avoided pain-related physician contacts. Another one-year follow-up (Vasudevan et al. 1985) of the first 78 patients to complete a multidisciplinary program found that employment had increased from 19 to 52 percent and analgesic use had declined from 92 to 45 percent.

A less optimistic view, which is more consistent with the long-term outcome of other chronic conditions, comes from an average two-year follow-up of 57 patients (Lutz et al. 1983). Patients were contacted to determine compliance with three daily regimens, of physical and occupational therapy exercises, relaxation and self hypnosis, and use of proper body mechanisms. Only 12.3 percent were doing all three regimens daily in a typical week and average overall compliance was only 42 percent.

All of the cited outcome studies suffer from methodological flaws, including the absence of any control group. A design that avoided this weakness (Sturgis et al. 1984) compared 14 individuals who completed a rehabilitative pain program with a comparable group matched for disease and demographic variables who were eligible for treatment but had declined. The survey was conducted two-and-a-half years after initial referral and showed the customary 50 percent pain reduction reported by the treated group. These patients also used significantly more self-control strategies than the untreated patients. However, their use was limited and far less than anticipated from the level of training they had received.

In evaluating overall success, it is difficult to tease apart the contributions to outcome of individual components of treatment. Once a multimodal approach appears to work, clinicians express reluctance to subject isolated components to controlled prospective evaluation. It is difficult to devise appropriate placebo controls for complex procedures and exceedingly difficult for the rater to remain unaware of which treatment the patient has had. Analyses are necessary that not only take multiple variables into account but also allow for additive or synergistic effects. For example, it is conceivable that a tricyclic compound prescribed alone may produce no significant benefit until administered with psychotherapy in conjunction with physical rehabilitation. The effects of one treatment also might be too small to yield statistically significant results. The type of research necessary to elucidate such interactions is illustrated by a study (Linton and Gotestam 1984) in chronic back and joint pain patients comparing the outcome of relaxation procedures alone, relaxation coupled with operant techniques, and a waiting list control. Both treatments were superior to the control group at termination and nine-month follow-up, but the addition of operant techniques did not significantly benefit pain reduction although it did improve activity levels and medication variables.

Comprehensive reviews of relaxation training, biofeedback, operant techniques, hypnosis, and cognitive behavioral strategies reveal scanty evidence of treatment specificity (Turner and Chapman 1982a,b).

Repeated single subject research designs and large sample studies using multivariate analyses and multidimensional scaling are ways to attempt answers, but we may be left with the paradox that while multimodal treatment programs for chronic pain seem to work (at least in uncontrolled studies), no one single variable appears to make a major contribution to outcome.

This paradox is not peculiar to pain research but has been noted in the literature on compliance in hypertension, where single interventions almost never outstrip control strategies but where complex multiple interventions usually produce demonstrable and worthwhile change (Haynes 1980). Finally, treatment results with groups may hide differences between the responses of individuals. Even if it can be shown conclusively that improvement with one method is, on the average, greater than with other methods, it does not mean it is the most suitable for all patients. This phenomenon cannot be adequately tested in conventional, controlled trials (Kellner 1976) but may be particularly relevant in the management of chronic pain which is so multiply determined.

Chapter 191

Hypochondriasis and Body Dysmorphic Disorder

The crucial features of hypochondriasis are either an unrealistic fear or a false belief of having a disease, or both, that persist despite reassurance. Hypochondriasis and functional somatic symptoms are different phenomena; however, they coexist in a large proportion of patients, and the principles of therapy, as outlined in the chapter on undifferentiated somatoform disorder, apply also to the management of patients with hypochondriasis.

The Hypochondriacal Reaction

It is beyond the scope of this section to discuss the research and the controversies on the nature of hypochondriasis. However, it is essential to detect the presence of another disorder, such as endogenous depression or panic disorder, which can mimic hypochondriasis; these disorders require different treatments. This is discussed again in the section on drug treatment.

A simplified scheme of the hypochondriacal reaction is presented first. It is based on empirical studies with hypochondriacal patients as well as on detailed case histories.

The patient may have had earlier experiences which predispose him to attend to bodily symptoms, such as disease in the family in childhood. The precipitating event can be any psychiatric disorder with anxiety or depression and somatic symptoms or an event which induces fear of disease, such as witnessing death with great emotional impact.

Some time after somatic symptoms are perceived, the idea of being ill may occur. Under fortunate circumstances the symptoms soon abate, or the patient is successfully reassured by his physician that they are harmless, so the reaction does not develop further and from then on the patient ignores the symptoms until recovery occurs. Such is the most common outcome of somatic functional symptoms. If the idea of personal illness persists—for example, because of persistence of somatic symptoms with unconvincing reassurance—the patient may become anxious over the serious consequences which physical disease can entail. Anxiety serves as a motive for selective perception; the patient may begin to notice his heartbeat or sensations associated with other functions. In some patients these sensations can dominate the perceptual field. Thus, an innocuous reaction begins to develop into a hypochondriacal neurosis.

The physicians' explanations that there is nothing wrong or that it is only imagination fail to convince the patient because he knows that he has distressing bodily symptoms; these explanations only persuade him that he has an undiagnosed disease. He may remember different diagnoses by various physicians and may be treated for these conditions. Throughout these experiences skills of perceiving somatic symptoms improve. Focusing attention on his body becomes an overlearned habit. Secondary conditioning may occur in which anxiety becomes conditioned to the perception of somatic sensations or to the thoughts of disease. These attacks lead to more somatic symptoms which in turn lead to more anxiety, more selective perception, and a vicious cycle. Depression is common, in part, because the patient suffers and feels helpless. Some patients become angry, apparently because of unmitigated distress and their belief that they encounter impatient, rejecting, or hostile physicians. The physician may be frustrated because the patient refuses to accept explanation or fails to benefit from repeated reassurance and makes irrational, egotistical demands. There are large differences among the personalities of individuals who share hypochondriacal beliefs and fears; inevitably these reactions interact with the patient's personality, and the clinical presentations of hypochondriasis vary considerably. Numerous other phenomena, such as a tendency toward depression, low pain threshold, and a dependent personality may complicate the neurosis but are not essential features.

Treatments

There are no adequate controlled studies of the treatment of hypochondriasis. Either the published studies deal with similar conditions, such as physical diseases with hypochondriacal tendencies (Cooper et al. 1975), or the design of the study was unsuitable to evaluate the effects of treatment (Kellner and Sheffield 1971). There are several uncontrolled studies of hypochondriasis in which the outcome of treatment was evaluated in a fairly large number of patients, and these show that a substantial proportion of patients had improved or had recovered (Kellner 1983; Kenyon 1964; Pilowsky 1968).

The recommendations presented here are based on controlled studies of similar disorders (these are summarized in the sections of undifferentiated somatoform disorder and somatoform pain disorder), on uncontrolled studies of hypochondriasis

(Kellner 1982), on research in psychotherapy in general, and on research findings on the psychopathology of hypochondriasis.

The reasons for choosing a particular therapeutic approach are briefly summarized, and the views of some of the authors who advocated a similar approach are quoted. The controversies in the literature are not discussed in detail; views on management, the rationale, and the research on which these recommendations are based have been described elsewhere (Kellner 1986). Alternate approaches are listed when there is some research evidence, or at least case histories, to support these methods.

The principles of the psychotherapeutic strategies can be summarized as follows: a physical examination repeated when necessary to assure the patient; concurrent treatment of coexisting psychiatric disorders; explanatory therapy that includes emphasis on the innocuousness of the phenomena; and accurate information about the psychophysiologic processes involved. The patient is made aware of his selective perception, and his perception is retrained; deliberate suggestion is used when this is in keeping with accurate information such as the excellent prognosis.

Physical Examination and Reassurance

Before psychotherapy is attempted, several steps should be taken: the patient should have a thorough physical examination, and previous physicians' records and hospital charts should be requested. This allows a review of previous treatments and avoids unnecessary new investigations. A few new laboratory investigations may need to be ordered because some patients, particularly those with conspicuous psychiatric disorders, have physical diseases that have been overlooked (Jamieson and Merskey 1985). These procedures also signify to the patient that his condition is taken seriously by the new therapist. If no substantial physical abnormality is found, the initial explanation should be brief and simple enough to be clearly remembered: for example, "You are in excellent physical health (as opposed to "there is nothing wrong with you" or "it is psychosomatic") and, "these cramps can be extremely unpleasant and they may take a long time to go away." It appears that in chronic hypochondriasis, physical examination is at best only temporarily effective; however, when combined with appropriate reassurance, it appears to have a cumulative effect (Kessel 1979; Mayou 1976; Pilowsky 1968; Salter 1972; Sapira 1972). A brief physical examination should be made when new symptoms appear, or the patient believes that he has developed a new illness since the last examination (Altman 1978; Drossman 1978; Gillespie 1928). Once therapy has progressed and rapport has been established, a telephone interview with explanation and reassurance is often adequate. With repetition, reassurances which were initially ineffective, or effective only for a short time, tend to have longer effects, appear to be more frequently recalled, and when recalled, carry more conviction than at the beginning of treatment.

Exploration

The psychological exploration should initially be aimed at the patient's fears and beliefs about his illness. These may be overwhelming, and attempts to discuss issues other than his fears may be regarded by the patient as irrelevant. Most writers recommend that a patient should be allowed, even encouraged, to talk about his physical symptoms and that the physician should pay close attention to his physical complaints (Adler 1981; Gillespie 1928; Kenyon 1978). Moreover, many hypochondriacal patients miss the opportunity to talk about their distress with someone who understands how they feel. In their usual encounters with physicians, the medical history has been limited to brief routine questions about symptoms, followed by orders of laboratory investigations and prescriptions of treatment. There are substantial differences among patients who display hypochondriacal behavior, and it is important to explore their fears and beliefs before specific treatment strategies are planned. The exploration helps in the choice of sequence of psychotherapeutic strategies and in their emphasis; however, a few general principles apply.

Persuasion

With a patient who believes that he suffers from an undetected physical disease, devising methods to convince him that his symptoms are innocuous and his beliefs are false is crucial to progress. Unless the patient's conviction that he suffers from a dangerous undiagnosed disease changes, it will continue to reinforce the psychopathology which is responsible for the heightened perception of somatic sensations and other phenomena of hypochondriasis.

Frequency of Sessions

Initially, the frequency of sessions should be at least once a week. Frequent sessions have a reassuring effect on the patient, especially if he's free to call for additional appointments when he is in a panic and believes that he has acquired a new disease. This approach can help avoid a visit to an emergency room, which often leads to the acquisition of another diagnosis, such as hypoglycemia, allergy, or menopause. Only at a later stage, when the patient's beliefs have changed and his fears abated, can sessions become infrequent for follow-up treatment. Only in patients who have chronic hypochondriasis and in whom all treatment has failed should the sessions be infrequent; regular, brief office appointments, usually a few weeks apart, are helpful in assuring the patient of the physician's care and attention even when he has no symptoms to report (Brown and Vaillant 1981; Busse 1956; Leonhard 1968; Turnbull 1974).

Explanation and Information

Most patients do not understand the relationship between emotions and somatic symptoms as it applies to them. The terms used and the examples given should be in keeping with the patient's ability to understand. Explanatory therapy can focus on topics as follows:

Accurate information. There is evidence from research in psychophysiology that accurate information about the relationship of a threatening stimulus and the somatic consequences can influence the severity of autonomic responses, subjective distress and behavior (Schachter and Singer 1962), conditioning of the heart rate (Lacey et al. 1955), and postoperative pain (Egbert et al. 1964). For example, the patient is told that somatic symptoms are exceedingly common: only a small proportion are caused by disease, and the rest are compatible with excellent physical health.

Selective perceptions. Once rapport has been established and the patient's belief that he has a serious disease has become intermittent, the patient may be willing to learn more about his psychophysiologic mechanisms. The therapist can explain that selective attention to one part of the body makes a person more aware of sensation in that part than in other parts. Examples can be given to show that a person may be distressed and complain about a vague ache around his heart, whereas he ignores a swollen and badly sprained ankle because he is not concerned about the injury, knowing it will heal. The therapist may emphasize a part of the patient's history: when distracted by an important event the patient was not aware, at that time, of discomfort.

It is important for the patient to understand that, just as learning to perceive a certain part of his body or certain symptoms took a long time, so will unlearning of this habit; initially, unlearning will frequently prove unsuccessful so that symptoms will recur for some time with their original intensity before mastery of the unlearning is obtained.

Counteracting iatrogenic beliefs.   Frequently diagnostic terms used by innumerable previous physicians are remembered but misunderstood, and many hypochondriacal patients believe that they suffer from a multitude of diseases. These may include terms like sinusitis, catarrh, chondritis, strained heart, and rheumatism. The patient may believe that his symptoms are caused by these various diseases though current symptoms may be obviously unrelated to the patient's physical abnormality, or the abnormality may be so trivial as to be out of proportion to the distress. If the patient has been given incorrect physical diagnoses by previous physicians, repeated explanation of the true nature of the symptoms is necessary as a form of counter propaganda since the patient must be persuaded that the previous diagnosis was in error.

Repetition, Suggestion, and Cognitive Exercises

Repetition

There is evidence that patients frequently either forget information or distort it (Ley and Spellman 1967; Mabry 1964). Psychophysiologic relationships are often difficult for the patient to grasp or to remember, and it is best to give a small amount of information at one time and to repeat the information. Even knowledgeable patients who are distressed may be unable to understand the physician's explanations. Repetition forms an essential part of working through and coaching because many patients find it difficult to learn new skills and habits.

Suggestion

Hypochondriacal patients have usually had varied treatments, including diverse psychoactive drugs, without responding to them; they also appear to be poor placebo responders. So, any suggestion in order to be helpful ought to have also another function, such as accurate information. For example, "If you manage to remain relaxed and manage to think of something else, the discomfort will be less noticeable than if you worry or panic." Examples from the patient's history can be given to emphasize this point.

Therapeutic Alliance and Empathy

There is evidence that empathy plays a part in nondirective psychotherapy. Many of these patients feel rejected by their previous physicians who were frustrated by their patients' frequent, irrational, and egotistical demands for attention. The new therapists, understanding that the patient really suffers and needs help, aids in establishing rapport and a therapeutic alliance.

Other Treatments

Physical Exercise

Several authors have suggested physical exercise in patients with psychophysiologic symptoms or hypochondriasis (Kulenkampff and Bauer 1960; Leonhard 1968). Several controlled studies suggest that physical exercise increases psychological wellbeing. In an uncontrolled study with neurocirculatory asthenia there was a substantial decrease in somatic symptoms after exercise (Shoenfeld et al. 1978). In an uncontrolled study of hypochondriasis, none of the patients participated in any regular exercise. They were advised to exercise regularly and, if feasible, to exercise when they felt anxious. Initially, most patients were reluctant to follow this advice, yet most of the improved patients greatly increased their physical activity as treatment progressed (Kellner 1982).

Disease Phobia

It is uncertain whether disease phobia requires different or additional techniques apart from those listed above for the treatment of disease convictions. If the patient clearly has only fear of disease without being convinced that he suffers from a disease, then several of the strategies enumerated above may be redundant. Kumar and Wilkinson (1971) successfully treated three cases of disease phobia with thought stopping. Floru (1973) treated two patients with disease phobia with systematic desensitization. O'Donnell (1978) treated a female patient with a severe cancer phobia and hypochondriacal behavior with a combination of hypnosis and implosion. Marks (1978) advocates flooding in imagery or by exposure to photographs of pathologic specimen as a treatment of choice in disease phobia. In an uncontrolled series of hypochondriacal patients treated with psychotherapy, two patients who had predominantly disease phobia were successfully treated with the psychotherapeutic strategies described (Kellner 1983).

Insight and Conventional Psychotherapy

Many patients with hypochondriacal preoccupations will reveal other psychopathology when their attitudes toward disease change. Rather than a process of symptom substitution occurring, the conflicts, previously overshadowed by dread of disease and somatic symptoms, become an object of attention and concern. Many of these patients require psychotherapy directed at these concerns. In other patients who initially appear to be hypochondriacal and have somatic complaints, it soon becomes apparent that neurotic conflicts, or environmental stress, were largely responsible for their distress and for some reason the somatic symptoms were presented to their physicians. These patients will choose to talk about topics other than their somatic complaints, and these will eventually remit as psychotherapy progresses. If hypochondriasis represents part of an atypical grief reaction, psychotherapy dealing with grief, such as described by Raphael (1975), should be incorporated in the treatment.

Treatment of Residual Somatic Symptoms and Pain

Some patients, despite abandoning their conviction of suffering from a severe physical disease, have residual somatic symptoms, including pain. Additional strategies, such as are described in the section on somatoform pain disorder, may have to be adopted.

Some patients in whom hypochondriasis has lasted for a long time appear to have adapted to a life of an invalid. Some have a physical disease, in addition to hypochondriacal beliefs and attitudes. The methods described are often inadequate to deal with the habit of being ill or the advantages of being regarded as disabled. Additional treatments may have to be adopted, perhaps such as those proposed by Cooper et al. (1975), and others aimed at changing the patients' habits, motivations, and goals (Ford and Long 1977; Wooley et al. 1978). Some of the methods described in the section on somatization disorder may be adopted.

If somatic symptoms persist or become worse, the diagnosis needs to be reconsidered.

Group Therapy

The comments about group therapy for somatization disorder probably apply also to hypochondriasis. With patients who are convinced they have a serious disease, the therapist should remain active, focusing on strategies as discussed in this section. In other words, the treatment should be similar to that of individual therapy, given for a group of patients together; moreover, group therapy may also have other advantages as discussed in the section on somatization disorder.

Therapeutic Emphases

To determine which of the recommended techniques are beneficial and which are superfluous, or perhaps even detrimental, will require several controlled studies to test individual hypothesis. Simple good doctoring is probably the best initial treatment. The patient should be treated with interest, compassion, and patience, and the therapist should have attributes which he would want his own doctor to possess if he suffered from the dreadful fears and beliefs of a hypochondriacal patient. If a trial of this approach fails to induce at least intermittent doubts and intermittent improvement, other treatment approaches need to be added, starting with strategies which seem to fit the patient's psychopathology and are the least time consuming. The optimal combination is likely to differ from one individual to another since there are large variations in personality, beliefs, and fears among the patients who share the diagnosis of hypochondriasis.

Drug Treatments

here is no evidence that drug treatment is effective in primary hypochondriasis, yet drug treatment is often indicated when the patient is severely distressed and not benefiting adequately from psychotherapy. If drug treatment is used, it is largely directed at coexisting anxiety or depression or at coexisting somatic symptoms such as caused by the fibrositis-myalgia syndrome or irritable bowel syndrome.

Most hypochondriacal patients referred for psychiatric treatment have had a variety of drugs to which they have not responded adequately. However, often these drugs were prescribed in inadequate doses or inappropriate combinations. Sometimes drug treatment is strikingly effective in these patients.

The first consideration is to determine whether the patient also suffers from a depression (Kenyon 1964; Pilowsky 1970) because hypochondriasis may be a symptom of an endogenous depression (major depression melancholic type), and may remit once the depression is effectively treated (Burns 1971; Kellner et al. 1987; Kenyon 1964; Ladee 1966; Lesse 1967). If there is evidence of depression, or at least a suspicion that it is a substantial contributing factor, the therapist should assume that the hypochondriasis is secondary to depression and treat it initially as such. In view of the added antianxiety effects of imipramine (Covi et al. 1974), which seem to occur without the risk of habituation and dependence, this drug may be a suitable choice even if there is a generalized anxiety state, especially if the patient has spontaneous panic attacks. Phenelzine has similar advantages (Sheehan et al. 1980) and offers the second choice for the patient who cannot tolerate the side effects of imipramine and those of other nonmonoamine oxidase inhibitor antidepressants. In an uncontrolled study, tranylcypromine appears to be effective in patients with somatic complaints and hypochondriacal tendencies (Lesse 1967). If hypochondriasis is secondary to panic disorder, effective drug treatment of this disorder will relieve hypochondriacal fears and beliefs (Noyes et al. 1986).

If anxiety is only intermittent, or if antidepressants are unsuitable, benzodiazepines may be tried. Most attacks of panic in hypochondriacal patients do not appear to be spontaneous but rather the effect of fear associated with beliefs about disease and the vicious cycle of fear, somatic symptoms, and more fear. Once this cycle has been interrupted with adequate doses of antianxiety drugs, the patient can be spared long periods of these dreadful episodes; this can, in turn, allay a great deal of anticipatory anxiety and appears to reduce the frequency of these attacks. Such treatment should always be given in conjunction with psychotherapy with an explanation of the effect of the antianxiety drugs.

In treating hypochondriacal patients, the patient is better advised to take the drugs only intermittently, unless there is a generalized state. In severe generalized anxiety, patients appear to benefit from high doses of continuous medication for a few weeks to allay anxiety as much as possible. The patient should be instructed to reduce the total amount, to take less when not feeling afraid and later to take the dose only if acutely distressed, "like aspirin for headaches." He must be told that the medication is not going to relieve all his physical symptoms, but it may help him to relax. Once relaxed, he should find it easier to avoid paying attention to physical discomforts or the belief that he is ill and to concentrate on other matters. With effective treatment and the passage of time, the patient takes drugs less frequently and in successful cases stops taking them altogether.

Electroconvulsive Therapy

There are several reports of hypochondriacal patients treated with ECT (Burns 1971; Kenyon 1964; Kreitman et al. 1965; Ladee 1966; Pilowsky 1968). Some studies show conflicting results; several authors found the presence of hypochondriasis to be an indicator of a poor prognosis with ECT (Carney et al. 1965; Hobson 1953; Roberts 1959), yet others reported striking improvements in a few patients (Burns 1971; Kreitman et al. 1965). The likeliest explanation for this discrepancy lies in the differences among hypochondriacal patients in the different studies. There is evidence to suggest that those with endogenous depression (melancholic type) respond well to ECT, whereas those with depressive neurosis and hypochondriacal features have poor responses; this would suggest that the response to ECT depends on the kind of depression rather than on the presence or absence of hypochondriacal features.

Psychosurgery

A few authors recommend psychosurgery in severe and intractable cases of hypochondriasis (Mayer-Gross et al. 1969; Bernstein et al. 1975; Kenyon 1976). There are only a few published case histories. Those who have written on this topic tend to agree that it should be the last resort, considered only in the seriously disabled patients tormented by symptoms that have failed to respond to other methods of treatment (Kenyon 1976). At present there is no evidence that it is an effective treatment in hypochondriasis.

Monosymptomatic Hypochondriasis and Dysmorphophobia

There are several terms for monosymptomatic hypochondriasis in the literature, such as circumscribed hypochondria. Delusions of parasitosis (or dermatozoiasis) or chronic tactile hallucinosis constitute a subgroup of this syndrome. The DSM-III-R (American Psychiatric Association 1987) term is delusional (paranoid) disorder—somatic. From the description of case histories it appears that various psychiatric disorders can present as monosymptomatic hypochondriasis (Hallen 1970; Kellner 1986; Ladee 1966; Munro and Chmara 1982; Skott 1978; Vacek 1972), and delusions of parasitosis appear to have etiologies largely different from those of other types of circumscribed hypochondriasis (Skott 1978). Sometimes a patient who is neurotic may present with a clinical picture resembling monosymptomatic hypochondriacal delusions (Hallen 1970); in these patients an attempt of psychotherapy should be made. In the patients who are delusional, pimozide has been reported to lead to striking improvements (Riding and Munro 1975). In a double-blind crossover study of patients with delusions of infestations, both itch, but delusions improved more with pimozide than with placebo (Hamann and Avnstorp 1982). There is one case report of a patient with delusions of parasitosis who failed to respond to several treatments but responded to treatment with parstelin (Roberts and Roberts 1977). Conversely, there is a case report of another monoamine oxidase inhibitor (phenelzine) causing these delusions (Liebowitz et al. 1978). Successful treatment of two cases described as monosymptomatic hypochondriasis with antidepressants was reported by Brotman and Jenike (1984); all previous treatments had failed.

Body dysmorphic disorder (300.700). There are no adequate studies of the treatment of body dysmorphic disorder (dysmorphophobia), only isolated case reports.

Patients with body dysmorphic disorder, a persistent false belief of being deformed or preoccupation with imagined defective physical appearance, are remarkably resistent to all kinds of treatments. The strategies outlined in the section on hypochondriasis may be tried, but psychotherapy is often unsuccessful and a good response to drug treatment is rare. A recent report suggests that exposure therapy and persuasion is helpful in some patients (Marks and Mishan 1988). Antidepressants and neuroleptics may be tried; there is one case report of a patient with dysmorphophobia having improved with doxepin (Brotman and Jenike 1984). The adjustment after cosmetic surgery is poor in a substantial proportion of patients (Connolly and Gibson 1978).

Chapter 192

Undifferentiated Somatoform Disorder and Somatoform Disorder Not Otherwise Specified

These new categories replace the 0057-14 category of atypical somatoform disorder. The latter was defined in the DSM-III (American Psychiatric Association 1980) as a residual category to be used when the predominant disturbance is a presentation of physical symptoms or complaints, not explainable on the basis of demonstrable organic findings or a known pathophysiologic mechanism and apparently linked to psychological factors.

In order to discuss the treatment of the symptom, a brief overview of the nature of these complaints is presented here. Somatic symptoms are extremely common (Kellner and Sheffield 1973; Wadsworth et al. 1972). About 60 to 80 percent of a normal population will experience at least one somatic symptom in any one week (Reidenberg and Lowenthal 1968). A large proportion of patients presenting to physicians and surgeons do not suffer from physical disease but from somatic complaints for which no organic cause can be found on routine investigations; the figures range from 20 to 84 percent (Christian et al. 1954; Gomez and Dally 1977; Katon 1982; Kellner 1965; Kessel 1960; Mayou 1973, 1976). Thus, taken as a group, functional somatic symptoms (FSS) constitute a major public health problem because a large part of physicians' time is spent examining, investigating, and treating these patients (Lowy 1976). Most of the patients are treated by nonpsychiatric physicians; they are usually referred to a psychiatrist only when the disorder is unusually distressing, does not remit with treatment, or is complicated by another psychiatric disorder.

For the purposes of this chapter, FSS—the bodily symptom of somatizing patients—are defined as somatic symptoms which are not caused by pathology detectable by physical examination or routine laboratory investigations although specific physiologic changes can be detected in some of these symptoms by special techniques. The term is not entirely satisfactory; however, it demarcates these symptoms from those caused by physical disease, and this criterion has been used in numerous published studies of somatization. These symptoms occur in normal individuals; they are common in psychiatric patients, and many would be regarded as a part of another syndrome, such as anxiety or depression, or classified as undifferentiated somatoform disorder. Not all symptoms can be labeled confidently as functional (for example, gastric discomfort associated with hyperemia and hyperactivity of gastric musculature precipitated by emotion is an example of a psychophysiologic symptom). Yet the distinction from gastric ulcers—a physical disease in which psychological factors may play a part (Psychological Factors Affecting Physical Condition 316.00)—is important. These diseases, unlike functional symptoms, can be life-threatening and usually require medical, and sometimes surgical, treatment; their etiology tends to be different and somewhat different psychotherapeutic strategies appear to be appropriate (Conte and Karasu 1981; Kellner 1975).

Somatic symptoms are decidedly more common at times of depression, anxiety, or other forms of arousal. Many of these symptoms are caused by excessive activity of the autonomic nervous system, with subsequent smooth muscle contraction, increased tension in voluntary muscle, or other disturbances of physiologic function, such as increased secretion of gastric juice (Kellner 1985). According to the DSM-III-R (American Psychiatric Association 1987) classification of an undifferentiated somatoform disorder includes only those physical symptoms or complaints that are not explainable on a known pathophysiologic mechanism. However, a large proportion of patients with functional somatic symptoms need to be classified in this category because the exact cause of the disorder is usually not known; on routine physical examination and laboratory investigation no adequate cause is found. So the detection of the exact mechanism—for example, whether there are increased contractions of smooth muscle—is often not feasible. Thus many patients with multiple somatic symptoms such as "diverse somatizers" (Cloninger et al. 1984), who do not have another psychiatric disorder such as depression or anxiety, do not satisfy the criteria for any other somatoform disorder and by definition belong to the category of undifferentiated somatoform disorder.

Studies of Psychotherapy

Patients with Somatic Complaints

Early outcome studies suggested that neurotic patients who had predominantly somatic symptoms responded less well to conventional psychotherapy than patients with predominantly emotional symptoms (Rosenberg 1954; Stone et al. 1961); yet several uncontrolled studies, as well as controlled studies, have shown good results of treatment. For example, a large proportion of patients in family practice with functional somatic symptoms completely recovered with the physician's explanation and reassurance only (Kellner 1963; Thomas 1978).

There are several controlled studies of patients with functional somatic symptoms. Some of these are with patients that might be classified retrospectively as undifferentiated somatoform disorder, and others might be classified in another category of the DSM-III-R (for example, Psychological Factors Affecting Physical Condition, 316.000). But the treatments employed are applicable to the disorders discussed in this section.

Draspa (1959) used a combination of psychotherapeutic techniques in patients who had muscular pain for which no organic cause was found. A group of 112 patients were matched with another 112 with the same complaint. Both groups had physical treatments, but the experimental group also had psychological treatments that consisted of the following: 1) teaching the patient passive and active relaxation; 2) reassuring him that the pain was only muscular and posed no dangers; and 3) giving insight into the causes of excessive muscular contraction and so "promoting self-adjustment to changed internal or external environmental situations." Almost twice as many patients in the experimental group as in the control group became free of pain. The mean numbers of attendances for the experimental group was only half that of the control group, and recovery took twice as long in the control group.

Cooper et al. (1975) carried out a study of veterans who had physical illnesses and hypochondriacal personalities and who regarded themselves as more disabled than their physical condition would justify. The experimental group was treated with an unusual therapeutic approach. Treatment consisted of sensory deprivation for two-and-one-half hours, preceded and followed by an interview designed to structure the interpersonal meaning of the experience to selectively reinforce social roles which were antithetical to the patient's characteristic maladaptive interpersonal behavior. For example, in treatment of patients with passive-dependent personalities, the interviewer assumed a role of active warmth before sensory deprivation, then afterwards changed to passive warmth to allow the patients to become more dominant. Veterans in a control group of 10 had only routine medical treatment. On a follow-up, the 10 experimentally treated patients attended medical clinics at a greatly reduced rate, whereas the patients in the control group visited the clinic as often as usual.

There are two studies of psychotherapy of the irritable bowel syndrome. Schenecke and Schüffel (1975) treated patients with an irritable bowel syndrome with brief psychotherapy consisting of six sessions of 20 minutes each and compared these with placebo treatment and with the effects of an experimental drug. Psychotherapy was no more effective than other treatments in this study. Svedlund et al. (1983) carried out a controlled study of psychotherapy in outpatients with irritable bowel syndrome. The patients in the control group had routine medical care; the patients in the experimental group were scheduled for 10 one-hour sessions of psychotherapy over three months, "aimed at modifying maladaptive behavior in finding new solutions to problems. The focus was on means of coping with stress and emotional problems. Sometimes the more educative or teaching strategy about relations between stressful life events and abdominal symptoms was used. . . ." At the end of this study, because of dropouts, the mean number of psychotherapy sessions was 7.4. Both groups improved, but improvement in the psychotherapy group was significantly greater for abdominal pain and bowel dysfunction; this improvement continued after 15 months, whereas the control group had deteriorated slightly.

There were several differences in design between the two studies of psychotherapy in the irritable bowel syndrome, and these may be the reasons for the differences in outcome; for example, in the Schenecke-Schüffel study the number of psychotherapy sessions was limited to six sessions of 20 minutes each, which appears inadequate for the treatment of a long-standing disorder.

Sjödin et al. (1986) carried out a controlled study of psychotherapy of patients with peptic ulcers. Apart from examining the course of the disease, they also examined the effect of psychotherapy on somatic symptoms that were unrelated to gastrointestinal disease. Over 100 outpatients with chronic peptic ulcers were allocated either to routine medical care alone or combined with dynamically oriented individual short-term psychotherapy. The mean number of psychotherapy sessions over three months was 7.6 with an upper limit of 10 sessions. The emphasis was on coping with stress and emotional problems. "Sometimes a more directive strategy was used to draw attention to associations between stressful life events and abdominal symptoms." The therapists also aimed to help find new solutions to the identified problems. There was a significantly greater improvement in the psychotherapy group of somatic symptoms in general as well as in ulcer symptoms, and these differences in outcome were maintained on a 15-month follow-up.

Headaches

Since many patients with functional somatic symptoms suffer also from various kinds of headaches, the studies of the treatment of headaches are briefly reviewed.

Muscle contraction or tension headaches have been treated largely with EMG biofeedback and deep muscular relaxation; migraine headaches have been treated with temperature biofeedback and deep muscular relaxation. Tarler-Benlolo (1978) suggested that a combination of relaxation and biofeedback would provide the best treatment in muscle contraction headaches. Several reviewers concluded that in muscle contraction headaches or tension headaches EMG biofeedback and muscle relaxation training were equally effective and both superior to placebo treatments (Editorial, Lancet 1980; Jessup et al. 1979; Nuechterlein and Holroyd 1980). Reinking and Hutchings (1981) concluded that the long-term outcome depended more on the continued practice of relaxation than on the initial method of treatment. Blanchard et al. (1980), in a detailed survey of published research on the treatment of headaches, concluded that for tension headaches: "Frontal EMG biofeedback alone, or combined with relaxation training, or relaxation training alone, were equally effective and significantly superior to medication placebo or psychological placebo."

Jessup et al. (1979) concluded that the application of temperature biofeedback in migraine headaches remains of unproven value; on the other hand, Prima et al. (1979) expressed the view based on their survey that temperature biofeedback is preferable to other methods. Johansson and Ost (1982) argued that research had not examined adequately the crucial elements in temperature feedback training, including whether the patient had learned to control his temperature even without feedback and whether he could apply temperature control in critical situations of everyday life. Blanchard et al. (1980) concluded that for migraine headaches, temperature biofeedback alone, relaxation training alone, or temperature feedback combined with autogenic training were equally effective and significantly superior to medication placebo.

Mitchell and Mitchell (1971) and Mitchell and White (1977) compared various methods of treating migraine headaches in three studies. Treatments included relaxation training, systematic desensitization, a method combining systematic desensitization and assertive training ("combined desensitization"), combined desensitization using written instructions together with an audiotape, and no-treatment control groups. The number of patients in each group was small. The findings suggest that the combination of desensitization and assertive training, whether supervised by a live therapist or learned from written instructions and audiotape, were superior to other treatments in reducing the frequency of migraine attacks.

In several studies, cognitive strategies, including stress inoculation and the teaching of coping skills, were compared to other methods. Some of these studies were carried out with only a few patients and require replications with larger samples. Holroyd et al. (1977) compared the treatment of tension headaches with stress-coping training (consisting of cognitive reappraisal of the situation, attention deployment, coping self-instructions, and imagery), EMG biofeedback, and a waiting-list control group, each group containing 10 subjects. Only the stress-coping training group showed significant improvement at the end of follow-up.

Discussion

These studies deal with diverse groups of patients who had only somatic complaints in common; however, it needs to be emphasized that all had chronic symptoms. It is not possible to assume that similar treatment will be effective in patients with all kinds of functional somatic symptoms. Judging by the low drop-out rates in some of these studies, it appears that these patients were motivated and persistent, which may have been one of the reasons for the successful outcomes.

The findings of studies of patients with somatic symptoms (some of these are listed in the section on somatoform pain disorder) suggest that a substantial proportion improve or recover with or without formal psychotherapy; however, psychotherapy accelerates improvement and, in some, may have aided recovery which would not have occurred with routine medical treatment alone.

There are several possible reasons why somatizing patients have been regarded as largely unsuitable for psychotherapy. Early studies with psychiatric patients suggest that patients with somatic symptoms had, on the whole, a worse outcome than neurotic patients or those with mainly affective disorders. Yet, controlled studies suggest that the outcome of psychotherapy is as good or better with somatizing patients as with patients who have other psychiatric disorders. Several authors—for example, Sifneos (1973), Nemiah (1975), and Ford (1983)—expressed the view that somatizing patients have alexithymia, are deficient in emotional expression, manifest their distress in body language, and therefore prove less accessible to verbal psychotherapy. However, it is also possible that some patients, who are distressed because they are preoccupied with somatic symptoms, may not attend to emotional intrapsychic processes, and may only be less suitable for psychotherapy that aims at insight and solution of internal conflicts. Conventional nondirective verbal techiques may be inappropriate for these patients, at least initially, because they do not address themselves to the patient's concern about somatic symptoms and his fear or conviction of having a serious disease. The poor outcome of the early studies appears to have been caused in part by the use of inappropriate methods of psychotherapy.

Antidepressants and Antianxiety Drugs

The principles of the choice of psychotropic drugs for the treatment of somatic symptoms are the same as in the treatment of anxiety disorders and depressive disorders as discussed elsewhere in this volume. Psychotropic drugs should be used in patients with functional somatic symptoms to treat the coexisting affective disorder or should be used if the bodily distress is clearly relieved by these drugs.

Tricyclic antidepressants are effective in the treatment of somatic symptoms; several studies show antidepressants reducing somatic symptoms in depressed patients more than placebo. Covi et al. (1974) and Kahn et al. (1981), in two large, well-designed double-blind drug trials, compared the effects of several drugs on anxiety and depression in nonpsychotic depressed and anxious outpatients. Imipramine proved more effective than diazepam and chlordiazepoxide (CDP) in reducing anxiety as well as depression, but differences between drugs in the reduction of somatic symptoms were inconsistent. Early in treatment, CDP appeared superior to imipramine, whereas imipramine became more effective later. Sheehan et al. (1980) found in anxious psychiatric outpatients a significantly greater decrease in the somatic symptom score of the Hopkins Symptom Checklist with imipramine and with phenelzine than with placebo. In patients with generalized anxiety disorder, alprazolam was more effective in relieving somatic symptoms than imipramine, whereas the reverse was true for psychic symptoms (Hoehn-Saric et al. 1985).

There is evidence from controlled double-blind drug trials that benzodiazepines reduce somatic symptoms in patients with anxiety disorders. Uhlenhuth et al. (1982) and Glass et al. (1985) surveyed placebo-controlled studies with benzodiazepines.

The main purposes of these surveys were to compare commonly used rating and self-rating scales and to determine which of these methods is more sensitive in detecting significant differences between an active psychotropic drug and placebo. However, the survey shows clearly that benzodiazepines were more effective than placebo in several studies in reducing anxiety symptoms as well as somatic symptoms regardless of whether they were rated by the psychiatrist or self-rated by the patient.

Propranolol has been found to decrease somatic symptoms in anxious patients and also to reduce anxiety somewhat (Cole et al. 1979; Kellner et al. 1974; Noyes 1982; Tyrer 1976). There is no conclusive evidence from controlled studies that effects of beta-blockers on functional somatic symptoms are substantially different from those of benzodiazepines, although at least some therapeutic differences seem likely because of the known differences in neuropharmacologic effects.

In one double-blind, placebo-controlled study, tybamate proved more effective in reducing somatic symptoms than emotional symptoms in anxious, neurotic patients (Rickels et al. 1968). However, this is the only study with tybamate in which this effect is reported, and it requires replication before it can be concluded that tybamate has these specific effects.

Chapter 193

Conversion Disorders

The Context of Treatment

Conversion disorders, by convention, are about a loss or change in bodily function. The classical conversion symptoms are paralysis of a limb, loss of sight, deafness, and glove and stocking anesthesias. They are diagnosed by the discovery of a discrepancy on physical examination. The discrepancy is that the patient can be shown to do things with his muscles or sensory system which he believes to be beyond his power. Dissociative disorders which are believed to be identical with them in regard to mechanisms and significance represent a loss or change in psychological function. Hysterical amnesia is the model of dissociative disorders. Besides the criteria given in DSM-III (American Psychiatric Association 1980), it is worth noting that the conflict may be essentially intrapsychic with the external stimulus serving only as a trigger for the illness. Further, the existence of a psychological problem is first indicated by neurologic or other examination which demonstrates that a response occurs in a part which a patient believes is not functioning (Head 1922). The latter finding is often not available for sensory complaints such as pain but can be very useful in motor symptoms.

The treatment of individual conversion symptoms depends greatly upon the context. Monosymptomatic conversion disorders may occur in several circumstances. The traditional case is a young patient, usually a dependent female, faced with a difficult emotional conflict; but male hysteria, first described in detail in relation to accidents (Reynolds 1869) was acknowledged, inescapably, after the "shell-shock" label of the First World War was better understood.

First, perhaps the most common circumstance in current North American practice is a hysterical exacerbation of physical illness. In its mildest form it may be no more than a reaction to physical examination based on anxiety. The patient is tense and resists or gives way inappropriately during physical examination, producing a hysterical sign. Neurologists or internists or orthopedic surgeons who find this symptom on physical examination tend to say that the patient is hysterical. Technically they are correct, but the patient is not really manifesting an established conversion complaint. He is merely showing a related psychological response in the specific circumstances of physical examination. Sometimes he is showing the response for a reason which must be counted as normal. He may have been asked to do something which will give him pain, and he refuses to use his arm or leg or back accordingly. This leads to a misdiagnosis of hysteria when the diagnosis should be "pain inhibition on physical examination."

Second, if the symptom is more persistent than discussed, and particularly with hysterical fits, it appears to represent an emphasis by the patient on a symptom which he does not feel is receiving adequate attention. Third, in a few instances like anticonvulsant drug intoxication, the symptom appears with the intoxication and remits with physical improvement such as reduction of the drug level, illustrating that impaired function of the brain can make a person more prone to conversion phenomena.

A fourth important circumstance is to be found when the conversion symptom occurs as part of another psychiatric syndrome. Occasionally, the conversion symptom is a precursor of schizophrenia but more often it is found as part of a depressive illness. Fifth, conversion symptoms are wont to develop in individuals with severe personality problems. Young and immature people and those under special stress may develop conversion symptoms without extreme personality difficulties. However, the chronic conversion symptom, for example, sustained paralysis with contractures, is frequently, if not always, associated with a severe personality problem, commonly a mixture of the classical hysterical (histrionic) personality and sociopathic traits. A history of childhood deprivation and abuse is frequent in these patients. The St. Louis group, incidentally, has arrived at a similar association from another direction, by demonstrating a relationship between somatization disorder in women and a family history of sociopathy in the male relatives.

Sixth, conversion symptoms are often part of an extensive somatization disorder with multiple other bodily symptoms, which is treated separately here. Seventh, conversion symptoms may be part of an epidemic. These diverse circumstances all influence the approach to treatment. Finally, conversion symptoms may occur in otherwise normal individuals under unbearable stress, such as that described in the trenches in the First World War or some of the more dreadful battle conditions in the Second World War.

Principles of Treatment

Cases of recent onset usually have a good outcome. This is a general principle in most psychiatric illness, albeit with a few exceptions. Hysterical complaints which arise in children usually have a a good prognosis with resolution of symptoms in approximately 63 percent (Proctor 1958). A worse long-term prognosis was found by Robins and O'Neal (1953), but they used a broader notion of hysteria and included cases of hypochondriasis and mixed psychoneuroses. On long-term follow-up of 23 patients who were reexamined, four had a state resembling somatization disorder and 11 had anxiety neurosis or other psychological or organic problems. Six more had other symptoms and only two were completely well. However, their basic concept of the illness was much broader. Hysterical symptoms or conversion symptoms in young persons under stress usually remit promptly (Ljungberg 1957; Slater and Glithero 1965) as do those in people under severe stress once it has been relieved (Carter 1949). Abnormal personality worsens the prognosis (Ljungberg 1957). Ciompi (1969), in a prolonged follow-up study with a mean duration of 34 years, found two patients with schizophrenia and two with epilepsy out of 38 patients. Conversion symptoms had largely disappeared, but two-thirds were mildly anxious, depressed, or hypochondriacal. Slater (1965) emphasized the emergence of organic disease on follow-up, but others (Merskey and Buhrich 1975; Whitlock 1967) showed it to be common and mostly recognizable at the time of diagnosis.

Overall, the general tendency of acute conversion symptoms is toward recovery with the emergence on follow-up of small numbers of patients with schizophrenia, bipolar disorder, and additional organic diagnoses (Ljungberg 1957; Merskey 1979; Ochitill 1982). Other signs of mild anxiety or depression are liable to be found in longer follow-up of patients who have had conversion symptoms (Ciompi 1969; Robins and O'Neal 1953).

It follows from psychoanalytical theory that the simple removal of the conversion symptoms by suggestion or by behavioral measures might lead to symptom substitution if the basic etiologic conflict or problem is not solved. This happens rarely in the practice of a neurologist (Carter 1949), perhaps because with acute illnesses the removal of symptoms by a procedure like hypnosis is often coupled with environmental change or alterations in the personal relationships which underlie the original mechanism of symptom production. Also, in cases of conversion symptoms secondary to drug intoxication, organic disease, or major psychiatric disorder, the treatment of the primary disorder can be sufficient to remove the patient's main problem. It is believed—though not documented in the research literature—that there is a risk of suicide or attempted suicide by patients from whom hysterical symptoms are removed abruptly, and this means that it is essential to provide an adequate structure for the treatment process so that if the patients' feelings and mood change, further support and help can readily be offered. This is necessary and good practice, whether the symptoms are removed abruptly or gradually.

Where symptoms arise against the background of a personality disorder or maladjustment, some response can be anticipated for the individual symptoms; but recurrences and other problems are usually inevitable so that long-term management of the personality problem or disorder has to be considered.

The largest number of cases was probably treated in the First World War (Merskey 1979). Experience in the Second World War favored both prompt sedation and acute abreactive techniques (Grinker and Spiegel 1943; Sargant and Shorvon 1945). Systematic reports of the results of treatment by suggestion (Carter 1949), by eclectic methods (Ljungberg 1957), or by psychoanalytic techniques (Fenichel 1930; Weber et al. 1967) are also available. However, there is a lack of standardized comparisons on the basis of descriptions of cases of comparable severity. Diagnoses, the presence of other illness whether organic or psychiatric, the duration of symptoms, the grouping of symptoms, the selection of samples, outcome criteria, and methods of treatment all vary enormously from sample to sample. No controlled prospective studies nor even adequate comparative studies have been done. Thus, recommendations for treatment are made against a background of clinical experience which has not been well organized and has scarcely been standardized.

Aims of Treatment

The removal of the symptom is usually the initial aim. If the symptom is neither unpleasant as with pain, nor disabling (e.g., blindness, paralysis), it may not matter to treat it. Thus, hysterical anesthesia of a limb, which is often iatrogenic and produced during examination, does not lead to obvious harm and ordinarily needs no direct attention. However, disabling symptoms and unpleasant ones clearly require resolution.

The second aim is no less important than the removal of symptoms. It is a review of the patient's overall adjustment, including his or her relationships at home, at work, and in the larger social environment as well as any intrapsychic difficulties that can be identified as important.

General Treatment and Management

The exclusion or recognition of concomitant organic disease is essential. For individual cases all the procedures suggested should occur in the context of a full initial interview with the patient and with other relevant persons like close family members. The following approaches may then be employed according to circumstances and preference.

Correction or Alleviation of Organic Disease

Since it is known that phenytoin and other drugs may cause hysterical symptoms when at a toxic level, it is important to review drug levels in the serum of any patient in whom this may be relevant to a hysterical symptom. A modest reduction of dosage is usually adequate to alter the situation although there is sometimes a delay of a few days, or a week or two following normalization of the level in the serum before the psychological symptom remits. Presumably, intracellular levels take longer to recover, just as serum measurements of thyroid function can normalize before the mental state will do so in hypothyroidism. Patients with epilepsy appear to be more prone to conversion seizures than patients without brain damage and are also liable to produce additional seizures if they think their existing condition is being inadequately treated, as well as for other reasons. Exploration of this aspect of the situation directly with the patient is normally desirable. Supporting evidence that fits are hysterical in type may be obtained through EEG studies or through the serum prolactin test with prolactin levels being considerably higher after an epileptic seizure than after a hysterical one (Trimble 1978). Other patients, for example, with multiple sclerosis, may have fears and uncertainties arising out of their experience of illness or may be acting at a regressed level because the disorder interferes somewhat with cerebral function. These elements of the patient's condition likewise may be managed either by discussion and review of the situation, or by appropriate nursing.

Psychologic support in tolerating chronic disability; arrangement of facilities or of work obligations; adjustment of the patients' expectations and the family expectations; and a revision of social commitments may all be necessary. These activities involve elements of psychological support and also of social support or practical help. Usually also, an approach of this type is assisted by a psychological explanation of the patients' major needs and inclinations, which can be adjusted internally or externally to adapt the individual to the situation in which he finds himself.

Indirect suggestion is inherent in this approach. A position is established that certain things will be done in consequence of which improvement is anticipated. This may happen overtly, covertly, and also unwittingly on the part of the therapist or the therapeutic team. Direct suggestion with or without hypnosis may also be employed.

Conversion Symptoms with Other Psychiatric Illnesses

Besides the search for organic illness, the clinician should also look for other psychiatric diagnoses, especially depression and sometimes schizophrenia, which may relate to the current complaint. If such disorders are found or are reasonably strongly suspected, the relevant treatment should be instituted with antidepressants or phenothiazines and other psychological and social techniques appropriate to those conditions. Principles of enquiry, support, and suggestion may also be applied.

Conversion Symptoms Without Other Conditions

In this situation too, the same psychological principles apply as in the other circumstances. Psychological support, social support, and practical help may all be employed, whether the patient is interviewed alone and a change of job is recommended, or whether marital or family therapy are instituted. The basic approach is one of support combined with indirect or direct suggestion initially, particularly for acute symptoms.

Direct suggestion may involve retraining or behavioral techniques. For example, aphonias have been cured by teaching patients that they can cough, then that they can say "ah" and then that they can manage more varied syllables (bah, pah) and so on until speech is resumed. This should always be undertaken with a background of psychological and social support.

Other Specific Treatments

Besides the treatments mentioned, which may be appropriate for any of the acute causes of conversion symptoms, a number of other specific measures have been employed. They may be noted as follows.

Hypnosis

There are essentially two views of hypnosis. One is that it is a special state, perhaps accompanied by altered consciousness but certainly physiologically different from normal waking or attention. In this state patients manage to do things they could not otherwise do to the same extent or receive suggestions which they would not otherwise follow. That view is challenged by the absence of relevant physiologic evidence which may distinguish hypnosis from other conditions of suggestion (Merskey 1971) and by the substantial work of Barber (1959) which indicates that task-motivating suggestions will produce as much effect in hypnosis as trance induction. The viewpoint preferred here is the latter one, but the former is also widely accepted. It can be said at a minimum that the procedure of offering hypnotic instructions or suggestions frequently results in the remission of acute conversion symptoms but not often in the improvement of chronic ones. It may well serve as an excellent face-saving maneuver for patients who believe in it—and encouragement for doctors who believe in it likewise. Apart from acute cases, it is open to question whether hypnosis has any place in the management of conversion disorder except as a means of establishing a relationship between the therapist and the patient. Other therapists will prefer to establish their relationship by interview techniques including formal face-to-face procedures and formal psychoanalytic measures.

Narcoanalysis

The injection of amylobarbitone sodium or other sedative medication, sometimes followed by an alerting substance like methylamphetamine, was widely used in acute cases of battle neurosis, many of them with hysterical features, following the Second World War (Sargant and Shorvon 1945). Simple sedation was also recommended by the same authors. The prognosis of these cases was good and the effects of the treatments apparently excellent. Currently, in civilian practice, there is little use for such measures although sometimes an acute stress-induced illness might be treated this way. Occasionally, narcoanalysis, and especially the injection of methylamphetamine, may serve as a means of encouraging the patient to feel able to talk about something on which his or her feelings have previously been inhibited. In established chronic conversion symptoms, these treatments seem to offer little.

Insight Psychotherapy

A single clinical interview or one or two more sessions of further communication between therapist and patient results in some patients developing striking insight into the background and origin of particular symptoms. Thus, this approach which is noninvasive, and may be minimally intrusive, is an excellent benign measure for the initial management of patients with hysterical symptoms. If acute symptoms do not respond to this approach, then some of the other more dramatic measures, like hypnosis and narcoanalysis, may be legitimately employed. However, if neither dramatic treatments nor brief, gentle treatments seem to work, there may be a case for prolonged psychotherapeutic management. Anecdotal evidence on single cases of hysteria treated in this fashion begins with Freud (Breuer and Freud 1893–95) and is common in the psychoanalytic and general psychiatric literature. Systematic studies or reports on groups of patients are less common. However, Fenichel (1930) reported 10 years' experience from the Berlin Psychoanalytic Institute involving 105 cases of conversion hysteria, of whom 74 continued in therapy for at least six months. Forty-six of those patients were cured or much improved while 28 were improved or without change. Weber et al (1967) reported on patients treated at the Columbia Psychoanalytic Clinic. Only approximately one-third of those patients with conversion symptoms were free of them at the time of discharge from treatment. It is fair to observe that these may well have represented relatively chronic cases.

Behavior Therapy

The management of hysteria has always included some behavioral elements, although these strategies were described by different terms. A variety of manipulations have been employed including removing patients from environments in which they were prone to symptoms (e.g., Carter 1853). Lazarus (1963) reported the outcome for 27 patients with conversion or dissociative symptoms, among some others treated with behavior therapy; a multimodal approach, sometimes involving the ancillary use of hypnosis, medication, or more than one therapist, produced marked improvement or recovery of 19 (71 percent) patients after an average of 14 treatment sessions. Lasting success was also obtained with patients who had been disabled for years despite other approaches (Liebson 1969; Munford et al. 1976). Yealland (1918) used electrical stimulation in a thoroughly aversive fashion, even though it may not have been admitted. Dickes (1974) reported a retrospective chart review comparing behavior therapy with traditional measures. He reviewed 16 patients altogether. Bird (1979) gives a detailed review of this topic and notes obvious flaws in Dickes' study including possible nonrandom allocation of patients and limited follow-up. Of the patients treated with behavior therapy, a substantially larger proportion appeared to have recovered. Scallet et al. (1976) reviewed 23 reports on the management of "chronic hysteria" which included patients with conversions. Sixty-two percent of outpatients from all sources and 65 percent of inpatients were improved although the duration of improvement is often not clear. This study is described later. This finding may apply as well to many patients with monosymptomatic conversion complaints, and more reports are emerging in the current literature. Of course, if conflicts are recognized and points can be identified where psychological management may make a difference, it would be very important to provide psychotherapy and alteration of personal relationships as well as behavior therapy to accelerate symptomatic improvement.

Somatic Treatments

Lithium treatment has been reported by Van Putten and Alban (1977) as being very successful in one protracted case. This raises the possibility of an affective disorder which is undiagnosed or difficult to diagnose. Reviews of electroconvulsive treatment (Milligan 1946; Sands 1946) report recoveries and improvements in hysteria after ECT, but the literature does not give adequate descriptions of the follow-up of conversion reactions treated in this way for conclusions to be drawn about its efficacy. However, since it is well accepted that a number of patients with hysterical symptoms may have depression which is sometimes poorly recognized, it is likely that at least some of the responses are due to the effective treatment of depression which has conditioned the appearance of the conversion symptom. We have also known ECT to be recommended in the form of a single shock; the patient, while still confused after the ECT, is kept walking or maintaining his apparently lost function until he is sufficiently aware to be able to continue with it in a clear state of consciousness. This could only be justified in an extreme case or after the failure of all other measures. Walter et al. (1972) reported the use of a combination of multiple somatic treatments (sedation, phenothiazines, ECT, and antidepressants concomitantly). The patients treated had failed other methods, and 39 percent showed symptomatic recovery or marked improvement. These approaches using rather potent combinations of drugs with a clear risk of toxicity would only be appropriate, if at all, in patients who had failed to respond to a careful trial of less hazardous measures.

Social Therapy

Certain social measures may be highly beneficial to patients with conversion disorder. These treatments may not be directly recommended for patients but can occur concomitantly with medical management. Anecdotal reports are quite common that a combination of suggestion and catharsis, such as experienced by participants in meetings of faith healers will lead to remission or perhaps to recovery in some patients with conversion disorder. Similarly, exorcism and other religious procedures may be associated with cures. Specific social maneuvers can also benefit the management of epidemics of hysterical symptoms. For example, Nitzkin (1976) reported that an outbreak at a local elementary school ceased with a public announcement of the diagnosis of "mass hysteria." Mohr and Bond (1982) managed a small group of girls at the heart of one chronic epidemic affecting 63 children by supervising them at one neurology clinic. Armstrong and Patterson (1975) managed an epidemic outbreak in a series of Cree villages by a combination of methods. Children were interviewed individually, parents were given an opportunity to ventilate their feelings, and both groups were reassured and given information on undramatic methods of handling attacks of hysterical fits. Liquid chlorpromazine was made available for administration (which is not a recommended treatment), and the procedures were reviewed with community leaders and other influential people. Social gathering around individuals having seizures was discouraged. Increased recreational programming was suggested for the groups, and the epidemic subsided.

The ending of an epidemic by means of a ritual procedure undertaken by a local healer (Pawang) is reported by Teoh (1975). Resolution of the problem by closing schools, although not a very satisfactory method, is noted by Dhadphale and Shaikh (1983) and by Adomakoh (1973). The latter author emphasizes the importance of segregation of leading or affected individuals in the epidemic. Sirois (1974) lists responses to epidemics of which isolation of affected individuals and the closing of schools are the most common.

Chapter 194

Factitious Disorder with Physical Symptoms

Factitious disorder is one category of abnormal illness behavior in which the individual deliberately produces signs of a disease or gives a false history of disease or both. This chapter deals with the physical variant of the disorder; the psychological form is described elsewhere in this volume. The main aim of patients with this disorder is to receive medical care, but sometimes other secondary motives, such as obtaining narcotics, may also play a part.

The history of factitious disorders extends for centuries. Hector Gavin (1843) wrote a treatise on these disorders. He advised that "The difficulty in the detection of untruth, fraud, and deceit is exactly in the ratio of ignorance and paucity of the resources of the observer." Asher (1951) described patients who traveled widely, telling dramatic medical histories. He termed their condition as "Münchausen's syndrome," after the Paul Bunyan-like storyteller, Baron Federick von Münchausen. Asher described variants of this condition, such as "laparotomophilia migrans," for patients seeking repeated abdominal surgery; these subcategories were dropped from most current usage.

DSM-III-R (American Psychiatric Association 1987) describes three categories of factitious disorders: those with physical symptoms, those with psychological symptoms, and a third with a combination of the two. This section will discuss factitious disorders with physical symptoms. The DSM-III-R category of Factitious Disorder with Physical Symptoms (301.51) contains the following criteria for this condition:

A. Intentional production or feigning of physical (but not psychological) symptoms.
B. A psychological need to assume the sick role, as evidenced by the absence of external incentives for the behavior, such as economic gain, better care, or physical well-being.
C. Occurrence not exclusively during the course of another Axis I disorder, such as schizophrenia.

Factitious illness patients can create signs and symptoms in any organ system. A plethora of laboratory abnormalities have been produced, including anemia, hypokalemia, hematuria, hypoglycemia, coagulopathy, and hyperamylasuria. Patients have injected themselves with bacteria, taken surreptitious doses of drugs, such as furosemide and insulin, and spat saliva into their urine to elevate amylase readings.

A typical patient comes to a hospital emergency room with a plausible history for a serious medical illness. Patients often are facile with medical terminology and may make specific suggestions for diagnostic tests and analgesics.

Differential Diagnosis

These disorders need to be differentiated from others in which the patient appears to be physically ill, but no disease can be found to account for his symptoms and signs; these include the other somatoform disorders and malingering. However, the most important differential diagnosis is a rare physical disease.

Other self-destructive acts, besides factitious disorders, may also result in medical care. These would not be classified as factitious, since the goal of these acts is not primarily to obtain medical care.

It is extremely difficult to establish a person's motives and goals unless rapport and trust have been established and even then the patient may be resistant to revealing his true motives or may not be fully aware of them. Factitious patients typically produce their signs and symptoms consciously. Their motivations, however, are believed to be primarily unconscious. The only overt goal an observer of factitious disorder patients could identify is that the individual wishes to assume the role of a medical patient. In patients with other abnormal-illness behaviors such as hypochondriasis, somatization disorder, conversion disorder, and somatoform pain disorder, the psychopathologies are believed to be different and are described in other chapters. Malingerers produce their complaints with both conscious awareness and motivation; the motive is some sort of gain, such as disability payments. Even if they do not admit their motivations, they are often apparent to an outside observer.

Factitious disease can be produced at three levels of enactment. The first is one of a fictitious history. The patient describes a history of disease, but there are no actual signs of illness. The second level involves the individual who simulates the signs of disease. An example of this level would be the patient who lances his finger and puts drops of blood into his urine. The third level of enactment is the individual who actually creates a physical disease state. For example, one patient admitted that she injected herself with urine to produce septicemia. Any level of enactment can be added by a patient who truly suffers a medical disorder. Such elaboration may be especially difficult to diagnose and manage.

Prevalence

The prevalence of factitious disorders is unknown because a substantial proportion is probably never diagnosed. Some studies have been carried out in tertiary referral centers which may yield misleadingly high prevalence rates; moreover, the findings have varied across centers. For example, at the National Institutes of Health, in a study of fever of unknown origin (FUO), 9.6 percent were diagnosed as factitious (Aduan 1979), whereas at Stanford University, a similar study found 2.2 percent of FUOs to be factitious (Rumans 1978). Although these studies are probably skewed to higher levels than might be found in community hospitals, the numbers suggest a serious encroachment on the medical staff's efforts since each case consumes many hours of diagnostic procedures and tests and may entail lengthy hospitalization.

One of the notable findings to emerge from the literature is the repeated observation that many factitious patients have worked in the health care field; nurses, ward clerks, physical therapists, and aides are common occupations.

Prognosis

Little is known of the prognosis of factitious disease because there are only a few studies that address this issue. Many of the patients with chronic factitious disorders have stable social relationships, an adequate work record, and are reasonable candidates for psychiatric treatment. The Münchausen syndrome is regarded as the most malignant end of the spectrum; these patients lack social support, have an itinerant life-style, and have sociopathic traits (including being impostors and liars) and do not persevere with psychiatric treatment. Munchausen patients are believed to represent less than 10 percent of the patients with factitious disorders (Reich 1983; Rumans 1978).

Etiology and Pathogenesis

Judging from published case histories, emotional and physical deprivation, including parental physical abuse, are common in the background of factitious disorder patients. Frequently the individual has been hospitalized in the early childhood years; this may have been traumatic or may have served as an escape from the abusive home situation. Views on the psychopathology of these patients are based for the most part on theoretical assumptions, derived from case reports. Various characteristics have been described by authors who have intensively evaluated patients with factitious disorders (Ford 1973; Reich 1983; Stone 1977). The features that have been suggested are a strong yearning for dependency, masochistic traits, anger over past deprivations, and the need for the feeling of mastery, including the need to defeat the physician. The patient fails to realize that his victory is an empty one since he pays the cost of debility and patienthood.

Treatment

The first step of treatment is recognition. The primary physician should suspect the possibility of a factitious disease when history, laboratory, and physical examination findings appear inconsistent. For example, when a patient repeatedly has an elevated thermometer temperature without other evidence of infection such as sweating, flushing, and increased pulse rate, the physician should consider factitious disease as a diagnosis. The level of suspicion should probably be increased if the individual has worked in some health-related field (Reich 1983; Rumans 1978). Contacting another source of information besides the patient may yield crucial information. Family members, old medical records, or friends may impart information that establishes the diagnosis before more time-consuming, invasive diagnostic procedures have been undertaken. Unfortunately, the factitious disorder patients are also aware of the utility of collateral information, so they may deny that any medical records, family, or friends exist. A perplexing seriously ill patient with no available friends or family is often a clue toward the presence of factitious disease.

There are no controlled studies of the treatment of this disorder so the recommendations here are based on the views of psychiatrists who have treated several such patients and on published case histories. Once the primary physician has identified that the disease is factitious, he or she should request a psychiatric consultation. There is no agreement among authors whether their patients should be initially confronted or not. Numerous authors (Bursten 1965; Ford 1973; Fras 1971) have advocated avoidance of confrontation. They suggest the psychiatric consultant develop a supportive relationship to learn from the patient what function the disorder serves as well as allowing the beginning of a therapeutic relationship. If later the consultant recommends psychiatric treatment, he has a better fund of information upon which to base his recommendations.

Conversely, some authors recommend that confrontation should be vigorous and at an early stage if the patient is to be helped (Jefferson 1982; Nadelson 1979; Stone 1977).

Hollender believes that confrontation is usually best handled conjointly with both primary physician and psychiatrist present.

The psychiatrist alone is in a weak position to confront the patient since his information has been obtained second hand from the primary physician; if the latter states his case in a straightforward manner, the psychiatrist has witnessed the diagnosis being imparted and is in a good position to develop an alliance with the patient. It seems helpful if the confrontation is carried out in a nonpunitive and nonhostile manner and the primary physician reassures the patient medical care will continue, parallel with psychiatric treatment (Ford 1973).

Usually, the confrontation is best done by making a statement similar to the following: "We know you must have been in distress to use the methods you did to get help; we'd like to offer you a better way of getting help for yourself—psychiatric treatment." Reframing the factitious act as a cry for help may diminish the staff's tendency to view the patient with moral opprobrium. Physicians should not expect that all patients will admit their actions during the confrontation process. Reich (1983) noted an admission in only one-third of the cases they (1981) surveyed. Hyler and Sussman (1981) similarly note that most patients will "refuse to be unmasked" or will leave the hospital against medical advice when challenged.

In a substantial proportion of cases the factitious etiology cannot be confirmed with certainty and remains only a strong likelihood, because the patient was not observed nor does he admit to the deception. It is probably best for the primary physician to make the diagnosis as accurate as possible and to pursue diagnostic procedures until he is reasonably certain that the patient does not have a serious disease. Only then can the confrontation include the statement that the physician believes that the disease is factitious.

In the in-hospital management of factitious disorder, an important consideration for the psychiatric consultant is the staff's response. Since the implicit foundation in the staff-patient relationship is honesty and the expectation that the patient will try to get well, it is little wonder that staff feel anger and outrage after learning that the patient's disease is factitious. The consultant's task is to initially allow staff a forum to discuss their feelings. An ad hoc staff meeting is often useful for this purpose. After their anger has been expressed it becomes more possible for the staff to consider the patient's motivations for self-destructive behavior. They can begin to see the behavior as a psychopathologic symptom, not just an act of sociopathy aimed at them personally. Once staff have recognized this, there is less likelihood that staff will act out angrily toward the patient, such as with abrupt discharge, which may interrupt the tenuous therapeutic relationship the psychiatrist has established with the patient.

Once confrontation has been completed and the staff's reactions have been explored, the consultant must address the therapeutic options. Inpatient psychiatric treatment may be the safest alternative for patients who have produced a life-threatening disease. It is often difficult, however, to have the patient with this disorder accept admission. When family members can be reached they may be helpful in encouraging hospitalization. If the patient refuses admission but consents to outpatient care with family members involved, a discussion with the family may make them better informed, more accepting, and more able to monitor the patient and perhaps set appropriate limits. The discussion with the family may require several sessions, because some family members may initially reject the information as a hostile and unfounded accusation.

With both in- and outpatient treatment, medication appears to be of some value, but there is no systematic study of this in the literature. One of the aims of treatment is to decrease the distress these patients experience. When the patient has another psychiatric disorder this may require drug treatment (Fras 1971). There have been case reports of antidepressants having been used advantageously in some of these patients (Ford 1983; Reich 1983; Stone 1977). The patient needs to be persuaded that several medications may have to be tried because it cannot be predicted which drug will help him most. As with most resistant patients, he is likely to be more accepting of the recommended treatment if the therapist has built an alliance before the medication is suggested.

Psychotherapy with a factitious disorder patient has been attempted in various forms. Fras (1971) saw one patient for 70 sessions of individual therapy while the patient's parents were in family therapy simultaneously with a social worker. He advocates supportive psychotherapy in treating the factitious disorder patient, and avoidance of insight as a goal. Mild confrontations produced decompensation in his patient, which required phenothiazine treatment.

Stone (1977) takes an opposing view to Fras in affirming that "the circle must be closed," if therapy is to be successful. In his female patient with aspirin-induced bleeding, a vigorous confrontation took place with the patient once she had been transferred to the protective environment of a psychatric ward from a medical floor. Upon confrontation, the patient demanded to be immediately released and was discharged. Sometime later the patient voluntarily contacted the therapist and arranged for an outpatient referral. She was able to stay in treatment for 10 months with antidepressants as an additional treatment. Stone believes that the family and staff must vigorously and repeatedly confront a factitious patient if change is to occur.

In a detailed review of a psychotherapy of another factitious disorder patient, Mayo and Haggerty (1984) describe psychoanalytically oriented psychotherapy over 70 weekly sessions with a young woman. Their findings suggest that factitious symptoms and fabrications can be seen as metaphorical communications related to the stability of object relationships in their patient.

Unfortunately, the few cases of intensive individual therapy do not offer an adequate guide for treatment. The recommendation for psychotherapy is based on the principles that follow: the therapist is likely to be the only person in the patients' life who will understand the problem and be an empathic mentor. He or she should remain supportive, aim at the establishment of a therapeutic alliance, and focus on disease, suffering, anger, and the need to be cared for. Attempts must be made to protect the patient from further injury by consulting and collaborating with the patient's physician so that while therapy is in progress the patient is not rejected by his or her physician and yet not subjected to time-consuming, expensive, or even dangerous investigations and treatments.

Behavioral methods have been tried with factitious disorders. Yassa (1978) reported successful treatment of factitious behavior in a female schizophrenic patient with operant conditioning over a three-year hospitalization. That case report is unusual in that most patients with factitious disorder do not have an overt psychosis and are not found among long-term inpatients. (Since the patient was schizophrenic, she might not be classified in the DSM-III-R in the the category of factitious disorder.) Obviously, the vast majority of factitious disorder patients would not be candidates for such a program. Klonoff et al. (1983) developed an outpatient behavioral program for a woman with seizures that appeared to be factitious. Her team provided biofeedback sessions as a face-saving way for the woman to reduce her seizure frequency without having to reveal the true nature of the disorder and to protect her from the scorn of her family. The therapists responded positively to the woman's conversation about nonseizure topics, and ignored any comments regarding her seizures. They deliberately voiced skepticism when the patient reported successes. Treatment consisted of once-weekly meetings over a nine-month period. At the end of treatment she was completely free of seizures.

In summary, various treatment approaches have been used in factitious disorders. Psychotherapy, as well as behavioral techniques, has been used with some success, and the usefulness of confrontation has been debated. There have been no prospective comparative studies that have established a particular approach as a treatment of choice. Further research might clarify the most appropriate strategies for the treatment of patients with factitious disorders.

Chapter 195

Factitious Disorder with Psychological Symptoms

The occasional practice of feigning insanity dates at least from King David (1 Samuel, Chap. 21, V. 11–15). The classical description by Ganser (1898) relates to prisoners under stress. The simulation of psychological illness is very rare (Jones and Llewellyn 1917), and when it occurs as Ganser's syndrome, there is either important environmental stress (Ganser 1898; Tsoi 1973), brain damage (Whitlock 1967), or other severe psychological illness (Anderson and Mallinson 1941). Scott (1965) has distinguished between Ganser symptoms and Ganser's syndrome, the former perhaps being common when there is another underlying cause and the latter when a stress situation is present. Other conditions which have been called hysterical psychoses or culture-bound syndromes such as Latah, Amok, Piblokto, Wittigo, Voodoo, and Phii Pob and Negi Negi all involve considerations of environmental stress or interpersonal problems as do psychogenic psychoses and folie familiale or folie partagée (Merskey 1979). Moreover, they may not be simulated insanity but illness produced unconsciously. These conditions with psychological symptoms are not part of the DSM-III-R (American Psychiatric Association 1987) category of factitious disorder because environmental factors are prominent in all of them.

The present DSM-III-R category of factitious disorder with psychological symptoms excludes the case of individuals under external stress and represents a parallel to factitious disorder with physical symptoms. These are described in another chapter.

Factitious disorder with psychological symptoms has been defined in DSM-III-R according to the same pattern and hence emphasizes that the patient's aim is to assume the patient role and is not explained by his environmental circumstances.

Jefferson and Ochitill (1982) questioned whether the present syndrome exists at all as a free-standing entity; nevertheless, there are a few reports which support the idea. Jones and Llewellyn (1917) mention a report of three criminal offenders who were condemned to death and reprieved. They had been thought not to be insane but to be feigning, but later became insane. Jones and Llewellyn state that paradoxically "feigned insanity only occurs in those more or less mentally deranged or predisposed by heritage to mental instability." They emphasize that there is always a motive—for example, a recovered patient wishing to remain in an asylum, or a link with litigation. However, their observations leave open the possibility that some patients with a tendency to psychotic illness will develop feigning of psychological illness, either as a precursor of their overt psychosis or subsequently. In such cases, the degree of environmental stress may not be particularly important, although it may be relevant that some environmental stress has occurred.

Hay (1983) describes the actual simulation of psychosis as a precursor of schizophrenia. Hopkins (1973) also describes pretended coma as a sign of personality disorder in some cases. Bleuler (1950) and Sim (1981) noted that occasional schizophrenic patients would show a "buffoonery syndrome" which is, however, associated with positive evidence of schizophrenia. The most substantial report of this condition was provided by Pope et al. (1982) who discovered nine such patients among a group of 219 consecutively admitted to a research ward for psychotic disorders. Although those authors do not give much information about the mental state of the individuals in question, they imply in two brief instances that patients preferred the research ward to being discharged or to being transferred to a state hospital. Nevertheless, the DSM-III-R criteria which those authors emphasized, require that the patient should be maintaining the symptom for the sake of status as a patient or treatment as a patient rather than for specific environmental purposes. Overall, however, those authors seem to have made a case that they could discover a number of patients who seemed to fit the DSM-III-R criteria. Accordingly, it appears that there are a few instances where the DSM-III-R category of feigned insanity without environmental cause may occur, although it is likely that even in those instances most patients will have had some environmental insult, albeit a minor one, and will be liable to unfeigned madness in addition.

Treatment

Virtually nothing is written on the treatment of these cases. The theoretical treatment may be derived as by Jefferson and Ochitill from a consideration of Ganser's syndrome and from the information we have from Hay. It will be important to search first for environmental causes and to change these if this is feasible, to examine the patient for physical illness affecting brain function, and to entertain the possibility of a diagnosis of schizophrenia or other major psychotic illness. Spontaneous remission may be anticipated sometimes, but if, in fact, the individual shows signs which indicate psychiatric disorder, this requires the appropriate treatment (Goldin and Macdonald 1955). For the rest, supportive care is indicated.

Chapter 196

Somatization Disorder

The diagnostic criteria for this disorder in DMS-III-R (American Psychiatric Association 1987) include:

A. A history of many physical complaints or a belief that one is sickly, beginning before the age of 30 and persisting for several years.

B. At least 13 symptoms from the list summarized below. To count a symptom as significant, the following criteria must be met:
    (1) no organic pathology or pathophysiologic mechanism (e.g., a physical disorder or the effects of injury, medication, drugs, or alcohol) to account for the symptom or, when there is related organic pathology, the complaint or resulting social or occupational impairment is grossly in excess of what would be expected from the physical findings.
    (2) has not occurred only during a panic attack.
    (3) has caused the person to take medicine (other than over-the-counter pain medication), see a doctor, or alter life-style.

Thirty-five possible symptoms are listed including conversion symptoms, various functional somatic symptoms, pain, psychosexual disorders, and others such as excessive menstrual bleeding and severe vomiting during pregnancy. Somatization disorder is derived from Briquet's syndrome (Briquet 1859) but differs from the latter on a few features. The treatments proposed in this section apply to both disorders.

Studies of Treatment and Prognosis

Guze and Perley (1963) followed up 25 female patients with hysteria (the authors used the term synonymously with Briquet's syndrome). They reported that all 25 women had been offered psychiatric treatment, few of them accepted its validity, and they nearly always discontinued the visits because they believed them to be unnecessary or ineffective; only six persisted with psychotherapy for several months. The authors reported that the disorder had a chronic course without appreciable remissions. After psychiatric referral, the patients continued to consult other physicians for the same complaints and continued to be hospitalized.

Coryell and Norton (1981) reviewed hospital charts of patients treated with various therapies for somatization disorder. The outcome on follow-up was decidedly worse than for depressives and "Non-Briquet hysteria" (a similar syndrome, but not satisfying the criteria for Briquet's syndrome), yet the outcome was better than that reported by Guze and Perley. After five years, 30 percent had recovered and this proportion of recoveries was maintained for another 10 years.

Scallet et al. (1976) surveyed the literature on the treatment of "chronic hysteria," but the patients were not limited to Briquet's syndrome. In this survey all the studies of psychotherapy were uncontrolled. Diverse treatment methods had been used and outcome varied across studies.

Most psychiatric treatments have been tried in chronic hysteria, but there is no adequate published prospective controlled study of psychotherapy of somatization disorder (see Note on page 2170). It is not possible to conclude from uncontrolled studies whether one treatment is more effective than another, since selection of treatment by patients and investigators makes it likely that different populations receive the different treatments. Patients referred to a psychiatrist are generally a subgroup who are more distressed and have responded less well to treatment than those managed adequately by their general physician's reassurance and treatment and may have a worse prognosis.

Scallet et al. (1976) carried out a small controlled study of patients with somatizing disorder. They compared two methods of electrosleep and used as a control a placebo treatment. All patients were treated initially with autogenic training. The number of patients in this study was too small for conclusions on the efficacy of treatments; it is mentioned here because it is the only controlled study in which patient selection was limited to those with the diagnosis of somatization disorder. The patients did not benefit from electrosleep but benefited, perhaps, from autogenic training.

Group Psychotherapy

Several authors have pointed out that somatizing patients are not suitable subjects for group psychotherapy; they tend to focus on their somatic complaints rather than on emotional and interpersonal difficulties. Yallom (1970) wrote that "patients who utilize denial or other self-deceptive mechanisms, who tend to somatize psychological conflicts or deal with them in a nonpsychological mode, are usually poor group referrals." He also quotes results showing that somatizing patients are overrepresented among the dropouts. These findings are similar to those of early studies of individual psychotherapy with somatizing patients which are briefly discussed in the chapter on atypical somatoform disorder.

Valko (1976) reported the only study of group therapy on six patients with Briquet's syndrome who fulfilled the DSM-III (American Psychiatric Association 1980) criteria for somatization disorder. There was no control group. The patients met weekly for one-and-one-half hours. Initially, the patients had an opportunity to talk about their problems, a need apparently felt by all the patients. After the second meeting the patients apparently became less concerned about their physical symptoms and after the third meeting spent little time talking about them. The patients appeared to be reassured to find that other people had similar problems, to learn that their physical symptoms were real and that they were "not crazy with imaginary symptoms," and to learn that their physical symptoms did not signify the onset of a physical disease. Later they learned to identify that stress made them feel nervous and then caused physical symptoms. The patients improved fairly rapidly, their relationships with their families improved, the use of medication decreased substantially in most patients, the number of attendances to nonpsychiatric physicians decreased, and the patients reported that they had more self-confidence and an improvement in mood. After four months the group was terminated; three of the patients who relapsed improved rapidly again when the group was restarted.

Although this is only a small study and without controls, the improvement in the patients was fairly quick, and several features in the patients' lives appeared to have changed for the better. This is in contrast to the generally gloomy prognosis by therapists based on outcome studies that indicate chronicity and poor response to treatment.

Psychotherapeutic Strategies

Several controlled studies of psychotherapy of somatizing patients are summarized in the sections on atypical somatoform disorder and psychogenic pain disorder. These studies do not deal with somatization disorder—a condition that appears to be more difficult to treat—but illustrate some successful psychotherapeutic methods in chronic somatizing patients.

In the absence of adequate studies, particularly controlled studies, any recommendations on treatment are, of course, tentative. These guidelines are based on the experiences of therapists who have reported their findings, on the outcome of uncontrolled studies, and from the outcome of treatment with patients with similar disorders.

The principles of psychotherapy with somatizing disorder can be outlined as follows:

1. The therapist must be prepared to accept the patient's descriptions of pain and suffering. It is unlikely that a therapist who cannot tolerate persisting and varied bodily complaints and lack of psychological sophistication will establish an adequate rapport with patients who are anguished, have had many treatments that have failed, and have had frustrating experiences with other physicians.

2. The patient may not believe that he or she is in need of psychiatric treatment. The therapist will need to convey initially to the patient that his or her role is to help with the emotional consequences of having distressing bodily symptoms in order to make the emotional symptoms less distressing rather than promising relief from bodily symptoms.

3. Some of the patients with somatizing disorder have, at least intermittently, hypochondriacal fears and beliefs, and these need to be addressed as outlined in the chapter on hypochondriasis.

4. Some patients have persistent or recurrent distressing somatic symptoms, including pain, and therapeutic approaches similar to those described in the section on psychogenic pain disorder may be helpful.

5. Coexisting disorders, such as anxiety and depression, need to be treated often with drug therapy, which is described later.

6. The therapist should try to persuade the patient to limit his or her visits to one physician, preferably one who is a conservative diagnostician and therapist, because if the patient seeks out several physicians, the number of diagnoses and treatments, including exploratory surgery, may increase (Ford 1983; Quill 1985; Woodruff et al. 1982).

7. It appears important for the primary physician to support the therapist's efforts, which may include weaning the patient from numerous medications. Preferably, the primary physician and the therapist should discuss changes in treatment whenever this becomes necessary.

8. At present there are no published studies on family therapy in somatizing disorder. There are reports of uncontrolled studies of family therapy in patients with chronic pain. Perhaps similar methods can be adopted for patients with somatizing disorder in order to help other members to understand the disorder, to help them to tolerate the patient's behavior, and to learn to respond more appropriately.

9. At present there are no studies that compare individual psychotherapy to group psychotherapy; the latter deserves a trial when several patients with somatizing disorder, chronic somatic complaints, or hypochondriasis present for treatment at the same time (Dwan and Nesbitt 1978; Mally and Ogston 1964; Melson et al. 1982). However, a somatizing or hypochondriacal patient may not be suitable for therapy with a group of nonsomatizing or nonhypochondriacal patients because therapy could easily neglect his main concerns (Leonhard 1979). Several introductory sessions of individual therapy before group therapy appear to be of advantage with chronic somatizing patients in order to establish rapport with the therapist and to prepare them for the experience of group therapy (Ford and Long 1977). The sharing of experiences with fellow sufferers in the group and learning that others have similar ordeals may be sources of additional consolation and support (Valko 1976).

Drug Treatments

There are no adequate studies of drug treatment of somatizing disorder. Studies of the effects of psychotropic drugs on somatic complaints are summarized in the sections on undifferentiated somatoform disorder and somatoform pain disorder.

The main role of psychotropic drugs is in the treatment of intercurrent or coexisting psychiatric disorders, such as depression or anxiety. Another therapist's role is the prevention of the unnecessary use of drugs, particularly long-term use of habit-forming drugs. Many of the patients with somatizing disorder have a multitude of medications, some of them apparently no longer necessary and some that probably never were. Conversely, psychotropic medications are sometimes prescribed in inadequate doses or in inappropriate combinations. The principles of prescribing should be similar to those described in the chapter on hypochondriasis. The therapist should aim at as few drugs as possible, preferably those that are not habit-forming. If antidepressants are prescribed, several trials may be needed to find one which has the best therapeutic effect and the least unpleasant side effects.

Electroconvulsive Therapy

Guze and Perley (1963) reported on two patients with Briquet's syndrome who received ECT during each of three psychiatric hospitalizations. These women reported that ECT helped with some of the symptoms only—chiefly depressed feeling and crying spells—but it was not possible to evaluate the duration and degree of improvements, because ECT had been administered several years before in each case. Bibb and Guze (1972), from a review of charts of 95 patients with somatization disorder, some of whom had been treated with ECT, concluded that ECT may have improved depression but did not reduce the severity or frequency of somatic symptoms. There are several reports in the literature on the treatment of acute, as well as chronic hysteria with ECT (Milligan 1946; Noreik 1970), but it is impossible to conclude from most of the descriptions of the patient what proportion had a somatization disorder. There is no evidence that ECT has any beneficial effects in this disorder unless the patient has a coexisting depression that requires such treatment.

Note

Since this chapter was written, a controlled study was published by Smith et al. (1986) which has bearing on the management of somatization disorder because it demonstrates the value of consultation with the patient's primary physician. Consultation may be the treatment of choice for some patients with somatization disorder who have no other psychiatric disorder; another referral to a psychiatrist may not become necessary unless the patient deteriorates or the progress is unsatisfactory. The authors randomly assigned 38 patients to either a consultation or a control group and studied them for 18 months. After nine months the control group was crossed over to receive the same intervention as the consultation group. The physicians in the consultation group were sent a detailed letter; this letter described the nature of the disorder, including its chronic relapsing course, its low mortality, and its morbidity. The physician was encouraged to serve as the primary physician; the consultant suggested that a regular scheduled appointment be made for the patient (possibly every four to six weeks) and that physical examination be performed at each visit to look for signs of disease so that the symptoms would not be taken at face value. The consultant also suggested that the physician should avoid hospitalization, diagnostic procedures, surgery, and the use of laboratory assessment unless these were clearly indicated. The physicians were encouraged not to tell the patients "It's all in your head." After the psychiatric consultation, the quarterly health care charges in the treatment group declined by 53 percent. In contrast, the charges in the control group showed wide variations but no overall change. After the control group was crossed over to receive treatment the quarterly charges declined by 49 percent. The reductions in expenditures in both groups were due largely to decreases in hospitalization. This study does not reveal the long-term outcome of the disorder but in the short term led to substantial decreases in cost and the inconvenience and risks of hospitalization and laboratory investigations.

References

Section 20
Somatoform and Facititious Disorders

Adler G: The physician and the hypochondriacal patient. New Engl J Med 304:1394–1396, 1981

Adomakoh CC: The pattern of epidemic hysteria in a girls' school in Ghana. Ghana Medicine Journal 13:407–411, 1973

Aduan RP, Fauci AS, Dale DC, et al: Factitious fever and self-induced infection. Ann Intern Med 90:230–242, 1979

Alexander F: Psychosomatic Medicine. New York, Norton Co, 1950, 263–271

Altman N: Helping the hypochondriac. Am Fam Physician 17:107–112, 1978

American Psychiatric Association: Diagnostic and Statistical Manual of Mental Disorders, 3rd ed. Washington, DC, American Psychiatric Association, 1980

American Psychiatric Association: Diagnostic and Statistical Manual of Mental Disorders, 3rd ed, revised. Washington, DC, American Psychiatric Association, 1987

Anderson EW, Mallinson WP: Psychogenic episodes in the course of major psychoses. Journal Mental Science 87:383–391, 1941

Armstrong H, Patterson P: Seizures in Canadian Indian children. Canadian Psychiatry Association Journal 20:247–255, 1975

Aronoff GM, Rutrick D: Psychodynamics and psychotherapy of the chronic pain syndrome, in Evaluation and Treatment of Chronic Pain. Edited by Aronoff GM. Baltimore-Munich, Urban and Schwarzenberg, 1985

Asher R: Münchausen's syndrome. Lancet 1:339–341, 1951

Banks MH, Beresford SHZ, Morrell DC, et al: Factors influencing demand for primary medical care in women aged 20–40 years: a preliminary report. Int J Epidemiol 4:189–255, 1975

Barber TX: Toward a theory of pain: relief of chronic pain by prefrontal leucotomy opiates, placebos and hypnosis. Psychol Bull 56:430–460, 1959

Bassett DL, Pilowsky I: A study of brief psychotherapy for chronic pain. J Pychosom Res 29:259–264, 1985

Bernstein IC, Callahan WA, Jaronson JM: Lobotomy private practice. Arch Gen Psychiatry 32:1041–1047, 1975

Bibb RC, Guze SB: Hysteria (Briquet's syndrome) in a psychiatric hospital: the significance of secondary depression. Am J Psychiatry 129:138–142, 1972

Bird J: The behavioural treatment of hysteria. Br J Psychiatry 134:129–137, 1979

Blackwell B, Galbraith JR, Dahl DS: Chronic pain management. Hosp Community Psychiatry 35:999, 1984

Blanchard EB, Theobald D, Williamson D, et al: Temperature biofeedback in the treatment of migraine headaches. Arch Gen Psychiatry 35:581–588, 1978

Blanchard EB, Andrasik F, Ahles TA, et al: Migraine and tension headache: a meta-analytic review. Behav Res Ther 613–631, 1980

Bleuler EP: The Group of Schizophrenias. New York, International Universities Press, 1950

Block A: An investigation of the response of the spouse to chronic pain behaviour. Psychosom Med 43:415–422, 1981

Blumer D, Heilbronn M: Antidepressant treatment for chronic pain: treatment outcome of 1,000 patients with the pain-prone disorder. Psychiatr Annals 14:796–800, 1984

Boyd D: Electroshock therapy in atypical pain syndromes. Lancet 76:22–25, 1956

Brena S: Chronic pain states: a model for classification. Psychiatr Annals 14:778–782, 1984

Breuer J, Freud S: Studies on Hysteria: Complete Psychological Works of Freud, vol 2. (1893–95) London, Hogarth Press, 1955

Briquet P: Traite Clinique et Therapeutique de L'hysterie. Paris, Bailliere and Fils, 1859

Brodsky CM: The Harrassed Worker. Lexington, Mass, Heath, 1975

Brotman AW, Jenike MA: Monosymptomatic hypochondriasis treated with tricyclic antidepressants. Am J Psychiatry 141:1608–1609, 1984

Brown HN, Vaillant GE: Hypochondriasis. Arch Intern Med 141:723–726, 1981

Burns BH: Breathlessness in depression. Br J Psychiatry 119:39–45, 1971

Bursten B: On Munchausen syndrome. Arch Gen Psychiatry 13:261–268, 1965

Busse EW: The treatment of the chronic complainer. Medical Record and Annals 50:196–200, 1956

Carron H: Primary care in pain management. Urban Health 8:16, 1979

Carron H: Compensation aspects of low back claims, in Management of Low Back Pain. Edited by Carron H, McLaughlin R. Boston, John Wright PSG Inc, 1982

Carter AB: The prognosis of certain hysterical symptoms. Br Med J 1:1076–1079, 1949

Carter RB: On the Pathology and Treatment of Hysteria. London, Churchill, 1853.

Catchlove R, Braha R: The use of cervical epidural nerve blocks in the management of chronic head and neck pain. Can Anaesth Soc J 31:2, 1984

Catchlove R, Cohen K: Effects of a directive return to work approach in the treatment of workman's compensation patients with chronic pain. Pain 14:181–191, 1982

Christian P, Hase B, Kromer W: Statistische Untersuchungen uber die sogenannten Nervosen Herz—und Kreislaufstorungen. Archiv Kreislauf Forschung 20:287–305, 1954

Cinciripini P, Floreen A: An evaluation of a behavioral program for chronic pain. J Behav Med 5:375–389, 1982

Ciompi L: Follow-up studies on the evolution of former neurotic and depressive states in old age: clinical and psychodynamic aspects. J Geriatr Psychiatry 3:90–106, 1969

Cloninger CR, Sigvardsson S, von Knorring A-L, et al: An adoption study of somatoform disorders, II: identification of two discrete somatoform disorders. Arch Gen Psychiatry 41:863–871, 1984

Cole JO, Altesman R, Weingarten C: Beta-blocking drugs in psychiatry. McLean Hospital Journal 4:40–68, 1979

Connolly FH, Gibson M: Dysmorphophobia—a long-term study. Br J Psychiatry 132:568–570, 1978

Conte HR, Karasu TB: Psychotherapy for medical review and critique of controlled studies. Psychosomatics 22:285–315, 1981

Cooper DG, Dickenson JB, Adams HB, et al: Interviewer's role-playing and responses to sensory deprivation: a clinical demonstration. Percept Mot Skills 40:291–303, 1975

Coryell W, Norten SG: Briquet's syndrome (somatization disorder) and primary depression: comparison of background and outcome. Compr Psychiatry 22:249–256, 1981

Covi L, Lipman RS, Derogatis LR, et al: Drugs and group psychotherapy in neurotic depression. Am J Psychiatry 131:191–198, 1974

Covino N, Warfield C: Hypnosis and the management of pain. Hosp Pract, Feb 15, 1985

Crasilneck H: Hypnosis in the control of chronic low back pain. Am J Clin Hypn 22:71, 1979

Davidson J: Monoamine oxidase inhibitors in patients with chronic pain. Arch Gen Psychiatry 42:635–636, 1985

Demirel T, Braun W, Reimers C: Results of spinal cord stimulation in patients suffering from chronic pain after a two year observation period. Neurochirurgia (Stuttg) 27:47–50, 1984

Dhadphale M, Shaikh SP: Epidemic hysteria in a Zambian school: "the mysterious madness of Mwinilunga." Br J Psychiatry 142:85–88, 1983

Dickes RA: Brief therapy of conversion reactions: an in-hospital technique. Am J Psychiatry 131:584–586, 1974

Doleys DM, Crocker M, Patton D: Response of patients with chronic pain to exercise quotas. Phys Ther 62:1111–1114, 1982

Draspa LJ: Psychological factors in muscular pain. Br J Med Psychol 32:106–116, 1959

Drossman DA: The problem patient: evaluation and care of patients with psychosocial disturbances. Ann Intern Med 88:366–372, 1978

Dwan C, Nesbitt J: Group approach to hypochondriasis. Am Fam Physician 18:23, 1978

Editorial: Biofeedback and tension headache. Lancet 898–899, 1980

Egbert LD, Bettit GE, Welch CE, et al: Reduction of postoperative pain by encouragement and instruction of patients. N Engl J Med 270:825–827, 1964

Engel G: Psychogenic pain and the pain-prone patient. Am J Med 26:899, 1959

Feinstein A: An additional basic science for clinical medicine, I: the constraining fundamental paradigms. Ann Intern Med 99:393–397, 1983

Fenichel O: Berlin Psychoanalytic Institute Report, 1929–30, 1930

Floru L: Verhaltenstherapeutische versuche durch systematische Desensibilisierung. Psychiatria Clinica 6:300–318, 1973

Follick MJ, Smith TW, Ahern DK: The sickness impact profile: a global measure of disability in chronic low back pain. Pain 21:67–76, 1985

Ford CV: The Munchausen syndrome: a report of four new cases and a review of psychodynamic considerations. Psychiatry Med 4:31–45, 1973

Ford CV: The Somatizing Disorders—Illness as a Way of Life. New York, Elsevier Biomedical, 1983

Ford CV, Long KD. Group psychotherapy of somatizing patients. Psychother Psychosom 28:294–304, 1977

Fordyce WE: Behavioral Methods for Chronic Pain and Illness. St. Louis, CV Mosby, 1976

France R, Krishnan K, Houpt J, et al: Differentiation of depression from chronic pain with the dexamethasone suppression test and DSM-III. Am J Psychiatry 141:1577–1579, 1984

Frank JD: Common features of psychotherapy. Aust NZ J Psychiatry 6:34–80, 1972

Fras I, Coughlin BE: The treatment of factitial disease. Psychosomatics 12:117–122, 1971

Ganser SJM: A peculiar hysterical state. Arch Psychiat NervKrankh 30:633–640 (1898). Translated by Schorer CE. British Journal Criminology 5:120–126, 1965

Gavin H: Feigned and Factitious Diseases. London, J and A Churchill, 1843

Getto C, Ochitill H: Psychogenic pain disorder, in Treatment of Mental Disorders. Edited by Greist J, Jefferson J, Spitzer R. New York, Oxford University Press, 1982

Gillespie RD: Hypochondria: its definition, nosology, and psychopathology. Guys Hospital Report 8:408–460, 1928

Gilson BS, Gilson JS, Bergner M: The sickness impact profile: development of an outcome measure of health care. Am J Public Health 65:1304–1310, 1975

Gingras M: A clinical trial of tofranil in rheumatic pain in general practice. J Int Med Res 4:41–49, 1976

Glass R, Uhlenhuth EH, Kellner R: The value of self-report assessment in studies of anxiety disorders. J Clin Psychopharmacol 7:215–221, 1987

Goldin S, MacDonald JE: The Ganser state. Journal Mental Science 101:267–280, 1955

Gomez J, Dally P: Psychologically mediated abdominal pain in surgical and medical outpatient clinics. Br Med J 2:1451–1453, 1977

Grinker RF, Spiegel JP: War neurosis, in North Africa: The Tunisian Campaign. New York, Josiah Macy Jr Foundation, 1943

Guze SB, Perley MJ: Observations on the natural history of hysteria. Am J Psychiatry 119:960–965, 1963

Hallen O: Uber circumscripte Hypochondrien. Nervenarzt (Berlin) 41:215–220, 1970

Hamann K, Avnstorp C: Delusion of infestation treated by pimozide: a double-blind crossover clinical study. Acta Derm Venereol (Stockh) 62:55–58, 1982

Hansen E, Hansen J: Acupuncture treatment of chronic facial pain—a controlled crossover trial. Presented at the 33rd Annual Meeting of the Scandinavian Neurosurgical Society, Aarhus, Denmark, 1981

Hart H: Displacement, guilt, and pain. Psychoanal Rev 34:259, 1947

Hay GG: Feigned psychosis—a review of the simulation of mental illness. Br J Psychiatry 143:8–10, 1983

Haynes R: A review of tested interventions for improving compliance with antihypertensive treatment, in Patient Compliance to Prescribed Regimens: A Report to the National Heart, Lung, and Blood Institute. Edited by Haynes R, Mattson M, Engerbretson T. National Institutes of Health Publication No 81–2102, pp 83–112, 1980

Head H: An address on the diagnosis of hysteria. Br Med J I:827–829, 1922

Heaton RK, Getto CJ, Lehman AW, et al: A standardized evaluation of psychosocial factors in chronic pain. Pain 12:165–174, 1982

Hoehn-Saric R, McLeod DR, Zimmerli WD: Differential effects of alprazolam and imipramine in generalized anxiety: somatic versus psychic symptoms. Presented at the Fourth World Congress of Biological Psychiatry. Philadelphia, Pa, 1985

Hohman L, Wilkinson W: Pain equivalents treated with electroshock. U.S. Armed Forces Journal 4:1025–1030, 1953

Holroyd KA, Andrasik F, Westbrook T: Cognitive control of tension headache. Cognitive Therapy and Research 1:121–133, 1977

Hopkins A: Pretending to be unconscious. Lancet pp 312–314, 1973

Hudgens A: Family oriented therapy of chronic pain. Journal of Marital and Family Therapy 5:67–68, 1979

Hyler SE, Sussman N: Chronic factitious disorder with physical symptoms (the Münchausen syndrome). Psychiatric Clin North Am 4:365–377, 1981

IASP. International Association for the Study of Pain: classification of chronic pain syndromes and definition of pain terms. Pain. Suppl 3, 1986

Jamieson WG, Merskey H: Representation of the thoracic outlet syndrome as a problem in chronic pain and psychiatric management. Pain 22:195–200, 1985

Jefferson JW, Ochitill H: Factitious disorders, in Treatment of Mental Disorders. Edited by Greist JH, Jefferson JW, Spitzer RL. New York, Oxford University Press, 1982

Jessup B, Neufeld R, Merskey H: Biofeedback therapy for headache and other pain: an evaluative review. Pain 7:225–270, 1979

Johansson J, Ost L: Self-control procedures in biofeedback: a review of temperature biofeedback in the treatment of migraine. Biofeedback Self Regul 7:425–440, 1988

Jones AB, Llewellyn LJ: Malingering or the Simulation of Disease. London, Heinemann, 1917

Kahn RJ, McNair DM, Covi L, et al: Effects of psychotropic agents on high anxiety subjects. Psychopharmacol Bull 17:97–103, 1981

Kahn RJ, McNair DM, Lipman RS, et al: Imipramine and chlordiazepoxide in depressive and anxiety disorders, II: efficacy in anxious outpatients. Arch Gen Psychiatry 43:79–86, 1986

Katon W: Depression: somatic symptoms and medical disorders in primary care. Compr Psychiatry 23:274–287, 1982

Katon W, Egan K, Miller D: Chronic pain: lifetime psychiatric diagnoses and family history. Am J Psychiatry 142(10):1156–1160, 1985

Kellner R: Neurotic Ill Health in a General Practice on Deeside. Doctoral Dissertation. Liverpool, England, University of Liverpool, 1963

Kellner R: Neurosis in general practice. Br J Clin Pract 19:681–682, 1965

Kellner R: Psychotherapy in psychosomatic disorders: A survey of controlled studies. Arch Gen Psychiatry 32:1021–1030, 1975

Kellner R: Psychotherapeutic strategies in hypochondriasis: a clinical study. Am J Psychother 36:146–157, 1982

Kellner R: The prognosis of treated hypochondriasis: a clinical study. Acta Psychiatr Scand 67:69–79, 1983

Kellner R: Somatization and Hypochondriasis. New York, Praeger, 1985

Kellner R: Somatization and Hypochondriasis. New York, Praeger-Greenwood, 1986

Kellner R, Sheffield BF: The relief of distress following attendance at a clinic. Br J Psychiatry 118:195–198, 1971

Kellner R, Sheffield BF: The one week prevalence of symptoms in neurotic patients and normals. Am J Psychiatry 130:102–105, 1973

Kellner R, Collins AC, Shulman RS, et al: The short-term antianxiety effects of propranolol HCl. J Clin Pharmacol 14:301–304, 1974

Kellner R, Fava GA, Lisansky J, et al: Hypochondrial fears and beliefs in melancholia: the response to amitriptyline. J Affective Dis 10:21–26, 1986

Kenyon FE: Hypochondriasis: a clinical study. Br J Psychiatry 110:478–488, 1964

Kenyon FE: Hypochrondriacal states. Br J Psychiatry 129:1–14, 1976

Kenyon FE: The hypochondriacal patient. Practitioner 220:245–250, 1978

Kenyon J, Knight C, Wells C: Randomized double-blind trial on the immediate effects of naloxone on classical Chinese acupuncture therapy for chronic pain. Acupunct Electrother Res 8:17–24, 1983

Kerns RD, Turk DC, Rudy TE: The West Haven-Yale multidimensional pain inventory (WHYMPI). Pain 23:345–356, 1985

Kessel N: Reassurance. Lancet 2:1128–1133, 1979

Kessel WIN: Psychiatric morbidity in a London general practice. Br J Prev Soc Med 14:16–22, 1960

Khatami M, Rush A: A one-year follow-up of the multimodal treatment for chronic pain. Pain 14:45, 1982

Kiser R, Gatchel R, Krishin B, et al: Acupuncture relief of chronic pain syndrome correlates with increased plasma met-enkephalin concentrations. Lancet 12:1394–1396, 1983

Klonoff EA, Younger SJ, Moore DJ, et al: Chronic factitious illness: a behavioral approach. Int J Psychiatry Med 13:173–183, 1983

Kreitman N, Sainsbury P, Pearce K, et al: Hypochondriasis and depression in outpatients at a general hospital. Br J Psychiatry 111:607–615, 1965

Kulenkampff C, Bauer A: Uber das Syndrom der Herzphobie: Schluss. Nervenarzt (Berlin) 31:496–507, 1960

Kumar K, Wilkinson JCM: Thought stopping: a useful treatment in phobias of internal stimuli. Br J Psychiatry 119:305–307, 1971

Lacey JI, Smith RL, Green A: Use of conditioned autonomic responses in the study of anxiety. Psychosom Med 17:208–217, 1955

Ladee GA: Hypochondriacal Syndromes. New York, Elsevier, 1966

Langley G, Sheppeard H, Johnson M, et al: The analgesic effects of transcutaneous electrical nerve stimulation and placebo in chronic pain patients. Rheumatol Int 4:119–123, 1984

Larbig W, Gerber W, Kluck M, et al: Therapeutic effects of delta-sleep-inducing peptide (DSIP) in patients with chronic, pronounced pain episodes. Eur Neurol 23:372–385, 1984

Large RG: The psychiatrist and the chronic pain patient: 172 anecdotes. Pain 9:253–263, 1980

Latimer P: External contingency management for chronic pain: critical review of the evidence. Am J Psychiatry 139:10, 1982

Lazarus AA: The results of behavior therapy in 126 cases of severe neurosis. Behav Res Ther 1:69–79, 1963

Leonhard K: On the treatment of ideohypochondriac and sensohypochondriac neuroses. Int J Soc Psychiatry 2:123–133, 1968

Leonhard K: Therapeutisches Versaumnis durch Unterlassung der Einzelbehandlung bei Sekundären Fehlentwicklungen. Psychiatr Neurol Med Psychol (Leipz) 31:723–729, 1979

Lesse S: Hypochondriasis and psychosomatic disorders masking depression. Am J Psychother 21:607–620, 1967

Lewis A: "Psychogenic": a word and its mutations. Psychol Med 2:209, 1972

Lewith G: How effective is acupuncture in the management of pain? Journal Royal College of General Practitioners 34:275–279, 1984

Lewith G, Machin D: On the evaluation of the clinical effects of acupuncture. Pain 16:111–127, 1983

Ley P, Spellman MS: Communicating with the Patient. Worchester and London, Staples Press, 1967

Liebowitz MR, Nuetzel EJ, Bowser AE, et al: Phenelzine and delusions of parasitosis: a case report. Am J Psychiatry 135:1565–1566, 1978

Liebson I: Conversion reaction: a learning theory approach. Behav Res Ther 7:217–218, 1969

Ljungberg L: Hysteria: a clinical, prognostic, and genetic study. Acta Psychiatr Scand 112:1–162, 1957

Lowy FH: Management of the persistent somatizer. Int J Psychiatry Med 6 (1/2): 227–239, 1976

Lundberg T: Vibratory stimulation for the alleviation of chronic pain. Acta Physiol Scand 523:2–51, 1983

Lutz R, Silbret M, Olshan N: Treatment outcome and compliance with therapeutic regimens: long-term follow-up of a multidisciplinary pain program. Pain 17:301–308, 1983

Mabry JH: Lay concepts of etiology. J Chron Dis 17:371–386, 1964

Mally MA, Ogston WD: Treatment of the "untreatables." Int J Group Psychother 14:369–374, 1964

Marks IM: Living with Fear: Understanding and Coping with Anxiety. New York, McGraw Hill, 1978

Marks I, Mishan J: Dysmorphobic avoidance with disturbed perception. Br J Psychiatry 152:674–678, 1988

Marlatt G, Gordon J: Determinants of relapse: implications for the maintenance of behaviour change, in Behavioural Medicine: Changing Health Lifestyles. Edited by Davidson P, Davidson S. New York, Brunner Mazel, 1980

Mayer-Gross W, Slater E, Roth M: Clinical Psychiatry, 3rd ed. Baltimore and London, Williams and Wilkins, 1969

Mayo JP, Haggerty JJ: Long-term therapy of Munchausen syndrome. Am J Psychother 38:571–578, 1984

Mayou R: Chest pain in the cardiac clinic. J Psychosom Res 17:353–357, 1973

Mayou R: The nature of bodily symptoms. Br J Psychiatry 129:55–60, 1976

Melson SJ, Rynearson EK, Dortzbach J, et al: Short-term intensive group psychotherapy for patients with "functional" complaints. Psychosomatics 23:689–695, 1982

Melzack R, Wall P: Acupuncture and transcutaneous electrical nerve stimulation. Postgrad Med J 60:893–896, 1984

Melzack R, Weisz A, Sprague L: Strategems for controlling pain: contributions of auditory stimulation and suggestion. Exp Neurol 8:239, 1963

Mendels J: Electroconvulsive therapy and depression, III: a method for prognosis. Br J Psychiatry 111:687–690, 1965

Mendelson G: Illness behaviour, pain, and personal injury litigation. Presented at the First International Conference on Clinical and Social Aspects of Illness Behaviour. Adelaide, Australia, 1984

Merskey H: An appraisal of hypnosis. Postgrad Med J 47:572–580, 1971

Merskey H: The Analysis of Hysteria. London, Bailliere Tindall, 1979

Merskey H: Psychological approaches to the treatment of chronic pain. Postgrad Med J 60:886–892, 1984

Merskey H, Buhrich NA: Hysteria and organic brain disease. Br J Med Psychol 48:359–366, 1975

Merskey H, Lau CL, Russell ES, et al: Screening for psychiatric morbidity, the pattern of psychological illness and premorbid characteristics in four chronic pain populations. Pain 30:141–157, 1987

Milligan WL: Psychoneuroses treated with electrical convulsions. Lancet 2:516–520, 1946

Mitchell KR, Mitchell DM: Migraine: an exploratory treatment application of programmed behavior therapy techniques. J Psychosom Res 15:137–157, 1971

Mitchell KR, White RG: Behavioral self-management: an application to the problem of migraine headaches. Behavior Ther 8:213–221, 1977

Mohr PD, Bond MJ: A chronic epidemic of hysterical blackouts in a comprehensive school. Br Med J 284:961–962, 1982

Monks R, Merskey H: Treatment with psychotropic drugs, in Textbook of Pain: Sec. 3A3. Edited by Wall PS, Melzack R. London, Churchill Livingston, 1984

Munford PR, Reardon D, Liberman RP, et al: Behavioral treatment of hysterical coughing and mutism: a case study. J Consult Clin Psychol 44:1008–1014, 1976

Munro A, Chmara J: Monosymptomatic hypochondriacal psychosis: a diagnostic checklist based on 50 cases of the disorder. Can J Psychiatry 77:374–376, 1982

Nadelson T: The Münchausen spectrum: borderline character features. Gen Hosp Psychiatry 1:11–17, 1979

National Commission for the Protection of Human Subjects of Biomedical and Behavioral Research: Psychosurgery. Washington, DC, U.S. Department of Health, Education, and Welfare, DHEW Publication No. (OS) 77-0002

Nemiah J: Denial revisited: reflections on psychosomatic theory. Psychother Psychosom 26:140–147, 1975

Ng LKY: A perspective on chronic pain: treatment and research, in New Approaches to the Treatment of Chronic Pain. Edited by Ng LKY. Rockville, Md, Alcohol, Drug Abuse, and Mental Health Administration, 1981

Nitzkin JL: Epidemic transient situational disturbance in an elementary school. J Fla Med Assoc 63:357–359, 1976

Noriek K: A follow-up examination of neuroses. Acta Psychiatr Scand 46:81–95, 1970

Noyes R Jr: Beta-blocking drugs and anxiety. Psychosomatics 23:155–170, 1982

Noyes R Jr, Reich J, Clancy J, et al: Reduction of hypochondriasis with treatment of panic disorder. Br J Psychiatry (in press)

Nuechterlein KH, Holroyd JC: Biofeedback in the treatment of tension headache. Arch Gen Psychiatry 37:866–873, 1980

Ochitill H: Conversion disorder, in Treatment of Mental Disorders. Edited by Greist JH, Jefferson JW, Spitzer RL. New York, Oxford University Press, 1982, pp 271–277

O'Donhell JM: Implosive therapy with hypnosis in the treatment of cancer phobia: a case report. Psychotherapy Theory, Research and Practice 15:8–12, 1978

Okasha A, Glaleb HA, Sadek A: A double blind trial for the clinical management of psychogenic headache. Br J Psychiatry 122:181–183, 1973

Painter J, Seres J, Newmann R: Assessing benefits of the pain center: why some patients regress. Pain 8:101–113, 1980

Pawl RP: Pain Primer. Lake Forest, Ill, Yearbook Medical Publishers, 1979

Pilowsky I: The response to treatment in hypochondriacal disorders. Aust N-Z J Psychiatry 2:88–94, 1968

Pilowsky I: Primary and secondary hypochondriasis. Acta Psychiatr Scand 46:273–285, 1970

Pilowsky I: Psychotherapy for chronic pain. Clinical Anesthesiology, 3:143–153, 1985

Pilowsky I, Hallett E, Bassett D, et al: A controlled study of amitriptyline in the treatment of chronic pain. Pain 14:169–179, 1982

Pinsky JJ: Chronic intractable benign pain: a syndrome and its treatment with intensive short-term group psychotherapy. J Human Stress 45:17–21, 1978

Pinsky JJ, Malyon AK: The eclectic nature of psychotherapy in the treatment of chronic pain syndromes, in Chronic pain. Edited by Crue BD. New York, SP Medical and Scientific Books, 1979

Pinsky JJ, Griffin SE, Agnew DC, et al: Aspects of long-term evaluation of pain unit treatment program for patients with chronic intractable benign pain syndrome: treatment outcome. Bulletin Los Angeles Neuroscience Society 44:53–69, 1979

Pond DA, Bidwell BH: A survey of epilepsy in 14 general practices, II: social and psychological aspects. Epilepsia (Amsterdam) 1:285–299, 1959

Pope HG, Jonas JM, Jonas B: Factitious psychosis: phenomenology, family history, and long-term outcome of nine patients. Am J Psychiatry 139:1480–1483, 1982

Prima A, Agnoli A, Tamburello A: A review of the applications of biofeedback to migraine and tension headaches. Acta Neurol 34:510–521, 1979

Proctor JT: Hysteria in childhood. Am J Orthopsychiatry, 28:394–407, 1958

Quill TE: Somatization disorder. JAMA 254 (21):3075–3079, 1985

Raphael B: The management of pathological grief. Aust NZ J Psychiatry 9:173–180, 1975

Reich P, Gottfried LA: Factitious disorders in a teaching hospital. Ann Intern Med 99:240–247, 1983

Reich J, Tupin JP, Abramowitz SI: Psychiatric diagnosis of chronic pain patients. Am J Psychiatry 140:1495–1498, 1983

Reidenberg MM, Lowenthal DT: Adverse non-drug reactions. N Engl J Med 279:678–679, 1968

Reinking RH, Hutchings D: Follow-up to: Tension headaches: what form of therapy is most effective? Biofeedback Self Regul 6:57–62, 1981

Reynolds JR: Remarks on paralysis and other disorders of motion and sensation, dependent on idea. Br Med J II:483–485. Discussion 378–379, 1869

Richardson D: Intracranial stimulation for the control of chronic pain. Clin Neurosurg 31:316–322, 1983

Richelson E: The use of tricyclic antidepressants in chronic gastrointestinal pain. J Clin Psychiatry 43:50–55, 1982

Rickels K, Hesbacher P, Vandervort W, et al: Tybamate—a perplexing drug. Am J Psychiatry 125:76–82, 1968

Riding J, Munro A: Pimozide in the treatment of monosymptomatic hypochondriacal psychosis. Acta Psychiatr Scand 52:23–30, 1975

Roberts A, Reinhardt L: Behavioral management of chronic pain: long-term follow-up with comparison groups. Pain 8:151–162, 1980

Roberts J, Roberts R: Delusions of parasitosis. Br Med J 1:1219, 1977

Robins E, O'Neal P: Clinical features of hysteria in children wth a note on prognosis: a two to seventeen year follow-up study of 45 patients. Nerv Child 10:246–271, 1953

Romano J, Turner J: Chronic pain and depression: does the evidence support a relationship? Psychol Bull 97:18–34, 1985

Rosenberg S: The relationship of certain personality factors to prognosis in psychotherapy. J Clin Psychol 10:341–345, 1954

Rosenblatt R, Reich J, Dehring D: Tricyclic antidepressants in treatment of depression and chronic pain: analysis of the supporting evidence. Anesth Analg 63:1025–1032, 1984

Rumans LW, Vosti KZ: Factitious and fraudulent fever. Am J Med 65:745–755, 1978

Rutrick D, Aronoff GM: Combined psychotherapy for pain patients. Hosp Pract, Sep 1983, pp 60E–60R

Salter RH: Coronary neurosis. Br Med J 1:245–246, 1972

Sands DE: Electro-convulsion therapy in 301 patients in a general hospital. Br Med J 2:289–293, 1946

Sapira JD: Reassurance therapy. Ann Intern Med 77:603–604, 1972

Sargant W, Shorvon HJ: Acute war neurosis. Arch Neurol 54:231–240, 1945

Savitz S: Hypnosis in the treatment of chronic pain. South Med J 76:319–321, 1983

Scallet A, Cloninger CR, Othmer E: The management of chronic hysteria: a review and double-blind trial of electrosleep and other relaxation methods. J Nerv Ment Dis 37:347–353, 1976

Schachter S, Singer JE: Cognitive, social, and physiological determinants of emotional state. Psychol Rev 69:379–399, 1962

Schenecke OW, Schüffel W: Evaluation of combined pharmacological and psychotherapeutic treatment in patients with functional abdominal disorders. Psychother Pyschosom 26:86–92, 1975

Scott PD: Commentary on: a peculiar hysterical state by S. J. M. Ganser. Brit J Criminol 5:127–131, 1965

Shanfield S, Heiman E, Cope D: Pain and the marital relationship in psychiatric distress. Pain 7:343–351, 1979

Sheehan DV, Ballenger J, Jacobsen G: Treatment of endogenous anxiety with phobic, hysterical, and hypochondriacal symptoms. Arch Gen Psychiatry 37:51–59, 1980

Shorer PG: A peculiar hysterical state by S.J.M. Brit J Criminol 5:120–126, 1965

Shoenfeld Y, Shapiro Y, Drory Y, et al: Rehabilitation of patients with NCA (asthenia) through a short-term training program. Am J Phys Med Rehabil 57:1–8, 1978

Sifneos PE: The prevalence of alexithymic characteristics in psychosomatic patients. Psychother Psychosom 22:255–262, 1973

Sim M: Guide to Psychiatry, 4th ed. Edinburgh, Churchill Livingston, 1981

Sirois F: Epidemic hysteria. Acta Psychiatr Scand, (Suppl) 252:1–46, 1974

Sjödin I, Svedlund J, Ottosson JO, et al: Controlled study of psychotherapy in chronic peptic ulcer disease. Psychosomatics 27:187–200, 1986

Skott A: Delusions of Infestation: Reports from the Psychiatric Research Centre. St. Jorgen Hospital, University of Goteborg, Sweden, 1978

Slater E: Diagnosis of "hysteria." Br Med J 1:1395–1399, 1965

Slater E, Glithero E: A follow-up of patients diagnosed as suffering from "hysteria." J Psychosom Res 9:9–13, 1965

Smith GR, Monson RA, Ray DC: Psychiatric consultation in somatization disorder. N Engl J Med 314:1407–1413, 1986

Spence N: Relaxation training for chronic pain patients using EMG feedback: an analysis of process and outcome effects. Aust N-Z J Psychiatry 18:263–272, 1984

Spiegel D, Bloom JR: Group therapy and hypnosis reduce metastatic breast carcinoma pain. Psychosom Med 45:333–339, 1983

Stone AR, Frank JD, Nash EH, et al: An intensive five-year follow-up study of treated psychiatric outpatients. J Nerv Ment Dis 133:410–422, 1961

Stone MH: Factitious illness: psychological findings and treatment recommendations. Bull Menninger Clin 41:239–254, 1977

Sturgis E, Schaefer C, Sikora T: Pain center follow-up study of treated and untreated patients. Arch Phys Med Rehabil 65:301–303, 1984

Svedlund J, Ottosson J, Sjödin I, et al: Controlled study of psychotherapy in irritable bowel sydrome. Lancet 2:589–592, 1983

Swanson D, Maruta T, Swenson W: Results of behaviour modification in treatment of chronic pain. Psychosom Med 41:55–61, 1979

Swerdlo M: Anticonvulsant drugs and chronic pain. Clin Neuropharmacol 7:51–82, 1984

Tann SY: Cognitive and cognitive behavioural methods for pain control: a selective review. Pain 12:201, 1982

Tarler-Benlolo L: The role of relaxation in biofeedback training: a critical review of the literature. Psychol Bull 85:727–755, 1978

Teoh JI: Epidemic hysteria and social change: an outbreak in a lower secondary school in Malaysia. Singapore Med J 16(4):301–306, 1975

Thomas KB: The consultation and the therapeutic illusion. Br Med J 1:1327–1328, 1978

Trifiletti R: The psychological effectiveness of pain management procedures in the context of behavioural medicine and medical psychology. Genet Soc Gen Psychology Monogr 109:251–278, 1984

Trimble MR: Serum prolactin in epilepsy and hysteria. Br Med J 1682, 1978

Tsoi WF: The Ganser syndrome in Singapore: a report on ten cases. Br J Psychiatry 123:567–572, 1973

Turk D, Meichenbaum D, Berman W: Application of biofeedback for the regulation of pain: a critical review. Psychol Bull 86:1322–1338, 1979

Turk D, Meichenbaum D, Genest M: Pain and behavioural medicine. New York, Guilford Press, 1984

Turnbull JM: The hypochondriacal patient, in Psychosocial Basis of Medical Practice. Edited by Bowden CL, Burstein AG. Baltimore, Williams and Wilkins, 1974, pp. 73–80

Turner J, Chapman CR: Psychological interventions for chronic pain: a critical review, I: relaxation training and biofeedback. Pain 12:1–21, 1982a

Turner J, Chapman CR: Psychological interventions for chronic pain: a critical review, II: operant conditioning, hypnosis, and cognitive-behavioural therapy. Pain 12:23–46, 1982b

Turner J, Calsyn D, Fordyce W, et al: Drug utilization patterns in chronic pain patients. Pain 12:357–363, 1982

Tyrer P: The Role of Bodily Feelings in Anxiety. London, Oxford University Press, 1976

Tyrer P: The role of the psychiatrist in the pain clinic. Bulletin of the Royal College of Psychiatrists 9:135–136, 1985

Ulenhuth EH, Glass RM, Haberman SJ, et al: Sensitivity of clinical measures in trials of antianxiety agents, in Quantitative Techniques for the Evaluation Behavior of Psychiatric Patients. Edited by Burdock EF, Sudilorsky A, Gershon S. New York, Marcel Dekker, 1982

Vacek J: K problému tzv. cirkumskriptních hypochondrií. Československá Psychiatrie (Praha) 68:312–317, 1972

Valko RJ: Group therapy for patients with hysteria (Briquet's disorder). Dis Nerv Syst 37:484–487, 1976

Van Hagen KO: Chronic intolerable pain. JAMA 165:773–777, 1957

Van Putten T, Alban J: Lithium carbonate in personality disorders: a case of hysteria. J Nerv Ment Dis 164:218–222, 1977

Vasudevan S, Lynch T, Grunert B, et al: Outpatient management of chronic pain: long-term results. Wis Med J 84:7–10, 1985

Wadsworth, MDJ, Butterfield WIH, Blarey R: Health and Sickness: The Choice of Treatment. London, Tavistock, 1972

Walker J: Relief from chronic pain by low power laser irradiation. Neurosci Lett 43:339–344, 1983

Walsh T: Antidepressants in chronic pain. Clin Neuropharmacol 6:271–295, 1983

Walter CJ, Mitchell-Heggs N, Sargant W: Modified narcosis, ECT, and antidepressant drugs: a review of techniques and immediate outcome. Br J Psychiatry 120:651–662, 1972

Walters A: Psychogenic regional pain alias hysterical pain. Brain 84:1–18, 1961

Watson CP, Evans RJ, Reed K, et al: Amitriptyline versus placebo in posttherapeutic neuralgia. Neurology 32:671–673, 1982

Weber JJ, Elinson J, Moss LM: Psychoanalysis and change. Arch Gen Psychiatry 17:687–709, 1967

Weinstein E, Kahn R, Bergman P: Effect of electroconvulsive therapy on intractable pain. AMA Archives Neurology and Psychiatry 81:37–42, 1959

Weiss D, Bloomburg W, Drew J: The use of electroshock as therapy for atypical and intractable pain (transcript). 82nd Meeting of the American Neurological Association. 1958, pp 166–168

White BWS, Donovan WH, Dwyer AP: A comprehensive programme for the assessment and treatment of low back pain in Western Australia, in Problems in Pain. Edited by Wallace M, Peck CL. London, Pergamon Press, 1980

Whitlock FA: The Ganser syndrome. Br J Psychiatry 113:19–30, 1967

Woodforde JM, Merskey H: Personality traits of patients with chronic pain. J Psychosom Res 16:167, 1972

Woodruff RA, Goodwin DW, Guze SB: Hysteria (Briquet's syndrome), in Hysteria. Edited by Roy A. Chichester, John Wiley and Sons, 1982

Wooley S, Blackwell B, Winget C: A learning theory model of chronic illness behaviour: theory, treatment, and research. Psychosom Med 40:379–401, 1978

Yallom ID: Theory and Practice of Group Psychotherapy. New York, Basic Books, 1970

Yassa R: Munchausen's syndrome: a successfully treated case. Psychosomatics 19:242–243, 1978

Yealland LR: Hysterical Disorders of Warfare. London, MacMillan Publishing Co., 1918

Dissociative Disorders (or Hysterical Neuroses, Dissociative Type)

Chapter 197

Introduction

The category of dissociative disorders is made up of five entities, the first three of which involve a disturbance in memory. Psychogenic amnesia and psychogenic fugue are regarded as distinctive free-standing disorders. A good case could be made, however, for subsuming psychogenic fugue under psychogenic amnesia. Also, there is a striking resemblance between psychogenic fugue and multiple personality.

Depersonalization disorder has been listed as a dissociative disorder because the feeling of one's own reality is lost. This inclusion has been questioned because a disturbance in memory is absent. Most significantly, in terms of our present concern, it will be seen that the treatment for depersonalization disorder is distinctively different than it is for either dissociative or conversion disorders, the so-called hysterical neuroses of DSM-II (American Psychiatric Association 1968).

In the past few decades, there has been a resurgence of interest in multiple personality. It has been suggested that the diagnosis of multiple personality was simply overlooked and consequently many patients, who might have been treatable, went undiagnosed and remained untreated. The position just stated has been firmly held by one camp. Another camp contends that the recent increase in the number of cases of multiple personality reflects a resurgence of interest on the part of psychiatrists who in turn have influenced suggestible patients. In other words, they maintain that we are witnessing the effect of iatrogenesis.

The subgroup of atypical dissociative disorders reflects the general unevenness of this overall category. Some of the atypical dissociative disorders are unquestionably dissociative in nature; others are open to question. Also, there are probably dissociative disorders not included here that are hidden in other parts of DSM-III (American Psychiatric Association 1980). One example might be pathologic intoxication, now referred to as alcohol idiosyncratic intoxication. There is reason to believe that what has been regarded as an idiosyncratic reaction to the ingestion of a small amount of alcohol is actually a dissociative disorder (Hollender 1979).

It has been implied or stated that psychogenic amnesia, psychogenic fugue, and multiple personality are disorders, but perhaps in fact they are only symptoms. No matter what they are labeled, however, they clearly serve a protective function. Accordingly, our therapeutic approach should be designed to determine the nature of the underlying threat and the best way to relieve it.

Chapter 198

Psychogenic Amnesia

Definition

The term, *psychogenic amnesia*, is used in DSM-III-R (American Psychiatric Association 1987) to describe a specific entity. It is a "dissociative disorder" in which a sudden temporary alteration in consciousness occurs and important personal events cannot be recalled. This disorder is not due to organic brain disease.

The most common feature is a temporally localized or circumscribed amnesia. In other words, there is total memory loss for a specific period of time. Typically, the amnesia involves the first few hours following an emotionally traumatic event. However, psychodynamic factors modify the clinical picture and ultimately determine the actual pattern of forgetting. Thus, specific islands of recall may punctuate the amnesic period. When these occur, the term used in DSM-III-R is *selective amnesia*. Memory loss may be total and extend backward from the traumatic event to encompass the patient's entire life up to and including the traumatic event, or the inability to recall may continue beyond the traumatic event into the present. The terms, *generalized amnesia* and *continuous amnesia*, have been adopted in DSM-III-R for the latter two patterns. These separate diagnostic designations are probably not of much significance from a practical clinical point of view.

Associated symptoms include perplexity, disorientation, purposeless wandering, and la belle indifference. In wartime this disorder often occurs in young men in the combat zone. In civilian life it may occur somewhat more frequently in adolescent girls. It rarely occurs in the elderly.

Attacks are more often associated with specific personality disorders, namely histrionic or borderline. An acute psychological trauma, that is, subjectively intolerable life situation, is the usual precipitating factor. Thus, a posttreatment stress disorder may also be present.

Patients with psychogenic amnesia are likely to seek help. They may present themselves at hospital emergency rooms or to police officers and complain of "lost memory."

Memory Functioning

Much of forgetting is purely or even partially psychogenic. Memory functioning is usually described in terms of the three "Rs"—registration, retention, and recall.

The first requirement for normal memory registration is a physiologically intact, alert central nervous system. Thus, substance abuse may lead to transient disturbances in registration. This is seen in the so-called "alcohol blackout" and in the impaired capacity to learn noted in benzodiazepine abusers. Diffuse brain disease from any cause may be associated with impaired registration. This may lead to permanent and irretrievable memory loss. Clouded states of consciousness following grand mal seizures or following electroshock therapy may be associated with patches of permanent memory loss.

On the other hand, events that take place during periods of severe negative emotional states such as depression, panic, rage, or shame may be securely registered, stored, and retained, but are not retrievable into consciousness except by special means such as hypnosis, intravenous barbiturate interviews (narcoanalysis), or psychoanalysis.

In relation to the function of retention, it should be noted that old memories tend to be retained better than recent memories. This pattern is characteristically intensified in the presence of diffuse organic brain disease.

In relation to the phenomenon of recall, it should be noted that vast quantities of stored data can be recalled potentially but are not available because some psychological mechanism is blocking access to consciousness. This is true of the physiologically intact brain. However, it is also true for the organically injured brain. The organically injured brain may fail to register an event. It may not retain registered events for very long, and recall in general is more difficult. However, even the brain-injured patient tends to recall selectively and a strong psychogenic factor is easily demonstrable in their amnesia.

Differential Diagnosis

First, one must rule out amnesia due to organic causes, for example: concussion, dementia, substance-induced intoxication, the alcohol amnestic disorders, and seizure-connected states of clouded consciousness.

Apart from the physical and laboratory evidence of organic brain disease, some amnesia patterns are characteristically organic. For example, recent memories tend to be more severely affected than remote memories, which tend to remain relatively intact. In addition, organic "forgetting" is commonly in the service of anosognosia (the syndrome of delusional denial of illness) (Weinstein and Kahn 1955). Patients think and act as if they are in a time and place and in circumstances preceding their present state of organic brain disease.

Often the response of the psychogenic amnesia patient to the precipitating traumatic event is to take physical flight. When first discovered by the police, for example, he or she may not only be suffering from psychogenic amnesia but may also be a long distance from home. He or she may have even adopted a new identity to some degree. When these additional dramatic features occur, the diagnostic term *psychogenic fugue* is applied (300.13).

Treatment

Because a subjectively intolerable life situation precipitates the disorder, disconnection from this life situation is the first step in treatment. Accordingly, hospitalizing such patients may be imperative and serve as a powerful anxiety-relieving procedure. The use of strong suggestion to remember may then suffice to lift the amnesia. In other instances, hypnosis with the suggestion to regress temporally to the period immediately preceding the memory loss will not only restore the lost memory but also identify the life stress that precipitated it.

With difficult-to-hypnotize patients, a small quantity of a 5 percent solution of an intravenous barbiturate (sodium amobarbital or sodium pentobarbital) may elicit an abreaction, that is, an emotionally charged recall of the lost memory. Although those subject to psychogenic amnesia are typically young adults in good physical health, certain precautions must be observed before proceeding with an intravenous barbiturate interview. Evidence of severe physical illness of any kind is a contraindication to the procedure. Because of the nature of psychogenic amnesia, obtaining "informed" consent from the patient would seem to be a meaningless gesture. Fortunately these patients are usually eager for help and readily accept this and other procedures. If, however, a patient refuses to accept a barbiturate interview, his or her wish must be respected. An underlying paranoid psychotic disorder might be intensified if the procedure is carried out without consent. If responsible relatives are on the scene, their cooperation and consent should be elicited. However, often they are not available until the amnesia has been lifted.

The 5 percent barbiturate solution must be injected slowly, not ever faster than 1.0 ml per minute. If speech becomes slurred, marked nystagmus is present, or mistakes are made in counting numbers backwards, it is likely that the optimal blood level has been exceeded. To titrate the dose for the interview, it is helpful to observe the patient's face. A skin flush is an important preliminary sign. The eyes may suddenly fill with tears, or, conversely, the patient may suddenly relax and make some jocular remark. These are delicate endpoints. When this point is reached, the abreaction may be precipitated by a sudden frightening noise created, for example, by striking a large empty tin can with a stick. A stern command given loudly in a startling manner also may touch off the abreaction. Prior to that point the interviewer's interventions should be scanty, brief, and neutral. Thereafter, he or she may enter actively into a psychodrama with the patient, encouraging the expression of all thoughts and feelings that have caused suffering. It should be noted that not all barbiturate interviews are successful. The patient should abreact with relative spontaneity. Persistent interrogation of a somnolent, nonresponsive patient usually is not productive.

It is important for the therapist to consider carefully the stressful reality, the traumatic event, that precipitated the psychogenic amnesia and take steps to reduce that stress. Failure to do so invites further episodes of amnesia and even dangerous acting out, including murder (Myerson 1966).

Case 1

The following case report illustrates some classical aspects of psychogenic amnesia. The patient, a 32-year-old married salesman, was found by a police officer sitting in his car parked at the edge of a highway. He seemed perplexed and bewildered. In response to the officer's questions, he revealed that he could not recall who he was, how he got to the spot on the road where he was found, or where he was going. Family contact revealed that he had left home abruptly on December 25, 1973, after his wife disclosed her intention to divorce him and, despite his pleas that she reconsider, had also ordered him out of the house. After an extensive medical workup failed to reveal significant organic pathology, he was admitted to a psychiatric ward on January 2, 1974.

In the admission mental status report, it was noted that the patient presented a bland facade out of keeping with his predicament (la belle indifference). He spoke slowly but calmly and revealed that he had full recall for events prior to 1959 but had a feeling of total estrangement from his present surroundings. He felt that his face looked older than he remembered it. He seemed totally out of touch with current events in the world and in his community.

The patient gave a history of a chaotic family background. He was born out of wedlock and never knew his father. His mother abandoned him at an early age, and he was raised until he was four years old by an alcoholic maternal grandmother. Until the age of seven years, he was with a maternal aunt whom he described as an alcoholic prostitute. Another maternal aunt provided a home for several years; this was a stormy home in which he was frequently called a "bastard" and was told that his mother was a prostitute. This aunt was hospitalized for a psychotic episode; she subsequently divorced and remarried. When the patient was 17 years old, he was ordered out of the house by the aunt's new husband.

The patient began working and, at the age of 20, he married a high school classmate. This marriage was stormy. His wife was repeatedly involved in infidelities, and they were separated twice. Nevertheless, they remained married for 12 years and had two sons, ages seven and nine.

In the sheltered setting of the hospital and with the help of two sodium amobarbital interviews, the patient was able to recapture his lost memory.

Comment.   The amnesia dating back to 1959 was a puzzle until it was learned during the sodium amobarbital interview that that was the year in which he was ordered out of his maternal aunt's home. Whatever the limitations of this home, it had nevertheless provided some sense of stability and continuity to his life. With his marriage to his high school classmate three years later, he was able to find a home again, a stormy one to be sure, but one to which he clung desperately. When his wife declared her determination to end the marriage and ordered him out of the house, it awakened the memory of the previous trauma when he was ordered out of the home of the maternal aunt.

Case 2

In May 1943, at the end of the Tunisian campaign, an American military policeman found an enlisted man wandering the streets of Algiers. When asked his name, the soldier fingered his dogtags with a perplexed expression and then stated that he could not remember. To all other questions, he responded with increased bewilderment and repeated insistently that he could not remember anything. He was admitted to a nearby army hospital where he continued to display these same clinical features, perplexity and amnesia.

Physical examination was entirely negative. In current terminology, he could be classified as a case of psychogenic amnesia. In response to a small quantity of intravenous sodium pentobarbital, the look of perplexity gave way to an expression of abject terror. In response to the strong suggestion to describe what was happening, he began trembling, his teeth chattered, he wept, and he spoke excitedly of a battle scene. In a state of full emotional abreaction, he reconstructed the details of his landing with the U.S. Army 1st Infantry Division on a beach in Algiers on November 8, 1942. At one point, he screamed that a shell exploded and killed all his buddies. He sobbed quietly for a while and then began enacting another scene. He was now on a park bench somewhere in Algiers weeping. A young woman came up to him and encouraged him to accompany her to her apartment. During the next several months, the soldier never left her apartment. She went off to work each morning and brought back food in the evening. This continued until the end of the Tunisian campaign when he believed he had to return to duty. He left her apartment, ostensibly to find his outfit. He stated that, as soon as he stepped out into the street, he lost consciousness and this loss persisted until the moment of the pentobarbital interview. During the abreaction and subsequent interviews, the soldier developed total recall. He was able to present a detailed and coherent account of his past life, including the period of seven months in Algiers during which he lived with the young French woman.

The patient, 21 years old, the oldest of seven children, had done odd jobs after finishing grade school at the age of 16. He was 18 years old when he enlisted in the regular Army. He had been in the service for over two years when he participated in the North African landing with the 1st Division.

After a discussion with the patient concerning his legal liabilities, the Judge Advocate's office was contacted. It was thought that this soldier had what we would now call a *borderline personality disorder* (301.83) and the amnesic state was a complication of the associated emotional instability. It was agreed that the soldier should not be charged with desertion. He served a brief prison sentence on a lesser charge; on completing the sentence he was reclassified to noncombatant status and given a limited duty assignment.

Comment.   It was noted earlier how important it is for the therapist to consider carefully the traumatic event that precipitated the amnesia and to protect the patient from further exposure to the intolerable situation. In this case, the brief prison sentence and a return to noncombat duty proved effective in rehabilitating this young soldier.

Chapter 199

Psychogenic Fugue

Symptoms such as alternating personalities, extended periods of amnesia, and assumption of new identities with loss of memory for the past provide rich material for novelists and screen writers. Because of their dramatic quality the general public is well aware of this fascinating group of psychiatric syndromes, now known as the dissociative disorders. However, following a period in the late 19th century, when every psychiatric expert seemed to have his favorite case, relatively little has been written about this diagnostic group (Nemiah 1980). Perhaps this is because there is little to add to the earlier, detailed clinical descriptions and because these disorders are difficult to study experimentally.

Before treatment is discussed, the diagnostic criteria for psychogenic fugue, the phenomenology of the syndrome, and the etiologic factors proposed to explain it will be reviewed. Treatment, as will become apparent, requires an understanding of what the fugue may represent in terms of its defensive nature and the possibility of underlying serious psychiatric/neurologic disease.

Diagnostic Criteria

In keeping with its Meyerian orientation, the DSM-I (American Psychiatric Association 1952) used the term *dissociative reaction* to include a wide variety of symptoms that reflected personality disorganization (pp. 32–33). These diagnoses were placed within the category of psychoneurotic disorders. The second edition of the manual (DSM-II) (American Psychiatric Association 1968) returned to the classification proposed by Janet (1907, pp. 39–40) and categorized the dissociative symptoms as a subtype of hysterical neurosis. A more recent diagnostic manual (DSM-III) (American Psychiatric Association 1980, pp. 244–249) placed the dissociative disorders in a separate category which includes the disorders discussed in this section. Specific DSM-III-R (American Psychiatric Association 1987) diagnostic criteria for psychogenic fugue are listed in Table 1. Psychogenic fugue differs from psychogenic amnesia in that with the latter there is only memory loss and with the former there is also a change in behavior that is inconsistent with the basic personality (assumption of a new identity, partial or complete).

An argument could be advanced that psychogenic fugue is not a "diagnosis" but rather a symptom of an underlying psychiatric disorder. Physicians no longer speak of "fever" as a diagnosis; similarly it probably is incorrect to speak of a symptom occurring in a wide variety of psychiatric illnesses as a distinct diagnosis. Psychiatric disorders associated with psychogenic fugue include depression, bipolar affective disorder, schizophrenia, personality disorders, intoxication states, metabolic disorders, and organic neurologic disease, particularly temporal lobe epilepsy (Akhtar and Brenner 1979).

Phenomenology

Psychogenic fugue is believed to be a relatively rare phenomenon. The psychiatric literature in regard to this disorder is anecdotal, based on case reports, either single or multiple. Despite some efforts to categorize features such as age or gender (see below), there have been no systematic studies of incidence or prevalence.

The following clinical vignettes, drawn from the clinical experience of the author, illustrate some commonly seen features.

Table 1. DSM-III-R Diagnostic Criteria for Psychogenic Fugue
A. The predominant disturbance is sudden, unexpected travel away from home or one's customary place of work, with inability to recall one's past.
B. Assumption of a new identity (partial or complete).
C. The disturbance is not due to Multiple Personality Disorder or to an Organic Mental Disorder (e.g., partial complex seizures in temporal lobe epilepsy).

Case 1

A 53-year-old married male technician was admitted to the medical service of a general hospital after being found, stuporous and dehydrated, sitting in his car parked at a truck stop 35 miles from his home. He denied knowing who he was but identification was readily established through his car registration. He then regained past memory except for the preceding 48 hours. The last thing he could remember was driving on the interstate highway.

No organic disorder could be identified as the cause of the amnesia but a drug screen was positive for barbiturates. Psychiatric consultation was requested. In a series of interviews the patient's memory gradually returned and he then "remembered" feeling overwhelmed by his teenaged daughter's sexual behavior and by increasing pressures at work. Upon detailed questioning it became evident that symptoms reflecting major depression (i.e., insomnia, anorexia with weight loss, anhedonia, decreased libido, and decreased concentration) had been present for several months.

The only prior psychiatric history was a depression which had resolved spontaneously without treatment. The patient, a "solid citizen," was a devoutly religious man belonging to a fundamentalistic sect. The fugue had permitted escape from his depressed mood and had allowed his apparent suicidal attempt, both of which were incompatible with his strict religious beliefs. The patient was treated with a tricyclic antidepressant and his depressive symptoms remitted. He dropped out of treatment as soon as there was relief from his depressive symptoms, but follow-up several months later indicated that there had been no further fugue states.

Case 2

A 33-year-old black male was hospitalized on the neurologic service of a large metropolitan hospital after "coming to" in an urban rescue mission. For two days he had participated in the activities of the mission as if he were one of the regulars. Upon coming to he professed a complete loss of memory for the past, including his name, but was identified by the information in his wallet. He claimed that he did not recognize his wife or children but did say that they must be related if everyone said so.

Neurologic evaluation was normal and the mental status examination revealed the patient to be pleasant and superficially cooperative but psychologically unsophisticated. Cognitive functions were intact with the exception of slow responses and lack of remote memory.

The patient was agreeable to the suggestion of an amytal interview. During the interview he had a return of memory and recalled that subsequent to some marital strife he had gone for a walk late one night, taking with him a personal stereo cassette recorder and a large sum of cash. He reported that he had been accosted by two men who robbed him, held a gun to his head, and threatened to kill him if he said anything. The next two days were remembered hazily until coming to at the mission.

Past history was significant in that he had experienced an episode of depression associated with transient suicidal ideation and memory problems nine years previously. He was hospitalized briefly at that time but then dropped out of treatment because he felt that his psychiatrist did not seem very interested in him. The patient also had a history of episodic abuse of ethanol and marijuana, and his wife reported that in response to marital arguments the patient had frequently "run home" to his mother.

Subsequent to the amytal interview the patient rapidly regained his past memory and was then discharged from the hospital. However, he repetitively missed scheduled outpatient psychotherapy appointments despite his overt stated motivation to resolve his life problems. A follow-up conversation with the wife indicated that he had experienced one additional brief period of memory loss and that he was continuing to "run home to his mother."

In summary, this man had prominent passive-dependent and immature personality characteristics. He literally "ran" from his marital problems and at times used chemical substances to facilitate repression. His psychogenic fugues were consistent with these characterologic features and his assumption of the role of a rescue mission derelict was to place himself into a totally dependent position.

Fugue states usually occur at times of turmoil and emotional stress. They are reported more frequently during periods of prolonged intensive stress such as war (Fisher 1945; Sargant and Slater 1940) or in populations in which there is high situational stress (Kennedy and Neville 1957).

A fugue may last only for hours and consist mainly of aimless wandering or behavior similar to that described in the clinical vignettes. One report indicated that about half of all fugues last less than 24 hours (Abeles and Schilder 1935). Others may be of long duration, during which the person assumes a new identity and maintains integrated behavior including the seeking of employment and the arranging of living conditions. In the latter case the differences between psychogenic fugue and multiple personalities might appear to be minimal. The majority of patients have more than one fugue episode (Berrington et al. 1956). Patients who experience fugue states also often have the symptoms of multiple personality and conversion (Abeles and Schilder 1935; Chancellor and Fraser 1982; Fisher 1945; Parfitt and Gall 1944). This phenomenological observation is consistent with Janet's (1907) opinion that dissociation and conversion are both symptoms of "hysteria."

Clinicians who have studied multiple patients with fugues report that some features are frequently seen. Although there is not universal agreement, most clinicians have been impressed that hysterical (and/or hysterical personality) mechanisms are often present. Berrington et al. (1956) found that a majority of these patients could best be described as "hystero-psychopathic." Also, these patients have been reported to be highly suggestible (Fisher 1945; Kennedy and Neville 1957) and prone to lie (Stengel 1941). Abeles and Schilder (1935) commented upon the high frequency of prior fainting episodes or suicidal attempts. These symptoms, along with the fugue, can be interpreted as attempts to escape from problems and thus define a specific coping style (Fisher 1945).

In one series of 63 patients with psychogenic fugues, the gender distribution was approximately equal (Abeles and Schilder 1935), while in another series of 74 patients, males predominated (Kennedy and Neville 1957). The type of hospital or clinical setting (e.g., military hospital) may create a bias in regard to gender. The age distribution for these patients is primarily in the second, third, or fourth decades (Abeles and Schilder 1935; Berrington et al. 1956).

Several authors believe that fugue is a symptom and that when it is relieved there is always an underlying disorder (Fisher 1945; Geleerd et al. 1945; Kennedy and Neville 1957; Parfitt and Gall 1944). According to Kennedy and Neville the underlying disorder is usually a serious organic disease, malingering with the objective of concealing a legal offense, or intolerable anxiety or depression. Schizophrenia has also been associated with psychogenic fugue (Abeles and Schilder 1935; Geleerd et al. 1945; Myerson 1966).

The importance of organic brain disease is raised repetitively in the differential diagnosis of fugue. Kennedy and Neville (1957) reported that of the patients with sudden loss of memory whom they studied, 37 percent had gross organic disease of the central nervous system. Epilepsy, head injury, chronic encephalitis, and senile dementia were the most common diagnoses. Highlighting the complicated nature of this symptom complex is the fact that many patients with proven organic disease had at least some restoration of memory with hypnosis! Stengel (1941), who investigated fugue from a psychoanalytic perspective, also found that epilepsy was related in some manner to 40 percent of a series of 25 patients. Berrington et al. (1956) found a history of head injury in about one-half of the 37 patients with fugue. Shenk and Bear (1981) reported that patients with temporal lobe epilepsy have a notably high incidence (33 percent) of dissociative episodes which are not seizures. Other factors such as the use of medications which can affect mental functioning (Gifford et al. 1977) or heavy use of alcohol (Berrington et al. 1956; Goodwin et al. 1969) may also facilitate the development of fugue states. In general it would appear that organic factors that affect memory or create altered states of consciousness may, in a nonspecific manner, be associated with an increased frequency of fugue states. A prior episode of an organically based amnesia may also promote a model of learned behavior for psychogenic disorders of memory (somatic compliance).

Another psychiatric disorder notably associated with fugue is depression (Berrington et al. 1956; Kennedy and Neville 1957; Stengel 1941). Stengel (1941) and Berrington et al. (1957) both found a "depressive setting" to be present in the majority of patients whom they studied. Other case reports (Abeles and Schilder 1935; Gudjonsson and Haward 1982; Myerson 1966), including the first case above, also point out that depression and fugue may coexist.

Psychogenic fugue has been interpreted as a partial suicide (Geleerd et al. 1945; Gudjonsson and Haward 1982) and, as in the first case above, the fugue may be used to make a suicidal attempt which is otherwise not consciously acceptable to the patient because of superego prohibitions.

Etiologic Concepts

Fugue states occur in a wide variety of psychiatric disorders. If a common thread exists, it is probably the trait of being highly suggestible and the capacity to use massive repression and escape as a coping style. This description suggests a hysterical cognitive style. The fact that these patients also frequently have conversion symptoms lends support to Janet's concept that the two phenomenon are closely linked. The presence of any current or past organic brain dysfunction may also facilitate the development of fugue.

A theoretical view of fugue as a nonspecific symptom has important implications in regard to treatment. First, the patient with fugue must be carefully evaluated neurologically and treatable neurologic disorders must be addressed. Secondly, alleviation of the symptom of the fugue itself must be regarded as only the first therapeutic step in addressing the overall problem which led to the fugue (Herman 1938). Because the fugue may be serving a protective function, it would be unwise to remove the symptom unless there is provision for comprehensive treatment and potential legal issues have been considered (see below).

Therapeutic Techniques

Before outlining treatment techniques for fugue, a note concerning an ethical issue is in order. The patient's behavior during a fugue state is often different from his or her usual behavior. During fugue states sexual behavior may be less inhibited and/

or the patient may engage in other activities, perhaps criminal in nature, which would be unacceptable to the individual in a normal state of consciousness. Therefore restoration of memories of the fugue period may elicit information that the patient might prefer to suppress, and in fact if the behavior was illicit the situation is one in which self-incrimination is possible (MacHovec 1982; Myerson 1966). Similarly, because these patients tend to be markedly suggestible it is entirely possible that, in response to cues from the interviewer, incorrect information may be reported as fact (Fisher 1945; Kennedy and Neville 1957). Members of the treatmemt team must keep these issues in mind in interpreting data and, in regard to persons suspected of criminal acts, may wish to consult with the patient's attorney before proceeding to restore memory for the fugue state.

Several techniques to restore memory for past events and personal identity have been described. Each has been reported by its advocate to be effective and therefore the choice of a technique may be regarded to be largely a matter of the therapist's preference. These techniques include the following:

Psychotherapy-anamnesis. When a patient is encouraged to talk about that which is remembered, there is a tendency for memory associations to gradually fill in the gaps. Free association may facilitate this process and the therapist can assist by making connections. It is useful to focus on those events immediately preceding the onset of the fugue. Not only will this assist in the restoration of memory but valuable psychodynamic material is often obtained and the groundwork is built for further psychotherapy, if indicated.

Automatic writing, which is free association with writing, consists of asking the patient to write automatically without paying attention to the content (Abeles and Schilder 1935). Review of the written productions may provide clues that in turn elicit memories.

Hypnosis. Amnesic patients are reported to be easy to hypnotize (Kennedy and Neville 1957) and many clinicians have used this method to restore memory in the patient with dissociation. One hypnotic technique described is the use of progressive relaxation followed by visual imagery (MacHovec 1981). The patient is encouraged to relive known events in his or her past and this is usually accompanied by emotional abreaction and the deepening of hypnosis (Kennedy and Neville 1957). The patient is encouraged to keep talking about past events. It is suggested to the patient that when awakening from the trance the amnesia will be gone. Memory may be restored in one hypnotic session but more usually several interviews will be required.

Amytal interview. The use of amobarbital sodium as a way of inducing a state of altered consciousness and successfully treating a psychogenic amnesia was first reported by Herman (1938). The basic principle is to titrate the injection of a barbiturate to the point where the patient is disinhibited but not asleep. The effect may be partially due to suggestion that includes the idea that the injection is a "truth drug" (Kennedy and Neville 1957).

Before proceeding to administer an amytal interview, certain precautions must be observed. Contraindications to the procedure include a history of porphyria; barbiturate allergy or addiction; severe liver, renal, or cardiac disease; upper respiratory infection or inflammation; concurrent intoxication with depressant drugs; and severe hypo- or hypertension (Sbriglio 1984). It is the author's policy to obtain informed consent when the clinical condition of the patient permits. Cardio-respiratory resuscitation equipment must be readily accessible in event of the rare complications of cardiac or respiratory arrest.

Several techniques for amytal interview have been described (McGraw and Oliver 1959; Sbriglio 1984). The technique used by the author is as follows. An intravenous infusion with normal saline is established and then a 5 percent solution of sodium amytal is injected in a "piggy-back" manner at a rate of no faster than 1 cc per minute (50 mg per minute). One method of determining when the proper level of barbiturate intoxication has been achieved is to ask the patient to count backward from 100. The point to begin the interview is when speech becomes slightly slurred or when the patient begins to make mistakes in counting. The presence of sustained rapid lateral nystagmus may also be used as a sign of the proper level of narcosis. The usual amount of barbiturate necessary to achieve this state ranges between 150 and 350 mg. The level of narcosis can be maintained if necessary by the infusion of 25–50 mg amytal every five minutes (Sbriglio 1984).

The interview should initially begin with emotionally neutral topics and then progress to a discussion toward areas of psychologic trauma and suspected repression. Emotional abreaction is not unusual and if the patient becomes severely agitated it may be necessary to terminate the interview with an additional dose of 50–100 mg of amytal. At the conclusion of the interview the interviewer may suggest that all that has transpired will be remembered or, if desired, the patient can be administered sufficient amytal to induce sleep and the interview will be forgotten.

The restoration of memory by one of the preceding techniques must not be interpreted as prima facie evidence that the fugue state was entirely of psychogenic etiology. Patients who have an organic etiology (41 percent of the series reported by Kennedy and Neville 1957) may have a symptomatic response and still have underlying organic pathology. Each patient with a fugue state requires a careful neurologic investigation even when psychodynamic factors apparently explain the symptom.

Following restoration of memory and personal identity and neurologic evaluation, one needs to be attentive to the underlying disorder which produced the fugue. This may be treatment for depression or schizophrenia, crisis intervention in reference to acute life problems, or attention to a concurrent neurologic disease.

Enlisting participation in the treatment process may be difficult because of the patient's coping style. Dissociation is a primitive and somewhat magical way of escaping from problems. In employing this defense the patient throws himself or herself at the mercy of the community and then may expect, in a dependent fashion, that someone else will assume responsibility for his or her life. Certainly neither of the two persons described in the cases mentioned above had any real recognition of their own personal responsibility to solve life problems.

Chapter 200

Multiple Personality Disorder

Multiple personality disorder (MPD) is currently the focus of renewed and expanding clinical and scholarly interest. Within a span of under a decade, a literature consisting largely of sporadic single case reports has been supplanted by a literature increasingly composed of studies of considerable numbers of MPD patients (Putnam 1986). These studies have generated findings that suggest that many long-standing beliefs about this condition must be revised or discarded altogether (Kluft, in press[b]). Because this newer literature is often at variance with traditional teachings, and rapidly has developed a language of its own, the authors will begin with a brief recapitulation of a widely held point of view that newer findings appear to disconfirm, and provide a glossary at the end of this chapter.

Diagnosis and Phenomenology

A disorder is characterized by a cluster of symptoms and/or signs and has a more or less predictable course (Woodruff et al. 1974). Until recently, the existence of more than one personality in a single individual was considered the essence of MPD, and the longitudinal course of the disorder was essentially unknown. Since it is quite easy for behavior characteristic of different personalities to be role-played or induced, with or without hypnosis (Harriman 1942, 1943; Kampman 1974; Kluft 1982, 1985d; Leavitt 1947; Spanos et al. 1985), the dramatic nature of the symptomatology often provides the condition with its own worst enemy in terms of scientific credibility (Goodwin 1985; Kluft 1984a), and it is well established that simulators often succeed in deceiving experienced observers (Orne 1959, 1979a), many have been inclined toward a skeptical stance toward MPD. It often is seen as an iatrogenic artifact, or as a patient's vehicle for achieving secondary gain. From these lines of reasoning has emerged a widespread belief that the correct treatment approach toward MPD is to decline to reinforce its manifestations by according them attention and to "debunk the patient's 'splitting' tendencies" (Linn 1986, p. 2). Follow-up studies of patients exposed to such treatments were not available.

Recent studies, however, offer a different perspective on both the symptoms and signs and the longitudinal course of MPD. Flamboyant presentations of MPD are the most easily diagnosed variants, but are atypical. Ninety-four percent of MPD patients try to hide or dissimulate their pathology; only 6 percent are clearly using their condition for secondary gain (Linn 1986). The core phenomena of MPD are usually covert, and embedded in the matrix of a polysymptomatic presentation suggestive of several types of emotional and physical disorder (Bliss 1980; Coons and Milstein 1986; Kluft 1985b; Putnam et al. 1986). This is why the average MPD patient acquires an average of 3.6 erroneous diagnoses over an average of 6.8 years between first evaluation of symptoms referrable to MPD and an accurate diagnosis (Putnam et al.

1986). Reviews of the literature suggesting that hypnosis creates MPD found no data to sustain this belief (Braun 1984a; Kluft 1982, 1985d). MPD patients approached with hypnosis are indistinguishable from those never hypnotized (Putnam et al. 1986). Hypnotic suggestion creates phenomena analogous to but different from clinical MPD (Kluft 1982, 1985d); those simulating MPD rarely endorse the wider complex of symptoms associated with clinical MPD (Kluft, in press[e]).

MPD has been studied in patients from childhood to senescence (Kluft 1985b). Cases have been reported of children who were assessed and showed no signs of MPD, who were traumatized (with confessions from the traumatizers), and who were found thereafter to have developed MPD (Kluft 1984c, 1984d). Studies indicate that 80 to 97 percent of MPD patients have experienced forms of child abuse (Bliss 1980; Putnam et al. 1986; Schultz et al. 1985). Those studies contradict the image of MPD as a flamboyant iatrogenic artifact. They suggest, instead, that MPD is most parsimoniously understood as a posttraumatic dissociative disorder of childhood onset (Kluft, in press[d]), in which a child, unable to evade or escape overwhelming events, flees inwardly by developing other personalities to encapsulate and cope with traumata he or she cannot otherwise avoid.

Furthermore, follow-up studies now allow a comparison of MPD patients treated with "benign neglect" of their separate personalities in contrast to those treated in therapies that address the separate personalities. Of 12 patients whose MPD was addressed by nonreinforcement/debunking treatments or no treatment, all had MPD on reassessment three to 10 years thereafter (Kluft 1985b). In contrast, of a cohort of 52 actively treated MPD patients reassessed over two years after unifying, only three or 6 percent continued to have diagnosable MPD (Kluft 1986a). It is on the basis of such findings that the authors will emphasize approaches to treatment congruent with the newer literature.

As a clinical entity, MPD is a severe dissociative psychopathology involving a disturbance of both memory and identity (Nemiah 1981), and distinguished from all other psychiatric syndromes by the existence of multiple amnestic episodes, together with the presence of alternating separate and distinct identities (Horevitz and Braun 1984). Signs and symptoms suggestive of concurrent or alternative diagnoses are almost invariably present (Bliss 1980; Horevitz and Braun 1984; Kluft 1985b; Putnam et al. 1984). Therefore, MPD should be diagnosed whenever its features are present, and regarded as a "superordinate diagnosis" that may encompass other manifestations (Putnam et al. 1984). The DSM-III-R (American Psychiatric Association 1987) acknowledges the clinical diversity of this condition (Kluft 1985b), and indicates that some cases with the structure of MPD but without fully developed classic features can be classified as a variant of atypical dissociative disorder.

Until recently, MPD was considered a rarity; its authenticity was questioned. The very drama and fascination which often surround it have detracted from its being considered a subject for serious scientific inquiry. In 1944, Taylor and Martin studied the world's literature and found 76 cases accessible for review. In 1980, Bliss reported over 200 cases. Since 1980, many authors or groups have reported series of 10 or more patients (Beahrs 1982; Bliss 1980, 1983; Clary et al. 1984; Coons 1985; Greaves 1980; Horevitz 1984; Kluft 1984e, 1985b; Putnam et al. 1986; Solomon and Solomon 1982). A series of 355 MPD patients from 355 separate therapists has been presented (Schultz et al. 1985).

The reasons for this abrupt rise in recognition and reportage are complex, and have occasioned considerable debate. Media and lay attention to celebrated cases, the illustration and exploitation of MPD in television and movie dramas, the reclassification of MPD as a free-standing entity in DSM-III-R, the recognition of the striking parallels between MPD and posttraumatic stress disorder (Coons and Milstein 1984; Spiegel 1984), excitement generated by neuropsychophysiologic research findings (Braun 1983; Brende 1984; Cocores et al. 1984; Coons et al. 1982; Mathew et al. 1984; Putnam 1984; Putnam et al. 1982; Silberman et al. 1985), and the educational efforts of a small group of dedicated clinicians and teachers are often cited as factors that have increased psychiatrists' awareness of MPD. Also, MPD is commonly the sequel to an abusive and/or overwhelming childhood (Coons and Milstein 1986; Kluft 1984e; Putnam et al. 1986; Schultz et al. 1985; Wilbur 1984b). An increased awareness of the prevalence of child abuse and incest and a sensitization to the mistreatment and exploitation of women have led to heightened interest in a condition associated with 97 percent incidence of child abuse among its victims (Putnam et al. 1986), and a 4:1 (Kluft 1984a) to 9:1 (Greaves 1980) predominance of women among its sufferers.

However, other voices suggest patients without the diagnosis are receiving it nonetheless. Victor (1975) has wondered if making the diagnosis can constitute a folie à deux. Kline (1984) is concerned whether patients with severe ego fragmentation are being erroneously mislabeled. Thigpen and Cleckley (1984) caution that patients may try to "achieve" the diagnosis and seek therapists who will "sanction" it. Orne warns against the diagnosis being suggested (Goleman 1985; Orne et al. 1984), and Spanos et al. (1985) suggest patients may respond to cues to enact MPD behaviors.

The Goals of Treatment of Multiple Personality Disorder

The scientific study of the treatment of MPD has barely begun (Kluft 1984e; Putnam 1986). Treatment approaches have been described but none has been subjected to rigorous or objective evaluation. Articles can be found that both advocate and countermand or question virtually every major therapeutic approach (Kluft 1984e, 1986a). Although the first successful treatment of MPD was reported by Despine in 1840 (Ellenberger 1970), very few articles on treatment appeared prior to the 1980s (Boor and Coons 1983; Kluft 1985c; Putnam 1986; Putnam et al. 1982). To this date, there are no controlled studies comparing the fates of treated and untreated cohorts, nor any comparing the efficacy of one approach to another. Single MPD cases have been followed (Cutler and Reed 1975; Lipton and Kezur 1948; Rosenbaum and Weaver 1980). One study reassessed patients who declined treatment for MPD, finding that their dividedness persisted and also discovering that for most patients overt dissociation diminished from middle age into senescence (Kluft 1985b). Kluft (1982, 1984e, 1986a) followed a series of MPD patients treated to the point of integration and periodically reassessed. These studies suggest that MPD patients can achieve stable integration, and sustain these gains over time.

It is generally agreed that MPD does not exist in the abstract, or as a free-standing target symptom. It is found in a diverse group of individuals with a wide range of Axis II or character pathologies, concomitant Axis I diagnoses, and many different constellations of ego strengths and dynamics (Kernberg, in press; Kluft 1984e). Consequently, treatment approaches must be individualized.

The tasks of therapy are those pursued in any intense change-oriented treatment, but are undertaken with a patient who lacks a unified personality. Consequently, one cannot rely upon a patient having an ongoing available observing ego, and may encounter massive disruptions in usually autonomous ego functions, such as memory. The personalities may have different perceptions, recollections, priorities, goals, and degrees of involvement with and commitment to the therapy, the therapist, and one another (Kluft 1984b, 1985c). Almost invariably, it becomes essential to replace this dividedness with agreements to work toward certain common goals, and to arrive at a degree of unity and purpose and shared motivation in order for any treatment to succeed. Effort to bring about such cooperation and facilitate the possible integration of the several personalities distinguishes the treatment of MPD (Kluft 1984b, 1984e).

Integration is usually considered a desirable goal although some argue that multiplicity should be transformed from a symptom into a skill (Beahrs 1982). In a given case, it is hard to argue with Caul's pragmatism: "It seems to me that after treatment you want a functional unit, be it a corporation, a partnership, or a one-owner business" (Hale 1983).

Integration is a pragmatic and desirable goal. It must be regarded as essential in the treatment of a youngster, who should be spared going through crucial developmental stages in a divided state (Fagan and McMahon 1984; Kluft 1984c, 1984d, 1986c.) Generally used as synonyms (Kluft 1985c), the terms unification, integration, and fusion are understood to connote the spontaneous or facilitated coming together of personalities after adequate therapy has helped the patient to see, abreact, and work through the reasons for being of each separate alter, erode their barriers, and allow mutual acceptance, empathy, and identification. It does not indicate the dominance of one alter, the creation of new "healthy" alter, or premature compression or suppression of alters into the appearance of a resolution (Kluft 1982, 1984e, 1985c).

In more specific usage, unification is a fairly neutral overall inclusive term. Integration connotes an ongoing intrapsychic process of undoing all aspects of dissociative dividedness that begins long before there is any reduction in the number or distinctness of the personalities, persists throughout the treatment of the divided individual, and continues at a deeper level even when the separate personalities have blended into one.

If therapy does not continue to work toward full integration, the achievement of apparent unity will prove transient (Kluft 1984e). Fusion has come to mean "three stable months of 1) continuity of contemporary memory, 2) absence of overt behavioral signs of multiplicity, 3) subjective sense of unity, 4) absence of alter personalities on hypnotic re-exploration (hypnotherapy cases only), 5) modification of transference phenomena consistent with bringing together of personalities, and 6) clinical evidence that the unified patient's self-representation included acknowledgment of attitudes and awarenesses which were previously segregated in separate personalities" (Kluft 1982, 1984e). Such stability usually follows the collapse of one or more shorter periods of what looks like fusion. If patients fulfill these criteria for an additional two years, relapse is uncommon, and relatively few additional or newly found alters are encountered. Hence, apparent fusion means fulfillment of criteria 1–6 for under three months, and stable fusion means this for a minimum of 27 months (Kluft 1984e, 1986a).

Although this discussion focuses on unification, unification is only one aspect of the overall treatment of the suffering individual. Treatment must address itself to the needs of the total human being. A therapy that treats MPD rather than the individual afflicted by it is countertherapeutic.

Modalities of Treatment

Many of the most experienced clinicians were unpublished until quite recently, and had passed on their methods in workshops, courses, and supervision, developing an "oral literature" (Kluft 1984e; Putnam 1986). In contrast, several available articles had offered general advices based on single cases or small or unspecified data bases.

In general, reports based on limited numbers of patients tend to explain MPD and its treatment in terms of the application of particular theories and techniques, and papers drawing on larger data bases offer recommendations inferred from clinical work, and are fairly atheoretical. Here, the literature on treatment methods will be reviewed, without regard to the articles' data base. Subsequent discussions will rely more heavily on the work of authors with extensive clinical experience with MPD.

Psychoanalytic formulations and treatments of MPD have been discussed (Berman 1981; Kluft, in press[c]; Lampl-De Groot 1981; Lasky 1978; Marmer 1980a, 1980b; Ries 1958; Wilbur 1986). A small minority of MPD patients are completely accessible without hypnosis, are minimally alloplastic, develop a good therapeutic alliance across personalities, and possess sufficient ego strength to undertake a relatively unmodified classical psychoanalysis. Some have undergone analysis without their diagnosis being suspected, and others have had their analyses interrupted by regressive phenomena that were not recognized as manifestations of a dissociative disorder (Kluft, in press[c]; manuscript submitted for publication).

Psychoanalytic psychotherapy, with or without facilitation by hypnosis, is widely recommended and practiced. Wilbur (1984d, 1986) has discussed aspects of transference and interpretation. Marmer (1980a) has explored the dreams of such patients. Bowers et al. (1971) offered ground rules for work within a psychoanalytic psychotherapy facilitated by hypnosis. Kluft (1982, 1983, 1984e) has described the difficulties in applying a purely intrapsychic approach to patients whose dividedness has impaired the ego functions usually relied upon in psychoanalytic treatments, and discussed ancillary hypnotherapeutic technique and crisis management (Caddy 1985; Kohlenberg 1973; Price and Hess 1979).

Behavioral treatments have been described (E. Kolonoff and J. Janata, personal communication, 1984). Such regimens can make dramatic transient impacts upon the manifest pathology of MPD, but Caddy alone describes achieving a long-term remission. In practice, many MPD patients experience behavioral protocols as punitive and respond poorly. Many workers think that simplistic applications of behavioral techniques may inadvertently replicate childhood traumata in which the patient's pain was not met with an empathic response. At this point in time, the behavioral treatment of the core pathology of MPD remains largely unexplored, although many associated symptoms such as phobias and inhibitions respond well to such measures as systemic desensitization and very gradual assertiveness training.

Family interventions have been described (Beale 1978; Davis and Osherson 1977; Kluft et al. 1984; Levenson and Berry 1983; Sachs 1986). Although MPD is often the reflection of and sequel to severe family pathology, family therapy is rarely successful as a primary treatment modality. Attempts to treat adult MPD patients within their traumatizing family of origin frequently retraumatizes rather than helps the patient. However, family interventions may be critical in work with a child or early adolescent with MPD (Kluft 1986c, in press[e]; Kluft et al. 1984). Conjoint work with the MPD patient, spouse, and/or children may preserve and strengthen relationships, and may prevent the children incorporating or being drawn into aspects of an MPD patient's psychopathology. The concerned others in an MPD patient's life space may require considerable education and support as they bear the brunt of the patient's difficulties on a day-to-day basis (Kluft et al. 1984; Sachs 1986).

Several workers (Caul 1984; Caul et al. 1986; Coons and Bradley 1985) have addressed problems involved with the group treatment of MPD patients. Unintegrated MPD patients in heterogeneous groups may be scapegoated, disbelieved, feared, or imitated and may require so much attention at times of switching or crisis as to incapacitate the group for productive work. Their materials and experiences may overwhelm other group members; in turn, the MPD patients are exquisitely sensitive and become engulfed in others' issues. They frequently dissociate in or run from sessions. The routine inclusion of MPD patients in traditional group therapy cannot be recommended. Clinical experience suggests MPD patients are more successful in task or project oriented groups such as occupational, art, movement, and music therapy may provide (Kluft 1984b). Anecdotal accounts describe their successful inclusion in groups with a shared experience (incest survivors, rape victims, adult children of alcoholics). Some workers (Caul 1984; Caul et al. 1986; Coons and Bradley 1985) have begun homogeneous groups of MPD patients, and find that they are difficult, but can be helpful.

Many clinicians have used videotape techniques to broach amnestic barriers and confront personalities with the existence of and repressed experiences of other personalities. Caul (1984) described the taping and therapeutic use of hypnotically facilitated interviews; Hall et al. (1975) wrote about retrieving material in amobarbital-facilitated sessions, which were then played back. Some patients can tolerate videotaped confrontation with memories and personalities from which they were profoundly dissociated but many are overwhelmed by such materials or rerepress them (Caul 1984). The use of such approaches cannot be advised uniformly.

Hypnosis is a facilitator of treatment, not a treatment per se (Frischholz and Spiegel 1983). The integration of judicious hypnotic work into a well-planned, thoughtful psychotherapy individualized to a particular MPD patient and oriented toward integration can be extremely productive. Such efforts are useful in exploration, gaining access to personalities from therapeutic work, facilitating abreaction, breaching amnestic barriers, and encouraging the personalities to communicate and in achieving integration. Approaches have been described by many authors (Allison 1974; Beahrs 1982; Brandsma and Ludwig 1984; Braun 1980, 1984b; Caul 1984; Confer 1984; Erickson 1939; Gruenewald 1971; Kluft 1982; Spiegel 1986; Watkins and Watkins 1981).

Several authors identified with the use of hypnosis have developed innovative approaches which are not readily classified. Caul (1984) has evolved a strategy of encouraging personalities to share contemporary awareness and emerge in succession to arrange a group therapy among them. Beahrs (1982) has tried to transform dissociation from a pathology to a skill. Watkins and Watkins (1981) have evolved an ego-state therapy which largely depends upon a model of negotiating with the personalities to resolve disagreements and differences. Several clinicians have advocated actively creating experiences within the therapy that regress the MPD patient and then nurture the patient through a more positive recapitulation of the various development phases. Treatment does not necessitate such extreme measures.

Useful Principles and Caveats

The patient who develops MPD has 1) the capacity to dissociate, which becomes enlisted as a defense in the face of 2) life experiences (usually of severe abuse) that traumatically overwhelm the nondissociative adaptive capacities of a child's ego. A number of 3) shaping influences, substrates, and developmental factors determine the form taken by the dissociative defenses (i.e., personality formation). Those who remain dissociated 4) receive inadequate stimulus barriers, soothing, and restorative experiences, are placed in double binds, and are exposed to pressures and further traumatizations that reinforce the need for and the shape of the dissociative defenses (Kluft 1984e). Elements of this Four-Factor Theory of Etiology have been confirmed empirically. Bliss (1983) and Lipman (1985) have shown the high hypnotizability of

MPD cohorts. Putnam et al. (1986) and Schultz et al. (1985) found a 97 percent incidence of abuse in MPD histories, and Kluft (1984d) and Fagan and McMahon (1984) have found that positive interventions and interdiction of pathologic influences rapidly reverse childhood MPD.

This theory has implications for treatment. Whether or not the clinician elects to use hypnosis in treatment, he or she should be aware of how dissociative manifestations may express themselves in clinical settings, especially as psychosomatic or quasipsychotic presentations (Kluft 1985b). The patient will bring his dissociative defenses into the therapy. One must "be gentle, gradual, and avoid imposing upon the patient any overwhelming experience that is not an inevitable concomitant of dealing with painful material. The material to be recovered brings with it the certainty of reliving anguish, and explains these patients' frequent evasiveness, protracted resistances, and mistrust of the therapist's motives" (Kluft 1984e). The patient needs to be empathically understood across and within all personalities; the therapist must deal with all with an "even-handed gentle respectfulness" (Kluft 1984e), but help the patient protect himself from himself. All personalities must be understood as parts of the total patient, and included in the treatment. A mutuality of working together and recognition of the difficult nature of the job to be done is essential. These treatments "sink or swim on the quality of the therapeutic alliance established with the personalities" (Kluft 1984e).

Bowers et al. (1971) advanced several principles of treatment, only one of which, the routine use of group therapy, has been supplanted. The therapist must remain within the limits of his or her competence and not rush to apply incompletely understood and partially mastered principles and techniques. Integration must take priority over exploring fascinating phenomena and differences. All alters should be helped to understand themselves as more or less dissociated sides of a total person. The personalities' names are accepted as labels, not as guarantees of individual rights to irresponsible autonomy. All alters must be heard with equal empathy and concern. Often one or more will be especially helpful in advising the therapist of the readiness to proceed into painful areas. "Encourage each personality to accept, understand, and feel for each other personality, to realize each is incomplete so long as it is separated from the rest of the individual, and to unite with the others in common interests." One must handle with respect the patient's distress about facing painful material, and the alters' misgivings about integration.

Within the context of psychodynamic psychotherapy, hypnosis may be valuable to deal with serious conflicts among alters, and to help the individual "recognize, consider, and utilize his various past and present experiences, impulses, and purposes for better self-understanding and increased self-direction." One must intervene therapeutically with concerned others when necessary. One need not dramatize amnesia. Assure the patient he will recover his past when he is able.

A General Outline of the Steps of the Treatment

Every stage of the treatment of MPD depends on the strength of the therapeutic alliance, both globally and with individual personalities. In the face of severe dysphoria, difficult material, frequent crises, challenging transferences, and the likelihood that the personalities may have grossly divergent perceptions of the psychiatrist and test him rigorously, the patient's commitment to the tasks of therapy and to collaborative cooperation are critical. This is implicit in the general treatment plan outlined by Braun (1980, 1986), which has sufficient universality to encompass most treatment formats.

Braun enumerates 13 steps, acknowledging that in practice they are overlapping and ongoing rather than neatly sequential. Step 1 involves the development of trust, and is rarely complete until the end of therapy. Operationally, it means "enough trust to continue the work of a difficult therapy." Step 2 includes making the diagnosis and sharing it with the presenting and other personalities. This is done in a gentle manner, soon after the patient is comfortable in the therapy and the therapist has sufficient data and/or has made sufficient observations to place the issue before the patient in a matter-of-fact and circumspect way. Only after the patient appreciates the nature of his situation can the true therapy of MPD begin.

Step 3 is establishing communication with the accessible alters. In many patients whose alters rarely emerge spontaneously in therapy and who cannot switch voluntarily, hypnosis or hypnotic techniques used without the formal introduction of hypnosis (Gruenewald 1971) may be useful. Upon gaining access to the alters, Step 4 is contracting with them to attend treatment and to agree not to harm themselves, others, or the body they share. Some helper personalities rapidly become allies, but it is the therapist's obligation to keep such agreements in force. Information gathering with each alter is Step 5, and encompasses learning of their origins, functions, problems, and relations to other alters.

In Step 6, the alters' problems are addressed. During such efforts, prime concerns are remaining in contact, sticking with painful subjects, and setting limits. Step 7 involves mapping and understanding the structure of the personality system. Hypnosis and other special procedures are of use (Braun 1986). With these as background, therapy moves to Step 8, enhancing interpersonality communications. Hypnotic interventions to achieve this have been described (Brende 1984; Kluft 1982, 1983), as has internal group therapy (Caul 1984). Step 9 is resolution toward a unity, and facilitating blending rather than encouraging power struggles. This often occurs in the process of therapy without specific interventions. Both hypnotic and nonhypnotic approaches have been described. (Braun 1980, 1984b; Kluft 1982, 1984e; Wilbur 1984d).

Integrated patients must (Step 10) develop new intrapsychic defenses and coping mechanisms, and (Step 11) learn adaptive ways of dealing interpersonally. A substantial amount of working through and support is necessary for (Step 12) solidification of gains; (Step 13) follow-up is essential.

Interventions and Techniques Which Facilitate Treatment

The treatment of MPD is generally an intense dyadic psychodynamic therapy, with two or more visits per week, and the occasional or regular use of extended sessions. However, the nature of the psychopathology is such that many clinicians have used various ancillary interventions and techniques to facilitate, structure, and support this primary vehicle. Most of these efforts are attempts to gain access to material and personalities that are often difficult to reach. Some personalities' spontaneous emergencies are too unlikely or infrequent to rely upon.

The patient may be asked to write whatever crosses his or her mind for 15–60 minutes per day. Often personalities unable or unwilling to express themselves in session make use of this modality. Many patients feel it facilitates both interpersonality communications and working through. Some patients are best able to express themselves, outline their conflicts, and retrieve memories most readily in some sort of artistic expression.

Many therapists involve colleagues to bring other modalities to bear or to share and distribute the intensity of the treatment process and the transference. Such approaches often are supportive of both the therapist and the therapy, but, failing clear role definitions and energetic efforts to keep communications open among the collaborators, counterproductive outcomes are not uncommon. Many therapists, hoping to lighten their burden by involving others, have found the effort involved in collaborative communication more demanding than the burden of solo therapy.

Several workers have tried to speed treatment by videotaping the separate personalities and showing the tapes of one personality to another, etc. In general, the use of videotape methods to "breach the dissociative barriers by storm" is associated with a high incidence of crises (Caul 1984). Taping for use later when the patient feels ready to see such materials can be helpful. In short, videotape methods are not a substitute for more traditional approaches to defensive structures, but can be a useful adjunct.

The use of drug-facilitated interviews to gain access to the various personalities and to repressed memories is frequently suggested, but not often undertaken. A review of Wilbur's work with "Sybil" illustrates the method's assets and liabilities (Schreiber 1973). Valuable materials were recovered, but "Sybil" rarely integrated what was thus recovered into her regular memory. She came to prefer her passivity in this approach to an active involvement in ongoing exploratory therapy. Many MPD patients request such interviews as a resistance to accepting painful truths they themselves have recalled, or to dissociate themselves from active efforts to recover and deal with their past. In brief hospital stays, drug-facilitated interviews may be useful. Some patients who refuse hypnosis will accept drug-facilitated inquiries.

Of the many facilitators of the treatment of MPD, hypnosis has stirred the most interest and the most controversy. While much theoretical concern has been expressed over whether or not to hypnotize MPD patients (Kluft 1982), it should be realized that they are going in and out of autohypnotic trance states on an ongoing basis (Bliss 1980). Therefore, "hypnotic" phenomena may occur without the formal induction of hypnosis (Gruenewald 1971). Several reviews have discussed the relationship of MPD and hypnosis (Braun 1984a; Gruenewald 1984; Kline 1984; Kluft 1982; Sutcliffe and Jones 1962). Although several authors continue to be concerned with the possibility of hypnosis and other interventions causing iatrogenic MPD (Kline 1984; Kluft 1982; Orne et al. 1984; Spanos et al. 1985; Thigpen and Cleckley 1984; Victor 1975); the emerging contemporary consensus is expressed by two quotations. Gruenewald (1984) wrote, "While it is highly unlikely that current situational variables—including hypnosis—are involved in creating the multiple personality syndrome, it is conceivable they may be instrumental in concretizing and possibly encouraging a pre-existing tendency." Kluft (1982) observed, "Phenomena analogous to and bearing dramatic but superficial resemblance to clinical multiple personality can be elicited experimentally or in a clinical situation if one tries to do so or makes technical errors . . . the phenomena described in the Hilgards' hidden observer work . . . and the Watkins' ego state articles . . . can be elicited by hypnosis and overinterpreted as multiple personality. . . . However, the evidence that skillful therapeutic hypnosis creates or worsens multiple personality remains to be presented." This optimistic view of the safety of judicious hypnosis does not extend to its application under forensic circumstances where other considerations prevail and special cautions need apply (Kluft, in press[e]; Orne 1979b; Orne et al. 1984).

It is difficult to speak of hypnotic or hypnotherapeutic interventions in the treatment of MPD without introducing certain considerations. First, it is difficult to determine what is intrinsic to hypnosis as a phenomenon (Frankl 1976; Orne 1959).

Second, hypnosis in and of itself is not a treatment (Frischholz and Spiegel 1983). To say a patient was treated with hypnosis or hypnotherapy is a convenient shorthand, the meaning of which must be determined by the context. Third, in treatments involving the use of hypnosis, it is difficult to be sure which aspects of a patient's response are due to the context of the treatment, preexisting or encouraged expectations, the patient's intrinsic hypnotic talent, the trance, or the interventions which precede, occur during, or follow the use of trance (Frankl 1976). Fourth, MPD is a dissociative pathology. Bliss (1980, 1983) has called it an "hypnotic pathology," involving the use of autohypnosis. Most workers concur that hypnosis, in some form, inevitably enters the therapy. Hence, many treatments of MPD proceed without the therapist's formal induction of trance in a patient (heterohypnosis), but there is no treatment of MPD without "hypnosis." It "comes with the territory."

When patients accustomed to being out of control, unable to gain access to aspects of their own minds, and mystified by their experiences see through their experience of therapeutic hypnosis that such control and access and understanding is feasible, they move toward becoming more active and optimistic partners in treatment. Some MPD patients learn to apply these approaches inwardly and do valuable therapeutic work between sessions.

Proceeding rapidly to formal hypnosis may be necessary in a case seen for consultation or in crisis, but, when circumstances permit, it is worthwhile to undertake both a baseline assessment of accessibility and directional awareness among the alters, and make a straightforward attempt to elicit their cooperation, prior to heterohypnosis. It is helpful to form an estimation of the patient's capacity for a therapeutic alliance and learn his or her characteristic nondissociative defenses and resistances.

In using hypnosis, it is effective to proceed very slowly, openly, and methodically, to explore resistances, respect anxieties, and create an atmosphere of safety. Initial hypnotic experiences should be benign and controlled, with the therapist intervening to prevent disruptions or rapid regressions. As work proceeds, the patient may associate hypnosis with the unpleasant material and affects it is used to uncover. It is important to introduce its use in a positive context and arrive at a way of working with it that is tolerable to a patient who may fear loss of control, vulnerability, or the abrupt emergence of unpleasant material. An apprehensive patient often will permit work toward either hearing inner vocalizations or the use of an ideomotor signal as a way of contacting alters whose full emergence they fear and resist. Indirect efforts may be preferable to the risk of precipitating an unnecessary crisis that could damage the overall course of therapy.

Some techniques associated with hypnosis will be discussed. Virtually all can be used without the formal induction of hypnosis in some MPD patients. Gruenewald (1971) first described this as the use of "hypnotic technique without hypnosis."

Hypnosis is useful in contacting alters. Many MPD patients, even if most alters are available on request, have some personalities not regularly accessible without such interventions. Also, it is rare for a full roster of alters to be known from the start. Stalemates often are related to unsuspected additional dividedness (Kluft 1985d). Usually, once an alter has been reached by hypnosis on a few occasions, it can emerge on request if the personality currently in control is cooperative, and is assured it will be "brought back." In many instances, the attenuated contact of inner vocalizations or ideomotor signaling is preferable, and can circumvent the anxiety some alters experience in yielding executive control of the body to others.

Hypnosis may facilitate information-gathering. Often this involves multilevel hypnosis, that is, the use of hypnosis in facilitating retrieval of data from a second alter that had been brought out by hypnosis. The trance for both alters must be ended separately. Otherwise, "hangovers" and passive influence experiences (as one alter continues to impact on another) may persist (Braun 1984b). Data retrieved under hypnosis, whether by direct inquiry, suggested recollection, or age regression, have widely recognized limitations (Orne 1979b). However, most allegations of child abuse prove fairly accurate. False withdrawals are common, while false accusations are rare (Goodwin 1982; Summit 1983). There often is no way to confirm or deny recovered material. Pragmatically, goodness of fit among data from many sources and in the transference are useful checks. In the authors' experience, patients with strong tendencies toward confabulation and/or pseudologia fantastica have inconsistencies in their accounts and bring these tendencies into the transference, where clarification can be achieved.

Hypnosis can facilitate abreaction or uncover repressed affects. Single interventions, however intense, rarely suffice. Abreaction by one alter may or may not affect another which had experienced the same events. During abreactions, many patients break from trance when upset, but most return to the work in a few moments or within a few sessions. The introduction of these techniques must be timed carefully and, whenever possible, begun in a session for which extra time is allotted. Patients generally fear leaving a session in a disorganized state more than they fear the abreaction of affect per se. Restoration of equilibrium is essential.

MPD patients suffer numerous severe and distressing symptoms, including the expression of aspects of traumata as somatoform discomfort, the experience of interpersonality conflicts as headaches or conversion symptoms, and acute phobias. Hypnotic interventions may be used to bring about symptomatic relief directly, or to discover which conflicts underlie the symptom. Usually, relevant alters can be reached and persuaded to discuss their conflicts, and to desist from expressing the conflicts in disabling symptoms. Relief is usually transient until the conflicts causing the symptoms are resolved (Kluft 1983).

A primary use of hypnosis is in facilitating integration. It is possible to challenge barriers by addressing comments to alters other than the one which is "out," and by suggesting "everyone" or "the entire mind" should listen. Alters can be elicited and encouraged to begin inner dialogues, speaking to one another across (and thereby eroding) amnestic and other barriers. In crises, one tries to reach those involved in the crisis, but in general, one begins by facilitating contact among alters that are congenial and/or minimally threatening to one another. Initial failure is common, but, with persistence, success is usually achievable. Alters can be taught to dialogue and spend time in contact both within and between sessions. Mutual identification and empathy and increasing cooperation erode differences. Alters can be elicited to interact in an "inner group therapy"(Caul 1984).

Many patients have had at least one alter that fused during an hypnotic ritual, even if many had integrated spontaneously in the course of therapy. Alters may fuse singly, in groups, or all at once. Lasting integrations follow extensive work on the erosion of dissociative barriers and substantial strides toward identification, empathy, and mutual acceptance. Alters with traumatic recollections and minimal narcissistic investment in separateness may fuse upon abreaction. Pressure toward premature fusion is associated with crises and obstructions. It is best to wait until alters begin to find being separate unnecessary, or uncomfortable, as their boundaries erode.

If fusion is not progressing smoothly without facilitation, hypnotic efforts are useful to contact the alters verging on fusion, to search for their remaining areas of conflict, and to work on resolving those issues. Then, an hypnotic ritual of fusion may be offered, using a combination of direct suggestion and the indirect suggestion of an imagery of joining. Clinical experience shows that images which imply elimination, subtraction, death, or going away are associated with poor results (Kluft 1982, 1984e, 1985d). Images of union, merger, or rebirth in which all are preserved by joining into one are much more successful. They convey the message "be present always, but as one." Images of streams joining a river, of snow on many mountains melting and flowing into the same lake, on whose surface the mountains are reflected, mirror-like, or of glowing lights coming together have been described (Kluft 1982). Many patients have favored a dance imagery, or one based on a light so bright it obscures vision entering a circle of personalities and flowing among them as a current of energy, which brings together those who have agreed to join. Imagery must be congenial to the patient, rather than practiced and "cook book" (Kluft 1986b).

Autohypnosis has been used to facilitate inner dialogues away from sessions, to work on symptoms, or to alleviate anxiety. However, it can become co-opted as a resistance. It probably should not be taught unless the therapeutic alliance is strong (Braun 1984b; Kluft 1982).

The use of extrusive or supportive techniques, in which a personality is commanded to leave or the curtailment of its function is suggested, was described by Allison (1974). Such techniques yield transient rather than lasting results, often followed by retaliation by the alter against which the suggestions were made. Their indifferent success and high cost benefit ratio relegate them to rare usage. They have a place in emergencies, when achievement of control will be followed by placement of the patient in a protected environment.

Occasionallly, MPD patients have alters whose self-perceived ages are different from the biologic patient's, and who either fail to change in perceived age, or need or insist upon help "growing up." For such patients, who often have some very youthful personalities, age progression fantasies under hypnosis may be useful. Series of "time machine" fantasies have been used in which alters who experience themselves at the actual age experience the normal passage of time, but those who are younger (for example) experience much more time passing in a comparable period (Kluft 1985a).

It must be emphasized that no hypnotically facilitated intervention has, in and of itself, free-standing utility and safety. The incidence of adverse sequelae in the judicious hypnotic facilitation of a well-planned treatment of MPD verges on nil.

Under certain circumstances, interventions involving hypnosis should not be undertaken without weighing additional considerations. This is the case for patients who are facing legal charges, who are involved in current litigation, or whose circumstances suggest they may become involved with the legal system (Orne 1979b).

Child abuse is found in most cases of MPD; as a consequence legal intervention may be necessary. Children with MPD should be assessed as accurately as possible prior to a hypnotic intervention, and their freely recalled accounts should be recorded. Therapeutically, first priority must be given to alleviating environmental stresses (Kluft, in press[a]). Beginning hypnotic work prior to this may both undercut later credibility and increase vulnerability at a difficult period.

Patients with coexisting affective disorder do not do well with hypnotic interventions until the mood disorder is controlled, usually pharmacologically (Kluft 1984b). Elderly patients' medical status should be assessed and stabilized prior to interventions which may unlock deeply distressing materials. Special techniques to attenuate the impact of these materials may be advisable (Kluft, in press[a]).

When a clinician skilled in the use of hypnosis with MPD is collaborating with another therapist or a team, it is crucial to have clarification of roles and prerogatives, and essential that each help the other anticipate the likely consequences of his or her work for the patient's management. The clinician using hypnosis must share all data and processes, and guard against 1) being perceived unrealistically as the "real" or "more powerful" therapist, or 2) unwittingly feeding into a splitting of the therapy team. The diagnostic use of hypnosis in consultation can prevent years of misdiagnosis and consequent unnecessary human tragedy.

Hospital Treatment

Hospitalization may be required for self-destructive episodes, severe dysphoria, fugues, or alters' inappropriate behaviors. Sometimes a structured inpatient environment is advisable for difficult phases of treatment. Stays of considerable length may prove necessary. MPD patients can be quite challenging, but if the hospital staff accepts the diagnosis and is supportive of the treatment, most can be managed adequately. MPD patients rarely split staffs. Rather, staffs split themselves by allowing divergent views about this controversial condition to influence their professional behavior; unfortunate polarizations ensue. MPD patients, especially the first few admitted to a unit, can be experienced as threatening to a milieu's sense of competence. Staff's sense of helplessness vis-a-vis the patient can engender resentment of both the patient and the admitting therapist. It is optimal for the therapist to help the staff in matter-of-fact problem-solving, explain his or her therapeutic approach, and be available by telephone.

The following advice emerges from clinical experience. 1) A private room offers the patient a place of refuge and diminished crises. 2) Staff should be instructed to treat all alters with equal respect, and address the patient as he or she wishes to be addressed. Insisting on a uniformity of name or personality may provoke crises or suppress critical data. Many of the advantages to be gained by 24-hour observation will be forfeited. 3) Make it clear that staff is not expected to recognize each alter. Alters must identify themselves to staff if they find such acknowledgment important. 4) Anticipate likely crises with staff; emphasize one's availability. 5) Explain ward rules to the patient personally, having requested all alters to listen, and insist on reasonable compliance. If problems emerge, offer warm and firm responses, and eschew punitive measures. 6) Such patients often have trouble with verbal group therapy, but do well in art, movement, or occupational therapy groups (Kluft 1984b). 7) Encourage a cooperative therapeutic thrust despite disagreement about MPD; emphasize the need to maintain a competent therapeutic environment. 8) Help the patient focus on the goals of the admission rather than succumb to a preoccupation with minor mishaps and problems on the unit. 9) Clarify each staff member's role to the patient, and emphasize all will not work in the same way. For example, it is not unusual for patients whose therapists elicit and work intensively with various alters to misperceive staff as unconcerned if they do not follow suit, even though it usually would be inappropriate if they did so (Kluft 1984b).

Medications

It is generally agreed that medication does not influence the core psychopathology of MPD, but may palliate symptomatic distress or impact upon a coexisting drug-responsive condition or target symptom (Barken et al. 1986; Kluft 1984b). Many MPD patients are treated successfully without medication. In six patients with MPD and major depression, Kluft found treating either disorder as primary failed to impact on the other. However, Coryell (1983) reported a single case in which he conceptualized MPD as an epiphenomenon of a depression. While most MPD patients manifest depression, anxiety, panic attacks, and phobias, and some show transient (hysterical) psychoses, the drug treatment of such symptoms may yield responses that are so rapid, transient, and inconsistent across alters, or that persist despite the discontinuation of the medication, that the clinician cannot be sure an active drug intervention rather than a placeboid response has occurred.

Hypnotic and sedative drugs are often prescribed for sleep disturbance. Many patients fail to respond initially or after transient success, and try to escape from dysphoria with surreptitious overdosage. Most MPD patients suffer sleep disruption when alters are in conflict and/or painful material is emerging. This problem may persist throughout treatment. Often, one must adopt a compromise regimen which provides "a modicum of relief and a minimum of risk" (Kluft 1984b). Minor tranquilizers are useful, but tolerance can be expected, and occasional abuse is encountered. Often, high doses become a necessary transient compromise if anxiety becomes disorganizing or incapacitating. In the absence of coexisting mania or agitation in affective disorder, major tranquilizers should be avoided. Most "psychotic" symptoms in MPD respond best to psychotherapy. Their major use in MPD is for sedation when minor tranquilizers fail, or abuse or tolerance has become problematic.

Many MPD patients have depressive symptoms, and a trial of tricyclics may be warranted. In cases without classic depressions, results are often equivocal. MAOI drugs may help atypical depressions in reliable patients. Patients with coexistent bipolar disorders and MPD may have the former disorder relieved by lithium. Two articles suggest a connection between MPD and seizure disorders (Mesulam 1981; Schenk and Bear 1981). Notwithstanding that the patients cited had, overall, equivocal responses to anticonvulsants, many clinicians have instituted such regimens.

The Course and Characteristics of Treatment

It is difficult to conceive of a more demanding and painful treatment, and those patients who must undertake it have many inherent vulnerabilities (Kluft 1983, 1984b). Dissociation and dividedness make insight difficult to attain. Deprived of a continuous memory, and switching in response to both inner and outer pressures and stressors, self-observation and learning from experience are compromised. The patients' alters may alienate support systems by their disruptive and inconsistent behaviors; their memory problems may cause them to appear to be unreliable at best. Traumatizing families may openly reject the patient and disavow everything the patient has alleged, endorsing a fraudulent but more congenial reality (Summit 1983).

The alters' switching and battles for dominance can create an apparently never-ending series of crises. Alters identifying with aggressors or traumatizers may try to suppress those who want to cooperate with therapy and share memories, or punish those they dislike by inflicting injury upon the body. Battles between alters may result in hallucinations and quasipsychotic symptoms (Kluft 1983, 1984b). Some alters may deny their condition and/or suddenly withdraw the patient from therapy.

Painful memories may emerge as hallucinations, nightmares, or passive influence experiences. In order to complete the therapy, longstanding repressions must be undone, and dissociative defenses and switching must be abandoned and replaced. Also, the alters must give up their narcissistic investments in separateness, abandon aspirations for total control, and "empathize, compromise, identify, and ultimately coalesce with personalities they had long avoided, opposed, and rejected" (Kluft 1984b).

In view of the magnitude of the changes required and the difficulty of the materials to be worked through, therapy may prove arduous for patient and therapist alike. Ideally, a minimum of two sessions a week is desirable, with the opportunity for prolonged sessions when advisable. Telephone accessibility is desirable, but firm nonpunitive limit-setting is very much in order. The pace of therapy must be modulated to allow the patient respite from an incessant exposure to traumatic materials. Some patients, once their amnestic barriers are eroded, will be in states of "chronic crisis" for long periods of time.

The following observations describe common aspects of the treatment process. The patient's baseline history is invariably incomplete. Much history is cloaked by amnesia. A history of abuse by significant others may not be disclosed in the initial interview. Inquiry about amnesia is crucial, but because patients may not recognize "blackouts" as amnestic episodes, and may "forget that they forget," they may deny amnesia on direct questioning. However, if asked whether, on occasion, time seems to "get away" or be discontinuous, they may acknowledge this. If they had been told they had done something they could not recollect, this may indicate a period of amnesia, and suggest a switching of personalities. Indirect inquires about amnesia, that is, asking if they have found strange clothing in their closet, or items in their grocery bag which they did not remember buying, may also provide clues. Sometimes patients appear frightened when these questions are asked, fearing that they have unknowingly "shoplifted" something instead of buying it.

On inquiring about experiences of discontinuous time, it is important to explore the circumstances under which they occurred. This may reveal what pressures or persons trigger switching. Investigating at what age these episodes of discontinuous time began offers information relevant to the onset of a dissociative process. For example, if a patient states that he found something strange in his closet when he was nine years old, it gives the therapist some indication to suspect that alteration of personalities was taking place at this age.

It is useful to inquire as to how long a particular personality has been functioning in the world or whether or not he or she has much memory of the early years of life. The absence of childhood memories and the use of a name other than one's legal name suggests the presenting personality is an alter that may not be the chronologically first personality, often termed the "original" or "birth" personality.

Presuming the diagnosis has been made, the therapist should undertake an explanation of the diagnosis, the treatment recommended, and a general introduction to treatment (Wilbur 1984a). This may cause some anxiety, usually because MPD patients fear they have done something "wrong" when they were not in control of their bodies. They can be assured that their illness is treatable and that both clinical experience and research (Kluft 1984e, 1986a) indicate that, if they stay with treatment, they are likely to enjoy a satisfactory outcome.

For therapy to be effective, trust must be established between the therapist and each of the personalities as they appear (Wilbur 1984d). It may take several interviews before trust is adequately established for any single alter. This may depend upon the therapist provisionally "believing" the patient, or making his or her open-mindedness apparent. Alternates will test to find out whether their reports are accepted. They may also endeavor to find out if the therapist approves or disapproves of them. They may regard the therapist as a punitive authority figure and expect reenactments of "punishment," which later turn out to have been abuse.

When psychoanalytic techniques are used in the course of treatment, patients may be encouraged to relate their thoughts, dreams, and memories (Wilbur 1984c, 1986). Alternates may have different thoughts, dreams, and memories, but may keep them submerged for the purpose of self-protection. The therapist should not be confused by the differences in the reports of alternates, which usually can be clarified over time. In some cases, alters who know much about the complex of personalities can offer a clear explanation.

An alternate may report the thoughts, dreams, and memories of another alternate in the complex of personalities. The therapist may ask who is telling what about whom. Interpretation of thoughts, dreams, and memories may be extremely effective in helping one alternate understand the emotional conflicts of others. Sharing of information among personalities should be encouraged as tolerated. For example, one alternate may be told to tell another alternate about what has been discussed. In the course of treatment in relating thoughts, dreams, and memories, one alternate may relate abuses endured by other alternates. This may facilitate the revelation of past traumas.

When accounts of abuses begin to surface, the therapist should clarify for the patient the inappropriateness of such mistreatment (Wilbur 1984b). It is important to help these patients understand that they were not "bad" children whose abuse was really well-deserved punishment. They may not realize that they were victimized, and need not continue to suffer the intense guilt and shame from the "blame" heaped upon them by their abusers. If they suffer amnesia as adults, they may be accustomed, even as adults, to being called liars and worse.

As alternates surface, their origin, their emotional state, and the conflicts which precipitated their becoming separate should be explored. Hypnosis may be quite valuable in uncovering the conflicts and traumatic events that may have led to the production of alternates. When the patient is cooperative, this is a relatively simple process. However, hypnotic inquiry is not a truth serum. In routine interviews, the average MPD patient withholds or is unaware of data relevant to making the diagnoisis, and Kluft (unpublished observation) has found that over 50 percent of his MPD patients had held back information during initial hypnotic inquiry. In clinical practice, it is difficult to conceal the purpose of hypnotic inquiries. Resistance may be mobilized as personalities try to block one another's emergence or to evade discovery. Often presenting personalities become anxious and break the trance; often other alters do not cooperate with the questioning. It may be necessary to ask the presenting personality to step back, enter a fantasy, or otherwise absent himself or herself. Then, the therapist can ask about the presence of other entities, and request their emergence, inner vocalization, or response to questions by ideosensory or ideomotor signals. The latter may be preferable at first, especially in emergencies. The patient is less likely to resist, and the experience is not likely to be disturbing. Of course, the diagnosis can only be suspected until an alter who fulfills diagnostic criteria is actually encountered. Not uncommonly, the diagnostic picture remains unsettled for fairly prolonged periods.

In the context of an overall psychoanalytic psychotherapy treatment, the therapist may speed up the process by using hypnosis to call other alternates forward to ask them to tell in turn what brought them into the life of the original or birth personality and when.

Because MPD is a dissociative process and the dissociations begin to occur early in life, usually during infancy or early childhood, as defenses against abuses that caused intolerable affects and conflicts, treatment depends on resolving these intolerable conflicts and diminishing the intensity of the affects. Abuse may have been physical, physiologic, psychological, sexual, nonnurturing, and/or neglect. The commonest significant abuses are sexual, physiologic, and psychological. Incest and incest-rape are also frequent in a history of MPD patients (Coons and Milstein 1986; Putnam et al. 1986; Saltman and Solomon 1982; Wilbur 1984b). Repetitive abuse tends to solidify the presence of an alternate who is formed to handle such difficulties.

The birth personality may not be available at the beginning of treatment or may not have been active for days, weeks, months,or even years. Personalities of all ages may occur. Alternates with every type of conflict and intolerable affect occur. They may have suicidal or homicidal tendencies toward another alternate or toward individuals outside; they may be violent. They may be of the opposite sex from the birth personality. Alternatives who believe in spirits may consider other alternates as manifestations of a possession state. Alternates may claim different backgrounds, educations, and languages. Incomplete personalities or fragments occur (Kluft 1984a).

When there are suicidal or homicidal tendencies, the therapist should contract with alternates harboring those tendencies not to act without consulting the therapist in depth and over time about the act that is planned. The contracts have to be renegotiated from time to time. Hospitalization may be necessary when such contracts are violated, or cannot be made.

In the course of therapy, it is helpful if the therapist observes and comments upon emotional overloads. Because MPD patients are usually neglected as well as abused within their families, such interest is deeply appreciated. It is important that the therapist be reasonably available to MPD patients. Many of them become markedly anxious and fearful, especially if they develop an amnestic period and get lost. With the therapist's acquiescence, they may carry the therapist's office and home telephone numbers. Then, if they find themselves in a strange place, they can call for reassurance and assistance in returning home.

MPD patients express every conceivable affect. Anxiety is usually severe and chronic. Sorrow, sadness, grief, and depression may be experienced by one, several, or all personalities. Fury, rage, and anger are usually relegated to one or more of the alternates. Such affects and their attendant conflicts are segregated within certain alternates so that the original personality as well as others in the complex do not need to feel fury, rage, and/or anger. Apprehension is frequent. Ambivalence may be expressed by two alternates disagreeing with one another. MPD patients show shame, embarrassment, apathy, coldness, and diminished affect. On occasion, a personality may express elation. This may occur when a problem is solved and either the birth personality or an alternate is "free." Apprehension, guilt, blocking, and psychic pain all occur. Wit and humor used as defenses may be expressed by at least one of the alternates and often by more than one.

When the therapist thinks that the patient is expressing inappropriate affect, it may be because the conversation is believed to be with alternate "A" when actually it is with alternate "B." The affect is found to be appropriate for each specific personality, given its assumptive world. Reactions to conflicting affects implicit in conflicting alternates distress the patient during sessions. Any or all affects may appear in transference relationships.

Conflicts involving dependence and independence are crucial. Because MPD patients rarely receive adequate nurturing and the type of support that encourages growth toward independence, many are intensely dependent. This must be accepted and analyzed so that they can grow from pathologic dependency to true autonomy.

Conflicts of love and hate (particularly toward a parent who was an abuser) are found in most MPD patients. Problems with self-worth and self-esteem are common.

Other conflicts include cruelty versus kindness, sensuality versus frigidity and impotence, seductiveness versus puritanism, and assertion versus inhibition. When any of these conflicts immobilize the patient, depression may ensue.

A major focus of treatment consists of dealing with these polarized and conflicting intolerable affects, experiences, and belief systems. When these are dealt with, the intensity of the affects diminishes, the conflicts approach resolution, and fusion may take place automatically. This sequence may occur throughout treatment. In the treatment situation, the therapist should never show favoritism to one or another of the alternates, even if one is much easier to deal with and talk to than another. It is of no value to try to "do away" with any personality, especially a personality that may have perceived itself to be bad and act consistent with that belief. Doing away amounts to repression. Each personality exists for specific reasons. Angry personalities, for example, may be extremely important as guardians of assertiveness.

Understanding the multiple transferences encountered in the treatment of MPD patients is of prime importance (Kluft 1984b; Wilbur 1984d), and can be quite challenging. At times, transference reactions have what the junior author has called a "post-traumatic" quality, and involve reliving of past experiences which are perceived as actually recurring, and include misperception of the therapist as the actual figure of someone from the past. This variety of transference has more the quality of an age regression with revivification than the quality of a reconstituted object relation.

As affects are defused and conflicts resolved, solid fusion may take place. Fusion may be encouraged by suggestion, but fusion that occurs through hypnotic suggestion may defuse more readily than fusion that takes place spontaneously. The final resolution of an MPD patient's condition is the result of total integration of all personalities with the original or birth personality. This occurs with the satisfactory resolution of all major conflicts. Treatment should be continued following this integration to assist in adjustments that the now-integrated birth personality still has to make. The solidification of newly learned behaviors and beliefs has to occur, giving the patient an opportunity to become a functioning individual free of symptoms.

Postfusion Therapy

Treatment does not end with unification. Patients who leave therapy at this point almost invariably relapse. Further working through is necessary, as is the development of non-dissociative coping strategies and defenses. Although newly integrated MPD patients often want to forget their past and rush to make up for lost time, and may be encouraged to do so by well-intentioned and/or impatient others, they are vulnerable neophytes. It remains advisable to suggest deferring major decisions and to offer anticipatory socialization to likely difficulties.

Positive developments include realistic goal-setting, clearer perceptions of others, increased anxiety tolerance, gratifying sublimations, and tolerance of painful material in the transference. A less hopeful sign is an avoidant adaptation. It is helpful to bear in mind that partial relapses and the discovery of other personalities are not infrequent (Kluft 1984e, 1985d, 1986a). An integration's failure is no more than an indication that its apparent occurrence was incomplete or premature, and reflects either an incomplete understanding of the total system of personalities, a flight into health, or an evasion of still further difficult material related to the experiences of the relapsed or previously unknown personalities. Many patients require prolonged periods of postfusion therapy.

The Therapist's Reactions

Work with MPD can be arduous and demanding. Certain initial reactions are normative: excitement, fascination, overinvestment, and interest in documenting the panoply of pathology. These often are followed by bewilderment, exasperation, and a sense of being drained. Many feel overwhelmed by the painful material, the high incidence of crises, the need to bring to bear a variety of clinical skills in rapid succession and/or novel combinations, and the skepticism of usually supportive colleagues. Many therapists, sensitive to their patients' isolation and the rigors of therapy, find it difficult to be both accessible and able to set reasonable and nonpunitive limits. They discover that the patients consume substantial amounts of time. Often the therapist is distressed to find himself unable to rely upon his preferred techniques and theories in work with MPD. It is easy to become exasperated with some alters' failure to cooperate with or value the goals of the therapy, and/or their incessant testing of the therapist's trustworthiness and goodwill.

The therapist's empathic capacities are sorely taxed. It is difficult to feel along with the separate personalities, and to remain in touch with the "red thread" of a session across dissociative defenses and personality switches. Furthermore, the material of therapy is often painful, and difficult to accept on an empathic level. Four reaction patterns are common. In the first, the therapist retreats from painful affect and material into a cognitive stance and undertakes an intellectualized therapy in which he or she plays detective, becoming a defensive skeptic or an obsessional worrier over what is real. In the second, the therapist abandons a conventional stance and undertakes to provide an actively nurturing corrective emotional experience, in effect proposing to "love the patient into health." In the third, the therapist moves beyond empathy to counteridentification, often with excessive advocacy. A fourth is masochistic self-endangerment or self-sacrifice on the patient's behalf. These countertransferential stances, however rationalized, undermine rather than advance the treatment.

Therapists who work effectively with MPD patients set firm but nonrejecting boundaries and sensible but nonpunitive limits. They safeguard their practices and private lives. They know therapy may be prolonged, and avoid placing unreasonable pressures upon themselves, the patients, or the treatment. They are wary of accepting an MPD patient whom they do not find likeable, because they are aware their relationship with the patient may become intense and complex, and extend over many years. As a group, successful MPD therapists are flexible and ready to learn from their patients and colleagues (Kluft 1985c).

Forensic Psychiatry Considerations

The clinician should be aware that there are many medical as well as legal ramifications of this disorder and it frequently is involved in the criminal/legal arena. This is especially so in battered wife syndrome, where this type of dissociative disorder is frequently used as an insanity defense or as a mitigating factor, and the clinician should attempt to be careful not to be drawn into presenting testimony in behalf of the patient while still trying to treat the patient. It is generally recommended that the clinician refer his patient to a forensic psychiatrist to handle the medical and legal aspects of any criminal defense.

Also, from time to time in the civil courts there are contractual disputes that involve contracts made by one of several multiple personalities and for which there is amnesia by the host personality. Again, it would be best to have forensic psychiatry consultants handle the forensic aspects of such a case.

Follow-Up Studies

Case reports and a recent study of the natural history of MPD show that untreated MPD patients do not enjoy spontaneous remission, but that many (70–80 percent) appear to show increased dominance by one alter with relatively fewer and more covert intrusions of the others as they go through middle age and the later years (Cutler and Reed 1975; Ellenberger 1970; Kluft 1985b; Lipton and Kezur 1948; Rosenbaum and Weaver 1980). Kluft (1982, 1984e, 1985c, 1985d, 1986a) has followed a group of MPD patients treated to the point of integration and periodically reassessed over the years. A study of a group of 52 patients who had been reassessed a minimum of 27 months after apparent fusion found that 49 (94 percent) had not relapsed into behavioral MPD and that 41 (78.8 percent) showed neither residual nor recurrent dissociative phenomena (Kluft 1986a).

It appears that MPD is responsive to intense psychotherapeutic interventions. The prognosis is excellent for those MPD patients who are offered intensive treatment and are motivated to accept it.

Glossary

1. **Alter:** A generic term for any personality or fragment, useful because in clinical situations it often is unclear, for protracted periods, which personalities are original, host, presenting, etc., or whether an entity is sufficiently distinct and elaborate for a more precise label.
2. **Alternate:** There are two usages: 1) synonym of alter; 2) denotes a personality other than the original, host, or presenting. Difference determined by context.
3. **Birth personality:** The identity that developed prior to the first split, and from which the first additional personality was split in order to survive some stress.
4. **Complex:** The overall system of personalities, including all alters.
5. **Fragment:** An entity resembling a personality, but with a more limited range of functions, emotions, and history.
6. **Fusion:** Defined in the text.
7. **Host personality:** The alter that has executive control of the body the greatest percentage of time during the given time under consideration.
8. **Integration:** Defined in the text.
9. **Original personality:** Synonym for item 3.
10. **Personality:** 1) In more precise usage, an entity with a firm, persistent, and well-founded sense of self and a characteristic and consistent pattern of behavior and feelings in response to given stimuli. It must have a range of functions, a range of emotional responses, and a significant life history (of its own existence). 2) Also, loosely, a synonym for items 1 and 2.
11. **Presenting personality:** Whichever personality "presents" itself for treatment.
12. **Primary personality:** An ambiguous term that has been used as a synonym for both 3, 9 and 7. Its meaning must be determined by context.
13. **Split:** Create a new personality.
14. **Switch:** Change of personality in executive control, occurring between personalities that already exist.
15. **Unification:** Defined in the text.

Chapter 201

Depersonalization Disorder (or Depersonalization Neurosis)

Subjectively experienced affective and cognitive states create dilemmas for both psychiatrists and patients. Their subjective nature means that the ability to communicate such an experience to others is influenced by the communicator's choice of and facility with words and the listener's interpretation of the selected words. Take, for example, the semantic confusion associated with the spectrum of terms and expressions used to communicate the various feeling states of depression (e.g., unhappy, discouraged, demoralized, down, sad, blah, low, blue). However, perhaps because depressed feelings are so often linked to loss, disappointment, and other frequently experienced situations, there is a collective sense of what is being described even though both the intensity of, and the situations which evoke, such feelings can be highly personal. In contrast to depression, the experience of depersonalization evokes no universally accepted picture.

Phenomenology

The following abbreviated vignettes convey the many faces of depersonalization and examples of the varied states to which it is linked:

"I was standing in this long hallway looking at the geometric designs in the rug. The fluorescent lights created an eerie blinking effect. I started to felt a sense of apprehension, and then everything began to feel strange. I felt removed from the situation, almost detached. It was as if I was watching myself. Time seemed suspended. I don't know how much time elapsed, but next I began to feel a sense of panic and thought I was going crazy." These are the words of a 30-year-old woman seen by one of the authors (RIS). She had panic disorder and responded to treatment with the monoamine oxidase inhibitor, phenelzine.

"I woke up with a peculiar feeling. I felt fuzzy. Nothing was like it usually was. My head felt full. I felt disconnected and strange. It lasted all morning." This patient of one of the authors (RIS) had been taking amitriptyline for 36 hours. The feelings cleared with a change in medication to desipramine.

The next two cases are reproduced with permission from the *DSM-III Casebook* (Spitzer et al. 1981).

"She began feeling panicky and having experiences in which she felt as if she were removed from her body and was in a trance . . . . " This 23-year-old woman was diagnosed borderline personality disorder.

"For the past two years he had experienced increasingly frequent episodes of feeling 'outside' himself . . . accompanied by a sense of deadness in his body . . . he felt a lack of easy, natural control over his body and his thoughts seemed foggy . . . " This 20-year-old man was diagnosed depersonalization disorder.

From these case vignettes, it is evident that at the core of the experiences of depersonalization is a subjective feeling of estrangement or detachment from one's sense of self, body image or representations, or surroundings. There is also a relationship to or overlap with the concept of derealization in which there is a detachment from or change in awareness of one's environment, creating a feeling of estrangement or unreality. In the former the person is saying, "I feel strange," while in the latter the person is saying, "My surroundings feel strange."

Although the experiences associated with depersonalization were described in 1872 by Krishaber (Lehmann 1974), the actual term was introduced into the literature by Dugas in 1899 (Shraberg 1977). What stands out from a review of the four score or more years of literature dealing with depersonalization is the inconclusiveness of the definitions and descriptions of this experience. Many patients have difficulty describing its frightening, strange, and bizarre nature. Moreover, because the symptom is so strange and unfamiliar, many patients are afraid to report it for fear they will be judged insane (Parikh et al. 1981; Shorvon 1946). In a study of 388 assumed to be "normal" undergraduate students, one-third reported at least one episode of depersonalization; of these only a small proportion sought professional help (Trueman 1984).

There is a debate in the literature as to whether depersonalization exists simply as a nonspecific experience occurring along with other psychopathologic symptoms or whether it is a distinct syndrome in which depersonalization occurs as the primary major presenting finding (Davison 1964; Harper and Roth 1962; Shorvon 1946; Torch 1978). We agree with Cattell (1966) who considered both perspectives to be valid.

Working Definition

Levy and Wachtel (1978) commented that "of the manifold problems related to the study of depersonalization, the most basic revolve around definition . . . . Various writers on the subject are . . . not writing about the same thing at all, but are instead confusing different sets of phenomena . . . calling them by the same name." Our review, however, suggests a reasonable degree of agreement with our working definition of depersonalization: a subjective feeling or experience of strangeness, alienation, unreality, disconnectedness or unfamiliarity with one's self (the sense of one's mind—personality, identity, perceptions, affects, emotions—or body image or boundaries), actions, surroundings, or environment. It is as if the familiar becomes unfamiliar, strange, or foreign, and because reality testing remains intact, there is an awareness that something is wrong. It is the sense of reality that is disturbed—not the reality testing. Individuals describing depersonalization use such phrases or words as: "as though," "as if," "just like," "dream-like," "unreal," or "different." There may even be an affective numbness, the so-called anesthesia psychica. It is not clear, however, whether this dulling is part of the experience of depersonalization or a response to it.

In DSM-III-R, depersonalization disorder (300.60) is classified as a dissociative disorder (American Psychiatric Association 1987). The criteria from DSM-III-R are listed in Table 1. Heightened self-observation is often an integral part of the depersonalization experience, and it may have an obsessional quality. Distorted perceptions of space and time, déja-vu and jamais-vu, altered or fugue-like states of consciousness (reported as being in a "fog," a "dream," "behind a veil"), anxiety with autonomic dysfunction, and the affective numbing described above are also common occurrences (Harper and Roth 1962; Renik 1978; Shorvon 1946).

Frequency and Linkages

Depersonalization is reported across a broad spectrum of both functional and organic psychiatric disorders. These include schizophrenia, bipolar illness, depression, panic disorder, hysteria, obsessive-compulsive disorder, epilepsy, tumor, intoxication, fever, delirium, hyperventilation, hypoparathyroidism, migraine, alcoholism, hallucinogen ingestion, carbon monoxide poisoning, and posttraumatic states (emotional or physical trauma). Curiously, we have never heard it reported by a manic patient. It also occurs in nonclinical populations following stress, calamity, fatigue, loneliness, sleep deprivation, sensory deprivation, emigration, and air travel (Davison 1964; McKellar 1978; Meares and Grose 1978; Shorvon 1946; Taylor 1982; Trueman 1984; Walsh 1975). Not infrequently, it begins in the "calm" following the "storm." Because of its presentation in such a broad range of settings, depersonalization per se is obviously a nonspecific entity and is not pathognomonic of any known clinical disorder.

Etiology

The etiology of depersonalization is unknown. Various biologic and psychoanalytic hypotheses have been proposed. We agree with Lehmann who wrote, "depersonalization is . . . a . . . behavior that is multidetermined, having both psychological and biological roots of differing comparative significance" (Lehmann 1974). The observation that depersonalization occurs in a wide variety of clinical conditions and settings (including in normals) has led many to speculate that it is a "preformed functional response of the brain" (Davison 1964; Shorvon 1946; Shraberg 1977; Torch 1981). Such a functional biologic response would be advantageous and adaptive to

---

Table 1. DSM-III-R Diagnostic Criteria for Depersonalization Disorder (300.60)

A. Persistent or recurrent experiences of depersonalization as indicated by either (1) or (2):
   (1) an experience of feeling detached from, and as if one is an outside observer of, one's mental processes or body
   (2) an experience of feeling like an automaton or as if in a dream

B. During the depersonalization experience, reality testing remains intact.

C. The depersonalization is sufficiently severe and persistent to cause marked distress.

D. The depersonalization experience is the predominant disturbance and is not a symptom of another disorder, such as Schizophrenia, Panic Disorder, or Agoraphobia without History of Panic Disorder but with limited symptom attacks of depersonalization, or temporal lobe epilepsy.

an organism threatened by the overwhelming, paralyzing, or disruptive effects of painful emotions and anxiety. It is when this "productive" response occurs autonomously, in the absence of stress, that it becomes maladaptive.

A neural substrate has been proposed, causing a nonspecific cerebral dysfunction resulting in the experience of a change in body image (Shorvon 1946). Both anosognosia and Gerstmann syndrome are examples of disorders with anatomic localization causing the subjective experience of an estranged, altered body image. The occurrence of depersonalization in toxic (e.g., drugs) and organic (e.g., tumor) conditions also points to a probable physiologic or anatomic basis for this phenomenon.

Several psychoanalytically oriented authors understand depersonalization as a defensive maneuver (Cattell 1966, 1975; Lehmann 1974; Levy and Wachtel 1978; Shraberg 1977; Stolorow 1979). Guilt, untamed id, aggression, anger and rage, painful affects, intense conflict, danger, primitive regression fusion fantasies, conflicting ego identifications, anxiety, and anal exhibitionism have all been thought to be defended against by depersonalization. A dissociation in ego functioning is postulated, in which the observing self is split off from the experiencing-participating self and thereby "protected." Shifting of libidinal cathexis and attention away from objects toward the self is another hypothesis. In this situation, the self becomes the object of intense scrutiny and hypercathexis.

Stolorow (1979) contended that depersonalization is likely to occur just when a psychosis might have emerged. Contrasting hypochondriasis and depersonalization, he postulated that in the former there is a fear of impending dissolution of the self, accounting for the hypercathexis of the body and self in an attempt at restitution. In the latter the dissolution and fragmentation of the self have proceeded so far that the self is experienced as strange and unreal. Thus, depersonalization is hypothesized to occur in patients whose self-representations are defective and incohesive because of developmental impairment in self-object differentiation.

Shapiro (1978) elaborated on this view, postulating that a sense of reality comes from a validation of experiences and feelings of an infant through empathic parental mirroring. If this does not occur, the sense of reality may be easily disrupted and affected. Cattell (1966) supported this: " . . . in the individual whose basic integrative capacity is impaired, . . . the ability to develop 'familiars' . . . is deficient. Identifications are less than stable . . . making the self-image vulnerable . . . the familiar, never solidly established, easily becomes unfamiliar, suddenly and unpredictably."

Our view of these models is that in susceptible individuals, any transition (e.g., physiologic, psychic, or environmental) can disrupt the sense of reality. At the present time, not one of the hypotheses about depersonalization is based on much more than speculation; they are not founded on systematically conducted studies.

Treatment

Effective treatment of a symptom or disorder usually follows from an understanding of etiology or at least from some sense of the mechanisms underlying symptom formation. As might be expected, the results of the treatment of depersonalization are not impressive. When depersonalization is a symptom occurring in a functional or organic illness, treatment of the primary underlying disorder will often, but not always, relieve the depersonalization as well. When it is the primary symptom in the syndrome of depersonalization disorder, it is often refractory to treatment. Those who advocate psychotherapy or psychoanalysis state that a minimum of five years of treatment may be required (Cattell 1966; Lehmann 1974; Torch 1981), perhaps because many of these patients are extremely obsessional. Family therapy (Dullinger

1983), directive therapy (Blue 1979), cognitive and assertive therapy (Levy and Wachtel 1978), and group therapy (Meares and Grose 1978) have been reported to be effective in single case studies, but no generalizations are warranted from this database.

In a study of 66 patients with depersonalization as a syndrome, the following somatic treatments were employed without substantial success: ECT, insulin coma, continuous narcosis, ether abreaction, vasodilators, benzedrine, and leucotomy (Shorvon 1946).

Of seven patients with a depersonalization syndrome treated by Davison (who considered impaired arousal as the etiologic mechanism) with a brief exposure to intravenous amphetamine, four patients attained immediate relief lasting as long as one year. Amobarbital was found to be helpful, while imipramine, amitriptyline, phenelzine, and chlordiazepoxide were not (1964). These findings contrast sharply with R.I. Shader's experience in treating over 200 patients, whose depersonalization experiences, occurring in the context of panic disorder, responded favorably to phenelzine, alprazolam, trazodone, imipramine, or amitriptyline (listed in order of frequency of use). Noyes et al. (1987) recently reported on the successful treatment of a 16-year-old male with desipramine at 200 mg.

Phenelzine is reported to have produced a positive response in a 36-year-old male with phobic anxiety depersonalization syndrome who previously had failed to respond to psychoanalytically oriented psychotherapy or to supportive psychotherapy and trials of thiothixene, perphenazine, trifluoperazine, diazepam, imipramine, and biofeedback (Hollender and Ban 1979).

Cattell (1959, 1966) mentioned that D-amphetamine and amobarbital "often neutralize depersonalization phenomena" but cited no data. Walsh (1975) also mentioned the usefulness of D-amphetamine, but again no study was cited.

Nuller (1982) found several drugs to be useful in patients who present with acute symptoms of the syndrome. In his study, 25 of 42 patients sustained a two-year remission on the benzodiazepine, phenazepam, and nine of 22 patients improved when treated with the neuroleptic, clozapine. The Roth group, in their series of patients with phobic anxiety depersonalization syndrome, treated one patient with intravenous thiopentone (a barbiturate), and the patient's remission lasted two years. Another patient, initially treated with D-amphetamine and amobarbital, went into a remission lasting four years (Harper and Roth 1962). If depersonalization were, for example, to involve a dysfunctional reticular activating system (i.e., impaired arousal) and/or disturbance in the investment of attention, then the few successful case reports in which D-amphetamine was used could reflect this drug's capacity to increase arousal and heighten the focusing of attention. That sedatives alone or in combination with D-amphetamine are occasionally successful points to the possible role of anxiety in depersonalization. However, we cannot escape the possibility (even probability) that depersonalization is a heterogeneous entity which responds to different treatment modalities in different settings.

These reports of somatic treatment are interesting but inconclusive. Most are single case reports. None employed double-blind or placebo-controlled conditions. Most did not even clearly define the clinical entity or the population studied. Such is the current state of the art in the treatment of depersonalization.

Future Directions

Any meaningful understanding of the etiology and treatment of depersonalization first requires the establishment of clear inclusion and exclusion diagnostic criteria. Once widely accepted diagnostic and symptom criteria are established, controlled, multicenter studies will be needed. Neurophysiologic studies of probands and controls, looking at skin resistance and EEG desynchronization during depersonalization episodes and during the intervals between them, could be revealing. In addition to sedatives and D-amphetamine, drugs such as phenelzine, trazodone, clomipramine, and alprazolam might be useful agents for study because of their potential value in patient groups who are prone to depersonalization (e.g., borderline disorder, panic disorder, obsessive-compulsive disorder).

Chapter 202

Dissociative Disorder Not Otherwise Specified

Dissociative disorder not otherwise specified (DSM-III-R 1987, 300.15) is defined as follows:

> Disorders in which the predominant feature is a dissociative symptom (i.e., a disturbance or alteration in the normally integrative functions of identity, memory, or consciousness) that does not meet the criteria for a specific Dissociative Disorder.
>
> *Examples*:
> (1) Ganser's syndrome: the giving of "approximate answers" to questions, commonly associated with other symptoms such as amnesia, disorientation, perceptual disturbances, fugue, and conversion symptoms.
> (2) cases in which there is more than one personality state capable of assuming executive control of the individual, but not more than one personality state is sufficiently distinct to meet the full criteria for Multiple Personality Disorder, or cases in which a second personality never assumes complete executive control.
> (3) trance states, i.e., altered states of consciousness with markedly diminished or selectively focused responsiveness to environmental stimuli. In children this may occur following physical abuse or trauma.
> (4) derealization unaccompanied by depersonalization.
> (5) dissociated states that may occur in people who have been subjected to periods of prolonged and intense coercive persuasion (e.g., brainwashing, thought reform, or indoctrination while the captive of terrorists or cultists).
> (6) cases in which sudden, unexpected travel and organized, purposeful behavior with inability to recall one's past are not accompanied by the assumption of a new identity, partial or complete. (American Psychiatric Association 1987)

This category presents many problems for those who would recommend correlative psychiatric treatments. First of all, it is described by only a few lines in DSM-III-R. To some extent it is a category of exclusion.

More specifically, there are special diagnostic and definitional problems associated with several of the examples cited in DSM-III-R. For example, brainwashing is regarded by Sadock (1980) as a "condition not attributable to a mental disorder"; if it is not attributable to a mental disorder, is it "treatable" and if so, in what sense? On the other hand, Nemiah (1978) suggested that many people subjected to brainwashing, thought reform, and the like suffer from secondary alexithymia—a functional regressive condition in which the victim is unable to find words for feelings, to recall dreams, or to fantasize. The psychopathologic nature of this condition is further supported by its similarity to the symptom picture shown by decommissurotomized patients (Hoppe and Bogen 1977).

Similarly, trance-like states may occasion widely varying perspectives and opinions about the proper treatment. This divergence is reflected in the provocative title of the Group for the Advancement of Psychiatry (GAP) report, *Mysticism: Spiritual Quest or Psychic Disorder?* (1976). Social, cultural, political, economic, and religious factors all play a role in the diagnosability and hence treatability of "trance" states.

"Indoctrination" may produce Orwell's automatons; it may also result in "good" citizens. And, in addition to good citizens, indoctrination by various sources may produce "good" consumers, churchgoers, atheists, family members, and others who, in their inflexible commitment, may be considered "dissociated." Thus, the dissociative disorder not otherwise specified category is a grey zone, and in perhaps no other category in this manual is more caution necessary on the part of the clinician who would offer treatment.

Trance-Like States

Once it is determined that the trance represents a dissociated state rather than an elected and autonomous altered state of consciousness, correct diagnosis is crucial. Trance states may be seen in conditions as diverse as hysterical attacks, schizophrenic disorder, and toxic delirium. In these cases, the treatment is essentially that of the underlying disorder. Feigned trance states may be described by criminals who wish to avoid prosecution. Psychological testing, particularly the use of the Minnesota Multiphasic Personality Inventory, can be very helpful in distinguishing bogus states from those based on genuine psychopathology. The well-disguised validity scales (L, F, and K) on the MMPI should alert the clinician to the possibility of malingering or support suspicions of such. Hypnotic and amytal interviews may also prove useful.

In those instances in which it is clear that underlying psychopathology is not predominant but there are reasons to be concerned (e.g., the emancipated adolescent who seeks a mystical life style and is brought to you by worried parents), the clinician must bear several factors in mind. First, because it is probable that only a small minority of those who meditate become psychiatrically disordered as a result and that only a few of these voluntarily seek psychiatric help, it is important to assess how the person got to you—that is, how he or she came to have the "patient" role, and how ego-dystonic the prospect of psychotherapy is to him or her; the answer to these questions may affect outcome much more than the "symptoms."

Secondly, the desire for mystical union—the achievement of at-oneness with forces transcendent and immanent—is, in the reasonably healthy person, counterbalanced by a desire to be individual, unique, separate, and autonomous. Indeed, genuine mystical experience may catalyze a fierce determination to be free and independent in worldly affairs: "When the man has gone through life dominated by one idea then he is approaching Yoga; he is getting rid of the grip of the world, and is beyond its allurements" (Besant, 1913 p. 41). Therefore, the clinician must begin by acknowledging with the patient-to-be that free choice in the matter of religious commitment is important and that you, as the clinician, would not wish to interfere with that prerogative.

Thirdly, the mystical quest is a quest for solace, psychological comfort, inner peace, tranquility (Horton 1973, 1974, 1981). It is a quest often undertaken at a time of separation from parents, family, or other accustomed relationships, when the need for solace and solacing substitutes is intense.

Trance states, meditation experiences, employment of a soothing mantra, and the like are sought, albeit unwittingly, as progressive transitional phenomena conferring both a sense of cosmic or universal at-oneness and a feeling of autonomy from ordinary external supplies of comfort, such as demanding, punitive, and restrictive parents. As with the use of other transitional objects and phenomena, the solution to their employment is usually not to try to wrest them away from their users. The best approach entails careful, empathic listening with particular emphasis on feelings about the self. This is because many mystically oriented persons are in severe conflict about the nature of their inner life and the quality of their subjective experience. The therapist may then become an orienting emotional touchstone, a safe-port-in-the-storm, for the fledgling mystic who incurs certain risks in practicing inner thought control that leads to trance states.

Occasionally, even an apparently healthy person—usually an adolescent who is a novice at meditation—has a frightening experience during or immediately following a trance state. For example, one young man who meditated by "clearing (his) mind" suddenly and totally unexpectedly had the experience of "seeing a snake." This was not an hallucination in the usual sense. Rather, it was more the experience of a deadly-snake-like presence that he could not shake off by vigorous efforts at reality testing. In the throes of this terrifying phenomenon—the experiential essence of which was the opposite of what he sought—he called an older man whom he knew had an interest in these phenomena and tearfully described his mental state. The advisor soothingly told him that "this sometimes happens" and "tell it to go away, keep telling it to go away; talk to it just like another person." This advice was remarkably calming and effective and the negative (primary process) presence disappeared from consciousness after a few minutes.

In other cases, reaction to the meditation experience may aggravate an already existing depression. A middle-aged woman who had been meditating daily for several years with the use of a mantra stated: "I get very high and see the light. It lasts for a while after I come down. Then, I crash. Sometimes I get so despondent that I think of suicide. I look for a lesson in it but I can't figure out what it is. It's like I expect something from having seen the light, for example, being loved, and when it doesn't happen I feel terrible."

In still other instances, the trance experience, or the effort to achieve it, may precipitate psychological decompensation. A meditation instructor and the members of her class became frightened when one of the class members suddenly became "catatonic" during a trance exercise and required emergency psychiatric treatment.

These cases are cited to emphasize two points: 1) People who meditate and seek trance states run risks that may be special to the resulting trance state rather than determined solely or mainly by preexisting psychopathology; 2) a solacing, non-threatening, nonjudgmental, genuinely inquiring attitude is singularly important in helping the trance state casualty to recover.

The presumptive diagnosis of "schizophrenia," psychotic depression, or "hysterical" dissociation may seriously interfere directly and indirectly with the clinician's ability to be helpful. However, this awareness should not preclude the giving of advice; for example, "Perhaps it would be a good idea if you took a time out from meditation until you are feeling more secure in what you are doing." A recommendation for at least a temporary return to a more structured, traditional form of religious observance is sometimes beneficial, as is the prescription of thoughtful readings, such as Jung's *Psychology and Religion* (1959), which details some of the psychological issues, including the hazards, involved in seeking individual enlightenment.

Derealization Unaccompanied by Depersonalization

Derealization is the sensation of changed reality or that one's surroundings have altered. This "includes distortions of spatial and temporal relationships so that an essentially neutral environment seems strangely familiar (deja vu) or strangely unfamiliar (jamais vu) or otherwise strange and distorted" (Linn 1980, p. 1026). An example of changed reality and surroundings was given by an anxious young man following his atttendance at a sporting event. Sitting high above the crowd, he was suddenly afflicted with the brief, unpleasant sense that the heads of hair of his fellow spectators were actually animal pelts, that he was looking at a sea of animal fur. Such states are thought to occur most often in schizophrenia but may be seen with hysteria, epilepsy, atypical depressive reactions, traumatic stress reactions, head injury, and normally, as in the seemingly ubiquitous deja vu experience.

Treatment consists of correcting the underlying disorder, with one precautionary note: Linn pointed out that it is important to separate derealization resulting from an atypical depressive reaction from that of schizophrenia, since use of major tranquilizers with the former may intensify the symptoms.

Dissociation Resulting from Brainwashing, Thought Reform, Cultism, and Other Forms of Thought Control

It is important to assess who it is that has been subjected to systematic efforts at indoctrination. A person's characteristic defensive structure, maturity, experience, intelligence level, typical ways of finding solace and relief from stress, and many other factors will influence the effect of manipulative techniques. It is generally assumed that virtually anybody will succumb to brainwashing given the right (or wrong) circumstances; Orwell's *1984* is a vivid example supporting this belief. Oriana Fallaci's *A Man* (1980) and Jeremiah Denton's *When Hell Was in Session* (1982) are graphic presentations of the ability of at least a few people to resist modern and vigorous efforts at mind reform.

Sadock (1980) recommends "supportive" psychotherapy, "re-education, restitution of ego strengths that existed before the trauma, and alleviation of the guilt and depression that are remnants of the frightening experience and the loss of confidence and confusion in identity that result from (brainwashing)" (p. 833). With respect to those young people who fall victim to cults, Ostow (1980) recommended maintenance of contact with the young person, the continued display of love and concern, and the expression of unconditional acceptance without concealment of opposition to the youngster's present course.

Exposure to extreme stress in the form of brainwashing, thought control, and cultism may leave one without words for feelings (Nemiah 1978). In addition to showing communicative incompetence, such people often look "spaced out" or shell-shocked. In such cases, the inability to be emotionally expressive with words and through dreams and fantasies is felt by the victim to be protective from further pain, humiliation, and over-stimulation.

Placement in a demonstrably safe atmosphere is the first step toward alleviating this syndrome. The provision of reassurance, love, and comfort may be necessary since the development and maintenance of the competent use of the language faculty is inextricably bound up with the ability to experience reliable soothing from others (Horton and Sharp 1984). Brainwashing has the opposite effect; there, solace, when it is offered, is manipulative and conditional and never reliable.

Following the re-establishment of a sense of safety, it may be months or years before the victim can begin to give words to his or her traumatic experience. A cautious, supportive, individual psychotherapy, approximately once weekly, may assist the patient to begin to once again connect feelings, words, and thoughts. Stress may need and respond to intensive dynamic psychotherapy. Often, it is necessary for the patient to retell his or her story many times as part of the working-through process.

References

Section 21
Dissociative Disorders

Abeles M, Schilder P: Psychogenic loss of personal identity. Arch Neurol 34:587–604, 1935.

Akhtar S, Brenner I: Differential diagnosis of fugue-like states. J Clin Psychiatry 40:381–385, 1979

American Psychiatric Association: Diagnostic and Statistical Manual of Mental Disorders. Washington, DC, American Psychiatric Association, 1952

American Psychiatric Association: Diagnostic and Statistical Manual of Mental Disorders, 2nd ed. Washington, DC, American Psychiatric Association, 1968

American Psychiatric Association: Diagnostic and Statistical Manual of Mental Disorders, 3rd ed. Washington, DC, American Psychiatric Association, 1980

Barken R, Braun BG, Kluft RP: The dilemma of drug therapy for multiple personality disorder, in The Treatment of Multiple Personality Disorder. Edited by Braun BG. Washington, DC, American Psychiatric Association, 1986

Beahrs JO: Unity and Multiplicity. New York, Brunner-Mazel, 1982

Beale EW: The use of the extended family in the treatment of multiple personality. Psychiatry 135:539–542, 1978

Berman E: Multiple personality: psychoanalytic perspectives. Int J Psychoanal 62:283–300, 1981

Berrington, WP, Liddell DW, Foulds GA: A re-evaluation of the fugue. J Mental Sci 102:280–286, 1956

Besant A: An Introduction to Yoga. Adyar, Madras, India, Theosophical Publish House, 1913

Bliss EL: Multiple personalities. Arch Gen Psychiatry 37:1388–1397, 1980

Bliss EL: Multiple personalities, related disorders, and hypnosis. Am J Clin Hypn 26:114–123, 1983

Blue FR: Use of directive therapy in the treatment of depersonalization neurosis. Psychol Rep 45:904–906, 1979

Boor M, Coons PM: A comprehensive bibliography of literature pertaining to multiple personality. Psychol Rep 53:295–310, 1983

Bowers MK, Brecher-Marer S, Newton BW, et al: Therapy of multiple personality. Int J Clin Exp Hypn 19:57–65, 1971

Brandsma JM, Ludwig AM: A case of multiple personality: diagnosis and therapy. Int J Clin Exp Hypn 22:216–233, 1984

Braun BG: Hypnosis for multiple personalities, in Clinical Hypnosis in Medicine, Edited by Wain HJ. Chicago, Year Book Publishers, 1980

Braun BG: Neurophysiologic changes in multiple personality due to integration: a preliminary report. Am J Clin Hypn 26:84–92, 1983

Braun BG: Hypnosis creates multiple personality: myth or reality? Int J Clin Exp Hypn 32:191–197, 1984a

Braun BG: Uses of hypnosis with multiple personality. Psychiatric Annals 14:34–40, 1984b

Braun BG: Issues in the psychotherapy of multiple personality disorder, in The Treatment of Multiple Personality Disorder. Edited by Braun BG. Washington, DC, American Psychiatric Association, 1986

Brende JP: The psychophysiologic manifestations of dissociation: electrodermal responses in a multiple personality patient. Psychiatr Clin North Am 7:41–50, 1984

Caddy GR: Cognitive behavior therapy in the treatment of multiple personality. Behav Modif 9:267–292, 1985

Cattel JP: Psychopharmacological agents: a selective study. Am J Psychol 115:352–354, 1959

Cattel JP: Depersonalization phenomena, in American Handbook of Psychiatry, VIII. Edited by Arieti S. New York, Basic Books, 1966, pp 88–102

Cattel JP: Depersonalization: psychological and social perspectives, in American Handbook of Psychiatry, 2nd ed. Edited by Arieti S. New York, Basic Books, 1975, pp. 766–799

Caul D: Group and videotape techniques for multiple personality disorder. 14:43–55, 1984

Caul D, Sachs RG, Braun BG: Group therapy in treatment of multiple personality disorder, in The Treatment of Multiple Personality Disorder. Edited by Braun BG. Washington, DC, American Psychiatric Association, 1986

Chancellor AM, Fraser AR: Dissociative disorders, conversion disorder and the use of abreaction in a 22 year old male. N Z Med J 95:418–419, 1982

Clary WF, Burstin KJ, Carpenter JS: Multiple personality and boderline personality disorder. Psychiatr Clin North Am 7:89–100, 1984

Cocores JA, Bender AL, McBride E: Multiple personality, seizure disorder, and the electroencephalogram. J Nerv Ment Dis 172:436–438, 1984

Confer WN: Hypnotic treatment of multiple personality: a case study. Psychotherapy and Psychosomatics 21:408–413, 1984

Coons PM: Children of parents with multiple personality disorder; in Childhood Antecedents of Multiple Personality. Edited by Kluft RP. Washington, DC, American Psychiatric Association, 1985

Coons PM, Bradley K: Group psychotherapy with multiple personality patients. J Nerv Ment Dis 173:515–521, 1985

Coons PM, Milstein V: Rape and post-traumatic stress in multiple personality. Psychol Rep 55:839–845, 1984

Coons PM, Milstein V: Psychosexual disturbances in multiple personality: characteristics, etiology, and treatment. J Clin Psychiatry 47:106–110, 1986

Coons PM, Milstein V, Marley C: EEG studies of two multiple personalities and a control. Arch Gen Psychiatry 39:823–825, 1982

Coryell W: Multiple personality and primary affective disorder. J Nerv Men Dis 171:388–390, 1983

Cutler B, Reed J: Multiple personality: a single case study with a 15 year follow up. Psychol Med 5:18–26, 1975

Davis DH, Osherson A: The concurrent treatment of a multiple personality woman and her son. Am J Psychother 31:504–515, 197X

Davison K: Episodic depersonalization. Br J Psychol 110:505–513, 1964

Denton JA Jr: When Hell Was in Session. Lake Wylie, Robert E. Hopper and Associates, 1982

Dullinger SJ: A case report of dissociative neurosis in an adolescent treated with family therapy and behavior modification. J Consult Clin Psychol 51:479–484, 1983

Ellenberger HF: The Discovery of the Unconscious. New York, Basic Books, 1970

Erickson MH, Kubie LS: The permanent relief of an obsessional phobia by means of communications with an unsuspected dual personality. Psychoanal Q 8:471–509, 1939

Fagan J, McMahon PP: Incipient multiple personality in children: four cases. J Nerv Ment Dis 172:26–36, 1984

Fallaci O: A Man. New York, Pocket Books, 1980

Fisher C: Amnesic states in war neuroses: The psychogenesis of fugues. Psychoanal Q 14:437–468, 1945

Frankl FH: Hypnosis. New York, Plenum Medical Book Company, 1976

Frischholz E, Spiegel D: Hypnosis is not therapy. Bulletin of the British Society of Clinical and Experimental Hypnosis 6:3–8, 1983

Geleerd EB, Hacker FJ, Rapaport D: Contribution to the study of amnesia and allied conditions. Psychoanal Q 14:199–220, 1945

Gifford S, Murawski BJ, Kline NS, et al: An unusual adverse reaction to self-medication with prednisone: an irrational crime during a fugue-state. Int J Psychiatry Med 7:97–122, 1977

Goleman D: New focus on multiple personality. New York Times: Science Times (C), C1 and C6, May 21, 1985

Goodwin DW, Crane JB, Guze SB: Phenomenological aspects of the alcoholic "blackout." Br J Psychiatry 115:1033–1038, 1969

Goodwin J: Sexual Abuse. Boston, John Wright-PSG, Inc, 1982

Goodwin J: Credibility problems in multiple personality disorder and abused children, in Childhood Antecedents of Multiple Personality. Edited by Kluft RP. Washington, DC, American Psychiatric Association, 1985

Greaves GB: Multiple personality: 165 years after Mary Reynolds. J Nerv Ment Dis 168:577–596, 1980

Gruenewald D: Hypnotic techniques without hypnosis in the treatment of dual personality: a case report. J Nerv Men Dis 153:41–46, 1971

Gruenewald D: On the nature of multiple personality: comparisons with hypnosis. Int J Clin Exp Hypn 32:170–190, 1984

Group for the Advancement of Psychiatry: Mysticism: Spiritual Quest or Psychic Disorder? Report No. 97. New York, Group for the Advancement of Psychiatry, 1976

Gudjonsson GH, Haward LRC: Case report–hysterical amnesia as an alternative to suicide. Med Sci Law 22:68–72, 1982

Hale E: Inside the divided mind. New York Times Magazine, Apr 17, 1983, pp 100–106

Hall RC, Le Cann AF, Schooler JC: Amobarbital treatment of multiple personality. J Nerv Ment Dis 161:138–142, 1975

Harper M, Roth M: TLE and the phobic anxiety depersonalization syndrome. Comp Psychiatry 3:215–266, 1962

Harriman P: The experimental production of some phenomena of multiple personality. Journal of Abnormal and Social Psychology 37:244–255, 1942

Harriman P: A new approach to multiple personality. Am J Orthopsychiatry 13:638–643, 1943

Herman M: The use of intravenous sodium amytal in psychogenic amnesic states. Psychiatr Q 12:738–742, 1938

Hollender MH: Pathological intoxication—is there such an entity? J Clin Psychiatry 40:424–426, 1979a

Hollender MH, Ban TA: Ejaculatio retarda due to phenelzine. Psychiatr J Univ Ottawa 4:233–234, 1979

Hoppe K, Bogen J: Alexithymia in twelve commissurotomized patients. Psychother Psychosom, 28:148–155, 1977

Horevitz RP, Braun BG: Are multiple personalities borderline? Psychiatr Clin North Am 7:69–88, 1984

Horton PC: The mystical experience as a suicide preventive. Am J Psychiatry 130:294–96, 1973

Horton PC: The mystical experience: substance of an illusion. J Am Psychoanal Assn 22:363–80, 1974

Horton PC: Solace—The Missing Dimension in Psychiatry. Chicago, University of Chicago Press, 1981

Horton PC and Sharp SL: Language, solace and transitional relatedness. Psychoanal Study Child, 39:167–194, 1984

Janet P: The Major Symptoms of Hysteria. New York, MacMillan, 1907

Jung CG: From psychology and religion, in The Basic Writings of CG Jung. New York, Modern Library, 1959

Kampman R: Hypnotically induced multiple personality. Int J Clin Exp Hypn 24:215–227, 1974

Kennedy A, Neville J: Sudden loss of memory. Br Med J Clin Res 2:428–433, 1957

Kernberg OF: Some clinical observations on multiple personality, in Multiple Personality and Dissociation. Edited by Braun BG, Kluft RP. New York, Brunner-Mazel (in press)

Kline MV: Multiple personality: facts and artifacts in relation to hypnotherapy. Int J Clin Exp Hypn 32:198–209, 1984

Kluft RP: Varieties of hypnotic interventions in the treatment of multiple personality. Am J Clin Hypn 24:230–240, 1982

Kluft RP: Hypnotherapeutic crisis intervention in multiple personality. Am J Clin Hypn 26:73–83, 1983

Kluft RP: An introduction to multiple personality disorder. Psychiatric Annals 14:19–24, 1984a

Kluft RP: Aspects of the treatment of multiple personality disorder. Psychiatric Annals 14:51–55, 1984b

Kluft RP: Childhood multiple disorder, in Childhood Antecedents of Multiple Personality. Edited by Kluft RP. Washington, DC, American Psychiatric Association, 1984c

Kluft RP: Multiple personality in childhood. Psychiatr Clin North Am 7:121–134, 1984d

Kluft RP: Treatment of multiple personality disorder: a study of 33 cases. Psychiatr Clin North Am 7:9–29, 1984e

Kluft RP: Hypnotherapy of childhood multiple personality disorder. Am J Clin Hypn 27:200–210, 1985a

Kluft RP: The natural history of multiple personality disorder, in Childhood Antecedents of Multiple Personality. Edited by Kluft RP. Washington, DC, American Psychiatric Association, 1985b

Kluft RP: The treatment of multiple personality disorder (MPD): current concepts, in Directions in Psychiatry, vol 5, Lesson 24. Edited by Flach FF. New York, Hatherleigh Press, 1985c

Kluft RP: Using hypnotic inquiry protocols to monitor treatment progress and stability in multiple personality disorder. Am J Clin Hypn 28:63–75, 1985d

Kluft RP: Personality unification in multiple personality disorder: a follow-up study, in The Treatment of Multiple Personality. Edited by Braun BG. Washington DC, American Psychiatric Association, 1986a

Kluft RP: The place and role of fusion rituals in treating multiple personality, newsletter, American Society of Clinical Hypnosis 26:4–5, 1986b

Kluft RP: Treating children who have multiple personality disorder, in The Treatment of Multiple Personality Disorder. Edited by Braun BG. Washington, DC, American Psychiatric Association, 1986c

Kluft RP: Children and other unexpected cases of multiple personality disorder, in Multiple Personality and Dissociation. Edited by Braun BG, Kluft RP. New York, Brunner-Mazel (in press)[a]

Kluft RP: Dissociative disorders, in An Annotated Bibliography of DSM-III. Edited by Skodol AE, Spitzer RL. Washington, DC, American Psychiatric Association (in press)[b]

Kluft RP: High Functioning multiple personality disorder. J Nerv Ment Dis (in press)[c]

Kluft RP: Reply to Paul Chodoff. Am J Psychiatry (in press)[d]

Kluft RP: The simulation and dissimulation of multiple personality disorder. Am J Clin Hypn (in press)[e]

Kluft RP: Unsuspected MPD: an uncommon source of protracted resistance, interruption, and failure in psychoanalysis. Manuscript submitted for publication

Kluft RP, Braun BG, Sachs RG: Multiple personality, intrafamilial abuse, and family psychiatry. International Journal of Family Psychiatry 5:283–301, 1984

Kohlenberg RJ: Behavioristic approach to multiple personality: a case study. Behav Res Ther 4:137–140, 1973

Lampl-De Groot J: Notes on multiple personality. Psychoanal Q 50:614–624, 1981

Lasky R: The psychoanalytic treatment of a case of multiple personality. Psychoanal Rev 65:355–380, 1978

Leavitt H: A case of hypnotically produced secondary and tertiary personalities. Psychoanal Rev 34:274–295, 1947

Lehmann LS: Depersonalization. Am J Psych 131:1221–1224, 1974

Levenson J, Berry S: Family intervention in a case of multiple personality. Journal of Marital and Family Therapy 9:73–80, 1983

Levy JS, Wachtel PL: Depersonalization: an effort at clarification. Am J Psychoanal. 38:291–300, 1978

Linn L: Classical manifestations of psychiatric disorders, in Comprehensive Textbook of Psychiatry, 3rd ed, vol 1. Edited by Freedman AM, Kaplan HI, Sadock BJ. Baltimore, Williams and Wilkins Co 1980

Linn L: Multiple personality disorder. Unpublished paper, 1986

Lipman L: Hypnotizability and multiple personality. Presented at the Annual Meeting of the American Psychiatric Association, Dallas, May 1985

Lipton SD, Kezur E: Dissociated personality: status of a case after five years. Psychiatr Q 22: 252–256, 1948

MacHovec FJ: Hypnosis to facilitate recall in psychogenic amnesia and fugue states: treatment variables. Am J Clin Hypn 24:7–13, 1981

Marmer SS: The dream in dissociated states, in The Dream in Clinical Practice. Edited by Natterson JM. New York, Aronson, 1980a

Marmer SS: Psychoanalysis of multiple personality. Int J Psychoanal 61:439–459, 1980b

Mathew RJ, Jack RA, West WS: Regional cerebral blood flow in a patient with multiple personality. Am J Psychiatry 142:504–505, 1984

McGraw RB, Oliver JF: Miscellaneous therapies, in American Handbook of Psychiatry, vol 2. Edited by Arieti S. New York, Basic Books, 1959

McKellar A: Depersonalization in a 16 year old boy. South Med J 71:1580–1581, 1978

Meares R, Grose D: On depersonalization in adolescence: a consideration from the viewpoints of habituation and identity. Br J Med Psychol 31:335–347, 1978

Mesulam M: Dissociative states with abnormal temporal lobe EEG. Arch Neurol 38:176–181, 1981

Myerson AT: Amnesia for homicide. Arch Gen Psychiatry 14:509, 1966

Myerson AT: Amnesia for homicide ("pedicide"). Arch Gen Psychiatry 14:509–515, 1966

Nemiah JC: Alexithymia and psychosomatic illness. J Cont Educ Psychiatry October 25, 1978

Nemiah JC: Dissociative disorders (hysterical neurosis, dissociative type), in Comprehensive Textbook of Psychiatry, 3rd ed, vol 2. Edited by Kaplan HI, Freedman AM, Bacock BJ. Baltimore, Williams and Wilkins, 1980

Nemiah JC: Dissociative disorders, in Comprehensive Textbook of Psychiatry, 3rd ed. Edited by Kaplan H, Freedman A, Sadock B. Baltimore, Williams and Wilkins, 1981.

Noyes R Jr, Kuperman S, Olson SB: Desipramine: A possible treatment for depersonalization disorder. Can J Psychiatry 32:782–784, 1987

Nuller YL: Depersonalization—symptoms, meaning, therapy. Acta Psychiatr Scand 66:451–458, 1982

Orne MT: The nature of hypnosis: artifact and essence. Journal of Abnormal and Social Psychology 58:277–299, 1959

Orne MT: On the simulating subject as a quasi-control group in hypnosis research: why, what, and how, In Hypnosis: Developments in Research and New Perspectives, 2nd ed. Edited by Fromm E, Shor R. New York, Aldine, 1979a

Orne MT: The use and misuse of hypnosis in court. Int J Clin Exp Hypn 27:311–341, 1979b

Orne MT, Dinges DF, Orne EC: On the differential diagnosis of multiple personality in the forensic context. Int J Clin Exp Hypn 32:118–169, 1984

Ostow M: Religion and psychiatry, in Comprehensive Textbook of Psychiatry, 3rd ed. vol 3. Edited by Freedman AM, Kaplan HI, Sadock BJ. Baltimore, William and Wilkins Co, 1980

Parfitt DN, Gall CMC: Psychogenic amnesia: the refusal to remember. 90:511–531, 1944

Parikh MD, Sheth AS, Apte JS, et al: Depersonalization. J Postgrad Med 24:226–230, 1981

Price J, Hess ND: Behavior therapy as a precipitant and treatment in a case of dual personality. Aust N Z J Psychiatry 13:63–66, 1979

Putnam FW: The psychophysiologic investigation of multiple personality disorder: a review. Psychiatr Clin North Am 7:31–39, 1984

Putnam FW: The treatment of multiple personality: state of the art, in The Treatment of Multiple Personality Disorder (MPD). Edited by Braun BG. Washington, DC, American Psychiatric Association, 1986

Putnam FW, Buchsbaum M, Howland F, et al: Evoked potentials in multiple personality disorder. Presented at the Annual Meeting of the American Psychiatric Association (as new research abstract #139), Toronto, 1982

Putnam FW, Loewenstein RJ, Silberman EK, et al: Multiple personality disorder in a hospital setting. J Clin Psychiatry 45:172–175, 1984

Putnam FW, Guroff JJ, Silberman EK, et al: The clinical phenomenology of multiple personality disorder: review of 100 recent cases. J Clin Psychiatry 17:285–293, 1986

Renik P: The role of attention in depersonalization. Psychoanal Q 47:588–605, 1978

Ries H: Analysis of a patient with a split personality. Int J Psychoanal 39:397–407, 1958

Rosenbaum M, Weaver GM: Dissociated state: status of a case after 38 years. J Nerv Ment Dis 168:597–603, 1980

Sachs RG: The adjunctive role of social support systems in the treatment of multiple personality disorder, in The Treatment of Multiple Personality Disorder. Edited by Braun BG. Washington, DC, American Psychiatric Association, 1986

Sadock VA: Other conditions not attributable to a mental disorder, in Comprehensive Textbook of Psychiatry, 3rd ed, vol 3. Edited by Freedman AM, Kaplan HI, Sadock BJ. Baltimore, Williams and Wilkins Co, 1980

Saltman V, Solomon RS: Incest and the multiple personality. Psychol Rep 50:1127–1141, 1982

Sargant W, Slater E: Acute war neuroses. Lancet 2:6097–6098, 1940

Sbriglio R: The amytal interview in emergency and psychiatric settings. 20(#10):91–99, 1984

Schenk L, Bear D: Multiple personality and related dissociative phenomena in patients with temporal lobe epilepsy. Am J Psychiatry 138:1311–1316, 1981

Schreiber FR: Sybil. New York, Henry Regnery, 1973

Schultz RS, Braun BG, Kluft RP: Creativity and the imaginary companion phenomenon: prevalence and phenomenology in MPD. Presented at the Second International Conference on Multiple Personality/Dissociative States, Chicago, 1985

Shapiro S: Depersonalization and daydreaming. Bull Menninger Clin 42:307–320, 1978

Shenk L, Bear D: Multiple personality and related dissociative phenomena in patients with temporal lobe epilepsy. Am J Psychiatry 138:1311–1316, 1981

Shorvon HJ: The depersonalization syndrome. 39:779–792, 1946

Shraberg D: The phobic anxiety depersonalization syndrome. Psychiatric Opin 14:35–40, 1977

Silberman EK, Putnam FW, Weingartner H, et al: Dissociative states in multiple personality disorder: a quantitative study. Psychiatry Res 15:253–260, 1985

Solomon RS, Solomon V: Differential diagnosis of multiple personality. Psychol Rep 51:1187–1194, 1982

Spanos NP, Weekes JR, Bertrand LD: Multiple personality: a social psychological perspective. J Abnorm Psychol 94:362–376, 1985

Spiegel D: Multiple personality as a post-traumatic stress disorder. Psychiatr Clin North Am 7:101–110, 1984

Spiegel D: Dissociation, double binds, and posttraumatic stress in multiple personality disorder, in The Treatment of Multiple Personality Disorder. Edited by Braun BG. Washington, DC, American Psychiatric Association, 1986

Spitzer RL, Skodol AE, Gibbon M, et al: DSM III Casebook, Washington, DC: 1981, pp. 85–87, 112, 113

Stengel E: On the etiology of the fugue states. Journal Mental Science 87:572–599, 1941

Stolorow RS: Defensive and arrested development aspects of death anxiety, hypochondriasis and depersonalization. Int J Psychoanal 60:201–213, 1979

Summit R: The child sexual abuse accommodation syndrome. Journal of Child Abuse and Neglect 7:177–193, 1983

Sutcliffe JP, Jones J: Personal identity, multiple personality, and hypnosis. Int J Clin Exp Hypn 10:231–269, 1962

Taylor FK: Depersonalization in light of Brentano's phenomenology. Br J Med Psychol 55:297–306, 1982

Taylor WS, Martin MF: Multiple personality. Journal of Abnormal and Social Psychology 39:281–300, 1944

Thigpen CH, Cleckley HM: On the incidence of multiple personality disorder. Int J Clin Exp Hypn 32:63–66, 1984

Torch EM: Review of the relationship between obsession and depersonalization. Acta Psychiatr Scand 58:191–198, 1978

Torch EM: Depersonalization syndrome: an overview. Psychiatr Q 53:249–258, 1981

Trueman DJ: Depersonalization in an non-clinical population. Psychol 116:107–112, 1984

Victor G: Sybil: Grand hysterie of folie a deux? Am J Psychiatry 132:202, 1975

Walsh RN: Depersonalization: definition and treatment. Am J Psychiatry 132:873, 1975

Watkins JG, Watkins HH: Ego-state therapy, in Handbook of Innovative Therapies. Edited by Corsini. New York, Wiley, 1981

Weinstein EA, Kahn RL: Denial of Illness. Springfield, Ill, Charles C Thomas, 1955

Wilbur CB: Creating a therapy situation for the multiple personality disorder patient. Presented at the First International Conference on Multiple Personality/Dissociative States, Chicago, September, 1984a

Wilbur CB: Multiple personality and child abuse. Psychiatr Clin North Am 7:3–8, 1984b

Wilbur CB: Psychoanalytic issues in the treatment of multiple personality. Presented at the First International Conference on Multiple Personality/Dissociative States, Chicago, September 1984c

Wilbur CB: Treatment of multiple personality. Psychiatric Annals 14:27–31, 1984d

Wilbur CB: Psychoanalysis and multiple personality disorder, in The Treatment of Multiple Personality Disorder. Edited by Braun BG. Washington, DC, American Psychiatric Association, 1986

Woodruff R, Goodwin D, Guze S: Psychiatric Diagnosis. New York, Oxford University Press, 1974

Sexual Disorders

Chapter 203

Introduction

DSM-III (American Psychiatric Association 1980) provided a radical departure from the DSM-II (American Psychiatric Association 1968) classification of psychosexual dysfunctions, which made very limited and rather vague reference to psychophysiologic disorders. The Task Force based the new classification on the phases of sexual response, namely desire, excitement, and orgasm.

There were (and continue to be) a number of controversial issues in the classification. Perhaps the most controversial was the exclusion of homosexuality in DSM-III (the decision to remove homosexuality from the list of mental disorders had been made by the American Psychiatric Association some years earlier) and the inclusion of ego-dystonic homosexuality. While it is possible to discuss the clinical aspects of ego-dystonic homosexuality without suggesting that homosexuality is pathologic, since ego-dystonic homosexuality has now been dropped from DSM-III-R (American Psychiatric Association 1987), that subject is not included in this section.

Other issues that have been "sticky wickets" involve decisions to separate sexual aversion from inhibited sexual desire and deal with it as a separate entity (not done in DSM-III, but included in DSM-III-R) and whether to include hyperactive sexual desire or arousal as a category unto itself. The decision has been not to do that, so it is not included in DSM-III-R, yet some brief discussion of this topic will be found in the chapter dealing with problems of sexual desire. Inhibited sexual desire has become hypoactive sexual desire disorder, e.g., ISD is now HSDD. The term "inhibited" was dropped because it implied a psychodynamic etiology to the problem. In maintaining the descriptive approach, the somewhat awkward term HSDD was coined.

One of DSM-III's unisex diagnoses, inhibited sexual excitement, has been modified to fit with better usage. Two diagnostic categories in DSM-III-R take its place, male erectile disorder and female sexual arousal disorder. The clinical literature kept referring to male inhibited sexual excitement (the DSM-III category) as erectile dysfunction, and there appeared to be little justification for deviating from this usage in the nomenclature. Although there have been attempts to separate the terms "arousal" and "excitement," most clinicians seem to use these terms interchangeably.

Sexual life is as varied and heterogeneous as life itself, so classification schemes require a category where cases impossible to classify can be placed. Examples of such hard to classify cases are included in "Atypical Psychosexual Disorders."

Not only are sexual problems heterogeneous, but so are methods of treatment. While most of the psychotherapeutic methods are discussed in various places in the volume, emphasis is on psychodynamic psychotherapy and behavioral therapy. Cognitive therapy, object relations therapy, and communications therapy are not completely slighted, but not particularly emphasized.

While no special chapter is devoted to the family therapy of sexual dysfunctions, the overwhelming approach to sexual problems is couple therapy. Among the debts to Masters and Johnson, perhaps the greatest one is that their treatment method switched the focus from individual to couple therapy, and that remains the principal orientation of the authors. As this scientific era is one of expanding knowledge about the neurosciences and psychopharmacology, the volume would not have been complete without a thorough discussion of drugs that influence sexual function (see "Drug Therapy"), a discussion of the surgical methods of alleviating erectile dysfunctions (see "Surgical Treatments"), and the basic research findings in the field.

Finally, a note of regret that a section on sexuality has nothing to say about AIDS. When this project was begun in 1983, AIDS was just being recognized. While AIDS is not necessarily associated specifically with any sexual dysfunction, had we an opportunity to re-write the chapter on "Special Populations," a lot of attention would have been given to the sexual behaviors associated with AIDS and to the special issues of prevention and of care for those who are sero-positive or who have developed symptoms of AIDS. In fact, in view of the frequency and variety of neuropsychiatric manifestations of AIDS, a separate chapter devoted to AIDS would have been in order.

Chapter 204

Evaluation of Sexual Disorders

Comprehensive and precise assessments of the determinants involved in sexual dysfunction are of primary importance to successful treatment. Accurate diagnosis, the cornerstone of all medicine, is equally critical in the treatment of sexual disorders. A wide range of psychogenic and organic disorders may produce identical symptoms, and treatment failures can frequently be linked to a failure to differentiate between organic and psychogenic causes.

Correct diagnosis must also comprehend the triphasic model of sexual disorders, as defined by the Diagnostic and Statistical Manual of the American Psychiatric Association (DSM-III-R). Impairments of desire, arousal and orgasm phases of sexual functioning each have various etiologies, and treatment plans must evolve accordingly.

Differentiating Between Organic and Psychogenic Sexual Disorders

In differentiating between organic and psychogenic sexual disorders, recent advances in the area of identifying organic causes of dysfunction have made the evaluator's task lighter. Sophisticated techniques such as the use of nocturnal penile tumescence monitoring to measure erections naturally occurring during REM sleep assist the clinician in ruling out organic erectile difficulties. This procedure, used in conjunction with other tests performed at specialized evaluation centers, can frequently detect the presence of organically caused impotence (Karacan and Moore 1985). However, these tests will not be called for in all cases, and a thorough evaluation including history taking and psychological assessment will frequently establish that the disorder is almost surely of psychogenic origin, and specialized testing is not called for.

The process of evaluating a sexual disorder begins with the clinical interview. The therapist initiates the diagnostic procedure by focusing on the chief complaint and its development over time, and determining which phases of the sexual response cycle are affected. The initial consultation serves as not only a "fact-gathering" medium, but establishes dialogue with the individual or couple and facilitates the patients' future willingness to cooperate with the treatment plan. The therapist must convey empathy and helpfulness to the patients, and the interview should optimally take place in a relaxed, private atmosphere. The therapist's attitude should be non-judgmental, and the language used in the sessions should be neither strictly clinical nor "street" terminology, as either extreme may be interpreted by the patients as condescending.

While a predetermined set of questions must be answered in a consultative interview in order to acquire the necessary information to make an accurate diagnosis, it is important to note that the interview should not be conducted in an overly structured fashion. In evaluating a sexual disorder it is important to examine the patient's history as it relates to the present complaint, rather than simply to develop a chronological or sequential set of events preceding the complaint. For example, asking a patient, "When did you first begin masturbating?" automatically elicits a chronological response, while suggesting that the patient "tell me about your experiences with masturbation" may provoke a more "telling" initial response covering a range of masturbatory experiences and anxieties. If necessary, the therapist can subsequently fill in the blanks by asking, "How young were you when that occurred?" Structured questionnaires about sexual function and the quality of the couple's relationship and personality, depression, and anxiety inventories can be helpful for research and screening purposes, but must be supplemented by detailed interviews.

The initial phase of the history-taking process should result in the following information:

1. The nature of the dysfunction(s)—lack of interest in sexual activity (desire), inability to achieve sufficient arousal or lubrication (arousal or excitement), inability to achieve orgasm, dyspareunia, vaginismus
2. When the sexual difficulty first became apparent—how long ago, in what situation, with what partner(s) (spouse, boyfriend/girlfriend, casual encounter, prostitute)
3. With what frequency the difficulty has been encountered—with each sexual contact (global), only with certain sexual partners or in certain sexual encounters (situational), only with a partner and not with masturbation

4. The course of the dysfunction—acute onset or gradual; progressive, static, or intermittent
5. The patient's view of the etiology of the problem—"maybe I'm just getting older," "my partner expects too much from me," "it must be something physical," "I'm always too tired," "I can't understand what he/she wants"
6. What attempts the patient and partner have made to correct the dysfunction and with what results

Further examination of a demographic nature will be helpful, such as length of time the couple has been married or together, past long-term marriages or relationships, occupation of both partners. Other factors which may influence sexual function are stressful work, long or irregular work hours, whether there are children or other family members at home. Information about these areas should be gathered during the initial evaluation.

Other information necessary during evaluation include the following:

1. Family attitudes about sex during patients' upbringing—degree of openness or reserve, feelings, about nudity/modesty
2. Sexual information—from parents, peers, books, etc.
3. Childhood sexual activity—age, feelings of guilt or pleasure, discovery by adults and consequences
4. Adolescent sexual experiences—necking, intercourse, feelings of guilt or pleasure
5. Adult sexual experiences—number of partners; gender of partners; accompanying feelings of pleasure, guilt, remorse, fear
6. Masturbatory experiences—what age, frequency, by what method (hand, pillow, vibrator, etc.), accompanying feelings
7 Traumatic sexual encounters—sexual abuse, incest, molestation, rape, disparaging or hypercritical partner, perceived inadequate performance, harsh or frequent rejection of sexual overtures
8. Sexual fantasies—nature of "favorite" fantasies, accompanying feelings
9. Sexual deviations—contact with animals, voyeurism, exhibitionism, pedophilia, fetishes, sadomasochism
10. Homosexual encounters—at what age, with how many partners, accompanying feelings

If the interviewer has been thorough in the history-taking phase of the evaluation, he or she often can make a reasonable determination as to whether the dysfunction is organic or psychogenic in nature. One indicator is whether the disorder is global (all the time, with all partners) or situational. A global disorder is one indicator that special clinical tests and examinations may be called for, while a situational disorder is more likely to be traced to psychogenic origins. The clinician should be aware that there are exceptions to the "rule" that situational dysfunctions are psychogenic. For example, physically based dyspareunia may occur only in certain positions, and a man with marginal penile vascular supply may at times be able to achieve and maintain erections or have occasional erections on awakening.

Another area of examination that may identify an organic sexual difficulty is that of alcohol and drug use. Alcohol, psychoactive drugs, antihypertensive medications, narcotics, and alpha and beta adrenergic blocking agents have all been linked to sexual problems, in particular to erectile failure and decreased desire; and it is important to establish in the initial interview whether the patient is undergoing a course of treatment with these medications, or has a history of excessive use of alcohol.

Clinical tests and examinations may be indicated based on the findings of the initial consultation. These include the following.

Physical Examination

A routine physical examination of the partner complaining of the sexual problem (or both partners if both have dysfunction) should be performed. Any chronic or debilitating disease may decrease sexual desire in men or women. In particular, patients should be examined for evidence of endocrinopathy, hypothalamic-pituitary axis dysfunction, hepatic and renal disease, and intracranial pathology. A wide range of medical problems can be associated with erectile failure, including cardiovascular, endocrinologic, neurologic, hematologic, hepatic, and genitourinary disease. Lesions of the spinal cord and autonomic neuropathies can cause orgasm phase problems in men and women. Prostatitis has been associated with premature ejaculation and impotence. Estrogen deficiency, and rarely, central or peripheral nervous system pathology, may cause impaired sexual excitement in women.

A genital examination (including pelvic examination in women) is critical. Many clinicians perform these in the format of a "sexological exam." A sexological exam simply means that the exams are done with both partners present and with attention to education, permission to touch the genitals, desensitization, and reassurance of normalcy (if this is the case) as well as attention to any abnormal findings. This adds an important dimension to the sex therapy as well as to the evaulation. Genital examinations are particularly important in the assessment of excitement phase disorders, dyspareunia and vaginismus because local pathology is not uncommon in these. (The ethical issues of a psychiatrist performing a physical involving the genitals are discussed in the chapter on "Special Approaches.") If the history or physical examination indicates possible organic pathology, further tests may be required.

Impaired sexual desire. Tests for liver and thyroid function and for blood urea nitrogen (BUN), creatinine, cortisol, testosterone, estrogen, leutinizing hormone (LH), follicle stimulating hormone (FSH), and prolactin levels are indicated if signs or symptoms of diseases in the relevant systems are present.

Male erectile disorder (impotence). Blood tests can be useful in documenting systemic (or testicular) disease states associated with impotence. In particular, hyperprolactinemia, low plasma free and bound testosterone levels, and (less well documented) abnormal LH and FSH levels can be associated with biogenic impotence. Unless erectile failure is clearly situational and the patient can have firm, long-lasting erections in certain other situations, biogenic impotence must be ruled out.

The most widely used laboratory procedure to determine whether erectile dysfunction is psychogenic or biogenic is nocturnal penile tumescence (NPT) monitoring. All healthy males from infancy to old age have NPT associated with rapid eye movement (REM) sleep, although there are some qualitative and quantitative changes with age (Karacan et al. 1975). Since monitoring occurs during sleep, negative effects are presumably at a minimum. While negative affects in dreams may be associated with transient periods of reduced erection, they do not inhibit erections over a full night or series of nights (see Karacan et al. 1975 for review). Psychiatric disorders such as depression and anxiety can inhibit NPT, primarily, but not exclusively, by interfering with REM sleep.

NPT monitoring is best done in a hospital or laboratory setting with concomitant monitoring of sleep EEG (to assure adequate REM sleep), penile circumference changes at base and tip, and penile rigidity during maximal erections. Rigidity is an important measure because some men can have good circumference increases but not enough firmness for penetration. Home NPT monitoring is much less expensive and more convenient, but because REM sleep and rigidity are not measured and artifacts and equipment malfunction cannot be detected as easily, it is less reliable.

NPT monitoring can determine if erectile capacity is impaired, but ancillary tests are needed to determine etiology. Careful examination of the penis in the flaccid and, if possible, erect or semierect states may reveal structural defects such as Peyronie's plaque, chordee, or cavernosal tissue abnormality. Bulbocavernosus and ischiocavernosus reflex latency (electrical stimulation of the glans penis and EMG recording of the muscle response) can reveal somatic nerve function abnormalities, and stimulation of the prostatic urethra with response recording may reveal autonomic neuropathy. Recording of sensory thresholds on the penis determines if there is a sensory deficit. Abnormal findings on systemic tests of autonomic nervous system function such as heart beat-to-beat variability during deep breathing can suggest the possibility of a systemic autonomic neuropathy. And sacral evoked response testing evaluates the integrity of the neural circuits from the sacral area through the spinal cord to the brain.

The most commonly used measure of vascular function is the Doppler examination of pulse volume and pressure in the penis. Pressures in the right and left dorsal and cavernosal arteries in the flaccid penis normally are about equal to or slightly lower than the brachial blood pressure. Normally, penile pressure should not be lower than 0.8 of the brachial pressure. The penile pressures should be measured at rest and again after buttocks and leg exercise. If there is a fall in pressure, a vascular "steal" phenomenon may be present which could cause the patient to lose erections during thrusting.

More invasive tests may be performed when indicated. A corpus cavernosogram, injection of contrast media into one corpus during fluoroscopy, can identify abnormalities of venous drainage or structural defects of the corporae. And arteriography is sometimes performed to determine the location of an arterial stenosis when vascular surgery is contemplated. The injection of papaverine or other vasodilator into the penis, thereby causing erection, can be used as a diagnostic as well as a therapeutic tool.

Female sexual arousal disorder. The most common biogenic cause for decreased vaginal vasocongestion and lubrication is atrophic vulvovaginitis due to estrogen deficiency, especially in postmenopausal women. Pelvic exam reveals a dry, thin vaginal mucosa, plasma estrogen levels are low while LH and FSH are often elevated, and a wet smear of vaginal mucosa reveals a predominance of parabasal cells. Serious endocrine, metabolic, vascular and neurologic disease presumptively may impair sexual excitement and are usually readily apparent on history and physical exam. Unfortunately, there are many unknowns about physical impairment of female sexual excitement (and orgasm), and proven valid and reliable laboratory tests of vascular and neurologic function in the genital region are unavailable or not generally used.

Premature ejaculation (PE). Primary PE is almost always psychogenic. PE developing after a period of normal ejaculatory control may be secondary to impotence (the patient learns to ejaculate rapidly before losing his erection), and may be due to neurologic conditions affecting the sacral spinal cord or its peripheral nerves, or to prostatitis or urethritis.

Retarded ejaculation (inhibited male orgasm). Retarded ejaculation (RE) must be distinguished from retrograde ejaculation and anejaculatory orgasm. In the latter two, the psychic and genital components of orgasm are present without the appearance of ejaculate, and they are virtually always due to physical or drug-related causes. Examination of a post-orgasm, spun urine sample can differentiate retrograde ejaculation (semen in sample) from anejaculatory orgasm (no semen). Primary RE and RE in a healthy young or middle-aged man not taking drugs are very likely psychogenic. Organic causes must be sought in secondary RE. Alpha adrenergic blockers, ganglionic blockers and thioridazine are common causes of RE; less commonly, drugs causing central nervous system depression, antidepressants, and buterophenones delay ejaculation. Since ejaculation is a spinal reflex mediated through the sympathetic nervous system, any medication or disease state disrupting this reflex arc may be causative. In such cases, other findings are usually evident, such as bowel and bladder dysfunction, neurologic findings, diabetes, etc. As men age, the latency from erection to ejaculation often increases; this is a normal age-related process and should be differentiated from retarded ejaculation.

Male dyspareunia. The male may have pain on intromission, thrusting, or ejaculation, and if physical causes exist, they are often apparent on physical examination or during history taking. The most common causes of pain on intromission or thrusting are dermatologic lesions, urethritis, and anatomical abnormalities. A careful examination of the penis can reveal conditions such as phimosis, balanitis, chordee, Peyronie's plaque, or other scar tissue in the penis which can lead to painful erections or pain during coitus. Urethritis can cause pain on intromission, thrusting, or ejaculation, and the history also reveals burning on urination and urinary urgency or hesitancy. Infectious causes of urethritis can be documented by urinalysis, while noninfectious urethritis is usually diagnosed by history alone. Painful ejaculation may be caused by inflammation or lesion of the prostate, seminal vesicles, vas deferens, epididymis, urethra, or testicles. Examination and culture of expressed prostatic secretions, ejaculate, and urine can be useful. Rarely, painful spasm of perineal and reproductive organ muscles causes ejaculatory dyspareunia.

Female dyspareunia. The physical causes of female dyspareunia are many and varied. Pain on penetration may be caused by an intact hymen; inflammation; scarring or trauma to the clitoris, vagina, vulva, Skene or Bartholin glands; vaginismus; urethritis; or inadequate lubrication. These causes can usually be readily determined by gynecologic examination and cultures and smears of the affected area if indicated. Mid-vaginal pain may be caused by vaginitis, urethritis, trigonitis, or cystitis; a short or scarred vagina; or anorectal disease. Again, these disorders are usually apparent on examination or smears of the affected area, and the pain can often be reproduced during the examination. Pain on deep thrusting is often due to pathology of the pelvic organs. Scarring, fixation, inflammation, and neoplasms of the uterus, adnexae, bladder, and bowel can be causative. Endometriosis and ectopic pregnancy may also cause pain on deep thrusting. Cervical disease and a vagina that is shorter than the erect penis may lead to pain, particularly if penile thrusting is forceful. Prolonged pelvic congestion due to arousal without orgasm causes discomfort in some women, particularly multiparous women with genital or pelvic varicosities. Painful orgasm is most often a result of uterine spasms or strong contractions during and after orgasm. Women with IUDs, which result in enhanced uterine contractility, and women with primary dysmenorrhea who have increased baseline uterine tone are most likely to suffer from painful uterine contractions with orgasm. Both men and women may have pain outside of the pelvic region during coitus due to such conditions as angina, post-orgasm vascular headaches, or orthopedic problems.

Vaginismus.   Vaginismus is the reflexive, painful spasm of perineal and para-vaginal muscles when penetration (during intercourse, gynecologic exam, or other manipulation) is attempted. Any physical condition that causes a dyspareunia can result in vaginismus as a protective reflex against pain. Secondary vaginismus is more likely due to painful physical conditions than is primary vaginismus.

If the tests and evaluations reveal the presence of an organic cause for the sexual disorder, psychological assessment and possible psychotherapy are not necessarily discarded as part of the treatment plan. For example, a case in which a patient has fully recovered from a central nervous system trauma which caused a temporary erectile dysfunction, but who is still experiencing erectile difficulties, may be responsive to a brief course of psychosocial therapy (Lobitz and Lobitz 1978). Another example is the patient with biogenic impotence who has received a penile prosthesis. Occasionally, the couple will have difficulty with sexual adjustment, and psychotherapy including exploratory, behavioral, and educational techniques can be helpful.

Psychological Assessment

Patients with psychological problems in addition to sexual dysfunctions may respond poorly to treatment plans until underlying psychiatric disorders have been treated. A psychiatric examination to assess psychogenicity of the sexual disorder, as well as patient's suitability as a candidate for possible psychotherapeutic approaches, is the next phase of the evaluation.

It is important to establish the level of psychopathology in the patients before determining a treatment plan. Many patients suffering from relatively minor psychological dysfunctions are good candidates for a course of brief sex therapy, while patients with more serious intrapsychic or interpersonal problems may require extensive psychotherapeutic treatment before, during, or instead of behavioral sex therapy.

Helen Singer Kaplan describes three mental "levels" of psychological causes of sexual dysfunction (Kaplan 1979), and suggests that the psychiatric examination phase of the evaluation focus on determining whether psychopathology exists at a "superficial level," "mid-level," or "deep" level.

On the superficial level are patients with performance anxiety, including fear of sexual failure, spectatoring, disparaging thoughts about their attractiveness or adequacy (common in overweight men and women, women who perceive their breasts as small, and men who perceive their penises as small), and inhibitions about communicating sexual preferences.

"Mid-level" conflicts may have their roots in negative family messages and roles and childhood emotional trauma resulting in success phobias. The "mid-level" category may also encompass power struggles between partners and parental transference to the partner.

The "deepest" conflicts include extremely negative consequences of childhood sexual discovery and experiences resulting from extreme religious or family prohibitions against sexual pleasures. Included in this category are oedipal and pre-oedipal conflicts, e.g., conflicts over trust, dependency, and control which undermine the patient's ability to form suitable romantic attachments in later years and cause serious marital conflicts.

Patients whose dysfunctions originate at the "superficial level" will be the best candidates for short-term psychosexual therapy. Anorgasmia in women and premature ejaculation in men are frequently rooted in this "superficial level" and are highly responsive to treatment. However, hypoactive sexual desire often has its psychogenicity in the "mid-" or "deep" levels and may respond better to longer-term psychotherapy, or a combined behavioral and exploratory approach.

A psychiatric examination of both partners may reveal psychological disturbance in one but not the other, or "superficial level" conflicts in one partner and "mid-level" conflicts in the other. The successful outcome of the treatment program may depend on establishing the more disturbed patient in individual psychotherapy before continuing with sex therapy.

The psychiatric examination may also identify psychopathology which is not fundamentally related to the sexual dysfunction. The decision to treat a couple in a psychosexual modality despite observable psychopathology in one or both partners may be based on two criteria (Lobitz and Lobitz 1978): 1) the problem should not interfere greatly with the person's everyday functioning, and 2) the problems should not be likely to interfere with treatment.

Treating patients with psychotic, affective, or panic disorders will generally require that the patient be maintained on medication, and often that the patient be seen concurrently in individual therapy to maintain the patient's functioning.

The evaluation of current sexual behavior is best accomplished by a detailed review of the sexual response cycle encompassing practices and problems in desire, excitement, orgasm, and resolution phases. Discerning both the physical changes and the subjective experience accompanying each of these phases enables the physician to make a phase-specific evaluation of the sexual disorder.

At the conclusion of the review of sexual systems, the therapist should have acquired a description of both the emotional and physical events which transpire during the couple's sexual interaction, and should be able to identify the "problem" phase or phases. At this stage, it should also become clear whether there are ineffective sexual behaviors that hinder the partners' ability to achieve sexual satisfaction. A detailed description of foreplay activities, for example, may indicate that physical caressing is either rough or non-existent, or that the partners are either ignorant of or fail to communicate their needs and desires in this area. At the extremes are the man who fondles his partner's breasts, but fails to stimulate her clitoris, or conversely, having learned that stimulation of the clitoris evokes pleasure in the partner, the man ignores other erotically sensitive parts of her body. Likewise, a woman may be inhibited about manual or oral stimulation of her partner's penis.

Unwillingness to assertively ask the partner to participate in specific sexual activities may also be identified during the review of sexual systems. Communication is paramount to healthy sexual activity, and failures in this area contribute to maintaining sexual disorders, and may even enhance the condition. For example, a woman with particular difficulty in asserting her needs in the relationship musters her courage and tells her husband that she desires stimulation of her clitoris. Her partner complies, but performs the stimulation in a manner so rough as to be painful. Rather than assert herself even further by offering him direction which he may perceive as criticism, she submits to the painful caress, and her initial problem of anorgasmia is now compounded by difficulties in the arousal and desire phases, anticipating that sexual activity will be painful.

In the same sense, incomplete information or negative messages in childhood may result in behavior that reinforces negative sexual experiences. For example, a patient caught by her morally rigid parents while engaged in adolescent petting and severely reprimanded is told that "nice girls don't," and that no man will be interested in a girl who "acts like a cat in heat." The patient may subsequently experience an inability to display sexual arousal as an adult, resulting in her partner's complaint that "she acts like she's not enjoying it at all." Another patient, from a devoutly religious family, cannot integrate his wife's obvious feelings of sexual excitement with her role as wife, mother, and member of the church, and is appalled by her display of arousal. Counteracting these early messages may require re-education of the couple regarding the appropriateness of his or her own and partner's responsiveness to sexual stimulation.

The final phase in the evaluation process is an examination of the couple's relationship. For this purpose, the couple should be interviewed both together and individually. Evidence exists that most couples who refer themselves for sex therapy are also experiencing considerable marital discord (Sager 1976). The evaluation of the couple's marriage should include the following determinations (Lobitz and Lobitz 1978):

1. Whether other relationship problems are so salient that they would interfere with sex therapy
2. Whether the couple's needs would be best served by being seen in a more broadly defined marital therapy program
3. Whether the equilibrium in the relationship would be upset severely by the process of sex therapy

It is virtually impossible to treat a couple in psychosexual therapy if the level of hostility is so great that it would be ludicrous to expect them to perform a series of sensate-focus exercises or adhere to a structured plan to increase communication of their sexual needs and desires. While the level of marital discord may become apparent through direct questioning, it may also become obvious in observing the patients' responses to the therapist's questions and to each other's comments. Do they frequently interrupt each other, arguing about who should answer the question, vehemently disagreeing with the partner's answer, sulking in response to a partner's assertion, making accusatory statements such as "It's not *my* problem—it's his/hers"?

Psychosexual therapy may prove to be a substantial stressor in an already dysfunctional marital system, and it is therefore advisable to determine the couple's commitment to the resolution of their sexual difficulties, and even to the continuation of the marriage. A highly motivated couple who admit to marital discord but are able to be open with the therapist and each other and express their feelings may be suitable for a combined course of marital and psychosexual therapy. Conversely, couples may express no overt marital discord but their unresponsiveness or coolness to each other and diffident attitudes make them poor candidates for sex therapy. The stressors involved in sex therapy may wreak havoc with a marital system which is based on maintaining a "truce" at a comfortable distance. Confronting sexual realities and exploring their own and each other's feelings may create a potentially explosive situation.

The Treatment Plan

Specific goals for treatment can now be established based on the findings of the medical and psychiatric examination results. Treatment should be directed toward modifying the immediate causes of the sexual dysfunction symptom, and any underlying causes which may be maintaining the symptom. Clinical evidence indicates that a significant proportion of patients can establish or resume normal, enjoyable sexual functioning once the symptom has been treated successfully.

An estimated 30 to 40 percent of cases of sexual dysfunction can be improved or eliminated without major psychodynamic changes (Lief 1981). Another 10 percent, Lief estimates, need individual therapy; 20 percent require marital therapy, with sex therapy not attempted until much later; and 30 percent will need a combined course of sex and marital therapy. Not every sexual disorder is curable, given that many cases result from intense marital discord or deeply rooted psychological maladies. There is hope, however, that referral to appropriate marital therapists and/or long-term treatment in psychotherapy may result in substantial improvement in the marital system and an eventual continuation of sex therapy. Patients with psychogenic sexual dysfunctions who are not coupled are treated with individual psychotherapy, which may be dynamic, cognitive, or behavioral.

Biogenic sexual dysfunctions are frequently amenable to treatment as well, e.g., steroid replacement therapy for atrophic vaginitis. Even if the disorder is caused by an untreatable illness or injury, a treatment program can be designed to engage the couple in other means of sexual fulfillment without intromission. Love-making techniques with an emphasis on sensuality and discovery of erotic body areas other than the genitals offer many organically impaired couples a welcome substitute for formerly non-existent or frustrating sexual interactions.

Medication may be helpful in some cases, particularly in instances of acute anxiety and panic evoked by sexual feelings and activities. Tricyclic antidepressants and monoamine oxidase (MAO) inhibitors have been found to be beneficial (Klein 1980) as well as alprazolam and trazodone (Sheehan 1982). Anxiety may then be reduced to a level at which the patient can begin to respond to other stages in the treatment plan.

In the least severe sexual dysfunction cases where incorrect or incomplete sexual information has been established as the primary cause of the sexual disorder, a treatment program of education and communication may be in order, including films, erotic literature, and play designed to increase the couple's awareness of their own and each other's sexual responses. Accompanied by supportive and helpful advice from the therapist, such cases have an excellent prognosis.

A wide range of therapies designed to alleviate sexual anxiety and conflict may be used in many cases, including behavioral therapy, which is frequently warranted in cases of sex phobia and avoidance, and anorgasmia or premature ejaculation. Behavioral therapy is frequently the treatment of choice for anorgasmic women, as the probability of the patient's learning to have orgasm in a relatively few sessions is high (Kaplan 1983), when treatment is geared towards modifying the specific and immediate causes of the orgasm inhibition. Conjoint insight-oriented psychotherapy may be used to promote communication in conjunction with structured sexual tasks. Individual insight-oriented therapy may produce a favorable outcome through the patient's awareness of underlying conflicts.

In summary, the treatment plan is a highly individualized plan formulated only after a complete and comprehensive evaluation including both medical and psychological testing, history taking, evaluation of current sexual behavior and its development, and assessment of the couple's relationship. The thoroughness of the evaluation may mean the difference between successful short-term treatment and failures in treatment at great cost to the patient, both financially and intrapsychically.

Chapter 205

Atypical Psychosexual Disorder

Human sexuality encompasses so many varying facets of life that it appears impossible to develop a diagnostic scheme that includes every variation or vicissitude. Sexual behavior is as varied as life itself, and sexual problems brought to the physician or other health professional are so heterogeneous that no single clinician in a lifetime will have seen every sort of sexual problem.

In order to have a category in which these otherwise unclassifiable cases can be placed, DSM-III (American Psychiatric Association 1980) included "Atypical Psychosexual Dysfunction," and, for good measure, added "Psychosexual Disorder Not Elsewhere Classified." DSM-III-R (American Psychiatric Association 1987) has modified this somewhat and is now labelling these difficult to place clinical situations in "Sexual Dysfunction Not Otherwise Specified (NOS)" and "Sexual Disorder NOS." This chapter will deal with a number of clinical entities, and because "disorder" is more generic than "dysfunction," these will be included under the general rubric of "Atypical Psychosexual Disorder."

Some cases included here will demonstrate the persisting confusion in classification. For example, sexual aversion was not included in DSM-III but is included in DSM-III-R. In the committee developing DSM-III-R, a spirited discussion also took place as to whether "Hyperactive Sexual Desire" should be included. The decision was to exclude it, but nonetheless, it is discussed in this section. Similarly, dyspareunia in men was not included in DSM-III, but is included in DSM-III-R, and this subject is discussed also. Even so, not all the issues dealing with sexual pain are included in DSM-III-R. Some of them will be discussed below.

While the major concern of this volume is the description and treatment of sexual dysfunctions, this chapter will exclude those and concern itself with sexual concerns, difficulties, and some that may be labelled as paradysfunctional in the sense that they cannot be definitely categorized in our nomenclature. An example of that would be sexual anhedonia or sexual anesthesia.

In general, sexual *concerns* involve questions about the person's concept of himself, and include such things as normalcy, body image, fears of rejection, and fears of aging. Sexual *difficulties*, on the other hand, involve issues causing conflicts between partners such as differing attitudes towards oral sex, timing of sex, amount of foreplay, and frequency of sex (Lief 1981).

Ellen Frank et al. (1978) in their study of couples who, by self report, regarded their marriages as happy, found that sexual difficulties create more sexual and marital dissatisfaction than do dysfunctions. This was particularly true of the wives. That investigation discovered that a stronger predictor of marital dissatisfaction than sexual dysfunction was the number of sexual difficulties reported by the wife. Apparently it was the wives' difficulties that were least well-tolerated. These researchers did not differentiate between concerns and difficulties, labelling them all "difficulties," but it is helpful to differentiate between issues dealing with self, namely "concerns" and issues dealing with conflict between the partners, namely "difficulties."

Sexual Concerns

Concerns only become problems if they lead to inhibition of performance or sexual dissatisfaction. If they create conflict with the spouse or other partner, they turn into difficulties.

Normalcy

The most common sexual concern is "normalcy." Concerns about normalcy are felt about any facet of sex, for example, parts of the sexual repertoire, such as oral sex; the frequency of sex; other sexual practices, such as masturbation; fantasies; body image, such as size and shape of breasts and penis. An example of a case that would have to be labelled as atypical psychosexual disorder would be that of a woman who came in complaining that she was frigid. On inquiry, she replied that she no longer had multiple orgasms, which she had had all her adult life, but merely one per encounter. There would be no way to label this patient dysfunctional, yet she was very distressed because her expectations of multiple orgasms were not being realized. Her definition of normalcy included being able to have multiple orgasms.

Body Image

Concerns about body image and their reflections on masculinity and femininity are ubiquitous among teenagers and common among adults of all ages. It is a rare male who in his teenage years did not have some concern about the size of his penis. Similarly, female adolescents place unusual emphasis on their breasts. These concerns are not limited to adolescents.

A 35-year-old physician discovered that his wife was having an extramarital relationship. In a bitter argument, she told her husband that her lover had a much larger penis than he did. The husband went into a profound depression believing that he had a penis too small to be effective in sexual relations. On two occasions, he sought to pressure a urologist into giving him a penile prosthesis even though the urologist explained that this would not increase the size of his penis. He was not at all reassured by the urologist's examination and statement that the penis was of normal size. He was so convinced that he had an unusually small penis that he became suicidal.

Body image concerns may be significant factors in producing inhibition of desire or of excitement. For example, after mastectomy a woman may be fearful that her husband will find her body repugnant, and this fear of his aversion, and perhaps his pity as well, may be perceived as a form of rejection reinforcing her feelings of deficiency, incompleteness, and worthlessness. All of this may interfere with her desire for sex and her capacity to respond. One study (Frank D. et al. 1978) demonstrated that changes in sexual behavior were significant after mastectomy. One-third of the women did not resume intercourse for as long as six months after hospitalization. There was a decrease in orgastic capacity and frequency of intercourse as well as female initiation of sexual activity. Breast stimulation as a part of foreplay decreased substantially, a change that lasted for years. Changes in coital position and in nudity indicated an increase in self-consciousness about their bodies.

Similar responses often occur after ablative surgery that leaves a patient with an ostomy. Some of the surgery often has biogenic consequences, but in addition, feelings of shame and concerns about the partner's reaction may cause or augment existing sexual dysfunctions.

Diagnostically, not all these cases would be labelled as atypical; they might indeed create definite dysfunctions although they are a consequence of the patient's sexual concerns. On occasion, however, the patient has no dysfunction, and yet is still sufficiently distressed about his or her body image that the problem is brought to the physician for help.

Sexual Difficulties

These cases also reveal the fluid boundary between concerns and difficulties. In a committed relationship, a concern often creates an actual or perceived partner conflict, and then would be labelled a "difficulty." Arguments between couples about what is "normal" are common. For example, a partner who desires a particular sexual behavior, such as oral sex, will label it normal, whereas the partner who has an aversion to it will label it abnormal. Conflicts over frequency, as well as sexual behaviors and desires, can be labelled as abnormal by one partner, leading to conflict.

Some of the most common difficulties revolve around conflicts over frequency of sex, timing of sex, the setting for sex, the type and amount of foreplay, what should be included in the sexual repertoire, coital position, timing of penetration, type and timing of orgasm, afterplay, degree of passion, and the amount and quality of affection.

In carrying out sex therapy, the sex therapist often discovers problems with initiation. This is one of the most common difficulties encountered. Misinterpretations of the intent of the partner or misreading of signals is quite common. On occasion, one finds a full-blown situational aversion based on problems of initiation. An example of this is the woman who almost invariably rejected her husband's advances on going to bed, but would be fully responsive if the initiation occurred in the morning or if she were the initiator. It wasn't immediately apparent why this pattern had evolved, but later in therapy it came out that she had been sexually molested regularly by an older brother who would approach her after she had gone to bed at night. The memory of this trauma still served to inhibit her responsivity to her husband 30 years later.

Many of these difficulties defy adequate categorization. For example, they are over what is permissible sexual behavior. One partner may wish to engage in troilism (three partners) or group sex and is opposed by the other partner. The only diagnosis that could be applied is one of those mentioned in the beginning of this chapter.

Atypical Ejaculatory Problems

While premature ejaculation and inhibited male orgasm, or retarded ejaculation, are discussed in other chapters, there are clinical situations that can only be called atypical. While relatively rare, there are men who have a full and complete ejaculation with adequate force and amount of ejaculate, yet have very little or no sensation of orgasm. This anesthetic ejaculation, or sexual anhedonia, is a puzzling entity. The only psychodynamic common denominator found is that this syndrome tends to occur in men with obsessive compulsive personality disorders where there is an excessive need for control. As far as it can be determined, the anesthesia, or loss of orgastic pleasure, is a conversion symptom, but found in obsessionals rather than in those with hysterical personalities (Williams 1985).

One patient who had had radiation for carcinoma of the prostate had an unusual ejaculatory problem. Fully five minutes after his orgasm, he would ejaculate. Ejaculation was full with adequate propulsion, and yet there was a marked delay between orgasm and ejaculation. Several urologists consulted had never seen this before, even in patients with physical disease.

Another ejaculatory problem that has been rarely reported is that of "paradoxical orgasm." These are men who ejaculate in non-sexual situations, most often in situations which are competitive in nature and might ordinarily bring forth some assertive or aggressive behavior. Men who have conflicts over self-assertion and aggression may paradoxically have an ejaculation, generally without erection, in a situation that would demand some forceful behavior.

Rapid Orgasm in the Female

On occasion, a woman has such a rapid orgastic response that it is equivalent to premature ejaculation in the male. While this might ordinarily be welcomed by men who have a tendency to premature ejaculation, it may cause distress. Segraves in a personal communication (1985) reported a case of rapid orgasm in the female which created considerable distress.

An American lawyer in his 30s married a Scandinavian car rental clerk in her early 20s during a two-week trip to Europe. This lawyer required approximately five minutes of coital thrusting to reach orgasm. His wife experienced orgasm almost immediately upon penetration and found further genital stimulation unpleasant, bordering upon discomfort. The dynamics were complicated, as the husband desired a pleasuring style of foreplay whereas the wife desired direct focus genital foreplay and disliked non-sexual foreplay. Common sense suggestions, such as more intense genital stimulation of the husband prior to penetration and delaying tactics for the wife, were minimally successful. It appeared that the wife had an intimacy disorder which was manifested in rapid orgasm. A combination of interpretation and sensate focus exercises appeared to help this woman find post-orgasmic coitus slightly less intolerable before she precipitously withdrew from therapy.

Pain Disorders

Dyspareunia in men, now part of DSM-III-R (not in DSM-III), is discussed in other chapters. However, there are other pain syndromes which cannot be called dyspareunia. For example, there are men and women who get coital headache. This syndrome in men is discussed later, yet it would have to be labelled as one of the atypical disorders.

There are others who have post-coital pain, usually genital pain which does not seem to be related to physical disorders such as pelvic disorders in the female or prostatitis in the male. In many of these instances, there seems to be a large conversion element. Some people complain of pain during sexual excitement prior to intercourse. This cannot always be related to physical factors, and again seems to be psychogenic in origin.

Sexual Aversion

Sexual aversion is not in DSM-III, but is now in DSM-III-R. Thus the current diagnosis would depend on which system of classification is used.

Cases of sexual aversion in which there is an intense revulsion or rejection of sexual activity can now be separated from hypoactive sexual desire disorder. These often include penetration anxiety due to a violence misconception of sex. Behind this fear are also often either pleasure anxiety or anxiety over loss of control or both. Other types of aversion to sex can occur because of a chronic illness. Patients with respiratory disease may avoid sex because of the fear of suffocation, as may patients with a history of myocardial infarction (M.I.) who are often afraid of dying during the sex act. Sometimes it is their partners who have intense anxiety about this.

A frustrating case of cardiac sexual neurosis was seen some years ago. This professional man had had a serious M.I. and thereafter was afraid to engage in coital sex because of the fear of dying during intercourse. With a great deal of reassurance and a combination of dynamic and behavioral therapy, he began to resume sexual relations with his wife when he had a serious attack of fibrillation during coitus. The impact on his physician, while not as bad as the effect on the patient, nevertheless was considerable.

Relationship Problems

Some relationship problems clearly involve atypical sexual behavior that have to be classified as such. This might include the Don Juan type of personality interested in multiple conquests, unable to form close intimate relationships. The madonna-prostitute complex, first described by Freud, usually leads to situational or partner-related hypoactive sexual desire. On occasion there is only a relative diminution of sexual desire, one that may not even cause distress to the partner, yet the patient may seek treatment because of depression or general dissatisfaction with this type of lifestyle.

There are peculiar relationship problems for which no definite categorization is possible. One such patient took great pride in the number of women he impregnated. He would put holes in the bottom of condoms, and when eventually seen by a psychiatrist, proudly claimed that he had impregnated over a dozen women. This need for revenge was connected to his discovery, when he was a pubertal boy, that his mother was engaged in an extramarital affair with the foreman who worked for the father's construction company.

Sadistic sexual behaviors are paralleled by masochistic ones. Problems of intimacy in which pain and humiliation are prominent features may be placed in the category of sexual disorder NOS. These cannot always be called true sexual masochism since there is absence of real or fantasied physical pain in the relationship.

Gender Orientation

Since ego-dystonic homosexuality has been removed from DSM-III-R, and thus from this monograph, the diagnosis for those people perplexed and confused over their gender orientation (obviously excluding transsexualism or other gender identity disorders) will have to be sexual disorder NOS. Space precludes the more complete discussion that these clinical issues deserve. For a fuller treatment, see Lief and Kaplan (1986). Also of interest is the paper by Ovesey and Woods (1980).

Chapter 206

Psychiatric Disorders and Sexual Functioning

A person may be sexually dysfunctional and mentally healthy at the same time. However, emotional and sexual health may as often be related. We have only the individual expert's testimony regarding primal cause. Did the psychological illness cause the sexual disability or was the sexual disorder unsettling to the psychic apparatus? Perhaps there is only one generalization: Sexual behavior, like all human behavior, represents a complex interplay among intrapsychic, interpersonal, biologic, and social factors (Woods 1981). Treatment requires selectivity according to the therapist's beliefs about cause, effect, and potential for recovery. This chapter will discuss current thinking about sexuality and affective disorders, schizophrenia, and personality disorders, and will offer a conceptual approach to the treatment of emotionally distressed individuals in sex therapy.

Major Depressive Episodes

We have no major studies of the precise correlations between depression and infantile, childhood, and pubertal sexuality. Clinicians hypothesize that an absence of normal curiosity and sexual interest may accompany depression in the early years. Conversely, an intense preoccupation with sexual concerns may also be present. Depending on individual response patterns and age of onset, depression may lead to social withdrawal, drugs, or promiscuity.

In the adult, most clinicians have historically agreed that the majority of depressed patients experience significant reduction of libido and desire (Lief 1977). A group at Columbia confirmed that all their hospitalized depressed patients noted decreased interest in sexual intercourse, especially those with bipolar depression (Dunner et al. 1976). A study of outpatient depressive females also demonstrated that they had sex less frequently and with less interest than non-depressed women (Clayton et al. 1965). At the start of the 1980s, Dunner wrote that "there are ample data to support the notion that decreased interest in and frequency of sexual intercourse are the usual changes in sexual functioning during depression" (Dunner 1980).

Working with a database of sexually dysfunctional patients (rather than a base of hospitalized depressives), Derogatis and Meyer (1979) found notable elevations in depression and guilt on their Affect Dimension Scores. In 1981, they found more specifically that impotent men and women suffering vaginismus, dyspareunia, and inhibited orgasm also ranked high in depression (Derogatis et al. 1981). Approaching the problem with physiologic tests, Roose et al. (1982) supported the likelihood of a connection between certain cases of impotence and depression. They reported that two hospitalized depressed men had no full nocturnal erections on sleep studies, but that this condition was reversible when the depression cleared. A similar observation had been made from a broad clinical base (Offit [1977] 1986).

From the analytic point of view, an extensive body of literature deals with factors in the etiology of depression such as "aggression, oral elements, introjection and identification, narcissism, nature of early object relations, splitting, the depressive superego, infantile phases, and paranoia" (Sunshine 1979). Practicing psychiatrists note that sexual expression of depressed feelings usually relates to some premorbid personality trait. When obsessiveness, guilt, and self-punitive ideation are part of the depressive syndrome, they are often reflections of these personality styles prior to the depression and extend to sexuality during it. Depressives may perpetuate their obsessional traits by pathologic sexual guilt, ruminating over past sexual transgressions, or by masturbation (Andreasen 1981). Paranoia and projection may emerge in delusions of sexual suspiciousness or fears of sexual attack. Rage during sex-play or coitus has been reported. The rage may be projected, displaced, or real (previously bound). Sexual inhibition can also be a depressed person's tool for expressing anger to a partner (Appleton 1982). Perhaps people demonstrate their sexuality in depression more often by their style of avoiding it than by their style of engaging in it.

Only anecdotal and clinical evidence support an infrequent increase in sexual interest among depressives (Woods 1981). Males impotent with their wives may frequent prostitutes or attempt extramarital relations to prove that they can perform; they may also do so to compensate for poor self image. Younger women become promiscuous or even prostitute themselves to shore up their self image through sexual acceptance or payment. Some have even found promiscuity a route to the comfort of "being held."

Thus, a current view is that sexual dysfunction, particularly erectile dysfunction, may be caused by depression of sufficient dimension. Such sexual dysfunction may also devastate a person enough to cause depression. Finally, a sexual symptom or behavior may be selected, consciously or not, in order to avoid depression.

Bipolar Disorder

According to DSM-III-R (American Psychiatric Press 1987) guidelines, the depressive phase of manic depressive disorder is considered to be short-lived and turbulent; sexuality at this time is likely to be vigorously avoided, perhaps even more so than in major depressive episodes. The sexual symptoms of mania may sometimes, but not always, consist of an increase in sexual thoughts, conduct, intercourse, and promiscuity (Liss 1982). However, we do not know why some people are stimulated and others are not. Nor do we know whether sexual expression in mania is related to earlier personality characteristics, although that seems likely.

Spalt comments that in individuals with secondary affective disorder, extramarital sex seems to be associated with the preexisting disorders: anti-social personality (68.4 percent), alcoholism (57.7 percent), and hysteria (22.7 percent) (Spalt 1981).

The relationship of manic sex to premorbid personality style may be inferred from case histories in the paper by Liss (1982). In one, an extravagant, workaholic businessman became manic and developed extensive interests in group sex, video-taping exploits, etc. One may connect his premorbid narcissism to the style of his manic grandiosity. Another young man with a previous anti-social personality engaged, during mania, in the anti-social behavior of homosexual prostitution.

Schizophrenia

The literature is quite inconsistent about changes in sexual behavior among schizophrenics. Recently the trend is toward finding a reduction, although one can find an article to demonstrate anything: that sex in schizophrenia increases, decreases, or becomes more or less satisfactory. The paradoxes and contradictions in the literature are noteworthy.

No significant differences were found in sexual behavior between 50 psychotic female outpatients and 100 non-psychiatric patients (Winokur et al. 1959). In a later study, there was an impression of increase in sexual desire, gratification, and auto-erotic activity in hospitalized schizophrenic men and "unrestrained and degraded behavior" in women (Lukianowicz 1963). A decrease on hospitalization was followed by an increase in sexual behavior later (Varsamis 1971). One study observed that schizophrenic women may have high orgastic capacity (Barker 1968); another affirms that basically schizophrenics are anhedonic (Rado 1962).

There seems to be some small agreement on two points: 1) schizophrenics tend to avoid intimate, close relationships (Cheadle, et al. 1978; Frank 1969); and 2) psychosis may cause hostile, impulsive, or bizarre behavior.

Wood tried to put order into the confusion by saying that the "effects of schizophrenia on sex depend on whether it develops early or late in life, and on the extent of disruption in the overall social functioning" (Woods 1981). This was corroborated in 1984 by a Czechoslovakian researcher who examined world literature and found a similar variety of opinion. His study suggested that female schizophrenics were retarded in their sexual development by some childhood biologic factor; in adult life sexuality was negatively affected by social isolation (Raboch 1984).

We have done little to establish connections between schizophrenic behavior and premorbid sexuality, with the exception of one remarkable study at the Psychiatric University Clinic in Berne, Switzerland. All instances of overt heterosexual interactions among acute psychiatric patients on mixed-sex treatment units were studied in depth. It was found that "the type of overt sexual interaction engaged in by inpatients depended more on each patient's history, including past sexual life, than on clinical diagnosis" (Hartcollis 1964).

Among the patients in this group, an acutely schizophrenic young woman was observed to use sex as a means of attaining communication, dependency, and security needs. An acute paranoid schizophrenic was found to use sex to satisfy dependency needs and express liberation from his mother. The conclusion to the study emphasized that the most important key to psychodynamics is frequently "expressed in concentrated form in the overt sexual behavior. Thus, such behaviors never should be neglected. Instead, they are to be investigated thoroughly in order to discern the central problems of the patient" (Hartocollis 1964).

The Personality Disorders

It has long been true that literature relating sexual behavior to character formation is scarce. Research has failed to make a specific connection between particular sexual dysfunctions and particular personality disorders. However, recent work has shown an important trend toward eliciting a connection between general sexual dysfunction and the types of psychological distress common to personality disorders. Anxiety, depressive ideation, feelings of inferiority, and self-deprecation are prominent in many people with sexual dysfunction (Deragotis and Meyer 1979). Hostility (Cooper 1968), guilt, and anxiety (Munjack et al. 1981) are significant in studies of psychogenically impotent men. In one study of married men, for example, it was found that males subject to erectile and/or ejaculatory difficulties exhibited great sensitivity to rejection and guilt, as well as high levels of hostility and intrapunitiveness (Rosenheim and Neuman 1981). Another study of personality style and sexual function among psychiatric outpatients revealed significant anxiety and impulsivity in dysfunctionals (Kupfer et al. 1977).

Some interesting characterologic research has begun to assist treatment of sexually dysfunctional couples. Employing a temperament analysis scale, Roffe and Hunt (1981) defined four types of marital interactions and discussed transactional dynamics in terms of their therapeutic implications. This study represents an important acknowledgment of the need for such integrative thinking in sex therapy.

Another study indirectly confirming a relationship between characterologic pain and sexual dysfunction found that prior to therapy, sexually dysfunctional patients lacked self-confidence, felt unattractive, and were easily irritated and depressed. They described themselves as obstinate, uncooperative, and reactive-aggressive. Female patients described themselves as inhibited, shy, timid, and distrustful. All these problems improved after therapy (Ulrich and Pfafflin 1980).

Treatment of Sexually Dysfunctional People with Personality Disorder

The trend of the past decade has been toward including a psychodynamic approach, but sparingly and only when necessary, in a task oriented sex therapy. The work of the next 10 years, for a more disturbed population, may rest in practicing a longer term insight oriented sex therapy that includes suggestions for sexual activity, mainly when their dynamic purpose is clear to the patient. Therapy usually needs to go on well past the point of symptom alleviation to be more permanently effective.

This position is held by Levay (1983), who even affirms that sex therapy produces lasting symptomatic change only through first producing character change. Although he does not describe a sex therapy specific to personality disorders, Levay clarifies the mission:

> It is the task of the sex therapist to thoroughly evaluate the ego strength and psychodynamics of prospective patient couples and to select those in whom brief focused psychotherapy can produce the kind of personality change necessary to alleviate the presenting symptom. Other patient couples, currently constituting a considerable majority, require much more prolonged intervention, more akin to psychodynamic couple psychotherapy, where therapeutic intensity is kept at a much lower level, and conflicts, transference, and resistance are mobilized much more cautiously by a more gradual introduction of the behavioral tasks. If such precautions are not taken, therapy may not only prove

fruitless, but may actually aggravate the patients' condition and even lead to negative character change.

This group of more fragile people includes both those with the major diagnosis of personality disorder and those who suffer such disorder between psychotic episodes. Treatment appropriate to these disturbed groups may also be effective in people with less intense psychological disorders.

Character Traits to Be Treated

There are perhaps five major areas of disturbance common to all personality disorders. They are

1. Impaired ability to express warm and tender emotions
2. Difficulty with rejection or criticism
3. Difficulty with exhibiting
4. Difficulty with perception of authority
5. Difficulty with basic self-esteem

We may approach the work of treatment by examining these common denominators in the different personality disorders.

1. Impaired ability to express warm and tender emotions

The majority of people with personality disorders have often developed strong defenses against the need to receive warmth and tenderness. Consequently, their ability to experience and express these feelings is usually constricted.

DSM-III finds that this trait is almost ubiquitous through the personality disorders. Paranoids show "restricted affectivity"; the schizoid personality demonstrates "coldness and aloofness, and absence of warm, tender feelings for others"; schizotypals possess "inadequate rapport in face-to-face interaction due to constricted or inappropriate affect, e.g., aloof, cold"; and narcissists have "a lack of empathy" (inability to recognize and experience how others feel) (p. 350). Avoidants restrain positive affectivity unless there are unqualified guarantees of acceptance. Compulsives "restrict warm and tender emotions"; and passive-aggressive personalities are, by definition, not generously expressive of active-affiliative drives.

At the other extreme, borderlines, histrionics, and dependents are impaired because they usually exaggerate expression of emotional concerns. They manipulate to receive the nurture they crave, but rarely succeed in getting it.

2. Difficulty with rejection or criticism

While anti-social and passive-aggressive personalities have difficulty because they appear to court negative responses, and schizoids defend by "indifference to social relationships" (American Psychiatric Association 1987), people with the rest of the disorders find rejection or criticism intolerable. Paranoids fear being harmed and have a "tendency to be easily slighted and quick to react with anger or counterattack" (American Psychiatric Association 1987). Dependents often lack self-confidence, fear responsibility, and accept too much criticism. Avoidants are easily hurt by criticism and are devastated by the slightest hint of disapproval. Borderlines frequently display temper at the slightest sign of criticism, while the compulsive often has "an inordinate fear of making a mistake." The entire range of hurt response may be exhibited by narcissists, from "cool indifference" to "rage, shame, or humiliation" (American Psychiatric Association 1987).

3. Difficulty with exhibiting

Problems related to " showing" also form an interesting thread through the personality disorders. The ability for sexual exhibition often parallels ways of demonstrating oneself to the world. Paranoids, of course, head the list of those who are fearful, with their hypervigilant expectations of harm. The aloofness of the schizoid requires exhibiting as little as possible, and the suspiciousness of the schizotypal, combined with social isolation, keep display to a minimum. Similar qualities in the avoidant personality make sexual display unlikely. Compulsives often have trouble allowing their physical imperfections to be observed, while passive-aggressives may stay quietly covered as a form of provocation.

Conversely, narcissists are the prime exhibitionists, requiring "constant attention and admiration." Histrionics, by definition, dramatize, often displaying their sexual wares whether they are sexually reactive or not. Borderlines may impulsively display any number of unattractive traits, and may arrange it so that their display of sexuality becomes equally unpalatable. Anti-social personalities, of course, are likely to display sexually for some illicit profit.

4. Difficulty with perception of authority

Problems with what constitutes authority and how to react to it run through all the personality disorders. Indeed, the response to authority may be more intimately related to, more pathognomonic of, character problems than any other trait. Authority, for the paranoid, is quite threatening and punitive, causing "avoidance of accepting blame, even when warranted." Schizoids often live privately to avoid the concept that any higher authority exists, while schizotypals are prone to "superstitiousness" and may have illusions of contact with higher "forces." Borderlines characteristically have shifting and unstable attitudes that reflect non-acceptance of control by anything but internal impulse; curiously, avoidants tend to think of authority as a positive source of good feeling—to which they are not entitled. Dependents, of course, overvalue authority, passively allowing "others to assume responsibility over major areas of life."

Again, on the other side of the ledger, compulsives often feel themselves to be the final authority. A compulsive may insist "that others submit to his or her way of doing things." Narcissists possess a similar grandiosity, feeling "entitlement" and acting exploitively. Anti-social behavior by definition involves flouting authority.

In dyadic relationships, authority is often projected on a partner, who may then be feared, avoided, placated, praised, despised, depended upon, obeyed exactly, or rebelled against; these behaviors are characteristic symptoms of personality disorders.

5. Difficulty with basic self-esteem

All personality difficulties are virtually founded on defective or distorted self-esteem. The personality type is easily recognizable by the problem: Those who are "easily slighted and ready to take offense" are paranoid; those who feel "chronic emptiness and boredom" and tend towards suicidal gestures are borderline. Avoidants clearly suffer "low self-esteem." Such a person "devalues self-achievements and is overly dismayed by personal shortcomings." The person who "lacks self-confidence, e.g., sees self as helpless, stupid," is dependent. Feeling inadequate and overwhelmed by the mass of work one sets oneself to accomplish is typical of compulsivity. An unusual indifference to being devalued by others is demonstrated by the passive-aggressive.

Conversely, narcissists have a "grandiose sense of self-importance"; anti-socials take the importance of their own wishes for granted. Schizoids avoid coping with the problem of whether they are worthwhile. A paradox is that compulsives are as often inflated in their estimation of themselves as they are deflated by their imperfections.

Additional Considerations in Treatment

1. Sensual skill

In lovemaking, the ability for sensual touch is often less related to personality type than one would expect. It is a common impression that dependent people touch with care, while schizotypals touch with a certain detachment and coldness. Yet many instances exist in which the extremely dependent person has no ability to be sensual, while the schizoid—distant though he or she may be—can caress with considerable skill. This deficiency may be more related to how a person was handled by parenting figures. Most often, training to be physically distant prevails; sometimes a person seeks a lot of touching to compensate for its absence in childhood.

Frequently, sensual skill may be taught; in refractory cases, a neuropsychiatric condition called "sexual dyskinesia" (Offit 1986) may destroy a partner's sexual pleasure. This may be a variant of dyslexia, clinically manifest in the inability to dance rhythmically or to perform small muscle tasks.

The capacity for true warmth and affection does not arise out of sensual skill, nor does an affectionate nature automatically imply an ability for sensual skill. Identifying whether one or both of these qualities exist in a person is essential to treatment.

2. Pleasure

The ability to experience pleasure, in general, frequently relates to sexual drive. Help in experiencing whatever sort of joy a person may be lacking can contribute to increased pleasure in sexuality. Hedonic inhibition is usually directly related to personality disorder since the distress due to character imbalance destroys joy and pleasure.

3. Meaning of sex

It is important to ask patients what sex means to them. What does it mean to give sexual satisfaction? Is it affection, aggression, submission, unity, acquisitiveness? In the same way, what does it mean to receive sexual pleasure? This meaning, too, is usually congruent with personality type. A moderately schizoid type, who thinks sex is an ideal act with an idealized object, will have great sexual difficulty with a paranoid person who basically experiences sex as an intrusion or a demand.

The level of sexual involvement that patients desire may or may not be related to character disorder. Some people without psychological disturbance want a transient and superficial relationship. Others want sex to express "everything." Whether people want sex as a quick release of tension or a peak experience, some equation has to be made between the purpose of sex and the possibility of achieving it.

Psychosexual Dysfunction and Personality

In a scheme that considers personality problems in tandem with sexual dysfunction, five classifications may be helpful:

1. Primary disorder, unrelated to the partner and apparently unrelated to personality traits
   Example: A young man may have a lifetime history of premature ejaculation. Clinical judgment may indicate that the cause of his prematurity may be a "highly tuned" nervous system, efficiently geared to multiply the human race. The dysfunction may not have been caused by a personality problem or been of long enough duration to result in one.
2. Primary disorder, unrelated to the partner but evidently bearing some relationship to personality traits
   Example: In impotence due to global shyness in a schizoid personality, a schizoid individual may idealize all women; he may feel inadequate to talk to them, much less make love to them. On sexual contact, if he can reach that point, he becomes impotent.
3. Primary disorder, related to both interpersonal and intrapsychic conflicts
   Example: A disorder of sexual excitement may exist in a person who fears loss of control of self and others. When a woman experiences feelings of fear as her excitement mounts, she may stop the sexual contact just as pleasure begins to summate. She may fear losing control of herself in orgasm; more than that, she may fear that she will lose psychological control of the relationship if she begins to depend on a man for sexual satisfaction. This union may be made all the more complex by the partner's requirement for a woman's sexual satisfaction and emotional dependence as conditions for his own comfort and self-esteem.
4. Secondary disorder, related to all partners and to an intrapsychic event
   Example: An obsessive-compulsive man finds he has no ability to perform sexually subsequent to his decision to become a physician. At medical school, his obsessional nature is severely reinforced. He tries to perfect his knowledge so that he will never make a mistake that will harm another human being. He puts aside his social life but feels that he ought to have sexual intercourse as a form of physical release so that his life-style is not altogether imperfect. All his attempts at sexual contact fail.
5. Secondary disorder, related to a specific partner or specific types of partners, reflecting interpersonal and/or intrapsychic conflict
   Example: A woman frequently loses sexual desire because her idealizations fail and argument replaces felicity. She usually chooses men whose qualities resemble those of her extraordinarily warm and generous father. Whenever these men display self-interest or request small self-sacrifice of her, however, she loses desire for sex. Her idol falls.

Areas of Intervention

There are five main areas of intervention:

1. Relief of inhibition due to misperceptions about sex
2. Affectional training

3. Physical and social skills training
4. Individual treatment of psychiatric disorder with a view toward alleviation of sexual difficulties
5. Treatment of interpersonal conflict with a view toward alleviation of affiliative and sexual difficulties

The first three categories are generally approached supportively and educationally to fill the gaps in patients' education or behavior. Therapy needs to be practiced in such a fashion that the patients' personality disorders do not interfere with acceptance.

One may approach giving education or instruction in three basic ways:

1. Gentle, straightforward teaching
2. Indirect suggestion
3. Direct suggestion, with verbalized anticipation of non-compliance

Dependent and passive people take supportive instruction best. Paranoids also take it well, providing the therapist is very straightforward. Schizoids need options for backing off. Obsessionals need indirect suggestion so that they can experience their own control of the work. People with authority problems and aggressive trends need to be shown that their non-compliance is automatic. At an appropriate time, the therapist may point out how an approach has been fashioned according to the patient's character. The patient can then decide upon continuing in the same pattern.

Psychotherapy with Couples

In the treatment of couples, most dyadic difficulties refer to the five major personality problems:

1. Restricted ability to express warm and tender emotions

This is most often interpreted by the partner as absence of those emotions. Training in defense recognition by the partner is necessary to give the restricted person the confidence to begin to change.

The most commonly perceived dangers of expressing warm feelings are: to be wrong in one's judgment (obsessive); to be overwhelmed by the demands of the respondents (avoidant, schizoid); to receive an insufficient response (borderline, passive-aggressive); to be hurt or abandoned by the respondent (paranoid).

In couples therapy where one partner cannot express close feelings, the other usually interprets this failure to demonstrate and particularly to verbalize emotion as an absence of it. The aggrieved usually needs to be helped to recognize not only a mate's major defenses but also the reason for their existence.

Case example: Catherine (age 51) and Michael (age 57) came to therapy because Michael developed impotence soon after marriage. It was the second marriage for both. Michael, the head of a large advertising firm, had ended his first marriage because he felt his wife was critical, domineering, and thoughtless towards him and their two daughters.

Catherine, a professor of history whose regal manner was striking, had ended her first marriage because she felt emotionally abandoned by her husband.

At the outset of therapy, Michael experienced his new wife as cold, selfish, and unexpressive. Her history revealed that she had been orphaned early and treated badly by a series of relatives. Expecting rejection and abandonment, she had ceased to proffer affection long before she met Michael. He had not been attracted by warmth but rather by a lusty, non-dependent attitude towards sex that now made him impotent.

The first step was to help Michael to understand that Catherine loved him but could not express it affectionately for fear of desertion. This point was made when Catherine cried—for the first time since childhood—as she remembered that her father had held her briefly and sentimentally before he left her and her mother.

At this point, sex therapy began with a suggestion for affectionate stroking—to see if Catherine could tolerate it. The psychological purpose of the suggestion was made clear so that the "resistance" of rage at potential abandonment and consequent anger at Michael would be understood before it happened. Catherine felt these emotions but kept them under control and was eventually able to tolerate stroking both passively and actively. In sex, the physical expression of warmth and tender feelings, or at least of sensual feelings, is generally necessary to function. Learning to do this may cure a large segment of many personality disorders. As Catherine learned to overcome her receptive and expressive inhibitions, she reported fewer difficulties in her teaching life, too. She began to express appreciation of her students.

2. Difficulty with rejection or criticism

This is often interpreted by the partner as weakness, hostility, or distance. It is frequently a failure of perception on the part of the person feeling criticized and is important in the discussion of specific sexual behavior.

Although she was learning to be more affectionate, Catherine spoke bitterly of Michael's perfectionism, his habits of order, his domineering behaviors, his rages, and his insistence that he was always right. She felt regularly and thoroughly criticized. In the years prior to becoming orphaned, it emerged that Catherine's mother had been regularly critical and cruel to her.

Michael's history revealed that he was raised overindulgently by parents who considered him messianic. His possessions, opinions, and actions were sacred. As a consequence, he behaved in an arrogant manner that was not designed for successful domesticity even though it was meant to express caring.

When she realized that Michael's arrogance was really an attempt to help as well as a defense of his childhood perfection, Catherine became able to control her hostile response. She was also able to stop projecting on him the image of her own critical mother. Instead of reacting defensively herself, she was able to reassure him about not being perfect in all areas, including sexual performance. Michael, too, began to control his rages because he saw that he did not have to be a perfectly gilded idol to deserve Catherine's love. Michael's impotence resolved spontaneously when Catherine's hostility noticeably lessened.

3. Difficulty with exhibiting

Too little is often interpreted as withdrawal or miserliness. Too much is often seen as domination or self-aggrandizement.

Even though they could now have intercourse, Michael felt that their intimate life was limited. Catherine's constricted life style had been that of an impoverished scholar. Although she was attracted by Michael's display of wealth, soon after marriage she began to resent it as his way of expressing dominance.

Catherine acted out this conflict by refusing to exhibit her body during sex play. She wore pajamas and declined to wear the expensive nightgowns that Michael bought. She said that even though she was a lusty woman in the dark and under the covers, she could never display her body seductively. She particularly could not wear lingerie because it made her feel like a whore.

After exploring Catherine's ambivalence and attractions to the many male parent figures she had experienced during her travels from one household to another, Catherine was encouraged to be more generous with her body. She did not have to fear that advantage would be taken—as well it might have been during her childhood. Rather than experiencing exposure as vulnerability, she was helped to see it as the safest way to give and receive love. As she began to experience showing her body as an altruistic act rather than a demeaning one, she began to be more generous with herself in other ways. She began to enjoy spending money on clothes and parties. On the other hand, Michael's compulsion to have the best of everything and to display its orderly perfection began to lessen as he felt appreciated even though he was fallible.

4. Difficulty with authority

This problem is often seen as a deliberate rebelliousness and failure to collaborate and cooperate.

Michael's potency ebbed and flowed, depending mainly on the state of his conflict with Catherine about authority. Both he and Catherine saw each other as arbitrary authority figures. He interpreted her aggrieved withdrawals as imperious and punitive rather than as hurt and self-protective. She saw his volatile outbursts as assertions of grandeur instead of childish tantrums. Each felt that the other was trying to attain autocratic control.

In sex, lovemaking foundered and recovered again and again because each felt that the other wanted it to proceed in a specific way based on inconsiderate desires. They fought and retired to their respective corners on a number of oral issues, such as kissing techniques, unattractive eating habits, alcohol odor, tobacco aura. On discharge, none of these issues was perfectly resolved, but both had learned that a perfectly reasonable wish was not an authoritarian command. For example, Catherine's request for lubricating jelly was neither a demand nor a complaint about Michael's imperfections as a lover.

Authority problems are almost always to be found in sexually dysfunctional relationships, and dealing with these in life as in sex may be immensely beneficial.

Considering Catherine's extraordinarily sensitive and paranoid responses to other people's wishes, and Michael's obsessive-compulsive need to be in control, it was fortunate that both were of high enough motivation and awareness to appreciate the irrationality of their positions. Constant therapeutic reminders of their equality enabled both to have non-combative periods when sexual function was good.

5. Difficulty with self-esteem

One partner often believes the other's low opinion of himself or herself, in spite of obvious evidence to the contrary. Low self-esteem is a feature of depression, which reduces sexuality in general.

Even when they were not fighting, Catherine and Michael were frequently too depressed to have sex. Catherine saw herself as a failure in her past marriage and as an underpaid, overworked teacher at an insignificant college. Michael saw himself as unable to fill the unusual destiny for which his parents had considered him chosen. Being a successful businessman was not a transcendental triumph. It was necessary to help to build this couple's self-esteem and their visions of each other as handsome, adaptive people who had done exceptionally well in spite of unique obstacles. Improved self-esteem is a core issue in most psychotherapy today, but it seems particularly important to nourish sexual happiness.

When these five major issues are explored and treated with insight and appropriate suggestions, one can alleviate considerable depression and much sexual distress. Reinterpretation (or cognitive relabelling) of each partner's behavior is the first goal. The second is to interrupt the destructive system through carefully selected (and thoroughly explicated) interventions. Frequently this procedure has to be performed in non-sexual contexts before sufficient harmony exists to bring it to the sexual relationship. (For a discussion of unrecognized transference issues leading to marital discord and sexual symptoms, see Chapter 213.)

Chapter 207

Hypoactive Sexual Desire and Other Problems of Sexual Desire

The Concept of Sexual Desire

Prior to the publication of *Human Sexual Inadequacy* (Masters and Johnson 1970), academic sexuality almost exclusively belonged to psychoanalysis. The psychoanalytic tradition had not specifically taken up the problem of sexual desire, (although Rado [1962] had described it in other terms as the "sexual motive state"). Like other sexual dysfunctions, it was subsumed under the terms "impotence" and "frigidity" and assumed to have vital determinants in psychosexual development. Sexual desire was, of course, discussed by Freud and other analysts, but these landmark papers had to do with the role of instincts and the ontogeny of intrapsychic development rather than desire in adult life (Compton 1981a, 1981b, 1981c).

Masters and Johnson's interpersonal and behavioral perspective on adult sexual life was revolutionary but focused no attention upon sexual desire. The clinical problem remained unappreciated until Kaplan (1976) realized that the unsuccessfully treated cases of sexual unarousability usually manifested a deficiency in sexual desire. She then postulated three basic components of sexual life—desire, arousal, and orgasm—stressing that sexual desire was an appetite, analogous to hunger and thirst, which had its neural basis in the limbic system (Kaplan 1979). Like other components, the expression of the activity of this limbic substrate was influenced by psychological factors. Kaplan's physiologic emphasis was attractive for its clarity and simplicity. Sexual desire was a limbic phenomenon, arousal a parasympathetic phenomenon, and orgasm a sympathetic one. Most important, however, was the insight that many clinical problems related basically to desire rather than to arousal or orgasmic difficulties. Today, for example, a conservative estimate might be that one-half of those seeking help for various sexual dysfunctions have a disturbance in their ability to generate sexual desire.

Sexual Desire as an Amalgamation

Sexual desire is an amalgamation of three reasonably separate phenomena—drive, motivation, and aspiration. Each of these however, is frequently referred to as sexual desire.

Sexual drive. Sexual drive is the product of a neuroendocrine generator of sexual impulses. The activity of this androgen dependent system in both males and females tends to have a frequency or rhythm over the life cycle (and during the menstrual cycle—see chapter on "Psychiatric Disorders and Sexual Functioning"). This is usually clinically stated as high, moderate, low, or absent drive. Drive per se, especially in males, has a gradual diminution from young to middle to older adulthood (Martin 1981). Sexual drive, what Freud sometimes meant by "libido" or "the sexual instinct," ensures the perpetuation of the species and, therefore, in all likelihood is genetically organized.

The "sexual drive" refers to the spontaneous manifestations of genital excitement. These include: 1) genital tingling; 2) a perceptual shift whereby the sexual attributes of others achieve a dominant place in the hierarchy of stimuli impinging upon consciousness; and 3) partner-seeking behavior or masturbation. These spontaneous endogenously stimulated changes occur in most, but not all, adolescents and young adults. Sexual drive is most dramatically manifested in adolescence because either its intensity is strongest or the capacities to control it are weakest. People commonly refer to drive manifestations as "horniness." "Horniness" is imprecise for our purposes because it also is used to indicate genital excitement stimulated by perceptual cues originating outside the individual.

Many biologic influences on drive are recognized. The most important inhibitors are elevations of prolactin from pituitary tumors or phenothiazines; diminutions of testosterone; antihypertensive medications; cardiac, renal, or respiratory failure; depression (Kaplan 1983). Possible augmentors of drive include mania, alcohol, amphetamine, and other drugs of abuse. (Excessive use of alcohol, amphetamines, or other drugs may lead to performance dysfunctions.)

It is a considerable clinical challenge to appraise correctly the drive component of sexual desire. The periodicity of spontaneous excitement is one indication. One can ask how long after an orgasm before the patient feels a physical need for another one. Erotic dreams, nocturnal orgasms, nocturnal and morning erections, and spontaneous erotic changes in perception may indicate the activity of this brain system. Women should be asked if they recognize a portion of their menstrual cycle when they are typically interested in sex. Masturbation may be a means of regulating sexual tensions due to drive, but caution is needed because other factors are often involved, that is, excitement arising from interaction with the environment, habit, or anxiety reduction.

Drive is a clinical assessment problem because it is more subjective than behavioral. When it is carefully evaluated, however, many individuals with inhibited desire are recognized as having manifestations of reduced drive. Of the three components of sexual desire, drive is the most likely to be measurable; for example, effects of pregnancy, lactation, menopause, medications, or grief on drive can be studied. The natural history of sexual drive through the life cycle for either sex has not been well studied, however. It may decline significantly during the 30-40 decade for many males, though the frequency of sexual behavior does not. Some older people lose their drive entirely; many evidence it only rarely. The neuroendocrine mechanisms for such changes have not been elucidated with any degree of certitude. There is no reason to assume that drive decline follows the same time course in both sexes (Pfeiffer and Davis 1972). In many women, sex drive persists longer than in their male partners. The relative contributions of hormones, dyadic, and individual factors have yet to be worked out.

Motivation.   Human sexual desire cannot be simply reduced to its biologic component. A more enduring component is motivational, that is, willingness. Herein lies the greatest complexity of sexual desire because present and past intrapsychic and interpersonal determinants interact to produce sexual motivation. Some vicissitudes in motivation may be explained by drive fluctuations, but a great deal more is involved.

Psychological motivation for sexual behavior can be induced by many stimuli. The most important of these involves combinations of nonverbal, verbal, and tactile interpersonal behaviors. Voyeuristic stimulation is most readily recognized by entrepreneurs for its ubiquitous power to generate arousal. Voyeuristic stimulation involves the hearing of, reading about, or sight of the sexual excitement of others. Attraction involves a perception of another that meets some need in the observer. Attraction to another does not require any actual interchange between two people. Each of the inducers of sexual motivation involves a transient fantasy. Fantasy, conscious or unconscious, may well be the intrapsychic mechanism for generating the earliest peripheral physiologic manifestations of arousal. It is of great interest that testosterone deficiency has recently been shown to limit arousal using fantasy (Bancroft and Wu 1983). Testosterone deficiency may therefore subvert this sequence: inducer, fantasy, motivation, arousal.

The motivation component of desire can be thought of as subserving the need for attachment. This places the subject of motivation in the realm of object relations. Drive, the biologic aspect of desire, and the motivation ideally work in concert.

Cognitive aspiration.   The third component of desire is ideational or cognitive. It is the wish for sex or the wish not to have sex. Cognitive aspiration does not predict drive, response to inducers, or arousal capacity. People who lack drive and motivation may wish to have sex because it is their concept of what is expected. People with drive, motivation, and arousal with a partner may represent themselves as not wanting to have sex because of the thought "sex is sinful." Cognitive aspirations are often in conflict with other aspects of desire. Some of these conflicts go beyond moral considerations to awareness of the potential dangers of an intimate relationship. Cognitive aspirations about sexual behavior function as a gating mechanism—an acceptance or rejection of what is happening. They can allow the sexual system to freely operate, impair it, or shut it down.

The Contexts of Sexual Motivations

Four larger contexts contribute to sexual motivation: Gender identity, quality of the nonsexual relationship, reasons for sexual behavior, transference from past attachments.

Gender identity consists of several closely related dimensions: sexual identity, gender role identity, sexual orientation, intention. Sexual motivation does not ever achieve any psychological independence from the dimensions of gender identity.

Sexual identity is the sense of maleness or femaleness. Gender role identity is the sense of oneself as masculine, feminine, ambiguous, or neuter. Depending upon the current form of gender role identity, drive-motivation either inconspicuously reinforces the gender sense or conflicts with and confuses it. For example, a male who feels more feminine than masculine may feel anxious and uncertain in response to his need for sexual expression.

Sexual orientation has two subtle different aspects. In its most important subjective aspects, orientation refers to the specific sex and gender characteristics of those images that elicit arousal through daytime or masturbatory fantasy and dreams. Based upon erotic attraction, an adult orientation can be thought of as heteroerotic, homerotic, or bierotic. In its more widely understood objective aspect, however, sexual orientation refers simply to the biologic sex of one's preferred, usually actual partners. Based upon the sex of partners, an adult can be thought of as heterosexual, homosexual, or bisexual. Erotic imagery and the sex of a partner are not invariably consistent. Conflict over homoerotic images or experience may diminish sexual desire.

Intention refers to the behaviors that adults wish to engage in with their partners. Conventional intentions involve a variety of sexual practices predicated upon a peaceable mutuality of pleasure. Unconventional intentions often involve a hostile relationship between an aggressor and a victim. The paraphilias—sadism, exhibitionism, masochism—involve hostility rather than affection and represent unconventional intentions.

For every adult, the subjective erotic response and its translation into arousing partner behavior involve an integration of preconditions based upon the person's gender identity, orientation, and intention. Many desire problems involve unconventional aspects of sexual identity which are either hidden from the partner or incompletely recognized by the patient. This intrapsychic context generates the first of four perspectives on the motivational component of sexual desire.

1. The presence of sexual desire indicates a willingness to recognize one's gender sense, orientation, and intention.

Most desire problems seen by clinicians derive from difficulties in the interpersonal nonsexual context. This context enables sexual behavior because, in an ultimate sense, each partner is genuinely willing to engage in sex. Unacceptable nonsexual relationship contexts render two otherwise sexually capable individuals asexual when one or both partners can no longer tolerate the actuality of the relationship. Clinicians must greatly respect motivations not to engage in sex. These motivations often arise before their source is recognized by the individuals involved. This interpersonal context leads to the second perspective on the motivational component of sexual desire.

2. The presence of sexual desire implies an acknowledgment that, all things consid-

ered, the relationship outside the bedroom is acceptable. (Exceptions to this rule occur; for example, couples who hate each other may still enjoy passionate sex.)

The third context derives from answers to why individuals behave sexually when they do. For any couple, the question of the specific motives for sex becomes why does he or she behave sexually at this time. It is probably quite rare that a couple simultaneously experiences drive per se. It is more common that couples share an arousing experience; for example, being with a couple that is fighting or spending a too long weekend with family makes the partners appreciate each other. Sex becomes the vehicle for nonverbal expression of such appreciation. Many individuals believe it is fundamentally important to have sex regularly, but don't know why. The answer may derive from the fact that sexual relationships are a means of reaffirming attachment.

Some episodes can be expressions of a wish for personal pleasure, a wish to give pleasure, or a desire to escape from an unpleasant preoccupation. Getting to sleep, relieving built up or anticipated tensions, relief from loneliness, or getting pregnant are easily recognized motives. Another frequent motive, obtaining reassurance that one is loved, brings up the issue of the conscious and unconscious meanings ascribed to sexual behavior (Scharff 1982). Much sexual behavior is simply compliance. Many of the specific reasons for sex may be traced to inducers outside the orbit of the couple, e.g., exciting interplay occurring between one spouse and someone at work. Most of the time the motive for sex arises in one partner; in order to be translated into sexual behavior, that motive must induce the partner to behave sexually.

Adult sexual motivation fluctuates along a spectrum ranging from driven, eager, willing, indifferent, uninterested, reluctant, and avoidant. Most waking moments are spent in a sexually indifferent state. Although some brief arousal may occur, by the time a sexual opportunity is available, lack of interest may again exist. When there is sexual interest, the task of the eager one is to engage the partner. Desire problems may stem from the process of negotiating a sexual relationship, rather than a lack of drive or motivation to behave sexually. Something goes wrong in the process whereby the interested one communicates that interest and entices the partner.

Men and women who occupy the driven end of the desire spectrum may be as problematic to themselves and their partners as those who are stuck at the avoidant end. Those who are always eager are not necessarily motivated by drive. One "high sex drive" patient desisted from his daily routine of intercourse with his coerced wife when it was suggested that he was substituting quantity for quality. He and his wife now readily distinguish making love from having sex. "Having sex" is done before a high tension day or if he is going to be out of town for a few days. They "make love" when they feel good about each other after spending time together. Otherwise she sees her role as helping him regulate his excitement and anxiety through sexual intercourse. This interpersonal context leads to a third perspective on the motivational component.

3. The presence of sexual desire implies the capacity to agree to behave sexually for any specific reason such as affection, sadness, anxiety, excitement, habit.

The transferential context, the fourth context in which sexual motivation is imbedded, has an explanatory power that is difficult to ignore. This context is best considered after the other ones have failed to yield a useful explanation for the motivational problem. Its essence is that sexual expression unconsciously mobilizes positive or negative attitudes toward the partners derived from previous experience with the love objects. Good sexual relationships presume a positive transference of trust and safety from the residue of childhood experience. Desire deficiencies or excesses may relate to unconscious expectations of harm or deprivation, that is, negative transferences.

One common form of a transferentially based motivational problem is exemplified by a person with drive manifestations who aspires to sexual behavior with his or her valued spouse, but who is only motivated to have sex with another person. This pattern begins only after the person develops a deep emotional attachment to the partner. For example, the clinician is told that everything was normal until the engagement or the marriage took place. Analytic perspective on such patterns often involves an oedipal explanation. The adult has failed to unite the sensual and affectionate trends of his or her sexual instinct. Originally combined and focused on the opposite sex parent, these trends are normally separated for a long period of post-oedipal development only to recombine when normal adult love occurs. Thus, such patterns represent a form of immaturity—specifically the developmental failure to direct love and lust toward the same love object (Freud 1912). Another explanation is that the motivation not to make love stems from the sense of vulnerability (and consequent fear of intimacy) that arises from the transference to the partner of the painful experience with parents.

In order to provide a loving attachment, the partner usually offers protection from pain, rejection, abuse, disrespect, torture, or harm. In many troubled couples the partner is, indeed, trustworthy. The archaic image of the parent is not; it is the childhood residue that is unconsciously bestowed upon the partner. The one who is motivated not to have sex acts as though sex will lead to the repetition of the painful aspects of past attachments. There are many unsolved childhood dilemmas that can be tranferred to the current partner. This intrapsychic context leads to a fourth perspective on the motivational component of sexual desire.

4. The presence of sexual desire implies the person is able to transfer positive internalized images of past important attachment figures to the partner (and is able not to contaminate the partner with negative transferences from those figures).

Diagnostic Assessment

At the end of diagnostic evaluations or, more important, upon the completion of therapies, problems of desire are thought to have one or more of the following causes:

1. Diminished or absent drive manifestations (hypoactive sexual desire)

- Depressive disorder
- Medication side effect
- Unrecognized or inadequately treated physical illness
- Aging
- Constitutional or lifelong pattern
     Klinefelter's syndrome
     No apparent disease
- Psychotic disorder—not medication induced
- Response to other sexual dysfunction

- Impact of being raised in vastly different culture
- Sexual abuse as a child; other sexual trauma, such as rape
- Androgen deficiency

2. High "drive" manifestations

- Psychotic disorder
    Mania or hypomania
    Schizophrenia
    Borderline personality disorder
- Substance abuse
- Sexual abuse as a child
- Perversion
- Low desire in partner
- Constitutional, no apparent problem

3. Diminished or low motivation for partner sexual behavior (situational hypoactive sexual desire)

- Nonsexual relationship deterioration
    "Secret"—extramarital affair or plan for divorce
    No secret
- Variation in sexual identity
    Fully known by the person but not partner
    Not well understood by the person
- Confusion of partner with parent
    Traumatic past relationship with parent
    Inability to love and have sex with same person
- Sexual relationship problems
    Significant other dysfunction in person or partner
    Difficulty with means and timing of initiating sex
    Deficiency in knowledge of sexual technique

It is not always a simple matter to distinguish a desire from an arousal or an orgasmic phase problem. Many desire problems begin with arousal or orgasmic symptoms. It is not always clear whether the desire problem is a response to helplessness in dealing with the original symptom or the original symptom is simply the early manifestation of the desire disorder.

Many people want their low frequency of genital contact and limited sexual desire to be due to physical factors other than age. Their search for a hormonal deficiency often delays a thorough evaluation of the physical and emotional health of the symptom bearer and partner. The therapist must be able to provide access to competent and selective medical evaluation to identify physiological impairments that limit sexual drive. Many physical problems affect sexual desire indirectly through the emotional response to the problem. The therapist must maintain a reasonable perspective in deciding when and how extensively to pursue the possible organic contributions to a problem. Unhelpful clinical encounters can result from over-emphasizing the organic or the psychological. When, for example, all men with low desire are investigated with testosterone and prolactin levels, the yield of hypogonadism and hyperprolactinemia is very low (Nickel et al. 1984).

Judgment is also necessary as to when to see the partner alone or the couple together. The data available to the therapist vary considerably depending upon whose perspective is sought. A thorough evaluation of a married couple ideally consists of interviews with each partner and with the couple together until the clinician is able to formulate a reasonable method of proceeding. Sometimes the first clue to the cause of the desire problem lies in the difficulty in scheduling the appointment with the spouse. Not all symptom bearers will accept their partner's involvement because they know they cannot talk freely in front of him or her. The therapist should feel free to respond to each clinical situation in an individual manner.

A convergence of multiple influences accounts for most desire problems. Ascribing a symptom to a single cause, for example, relationship deterioration, is accurate but not thorough. Age, stage of development, personality characteristics, past experience, values, and many other factors enter into the pathogenesis of a problem. Clinicians, however, must vigilantly pursue etiologic hypotheses and make sense to the couple and to themselves. By the end of therapy, few believe it was as simple as the hypothesis that emerged after the "complete" evaluation. The appreciation of the complex role the desire difficulty plays in the couple's mental life requires more than a few visits. Where there is a significant motive present not to have sex, the individual or the couple presents the cognitive aspiration to have sex. Often the shrillest complainer about the partner's deficient desire will be the most resistant to recovery. Therapy of psychological desire problems requires recognizing the motive not to have sex.

Treatment

Conditions That Begin as Organic

The patient and the spouse must be accurately informed of the source of the problem and their unique emotional response to it. The therapist assiduously attempts to identify and ameliorate the organic source of the drive impairment, but often confronts an unchangeable medical situation. The therapist does what is in his or her power to do—attend to the affectual and coping responses of the couple, keep the organic origin in sharp focus, and outline what is possible sexually. Unfortunately, the motivational and the erectile responses of a significantly drive-impaired individual are limited. Orgasm is still possible if intense persistent stimulation is provided.

Case 1. A 53-year-old man and 50-year-old woman, both divorced, decided to marry after a one-year courtship. Their relationship, including sex, was the most satisfying either had ever experienced. Two months before the wedding he developed a urinary obstruction. A TUR for benign prostatic hypertrophy quickly turned into a radiation treatment for carcinoma of the prostate. Shortly after the course of radiation, he lost his sexual desire and potency. His testosterone levels were consistently less than 80 ng/dl. The urologist and oncologist felt that the tumor within the prostatic capsule had been destroyed, but thought it dangerous to administer testosterone. (Radiation to the pelvis may, in addition to destroying the Leydig cell function, induce fibrosis of some arteries supplying the penis.)

Although frightened by the prospect of a recurrence of the cancer and continued impotence, they decided to marry. One year later, both viewed the decision as good, but almost no sexual interaction was occurring. He was mortified by his loss of potency and could barely stay in the room whenever she referred to their sexual experience. It became increasing difficult for her to be simply relieved that all the cancer was removed. She was also feeling deprived. He, who could not get enough of her prior to the operation, seemed to even rarely initiate conversation, let alone sex. She knew he too was terribly distressed about their unnatural relationship. Talking about their responses to their horrible luck in front of one another enabled them to talk and relate more freely outside of therapy. They began to have mutually orgasmic experiences after seeing the therapist but the frequency was limited. They have their hopes pinned upon the recovery of his Leydig cell function.

Case 2.   Two years ago a 25-year-old man fell off a roof. After several months of paraplegia, a thoracic decompression initiated a gradual improvement which left him with paraparesis. He was able to walk with a cane and return to work. As recovery continued, his erectile and ejaculatory capacity reappeared, albeit in a muted unpredictable fashion. The attempts to reinitiate sexual experiences with his wife of four years led to great frustration. He was delighted he could still have some sexual responsiveness. She cried during lovemaking complaining that he was too mechanical, rushing only to insert his semihard erection before it was lost. Although he could ejaculate, he required more stimulation than was possible in the vagina. After several months of unsatisfying attempts, she maintained, "I lost my sex drive entirely!" Her recent sexual history revealed she masturbated several times a week and was having fantasies of grabbing men off the street. The major intervention was to discuss her feelings about her new life situation—especially her rage—and to clarify for both of them how important the acknowledgment of her losses were. He realized that he had been "self-centered," endlessly discussing his zones of sensation and strategies for erectile maintenance. Her sexual motivation immediately improved, she was again orgasmic, and she did what she could for her husband without interfering anxiety, sadness, and anger.

Low Motivational State Due to Relationship Problems

Difficulties relating to one another outside the bedroom diminish sexual desire for most, but not all, individuals. Men and women "just don't feel like sex" after objectionable behavior occurs yet another time. The aspiration for sex with the partner may continue; carrying it off is difficult and emotionally unsatisfying. Often the aspiration for sex with another increases. Deteriorated relationships do not have a uniform impact upon sexual drive. Drive may seem to disappear entirely, misleading the clinician into considering an organic explanation for the lack of sexual desire.

The explanation for the couple's relationship problem is often not very clear. The offended spouse is quick to point out the limitations of the partner and now responds to these much more strongly than to the positive attributes. It is not so much the behavior of the spouse that offends as it is the meaning attributed to that behavior. Relationships involve perception and interpretation of behavior. The therapist does not know what the past has been. The therapist has access only to each spouse's view about what happened, why, and what was its meaning. Often, the behavior that is now unbearably objectionable has been present from the premarital relationship. While both the therapist and the couple seek to understand how the relationship deteriorated, it is important for the therapist to privately remain skeptical about even the most cogent explanation. People sometimes are relieved not to have to bring everything that has transpired to their therapy.

Much of the work with couples whose chief complaint involves limited desire (nonconsummation, infrequent sex, one partner's avoidance) involves marital therapy. Just what marital therapy is, and how it is done, depends upon the therapist and the couple (Gurman and Knisherman 1981). It is relatively easy to deal with a couple with the following characteristics:

1. Genuinely motivated to maintain the relationship
2. No understanding of cause of disagreement
3. Capacity to talk rather than behave
4. No big secrets
5. Basically honest

The therapist provides such a couple with the opportunity to remove some of the mystery and confusion about their emotional response to one another. Therapy is a shared intense affectual experience which provides more intimacy than the couple can usually generate on their own. It often leads to a new appreciation of the partner's behavior and motives. Hostile interpretations give way to benign ones. The sexual motivational problem is afforded a respectable position as a means of coping with a situation that could not be clearly identified, discussed, appreciated, and changed. The motivational component of desire often improves dramatically as long as the therapy promises to continue dealing with the underlying interpersonal problem. Such are the cases and the course of relatively brief conjoint therapies that give sex and marital therapy their good name and respected place in the mental health community. Therapists need these cases to maintain their self-esteem and to fortify themselves for the more common cases of low sexual motivation that are not "easy."

Case 3. A 30-year-old mother of two preschool children refused to have sex with her husband because he was insensitive to her. She complained that his preoccupation with work, lack of intuitive grasp of feelings and their importance to life, unfriendliness to her friends, and self-centered rapid ejaculation made her feel alone in her marriage. He was quite frightened by these increasingly vociferous comments, in part, because his previous wife also complained how unfeeling he was as a partner. Simultaneously, his boss was informing him that his perfectionistic style caused problems for the many people who worked for him. He entered individual psychotherapy, and after several months, began marital therapy. Much of his behavior changed. Although now more pleased with her husband, the wife remained sexually unreceptive. He realized that her lack of desire was not simply tied to his "lack of feelings." She still spoke of his hopelessness as a husband and gravitated to opportunities to criticize him. His explanation that her sexual refusals made it difficult to want to please her fell on deaf ears.

The therapist had thought her ne'er-do-well father who committed suicide when she was five, leaving the family in financial ruin, explained some of her negative perceptions of her husband. She was unable to grasp the possibility. When her husband continued to press for her reason for sexual avoidance, she asked to speak to the therapist alone. She then announced that she had decided to leave him. During the first full individual session, she steadfastly reiterated her intent to divorce even though she valued the close relationship between her children and her husband and felt that her husband might kill himself. At the end of the session, however, she suddenly cried saying she was not the strong person she had imagined herself to be. Before the next session she had a flood of memories and came prepared to tell "her secret." She described herself as a much loved child who was aware, from an early age, that her younger sister was unwanted, less loved, and always very difficult. Unlike the patient, who always was highly regarded, the sister had forever been in trouble—including psychiatric hospitalizations as a teenager and an adult. The patient's husband (a very successful man) reminded her of her sister. The patient has always felt guilty about her sister's misery. She cried over her helplessness to relieve her suffering. Pity was her predominant emotion about her sister. Over the next few sessions she was able to acknowledge her occasional subtle pleasure in her sister's misfortune. She described her guilt over the comfortable economic circumstances she had achieved through marriage, while her sister barely survived economically, and wondered how much her willingness to destroy the family's structure had to do with her own family's misfortune when she was her daughter's age. Her husband was grateful when she was able to resume sexual relationships but remained wary of her capriciousness. She was unable to subjectively love him in the free intense manner that was her ideal. This was based upon a love affair she had had with a man 30 years her senior.

Low Motivation Due to Sexual Identity Problems

Many gender dysphoric, homoerotic, and perverse men and women aspire to relate sexually in a conventional manner to their partners. The presence of a sexual identity problem is often a profound surprise to the spouse. This is both because the partner has never shared the information and the spouse has not seemed to want to know. Interventions with such couples should include attention to the partner's reactions to the information. Considerable emotional instability is likely to occur as the partner gives personal meaning to the information. The therapist's calm manner can be quite useful in educating the couple about sexual identity development. There are many myths to be dispelled—especially that if a person has an atypical sexual identity, a satisfying heterosexual relationship is impossible. The exploration of feelings about the sexual identity issues should be done regardless of when the spouse learned about it. The "normal" spouse's sexual identity concerns invariably arise.

Case 4.   A frantic woman sought an emergency visit after discovering her husband's cache of answered ads for pictures of men in their underwear. She had not known of his homosexuality. Now suddenly his years of sexual avoidance and uncommunicative behavior had an explanation. Her panic was made worse by her therapist who suggested she would have to choose whether she wanted to stay married to a homosexual. Upset by this advice, she sought help from another therapist. She was relieved by her second therapist's skepticism about having to leave the marriage and separate her husband from his two children. The interview with him and the conjoint marital therapy that ensued led to a remarkable improvement in the couple's sexual and nonsexual relationship. He was eventually able to discuss some aspects of his homosexuality. He no longer had to make lame excuses for his late nights and began spending more time at home. She bravely coped with the knowledge of her husband's infidelity. This pain was offset, however, by his greater emotional availability. In surviving this crisis, the self-confidence of both spouses was enhanced. They have been reluctant to give up the twice monthly conjoint therapy so it continues into its second year. The frequency of marital sex has gone from three to four times per year to approximately three times a month.

The sexual history of desire problems must always include an opportunity to learn about sexual identity issues. Approximately 10 percent of the population has an atypical sexual identity (more, if one includes bisexuals). Most people with subtle sexual identity problems do not readily volunteer them, sometimes because they do not want to acknowledge it to themselves, and sometimes because they are fearful of the therapist's response. The danger of not evaluating the sexual identity of each partner is that the therapist's politely received comments may be too superficial to be helpful. However, sometimes helping the couple to relate better to one another strengthens their bond and generates more frequent sex, even without knowing the intrapsychic details of sexual identity.

Case 5. A 28-year-old swaggering woman and her 23-year-old passive nervous husband sought help for nonconsummation of their three-year marriage. She had not worn a dress since early adolescence. He had showered with his mother till he was 13. The wife portrayed herself as having a feminine gender identity and a heteroerotic orientation with images of conventional intercourse, but was unable to discuss the topic except by nodding assent. She seemed to have all three components of desire. He had limited drive manifestations and aspired to have sex, but had not attempted to relate physically to his wife before or during the marriage. They both were quite resistant to engaging in caressing and holding, but would not acknowledge that it was not simply that they were so busy with their careers. When they did touch one another, it was pleasant but did not improve their motivation to repeat the experience. A job change provided a face-saving means of ending therapy.

Knowing that many people with gender identity, orientation, or intention disorders have a regular sexual relationship with a partner guards against the pessimistic assumption that such disorders preclude heterosexual relationships. The key question remains what enables some individuals with these mental patterns to function sexually while others are paralyzed by their conflicts. Recent work by Schwartz and Masters (1984) has shown that many homoerotic men can be helped to comfortable heterosexual experiences with a multimodal therapy. Therapy can make a great difference, but it is not likely that any one technique is the sine qua non of change.

When sensate focus exercises were introduced in 1970 they were thought to have a very strong therapeutic impact on couples regardless of their specific dysfunctions. With further use, the exercises were appreciated for their capacity to rapidly identify the partner who was harboring a significant emotional obstacle to engaging in sexual behavior (Levine 1976). This technique was employed less when therapists recognized during evaluations where the resistance resided (Kaplan 1983). Today, sensate focus exercises, especially those involving holding, caressing, and exploring the nongenital surfaces, can be occasionally therapeutic for desire problems if introduced in the therapy when the couple has the willingness to engage in the experience.

Lifelong Low Sexual Desire

One of the many mysteries about sexual desire is why it is infrequent or absent in some physically and emotionally healthy individuals. The possible answers are various combinations of

1. Constitutional endowment—the drive mechanism is poorly developed. There is evidence that men with Klinefelter's syndrome, a chromosomal disorder affecting testosterone production and brain development, have weak, late onset drive manifestations and loss of sexual desire in their early 30s (Rabach et al. 1983). Clinically, however, it appears that low constitutional endowment is more common among women.
2. Cultural impact—certain subcultures may present a powerful antisexual message that many children incorporate into their psyches at an early age. The result can be a lifelong repressive attitude towards intra-psychic sexual manifestations.

3. Resolution of childhood sexual conflict—the unique developmental experience of the child may leave it overwhelmed by sexuality. The person avoids intimacy as a result of fears and never generates the conditions that enable most people to come to grips with the sexual dimensions of their being.
4. Problematic intimate relationship—many repressed young people discover their intra-psychic sexual manifestations only after falling in love and being married. Some of these people may marry similarly repressed partners or have interpersonal difficulties from the start of their relationship so that their sexual unfolding never occurs.
5. Defense against psychosis—occasionally therapy with a person without desire precipitates a major psychological decompensation. The behavior or the thought content during mania, psychosis, or the depression which ensues, demonstrates that sexual interest is present but unable to be managed. Therapists who have witnessed these reactions quickly become convinced that everyone need not have sexual desire.

Case 6. A woman and her recently retired husband, both in their early 50s, sought help to improve their rarely occurring sexual relationship. Her sexual experience consisted of providing for him when he returned from his travels. She obtained no pleasure. Secretly angry at his turning over all responsibility for their children to her, she felt generally abandoned. He was a cheerful energetic man who loved sex and endlessly "pestered" her. She could not recall ever having sexual desire, masturbating, being aroused, having a sexual fantasy, or achieving orgasm. She did not ever think about sex and could not comprehend her husband's interest in the physical experience. Now that he was retired, their children out of the house, and the anger over her abandonment dissipating, she was interested in seeing if she could discover what her husband insisted she was missing.

She was an athletic, strikingly beautiful woman who became an award-winning dancer in the last five years. The pleasure in dancing was enormous: grace in movement, admiration of others, and the costumes. Her husband encouraged her even though he was not skilled enough to be her partner.

Therapy was very useful to this couple. Using sensate focus exercises, she was able to concentrate on sensation and learn to pursue pleasure for herself. He was delighted with his wife's new motivation and did all he could to stimulate her. Within two months she began to be regularly orgasmic. She aspired to have sex, she was willing to have sex both to please her husband and herself, but she did not evidence any spontaneous drive manifestations.

Problems of Increased Desire

These problems are only now beginning to attract clinical and research attention (Barlow and Abel 1976; Berlin and Meineche 1981; Levine 1982). Human sexuality specialists are sensing their potential for illuminating biologic and mental mechanisms underlying sexual desire. The study of high sexual desire not linked to paraphilias (not yet an acceptable DSM-III-R [American Psychiatric Association 1987] diagnosis) is a frontier concept in the same manner that low sexual desire was eight years ago.

Currently it is not clear whether these problems represent high sexual drive which is presumably due to a biologic abnormality, or high sexual motivation which is the result of psychological processes. Most of these patients aspire to have less sexual desire because their lives are dominated by recurrent erotic images and sensations.

Many masturbate 10 or more times a day, at times. Their erotic preoccupation precludes concentration on learning and work, and interferes with object relationships.

These problems are seen more commonly among men, many of whom have a well-defined sexual intention disorder. Such men are often diagnosed as impulse ridden characters and are thought to have little capacity to benefit from traditional forms of psychotherapy. Many have soft, nonspecific neurologic signs (Berlin and Meineche 1981). Such men are currently treated at a few centers with a testosterone depleting hormone, depo-Provera. The ability of this intramuscular medication to lessen the frequency and intensity of erotic imagery, masturbation, and inappropriate sexual behavior is quite dramatic in some patients. The men with the least control over their impulses who are available for treatment (not going to prison), tend to be given the drug. The milder cases tend to be dealt with by other means.

When less severe cases are treated in psychotherapy or when men on depo-Provera are seen in concomitant individual psychotherapy, the therapist often develops the conviction that sexual excitement has a defensive function. When a painful emotional experience is discussed, the patient has an impulse to act out sexually rather than experience the affect. If acting out becomes impossible, the patient may develop a profound depression, rage, or anxiety state. These dramatic experiences suggest that sexual behavior has come to substitute for dysphoria. The origins of this defensive use of excitement are assumed to reside in early life chaotic object relationships. But it is equally plausible that some of the problem may be generated by the child's unusual brain function.

Abel and his co-workers have developed a multimodal behavioral paradigm that is effective in helping paraphiliac men gain control over their perverse erotic experiences (Abel et al. 1978). Key elements of this program are a masturbation satiation technique, group therapy for confrontation of the rationalizations that are ubiquitous among frequent sex offenders, social skills training, and isolation from the judiciary system. The same techniques may be used with patients who have a non-paraphiliac sexual addiction.

The differential diagnosis of non-paraphiliac men and women with elevated sexual desire includes psychoses, affect disorder, personality disorder, substance abuse, sexual abuse as children, and structural brain disease. Diagnostic and treatment difficulties can be formidable.

Case 7. A 45-year-old chronically depressed woman, an incest partner of her father for many years, was referred because of the development of a relentless genital excitement 18 months previously. Masturbation provided only about an hour's relief. She became paralyzed with depression, unable to work or keep house, shortly before the symptom appeared. Her therapist discovered her incest experience during hypnosis; she had no conscious memory of such. When initially seen, it was apparent that reality testing was intermittently poor. She demonstrated many signs of borderline personality organization. Weekly psychotherapy with concomitant lithium therapy improved her vocational and domestic paralysis but did not change her genital sensations. As more of the incestuous memories became conscious she showed more frequent intermittent psychotic perceptions. Eventually the psychotic transference became a full blown paranoid psychosis necessitating hospitalization. Months later when the therapist realized that discussions of her incestuous experiences were not in her best interests, the symptom gradually became weaker and disappeared for days at a time. Just as the therapist began to think it might give way permanently, the genital excitement returned as she prepared to take a two-week vacation.

Case 8. An intermittently alcohol-abusing middle-aged divorced woman with a constant, cheerful style had 18 years of continuous genital urges. She claimed that on certain days these led her to achieve 100 or more orgasms. Lithium dramatically changed her life. For the first time in recent memory she was able to not masturbate. Some days she even felt no sexual urge. Even on her "bad" days she only masturbated for an hour and could work eight hours. During this sexually quiescent phase, the therapist asked her to close her eyes and image the saddest moment in her life. Within seconds she was having her typical clitoral sensation. After several months of sexual quiescence, she began to drink uncontrollably.

These two cases are typical of the severe desire excesses. They force the clinician to confront major mental illness. Less severe desire excesses not only are easier to deal with but have a better prognosis. Couples often have such discrepant drive and motivational patterns that they are not clear who is "oversexed" and who is "undersexed." Individuals may experience an enigmatic transient motivational surge after object loss that the therapist may be able to explain. Many men feel they need to have sex so frequently their partners come to dread any physical contact. Their desire problem can be decreased or removed by discussing the process of enticing the partner. Improving the quality of sexual relationships by helping a man to be attentive to his partner, educating both partners about pleasure giving and pleasure receiving dimensions, and discussing what each partner likes about sexual behavior may dramatically cure the "oversexed" person. Some individuals can use sexual behavior as a sanctuary from their anger, disappointment, and worry. The demand for sex represents an attempt to relieve tensions that are not sexual in origin.

Therapeutic Effectiveness with Desire Disorders

Therapy of sexual dysfunction was warmly welcomed to the therapeutic community because there were indications that more direct discussion of sexual behavior, a couple treatment format, and the use of sexual behavioral prescriptions helped people. The data suggesting that a definable percentage of patients in a particular dysfunction category could be helped in an innovative, relatively inexpensive treatment gave birth to the clinical field of human sexuality. This optimism occurred, however, before sexual desire was even conceptualized as a component of sexual life. Today, even the simple cases of arousal and orgasmic component problems do not seem simple to most therapists.

In this chapter techniques were not emphasized, per se. The basic psychotherapeutic skills possessed by competent professionals are more important than the instructions about how to do something. Moreover, it is the timing and the tact of their application rather than the technique itself that is crucial. The style, the judgment, and the creativity of the therapist is one issue. Therapists interact with the specific dilemmas of their patients. The treatment must come to grips with these dilemmas to enable one or both partners to change something—give up the secret, admit one's fears, treat the partner in a supportive manner, stop the medication, etc. How the therapist catalyzes these changes is often only incompletely known by the therapist.

Any data on treatment effectiveness of desire problems need to be carefully scrutinized with a series of critical questions.

1. What desire problem was being treated?

2. What other sexual and emotional problems existed in the symptom bearer and in the relationship?
3. What was the format of the treatment? Frequency? Duration?
4. What were the major elements of the treatment process as conceived by the therapist?
5. How many patients had to be screened to find the sample?
6. What was the dropout rate?
7. What were the criteria of improvement and how were they measured?
8. What was the difference between the end of treatment results and the post-treatment results?

Chapter 208

Female Sexual Arousal Disorder and Inhibited Female Orgasm

Excitement and Orgasm Phases of the Sexual Response in Women

The sexual response cycle can be divided into four phases: desire, arousal, orgasm, and resolution. The arousal and orgasm phases in women consist of both genital and extragenital events described in exquisite detail by Masters and Johnson (1966). With adequate sexual stimulation blood rushes to the pelvic area, leading to vasocongestive changes such as swelling and deepening of color of the labia minora and glans clitoris. The labia majora of multiparous women may also engorge with blood, while in nulliparous women they flatten against the perineum and elevate away from the vaginal outlet. Vaginal vasocongestion leads to lubrication, a transudate through the vaginal wall. The upper two-thirds of the vaginal barrel expands, and the uterus and cervix elevate. Extragenital responses include increased muscle tension throughout the body, nipple erection and breast swelling, skin flush, hyperventilation, tachycardia, and elevated blood pressure.

With continued sexual stimulation, the plateau stage of sexual excitement is attained; the labia minora becomes more deeply colored, the clitoris retracts and elevates under the clitoral hood, and the lower one-third of the vagina becomes so engorged with blood that the central lumen decreases. Women's descriptions of the subjective experience reflect increasing sexual tension with desire for orgasm and at the same time increasing pleasure. Descriptions of mental states during increasing arousal include more involvement with exciting fantasy, more focus on and appreciation of pleasurable genital sensations or a more free-floating mental state, and an increasing sense of "connectedness" with the partner.

When orgasm is reached there are involuntary muscle contractions in various parts of the body, in particular, of the pelvic and perineal muscles, including the uterus. These contractions hasten the disappearance of vasocongestion from the genital area. For most women, orgasm is considered a peak experience of pleasure. Although orgasm descriptions vary, many women describe a sense of suspension of sensation followed by intense awareness of the genital area, a spreading warmth and a throbbing in the genitals (Masters and Johnson 1966).

Aging and Female Sexual Responsivity

Enhancement of sexual arousal and orgasm by learning and/or maturity is frequent in women—for many, the height of responsiveness and enjoyment is in the fourth and fifth decades of life (Kinsey et al. 1953; Masters and Johnson 1966). Some women first achieve coital orgasm during these years. Lessening of inhibitions, learning, comfort in the marital relationship, and absence of children in the household may all contribute. Another possible factor is the necessity for longer foreplay for the man to achieve an erection, also providing the woman more time to become aroused.

Postmenopausally, there is a definite decline in the woman's ability to vaginally lubricate because of a drop in circulating estrogen. The vaginal wall becomes thinner, shorter, and less expandable; intercourse may be painful without lubrication. Vaginal transudation is slower to appear. Muscle contractions during orgasm are less intense and frequent. Sexual desire, arousal, and ability to achieve orgasm, however, may or may not decline in a given woman. Factors such as availability of a sexual partner and previous sexual activity and responsiveness appear to be more important than the physical changes associated with age.

Vaginal versus Clitoral Preference

Except in those times in history and those cultures in which proper women were expected not to enjoy their sexuality, the woman who reached orgasm quickly through intercourse has been valued (just as the man who did not reach orgasm quickly through intercourse has been valued). Many authors attribute this praise of the "vaginal orgasm" to Freud's view of female psychosexual development; however, the perceived desirability of orgasm with intercourse is more likely rooted in the human beliefs that a man is more virile if he can bring a woman to orgasm with intercourse and in the pleasure and closeness many couples describe with mutual coital satisfaction. Actually, Freud did not discuss either clitoral or vaginal orgasms (Jayne 1984; LaTorre 1979), but rather the concept of transfer of the chief erotogenic zone from the clitoris to the vagina, and that clitoral preference represents a fixation in female development and may result in sexual dysfunction (Freud 1953).

There are currently two major controversies surrounding coital versus direct clitoral stimulation in attaining orgasm. First, is there a difference in orgasms produced via clitoral stimulation from those achieved during intercourse? Coitus provides indirect stimulation by rubbing of genitals against the partner. It also provides the psychological stimulation of closeness to a partner, stimulation of the outer one-third of the vagina, and with deep penetration, pressure on and movement of the cervix (and thus uterus). Thus, it generally provides more global stimulation with less intense stimulation of the clitoris than does clitoral masturbation. Masters and Johnson (1966) found no physiologic differences in their measurements of coitally achieved versus clitoral masturbation-achieved orgasms, except perhaps in the intensity of muscle contractions (greater with masturbation). Subjectively, there is a difference for many women (Fisher 1973; Hite 1976; Singer and Singer 1972). Coitally achieved orgasms are generally described as more diffuse and less intense than those with masturbation, but are preferred by many women because of the sharing and love.

The second controversy is of even more importance to the clinician who refers or treats patients for sexual problems. Is the inability to achieve coital orgasm pathologic? If a woman can orgasm only with masturbation, should she be treated; and what about the woman who has coital orgasms only with concurrent manual stimulation? One method of attempting to answer these questions is by studying the anatomy. There is little question that in healthy women the clitoris is a highly sensitive organ, one that when sufficiently stimulated in a psychologically responsive woman can trigger orgasm. There is some question about the sensitivity of the vagina and the possibility of its stimulation triggering orgasm. Kinsey et al. (1953) and Masters and Johnson (1966) believed the vagina made relatively little contribution to sexual stimulation. Their measurement techniques have been criticized (Alzate 1985; Hoch 1980; Perry and Whipple 1981). However, it is clear that the clitoris is the more sensitive of the two organs.

Survey data also support the notion that clitoral stimulation is the most effective means of achieving orgasm. In all major studies of the subject, it has been found that women are more likely to achieve orgasm through clitoral stimulation than through intercourse alone. In fact, about 30 to 45 percent of women regularly have orgasms during intercourse (Fisher 1973; Hite 1976; Kinsey et al. 1953; Terman 1951), and studies specifically evaluating orgasm and simultaneous manual clitoral stimulation suggest that only 20–30 percent of women can climax regularly from intercourse without such stimulation (Fisher 1973; Hite 1976).

A number of studies have been done to determine if women who are anorgasmic are more psychologically disturbed than orgasmic women, or if coitally anorgasmic women are more disturbed than coitally orgasmic women. With the possible exceptions of mania (Allison and Wilson 1960), depression (Winokur 1963), hysteria (Purtell et al. 1951), and dementia (Winokur 1963), no consistent differences have been found. In one study of 306 women, it was found that women who preferred direct clitoral stimulation during lovemaking to penile intromission were more assertive, which was interpreted as more masculine. However, these women were also more likely to be younger. An alternative interpretation of the data is that the enjoyment of and ability to achieve orgasm during intercourse is related to learning and experience over time.

In summary, most women do not achieve orgasm regularly through coitus alone and there is no evidence that this is pathologic per se. Kaplan (1974) describes a continuum of female orgasmic response. At the one end is the rare women who can orgasm without genital stimulation, then the 20–30 percent of women who climax during intercourse without simultaneous clitoral stimulation; next, there are the women who require additional clitoral stimulation during coitus. Some women achieve orgasm with noncoital clitoral stimulation but lose this capacity during intercourse. At the more dysfunctional end of the spectrum are women who cannot reach orgasm in the presence of a partner, but can with solitary masturbation, and finally the anorgasmic woman. Many couples present for treatment to attain female coital orgasm. Reassurance that the necessity for direct clitoral stimulation during or outside of intercourse is a variant of normal sexual functioning is sometimes all that is necessary. For other couples, who are particularly distressed by this, or in whom there are relationship conflicts or intrapsychic conflicts in the woman believed to be contributory to the coital anorgasmia, sex therapy can be helpful.

The Menstrual Cycle and Sexual Responsivity

A number of studies have attempted to discern whether the menstrual cycle and its associated hormonal changes affect sexual desire and arousal, including genital physiologic changes, in women. Except for women with marked cyclical mood change ("good mood" or "general well being" associated with increased sexual interest and feelings), there have been no consistent findings correlating reported sexual interest and activity with the phase of the menstrual cycle. (For a review of 32 of these studies, see P. Schreiner-Engel: Female Sexual Arousability: Its Relation to Gonadal Hormones and the Menstrual Cycle. Ph.D. thesis, State University of New York, 1980.) However, many studies have the methodological problems of retrospective reporting, differing definitions of sexual desire and arousal, not distinguishing self-initiated from partner-initiated activity or masturbatory from coital activity, not measuring hormone levels, and so forth. One study monitoring vaginal blood volume responses to erotic stimuli during the menstrual cycle found no significant changes in subjective arousal or vasocongestion across the cycle (Hoon et al. 1982). A larger study which also determined estradiol, progesterone, and testosterone levels in the follicular, ovulatory, and luteal phases found no difference in subjective arousal, but vaginal vasocongestive responses were significantly lower in the ovulatory phase than in the follicular or luteal phases (Schreiner-Engel 1981).

Female Sexual Arousal Disorder

Sexual arousal can be defined as the combination of psychological and physiologic responses which occur during a sexually stimulating situation, whether it be externally (visual, tactile, auditory, olfactory, gustatory) or internally (fantasy) induced. Sexual arousal is definitionally differentiated from sexual desire, but in clinical situations it may be difficult to distinguish. For example, a woman who lacks sexual desire often does not respond with excitement to what most would consider sexually stimulating; or if she consistently fails during the arousal phase of sexual response, she may begin to inhibit her desire.

DSM-III (American Psychiatric Association 1980) defined inhibited sexual excitement (ISE) as "recurrent and persistent inhibition of sexual excitement during sexual activity, manifested by partial or complete failure to attain or maintain the lubrication-swelling response . . . until completion of the sexual act," and specified that it may not be due to organic factors, inadequate stimulation, or mental disorder. Thus, DSM-III did not mention that hard-to-define psychic component of arousal in its definition of impairment. To the woman, however, the psychic component is of utmost importance and there are patients who complain of not feeling arousal or enjoyment despite vaginal lubrication and vasocongestion. There are some research data to support this complaint (Hoon and Hoon 1978; Hoon et al. 1976; Steinman et al. 1981). Apparently, there is less correlation between physiologic and subjective measures of sexual excitement in women than in men, and women who achieve orgasm more consistently are more aware of physiologic changes during sexual excitement than those who are less frequently orgasmic. In a study of vaginal pulse amplitude responses to erotic stimuli in sexually nondysfunctional women, there were groups of women whose subjective and physiologic measures of arousal did not correlate positively during some or much of the stimulus time (Heiman 1980). There is also some evidence that women complaining of sexual dysfunction are less attuned to the vasocongestive changes during sexual excitement and less subjectively aroused (Heiman 1975). Instruction about recognizing and focusing on the genital sensations can improve the correlation between subjective and objective sexual arousal (Korff and Geer 1983). Fortunately DSM-III-R (American Psychiatric Association 1987, p. 294) not only changed the name of the disorder, it also includes a psychic component, namely "persistent or recurrent lack of subjective sense of sexual excitement and pleasure in a female during sexual activity."

Prevalence of Female Sexual Arousal Disorder

The prevalence of this disorder in women is uncertain. Although there is much literature about desire, erection, and orgasm disorders in men, and about desire and orgasm problems in women, there is little discussion of psychogenic arousal disorders in women. In fact, some excellent sex therapy manuals do not discuss this dysfunction or do so only cursorily (LoPiccolo and LoPiccolo, 1978; Meyer et al. 1983), or the authors do not specifically diagnose such patients in their clinical populations (Meyer et al. 1983). Kaplan (1983) states that failure of excitement in women is relatively rare, at least rare as an isolated problem not associated with inhibited desire or orgasm. But it is not unusual for a psychotherapist to hear a patient talk about having sexual desire, being able to reach orgasm if the circumstances are right for her, but frequently "shutting off" arousal during the sex act. She may describe being aroused but suddenly becoming angry, anxious, or distrusting of the partner or thinking about nonerotic material. One possible reason for the relative lack of specific information about this syndrome in women is that, prior to DSM-III (1980), the term or one equal in definition was not uniformly used, and an arousal disorder was often included in desire or orgasm disorders.

Another reason was the focus of the DSM-III definition of the disorder, which stressed the genital lubrication response to the exclusion of the psychic component of sexual excitement. This may have tempted some clinicians to ignore subjective complaints or diagnose them as some other disorder. As mentioned earlier, this has been corrected in DSM-III-R. Finally, it may be difficult in some cases to distinguish by history an arousal phase from an orgasm phase problem. A case history will be presented later to exemplify this diagnostic dilemma.

As with other psychosexual dysfunctions, diminished sexual arousal may be situational, that is, occurring only in some situations, only with masturbation, only with a partner, or only with a certain partner; or it may be global (total). Theoretically, psychogenically impaired sexual excitement in women can exist in a primary form— that is, the woman has never experienced excitement from any form of sexual stimuli— but no clear case reports of such exist.

Identifiable physical causes of impaired genital vasocongestion are not rare. By far the most common is postmenopausal estrogen deficiency, because adequate levels of estrogen are required for the vasocongestion-lubrication response. Other conditions affecting the vaginal wall; central and peripheral neurologic disorders affecting the genital area; less often, drugs (anticholinergic and antihistaminic "drying" medications, antihypertensive medications); or pelvic vascular disorders may decrease lubrication and vasocongestion (Kaplan 1983). Dyspareunia (see Chapter 209), because sexual activity is painful, may lead to a secondary inhibition of sexual arousal, desire, or orgasm.

The psychological antecedents of an arousal disorder are nonspecific in the sense that the same conflicts can inhibit other phases of the sexual response. Kaplan (1979) suggests that, in general, the more serious and deep-rooted the conflict, the earlier the phase of sexual response that is affected. That is, desire phase dysfunctions are, in general, related to the more serious and deep-rooted conflicts. In this scheme, an arousal disorder would fall midway. Among the possible psychological correlates are obsessive self-observation ("spectatoring"), performance anxiety, sexual guilt and other conflicts about intercourse, marital discord, anger at the partner, fear of pregnancy, and fear of orgasm.

And finally, a few situations should be distinguished from a disorder of arousal. Women require relatively continuous psychological or physical stimulation to maintain arousal and lubrication. If there is inadequate stimulation or if stimulation ceases, vasocongestion/lubrication may be lost. Also, in the supine position, the vaginal transudate may gravitate toward the vaginal vault—so that the woman and her partner may be unaware of the lubrication.

Inhibited Female Orgasm (IFO)

Inhibited female orgasm is defined in DSM-III-R as "persistent and recurrent delay in, or absence of, orgasm in the female . . . following a normal sexual excitement phase during sexual activity that is . . . adequate in focus, intensity, and duration (p. 294). Anorgasmia due to organic factors or psychiatric illness is excluded from IFO. The anorgasmia may be primary, the woman never having had an orgasm, or secondary; it may be situational, such as an inability to achieve coital orgasm but ability to achieve masturbatory orgasm, or it may be global (total).

Anorgasmia and desire for improved orgasmic capacity are common. The majority of women report not routinely achieving coital orgasm; estimates of prevalence of primary global anorgasmia range from about 5 to 12 percent of sexually active women (Fisher 1973; Hite 1976; Hunt 1974; Kaplan 1974; Kinsey et al. 1953).

Many studies have sought to determine what factors play a role in anorgasmia, often with conflicting results or the finding of few significant correlations. The following will summarize some of the findings.

Practice Effects

There are convincing clinical data demonstrating that the ability to have an orgasm and increased orgasm frequency can be attained with learning and practice. In fact, behavioral sex therapies are grounded in the belief that becoming familiar with one's body and practicing self-stimulation are methods of improving orgasmic capacity. Success in acquiring orgasm with these methods is high. Of course, the effects of relaxation, decreased pressure to perform, encouragement and permission from the therapist, increased information about sexuality, and other factors are also part of the therapy. Surveys report mixed results. Kinsey et al. (1953) found that 49 percent of women attained orgasm after one month of marriage, 75 percent after one year, 84 percent after five years, and 89 percent after 20 years. Chesser (1956) reported a negative correlation between duration of marriage and orgasm, and Terman (1951) found no relationship. These surveys are not particularly useful in determining practice effects because increasing duration of marriage may be associated with many other changes in the woman and the couple's relationship which affect sexuality and attitudes.

Age Effects

For most women, increasing age over 50 has no dramatic effects on ability to climax or on the pleasure experienced, although the vasocongestion and muscle contractions decrease somewhat after menopause (Kinsey et al. 1953; Masters and Johnson 1966; Terman 1951).

Sociocultural and Religious Effects

Extremes of religious or societal attitudes may affect orgasmic ability. Highly devout Catholics and Jews in some instances have reported being less frequently orgasmic than their religiously inactive cohorts (Cashin-Gottstein 1966; Hamblin and Blood 1957; Kinsey et al. 1953). On the opposite end of the spectrum, in one isolated island community anorgasmia was nonexistent (Marshall 1971). The mores of this culture included a high value placed on female sexual satisfaction, encouragement of female sexual activity with multiple partners, and devaluation or ridicule of men who did not "bring" their partner to orgasm. Although there are conflicting reports, there is no clear general effect of other factors, such as education, socioeconomic class, parity, and sexually traumatic childhood experiences on the attainment of orgasm (Chesser 1956; Hunt 1974; Kinsey et al. 1953; Terman 1951).

Many popular publications stress that the key to orgasm is longer and stronger foreplay and coitus. This is only sometimes true. Certainly it is clear that very brief foreplay or foreplay ignoring the clitoris can be inadequate. But Huey et al. (1981) found no differences in duration of foreplay and intromission between groups of primary globally, primary coitally, and secondary coitally anorgasmic women. However, a retrospective review of structured interviews of married white women revealed that, within 1 to 10 minutes of foreplay about 40 percent of the sample almost always achieved orgasm, with 15–20 minutes 50 percent did, and with longer foreplay about 60 percent did. Wives with lesser orgasm rates received shorter periods of foreplay. Women who never reached orgasm constituted a separate group. On the average they received more foreplay, likely due to the partner's attempts to induce orgasm (Gebhard 1978). This same study found a similar trend in duration of intromission to orgasm frequency.

Those studies suggest a separate group of dysfunctional women who have a high orgasmic threshold, and in whom no duration, level, or focus of stimulation may be useful. Such a group may exist, but if so, they have not been thoroughly studied to determine sensory threshold, couple interaction, or sexual techniques. It should also be noted that subjective reports of duration of sexual activity are subject to large error.

One might expect that anorgasmic women would be less mature and more neurotic than orgasmic women, but the results of several major studies have revealed little difference, and even when a difference was found, cause and effect could not be assumed. Further, because so many variables were studied, a few positive correlations could occur by chance. Large studies were done by Terman (1938, 1951). Orgasm consistency was not correlated with reported attachment to, conflict with, attitudes of, or happiness of either parent. He did find that anorgasmic women viewed themselves as more lonely, grouchy, miserable, and pessimistic. Fisher's extensive study (1973) was not able to differentiate orgasmic from anorgasmic women by similar reported feelings, and he also found no correlations with the above mentioned parental factors. Orgasm consistency was not related to aggressiveness, passivity, femininity, narcissism, guilt, impulsivity, affectionateness, or a number of other characteristics. The most predictive trait he found was that anorgasmic women viewed love objects as less dependable. The one psychological characteristic that has been correlated with orgasm consistency in a number of studies is marital happiness; cause versus effect has not been determined.

Physical causes for anorgasmia are not nearly so common as other causes, but they deserve evaluation if the history or physical exam suggests medical illness. A number of drugs have been associated with delayed or absent orgasm in a small percentage of patients. These include tricyclic antidepressants and to a greater extent monoamine oxidase (MAO) inhibitors; CNS stimulants in high doses and CNS depressants; antihypertensive medications, especially those affecting sympathetic neurotransmission; and antianxiety drugs. Certain neurologic conditions affecting the genital nerves, endocrine disorders including those with elevations or decreases in cortisol, hypothyroidism and diabetes, and on rare occasion vascular pathology or anatomical genital defect can affect orgasm (Kaplan 1984). Women with secondary and those with global anorgasmia are more likely to have biological problems than those with primary or situational anorgasmia. Kegel (1956) proposed that weak pubococcygeal muscles may decrease sexual arousal and orgasm. Although the studies about this are not conclusive, the preponderance of evidence suggests that weak muscles have little to do with inhibiting orgasm (Chambless et al. 1982; Chambless et al. 1984; Roughan and Kunst 1981). Another anatomic area purported to increase or enhance orgasm is the Grafenberg spot (1950), a spot on the anterior wall of the vagina which is proposed to trigger orgasm and female ejaculation (Ladas et al. 1982). There are no substantive anatomical or microscopic data that support the existence of such a distinct spot or of female non-urinary ejaculation, although in some women the anterior wall of the vagina is quite sensitive (Alzate 1985; Hoch 1980).

Although large surveys of orgasmic and anorgasmic women fail to reveal neurotic or personality correlates of anorgasmia, clinical evaluation reveals that certain conflicts or psychological states may be associated. Among these are performance anxiety, obsessive self-observation, anger at the partner, detachment from the sexual situation, negative fantasies or inhibited fantasy, guilt, fear of sexual success or of loss of control, marital discord, deliberate withholding, and ambivalence about intimacy or intercourse.

Case history

Jamie, age 29, and Rick, age 28, have been married four years, have had no children or previous marriages, and present with the complaint of her never having reached orgasm. They have a warm and mutually supportive relationship, but have recently been avoiding touching for fear of its leading to frustrating intercourse. Rick has no problem with erection or ejaculation, but he and Jamie are demoralized because she doesn't climax. They always make love in the dark and in the male superior ("missionary") position and are both comfortable with that.

Rick is a quiet, intelligent man who works in electronics. He had only one short-lived sexual relationship prior to Jamie and describes no sexual dysfunctions in himself or his previous partner. Jamie is a personnel manager for a moderate-sized business. She has a B.A. in psychology, is socially outgoing, and is knowledgeable about sexuality. She has had four previous sexual relationships. The first was traumatic. It was their first date, and she says she verbally resisted and also pushed him away, but he continued undressing her. She became terrified and passive. He penetrated her and ejaculated. She describes no sexual excitement. She is not sure whether she considered it rape. She never saw him again.

Rick grew up in a devoutly religious family. His mother was the more dominant of his parents. She was "hovering and expected a lot" of Rick. His father was jovial when at home, but rarely interacted closely with Rick. Jamie's parents divorced before she was born, and she never knew her father. Her mother did not remarry. Jamie described her mother as hardworking, busy, but caring. Jamie says she was overweight as a child and still has body image problems, although she is only slightly above ideal weight.

Both currently have desire for lovemaking three or four times a week, and for the first two or three years of marriage would have intercourse during those times; now it is attempted about once every week or two. Foreplay mainly focuses on genital stimulation, and each in turn "works" on the other. Rick achieves erection but Jamie is not aroused or lubricated. He gives her cunnilingus, which at times results in her vasocongestive response, but this is more duty than excitement for him. By the time he achieves an erection, she has lost arousal. During foreplay she becomes worried about failure and frustrated.

Jamie thinks she has never had an orgasm. Her descriptions of her responses lead the therapist to believe that, on rare occasions, she has reached the plateau phase, but not orgasm. Most of the time she does not feel aroused or notice lubrication. She does not masturbate and reacts with distaste to questions about masturbation. She also expresses the idea that fantasy during lovemaking is disloyal to her husband. She has no physical diseases, and her pelvic exam is within normal limits.

Evaluation: diagnoses, etiologies, prognoses.   The first question for the clinician is: Is there a sexual dysfunction and, if so, which one(s)? Sometimes there are multiple diagnoses—for example, inhibited female orgasm which has led to inhibited arousal in the woman—and there may be prior, concurrent, or subsequent development of dysfunction in the partner. Or there may be no sexual dysfunction, but rather inadequate foreplay, unsuitable partner, deliberate withholding of sex, depression, or other problems. In the case of Jamie and Rick, the diagnosis of inhibited female orgasm seems in order. She has never reached orgasm (although she has not attempted orgasm through masturbation). A second diagnosis of female sexual arousal disorder (FSAD) is made, because she generally fails to become aroused and lubricated or becomes only minimally or briefly so.

What are the etiologies? The state of the art evaluation for female sexual dysfunctions has progressed little past the history and routine physical exam (in contrast to evaluation for impotence). Assessment of vaginal and clitoral blood flows, sensory thresholds in the genitals, and perineal muscle activity have not been studied thoroughly enough to determine whether they may be useful in diagnosing biogenic sexual problems in women. However, many known physical causes of FSAD and IFO can be ruled out by the history and sexologic (pelvic) exam. Jamie has no evidence of biogenic sexual dysfunction.

If the dysfunction is psychogenic, what are the likely conflicts and behaviors involved? Determination of the immediate antecedents, such as performance anxiety or spectatoring (Kaplan 1979), is usually simple and may be all that is needed to conduct a successful sex therapy. Often the clincian detects more deeply rooted unconscious conflicts which are presumed to be causative or contributory, such as ambivalence about intimacy, guilt about pleasure, or Oedipal conflicts. It may or may not be necessary to uncover these conflicts for resolution of the psychosexual dysfunction. Discord between the partners may also be contributory, and when present, usually requires exploration in the therapy.

Even the most dysfunctional couples can be helped by sex therapy, but some factors are of prognostic value (Kaplan 1979; Meyer et al. 1983). Among these are motivation and desire for change in both partners, commitment to the relationship, short duration of symptoms, absence of major psychopathology, and absence of serious couple conflicts. Secondary gain, substance abuse, incompatible sexual orientation or desires (e.g., fetishes, sadomasochism), and a secret affair are unfavorable prognostic signs. Many but not all studies have shown that focused sex therapy of the Masters and Johnson type (or a modified form) and group therapy of anorgasmia are more successful in treating primary than secondary anorgasmia (Kilmann 1978; Mills and Kilmann 1982). One explanation for this difference is that marital problems may contribute more heavily in secondary anorgasmia, and that symptom-focused treatment may be inadequate.

Relative to many couples that sex therapists treat, the case of Jamie and Rick is an uncomplicated one. They do not have a hostile relationship, psychiatric disorders, or major character pathology. They are committed to each other and there are no known outside affairs. Despite this, it is not simple to determine what factors may be causal in the dysfunctions. Part of the difficulty is that there are few data that links remote traumas and conflicts to specific sexual dysfunctions. Many women who have significant Oedipal or pre-Oedipal conflicts, have been victims of incest or rapes, or have schizophrenia or serious character pathology do not have sexual dysfunctions. Determining immediate antecedents is usually simpler. In Jamie's case, during sexual attempts, she begins wondering if she will climax this time and becomes anxious that she will not (performance anxiety). She begins to switch from sensual thoughts and enjoyment to cognitive mentations (spectatoring): Will I become lubricated? If I don't have an orgasm, will Rick feel hurt, or will I have that lingering discomfort in my pelvis? She begins having negative fantasies, reruns of previous failures. Arousal and vasocongestion are blocked. Foreplay and intercourse seem like a chore.

The treatment of Jamie and Rick.   Our initial assessment indicates that focused sex therapy with this couple is indicated. The marriage seems basically solid so that general marital therapy will likely not be required for symptom reversal. Also, neither Jamie nor Rick appear to have serious neurotic, psychotic, or character pathologies that suggest the necessity of longer term individual therapy. The treatment techniques that may prove helpful to this couple are:

1. Sex education and permission giving. Discussions, films, and readings about genital anatomy, the sexual response cycle and its differences in men and women, lovemaking techniques, and masturbation will serve several purposes for Rick and Jamie. First, it provides accurate sexual information and helps negate myths, something that Rick in particular may need considering his limited background in sexual matters. Second, it gives permission to discuss sexual matters and enjoy sexuality. Repeated discussion between patients and a therapist gradually diminishes the couple's inhibitions (desensitization). Third, it demonstrates new techniques; and

fourth, it reduces isolation and shame. Some couples believe they are alone in having sexual difficulties or that their symptoms mean they are "freaks." Learning that many other couples have had the same problems (and have been helped) provides relief of anxiety and renewed hope.

2. Communication techniques training. Most couples with sexual problems do not communicate well in or outside of the bedroom. Training focuses on nonblaming, nonaccusing expression of feelings, needs, desires, and dislikes.

3. Prescription of masturbation and mutual pleasuring exercises at home (sensate focus, see chapter on "Inhibited Sexual Excitement in the Male"). These bring the couple together in a nondemanding, pleasurable atmosphere and help them undo old, dysfunctional approaches to lovemaking and learn new approaches. The in vivo graded exposure tasks treat performance anxiety.

4. Meetings with the therapist (usually weekly) to discuss problems and progress. The home exercises often become the focus of resistance, and as such, are a tool to help make conflicts and feelings accessible to the therapist and couple. Exploratory psychotherapy may be used to address the resistance and its underpinnings as needed for therapy to progress (Kaplan 1974). These sessions also allow the therapist to access the emotional state of each partner and any developing crises in the relationship, to provide encouragement, and to give a new assignment for the next session.

Jamie was given reading material about masturbation, and the couple was shown a film about a woman sexually exploring her body. She was then asked to explore her own body in private and to discover what felt pleasurable. She had reservations about this but agreed to try. She was encouraged to use fantasy during self-stimulation and during the sensate focus exercises.

The couple was then given sensate focus I and II exercises, beginning with mutual nongenital body pleasuring and later, nondemanding genital touching. They were told to stop if Jamie felt near to orgasm. Intromission was prohibited, but Rick could masturbate to orgasm if he desired. The couple was told to communicate verbally and nonverbally what was pleasurable for each.

Jamie found that she became aroused with the self-stimulation but pulled back before orgasm. This continued for a few weeks, and the therapist chose to explore more deeply Jamie's anxiety about letting go. During the next sessions, connections were made between the anxiety and her guilt about masturbation; her belief that she would appear ridiculous or undignified during orgasm; and her first traumatic sexual experience, which left her feeling out of control, angry, and frightened.

At the following session, Jamie reported she had not yet reached orgasm during masturbation; she would either not become very aroused or would stop before orgasm. She did report "almost" climaxing during Rick's stimulation of her clitoris. Although for many women orgasm with a partner is more anxiety-provoking than orgasm alone, it seemed to be different for Jamie. Perhaps her resistance to masturbation was more tenacious than her anxiety about letting go with Rick.

The therapist decided that learning of orgasm through masturbation, for most women the most successful technique, should be bypassed for the time being, and proceeded to prescribe mutual (not necessarily concurrent) genital stimulation without prohibiting orgasm.

Over the next few weeks, Jamie climaxed during both Rick's oral and manual stimulation of her. Treatment proceeded through the steps of nondemanding intromission, female superior position without orgasm, to the bridge maneuver, which consisted of intercourse with Rick concurrently stimulating her clitoris. Later, Jamie was able to do this for herself during intercourse but did not continue to try to climax by masturbation. Rick and Jamie felt successful with the gains they had made, and therapy was stopped.

Summary of Treatment Approaches

Volumes have been written about the defects in assessing outcome of the many psychotherapies used to treat psychiatric disorders. Treatment of psychosexual dysfunctions is no exception (Kilmann 1978). Confounding variables include lack of uniformity and specificity of 1) diagnosis; 2) characteristics of the patient, partner, couple relationship, and therapist; 3) time format; and 4) criteria for success. Inadequate follow-up and noncomparable control subjects and conditions or lack of controls also causes confusion. Thus, it is premature to claim that a specific technique is clearly superior to another in the treatment of IFO or IFE.

Despite this, it is clear from a number of studies that IFO has a good prognosis and can often be treated in brief therapies. The most frequently used brief therapy is in vivo systematic desensitization in a modified Masters and Johnson (1970) approach. Jamie and Rick were treated in this manner. The most common modifications include 1) weekly sessions rather than an intense, daily experience for two weeks; 2) one therapist or two same-gender therapists rather than a male and female therapist; and 3) more attention to psychodynamic psychotherapy techniques to work through resistant behavior.

Group treatment of primary anorgasmic women focusing on education and masturbation training is also effective in teaching them to have orgasm with masturbation. A higher emphasis on communication techniques is believed more effective for women with secondary anorgasmia, whether they are treated in a group or couple setting (Kilmann 1978). A possible reason for this is that dysfunctional marital communication is more likely to be contributory to the sexual problem in these women. All-female groups or groups including the partners are both effective.

The issue of when to use therapies other than those just described is unresolved. Long-term individual psychodynamic psychotherapy may be indicated for those women who have serious neurotic or characterologic problems that directly interfere with their sexual functioning. Couple therapy is sometimes required for those who have serious marital discord. Anxiolytics can be a useful adjunct to behavioral sex therapies when the woman has a high anxiety level or phobic avoidance of sex (Kaplan 1979).

Chapter 209

Dyspareunia and Vaginismus

DSM-III-R (American Psychiatric Association 1987) indicates that dyspareunia is the appropriate diagnosis when sexual activity is associated with recurrent and persistent genital pain in either a male or a female and the cause is not exclusively a lack of lubrication or vaginismus.

DSM-III-R states that vaginismus is the diagnosis when there is a history of recurrent and persistent involuntary spasm of the musculature of the outer third of the vagina that interferes with coitus and is not caused exclusively by a physical disorder or another mental disorder. In our discussion of vaginismus, we will describe a spectrum from mild (some discomfort and tightness at the time of penetration) to severe (penetration is impossible). When mild to moderate vaginismus is recognized, one finds that it is perhaps the single most common sexual problem in women.

Vaginismus should be considered a subcategory of dyspareunia since it produces recurrent and persistent genital pain associated with coitus. Dyspareunia not the result of vaginismus can almost always be traced to a specific physical cause or to total lack of sexual arousal. Therefore, unless female coital discomfort is caused by vaginismus or lack of arousal, it should be the province of the physician, preferably one who is sensitive to the emotional complications which may result from dyspareunia. Of course, when emotional sequelae are great, the help of a psychotherapist may be indicated. Where lack of sexual arousal is the problem, sex therapy should be suggested.

In the past, dyspareunia has not been carefully defined and diagnosed. For example, in an otherwise excellent chapter on dyspareunia, Lazarus (1980) cites a number of case examples where the coital pain is most likely attributable to vaginismus, but this diagnosis was not made. In fact, the diagnosis of vaginismus is often missed. We hope to provide enough information in this chapter to help practitioners become more skillful in the diagnosis of vaginismus.

We will begin with a brief overview of dyspareunia (including vaginismus), including a discussion of organic problems since it is essential that the mental health professional be alert to the presence of organic etiologies in order to prescribe appropriate treatment. This discussion is also important in helping practitioners distinguish between the pain caused by vaginismus or other causes since sometimes both an organic cause and vaginismus are simultaneously present.

Dyspareunia

Organic Causes

A variety of medical conditions affecting both external and internal genitalia can lead to pain during sexual activity in both men and women.

External Genitalia

External female genitalia include the structures of the vulva (Bartholin's glands, major and minor labia, clitoris), the urethral opening, and the vaginal outlet which includes the hymen and its remnants and the glands and mucous membrane of the vestibule. All of these structures are affected by sex response as increased blood flow during sexual arousal leads to vasocongestion. If irritation or swelling is present, the vasocongestive changes can lead to a burning or more painful sensation. The discomfort may be present with any sexual arousal or only during intercourse.

Infections, chemicals and allergies. The external genitalia are subject to infections, the most common of which are due to monilial organisms. Herpes, trichomoniasis, and clostridial infections are also common. Most often, infected tissues are readily recognized. However, unless a very careful examination is done, small but significant areas of irritation beneath the labial folds, the clitoral hood, and the posterior vestibule in the mid-line can be missed.

Anatomic conditions. Congenital and acquired anatomic disorders of the external genitals include partial or complete hymeneal obliteration, absence of the vagina, and scarring after traumatic injury or surgery including episiotomy repair after childbirth. Perhaps most common, and often overlooked by examining physicians, is a fibroepithelial strand subdividing the hymeneal opening. A byproduct of normal embryologic development, the strand can persist into adulthood. Rupture of the strand, which can occur with tampon insertion, genital petting, or masturbation, can be painful and frightening and lead to subsequent fear of penetration. The finding of either an intact strand or the stump of a ruptured one may suggest a direct cause of dyspareunia or a significant factor in the development of vaginismus.

Estrogen deficiency. Decreased estrogen leads to vulva atrophy (Lang and Aponte 1967), decreased blood flow (Sarrel 1977), and increased vulnerability to infection and irritation. Such changes occur most often after menopause. However, any woman who complains of dyspareunia and who shows evidence of decreased estrogen effects (e.g., amenorrhea) should be suspected of having pain secondary to hypoestrogenic effects.

Internal Genitalia

Female internal genitalia include the vagina, cervix, uterine body, fallopian tubes, and ovaries. Infection in any of these areas can cause pain during sexual activity. In particular, gonococcal infection of the cervix and fallopian tubes leading to both acute and chronic pelvic inflammatory disease frequently causes deep dyspareunia. Anatomic conditions of internal genitalia which can cause dyspareunia include vaginal septa and narrowing or shortening of the vagina after gynecologic surgery or radiation treatment. Endometriosis implants in any of the internal pelvic organs can cause sharp pain either during the increase in sexual excitement or when struck during coitus. Other gynecologic conditions affecting internal genitalia and causing dyspareunia include fibromyomata uteri, ovarian cysts, and prolapse of the uterus. A more complete discussion of gynecologic causes of dyspareunia can be found in Sarrel (1983).

Genital Pain in Men

Men may experience genital pain during sexual activity for a variety of reasons. Sexual arousal which does not culminate in orgasm can lead to testicular congestion which can be painful. More common among younger men, it can occur in men of all ages. However, its incidence is not nearly as common as folklore would lead one to believe. Congestion of the prostate during sexual arousal can lead to referral pain in the tip of the penis. During sexual response testicular rotation occurs and testicular torsion can be a complication of sexual arousal, particularly in young adolescent males.

Anatomic conditions which can produce symptoms include adherence of the foreskin and phimosis. Sharp angulation of the penis can occur as a result of congenital malformation or as a complication of Peyronie's disease and lead to pain with arousal or with attempts at coitus.

Gonorrheal infections can lead to burning or sharp penile pain during ejaculation. Prostatitis can cause pain in the tip of the penis during sexual activity. Balanitis and herpetic infections on the penis are frequently painful.

Men who have had pain associated with sex can develop perineal muscle spasms. As a result they may experience pain or a burning sensation with any kind of sexual arousal or at any attempt at genital manipulation. Although a rare syndrome in men, this reaction is a counterpart to vaginismus in the female and can be diagnosed and treated in a way analogous to vaginismus treatment in the female.

Psychological Reactions to Dyspareunia

Part of the evaluation of dyspareunia involves an appreciation for psychological mechanisms which influence the meaning of this presenting symptom. Some women have pain for years before they seek professional help. Others have the experience of pain, seek help, but are not helped and eventually, after repeating such experiences, become unable to ask for help. Still others react to the painful experience in ways that make subsequent intercourse impossible. Finally, there are those who lose sexual desire or even become aversive to further sexual experiences.

The defense mechanism of denial is commonly used to cope with dyspareunia. As a result there can be injury to tissues, repeated episodes of infection, post-coital bleeding, etc. Frequently, a woman will not present her dyspareunia history but only appear for help when some other manifestation has developed such as sexual dysfunction in her male partner.

"Learned helplessness" (Seligman 1975) is relevant to the reactions to dyspareunia. The model of learned helplessness is that of a dog trapped in a cage and exposed to electro-shock from which it cannot escape. At first, the dog tries to escape but, eventually, faced with the impossibility of getting away from the pain, stops its efforts. Barriers can then be removed, but when the dog is shocked it will no longer try to move from the platform on which the shock is given. Only after repeated help in getting off the platform and being rewarded for leaving the painful environment will the dog begin to relearn how to protect itself. The dyspareunia patient who has had multiple experiences in which she felt she could not stop the pain is in an analogous situation. Psychologically, she too may not be able to help herself. Evaluation of the dyspareunia therefore must also consider the capacity of the patient to help herself. When there is evidence of a state of learned helplessness, an appropriately supportive regimen is necessitated and psychotherapy may be indicated.

Vaginismus

Etiology

The most important etiologic factor in vaginismus is the woman's fear that vaginal penetration will be uncomfortable or painful. The origins of this fear are slightly different in each case but many themes recur. Typically there have been sensitizing experiences in childhood, associating bodily or genital penetration with pain, followed by further negative experiences in adolescence and adult life. The end result is a fear of vaginal penetration which causes involuntary tensing of vaginal muscles when penetration is anticipated.

Penetration anxiety.   We assume that there is a degree of penetration anxiety in all females from childhood on. Without this assumption it would be very difficult to explain the female's extreme sensitivity to life experiences associating pain, anxiety, and vaginal penetration. The literature supports the notion that little girls fear (as well as desire) penetration. An alternative hypothesis would be that all humans are "instinctively" afraid of body penetration of any sort. In support of this hypothesis is Fisher and Cleveland's (1968) finding that men are more upset than women by a penetration of their body boundary (e.g., by surgery). Fisher postulates that women are gradually acclimated to body penetration through experiences such as menstruation, sexual intercourse, and the delivery of a baby.

Childhood and adolescent events which we have observed to increase penetration anxiety fall into three categories. The first is non-genital experiences. In this category we have elicited relevant histories of repeated "needles"; unusually painful or frightening dentistry, often including local anesthesia injection; frequent throat cultures; one or more urethral dilations done without anesthesia. In each case the little girl experienced a combination of pain and extreme anxiety. Many were chronically afraid of doctors and/or medical procedures and often had greater than average anxiety about pain.

Females of small stature who viewed themselves as frail, petite little girls often carry a distorted image of their bodies into adolescence and adulthood. They picture their vagina as tiny and frail and see an erect penis as huge and threatening. They may perceive a finger or tampon as similarly frightening. Of course, a violence misconception of coitus is not necessarily restricted to small women.

Genital trauma.   The second category of relevant, predisposing childhood and adolescent experiences is that of genital trauma. This might include excision of a labial boil, accidental injury to the vulva (most often when riding a bicycle or climbing a fence), unusual pain and difficulty inserting tampons (sometimes caused by a hymeneal strand), and difficult experiences during early pelvic examinations.

In every case, it is less the experience itself than the affect surrounding it which matters. Variables such as the girl's personality; her parents' ability to reassure or their tendency to overreact; the attitude of the doctors, nurses, or dentists involved are all crucial.

We will look at one of the above-mentioned factors, tampon usage, in some greater detail because this is one of the most common predisposing events in the histories of women with vaginismus.

When tampon insertion is unusually difficult or impossible or when it is associated with pain the girl will miss out on most of the opportunities for positive learning and will, at the same time, incorporate negative ideas about her vagina. Girls who try repeatedly to insert a tampon, but continue to fail (often in spite of very determined efforts and the assistance of an older sister or friend), tend to believe that they are not anatomically normal. At pubarche (the time at which the earliest pubertal changes begin), the vagina and uterus are small structures, not very changed from their earlier size. By the time of menarche, enlargement has begun, but the vagina is still smaller than it will eventually be at the end of the teenage years. Thus, if a girl tries to insert a tampon in the first year or so of her periods, she may have difficulty because of the small size of the vagina. At a later time there may be so much apprehension and tension associated with the attempts at insertion that, in addition to ordinary difficulties such as correct angling, the girl's pubo-coccygeus muscles may involuntarily tighten, making the vaginal opening too small for the tampon to enter. This is an early experience of vaginismus; in the histories taken from women with the problem of vaginismus, difficulty with tampon insertion is frequently elicited (Sarrel and Sarrel 1984).

Sometimes a girl will be able to insert her first tampon with relative ease but when she tries to remove it, it seems to be stuck. In pulling more strenuously the tampon comes out but she experiences very sharp pain and local bleeding. This may be caused by a strand of epithelial tissue which bisects the vaginal opening which is present in approximately 4.5 percent of adolescent females. A tampon may go in easily enough to one side of the strand but tends to push against it with attempted removal. Here the important factor is the early association between an object in the vagina and severe pain. Although it is usually only a single incident, it often has a lasting impact, perhaps because it is in the context of a new experience.

Child abuse.   The third category of childhood and adolescent experience that may predispose to vaginismus is child abuse. Professionals should inquire carefully about beatings, inappropriate and frightening sexual advances, actual molestation, or rape. Where these experiences involved vaginal penetration by finger, object, or penis, the sensitizing effect is that much greater.

Readiness for first intercourse.   In addition to fear of pain with vaginal penetration another important factor in vaginismus is conflict or ambivalence about sexual intercourse. First intercourse is a significant event, part of what has been called sexual unfolding—the process of moving toward adult sexuality. Psychological readiness for first intercourse is influenced by many variables. Some young women are still too libidinally tied to their parents and siblings to take this step which so dramatically symbolizes independence. However, their very conflict over dependence/independence may lead them to try to have intercourse only to find that the vaginal muscles make penetration impossible or difficult and painful. Other common sources of anxiety include: behavior which is contrary to strongly held cultural or religious prohibition; fear of pregnancy or venereal disease; anxiety about being discovered and reprimanded; fear of becoming promiscuous; confused sexual identity. Conflict may also derive from ambivalence about the immediate situation, for example, lack of privacy.

Interpersonal conflict.   Interpersonal conflict may also be a factor in vaginismus. The symptom may appear due to anger at the partner, a power struggle between partners, specific resentment about being "used" sexually by the partner, or mistrust about the partner's caring and commitment.

The partner's personality and behavior may contribute to the development of vaginismus. If he is rough, fast, insensitive, or forces intercourse, he may instill or exacerbate fear in a woman. In some cases the size of a man's penis may be a factor if the woman, already anxious about penetration, perceives him as unusually large.

In an unconsummated relationship the partner's fear of hurting and/or his own anxieties about vaginal penetration may be important etiologic factors. These men are tentative and pull back at the first sign of any anxiety in the female. The man and woman mutually reinforce one another's anxieties about intercourse.

A man's sexual dysfunction may contribute to the development of vaginismus in a partner although, more commonly, men develop erectile problems or premature ejaculation in response to the woman's vaginismus.

There is no evidence that any one personality style or psychiatric disorder predisposes a woman to vaginismus although clinical impression supports the hypothesis that anxious and fearful women are over-represented among vaginismus patients. Vaginismus may also be associated with psychotic delusions about vaginal penetration by disembodied penises, with phobic anxiety syndrome, and hypochondriasis. Since vaginismus is so often secondary to organically caused dyspareunia, it is not surprising that it occurs in women who have no diagnostic psychiatric disorder.

Diagnosis

The diagnosis of vaginismus is made through history taking and physical examination. The history may elicit a description of differing degrees of vaginismus:

1. Mild vaginismus is usually described as pain or discomfort during penile insertion (often said to be a burning sensation) which subsides after 30 to 60 seconds, although the pain or discomfort may continue throughout intercourse and some soreness may persist afterwards.
2. Moderate vaginismus involves pain or discomfort as in mild vaginismus plus difficulty inserting the penis, which may only partially penetrate the vagina.
3. Severe vaginismus is present when muscle spasm is so severe that any kind of vaginal penetration is impossible and pressure against the opening is painful.

The history often includes a complaint of vaginal dryness which may be due to complete lack of arousal or to the trapping of vaginal lubrication behind the tensed orifice. Once the penis (or a finger) has penetrated, lubrication is often found within the vaginal barrel.

Although, as described in DSM-III-R, vaginismus ordinarily involves tensing of muscles in only the outer third of the vagina, there are cases in which other pelvic muscles caused deeper vaginal contractions as well. It is helpful to understand this phenomenon, which can be observed during pelvic examination, but it does not alter treatment.

The majority of women with vaginismus have it in response to all attempts at vaginal penetration whether by a penis, tampon, finger, or speculum. However, it is sometimes situational. It may be present with one partner but not another. Spasm may be present only in sexual situations or in non-sexual ones as well.

Vaginismus may be primary (life-long) or secondary (acquired). Women with primary vaginismus have always had muscle spasm and difficulty with penetration starting with their first intercourse experience. Women with secondary vaginismus have previous histories of non-painful intercourse typically followed by experiences of pain due to organic causes which in turn have led to the development of muscle spasm. Secondary vaginismus may reflect conflict in a relationship as well as a wide variety of intrapsychic causes (Fertel 1977; Fordney 1978; Masters and Johnson 1970). There are certain points in the life cycle when women are more vulnerable to developing vaginismus. For example in the postpartum months (Sarrel and Sarrel 1984) and at the time of menopause (Sarrel and Whitehead 1985).

On physical examination, the muscle contraction is usually elicited by the examiner's approaching the patient and placing his or her hand on the inner aspect of the patient's thigh or by touching anywhere in the genital area. The patient herself is often completely unaware that this contraction is taking place but she can see it for herself in a hand-held mirror.

The physical examination and diagnosis is also the first step in treatment. Wherever possible the woman's sexual partner should be present for this examination. For the partner, seeing the vaginismus response elicited by the doctor's approach helps to allay his feelings of personal rejection. In cases where there is pronounced vulvitis he is often amazed to see the extent of reddening and obvious soreness and this too is helpful. From a vague and amorphous problem which has often been interpreted as "psychological" or interpersonal, the difficulty can be seen as having a genuine physical basis, albeit with important psychological and interpersonal aspects.

Treatment

The literature describes several approaches to the treatment of vaginismus—surgery, the use of drugs for relaxation, hypnosis, psychodynamic and other types of psychotherapy, and vaginal dilators (Abarbanel 1978; Bancroft 1983; Fuchs et al. 1978; Leiblum et al. 1980). The use of surgery is not recommended except in the rare instances of a very thick, tight hymen. Even then, dilators may be preferable because they do not cause yet another sensitizing trauma to the vaginal entrance. Hypnosis and the use of drugs to induce relaxation can succeed on their own or in combination with behavioral treatment using dilators.

Psychotherapy alone may be effective if the causal factors are intrapsychic or interpersonal and if the woman does not have a deeply entrenched fear that penetration will hurt.

Symptom focused behavior therapy, utilizing dilators or fingers to systematically desensitize the woman to vaginal penetration, is very often all that is required to treat vaginismus successfully. Where the primary factor is fear of painful penetration, this approach is well-justified. Generally one uses the approach of treating the symptom unless and until resistance is encountered and, at the point of resistance, using psychotherapeutic tools to uncover and/or bypass the resistance.

Dilators are probably the most widely used treatment modality for vaginismus. Vaginismus does not require anatomical stretching of tissues. The dilators are simply a tool used to eliminate fear of penetration and to recondition the learned reaction of muscle tightening in response to this fear. By starting with a small pre-lubricated dilator a woman can experience vaginal penetration which is comfortable and entirely under her control. Therapy is designed to facilitate relaxation, via general relaxation training. She may be instructed to tense and relax her vaginal muscles voluntarily several times before attempting insertion. Insertion should be slow and gentle and must not proceed if there is any pain. If there is pain, she should stop and try again later. When insertion has been accomplished, the dilator should be left in place for 45 minutes without movement.

After becoming comfortable with the first dilator and using it four to seven times, she proceeds to the next size. She prepares, as above, but in addition, she inserts the first dilator for approximately thirty seconds just prior to inserting the second. At each step, the one-step-smaller dilator is used in this preparatory fashion.

Dilators may be used in the presence of the sexual partner but the woman must feel in total control of the penetration experience. By the time she gets to the third or fourth dilator, a woman may want to allow her partner to insert the dilator some of the time. If the partner is willing to accept her being in control of the situation, this may work well.

During the weeks when dilator treatment is in progress, there should be no other vaginal penetration (including tampons, if they elicit muscle tensing). The transition to intercourse should involve the female-above position and the same principles as dilator insertion, i.e., the woman is in control and she is not to allow penetration if there is pain.

The majority of reports in the literature which describe combining some kind of progressively graded vaginal insertion with psychotherapeutic support are extremely optimistic about treatment outcome, most stating success in all or almost all cases (Fuchs et al. 1978; Lazarus 1980; Leiblum et al. 1980; Masters and Johnson 1970). It is the rare case of vaginismus which cannot be treated successfully. When failure occurs, it is usually due to premature termination and/or the fact that there are other sexual problems complicating the picture—either in the woman or her partner.

Although the treatment of vaginismus is usually successful, it is not always easy. Therefore, it is appropriate to discuss some commonly encountered resistances and suggest strategies for overcoming them.

1. Inability to relax. Many women with vaginismus are tense persons with generalized muscle tension, including their vaginal muscles. The following may be helpful in these cases: systematic relaxation training, yoga or transcendental meditation, decreasing life stresses, warm baths, music or other environmental soothers, avoiding dilator insertions when generally tense, Kegel exercises, relaxing imagery, and anxiety-reducing medication.

2. Resistance to all "homework." This may be due to fear of failure, in which case increased support and encouragement from the therapist and the partner are called for. Global resistance may be due to resisting authority in which case paradoxical suggestions such as, "Don't do any homework this week. It is too much for you," is sometimes useful.

3. Resistance associated with use of dilators. Some women cannot progress in treating vaginismus because they have neurotic fantasies of damaging themselves with dilators. Fears about infection or tearing vaginal tissues are not uncommon sources of resistance. These fears must be delineated and countered, if possible. Some women find the sexual arousal they experience with dilation to be frightening or objectionable. These feelings need to be dealt with before they can progress. Using dilators may arouse suppressed or repressed feelings, e.g., rage at her husband's abuse as she tries to insert the dilator. The therapist can utilize this reaction to help her recognize her anger. It is also not unusual for dilator insertion to trigger repressed memories of genital trauma. In many instances, after recall of the repressed event, the treatment proceeds smoothly.

4. Partner undermines therapy. As a woman begins to have success inserting dilators, her partner's anxieties may intensify. He may become anxious about her increasing autonomy and assertiveness and/or about her potential sexual "demands" once she can have comfortable penetration. In fact, at this point in therapy one is often

reminded of Masters and Johnson's principle that there is no such thing as an uninvolved partner, as a longstanding but unrecognized male dysfunction becomes apparent.

Chapter 210

Premature Ejaculation and Inhibited Male Orgasm

Through the centuries, there has been so much spotlight on erectile disorders that those of ejaculation have received limited attention. While erectile difficulties may be devastating to a man's sexual self-esteem, difficulties due to ejaculation can be frustrating to him as well as his partner. Persistence of ejaculatory symptoms not uncommonly (often needlessly) lead to erectile problems followed by sexual disinterest— quite literally a complex "giving up" syndrome to be disentangled by the clinician. Another feature is that many men with severe recurrent premature ejaculation, lacking a sexual vocabulary, label it as a "touch of impotence." Too often this is accepted by the clinician without further history taking.

The professional's challenge will be to seek the chronology or sequence of the sexual symptoms. Depending on the sophistication of the patient and the geographical setting, the patient may or may not have been to a specialist urologist for a thorough evaluation of his genital function. He may need such a referral so that the psychiatrist is sure there is no somatic pathology. If there is, the patient can be assisted to understand and adjust to the physical realities. Modified sex therapy may be incorporated when so indicated by the physical findings.

Ejaculation

The actual process of ejaculation involves two phases (Figure 1). The first, emission, consists of the filling of the prostatic urethra with sperm and seminal fluid, from the ampullae of the vasa and the seminal vesicles. The emission results from the smooth muscle contractions in these structures as well as in the prostate. This creates a "pressure chamber" (Newman et al. 1982) dilation of the prostatic urethra under high pressure, causing the man's normal feeling of impending ejaculation. During emission, both the proximal smooth muscle (bladder neck) and the distal striated muscle

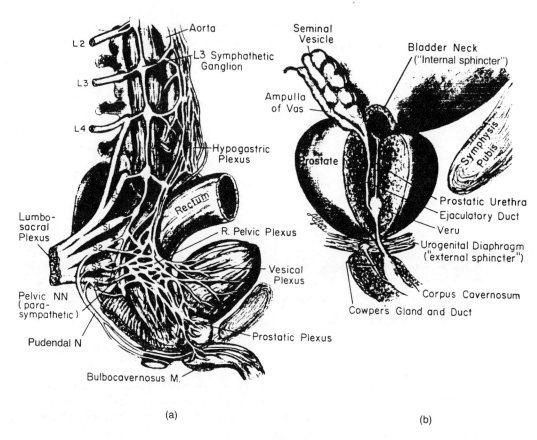

(a)   (b)

Figure 1. Composite Picture of Nerves and Close-up of Seminal Vesicles. (a) Anatomy of the nerve supply to the male genitourinary structures; (b) Anatomy of the seminal tract.

urinary sphincters are tightly closed. This part of the process is mostly under alpha-adrenergic sympathetic control.

The second phase, ejaculation, consists of the propulsion of the semen out of the urethra by clonic contractions of the striated pelvic and perineal muscles, especially the bulbocavernosus and ischiocavernosus. During this phase the bulbous urethra alternately fills and enlarges and then empties forcefully. This is mostly under somatic efferent control.

Orgasm, then, is the combination of all the various muscle contractions, both smooth and striated, plus the pressure changes during emission and ejaculation. Subjectively, the pleasure of an orgasm comes from the build-up of both the pressure chamber and the tension resulting from the strong contractions of the body's striated muscles. This is accompanied by the sudden release of the high intraurethral pressure, and then the total relaxation. The orgasm can be produced by coitus, masturbation, or any other form of sex play. The emotional pleasure of the orgasm is enhanced by the closeness to the loved partner; that differentiates "making sex" from "making love" (Renshaw 1983). Details of the other body changes during all phases of sexual arousal can be found in Masters and Johnson's work (1966).

Premature Ejaculation (PE)

It is possible that the family physician, the urologist, endocrinologist, and sex therapist each see a different and selected population of men with sex problems. Table 1 describes men presenting at the small Chicago Loyola Sexual Dysfunction Training Clinic over an 11-year period (1972-1983). Most of these patients were self-referred, and nearly all the men had seen at least one or more urologists at some time before seeking sex therapy. One study of 100 selected educated white "normal" happily married couples reported that 36 percent of the men expressed dissatisfaction because they ejaculated too quickly (Frank et al. 1978).

There is little academic agreement on what constitutes premature ejaculation. Some urologists state that if the man ejaculates in less than one minute after vaginal penetration or after fewer than eight strokes, it constitutes premature ejaculation. Admitting to the difficulty of defining the syndrome of premature ejaculation due to the many sociocultural elements, the Masters-Johnson Foundation at St. Louis considers a man a premature ejaculator "if he cannot control his ejaculatory process for a sufficient length of time during intravaginal containment to satisfy his partner in at least 50 percent of their coital connections" (Masters and Johnson 1970). They also admit that this definition is not valid if his partner is non-orgasmic, but the approach was an attempt to correct a "stop-watch" concept. In their landmark study of about 8,000 men Kinsey and co-workers (1948) reported that their subjects subjectively reported an average between intromission and ejaculation of one and one-half minutes. The definition in the DSM-III-R (American Psychiatric Association 1987, p. 295) emphasizes the patient's subjective feelings of satisfaction. "Ejaculation occurs before the individual wishes it." This removes an objection to the DSM-III definition which emphasized voluntary control. The difficulty of using timing alone for diagnostic purposes highlights that this syndrome is usually noted as "relative to the partner" unless it is so severe that a man recurrently ejaculates prior to intromission. Also the emphasis is on persistence and recurrence of the symptom rather than as an occasional transient manifestation.

Sometimes a man does not consider that he has a problem with premature ejaculation. He may blame his wife for being "frigid," thinking his speediness means sexiness. He may even divorce her and search for a "more sexual" woman. Then a second or third (usually a more experienced) partner may express sexual discontent and say to him: "What's the matter with you? Why do you come so quickly?" For

Table 1. Males Presenting at a Sexual Dysfunction Clinic (n = 723)

Diagnosis	Number	Percentage
Secondary Impotence	227	31.4
Premature Ejaculation	138	19.1
PE and Secondary Impotence	60	8.3
Inhibited Sexual Desire	153	21.2
(68 also had PE or Impotence or both)		
Retarded Ejaculation	16	2.2
Primary Impotence	19	2.6
Symptom-Free (attending with symptomatic spouse)	110	15.2

the first time he may then inquire, compare, and define his rapid ejaculation as a sexual dysfunction, namely, sexual dissatisfaction is in the partner context only. It is possible that another partner may not be distressed but accepting, due to ignorance or even lack of coital interest. For him, with arousal, tension release, and relaxation the premature ejaculation may be quite ego-syntonic. Only in wanting to please his partner (by knowing what she wants) does he realize that sustaining his erection and delaying ejaculation can be enhancing to both of them.

Premature ejaculation must be examined for two distinctly different groups: 1) transient, and 2) chronic. Transient premature ejaculation may be far more common than clinicians realize simply because being transient and reversible, it is rarely reported and only distressing if it proceeds to a chronic symptom. Causes of transient PE are usually: inexperience or adolescence (non-learning); high excitement; feeling awkward or unfamiliar in a situation or with a partner; fear of being seen (motel, drive-in, back seat, living room, etc.); return after a long absence from a regular partner (continence); very infrequent coitus (less than monthly). These are emotional or interactional causes.

No specific physical factors such as infections or use of medications or street drugs are noted to be causative of PE, although very occasionally a man may say that a very cold room temperature or certain foods causing gastric distress may be related. Whether this is factual and valid would require further observation.

Reversal of transient PE is often spontaneous by a second attempt at coitus that same evening (the second erection lasts longer anyway). Diffusing tension with shared laughter; teasing ("I just couldn't wait to love you!"), relaxation; and repeating their love play and coitus in a more secure, comfortable setting later often deals with PE by focusing attention on the loved person rather than on performance.

In nearly all instances, chronic premature ejaculation is due to faulty learning (conditioned rapid responses). These stem from 1) ignorance: thinking ejaculate is pus or otherwise pathologic; not knowing about coitus and a woman's responses; 2) emotional factors: a partial list includes sexual and social inhibitions; religious or moral concerns; fear of not knowing how, or of not performing well (solo or dyadic); traumatic first experiences; fear of being discovered during coitus or of being hurt or punished; 3) interpersonal factors: fear of displeasing the partner; of being ridiculed by her or by peers; concern about impregnation or contracting venereal disease; being blamed and rejected later; being discovered and punished, etc.

Masturbation does not cause PE despite the enduring myth. No known biologic or chemical factors have as yet been shown to cause sustained recurrent premature ejaculation.

Performance failure aggravates the condition. Literally, until corrected, the worse it gets, the worse it gets. Also, sexual abstinence often makes PE worse, a truly distressing cycle for both partners.

The premature ejaculator, much as he yearns for loving sexplay, may ejaculate at the sight of his partner unclothed, may ejaculate as she embraces him, may become almost phobic about genital touch since he finds he ejaculates speedily with a partial erection or even with a flaccid penis.

Secondary impotence and/or inhibited sexual desire may follow PE and may even years later, be the only presenting complaints when sex therapy is sought. Often the early PE is forgotten or not considered relevant. It is important to elicit the history of PE since this triad of symptoms responds well to brief couples sex therapy, using the same treatment techniques as for PE.

The "frigid wife" as etiology of premature ejaculation does not hold up in clinical studies. A man with PE may indeed have a partner with primary anorgasmia—more as a coincidence than a cause. Usually the premature ejaculation preceded this union and often persists in another coupling unless treated.

Medical Work-Up

(*Note*: Not all of these are applicable in the psychiatrist's office.) For PE, the medical work-up is that routinely needed for sex therapy: a complete physical (and neurologic) examination with special attention to and explanation of the genital organs (Masters and Johnson 1970). This is called a sexological examination (touch and tell) about the penis, foreskin, scrotum, testes, vasa, pudendal innervation; position of the fingers of the partner on the frenulum and coronal ridge to teach the squeeze technique (the root or midshaft of the penis squeezed for solo practice). The sexological examination gives the patient as well as his partner basic body knowledge, permission to look, plus PE treatment directives from the physician authority: how, when, and where to touch the penis to assist sexual function (in the privacy of home).

Urine analysis, complete blood count, testosterone, prolactin, thyroid levels (and other tests) are done if indicated by findings on history or the physical exam.

If there is prolonged erectile dysfunction as well, the clinician has two options for the medical work-up: to use the first several weeks of brief sex therapy as a diagnostic test for the appearance of erotic erections, solo (with masturbatory fantasy), or during the couple's preliminary loveplay (sensate focus home exercises). If these are satisfactory to the patient and his partner, then no further lab tests are needed. If the patient cooperates sincerely with self-pleasuring and/or has loveplay erections that are lost on penetration then after six visits further tests are indicated, e.g., penile blood flow (oscillometry). The penile blood pressure is normally 80 percent that of the brachial blood pressure. Nocturnal penile tumescence (NPT) studies (also now done on day sleep for nightshift workers) can determine whether, during sleep, there are erections during the rapid eye movement (REM) phases. A simultaneous EEG reading is, therefore, as essential as the penile measurement to ensure the man has indeed attained REM phase sleep. An agitated, anxious man in the unfamilar experience of all the wires, straps, or snap gauges on his penis in a strange bed may not have REM episodes. Therefore, a "negative" (no sleep erections) may only mean no REM stage sleep. If there are REM episodes with partial erections, the difficult somatopsychic interface of emotional reaction to some organic change is there to be dealt with clinically. Sleep studies measure potency, not ejaculation.

There may be natural improvement of PE after attaining the age of 50 years. Due to arteriosclerotic changes, there is slower filling and more rapid emptying of the erect penis, yet the plateau phase of erection may be maintained for long periods for sensual pleasure if the man has learned to understand and control the sensation of ejaculatory demand (Masters and Johnson 1970).

Self-help measures for PE (often these are only partially successful, if at all) may have been distraction in fantasy (usually of non-sexual content such as sports or mathematics, etc.); visual or auditory distraction such as TV or radio during coitus (this may upset the partner unless she understands why it is used); using concurrent pain stimulus during coitus (tugging the scrotum, pinching the perineum, a full bladder, biting the tongue or lip, tugging an ear lobe are some of many reports); masturbating to ejaculation before intercourse; trying for a second coitus within hours after a PE. The latter two may be easier for a younger man, since the refractory phase may be somewhat longer for a man over 50 years. Believing in a particular local anesthetic cream on the penis is another reported self-help for PE although the majority of PE-treated report this became ineffective after one or two applications.

Understanding and controlling the ejaculatory reflex is a matter of learning for each developing adolescent. With practice of ejaculatory control, confidence occurs (like shooting a basket that makes a successful team player later). Practice of masturbation squeeze technique will lead to greater skill at extending the plateau of erection. Allowing his entire body to enjoy relaxed sensations of total body touch and closeness prevents feeling overwhelmed by focal penile stimulation and is of great help to a man with PE. Some young men deliberately practice solo at home to lessen and then regain an erection to obtain more deliberate mastery of the reflex. They are able to take pleasure in deliberately losing an erection. Many men panic at this very thought, yet it is a matter of practice with a relaxed state of mind that overcomes PE anxiety. By reading a self-help sex manual many men have learned, alone or with a partner, the penile squeeze for reversing PE (Masters et al. 1986). The experience, even enjoyment of the sustained tension (plateau), is in later days followed by relief of the ejaculatory discharge and post-climactic relaxation. This latter afterglow of togetherness is an invaluable time of great closeness and also openness for sharing positive, tender recognition. It is also a defenseless and highly vulnerable time for both. A man may be anxiously concerned that his partner be sexually satisfied too. If she realizes this, she can let him know rather than wait to be asked. If abrasive comments are exchanged in this phase, the pain may be great for both partners. If this afterplay time of optimum closeness and sharing is either not understood or not experienced due to the disappointment of PE it can become destructive due to postcoital exchange of negative comments, smoking, drinking, turning on a TV or rushing off to wash up, etc.

There may be progression from PE to impotence or to hypoactive sexual desire or to all these after some years if ejaculatory control has not been learned.

If there is emotional conflict instead of confidence, the sexually emerging young man with PE develops anxiety, fear of failure, guilt, shame, and self-blame. Even the prospect or thought of intercourse can then be upsetting, yet his thoughts are preoccupied with it. Avoidance of sexual encounters or a desperate search for "cures" may ensue—ointments, pills, mechanical devices, circumcision, alcohol, etc. Sometimes to check out "is it her (spouse) or me?" he may have an affair and be highly distressed with himself that he has taken his PE symptom with him. Moreover, discovery of infidelity, herpes, or venereal disease may then cause or aggravate a couple's marital distress.

A few pockets of contemporary physicians steadfastly refuse to recognize that PE is a valid symptom. They cite the fact that since primate males ejaculate in less than 50 seconds, both men and their partners should accept rapid ejaculation as "natural." Not considered in this hypothesis are these elements: 1) in the wild, where brief periods of estrus prevail, copulatory opportunity is limited to the strongest males, and vulnerability is highest during coitus (from competing male peers or from predators); for estrus-free humans there is unlimited potential for year-round coitus and locked doors provide greater safety than open plains or bushes; 2) the "natural" rectal sphincter reflex is conditioned in babyhood for improved learned control of fecal soiling as part of human socialization. Thousands of men through the ages have gradually learned to control their ejaculatory reflex in the interest of their sociosexual satisfaction and adjustment.

Certain cultural groups set up specific expectations for men to have coital rituals such as eating during coitus to extend the time of coital erections and delay ejaculation (Vastayana [A.D. 400] 1963). However, only a fraction of India's masses today have read the Kama Sutra, and Indian physicians report that PE is a prevalent symptom for which herbal, magic, and medical remedies are sought. Inflammation such as prostatitis or other genitourinary infections as an organic cause for chronic PE has not stood up to examination of large series of patients (Cooper 1969; Kolodny et al. 1979; Levine 1976).

Division into primary PE (life-long) and secondary PE (Munjack and Oziel 1980) where the man describes onset of PE after emotional, marital, or job problems with a previously satisfactory sexual adjustment is an approach that merits further study. It would seem to imply that PE overcome by learned control may show temporary regression under stress with return of the learned control with adaptation to the stress.

However, in 198 cases evaluated at Loyola, the history was of life-long PE. Further observation is needed to determine if secondary (and sustained) PE occurs, and, if so, how often and under what conditions.

Partner-specific PE is still described by some contemporary British professionals (Cole 1984) while secondary and partner-specific PE as a result of marital stress was noted in one text (Munjack and Oziel 1980). It may also occur with extramarital sex because of guilt.

Treatment

Phase I. Management begins with and cannot be separated from an explicit general and sexual history taking during which must be discussed: 1) the patient's reactions to the PE; 2) his first awareness of it; 3) any ridicule or negative reaction from a partner; 4) his personal or learned cultural attitudes toward a woman's role and her responses during lovemaking and coitus; 5) his responses to petting and foreplay; 6) his knowledge of the difference in the average timing between a woman's sexual arousal to climax response (about 13 minutes) and a man's sexual arousal to climax response (about 2½ minutes); 7) his masturbatory frequency, first masturbatory episode, attitude, shame, guilt, discovery, trauma, and solo experimentation to attain delay of his ejaculatory reflex; 8) his sexual fantasies, shame, guilt about them, their range, incidence, and use during masturbation and coitus; 9) his dating history, social activity, sexual approach patterns, and pre-coital preparations and thoughts (anxiety, failure fears, pregnancy worries, etc.); 10) previous help: drugs, salves, etc. Such an explicit sexual history inevitably provides basic sex education.

Phase II. Recapitulation of the pattern of the given history is an essential next step to help the PE patient to hear and help himself and to gain perspective with the physician's assistance. For example: PE is a very common problem related to anxiety and to not knowing about sexual performance. You were only 15 years and totally inexperienced when your classmates dared you for your very first try out. You were scared, the girl yelled at you, then some joker said the police were on their way. You didn't practice after that, you really didn't learn, and had years of feeling sexually inadequate and guilty. You've tried sex again and again but without new learning. You're 34 years old and this is your third marriage. But you haven't given up and still try to have intercourse. That's a good attitude.

Phase III. Reassurance is in order after the physical exam. For example, "There is hope and a strongly favorable outlook. You're healthy physically. Emotionally, you'll have to freeze the failure messages and now learn a new way to relax and to last longer."

Phase IV. The treatment options all include some practice at home. This will depend upon what the clinician can offer and the patient's relationship resources.

Solo Male Patient and Solo Therapist

After the initial interview, history, physical, sexological examination, and integrative recapitulation then five or six follow-up weekly sessions can be the contract.

Give these instructions: "On awakening, empty your bladder, return to bed. Practice a few long very slow deep breathing exercises to relax. Use sexual fantasy, then masturbate. Enjoy the erection. The moment before you have an urge to ejaculate (when you can no longer hold) squeeze firmly (not painfully) for 15 seconds at the root or on the shaft of the penis. If the urge to ejaculate comes the moment you erect, then squeeze the moment you erect. Let go after 15 seconds and about half the erection will be lost. Let it go down and feel satisfaction in your control of letting the erection go down. Experiment with an optional squeeze: with your second and third fingers squeeze firmly for four seconds between your scrotum and anus (Chang 1977). This "ancient Chinese secret squeeze" can be applied privately in any position with your non-dominant hand. Fantasize and masturbate again then squeeze either way as before. Repeat twice more then ejaculate. You will find the length of erection time gradually increases. Practice daily for about 10 days to attain skill and confidence. Practice deep slow breathing each time you get old anxieties or old failure messages creeping back. When you bathe or shower, take extra time afterwards to self-massage your whole body by hand or by towel just for sensual pleasure. Enjoy it.

Talk to your spouse or special partner about this practice prescription, if you think she'll understand. If not, then keep it private. Pleasure your partner by kissing, massaging her face and body in loving play. Then you lie supine. Non-verbally position her to sit astride on top of you. Caress her. Use your slow deep breathing exercises and relax yourself. Let the erection go down; squeeze at the root if you want to. Don't be upset if you lose an ejaculate. Use relaxed humor, go on caressing. A second erection will be harvested. Ask your partner to mount and insert the soft penis into her vagina—using saliva, baby oil, or KY jelly. This may be awkward but is possible and needs a little practice. Ask her to contract her lower circular vaginal muscles several times. This feels good for both. Relaxed deep breathing helps to extend and enjoy this experience. Continue caressing her. Using written instructions from the physician is often a great help to both partners. You can read and smile, re-reading it when you fumble. Just try again.

This is a matter of new learning. First the knowledge, then practice gives skill which gives confidence and comfort that your reflex is under voluntary control.

With partner mounted on top she can make thrusting movements. You can, moments before your ejaculatory urge, squeeze at the root of the penis, or she can do the same, or you can signal her to stop and squeeze the lower vagina tightly for 15 seconds, or she can dismount and squeeze for 15 seconds. You will lose half the erection. She mounts again to repeat the cycle.

Having humor, goodwill, and patience all help to bond you as a couple and turn the sex act into a loving exchange."

Leave an open door to return for one or two visits should the problem recur under stress. Remind him also if PE recurs to practice the slow breathing and relaxed solo squeeze exercises meantime until the appointment.

Solo Male Patients in Brief Men Sex Group Therapy

Initial individual interview history, physical and sexological examination and integrative recapitulation, then six group sessions can be the contract.

Instructions for practice at home solo and with his partner are as described above.

The men in the group meet weekly with you for an hour for six visits to discuss feelings and practical experiences. Provide clarification and sex education at each visit. The time-limited format is a deliberate attempt to provide an action-oriented behavioral approach, with a sense of community in a supportive group. The symptoms do not have to be limited to PE. Myths, "macho" attitudes, early sex pressures, and personal hurts will surface in the group. Either a male or female group leader has been successful. This modality also may be an excellent learning experience for a trainee therapist, while providing extra eyes and ears for the group leader. Termination issues must be dealt with from weeks one to six. Therefore, always leave an option to return if needed. If they wish to recontract for a further six weeks, fine. Slow breathing and relaxed squeeze exercises might be enough to use at home to reverse the anxiety, and they can be reminded to return to this step should stress cause recurrence of PE.

Couples Sex Therapy with Solo or Dual Sex Therapists

Begin with an initial individual interview, explicit history and thorough physical, then an educational sexological examination for each, done in the presence of the partner (Masters and Johnson 1970). End each session with an integrative recapitulation of their problems—physical, general, sexual and marital, and the home tasks for the coming week.

Give instructions for home loveplay and sex exercises (solo and together) as described above.

Contract for four to six weekly follow-up visits, encouring them to make the time for home pleasuring. Below is the Loyola home instruction sheet given to a couple on the first visit to take home. It may be duplicated without requesting permission.

Loyola Sensate Focus (modified from Masters and Johnson [1970])

This is a new phrase for "petting," massaging, intimate touch, foreplay, both sensual (desexualized) and sexual. Note the difference in yourself.

Sex feelings are a natural, normal, healthy part of each of us. These suggestions are for you at home. Bathe, undress totally. Lock door, phone off the hook. Music if you like it. The early emphasis is on the sensual rather than the sexual, i.e., sound, sight, smells, thoughts, taste, and touch that are pleasing to each. Freely tell your partner. Become self-aware. Relax and enjoy these sexual perceptions. Avoid, if possible, pressures of time and performance. Relax, select a preferred position. Allow each in turn to be receptive to pleasure from the giver, then switch so that the receiver may provide enjoyment in turn. Each be acutely SELF-AWARE of your feelings, both as giver and as receiver. Express your pleasure—it is a wonderful gift to your partner to know you are enjoying his or her touch, words, or sounds. If you are solo, simply use fantasy and do the same pleasuring. Being rested is preferable to being fatigued.

STEP I. (A) Face exploration, with fingertips and lips, eyes open and closed, also ears and neck. Light, firm, brush, feather, etc. Be creative.

(B) *Explore body*: Stroke lightly and firmly, massage, caress, kiss areas of pleasurable sensation on entire back, arms, chest, abdomen, legs, etc. Take turns. Guide with words, own hand, or sounds. Say how it feels. RELAX. Breathe in and out slowly. Use fantasy, enjoy.

(C) Avoid the breast and genital area. No intercourse. If arousal or erections occur, simply stop, hug. Tell your partner, embrace awhile, let the arousal subside deliberately. Then start to play again. This gets in touch with your sexual self and builds confidence.

STEP II. I(A) and (B) again. Think of last week, remind each other of pleasure areas. RELAX.

(B) Light, teasing, non-demanding genital and breast stroking. Explore, caress, massage, kiss, tell each other how it feels, verbally or non-verbally. Give the gift of a smile and sounds.

(C) No intercourse yet. Enjoy arousal, erections. Climax, if you're close. Embrace, pause. Start again.

STEP III. (A) All of Steps I and II.

(B) Male lying, female sitting facing him. Squeeze Technique: Stroke penis until he signals his point before ejaculation. Squeeze at the ridge of the tip for 15 seconds. Release, lose 30 percent erection. Wait 50 seconds. Play again to full erection. Squeeze again. Repeat four times. *Solo male*: Lie down, same steps. Squeeze root or shaft of penis for 14 seconds yourself, or with second and third fingers, squeeze firmly for 4 seconds between your scrotum and anus.

STEP IV. (A) All of Steps I and II.

(B) Female superior. Lubrication (saliva, etc.). Vaginal containment of the flaccid penis. Use lubrication. Clamp lower vaginal muscles, or either partner squeeze at the root of the penis between your bodies, or dismount and squeeze for 15 seconds, or man with second and third fingers squeeze firmly for 4 seconds between your scrotum and anus. Experiment, laugh, enjoy, relax. Then short contractions. Then sit still. Male passive, no thrusting. Be aware of your feelings each and tell. Enjoy. RELAX. Take 10 minutes. Kiss, touch, love, talk.

(C) When male ready, female begin friction movements. Find optimum position for self, each. No martyrs necessary! Savor the afterglow together.

STEP V. (A) All of Steps I, II, III.

(B) Play to intercourse and climax. Savor the afterglow.

STEP VI. Your own innovations. Don't let horseplay interfere with foreplay, loveplay, and afterplay.

Termination issues are always there to be dealt with as the patients' separation anxieties surface. Leave them the option to return for one or two visits should the symptom recur. (Many sex therapists advocate routine follow-up visits at six weeks, three months, six months, and a year later.) Tell them that a return to the relaxed Step I and II loveplay may be enough to reverse anxiety or a regression to PE.

Medication

Alcohol is perhaps the most frequently used over-the-counter antianxiety agent. However, excess use is more likely to lead to erectile problems; it is difficult to adequately titrate alcohol to reverse PE. The minor tranquilizers have been singularly unsuccessful in assisting PE. Phenothiazines, especially thioridazine, have been tested for PE since delayed ejaculation is a known side effect (Mellgren 1967). However, sustained drowsiness, lowered libido, and retrograde ejaculation make its use unreliable and undesirable (Shader 1964). Clinically, haloperidol and monoamine oxidase inhibitors (MAOI) have been noted to cause ejaculation delays. However, in a man who is non-psychotic or not depressed the use of the haloperidol has risks of dystonia while the drowsiness and dietary restrictions of the MAOI make regular use questionable. Also with sedation as possible side effects of both, general sexual arousal may be compromised. In conjunction with brief sex therapy, a three- to eight-week trial of thiothixene, 2 mg daily, may interrupt the "panic cycle" and facilitate relaxation (Renshaw 1978), and has been used with 50 highly anxious PE patients with good results.

Homosexuals and PE

Clinicians report occasionally a well-adjusted homosexual will present for help with PE due to frustration that his partner lasts longer than he does. The same procedures followed with heterosexual couples work with gay couples, and the individual homosexual can be treated with safe sex instructions in the same way too, in this AIDS era. If group therapy is available as an adjunctive method, the group should be homogeneous, that is, restricted to gay men.

Follow-Up

Even with entrenched, progressive PE of over 20 years' duration, the Loyola experience over a 12-year period is positive for immediate symptom reversal (coital satisfaction) (77 percent for PE with impotence, up to 90 percent for PE). Does PE recur and with what frequency? Some do (about 5 percent). Usually only two visits with direction to start once more with "step one" of relaxed nongenital touching has helped. Those who return are well-motivated.

Follow-up is admittedly extraordinarily difficult. Loyola has done a mail follow-up annually since 1972. A smaller and smaller percentage of replies are received with a larger and larger batch of envelopes marked "moved." Completed follow-ups are rarely matter-of-fact reports. There are two groups. Fortunately the first and largest group is highly positive. The second and smaller batch says 1) problem returned or 2) divorced (often the latter will nonetheless mention that sex remains improved although they want no more Loyola follow-ups).

Of the symptomatic males who return a negative mail follow-up, it is more likely to be one with impotence than with PE. The PE patient is much more likely to phone for a visit than to wait for the annual mail. Often a telephone directive to try two weeks again on relaxed pleasuring without coitus and an appointment in three weeks time results in a cancellation call.

If not, the approach for return of PE is to reapply the basic treatment techniques, the sex therapist working carefully to deal with his self-esteem erosion. Mention that learning can be lost as in a new language or a new skill such as piano playing.

Reassurance, more practice, and checking for relationship problems that may be of key importance will be the approach (Renshaw 1983). Ask whether the PE is serving a purpose, namely to distance him from nonsexual bedroom conflicts that arouse excess anxiety. Suggest problem solving outside the bedroom. Additional marital therapy may be indicated in some cases.

Orgasm with Flaccid Penis

Inclusion as a separate entity of this symptom is to give it credence since too few non-medical clinicians believe the patient. Orgasm with a flaccid penis is not uncommon. In a patient who has a patent urethra and seminal tract, as well as a normal bladder neck and normal sympathetic innervation of those structures, ejaculation is possible despite his inability to achieve an erection which is adequate for penetration. Various conditions that interfere with erection need not prevent spermatogenesis, seminal fluid production and secretion, or propulsion of the ejaculate if the man is motivated enough to continue participating in sexual intercourse and masturbation. The cause of the flaccidity may be organic, vascular, or neurologic; and these must be excluded first by history, examination, and lab tests. All of the etiologic considerations for impotence are relevant in the differential diagnosis.

While it is not conclusive by any means, the presence of ejaculation and orgasm with a flaccid penis, if it occurs with masturbation as well as with coitus, may be suggestive of a physiologic (organic) rather than an emotional etiology of a patient's erectile dysfunction.

If the flaccidity is present in only certain specific sexual situations, while the patient has normal erections with ejaculations at other times, then the etiology is more likely emotional or interactional. High anxiety and severe premature ejaculation are commonly antecedents to a selective or situational symptom.

The medical evaluation of this condition involves the basic work-up as for PE or erectile dysfunctions: a careful, explicit sexual and medical history; a good physical, neurological and sexological examination, and laboratory studies (Masters and Johnson 1970). Evaluation of genital blood flow and sleep tumescence may in some cases also be necessary.

If the etiology is not organic then brief sex therapy is the treatment of choice, offering the same options outlined in segment II on premature ejaculation.

Orgasm with a flaccid penis may be reversed depending on the patient and partner's more relaxed and open attitudes; their willingness to learn sensual loveplay; non-demanding genital play; enjoying and not using erections for a few weeks until control and confidence occur, then proceeding to female superior coitus.

Many patients with this problem (if it is of several years' duration) are unwilling or too anxious to be able to cooperate with such a program. They may opt to have a "quick and easy" penile prosthetic implant instead. They must be told that the prosthesis provides an artificial erection and that such surgery will have no effect on their already described powers of ejaculation and orgasm. Their coital anxiety may remain and still prevent the use of the prosthesis post-implant, especially if there are unresolved interpersonal conflicts. It would be important in such couples to consider both pre- and post-prosthesis sex therapy, rather than an either/or (surgery or sex) treatment approach.

Coitus Interruptus and Coitus Reservatus

The Latin term coitus interruptus (CI) describes a man's withdrawal from the act of intercourse as a contraceptive attempt. It is possibly the most ancient form of contraception, and is described in many cultures and recorded in Genesis 38:8–9 in the much quoted story of Onan who was instructed by God to impregnate his brother's widow so her offspring might inherit the land. However, greed (for the inheritance) obstructed obedience, he withdrew and ejaculated on the ground. His act of coitus interruptus (disobedience) cost Onan his life—he was killed instantly. Somehow this biblical story of CI became confused with punishment for masturbation. Since the 18th and 19th centuries, the term "onanism" has been used synonymously and inaccurately with masturbation, even in medical texts.

The act of coitus interruptus is still commonly used to avoid impregnation, especially by adolescents. The act, however, takes self-control, a strong body awareness, and a willingness to interrupt the rhythm of thrusting a few seconds before a man is ready to reach his orgasmic pinnacle. This too often results in forgetting his proposed caution. An inexperienced teen is flooded with sexual hormones, has a high drive, and still has rudimentary sexual learning about his point of orgasmic inevitability before which he must withdraw. For a neophyte, CI contraception may be difficult; the chances are great that he will leave some semen in the vagina.

One often quoted estimate of the effectiveness of CI as a contraceptive is 15 to 40 percent (Kolodny et al. 1979). A scientific study to verify these subjective figures would be difficult to conduct. If a couple build up high desire and both agree to use CI, it may still be quite frustrating for the partners when the vagina becomes a fleeting stimulus followed by a hasty withdrawal, a fuss about where to ejaculate, and then the worry about whether "it" (CI) was successful. Mutual closeness and caring may not be easy in such circumstances. A man who uses CI may be sensitive to his partner's incomplete sexual response and assist her to climax. If he is totally self-preoccupied she may be frustrated and upset, unless she feels free enough to complete her own stimulus to orgasm.

The clinician taking a sexual history where CI is or was used will need to be explicit in questions such as: When did you begin to use CI? Where did you hear about it? What was the first time like? How many thrusts could you make before withdrawal? How did your partner react? Do you think she had an orgasm? Did you tell her before? Did you talk about it afterwards? What did she say? How did you handle the ejaculate? Did you ever impregnate a partner using CI? How long did you continue to use CI? Do you think you learned to control yourself better? How long (now) do you think your erections last during intercourse? What other contraceptive method have you used? What was intercourse like (with other contraceptives) for you and for your partner? Did (do) you have religious concerns about using CI? Did (does) your partner have religious concerns about using CI? Do you have any questions about CI?

The concern exists that CI may actually be a factor that conditions a man to PE (Masters and Johnson 1970).

Coitus Reservatus

Coitus interruptus is not to be confused with coitus reservatus (CR) which is the opposite end of the continuum. The Latin nomenclature is all they have in common. In several cultures the ability to sustain erections for a prolonged time is considered the epitomy of virility and the mark of a great lover thus able to enhance his partner's sexual enjoyment as well as his own. In some circumstances, the pursuit of a sustained erection has taken on cultist proportions, where techniques to modulate excitement while retaining an erection were allegedly taught and learned to the point of a man's being able deliberately to ejaculate (retrograde) into his bladder. Physiologically this would entail being able to close the external sphincter while relaxing the internal (bladder neck) sphincter.

The Oneida community in its 19th century format practiced eugenics with strict rules on who could mate to pregnancy. However, members were permitted to have intercourse freely provided they used coitus reservatus (Bishop 1969; Noyes 1866). Sustaining erections was for the pleasure of both partners. Not ejaculating was for natural contraception. Oneida founder, John Humphrey Noyes, in 1844 thought his idea of "male continence" (also coitus reservatus or coitus obstructus, a synonymous term) was an original one. He also noted when he first mentioned it in print in 1866, that after 22 years of coitus reservatus practice none of the predicted negative bodily effects had been noted in his Oneida community (Bishop 1969; Noyes 1866). His was a religious sect, practicing omnigamy—all members were allowed sexual access. Since the latter practice became a legal issue, it is no longer part of contemporary Oneida community life.

In India, karezza (deliberate indefinite delay of ejaculation) represented a form of spiritual enrichment to those who practiced the technique in the 10th century. Some males claimed they attained by quiet, passive coitus a dozen sexual climaxes without ejaculation, others that they pleasurably experienced retrograde ejaculation during coitus using the karezza method, considered similar to but different from the Tao art of coitus reservatus described in an earlier century (Chang 1977).

Ancient Chinese "Bedchamber" books of the seventh century were designed as sex instructions for women and men so they might combine the inexhaustible "yin" (female essence) with the "yang" (semen). The ideal was for the man to remain intravaginally for maximum absorption of yin essence (most potent during her orgasm). Therefore, to informed Chinese men who abided by this classic Taoist belief, the woman's orgasm was as important to him as to her. There was also advice about how much semen a man could ejaculate per day, per season, per size and height. Careful instructions were given to the man so that the yang essence could ascend to and nourish his brain (coitus reservatus).

It is also noted that Arabian medicine wrote of "Imsak" or "Ismak," a practice for a man to learn to hold his ejaculate and only release biweekly no matter how often he had coitus.

In summary, it is of assistance to every clinician to have some historical background regarding the very old practice of coitus interruptus. A man skilled at coitus reservatus will prize the skill and not present with this as a complaint. His partner may if she does not understand or enjoy it. Occasionally a patient may report he has read and practiced either of these techniques. CI is to be considered in the differential diagnosis of PE and coitus reservatus in that of delayed ejaculation. Both CI and CR are deliberate practices. Questions about the aware use and the duration of use of each will assist in clinical differentiation.

Absent or Inhibited Male Orgasm, Alias Retarded Ejaculation

Incidence

There are few large series noted in the literature of persistent non-organic retarded ejaculation (RE). Masters and Johnson (1970) reported 17/510 couples with RE. Loyola

Sexual Dysfunction Clinic treated 16/723 couples with RE between 1972-1983. Others on the east and west coasts, respectively, have reported somewhat more frequent presentation (Kaplan 1974; Munjack and Oziel 1980). Transient reversible RE may be exceedingly common considering the alcohol consumption of U.S. men, most of whom make the causal connection and do not usually present for sex therapy. Needed medications may also increase the incidence of transient RE, reversible when the medication is discontinued. Both of these are chemical organic factors to be excluded before a diagnosis of recurrent non-organic RE is made. If a man prizes his RE, however, it is not wise to use a diagnostic tag since this would imply distress with a symptom.

The definition in DSM-III-R (American Psychiatric Association 1987, p. 295) is "persistent and recurring delay in, or absence of, orgasm" following an adequate phase of sexual excitement. The same individual may also meet the criteria for Male Erectile Disorder if at other times there is a problem with the excitement phase during sexual activity. In such cases, both categories of psychosexual dysfunction should be noted. The disturbance is not caused exclusively by organic factors and is not symptomatic of another clinical psychiatric syndrome.

Since the term inhibited male orgasm (IMO) is so rarely retrievable in urological or psychiatric research, or even in recent textbooks, the more commonly used synonym retarded ejaculation will be used in this chapter.

Two key elements to note in this definition are:

1) the recurrence of the symptom;
2) the cause is not exclusively organic.

Organic causes of RE can be mechanical, endocrine, neurologic, or chemical. Mechanical factors may bring about the obstruction to the flow of semen. These factors include stricture, trauma, malignancy, or benign prostatic hyperplasia. The most common clinical problem that has to be differentiated from RE is retrograde ejaculation following surgery for benign prostatic hyperplasia. Occasionally one finds congenital absence of one or all of the seminal tract structures.

Endocrine factors are mediated through a decrease in androgens or a decrease in androgen sensitivity. One example is hyperprolactinemia, the most common causes of which are medication use and prolactin-producing adenomas of the pituitary.

Neurologic factors include peripheral nerve damage through trauma or surgery or the various illnesses that may cause neuropathy, such as diabetes, uremia, and alcoholism. Spinal cord pathology may affect ejaculation and may include vascular insufficiency, neoplasia, inflammation, infection, and degenerative conditions. In a series of 50 spinal cord patients, only 20 percent reported having achieved ejaculation with intercourse at least once (Phelps et al. 1983).

With respect to cerebral factors, the temporal and frontal lobes seem to be particularly important. Patients with Parkinson's disease, for example, have difficulty with both erection and ejaculation possibly because of decreased dopamine.

Chemical factors affecting ejaculation have been discussed earlier. However, since alcohol is so important, it is worthwhile to emphasize its importance in ejaculation as well as in erection; 50 percent of alcoholic men have sexual performance problems, and 10 percent or more have inhibited or absent ejaculation (Levere and Smith 1973). The pathogenesis of erectile problems may be due to a combination of factors, such as occlusive vascular disease, peripheral neuropathy, testicular damage, or liver disease. Approximately 25 percent of patients who abstain from alcohol for about four weeks will have remission of their sexual problems without any other treatment, unless there is liver damage or other complications. One prognostic indicator is normal gonadotrophin response to pituitary stimulation with clomiphene (Van Thiel et al. 1982).

Medical Work-Up

For inhibited or absent male orgasm the basic medical protocol is followed as outlined in the earlier segment on premature ejaculation.

In addition, during the careful physical and sexological examination, specific added attention must be focused on: 1) liver size, the breasts for gynecomastia or galactorrohea (alcohol or drug effects, also hyperprolactinemia); 2) general and specific neurologic responses:

- Peripheral sensation to touch, pinprick and vibration will establish gross neuropathy in the lower limbs. Nerve conduction may be measured.
- Perianal saddle area must also be checked for touch and pinprick.
- The mucocutaneous junction touched with a pin should result (during a rectal) in a brisk anal sphincter contraction on the examiner's finger.
- A light stroke or sudden squeeze of the glans penis also normally results in quick contraction of the anal sphincter on the examining finger (bulbocavernous reflex).
- The cremasteric cutaneous reflex elevates the testis on the same side when the upper inner thigh is stimulated briskly and tests the ilioinguinal and genitofemoral nerves (from L1 and L2).
- The scrotal reflex tests the contraction of the dartos smooth muscle bundle when a cold object is applied to the scrotum—a help to evaluate the autonomic nervous system.
- Instability of sweating, temperature, lachrymation, bowels (diarrhea-constipation), and blood pressure (a drop) with postural change from lying horizontal to standing up (postural hypotension) will all provide further clues to possible autonomic nervous system problems.

Since the urinary and genital systems share a sizable amount of their innervation, difficulties related to urine control and flow must be followed with further tests such as cystometry, cystourethroscopy, or sphincter electromyography done by a urologist.

To distinguish between retarded and retrograde ejaculation, a relatively easy test may be carried out: a microscopic examination of centrifuged post-ejaculation urination (after masturbation or intercourse). If there was retrograde ejaculation, great numbers of sperm will be visualized.

To screen out possible endocrine pathology as a cause for absent ejaculation, serum prolactin, testosterone, and luteinizing hormone levels must be done. Thyroid and adrenal function tests may be needed, especially if there is also a reported libido loss and other suggestive symptoms. Macro or micro pituitary tumors may be a cause of absent libido and absent ejaculation. Positive findings require referral for further work-up (x-rays, CAT scan, etc.) and long-term medical or surgical treatment which may reverse the sexual symptoms. In some cases additional brief sex therapy may assist general and marital adjustment for both partners.

If cirrhosis is suspected as causing some of the physical findings then blood tests for liver function tests will be indicated.

For a man who complains of absent ejaculation, although his gross general physical exam reveals no pathology, but by history is clinically depressed, has renal or hepatic problems, or is on long-term phenothiazine maintenance for psychiatric reasons or for pain control, a blood prolactin is indicated since these factors can cause hyperprolactinemia that may contribute to the sexual problem. Reduce, remove, or change medication to see whether this has a positive effect on the ejaculation problem (Dela Fuente and Rosenbaum 1981).

A careful repeat history taking regarding alcohol, medications, over-the-counter and street drugs is worthwhile because on a second or third visit the patient may be more honest and open. Correlating the possible sexual side effects of alcohol and/or medication is important patient education.

When the medical work-up is completed, a working diagnosis of organic, psychogenic, or "a little of both" will assist further management. Progression of RE (psychogenic inhibited orgasm) with age is not specifically reported in the literature. Reported experimentation and ejaculatory success with a different partner is difficult to assess without validation from that partner. If accurate, help the patient to understand the disinhibiting factors that have freed him of his symptoms. He may thus be able to succeed with marital coitus.

Retarded ejaculation (RE) or involuntary delay is a diagnosis to be made by exclusion of deliberate control (coitus reservatus or obstructus) or of organic pathology. What are the possible underlying features of psychogenic RE? Some may relate to sexual inhibitions, to anxiety that sex is dirty (ejaculate seen as messy) or sinful, or fear of urinating during coitus (sometimes with early enuresis history). Some men have, in religious instruction, learned that it is a venial sin to masturbate short of ejaculation, but a mortal sin to go all the way, thus programming themselves for RE. In others, the anxiety may be about parenting, with fear of pregnancy. The financial or emotional cost of child rearing is one of several areas where he finds it difficult to "let go"—of his money, of his time, of his control, of his habits, and of his ejaculate. For many persons early sexually restrictive rearing may relate to current difficulty with fully allowing himself to enjoy, to play, to be deserving of sexual relaxation, or to be emotionally close to his partner. RE is sometimes seen in men with severe fears of intimacy and/or loss of control. Severe interpersonal conflict may result from RE, as the wife struggles with self-blame or feels anxious when unable to find an answer to their sexual questions. At times she may be even more upset than he about the RE. Educating her will greatly reduce her anxiety and allow a better clinical assessment of how to direct the relationship and provide needed sex therapy.

Couples Sex Therapy with Solo or Dual Sex Therapists

Begin with an initial individual interview, explicit history, and thorough physical then an educational sexological examination for each, done in the presence of the partner (Masters and Johnson 1970). End each session with an integrative recapitulation of their problems—physical, general, sexual and marital, and the home tasks for the coming week.

Give instructions for home loveplay and sex exercises.

Contract for four to six weekly follow-up visits, encouraging them to make the time for home pleasuring. Give them permission to enhance affectionate and sexual fantasies and feelings. The home instruction sheet is given to a couple on their first visit to take home. They are asked to follow all the steps except the squeeze technique (unless they would like to try it for fun or novelty). When the male feels ready in Step V, he is told to relax as completely as possible and his partner (on top) to "ride" as vigorously as possible. The sexual role reversal of passive-receptive male and active female is discussed beforehand. Also the possible "blocks" regarding sinfulness, sharing, closeness, pleasing his partner, parenting (impregnation), or other fears are to be explored and dealt with in the visits preceding their trial of Step V. Self-relaxation and slow breathing are discussed. "Think of floating or gliding" are other relaxation helps. In the Loyola seven-week program, 11 of 16 RE men allowed themselves to let go and ejaculate, first by his partner's manual stimulation, then intravaginally at least once in week 6 or 7. There was great relief in the successful ones, optimism in the other five, but they did not keep their scheduled follow-up. Only four of the 11 men with RE reversal responded to long-term mail follow-up and these had sustained improvement.

Some programs use a more elaborate and slower program but no outcome statistics are given (Munjack and Oziel 1980). Individual psychotherapy for men whose RE is part of a distancing operation is recommended by others.

Medications of a specific nature may or may not be successful (see Chapter 214). The short-term use of a small dose of an anxiolytic used an hour pre-coitus may be of possible help to the man so fearful that slow breathing and relaxation cannot settle him. Once he has "broken through the barrier" and ejaculated coitally, his anxiety should be allayed.

Ejaculatory Pain

The scientific literature is replete with hypotheses, analyses, and case reports about the neurophysiologic and psychological aspects of pain. This symptom is so subjective a perception that each patient, depending on his medical condition and his emotional state, will experience and react to similar stimuli in very different ways. Thresholds of pain appreciation may cause one patient great disability while another patient may be barely conscious of a particular pain. Complicating this picture even further is the emotionally charged issue of sexuality and ejaculation. When sex is involved, a sensation that may otherwise be overlooked can conceivably be magnified due to strong personal emotional factors.

All of the factors mentioned under delayed ejaculation must be known—how often he ejaculates with coitus, conflicts about parenting, onset, and inter-partner variation. Painful ejaculation may have many causes. It also may be perceived in many different locations in the body and described as "tearing," "burning," "throbbing," "sore," "shooting," "shifting," "deep," "like ice," "heavy," "uncomfortable," "spasmodic," and just plain "painful." The location of ejaculatory pain may be perplexingly noted as: the urethra, glans penis, perineum, rectum, buttocks, testicle, whole penis, suprapubic area, extremities, chest, and even the head. The timing of the pain—before, beginning of, midway, and after ejaculation—may assist the clinician to establish whether the cause is peripheral (meatus, urethra) or deeper (prostate, seminal vesicles) or other (vas, anal fissures, muscles, sciatica, etc.). Bowel habits may be related; one patient connected a long period of chronic constipation to post-ejaculatory pain. The pain was totally relieved when a daily regimen of roughage in his diet was followed.

Various medications have been reported to be associated with painful ejaculation. Pain on ejaculation was described after taking the following: imipramine—midshaft penile pain; protryptyline—pain in the glans penis; desmethylimipramine—deep perineal pain plus urethral burning (Simpson et al. 1965). Kotin et al. (1976) described sexual problems in 60 percent of patients taking thioridazine, of whom 49 percent had difficulties with ejaculation; two patients (3.5 percent) complained of pain at the time of ejaculation: one had suprapubic pain and the other claimed that he "felt like his legs and muscles were being pulled apart." Interestingly, one of the authors took 50 mg of thioridazine orally once and masturbated four hours later. He experienced a "tearing suprapubic pain at orgasm and had no seminal fluid to ejaculate." The authors postulated that this effect could be due to specific alpha adrenergic blockage of the genitourinary system with no other sympatholytic side effects.

Amoxapine also has been implicated as a cause of painful ejaculation. One patient claimed to have slow, painful muscle contractions during ejaculation "with persisting n uscle tension for several hours," while another patient reported "abnormally protracted, spasmodic ejaculation" that he characterized as painful and burning (suprapubic); occasionally, the pain radiated to his testicle (Kulik and Wilbur 1982; Schwarcz 1982). The proposed mechanism of action is an inhibition of nonadrenalin uptake and, therefore, potentiation of its effects. This may interfere with the coordinated contractions of the seminal tract smooth muscle, causing "painful spasticity." Not all drugs of the same class and action have been associated with such painful symptoms. Thus, the full explanation of the ejaculatory pain is still unknown.

Trifluoperazine and haloperidol are additional medications that have been reported to cause painful ejaculation; one patient reported "deep, sharp pain" when his muscles contracted during orgasm" (Berger 1979).

Urethral pain on ejaculation may be caused by prostatitis (a relatively common cause of transient ejaculatory pain); benign prostatic hyperplasia (BPH); urethral obstruction (benign or malignant); and urethritis (itself having many causes). Rectal and perineal ejaculatory pain also can be caused by both BPH and seminal vesiculitis. Patients with epididymitis and vasitis may experience scrotal or inguinal pain upon ejaculation. Some patients complain of painful ejaculation after vasectomy. The cause is thought to be either inflammation of the spermatic nerve if the pain is associated with a sperm granuloma (Shapiro and Silber 1979) or "congestive epididymitis" if there is no sperm granuloma (Schmidt 1979). Treatment involves vasovasostomy or draining the stump of the vas that is still in continuity with the epididymis (Edwards and Erry 1982). Occasionally patients will complain of painful ejaculation (mostly rectal and urethral) after prostatectomy for benign disease. It is thought that post-surgical ejaculatory duct obstruction may be the cause.

Other Types of Coital Pain

Patients with severe cardiac or pulmonary disease may experience symptoms of chest pain or shortness of breath during intercourse and during the heightened excitement of climax may have particularly intense chest pain. The same may be true with patients suffering from painful chronic musculoskeletal or neurologic conditions. If general body pain does not interfere with their ability to achieve erection, it may heighten at the time of ejaculation, yet for many men the pleasure of closeness and sexual release is an affirmation of vitality and virility, so they continue their sex life despite the pain. For a man who has sex inhibitions or interpersonal conflict, the pain may be a welcome reason to avoid all sexual or affectionate contact.

"Orgasmic cephalgia" is a very interesting phenomenon. One type of this head pain is bilateral, dull, and secondary to normal generalized orgasmic contraction of the neck and facial muscles. A second type of orgasmic headache is described as explosive, throbbing, and unilateral, occurring before or right at the time of ejaculation. These seem to be more common in men but may occur in both sexes. The headache does not occur in the affected individual with every coital event; it is random but more likely to occur at times of increased stress such as during "illicit activity" and at high altitudes (Appenzeller et al. 1979). The pain is associated with increase in heart rate and blood pressure. If sexual activity is terminated at the beginning of the headache then the head pain generally subsides in a few minutes. If orgasm is achieved, then the headache may persist for several hours. Some of these patients also have a history of migraine headaches.

Ordinarily, orgasmic cephalgia is considered a benign condition. More serious problems may become apparent during orgasm, however. Congenital aneurysms of the brain can rupture (subarachnoid hemorrhage) during the stress of sexual activity, a cause of sudden death (Lundberg and Osterman 1974). Cerebral ischemia as well as aortic ischemia may be manifested by coital headaches (Levy 1981; Staunton and Moore 1978). If orgasmic headaches become persistent, regularly recurrent, associated with vomiting or other neurologic symptoms or signs, then careful medical investigation is indicated.

The pathophysiology of coital headaches is not fully understood. Many believe that it is a vascular phenomenon (Paulsen and Klawans 1974), which may or may not be associated with a neurohumoral influence (Levy 1981). The treatment of benign coital cephalgia is first a trial of muscle self-relaxation techniques or a small dose of a minor tranquillizer pre-coitally if the headache appears to be of the tension type. If these are unsuccessful, a small pre-coital dose of propranolol, a beta-adrenergic blocker, is successful in many patients, suggesting that the headache and the sympathetic nervous system may be related. The lowest possible dose of any medication must be prescribed because it may cause difficulties with the patient's ability to achieve an erection.

Chapter 211

Male Erectile Disorder

Prevalence

There is minimal evidence concerning the prevalence and natural history of male erectile disorder in the human.

Frank et al. (1978) in a questionnaire survey of volunteer married couples reported that 7 percent of the males (average age 36) complained of difficulty obtaining erections. Nine percent reported difficulty maintaining an erection. Nettelbladt and Uddenberg (1979) reported similar findings in an interview study of a representative sample of 58 Swedish married men with an average age of 31. Seven percent of this sample reported chronic erectile problems. In a questionnaire study of British university students, Eysenck (1976) found that 42 percent of the males who were sexually experienced reported at least one incident of erectile failure. Segraves et al. (1982)

examined the spontaneous remission rates in 66 men complaining of erectile failure who refused psychiatric treatment of the symptoms. At one year follow-up, nine (14 percent) were asymptomatic without formal treatment. This group of men was approximately 50 years old and had been symptomatic for over one and one-half years prior to seeking medical consultation. A subsequent study (Segraves et al. 1985a) found a spontaneous remission rate of 30 percent in men with psychogenic impotence who refused psychiatric treatment.

The prevalence of erectile dysfunction in certain medical subpopulations exceeds that of the general population. Recent surveys by various investigators suggest that the prevalence of impotence in diabetics approaches 50 percent (Ellenberg 1971; Kolodny et al. 1974; Rubin and Babott 1958; Rundles 1945; Schoffling et al. 1963). Other medical conditions with a high prevalence of erectile disturbance include renal failure (Bonner et al. 1975; O'Brien et al. 1975; Salvatierra et al. 1975; Schmitt et al. 1968), multiple sclerosis (Ivers and Goldstein 1963; Lilius et al. 1976; Vas 1969), and arterial hypertensive disease (Bulpitt and Dollery 1973; Segraves 1977). Slag et al. (1983) reported the results for a survey of 1,180 outpatients at the Minneapolis Veterans Administration Medical Center. In this sample of men with an average age of 59, 401 (34 percent) were found to be impotent.

Erectile function is the end product of complicated, interactive biologic and psychological influences, and erectile failure can have its etiology in a myriad of biologic and psychological systems. Although the actual percentage of patients with biogenic impotence presenting for psychiatric treatment is probably low (Segraves et al. 1981a) (this is still controversial—see chapter on Drug Therapy), the psychiatric clinician needs to be certain that an adequate biomedical assessment has been performed before embarking on the psychiatric treatment of these syndromes. The necessary evaluation required to ascertain if the difficulty is psychogenic in etiology has been reviewed in previous chapters in this text. It is important for the clinician to realize that all cases cannot be neatly dichotomized into biogenic and psychogenic etiologies. Many patients have mixed etiologies and require special treatment considerations.

Etiology

Most of the current treatment formats for the therapy of erectile disorder are based on assumptions regarding the etiology of this syndrome.

The predominant theoretical hypotheses concerning the pathogenesis of erectile failure can be grouped into psychodynamic, behavioral, and systems approaches. Psychodynamic theorists have tended to emphasize the role of underlying unconscious conflicts in the genesis of erectile problems and have hypothesized that erectile failure is often a manifestation of a generalized personality problem (Reynolds 1981). Unresolved oedipal conflicts and anger toward women have been two commonly expressed hypotheses (Noy et al. 1966). Behavioral therapists have hypothesized that learned anxiety maintained by current environmental stimuli is the major etiologic variable (Dengrove 1971). These approaches tend to focus on direct modification of the presenting symptom without consideration of individual or couple psychodynamics. Masters and Johnson's (1970) therapeutic approach, with its emphasis on decreasing "performance anxiety" (fear of inadequate performance) and "spectatoring" (obsessive self-observation), is behavioral in its treatment focus. The prescribed sexual homework assignments are clearly analogous to the behavioral therapy technique of in vivo desensitization (Murphy and Milulas 1974). Marital therapists have emphasized that sexual problems are often a manifestation of underlying couple dynamics (Segraves 1982). In a comprehensive review of the literature concerning factors in male sexual inadequacy, Cooper (1969a) emphasized that there is minimal firm evidence to support any of the hypotheses concerning psychological causation of erectile problems. "In most cases, etiological generalizations have been made on inadequate nonspecific data, often derived from single or a few case studies. Another serious criticism related to interpretation of observations, for example, that anxiety, hostility, and disgust coexist with other such factors or a functional psychosis might coexist with a potency disorder is incontestable, but to assume causality may only rarely be admissible; more often these may be its consequence or a mere coincidence" (Cooper 1969, 337). Cooper also emphasized that the current conceptualization of sexual disorders as psychosomatic exists in the absence of supporting empirical investigation.

The prevailing view among clinicians experienced in the treatment of psychogenic erectile problems is that this disorder does not have a universal pathogenesis (Kaplan 1974; Kolodny et al. 1979; Levine 1984; Segraves et al. 1985b). This clinical impression is supported by the failure of clinical investigation to find a reproducible personality profile descriptive of men with psychogenic erectile failure (Segraves et al. 1981b).

Anxiety as a Final Common Pathway

Most contemporary clinicians assume that anxiety associated with coital attempts (performance anxiety) is the final common pathway by which a multiple of psychological influences interrupt the erectile process (Levine 1985). If this anxiety is severe enough to distract the man from the usual sexual stimuli which elicit erections, impotence results. A self-perpetuating mechanism has been described by numerous clinicians (Segraves 1978). After the initial erectile failure, a vicious cycle of performance anxiety contributing to future erectile failure is possible. The man may become so anxious about erectile failure at his next intercourse opportunity that he is too anxious to become sexually aroused and consequently does not have an erection. He will then become even more anxious on future coital opportunities. This cycle has also been described as a self-reinforcing mechanism (Arentewicz and Schmidt 1983) or a demand-negative expectancy cycle (Beck et al. 1983). Factors maintaining the cycle include self-monitoring (spectatoring); an expectation of failure; and, to various degrees, the partner's reaction.

Some evidence suggests the importance of coital anxiety in psychogenic impotence. Cooper (1969b) found that 94 percent of patients with male potency disorders reported anxiety related to the act of coitus. Fear of failure was the most frequent specific anxiety reported. In a study of four groups of men, those with psychogenic erectile problems, normals, men with organic impotence, and men with premature ejaculation, Kockott and associates (1980) reported that men with psychogenic impotence reported the highest sexual anxiety and exhibited sexual avoidance behavior. In a study of the effect of attentional focus on erectile response, Beck et al. (1983) measured penile circumference changes during erotic film presentation in normals and in men with erectile problems. Two different instructional sets were utilized: in one the subject was asked to focus on the women in the film; in the other, on the man. Sexually dysfunctional men, as compared with controls, had less erectile response to highly erotic material when instructed to focus on the female. Post-session interviews indicated that many of these men reported that when their sexual partners are highly aroused, they feel great pressure to perform.

A study by Sakheim et al. (1984) offers partial support to the role of "spectatoring" in maintaining psychogenic impotence. They reported that observing one's own state of erectile turgidity inhibited the erectile response only at states of low to moderate arousal. Under conditions of high arousal, self-observation augmented the erectile response. These results were interpreted as indicating that focusing on minimal erectile response under conditions of low arousal may decrease arousal whereas focusing on one's erection under states of high arousal may facilitate greater arousal.

Even if one assumes that coital anxiety is the major mechanism underlying erectile failure, one still wonders why the self-reinforcing mechanism remains operative in some men and not others. Presumably, many men have episodic erectile failure without progressing to persistent failure. Similarly, the effectiveness of behavioral sex therapy with its focus on decreasing coital anxiety does not prove that anxiety was the etiologic factor.

Clinical Subgroups

Men with inhibited sexual excitement are an extremely heterogeneous population (Segraves et al. 1981b). The presence of psychogenic erectile problems appears to be related to a variety of causes ranging from individual psychopathology to marital discord in otherwise healthy individuals. In some men, the onset of impotence appears to be clearly related to an identifiable psychosocial stress such as widowhood, divorce, or the death of a child or parent. Efforts to identify etiologic factors are unlikely to be successful until we achieve some meaningful subdivision of this clinical position.

Primary Impotence

Masters and Johnson (1970) suggested that impotence be subdivided into primary and secondary subtypes. Primary impotence was the term employed to describe men who had never been coitally successful; secondary impotence referred to erectile failure in men with at least one coital success. Clinical experience suggests that this subdivision into primary and secondary subgroups is meaningful if one uses age or chronicity modifiers to limit the diagnosis of primary impotence to men with chronic erectile failure (i.e., excluding young males with transitory anxiety and erectile failure during initial attempts at coitus). Treatment success rates are generally lower in men with primary impotence (Glover 1983) and associated psychiatric disorder is more common in this group of patients (Levine 1985). Schiavi et al. (1984) recently reported that patients with primary impotence differed from those with secondary impotence on nocturnal penile tumescence and sleep-hormonal parameters. Men with primary impotence spent significantly less time at full or nearly full tumescence during sleep and did not demonstrate the significant increases in testosterone during rapid eye movement sleep and during full tumescence noted in normals and men with secondary impotence. This finding is interesting in view of an earlier report by Johnson (1965b) that men with early onset impotence (primary impotence) have marked tendencies toward gynandromorphy (femaleness) in skeletal structure.

Secondary Impotence

There is suggestive evidence that secondary impotence can also be meaningfully subdivided. One suspects that men with a history of recurrent episodes of erectile failure are distinct from patients presenting with a single period of erectile failure. In patients with recurrent bouts of erectile failure, the likelihood of characterologic issues, constitutional factors, or marital conflict being operative is high. In patients with a single bout of impotence and good premorbid sexual function, a causation in the immediate past or present is more likely. Early childhood trauma and other putative psychiatric variables are less likely to be a factor if the man performed successfully for a long period of time before becoming symptomatic.

There is also suggestive evidence that secondary impotence may be meaningfully subdivided in terms of symptom onset and duration. Patients with an acute onset of symptoms preceded by a clear precipitant have been reported to have more favorable outcomes to a variety of interventions than patients with insidious onsets to their difficulties (Ansari 1976; Cooper 1969c; Johnson 1965b). It appears that the onset of impotence in a man with good premorbid sexual function is often related to unrecognized affects associated with a major life change (Levine 1985). For example, erectile concerns and difficulties are quite common in widowed or divorced men and may indicate an unresolved grief reaction or ambivalence about reattachment. Another common precipitant is a change in the marital situation. Many men fail to consciously appreciate changes in the interpersonal milieu which affects the overall attractiveness of the spouse. Chronicity of the complaint may also affect treatment responsivity. Impotence of a briefer duration (for example, three years or less) has a much more favorable prognosis than chronic impotence (Cooper 1969c; Cooper 1971; Johnson 1965b; Segraves et al. 1982).

The importance of this section on subtypes is the possibility that differential responses to treatment are dependent upon the clinical presentation. In other words, a first bout of psychogenic erectile failure in a man with good premorbid sexual function is very likely to respond to brief symptom-oriented therapy. If the symptom is of brief duration and the onset was abrupt, the prognosis is further improved. At the other end of the spectrum, primary impotence, recurrent erectile problems, problems of insidious onset, and problems of long duration are less likely to respond to brief directive therapy without the inclusion of other treatment techniques.

Treatment

The efficacy of behavioral sex therapy is fairly well established for most of the psychosexual disorders (Marks 1981). However, the effectiveness of such treatment approaches for inhibited sexual excitement in the male is not as clearly established, and varying success rates have been reported in the literature. Although several authors have reported high success rates using symptomatic treatment approaches (Arentewicz and Schmidt 1983; Masters and Johnson 1970), other investigators have reported less encouraging results. Everaerd (1977) reported minimal effects of behavioral sex therapy on reversing erectile complaints. Similarly, Heiman and LoPiccolo (1983) reported that behavioral sex therapy did not produce symptom remission to a statistically significant degree in men with erectile problems. The results of several other investigations raise questions regarding the specificity of behavioral sex therapy for the treatment of erectile dysfunction. For example, Ansari (1976) reported that simple reassurance was as effective as sex therapy in the treatment of chronic impotence, and Crowe et al. (1981) reported that marital therapy was as effective as sex therapy in relieving complaints of erectile failure. It is also of note that Levine and Agle (1978) reported a very high relapse rate in men previously successfully treated for impotence.

Although there is more substantiation of the effectiveness of behavioral sex therapy than alternative treatment approaches, the clinician needs to be cognizant that the evidence is far from conclusive. Similarly, the bulk of the studies to date have been conducted with heterogeneous groups of patients. It is possible that the inconsistent reports of treatment efficacy are related to differences in patient populations. Unfortunately, most of the published controlled outcome studies to date do not include adequate descriptions of patient characteristics to permit an analysis of outcome related to patient characteristics.

The treatment approaches which will be described in this chapter refer to patients with inhibited sexual excitement as the primary or sole diagnosis. If the sexual difficulty is secondary to another disorder (for example, affective disorder), that disorder should be treated first. Similarly, the treatment approach may require modification if the erectile disorder coexists with marital discord or a personality disorder. As previously mentioned, patients with mixed organic and psychogenic etiologies will also require specialized treatment approaches.

The rationale for the suggested treatment approaches is to choose the minimum intervention shown to be effective for the complaint. In certain subgroups of impotent men (secondary, good premorbid adjustment, acute onset, brief duration), behavioral sex therapy is known to have a high likelihood of success. In other subgroups (primary or insidious onset), the prognosis with behavioral sex therapy is more guarded. However, favorable outcomes have been reported using this approach and cost-effectiveness concerns probably dictate that it should be the initial therapeutic endeavor.

Secondary Impotence, Acute Onset, Brief Duration

Patients with good previous sexual functioning who experience the sudden onset of erectile failure after an identifiable stress respond favorably to a variety of psychiatric interventions (Annon 1974; Ellis 1980). In monosymptomatic patients with good hetereosexual relationships, behavioral sex therapy is likely to have a good outcome. One suspects that treatment gains in such cases are likely to be sustained as characterological problems are seldom involved and the environmental events responsible for symptom onset are frequently transitory. Probably many of these complaints would remit with interventions briefer and less formal than structural behavioral sex therapy. Unfortunately, we have minimal firm evidence as to when formal therapy versus brief reassurance is indicated.

For example, an unmarried cardiologist requested psychiatric consultation because of repeated erectile failure with a nurse he was dating. Questioning quickly revealed the probable absence of an organic etiology, the absence of any major life stress or change, the absence of major psychopathology, and a history of numerous successful sexual encounters with other partners. By exclusion, it appeared likely that his difficulty was related to some aspect of his relationship with the nurse. He refused to involve the nurse in treatment. It was then suggested that he desist in his repeated coital attempts until we could determine the reason for his problem. The next session was focused on understanding his relationship with his partner. The relationship had developed over three to four dates, and on the fourth date, he had asked her to spend the night at his apartment. She agreed and told him how much she liked him. However, on the drive back to his apartment, she casually mentioned that she was dating a lawyer who had asked her to marry him. She told the cardiologist that she couldn't decide whether or not to marry the lawyer. His erectile problem began shortly thereafter. The cardiologist was asked whether his erectile problem might be related to his anger concerning the uncertainty of her involvement with him. In the next meeting, the cardiologist reported that he and the nurse had had a long argument on their next date followed by successful coitus.

Many patients present to non-psychiatric physicians and resist referral to psychiatrists (Segraves et al. 1981a). Fortunately, many of these patients will respond to very brief contact and minimum intervention. In one series, approximately 14 percent of such patients had a remission of symptoms after a single interview with a urologist or psychiatrist (Segraves et al. 1981a). This interview stressed that the patient's problem appeared to be environmentally rather than biologically induced and that such problems often remit with the passage of time. More recently, Segraves et al. (1982b) experimented with an alternative approach for men with psychogenic impotence who refuse a referral to a psychiatric setting. These patients were seen in the urology clinic for an average of four sessions by a psychiatrist. The patients were informed that the problem appeared stress related and that such problems often resolve in time. The patients were advised to continue to have foreplay, but coitus was strictly forbidden. Spouses were not seen and structured sensate focus exercises were not employed. Follow-up revealed that slightly more than 50 percent of such patients reported a restoration of erectile function after this brief intervention. It is of note that a similar approach was advocated by Tuthill in 1955: "When intercourse has failed, the patient must stop trying, and retrace the steps of courtship, which in some cases he may never have trod at all. . . . Often the first problem is to persuade them to spend enough time in bed together for spontaneous contact to take place. . . . After a time the search for pleasure becomes his objective, and he forgets that he is trying to achieve intercourse. . . . . The essence of treatment is the simple lesson that intercourse is a sensual pleasure or nothing" (Tuthill 1955, 124–125).

Secondary Impotence, Insidious Onset, and/or Long Duration

Many patients will report the insidious onset of erectile problems or will report that the problem began so long ago that they cannot recall a precipitating event. Spontaneous remission appear to be less common in this group of patients (Segraves et al. 1982). Similarly, these types of patients are often difficult to successfully treat in behavioral sex therapy (Ansari 1976). In such cases, the stimuli maintaining the disorder (whether intrapsychic or environmental) have been relatively resistant to change in spite of the passage of time. In such situations, the most likely source for the reinforcing stimuli lies within the intimate interpersonal environment (Heiman and LoPiccolo 1983). The nature of these interpersonal systems which operate to maintain the symptom may not become obvious until therapy is well underway. In other words, one utilizes the prescription of physically intimate activities both as a diagnostic device and as a therapeutic procedure.

For example, a recently remarried widower in his 60s reported that he had not experienced erections under any circumstances since his previous wife's death five years ago. The previous marriage was sound both sexually and interpersonally. He reported a seemingly normal grieving period. A complete biomedical assessment did not reveal an organic component to his problem, and there was no evidence of marital dysfunction in his current marriage. The therapist prescribed non-sexual sensual exploration of one another (sensate focus exercises). In the subsequent sessions, the couple reported numerous plausible reasons why the exercises could not be completed. At this point, psychotherapeutic exploration could not detect the origin of the resistance to the sensual exercises. The therapist indicated that completion of the exercises was necessary for therapy to be successful. In subsequent sessions, the man appeared increasingly anxious and his wife reported that her husband was unusually tense during intimate caressing. In the next session with the therapist, the couple reported that the husband had begun to become more relaxed during touching exercises, experienced sexual excitement and a full erection before becoming overwhelmed with sexual memories of his deceased wife and severe psychological pain. The exercises were interrupted by his intense sobbing. It became clear that an incomplete grief reaction had interfered with his sexual arousal and excitement with his new partner. He and his deceased wife had experienced an unusually intimate and mutually satisfying sex life. Fortunately, his new wife was also a widow and could understand her husband's pain. Continuation of the sexual exercises with discussion of the evoked affect helped this man to complete his grieving period and to become coitally active with his new partner.

Interactional Pattern Maintains Problem

A common interpersonal pattern in couples has been described by many clinicians (Kaplan 1974; Levine 1985; Masters and Johnson 1970):

1. The husband, because of his fear of failure, avoids all physical intimacy—even a casual caress reminds the man of his inadequacy
2. The spouse or partner at first attempts not to pressure the man as his emotional pain is obvious; subsequently, the spouse begins to resent the rejection and interpersonal distance
3. The emotional distance between the couple widens and episodes of emotional and/or physical intimacy become infrequent

In other words, the couple inadvertently evolves an interactional system that maintains the problem. The absence of physical intimacy decreases the likelihood of sexual excitement spontaneously occurring and resulting in a "spontaneous remission." The anxiety associated with physical intimacy persists and is not allowed to undergo natural extinction. The absence of intimacy contributes to an interpersonal climate of pain and resentment and thus is not conducive to natural experiments which might be successful. This pattern and minor variations thereof have been described by numerous clinicians and is probably reflective of the conscious experience of many patients and their spouses. What is unclear is why some couples seemingly get "stuck" in this pattern and are resistant to environmental events which might disrupt the sequence. Some clinicians have postulated that clinical couples differ from normals in that the problem isn't discussed (Masters and Johnson 1970). Another possibility is that many couples ineffectively attempt to discuss and resolve the problem before retreating to silent withdrawal. In my opinion, problems like this tend to be self-sustaining in couples in which one or both are unusually sensitive to rejection. The absence of physical interest is internally construed as evidence of rejection of self. The anger so effectively mobilized inhibits efforts by the other to resolve the difficulty. An impotent male with a fear of failure needs an unusually supportive and understanding female to be able to relax sufficiently to again experience full sexual arousal, obtain erections with some reliability, and thus regain self-confidence.

Goals of Behavioral Therapy

The goals of behavioral therapy of erectile problems are:

1. To engender an atmosphere of safety within the couple unit
2. To decrease the fear of failure
3. To shift attention away from the fear of failure to the experience of sensory pleasure

These objectives can usually be achieved in brief directive conjoint behavioral sex therapy. Although a variety of modifications from the basic Masters and Johnson program have been described (Cooper 1978), the essential components in this treatment package include:

1. A prohibition of coital attempts
2. Facilitation of frank discussion concerning sexual activities
3. The prescription of sexual exercises of increasing physical intimacy

The prescription of exercises for the treatment of erectile dysfunction may consist of the following:

1. Taking turns in the exploration of the other's body excluding breasts and genitals (alternating giving and receiving sensual pleasure)
2. Genital or breast exploration allowed (patients instructed to focus on personal pleasure, not erection or arousal level of the partner)
3. Intermittent penile caressing resulting in the repeated tumescence and detumescence of the penis
4. Vaginal containment with minimal thrusting; female superior position
5. Thrusting to orgasm, man supine
6. Intercourse with woman supine

A variety of interventions other than the rote prescription of behavioral exercises are required for the successful therapy of inhibited sexual excitement. Many of these interventions have to be individualized for each case and require considerable psychotherapeutic skill. However, certain inventions are almost universal. Most men with persistent erectile problems suffer from a loss of self-esteem and a sense of helplessness. A certain degree of reassurance is usually attempted. For example, most patients are informed that erectile problems are quite common and are usually time limited. Whenever possible, a cognitive framework for the genesis of the problem and the goal of the therapy is offered. Most men can identify with the concept of the vicious cycle of failure and performance anxiety augmenting one another and the need to interrupt this cycle by prohibiting coitus and focusing on physical pleasure. Similarly, a large number of widowed and divorced men can identify with the hypothesis that part of their difficulty may reflect a fear of re-involvement; thus, the therapy will approach sexual intimacy in small graduated steps.

Certain therapists have recommended the use of erotic films and literature in the treatment of sexual disorders in spite of the absence of evidence concerning their efficacy (Bjorksten 1976). It is doubtful that such materials are necessary to augment sexual arousal. The repetitive exposure to sexual stimulation and the continual focus on sexuality in sex therapy is usually sufficient to mobilize sexual arousal.

Treatment Formats

Current evidence suggests that the use of once a week sessions is as effective as the daily treatment program originally described by Masters and Johnson and that a solo therapist is probably as effective as a co-therapy team (Arentewicz and Schmidt 1963; Heiman and LoPiccolo 1983). If a once a week treatment format is utilized, the usual treatment length is 12–14 sessions. The couple is instructed to set aside at least two one-hour periods per week during which they will be rested and unrushed. Therapy sessions focus predominantly on the prescribed exercises and the couple's reactions to these. Throughout the treatment program, the therapist attempts to shift the couple's focus away from performance and toward the experience of pleasure without performance expectations.

In certain cases, progress will be extremely rapid and not require the usual sequence of 10–12 outpatient interviews. An example of such a case follows.

A highly successful and ambitious businessman in his 60s had been impotent for approximately five years. His erectile difficulties had begun during a period of economic setbacks that he subsequently overcame. Being unable to tolerate failure, he totally ceased attempts at coitus and shunned physical intimacy, which reminded him of his failure. He entered therapy at his wife's insistence, being afraid that she would leave him or take a lover. His wife, although sexually responsive, missed the signs of physical intimacy more than coitus itself. In the initial sessions, she was quite explicit in telling her husband how she missed the physical intimacy. She stated clearly that his absence of erections was not a failure from her perspective but that he was failing her as a husband by withholding physical intimacy. The therapist made certain that the businessman heard and incorporated his wife's subjective experience of the situation. His wife also spoke of her husband's impending retirement and their need to reestablish intimacy for their future time together when work successes would not be present for her husband. Playing on the husband's task-oriented approach to life, the therapist suggested that the reestablishment of intimacy at home was his next developmental challenge. The therapist also emphasized his wife's need for physical intimacy and the much lower priority of coitus per se. Sensate focus exercises were prescribed. By the fifth week of sensual exercises, the businessman had begun to experience full sustainable erections. Successful intercourse was resumed contrary to the therapist's instructions. The therapist felt that it was important for this competitive businessman to disobey the younger physician's instructions. The husband's potency continued, and the remaining sessions were devoted to their discussing ways to prepare for retirement.

Primary Impotence

Older males who have never been coitally successful are relatively infrequent clinical phenomena, and minimal evidence covering the preferred treatment approach is currently available. The presence of associated psychopathology may be unusually high in this group and careful psychiatric screening should be performed before behavioral sex therapy is recommended (Levine 1985). In clinical practice, these patients are frequently unmarried and enter therapy without a partner. If a "behavioral" approach is utilized, early therapy may need to focus on social skills training and exploring cognitions related to relationships with the opposite sex. Considerable generalized anxiety concerning females and avoidance of females in multiple contexts is often present. This anxiety and related behavioral pattern may need modification before sex therapy is possible. In patients with partners, behavioral sex therapy is often successful although less successful than in secondary impotence.

Younger males who have never had intercourse and who have failed at their initial coital attempts are also a heterogeneous group. Many of these males respond to simple reassurance. Only a minority of such cases are candidates for behavioral sex therapy.

Other Considerations

In patients with erectile dysfunction of long duration, it may be impossible to identify the forces responsible for the problem. One may erroneously assume that the problem is maintained by current interpersonal events. The turmoil secondary to the difficulty may obfuscate a search for remote causes which are still operative. It is not unusual to begin behavioral sex therapy and subsequently discover that the wrong treatment was prescribed. The early sign of this is resistance to complying with the recommended sexual exercises. If exploration of the reasons for the resistance and/or reinforcement of the necessity to complete the exercises are insufficient, one's suspicion that an alternative treatment might be indicated should be heightened. In other cases, the resistance is more subtle—the behavioral steps are completed in an emotionally detached manner. Usually, non-verbal cues in the session will alert the therapist to this possibility. It is usually prudent to first assume that the therapy is progressing too rapidly for one or both of the patients and thus to slow the pace. If by the fifth or sixth session, some progress in experiencing sexual intimacy has still not been accomplished, behavioral sex therapy will probably be unsuccessful unless alternative approaches are also utilized.

The most common problem is for marital disharmony to be so severe that behavioral sex therapy will not work. In these instances, it may be most profitable to straightforwardly inform the couple that marital therapy work needs to be completed before continuing sex therapy. Less frequently, one of the spouses will experience too much individual discomfort to complete behavioral sex therapy. In these cases, sex therapy can be temporarily interrupted for brief focused individual psychotherapy before continuing conjoint sex therapy (Kaplan 1974), or the therapist may continue the individual psychotherapy in the conjoint treatment format before continuing sex therapy.

Cases with Mixed Etiologies

It is clear that not all cases of erectile failure can be clearly diagnosed as organic or psychogenic in etiology (Renshaw 1978; Schiavi 1980). In many patients, the erectile failure reported will be the result of an admixture of biogenic and psychological factors, and a premature attempt to arrive at an exclusive etiologic diagnosis may be a disservice to the patient. Attempts to estimate the relative balance of organic and psychological factors may lead to more effective interventions.

It is not uncommon for men with similar degrees of organically based decrements in erectile capacity to respond quite differently. One diabetic male with semi-turgid erectile capacity (as confirmed by nocturnal penile tumescence testing and spouse report) may become extremely discouraged, cease all coital attempts, and become functionally impotent. Another diabetic with a seemingly more severe biogenic impairment may continue to be coitally active albeit with a reduced frequency and with modification of technique. In cases of partial decrement in biologic capacity and total decrement in activity, psychiatric treatment may be indicated. In clinical practice, one also encounters patients for whom a complete biomedical assessment does not lead to a definitive conclusion. For example, nocturnal penile tumescence recording in a neurophysiology laboratory may reveal three rapid eye movement related tumescence periods. One of these tumescence periods may be rated as 80 percent of normal and sufficient for vaginal penetration whereas the other two erections may be rated as only 30 percent of normal and clearly insufficient for penetration. Most vascular laboratories are now capable of using Doppler assessment of penile blood flow to identify cases of vasculogenic impotence. Determinations of penile blood flow in certain patients may indicate a marked decrement in penile perfusion yet it may be unclear whether the vascular occlusion is sufficient to account for the erectile impairment.

In cases where there is a marginal decrement in biologic erectile capacity or where laboratory procedures render inconclusive results, there is a possibility that psychiatric intervention may lead to a partial restoration of function. In such cases, sex therapy can be utilized to maximize the remaining function. A major portion of the intervention is educational. Both the patient and spouse need to realize that failures will occur and are not necessarily reflective of their feelings toward one another. Certain practical suggestions may also be helpful. For example, the couple may be advised to restrict sexual activity to times when the male is well rested and to avoid such activities at times of interpersonal stress. The possible need for increased amounts of direct manual stimulation should be emphasized, and the use of coital positions requiring less male movement and allowing for easier penetration might be recommended. At the same time, the therapist would attempt to engender a relaxed pleasure oriented approach to sex and to identify and modify factors which might interfere with full arousal and satisfaction. Some patients with partial organic impairment are able to resume satisfactory coitus on a once every other week basis after psychotherapy. In other patients, an organic basis for the erectile dysfunction will be discovered and corrected and the patient will remain sexually impaired. Because of the anxiety and demoralization induced during the biologically induced erectile failure, the patient remains dysfunctional. In these situations, the psychiatrist may need to work closely with the non-psychiatric physician in order to restore erectile function in the patient. Certain patients may become impotent on hypotensive drugs and remain so because of performance anxiety after the offending agent is discontinued. A similar situation can sometimes occur in men who receive exogenous testosterone for primary hypogonadism.

Other Treatment Approaches

The treatment formats described in this chapter are basically pragmatic and behavioral in focus. This reflects the conviction that behavioral sex therapy should be the first line therapy for such disorders and that longer therapies of unproven efficacy should be employed only as a last resort. Clearly, behavioral sex therapy even with considerable modification to fit individual couples' needs is neither acceptable nor effective with all couples. The questions of when to use other therapies and what these therapies should be remain unclear. If the variables maintaining the difficulty appear to be predominantly interpersonal, one of the marital therapy approaches would be indicated. (If the sexual problem is one of a number in a patient whose major diagnosis is a personality disorder, dynamic or cognitive psychotherapy should be considered.)

It is not uncommon to encounter patients who remain symptomatic after considerable psychiatric treatment including behavior therapy, marital therapy, and psychoanalytically oriented psychotherapy. Certain centers have reported using penile prosthesis implantation for men with psychogenic impotence who fail to respond to psychiatric treatment. As minimal information is currently available concerning the psychiatric sequelae of such intervention (Goldman and Segraves 1985), considerable caution must be exercised before considering such a treatment approach. (See Chapter 212.)

Chapter 212

Surgical Treatment of Impotence

Diagnosis of Impotence

The appropriate selection of candidates for surgical treatment of impotence is essential to obtain optimum patient satisfaction. The decision to proceed with surgery must be based on the overall assessment of the patient and the results of previous treatment. Success rates are enhanced if a psychiatrist or sex therapist participates in the evaluation.

The history of sexual dysfunction must be carefully explored (Malloy and Wein 1978). Many conditions such as infectious processes of the bladder, prostate, and seminal vesicles can lead to temporary sexual dysfunction. The time, onset, and duration of the impotence must be carefully determined.

The physical examination is extremely important. The patient's overall physical condition must be assessed with special emphasis being placed on the examination of the genitourinary tract. The penis and scrotum have to be carefully assessed for the appropriate type of prosthesis that must be used. The prostate has to be carefully evaluated to rule out conditions which could affect potency such as infection or malignancy. Benign enlargement must be assessed since this should be corrected before any surgical intervention for impotence is attempted.

The laboratory evaluation of the patient should include a complete blood count; SMA-12; and tests for serum acid phosphates, serum testosterone, and prolactin. Low serum testosterone is one of the few medical conditions that is easily treated and will provide improvement in sexual functions.

After the complete history, physical, and laboratory evaluation, special diagnostic tests may be indicated (Wein et al. 1984). The evaluation of vascular conditions can be done with Doppler blood pressure assessments of the penile arteries. In special instances vascular assessment, including arteriography, should be considered if penile revascularization is a possible therapy. In the overwhelming majority of patients suffering with erectile impotence, vascular reconstruction has not been successful. However, an exact etiology for organic impotence is important not only for the medical assessment of the patient but for legal purposes as well.

Nocturnal penile tumescence studies are the most accurate diagnostic tests of erectile dysfunction. The study in more than 90 percent of cases will determine whether the sexual dysfunction is on an organic or functional basis. The study should be done in a monitored environment for at least two nights and possibly three nights. If there is any question of disability claims from previous accidents, surgery, or trauma, the tests should be done in conjunction with EEG monitoring in a sleep laboratory to assure that the patient is having adequate REM sleep. If the patient is not sleeping well or does not have sufficient REM episodes on EEG, the test may not be valid. Alternate assessment of penile function while patients are sleeping, such as the stamp test or snap gauges, are not accurate. They leave the patient and doctor at risk in claiming the impotence was of an organic nature.

Psychological testing should be considered in all patients. The Minnesota Multiphasic Personality Index (MMPI) has proved helpful in many series in the initial screening of patients for the presence of psychosis or other severe personality disorders. In any patients with organic impotence in which the diagnosis is not clearly established or in which there may be a personality disorder, consultation with a psychiatrist is essential. He or she will help in the evaluation of the patient (and often of the spouse) and in counseling the patients as to alternative forms of sexual therapy. The surgeon should always consider a conservative course of sexual therapy if the patient has any hesitation regarding surgery.

Indications for Penile Prosthesis

The surgical correction of impotence is basically that of insertion of a penile prosthesis. Penile vascular reconstruction is only appropriate in selected patients (Michal et al. 1974), usually in the younger patient who on vascular assessment has a definitive vascular obstruction as seen, for example, in trauma cases and in certain congenital conditions. Even in these cases the long-term results of vascular reconstruction have not been encouraging. At two years post-op the vast majority of these patients are again having sexual dysfunction.

Patients who are appropriate for penile prostheses are those that have failed conservative medical therapy. Patients with diabetes mellitus have a high incidence of erectile dysfunction. More than 50 percent of males who have had diabetes for more than 15 years will have some form of erectile dysfunction. Patients who have failed conservative treatment of testosterone deficiency are also candidates. Patients with renal failure on dialysis also are appropriate candidates. Another large series of patients requiring surgical correction are those that require hypertensive medications for control of their blood pressure. A side effect of many of the medications is erectile impotence. The prosthesis allows good control of their medical condition without loss of erectile function. Patients who required radical pelvic surgery such as total cystectomy, radical prostatectomy, or abdominal perineal resections are also candidates for the prosthesis. Trauma to the penis, scrotum, perineum, or spine may also produce impotence.

Patients with psychogenic impotence who have not improved on adequate sex therapy may also be considered for penile prosthesis, particularly those patients 50 years of age or older, and those patients in whom the impotence has lasted for more than two years.

All patients must thoroughly understand what the prosthesis can and cannot do (Malloy et al. 1980). They should have an understanding of the advantages and disadvantages of all types of prostheses and the expected survival of the various types of prostheses. A full informed consent must be provided so the patient can participate in the decision as to what type of prosthesis he wishes. If possible, it is extremely important to have the sexual partner participate in the discussions so she also understands what the surgery can accomplish. If the surgeon cannot implant all types of prostheses, he still should give a complete evaluation to the patient.

Types of Prostheses

Penile prostheses are divided into essentially two major groups: semi-rigid rod types of prostheses and the inflatable types of prostheses.

The semi-rigid rod prostheses are those that do not have fluid or an inflatable nature. The most common types of prostheses in use at this time are the Small-Carrion prosthesis (Small and Carrion 1975), the Finney flexi-rod prosthesis (Finney 1977), the Jonas flexible prosthesis (Jonas and Jacobi 1980), and the AMS (American Medical Systems) model 600 flexible prosthesis.

The Small-Carrion prosthesis consists of two semi-rigid medical-grade silicone rods. The penile portions have interiors of silicone sponge. The paired rods fit into the corpora cavernosa from the crus extending to the glans penis. The prosthesis is available in various lengths and diameters. The proper size for the patient has to be estimated at the time of the surgery by measuring the entire length of the tunnel that is dissected in the corpora cavernosa. The surgeon should have all sizes available to him at the time of the surgery. If a prosthesis is improperly sized, it may cause the so-called "SST" deformity where the glans sags over the tip of the prosthesis. If a prosthesis is too long it can cause undue pressure on the glans or urethra causing an erosion (Malloy et al. 1980). The prosthesis may be inserted through a perineal or scrotal incision, a suprapubic incision, or a penile incision. Care must be taken with penile incisions so that damage to the neurovascular bundle is not a complication. The incision is contraindicated in diabetics since the scar can cause neuroma or potential anesthesia of the glans penis.

The Finney flexi-rod prosthesis is similar to the Small-Carrion except the proximal end can be trimmed for exact sizing at surgery. It is somewhat more flexible and easier to conceal under clothing. The surgical incisions are the same and care must be taken to assure proper fit at the time of surgery.

The Jonas flexible prosthesis has the advantage of a malleable silver core wire center which allows the penis to be bent downward for concealment. At intercourse it can be bent into an erect state. This type of prosthesis has become increasingly popular with surgeons since it does allow easier concealment.

In 1983 the AMS model 600 flexible semi-rigid rod prosthesis was introduced. It also has a flexible steel wire core which allows for bending the penis into the appropriate position. The advantage of the AMS model 600 prosthesis is that it comes in three basic sizes with rear tip extenders for proper length. This allows the hospital to carry a smaller inventory of prostheses to reduce cost. The prosthesis may be trimmed to a smaller diameter if this is appropriate for the patient.

All semi-rigid rod prostheses have the advantage of a simpler operative procedure with a shorter hospital stay and fewer complications requiring additional surgery. The overall cost is slightly less. The distinct disadvantage of the semi-rigid rod type prostheses is the cosmetic concealment. The penis is permanently semi-erect with the Small-Carrion and Finney prostheses. The Jonas and AMS model 600 prostheses can be concealed more easily but the prosthesis is still palpable within the penis. The sexual partner is aware of the prosthesis. This makes the situation somewhat more difficult for single men who are not dealing with one sexual partner. Urologic instrumentation is much more difficult through semi-rigid rod prostheses in that the penile length cannot be compressed. Transurethral resections of the prostate or transurethral resection of bladder tumors are very difficult if not impossible with this prosthesis in place. These possible conditions should be carefully considered in advising a patient to have this type of prosthesis.

The overall results of all types of semi-rigid rod prostheses have been good. Most patients are satisfied with the results and the complication rates have run between 15 and 20 percent (Jonas 1983; Small 1978). It should be emphasized to all patients, however, that there is no guarantee that any type of prosthesis will last throughout their entire lifetime. The wire cores of the Jonas or AMS model 600 prostheses may break. The Small-Carrion or Finney prostheses may become dislodged or have mechanical problems. All patients should be informed that they may need a revision in the future.

Inflatable Penile Prostheses

The inflatable penile prosthesis, first introduced by Scott et al. (1973), has unique features that are very appealing to the physician and the patient. The prosthesis consists of two hollow cylinders that are implanted into the corpora cavernosa of the penis. These cylinders are connected by tubings to an inflate-deflate mechanism that is placed in the scrotum subcutaneously. This device is connected in turn to a reservoir that is secured in the space of Retzius or in the pelvis. When the patient desires an erection he can squeeze the inflate-deflate mechanism to transfer fluid from the reservoir into the cylinders, which will increase in length and circumference. The erection obtained has a natural physiologic appearance. The device is not palpable to the sexual partner. The device will stay rigid as long as the patient desires even after he ejaculates. Therefore, it allows completion of coitus to the satisfaction of both partners. When intercourse is finished, the deflate mechanism can be activated, returning the fluid to the reservoir. The penis then assumes a natural flaccid configuration. This is extremely important for cosmetic reasons since there is no embarrassment in public places such as locker rooms. There are no problems with concealment under clothing. There is not constant pressure on the glans penis or urethra, which greatly decreases the chances of erosion. Urologic endoscopy can easily be performed through the penis if the patient requires cystoscopy or transurethral resections of the bladder or prostate.

The disadvantage of all types of inflatable prostheses has been mechanical failure of component parts. The initial type of prosthesis had problems with leakage from the cylinders in the penis plus the reservoir (Furlow 1979; Mallow 1977). In the ensuing years the American Medical Systems models have been improved with redesign so that the cylinders are stronger (Mallow et al. 1983). The reservoir has been changed to a spherical, dip-coated type that has prevented leakage. Non-kinking tubing has been used from the reservoir to pump to prevent mechanical obstruction. In 1983

American Medical Systems initiated its model 700 prosthesis that incorporated these improvements.

In the same year, the Mentor Company produced its inflatable prosthesis featuring polyurethane cylinders. The ostensible advantage of this type of prosthesis has been the strength of the polyurethane cylinders with lessened chance of cylinder failure (Malloy et al. 1982). The advantages and disadvantages of this prosthesis are basically the same as the American Medical Systems inflatable penile prosthesis. What the potential problems of polyurethane are is a question that has to be resolved with time in the use of this prosthesis. Polyurethane in other prostheses has not been as bio-compatible as silicone rubber implants.

The success rates of the American Medical Systems inflatable penile prostheses have been excellent. From the early models which had mechanical failure rates as high as 35 percent there has been vast improvement.

The Mentor inflatable prosthesis has also had excellent results (Merrill and Javaheri 1984).

Newer types of inflatable prostheses are presently being tested. These types of prostheses are two cylinders with self-contained fluid that are implanted into the corpora cavernosa. The cylinders are inflated by squeezing the cylinders at various positions on the penis. There is no need for a separate inflate-deflate mechanism or a reservoir to contain the fluid. These cylinders will allow an erection but will not give the increase in diameter that is seen with the other types of inflatable prostheses. Since these devices are still in the developmental stage, long-term assessment will have to be awaited.

(Roles of the psychiatrist are in pre-operative evaluation, interviews with the spouse and in post-operative sessions with the patient or couple dealing with psychological concerns.)

Chapter 213

Individual and Couple Therapy

Prevalence

Considerable evidence suggests that sexual disorders are psychiatric syndromes with a high prevalence. This statement has to be tempered with the observation that research concerning sexual behavior is fraught with methodological difficulties. Clearly, "social desirability" may shape responses to questionnaires. More important, population parameters can be properly estimated only on the basis of reasonably random samples of the population (Eysenck 1976). Unfortunately, most of the published research to date including Kinsey's research (Kinsey et al. 1948, 1953) does not involve random sampling of the general population. A third problem concerns how recently the study was performed. There clearly have been changes in mores concerning sexual behavior, especially of females, within this century (Leiblum and Pervin 1980). It is quite possible that a more "permissive" attitude toward female sexuality has influenced the prevalence of female sexual disorders. It has even been suggested that newly sexually liberated females may adversely affect the potency of contemporary men (Kaplan 1974). Although it is unproven that changes in social mores influence the prevalence of sexual disorders, one should perhaps exercise caution in extrapolating from data published as long as 10 or 20 years ago. Another problem in interpreting older data concerns definition of terms. With the publication of DSM-III (American Psychiatric Association 1980), the psychosexual dysfunctions have been precisely defined. In some of the older studies, terms such as impotence and frigidity were often unclearly defined. All studies of the prevalence of sexual disorders rely on patient self-reports of difficulty and thus are subject to the possibility that the patient has an exaggerated fantasy of what normal sexuality should be. For this reason, studies that report the prevalence of discrete observable dysfunctions are more valuable than studies of self-reported satisfaction.

Frank and associates (1978) published one of the most recent surveys of the prevalence of sexual dysfunction in the general population. One hundred volunteer married couples (average age 36) in Pittsburgh completed a lengthy questionnaire containing questions regarding sexual difficulties. The results were striking in that 63 percent of the women and 40 percent of the men surveyed listed at least one sexual difficulty. The data for the females were: 48 percent complained of difficulty becoming aroused; 33 percent complained of difficulty maintaining arousal; 46 percent reported difficulty reaching orgasm; and 15 percent complained of total inability to reach orgasm. The data for males were: difficulty obtaining erections, 7 percent; difficulty maintaining erections, 9 percent; rapid ejaculation, 36 percent; difficulty ejaculating, 4 percent. This study did not employ good sampling procedures, and one is uncertain of the meaning of the answers to the questions in terms of defining syndromes. However, Nettelbladt and Uddenberg (1979) reported similar data concerning the prevalence of male disorders in a semi-structured interview study of a representative sample of married Swedish men. Again, 40 percent of the male sample reported a tendency toward sexual dysfunction, with 39 percent experiencing premature ejaculation, 7 percent impotence, and 10 percent retarded ejaculation. The median age of this sample was 31 years.

In a recent study of the use of sexual histories in general medical practice, Ende et al. (1984) reported the frequency of sexual problems and concerns in 228 outpatients at the Boston University Medical Center. Fifty-three percent had one or more sexual problems. Among female patients, the most frequently reported difficulties were: lack of sexual desire (27 percent), lack of orgasm (25 percent), concern about coital frequency (23 percent), and painful intercourse (20 percent). The most frequent male concerns were: concern about coital frequency (18 percent), relationship problems (15 percent), premature ejaculation (14 percent), impotence (12 percent), and health-related sexual problems (12 percent). It is of note that the overall prevalence of sexual concerns was similar for both sexes and unrelated to the patient's age.

There have not been any recent well-designed studies of the prevalence of female sexual dysfunction in the general population. Numerous older studies reported that approximately 30 percent (Kinsey et al. 1953; Slater and Woodside 1951; Terman 1938, 1951) of married females either never achieve orgasm or do so only occasionally. In a more recent investigation, Fisher (1973a, 1973b) reported that 60 percent of the women investigated (volunteers, non-randomly selected) reported that orgasm did not occur consistently. Approximately 5–6 percent of his sample reported never achieving orgasm. Catalan and associates (1981) interviewed all new admissions to a clinic for sexually transmitted diseases at Radcliffe Infirmary. Among a population of 70 female patients (average age 24, 60 percent unmarried), 37 percent had coital orgasmic dysfunction. Other disorders noted were vaginismus, 4 percent; dyspareunia, 11 percent; loss of libido, 13 percent. Levine and Yost (1976) interviewed every third admission to a gynecology clinic in Cleveland. In this population (black, lowest socioeconomic group, average age 34, 70 percent unmarried), 71 percent reported reaching orgasm on at least 50 percent of coital occasions. Seventeen percent reported total inability to reach orgasm with a partner. Seven percent were diagnosed as having excitement phase dysfunction and three percent orgasm phase dysfunction.

Psychiatric Disease and Sexual Impairment

Rather surprisingly, there is minimal evidence of an association between other psychiatric disease and sexual impairment. Maurice and Guze (1970) independently assessed 20 consecutive admissions to the Reproductive Biology Research Foundation in St. Louis and found evidence of psychiatric disorder separate from the sexual symptom in only a minority of these patients. Numerous studies have failed to find differences between female psychiatric patients and normals in their orgasmic capacity (Burton and Kaplan 1968; McCulloch and Stewart 1960; Schaefer 1964; Slater and Woodside 1951; Winokur et al. 1959; Winokur 1963). However, a minority of studies have reported that married normal females tend to have more frequent orgasms than neurotic outpatients (Coppen 1965; Landis et al. 1940). Purtell and co-workers (1951) reported decreased sexual responsiveness among conversion hysterics, although this was not replicated by Roy (1981). Numerous studies have failed to find consistent personality patterns in men with psychogenic erectile problems (Segraves et al. 1985), and studies have failed to find consistent personality correlates of decreased orgasmic capacity in females (Fisher 1973a). Recent work has provided suggestive evidence of decreased coital activity, decreased orgasmic capacity, and reduction of erectile capacity in patients with depressive disorders (Tamburello and Seppecher 1977), as well as evidence of increased neuroticism in students with sexual difficulties (Eysenck 1976). There is also tentative evidence of increased anxiety levels (especially coital anxiety) in people with sexual dysfunctions (Norton and Jehu 1984).

Marital Discord and Sexual Dysfunctions

The relationship between marital discord and sexual dysfunction remains unclear. The prevailing clinical impression is that the two factors are closely interrelated (McGovern et al. 1975; Perrault et al. 1979; Sager 1976), and most sexual dysfunction treatment programs include a marital therapy component (Haslam 1971; Segraves 1976; Verhulst and Heiman 1979). Many clinicians believe that sexual problems are often secondary to relationship dynamics and the result of other problems in the relationship. Data consistent with this viewpoint include the observation that couples seeking sex therapy often present with considerable marital discord (Frank et al. 1976), that female marital happiness is highly correlated with orgasm frequency (Clark and

Wallin 1965), and that cessation of marital coitus is often related to marital discord (Edwards and Booth 1976). However, other investigators have reported differences between couples seeking treatment of sexual difficulties and those seeking marital therapy (Frank et al. 1981; Hartman 1980). Couples seeking treatment of sexual difficulties alone are characterized by less antagonistic relationships. Sexual difficulties can occur in the context of functional marriages and "sexual dysfunction and marital distress may operate independently of one another" (Hartman 1980, p. 576).

Treatment

The history of the treatment of sexual dysfunction can be grouped into three eras: before Masters and Johnson, the Masters and Johnson era, and the post Masters and Johnson era (Crown and D'Ardenne 1982). Another way of restating the same premise is that the therapies of sexual dysfunction can be classified as indirect, direct, and combined approaches.

Indirect Approaches

Prior to 1970, the predominant psychiatric treatment approach for sexual dysfunction was psychoanalytically oriented individual psychotherapy (Wright et al. 1977). This approach was based on the assumption that the etiology of the sexual difficulty was related to psychological events remote in time from the current difficulty and related to intrapsychic conflict. A close interrelationship of sexual difficulties and personality and neurotic disorders was assumed. In particular, sexual difficulties might be related to oedipal or pre-oedipal issues. Oedipal conflicts might be suspected if the patient experienced sexual difficulties in settings construed to have a competitive theme. Sexual excitement and behavior might evoke unconscious incestuous wishes and the attendant castration anxiety and guilt. Pre-oedipal conflicts would refer to the patient's inability to trust sufficiently for mature sexual intimacy; the lack of trust may be due to deprivation, inconsistent nurturance, excessive dependency, inadequate self-esteem, etc. In either case, the psychic conflict underlying the sexual difficulty would be assumed to be unconscious and thus not modifiable by rational discourse (Meyer 1976). The treatment thus recommended was individual insight-oriented psychotherapy. The therapeutic efficacy of such an approach is unclear (Cooper 1971). The largest clinical series reported was by O'Connor and Stern (1971) in which a retrospective analysis of outcome was performed in 96 patients seen in psychoanalysis or psychoanalytically oriented psychotherapy over a 17-year period. Unfortunately, methodological problems with this study render the data difficult to interpret (Reynolds 1977).

Direct Methods

Beginning in the late 1950s, behavior therapists of the classical conditioning school described promising results treating sexual disorders with novel, brief, system-oriented counseling techniques (Brady 1966; Cooper 1969a, 1969b; Friedman 1968; Garfield et al. 1968; Haslam 1965; Kraft and Al-Issa 1967, 1968; Lazarus 1963, 1965; Wolpe 1958). These treatment approaches were similar to those advocated for the treatment of phobias and assumed that sexual disorders were the result of sexual stimuli having been associated with anxiety. The goal of therapy was to extinguish the anxiety associated with sexual behavior. Because of the small number of cases reported and the radical departure from standard psychiatric practice, these early reports had minimal impact on the psychiatric treatment of sexual disorders. Another factor which may have diminished their impact was the political climate at that time. The psychological literature was replete with polemical attacks and counterattacks by behavior therapists and psychodynamic therapists on the treatment results and theoretic flaws of the opposing school of thought (Segraves and Smith 1976). This climate did not foster the acceptance of radical departures from standard treatment approaches by psychiatric physicians.

This changed considerably with the publication of *Human Sexual Inadequacy* by Virginia Johnson and William Masters in 1970. They reported their clinical results in 790 cases with extensive follow-up data, supporting their claim that most psychosexual dysfunctions respond favorably to brief symptom-oriented counseling methods. Their work had a profound impact on the psychiatric treatment of sexual disorders (Segraves 1978), and behavioral treatment of sexual dysfunction gained rapid popularity in advance of hard evidence supporting its efficacy (Marks 1981). Their treatment approach emphasized contemporary as opposed to historical causes of sexual difficulties and focused on the roles of performance anxiety, lack of information, and poor marital communication. Treatment consisted mainly of education, facilitating communication, alleviating performance anxiety, and graduated sexual exercises. These graduated sexual exercises appear to be a variant of in vivo desensitization, a technique previously advocated by behavior therapists (Franks and Wilson 1974). One of their major contributions was the evolution of a "therapy manual" for sexual disorders. Their approach specifies the need for a dual-sex therapist team, the couple as the treatment unit, brief intensive therapy (daily for two to three weeks), and immediate feedback from the therapists. The major therapeutic agent consists of a sequence of behavioral exercises that the couple performs between therapeutic sessions. These exercises are arranged in terms of progressive physical and then sexual intimacy. It is important to note that the exercises are utilized to provide a progressive experience of sexual intimacy and that rote performance of the exercises is not a sufficient therapeutic endeavor. Their treatment orientation could perhaps best be described as a combined behavioral-systems approach, stressing the modification of interactional behavior in the couple. Their approach is not psychotherapeutic in the usual psychiatric use of that term in that insight and personality restructuring are not attempted.

The Masters and Johnson approach to the treatment of sexual disorders has been adopted by numerous centers and therapists (Annon 1974; Bancroft 1983; Everaerd 1977; Hartman and Fithian 1972; Kaplan 1974; McCarthy 1973; LoPiccolo 1975). In many centers, minor modifications of the basic treatment approach have been incorporated, such as the use of spaced rather than massed interventions (e.g., once a week therapy for 8 to 10 weeks instead of daily sessions for two weeks) and the use of a solo therapist rather than a dual sex co-therapy team. Outcome data reported by other investigators have varied widely, although most are reporting lower success than that obtained in the original Masters and Johnson report. In a review of the outcome literature, Wright and associates (1977) concluded that the therapeutic success of this approach appeared to co-vary with the stringency of the screening criteria. Programs using stringent screening procedures and thus utilizing a highly select population (e.g., Masters and Johnson 1970) reported higher success rates than studies of unselected psychiatric outpatients. The presence of associated psychopathology (Meyer et al. 1972) and the presence of significant marital discord (Crowe 1977) decrease the likelihood of a successful outcome from behavioral sex therapy. Another problem in evaluating the effectiveness of behavioral approaches to sexual dysfunction concerns the handling of dropouts. Several investigators have noted the presence of dropout rates exceeding 40 percent (Mathews 1981; Segraves et al. 1981, 1982). The growing realization that the behavioral treatment approach might be appropriate for only highly select patients led many clinicians to explore treatment approaches incorporating behavioral techniques with techniques derived from psychodynamic psychiatry.

Combined Approaches

Although there is literature on the use of combined behavioral and psychodynamic treatment techniques for neurotic disorders (Goldfriend 1982), the literature on combined approaches for sexual disorders is less extensive. Levay and associates (1976) discussed the problems of combining conjoint sex therapy with individual psychoanalytically oriented psychotherapy with one of the spouses and concluded that the dual therapy approach had considerable benefits and deserved wider application. Numerous other therapists have discussed the use of both approaches by the same therapist (Arentewicz and Schmidt 1983; Crown and D'Ardenne 1982; Frank 1982; Levay and Kagle 1977; Sollod 1975). The leading synthesizer of psychoanalytic and behavioral approaches to the treatment of sexual disorders is Kaplan (1974, 1975, 1983). She emphasizes a multicausal conception of etiology, giving equal emphasis to remote (i.e., psychodynamic) and immediate factors, such as performance anxiety, in causation and advocates an eclectic approach to treatment combining behavioral assignments with marital therapy and individual dynamic psychotherapy. Her approach is unique in that she deals with remote causes of sexual dysfunction only to the extent necessary to cure the target symptom. For example, psychodynamic insight might be utilized to overcome resistance to performing the behavioral assignments. Kaplan has had a far-reaching influence on clinicians who are impressed that many patients simply do not respond to a simplistic model of behavioral sex therapy. Her model is certainly useful to clinicians who need a conceptual framework that will allow them to utilize all possible effective interventions within a coherent conceptual model. Another major influence in the use of integrated approaches to sex therapy has been the work of David Scharff (1982). In his recent text, he has developed a framework for understanding sexual dysfunction within objects relation theory.

However, two notes of caution need to be raised concerning amalgamated treatment approaches. First, there is minimal evidence to date that such multi-theoretical approaches significantly enhance treatment outcome. Second, a loose combination of procedures from different theoretic orientations can lead to a situation where it is virtually impossible to isolate the effective treatment procedures or the appropriate theoretic system. In 1971, Eysenck and Beach strongly deplored integrated approaches to therapy: " . . . We believe that it results in a gigantic mish-mash of theories, methods, and outcomes that is forever beyond the capacity of scientific research to resolve. Theoretical differences should be recognized and their practical and applied consequences differentiated as clearly as possible; only in this way can the good and bad points of each theory be disentangled" (Eysenck and Beach 1971, 602). Given the complexities of clinical care, Eysenck and Beach's warning, although sound, is often difficult to follow.

Integration of Psychodynamic and Behavioral Treatment

Within the field of general psychotherapy, considerable attention has been focused on the conceptual integration of psychodynamic and behavioral approaches to a variety of neurotic disorders (Birk and Brinkley-Birk 1974; Hunt and Dyrud 1968;

Segraves 1982). The past climate of polarization between psychodynamic and behavioral schools of therapy has been replaced by the current climate of rapprochement as evidenced by such developments as mediational behaviorism (Bandura 1977) and cognitive behaviorism (Mahoney 1974). Much of this work can be transposed to the treatment of sexual disorders.

Part of the difficulty in conceptual integration resides in the language and basic assumptions employed by the differing orientations. Psychoanalytic theory tends to emphasize the role of remote causes of current difficulties, to focus on subjective experience and unconscious motivation, to use higher level abstractions and molar units of explanation, and to view a favorable outcome as the modulation of subjective events within the organism and the transfer of this new learning to interactions with significant others outside of the psychotherapy context. Resolution of the transference is considered to be one of the major agents of change. Behavioral therapies, by contrast, tend to emphasize that the determinants of behavior reside outside the individual in the interpersonal environment, tend to utilize operationally defined molecular units of explanation, to focus on modification of current observable behavior, and to pay scant attention to inner symbolic events within the orgasm.

Many modern clinicians have suggested that the seemingly irreconcilable chasm between the opposing schools of thought can be bridged by the adoption of a few basic assumptions:

1. There is a reciprocal interaction between inner symbolic events and behavior such that significant psychotherapeutic change can be elicited in either sphere and will influence the other (Birk and Brinkley-Birk 1974; Segraves and Smith 1976).
2. The assumption that transference reactions (learned expectations of significant others and the carry-over of this to new relationships) often manifest themselves between spouses rather than between the couple and therapist (Gurman 1978; Meissener and Nicholi 1978; Sager 1967).
3. The assumption of eliciting self-confirmatory behavior from others (Bandura 1977; Carson 1969; Leary 1957). In other words, patients tend to restrict the range of their spouse's behavior by the contingencies they provide for that behavior.
4. The concept of "acting-in" (the development of new patterns of behavior that are incongruent with the usual defensive structure and thus lead to intrapsychic change) (Ackerman 1977; Birk and Brinkley-Birk 1974; Carson 1969; Marmor 1971; Wachtel 1977).

Another difficulty in conceptual integration is that psychoanalytic theory is basically a theory of individual psychology. The conceptual system evolved from Ezriel (1952) allows a translation of this individual psychology into an interpersonal environment. According to Ezriel, the psychoanalytic triad of impulse, anxiety, and defense can be translated into an interpersonal context by referring to these concepts as the required relationship, the feared catastrophe, and the avoided relationship. For example, a male patient who is afraid of his own sexual impulses may subtly and unknowingly provoke his wife to act in a non-sexual manner and evidence considerable discomfort if his wife responds outside this restricted range of behavior. In such a situation, the therapist can either attempt to change the behavior of the couple such that the avoided relationship becomes manifest and the husband learns that the feared catastrophe is not operative in this current relationship or the therapist can treat the husband in individual psychodynamic psychotherapy. The choice of the therapeutic approach is pragmatic and made in terms of which approach appears to be most cost-effective in producing the required change.

Conjoint versus Individual Therapy

Masters and Johnson strictly advocate treating the couple as a unit, stressing that there is no such thing as an uninvolved partner. This has led to the adoption of the conjoint treatment technique in most sexual dysfunction clinics. It should be noted that there is minimal empirical support of the improved efficacy of conjoint over individual therapy and that some patients find the conjoint treatment format totally unacceptable. The decision concerning whether a conjoint or individual approach should be utilized can be made on practical, as contrasted with theoretic, grounds. In any given disorder, the degree of partner participation in eliciting and/or maintaining the symptom is often unknown and may even remain unclear until there is clear evidence of symptom remission (Kaplan and Kohl 1972; Segraves et al. 1982). The practical implication of this is that it is preferable to include the partner in diagnostic and treatment sessions whenever possible. In some cases, the symptom may serve to protect the other spouse or to maintain equilibrium in a precarious relationship. Even in a healthy relationship, the partner may have adapted to the problem and be fearful of change and unwittingly interfere with progress. In almost all situations, the partner's cooperation is essential to progress. In certain situations, spouse involvement may prove impossible. Therapeutic success is still possible although treatment of the identified patient alone is usually the less preferred treatment alternative.

Patient Selection

The clinician will encounter many self-referred sex therapy patients, and considerable clinical skill may be required to judge the appropriateness of this therapy approach for any individual or couple. The first task with many self-referred patients is to decide whether other treatment approaches might be more appropriate. Various factors including faulty self-assessment, severe marital discord, and severe co-existing psychopathology may mitigate against the effectiveness of sex therapy. Many patients may be aware of longstanding interpersonal difficulties and conclude that sexual difficulties are the source of their plight in life. In many of these cases, alternative therapies may be more appropriate. Severe marital discord (Lobitz and LoPiccolo 1972; Sager 1976) and severe psychopathology (Lansky and Davenport 1975; Munjack and Kanno 1977) are both relative contraindications to behavioral sex therapy. If significant marital discord is present, the therapist needs to assess whether the discord is so severe that the couple will not comply with the treatment program (Segraves 1981). Although the presence of co-existing psychopathology is not an absolute contraindication to sex therapy, it does appear to decrease the likelihood of a successful outcome (Wright et al. 1977).

Conjoint Treatment Approach

Current evidence suggests that the preferred treatment approach for most psychosexual dysfunctions is a minor modification of the approach originally described by Masters and Johnson (Marks 1981). Their therapy approach can be modified by the use of a single therapist (Arentewicz and Schmidt 1983; LoPiccolo 1982) and the use of spaced sessions (Heiman and LoPiccolo 1983; Mathews 1981) without demonstrable loss of effectiveness. This approach combines the prescription of sexual exercises of progressive intimacy with psychotherapy sessions. The prescribed steps have been adequately described elsewhere (Levine 1985; Masters and Johnson 1970).

It is rapidly becoming clear that the simple prescription of sexual exercises is frequently inadequate to achieve therapeutic success and that the effective sex therapist needs to possess a wide repertoire of psychotherapeutic skills (Kaplan 1974). The organizing principle of sex therapy is that the therapist's major goal is to foster the progressive experience of emotional and sexual intimacy between the sexual partners. The prescribed exercises are a means to the end, and there is not an "approved" list of correct exercises. The therapist can improvise as necessary as long as he (or she) maintains the goal of gradual escalation of sexual intimacy at a pace tolerable to both partners. The artistry of the therapist comes into play around several issues. The therapist needs to orchestrate the experience of sexual intimacy in such a manner that the couple experiences a sense of progress while not progressing so rapidly that the anxiety becomes intolerable. A second issue requiring some degree of therapeutic skill concerns when the therapist should divert from direct discussion of feelings concerning the sexual exercises to focus on issues less directly related to the presenting complaint. Such a decision can be extremely difficult when marital discord erupts or one of the patients clearly has other psychological problems which appear to be linked to the sexual complaint. In such instances, the "rule of thumb" is to divert only when other issues are clearly interfering with the experience of sexual intimacy. At this time, the diversion should be of the minimum length necessary to bypass the obstacle to the experience of intimacy. It is clear that discussion of sexual feelings in early childhood can serve as a defense against the experience of sexual intimacy in adult life. As a general rule, it is preferable to postpone discussion of other interpersonal or intrapsychic problems until the successful completion of behavioral sex therapy.

Individual Therapy

Individual therapy of sexual dysfunction would be considered when a partner is unavailable, when the patient absolutely refuses to involve the partner, and when the partner refuses to be involved. There is minimal evidence concerning the differential effectiveness of behavioral versus psychodynamic treatment of the individual patient. In such situations, the decision regarding the preferred treatment approach involves the presenting symptom and its social context, the relative skills of the therapist, and the patient's manner of conceptualizing the difficulty.

In patients with the sudden onset of symptoms after a long period of good premorbid function, the therapist may elect to employ simple education and reassurance, realizing that many sexual disorders undergo spontaneous remission without formal treatment (Nathan 1984; Segraves et al. 1982). The presence of a long period of adequate functioning before the development of symptoms, of course, suggests that the etiology is probably related to changes in the immediate environment. In patients with a clear precipitant (a stressful event preceding the onset of symptoms), the preferable approach might be to explore the meaning of the precipitant for the patient and to relate this to his or her current symptomatology (Butcher and Kass 1978).

Many of the approaches utilized in the treatment of couples can be successfully adopted to the treatment of singles without partners in treatment. The patient can be given the behavioral assignments to complete with the partner who refuses to enter treatment. Alternatively, the assignments may be completed with multiple partners. Females with difficulty in sexual excitement and orgasm have been successfully treated without their partner's active participation in therapy (Barbach 1975). The female patient is instructed in fantasy elaboration and masturbatory training. Certain bridging exercises are included to facilitate the transfer of this new skill to partners.

Single males with erectile problems and the absence of requisite skills to obtain a sexual partner often present therapeutic challenges. The usual behavioral treatment for such men involves social skills and assertiveness training prior to sex therapy. Graduated homework assignments can be employed.

Psychodynamic therapy can also be utilized in singles without partners. If an identifiable focus (core conflict) can be related to the presenting symptom, the patient may be an appropriate candidate for brief dynamic psychotherapy (Malan 1976). In patients with more extensive characterologic issues and without an identifiable core conflict, long-term exploratory psychotherapy may be the preferred treatment.

In the last two decades, we have witnessed considerable progress in our understanding of the prevalence, etiology, and treatment of the psychosexual disorders. These disorders have been found to have a higher prevalence in the general population than previously thought, and there is minimal evidence that other psychiatric disorders are associated with the psychosexual disorders. Treatment approaches have evolved from individual psychodynamic psychotherapy to conjoint behavioral sex therapy and to combined approaches utilizing both psychoanalytic and behavioral techniques. This emphasis on developing effective psychiatric interventions has led to a climate of conceptual integration of both psychodynamic and behavioral principles of treatment. The philosophy of the contemporary sex therapist appears to be that of technical empiricism rather than theoretical orthodoxy. It is encouraging that a database is beginning to accumulate concerning patient selection for the new sex therapies and concerning how to select the appropriate form of intervention for a given patient. The last two decades have produced considerable gains in knowledge in this relatively new psychiatric subspecialty which are valuable to the practicing clinician.

Chapter 214

Drug Therapy

A New Understanding of the Causes of Sexual Dysfunction

The medical treatment of sexual dysfunction with drugs is in its infancy. Far outdistancing this positive therapeutic effort is the widespread incidence of sexual dysfunction induced by prescription drugs—especially psychotropics.

The treatment of sexual dysfunction has until recently been almost exclusively in the purview of psychotherapists. However, a growing body of research is demonstrating that a higher percentage of sexual dysfunction than previously appreciated is caused by medical conditions. The advent of nocturnal penile tumescence monitoring and Doppler studies of genital blood flow has provided more sophisticated technical resources for detecting physiologic dysfunction. Endocrine function is now readily assessable by use of plasma hormone assays. These resources have improved our ability to identify medical causes of sexual dysfunction previously undetectable.

It is now estimated that 50–60 percent of impotence is due to organic disease (Smith 1981). This percentage may even increase as additional diagnostic research is reported. The figure varies depending on the type of specialist and the kind of clinic reporting. Much painful intercourse previously considered psychological has been found to be physically induced. The percentage diagnosed as due to physical causes continues to increase.

These medical conditions have psychological factors that contribute to the sexual problems or result from them, but the medical aspects can no longer be disregarded. In addition to commonplace medical complications such as diabetes and arteriovascular disease, another body of knowledge is emerging—the possibility that sexual dysfunction might be related to biochemical disorders of our CNS neurotransmitter systems.

The interrelationship among biochemistry, pharmacology, psychology, and medicine must be considered in the diagnosis and treatment of sexual dysfunction. The psychiatrist needs to be conversant with the overlapping areas of the metabolic process, disease, and psychological sexual dysfunction, as well as with the iatrogenic (drug-induced) sexual dysfunctions before considering the use of medications as therapeutic agents for psychiatric disorders. The more information he assimilates, the more increasingly complex the situation becomes. However, as data accumulates, diagnostic and therapeutic patterns emerge that are exceedingly valuable to the clinician.

The Effect of Commonly Prescribed Drugs on Sexual Function

It is impossible to discuss the positive sexual effects of drugs without first considering and understanding the sexual side effects of drugs already in use and their interactions. Many commonly used medications can interfere with sexual function in both men and women. For example, almost all drugs used for the treatment of depression have been reported, at one time or another, to have negative sexual side effects. In some cases, the dysfunction is dose-related, and in other cases it appears to be independent of dosage level. However, some of the very drugs reported to cause sexual dysfunction have also been reported to improve sexual function in certain cases—a perplexing situation. Once the mechanisms for sexual function are better understood, this seemingly paradoxical phenomenon will become more clear.

Commonly prescribed drugs that have been reported to cause sexual dysfunctions are diuretics, antihypertensives, antiarrhythmics, antihistamines, antiandrogens, anticholinergics, central nervous system depressants, antiulcer medications, anticancer drugs, sedatives, hypnotics, antidepressants, monoamine oxidase (MAO) inhibitors, antipsychotics, alcohol, and illegal drugs, including but not limited to cocaine, amphetamines, marijuana, and heroin. In recent years, there has been increasing recognition of the variety of drugs that can have adverse effects on the human sexual response cycle. More information is accumulating each year, so this list cannot be considered complete.

Due to the large number of commonly prescribed drugs, especially the psychotropics that adversely affect sexual function, an accurate diagnosis of the sexual problem becomes complex. First of all, the physician must assess whether there is a pre-existing sexual dysfunction. Second, careful questioning and screening techniques must be used to assess iatrogenic sexual dysfunction. Third, with 50 to 60 percent of impotence considered medical and an increasing percentage of dyspareunia considered medical, the physician must attempt to discriminate between the psychological factors involved in the sexual dysfunction and the medical factors.

A common medical misunderstanding results from the unsuccessful substitution of prescription drugs. There is the erroneous assumption that if you remove the offending drug, the sexual symptoms will disappear if the drug was responsible. This is often not the case, however, because a sexually depressing drug often induces a persistent psychological sexual dysfunction. Consequently, the drug can be removed, but the sexual problem will remain even though the drug was responsible for precipitating the sexual problem.

When a man becomes dysfunctional due to a prescribed drug, he doesn't necessarily connect the two events. He gets upset and worried about his change in sexual function. After a few experiences that he considers failures, he acquires all the fears of performance characteristic of psychologically impotent men. Even if the drug is discontinued or changed, the fear of failure persists. Consequently, the termination or substitution of medication gives a false negative response. The drug history must be evaluated with this dynamic in mind.

Many physicians are hesitant to suggest that a drug they are prescribing could interfere with sex, because they do not want to precipitate a self-fulfilling prophecy. Instead, they say nothing and assume the patient will report any sexual problems should they occur. This is not a realistic position.

It is best to say something to the effect that, "This medication causes sexual difficulties in some patients, not most. It is related to the dose and the individual. Please let me know if you experience any changes in your sex life."

Sex is important, and so is compliance with your prescribed drug regimen. Since both of these factors can be jeopardized by drug regimens, the physician faces a difficult challenge. An understanding of sexual psychopharmacology has become essential for responsible patient care.

Limitations of Available Data on Drug Effects on Sex

It must be emphasized that the mechanisms for sexual response and their interrelationship are complex. Data are derived from reported drug effects, mostly anecdotal, anatomical cadaver studies which are naturally limited, and animal studies which are difficult to translate to human behavior. We cannot study arousal or orgasm in either of those two circumstances. The study of patients with neurologic compromise due to disease, injury, or surgery has been particularly valuable, but handicapped by the fact that many investigators analyze every physical consequence but sex.

It must be noted that much more is known about male sexual response and how it is affected by drugs than is known about the female response. There are several reasons. Male sexual functioning is more obvious than female sexual functioning and, consequently, easier to observe and evaluate. Definitions of normal are clearer for the male than for the female. Experts are still debating whether there are one or two neurologic pathways for the female orgasm. Since the female sexual response is less apparent to a partner, interference with her sexual function can remain her secret. Women do not volunteer sexual data as readily as males, especially to physicians of the opposite sex. Some have been intimidated by an authority figure's making negative comments or judgments when they have attempted to discuss the matter. Some male therapists do not ask details about a woman's sexual responsiveness due to discomfort in communicating with someone of the opposite gender about sex, or due to the fear that their inquiries may be misunderstood as a personal overture. In addition, the exhaustive research on the female menstrual cycle and reproductive system may have overshadowed any direct interest in female sexuality itself.

Most papers on drug effects study the male and simply add "no information is available on the female, but the effects on the female are probably similar to those on the male." This conclusion is not warranted, especially in view of recent evidence on anatomic and biochemical differences between the human male and female brain (Durden-Smith and De Simone 1983), and the distinct difference in our sexual hormones. It could develop that drugs in general—not only sexual hormones—have different influences on men and women.

The majority of information we have about the sexual side effects of drugs, positive or negative, is anecdotal and based on information from a single or at most a few patients. Research studies have been small and often insufficient to draw definitive conclusions. There are very few double-blind studies. Most of the anecdotal drug reports do not take into consideration concurrent drug use, including nicotine and alcohol; underlying organic problems such as cardiovascular disease; psychological impotence; or sexual dysfunction in the partner. In the few controlled studies that exist, the number of subjects studied have been small. Well-designed research studies on the effect of drugs on the sexual response cycle are sorely needed.

The Sexual Effects of Psychotropic Drugs

Adverse sexual effects have been reported with all the tricyclic antidepressants, the MAO inhibitors, as well as most of the newly marketed or about to be marketed second generation antidepressants. Most of these drugs induce sedation to some degree, and some patients report some reduction in libido.

The human sexual response represents the manifestations of a series of complex interactions between the central and peripheral neural systems and involves a wide variety of neurohormones and neurotransmitters. In both males and females, sexual dysfunction can occur at one or more points in the sexual response cycle. Drugs which alter neuronal interactions may:

1. Decrease libido
2. Interfere with erection, orgasm, or ejaculation in men
3. Interfere with lubrication; delay, alter, or inhibit orgasm in women

For example, it is possible that a drug that produces parasympathetic blockade may inhibit erections and vaginal lubrication. The sympathetic system controls the vasoconstrictor impulses to the penile arterioles, so a drug that produces agonist effects at this level might cause loss of erection. Central dopamine blockade decreases sexual desire. Alpha-adrenergic blockade inhibits orgasm.

The following is a brief review of how the various medications can adversely affect sexual function.

Antianxiety Drugs

Antianxiety drugs (minor tranquilizers and sedatives) have been implicated as a cause of sexual dysfunction due to a depressant action on the central nervous system. Chlordiazepoxide (Librium) has been associated with impotence in one case report (Usdin 1960), or with inhibited orgasm in the male (Hughes 1964).

O'Connor and Scavone (1982), in their review article, attribute a decrease in libido and altered sexual response as side effects produced by barbiturates, benzodiazepines, and other sedative hypnotics. Despite there reports, diazepam is often used to treat psychologically induced sexual dysfunction inhibitions, i.e., sex-related performance anxiety.

Antidepressants

Tricyclic antidepressants have peripheral and central anticholinergic effects. They also cause central nervous system sedation which can affect desire and erection. Ejaculation can also be delayed or inhibited. Amoxapine, desipramine, imipramine, and protriptyline have all been associated with reports of retrograde or painful ejaculation (DeLeo and Magni 1983; Kulik and Wilbur 1982; Schwartz 1982). Amitriptyline can also cause retarded ejaculation (Nininger 1978).

In the female, sexual response can also be subdued but there is little in the literature on this subject.

The adverse actions of tricyclic drugs are probably caused by their interference with cholinergic or adrenergic neurotransmission. The drugs that cause painful ejaculation block alpha-adrenergic receptors and inhibit norepinephrine reuptake (Kulik and Wilbur 1982). Both of these actions may lead to spasticity of smooth muscle contractions.

Clomipramine (a drug that is not available in the United States) has been reported to cause impotence, delayed ejaculation, a low sex drive, but has also been reported to have positive sexual effects. A paper titled "The Unusual Side-Effects of Clomipramine Associated with Yawning" (McLean et al. 1983) studied four cases in whom the use of clomipramine for the treatment of depression increased sexual responsiveness. One patient noted that "since taking the medication, every time I yawn, I have an orgasm." She found she was able to experience orgasm by deliberate yawning. With discontinuation of the medication several weeks later, this phenomenon disappeared. In another case, a man had noted frequent intense urges to yawn without tiredness, and on many occasions when he yawned, he experienced orgasm with ejaculation. He denied increased libidinal drive or related fantasy. His awkwardness and embarrassment was overcome by continuously wearing a condom (McLean et al. 1983, p. 569). Another patient began to complain of what she termed "yawning spells," during which she experienced irresistible sexual urges. All sexual symptoms disappeared with discontinuation of the drug.

Paradoxically, several studies have been performed to evaluate the value of clomipramine as a treatment for premature ejaculation. The results have been inconclusive. The contradictions of this drug in particular demonstrate the challenge of interpreting the psychopharmacology of sexual response.

MAO Inhibitors

MAO inhibitors (tranylcypromine, isocarboxazid, phenelzine) increase the concentration of several neurotransmitters (serotonin, histamine, norepinephrine, dopamine). Their most specific reported sexual side effect is delaying or inhibiting ejaculation.

MAO inhibitors may cause sexual dysfunction by their enhancing effect on the central sympathetic neural system. They produce an effect on the peripheral system as well which overlaps that of the tricyclics. While MAO inhibitor drugs have been reported to cause an increase in libido (Simpson et al. 1965), they also produce an inability to develop or maintain an erection, ejaculatory dysfunction, inhibition of vaginal lubrication, and an inability to achieve orgasm. Reports of sexual dysfunction occur frequently with the use of phenelzine. Fewer reports of sexually related adverse effects are associated with isocarboxazid, pargyline, and tranylcypromine; however, these drugs are used less frequently than phenelzine.

Antipsychotic Drugs

Antipsychotics might interfere with sex through several mechanisms:

1. The anticholinergic properties of these agents cause ganglionic blocking, or central effects.
2. Antimuscarinic effects can produce sedation.
3. Some stimulate the release of prolactin, or cause effects on the thyroid or other endocrine systems.
4. They may cause alpha-adrenergic antagonism.
5. They antagonize dopamine neurotransmission.

These mechanisms may result in decreased libido, inhibition of vaginal lubrication, or difficulty in developing or maintaining an erection. The phenothiazines, thioxdanthenes, and butyrophenones also block dopamine and alpha-adrenergic receptor sites. The literature contains many documented cases showing that piperidine, phenothiazine, butyrophenones, and thioridazine cause a high incidence of ejaculatory dysfunction (Buffum 1982). Thioridazine (Mellaril) can decrease or eliminate ejaculation without affecting orgasm. It was once thought that thioridazine induced retrograde ejaculation, but this assumption has been disproved since post-orgasmic urine samples rarely contained sperm (Buffum 1982). The machanism for ejaculatory inhibition is not understood. Ejaculatory problems exist in as many as 57 percent of patients on thioridazine, and erectile problems have been reported in 54 percent (Buffum 1982; Kotin et al. 1976). Thioridazine may also impair orgasm in women (Segraves 1985).

Chlorpromazine also causes sedation, which can result in decreased libido. Haloperidol (Haldol) appears to be the available antipsychotic drug least likely to cause sexual dysfunction (O'Connor and Scavone 1982), perhaps because it lacks anticholinergic effects.

Lithium has also been implicated as the cause of sexual dysfunction. Lithium decreases sex drive when it is used to treat the manic phase of a bipolar disorder. This effect has been considered an indirect result of successful resolution of the manic condition that can be associated with the symptom of hypersexuality. However, lithium has also been reported to decrease libido and responsiveness in patients not having manic episodes, possibly due to a mild inhibitory effect on adrenergic function (Blay et al. 1982), or by its antagonistic effect on the dopamine system.

Ghadirian et al. (1982) assessed sexual dysfunction in 55 schizophrenic outpatients, all of whom were taking antipsychotic drugs including fluphenazine, trifluoperazine, and chlorprothixene. Fifty-four percent of the men reported moderate to moderately severe difficulties in sexual functioning. Most complained of a "decreased ability to achieve orgasm and changes in the quality of orgasm."

Summary of Mechanisms for Action of Sexually Depressive Drugs

1. Anticholinergic side effects
2. Dopamine blockade
3. Alpha-adrenergic antagonism
4. Interference with central nervous system transmitter system regulating the hypothalamic-pituitary-gonadal axis
5. Central nervous system depression
6. Endocrine or peptide system interference
7. Increased serotonin

Drugs to Avoid if a Pre-existing Sexual Condition Exists

If there is a pre-existing sexual disorder, there are certain drugs one should not prescribe unless the need for them outweighs sexual considerations. Two of the greatest causes of patient noncompliance with drugs are weight gain and negative sexual side effects. If the patient considers the sexual side effect important, even if the physician does not, he or she may refuse to take the drug or not take it regularly, thereby neutralizing therapeutic intentions.

Selecting the best prescription drug can involve many considerations. If the patient has vaginismus and is also depressed, amitriptyline might be selected for its muscular antispasmodic properties. If there is premature ejaculation in the history, thioridazine or any of the other psychotropics that inhibits or delays ejaculation could be appropriate, but they should be avoided if the patient complains of difficulty ejaculating.

If there is impotence or difficulty lubricating, do not use anticholinergics. If there is difficulty with arousal, the majority of psychotropic drugs will have an adverse influence: central nervous system depressants, tricyclics, antipsychotics, sedatives, etc. If there is ejaculatory incompetence or difficulty having orgasms in the woman, avoid MAO inhibitors and antipsychotics, particularly thioridazine.

Drugs with Positive Sexual Side Effects

L-Dopa

L-dopa, a dopamine precursor, has been reported to increase sex drive and activity in older patients when used in the treatment of Parkinson's disease (Hyyppa et al. 1975). Under close scrutiny, this effect was apparently transient and occurred in only a small percentage of patients treated with L-dopa. After these initial anecdotal reports of hypersexuality among Parkinson's patients treated with L-dopa, attempts to show specific beneficial changes of sexuality in such patients were unsuccessful (Benkert 1972; Hyyppa et al. 1975). Brown et al. (1978) put seven patients into a sequence of L-dopa and placebo and found improvement in sexual functioning in four out of seven patients, but the results were not clinically significant, and the number too small to draw useful conclusions.

Dopamine itself seems to modulate ejaculation latency. Rats can be made to ejaculate prematurely by giving them L-dopa with apomorphine so that DA receptors are stimulated at an exaggerated rate (Paglietti et al. 1978). The consequent premature ejaculation can be completely blocked by pretreatment with drugs that specifically block DA transmission in the brain (Napoli-Farris et al. 1984). These DA-blocking drugs include haloperidol (Haldol), commonly used as an antipsychotic; and meto-clopramide (Reglan), commonly used as an antinauseant. This work has been extended to human studies. Premature ejaculators were treated with metoclopramide in a double-blind crossover drug-placebo study (Falaschi et al. 1981). Metoclopramide significantly extended the time to ejaculation. In acute tests, premature ejaculators given metoclopramide two hours before testing took longer to ejaculate (lasted longer) than when given placebo (Falaschi et al. 1981).

Bromocriptine

Bromocriptine, an ergot dopamine agonist, has been used successfully in the treatment of patients with hyperprolactinemia, and to treat sexual dysfunction in uremic patients (March 1979). During effective treatment, there is usually an increase in libido and firmness of erection.

Bromocriptine has been tested for positive sexual side effects within a double-blind placebo-controlled study by Ambrosi et al. (1977) on 30 impotent male subjects. Improvement was noted in 52 percent of those subjects on bromocriptine and in 44 percent of those on placebo. Consequently, the improvement among bromocriptine users was not statistically significant, because the presence of an effect was confounded by a high placebo response. Moreover, uncontrolled studies in impotent men by Benkert (1980) and Cooper (1977) failed to show significant improvement with the use of bromocriptine.

Decreased sexual desire and orgasmic-ejaculatory difficulties could theoretically respond to treatment with drugs, but subjects with these dysfunctions are rarely the focus of drug therapy studies. It is possible that DA-specific drugs have positive effects only on sexual desire and orgasm. A beneficial effect upon erection could occur secondarily.

Testosterone

Testosterone has been used to increase sex drive in women and in testosterone deficient males (Bancroft 1978). It appears to have no effect on men with adequate levels of testosterone, but has been reported to increase libido and responsiveness in women (Greenblatt et al. 1983). Though a larger placebo-controlled investigation has shown no benefit of testosterone treatment for sexually unresponsive women (Mathews et al. 1983), other excellent studies have shown positive correlations between testosterone levels and female sexual drive and response (Persky et al. 1982), and an extensive placebo-controlled trial has shown strong positive effects on sexual drive with testosterone treatment of surgically menopausal women (Sherwin et al. 1985). Unfortunately, virilizing side effects could prohibit long-term use in some women.

The use of testosterone to treat male sexual problems is common, far more common than warranted by serum testosterone levels. This medical habit is not innocuous. Overloading the system with exogenous testosterone in the long term can decrease natural testosterone production. Because testosterone is an anabolic steroid, it can cause or aggravate high blood pressure and related cardiac problems. Exogenous testosterone can activate a testosterone dependent prostatic or testicular cancer. A high percentage of older men have undiagnosed prostatic cancer. These men often die of other causes before the prostatic cancer has had an opportunity to impair their general health.

Testosterone replacement should not be used in men with testosterone levels over 300 nanograms per deciliter (NG/DL). Prostatic examination and blood pressure evaluation should be done prior to initiation of treatment and periodically for follow-up during treatment. Testosterone should be given by injection. The optimum rhythm of injections is every two weeks (instead of the common practice of every three to six weeks). The oral route is not generally effective, although there are now compounds being studied in Europe that bypass intestinal degradation.

If a patient gives a history of having had a trial of testosterone injections, ask how soon following the first injection he or she noticed a response. If the response occurred immediately after the shot or within the first few days following the injection, it is probably due to a placebo effect, not the hormone. It generally takes between one and three weeks for clinical improvement to be noticeable.

It is now possible to measure both free and bound serum testosterone levels. The relationship of free testosterone to sex parameters is still difficult to define since there are few clinical trials. It is possible, even probable, that the free testosterone is the active agent in sex drive and the protein-bound testosterone the inactive agent, similar to the thyroxin model. Further research on free and bound testosterone may help to explain the poor correlation of total testosterone levels and sexual function. There are men with total testosterones of 150 NG/DL with no overt sexual dysfunction and men completely impotent with total testosterone levels of 1,000 NG/DL or more. Had we been able to isolate the free testosterone in these cases, it might have correlated with drive.

LHRH

Luteinizing hormone releasing hormone (LHRH) has been used in Europe to increase sex drive and improve erections. LHRH, also known as gonadotropin releasing hormone (GnRH), is a hypothalamic hormone. It triggers the release of the adenohypophyseal anterior pituitary hormones known as luteinizing hormone (LH) and follicle stimulating hormone (FSH). LH stimulates the testes to secrete testosterone. These hormones interact in a negative feedback loop so that increased levels of testosterone decrease LHRH secretion, resulting in the modulation of LH secretion.

Interest in LHRH as a possible enhancer of sexuality in human beings was initiated by reports that the LHRH peptide increased sexual behavior in estrogen-primed ovariectomized or hypophysectomized female rats and in testosterone-primed castrated male rats (Moss and Dudley 1979). It stimulated both male and female mating behaviors (mounting and lordosis). Subsequently, positive sexual effects were also found in the mouse, pigeon, lizard, and frog, indicating the essential nature of this hormone in sexual control.

Uncontrolled human studies with LHRH have suggested an aphrodisiac role in normal and secondarily impotent men. However, definite improvement in sexuality has only been shown in hormonally deficient men where LHRH resolved the deficiency. Controlled trials have shown various individual indications of positive sexual effects. However, overall differences from placebo have been nonsignificant, and consistent improvement due to LHRH treatment has been slight (Benkert et al. 1975; Kastin et al. 1979; Moss and Dudley 1979). Nevertheless, LHRH sniffers became popular in Europe among men for restoration of potency.

The breakthough in the use of LHRH was the finding that only pulsatile delivery of LHRH at its proper physiologic frequency (e.g., one pulse per hour in the rhesus monkey) was effective in correcting improper functioning of the sex hormone system (Knobil 1980). Currently, portable infusion pumps are used to stimulate ovulation in women (Filicori and Crowley 1983) and sexual maturity and potency in men (Hoffman and Crowley 1983). The effect can be dramatic. Within a few months of pulsatile LHRH treatment, idiopathic hypogonadotropic hypogonadal men noted accelerated puberty, increase in serum testosterone to adult levels, increase in testes size, spontaneous erections, nocturnal emissions, and even the appearance of acne vulgaris and increased sebaceous activity of the skin (Hoffman and Crowley 1984).

When LHRH is administered in greater than normal amounts, it can suppress its own response. Essentially, the LHRH receptors become saturated and stop working so that LH and FSH are not secreted and testosterone and sperm production decreases. Administration of LHRH super-agonist analogs (e.g., buserelin) can reduce testicular steroidogenesis and spermatogenesis (Labrie et al. 1983). Resourceful scientists quickly saw the possibility of using LHRH as a contraceptive. However, when LHRH is used in this way, the libido fades with the decrease in testosterone. The solution to this problem would be to give the males supplementary testosterone; but supplementary testosterone can revive spermatogenesis.

Contrary to the desensitization brought on by too much exogenous LHRH, the endogenous pulsatile rhythm of LHRH stimulates its own receptor. LHRH release is controlled by various neurotransmitters and neuropeptides and may be expected to be sensitive to various changes in the environment due to their interplay. The presence of a female or an intruder can alter a male's LHRH activity. Women's menstrual cycles can become irregular with emotional upset and men's testosterone levels are surprisingly dependent on how they are coping with the outside world. LHRH is crucially involved in such changes (Moss and Dudley 1984).

In the rat, LHRH receptors are concentrated in the medial preoptic area and arcuate nucleus of the brain. The same areas govern mating behavior of both male and female rats. Conditions that possibly suppress sexual functioning, such as hyperprolactinemia and stress-induced endogenous opioid and cortisol release, have been shown to supress LHRH secretion. Administration of substances that stimulate sexual behavior in animals, such as naloxone (Abbott et al. 1984) and L-dopa (Pucci et al. 1981), stimulate LHRH release. These same relationships may apply to humans.

La Ferla et al. (1978) have shown that LHRH is stimulated in male subjects during sexual arousal either during coitus or while viewing sexually explicit films. LHRH pulses result in increased testosterone, but there is evidence that LHRH also has a sexually stimulating effect through its own receptors in the brain so that its secretion can increase libido and erections even before levels of circulating testosterone are affected (Besser 1984). In sum, LHRH controls directly or indirectly, essential sexual and reproductive events. It has been made available in sniffers and portable infusion pumps so that it can be administered periodically for its positive sexual effects (LHRH cannot be taken orally because its peptide structure would be digested prior to absorption).

Vasoactive Intestinal Polypeptide

Vasoactive intestinal polypeptide (VIP) is a neuropeptide originally labeled as a gut peptide, but subsequently identified within the human brain and urinogenital tract. It has been reported to be a neurotransmitter in penile erection, and may have a clinical use in the treatment of impotence. Ottesen et al. (1984) have shown that VIP is released during erection, and intracavernous injection of VIP produces erection. Within the brain, VIP is concentrated in hypothalamic areas known to influence sexual excitation and has been implicated in the neuroendocrine control of pituitary function (Nicosia et al. 1983). Increases in prolactin during coitus could be due to VIP action since VIP is a potent prolactin releasing factor (Shimatsu et al. 1984). VIP has also been shown to be highly concentrated within the female vagina, uterus, and clitoris (Ottesen 1983). It exists as a co-transmitter in cholinergic neurons (Stahl 1984) and parasympathetic stimulation of the cat uterus involves VIP release that is not reduced by the cholinergic antagonist atropine or various adrenergic blocking agents (Ottesen 1983). Conceivably, VIP is the parasympathetic neurotransmitter primarily responsible for erection and lubrication. This could account for the apparent lack of a negative effect of atropine on physical arousal, despite the assumed control of arousal by parasympathetic innervation.

Intracavernous injection of the adrenergic blocking drug phenoxybenzamine and the vasodilators papaverine and phentolamine has also been used successfully to generate usable erections in organically impotent men. One should be aware that continued use of these vasodilators for months may cause priapism.

Dopamine Enhancing Antidepressants

Bupropion (Wellbutrin) is an investigatory antidepressant recently tested in clinical trials. It has been studied for sexual side effects and has been found to have no negative influence on sexuality in males treated for depression (Gardner and Johnson 1985). Bupropion has a novel chemical structure that does not act in traditional antidepressant ways. Its antidepressant mechanism is not understood, but it has been noted to inhibit dopamine uptake (Ferris et al. 1983). A large double-blind controlled study with 60 subjects, male and female, conducted at the Crenshaw Clinic has shown that bupropion significantly improves sex drive and performance in non-depressed men and women (Crenshaw et al. 1987).

Viloxazine significantly increased sex drive and libido in an open study with 20 mildly depressed patients (DeLeo et al. 1983). Sexual improvements due to these antidepressants might be due to their positive dopamine effect.

Serotonin Enhancing Antidepressants

Antidepressants, including MAO inhibitors, that prolong 5-HT activity include clomipramine (Anafranil), amitriptyline (Elavil), trazodone (Desyrel), phenelzine (Nardil), and isocarboxazid (Marplan). They have all been found to inhibit or retard ejaculation (Buffum 1982; Fraser 1984; Jones 1984; Segraves 1982). This ejaculatory delay effect has been used successfully to treat premature ejaculation (Bennett 1961; Goodman 1980; Porto 1980).

There have been few articles published on the treatment of premature ejaculation with antianxiety agents. Clinical trials with the antianxiety beta blocker drug propranolol (Inderal) failed to show efficacy in treatment of premature ejaculation (Cooper and Magnus 1984). Serotonergic drugs appear to delay ejaculation directly rather than just treat anxiety; consequently, they should be more effective than antianxiety drugs in the treatment of severe premature ejaculation. Such treatment is an excellent example of how an apparently negative sexual side effect can be used positively in the course of sexual therapy.

Trazodone

Given that trazodone presumably works through a serotonergic process, it could potentially retard ejaculation. No reports of retarded ejaculation as a side effect of trazodone occurred for quite a while, but recently a case study of inhibited ejaculation was published (Jones 1984) and more such reports of retarded or inhibited ejaculation can be expected. The side effect of priapism resulting from trazodone is produced by an unknown mechanism (Lansky and Selzer 1984).

Yohimbine

Yohimbine, a natural indole alkaloid that functions as an alpha-2-adrenergic antagonist, stimulates postsynaptic norepinephrine (NE) activity. It has a popular reputation as an aphrodisiac, and recent medical studies have shown it to have some value in the treatment of impotence (Morales et al. 1982). A preparation of yohimbine, testosterone, and nux vomica (Afrodex) showed efficacy for treatment of impotence (Margolis et al. 1971), but was banned by the FDA in 1973. Clark et al. (1984) have shown low dose yohimbine to have a stimulating action on male rat sex behavior. Controlled studies are being conducted to test the efficacy of yohimbine in the treatment of sexual dysfunction in man.

Since yohimbine can produce anxiety and has cardiac effects as well, it must be prescribed with caution.

Phenylethylamine

Since DA decreases with aging, particularly in sexually important areas of the hypothalamus, dopaminergic drugs should show significant sexual benefits in older subjects. An excellent study in "sexually sluggish old male rats" (Knoll et al. 1983) found that (-) -deprenyl (Segeline) restored normal sexual behavior and maintained this increased level of activity. ($-$)-Deprenyl is a new type of MAO inhibitor which at low levels is selective for dopaminergic amines (Zsilla and Knoll 1982). All MAO inhibitors presently available in the United States are non-selective MAO-A and MAO-B inhibitors or selective MAO-A inhibitors, indicating that they increase the levels of both 5-HT and NE. The negative sexual side effects of these MAO-A inhibitors (retarded ejaculation and impotence) are conceivably due to the elevation of serotonin activity by these drugs. (-) -Deprenyl is a MAO-B inhibitor, indicating that it is selective for phenylethylamine activity. Phenylethylamine (PEA) has been promoted in the popular press as the "Molecule of Love." PEA is the alleged aphrodisiac ingredient found in chocolate. Liebowitz (1983) has written a popular book called *The Chemistry of Love*, wherein PEA is said to be the endogenous chemical transmitter active in ecstatic and romantic sexual relationships. The direct precursor of PEA, D-phenylalanine, has been reported to stimulate mounting behavior in male rats (Segal et al. 1984). Segal et al. (1984) showed that PEA increased norepinephrine in the medial preoptic region of the rat brain, an area known to be crucial for regulation of sexual behavior.

Cocaine and Amphetamines

Cocaine increases sex drive and delays ejaculation. At higher doses, erection and orgasm become impaired.

Amphetamines and cocaine stimulate both DA and NE activity. Their positive sexual effect could be due to stimulation of DA, and their negative sexual effects, such as loss of erection, could be due to stimulation of NE. In order to test for effects due solely to dopaminergic processes, we need to use drugs that stimulate or inhibit DA alone.

Pheromones

In animals, there have been promising studies, not yet confirmed in humans, concerning the investigation of sexual pheromones and sexual scents, such as copulins (Doty 1977).

Pheromones are substances produced by one member of a species which influence the behavior and/or endocrine system of another conspecific. There are two specific classes of pheromones, primer and releaser (Vandenberg 1984). The releaser pheromones produce a quick behavioral change such as might be caused by a sexual attractant. The primer pheromones, in contrast, have their influences in altering the ovarian endocrine or behavioral status through chronic exposure. Thus, pheromones are substances which act between conspecifics to promote reproductive system alterations.

Sexual pheromones have been identified in animals from the cockroach to the boar. The best known sexual scents are those released by cats and dogs in heat. No sexual pheromone has yet been confirmed in the human, although research is active in this area.

Anti-Estrogenic Fertility Drugs

Clomiphene (Clomid, Serophene) and tamoxifen (Nolvadex) are anti-estrogens used to treat male infertility and stimulate female ovulation. Tamoxifen is predominately used to treat breast cancer. Both of these drugs stimulate the action of LHRH within the hypothalamo-pituitary-testicular axis so that testosterone is increased, the testes grow, and spermatogenesis may be generated. Increased libido was noted in five of 16 patients treated with clomiphene for infertility (Reyes and Faiman 1974) and increased libido was noted as a prominent side effect by Schellen (1975). Cooper et al. (1972) failed to find any significant improvement in psychogenically impotent males treated with clomiphene, despite following patient progress with a daily sexual questionnaire.

Clomiphene or tamoxifen treatment could generate the same sexual benefits as LHRH treatment without the difficulties inherent in pulsatile drug delivery. It possibly could be valuable in men with deficient sexual function due to borderline testosterone or hypogonadal conditions.

Imipramine

Imipramine has been used in conjunction with psychotherapy for the treatment of post-traumatic stress disorders (Burstein 1984), panic attacks, and sexual phobias associated with inhibited sexual desire (Kaplan et al. 1982). A patient with post-traumatic stress disorder (PTSD) is often incapacitated by anxiety, sleep disturbances, and other symptoms. Two or three weeks of treatment with imipramine significantly decreases the severity of forced recollections, sleep and dream disturbances, and flashbacks. This drug could be particularly valuable in the management of the rape trauma syndrome (Crenshaw 1978). While imipramine may effectively block panic attacks related to sexual issues, it appears to have no effect on the anticipatory dread or avoidance behaviors. MAO inhibitors and other tricyclics, particularly clomipramine, have also been used in the treatment of phobia and panic reactions.

Therapeutic Reduction of Sex Drive

Many drugs have been used successfully to modulate hypersexuality and to control deviant sexual behavior. Drugs have been used as an alternative to incarceration, castration, or brain surgery. Estrogens were once used to reduce sex drive in men, but caused disturbing side effects such as nausea, gynecomastia, and thrombosis. Currently, progestagens (e.g., Provera, Megace) and the antiandrogen cyproterone acetate are the drugs of choice (Freund 1980). Antipsychotics and tranquilizers such as benperidol and fluphenazine have been used successfully, and antidepressants such as amitriptyline and imipramine can sometimes be used for mild cases. Diethylstilbestrol has also been used to treat sex offenders.

The only drug currently available in the United States for sex drive reduction is medroxyprogesterone (Provera). It has been used successfully for a variety of deviant sexual behaviors (Berlin and Meinecke 1981).

Cyproterone (Androcur) is widely used in Europe. It has been reported that cyproterone chiefly reduces libido and leaves erection and ejaculation undisturbed so that only the undesirable motivation is decreased.

Few controlled studies have been done with antiandrogens or other drugs used to reduce sex drive. One would expect some direct or indirect depression of the sexual response due to these drugs, and more careful study may reveal these side effects. Use of medroxyprogesterone in lower doses in women for menstrual disturbances and treatment of menopause is assumed not to have negative sexual effects; but given progestagens' severe negative effect on libido in men, this assumption is highly questionable and should be rigorously tested. Although there is general agreement that androgens are the stimulating sex hormone in women (see chapter on psychiatric disorders and sexual functioning), the use of antiandrogens to control undesirable sexuality in women has not been reported; instead, psychoactive drugs are generally used.

Speculations

With the numerous chemical substances influencing sexual response and behavior in various ways, one can begin to see how body chemistry can be altered therapeutically to affect sexuality.

Sex Drive

Dopaminergic drugs could be used to improve low sex drive. Unfortunately, some of them, like cocaine, are often abused. Drugs like tranylcypromine, yohimbine, and viloxazine are potentially useful for increasing sex drive. New dopamine agonists are being tested currently, although side effects (as with nomifensine) may make them dangerous.

Orgasmic Dysfunctions (Including Ejaculatory Incompetence)

Certain drugs could help women reach orgasm more easily and assist men in the treatment of ejaculatory incompetence (retarded ejaculation). Sympathomimetics or alpha-adrenergic stimulating drugs are good candidates. A dopaminergic drug might trigger the signal for ejaculation or orgasm earlier through a general improvement in sex drive as well as by increasing the perception of physical sensations during intercourse. However, to date, efforts to treat ejaculatory incompetence with drugs have been ineffective.

Premature Ejaculation

Preventing premature ejaculation in men could be governed by drugs that inhibit the sympathetic nervous system. Serotonergic drugs could also be useful in regulating or retarding ejaculation. MAO inhibitors probably retard ejaculation by increasing serotonin levels. Phenelzine (Nardil), for example, usually does not inhibit erection but may inhibit orgasm. Isocarboxazid (Marplan) probably works in the same manner. Other tricyclic antidepressants that work chiefly through blocking 5-HT uptake could also be used. These include amitriptyline (Elavil) and trazodone (Desyrel).

Thioridazine (Mellaril) and other antidopaminergic tranquilizers and antipsychotics such as haloperidol (Haldol) could be tried over a short course of therapy. Over longer periods of time, milder serotonergic drugs such as lithium or the investigational antidepressant drug fluoxetine could be tried to prevent premature ejaculation. These could be used as adjuncts to psychotherapy.

Phenoxybenzamine (Dibenzeline) has been reported by some of my patients to delay or inhibit ejaculation and orgasm. It is an antispasmotic usually prescribed for lower urinary tract spasm. One patient had to interrupt taking it periodically in order to ejaculate.

Some drugs may inhibit ejaculation while not inhibiting orgasm (e.g., thioridazine), and some drugs may precipitate ejaculation without the presence of an erection. There is much research and careful observation that needs to be performed before these preparations can become clinically useful.

Impotence

There are four classes of drugs that could assist in sustaining erections. Antianxiety drugs that are not so powerful that they interfere with erections but sufficiently strong to inhibit the fears of performance that precipitate the loss of erection through sympathetic response could be helpful. Sympatholytics could assist in sustaining erections through delaying ejaculation. Parasympathomimetics could perpetuate erections and conceivably increase firmness, although recent studies are discrediting the relationship of erection and the parasympathetic nervous system. Dopaminergic drugs that improve sex drive could improve erections through this drive mechanism. Alpha 2 blockers such as yohimbine appear to delay ejaculation but also, through some mechanism not yet identified, may improve erections. It has been speculated that the effect is mediated through vasodilation or urinary tract irritation. Vasodilators with precise mechanisms yet to be discovered might assist in sustaining erections, although most cardiac drugs now in use may eliminate them. It will probably be demonstrated in future studies that some of the drugs now known to interfere with sexual function can be potentially useful at lower doses.

Vaginismus

Amitriptyline and Valium can be used during treatment of vaginismus both for antianxiety and muscle relaxant effects. Also indomethacin is often effective in the treatment of vaginismic women with primary dysmenorrhea.

Transient and Sustained Effects

Some drugs will be demonstrated to have transient sexual side effects such as L-dopa; others will have sustained effects. Both types of effects are valuable. A transient effect can be useful as a frame of reference, and to assist a patient in overcoming a learned sexual impairment. A sustained effect may be necessary if the medication is treating a biochemical deficit which is the cause of the sexual dysfunction. It is important to realize, however, that the drugs being discussed all have certain significant and undesirable systemic side effects and a risk benefit judgment can be difficult.

Ethics of Prescribing Sexually Potentiating Drugs

Medication and Psychotherapy

As in the treatment of depression, a pill alone is usually not sufficient. Psychotherapy is also required and the medication should only be prescribed under the supervision of a qualified physician. There is the question of symptom substitution versus definitive treatment. If you treat with medication, have you addressed the underlying problems responsibly? Will symptom substitution occur and leave the patient worse off than before? There are some symptoms that are preferable to others, so in certain cases being pragmatic can be relevant. However, there are often other issues that require psychotherapy.

Consider patients who have fear of success and difficulty dealing with it. They may enter therapy already convinced nothing will work. Often when they begin to get positive results, psychologically they do not cope well with these results. These patients need therapeutic help in order to adjust to their improved biologic sexual function. A sexually repressed individual may not like the feelings that the medications precipitate.

If there is a significant psychological component to the sexual dysfunction in addition to the medical problem, drug adjustment or withdrawal may not help without concomitant psychotherapy.

Relationship Impact

Also consider the relationship. When one partner improves, a pathologic symbiotic relationship may be disrupted, and the change may precipitate a separation or a divorce. There may be such pressure on the partner that new relationship problems are created.

If a medication increases sex drive, some individuals with poor impulse control may choose to have affairs that they would otherwise not consider.

Hypersexuality

Drugs that potentiate sexual function could cause hypersexuality or trigger criminal sexual acts in sex offenders or inappropriate sexual behavior in individuals with poor impulse control. It is not always known to the treating physician if a patient is engaging in sexually criminal behavior. Consequently, medication could aggravate obsessive or compulsive sexual behavior, sexual addiction, and paraphilias.

Fertility, Gender, Sexual Preference

It should be considered as a theoretical possibility that any drug affecting sex drive or performance may also influence the offspring of the treated patient. As in DES babies, if drugs are taken inadvertently or intentionally during pregnancy, there can be an influence on the health and sexuality of the progeny. Should a woman become pregnant on some of these new drugs without realizing it, the effects on the fetus could be serious, not only medically but perhaps with regard to sexual orientation and gender development.

Chapter 215

Special Approaches

While there is still a vigorous research effort to understand the causes of psychosexual dysfunctions, much more understanding is available than there was a generation ago. Ignorance about sexual functioning is a major contributor to dysfunction. Educational approaches, developed to counteract sexual ignorance, are effective in a variety of ingenious formats to supply information, modify attitudes, and improve skills. Anxiety from any cause contributes to psychosexual dysfunctions, so techniques to diminish anxiety, such as systematic desensitization and hypnosis, are useful in therapy. The role of one's sexual partner in causing and maintaining a psychosexual dysfunction is very important. When a partner is unavailable or unwilling to participate in therapy, specialized approaches, like the use of sexual surrogates, exist to solve the problem. The use of surrogates and some other approaches may be controversial because of real or potential ethical conflicts; these include the use of sexual aids, of which vibrators are the most important, and the use of the sexological exam. Each of these specialized approaches to treatment of psychosexual dysfunctions will be discussed in the sections that follow.

Educational Techniques

With the realization that psychosexual dysfunctions were common and treatable, there was a recognition of the necessity to train therapists. A wave of enthusiasm for teaching about human sexuality began in the early 1970s and spread throughout the decade to medical schools and other treatment facilities. There were few qualified teachers and a great many eager, curious students. Edward Tyler, M.D. (personal communication), a psychiatrist then teaching at Indiana University's Medical School, was assigned to teach human sexuality to about 250 students. In an effort to learn what might be useful to teach, he turned to the Archives of the Kinsey Institute for Sex Research on the Indiana University campus. They had an extensive collection of pornographic films, and Dr. Tyler happily devoted himself to two full days of reviewing them. The experiment surprised him. The deluge of sexually explicit materials turned his titillation into boredom very quickly. The repetitious exposure to the full range of sexual activities depicted in the films changed his initial reactions of shock and sexual arousal into jaded acceptance within hours.

Necessity bred invention. Tyler had no teachers; too many students; a mountain of "irresistibly boring," sexually explicit films; and an awareness that intensive exposure rapidly "desensitized" most observers to the sexually stimulating material. He conscripted discussion leaders into his course faculty and exposed his students to a learning experience similar to his own. Adding discussion groups to allow the students to explore their feelings on a more individualized basis was helpful. It not only made the students aware of their own sexual biases, values, and misconceptions, it made them realize that there was a wide range of sexual attitudes and values in the population.

At the same time, similar but independent educational approaches were being developed, refined, and applied widely to a broad range of target populations, propelled to a large extent by the organization of the Center for the Study of Sex Education in Medicine at the University of Pennsylvania (Lief and Karlen 1976). Sexual attitude restructuring (SAR) programs have been used with audiences of health care professionals, counselors, sex educators, and groups of lay people. A cottage industry devoted to making sexually explicit, educationally motivated films, tapes, videocassettes, pamphlets, and books sprang up to tap the commerical potential of a huge audience seeking explicit sexual information. As programs to treat psychosexual dysfunctions grew, the waiting lists of prospective patients grew longer. Educational programs, using sexually explicit materials created for the purpose, are efficient ways of exposing large groups of patients to attitudes and information that may help some of them to overcome their dysfunctions. It is an approach that requires relatively little professional time. One lecturer or discussion leader can interact with a large audience. As techniques of production grow more sophisticated, the materials available for education become better, requiring less time contribution from teachers or therapists.

The results of educational approaches seem promising. Objective scientific studies are few and limited in scope. It appears that many people with psychosexual dysfunctions caused wholly or partly by sexual ignorance or repressive attitudes can and do benefit from educational approaches (Mathews et al. 1976). For some people, the experience of participating in sexually educational activities with one's partner leads to more effective communication between the partners, and that is helpful. Clearly, there are many people for whom educational approaches are not sufficient, and those people need more extensive psychotherapy.

Systematic Desensitization

Anxiety is a major factor causing psychosexual dysfunction. The anxiety may be from any source. For example, it may be anxiety about one's ability to perform sexually up to one's expectations; it may be anxiety about death, injury, disease, or pregnancy resulting from sexual activity; or it may be anxiety about being discovered in sexual activity by one's parent, one's spouse, one's partner's parent, or one's partner's spouse. The anxiety, from whatever source, can be a contributing cause to any of the psychosexual dysfunctions. The effort to diminish anxiety to facilitate sexual functioning has a long history. Charms, love potions, and talismans to assure success in sexual conquest were the ancient equivalents of alcohol, methaqualone (Quaalude), marijuana, and cocaine taken in current times to diminish anxiety and stimulate performance. Their effects may be partly placebo and partly pharmacologic.

The psychotherapeutic approaches to controlling anxiety in treating sexual dysfunctions are usually a form of systematic desensitization. Based on the work of Wolpe and Lazarus (1958, 1966) the principle is that one cannot be both relaxed and anxious simultaneously. A patient is taught how to relax using a variety of related techniques (Benson 1976). Once relaxation has been mastered, the patient is systemically exposed to those thoughts or experiences which elicit his anxiety. Usually, he would begin the exposure to an aspect of the sexual situation which would evoke only moderate anxiety. He would experience the anxiety, then induce relaxation until the level of anxiety grew tolerable, then refocus his conscious attention on what was anxiety provoking. By repeated exposure to the anxiety, using relaxation, he would grow accustomed, i.e., not anxious, with that formerly anxiety-provoking circumstance. He would then progress to the next level or situation which would make him anxious and repeat the process. There are a number of innovative uses of various forms of systematic desensitization in sex therapy.

One common approach to the treatment of rapid ejaculation is the method of Lobitz and LoPiccolo (1972) which uses a form of systematic desensitization. Most men who ejaculate without adequate control do so after penile penetration of the vagina. Most men are better able to control ejaculation when masturbating alone. Lobitz and LoPiccolo advocate a series of steps between masturbating alone at one extreme and vigorous thrusting of the penis in the vagina at the other extreme. These steps include having the partner masturbate the man, perhaps using a lubricant, and vaginal penetration with the man on his back, no thrusting and the woman astride him. The patient begins at the first step where he feels more ejaculatory control. He will stimulate himself close to the point of ejaculatory inevitability, stopping before orgasm occurs. After repeating the procedure until he can tolerate the stimulation without experiencing orgasm, he then proceeds to the next intermediate step. In systematic fashion, he would progressively master the most anxiety-provoking situation after first learning ejaculatory control in less anxiety-provoking circumstances.

Another example of using systematic desensitization in treating psychosexual dysfunctions was the therapy of a 40-year-old man with inhibited sexual desire for his wife. He had grown up in a religious, sexually repressive household. If he would get drunk he could function sexually with his wife, although she abhorred having sexual contact with him when he drank. On the other hand, he experienced desire and would become involved with women he met while traveling in his work. He would also drink to reduce his anxiety and inhibitions.

Looking at his wife when she was naked made him very anxious, and he could not get sexually aroused. After teaching him to relax, the therapist instructed the wife to hold a sheet before her naked body at eye level. Her husband would look at her and ask her to lower the sheet to the point where his anxiety was no longer tolerable. She would hold the sheet at that point while he attempted to relax. When he was no longer anxious, he would instruct her to lower the sheet. By giving him, effectively, control over the amount of anxiety he would experience, and a means of diminishing it, he rapidly overcame the problem within a few days.

Hypnosis

Hypnosis has a long history as a psychotherapeutic technique. Unfortunately, hypnosis, like sex therapy itself, still suffers from a reputation as a questionably valid technique practiced by questionably legitimate therapists. It is important to acknowledge that while hypnosis and sex therapy may be practiced by some who lack personal or professional qualifications, there are many competent and innovative practitioners.

Hypnosis has three main uses in the treatment of psychosexual dysfunctions. It is an effective and powerful tool for achieving relaxation and therefore for relieving anxiety. Its use of visual imagery allows for mental rehearsal of sexually difficult situations. With reassurance and positive post-hypnotic suggestions, it may lead to increased confidence, and thereby improved sexual functioning. The third use of hypnosis is as an exploratory, diagnostic tool, enhancing understanding of psychodynamic motivation and conflict. For example, the reasons for resistance to sex therapy may be revealed during hypnosis.

Currently we are seeing another in the cycle of periodic resurgences of interest in hypnosis among mental health professionals. There have been some recent attempts to use hypnosis in systematic ways to treat psychosexual dysfunctions (Araoz 1982).

Sexual Aids

Perhaps the commonest and most readily available sexual aids are the perfumes, soaps, lotions, and lubricants used for sexual purposes. In recent years there has been a transition from the use of heavy, petroleum-based ointments to water soluble, lightly scented, non-irritating, easily dispensed lubricants to be applied to the genitalia or elsewhere.

Vibrators are useful to evoke orgasm, particularly in women. The stimulation is intense, and receptors are abundant and significant in the clitoris and penis. For those who are reluctant to touch their genitalia with their own hands, using vibrators, streams of water, or other objects may be easier and more acceptable ways of feeling pleasure.

While there is a surprisingly general acceptance of lubricants, lotions, vibrators, magazines, books, and films, more exotic paraphernalia is still marginally acceptable. Objects to enhance fantasy, such as restraints, whips, chains, dildoes, and a remarkably large array of sexual "aids" are available. No data exist about the extent of their use, but there are no indications it is diminishing. There are objections to using sexual aids because they are "unnatural," perverse, or because people fear that they will come to prefer using aids to interacting with a partner, or become addicted or dependent on the aids, becoming "vibrator junkies." Such addiction, however, is relatively rare. For most who use sexual aids to provide variety, excitement, and additional pleasure in sexual activities, there seems to be no adverse effect. On the other hand, many who seek sexual aids because of real or perceived sexual inadequacies might be better helped by competent sexual education or therapy, if only because the latter avenues would be more likely to help build knowledge and sustain confidence.

Surrogates

People with psychosexual dysfunctions have routinely sought other sexual partners when difficulties arise with their regular partner. Prostitutes have always met that need. As social mores change, amateurs rather than professionals have been the sexual partners of dysfunctional people.

As therapy for psychosexual dysfunctions developed in the past two decades, there was an important conceptual realization—the relationship was the preferred object of treatment rather than the separate individuals in the relationship. If no partner were available to cooperate in treating a psychosexual dysfunction, a surrogate partner might help.

The use of sexual surrogates by Masters and Johnson brought into the open a practice that had been going on surreptitiously. For some dysfunctional patients without available partners they found partners who would participate in sexual therapy. If a male patient had no available sexual partner, a woman would participate with the patient in the prescribed treatment. (In some areas of the country, male surrogates are used.) Ideally, the surrogate partner is an emotionally stable, sexually experienced, competent, and secure person whose own emotional needs are fulfilled in relationships other than with the patient. While surrogates do what they do expecting payment, they differ from prostitutes in their role expectations. Surrogates are teachers, not objects for sexual exploitation. The relationship with their clients is a quasi-psychotherapeutic one. Preferably the surrogate is directed in the psychosexual therapy by a therapist who conducts the treatment; the surrogate is a cotherapist. As with other psychotherapeutic relationships, the surrogate's involvement with the patient is to be confined to the psychotherapy situation, without expectation of a relationship to continue following the therapy. The premise underlying the use of surrogates in psychosexual therapy is that a patient may be able to overcome his dysfunction with the surrogate. Through gaining knowledge, confidence, or both, and with less anxiety, the patient can then function effectively with his non-surrogate partners.

The use of sexual surrogates in a legitimate, prescribed treatment program has provoked remarkable public interest and controversy. Surrogates are readily available in only a few of the major cities of the United States. Perhaps it is because sexual relations between unmarried and uncommitted people offends many people's morality that the use of surrogates is an issue. Certainly, there is rarely prosecution for sexual relations between consenting adults even when laws exist against the practice. The exchange of money for sexual services between patient and surrogate might be considered a form of prostitution and therefore illegal, but there are no documented prosecutions of surrogates, clients, or therapists by legal authorities. Neither have there been any malpractice suits known against surrogates or the therapists employing them.

A major concern is with selection and training of surrogates. Most candidates are women, although male surrogates also work as partners for women or for homosexual men. The motivations for becoming a surrogate vary. There are no clearly defined criteria for selection. Presumably, surrogate candidates are sexually experienced, without significant dysfunctions; personally secure about their sexual competence and desirability; and motivated by a desire to help others as well as by a desire to earn money. Many are in middle age, ranging from their 30s to their 60s, although a few are in their 20s. What, if any, exclusionary criteria there are is not known. Unlike other psychotherapeutic trainees, there are no formal intellectual, educational, experimental, or mental health standards. Training of surrogates is usually done by other surrogates. The length of training varies from weeks to months, and consists of supervised work as a surrogate, with a variety of partners, most of whom are also surrogate trainees. Obviously, the quasi-legal status of surrogates precludes any form of official licensure or certification. Some people licensed as psychotherapists also work as surrogates, but rarely; ethical standards precluding therapist-patient sex make this a dubious practice.

Ideally, in treating a psychosexual dysfunction, a therapist would use the surrogate just as he would use the partner of any patient. The patient and the surrogate would meet regularly with the therapist who would evaluate the problems and prescribe some activities for the couple to practice between meetings. As therapy progresses, the participants devise treatment strategies, flexibly, to contend with the resistances of the patients and to overcome specific deficiencies. The costs of treatment are substantial because the patient must pay for the therapist's time as well as the surrogate's time, both in meeting with the therapist and working with the surrogate. The therapy is expensive, logistically cumbersome, and therefore restricted to patients who can afford a substantial commitment of time and money.

In practice, there are several compromising and complicating issues. Many therapists who employ surrogates to work with patients are not well-trained or competent sex therapists. The surrogate, who often has more experience treating psychosexual dysfunctions, may take over the major responsibility for directing the therapy. Notwithstanding the fact that "training" as a sexual surrogate does not correspond to training as a psychotherapist, there are potential problems in the surrogate's being both partner and therapist simultaneously. The usual ethical constraints against therapists engaging in sexual relationships with patients might also apply. There is a danger of the surrogate's exploiting the patient; doing psychological harm to the patient; or failing through lack of training, experience, and objectivity to recognize dangerous circumstances.

Surrogate work is intense and emotionally demanding. Many surrogates, while lacking formal, academically based psychotherapy training, are sensitive, intuitively effective therapists. Whether they are or are not, most people in a surrogate role aspire to the higher status of the therapist role. There are frequently conflicts among therapist, surrogate, and client as to how treatment should progress. These should be resolved through discussion and guidance from a qualified, objective professional.

Other problems include the unwillingness of some married patients to notify their spouse of their wish to be treated with a surrogate. Most therapists will not risk a lawsuit by treating, knowingly, a married patient without getting informed consent to use a surrogate from the nonparticipating spouse. There are few treatment outcome studies of the efficacy of sex therapy. Outcome studies of surrogate sex therapy are very limited (Greene 1977; Johnston 1978; Minson 1980). The three studies, all disappointingly based on a few cases, support the need of surrogates to have more extensive therapy skills. One study emphasizes the need for close, effective collaboration among therapist, surrogate, and patient. The third suggests that the gains a patient makes from work with a surrogate are likely to generalize to sexual activities with other partners.

Sexological Examination

Another specialized approach in sex therapy is the sexological examination. Because so many people grow up unfamiliar with their own genitalia, and ignorant about the sexual anatomy of the other sex, it is often necessary. The sexological exam is one way of learning. It may be part of homework or it may be "orchestrated" by the physician. Each partner identifies the parts of their genital anatomy and demonstrates it to his or her partner. They may refer to diagrams. Commonly, the partners will touch or explore one another's genitalia with feedback and demonstration of what caresses are most pleasurable. The procedure educates, facilitates communication between partners, and places the responsibility for receiving pleasure where it belongs, on the person being pleasured. Like other behavioral assignments, the successful achievement of a sexological examination builds confidence and decreased inhibition.

Some modifications of the procedure are controversial. When a therapist is present at the time of a sexological exam, he may be the one to demonstrate the genital anatomy of the partners, including caresses to arouse sexual excitement. (This should never be done without the partner or other suitable third person present.) When a therapist is sexually stimulating a patient, the potential for sexual exploitation is great. Most of the leaders in the field of sex therapy recommend against direct sexual contact between patients and therapists under any circumstances. Since there are reliable, effective ways of treating psychosexual dysfunction without patient-therapist sexual contact, it is never advisable.

From a perspective of almost two decades one can see that progress in sex therapy has been due to a combination of evolving social attitudes and advancing scientific knowledge. In considering special approaches to treating sexual problems, it seems likely that the future will resemble the past. The subject of sexual fantasy is now being investigated, and the previously prevalent attitudes about fantasy being deviant or perverse will give way to the systematic, more effective use of fantasy to enhance sexual responses. Once freed from their inhibitions about sexual fantasy, sex therapists and others will try to understand and harness this natural force to people's sexual advantage.

Chapter 216

Special Populations and Sexual Dysfunctions

The purpose of this chapter is to provide a framework for understanding the treatment of psychosexual dysfunctions in populations that we have designated as "special." Clearly, it is not their sexuality that is different; rather, our attitudes and approaches to it at times require special consideration and understanding. It is within this conceptual framework that we have included widely disparate groups with very different needs, experiences, and concerns. Common to all is the requirement that the therapist be aware and sensitive to the specific needs of these patients in their evaluation and treatment approaches.

Specific techniques for treatment will only be described if they differ substantively from those techniques elsewhere in this section. Obviously, all contingencies cannot be addressed. We will attempt to provide a framework from which approaches and understanding can be derived and techniques applied.

Sexuality and Adolescence

In reviewing the various determinants and consequences of adolescent sexuality and pregnancy, we must emphasize that not all adolescent sexuality is dysfunctional. We include it in this discussion, rather, to elucidate the context and implications of sexuality during this life phase in order for appropriate treatment approaches to be instituted, where indicated.

It has been estimated that half the population of 15 to 19 year olds and a fifth of the 13 and 14 year olds in the United States are sexually active. Of the 10 million 15 to 19 year old females in this group, over 1 million become pregnant each year; 17 percent are postmarital conceptions, 22 percent continue their pregnancies and bear children out of wedlock, 10 percent marry, 13 percent have spontaneous abortions, and 38 percent have induced abortions (Psychiatric News 1982).

Adolescent Contraceptive Use

The increasing numbers of sexually active adolescents do not appear to use effective means of contraception. Thus, today more teens are at risk of becoming pregnant, and 80 percent of premarital pregnancies among teens are unintended. Although teenagers represent about one-fifth of those sexually active women who are capable of becoming pregnant, they account for almost half of the out-of-wedlock births and one-third of the abortions.

Moreover, fewer than 10 percent of today's youth receive comprehensive sex education programs in school (Kirby et al. 1979). Currently, less than half of U.S.

high schools have specific sex education courses. Some sex education is provided in most schools but Kirby et al. (1979) emphasize the need to teach related topics including the physical and emotional aspects of sexual intercourse as well as information regarding the sexuality of children.

While knowledge of sexuality does make a difference with regard to contraceptive use, it is not the only important variable affecting the incidence of teenage pregnancy. There does not seem to be a clear correlation between sexual knowledge and prior exposure to sex education courses, nor between contraceptive knowledge and use (Nadelson and Notman, 1985; Notman 1975; Schaffer and Pine 1975). Most adolescents do not use contraceptives with their first sexual intercourse (Notman 1975). Further, when adolescents do begin to use contraception, they demonstrate a high rate of discontinuance despite ongoing sexual activity. Peer and social pressure and fear of illness are often important factors in the cessation of contraceptive use. In addition, guilt about sexual activity, fear of discovery, impulsivity, denial, and conscious and unconscious wishes for pregnancy may favor discontinuity. Although the feeling that "it can't happen to me" may contain an ambivalent wish to become pregnant and demonstrate "femininity," it is important to remember that non-use of contraception is not the same as the wish to become pregnant. Several authors have also pointed to cognitive developmental factors as important aspects of adolescents' capacities for contraceptive planning and use. Certainly, the inability to plan for the future or to negotiate with parents or the health care system may be substantial barriers.

Earlier literature linked adolescent pregnancy with psychopathology, describing sexual activity as "acting out," a manifestation of intrapsychic disturbance. Recent work on this subject has suggested that psychopathologic factors exist in some teenagers, but for many there are family, peer, and social pressures favoring early sexual activity and even supporting pregnancy (Cobliner 1981; Nadelson and Notman 1985). In addition, unavailability or ambivalence about contraception or lack of accurate knowledge may increase the likelihood of pregnancy (Notman 1975).

Developmental Stage and Sexuality

Effective use of contraception requires acknowledgment of one's sexuality and an orientation toward future planning. Developmentally, adolescents often deny the consequences of their acts as a defense against conflict. Moreover, impulsivity is characteristic of many adolescents. Pressured activity, apparently inconsistent views, and swings between responsibility, constraint, thoughtfulness, and indulgence are aspects of the developmental process. Thus, the consistency, responsibility, and planning involved in effective contraceptive use may be at variance with the developmental stage of many adolescents, who are nevertheless sexually active. A pregnancy may even be perceived as appropriate punishment for a guilty adolescent (Deutsch 1945).

Since adolescents are in the midst of a process of changing the nature of their ties to parents and turning more to peers and other adults, distancing can be marked by rebellion and challenge, a manifestation of which may be the inception of sexual activity. Since peer support and approval are so important and self-esteem may depend on it, many adolescent girls become sexually involved despite their ambivalence. They may also be pushed into sexual activity to distance themselves when they feel pulled towards dependent attachments that they perceive to be regressive and unacceptable. The closeness of a sexual relationship and/or a baby may be seen as providing love and a less lonely life for many who may not perceive a baby as a separate person, but as an integral and lifelong companion. A pregnancy may express a longing to be cared for, both as a mother and as a baby (Cobliner 1981; Nadelson and Notman 1985; Schaffer and Pine 1975).

Pregnant Teenagers

Pregnancy in a teenager may be motivated by the need to replace a loss, cope with an uncertain identity, hold on to a love object, or regain closeness with the mother. Deutsch (1945) noted a flight from incestuous fantasies by means of sexual intimacy with another man. The acting out of unconscious Oedipal fantasies, a wish for revenge, and defective ego function have also been mentioned in the literature as motivational factors (Cvetkovitch and Grote 1975; Deutsch 1945; Schaffer and Pine 1975).

Blos (1962) and others (Nadelson 1975; Schaffer and Pine 1975) have stressed the importance of attachment of the girl in the pre-Oedipal mother-child relationship and the strength of this pull. Whether seeking some reestablishment of this contact through a pregnancy is to be considered "infantile" or "regressive," or a part of the uneven process of growth and development, without the pejorative implications of a term such as regressive, cannot be clearly resolved.

Family studies provide another perspective, suggesting that covert messages expressed by a family may be very important determinants of teenage pregnancy. The teenager may consciously or unconsciously carry out the family wish and provide a baby, especially as a replacement for a lost sibling, for the mother's loss of reproductive capacity, or in some other way to reflect family issues.

An adolescent's relationship with her family also influences the choice made if pregnancy occurs, e.g., whether an abortion is obtained. One study compared teenagers who chose abortion with those who chose to carry their pregnancy to term, and found that those who chose abortion reported greater conflict with their mothers prior to the pregnancy (Kane 1973). This might suggest that they also experienced greater autonomy reflected by greater freedom to act.

Other aspects of family and societal dynamics suggest that in some subcultures an adolescent may be fully integrated into the role of a sexually functioning woman and a pregnancy may be consistent with perceived expectations. The importance of maternal support systems and the devaluing of fathers and men are factors in etiology and outcome.

Those families who incorporate an adolescent mother and child into the household may, by their interactive pattern, support the relinquishing of adolescent developmental tasks and restrict the young mother's social, educational, and economic options (Smith 1983). On the other hand, when the adolescent does not assume a maternal role, it may be in part as a result of the young mother's abdication of the role and/or the usurping of the role by another family member. This may interfere with the young mother's assumption of the maternal role and the development of her competence in child rearing.

While not necessarily pathologic, adolescent development is complicated by the addition of a child. Fraiberg (1972) studied a severely disturbed group of adolescents, each of whom became pregnant when attachment and detachment from the primary family figures had produced considerable conflict. She found that these unresolved conflicts became the focus of new conflicts which embraced the child. She reported disorders of attachment in the babies, who represented past conflicts and were also a symbol of hope and self-renewal for the mother. Many of the typical conflicts of adolescence had become intensified and magnified for each of the girls before she became pregnant. However, Fraiberg also noted, "We can find a fair amount of adequate or excellent mothering."

We have increasingly come to understand the complexity of etiology and outcome when considering teenage pregnancy. Since it has been associated with an increased incidence of complications most often due to poor prenatal care, many intervention programs focus on this aspect. Negative consequences, however, are not inevitable, although pregnant teenagers are more likely to be without support and adequate resources, thus increasing their chances for greater difficulty and poorer outcome.

The teenage father has recently received attention, and programs have been directed toward defining the importance of the father's relationship with the mother, the impact of this relationship on parenting, and techniques to effectively engage these young men.

Intervention Programs

With regard to preventive and intervention programs after a pregnancy has occurred, a number of approaches have been proposed. Hospital-based prenatal care programs have been compared with school-based prenatal care. Although the care provided by the school resulted in earlier and higher frequency of prenatal visits, there were no substantial differences in outcome. (Taylor et al. 1983) Thus, it was not clear that greater involvement in prenatal programs was correlated with better outcome.

A comparison between specialized teenage prenatal services and regular obstetric clinics, using birth weight of infants as an outcome measure, found that those adolescents who were followed in the specialized obstetrical units reported low birth weight in only 9 percent of the infants followed, compared to 20.9 percent of the infants followed in the regular obstetrical clinic (Felice et al. 1981). Another study compared comprehensive adolescent pregnancy programs with regular health care provided at a hospital and reported that the two groups had similar medical and social outcomes, although the two programs served different patients (Aries and Klerman 1981). This emphasizes the need for a "good fit" for different teenagers' needs including multiple models of delivery of services.

A number of programs have focused on enhancing the adolescent's development after her child's birth. These include classes to facilitate the realization of educational and employment goals, and to foster future family planning. This is critical since one of the major long-term problems for adolescent mothers is the impact of pregnancy on formal education and subsequent employment. Teenage parenthood significantly reduces educational attainment, particularly for the young mother, and her employment prospects thus are also reduced. Women who start childbearing in their teens have more children, have them closer together, and have more unintended pregnancies than women who delay first births until their twenties (Mecklenburg and Thompson 1983). Further, the probability of separation and divorce is greater for teenage couples than those who marry later (Friedman and Phillips 1981). These various factors combine to heighten the prospect of welfare dependency for families that are initiated by a birth during the teen years (Trussel 1976).

Teenage Parenting

There have been a number of studies of parenting by teenagers. Sandler et al. (1980) reported that the pregnant adolescents who received adequate prenatal care were at no greater obstetric risk than older mothers. They concluded that comprehensive health care for pregnant adolescents may eliminate some of the negative consequences of childbearing at this young age.

Nelson et al. (1982) demonstrated an improvement in teenagers' parenting skills and health care when seen in a traditional health care facility, and Cappleman et al. (1982), looking at a home-based intervention program for infants of adolescent mothers, found that only 11 percent of the children remained at risk biomedically and environmentally after this intervention, while 50 percent of the children in a control group remained at risk. Sung and Rothroth (1980) found that setting up separate schools for pregnant teenagers encouraged completion of high school, entry into employment, and avoidance of repeated pregnancies.

Thus, it appears that if specialized services are provided, taking into account the developmental needs of adolescents, many of the risk factors associated with teenage pregnancy can be eliminated. There is a need for variety in the types of programs offered since no one program meets the needs of all pregnant and parenting teenagers. It is important for programs to provide comprehensive services including medical care, developmental information, educational assistance, and parenting skills. Since most teenagers who continue their pregnancies keep their babies, these services are essential for mothers and infants (Cappleman et al. 1982; Sandler et al. 1980; Sung et al. 1980).

Sexuality and Aging

In order to begin to consider sexuality and aging we must be aware of the concept of aging as a culturally determined one. Bengston et al. (1977), comparing Chicano, black, and white attitudes about what is considered "old," found that the ages given were in the 50s, 60s, and 70s, respectively. While sexuality has become a popular media topic, the paucity of literature on geriatric sexuality is striking. Even the pithy quotes or clever humor that do appear evoke the image of the dirty old man or disturbed old woman. This may be a form of denial, reflective of our anxiety about our own aging, our losses of loved ones as well as aspects of our own selves, and our fear of rejection. Sexuality, in contemporary U.S. culture, is seen as the province of youth.

It has been suggested that what is often seen as aggressive sexual behavior in some elderly people is motivated by their desire to regain mastery and a self-concept held earlier in life (Burg 1969). These efforts may be misinterpreted, disapproved of, or rejected. Sontag (1972) indicated that the most popular metaphor for happiness in our culture is youth. It is a metaphor for energy, restlessness, mobility, appetite: "for the state of wanting." This emphasis on youthful sexuality also narrows the definition of sexuality and fails to encompass the needs or behavior of people throughout their life cycle. It does not acknowledge the affection and intimacy of long-standing relationships, and physical aspects that may not be specifically coital, including touching and holding, which assume greater importance as people grow older. Sontag (1972) observed that aging might not actually interfere with physical or sexual functioning, but that a view of aging is incorporated into a self-image that may reject sexuality as inappropriate.

Case example.   For the first time in his life, a professional man in his 40s found himself drawn to public bathrooms where he tried to catch sight of other men's penises. This situation progressed to one of homosexual entrapment and arrest by the police. When he came to treatment, it emerged that he had been devastated by the loss of his youthful appearance and several episodes of impotence. His behavior was felt to be an attempt to deny normal aging and achieve a magical repair of the sense of inadequacy he felt in his body as a whole and his penis in particular.

Case example. A middle-aged woman came to treatment because of a strong urge to have a number of sexual partners other than her husband. She said it was "like being in an ice cream store; if you can have five flavors, why only one?" She verbalized a sense of urgency and a feeling that time was running out on her. Among a number of issues, a definite theme about bodily changes emerged. She had decided to have a hysterectomy but was terrified that loss of the capacity to have children would leave her "dried up, empty and old." In addition, she expressed the wish that through her affairs the vital, nurturing penises of young men would arrest her aging process and be her fountain of youth (Colarusso and Nemiroff 1981).

Sontag (1972) eloquently spoke of the "double standard of aging" and wrote "that old women are repulsive is one of the most profound esthetic and erotic feelings in our culture." Moreover, a sexual relationship between an older man and a younger woman is seen positively, as a sign of vigor and vitality; however, when an older woman and a younger man are paired, it is generally viewed as pathologic. Sontag (1972) also notes "women become ineligible much earlier than men do. A man, even an ugly man, can remain eligible well into old age . . . for most women, aging means a humiliating process of gradual sexual disqualification."

The role most identified as suitable for the aged is the sick role, not the sexual role (Weg 1983). Despite the "double standard," however, both men and women do fear loss of sexual adequacy and attractiveness. Human history is replete with magic, sorcery, and alchemy to find means to enhance the sexual capacity of those who are aging. The Bible tells us that King David required a young virgin to revive his aging body, and aphrodisiac recipes have been found on early Babylonian cuneiform tablets (Gruman 1966).

The equation of youth, vigor, and rejuvenation with sexuality is pervasive. Taoist philosophy teaches that sexual activity is a sacred duty and a rejuvenator, to be exercised often in order to achieve the goal of spiritual harmony (Tannahill 1983). Over the centuries, elaborate techniques were developed to augment and conserve semen since semen was equated with youth and "essence" (Steinbach 1963). Sexual rejuvenators have included sweet potatoes, orchids, mandrake, ginseng, partridge brains, and Chinese bird's nest soup. In 1889, Brown-Sequard (Weg 1983), a French physician, injected himself with guinea pig testes extract and reported that it had turned the clock back 30 years for him. There was also a period of time when "monkey gland" grafting was the vogue. This involved the insertion of slices of chimpanzee testes into the bursae of male patients. Steinbach (1963) suggested that an internal accumulation of sex hormones released into the blood could be achieved by tying off the vas deferens. This, he indicated, would restore youthful potency. Currently, sex hormone replacements are widely used for this purpose, despite their potential dangers and complications and the lack of substantial evidence of effectiveness.

Sexual Interest and Activity

Kinsey's work provided a "normative standard" (Hotvedt 1983) which paved the way for research into sexuality. Unfortunately, however, "numbers" research documents the "how many times do you?" question, but it does not place sexuality in the context of relationships, nor does it deal with its wider scope and expression. In addition, cross-sectional surveys report differences between old and young individuals, which can be misinterpreted as reflections of change over time as people grow older. The differences reported may actually be cohort differences, but an accurate portrayal of age-related differences. Likewise, while longitudinal research provides a better perspective on change, it does not address the relevance of the data for future generations.

With these caveats in mind, let us review some relevant data. Kinsey indicated that for the male the frequency of morning erections does not appreciably change until after age 65, and that among males over 70, 70 percent of those who were married reported a mean sexual frequency of 0.9 coital encounters per week. Pfeiffer (1974) found that at age 68, about 70 percent, and at age 78, about 25 percent of men were still sexually active. For men, being married was not a necessary factor, whereas for the majority of women, the availability of a sanctioned sexual partner appeared to be more important for continued coital activity. Another study reported that sexual activity declined most sharply after age 75 (Newman and Nichols 1960). Pfeiffer and Davis's (1972) longitudinal study of 60 to 94 year olds, most of whom were married and in good health, indicated that although sexual interest declined with age, half of those in their 80s and 90s reported continued sexual interest, and there was greater interest reported among women.

Further, elderly women continued to have the capacity for multiple orgasms, and post-menopausal women may actually increase their sexual interest and activity although vaginal lubrication may diminish. One explanation for this finding is that they are no longer fearful of pregnancy, another is that there is unopposed adrenal androgen activity, since estrogen activity decreases post-menopausally (Kaplan 1983). Widowed and divorced women over 70 also report a 25 percent incidence of masturbation (Christenson and Gagnon 1965). The frequency and intensity of sexual daydreams, however, has been reported to decline with increasing age (Giambra and Martin 1977).

Thus, we can assume that sexual capacity and interest do continue later on in life. While there do appear to be some differences in sexual interest and behavior with age, the lack of opportunity may be an important determinant. The ratios of older men and women present in the population make it clear that women are more likely to lack partners. For those between the ages of 64 and 74 the ratio of women to men is 130 to 100, and for 75 years and older, it is 178 to 100 (Pfeiffer 1974). Interestingly, among those who are married, studies suggest that women generally attribute cessation of sexual activity to their male partners, and men confirm this view.

The concept of "androgynization" with age has important implications for sexuality (Guttman 1977). Kaplan (1974) states:

As the biologic urge lessens with age, older males become more like women in their sexual behavior, in that fantasy and ambiance become more important in lovemaking, and there is relatively less preoccupation with orgasm. In older men, as the physical factors that motivate sexuality decline, psychic determinants become heavier contributors to the final sexual response.

Sexual Performance

With regard to specific aspects of sexual performance, there are reported changes in the sexual response cycle with age (Kaplan 1974). In the excitement phase, the capacity for erection becomes slower and more vulnerable as a man ages. Kaplan

(1974) believes that two factors are responsible: 1) the aging process; and 2) diseases with sexual side effects.

Kaplan (1974) indicates that erection and ejaculation are the most sensitive aspects of male sexual response. The refractory period increases in men and may result in a perception of lowered interest or potency and cause sufficient anxiety to affect performance. The pleasurable sensation associated with the plateau stage of the sexual response cycle does not decrease with age; however, the firmness of an erection or, in women, the fullness of the labial folds, will be less. For men, the plateau phase is lengthened. This could permit longer pleasuring and better control of ejaculation. For some men, a "paradoxical" refractory period may occur. The erection may be lost during the plateau period and these men have neither the desire nor capacity for an erection. Although this is a fairly common occurrence, it is not often discussed; thus, when a man experiences it he may find it quite disturbing (Dagon 1983).

The combination of declining physical capacity and a maintained or increased psychological need, which often has to do with countering a sense of disappointment in other areas of life, may make men more vulnerable sexually. Partner demands, Kaplan (1974) suggests, are a primary cause of impotence. Changes in sexual capacity may be misread as lack of interest and rejection, and this may cause the partner to increase demands.

Sexuality Disorders of Aging

With regard to the effect of diseases on sexuality, it has been estimated that 50 percent of those over 60 and 80 percent of those over 70 have some chronic health problem. Physicians often erroneously assume that these people are "too ill" to care about sex or that, if it is important, they will ask. Unfortunately, this view often leads to a "conspiracy of silence," and patients as well as physicians do not volunteer to discuss sexuality (Dagon 1983). The use of medications, particularly tranquilizers, autonomic blockers, antihypertensives, and anticholinergics, can interfere with sexual performance. Since the use of many of these medications increases with age, this effect is a likely etiologic factor.

Over one-half of older men develop benign prostatic hypertrophy (Dagon 1983), and surgery is often recommended. Almost invariably men fear that surgery will end their ability to be sexually active. The physician has an important role in educating and reassuring the patient. While transurethral resection of the prostate (TURP), retropubic, and suprapubic prostatectomy can produce some degree of incompetence at the bladder neck with retrograde ejaculation of semen into the bladder, this interferes with fertility, not necessarily with erection or physical sensations. Damage to the innervation of the erectile system, causing impotence, does sometimes occur with perineal surgical approaches to the prostate. This procedure is preferred for some cancer patients. However, men who are seen as "too debilitated" or "too old" to care about sex are often seen as candidates for these approaches. This assumption clearly should not be made without discussion with the patient and partner. The majority of instances of post-surgical erectile failures following prostatectomy procedures, however, are psychogenic.

The most common disorders affecting aging women are those associated with decreased production of estrogen. Thinning of the vaginal mucosa secondary to estrogen deficiency predisposes to infection, bleeding, and itching, and these are common causes for secondary dyspareunia and vaginismus. The loss of tissue support also predisposes to cystitis, stress incontinence, and dyspareunia. Since many women fear the development of endometrial cancer with hormone replacement, they may not take replacement estrogens and may develop sexual symptoms. At times, steroid replacement therapy is not suggested or advised, although taking estrogens and progestins reduces the risk of cancer in most women.

Masturbation is effective in preserving tone and lubricating ability. However, since older women are not as likely to masturbate as younger women, they may need permission and information, unless there are specific religious prohibitions. Local vaginal use of estrogen creams and suppositories may alleviate some of the atrophic vaginal changes, and other lubricants may significantly improve sexual functioning.

Hysterectomy should not alter sexual desire based on endocrine factors. Following hysterectomy, testosterone continues to be produced by the adrenal gland. This is associated with sexual arousal. Many women, however, are placed on hormone replacement and often on progestational compounds which may decrease sexual desire and cause mood disturbances. While it is clear that preservation of the pudendal nerves is critical in any pelvic surgical procedure, there is evidence suggesting that innervation may be interfered with when procedures, including vaginal hysterectomy, are performed (Weg 1983).

Mastectomy may result in sexual problems because of concerns women may have about their desirability and identity, and they may, because of feelings of shame, avoid nudity, sexual activity, or discussing their feelings with their partner. Supportive therapy actively involving a partner in reassurance, sharing of feelings, as well as participation in rehabilitation (e.g., dressing changes, exercise, and massage) may facilitate the grieving process and speed the return to normal sexual functioning.

Homosexuality and Aging

Homosexuality in older populations is rarely discussed. In a study of aging male homosexuals it was found that older men generally desired contact with men of their own age and that 50 percent of those between the ages of 50 and 65, and 83 percent of those over 65 reported satisfaction with their sex lives (Kelly 1977). These data certainly counter the prevalent view that the homosexual male is heavily youth-oriented. Aging for the lesbian has been seen as less problematic than for the gay male. This is said to relate to the greater focus on interpersonal aspects of relationships for women. That the number of eligible partners available to older lesbians is higher than the number available to heterosexual partners may be an important factor. Weg (1983) suggests "when Victorian social mores can be put aside, older women may find it possible to seek and share not only support, friendship and warmth with other women but also physical love."

Institutionalization and Sexuality

The few nursing home studies that have looked at sexuality have defined it in a narrow way, focusing on coital activity, fantasy, or masturbation. Sexual behaviors such as handholding, touching, hugging, or kissing are not considered. Kassel (1976) indicated that a significant portion of what is called disturbed behavior in nursing home patients results from sexual needs that are not permitted expression.

Nursing homes vary tremendously in their "tolerance" for sexual behavior, but even tolerant ones are often demeaning, voyeuristic, or infantilizing to the patients. Overtly negative staff attitudes may view any sexual behavior in older persons as inappropriate. This feeling is often more strongly held for women, who outnumber men by three to one in nursing homes. Masturbation may be dealt with by hand restraints, gerichairs, or drugs. Anxiety about reputation or criticism by relatives may promulgate and support policies of sexual suppression out of expediency (Kassel 1976).

Sexuality and Physical Health

There are a number of disorders and disabilities that occur at all ages and affect sexual functioning. It is important to emphasize at the outset, however, that most of these change the patterns or performance of sexual activity but do not exclude it. In considering the range of sexual disorders in people with physical illness and disabilities, we must, as in those without physical problems, distinguish among dysfunctions that have primarily an organic etiology, those with a psychogenic etiology, and those which occur at the interface between organic and psychogenic factors.

In this section, specific suggestions will accompany the discussion to illustrate the range of problems and solutions that may be possible. It is not possible to be all-inclusive, but suggestions can be extrapolated to physical disorders that have not been specifically delineated.

Again, at the outset we emphasize that cultural, ethnic, and religious factors have a significant impact on sexual functioning. This is particularly true following an illness or disability since previously defined "proper" sex acts may no longer be possible and alternative methods may be considered unacceptable (Griffith and Trieschmann 1983).* Further, since early experiences with parental figures and peer groups also influence and shape attitudes towards relationships and sexuality, problems may arise after physical illness or disability. Past experience and self-confidence are crucial factors in determining individual adaptation to illness and disability and pre-existing problems may become exacerbated. For example, the male with a pre-morbid history of intermittent secondary impotence may be more troubled by this symptom following a myocardial infarction.

Further, following the onset of an illness, an individual is vulnerable to secondary responses because devaluation and desexualization by the patient and by others frequently occur. A handicap may be incorporated into the identity of the individual, rather than seen as one component of the individual's personality and relationships.

Anxiety and fear about the illness or handicap itself and its implications may also inhibit sexuality. For example, those with severe cardiovascular disease, renal disease, diabetes, cancer, etc., must deal with potentially life-threatening illnesses; and for the illness that occurs later in life there are accompanying fears of aging, loss of status, etc.

Disabilities in Children and Adolescents

For those with congenital or early onset disabilities, developmental and family responses are critical to adaptation. Families may become overprotective in some situations but they may also be less demonstrative, particularly if the disability evokes feelings of revulsion or anxiety. Parents generally tend to avoid the issue of sexuality in children but even more so in disabled or ill children. This may foster feelings of inadequacy and conflict regarding sexuality.

In considering the treatment of any illness, generally, consideration of sexuality should be part of the plan. It should be thought of in terms of appropriate timing as

---

* This is an overview article on which this section is based. The interested reader can find references to the relevant original research cited in that article.

well as necessity for referral for specific concerns and instruction. Whenever possible, a partner should be involved. The range and type of issues to be addressed depends on the particular physical problems as well as the life situation and age of the patient, both at the time the physical disability occurred as well as currently.

There are a number of congenital defects which occur in children and affect their later sexual functioning. Often, although these may have been present from birth, it is not until after puberty that attention is paid to their effect on sexual functioning. Concerns about these may inhibit attempts at sexual involvement and activity. A child born with an observable disability such as cerebral palsy or the absence of an extremity grows up with this deficit incorporated into his or her self-image and this may impact on the development of self-esteem. Further, he or she may be rejected by peers and feel inadequate or uncertain about the possibility of sexual activity.

Accidents that occur in childhood or adolescence may necessitate changes in self-perception and behavior that can be extraordinarily stressful. Since spinal cord injury occurs frequently in the teens and 20s, often associated with accidents, there may have been prior sexual experience that may or may not make learning new modes easier. The depression and profound alteration in self-image that can occur may make it difficult to learn new patterns and behaviors.

Those with spinal cord abnormalities have different degrees of sexual and procreative capability, and they are often unaware of the sexual implications until later. For example, spasticity, contractures, and dislocations make sexual activity difficult, even when there is a partner. At times, symptoms such as spasticity can be treated with antispasmodic drugs although these can have side effects such as impotence.

For those who are congenitally blind or deaf, it may be difficult to develop a body image or perception of sexual anatomy, physiology, or functioning, even when information is provided. The loss of eye contact, and auditory cues, coupled with the absence of the kind of gestures and nonverbal communication that occur so often in interpersonal relations, may inhibit the ability to interact. Further, since motor activities, e.g., grimacing or nodding, are often found in this group, potential partners may be distanced. Very basic lessons in anatomy and physiology may be necessary. This might include life-sized models so that the patient is not confused by discrepancies in size and texture. While those whose disabilities occur later often have a history of sexual activity, the assault to their self-image may make it difficult to reengage in sexual relationships.

There are a wide variety of other disorders that may affect children and adolescents and can affect sexual functioning. These include malignancies, for which treatment with chemotherapy or radiation will affect reproductive capacity or cause symptoms such as hair loss, anorexia, etc., and also will profoundly affect self-image and self-esteem. Likewise, disorders such as rheumatoid arthritis can produce pain, weakness, and disability. Children and adolescents also suffer from chronic disorders such as renal and cardiac disease that may limit many activities by virtue of the disability itself or because of the psychic consequences.

Disabilities in Adulthood

To evaluate sexual problems in people with major illness or disability, the current level of sexual functioning must be placed in the context of prognosis and characteristics of relationships must also be considered. This, coupled with a thorough medical history and examination including any associated medical conditions (cardiac disease, hypertension, pulmonary disease, diabetes, etc.) that might interfere with sexual function, should be evaluated.

The history should include assessment of self-image and social networks prior to the onset of the disability or illness as well as cultural, ethnic, and religious influences in order to understand potential conflict with values or beliefs. It is necessary to learn about the degree of change in sexual pattern brought on by the disability. This includes what has been lost and what assets and liabilities remain. The impact is greater when the change from prior activities is greater. Specific measures of physical capacity may be indicated. This might include cardiac and blood pressure monitoring and/or pulse measured during sexual activity. Objective measures of strength, range of motion of the joints, and endurance may be important in some disorders, e.g., arthritis. Assessment for those with neurologic, neuromuscular, or orthopedic problems might include walking, wheelchair transfers, capability of positional changes, and self-care activities such as dressing, bowel and bladder management, and personal hygiene. Urologic assessment in spinal cord diseases or injury, and radiologic studies may be required to determine the structural integrity of bone in patients with cancer or osteoporosis.

Management and Treatment

Many sexual dysfunctions are not identified as related to a specific disability. Even when identified, however, consultation is not obtained or treatment may not be seen as possible so that it may not be recommended. There are a number of issues that must be taken into account in considering the management of sexual dysfunctions. These include:

1. Transfer activities (movement from bed to wheelchair, etc.).
2. Preparation for sexual activity (bowel and bladder care, positioning, contraceptives, etc.).
3. Stimulation of erection. For those neurologic disorders in which erection is not under cerebral control, regional tactile stimuli may need to be applied. Erections may also be elicited as a component of a mass reflex produced by scratching the sole of the foot, for example, in spinal cord patients with upper motor neuron lesions. By using the stuffing technique (direct insertion of semi-turgid penis), it may further engorge. Vibrators may also be helpful.
4. Positions for sexual activity. Support with pillows or padding may be helpful for those with various paralyses and limitations. In addition, the cardiac or hypertensive patient should probably avoid positions that require sustained isometric contraction and, therefore, they may be more comfortable in a nonmissionary position.
5. Variety of sex acts.
6. Precautions in sexual activity. The full healing of various lesions may preclude pressure on ulcers or surgical incisions. Spinal cord injury patients with lesions above the midthoracic level may experience autonomic dysreflexia during sexual activities.
7. Penile prostheses.
8. Drug management. Testosterone and its derivatives have been used to treat injured male spinal cord victims who have gynecomastia and testicular atrophy. There is evidence, however, that the reduction in endogenous androgen is temporary and is generally limited to quadraplegics. There is no evidence that the extrinsic testosterone will modify sexual performance or affect eventual testicular function.
9. Sperm banks.

10. Exercise.
11. Surgery. This may correct muscular skeletal deformities or deformities caused by previous surgery. Prostheses following a mastectomy have enormously beneficial effects.
12. Adaptive devices (splinting).
13. Contraceptives. It is important to attend to potential thromboembolic and vaso-constrictive possibilities as well as the fact that women with sensory defects may be unaware of perforations or pelvic infections and, therefore, intrauterine devices may be inappropriate.
14. The timing of sexual activity. Patients with some chronic diseases feel better in the early part of the day whereas arthritics may feel worse in the morning or late evening. Likewise, patients taking medications may have side effects that affect them at certain times of the day.

Films, including *Like Other People*, may be particularly helpful for use with special populations. In addition to its message of acceptance, it suggests alterations of sexual positions and preparation for sexual activities. While most women with spinal cord injuries are fertile, pregnancy may be complicated because of an increased incidence of urinary tract infections. Those men who do have erections may have retrograde ejaculation into their bladders and thus have reduced fertility. Orgasm in both sexes may be altered or absent.

One of the most difficult problems experienced by those with spinal cord injuries is the interference of bowel and bladder functions with sexual activity. Likewise, positioning and other preparation such as placement of contraceptives may be necessary depending on the nature of the problem, e.g., a quadraplegic will have to be positioned to achieve coitus.

Concerns about role reversal, especially as it affects self-esteem, may be important. Some believe that a dual-sex treatment team is better able to address these issues. Clinicians must be aware of a patient's desire to discuss sexuality, as well as those cues that indicate that he or she is neither ready nor interested. Some disabilities may provide an individual with an excuse to avoid sexual contacts, a wish that should be respected.

Specific Issues

This section will discuss some of the specific sexual issues to be considered for common disorders.

Diabetes

The most problematic symptoms related to diabetes of long-standing are the neuropathies and vascular problems that appear to be important etiologic factors resulting in impotence and ejaculatory difficulties in men. It is estimated that 50–60 percent of diabetic males experience this symptom, and, for some, impotence may be the first symptom of diabetes. Early and less severe symptoms may be treated by altering sexual position and modifying technique, but penile implants are currently the major mode of therapy for persistent impotence.

Renal Disease

Those with chronic renal disease do experience some improvement in many areas of functioning when on dialysis. Sexual dysfunctions, however, tend to continue and, for males, reduced sperm counts, decreased testosterone and testicular atrophy may occur. For women, amenorrhea and infertility may result.

Cardiovascular Disease

It is generally estimated that those who have had a mild myocardial infarction, without complications, may resume sexual activity within six weeks to two months. This depends, however, upon careful medical evaluation and monitoring. There does not seem to be any evidence to support the alternate view that sexual position will affect cardiac functioning. Masturbation consumes less energy than coitus.

Anginal attacks do occur during sexual activity and nitroglycerine has been used preventively. Other precautions include limiting food and alcohol intake immediately prior to sexual activity. While cardiac arrhythmias are a cause of some concern, there does not seem to be any evidence to support the view that they are likely to cause sudden death.

With regard to hypertension, many of the sexual problems attributed to the disease are probably related to the side effects of the medications used for control by both men and women. Since a wide range of medications has been reported to produce changes in libido and potency, it is sometimes possible to change a medication and reduce the sexual side effects.

For those who have had cerebral vascular accidents, sexual problems frequently relate to both the associated medical problems or causes of the stroke, e.g., hypertension, or to the disability which results, e.g., hemiparesis. Emotional problems may, however, contribute substantially to decreased functioning.

Cancer

One of the most important concerns of cancer patients, in addition to the disease itself, is the mutilation that surgical procedures or radiation cause, or the systemic effects of chemotherapy. For example, a woman with breast cancer may have a severely damaged self-image following a mastectomy if no prosthesis is provided. Likewise, the use of drugs and hormones such as testosterone in women may produce masculinizing effects, as well as increased libido, and men treated with estrogens may be distressed by gynecomastia. Pain from metastatic lesions together with systemic symptoms may affect sexual desire and/or specific problems may occur as a result of procedures that affect sexual organs. This includes adhesions, stenosis, or ostomies. Clearly, surgical procedures in the lower pelvis may interfere with sexual functioning because of the neurologic or vascular effects.

Frequently, the surgeon who has just performed a life-saving procedure is baffled by a patient who is upset about disfigurement or functional impairment. It is essential that whenever possible the nature and results of the procedure be discussed before it occurs, with both patient and family.

Neuromuscular and Joint Diseases

Degenerative joint diseases may cause pain and contractures limiting motion. At times, aspirin, heat, and exercise may be sufficient to increase mobility, but often alternative positions for coitus are the only possible approaches.

For those with neurologic disorders in which there are erectile problems, direct stimulation or trigger-point stimulation may be necessary. For some, erection will occur when perineal or adjacent areas are touched or massaged. The most difficult aspect of this is the acceptance of the need for alternatives.

Attention must also be paid to medication since any type potentially has a sexual side effect and patients are frequently on combinations and high doses. Films, group sessions, and support groups, as well as direct instruction with specific illustration, may be helpful for many.

Special Treatment Approaches

Some authors recommend the PLISSIT Model for treatment (Annon and Robinson 1981). This anagram refers to Permission-Limited Information-Specific Suggestions-Intensive Therapy. While this may over-focus on a behaviorally oriented approach, good results have been reported. Since the person may be fearful and misinformed, permission is particularly important and the clinician can introduce the topic of sexuality, acknowledge that he or she understands that the patient is worried, and that sexuality is a legitimate area of focus. The patient is also provided with factual information directly relevant to his or her specific sexual concern. Thus, it is possible to dispel unwarranted anxieties, for example, the fear of producing another stroke or coronary by engaging in coitus. Specific suggestions include problem-oriented strategies, prevention of pain or symptoms during sexual activity, or the use of alternative sexual activity to achieve sexual satisfaction. Practice and feedback are important components.

To conclude, it is important to reemphasize that most disabilities do not affect the sex drive any more than they would affect hunger or thirst, but disabilities often influence the type of sex acts that are feasible or advisible. Few disabilities preclude all sex acts. Likewise, this implies an appreciation of the values of the patient and partner and avoidance of an intervention that is inconsistent with these values.

Sexuality and Culture

Little attention has been paid to specific sexual concerns of racial, ethnic, or other minority groups. Cultural stereotypes tend to portray the sexual values, interests and activities of white, middle-class America as the norm. While it is not possible to consider each group specifically, this section will attempt to delineate salient issues by highlighting specific concerns. Further, it is important to be constantly aware of subcultural differences, and the enormous heterogeneity of each group. Each person's cultural background provides a contextual definition of normality.

In doing cross-cultural work, the pitfalls with regard to countertransference have been well described. They include over-identification, over-compensation, condescension, and flight (Bradshore 1973).

Blacks

Myths about unbridled black sexuality, in part, derive from the history of slavery and the experiences that grew out of it. Families were torn apart, avenues for sexuality were not readily available, and sexual patterns were imposed. Out of this evolved differences in perceptions and attitudes toward sexuality. The projection by whites of enormous sexual prowess and activity on the part of blacks must be seen from the context of its social structure and generally as a misrepresentation based on fear (Poussaint 1983). Others (Pinderhughes 1964) have described how American blacks had to conform to false beliefs about themselves that included the belief that they were less worthy, must surrender themselves and defeat themselves, and must accept persecution and seek direction from others. This also is incorporated into sexual patterns of behavior.

Orientals

The history of Orientals in the United States has also affected our views about their expressions of sexuality. For the Chinese, males in the late 19th century came to work in the western states and women did not. This disrupted family structure and was coupled with the idea that romantic love is a western and not an Oriental concept.

Although changes have occurred in recent years, marriages were traditionally arranged and women were subservient. Further, the principle of maintaining concubines was widely practiced and recognized, and the children of concubines were considered to be legitimate, although not entitled to full benefits of legitimate children. Many current sexual attitudes also derive from beliefs such as "too frequent intercourse drains a man's 'vital essence' " making him more vulnerable to disease. Thus, men were expected to avoid "excessive" ejaculation, clearly affecting masturbatory and other sexual practices. Although Taoist thinking focused extensively on women's rights to sexual pleasure, Confucianism saw procreation as the primary goal of sexuality (Ishihara and Levy 1970), and many of these attitudes have persisted to the present day.

Asians continue to be reluctant to divulge sexual experience although psychosexual dysfunctions have been reported (Tan 1981). The problems described range from guilt following masturbation or contact with a prostitute to the generally described range of sexual dysfunctions. The view that sexual function is a manifestation of emotional conflict persists as does the belief that sexual excess in men leads to disease. Little is known about female concerns and symptoms.

An interesting syndrome, koro, which consists of a sudden onset of complaints about the sensation of penile retraction into the body, has been described. According to Small (1983) it is similar to castration anxiety associated with feelings of guilt about sexuality. Its treatment is based on the view of its etiology and involves avoidance of foodstuffs that contain an excess of the "yin," and then a balance of "yang" foods. This syndrome has also been described in women, who experience sensations of nipple, breast, or labia retraction (VanWulfften 1936).

Because of the widespread Asian belief that sexual dissipation and excess loss of seminal fluid leads to emaciation and death, the syndrome of spermatorrhea can cause enormous anxiety. This includes excessive masturbation and nocturnal emissions.

Hispanics

As with other groups, Hispanic-Americans have been grouped together so that enormous cultural and attitudinal differences are often ignored. Those who come from different backgrounds as well as those who have migrated to different areas of the U.S. exhibit different attitudes and patterns. Generally, however, sexual discussion, particularly by women and in public, is not supported. A recent discussion with the Human Sexuality Planning Committee of a medical school with a large number of Hispanic students emphasizes the point. Both in curriculum planning and teaching methodology the faculty was very sensitive to the difference in attitudes between the Anglos and the Hispanics. Some of the explicit sexual material presented in such a course was quite acceptable to one group but was seriously resented by the other. Likewise, students' attitudes toward patient sexual practices differed enormously.

The culture of "machismo" and "marianismo" captures sexual and gender role definitions of male and female functioning (Wilkeson et al. 1983). Machismo is a powerful image of men and implies pressure toward aggressive sexual activity. Marianismo is the virginal, idealized view of women as sexually pure and spiritual. The reality of behaviors may vary enormously from this idealized image, and sexual problems frequently relate to the discrepancy between the ideal and the real.

Case example. A middle-aged Hispanic male who noticed some decrease in the strength of his erections became impotent because of feelings of failure. He could not tolerate the loss of his "macho" self-image and was explicit about this when seen in consultation. He was too uncomfortable to tell his family physician about the problem or to seek help. When his wife confronted him with it, he initially became extremely angry and left home for a week. During this time, he had a brief sexual affair and was asymptomatic. He concluded that the problem was his wife's and insisted she seek help. He was convinced by his wife, however, to see a urologist. The urologist, after finding no physical abnormalities, suggested that he seek a consultation with a person experienced in sexual therapy. The patient was willing to do so on the condition that his wife participate. Both partners were evaluated.

A brief course of combined sexual and marital therapy using behavioral and dynamic principles was instituted. During the course of treatment the couple revealed that their sexual life was somewhat inhibited because they lived in close quarters with their four adolescent children and kept their bedroom door open. The children felt free to enter their parents' bedroom. The wife accepted this because she believed that a mother must be available to her children at all times.

The couple was able to recognize the contributions of attitudes and background, and to work successfully in sexual therapy. For Hispanic families, in addition to the male macho image, a high value is place on children's needs. For this couple, there was enormous pressure on the wife to have children and to be constantly available. This placed her in conflict with her husband's demands and contributed to the problem.

In many Hispanic cultures the dichotomy between male expectations of experience and female expectations of inexperience reinforces a split so that men and women are expected to behave differently. Men are either seen as macho or they are considered ineffective. Women are viewed as either the good/madonna or bad/prostitute. During courtship, girls are closely supervised and virginity is highly prized. Although aspects of the chaperone system have disappeared in recent years, similar expectations of men and women continue. As a result, Hispanic women often find marital sexuality difficult. When they seek help, it is often because their husband makes demands that they find intolerable, e.g., oral sex.

Therapists working with Hispanic couples may find it difficult to deal with attitudes and patterns that seem to undermine contemporary women. Aspects of the role of women in Hispanic culture are also controversial within the culture. Family ties and loyalties are among the most important aspects of Hispanic cultures, although the degree of acculturation or adaptation to the particular "majority" culture is an important variable. Likewise, there may be generational issues. Children tend to adapt to culture and language more quickly than adults and this may cause disagreement and friction between generations.

Family members, however, do provide the kinds of supports that are necessary for problem solving and the value system may preclude turning to outsiders, particularly for problems that are seen as more "personal." This clearly affects help-seeking behavior as well as compliance. It is generally believed that Hispanics underutilize mental health resources because of their adherence to folk beliefs and reliance on folk healing methods, although this is not clearly documented to be related to service utilization.

In working with Hispanic families, as with families in all cultures, the entire family system must be understood. Since exposure of sexual difficulties on the part of both men and women is not generally acceptable, symptoms are often masked. For some men it may be easier to seek female physicians since the "loss of face," or self-esteem, is not as problematic in that relationship (Wilkeson et al. 1983). They may also have a higher expectation of the responsiveness of women.

Homosexuality

It is estimated that about 10 percent of the population in the United States is predominantly homosexual and a far larger number of people are bisexual. If one accepts the early Kinsey studies suggesting a continuum of sexual behavior and fantasy, it becomes apparent that homosexual thoughts, feelings, fantasies, and behavior are widespread.

Sexual dysfunctions in homosexuals are often ignored. The sexual problems of homosexuals differ very little from those of heterosexuals. Gays, however, experience a great deal of anxiety communicating with physicians, particularly if they have not yet publicly revealed their sexual orientation.

In a general medical evaluation of any patient it is important to ask specifically about sexual orientation in the sexual history since there are specific medical concerns and also because it gives the patient permission to discuss sexual problems more openly if they exist.

Since the range of sexual behaviors of homosexuals is extensive, one can expect that sexual dysfunction will exhibit the same range as in heterosexuals. It is important that assumptions about sexual practice are not made but that a detailed history is taken. It is clear, for example, that not all gay men engage in oral or anal intercourse. Likewise, mechanical devices might be used by some but not others. The etiologies of sexual dysfunction found in gays are similar to those found in heterosexuals.

Gartrell (1983) reports that the most common sexual problem in gay women is orgasmic dysfunction, as is true for heterosexual women. Vaginismus, she notes, occurs infrequently, probably due to the fact that lesbian lovemaking does not require the insertion of a large object into the vagina (Gartrell 1983). Gay men report problems with impotence and premature ejaculation which may be related to time-pressured sexual encounters. Gartrell also notes that rectal pain during anal intercourse is a frequent complaint.

In considering interventions there is no reason to consider these in a different way than with heterosexuals. The patient's partner should be included when appropriate and therapists can adapt techniques that are used with heterosexuals. Gartrell, for example, points out that the squeeze technique for treating premature ejaculation can be used as successfully with male homosexuals as with heterosexual couples.

Likewise, she notes, vibrators can be utilized in lovemaking between gay women to increase clitoral stimulation of those who are inorgasmic. The most important difficulties are attitudinal and this occurs with regard to patients as well as therapists.

Chapter 217

Basic Research Relevant to Treatment of Psychosexual Dysfunctions

Considerable research has been done in recent years on the psychobiologic processes that mediate sexual function and dysfunction. A body of rapidly evolving information is being gathered that has considerable significance for the etiologic understanding as well as the evaluation and treatment of sexual disorders. This chapter will present a brief and selective overview of relevant physiologic research on normal and dysfunctional human sexual behavior. The emphasis will be on basic psychophysiologic and endocrine aspects; no attempt will be made to encompass the wide range of pathologic conditions that are known to influence human sexual responses.

Psychophysiology of Sexual Function

Studies in the Male

Sexual arousal.   Three components of sexual arousal will be considered: genital changes, peripheral autonomic responses, and central processes associated with sexual excitement.

Animal experimentation and studies of patients with spinal cord injuries have suggested two distinct but interacting neurophysiologic pathways: a sacral parasympathetic component that mediates reflexive erections; and a thoracolumbar component that, via cholinergic fibers, mediates pyschologically induced erections (deGroat and Booth 1980). The traditional view that cholinergic mechanisms are responsible for erectile activity has been challenged, however, by the observation that atropine infusion does not prevent penile tumescence in primates and normal subjects (Wagner and Brindley 1980). (Atropine effects may be blocked by vasoactive intestinal poly-peptide (VIP)—see chapter on Drug Therapy.) There is increasing evidence that ad-renergic processes participate in the modulation of erectile function. Extensive adrenergic innervation, high norepinephrine concentration and both alpha- and beta-adrenergic receptors have been found in the corpora cavernosa of various species including men (Baumgarten et al. 1969; McConnell et al. 1979; Melman and Merry 1979). Erections may be enhanced by beta-2-adrenergic stimulants as well as by alpha-adrenergic blocking agents (Domer et al. 1978). Although the precise role of cholinergic and adrenergic neurotransmission remain unclear, this research has obvious significance for the understanding of the effects of drugs on sexual potency. In addition to au-tonomic agents, other substances such as VIP found in high concentrations in erectile tissues may also participate in the regulation of erectile processes (Larsson and Fah-nenkrug 1977).

Considerable attention has recently been placed on the vascular mechanisms of erection. Conti (1952) in a classic histologic study postulated that erections occur when pads (polsters) located between the arterioles and the erectile bodies relax under autonomic control resulting in an increased rate of arterial inflow into the intracav-ernous spaces. This notion was challenged by Newman and Tchertkoff (1980) who, based on anatomic evidence, suggest that the polsters are an age-related pathologic finding. There is little doubt, however, that increased arterial inflow to the cavernosus bodies, possibly modulated by the activity of perineal muscle structures (Karacan et al. 1983), is the primary determinant of erection. Actively controlled resistance to venous outflow may also contribute significantly to the sustaining of penile tumesc-ence (Wagner and Green 1981). In addition, relaxation of the smooth muscle within the cavernous tissues also contribute to the erectile process.

Sexual excitement is frequently accompanied by peripheral, autonomically me-diated responses such as increases in heart and respiratory rate, elevations in blood pressure and skin temperature, and pupillary dilation. Since these changes may also occur in response to non-sexually arousing states, current psychophysiologic research focuses on the assessment of penile tumescence as the most valid and reliable indicator of sexual arousal (Zuckerman 1971). Penile tumescence is measured by an elastic mercury-filled strain gauge that is placed around the penis. Changes in penile cir-cumference induce changes in electrical resistance that are recorded on a polygraph. A large body of empirical research has assessed penile tumescence as an objective measure of sexual attitudes, interest, and orientation in men (Abel et al. 1977; Bancroft 1974). This research has been based, at least in part, on the assumption that genital responses are not under voluntary control. Other studies have demonstrated, how-ever, that under certain conditions some degree of voluntary facilitation and inhibition of erections is possible (Barlow et al. 1975; Csillag 1976; Henson and Rubin 1971; Rosen et al. 1975).

The relation between cortical electrophysiologic activity during the waking state and sexual excitement remains largely unexplored. During sleep, the phenomenon of nocturnal penile tumescence (NPT) does provide an approach for the study of CNS processes relative to erectile function. NPT is a stable physiologic event that occurs in close temporal relation with REM sleep and is consistently observed from infancy to old age (Karacan et al. 1975). REM erections appear to be non-erotic in nature; only a minority has been associated with overt erotic dreams. Recency or amount of sex activity does not seem to influence NPT (Karacan 1979). Anxiety manifested in dream content or induced by the experimental situation, on the other hand, tends to inhibit sleep-related erectile activity (Fisher 1966; Karacan et al. 1966). The functional significance of NPT, as well as the nature of the relationship between the central processes that subserve erotically induced arousal and REM-related erections are presently unknown.

Orgasm. Orgasm is a poorly understood psychophysiologic event that is usually accompanied by increases in heart and respiration rate, a rise in blood pressure, changes in skeletal muscle activity, and a variably described subjective state. Our understanding of the spinal mechanisms that control emission and ejaculation is primarily based on animal experimentation with limited verification in humans. Emission of the sperm into the bulbar urethra is thought to be under thoracolumbar sympathetic control (deGroat and Booth 1980). Pharmacologic evidence suggests that the emission phase is mediated by release of norepinephrine acting on alpha-adrenergic receptors and that it is also influenced by cholinergic nervous activity (Anton and McGrath 1977; Kedia and Markland 1975; Sjostrand and Klinge 1977). Ejaculation is mediated by a sacral spinal reflex which results in clonic contractions of the striated muscles that surround the bulbar urethra. The participation of supraspinal processes in the orgastic response of humans has been the focus of limited experimental work. Electrophysiologic brain recordings with scalp electrodes (Mosovich and Tallafero 1954) or with implanted electrodes in the septal region (Heath 1972) have identified epileptiform brain activity during orgasm. Recently, Cohen et al. (1976) reported a left to right shift in hemispheric dominance during self-induced orgasm in both sexes. The extent to which these central neurophysiologic events are related to the nature and intensity of orgastic experiences as well as to the refractory period is not known.

Studies in the Female

Sexual arousal. Very little basic research has been done on the neurophysiologic and vascular processes that mediate female sexual arousal. It has been proposed that, in a manner similar to men, genital vasocongestion is due to increased arterial inflow following relaxation of polsters in supplying arteries and to the contraction of venous polsters that limit the outflow of blood from female erectile tissues (Levin 1980). The assumption that cholinergic mechanisms control female vasocongestion has been challenged by the observation that atropine administration does not prevent the normal vaginal hemodynamic changes that accompany sexual arousal (Levin and Wagner 1980).

Wagner and Levin (1978) have studied the physiology of vaginal fluid production in the non-stimulated and sexually aroused state. Studies of ionic composition support the notion that the lubrication fluid is a modified plasma transudate that emerges between the intercellular spaces of the vaginal epithelium during pelvic vasocongestion. The role of circulating hormones or neurotransmitters in the mechanism of vaginal lubrication is not known.

As in males, peripheral psychophysiologic measures such as skin temperature, blood pressure, heart rate, and finger pulse volume are not valid or reliable indicators of female sexual arousal. Since the most specific physiologic responses to erotic stimuli are changes in genital tissues, considerable efforts have been made to develop non-invasive approaches for genital assessment (Hoon 1978). Presently, the most frequently utilized method is vaginal photometry. It measures genital vasocongestion by means of a tampon-shaped device inserted into the vagina that contains a light source and a photosensitive receptor that records the light reflected back by the vaginal mucosa. Other assessment methods include the measurement of vaginal blood perfusion with a heated oxygen electrode or with an isothermal blood flow transducer, labial temperature recording, and vaginal electromyography. These measures usually demonstrate rapid and predictable increases during sexual arousal. However, differences in the pattern of change following termination of erotic stimulation, after orgasm or during the resolution phase, suggest that they measure different hemodynamic responses (Henson et al. 1979).

Studies on the relation between subjective and genital measures of female sexual arousal have given rise to conflicting results. The degree of subjective genital correlations in women has varied greatly across studies (Osborn and Pollack 1977; Schreiner-Engel et al. 1981; Wincze et al. 1977). It has been suggested that women having less evident genital responses than men are more influenced by culturally induced expectations in determining their subjective perception of sexual arousal. Wilson and Lawson (1978) found, for instance, that women's expectations of the effect of alcohol markedly influenced their subjective assessments of sexual arousal regardless of their genital vasocongestive responses following alcoholic intake. In a recent study, Korff and Geer (1983) demonstrated that instructions to attend to bodily cues significantly increased the relation between subjective and genital measures. The authors concluded that reduced attention to bodily cues may have contributed to the low subjective physiologic correlations of earlier studies in women. Lack of attention to physiologic signals in the determination of the level of arousal may be a significant factor in the pathogenesis of female sexual dysfunction.

As with men, we know little about the central neurophysiologic processes that mediate female sexual arousal. The study of brain electrophysiologic activity during sleep has revealed that women have periods of genital arousal during REM sleep similar to the cycle of penile erections in the male (Abel et al. 1979). Fisher et al. (1983) utilizing a thermoconductance method for assessing vaginal blood flow demonstrated that, in comparison to men, vaginal vasocongestive episodes show a less tight linkage to REM periods and are of shorter duration. The vasocongestive episodes measured during REM sleep were similar in magnitude to increases measured during masturbation to orgasm. In contrast to the increases in heart and respiration rates that accompany arousal induced by genital stimulation, there were only minor cardiorespiratory fluctuations during the vasocongestive episodes that occurred during sleep.

Orgasm. Although the scientific literature about female orgasm is extensive, we continue to know little about the physiologic aspects of this experience. Following the pioneering work of Masters and Johnson, recent research has focused on the quantitative characterization of pelvic muscular activity during orgasm (Bohlen et al. 1982; Gillan and Brindley 1979). The notion that there are no differences in physiologic responses to vaginal and clitoral stimulation has been challenged (Singer 1973), but evidence in support of the existence of different types of orgasm remains meager and inconclusive.

Considerable controversy has been generated by the report that stimulation of a more or less circumscribed area on the anterior vaginal wall, labeled the Grafenberg spot, induces intense erotic sensations and may trigger orgasm without concomitant clitoral stimulation (Ladas et al. 1982). It has been claimed that stimulation of this zone also results in some women in the emission of fluid at orgasm that is different from urine (female ejaculation). Controlled data in support of these claims are largely lacking (Goldberg et al. 1983).

Hormonal Aspects of Sexual Function

Studies in the Male

The significance of androgens for the sexual behavior of subhuman males is well-known, but only recently experimental work has begun to delineate their role on the sexuality of men. Plasma testosterone is characterized by irregularly occurring abrupt increases superimposed on a circadian rhythm with rising concentrations during sleep reaching maximum levels towards early morning. About 5 percent of circulating testosterone, the most important androgen, is free and presumed to be physiologically active at the target cell levels; the remainder is bound to plasma proteins. Evidence, primarily from animal studies, suggests that testosterone requires conversion to dihydrotestosterone and aromatization to estradiol to exert physiologic and behavioral effects. These effects take place following coupling at receptor sites located in central and peripheral target tissues. Sexual functioning may not only reflect variations in plasma testosterone, but also molecular mechanisms such as threshold changes at receptor sites. There is virtually no information on factors involved in receptor site sensitivity and on intracellular events within the brain that accompany behavioral activation.

The effect of androgens on male sexual function has been clearly documented in two recent double-blind studies on hypogonadal men (Davidson et al. 1979; Shakkebaek et al. 1981). Androgen withdrawal resulted in a rapid decrease in sexual interest and in a reduction in sexual activity while replacement therapy significantly increased sexual thoughts and reestablished sexual desire within a few weeks. Unexpectedly, erectile capacity measured by responsiveness to erotic films was not affected by androgen withdrawal suggesting that, at least on a short-term basis, androgens may be more important to maintain sexual desire than erectile function (Bancroft and Wu 1983). It is not clear, however, whether androgens influence sexual desire by a central effect on cognitive processes such as fantasy production or by a peripheral action on genital structures enhancing sensitivity and pleasurable sexual responses.

There are wide individual differences in circulating testosterone among normal adult men, but there is no convincing evidence that testosterone levels account for differences in sexual behavior. It is assumed, without much experimental evidence, that men normally have plasma androgens at concentrations substantially higher than the threshold levels required for physiologic and behavioral activation. Endogenous variations or exogenously induced androgen changes above this threshold would, therefore, not have behavioral consequences.

An important and related question is the effect of aging on pituitary-gonadal activity and on male sexual function. Several investigators have reported decreases in total and free plasma testosterone, a loss of circadian rhythmicity in testosterone, and elevated circulating estrogens in aged men (Bremmer et al. 1983; Dai et al. 1981; Drafta et al. 1982). The lower testosterone concentration may reflect a testicular defect since plasma LH and FSH increase with age and testosterone response to exogenous HCG is reduced in older men (Longcope 1973; Winters and Troen 1982). These observations have led to the hypothesis that androgen deficiency is responsible for the decline in sexual interest and activity frequently noted in older men. Remarkably few studies have assessed directly the role of hormones in age-related changes in sexual behavior. Tsitouras et al. (1982) recently found a modest association between plasma testosterone and frequency of sexual activity in aging men. Davidson et al. (1983) in a cross-sectional investigation of men aged 41–93 observed age-related declines in reported frequency of sexual activity, nocturnal erections, and sexual thoughts and fantasies; significant decreases in total and free testosterone; increases in plasma LH and FSH and no changes in estradiol and prolactin. Endocrine behavioral correlations for free testosterone and LH were low but significant. Total testosterone, estradiol, and prolactin were not related to any measure of sexual behavior.

Prolactin, LHRH, and endorphins have also been implicated in the modulation of sexual desire and arousal in men (Evans and Distiller 1979; Franks et al. 1978). The physiologic meaning of these observations derived mainly from pathologic conditions or pharmacologic interventions is not clear.

Studies in the Female

The cyclic hormonal variations associated with the menstrual cycle offer a unique opportunity to assess the effect of reproductive hormones on female sexual function. Although research efforts have been extensive, data on the relation between the menstrual cycle and female sexuality remain inconclusive. Schreiner-Engel (1980), in a review of 32 studies of sexual behavior during the menstrual month, did not observe a consistent relation between peaks of sexual activity and specific menstrual cycle phases. Among the methodological issues that may contribute to the discrepant findings are: differences in the definition of menstrual cycle phases, lack of assessment of circulating gonadal hormones, lack of control for the role of the male partner in the initiation of sexual activity, and the use of vague and discrepant criteria for the assessment of sexual behavior.

Studies on the relation between endogenous gonadal hormones and female sexual behavior are few. Persky et al. (1976) and Abplanalp et al. (1979) divided the menstrual cycle into three and five phases, respectively, based on hormonal criteria and were unable to identify cyclic variations in sexual behavior. Schreiner-Engel et al. (1981) evaluated, during different phases of the menstrual month, the relation between sexual arousability and plasma gonadal hormones, sampled at the time of the arousal experience. Sexual arousability was measured in the laboratory by self-report and by vaginal photometry in response to sexual fantasy and presentation of an erotic audio tape. Subjective reports of sexual arousal did not differ among menstrual cycle phases but physiologic arousal did vary with significantly higher mean arousal levels during the follicular and luteal phases than during the ovulatory phase. Evidence of a cyclic pattern of increased sexual feelings during the mid-follicular and late luteal phases has been provided by Bancroft et al. (1983) in a behavioral hormonal study of 55 women with normal ovulatory cycles. The perimenstrual increases in subjective sexuality were partially independent of the cyclic mood changes and sense of well-being that were also noted in the same women.

To what extent do gonadal hormones contribute to behavioral variations during the menstrual cycle or to individual differences in sexual interest in women? The prevailing notion is that androgens are the hormones primarily responsible for female sexual behavior. Until recently, the evidence was largely inferential and derived from the reported loss of sexual responsivity following adrenalectomy and the observation that sexual drive increases in response to therapeutic administration of androgens (Waxenberg et al. 1959). Persky et al. (1978b) found a significant positive relation between plasma testosterone and coital frequency and self-rated sexual gratification. In the Schreiner-Engel et al. study (1981), correlations within the group between testosterone and either subjective or physiologic measures of arousability were mainly low and insignificant. However, when two subgroups of women who had consistently high and low plasma concentrations of testosterone were compared, women with higher mean testosterone responded to controlled presentations of erotic stimuli with significantly greater physiologic arousal for longer periods of time (Schreiner-Engel et al. 1981). It was of interest that the increased arousability shown by the high testosterone women was not reflected in their general behavior. In fact, the high testosterone women had had significantly fewer sexual partners in the past and fewer of them lived with sex partners at the time of the study. Low testosterone women had significantly higher coital frequency and reported more sexual desire, responsiveness, and satisfaction. Bancroft et al. (1983) also observed that mean testosterone levels were positively related with masturbation frequency, but tended to be negatively associated with partner-related sexual activity. Clearly, the role of testosterone on female sexual behavior is complex. Sexual functioning may be directly influenced by androgens or indirectly affected by hormonal actions on personality variables or mood. Bancroft (1983) has proposed the provocative hypothesis that in addition to directly enhancing sexual responsiveness, androgens may influence female sexual behavior indirectly by contributing to the development of personality characteristics that are less likely to conform to traditional female roles. Although evidence in support of this hypothesis is limited, it is important to remind ourselves that sexuality is a multidimensional concept and that we cannot assume a priori that hormones will affect each dimension in the same manner.

The role of other gonadal hormones on female sexual function remains largely speculative. Exogenous administration of estrogens or progesterone for therapeutic purposes or for oral contraception suggests that estrogens may enhance sexual desire and responsiveness while progestational agents have a depressive effect on female sexuality (Bancroft 1983). Studies that have related estrogen fluctuations during the menstrual cycle to sexual behavior have provided negative results (Persky et al. 1978a).

In the menopausal woman a decrease in ovarian response to gonadotropins usually occurs with considerable individual variations in circulating estrogen levels. Decreased lubrication and vaginal atrophy due to low circulating estrogens may lead to dyspareunia and to a secondary decrease in sexual desire and responsiveness. Sexual desire may also decrease independently from trophic genital changes, but the role of central hormonal effects in this decline have only begun to be studied (Dennerstein and Burrows 1982; Leiblum et al. 1983). Recently, Sherwin et al. (1985) conducted a prospective crossover investigation of sex steroid administration on surgically menopausal women. They obtained evidence that androgen, but not estrogens, increased the intensity of sexual desire, arousal, and frequency following hysterectomy and oophorectomy. In keeping with the previously mentioned findings of Schreiner-Engel et al. (1981) and Bancroft et al. (1983), the androgen-related enhancement of sexual interest and arousal was not associated with a corresponding increase in interpersonal sexual activity.

Psychophysiology of Sexual Dysfunction

Male Dysfunctions

Several investigators have utilized psychophysiologic methods to explore in the laboratory the possible effects of anxiety, performance demands, attentional focus, and distraction on male sexual arousal. The experimental induction of anxiety was found to facilitate penile tumescent responses to erotic stimulation in non-dysfunctional individuals (Barlow et al. 1983). Normal men also exhibited greater erectile response to erotic audio tapes when they were preceded with instructions that emphasized performance. In contrast, men with erectile problems showed significantly less genital arousal to tapes preceded by performance demands than non-demand instructions (Heiman and Rowland 1983). Evidence of differential erectile responses to an erotic film presentation between functional and dysfunctional men was also recently provided by Beck et al. (1983). This study demonstrated that the arousal responses of both groups were influenced in a complex manner by instructions concerning attentional focus (self versus partner) and the level of partner arousal (high, low, and ambiguous).

The observation that some degree of voluntary control over sexual arousal responses is possible led to response-contingent biofeedback studies in a effort to increase the voluntary facilitation of erection. Results, although inconsistent, suggest that feedback, under certain conditions, may enhance penile tumescence in some men with erectile dysfunctions (Hatch 1981). The value of this approach for the treatment of impotent men, however, remains unproven.

An important application of psychophysiology to sexual dysfunction is the recording of penile tumescence as a diagnostic approach to differentiate psychogenic from organic erectile disorders. A growing body of information has demonstrated the value of monitoring penile tumescence during sleep, but evidence reviewed elsewhere (Schiavi and Fisher 1982) provides a cautionary note about the non-critical approach of this widely used diagnostic procedure. The measurement of erectile responses to controlled presentation of visual sexual stimuli in the laboratory has also been used clinically for the purpose of differential diagnosis (Wagner and Green 1981). It is not certain, however, that men with psychogenic and organic erectile disorders show reliable differential responses to psychological stimuli. It has been reported, for example, that functionally impotent patients may demonstrate a pattern of increased systolic blood pressure and depressed erectile activity to erotic stimulation that is similar to diabetic impotent men (Kockott et al. 1980). There is a need for more systematic research on the validity, reliability, and precision of these diagnostic approaches.

Female Dysfunctions

The application of psychophysiologic measures to characterize the genital responses of women with arousal dysfunction and to assess sex therapy outcome have provided disappointing results. Wincze et al. (1976) observed that the vaginal blood volume and dyastolic blood pressure changes to an erotic video tape in women with arousal and orgastic problems were significantly lower than a comparable group of normal subjects. The subjective arousal responses were rated similarly, however, by the normal and dysfunctional groups. These observations were not confirmed by Morokoff and Heiman (1980) who found that the vaginal responses to erotic stimuli of women with reported arousal difficulties were not different from a group of control women matched for age and years married. There is no evidence that sex therapy significantly increases genital arousability assessed by vaginal photometry. In the Morokoff and Heiman study mentioned above, for instance, sex therapy resulted in enhanced sexual responses in the laboratory in the absence of changes in physiologic measures of sexual arousal.

These studies, albeit few and on small subject samples, underscore the complexity of evaluating female sexual dysfunction. Morokoff and Heiman (1980) have discussed the discrepant subjective and physiologic responses of sexually dysfunctional females in relation to individual differences in perceptual acuity, faulty labeling, or lack of awareness of genital cues and problems in accurately reporting subjective experiences to the investigator. It would appear that since a woman's self assessment of arousal cannot be assumed to concur with her physiologic changes, both variables need to be considered as independent dimensions of her sexual responses.

It has been suggested by Abel and collaborators (1979) that the recording of vaginal arousal during sleep may minimize individual differences in expectations and attitudes; and therefore, it may more accurately reflect the physiologic capacity of women to become sexually aroused. Research on the diagnostic value of this approach is in progress in several laboratories.

Hormonal Aspects of Sexual Dysfunction

Male Dysfunctions

Studies of pituitary gonadal function in physically healthy men with erectile disorders have furnished inconsistent evidence. Although lower urinary or plasma testosterone has been reported by some investigators, most have been unable to detect hormonal differences between impotent men free from organic problems and non-dysfunctional subjects (Schiavi and White 1976). As discussed in a previous section, it may well be that circulating androgens need to fall under a relatively low threshold level before behavioral effects become evident.

Few studies have explored endocrinologically the possible existence of subgroups of physically healthy impotent men characterized by degree of sexual desire or by the history of the sexual problem. Studies of hypogonadal men (Davidson et al. 1979; Shakkebaek et al. 1981) have suggested that, at least on a short-term basis, the physiologic processes that subserve sexual drive are more sensitive to androgen deprivation than the mechanisms that mediate erectile capacity. In a study of pituitary gonadal variations during sleep (Schiavi et al. 1984) healthy men who had never been able to achieve intercourse differed from age-matched patients who had had a lifelong history of erectile failures and from normal controls on NPT and sleep hormonal parameters. In a similar investigation (Schiavi et al. 1988) men with hypoactive sexual desire had significantly lower plasma testosterone measured hourly through the night than controls, and there was a positive relation between testosterone and frequency of sexual behavior. The NPT parameters of the men with hypoactive sexual desire and secondary erectile difficulties were consistently and significantly lower than those of the non-dysfunctional men. Detailed clinical characterization of patients and the application of psychophysiologic and hormonal methods of evaluation may be required to identify biologically distinct subgroups within the population of patients broadly described as "psychogenically impotent."

The possibility that functionally impotent eugonadal patients may be responsive to androgen or LHRH has been explored with negative results (Benkert et al. 1979; Davies et al. 1976). It has been suggested that androgen administration may restore sexual drive and erectile capacity of healthy aging men with a verified decrease in gonadal function (Heller and Myers 1944). Assessment of the effectiveness of this approach awaits controlled evaluation.

In recent years, an association among hyperprolactinemia, diminished testosterone secretion, erectile impotence, and impaired sexual desire has been frequently reported. In contrast with a consistently high prevalence of erectile impotence in patients with elevated blood prolactin associated with pituitary tumors (Carter et al. 1978; Franks et al. 1978; Lundberg and Wide 1978), the hormonal screening of men with sexual difficulties unselected with regard to organic pathology have provided discrepant results (Schiavi et al. 1986; Spark et al. 1980; Swartz et al. 1982). The occurrence of hyperprolactinemia and/or pituitary tumor in this population has ranged between 0 and 60 percent. Some sexually dysfunctional men have shown abnormally high prolactin levels in the absence of identified pathology (Ambrosi et al. 1980) while others have had non-functional pituitary adenomas and normal prolactin secretion (Batrinos et al. 1981).

The pathogenesis of diminished sexual desire and erectile impotence in hyperprolactinemic men is not known. Decreased testosterone secretion may not be the sole determining factor because androgen administration fails to restore adequate sexual function in the presence of elevated prolactin levels (Carter et al. 1978). The behavioral effects associated with hyperprolactinemia may reflect the effect of central monoaminergic processes on sexual function. This is suggested by the observation that administration of bromocriptine, a dopaminergic agonist, to hyperprolactinemic patients may result in enhanced sexual desire and restoration of erectile capacity before normalization of testosterone levels (Magulesparen et al. 1978; McGregor et al. 1979).

Female Dysfunction

There is a lack of hormonal investigation in regularly cycling sexually dysfunctional women. Under the assumption that androgens contribute to female sexual desire and responsiveness, Carney et al. (1978) conducted a study comparing the effects of testosterone and diazepam each in combination with sex therapy, in the treatment of women with problems of sexual interest and enjoyment. Their observation that testosterone plus counseling had a therapeutic effect on orgasmic frequency and subjective quality of the sexual experience was not supported by a controlled study that compared testosterone with placebo (Mathews et al. 1983). The conclusion that testosterone is without therapeutic benefit is premature, however, because of the small dosage used; the sublingual mode of administration, with compliance problems; and the lack of verification of plasma hormonal levels. Obviously, administration of higher testosterone amounts needs to be balanced against greater risks of virilization.

The role of endocrine factors in problems of sexual desire, arousal, and orgasm frequently noted in the post-menopausal period have also received limited research attention. Presently, there is no direct evidence that variations in gonadal hormones during the menopause contribute to the onset of sexual difficulties other than when atrophic vaginal changes occur due to estrogen deficiency. Double-blind placebo controlled studies of the effect of gonadal steroids in sexually dysfunctional post-menopausal women suggest that estrogen alone or in combination with androgens may have therapeutic benefits (Campbell 1976; Dow et al. 1983). It is not clear, however, the extent to which the enhanced sexual desire and responsiveness noted following replacement therapy reflects improved general well-being, vaginal trophic changes, or a decrease in vasomotor symptoms.

Conclusions

Although the DSM-III-R (American Psychiatric Association 1987) classification of sexual dysfunctions has a psychophysiologic basis, there has been, until recently, an abysmal lack of knowledge on the processes that mediate human sexual responses. Extensive psychobiologic research on sexual behavior has been conducted during the past 10 years. This review demonstrates, however, that important gaps of information still exist. This lack of data is particularly obvious as it relates to an understanding of male and female sexual disorders.

Psychophysiologic research has already played a valuable contribution to the evaluation of inhibited sexual excitement in the male. The extent to which basic physiologic investigation may also contribute to the evaluation of female sexual dysfunctions and the treatment of sexual disorders remains to be determined. It seems likely that the increased understanding of the biologic processes that mediate sexual function will enhance our therapeutic capacity, particularly for the large number of patients in whom organic and psychological factors co-exist in the determination of their sexual symptoms.

References

Section 22
Sexual Disorders

Abarbanel A: Diagnosis and treatment of coital discomfort, in Handbook of Sex Therapy. Edited by LoPiccolo J, LoPiccolo L. New York, Plenum Press, 1978

Abbott DH, Holman SD, Berman M, et al: Effects of opiate antagonists on hormones and behavior of male and female rhesus monkeys. Arch Sex Behav 13:1–24, 1984

Abel GE, Blanchard ED, Becker JV: An integrated treatment program for rapists, in Clinical Aspects of Rape. Edited by Rada R. New York, Grune & Stratton, 1978

Abel GG, Murphy WD, Becker JV, et al: Women's vaginal responses during REM sleep. J Sex Marital Ther 5:5–14, 1979

Abel GG, Barlow DH, Blanchard EB, et al: The components of rapists' sexual arousal. Arch Gen Psychiatry 34:895–903, 1977

Abplanalp JM, Donnelly AF, Rose RM: Psychoendocrinology of the menstrual cycle, II: the relationship between enjoyment of activities, moods and reproductive hormones. Psychosomatic Med 41:605–615, 1979

Ackerman NW: Treating the Troubled Family. New York, Basic Books, 1977

Allison J, Wilson W: Sexual behavior in manic patients. South Med J 53:870–874, 1960

Alzate H: Vaginal eroticism: a replication study. Arch Sex Behav 14:529–537, 1985

Ambrosi B, Bara R, Travaglini P, et al: Study of the effects of bromocriptine on sexual impotence. Clin Endocrinol 7:417–421, 1977

Ambrosi B, Gaggini M, Moriondo P, et al: Prolactin and sexual function (letter to the editor). JAMA 244:2608, 1980

American Psychiatric Association: Diagnostic and Statistical Manual of Mental Disorders, 2nd ed. Washington, DC, American Psychiatric Association, 1968

American Psychiatric Association: Diagnostic and Statistical Manual of Mental Disorders, 3rd ed. Washington, DC, American Psychiatric Association, 1980

American Psychiatric Association: Diagnostic and Statistical Manual of Mental Disorders, 3rd ed, revised. Washington, DC, American Psychiatric Association, 1987

Andreasen NC: Sexual problems and affective disorders. Med Aspects of Hum Sex, 15:134–152, 1981

Annon JS: The behavioral treatment of sexual problems, in Brief Therapy, vol. 1. Honolulu, Enabling Systems, 1974

Annon J, Robinson C: Behavioral treatment of sexual dysfunctions, in Human Sexuality and Rehabilitation Medicine: Sexual Functioning Following Spinal Cord Injury. Edited by Sha'Ked A. Baltimore, Williams and Wilkins, 1981, pp 104–118

Ansari JMA: Impotence: prognosis, a controlled study. Br J Psychiatry 128:194–198, 1976

Anton PG, McGrath JC: Further evidence for adrenergic transmission in the human vas deferens. J. Physiol 273:45–55, 1977

Appenzeller O, Feldman RG, Friedman AP: Migraine, headache, related conditions. Arch Neurol 36:784, 1979

Appleton WS: How depressed patients adversely affect their marriages. Med Aspects of Hum Sex 16:154–157, 1982

Araoz D: Hypnosis and Sex Therapy. New York, Brunner/Mazel, 1982

Arentewicz G, Schmidt G: The Treatment of Sexual Disorders. New York, Basic Books, 1983

Aries N, Klerman L: Evaluating service delivery models for pregnant adolescents. Women Health 6:91–107, 1981

Bancroft J: Deviant Sexual Behavior: Modification and Assessment. Oxford, Clarendon Press, 1974

Bancroft J: The relationship between hormones and sexual behavior in humans, in Biological Determinants of Sexual Behavior. Edited by Hutchison JB. New York, John Wiley and Sons, 1978, pp. 493–519

Bancroft J: Endocrinology of sexual function. Clin Obstet Gynecol 7:253–281, 1980

Bancroft J: Human Sexuality and Its Problems. Edinburgh, Churchill Livingstone, 1983

Bancroft J, Wu FCW: Changes in erectile responsiveness during androgen replacement therapy. Arch Sex Behav 12:59–66, 1983

Bancroft J, Sanders D, Davidson D, et al: Mood, sexuality, hormones and the menstrual cycle, III: sexuality and the role of androgens. Psychosom Med 45:509–516, 1983

Bandura A: Social Learning Theory. Englewood Cliffs, NJ, Prentice Hall, 1977

Barbach L: For Yourself: The Fulfillment of Female Sexuality. New York, Signet, 1975

Barker WJ: Female sexuality. J Am Psychoanal Assoc 16:123–245, 1968

Barlow DH, Abel GG: Recent developments in the assessment and treatment of sexual deviations, in Behavior Modification: Principles, Issues and Applications. Edited by Kazdin A, Mahoney M, Craighead E. Boston, Houghton, Mifflin, 1974

Barlow DH, Agras WS, Abel GG, et al: Biofeedback and reinforcement to increase heterosexual arousal in homosexuals. Behav Res Ther 13:45–50, 1975

Barlow DH, Sakheim DK, Beck JG: Anxiety increases sexual arousal. J Abnorm Psychol 92:49–54, 1983

Batrinos ML, Panistsa-Faflia C, Anapliotou M, et al: Prolactin in impotent men. Psychoendocrin 6:341–345, 1981

Baumgarten HG, Falck B, Lange W: Adrenergic nerves in the corpora cavernosa penis of some mammals. Z Zellforsch 95:58–67, 1969

Beck JG, Barlow DH, Sakheim DK: The effects of attentional focus and partner arousal on sexual responding in functional and dysfunctional men. Behav Res Ther 21:1–8, 1983

Bengston V, Cuellar J, Ragan P: Contrasts and similarities in attitudes toward death by race, age, social class and sex. J Gerontol 32:204–216, 1977

Benkert O: Pharmacotherapy of sexual impotence in the male. Mod Probl Pharmacopsychiatry 15:158–173, 1980

Benkert O, Jordan R, Dahlen HG, et al: Sexual impotence: a double blind study of LHRH nasal spray versus placebo. Neuropsychobiology 1:203–210, 1975

Benkert O, Watt W, Adam W, et al: Effects of testosterone undecanoate on sexual potency and the hypothalamic-pituitary-gonadal axis of impotent males. Arch Sex Behavior 8:471–480, 1979

Bennett D: Treatment of ejaculation praecox with monamine oxidase inhibitors. Lancet 2:1309, 1961

Benson H, Klipper MA: The Relaxation Response. New York, Avon Books, 1976

Berger SH: Trifluoperazine and haloperadol—sources of ejaculatory pain? Am J Psychiatry 136:350, 1979

Berlin FS, Meinecke CF: Treatment of sex offenders with antiandrogenic medication. Am J Psychiatry 138:601–607, 1981

Besser CM: Sex hormones and the hypothalamus, in The Hypothalamus. Edited by Givens JR. Chicago, Yearbook Medical Publishers, 1984

Birk L, Brinkley-Birk AW: Psychoanalysis and behavior therapy. Am J Psychiatry 131:499–510, 1974

Bishop N: The great Oneida love-in. American Heritage 20:14–17, 86–92, 1969

Bjorksten OJW: Sexually graphic material in the treatment of sexual disorders, in Clinical Management of Sexual Disorders. Edited by Meyer JK. Baltimore, Williams and Wilkins, 1976

Blay L, Ferraz MPT, Calil HM: Lithium-induced male sexual impairment: two case report. Clin Psychiatry 43:497–498, 1982

Blos P: On Adolescence. New York, MacMillan Publishing Co., 1962

Bohlen JG, Held JP, Sanderson MO, et al: The female orgasm: pelvic contractions. Arch Sex Behavior 11:367–386, 1982

Bommer J, Ritz E, Tscjope W: Life on hemodialysis. Lancet 2:511, 1975

Bradshore W: Training psychiatrists for working with blacks in basic residency programs. Am J Psychiatry 135:1520, 1973

Brady JP: Brevital-relaxation treatment of frigidity. Behav Res Ther 4:171–177, 1966

Bremmer WJ, Vitiello MV, Prinz PN: Loss of circadian rhythmicity in blood testosterone levels with aging in normal men. J Clin Endocrinol Metab 56:1278–1281, 1983

Brown E, Brown GM, Kofman O, et al: Sexual function and affect in Parkinsonian men treated with L-dopa. Am J Psychiatry 135:1552–1555, 1978

Buffum J: Pharmacosexology: the effects of drugs on sexual function. J Psychoactive Drugs 14:5–44, 1982

Bulpitt CJ, Dollery CT: Side effects of hypotensive agents evaluated by self-administered questionnaire. Br Med J 3:485–490, 1973

Burg L: Sexual behavior in old age. Am J Psychiatry 126:159–162, 1969

Burstein A: Treatment of post-traumatic stress disorder with imipramine. Psychosomatics 25:681–686, 1984

Burton G, Kaplan HM: Sexual behavior and adjustment of married alcoholics. Quarterly Journal of Studies on Alcohol 29:603–609, 1968

Butcher JN, Kass MP: Research on brief and crisis-oriented therapies, in Handbook of Psychotherapy and Behavior Change: An Empirical Analysis, 2nd ed. Edited by Garfield SL, Bergin AE. New York, John Wiley and Sons, 1978

Campbell S: Double blind psychometric studies on the effects of natural estrogens on post-menopausal women, in The Management of the Menopausal and Post-Menopausal Years. Edited by Campbell S. Lancaster, Pa, MPT Press, 1976, pp. 149–158

Cappleman M, Thompson R, DeRemer-Sullivan P, et al: Effectiveness of a home-based early intervention program with infants of adolescent mothers. Child Psychiatry Hum Dev 13:56–65, 1982

Carney A, Bancroft J, Mathews A: Combination of hormonal and psychological treatment for female sexual responsiveness: a comparative study. Br J Psychiatry 133:339–346, 1978

Carson RC: Interaction Concepts of Personality. Chicago, Aldine, 1969

Carter JN, Tyson JE, Tolis G, et al: Prolactin-secreting tumors and hypogonadism in 22 men. N Engl J Med 299:847–852, 1978

Catalan J, Bradley M, Gallway J, et al: Sexual dysfunction and psychiatric morbidity in patients attending a clinic for sexually transmitted diseases. Br J Psychiatry 138:292–296, 1981

Chambless DL, Stern TE, Sultan FE, et al: The pubococcygeous and female orgasm: a correlational study with normal subjects. Arch Sex Behav 11:479–490, 1982

Chambless DL, Sultan FE, Stern TE, et al: Effect of pubococcygeal exercise on coital orgasm in women. J Consult Clin Psychol 52:114–118, 1984

Chang J: The Tao of Love and Sex. New York, EP Dutton Co, 1977

Cheadle AJ, Freeman HL, Korer J: Chronic schizophrenic patients in the community. Br J Psychiatry 132:221, 1978

Chesser E: The Marital and Family Relationships of the English Women. London, Hutchison's Medical Publications, 1956

Christenson C, Gagnon J: Sexual behavior in a group of older women. J Gerontol 20:351–356, 1965

Clark AL, Wallin P: Women's sexual responsiveness and the duration and quality of their marriages. American Journal of Sociology 71:187–196, 1965

Clark JT, Smith ER, Davidson JM: Enhancement of sexual motivation in male rats by yohimbine. Science 225:847–849, 1984

Clayton PJ, Pitts FN Jr, Winokur G: Affective disorder, IV: mania. Compr Psychiatry 6:313, 1965

Cobliner W: Prevention of adolescent pregnancy: a developmental perspective. Birth Defects 17:35–47, 1981

Cohen HD, Rosen RC, Goldstein L: Electro-encephalographic laterality changes during human sexual orgasm. Arch Sex Behav 5:189–199, 1976

Colarusso C, Nemiroff R: Adult Development: A New Dimension in Psychodynamic Theory and Practice. New York, Plenum Press, 1981

Cole MJ: Drugs and sexual dysfunction. Consultant 20:280, 1976

Cole MJ: Sex therapy—a critical reappraisal. Br J Sex Med 11:18–25, 1984

Compton A: On the psychoanalytic theory of instinctual drives, I: the beginnings of Freud's drive theory. Psychoanal Q 50:190–218, 1981a

Compton A: On the psychoanalytic theory of instinctual drives, II: the sexual drives and the ego drives. Psychoanal Q 50:219–237, 1981b

Compton A: On the psychoanalytic theory of instinctual drives, III: complications of libido and narcissism. Psychoanal Q 50:345–362, 1981c

Conti G: L'erection du penis humain et ses bases morphologicovasculaires. Acta Anat 14:217–262, 1952

Cooper AJ: Hostility and male potency disorders. Compr Psychiatry 9:621, 1968

Cooper AJ: Factors in male sexual inadequacy: a review. J Nerv Ment Dis 149:337–359, 1969a

Cooper AJ: A clinical study of coital anxiety in male potency disorders. J Psychosom Res 13:143–147, 1969b

Cooper AJ: Disorders of sexual potency in the male: a clinical and statistical study of some factors related to short term prognosis. Br J Psychiatry 115:709–719, 1969c

Cooper AJ: An innovation in the behavioral treatment in a case of non-consummation due to vaginismus. Br J Psychiatry 115:21–722, 1969d

Cooper AJ: Clinical and therapeutic studies in premature ejaculatory disorders. Compr Psychiatry 10:285–295, 1969e

Cooper AJ: Treatments of male potency disorders: the present status. Psychosomatics 12:235–244, 1971

Cooper AJ: Treatments of male potency disorders: the present status, in Handbook of Sex Therapy. Edited by LoPiccolo J, LoPiccolo L. New York, Plenum Press, 1978

Cooper AJ, Magnus RV: A clinical trial of the beta blocker propranolol in premature ejaculation. J Psychosom Res 28:331–336, 1984

Cooper AJ, Ismail AAA, Harding T, et al: The effects of clomiphene in impotence. Br J Psychiatry 120:327–30, 1972

Coppen A: The prevalence of menstrual disorders in psychiatric patients. Br J Psychiatry 111:155–167, 1965

Crenshaw T: Rape: helping the victim, in Counseling of Family and Friends. Edited by Medical Economics. Oradell, NJ, 1978

Crenshaw TL, Goldberg JP, Stern WC: Pharmacologic modification of psychosexual dysfunction. J Sex and Marital Therapy 13:239–252, 1987

Crowe MJ: Evaluation of conjoint marital therapy (abstracts). Sixth World Congress of Psychiatry. Honolulu, 1977. Washington, DC, American Psychiatric Association, 1977

Crowe MJ, Gillan P, Golombok S: Form and content in the conjoint treatment of sexual dysfunction: a controlled study. Behav Res Ther 19:47–54, 1981

Crown S, D'Ardenne P: Symposium on sexual dysfunction: controversies, methods, results. Br J Psychiatry 140:70–77, 1982

Csillag ER: Malfunction of penile erectile response. J Behav Ther Exp Psychiatry 7:27–29, 1976

Cvetkovitch G, Grote B: On the psychology of adolescents' use of contraception. J Sex Res 11:256–270, 1975

Dagon E: Aging and sexuality, in Treatment Interventions in Human Sexuality. Edited by Nadelson C, Marcotte D. New York, Plenum Press, 1983

Dai WS, Kuller LH, LaPorte RE, et al: The epidemiology of plasma testosterone levels in middle-aged men. Am J Epidemiol 114:804–816, 1981

Davidson JM, Camargo CA, Smith ER: Effects of androgens on sexual behavior in hypogonadal men. J Clin Endocrin Metab 48:955–958, 1979

Davidson JM, Chen JJ, Crapo L, et al: Hormonal changes and sexual function in aging men. J Clin Endocrinol Metab 57:71–77, 1983

Davies TF, Mountjoy CQ, Gomez-Pan A, et al: A double blind crossover trial on gonadotrophin releasing hormone (LHRH) in sexually impotent men. Clin Endocrinol 5:601–608, 1976

deGroat WC, Booth AM: Physiology of male sexual function. Ann Intern Med 92:329–331, 1980

Dela Fuente JR, Rosenbaum AH: Prolactin in psychiatry. Am J Psychiatry 138:1154–1159, 1981

DeLeo D, Magni G: Sexual side effects of antidepressant drugs. Psychosomatics 24:1076–1082, 1983

DeLeo D, Magni G, Pavan L: Modifications of libido and sex drive during treatment of minor depression with viloxazine. Int J Clin Pharmacol Ther Toxicol 21:4, 176–177, 1983

Dengrove E: Therapeutic approaches of impotence in the male, III: behavior therapy of impotence. Journal of Sex Research 7:177–183, 1971

Dennerstein L, Burrows GD: Hormone replacement therapy and sexuality in women. J Clin Endocrinol Metab 11:661–679, 1982

Derogatis LR, Meyer JK: A psychological profile of the sexual dysfunctions. Arch Sex Behav 8:201–223, 1979

Derogatis LR, Meyer JK, King KM: Psychopathology in individuals with sexual dysfunction. Am J Psychiatry 138:757–763, 1981

Deutsch H: Psychology of Women, vol 2. New York, Grune & Stratton, 1945

Domer FR, Wessler G, Brown RL, et al: Involvement of the sympathetic nervous system in the urinary bladder, internal sphincter, and in penile erection in the anesthetized cat. Invest Urol 15:404–407, 1978

Doty RL: Chemical communication of sex and reproductive state in humans, in Chemical Signals in Vertebrates. Edited by Muller-Schwarze D, Mozell MM. New York, Plenum Press, 1977, pp 273–286

Dow MGT, Hart DM, Forrest CA: Hormonal treatment of sexual unresponsiveness in post-menopausal women: a comparative study. Br J Obstet Gynaecol 90:361–366, 1983

Drafta D, Schindler AE, Stroe E, et al: Age-related changes of plasma steroid in normal adult males. J Steroid Biochem 17:683–687, 1982

Dunner DL: Changes in libido and sexual behavior associated with depression. Med Aspects Hum Sex 14:109–110, 1980

Dunner DL, Dwyer T, Fieve RR: Depressive symptoms in patients with unipolar and bipolar affective disorder. Compr Psychiatry 17:447, 1976

Durden-Smith J, DeSimone D: Sex and the Brain. New York, Arbor House, 1983

Edwards IS, Errey B: Pain on ejaculation after vasectomy. Br Med J 284–1710, 1982

Edwards JN, Booth A: The cessation of marital intercourse. Am J Psychiatry 133:1333–1336, 1976

Ellenberg M: Impotence in diabetes: the neurologic factor. Ann Intern Med 75:213–219, 1971

Ellis A: Treatment of erectile dysfunction, in Principles and Practices of Sex Therapy. Edited by Leiblum SR, Pervin LA. New York, Guilford Press, 1980

Ende J, Rockwell S, Glasgow M: The sexual history in general medicine practice. Arch Intern Med 144:558–561, 1984

Evans IM, Distiller LA: Effects of luteinizing releasing hormone on sexual arousal in normal men. Arch Sex Behav 8:385–396, 1979

Everaerd W: Comparative studies of short-term treatment methods for sexual inadequacies, in Progress in Sexology. Edited by Emme R, Wheeler CC. New York, Plenum Press, 1977

Eysenck HJ: Sex and Personality. Austin, University of Texas Press, 1976

Eysenck HJ, Beach R: Counterconditioning and related methods in behavior therapy, in Handbook of Psychotherapy and Behavior Change: An Empirical Analysis. Edited by Bergin AE, Garfield SL. New York, John Wiley and Sons, 1971, p 602

Ezriel H: Notes on psychoanalytic group therapy, II: interpretation and research. Psychiatry 15:119–127, 1952

Falaschi PA, De Giorgio RG, Frajese G, et al: Brain dopamine and premature ejaculation: results of treatment with dopamine antagonists, in Apomorphine and other Dopaminomimetics, vol 1. Edited by Gessa GL, Corsini GU. New York, Raven Press, 1981, pp 117–121

Felice M, Granados J, Ances I, et al: The young pregnant teenager. J Adolesc Health Care 1:193–197, 1981

Ferris RM, Cooper BR, Maxwell RA: Studies of bupropion's mechanism of antidepressant activity. J Clin Psychiatry 44:74–78, 1983

Fertel N: Vaginismus: a review. J Sex Marital Ther 3:113–121, 1977

Filicori M, Crowley WF Jr: Hypothalamic regulation of gonadotropin secretion in women, in Neuroendocrine Aspects of Reproduction. Edited by Givens JR. New York, Academic Press, 1983

Finney R: New hinge silicone implant. J Urol 118:585, 1977

Fisher C: Dreaming and sexuality, in Psychoanalysis—A General Psychology: Essays in Honor of Heinz Hartman. Edited by Loewenstein RM, Newman LM, Schur M. New York, International University Press, 1966

Fisher C, Cohen HD, Schiavi RC, et al: Patterns of female sexual arousal during sleep and waking: vaginal thermo-conductance studies. Arch Sex Behav 12:97–122, 1983

Fisher S: Understanding the Female Orgasm. New York, Basic Books, 1973a

Fisher S: The Female Orgasm: Psychology, Physiology, Fantasy. New York, Basic Books, 1973

Fisher S, Cleveland SE: Body Image and Personality. New York, Dover Publications, 1968

Fordney DS: Dyspareunia and vaginismus. Clin Obstet Gynecol 21:205, 1978

Fraiberg S: The adolescent mother and her infant. Adolesc Psychiatry 10:7–23, 1982

Frank D, Dornbush RL, Webster SK, et al: Mastectomy and sexual behavior: a pilot study. Sexuality and Disability 1:16–26, 1978

Frank E, Anderson C, Kupfer DJ: Profiles of couples seeking sex therapy and marital therapy. Am J Psychiatry 133:559–562, 1976

Frank E, Anderson C, Rubinstein D: Frequency of sexual dysfunction in normal couples. N Engl J Med 299:111–115, 1978

Frank L: Humanizing and dehumanizing aspects of human sexuality. Dis Nerv Syst 30:781, 1969

Frank OS: Symposium on sexual dysfunction: the therapy of sexual dysfunction. Br J Psychiatry 140:78–84, 1982

Franks CM, Wilson GT: Behavior therapy and sexual disorders: commentary, in Annual Review of Behavior Therapy. Edited by Franks CM, Wilson GT. New York, Brunner/Mazel, 1974

Franks S, Jacobs HS, Martin N, et al: Hyperprolactinemia and impotence. Clin Endocrinol 8:277–287, 1978

Fraser AR: Sexual dysfunction following antidepressant drug therapy. J Clin Psychopharmacol 4:62–63, 1984

Freud S: Three Essays on the Theory of Sexuality, in Complete Psychological Works of Sigmund Freud, standard ed, vol 7. Edited by Strachey J. London, Hogarth Press, 1953

Freud S: On the universal tendency to debasement in the sphere of love (1912), in Complete Psychological Works of Sigmund Freud, standard ed, vol 2. Edited by Strachey J. London, Hogarth Press, 1957, pp 177–190

Freund K: Therapeutic sex drive reduction. Acta Psychiatr Scand 62:6–317, 1980

Friedman DE: The treatment of impotence by brevital-relaxation therapy. Behav Res Ther 6:257–261, 1968

Friedman S, Phillips S: Psychosocial risk to mother and child as a consequence of adolescent pregnancy. Semin Perinatology 5:33–37, 1981

Fuchs K, Hoch Z, Paldi E, et al: Hypnodesensitization therapy of vaginismus: in vitro and in vivo methods, in Handbook of Sex Therapy. Edited by LoPiccolo J, LoPiccolo L. New York, Plenum Press, 1978

Furlow WL: Inflatable penile prosthesis: Mayo Clinic experience with 175 patients. Urology 13:166, 1979

Gardner EA, Johnson JA: Bupropion: an antidepressant without sexual pathophysiological action. J Clin Psychopharmacol 5:24–29, 1985

Garfield AH, McBready JF, Dichten M: A case of impotence successfully treated by desensitization combined with in vivo operant training and thought substitution, in Advances in Behavior Therapy. Edited by Rubin R, Franks CM. New York, Academic Press, 1968

Gartrell N: Gay patients in the medical setting, in Treatment Interventions in Human Sexuality. Edited by Nadelson C, Marcotte D. New York, Plenum Press, 1983

Gebhard PH: Factors in marital orgasms, in Handbook of Sex Therapy. Edited by LoPiccolo J, LoPiccolo L. New York, Plenum Press, 1978

Gessa GL, Tagliamonte A: Serotonin and sexual behavior, in Serotonin in Health and Disease, vol 5. Edited by Essman WB. New York, SP Medical and Scientific Books, 1978, pp 51–67

Ghardirian AM, Chouinard G, Annable L: Sexual dysfunction and plasma prolactin levels in neuroleptic treated schizophrenic outpatients. J Nerv Ment Dis 170:463–467, 1982

Giambra L, Martin C: Sexual daydreams and quantitative aspects of sexual activity: some relationships for males across adulthood. Arch Sex Behav 6:497–505, 1977

Gillan P, Brindley GS: Vaginal and pelvic floor responses to sexual stimulation. Psychophysiology 16:471–481, 1979

Glover J: Factors affecting the outcome of treatment of sexual problems. British Journal of Sexual Medicine 28–31, 1983

Goldberg DC, Whipple B, Fishkin RE, et al: The Grafenberg spot and female ejaculation: a review of initial hypothesis. J Sex Marital Ther 9:27–37, 1983

Goldfriend MR: On the history of therapeutic integration. Behav Res Ther 13:572–593, 1982

Goldman L, Segraves RT: Psychiatric evaluation of penile prosthesis candidates, in Diagnosis and Treatment of Erectile Problems. Edited by Segraves RT, Schoenberg HW. New York, Plenum Press, 1985

Goodman RE: An assessment of clomipramine (Anafranil) in the treatment of premature ejaculation. J Int Med Res 8:53–59, 1980

Grafenberg E: The role of the urethra in female orgasm. Int J Sexology 3:145–148, 1950

Greenblatt RB, Verheugen C, Chaddha J, et al: Aphrodisiacs—in legend and in fact, in Psychopharmacology and Sexual Disorders. Edited by Wheatley D. New York, Oxford University Press, 1983, pp 148–164

Greene S: Resisting the pressure to become a surrogate: a case study. J Sex Marital Ther 3:40–49, Spring 1977

Griffith E, Trieschmann R: Sexual dysfunctions in the physically ill and disabled, in Treatment Interventions in Human Sexuality. Edited by Nadelson C, Marcotte D. New York, Plenum Press, 1983

Gruman G: Sexual rejuvenation: a brief look at history. Trans Am Philos Soc 56:74–78, 1966

Gurman AS: Contemporary marital therapies: a critique and comparative analysis of psychoanalytic, behavioral and systems theory approaches, in Marriage and Marital Therapy. Edited by Paolino TJ, McCrady BS. New York, Brunner/Mazel, 1978

Gurman AS, Knishern DP: Handbook of Family Therapy. New York, Brunner/Mazel, 1981

Guttman D: The cross-cultural perspective: notes toward a comparative psychology of aging, in Handbook of the Psychology of Aging. Edited by Birren J, Schaie K. New Jersey, Van Nostrand Rheinhold, 1977

Hartman LM: The interface between sexual dysfunction and marital conflict. Am J Psychiatry 137:576–579, 1980

Hartman WE, Fithian MA: Treatment of Sexual Dysfunction. Long Beach, Calif Center for Marital and Sexual Studies, 1972

Hartocollis P: Hospital romances: some vicissitudes of transference. Bull Menninger Clin 28:62–71, 1964

Haslam MT: The treatment of psychogenic dyspareunia by reciprocal inhibition. Br J Psychiatry 111:280–282, 1965

Haslam MT: Psychosexual Disorders: A Review. Springfield, Ill, Charles C Thomas Publishers, 1971

Hatch JP: Psychophysiological aspects of sexual dysfunction. Arch Sex Behav 10:49–64, 1981

Heath RG: Pleasure and brain activity in man. J Nerv Ment Dis 154:3–18, 1972

Heiman JR: Use of the vaginal photoplethysmograph as a diagnostic and treatment aid in female sexual dysfunction. Presented at the Meeting of the American Psychological Association, Chicago, 1975

Heiman JR: Female sexual response patterns: interactions of physiological, affective and contextual cues. Arch Gen Psychiatry 37:1311–1316, 1980

Heiman JR, LoPiccolo J: Clinical outcome of sex therapy. Arch Gen Psychiatry 40:443–449, 1983

Heiman JR, Rowland DL: Affective and physiological sexual response patterns: the effects of instructions on sexually functional and dysfunctional men. J Psychosomat Res 27:105–116, 1983

Heller CG, Myers GB: The male climateric, its symptomatology, diagnosis and treatment. JAMA 126:472–477, 1944

Henson C, Rubin HB, Henson DE: Women's sexual arousal concurrently assessed by three genital measures. Arch Sex Behav 8:459–469, 1979

Henson DE, Rubin HB: Voluntary control of eroticism. J Appl Behav Anal 4:37–43, 1971

Hite S: The Hite Report. A Nationwide Study on Female Sexuality. New York, MacMillan Publishing Co, 1976

Hoch Z: The sensory arm of the female orgasmic reflex. J Sex Ed Ther 6:4–7, 1980

Hoffman AR, Crowley WF Jr: Chronic low-dose pulsatile gonadotropin-releasing hormone treatment of idiopathic hypogonadotropic hypogonadism in men, in Recent Advances in Male Reproduction. Edited by D'Agata R, Lipsett MB, Polosa P, et al. New York, Raven Press, 1983

Hoffman AR, Crowley WF Jr: Chronic administration of low-dose pulsatile gonadotropin-releasing hormone in idiopathic hypogonadotropic hypogonadism, in The Hypothalamus. Edited by Givens JR. Chicago, Yearbook Medical Publishers, 1984

Hoon EF, Hoon PW: Styles of sexual expression in women: clinical implications of multivariate analysis. Arch Sex Behav 7:105–116, 1978

Hoon PW: The assessment of sexual arousal in women. Prog Behav Modif 7:1–61, 1978

Hoon PW, Wincze JP, Hoon EF: Physiological assessment of sexual arousal in women. Psychophysiology 13:196–204, 1976

Hoon PW, Bruce K, Kinchloe B: Does the menstrual cycle play a role in sexual arousal? Psychophysiology 19:21–27, 1982

Hotvedt M: The cross-cultural and historical context, in Sexuality in the Later Years: Roles and Behaviors. Edited by Weg R. New York, Academic Press, 1983

Huey CJ, Kline-Graber G, Graber B: Time factors and orgasmic response. Sex Behav 10:111–118, 1981

Hughes JM: Failure to ejaculate with chlordiazepoxide. Am J Psychiatry 121:610–611, 1964

Hunt HF, Dyrud JE: Commentary: perspective in behavior therapy. Research in Psychotherapy 3:140–152, 1968

Hunt M: Sexual Behavior in the 70s. Chicago, Playboy Press, 1974

Hyyppa MT, Falck SC, Rinne UK: Is L-dopa an aphrodisiac in patients with Parkinson's disease?, in Sexual Behavior: Pharmacology and Biochemistry. Edited by Sandler M, Gessa GL. New York, Raven Press, 1975

Ishihara A, Levy H: The Tao of Sex: A Chinese Introduction to the Bedroom Arts. New York, Harper and Row, 1970

Ivers R, Goldstein N: Multiple sclerosis. Mayo Clin Proc 38:457, 466, 1963

Jayne C: Freud, Grafenberg, and the neglected vagina: thoughts concerning an historical omission in sexology. J Sex Res 20:212–215, 1984

Johnson J: Prognosis of disorders of sexual potency in the male. J Psychosom Res 9:195–200, 1965a

Johnson J: Androgyny and disorders of sexual potency. Br Med J 3:572–573, 1965b

Johnstone D: Some Current Practices in Sex Therapy with Surrogates. Doctoral dissertation. Los Angeles, California School of Professional Psychology, 1978

Jonas U: Five years' experience with the Silicone-Silver penile prosthesis: improvements and new developments. World J Urol 1:251, 1983

Jonas U, Jacobi GH: Silicone-Silver penile prosthesis: description, operative approach and results. J Urol 123:865, 1980

Jones SD: Ejaculatory inhibition with trazodone. J Clin Psychopharmacol 4:279–281, 1984

Kane F: Motivational factors in abortion patients. Am J Psychiatry 130:290–293, 1973

Kaplan HS: The New Sex Therapy, vol 1. New York, Brunner/Mazel, 1974

Kaplan HS: Sex therapy: an overview, in Sexuality and Psychoanalysis. Edited by Adelson ET. New York, Brunner/Mazel, 1975

Kaplan HS: Towards a rational classification of the sexual dysfunctions (editorial). J Sex Marital Ther 2:83–84, 1976

Kaplan HS: Disorders of Sexual Desire: The New Sex Therapy, vol 2. New York, Brunner/ Mazel, 1979

Kaplan HS: The Evaluation of Sexual Disorders: Psychological and Medical Aspects. New York, Brunner/Mazel, 1983a

Kaplan H: Sexual relationships in middle age. Physician and Patient, Oct 1983b, pp 12–20

Kaplan HS: The Evaluation of Sexual Disorders: Psychological and Medical Aspects. New York, Brunner/Mazel, 1984

Kaplan HS, Kohl RN: Adverse reactions to the rapid treatment of sexual problems. Psychosomatics 13:185–190, 1972

Kaplan HS, Fyer AJ, Novick A: The treatment of sexual phobias: the combined use of anti-panic medication and sex therapy. J Sex Marital Ther 8:3–28, 1982

Karacan I: Sexual arousal and activity: effect on subsequent nocturnal penile tumescent patterns. Sleep Research 8:61, 1979

Karacan I, Moore CA: Objective methods of differentiation between organic and psychogenic impotence, in Male Sexual Dysfunction and Impotence. Edited by Swerdloff RS, Santen RJ. New York, Marcel Dekker, 1985

Karacan I, Goodenough DR, Shapiro A, et al: Erection cycle during sleep in relation to dream anxiety. Arch Gen Psychiatry 15:183–189, 1966

Karacan I, Williams RL, Thornby JI, et al: Sleep related penile tumescence as a function of age. Am J Psychiatry 132:932–937, 1975

Karacan I, Aslan C, Hirshkowitz M: Erectile mechanisms in man. Science 220:1080–1082, 1983

Kassel V: Sex in nursing homes. Medical Aspects Hum Sex 10:244–247, 1976

Kastin AJ, Ehrensing RH, Coy DH, et al: Behavioral effects of brain peptides, including LHRH, in Psychoneuroendocrinology in Reproduction. Edited by Zichella L, Pancheri P. New York, North Holland Biomedical Press, 1979

Kedia K, Markland C: The effect of pharmacological agents on ejaculation. J Urol 114:569–573, 1975

Kegal AH: Sexual functions of the pubococcygeous muscle. Western J Surg 60:521–524, 1956

Kelly J: The aging homosexual: myth and reality. Gerontologist 17:328–332, 1977

Kilmann PR: The treatment of primary and secondary orgasmic dysfunction: a methodological review of the literature since 1970. J Sex Marital Ther 4:155–176, 1978

Kinsey AC, Pomeroy WB, Martin CE: Sexual Behavior in the Human Male. Philadelphia, WB Saunders Co, 1948

Kinsey AC, Pomeroy WB, Martin CE, et al: Sexual Behavior in the Human Female. Philadelphia, WB Saunders Co, 1953

Kirby D, Alter J, Scales P: An analysis of US sex education programs and evaluation methods. Bethesda, Md, Mathtech, June 1979

Klein DF: Anxiety reconceptualized, in Anxiety: New Research and Changing Concepts. Edited by Klein DF, Rabkins JG. New York, Raven Press, 1980

Knobil E: Neuroendocrine control of the menstrual cycle. Recent Prog Horm Res 36:53–88, 1980

Knoll J, Yen TT, Dallo J: Long-lasting, true aphrodisiac effect of (−)-deprenyl in sexually sluggish old male rats. Mod Probl Pharmacopsychiatry 19:135–153, 1983

Kockott G, Feil W, Revenstorf D, et al: Symptomatology and psychological aspects of male sexual inadequacy: results of an experimental study. Arch Sex Behav 9:457–475, 1980a

Kockott G, Feil W, Ferstl R, et al: Psychophysiological aspects of male sexual inadequacy: results of an experimental study. Arch Sex Behav 9:477–493, 1980b

Kolodny RC, Kahn CB, Goldstein H, et al: Sexual dysfunction in diabetic men. Diabetes 23:306–309, 1974

Kolodny RC, Masters WH, Johnson VE: Drugs and Sex, Textbook of Sexual Medicine. Boston, Little, Brown and Co, 1979

Korff J, Geer JH: The relationship between sexual arousal experience and genital response. Psychophysiology 20:121–127, 1983

Kotin J, Wilbert D, Verburg D, et al: Thioridazine and sexual dysfunction. Am J Psychiatry 133:82–85, 1976

Kraft T: The use of methohexitone sodium in the systematic desensitization of premature ejaculation. Br J Psychiatry 114:351–352, 1968

Kraft T, Al-Issa I: Behavior therapy and the treatment of frigidity. Am J Psychother 21:116–120, 1967

Kulik FA, Wilbur R: Case report of painful ejaculation as a side effect of amoxapine. Am J Psychiatry 139:234–235, 1982

Kupfer DJ, Rosenbaum JF, Detre TP: Personality style and sexual functioning among psychiatric outpatients. J Sex Research 13:257–266, 1977

Labrie F, Belanger A, Carmichael R, et al: Inhibition of the testicular steroidogenic pathway in experimental animals and men, in Recent Advances in Male Reproduction. Edited by D'Agata R, Lipsett MB, Polosa P, et al. New York, Raven Press, 1983, pp 239–248

Ladas A, Whipple B, Perry JD: The G Spot and Other Recent Discoveries about Human Sexuality. New York, Holt, Rinehart and Winston Co, 1982

La Ferla JJ, Anderson DL, Schalch DS: Psychoendocrine response to sexual arousal in human males. Psychosom Med 40:166–172, 1978

Landis C, Bolles M, D'Esopo DA: Psychological and physical concomitants of adjustment in marriage. Hum Biol 12:559–565, 1940

Lang WR, Aponte GF: Gross and microscopic anatomy of the aged female reproductive organs. Clin Obstet and Gynecol 10:454–465, 1967

Lansky MR, Davenport AE: Difficulties in brief conjoint treatment of sexual dysfunction. Am J Psychiatry 132:177–179, 1975

Lansky MR, Selzer J: Priapism associated with trazodone therapy: case report. J Clin Psychiatry 45:232–233, 1984

Larsson LI, Fahrenkrug J, deMuckadell OBS: Occurrence of nerves containing vasoactive intestinal polypeptide immunoreactivity in the male genital tract. Life Sci 21:503–508, 1977

LaTorre RA: Psychological correlates of preferences for clitoral or vaginal stimulation. Am J Psychiatry 136:225–226, 1979

Lazarus AA: The treatment of chronic frigidity by systematic desensitization. J Nerv Ment Dis 136:272–278, 1963

Lazarus AA: The treatment of a sexually inadequate man, in Case Studies in Behavior Modification. Edited by Ullmann LP, Krasner L. New York, Holt, Rinehart and Winston Co, 1965

Lazarus AA: Psychological treatment of dyspareunia, in Principles and Practices of Sex Therapy. Edited by Leiblum SR, Pervin LA. New York, Guilford Press, 1980

Leary T: Interpersonal Diagnosis in Personality. New York, Ronald Press, 1957

Leiblum SR, Pervin LA: Introduction: the development of sex therapy from a sociocultural perspective, in Principles and Practice of Sex Therapy. Edited by Leiblum SR, Pervin LA. New York, Guilford Press, 1980

Leiblum SR, Pervin LA, Campbell EH: The treatment of vaginismus: success and failure, in Principles and Practices of Sex Therapy. Edited by Leiblum SR, Pervin LA. New York, Guilford Press, 1980

Leiblum S, Bachmann G, Kemmann E, et al: Vaginal atrophy in the post-menopausal woman. JAMA 249:2195–2198, 1983

Levay AN: Personality change in sex therapy. J Am Acad Psychoanal 11:425–433, 1983

Levay AN, Kagle A: Ego deficiencies in the areas of pleasure, intimacy, and cooperation: guidelines in the diagnosis and treatment of sexual dysfunctions. J Sex Marital Ther 3:10–18, 1977

Levay AN, Weissberg JH, Blaustein AB: Concurrent sex therapy and psychoanalytic psychotherapy by separate therapists. Psychiatry 39:355–363, 1976

Levere F, Smith JW: Alcohol-induced sexual impotence. Am J Psychiatry 130:212, 1973

Levin RJ: The physiology of sexual function in women. Clin Obstet Gynecol 7:213–252, 1980

Levin RJ, Wagner J: Influence of atropine on sexual arousal and orgasm in women—a pilot study, in Medical Sexology: Proceedings of Third International Congress of Medical Sexology, Rome. Edited by Forleo R, Pasini W. Mass, PSG Publishing, 1980

Levine SB: Marital sexual dysfunction: ejaculatory disturbances. Ann Intern Med 84:575–579, 1976a

Levine SB: Marital sexual dysfunction: introductory concepts. Ann Intern Med 84:448–453, 1976b

Levine SB: A modern perspective on nymphomania. J Sex Marital Ther 8:316–324, 1982

Levine SB: The psychological evaluation and therapy of psychogenic impotence, in Diagnosis and Treatment of Male Erectile Dysfunction. Edited by Segraves NT, Schoenberg HW. New York, Plenum Press, 1985

Levine SB, Agle D: The effectiveness of sex therapy for chronic secondary psychological impotence. J Sex Marital Ther 4:235–258, 1978

Levine SB, Yost MA: Frequency of sexual dysfunction in a general gynecological clinic: an epidemiological approach. Arch Sex Behav 5:229–238, 1976

Levy RL: Stroke and orgasmic cephalgia. Headache 21:12, 1981

Liebowitz MR: The Chemistry of Love. Boston, Little, Brown and Co., 1983

Lief HI: Commentary: Current thinking on sex and depression. Med Aspects Hum Sex 11:22–23, 1977

Lief HI: Sexual concerns and difficulties and their treatment, in Sexual Problems in Medical Practice. Edited by Lief HI. Monroe, Wis., American Med Assn, 1981

Lief HI, Kaplan HS: Ego-Dystonic Homosexuality. J Sex Marital Ther 12:259–266, 1986

Lief HI, Karlen A: Sex Education in Medicine. New York, Spectrum, 1976

Like Other People (film): Highland Park, Ill, Perennial Educ, Inc

Lilius H, Valtonen E, Wilkstrom J: Sexual problems in patients suffering from multiple sclerosis. J Chronic Dis 29:643–647, 1976

Liss JL: Compulsive manic sexuality. Med Aspects Hum Sex 4:80–84, 1982

Lobitz WC, Lobitz GK: Clinical assessment in the treatment of sexual dysfunctions, in Handbook of Sex Therapy. Edited by LoPiccolo J, LoPiccolo L. New York, Plenum Press, 1978, pp 85–102

Lobitz WC, LoPiccolo J: New methods in the behavioral treatment of sexual dysfunction. J Behav Ther Exp Psychiatry 3:265–271, 1972

Longcope C: The effect of human chorionic gonadotropins on plasma steroid levels in young and old men. Steroids 21:583–592, 1973

LoPiccolo J: A program for enhancing the sexual relationship of normal couples. Counseling Psychologist 5:41–46, 1975

LoPiccolo J: Effects of variations in format on sex therapy outcome. Presented at the Society for Sex Therapy and Research. Charleston, SC, 1982

LoPiccolo J, LoPiccolo L (eds): Handbook of Sex Therapy. New York, Plenum Press, 1978

Lukianowicz N: Sexual drive and its gratification in schizophrenia. Int J Soc Psychiatry 9:250, 1963

Lundberg PO, Osterman PO: The benign and malignant forms of orgasmic cephalgia. Headache 14:164, 1974

Lundberg PO, Wide L: Sexual function in males with pituitary tumors. Fertil Steril 29:175–179, 1978

Magulesparen M, Ang V, Jenkins JS: Bromocriptine treatment of males with pituitary tumors, hyperprolactinemia and hypogonadism. Clin Endocrinol 9:73–79, 1978

Mahoney MJ: Cognition and Behavior Modification. Cambridge, Mass, Ballinger, 1974

Malan DH: The Frontier of Brief Psychotherapy. New York, Plenum Press, 1976

Malloy TR, Wein AJ: The etiology, diagnosis and surgical treatment of erectile impotence. J Reprod Med 20:183, 1978

Malloy TR, Wein AJ, Carpiniello VL: Comparison of the inflatable penile and the Small-Carrion prostheses in the surgical treatment of erectile impotence. J Urol 123:678, 1980

Malloy TR, Wein AJ, Carpiniello VL: Improved mechanical survival with revised model inflatable penile prosthesis using rear-tip extenders. J Urol 128:489, 1982

Malloy TR, Wein AJ, Carpiniello VL: Revised surgical technique to improve survival of penile cylinders for the inflatable penile prosthesis. J Urol 130:1105, 1983

March CM: Bromocriptine in the treatment of hypogonadism and male impotence. Drugs 17:349–358, 1979

Margolis R, Prieto P, Stein L, et al: Statistical summary of 10,000 male cases using Afrodex in treatment of impotence. Curr Ther Res 13:616–622, 1971

Marks IM: Review of behavioral psychotherapy, 2: sexual disorders. Am J Psychiatry 138:750–756, 1981

Marmor J: Psychoanalytic therapy and theories of learning, in The Interface between the Psychodynamic and Behavioral Therapies. Edited by Marmor J, Woods SM. New York, Plenum Press, 1980

Marshall DS: Sexual behavior on Mangaia, in Human Sexual Behavior: Variations in the Ethnographic Spectrum. Edited by Marshall DS, Suggs RC. New York, Basic Books, 1971

Martin CE: Factors affecting sexual functioning in 60–79 year old married males. Arch Sex Behav 10:399–420, 1981

Masters WH, Johnson VE: Human Sexual Response. Boston, Little, Brown and Co, 1966

Masters WH, Johnson VE: Human Sexual Inadequacy. Boston, Little, Brown and Co, 1970

Masters WH, Johnson VE, Kolodny RC: Sex and Human Loving. Boston, Little Brown and Co., 1986

Mathews AM: Treatment of sex dysfunction: psychological and hormone effects, in Learning Theory Applications in Psychiatry. Edited by Boulogouris JC. New York, John Wiley and Sons, 1981

Mathews A, Bancroft J, Whitehead A, et al: Behavioral treatment of sexual inadequacy: a comparative study. Behav Res Ther 14:427–436, 1976

Mathews A, Whitehead A, Kellett J: Psychological and hormonal factors in the treatment of female sexual dysfunction. Psychol Med 13:83–92, 1983

Maurice WL, Guze SB: Sexual dysfunction and associated psychiatric disorders. Compr Psychiatry 11:539–543, 1970

McCarthy BW: A modification of Masters and Johnson sex therapy model in a clinical setting. Psychotherapy Theory Research and Practice 10:290–293, 1973

McConnell J, Benson GS, Wood J: Autonomic innervation of the mammalian penis: a histochemical and physiological study. J Neural Transm 45:227–238, 1979

McCulloch DJ, Stewart JC: Sexual norms in a psychiatric population. J Nerv Ment Dis 131:70–73, 1960

McGovern L, Stewart R, LoPiccolo J: Secondary orgasmic dysfunction, I: analysis and strategies for treatment. Arch Sex Behav 4:265–275, 1975

McGregor AM, Scanlon MF, Hall K, et al: Reduction in size of a pituitary tumor by bromocriptine therapy. N Engl J Med 300:291–293, 1979

McLean JD, Forsythe RG, Kapkin JA: Unusual side effects of clomipramine associated with yawning. Can J Psychiatry 28:569–70, 1983

Mecklenburg M, Thompson P: The Adolescent Family Life Program as a Prevention Measure. Public Health Reports, vol 98, no 1. Washington, DC, US Department of Public Health, Jan–Feb 1983

Meissener WW, Nicholi AM: The psychotherapies: individual, family and group, in The Harvard Guide to Modern Psychiatry. Edited by Nicholi AM. Cambridge, Mass, Harvard University Press, 1978

Mellgren A: Treatment of ejaculation praecox with thioridazine. Psychother Psychosom 15:454–460, 1967

Melman A, Henry MD: The possible role of the cathecolamines of the corporal bodies in penile erection. J Urology 121:419–421, 1979

Merrill DC, Javaheri P: Mentor inflatable penile prosthesis: preliminary clinical results in 30 patients. Urology 13:72, 1984

Meyer JK: Psychodynamic treatment of the individual with a sexual disorder, in Clinical Management of Sexual Disorders. Edited by Meyer JK. Baltimore, Williams and Wilkins, 1976

Meyer JK, Schmidt CW, Lucas MJ, et al: Short term treatment of sexual problems. Am J Psychiatry 132:172–176, 1972

Meyer JK, Schmidt CW, Wise TN: Clinical Management of Sexual Disorders. Baltimore, Williams and Wilkins, 1983

Michal V, Kramar R, Pospichal J: Femoro-pudendal bypass, internal iliac thromboendarterectomy and direct arterial anastomosis to the cavernous body in the treatment of erectile impotence. Bull Soc Int Chir 34:343, 1974

Mills KH, Kilmann PR: Group treatment of sexual dysfunctions: a methodological review of the outcome literature. J Sex Marital Ther 8:259–280, 1982

Morales A, Surridge DHC, Marshall PG, et al: Nonhormonal pharmacological treatment of organic impotence. J Urol 128:45–47, 1982

Morokoff PJ, Heiman JR: Effects of erotic stimuli on sexually functional and dysfunctional women: multiple measures before and after sex therapy. Behav Res Ther 18:127–137, 1980

Mosovich A, Tallafero A: Studies on EEG and sex function. Diseases Nerv System 15:218–220, 1954

Moss RL, Dudley CA: Sexual function and brain peptides, in Brain: A New Endocrinology. Edited by Gotto AM Jr, Peck EJ Jr, Boyd AE. New York, North Holland Biomedical Press, 1979

Moss RL, Dudley CA: The challenge of studying the behavioral effects of neuropeptides, in Handbook of Psychopharmacology, vol 18. Edited by Iverson LL, Iverson SD, Snyder SH. New York, Plenum Press, 1984, pp 397–454

Munjack D, Kanno PH: Prognosis in the treatment of female sexual inhibition. Compr Psychiatry 18:481–488, 1977

Munjack DJ, Oziel LJ: Sexual Problems in Medical Practice. Boston, Little, Brown and Co, 1980

Munjack DJ, Oziel LJ, Kanno PH, et al: Psychological characteristics of males with secondary erectile failure. Arch Sex Behav 10:123–131, 1981

Murphy CV, Mikulas WL: Behavioral features and deficiencies of the Masters and Johnson program. The Psychological Record 24:221–227, 1974

Nadelson C: The pregnant teenager: problems of choice in a developmental framework. Psych Opinion 12:6–12, 1975

Nadelson C, Notman M: Behavioral psychological aspects of pregnancy and abortion, in Sexuality: New Perspectives. Edited by DeFries Z. Westport, Conn, Greenwood Press, 1985

Napoli-Farris L, Fratta W, Gessa GL: Stimulation of dopamine autoreceptors elicits "premature ejaculation" in rats. Pharmacol Biochem Behav 20:69–72, 1984

Nathan SG: Spontaneous remission of sexual dysfunction, in Emerging Dimensions in Sexology. Edited by Segraves RT, Haeberle EJ. New York, Prager, 1984

Nelson K, Key D, Fletcher J, et al: The teen-tot clinic: an alternative to traditional care for infants of teenaged mothers, adolescent fathers: an exploratory study. J Adolesc Health Care 4:117–120, 1982

Nettelbladt P, Uddenberg N: Sexual dysfunction and sexual satisfaction in 58 married Swedish men. J Psychosom Res 23:141–147, 1979

Newman G, Nichols C: Sexual activities and attitudes in older persons. JAMA 173:33–35, 1960

Newman HF, Tchertkoff V: Penile vascular cushions and erection. Invest Urol 18:43–45, 1980

Newman HF, Reiss H, Horthrup JD: Physical basis of emission, ejaculation, orgasm in the male. Urology 19:341–350, 1982

Nickel JC, Morales A, Condra M, et al: Endocrine dysfunction in impotence: incidence, significance and cost effective screening. J Urol 132:40–43, 1984

Nininger JE: Inhibition of ejaculation by amitriptyline. Am J Psychiatry 135:750, 1978

Norton GR, Jehu D: The role of anxiety in sexual dysfunctions: a review. Arch Sex Behav 13:165–183, 1984

Notman M: Teenage pregnancy: the nonuse of contraception. Psych Opinion 12:23–27, 1975

Noy P, Woolstein S, Kaplan-de-Nour A: Clinical observation on the psychogenesis of impotence. Br J Med Psychol 39:43–53, 1966

Noyes JH: Male continence or self-control in sexual intercourse: a letter of inquiry answered (pamphlet). New York, Oneida, 1866

O'Brien KM, Rawls J, Brinkley L: Sexual dysfunction in uremia. Proceedings of Clinical Dialysis Transplant Forum 5:98–101, 1975

O'Connor JF, Stern LO: Results of treatment in functional sexual disorders. New York State J Med 72:1927–1934, 1971

O'Connor TW, Scavone JM: Drug-related sexual dysfunction. Apothecary, Jan 1982, pp 20–30

Offit AK: The Sexual Self. Philadelphia, JB Lippincott and Co, 1977. Revised, New York, Congdon & Weed, 1983. Republished, Chicago, Contemporary Books, 1986

Osborn CA, Pollack RH: The effects of two types of erotic literature on physiological and verbal measures of female sexual arousal. J Sex Res 13:250–256, 1977

Ottesen B: Vasoactive intestinal polypeptide as a neurotransmitter in the female genital tract. Am J Obstet Gynecol 147:208–224, 1983

Ottesen B, Wagner G, Virag R, et al: Penile erection: possible role for vasoactive intestinal polypeptide as a neurotransmitter. Br Med J 288:9–11, 1984

Ovesey L, Woods SM: Pseudohomosexuality and homosexuality in men: psychodynamics as a guide to treatment, in Homosexual Behavior: A Modern Reappraisal. Edited by Marmor J. New York, Basic Books, 1980

Paglietti E, Pellegrini-Quarantotti B, Mereu G, et al: Apomorphine and L-dopa lower ejaculation threshold in the male rat. Physiol Behav 20:559–562, 1978

Paulson GW, Klawans HL, Jr: Benign orgasmic cephalgia. Headache 13:181, 1974

Perrault R, Wright J, Mathieu M: The directive sex therapies in psychiatric outpatient settings. Can J Psychiatry 24:47–54, 1979

Perry J, Whipple B: Pelvic muscle strength of female ejaculators: evidence in support of a new theory of orgasm. J Sex Res 17:22–39, 1981

Persky H, O'Brien CP, Kahn MR: Reproductive hormone levels, sexual activity and moods during the menstrual cycle. Psychosom Med 38:62–63, 1976

Persky H, Charney N, Lief HI, et al: The relationship of plasma estradiol level to sexual behavior in young women. Psychosom Med 40:523–535, 1978a

Persky H, Lief HI, Strauss D, et al: Plasma testosterone level and sexual behavior of couples. Arch Sex Behav 7:157–173, 1978b

Persky H, Dreisbach L, Miller WR, et al: The relation of plasma androgen levels to sexual behaviors and attitudes of women. Psychosom Med 44:305–319, 1982

Pfeiffer E: Sexuality in the aging individual. J Am Geriatr Soc 12:122–125, 1974

Pfeiffer E, Davis G: Determinants of sexual behavior in middle and old age. J Am Geriatr Soc 20:151–158, 1972

Phelps G, Brown M, Chen J, et al: Sexual experience and plasma testosterone levels in male veterans after spinal cord injury. Arch Phys Med Rehabil 64:47, 1983

Pinderhughes C: Effects of ethnic group concentration upon educational process, personality formation and mental health. J Natl Med Assn 56:407–411, 1964

Porto R: Double-blind study of clomipramine in premature ejaculation, in Medical Sexology. Edited by Forleo R, Pasini W. Amsterdam, Elsevier/North Holland, 1980, pp 624–628

Poussaint A: Black sexuality: myth and reality, in Treatment Interventions in Human Sexuality. Edited by Nadelson C, Marcotte D. New York, Plenum Press, 1983

Psych News: Pregnancy seen in teens least able for motherhood, 15:20, Aug 20, 1982

Pucci E, Franchi F, Kicovic PM, et al: Amplification of LH response to LHRH by dopamine infusion in eugonadal women. J Endocrinol Invest 4:55–47, 1981

Purtell JJ, Robins E, Cohen M: Observations of clinical aspects of hysteria. JAMA 146:902–909, 1951

Raboch J: The sexual development and life of female schizophrenic patients. Arch Sex Behav 13:341–349, 1984

Raboch J, Mellan J, Starka L: Kleinfelter's syndrome: sexual development and activity. Arch Sex Behav 12:59–66, 1983

Rado S: Psychoanalysis of Behavior, vol 2. New York, Grune & Stratton, Inc, 1962

Renshaw DC: Impotence in diabetes, in Handbook of Sex Therapy. Edited by LoPiccolo J, LoPiccolo L. New York, Plenum Press, 1978

Renshaw DC: Premature ejaculation. Consultant 13:99–100, 1978

Renshaw DC: Relationship therapy for sex problems. Compr Ther 9:32–39, 1983

Reyes FJ, Faiman C: Long-term therapy with low-dose cisclomiphene in male infertility. Int J Fertil 19:49–55, 1974

Reynolds BS: Psychological treatment models and outcome results for erectile dysfunction: a critical review. Psychol Bull 84:1218–1238, 1977

Reynolds BS: Erectile dysfunction: a review of behavioral treatment approaches, in Clinical Behavior Therapy and Behavior Modification, vol 2. Edited by Daitzman RJ. New York, Garland, 1981

Roffe MW, Hunt CH: A typology of marital interaction for sexually dysfunctional couples. J Sex Marital Ther 7:207–222, 1981

Roose SP, Glassman AH, Walsh BT, et al: Reversible loss of nocturnal penile tumescence during depression: a preliminary report. Neuropsychobiology 8:284–288, 1982

Rosen RC, Shapiro D, Schwartz GE: Voluntary control of penile tumescence. Psychosom Med 37:479–483, 1975

Rosenheim E, Neuman M: Personality characteristics of sexually dysfunctioning males and their wives. J Sex Res 17:124–138, 1981

Roughan PA, Kunst L: Do pelvic floor exercises really improve orgastic potential. J Sex Marital Ther 7:223–229, 1981

Roy A: Sexual dysfunction and hysteria. Br J Med Psychol 54:131–132, 1981

Rubin A, Babott D: Impotence and diabetes mellitus. JAMA 168:498–500, 1958

Rundles RW: Diabetic neuropathy. Medicine 24:111–116, 1945

Sager CJ: Transference in the conjoint treatment of married couples. Arch Gen Psychiatry 16:185–193, 1967

Sager CJ: The role of sex therapy in marital therapy. Am J Psychiatry 133:555–559, 1976

Sakheim DK, Barlow DH, Beck SG: The effect of increased awareness of erectile cues on sexual arousal. Behav Res Ther 22:151–158, 1984

Salvatierra O, Fortmann JL, Belzer FO: Sexual function in males before and after renal transplantation. Urology 5:64–66, 1975

Sandler H, Vietze P, O'Connor S: Obstetric and neonatal outcomes following intervention with pregnant teenagers, in Teenage Parents and Their Offspring. Edited by Scott K, Robertson E. Springfield, Ill, Charles C. Thomas Publishing, 1980

Sarrel L, Sarrel P: Pregnancy, in Sexual Turning Points: The Seven Stages of Adult Sexuality. New York, MacMillan Publishing Co, 1984

Sarrel PM: Biological aspects of sexual function, in Progress in Sexology. Edited by Gemme R, Wheeler CC. New York, Plenum Press, 1977

Sarrel PM: Dyspareunia, in Signs and Symptoms in Gynecology. Edited by Peckham BM, Shapiro SS. Philadelphia, JB Lippincott Co, 1983

Sarrel P, Whitehead M: Sex and menopause: defining the issues. Maturitas 7:14–19, 1985

Schaefer LC: Sexual Experiences and Reactions of a Group of 30 Women as Told to a Female Psychotherapist. Doctoral dissertation. Columbia University, 1964

Schaffer C, Pine F: Pregnancy, abortion, and the developmental tasks of adolescents. J Child Psychol Psychiatry 14:511–536, 1975

Scharff DE: The Sexual Relationship: An Object Relations View of Sex and the Family. Boston, Routledge and Kegal Paul, 1982

Schellen AM: Effects of gonadotropic hormones, clomiphene and releasing factors on human spermatogenesis, in Gonadotropins in Modern Therapy. Edited by Beric BM, Lunenfeld B, Kovac T, et al. Novi Sad, 1975, pp. 66–83

Schiavi RC: Psychological treatment of erectile disorders in diabetic patients. Ann Intern Med 92:337–339, 1980

Schiavi RC, Fisher C: Assessment of diabetic impotence—measurement of nocturnal erections. J Clin Endocrinol Metab 11:769–784, 1982

Schiavi RC, White D: Androgens and male sexual function: a review of human studies. J Sex Marital Ther 2:214–228, 1976

Schiavi RC, Fisher C, White D, et al: Pituitary-gonadal function during sleep in men with erectile impotence and normal controls. Psychosom Med 46:239–254, 1984

Schiavi RC, Fisher C, White D, et al: Plasma prolactin and estradiol during sleep in impotent men and normal controls. Arch Sex Behav 15:285–291, 1986

Schiavi RC, Schreiner-Engel P, White D, et al: Pituitary-gonadal function during sleep in men with hypoactive sexual desire and in normal controls. Psychosom Med 50:304–318, 1988

Schmidt SS: Spermatic granuloma, an often painful lesion. Fertil Steril 31:178, 1979

Schmitt GW, Shchadeh L, Swain CT: Transient gynecomastia in chronic renal failure during intermittent hemodialysis. Ann Intern Med 69:73–79, 1968

Schoffling K, Federlin K, Ditschuneit H, et al: Disorder of sexual function in male diabetes. Diabetes 12:519–527, 1963

Schreiner-Engel P: Female Sexual Arousability: Its Relation to Gonadal Hormones and the Menstrual Cycle. Doctoral dissertation. State University of New York, 1980

Schreiner-Engel P, Schiavi R, Smith H, et al: Sexual arousability and the menstrual cycle. Psychosom Med 43:199–214, 1981a

Schreiner-Engel P, Schiavi RC, Smith H: Female sexual arousal: relation between cognitive and genital assessments. J Sex Marital Ther 7:256–267, 1981b

Schreiner-Engel P, Schiavi RC, Smith H, et al: Plasma testosterone and female sexual behavior, in Excerpta Medica Proceedings of the Fifth World Congress of Sexology. Edited by Hoch Z, Lief HI. 1981c.

Schwarcz G: Case report of inhibition of ejaculation and retrograde ejaculation as side effects of amoxapine. Am J Psychiatry 139:233–234, 1982

Schwartz MF, Masters WH: The Masters and Johnson treatment program for dissatisfied homosexual men. Am J Psychiatry 141:173–281, 1984

Schwartz MF, Bauman JE, Masters WH: Hyperprolactinemia and sexual disorders in men. Biol Psychiatry 17:861–876, 1982

Scott FB, Bradley WE, Timm GW: Management of erectile impotence: use of implantable inflatable prosthesis. Urology 2:80, 1973

Segal M, Shohami E, Jacobowitz DM: Phenylethamine, norepinephrine, and mounting behavior in the male rat. Pharmacol Biochem Behav 20:133–135, 1984

Segraves RT: Primary orgasmic dysfunction: essential treatment components. J Sex Marital Ther 2:115–123, 1976

Segraves RT: Pharmacological agents causing sexual dysfunction. J Sex Marital Ther 3:157–176, 1977

Segraves RT: Treatment of sexual dysfunction. Compr Ther 4:38–43, 1978

Segraves RT: Female sexual inhibition, in Clinical Behavior Therapy and Behavior Modification, vol 2. Edited by Daitzman RJ. New York, Garland, 1981

Segraves RT: Marital Therapy: A Combined Psychodynamic-Behavioral Approach. New York, Plenum Press, 1982a

Segraves RT: Male sexual dysfunction and psychoactive drug use. J Postgrad Med 71:227–233, 1982b

Segraves RT: Female orgasm and psychiatric drugs. J Sex Educ Ther 11:69–71, 1985

Segraves RT, Smith RC: Concurrent psychotherapy and behavior therapy. Arch Gen Psychiatry 33:756–763, 1976

Segraves RT, Schoenberg HW, Zarins CK, et al: Characteristics of erectile dysfunction as a function of medical care system entry point. Psychosom Med 43:227–234, 1981a

Segraves RT, Schoenberg HW, Zarins CK, et al: Discrimination of organic versus psychological impotence with the DSFI: a failure to replicate. J Sex Marital Ther 7:230–288. 1981b

Segraves RT, Knopf J, Camic P: Spontaneous remission in erectile impotence. Behav Res Ther 20:89–91, 1982a

Segraves RT, Schoenberg HW, Zarins CK, et al: Referral of impotent patients to a sexual dysfunction clinic. Arch Sex Behav 11:521–528, 1982b

Segraves RT, Schoenberg HW, Zarins CK: Psychosexual and adjustment after penile prosthesis surgery. Sexuality and Disability 5:222–229, 1982c

Segraves RT, Camic P, Ivanoff J: Spontaneous remission in erectile dysfunction: a partial replication. Behav Res Ther 23:203–204, 1985a

Segraves RT, Schoenberg HW, Segraves KAB: Evaluation of etiology of erectile failure, in Diagnosis and Treatment of Erectile Problems. Edited by Segraves RT, Schoenberg HW. New York, Plenum Press, 1985b

Seligman M: Helplessness: On Depression, Development, and Death. San Francisco, WH Freeman and Co, 1975

Shader R: Sexual dysfunction associated with thioridazine hydrochloride. JAMA 188:1007–1009, 1964

Shapiro EI, Silber SJ: Open ended vasectomy, sperm granuloma, and post vasectomy orchalgia. Fertil Steril 32:546, 1979

Sheehan DV: Panic attacks and phobias. N Engl J Med 307:156–158, 1982

Sherwin BB, Gelfand MM, Brender W: Androgen enhances sexual motivation in females: a prospective, crossover study of sex steroid administration in the surgical menopause. Psychosom Med 47:339–351, 1985

Simpson GM, Blair JH, Amuso D: Effects of antidepressants on genitourinary function. Dis Nerv Syst 26:787–789, 1965

Singer I: The Goals of Human Sexuality. London, Wildwood House, 1973

Singer J, Singer I: Types of female orgasm. J Sex Res 8:255–267, 1972

Sjostrand NO, Klinge E: What function have cholinergic nerves in the smooth muscle of the male genital tract. Acta Physiol Scand (Suppl) 452:89–91, 1977

Skakkebaek NE, Bancroft J, Davidson DW, et al: Androgen replacement with oral testosterone undecanoate in hypogonadal men. Clin Endocrinol 14:49–61, 1981

Slag MF, Morley JE, Elson MK, et al: Impotence in medical clinic outpatients. JAMA 249:1736, 1983

Slater E, Woodside M: Patterns of Marriage. London, Cassell, 1951

Small E: Psychosexual issues in Asian culture, in Treatment Interventions in Human Sexuality. Edited by Nadelson C, Marcotte D. New York, Plenum Press, 1983

Small MP: Small-Carrion penile prosthesis: a report on 160 cases and review of literature. J Urol 119:365, 1978

Small MP, Carrion HM: A new penile prosthesis for treating impotence. Cont Surg 7:29, 1975

Smith AD: Causes and classification of impotence. Urol Clin North Am 8:79–89, 1981

Smith L: A conceptual model of families incorporating an adolescent mother and child into the household. Adv Nurs Science, Oct 1983, pp 45–60

Sollod RN: Behavioral and psychodynamic dimensions of the new sex therapy. J Sex Marital Ther 1:335–340, 1975

Sontag S: The double standard of aging. Saturday Review 55:29–38, 1972

Spalt L: Commentary. Med Aspects Hum Sex 15:151, 1981

Spark RF, White RA, Connolly PB: Impotence is not always psychogenic. JAMA 243:750–755, 1980

Staunton HP, Moore J: Coital cephalgia and ischemic muscular work of the lower limbs. J Neurol Neurosurg Psychiatry 41:930, 1978

Steinach E: Preserving sexual capacity, in Longevity. Edited by Guillerme J. New York, Walker Publishing Co, 1963

Steinman DL, Wincze JP, Sakheim et al: A comparison of male and female patterns of sexual arousal. Arch Sex Behav 10:529–547, 1981

Sung KT, Rothrock D: An alternative school for pregnant teenagers and teenage mothers. Child Welfare 59:427–436, 1980

Sunshine RF: Observations on the role of the libido in the psychoanalytic treatment of severely depressed patients. Int J Psychoanal 60:329–344, 1979

Tamburello A, Seppecher MF: The effects of depression on sexual behavior: preliminary results of research, in Progress in Sexology. Edited by Gemme R, Wheeler CC. New York, Plenum Press, 1977

Tan E: Culture-bound syndromes, in Normal and Abnormal Behavior in Chinese Culture. Edited by Kleinman A, Lin T. Dordrecht, Reidel, 1981

Tannahill R: The physiological perspective, in Sexuality in the Later Years: Roles and Behaviors. Edited by Weg R. New York, Academic Press, 1983

Taylor B, Berg M, Kapp L, et al: School-based prenatal services: can similar outcomes be attained in a non-school setting? JOSH 53:480–486, 1983

Terman LM: Psychological Factors in Marital Happiness. New York, McGraw Hill, 1938

Terman LM: Correlates of orgasm frequency in a group of 556 wives. J Psychol 32:115–172, 1951

Trussel T: Economic consequences of teenage childbearing. Fam Plann Perspect 8:184–190, 1976

Tsitouras PD, Martin CF, Harman SM: Relationship of serum testosterone to sexual activity in healthy elderly men. J Gerontol 37:288–293, 1982

Tuthill JF: Impotence. Lancet 124:128, 1955

Ulrich C, Pfafflin F: Changes in personality scores subsequent to sex therapy. Arch Sex Behav 9:235–244, 1980

Usdin GL: Preliminary report on Librium: a new psychopharmacologic agent. J Louisiana St Med Soc 112:142–147, 1960

Vandenberg JG: Pheromones and Reproduction in Mammals. New York, Academic Press, 1984

Van Thiel DH, Gavaler JS, Saughvi A: Recovery of sexual function in abstinent alcoholic men. Gastroenterology 84:677, 1982

VanWulfften PP: Neuropsychiatry, in Textbook of Tropical Medicine. Edited by deLangen C, Lichtenstein A. Batavia, New York, Kloff, 1936

Varsamis J, Adamson JD: Early schizophrenia. Can Psychiatr Assoc J 16:487, 1971

Vastayana: Kama Sutra (c AD 400). Translation. New York, Putnam and Sons, 1963

Verhulst J, Heiman JR: An interactional approach to sexual dysfunction. American Journal of Family Therapy 7:19–36, 1979

Wachtel PL: Psychoanalysis and Behavior Therapy. New York, Basic Books, 1977

Wagner G, Brindley GS: Effect of atropine and blockers upon human penile erection—a controlled pilot study, in First International Conference on Vascular Impotence. Edited by Zorgniotti A. New York, Charles C Thomas Publishers, 1980

Wagner G, Green R: Impotence: Physiological, Psychological, Surgical Diagnosis and Treatment. New York, Plenum Press, 1981

Wagner G, Levin RJ: Vaginal Fluid in the Human Vagina. Edited by Hafez ESE, Evans TN. Amsterdam, North Holland Publishing, 1978

Waxenberg SE, Drellich MG, Sutherland AM: The role of hormones in human behavior, I: changes in female sexuality after adrenalectomy. J Clin Endocrinol Metab 19:193–202, 1959

Weg R (ed): Sexuality in the Later Years: Roles and Behaviors. New York, Academic Press, 1983

Wein AJ, Van Arsdalen K, Malloy TR: Evaluation and treatment of impotence: the urologist's viewpoint, in Sexual Arousal: New Concepts in Basic Sciences, Diagnosis and Treatments. Edited by Fisher M, Fishkin R, Jacobs J. Springfield, Ill, Charles C Thomas Publishers, 1984, pp 101–115

Wilkeson A, Poussaint A, Small E, et al: Human sexuality and the American minority experience, in Treatment Interventions in Human Sexuality. Edited by Nadelson C, Marcotte D. New York, Plenum Press, 1983

Williams W: Anesthetic ejaculation. J Sex Marital Ther 11:19–29, 1985

Wilson G, Lawson D: Expectancies, alcohol, and sexual arousal in women. J Abnorm Psychol 87:358–367, 1978

Wincze JP, Hoon EF, Hoon PW: Physiological responsivity of normal and sexually dysfunctional women during erotic stimulus exposure. J Psychosom Res 20:445–451, 1976

Wincze JP, Hoon PW, Hoon EF: Sexual arousal in women: a comparison of cognitive and physiological responses by continuous measurement. Arch Sex Behav 6:121–133, 1977

Winokur G: Sexual behavior: its relationship to certain affects and psychiatric diseases, in Developments of Human Sexual Behavior. Edited by Winokur G. Springfield, Ill, Charles C Thomas Publishers, 1963

Winokur G, Guze GR, Pfeiffer E: Developmental and sexual factors in women: a comparison between control, neurotic and psychotic groups. Am J Psychiatry 115:1097–1110, 1959

Winters SJ, Troen P: Episodic LH secretion and the response of LH and FSH to LH-releasing hormone in aged men. J Clin Endocrinol Metab 55:560–565, 1982

Wolpe J: Psychotherapy by Reciprocal Inhibition. Stanford, Calif, Stanford University Press, 1958

Wolpe J, Lazarus AA: Behavior Therapy Techniques. New York, Pergamon Press, 1966

Woods SM: Sexuality and mental disorders, in Sexual Problems in Medical Practice. Edited by Lief HI. Monroe, Wis, American Medical Association, 1981

Wright J, Perreault R, Mathieu M: The treatment of sexual dysfunction. Arch Gen Psychiatry 34:881–890, 1977

Zsilla G, Knoll J: The action of (−)-deprenyl on monoamine turnover rate in rat brain, in Typical and Atypical Antidepressants. Edited by Costa E, Racagni C. New York, Raven Press, 1982, pp 211–217

Zuckerman M: Physiological measures of sexual arousal in the human. Psychol Bull 75:297–329, 1971

SECTION 23

Sleep Disorders

Chapter 218

Introduction

Perhaps more than other medical specialists, psychiatrists of the 1990s will need to be expert in the differential diagnosis and treatment of sleep/wake disorders. This is so for several reasons. First, the history of contemporary sleep research and the development of sleep disorders medicine has been substantially fostered by psychiatric investigators and practitioners. Second, a substantial percentage of sleep/wake complaints have psychiatric determinants; and many of the drugs currently used to treat sleep/wake disorders fall primarily within the pharmacologic armamentarium of the psychiatrist. Finally, even in those sleep/wake disorders that are not primarily psychiatric in etiology, clinically significant psychopathology is frequently prevalent as part of the presentation or as a sequela to the primary disorder.

In this chapter, we will review the most current and generally used approaches to the patient with a sleep disorder. Controlled clinical trials are still much needed in this field. Presentation of the major clinical and treatment aspects of sleep disorders will be organized around the DSM-III-R (American Psychiatric Association 1987) nosology. We have taken primarily a developmental and clinical management point of view in organizing this presentation, beginning with childhood sleep disorders, then progressing to childhood-onset and other forms of primary insomnia, to medically related insomnia, narcolepsy, sleep/wake schedule disorders, and concluding with sleep disturbances in late life.

Chapter 219

Parasomnias in Children

Parasomnias are abnormal behaviors that occur during sleep. Examples include nightmares, night terrors, sleep walking, enuresis, bruxism, sleep talking, and head banging (jactatio capitis nocturna). Some of these disorders, such as somnambulism, enuresis, and night terrors, are more common in children than in adults; others, such as nightmares, bruxism, and sleep talking, occur in both adults and children.

In most instances, the etiology of these disorders probably reflects a combination of genetic, developmental, psychological, and experiential factors (Kales et al. 1980a). Parasomnias frequently run in families, and a patient with one disorder often has an increased risk for other forms of parasomnia. For example, somnambulists suffer from bedwetting or night terrors. The disorders often disappear or decrease in frequency as the child matures. Stress, anxiety, and excitement may increase the number of episodes in a predisposed individual; and some studies indicate increased measures of psychopathology in affected individuals based on such instruments as the Minnesota Multiphasic Personality Inventory (MMPI). Nevertheless, these symptoms rarely result from mental and neurologic symptoms and are not usually associated with EEG abnormalities.

Parasomnias are sometimes considered disorders of arousal (Broughton 1968). The patients may be difficult to awaken and may sleep through an event or behavior that should arouse them; furthermore, specific disorders typically occur during sleep stages 3 and 4 (night terrors, sleep walking) or the first third of the night (enuresis, bruxism, head banging), when arousal is normally most difficult.

Nightmares and Night Terrors

Nightmares and night terrors may not be recognized as separate, distinct sleep problems. Parents will often say their child is having a bad dream when in fact the child suffers from night terrors. Clinicians should, however, make a differential diagnosis by history and other clinical features because different treatments may be indicated (see Table 1). Individuals who have nightmares generally recall in detail the fright-

Table 1. Nightmares and Night Terrors

	Nightmares	Night Terrors
Description	A scary, "bad" dream. Vivid recall of frightening scene	An attack of terror. Little or no mental content. No dream or frightening scene
Stage of sleep	REM sleep	Stage 4 sleep, NREM sleep, partial arousal
Typical time of night	Last half of night, when REM is common	First half of night, when stage 4 occurs
Appearance of child	Frightened, perhaps crying after nightmare	Screaming, thrashing, and bizarre behavior during and after event. Profuse sweating, tachycardia
Responsiveness	Usually oriented. Reassured by parent	Disoriented. Difficult to awaken and to calm. May be resistant
Return to sleep	May be delayed because of fear	Usually rapid
Recall of next day	Excellent	Little or none

ening content of the dream and, on awakening, rapidly become oriented and alert. By contrast, individuals who experience night terrors awaken abruptly, usually with a panicky scream, and recount having had a sense of terror but rarely recall detailed dream content. It may take as much as 10 minutes to calm an individual who has experienced a night terror.

Nightmares are not uncommon in the general population or during the course of normal child development. According to Ferber (1985), nightmares are relatively common before the age of seven, reflecting age-related emotional concerns about loss of love, separation, toilet training, and aggressive and sexual impulses. They may be less common between the ages of seven and 11 if these conflicts have been handled earlier, but nightmares tend to occur more often during adolescence and early adulthood with the stresses of growing up. Estimated prevalence of nightmares varies widely (Hartmann 1984), ranging from 5 to 29 percent of elementary school children to 4 to 5 percent of the general adult population.

Less is known about the prevalence of night terrors. It is estimated that about 1 to 4 percent of the population has had a night terror (Parkes 1986) and that the phenomenon is most common between the ages of three and eight (Hartmann 1984).

Clinicians, however, should not neglect two aspects of the clinical management of the child with frequent nightmares: 1) the search for stressful and traumatic forces in the child's experience, family dynamics, and health; and 2) the effect of the child's nightmares and behavior on the family itself. In most instances, occasional nightmares are part of the normal process of growing up and do not come to, or need, the attention of a clinician. If they do, they can often be handled by reassurance and family counseling.

Frequent nightmares, however, should prompt a more thorough psychiatric evaluation. Hartmann (1984) has suggested that they may be a marker of vulnerability to schizophrenia. Likewise, in a study of adults with chronic nightmares, Kales et al. (1980b) found that the nightmares usually began in childhood or adolescence after major life events and did not go away. These patients tended to be unusually suspicious as well as socially and emotionally isolated.

As part of the differential diagnosis of a patient whose symptom picture includes nightmares, nocturnal panic attacks should be considered as a possibility. Although we do not yet know whether nocturnal panic attacks occur in children, in adults they do occur and are similar to night terrors in children, although recall is good and subsequent confusion is lacking (Lesser et al. 1985).

In addition, recurrent nightmares may develop in children, as in adults, as part of the posttraumatic stress syndrome. For example, in an important longitudinal study of children who had been kidnapped and held captive in an underground trailer for 16 hours in Chowchilla, California, Terr (1983) described nightmares in a high proportion of the children up to four years later; many, for example, continued to dream of their death throughout this period of time.

Interestingly, some recent studies of nightmares in combat veterans suffering from PTSD indicate that these troubling events may occur in NREM as well as REM sleep (Hartmann 1984). Compared with veterans with a life-long history of nightmares, the veterans with PTSD nightmares had a better psychological health history prior to military service and had less evidence of psychopathology at the time of evaluation. They were more likely to dream of actual events, to have repetitive nightmares, and to experience body movements with the nightmare.

Although the cause of night terrors is not fully known, the risk appears to be increased within families, suggesting a genetic predisposition. In a study of adults with night terrors, Kales et al. (1980c) reported that one-third of the patients had

had a major life event that preceded or may have initiated the night terror episodes. Individuals with night terrors may also be more susceptible to migraine headaches, sleep walking, and enuresis.

Occasional night terrors usually do not require specific treatment. The parents or others who observe the episode may be much more upset by the event than the patient, who frequently has no memory of it. Nonetheless, the child may be deeply embarrassed if his friends tease him about screaming and carrying-on during sleep. The child and family should be reassured and encouraged to live with the problem until the night terrors are outgrown. Because daytime stress, anxiety, and irregular sleep patterns may increase the risk of a night terror in a susceptible individual, every effort should be made to minimize these potential factors. In addition, nighttime administration of diazepam (2.5–10 mg) or another benzodiazepine may reduce symptoms, presumably by reducing the amount of stage 4 sleep. In more severe adult cases, psychotherapy has been reported to be helpful.

Sleepwalking (Somnambulism)

Sleepwalking usually occurs during NREM sleep, typically during stage 4 sleep within the first three to four hours of sleep (Kales et al. 1966). In predisposed individuals, the actual episode may occur without obvious stimulation, but it may sometimes be initiated by a loud noise or by standing the child on his feet. Often the child may only sit up in bed with a glassy, undirected stare and then return to sleep. Alternatively, the child may wander around the room in a stereotyped fashion, demonstrating repetitive, clumsy movements; in some instances, individuals may leave the house or apartment and even drive an automobile. If awakened, the patient may be disoriented, frightened, and unaware that he or she was sleepwalking; dreams are not usually recalled. The next day, total amnesia for the event is common. Some authorities estimate that about 15 percent of all children have at least one sleepwalking episode (Parkes 1986).

Although sleepwalkers may maneuver around rooms and through doors without bumping into furniture or walls, they often injure themselves, for example, by falling through a window or off a balcony, by stumbling, or by thrashing out against the wall or window in their confusion. Although they are not dangerous per se, sleepwalkers have injured or even murdered others in an apparent state of partial wakefulness, confusion, and disorientation, particularly if drugs or alcohol are involved (Luchins et al. 1978). Some adolescents may become agitated during sleepwalking periods (Ferber 1985).

Genetic factors may be involved in somnambulism. Kales et al. (1980a) reported that the incidence of sleepwalking was increased tenfold in the first-degree relatives of a sleepwalker, and Bawkin (1970) found this concordance rate to be six times greater in monozygotic twins than in dizygotic twins. Sleepwalking has also been induced by drugs such as hypnotics or lithium-neuroleptic combinations in some predisposed patients.

Stress has been reported to increase the frequency of sleepwalking episodes in some patients. For example, Kales et al. (1966) reported that episodes occurred in spurts related to emotional situations. Somnambulists often have elevated scales on the MMPI when compared with normals but lower scores than psychiatric patients (Kales et al. 1980b; Spinweber and Greenberger 1984). In a study of 27 Navy recruits who were somnambulists, Spinweber and Greenberger (1984) found that subjects described themselves as poor or very poor sleepers; 25 of the 27 had a childhood history of sleepwalking, and 13 had a history of other parasomnias (enuresis, night terror, jactatio capitis nocturna, bruxism). The subjects averaged 1.6 sleepwalking episodes per week during their Navy careers.

No specific treatment is usually required for sleepwalking. The patient and family can be reassured that the child will usually outgrow it. The patient must, however, sleep in a safe environment. No established pharmacologic treatment has been accepted, but some patients respond to diazepam, anticonvulsants, or tricyclic antidepressants. Behavioral treatment and hypnosis may be useful in some patients. In evaluating a sleepwalker, the clinician should consider the possibility of a convulsive disorder.

Bedwetting (Enuresis)

About 15 percent of all five-year-olds and 5 percent of all 10-year-olds still wet their beds. By adolescence, about 1 to 2 percent of children still have occasional wet nights. About 60 percent of all enuretic children are boys (Ferber 1985). Some enuretic children, so-called "primary enuretics," have never achieved continence, while others (so-called "secondary enuretics") have resumed bedwetting after a period of dryness.

Unlike some of the other parasomnias, where the parent is more disturbed by the disorder than the child, in the case of enuresis it is usually the patient who is most upset. The attitudes of parents, siblings, and others, however, may greatly influence how the child feels about himself and the bedwetting. As told by George Orwell, a self-described enuretic, "I knew that bedwetting was a) wicked, and b) outside my control. The second fact I was personally aware of, and the first I did not question. It was possible, therefore, to commit a sin without knowing you committed it, without wanting to commit it, and without being able to avoid it."

Although medical causes of enuresis are probably uncommon, enuretic children over age five should have a medical examination and history, laboratory tests, urinalysis, and urine culture to rule out metabolic, neurologic, congenital, infectious, and other abnormalities. Detailed urological examination is not indicated unless prior evidence suggests pathology. Genetic factors play an important etiologic role in many cases (Mikkelsen et al. 1980). Although only 15 percent of all children have enuresis, the incidence increases to 45 percent if one parent has a history of bedwetting and to 75 percent if both parents do (Ferber 1985).

The pathophysiology of enuresis remins obscure and has been attributed to various factors, including a small, hyperactive bladder, increased volume output, excessively deep sleep, and delayed maturation. Although psychopathology can certainly occur in enuretic children, there is no a priori reason to assume that emotional factors are always causative (Mikkelsen et al. 1980). Enuretic episodes typically occur about three to four hours after the onset of sleep or following an episode earlier in the night; they are not preferentially associated with a particular stage of sleep (Mikkelsen et al. 1980).

Numerous treatment approaches have been advocated for enuresis, but all must involve education of the family, reassurance, and undoing excessive concern and blaming. Praise, reinforcement, and responsibility can be encouraged. Bladder training has been suggested to increase bladder capacity, detrusor strength, and appreciation of proprioceptive cues. The bell and pad method of conditioning has been successful in many studies. Although the clinical effectiveness of tricyclic antidepressants is well established in enuresis (Rapoport et al. 1980), these drugs should not be prescribed routinely. They may be dangerous (death has occurred in some cases), and side effects are often troublesome. Furthermore, tolerance frequently develops after an initial period of success, and the dose must be increased. Because the clinical benefits usually develop within a night or two of starting the tricyclic, drugs can be used successfully for short periods when children sleep over at a friend's house or go to camp.

Head Banging (Jactatio Capitis Nocturna)

Patients with this disorder exhibit rhythmic head or body rocking just before or during sleep, particularly during stages 1 and 2 of sleep (Ferber 1985; Parkes 1980). Delta sleep (stages 3 and 4) and REM sleep tend to inhibit it. Head banging is more common in boys than girls and may begin as early as age four months although it usually disappears during adolescence. Although head banging may be a habit that, like thumb sucking, comforts or soothes the patient, it may be hereditary in some cases. Usually head banging is not secondary to physical or psychological disorders. Some children may, however, develop calluses or wounds on their heads from the constant movement and trauma. No well-established treatment exists; but reduction of emotional stress, behavior modification, benzodiazepines, and imipramine have been reported to be helpful in some cases.

Bruxism (Tooth Grinding)

Bruxism occurs mostly in sleep stages 1 and 2 and is often related to emotional stress, although it has been reported in head injury and even in coma (Parkes 1986). Bruxism may seriously erode tooth surfaces and annoy bed partners or roommates. Mouth guards are sometimes worn to protect the teeth.

Other Parasomnias

In addition to the parasomnias mentioned earlier, some of the other abnormal behaviors during sleep listed by Parks (1986) in his review of parasomnias include hypnic jerks, fragmentary sleep myoclonus, benign neonatal sleep myoclonus, paroxysmal sleep dystonia, cluster headaches and paroxysmal hemicrania during REM sleep, and isolated or familial sleep paralysis.

Chapter 220

Primary Insomnia

Typically, insomnia is secondary either to some psychiatric distress, such as anxiety or depression, or to a medical condition such as sleep-related myoclonus, sleep-related apnea, pain, or allergies (Hauri 1982). Admittedly, it is often difficult to find these underlying psychiatric or medical causes of insomnia. Patients who complain about insomnia when the root problem is psychiatric distress have, by this behavior, already signaled that they are repressors, i.e., they do not see their problem in emotional terms. Similarly, many medical causes of insomnia are hard to find because they do not occur in the doctor's office but only when the patient is sleeping (e.g., myoclonus or sleep apnea). There is, however, a subgroup of insomniacs for whom poor sleep is the primary disturbance, not a symptom of something else. This chapter deals with these primary disturbances. However, a primary insomniac does not have to be completely free of all other problems or diseases. Rather, insomnia is defined as primary if, in the opinion of the clinician, the patient's insomnia cannot be adequately explained by any of the other problems that may be present. Mild depression or mild anxiety, for example, may well be present in a primary insomniac as a result of poor sleep, rather than being a cause of it.

Depending on numerous factors, such as patient population and diagnostic preferences, sleep disorder centers typically classify 15 to 30 percent of their insomniacs as primary. However, the true incidence rate in the general population is unknown.

Diagnosis

Primary insomnia (to use the DSM-III-R [American Psychiatric Association 1987] terminology) can be grouped into three subcategories: childhood-onset insomnia, persistent psychophysiologic insomnia, and insomnia complaint without objective findings.

Child-Onset Insomnia

Mr. O, a 35-year-old small businessman with serious insomnia, had already spent "a fortune" on diagnostic evaluations and tests in various well-reputed medical centers before he was referred to a sleep disorders center. Similarly, he had already undergone two lengthy courses of psychotherapy. He claimed he took two to three hours to fall asleep each night and that he then awoke frequently. He felt he rarely could sleep more than four hours. He was extremely slow getting started in the morning, dragging himself through most of the day, although he could not take naps. He felt that evenings were his best time. Although the insomnia became worse when he was under tension, he slept poorly even when things went well or when he was on vacation. He found that he was extremely sensitive to coffee and chocolate. Even a cola drink could keep him awake "for hours."

Mr. O had been tried on most hypnotics, sedatives, and antidepressants, with little effect. Each hypnotic had helped for a few days, then diminished in its efficacy.

Despite his excessive fatigue, Mr. O was relatively successful in his business mainly because he was well-organized, very careful, deliberate in his decisions, and well-controlled. He reported that any disorganized "hustle-bustle" or any sudden stimulus such as a sudden bright light or a clap behind his head made him very jumpy. A psychophysiologic evaluation confirmed this subjective report: Mr. O responded with much more arousal to stimuli than normal, and he showed a much slower recovery time than is typical.

Mr. O's problem had been long-standing. Indeed, he remembered vividly the uproar caused in his family when his parents discovered that, as a kindergartner, he often played for hours at night while they were sleeping. Grade school and high school were "a blur." He was poorly coordinated, irritable, and "hyperactive," although he was always tired.

Mr. O slept very poorly on all three nights in the laboratory. On average, he took about two hours to fall asleep, slept for less than five hours, and woke frequently. His sleep record contained long stretches that were difficult to score because sleep spindles were rare in stage 2 and eye movements rare during REM sleep.

Mr. O was told that he apparently suffered from "childhood-onset insomnia," i.e., an inherited neurologic-neurochemical imbalance in the sleep-wake system. He was then tried on a number of possible medications, but he responded only to relatively high doses of opiates. He now takes them every second or third night, and he simply does not sleep much during the intervening nights. In addition, he practices impeccable sleep hygiene (see below), and he sees a therapist for supportive work about twice a month.

Two very complex systems are involved when changing from wakefulness to sleep: the ascending reticular activating system (ARAS), which promotes wakefulness, and a far flung sleep-promoting system (the hypnagogic circuits) which interacts with the ARAS on multiple levels—on the level of the solidary tract nuclei, on the level of the raphe nuclei, and in the medial forebrain area. To fall asleep, stimulation in the ARAS first has to decrease passively to a relatively low level. This destimulation results in stage 1 sleep, the transition between waking and sleeping. Under normal circumstances, the sleep-promoting (hypnagogic) circuits will then become dominant, and this shift is indexed by stage 2 or deeper sleep.

In a system as complex as the sleep/wake cycle, the equilibrium between sleep and wakefulness does not lie at the same level in all humans. Childhood-onset insomniacs may simply be persons at the tail end of the normal curve, or they may actually have some biochemical or anatomic abnormality in the sleep/wake system. The etiology probably varies from case to case. The thought of an abnormality or lesion is supported by the fact that childhood-onset insomniacs often show soft neurologic signs during wakefulness; these symptoms include dyslexia, hyperactivity, and mild diffuse abnormalities on the clinical EEG (Hauri and Olmstead 1980).

Psychologically, childhood-onset insomniacs are typically repressors. Thus, many are mildly suspicious or unwilling to talk about their insomnia, possibly because so many of them have been unjustly accused of having serious, denied psychological problems.

Not all poor sleep in the young should be diagnosed as childhood-onset insomnia because only a limited number of childhood sleep problems are based on this presumed neurologic imbalance. Behavioral problems such as power struggles, fears of being alone or in the dark, and other psychological issues are much more likely to be the causes of insomnia in the very young (Regestein and Reich 1983).

Unfortunately, little progress has been made in treating childhood-onset insomnia. Impeccable sleep hygiene and excellent relaxation skills are required to help the already weak sleep system overcome the hyperaroused waking system. Medications have to be tried on a highly individual level. Some patients benefit from sedating tricyclics, others respond to neuroleptics, whereas others only gain relief from opiates. Benzodiazepines are rarely effective. No controlled treatment trials using medication have been conducted.

Persistent Psychophysiologic Insomnia (PPI)

Mrs. R, a 52-year-old widow, sought help for her insomnia after she had dozed off at the wheel and caused a near fatal accident. During the interview, she made a very controlled, polite, somewhat grim and tired impression. She stated that when her husband's lung cancer had been diagnosed eight years ago, she quit her job as a lawyer to take care of him for the last three months of his life. Insomnia had started during that time; when it did not disappear after his death, she sought intensive psychotherapy and underwent "grief work." This therapy brought much psychological benefit but no improvement in sleep. Now she was back at her profession and involved in a new relationship but still sleeping extremely poorly.

During the interview, Mrs. R related that she had never been a "champion" sleeper, having had difficulties with falling asleep once or twice per month throughout her adult life. She had worried little about her intermittent insomnia but had occasionally taken a prescription hypnotic during those few nights a month when she could not sleep.

Following her husband's death and during her three years of psychotherapy, she had been placed on a number of hypnotics. Each had helped for a few months, but she had become habituated to each of them. She reported some rebound insomnia when withdrawing from hypnotics but nothing very serious.

During her three consecutive nights in the laboratory, Mrs. R slept poorly, taking about an hour to fall asleep and then sleeping for about six hours each night, with multiple, prolonged awakenings. She showed more stage 1 and less deep (slow wave) sleep than expected and, according to her morning questionnaire, felt that she had slept at least as well in the labs as she had at home.

Under the assumption that Mrs. R's previous psychotherapy had left some unfinished business, she was first treated with short-term psychotherapy in a relatively dynamic mode. When little benefit developed from this approach, she was switched to a more behavioral treatment including cognitive restructuring, sleep hygiene, and relaxation training through biofeedback. In addition, she was given occasional hypnotics, to be used no more than twice a week. This process gradually improved her sleep, although she still slept poorly when excited or stimulated. However, she felt that this pattern had been typical all her life, even before the disease of her husband; and was quite satisfied with the outcome of her treatment.

Persistent psychophysiologic insomnia (PPI) has also been called "learned" or "behavioral" insomnia. Two main factors seem to operate in this condition: a predisposition toward poor sleep and maladaptive sleep habits, which are typically learned during a period of stress (Hauri and Olmstead 1986).

The typical predisposition toward poor sleep that is found in PPI may well be considered a mild form of childhood-onset insomnia, leading to occasional adult sleep difficulties. The learned component is usually established during a period of stress, when one's ARAS is stimulated and poor sleep is a natural result. Two maladaptive sleep habits then often develop. First, one becomes excessively concerned about one's poor sleep and then tries too hard to sleep. The more one needs to sleep, the harder one tries, and the more aroused and frustrated one gets. Second, the bedroom environment, where one has been frustrated by so many sleepless nights during the period of stress, becomes a trigger for frustration and arousal by a simple process of association (conditioning). These two bad habits disappear in most individuals as the crisis is resolved because any habit that is not occasionally reinforced will finally extinguish. However, in the person with an organic predisposition toward poor sleep, these habits cannot extinguish because they are occasionally reinforced. Thus, the insomnia that was learned in a period of stress may continue for months, years, or decades after the initial stress has been resolved.

Some patients with PPI may report that they fall asleep in inappropriate circumstances when they are *not* trying to sleep (e.g., in lectures or while driving). This problem typically occurs in those patients for whom the habit of trying too hard is the main culprit. Others report that they sleep poorly only in their own bedroom but better anywhere else, e.g., in the den, on the living room couch, during vacation away from home, or even in the sleep laboratory. In those cases, the conditioning against the bedroom may be the main problem. However, in many patients one finds a mixture of both.

Patients with PPI typically are sensation avoiders and they repress emotional material. Because of the increased tension and physiologic arousal experienced by these patients, they also often show other stress-related problems such as headaches or Reynaud's phenomenon.

By the time most patients seek help, other factors may further confuse the picture.

The patients may be excessively dependent on hypnotics, may have developed low self-esteem, which becomes aggravated every time they cannot sleep, or their chronic fatigue may have caused them to withdraw from most social contacts. One cannot be an insomniac for long without the insomnia affecting many other spheres of life as well.

Insomnia Complaint Without Objective Findings

Some patients complain about insomnia, whereas others, such as their spouses, report that the alleged insomniacs sleep quite well. Until recently, such patients were typically labeled as "pseudoinsomniacs," "manipulators," or worse (Borkovec 1979).

Although some patients undoubtedly use a complaint of insomnia frivolously to their own advantage, some recent evidence suggests that spurious complaints may actually be quite rare in the group of patients classified as insomnia complaint without objective findings. Patients who are so classified typically do not show the presumed character traits in areas other than sleep. For example, they do not manipulate around meals or work. Also, when awakened from stage 2 sleep, some of these patients can tell with much detail what they have been thinking about for the last half-hour, suggesting that their minds do not stop as much during sleep as is typical for other people. The mechanism for this perplexing finding is not understood, but it is interesting to note that the complaints of insomnia in such patients often stop when their (supposedly nonexisting) insomnia is treated, either with hypnotics or with behavioral therapy.

Overall Comments Concerning Diagnosis

Although the different subtypes of primary insomnia have been described as if they were separate entities (e.g., 1979 Association of Sleep Disorders Centers nosology), in practice they often shade into each other and into the other insomnia disorders. For example, whereas it may take a fair amount of stress to cause insomnia in a person with a very mild organic predisposition toward poor sleep, it will take less and less stress to cause insomnia as the underlying problem in the sleep/wake circuitry becomes worse, until, at the other end, no stress at all is needed in the childhood-onset insomniac. Thus, the PPI gradually shades into childhood-onset insomnia. Similarly, it is customary at this time to label as persistently psychophysiologic those insomniacs who in the sleep laboratory show either a sleep latency of 30 minutes or more or a sleep efficiency of 85 percent or less. Those who sleep better than that are labeled as insomnia complaint without objective findings. Obviously, the cutoff criteria are arbitrary, and one situation gradually shades into the other. Also, a serious loss of sleep may cause agitation, depression, and tension even in an otherwise well-functioning person; however, these same psychological parameters of agitation, depression, and tension may actually cause poor sleep. Which is the chicken and which is the egg? Likewise, periodic movements of the legs may not disturb a sound sleeper but may cause insomnia in someone who has lighter sleep, i.e., a person who has weaker sleep/wake neurologic circuits. Whether a given person's insomnia is secondary to psychiatric disorder, secondary to medical disease, or primary is often a matter of clinical judgment and a matter of degree, not absolute.

Treatment

Treatment of primary insomnia is highly individualized, as is typical for most disorders in which patterns of lifestyle and learning interact with physiologic parameters. However, there are some distinct methods and approaches from which one selects the appropriate building blocks for treatment.

Sleep Hygiene

It is surprising how often the simplest rules of sleep hygiene are violated. A patient may be drinking 15 cups of coffee a day and then complain about insomnia "coming out of the blue." Another patient may take two stressful jobs, finish the second one around midnight, and be surprised when unable to sleep by 12:30 A.M.

The major rules of sleep hygiene, based on current research, are summarized in Table 1. However, it is rarely useful to hand a patient this or any other list of sleep hygiene rules and expect positive results. Such a procedure would be akin to handing neurotic patients a sheet of rules for healthy living and then expecting them to dissolve their neuroses by themselves. Rather, these sleep hygiene rules need to be in the minds of the therapists who explore their patients' current lifestyles with them and try to understand why certain rules are violated and how unhealthy patterns might be changed. Behavioral shifts and lifestyle changes rarely come about by simply telling a patient to change.

Table 1. Eleven Rules for Better Sleep Hygiene

1. Sleep as much as needed to feel refreshed and healthy during the following day, but not more. Curtailing the time in bed seems to solidify sleep; excessively long times in bed seem related to fragmented and shallow sleep.

2. A regular arousal time in the morning strengthens circadian cycling and leads to regular times of sleep onset.

3. A steady daily amount of exercise probably deepens sleep; occasional exercise does not necessarily improve sleep the following night.

4. Occasional loud noises (e.g., aircraft flyovers) disturb sleep even in people who are not awakened by noises and cannot remember them in the morning. Sound-attenuated bedrooms may help those who must sleep close to noise.

5. Although excessively warm rooms disturb sleep, there is no evidence that an excessively cold room solidifies sleep.

6. Hunger may disturb sleep; a light snack may help sleep.

7. An occasional sleeping pill may be of some benefit, but chronic use of medications is ineffective in most insomniacs.

8. Caffeine in the evening disturbs sleep, even in those who feel it does not.

9. Alcohol helps tense people fall asleep easily, but the ensuing sleep is then fragmented.

10. People who feel angry and frustrated because they cannot sleep should not try harder and harder to fall asleep but should turn on the light and do something different.

11. The chronic use of tobacco disturbs sleep.

Note. Reprinted by permission from P. Hauri, *The Sleep Disorders*, Second Edition. Kalamazoo, Mich., The Upjohn Company, 1982.

As indicated elsewhere in this chapter, the chronic, nightly use of hypnotics and sedatives is rarely justified. Patients habituate to the drugs and then face rebound insomnia when they try to stop. On the other hand, there is rarely a primary insomniac who does not need an occasional hypnotic for those nights when sleeping is "a must," say, because of a very important upcoming day, or because scores of poor nights threaten to reactivate the old overconcern with inability to sleep. After discussing the problems with chronic use of hypnotics with these patients, it appears that most should be given a few hypnotics, to be used no more than once or twice a week in the circumstances described.

If benzodiazepines are not appropriate for various reasons, a number of alternate medications are occasionally useful. Very low levels of sedating tricyclic antidepressants (e.g., 10–25 mg of amitriptyline) seem helpful and less prone to habituation than the benzodiazepines. However, insomniacs often become extremely sedated and groggy for the first two or three days from even the most minute doses of these tricyclics. They then typically habituate and seem to sleep much better for many weeks or months.

Over-the-counter (OTC) hypnotics induce grogginess, not sleep. However, they may be useful if a patient's insomnia is caused by trying too hard to sleep. Feeling the increasing grogginess after the OTC medication may help calm the fears of such patients. They then relax, try less hard, and fall asleep naturally.

Two aspirin tablets or similar salicylates are also frequently effective for an occasional poor night of sleep, even in those types of insomnia that are not related to pain. However, not all insomniacs respond to aspirin, and its effects habituate rapidly.

Finally, L-tryptophan, in doses of about two grams per night, seems effective in many cases. Patients should be instructed to take this medication on an empty stomach (at least three hours after the last meal), about 30 minutes before going to bed, and with a carbohydrate such as orange juice. Milk should be avoided when taking tryptophan because it introduces other amino acids that compete with tryptophan for active transfer through the blood-brain barrier. Some experts recommend that patients take L-tryptophan for three nights a week, then stop for four. The opinions vary. In any case, L-tryptophan treatment is relatively expensive even if the drug is obtained in a health food store rather than a pharmacy.

Relaxation Therapy

Teaching insomniacs how to relax is probably the most common behavioral technique that is used to treat insomnia. The training is thought to be useful on the theory that all insomniacs are assumed to be muscularly tense or physiologically aroused. It is true that most normal sleepers show increased muscle tension and physiologic arousal during those few nights when they happen to sleep poorly. However, it is less often true for those with chronic insomnia. Therefore, before embarking on relaxation training, one needs some evidence that the patient is actually tense and nervous around sleep onset. This verification is important because there is evidence suggesting that if one teaches relaxation skills to an insomniac who is already quite relaxed around sleep onset, the training is not only ineffective but may cause frustration, anger, and a deterioration in sleep.

The type of relaxation training one uses is relatively unimportant. Progressive muscle relaxation, diaphragmatic breathing, hypnosis, certain types of meditation, biofeedback of EMG, GSR, or theta waves, and many other forms of relaxation have all been proven effective. It is important, however, that relaxation be taught very thoroughly under the supervision of an experienced trainer. Relaxation tapes, or a quick practice session in the physician's office, are rarely enough. This is so for two reasons. In general, insomniacs seem to be much slower in learning relaxation techniques than patients with other psychophysiologic disorders. Also, insomniacs need to use their relaxation skills around sleep onset, i.e., around a time when conscious, voluntary control is waning.

Some evidence suggests that relaxation training does not exert its main effect on insomnia by initiating an actual decrease in muscle tension or physiologic arousal. Whether or not one's heart rate, body temperature, or muscle tension is high or low when one goes to bed seems to have little effect on sleep onset. Rather, it appears that these relaxation techniques are effective mainly because they focus the insomniac's attention away from tension-inducing thoughts and onto a repetitive, nonthreatening stimulus.

Cognitive Therapy

To understand the goals of cognitive therapy in treating insomnia, several characteristics of the (neurologic) sleep/wake system need to be considered. As discussed earlier, whether a person is awake or asleep depends on the balance between the ARAS and the sleep-inducing system. Cognitive therapy cannot reach the components of the sleep-inducing system, but cognitions have definite effects on the ARAS. The ARAS has a very fast rise time. For example, if a gun is pointed at someone, this individual will rise to maximum arousal within a few seconds. On the other hand, the ARAS has a much slower fall time. In the example, if this individual finds that the gun is not loaded, it will still take five to 15 minutes, not a few seconds, to calm down. Because of these fast-rise, slow-fall characteristics, overall tonic levels of relaxation are easily overridden by episodic, short, arousal-inducing events such as an occasional worrisome thought. Insomniacs may well be deeply relaxed when trying to sleep, however, if only one anxious or arousal-producing thought occurs to them every five to 10 minutes, they still cannot fall asleep all night.

Based on these fast-rise, slow-fall characteristics of the ARAS, it appears that very detailed knowledge of the kinds of thoughts and stimuli that occur while an insomniac is trying to fall asleep is necessary. One then works behaviorally with these highly specific thoughts and stimuli, not with general arousal. For example, if there are simply too many tension-inducing thoughts, a distraction procedure might be used. One may advise the patients to read in bed until they are so tired that they simply cannot read anymore, or one may advise them to watch TV in bed until sleep overcomes them while watching. Similarly, if an insomniac typically looks at the illuminated bedroom clock every five to 10 minutes and then becomes upset about the precious time ticking away while sleep is not forthcoming, the removal of this clock is more crucial than 10 hours of relaxation training. On the other hand, if specific anxious thoughts keep the insomniac awake, these thoughts need to be dealt with individually. One might prescribe a presleep worry time lasting for about 30 minutes, during which the patient sits alone, undistracted, and writes down all the random thoughts that occur and then deals with and thinks about each troubling thought. If patients become angry or hyperaroused if they find themselves awake in the middle of the night, they need to be taught that even the best sleepers awaken five to 15 times each night. Good sleepers, however, do not become aroused when they become conscious. Rather, they think some nonthreatening thoughts and promptly fall asleep again within a few seconds. Poor sleepers, on the other hand, immediately become angry and upset that they are, once again, awake; these arousing thoughts then turn a short five-second arousal into a two-hour catastrophe. In this instance, and in many other cases, cognitive reframing techniques are quite effective, whereas other cognitive methods such as thought stopping are contraindicated when a patient is at the threshold of sleep.

In those patients in whom the maladaptive, conditioned association between bedroom stimuli and arousal is the main problem, stimulus control may be effective. Remember that this association is typically diagnosed in patients who sleep well away from their own bedrooms but poorly in their usual environment. In short, one explains first to the patient the mechanisms that keep them awake. One then gives them the following instructions:

1. For tonight, and for the next few weeks, go to bed only when you are really tired and when you think that you can fall asleep easily.
2. If you find that you cannot fall asleep easily once you are in bed, you are doing yourself harm because you strengthen the association between your own bedroom and arousal. Thus, you must get out of your bedroom. It does much less harm if the frustration about your inability to sleep is experienced in the kitchen or in the living room. Engage in some quiet activity away from the bedroom until you really feel very sleepy.
3. Once you are very sleepy, go to bed and fall asleep easily. If you are not able to do so, repeat step 2 as often as necessary until you can fall asleep easily.
4. In the morning, you must get up at your usual wake-up time, no matter how little you slept. Also, do not take any naps during the day.

It is easy to see what will happen. During the first few nights, the patients will sleep little as they spend most of their time away from their bedroom. However, two situations then develop. As sleep deprivation increases, the patients' sleep-inducing circuits become more powerful and they fall asleep more easily. Also, because, on every night, they eventually do have the experience of going to bed and falling asleep easily, the maladaptive conditioning between bedroom and frustration is weakened.

Typically, it takes a few weeks to treat a patient with stimulus control therapy. During these weeks, patients are often frustrated and willing to give up. Thus, daily support is usually required to keep insomniacs in this program. Certainly, one does not give this program to patients and then expect them to carry it through to completion without support. Stimulus control therapy is probably one of the best researched treatments for this type of problem and has been shown to be effective not only in young adults but also in the elderly. However, it needs a skilled therapist, time, and patience.

Insomniacs typically stay in bed much too long, trying to "squeeze the last drop" of sleep out of each night. The longer one stays in bed, the more shallow and fragmented sleep becomes. Curtailing sleep to fewer hours typically increases uninterrupted sleep and causes fewer awakenings.

In a form of behavior therapy called "sleep-restriction therapy," the patient first fills out one or two weeks of sleep logs describing each night at home. Patients are then instructed to stay in bed only for as long as they have actually recorded that they are sleeping. Say that an insomniac reports on his sleep logs that he sleeps about 2½ hours per night and that he typically gets up around 7:00 A.M. In that case, during the first week of treatment, this person would be asked to remain out of bed and awake until 4:30 A.M. He would then still have to rise at 7:00 A.M., and he would not be allowed to take any naps.

Each morning, patients on the sleep restriction regime report their sleep to their therapist or at least to the therapist's answering machine. When they report at least

90 percent sleep efficiency, that is, when they spend at least 90 percent of their restricted time in bed actually sleeping, their bedtime is lengthened in 15-minute intervals until they sleep normal amounts again.

This method is similar to stimulus control therapy. Initially, patients are severely sleep deprived in both methods. This factor helps them to fall asleep when they finally get to bed, and it breaks the maladaptive association between bedroom and arousal.

Surprisingly, the sleep restriction regime works poorly if there is only mild sleep restriction. The more severely bedtime is initially curtailed, the more effective the treatment seems to be. However, there are large dropout rates. Not all insomniacs can tolerate the long hours of staying out of bed during the night when they are extremely fatigued and sleep deprived.

Conclusion

Treating patients with primary insomnia is similar to treating patients with other physiologic problems that are strongly affected by lifestyle and learning. Dramatic cures are rare and the recommended behavioral treatments are time consuming. An occasional 15-minute visit to the therapist will not result in much improvement. Therefore, it is often better to refer such patients to the appropriate behavior therapists who specialize in such techniques. On the other hand, using the methods described and a fair amount of common sense in a creative and individually tailored approach will often result in marked sleep improvements. At least one-third of appropriately selected and treated primary insomniacs claim to be cured three months after treatment, many more claim that they received major benefits, and even the few who are not helped typically report that they worry much less about their sleep. Thus, some skilled time spent treating primary insomniacs is clearly worthwhile.

Chapter 221

Insomnia Related to Medical Conditions: Sleep Apnea and Nocturnal Myoclonus

Sleep may be disturbed by medical conditions that are evident in the awake patient or by disorders that are manifest primarily during sleep. Examples of the former include congestive heart failure, diabetes mellitus, and painful arthritic conditions.

In general, the best therapeutic approach in these around-the-clock disorders is to address the basic medical condition rather than the consequent poor sleep. With congestive heart failure, for instance, therapy is best oriented to cardiac drugs and diuretics that will eliminate dyspnea when the patient lies down, as opposed to treatment for the sleep problem that follows from the dyspnea. In contrast, a number of conditions are characterized by pathophysiology that appears only during sleep. Two major examples are sleep apnea syndrome and nocturnal myoclonus. Although they are very different disorders, they share a common quality. In both cases, disturbed physiology during sleep results in multiple short arousals at night (of which the patient may be unaware) that result in a sensation of poor sleep quality or daytime sleepiness.

Sleep Apnea Syndromes

Sleep apnea has two major forms: obstructive and central. Originally these were viewed as very different processes, with the former resulting from the collapse of the oropharynx and the latter due to a periodic failure of the nervous system to stimulate contraction of the diaphragm and the accessory muscles of respiration. Subsequently, a number of findings have indicated that the two forms may be more closely linked than was originally supposed. It has been observed, for instance, that diaphragmatic and genioglassal activity increase and decrease in a cyclic manner during sleep; the obstructive apneas tend to occur at the nadir of this cycle (Onal et al. 1982). Similarly, a reflex inhibition of respiration may result from activation of supraglottic mucosal receptors when the oropharyngeal airway is passively closed (Issa and Sullivan 1986). Thus, airway obstruction might be manifest as an ostensibly central apneic event. The clinical presentations of the two syndromes have traditionally been viewed as rather different, with obstructive sleep apnea syndrome considered to result primarily in daytime sleepiness, whereas central apnea syndrome has been thought to cause insomnia. Once again, this distinction is becoming less clear. With these cautions in mind, however, we will retain this classification for didactic purposes as we discuss treatment.

Treatment: Obstructive Sleep Apnea

Obstructive sleep apnea syndrome tends to be most common in men and in middle age. Patients often have histories of loud snoring and may manifest cardiovascular complications, including pulmonary hypertension, cor pulmonale, or systemic hypertension. In addition to complaints of poor sleep or daytime sleepiness, patients may report histories of memory difficulty, irritability, depressed affect, and sexual dysfunction. The available treatments, which are oriented to minimizing the number and severity of apneic episodes, range from very conservative steps involving body position and weight loss to major surgical interventions.

Weight loss may be of some benefit in treating obstructive sleep apnea, although it may be more likely to help patients with apneas in both NREM and REM sleep than those in whom the events occur primarily in REM. Most practitioners have had some cases in whom dramatic improvement occurred, and it is certainly good practice to recommend weight loss to all patients. Its utility is limited, however. In one study, patients with tracheostomies lost an average of 15 kg but were still unable to manage without the tracheostomies (Guilleminault et al. 1981). Body position should also be considered. Less negative inspiratory pressure is required to close the airway in the supine than in the prone position. Cartwright (1984) has observed that the number of apneas and hypopneas declines when patients sleep on the side compared to the back, although there was relatively less benefit in more obese persons. Because change in sleep position is such a benign intervention, it seems appropriate to recommend it as a rule to apnea patients.

Pharmacologic treatments. Since the early 1970s, case reports have appeared indicating that sleep apnea is reduced by antidepressants; subsequently most interest has centered around the use of protriptyline, often given in doses of 5 to 20 mg. One aspect of protriptyline's benefit is that it reduces REM sleep, during which particularly severe apneic episodes appear. There is also some evidence that protriptyline may be useful for apneic episodes in NREM sleep, although this is still a subject of inquiry. Side effects are those typical of tricyclics, including dry mouth, blurred vision, urinary hesitancy, and tachycardia. There is some suggestion that doses over 20 mg may be sedating in these patients. It seems wise to obtain an EKG to rule out conduction defects before embarking on long-term protriptyline therapy.

Progesterone has respiratory stimulant properties in normal subjects and has been reported to reduce pCO_2 in patients with obesity-hypoventilation syndrome. Clinical studies have tended to find little or no benefit in terms of number of apneas in the patient groups as a whole, although there are reports of improvement in heart failure and daytime alertness. Again, individual patients have sometimes been responsive. Typically, doses start at 20 mg and go up to 60 mg. Patients should be cautioned about possible alopecia or changes in libido, although these are very rare at the doses used for this condition.

Other pharmacologic agents have also been used in sleep apnea. Nomifensine was found to be of limited help in one study, although it has now been taken off the market. There is one report of benefits for obstructive, but not central, apnea from L-tryptophan in an average dose of 2,500 mg. It seemed most effective in patients whose apneas were primarily in NREM sleep and in those with fewer than 70 apneas or hypopneas per hour (Schmidt 1983).

Nasal oxygen has been given to apnea patients, usually at rates of 2 to 10 liters per minute although, in general, results have been modest. There have also been individual patients in whom oxygen appears to prolong apnea and increase pCO_2. The utility of this approach, thus, seems to be fairly limited.

Continuous positive air pressure (CPAP). A number of studies have examined the use of continuous positive air pressure (CPAP), in which a machine placed at the bedside applies room air at a pressure of 5 to 15 cm of H_2O into the oropharynx via a nasal mask. In general, results have been encouraging. A small percentage of patients find the mask uncomfortable or feel a sense of being closed in; some investigators are trying to determine whether classical desensitization measures may help these patients. Other complaints include excessive drying of the nasal mucosa. However, in general, CPAP appears to be a beneficial procedure and a useful alternative to surgery. Long-term follow-up studies of CPAP therapy are limited at this time. One group found that only 40 percent of patients were still using CPAP 18 months after initiation of therapy (Schweitzer et al. 1987), and long-term efficacy still needs to be explored.

Surgery. Two types of surgical procedures are usually used for obstructive sleep apnea: the uvulopalatopharyngoplasty (UPPP) and chronic tracheostomy. The UPPP, which was pioneered for sleep apnea by Fujita et al. (1981), has been of significant benefit for the complaint of snoring. Its utility for sleep apnea syndrome per se is somewhat less. Interpretation of the data is difficult because of differing standards of effectiveness, but the general impression is that UPPP significantly reduces number and severity of apneas in roughly 50 to 70 percent of patients in the short term. Complications, which are relatively unusual, include nasal regurgitation of liquids and alterations in voice. A certain percentage of patients—perhaps up to one-third—may require a temporary tracheostomy, which is usually closed in a few weeks.

The chronic tracheostomy is a highly effective, although very invasive, procedure. In one long-term follow-up of 50 patients, virtually all had dramatic decreases in number of apneas; 45 percent of patients felt that they were greatly helped in terms of daytime sleepiness and fatigue (Guilleminault et al. 1981). Complications from chronic tracheostomy involve infections and related maintenance issues. It should be noted that some patients remain hypercapnic after this procedure, perhaps as a result of a primary dysfunction resulting in hypoventilation in addition to obstructive sleep apnea.

Treatment: Central Sleep Apnea

Pharmacologic. There are fewer, and perhaps less satisfactory, treatments available for central sleep apnea. In practice, protriptyline is often given, and some tentative evidence suggests that the carbonic anhydrase inhibitor acetazolamide 250 mg qid may be of benefit in the short term.

Diaphragm pacing. A nonpharmacologic approach involves stimulation of the phrenic nerve in the lower neck. Often stimulation is done unilaterally, so that inspiration results from maximal contraction of a hemidiaphragm. Studies of this treatment for central alveolar hypoventilation syndrome (Ondine's curse) have been promising. Among the drawbacks is the relatively limited availability of facilities for diaphragm pacing at this time. There is also a possibility that in some patients diaphragm pacing may convert central apneas into obstructive events. This problem presumably results if strong contractions of the hemidiaphragm are out of phase with the normal mechanism maintaining patency of the upper airway during inspiration.

CPAP. CPAP has traditionally been used as a treatment for obstructive sleep apnea. One recent report by major investigators in this area has described benefits of CPAP for eight patients with primarily central apneas (Issa and Sullivan 1986). This observation strengthens the argument that central and obstructive sleep apnea syndromes may be more similar than was originally supposed. Many clinicians find CPAP useful only in obstructive apnea, however, and further research will be needed to clarify this issue.

Other precautions. In both central and obstructive sleep apnea syndromes, the patient should avoid alcohol and drugs that are respiratory suppressants. These include traditional anxiolytics and hypnotics as well as opiate analgesics. Surgical anesthesia should be given in the lowest possible dose and with great attentiveness to the patient's respiratory status. The safety of benzodiazepines in patients with sleep apnea syndromes is a matter that continues to be evaluated. Enough studies and case reports have found that these agents suppress respiration in chronic obstructive pulmonary disease and sleep apnea to suggest that the most prudent course is to avoid their use for sleep apnea (Mendelson 1987).

Nocturnal Myoclonus

Since the 1950s, case reports have appeared describing patients with regularly occurring myoclonic movements during sleep, and by the 1970s a syndrome of clonic leg movements resulting in insomnia was recognized (Guilleminault et al. 1975). Typically the movements involve dorsiflexion of the ankle and fanning of the knee and hip. In practice, movements are recorded by electromyographic electrodes placed over the anterior tibialis. Criteria for their occurrence continue to be discussed, but the most commonly accepted standard is that the movements last 0.5 to 10 seconds and appear every 20 to 40 seconds. The Association of Sleep Disorders Centers criteria (ASDC 1979) for diagnosis call for the presence of at least three myoclonic periods, each containing at least 30 such events. The movements themselves must be accompanied by EEG evidence of arousal (alpha activity or K-complexes); it is presumably these frequent interruptions in sleep continuity that lead to the complaint of poor sleep or excessive daytime sleepiness.

Nocturnal myoclonus should be distinguished from several other sleep-related movements. The first is hypnic jerks, brief generalized movements that often occur at sleep onset and are considered normal phenomena. Myoclonic and other types of seizures may occur during sleep; in contrast to nocturnal myoclonus, the EEG will show spiking activity in these conditions. In partial complex seizures, if the patients should awaken there will also be a history of seizure phenomena similar to those that occur in waking, including an aura, confusion, and possible automatic behavior. Nocturnal myoclonus should also be distinguished from the restless legs syndrome, in which patients describe a dysesthesia of the legs that occurs at rest and is relieved by moving about. In contrast, most nocturnal myoclonus patients are unaware of their movements unless informed by an unhappy bed partner. The majority of patients with restless legs syndrome also have nocturnal myoclonus. On the other hand, nocturnal myoclonus (which is much more common) usually occurs without any evidence of restless legs syndrome.

Myoclonic movements frequently appear in certain other disorders. These include narcolepsy, uremia or other metabolic disorders, and leukemia (although the relation to radiation and chemotherapy in the latter group is not clear). Newborns and infants may manifest myoclonic movements, although these usually disappear after the first few months of life. Some authors have pointed to the similarity of nocturnal myoclonic movements to the Babinsky sign, which of course occurs naturally in infants. The nocturnal myoclonus syndrome per se can occur at any age but becomes more frequent in middle age and is most common in the elderly.

Treatment

The major pharmacologic treatment for nocturnal myoclonus has been clonazepam, 0.5 to 1.5 mg. Results have been variable. It is also difficult to choose the appropriate endpoint in evaluating effectiveness. Mitler et al. (1986), for instance, found that 1.0 mg improved sleep without reducing the number of leg movements. The major side effect is excessive daytime sleepiness. In patients who also have a small number of disordered breathing events, or in those with true sleep apnea syndrome, there is the additional possibility that clonazepam might compromise respiratory function. For this reason, it may be wiser to use a short-acting benzodiazepine in these patients and to give the first bedtime dose in the sleep laboratory where respiration can be carefully monitored. The only available systematic study of a short-acting benzodiazepine for nocturnal myoclonus tested a dosage of 30 mg temazepam, which was found to be as effective as clonazepam; many clinicians have also used triazolam for this purpose. Baclofen (20–40 mg) has been reported to decrease EEG signs of arousal (Guilleminault and Flagg 1984); in NREM sleep it was found to increase the number of leg movements but decrease their amplitude.

In taking the medical history of a nocturnal myoclonus patient, one should inquire about drugs that can cause or exacerbate the condition. Some evidence suggests that this is true of tricyclic antidepressants. There have been individual case reports of nocturnal myoclonus and restless legs syndrome induced by lithium, and of myoclonus, hyperreflexia, and diaphoresis from the combination of L-tryptophan and phenelzine. Myoclonic movements also often appear during withdrawal from anticonvulsants and hypnotics.

Finally, many clinicians have the impression that nocturnal myoclonus is exacerbated by stress and anxiety. In addition to instituting pharmacologic treatment, it is good practice to look for sources of stress in the patient's life and consider whether any adjunctive nonpharmacologic measures are also indicated.

Summary

Many illnesses that are evident in the waking patient may disturb sleep. In addition, there are a number of disorders whose pathophysiology is manifested only during sleep and which lead to the complaint of insomnia or daytime sleepiness. Among these are the sleep apnea syndromes and nocturnal myoclonus. In both of these disorders, abnormal physiologic events cause multiple arousals throughout the night, resulting in disturbed sleep. Sleep apnea syndromes are generally divided into obstructive and central types, although the distinction is becoming less clear as knowledge of the pathophysiology increases. Treatments for obstructive sleep apnea include pharmacologic measures, use of CPAP, and surgical procedures. Pharmacologic treatments for central sleep apnea are available, although perhaps not completely satisfactory at this time. A number of conservative measures and common sense precautions should be followed for all sleep apnea patients.

Nocturnal myoclonus should be distinguished from a number of related conditions. One should also be aware that it may be exacerbated by some medications including tricyclic antidepressants. Once the diagnosis is made, pharmacotherapy with benzodiazepines is often useful, although one should be aware of possible enhanced sleepiness or interaction with any coexisting respiratory disorder.

Chapter 222

Narcolepsy

The essential feature of "hypersomnia disorders," as designated in DSM-III-R (American Psychiatric Association 1987), or "disorders of excessive sleepiness," as designated in the 1979 Association of Sleep Disorders Centers (ASDC) nosology, is daytime sleepiness or sleep attacks sufficiently severe to result in impaired social or occupational functioning. Typically, excessive daytime sleepiness manifests itself by the individual's falling asleep unintentionally at work, while driving, or during social occasions. Pathologic daytime sleepiness is typically a daily occurrence, regardless of the amount of sleep obtained at night (for example, sleep apnea of the obstructive type and narcolepsy-cataplexy both produce excessive daytime sleepiness). More rarely, the hypersomnia is episodic, as with premenstrual hypersomnia, Kleine-Levin syndrome (episodic hypersomnia with megaphagia, a rare idiopathic syndrome occurring in young men), and some forms of major depression (including the atypical and bipolar forms).

Together, obstructive sleep apnea syndrome and narcolepsy-cataplexy account for 80 to 90 percent of patients with hypersomnia seen in sleep disorders centers (Coleman et al. 1982). The remaining 10 to 20 percent of sleepy patients are diagnosed, variously, as having affective disorder, idiopathic CNS hypersomnolence (independent hypersomnia in DSM-III-R, i.e., excessive daytime sleepiness unrelated to another mental or physical disorder, occurring either in a familial or in a sporadic pattern), drug abuse, Kleine-Levin syndrome, or premenstrual hypersomnolence.

Because the preceding section dealt with treatment of sleep-induced respiratory impairment, the following material will be restricted to a consideration of narcolepsy.

After obstructive sleep apnea syndrome, narcolepsy-cataplexy is the second most common disorder of excessive daytime sleepiness (hypersomnia disorder) in patients referred to sleep disorders centers. Narcolepsy is equally prevalent in men and women and has usually declared itself clinically by the age of 30 and more typically becomes apparent during adolescence. The term narcolepsy means literally "sleep seizure" and refers to the occurrence of many unintentional or irresistible sleep attacks during any given day. These represent abnormal manifestations of REM sleep, including cataplexy, sleep paralysis, and hypnagogic hallucinations (Guilleminault et al. 1976). In 60 to 75 percent of cases, narcolepsy eventually is associated with cataplexy, the brief, sudden loss of skeletal muscle tone or posture temporarily, triggered by specific emotional stimuli. The severity of cataplexy varies considerably, e.g., a drop of the jaw, buckling of the knees, or falling. Generally, patients remain alert during attacks, even if unable to move, unless duration extends to 45 or 60 seconds. Such a prolonged cataplectic attack will often issue in a complete REM sleep attack.

Narcolepsy-cataplexy is a life-long disorder that often leads to considerable social, vocational, and psychiatric disability (Kales et al. 1982). With advancing age, narcoleptics are also subject to extreme fragmentation of nighttime sleep. Approximately 15 to 30 percent of narcoleptics show at least some nocturnal myoclonus and sleep apnea when recorded in the sleep laboratory (Van den Hoed et al. 1981). The most specific finding of narcolepsy, however, is repeated sleep onset REM periods (SOREMPs). Thus, a rapid descent from wakefulness to REM sleep is the characteristic and indeed pathognomonic finding of narcolepsy. This symptom can be most readily demonstrated during the multiple sleep latency test (MSLT).

The MSLT consists of a series of four or five daytime nap recordings spaced at two-hour intervals, lasting 20 minutes each, and beginning at 10 A.M. and running until 4 or 6 P.M. At the start of each nap, the patient is instructed to try to fall asleep. Narcoleptics usually fall asleep in under five minutes on each of these occasions and typically demonstrate two or more sleep onset REM periods.

It is vital that the diagnosis of narcolepsy be confirmed with polysomnography so that patients can get the treatment that is indicated and not be accused of malingering, and so the physician is appropriately protected from wrongful accusation of irresponsible prescription of controlled substances. Thus, the mainstay of symptomatic treatment of narcolepsy has been the use of stimulant medication or alerting tricyclic antidepressants, particularly methylphenidate, pemoline, or protriptyline (Schmidt et al. 1977; Zarcone 1973). Using the lowest dose necessary to control symptoms of daytime sleepiness, with frequent drug holidays, helps to prevent both the occurrence of side effects and the development of tolerance. Cataplexy can often be treated on a prn basis since this symptom waxes and wanes. It is usually best treated with low doses of tricyclic antidepressant, such as imipramine. Recent preliminary reports have also suggested other pharmacologic approaches to the treatment of narcolepsy-cataplexy, including gamma-hydroxybutyrate (GHB) (Mamelak and Webster 1981). The MAOI tranylcypromine may be helpful in some narcoleptics who have grown refractory to tricyclic antidepressants or to stimulants.

Chapter 223

Sleep-Wake Schedule Disorders

The Circadian System

A major function of the biologic clock, or circadian system, is to generate the circadian rhythms that provide the correct physiological and psychologic milieu for a restful night of sleep and day of activity. Such rhythms are not simply reactions to changes in posture, state, or surrounding environment but are self-sustaining, relying on external factors for their orientation and period, but not relying on them for the expression of the rhythms themselves (Aschoff 1981). Thus, circadian rhythms in physiology, subjective activation, and performance efficiency will persist, even when sleep is forbidden, activity limited, diet controlled, and time cues completely eliminated (Froberg 1977).

The oscillator responsible for generating circadian rhythms has a natural rhythm that is rather longer in period (usually by about an hour) than the 24 hours of earth's rotation and the time pieces of human society (Wever 1979). The entrainment mechanism is, thus, continually at work using time cues, or zeitgebers, to keep the oscillator running at exactly 24 hours and oriented toward sleep at night and wakefulness during the day. Usually, for an individual on a stable day-oriented routine, the presence of a circadian system reaps a considerable biologic advantage. There are certain situations and pathologic states, however, for which the circadian system can act as a liability rather than as an asset. Such problems often relate to a mismatch between the outputs, or temporal orientation, of the circadian system, and the particular routine to which the individual is required to conform. That mismatch can either result from an abrupt change in routine with which the circadian system has not yet caught up (jet-lag, shift work) or pathology in the circadian system or its entrainment mechanism (phase advance syndrome, phase delay syndrome), which causes it to be misaligned relative to the normal routine that the individual is trying to follow.

Shift Work

Patients with sleep-wake schedule disturbances related to shift work will typically present with a variety of symptoms, including sleepiness and malaise on the job, various forms of insomnia, irritability, and dissatisfaction with the social and domestic environment (Rutenfranz et al. 1977). Three factors contribute to these symptoms. The first relates directly to the phase of the patient's circadian rhythms at which sleep and wakefulness are taking place. Until the circadian system realigns to a nocturnal routine (and Knauth and Rutenfranz [1976] and Monk [1986] suggest that in most cases this never actually occurs), the patient is required to be awake and working at a circadian phase normally associated with sleep and trying to sleep at a phase normally associated with wakefulness. This situation can not only interfere with the patient's acquisition of sufficient sleep but also places him (and those around him) at personal risk if the task to be performed is a monotonous one requiring vigilance (e.g., driving) (Folkard and Monk 1979).

The second factor is closely related to the first, namely the chronic partial sleep deprivation that many shift workers experience (typically about seven hours less per week than their day working counterparts) (Knauth et al. 1980). One major source of this deprivation is the circadian system misalignment discussed earlier. Other sources are secondary effects springing from poor sleep hygiene practices (e.g., napping, excessive caffeine use) that the weary shift worker might adopt, as well as the more obvious effects of daytime traffic and household noise. The sleep of the night worker is much less protected by society's taboos than that of a day worker. Although no one would call a day worker on the telephone at 2 A.M., few would hesitate to call a night worker at 2 P.M.. The physician should, however, bear in mind that these exogenous noises may often be a scapegoat used by the patient to account for sleep disruption that is primarily endogenous in origin, resulting from a lowering of arousal thresholds associated with a misaligned circadian system (Folkard et al. 1978).

The third factor contributing to the symptoms of shift work comprises the social and domestic tensions and conflicts that often arise for the shift worker. One can all too easily regard the shift worker's problems as existing solely in the domains of sleep hygiene and circadian rhythms. This assumption, however, neglects an area of difficulty that can be very troublesome for the patient personally (Walker 1978, 1985) and can negate any coping or treatment strategies prescribed for the two other domains. For example, the domestic demands of women shift workers (who are often required to run a household and care for children) may completely overrule any patterns of behavior suggested by good sleep hygiene or circadian principles (Gadbois 1981). Likewise, the evening shift, which has minimal impact on sleep and circadian factors, can have a crushing impact on the shift worker's role as social companion (ruling out evening social activities with the spouse) and parent (only seeing school age children when they are asleep in bed).

Treatment strategies for the shift worker should thus proceed on a broad front, including good sleep hygiene (discussed elsewhere in this chapter), the application of circadian rhythm principles (Czeisler et al. 1982), and perhaps some family therapy to lessen the domestic tensions. The sleep/wake routine to be encouraged is one in which sleep follows as soon as possible after the night or evening shift, in a single consolidated episode. Daylight can be a potent zeitgeber working against a nocturnal realignment (Lewy et al. 1984), and shift workers would probably be well advised to avoid daylight exposure during the morning. (The efficacy of this approach remains to be tested, however.) Once a nocturnal circadian alignment has been achieved, efforts should be made to retain it, even on days off, though this is often not feasible (Van Loon 1963). It is important to strongly impress upon the patient that the quality and duration of sleep will be as much an outcome of adherence to the necessary circadian phasing strategies as it is to other factors (such as bedroom soundproofing and caffeine use) that are more obviously linked to sleep behavior.

Jet Lag

Sleep disorders related to transmeridian travel (jet lag) arise from the same circadian system difficulties that plague the shift worker and often appear with a very similar cluster of symptoms (Klein et al. 1972; Winget et al. 1984). The difference, however, is that jet lag symptoms are usually acute and short-lived compared to those of the shift worker because both physical (daylight/darkness) and social (clock time/traffic noise) zeitgebers are encouraging a circadian realignment.

Treatment for jet lag thus proceeds on two fronts. First, the sleep is consolidated and protected by pharmacologic (e.g., triazolam or a similar short acting hypnotic) (Seidel et al. 1985) or behavioral (avoidance of caffeine, good sleep hygiene, etc.) approaches (Mong 1987). Second, the circadian system must be encouraged to realign to the new time zone by maximizing the duration and intensity of exposure to both physical and social zeitgebers. Klein and Wegmann (1975) significantly worsened the amount of jet lag experienced by requiring subjects to stay within the confines of their hotel during the first few days after arrival.

Although jet lag sleep disorders are usually thought of as an acute, rather than chronic, problem, this is not always the case. With the rise of multinational corporations, there has developed a subgroup of the business community for whom jet lag has become a chronic complaint, similar to that experienced by the shift worker. These individuals very often find themselves spending one or two weeks out of every month in a radically different time zone than that of their home base. Thus, the jet lag effects from one trip may only just have dissipated when a new trip starts. Many patients who are involved in this level of travel report chronic irritability, below-par mental performance, and domestic or social difficulties, in addition to the more obvious factor of sleep disruption.

These effects are not always apparent to the patient, however, and the frequent inability of the patient to track such changes as they occur may be rather insidious. Some executives report that they only realize how debilitated they become when they cease traveling awhile and can regain their normal levels of mood and mental functioning. Treatment for such patients (who are often late middle aged and thus at extra risk for medical and psychiatric complications) must very often exclude hypnotic use, concentrating more on behavioral and psychosocial strategies, which are more appropriate for the chronic disorder.

Delayed Sleep Phase Syndrome

This syndrome, reported by Weitzman et al. (1982), primarily affects younger people (18 to 30 years of age). It is characterized by sleep that occurs at satisfactory levels of duration and efficiency but at wholly inappropriate times of day. Patients with this disorder often present with a sleep episode that can only start at four or five o'clock in the morning and thus grossly interferes with their ability to attend school or earn a living. It is different from a simple sleep onset insomnia in that when the subject retires at that inappropriate bedtime, sleep latencies are short, and a restful, apparently normal seven or eight hours of sleep are obtained.

Delayed sleep phase syndrome is a disorder of the circadian entrainment mechanism; and therapy must thus proceed along two fronts, attacking both ends of the entrainment process. At the circadian oscillator end, it appears that these individuals find themselves, as it were, only able to phase delay their circadian system to later bedtimes but not to phase advance it. Using an analogy, the therapy is to have them "drive around the block," i.e., acquire a phase advanced position by a series of phase delay steps. This process, termed "chronotherapy," requires each bedtime to be three hours later than the one before it, until the individual has acquired a socially acceptable phase position (e.g. bedtimes of 5 A.M., 8 A.M., 11 A.M., 2 P.M., 5 P.M., 8 P.M., and 11 P.M., ending there).

Following the acquisition of an appropriate sleep timing, attention must then be applied to the other end of the entrainment process, ensuring that exposure to social and physical zeitgebers is maximized (often using the social zeitgeber of an individual whose role is to enforce the required bedtimes). Any backsliding by the patient to a later bedtime must be scrupulously avoided, or the whole process has to be repeated.

Advanced Sleep Phase Syndrome

In contrast to delayed sleep phase syndrome, advanced sleep phase syndrome (Czeisler et al. 1986) tends to afflict the old rather than the young. Here the problem is one of an unacceptably early onset of sleep (e.g., at 7 or 8 P.M.) that, coupled with a reduced sleep duration, often leaves the patient wide awake during the early hours of the morning with nothing to do. Very often the patient will perceive this problem as insomnia. However, careful examination using a sleep diary will often reveal that acceptable amounts of sleep are being obtained, but that, like the delayed sleep phase situation, the sleep is occurring at the wrong time of day (see the next chapter for a further discussion of this general area).

The mechanisms producing advanced sleep phase syndrome are both biologic and psychosocial in origin. Biologically, there is a change in the circadian system with age, tending to flatten the amplitude of circadian rhythms, shorten the natural period length of the biologic clock, and advance the phase position of various circadian rhythms (Weitzman et al. 1982). Thus, from biologic factors alone, there is a natural tendency for older people to want to go to bed and get up earlier than their younger counterparts. Psychosocial factors will tend to exacerbate these tendencies. Many old people are bored, lonely, and house bound, not only missing out on social and physical zeitgebers that might aid in their circadian entrainment but also feeling that they might as well go to bed because there's nothing else to do.

Therapy for such patients is thus difficult and, again, mostly depends upon sleep hygiene principles. Spielman et al. (1983) have shown that progressive sleep restriction can have a beneficial effect on such patients. Usually, though, giving the patient a zeitgeber (e.g., the 11 P.M. television news) to work to, will help reduce the amount of wakefulness occurring between 2 and 5 A.M. and, thus, the amount of distress experienced by the patient.

Conclusion

Sleep/wake schedule disturbances occur primarily as a mismatch between the sleep/wake cycle timing expected by the endogenous circadian system and that required by society or one's job. Even without the complications of shift work, jet lag, or a pathology of the circadian system, sleep disorders can arise as a function of failing to expose oneself to sufficient social and physical zeitgebers and adopting a cavalier attitude toward the timing of sleep. Very often a common sense approach, based on the realization that the circadian system needs information to tell it the required timings of sleep and wakefulness, will suggest the strategies most helpful in ameliorating the patient's problems.

Chapter 224

Sleep Disturbances in Late Life

Etiology of Sleep Disturbances in Late Life

Almost 90 percent of persons aged 60 to 90 complain of insomnia at one time or another (Miles and Dement 1980). Although the elderly comprise only about 10 percent of the U.S. population, they take 25 to 40 percent of the nation's prescription drugs, including sleeping pills. Among the institutionalized elderly, survey evidence indicates that over 90 percent are prescribed hypnotic drugs (U.S. Public Health Service 1976).

Sleep disturbances in late life, regardless of clinical presentation, generally reflect a number of factors. Paramount among these are age-dependent decreases in the ability to sleep, sleep phase alterations (particularly advancement of the major sleep period to an earlier time of day), neuropsychiatric disorders (especially depression and dementia), pain and limitation of mobility (with excessive time in bed and with resultant decay of sleep/wake rhythm amplitudes), and poor sleep habits or negative conditioning. The increased prevalence with age of sleep-disordered breathing, nocturnal myoclonus, gastroesophageal reflux associated with hiatal hernia, and adverse environmental factors (such as excessive noise or temperatures outside the thermoneutral zone) also play a role. These factors and their interaction are depicted in Figure 1, which illustrates the multifaceted nature of sleep disturbance in late life and of insomnia in particular. These factors also determine the overall strategy of clinical assessment and treatment.

Clinical Assessment of Sleep Disturbances in Late Life

Keeping in mind the age-dependent decreases in the ability to sleep (particularly to achieve depth of sleep and to have long uninterrupted periods of sleep), the clinician should investigate several possibilities when approaching the older patient with a sleep disturbance. First, the clinician should inquire about poor sleep hygiene practices, for example, irregular sleep/wake scheduling; excessive environmental noise; temperature outside the thermoneutral zone; or evening self-medication with nicotine, alcohol, or caffeinated beverages. If the older patient shows evidence of obsessive worry about sleep or the use of the sleep setting for activities not conducive to sleep, these adverse conditioning factors may be playing an important role in the etiology and perpetuation of the complaint. Further, many older people have developed dependency on sleeping pills or other central nervous system depressive drugs and require detoxification. Another factor affecting sleep disturbance in late life is the temporal redistribution of the major sleep period, as evidenced by phase advancement or excessive daytime napping. The clinician should ask the patient's bedpartner about the presence of heavy snoring or obstructive breathing during sleep, which may well indicate sleep apnea. Similarly, feelings of restlessness in the legs at sleep onset may be a clue to the presence of nocturnal myoclonus. It is well known, also, that neuropsychiatric disorders of late life, particularly depression and dementia, are often associated with prominent disturbances of nighttime sleep and daytime alertness. Medical causes of pain, such as nocturnal angina and arthritis, may also play a role in disturbing sleep. Finally, but of great clinical importance, the use of sedating medication (not only sleeping pills, but also antihypertensives, antihistamines, and anxiolytics), its timing, and dosage should be reviewed for potential adverse effects on sleep and on daytime alertness.

To understand thoroughly an older person's sleep complaint, it is necessary to place it within the context of his or her daily schedule of activities or that of the institution in which he or she resides. As is well known, if the patient is a nursing home resident, wakefulness, wandering, or nighttime confusion (i.e., "sundowning") may be a major management problem that, unfortunately, often leads to excessive sedation, falls, further deterioration of mental status during the day, and accidents.

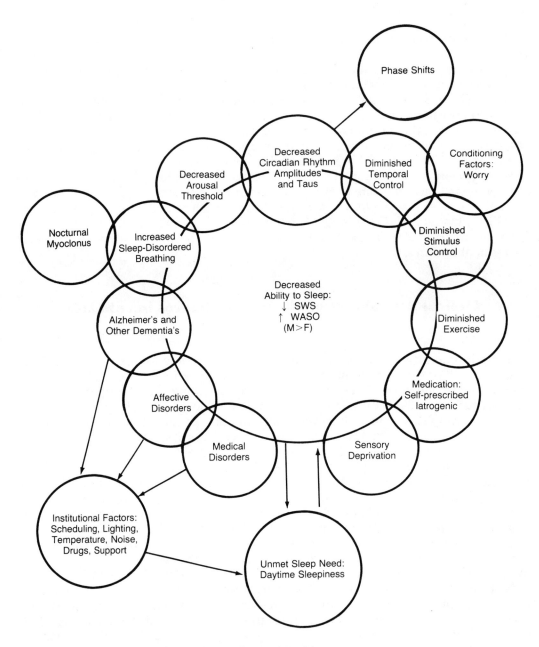

Figure 1. Geriatric Insomnia: A Multifaceted Problem

General Guidelines for the Treatment of Late-Life Sleep Disturbances

Routine treatment of sleep disturbances in late life must include consistent attention to regulation of the sleep/wake schedule and a comfortable sleep environment, with diminution of noise and maintenance of temperature in the thermoneutral zone. Reduction or omission of nicotine, alcohol, and excessive liquid ingestion in the evening (including caffeine) is likewise indicated. Use of the bedroom for sleep only and avoidance of activities in the bedroom that are not conducive to sleep will be helpful in many instances, as will careful attention to the timing of daily activities, meals, medication, and sleep periods. The physician may need to prescribe detoxification from CNS depressant or stimulant drugs as well as appropriate nonpharmacologic treatment such as behavioral therapy or chronotherapy when indicated. Finally, judicious use of antidepressant medication for the treatment of associated affective disorders is often indicated.

Guidelines for Pharmacologic Approaches to Late-Life Sleep Disturbances

Diagnosis is the most salient of all clinical considerations involved in the decision to prescribe medication for a late-life sleep disturbance. Sleeping pills have some place in the management of transient or situational insomnia, in persistent sleep loss associated with negative conditioning or bad habits, and in persistent insomnia associated with nonpsychotic psychiatric disorders (for a review, see Chapter 220). Additional considerations involved in prescribing sleeping pills for the elderly include 1) a review of the relative indications and contraindications for using low-dose sedating tricyclic antidepressant drugs, benzodiazepines, or sedating antipsychotic compounds; 2) changes in rate of metabolism; 3) effects on daytime alertness and performance; 4) other concurrent medications that might potentiate the sedative effects of sleeping pills; and 5) the potential effects on borderline or full-blown sleep apnea syndrome. In general, long-term prescribing is not recommended.

With respect to the appropriate class of compound, there is a paucity of data from controlled pharmacotherapeutic trials on well-diagnosed samples of geriatric patients to guide clinical decision making. For example, we could find only six controlled studies of sleeping pill use in elderly patients with dementia or organic brain syndrome published during the last 15 years (Linnoila and Viukari 1976; Linnoila et al. 1980a, 1980b; Schubert 1984; Stotski et al. 1971; Viukari et al. 1978). These studies involved a total of 134 inpatients, some with mild to moderate dementia, and others diagnosed as having organic brain syndrome with agitation. None of the studies used sleep laboratory or objective methods to assess drug effects. With the exception of the study by Schubert (1984), all studies employed a placebo control and were double blind. The major dependent measures in the studies reviewed were nursing observations of sleep onset time, sleep duration, and number and duration of arousals during the night. The studies investigated the effects of several different psychoactive agents on sleep in institutionalized demented patients, including butabarbital (50–100 mg), nitrazepam (10 mg), thioridazine (25 mg), flurazepam (15 mg), chloral hydrate (500 mg), lorazepam (2 mg), oxazepam (30 mg), temazepam (15 mg), and hydroxyzine (50–200 mg).

In general, the studies reported that, as compared with placebo, the use of active compounds was associated with nursing observations of increased sleep time, via a reduction in sleep onset and in the number of intermittent awakenings. In the study by Linnoila et al. (1980b), however, the use of lorazepam (2 mg), oxazepam (30 mg), and temazepam (15 mg) was not associated with a reduction in sleep latency but did result in improved sleep maintenance. In the study by Linnoila and Viukari (1976), low-dose thioridazine was reported to be superior to nitrazepam, with the use of the latter leading to increased daytime memory impairment, incontinence, diminished activities of daily living, and daytime sleepiness. Viukari et al. (1978) likewise reported decreased motor performance following the use of flurazepam and nitrazepam, as well as rebound insomnia following the use of nitrazepam. Similarly, Linnoila et al. (1980a) observed significant withdrawal insomnia with chloral hydrate when used in elderly inpatients with dementia. Finally, Schubert (1984) observed the development of tolerance to the sedating effects of hydroxyzine.

At this writing, we are reluctant to recommend the use of benzodiazepines to manage sleep disturbance associated with dementia. From the published studies, it is not clear that the use of benzodiazepines is a viable long-term strategy for successful maintenance of sleep disturbance in dementia; moreover, published studies suggest the development of either withdrawal effects, tolerance, or unacceptable side effects, including daytime sleepiness. Given the possibility that sleep apnea may occur significantly more often in dementia than in other types of late-life mental disorder, an interaction between sleep-disordered breathing and cognitive deterioration in dementia must be considered. In this context of uncertainty, therefore, we generally recommend the use of sedating antipsychotic compounds (for example, thioridazine 25–75 mg hs) for patients with marked behavioral disturbances at night who also have dementia (generally of the Alzheimer's type) associated with psychosis or delirium.

In other older patients with chronic insomnia who cannot function without maintenance sleep promoting medication, we generally favor the use of a low-dose sedating tricyclic antidepressant rather than a benzodiazepine. We believe that antidepressant medication may retain sedating effects longer than benzodiazepines, without the development of tolerance, daytime sequelae, or withdrawal syndromes. Moreover, such patients often have diagnosable affective disorders; they not infrequently also have low-grade sleep apnea, which might be diminished by tricyclic antidepressants but exacerbated by benzodiazepines. We would consider a benzodiazepine as maintenance therapy in chronic insomnia associated with a diagnosable anxiety disorder, if there is no sleep apnea, but controlled evidence in support of this is lacking.

When using benzodiazepines in the elderly, the key pharmacokinetic consideration is the half-life of the compound. (For a review, see Greenblatt et al. 1981.) It is well known that long-lasting sleeping pills are more likely to produce daytime sedation, the desirability of which will vary for specific patients. Related contraindications to sleeping pill use in the elderly include heavy snoring (which suggests sleep apnea), systemic illnesses that diminish the patient's ability to eliminate these compounds, the use of other medications (including alcohol) with potentially dangerous interactions, a history of drug abuse, jobs requiring alertness, and suicidal risk. If the physician determines that a benzodiazepine is indicated in an older patient, for example, to help with acute sleep disturbance in association with a major life change, the physician should establish the least effective dose (often one-third to one-half that prescribed in younger patients), tell the patient to take the medication about 30 minutes before bedtime, monitor daytime consequences (especially daytime sleepiness), follow the patient regularly, try to limit the use of the compound to fewer than 20 doses per month and for not more than three months total, and encourage the patient to increase reliance on nonpharmacologic approaches to sleep disturbance.

With respect to the use of tricyclic antidepressants to treat late-life sleep disturbances associated with depression, a recent review of experience with the tricyclic drug nortriptyline (Reynolds et al. 1987) found that the use of this agent, in doses ranging from 20 to 75 mg hs, was helpful in reducing depressive symptoms, including sleep disturbance, in late-life depression with or without associated cognitive impairment. In general, avoid tertiary amine tricyclic antidepressants in the elderly because of unacceptable side effects, such as orthostasis, anticholinergic delirium, and peripheral atropinic effects (Reynolds et al. 1987).

Guidelines for Nonpharmacologic Approaches to Late-Life Sleep Disturbances

Elderly persons and their families need to be told that some sleep disturbance may be an unavoidable consequence of aging; not that they need less sleep but, rather, that their ability to sleep diminishes with age. Reinforcement of the sleep/wake rhythm becomes extremely important in order to combat the age-related tendency to lose the consolidation of sleep and to develop a polyphasic sleep/wake cycle. The use of strong and consistent external time cues might achieve this goal without the side effects associated with sleeping pill use. In practical terms, the elderly person should be encouraged to maintain temporal control by going to bed only when sleepy, by getting up at the same time each morning, and by reducing or eliminating naps; and to maintain stimulus control by avoidance of using the bedroom for activities other than sleep. The latter will serve to keep the bed as a powerful stimulus to sleep. We emphasize the importance of strengthening temporal and stimulus control, together with education and reassurance, to give the elderly person a sense of increased control and to diminish the perceived need for sleeping pills.

In our studies of healthy older sleepers, we have also noted that elderly persons who habitually sleep will restrict themselves to six and one-half or seven hours' time in bed nightly and tend to have sleep continuity superior to that observed in persons who remain in bed eight hours or longer and whose lives are generally less active and structured. Our observation is consistent with Spielman's (1983) earlier claim that sleep restriction may be appropriate treatment in some types of insomnia, notably, conditioned or psychophysiologic insomnia.

Summary

We suggest that the clinician treating late-life sleep disturbances first needs to identify specific etiologic factors. Often multiple factors are operating in the same patient to produce a sleep/wake complaint. Second, it is important to recognize and educate the patient about age-dependent decreases in the ability to sleep. Third, given the apparent fragility and brittleness of the older person's circadian timekeeping system, it is important to reinforce sleep/wake rhythms by strengthening zeitgebers (time cues) and by enhancing stimulus control. Often, modest habitual restriction to six and one-half or seven and one-half hours' time in bed will help improve sleep continuity. At the same time, mild daytime sleepiness may be alleviated by a regularly scheduled brief nap. Fourth, chronopharmacologic issues must be addressed, particularly the timing of both psychotropic and nonpsychotropic drugs with respect to adverse effects on sleep and wake. Finally, pharmacotherapy should be used for specific indications only, for limited periods of time, and with attention to possible adverse effects on breathing during sleep.

References

Section 23
Sleep Disorders

American Psychiatric Association: Diagnostic and Statistical Manual of Mental Disorders, 3rd ed, revised. Washington, DC, American Psychiatric Association, 1987

Aschoff J, et: Handbook of Behavioral Neurobiology, vol 4. New York, Plenum, 1981

Bawkin H: Sleepwalking in twins. Lancet ii:446–447, 1970

Borkovec TD: Pseudo (experiential) insomnia and idiopathic (objective) insomnia: theoretical and therapeutic issues. Adv Behav Res Ther 2:27–55, 1979

Broughton R: Sleep disorders: disorders of arousal? Science 159:1070–1087, 1968

Cartwright RD: Effects of sleep position on sleep apnea severity. Sleep 7:110–114, 1984

Coleman RM, Roffwarg HP, Kennedy SJ, et al: Sleep-wake disorders based on a polysomnographic diagnosis. JAMA 247:997–1003, 1982

Czeisler CA, Moore-Ede MC, Coleman RM: Rotating shift work schedules that disrupt sleep are improved by applying circadian principles. Science 217:460–463, 1982

Czeisler CA, Rios CD, Sanchez R, et al: Phase advance and reduction in amplitude of the endogenous circadian oscillator correspond with systematic changes in sleep/wake habits and daytime functioning in the elderly. Sleep Res 15:268, 1986

Ferber R (ed): Solve Your Child's Sleep Problems. New York, Simon & Schuster, 1985

Folkard S, Mont TH: Shiftwork and performance. Hum Factors 21:483–492, 1979

Folkard S, Mont TH, Lobban MC: Shift and long-term adjustment of circadian rhythms in "permanent" night nurses. Ergonomics 21:785–799, 1978

Froberg JE: Twenty-four-hour patterns in human performance, subjective and physiological variables and differences between morning and evening active subjects. Biol Psychiatry 5:119–134, 1977

Fujita AS, Conway W, Zorick F: Surgical corrections of anatomic abnormalities in obstructive sleep apnea syndrome: uvulopapatopharyngoplasty. Otolaryngol Head Neck Surg 89:923–934, 1981

Gadbois C: Women on night shift: interdependence of sleep and off-the-job activities, in Night and Shift Work: Biological and Social Aspects. Edited by Reinberg A, Vieux N, Andlauer P. Oxford, Pergamon, 1981

Greenblatt DJ, Shader RI, Divoll M: Benzodiazepines: a summary of pharmacokinetic properties. J Am Geriatr Soc 11:11S–16S, 1981

Guilleminault C, Flagg W: Effect of baclofen on sleep-related periodic leg movements. Ann Neruol 15:234–239, 1984

Guilleminault C, Raynal D, Weitzman ED, et al: Sleep-related periodic myoclonus in patients complaining of insomnia. Trans Am Neurol Assoc 100:19–22, 1975

Guilleminault C, Dement WC, Passovant P, eds: Narcolepsy: Advances in Sleep Research. New York, Spectrum, 1976, p 689

Guilleminault C, Simmons FB, Motta J, et al: Obstructive sleep apnea syndrome and tracheostomy: long-term followup experience. Arch Intern Med 141:985–988, 1981

Hartmann E (ed): The Nightmare. The Psychology and Biology of Terrifying Dreams. New York, Basic Books, 1984

Hauri P (ed): The Sleep Disorders, 2nd ed. Kalamazoo, Mich, Scope Publications, The Upjohn Company, 1982

Hauri P, Olmstead E: Childhood onset insomnia. Sleep 3:59–65, 1980

Hauri P, Olmstead E: Persistent psychophysiologic (learned) insomnia. Sleep 9:38–53, 1986

Issa FG, Sullivan CE: Reversal of central sleep apnea using nasal CPAP. Chest 90:165–171, 1986

Kales A, Jacobson A, Paulson M, et al: Somnambulism: psychophysiological correlates, all night EEG sleep studies. Arch Gen Psychiatry 14:586–594, 1966

Kales A, Soldatos C, Bixler E, et al: Hereditary factors in sleep walking and night terrors. Br J Psychiatry 137:111–118, 1980a

Kales A, Soldatos CR, Caldwell AB, et al: Nightmares: clinical characteristics and personality patterns. Am J Psychiatry 137:1197–1201, 1980b

Kales JD, Kales A, Soldatos CR, et al: Night terrors: clinical characteristics and personality problems. Arch Gen Psychiatry 37:1413–1417, 1980c

Kales A, Soldatos CR, Bixler ED, et al: Narcolepsy-cataplexy, II: psychosocial consequences and associate psychopathology. Arch Neurol 39:169–171, 1982

Klein KE, Wegmann HM: The resynchronization of human circadian rhythms after transmeridian flights as a result of flight direction and mode of activity, in Chronobiology. Edited by Scheving LE, Halberg F, Pauly JE. Tokyo, Igaku Shoin Ltd, 1975

Klein KE, Wegmann HM, Hunt BI: Desynchronization as a function of body temperature and performance circadian rhythm as a result of outgoing and home coming transmeridian flights. Aerospace Med 43:119–132, 1972

Knauth P, Retenfranz J: Circadian rhythm of body temperature and re-entrainment at shift change. Int Arch Occup Environ Health 37:125–137, 1976

Knauth P, Landau K, Droge C, et al: Duration of sleep depending on the type of shift work. Int Arch Occup Environ Health 46:167–177, 1980

Lesser IM, Poland RE, Holcomb C, et al: Electroencephalographic study of nighttime panic attacks. J Nerv Ment Dis 173:744–746, 1985

Lewy AJ, Sack RA, Singer CL: Assessment and treatment of chronobiologic disorders using plasma melatonin levels and bright light exposure: the clock-gate model and the phase response curve. Psychopharmacol Bull 28:553–557, 1984

Linnoila M, Viukari M: Efficacy and side effects of nitrazepam and thioridazine as sleeping aids in psychogeriatric inpatients. Br J Psychiatry 128:566–569, 1976

Linnoila M, Viukari M, Numminen A, et al: Efficacy and side effects of chloral hydrate and tryptophan as sleeping aids in psychogeriatric patients. Int Pharmacopsych 15:124–128, 1980a

Linnoila M, Viukari M, Lamminsivu U, et al: Efficacy and side effects of lorazepam, oxazepam, and temazepam as sleeping aids in psychogeriatric inpatients. Int Pharmacopsych 15:129–135, 1980b

Luchins D, Sherwood PM, Gillin JC, et al: Filicide during psychotropic-induced somnambulism: a case report. Am J Psychiatry 135:1404–1045, 1978

Mamelak M, Webster P: Treatment of narcolepsy and sleep apnea with gamma-hydroxybutyrate: a clinical and polysomnographic case study. Sleep 4:105–111, 1981

Mendelson WB, ed: Human Sleep: Research and Clinical Care. New York, Plenum, 1987, pp 183–220

Mikkelsen EJ, Rapoport JL, Neel L, et al: Childhood enuresis, I: sleep patterns and psychopathology. Arch Gen Psychiatry 37:1139–1144, 1980

Miles LE, Dement WC: Sleep and aging. Sleep 3:119–220, 1980

Mitler MM, Browman CP, Menn SJ, et al: Nocturnal myoclonus: treatment efficacy of clonazepam and temazepam. Sleep 9:385–392, 1986

Monk TH: Advantages and disadvantages of rapidly rotating shift schedules—a circadian viewpoint. Hum Factors 28:553–557, 1986

Monk TH: Coping with the stress of jet-lag: Work and Stress, 1:163–166, 1987

Onal E, Lopata M, O'Connor T: Pathogenesis of apneas in hypersomnia-sleep apnea syndrome. Am Rev Respir Dis 125:167–174, 1982

Parkes JD: The parasomnias. Lancet ii:1021–1025, 1986

Rapoport JL, Mikkelsen EJ, Zavidil A, et al: Childhood enuresis, II: psychopathology, plasma tricyclic concentrations, and antienuretic effect. Arch Gen Psychiatry 37:1146–1152, 1980

Regestein QR, Reich P: Incapacitating childhood onset insomnia. Compr Psychiatry 24:244–248, 1983

Reynolds CF, Perel JM, Kupfer DJ, et al: Open-trial response to antidepressant treatment in elderly patients with mixed depression and cognitive impairment. Psychiatry Res, 21:95–109, 1987

Rutenfranz J, Colquhoun WP, Knauth P, et al: Biomedical and psychosocial aspects of shift work: a review. Scand J Work Environ Health 3:165–182, 1977

Schmidt HS: L-Tryptophan in the treatment of impaired respiration in sleep. Bull Eur Physiopathol Respir 19:625–629, 1983

Schmidt HS, Clark RW, Hyman PR: Protriptyline: an effective agent in the treatment of narcolepsy-cataplexy syndrome and hypersomnia. Am J Psychiatry 134:183–185, 1977

Schubert DSP: Hydroxyzine for acute treatment of agitation and insomnia in organic mental disorder. Psychiatr J Univ Ottawa 9:59–60, 1984

Schweitzer PK, Chamber GW, Birkenmeier N, et al: Nasal continuous positive airway pressure (CPAP) compliance at six, twelve and eighteen months. Sleep Res 16:186, 1987

Seidel WF, Roth T, Cohen SA, et al: Phase shift of REM distribution with triazolam. Sleep Res 14:311, 1985

Spielman AJ, Saskin P, Thorpy MJ: Sleep restriction: a new treatment of insomnia. Sleep Res 12:286, 1983

Spinweber CL, Greenberger D: Somnambulists and enuretics in the navy: MMPI, sleep questionnaire and case history data. Sleep Res 13:168, 1984

Stotsky BA, Cole JO, Tang YT, et al: Sodium butabarbital as an hypnotic agent for aged psychiatric patients with sleep disorders. J Am Geriatr Soc 19:860–870, 1971

Terr LC: Chowchilla revisited: the effects of psychic trauma four years after school bus kidnapping. Am J Psychiatry 140:1543–1550, 1983

U.S. Public Health Service: Physicians Drug Prescribing Patterns in Skilled Nursing Facilities. Dept. of Health, Education, and Welfare Publication 76-50050. Bethesda, Md, 1976

Van den Hoed J, Kraemer H, Guilleminault C, et al: Disorders of excessive daytime somnolence: polygraphic and clinical data for 100 patients. Sleep 4:23–37, 1981

Van Loon JH: Diurnal body temperature curves in shift workers. Ergonomics 6:267–272, 1963

Viukari M, Linnoila M, Aalto U: Efficacy and side effects of flurazepam, fosazepam, and nitrazepam as sleeping aids in psychogeriatric patients. Acta Psychiatr Scand 57:27–35, 1978

Walker J: The Human Aspects of Shiftwork. Bath, The Pitman Press, 1978

Walker J: Social problems of shift work, in Hours of Work—Temporal Factors in Work Scheduling. Edited by Folkard S, Monk TH. New York, John Wiley and Sons, 1985

Weitzman ED, Czeisler CA, Zimmerman JC, et al: Chronobiological disorders: analytic and therapeutic techniques, in Indications and Techniques. Edited by Guilleminault C. Calif, Addison Wesley, 1982a

Weitzman ED, Moline ML, Czeisler CA, et al: Chronobiology of aging: temperature sleep/wake rhythms and entrainment. Neurobiol Aging 3:299–309, 1982b

Wever R: The Circadian System of Man: Results of Experiments Under Temporal Isolation. New York, Springer-Verlag, 1979

Winget CM, DeRoshia CW, Markley CL, et al: A review of human physiological and performance changes associated with desynchronosis of biological rhythms. Aviat Space Environ Med 55:1085–1096, 1984

Zarcone VP: Narcolepsy. N Engl J Med 288:1156–1166, 1973

Impulse Control Disorders Not Elsewhere Classified

Chapter 225

Introduction

DSM-III-R (American Psychiatric Association [1987]) characterizes an impulse disorder as a failure to resist the urge to perform an act that is harmful to the person himself/ herself or to others. The urge may or may not be conscious and the behavior may or may not be deliberate. The individual experiences a buildup of inner tension which the behavior relieves; the behavior may or may not be ego syntonic and may or may not be accompanied by regret, self-reproach, shame, or guilt. Such syndromes are usually chronic and progressive, leading to considerable social impairment, with a gradual change in life-style, values, and risk taking.

An impulse disorder involves problems in tension regulation, affect intensity, action propensity, absence of fantasy, and difficulties in sublimating and channeling. Many persons with impulse disorders exhibit alexithymia, the inability to experience, name, and use affect, and they demonstrate many of the behavioral characteristics of borderline patients and patients with narcissistic disorders.

Clustered here are a seemingly unrelated group of syndromes and behaviors "not elsewhere classified." Yet, patients with these disorders share a propensity to behave, rather than think and feel. In many ways, their behavior resembles adolescent behavior perpetuated, and these disorders have their origins in childhood and adolescence; consequently, in discussing some of these impulse disorders, one cannot ignore pre-adulthood. For example, Meeks (1979) describes in considerable detail, with treatment recommendations, a number of childhood conduct problems—stealing, running away, vandalism, cruelty to animals, sexual assault, lying, firesetting, provocative behavior, defiance and disobedience, outbursts of rage and violence, and manipulative behavior—that foreshadow the impulse disorders of adolescence and adulthood.

Understanding the etiology of these disorders is difficult and complex, involving genetic and constitutional factors, temperament, and psychosociobiologic maturation and development. Such complexity is compounded by this clustering of the "not elsewhere classified." Thus, the reader or student must not view our work here as definitive or complete. Many of these syndromes have not been studied in depth. Cases have been reported not to prove a particular etiology but to illustrate a concept or model, and treatment recommendations are neither uniform nor consistent. In what follows, for example, we recommend psychotherapy and/or pharmacotherapy unevenly—not because we favor inconsistency, or are purposefully incomplete, but because these divergent disorders have been inconsistently studied and treated. We do not believe our efforts here to be exhaustive, and do not want them to be taken as the final authority in contemporary psychiatry. Rather, we are presenting our particular viewpoints, with the hope that the reader and practicing clinician will be stimulated to test out his or her own hypotheses; we trust that clinical work allows for individual innovations and styles of treatment.

Psychodynamic formulations and illustrations are, at best, descriptive explanations, not causal. Yet, the practicing psychiatrist usually attempts to formulate impulsive behavior in some sort of psychological or psychopathologic framework. He or she recognizes the significance of family pathology—the parents, for example, permitting, encouraging, or finding gratification in deviant behavior. The practitioner usually attempts some sort of psychotherapeutic intervention, with or without medication; and he or she generally believes that addressing symptoms or behavior alone will not suffice in those people in whom underlying psychodynamic issues are crucial. In some of the impulse disorders, we can be more specific about the efficacy of various psychological and biologic interventions; in others, we have little clinical research data.

General Comments

Freud ([1905] 1958) taught that in the perversions and certain character disorders, psychological problems are externalized instead of being experienced internally or resulting in symptoms, as in the psychoneuroses—an alloplastic rather than autoplastic outcome. The impulsive person causes trouble with others and the environment, rather than experiencing painful affect or disabling symptoms; he attempts to change his environment or a relationship, or to discharge internal tension through behavior, often delinquent or criminal in nature. Freud's concept of "acting out" refers to a similar process in treatment in which the patient behaves outside the treatment relationship in order to prevent himself from remembering the original trauma and experiencing the accompanying pain. Today, "acting out" has developed looser connotations and refers to various kinds of impulsive behavior, not the precise sense of doing instead of remembering. "Acting out" does suggest, however, the sense that these people seek to eliminate internal psychic distress by externalizing it onto the outside world.

The earliest and most significant work with impulsivity was done with delinquent adolescents, and, even today, an understanding of adolescent behavior disorders leads the clinician to a more comfortable awareness of adult behavior problems. August Aichhorn ([1925] 1935) was greatly impressed with Freud's teachings and tried to apply them to his work with wayward youth in Vienna. He viewed delinquency as the result of an early childhood deprivation, and attempted to find the psychic imbalance responsible for delinquent behavior, searched for the unconscious conflicts responsible for the symptomatic behavior, visualized the delinquent's behavior as the interactions of ego and superego, and focused on the youth's attempts to master external reality through his behavior. Such children have a weak ego and superego and are structurally deficient because they are still too attached to their ambivalently held parents. Psychic trauma causes wayward behavior, and the goal of treatment is to remove the cause rather than simply to eliminate the symptomatic behavior. Aichhorn taught that the underlying causes of delinquency can be uncovered only within a transference relationship. He understood deviant behavior as the expression of a wished-for gratification and trained his residential staff to understand this approach, and, if possible, nurture the child and gratify him psychologically. Such gratification would then result in a neurotic conflict between the wish to be gratified and a prohibition, and the staff member or therapist would become a transference figure for the delinquent, reenacting the wishes, conflicts, fears, and prohibitions of early childhood. These could then be understood and analyzed, and the symptomatic "acting out" behavior would resolve.

Aichhorn (1964) noted, however, that a therapeutic relationship could be established only with great difficulty with a certain kind of delinquent, like the "juvenile impostor" (Marohn 1977). Here, the delinquent did not experience the therapist as a separate person, but rather as an idealized part of himself, the ego ideal, ascribing to the therapist certain qualities that the child fantasized he had or wanted to achieve. Aichhorn recommended working with this type of delinquent by quickly establishing a narcissistic transference bond, foreshadowing later work by Kohut with narcissistic disorders. Aichhorn and followers such as Willie Hoffer (1949) recommended that the therapist actively encourage the establishing of such a transference, usually the idealization of a charismatic therapist, which they both believed was a defense against the deeper, more painful problem of unattended primitive grandiosity; their purpose was to intrude into the ego ideal, unmask it, and prove its inferiority by proving the therapist's own superiority. Thus, the psychiatric trainees of 25 years ago would be advised to impress the delinquent with how poorly he had functioned as a criminal and how much smarter the therapist was. Such efforts may encourge the delinquent to further misdeeds. These primitively organized patients, including those with impulse disorders, can often be understood as having narcissistic personality or behavior disorders (Kohut 1971, 1972, 1977), and the properly trained psychotherapist can use his or her empathic capacity to be sensitive to emerging narcissistic or selfobject transferences.

Alexander and Staub (1931), like Freud, observed that certain criminals act out of a sense of neurotic guilt, which plagues them because of forbidden wishes, desires, or fantasies of an aggressive or sexual nature. Their behavior is an attempt to provoke the external world to punish them and set their consciences at ease, a well-known example being the person who confesses to crimes he has not committed. Psychotherapy is directed at uncovering the psychological "crime" of which the patient feels guilty and resolving the neurotic conflict.

Also influenced by Freud's formulations about character disorders, Kate Friedlander (1960) proposed converting behavior disorders into neuroticism by blocking the avenues for impulse discharge, causing internalized psychic pain which can then be worked with therapeutically. While Aichhorn recommended creating conflict by gratifying the infantile wishes, Friedlander tried to reverse the process by reinternalizing an externalized internal conflict, by converting motor behavior to affect, thought, or fantasy. In like manner, Anna Freud (1965) conceptualized delinquency as a failure of the socialization process, a failure of the child to internalize the controls placed on him initially by his parents and other authority figures, an "identification with the aggressor." The child identifies with the aggressor-parent, and with the aggressor-therapist as well, and this provides the psychotherapist with the leverage he needs to begin to modify the child's values and behavior.

Many hospital and residential treatment programs for behavior disorders are based on these pioneering concepts of setting limits on behavior, both to create internal distress and to teach socialization and controls (Marohn et al. 1980).

Johnson and Szurek (1952) described delinquent children who were responding to and gratifying the unconsciously transmitted, deviant, but disowned urges and wishes of their seemingly upright parents; the child would then behave delinquently and gratify the parents vicariously. These motives are often uncovered in family therapy sessions. Brian Bird (1957) added to this paradigm the observation that, although able to respond to the parental unconscious, the delinquent has no psychological capacity to cope with his own unconscious wishes and urges, and presents a picture of driven impulsivity.

Glover's (1950, 1960) classification of juvenile delinquents into the structural and the functional provides an interesting and useful way of approaching the etiology of impulse disorders. A behavior pattern that is an entrenched part of the character structure, even though seemingly impulsive, such as stealing or setting fires repeatedly in defensive response to certain kinds of psychic stress, is structural. Behavior that represents a discharge of occasionally overwhelming inner tension, in an almost random manner, such as occasional purposeless outbursts of violence, is functional; functional problems result from temporary periods of developmental imbalance and stress, such as adolescence, and are not likely to persist as behavioral patterns. We must not assume that violent behavior necessarily expresses rage or destructiveness; often, adolescents and adults will behave violently because they are transiently fragmented or disorganized and because of the intense psychic stimulation of strong longings for affection and intimacy which overwhelm them, creating a traumatic state (Marohn 1974). Baittle and Kobrin (1964) studied a delinquent gang in psychoanalytic and sociologic depth, and were able to correlate structural and functional delinquents with social and community position and status. Peter Blos (1966) has emphasized that the adolescent who behaves impulsively is not only demonstrating the adolescent's tendency to use action instead of verbal communication, but also communicating symbolically an underlying wish or conflict, even though the behavior may appear meaningless or random. Furthermore, this underlying symbolism may be highly personalized and often represents a problem with another person (Bloch 1952).

Redl's (1966) and Redl and Wineman's (1957) monumental contributions have emphasized the child's ego deficits, their developmental origins, the functional impairment they produce in everyday activities, and the importance of treatment staff and other helpers providing external ego functions. His and similar work has structured much of the residential treatment of children and adolescents in this country; however, impulse-ridden adults are not provided the same opportunities for milieu therapy. The therapeutic community era has passed, and prisons no longer aspire to be therapeutic and rehabilitative in their mission. The idea of structuring an environment to confront, uncover, and give meaning to an adult's behavior is considered obsolete by many practitioners.

Winnicott (1958, 1973) saw deviant behavior as early and primitive hunger for the mother who was once possessed, but later lost, and whom the child hopes to recapture through behavior. Although impulsive behavior may seem purposeless, it is a sign of hope because the antagonist has not given up and is still searching, and the therapist may well become the target of his or her search.

These comments about adolescent psychopathology, impulsivity, and delinquency are relevant to an understanding of the adult impulse disorder and its treatment because the adult personality disorder is heir to the closure of adolescence. Often, in adolescence, we can begin to recognize some fairly well established delinquent behavioral patterns (Offer et al. 1979) that may foreshadow later impulsivity. The closure of adolescence, if it proceeds satisfactorily, involves a quieting down of the often-prevalent turmoil, some ability to regulate one's own inner psychological world, the development of a sense of self with continuity in time and space, a capacity for intimacy, the integration of genital sexuality into the personality structure, and the capacity to experience affect as part of oneself. Structurally impulsive adults persist, with the ego distortion of the adult who acts out repressed, conflictual sexuality in stealing; the primitive narcissism of the firesetter enraged at a seemingly unempathic world; or the person who strikes out violently because he is traumatically overstimulated by intense affectionate longings.

Many of these people lead risky lives and face violent death more frequently than the average individual (Marohn et al. 1982). When they face us in treatment, they are usually difficult. They are resistant; they frustrate us. They, and we, do not understand their motives or their behavior; and because they are often psychologically damaged and severely deficient individuals, they are not "attractive" patients. When they appear in the public sector, they are usually being shunted out of the mental health system and into the correctional system, where they are faced with no or uncertain diagnosis, little or no psychotherapy, poorly monitored psychopharmacology (if provided at all), and an attitude that behavior is consciously determined and under one's voluntary and moral control. If psychotherapy is attempted, the therapist is often confronted with a negativistic and hostile, sometimes violent patient, and such is usually equated with the absence of a treatment alliance or an untreatable patient (Marohn 1981). Psychotherapists often prefer agreeable, compliant, and rapidly improving patients.

Psychoanalytic drive and conflict psychology have helped us understand much about impulse and behavior disorders. Impulse disorders share certain psychological characteristics, e.g., the perversion, which is involved in many such disorders, and sadomasochism which is part of all perversions. These patients have more trouble and are less able to get control of the object even to act out the perversion effectively. Thus, they settle for very temporary control which results in a picture of impulsivity mixed with anger, violence, and sadism or a passive retreat toward firesetting, kleptomania, and hair pulling, making them similar to fetishists. For example, the kleptomaniac may look through the clothes of the admired/envied victim, with a clearly expressed sexual component to the relationship. Often, a patient of this sort would rather be accused of a crime than acknowledge the underlying perversion.

These patients cannot use their fantasies either to provide themselves substitute gratification or in treatment, because these fantasies awaken childhood feelings with shame, anger, and fear of others' reactions. They bring that fear into treatment and expect the therapist to react with disgust; they are often right, because many therapists find the fantasies which lie behind the impulsive behavior to be unacceptable and evocative of difficult countertransference problems. Patients with an impulse disorder often hide their shame over their fantasies with outbursts, creating a displacement, and then are angry at those who might detect their fantasies and feel disgust, contempt, and superiority toward them. This is a paranoid reaction, but somewhat realistic, because reactors are often enraged at such patients and act against them. These patients are very sensitive to contempt; their tendency is to show how big, strong, and threatening they can be to achieve equality. Of course, this breaks down, and the patient goes through the cycle of retreating to fantasy, acting out, feeling shame, and being punished. The punishment shifts away from the shame and repeats the childhood experience in which they were first punished for "shameful deeds." One needs to look closely at the precipitant of each incident of acting out to see how the old pattern is reawakened by recent events, but this is difficult to accomplish.

All these patients are difficult to treat, especially those who are violent and set fires; when threatened, they may well act out, and they are threatened by being humiliated or made an object of contempt. Thus, treatment is complex; the therapist has to understand both the psychodynamic issues and himself. Many therapists, like most people, feel some contempt and are disgusted by hair pulling, perversions that are clearly sexual, and violence. Even when the disorder seems clearly "medical," such as an ictal explosive disorder being treated pharmacologically, careful psychotherapeutic attention must be paid to a number of significant issues: how the patient may deny that he or she has any emotional problems, or that he or she derives any gratification from his or her behavior; how the patient adapts when he or she is not explosive; what changes take place in his or her family because of his or her behavior; how responsible he or she is for his or her behavior; and the problem of premature termination of medication because the problem is treated as an externally imposed disease, not as part of one's responsibility to oneself and others.

The therapist's own philosophy about volition, responsibility for behavior, and social control may complicate his or her therapeutic stance. Society has now entered the scene, with more frequent malpractice suits and the expectation that the therapist will warn the potential victim of a violent patient, and has complicated the therapist's role even more.

Family therapy can be helpful for certain children and adolescents, but an adult is usually no longer responding to the unconsciously transmitted messages of the parents, and his or her propensity for impulsivity needs to be understood as part of the personality structure, or lack of it. Treatment is difficult and requires sensitivity; one must constantly reject the attitude that these patients are different from us. It is difficult to work on the issues the patient presents; for example, the precipitating event gets lost because it reflects ordinary human conflicts like ours, especially clinging to childhood wishes and acting on them and resistances to growing up. The essence of the perverse and regressive behavior of these patients threatens our adjustment. These patients sense our ambivalence about being endlessly adult and responsible, touch off deeper levels of our own ambivalence, and attack our motives in becoming therapists to deny such wishes and our tendency to see them in others, while we present ourselves as adult, responsible, and in control at all times. The effective psychotherapist guards against sanctioning, condoning, or enjoying the antisocial behavior, and his or her most effective weapon is his own self-awareness and use of himself.

Those with impulse disorders, especially explosive disorders, can benefit from group activity. Because of their lack of structure, they can derive it from the group, sometimes sharing fantasies, though several may act out for the group. Group therapy is a good approach when shame is a big factor; here, one can encourage sharing fantasies while maintaining control. In individual therapy, the therapist has to be cautious sharing fantasies because such can be experienced as encouraging acting out, and that may be true when the therapist needs to deny the wish to maintain distance from his patient, leading to acting out, rage, and then separation.

The recent development of self psychology (Kohut, 1966, 1968, 1971, 1972, 1977, 1984) has given psychoanalysis and psychoanalytic psychotherapy new hope in working with the primitively organized individual. Often, for example, "acting out" behavior is not the result of some "inner" wish being expressed "outside" because the patient's experience is that he is at one with the world, which should be under his omnipotent control as a part of himself. Rather, "acting out" represents a state of psychic life where thought, word, and deed are one and inseparable, and the patient does not distinguish an "inside" from an "outside" reality. Those are concepts of the healthier observer, not of the inner experience of the impulse-ridden person. By persisting in his attempts to empathize with the psychological world of the impulse disordered patient, the psychotherapist will ultimately help the primitive selfobject transference unfold. Then, the reparative process can begin (Kohut 1984).

Because this section of DSM-III (American Psychiatric Association 1980) is constantly being reevaluated and modified, comments about each of these disorders may not stand the test of time, because the use of the individual categories may pass.

Others may be added, for example, our inclusion of trichotillomania, which is included in DSM-III-R. Nonetheless, each of these disorders represents a failure of tension regulation, deriving from psychological deficit or biologic deviation, which may be two aspects of the same fundamental pathology. Our science has not progressed enough that we can point with certainty to etiology; yet, accumulated clinical evidence, and some research reports, help us define some principles of therapy and management. Every treatment technique has been tried with the impulse disorders, but usually to address only the symptomatic behavior is inadequate, and underlying psychodynamic factors must be confronted.

Our purpose in this is not to present clear and rigid guidelines of treatment, but rather to stimulate the reader's and practitioner's interest, curiosity, and creativity in trying to understand and establish a therapeutic working alliance with these difficult patients. They are difficult because successful treatment invariably involves experiencing dysphoria and psychic pain, often defended against or relieved by action: gambling, stealing, firesetting, hair pulling, or "exploding" in sudden and often violent behavior.

Nonetheless, a chapter that offers no suggestions or thoughts about treatment unless there exist convincing controlled studies would be of little help to the clinician, because progress in psychiatry and medicine in general often relies on clinical impressions, findings, and inferences, without the benefit of controlled research studies.

> In treating disorders of impulse control which give pleasure or lead to a relief from tension, the therapist frequently needs patience and persistence because relapses tend to be common. Patients with these disorders who recovered may relapse a few times before they finally abstain. It may be that the patient needs the experience of a relapse to learn to resist the impulse. When the patient relapses, the treatments have to be repeated and he can be assured that this is a stage in his progress. Subsequent attempts at treatment appear to be more successful in that they can be shorter and lead to longer periods of abstinence before the patient finally desists altogether (Kellner 1982, p 407).

Chapter 226

Pathologic Gambling

Problems of Diagnosis Affecting Treatment

As in other impulse disorders, the gambler fails chronically to resist an impulse, in this case, to gamble. Often, he is also involved in committing illegal acts—usually nonviolent in nature—in order to get money with which to gamble, such as forgery, fraud, embezzlement, and income tax evasion. The impulse to gamble leads to difficulties in personal, vocational, and/or family pursuits. Because a number of the diagnostic criteria are the result of gambling losses, it is difficult to apply this diagnosis to the successful gambler or winner. How useful this diagnosis is in certain subcultures where gambling is practically normative remains to be defined. The proliferation of legalized gambling in the United States adds to the confusion over diagnosis.

Gambling leads to alienation of family and friends, marital discord, legal difficulties, vocational problems, and personal symptoms of anxiety and depression. The degree of severity and the impact on the treatment process are directly related to the number and intensity of the above, particularly the degree of depression.

History of Treatment

Most psychiatric treatment modalities have been utilized with the pathologic gambler: support groups, such as Gamblers Anonymous, founded in 1957 and similar in structure and ideology to Alcoholics Anonymous (Gamblers Anonymous 1977); marital therapy (Boyd and Bolen 1970; Victor and Krug 1967); psychoanalytic psychotherapy (Bergler 1985); and psychopharmacology. Inpatient treatment was first attempted in a systematic fashion at the Brecksville Veterans Administration Center near Cleveland, Ohio, in 1972; follow-up studies are currently being pursued (Russo et al. 1984). To date, no outpatient programs have reported follow-up studies; and, in general, there have been few controlled efficacy studies and few thorough follow-up studies which would permit a comparison of various treatment options.

There are three phases in the history of the treatment of the pathologic gambler. The first was the psychoanalytic which began in the early to mid-1920s. The second phase began in 1957 with the beginning of the self-help group, Gamblers Anonymous. The third phase began in 1972 with the Veterans Administration's first inpatient treatment program and has emerged in a bio-psycho-socio-cultural model. Much of the literature on treatment of pathologic gambling revolves around the work of Custer (1982a, 1982b, 1984; Custer and Milt 1985) and Gamblers Anonymous (Kellner 1982).

Recently, a court would not permit using the diagnosis of pathologic gambling as a defense against a charge of tax evasion (Psychiatric News 1985). Nonetheless, society is beginning to recognize the presence of the compulsive gambler in sports betting, and Gamblers Anonymous and private and public treatment programs have begun to see psychiatric casualties from this sector (Gammon 1986).

Clinical Experience and Research Studies

In addition to the experiences already described in the psychiatric literature, there are important contributions from the sociological literature (Lesieur 1979). Pathologic gambling has been viewed as related to a personality disorder, an addictive disorder, a neurotic disorder, or a variation of a major affective disorder, and appropriate treatment philosophies have developed.

Research studies of pathologic gamblers using structured clinical interviews and standardized diagnostic schema, like the Research Diagnostic Criteria and DSM-III-R, have evaluated, for example, the presence of other psychiatric disorders, such as major depression, bipolar illness, alcohol abuse, and antisocial personality, in pathologic gamblers.

McCormick and others (1984) have found a greater than 75 percent incidence of major depressive illness in a group of pathologic gamblers seeking hospital treatment. Similar findings, including recurrent episodes of major depression and mania, as well as a high prevalence of panic disorder and obsessive-compulsive disorder have been noted in members of Gamblers Anonymous who have not sought inpatient treatment (Linden et al., in press).

As in all these disorders, one must look closely at what sets off the cycle of gambling. A man may react to rejection by a woman or fear domination by her, and then act out his anger or reestablish mastery by self-involved gambling, like the child who turns to his body to master the loss of mother. He may try to soothe himself by gambling, discharging anger as he loses money that belongs to the woman and pleased that she is not getting it, because he does not want to share it with her. This cycle reflects the belief that the woman is all powerful and will not share power. When interviewed, such a man feels intimidated by the woman, projecting onto her his early fears of the mother. Pathologic gamblers may steal a stake with which to gamble, thus fulfilling fantasies of obtaining money magically. Gambling, of course, may be symptomatic behavior seen in a variety of psychiatric disorders. It may not represent the primary psychopathology, but be symptomatic of depression, for example.

Specific Treatment Modalities

To date, there has been only one report of the use of psychopharmacologic agents in the treatment of pathologic gambling, the successful use of lithium carbonate in the treatment of three cases (Moskowitz 1980). While there is considerable evidence for depressive illness in pathologic gambling, there have been no controlled studies of antidepressant medication.

Although there are case reports of gamblers treated in psychoanalytic psychotherapy, there are no controlled studies of such treatment, just as there have been no controlled studies of behavioral and family treatment even though satisfactory results have been reported. Group therapy and self-help programs like Gamblers Anonymous have benefited some, and such treatment is used in most comprehensive inpatient and outpatient treatment programs for pathologic gamblers, though again no controlled follow-up studies isolate this treatment modality. Outpatient treatment is effective when the patient is able to admit that gambling is a serious problem and receives emotional support from his family, from a group like Gamblers Anonymous, and from his job. Sometimes, referral to Gamblers Anonymous may be all that is necessary for treatment (Custer 1982a, 1982b, 1984).

With the high prevalence of major depression and other psychiatric disorders in pathologic gamblers, inpatient treatment is often required. There was a greater than 10 percent prevalence of serious suicide attempts in one group of gamblers who sought hospitalization (McCormick et al. 1984). Inpatient treatment is indicated when the depression is of suicidal proportions or after a suicide attempt. This approach is also indicated when the anxiety is so intense as to interfere with rational perceptions or reality testing. Referrals by Gamblers Anonymous strongly suggest the individual's need for inpatient therapy because they are experienced at recognizing the more severely disturbed gambler. The safe environment of an inpatient setting provides an opportunity for ventilation and interrupts the pervasive cycle of gambling and gambling-related behaviors.

To summarize, pathologic gambling is a relatively common, disabling, and persistent disorder about which to date there has been little research, in part because gambling often occurs in the presence of other, more familiar pathology. In addition, gambling is usually a "silent" disorder, not presenting with, for example, the medical sequellae of alcohol abuse.

Virtually all treatment modalities currently employed in psychiatry have been utilized with this disorder, and there are as yet no research studies to allow for the assessment of the relative merits of these different treatments. In general, an approach which utilizes several treatment modalities, including participation in Gamblers Anonymous, appears warranted at the present time. Evaluation for the presence of other psychiatric disorders, such as major depression, panic disorder, or alcohol abuse, may suggest specific treatment modalities to be pursued.

Treating the pathologic gambler effectively will interrupt the gambling, secure reemployment, improve interpersonal and marital relationships, repair financial deficits, and enhance impulse control.

Chapter 227

Kleptomania

Kleptomania, or "pathologic theft behaviors," is not synonymous with shoplifting, because, as defined in DSM-III-R, it refers to episodes of stealing which are characterized by a recurrent failure to resist impulses to steal objects that have no immediate use or monetary value to the thief. Kleptomania is apparently present in only a tiny percentage of female shoplifters referred for treatment; the incidence of kleptomania may be higher in persons not referred for psychiatric assessment. The recidivism rate associated with kleptomania may mean that it is more likely to be viewed as criminal (Psychiatric News 1985).

An increasing sense of tension before the act and an experience of either pleasure or release at the time of committing the theft are also required. Finally, the stealing must be done without long-term planning and assistance from or collaboration with others and cannot be due to a conduct disorder or antisocial personality disorder. In terms of differential diagnosis, the stealing must be differentiated from "ordinary" stealing, malingering (that is, claiming a psychological compulsion to steal when such does not exist), conduct disorder, manic episodes, and other psychiatric diseases that might lead to thievery in order to be correctly diagnosed as kleptomania.

As described above, most clinicians do not see patients presenting with kleptomania, but forensic psychiatrists do. There are also many adolescents and adults who steal for emotional reasons that clearly have little to do with efforts to gain material advantage. Even in cases in which thievery seems clearly related to material issues, as in situations where poor children are bused into affluent areas in an effort to obtain racial integration and become much involved in stealing from their more affluent classmates, the issues are obviously much more complicated than practical financial questions. For example, the question of personal worth, parental evaluation (often shown by gifts), social acceptance by peers and teachers, etc., all produce powerful incentives to anger, envy, and a wish to "even the score" in the deprived youngsters.

Stealing begins as a developmentally normal behavior, that is, the small child does not have a clear sense of personal property and is likely simply to appropriate things that please him. Later, the child develops a recognition of his right to his own possessions (frequently signaled by a very loud "mine"), but only gradually permits others the same rights. Much pathologic stealing also starts early in childhood, particularly when the child feels deprived of parental affection or feels that a sibling rival is favored with material benefits. In these situations, stealing not only redresses the perceived inequity but also soothes the child by making the good will and affection of the adult "unnecessary." In other words, the child says in essence, "It does not bother me that you will not give to me, since I will simply take what I want in any case."

Somewhat later in development, there are cases of stealing that do resemble classic kleptomania in that the youngster takes objects which seem to have primarily symbolic value and which produce an eroticized arousal and relief experience for the patient. However, almost every youngster who steals under any circumstances will admit to a rush of excitement related to the risk, a sense of outsmarting others, and the triumph of successful theft even in cases which most people would characterize as "ordinary stealing."

It should be noted that stealing is an especially persistent symptom which is very difficult to reverse in a permanent way. The reasons for this are very complex, including our society's ambivalent attitude toward theft. For example, many movies focus on heroes who are involved in imaginative and daring thefts and who gain the sympathy and support of wide portions of the population, even if the audience themselves would not be likely to engage in theft personally. In addition, persistent stealing does serve as a defense and guards against intense dependency conflicts. To ask these defended youngsters to risk a dependent relationship which they view as dangerous and unsatisfactory to replace an exciting and daring avoidance of those conflict areas is expecting a great deal.

Some kleptomaniacs struggle with sexually perverse dynamics. For example, a woman in psychoanalysis who liked to look through other women's clothing and feel them would then go out and steal the same kind of clothes from department stores; her fantasy was that her mother or sister was ambivalent about her having the same clothes that they had. Her perversion was hidden in the stealing. Some preadolescent boys break into houses, look through drawers at underthings, and then steal objects to mask their perversion. It is difficult to get them to describe their behavior and fantasies in detail, but it can be done. They do not steal from need.

Shoplifting involves a range of fantasies from stealing for need to perversion; by definition, kleptomania should be used with those people who are closest to perversions. An example is the well-to-do housewife who steals from a neighbor with whom she is fascinated or who steals from the department store because of her idealization of another woman. On some level, kleptomaniacs want to get caught, so that their activity can be exposed; they often call attention to themselves, unlike the "real" thief. After being caught once, they often give up the behavior, typical of that white collar crime where perversion plays a role. Many cannot stop without extensive treatment. Storekeepers see many women and children who steal until they are caught once and then get scared enough to give it up. Thieving behavior threatens everyone, because such behavior is typical and almost universal during preadolescence; in these adult patients, it represents a true developmental arrest.

Glover (1985) reports a patient with a history of daily compulsive shoplifting of 14 years' duration who was successfully treated by the aversive imagery of nausea and vomiting which the patient preferred to imagery of arrest. Gauthier and Pellerin (1982) describe a patient with "compulsive shoplifting" of four years' duration treated by thought-stopping and convert sensitization.

Several investigators (Casper et al. 1980; Hudson and Pope 1983) report associations between anorexia nervosa and bulimia and kleptomania. Other recent work confirms the impression that shoplifting in women results from depression and efforts to replace a loss (D'Elia and Fugere 1986); this dynamic is often seen in the forensic psychiatric clinic.

Tolpin (1983, p 482) described a 40-year-old divorcee who was analyzed for five years because she had "sought treatment for recurrent depressive states, insomnia, overuse of sleeping medication, and occasional kleptomania." Her idealizing transference pointed to a need for psychologically nourishing selfobjects because she had been unable to form a stable cohesive self. The importance of an empathic immersion in the psychological life of the compulsive shoplifter and of the resultant self psychological formulations and treatment strategies is demonstrated in the case reports of Ornstein et al. (1983). They emphasize how crucial it is to determine the precipitants to the stealing episodes, and they frequently found either some form of narcissistic injury or the actual or threatened loss of a necessary selfobject precipitating the theft.

Chapter 228

Pyromania

Pyromania is a disorder with great destructive potential that produces anxiety in therapist and society. Psychiatry's interest in pyromania began early in the 19th century when papers about firesetting behavior began to appear in the scientific literature. Marc (1833) classified firesetters as monomanie incendiare or pyromania in 1833. His use of the term is similar to the current DSM-III criteria for pyromania. These criteria include a recurring failure to resist the impulse to set fires; an increasing tension before setting the fire and an intense pleasure or release when the fire is set; a lack of motivation such as monetary gain or sociopolitical ideology; and firesetting not due to organic or mental disorders such as schizophrenia, antisocial personality disorder, or conduct disorder. The last two criteria correctly conclude that all firesetters should not be diagnosed as pyromaniacs. DSM-III-R adds that some patients have been described who are sexually aroused by fires, but caution should be used to determine if they meet the other criteria for pyromania since a diagnosis of fetishism (Lande 1980) may be more accurate. Firesetting may occur as a part of normal development in small children (American Psychiatric Association 1980; Kaufman et al. 1961; Nurcombe 1969). The diagnosis of pyromania is often overlooked in small children, however, as firesetting is misinterpreted as resulting from curiosity or accidents. Meeting the criteria for pyromania does not exclude a second diagnosis (Gruber et al. 1981; Heath et al. 1976; Jasper et al. 1909; Stewart and Culver 1982; Vandersall and Wiener 1970). If the patient meets the criteria for another disorder, both diagnoses should be made on the appropriate axis.

Review of the Literature

Many papers were written before the criteria for pyromania were outlined in DSM-III. Some publications include all firesetters, and not just pyromaniacs. Most of the recent observations are about children, and this must be considered when reviewing the literature. Publications about adults are usually limited to hospitalized psychiatric patients or arsonists in the penal system.

The prevalence of pyromania is difficult to determine. Meeks's (1979) comment that it is rare may be as accurate as we can be at this time. Prevalence is usually reported as a percentage of a clinical population ranging from 2.3 to 15.5 percent. The age of onset has been observed from three years of age to adulthood. Yarnell (1940) stated that the peak age of incidence for juveniles occurred at 13 years with a rapid drop-off afterwards. Most reports indicate that over 90 percent of firesetters are male.

Family pathology and social disorganization have been described by numerous authors. Divorces are common and an increase in the frequency of adoption (Kuhnley et al. 1982) has been reported. Families of firesetters tend to be larger than families of non-firesetters; ordinal position is less important. Lower and middle socio-economic levels are more commonly reported, but pyromania can be found in all socio-economic groups. Heath et al. (1983) concluded that lower income was one of the few factors that differentiated firesetters from non-firesetters. Kuhnley et al. (1982) and Ritvo and Shanok (1983) found that abuse did not discriminate firesetters and non-firesetters, but Jayaprakash et al. (1984) disagreed, stating that physical abuse was the only discriminating variable.

Patients with pyromania may also discharge tension through other behaviors (Kaufman et al. 1961; Lewis and Yarnell 1951; Nurcombe 1969; Royers et al. 1971; Vandersall and Wiener 1970), such as stealing, running away, truancy, sexual activity, alcohol intoxication, psychosexual dysfunction, and resentment of authority figures. A significant number of patients display poor academic performance, learning disabilities, attention deficit disorders, speech problems, visual and other physical defects, neurologic disorders, enuresis, and cruelty to animals (Eissler 1972; Fras 1979; Lande 1980; Lewis and Yarnell 1951; Michaels 1955; Michaels and Steinberg 1952; Nurcombe 1969; Robbins and Robbins 1967; Vandersall and Wiener 1970). While many pathologic findings are commonly observed, recent studies concluded that they do not differentiate firesetters from other psychiatric disorders (Heath et al. 1983). The literature is mixed about whether the IQ is low in pyromania, but IQ does not differentiate firesetting from non-firesetting patients. Hellman and Blackman (1966) suggested that the triad of enuresis, firesetting, and cruelty to animals could be a predictor of adult aggressive crimes. Others have failed to validate this hypothesis (Justice et al. 1974; Ritvo and Shanok 1983). Externally, rather than internally directed aggression does differentiate firesetters from non-firesetters (Heath et al. 1983; Kolko et al. 1985; Kuhnley et al. 1982).

Psychodynamic Formulation

Formulations about pyromania have varied. Excellent reviews can be found in Lewis and Yarnell's (1951) classic monograph, and in more recent articles by Heath et al. (1976), Mavromatis and Lion (1977), Vreeland and Waller (1978), and Fineman (1980). Many authors have focused on the relationship of feelings such as anxiety, depression, aggression, revenge, sexual feelings, and various stresses to pyromania. Increasing tension prior to setting the fire and a reduction afterward have been reported. Kaufman et al. (1961) stated that firesetting was part of a restitutive process.

Several articles have been published in the psychoanalytic literature that include formulations about pyromania (Fenichel 1945; Freud [1905] 1958, 1932; Grinstein 1952; Klein 1932; Schmid 1914; Simmel 1949; Stekel 1924; Stone 1979). In classical psychoanalytic theory, pyromania includes a sexual perversion; children often masturbate while they watch the fire. Both boys and girls may set fires out of rage at a rejection, just as an adult may strike back when rejected by a lover, who, whether homosexual or heterosexual, usually represents a mother figure. Doing and undoing is seen in setting the fire followed by fantasies of being a fireman or extinguishing the fire. Often these patients' ambitions exceed their perceived abilities, and they fear that they cannot compete in the world. Yarnell (1940) and Lester (1975) emphasized aggression directed toward a family member who withheld love or who was a rival for parental love. Yarnell also noted that all had some sexual conflict. More recently there has been an increasing emphasis on earlier developmental periods. Kaufman et al. (1961) concluded that the level of instinctual development was primarily oral in the 30 children they studied. Vandersall and Wiener (1970) found the expression of primitive, destructive, aggressive drives but were unable to demonstrate erotic-libidinal wishes expressed in the act of firesetting.

Focusing on the relationship among events, Bumpass et al. (1974, 1983, 1985a, 1985b) emphasized how feelings and behavior provide an additional perspective. Firesetting behavior usually begins during a period of personal or family stress when the need for support is increased and the adaptive skills are compromised. Fires are set as part of a predictable, repetitive sequence that includes events, feelings, and firesetting behavior. This sequence is set in motion in children and some adolescents and adults when there is an increased need for nurturing, and a triggering event makes it obvious that this need will not be met. This evokes an initial feeling of displeasure that is usually described as a sad-lonely feeling. The child does not use the initial feeling as a signal affect and is often unaware of this feeling until it is explored with the therapist. The ego does not mobilize adaptive mechanisms and self-comforting does not occur. As a result, the initial feeling progresses rapidly to an intolerable level and is replaced by rage. A severe, temporary regression occurs in several areas of the personality resulting in motor restlessness and object splitting. The rage is directed toward the split, bad, or frustrating object, with intent to destroy the object. Trial action through fantasy may reduce the intensity of the rage, but the rage is only discharged when the fire is set. The rage is usually displaced onto a safer, inanimate object. Anxiety before setting the fire suggests an awareness of potential danger and punitive consequences. This does not alter the firesetting behavior, nor does subsequent guilt or remorse prevent setting fires in the future. In some adolescent and adult patients, the sequence is more likely to be precipitated by events that result in disappointment in the self and is associated with feelings of shame, inadequacy, and helplessness. This sequence occurs over a longer period of time, and the firesetting fantasies may persist for days before they are acted upon. These patients may report the fire or actively participate in bringing it under control. There is often a feeling of pride or power resulting from setting the fire, extinguishing the fire, or the response of others to the fire. This helps to restore self-esteem.

No pyromaniacs utilize the initial feeling as a signal affect. They demonstrate many of the characteristics of alexithymia (Krystal 1979; Lesser 1981; Nemiah 1970; Sifneos 1974). They also have difficulty recognizing and describing feelings in themselves and others. Feelings are often poorly differentiated, thinking tends to be concrete, and creative and synthetic functions seem diminished. There is less symbolic play by children, and play lacks creativity. Fantasies are not shared, and when they are, they are frequently primitive and destructive.

The differences in formulations about pyromania may reflect different theoretical orientation by the authors, but Meeks (1979) suggests it may be because the disorder is rare. He adds that children may represent an entirely different syndrome. Yarnell (1940) noted behavioral differences between older adolescent and younger firesetters. Children and young adults may suffer from different development arrests and deviation than older adolescents and adults, but it may be that development during adolescence has modified the picture.

Interventions

Publications about the treatment of pyromania were uncommon before 1970. Although many of the earlier papers described patients in hospital settings, there was little description about their therapy. Lewis and Yarnell (1951) stated treatment should be in a hospital suitable for such patients, but added that the ideal institution had not been organized. Others suggested that a restricted environment might be necessary in the initial phase of therapy.

Much of the treatment of pyromania described is behaviorist in orientation (Kellner 1982). Holland (1969) described a positive reinforcement program and threat of punishment by the father. Carstens (1982) used a work penalty threat. Royers et al. (1971) selected an aversive therapy model. Welsh (1974) and Jones (1981) used stimulus satiation. Stawar's (1976) technique included operantly structured fantasies and positive reinforcement. McGrath et al. (1979) incorporated social skills training, overcorrection, covert sensitization, and fire safety training. Kolko (1983) trained the mother to implement a program consisting of negative practice with corrective consequences and token reinforcement in order to satiate and teach proper control of behavior.

Morrison (1969), Eissler (1972), and Minuchin (1974) each described successful intervention with crisis-oriented family therapy. Each author reported on one patient, and follow-ups varied from four months to two years. Bumpass et al. (1983) reported a series of 29 consecutive firesetters treated in an outpatient setting utilizing a graphing interview technique. Simmel (1949) reports the psychoanalytic evaluation of a patient with pyromania and therapy by a probation officer utilizing psychoanalytic theory, and Stekel (1924) describes the psychoanalytic treatment of a pyromaniac. However, a computerized search of the literature finds no studies describing traditional outpatient psychotherapy as the primary method of intervention in pyromania. No reports are found about the use of medication except in relation to associated disorders such as attention deficit disorder.

The development of effective community-based intervention programs for juvenile firesetters began in the mid-1970s. Little has been published in the scientific journals about these programs. A handbook published by the Federal Emergency Management Agency (n.d.) lists a total of 64 programs and briefly describes eight of them. Many of these programs are based on the U.S. Fire Administration/National Fire Academy manual "Interviewing and Counseling Juvenile Firesetters" (1979) with additional supplemental techniques reflecting the orientation of members of the individual agencies. The Firehawk Program in San Francisco (Herbert 1985; Wooden 1985) is one of the better publicized programs. Sixty percent of their firesetters are young children who have accidentally set a fire. Intervention for this group includes working three hours with a firefighter, learning such skills as designing an escape route from the home and using a fire extinguisher. The 35 percent who have set multiple fires are provided long-term companionship with a male firefighter who sees the child for a few hours every week. The goal is to rechannel the child's energy and to help the child regain self-esteem.

The graphing interview technique is the basis for intervention programs in three major cities in Texas. It can also be used in an outpatient setting and requires no special equipment. It is not difficult to learn, and the therapists can become proficient with minimal experience. Details of the technique have been published previously (Bumpass et al. 1974, 1983, 1985a). Conceptually, it is similar to Arieti's (1963) method of intervention with hallucinations, delusions, and ideas of reference in patients with schizophrenia.

The goal of the graphing technique is to stop the firesetting behavior. Although firesetting may not be ego-alien at the time of the act, most state they wish they had not set the fire and want to stop the behavior. The patient is encouraged to express this desire during the initial contact. The graph is constructed with the assistance of the patient by taking a detailed history of the events, behaviors, and feelings associated with the firesetting behavior. These are correlated in chronological sequence on a line graph. This process is utilized to help the patient become aware of the cause-effect relationship between feelings and behaviors. The patient is told he or she must become aware of the initial feeling and utilize it as a signal that he or she is at risk to discharge his feelings through inappropriate behavior. When the initial feeling is utilized as a signal, the patient can substitute more adaptive methods of dealing with the feelings. He is also told that everyone has intense feelings at times, and that he must learn to tolerate them. If the patient understands and can describe these concepts, there is a high probability that the firesetting behavior will not recur. Other forms of inappropriate behavioral discharge of tension often stop. Although the firesetting behavior usually stops, this technique does not alter many of the underlying problems. The graphing technique should be thought of as a preparatory phase of therapy, and additional forms of therapy may be indicated. The graphing technique also helps determine if the DSM-III-R criteria for pyromania are met. Since outpatient intervention is so effective, firesetting is not an indication for a restricted environment unless the associated psychopathology is severe.

Follow-up Studies

There are few reports of follow-up studies. A recidivism rate of 28 percent was reported by Yarnell (1940) and 23 percent by Stewart and Culver (1982) in hospitalized firesetters. The behavioral approach and the family crisis methods are successful interventions, but the papers usually describe only one patient, and follow-up studies are of brief duration. A telephone follow-up evaluation of 26 out of 29 patients from an earlier study of the graphing technique (Bumpass et al. 1983) found that only two had set subsequent fires; the average period of follow-up was two and one half years, with some patients followed as long as five years. There was also a significant reduction in other types of acting-out behavior. Fine and Lourie (1979) reported that the city agencies in Vancouver were unable to coordinate efforts to control firesetting. Follow-up for the other community based programs have reported recidivism from 0 to 10 percent. Known recidivism for the Texas programs is less than 2 percent with the number of interventions nearing 1,000. Follow-up methodology in many of these programs is not good, but improvement in recidivism, comparing present methods with earlier methods, is impressive. Reduction in property loss related to fires set by children is another indicator of their success. Dallas had a reduction of $536,102 (48 percent) during the first six months of operation and a 38 percent reduction in the number of fires set. Houston had a reduction of $8,000,000 from all fire-related property damage during its first year, but did not separate fires by children from the total and acknowledges that other factors may have contributed to this reduction. Fire-related property loss increased in the areas not served by this program during the same period. When the program was extended to those areas, their property damage also dropped (Bumpass et al. 1985b).

Strachan (1981) reviewed the charts of 79 firesetters seen in a Scottish juvenile court and found that over 90 percent had not set subsequent fires. However, seventy-two had previously set only one fire, and their other disruptive behaviors continued.

The effectiveness of interventions in pyromania is difficult to evaluate, because the number of those who would have stopped setting fires spontaneously has not been adequately studied. It is clear, however, that many would continue to set fires without intervention. The recent literature suggests that recidivism in an out-patient population is usually 5 percent or less in children. The data about older adolescents and adults is scarce, as they are fewer in number and often channeled through the legal system. Higher recidivism in hospitalized patients may reflect a greater degree of impairment (Pfeffer 1983), rather than ineffectiveness in the approach to treatment.

Chapter 229

Intermittent Explosive Disorder

This syndrome refers to patients who present with "tempers" and who relate the occurrence of sudden and paroxysmal outbursts of aggression. These outbursts occur abruptly and seemingly without warning, though a thorough history often reveals premonitory signs and symptoms. Precipitating stimuli are present in the environment but rarely account for the severity of the rage. The attack usually subsides quickly, and the patient at this point is calm and remorseful. Generally, patients presenting with this syndrome have a long history of the disorder and are known in the community or by their families or employers to demonstrate temper-prone personalities. The diagnosis is rarely made during the aggressive phase, and by the time such patients are seen in the office or hospital, they are typically penitent or passive. The diagnostic criteria of the illness as described in DSM-III-R (American Psychiatric Association 1987) are shown in Table 1. Aggression is a common symptom among certain personality disorders, such as the borderline and antisocial personality. It may be seen in affective and thought disorders as well, such as during the acute phase of manic illness, or during a paranoid psychotic episode. These conditions must be ruled out in making the diagnosis of the intermittent explosive disorder. The aggressiveness seen in the intermittent explosive disorder is phenomenologically linked to the episodic nature of the illness and is not seen as part of a premorbid state or as part of characterological states. Certain conduct disorders in childhood, such as the attention deficit disorders, seem related to the intermittent explosive disorder because in both conditions tempers are a prominent behavior; the same is true of certain organic brain syndromes in which there is documented cerebral dysfunction, often accompanied by impulsivity and aggressiveness.

DSM-III (American Psychiatric Association 1980) placed diagnostic emphasis upon neurologic parameters within the associated features of the syndrome. Thus, the temper outbursts were viewed as "ictal" in nature, possibly reflective of limbic dysfunction or frank psychomotor epilepsy. Reference was made to EEG findings suggestive of such disease or to psychometric findings of organicity or neurological impairment, such as the "soft" signs often associated with brain dysfunction involving temporal or parietal lobe dysfunction. From the standpoint of history, emphasis was also placed upon the patient's description of head injury and episodes of unconsciousness or other trauma in infancy such as febrile convulsions which may have predisposed the patient to brain dysfunction.

The intermittent explosive disorder was reviewed for inclusion in DSM-III-R. At that time, it was felt by clinicians that the limited scientific literature on the condition did not warrant inclusion of the above neurologic parameters. Accordingly, the syndrome is simply described by itself as a disorder of impulse control. The more neurologically flavored aspect of temper proneness was shifted to the organic personality disorders where rage attacks can be diagnosed as manifestations of an explosive type of such a disorder.

Table 1.   DSM-III-R Diagnostic Criteria for Intermittent Explosive Disorder
A. Several discrete episodes of loss of control of aggressive impulses resulting in serious assaultive acts or destruction of property.
B. The degree of aggressiveness expressed during the episodes is grossly out of proportion to any precipitating psychosocial stressors.
C. There are no signs of generalized impulsiveness or aggressiveness between the episodes.
D. The episodes of loss of control do not occur during the course of a psychotic disorder, organic personality syndrome, antisocial or borderline personality disorder, conduct disorder, or intoxication with a psychoactive substance.

History of the Disorder

The earliest presentation of this disorder is by Menninger (1963) who described the third order of dyscontrol in *The Vital Balance*. The most systematic work on the disorder of aggression has been carried out by Monroe (1970) in *Episodic Behavior Disorders*; Monroe analyzed not only the behavior disorders but also affective and mood disturbances which he felt reflected limbic systems dysfunction. In DSM-I (American Psychiatric Association 1952), temper was a prominent part of the emotionally unstable personality, while in DSM-II (American Psychiatric Association 1968), temper proneness appeared among the explosive personality. DSM-III is the first time that temper proneness itself appears as a separate category within a larger group of impulse control disorders.

Clinical Experience

Violence is common in many psychiatric disorders and may be directed or unfocused, the product of willfulness or the accompaniment of cerebral disorganization. The intermittent explosive disorder is one specific form of aggression reflected in temper proneness; as such, it is usually repetitive and stereotyped in nature. Patients with the disorder typically relate recurring rage attacks which interfere with jobs or family relationships. Temper proneness is often longstanding in nature, and comes to clinical attention only after the violence has led to some threshold event, i.e., acute disruption of a marriage, legal difficulty, loss of a job. Patients with this disorder have often deferred treatment of the condition, and may or may not view it as dystonic. Spouses or employers, on the other hand, perceive the behavioral outbursts as intolerable. At the same time, all parties attest to the "Dr. Jekyl/Mr. Hyde" quality of the patient, that is, his good demeanor and gentleness when the outburst is over. This duality can be seen in some cases of spouse abuse where the patient is remorseful subsequent to the temper outburst.

A sole diagnosis of the intermittent explosive disorder is rare. There is usually coexisting character pathology and patients with the disorder typically have difficulty expressing aggression. Obsessive compulsive personalities, for example, may react to stress by showing all-or-none temper outbursts. Other concomitant diagnoses include alcoholism.

Research

The literature on the intermittent explosive disorder is sparse. Monroe (1970) has furnished the most comprehensive accounts of patients with episodic behavior disorders, including those with problems of aggression. Among his descriptions are many patients who manifest what would now formally be labelled as the intermittent explosive disorder.

Bach-y-Rita et al. (1971) studied a group of 130 violent patients seen in a general hospital psychiatric service. A certain subgroup of these patients had temper proneness and the authors have commented on the clinical features of their rages, including suicidal behavior.

Monopolis and Lion (1983) studied 20 cases of the intermittent explosive disorder as it appeared among 830 admissions to a general hospital. They found an incidence of the disorder of 2.4 percent. Cases were diagnosed chiefly on the basis of simple description as listed above and not on the basis of the many neurological parameters found in DSM-III.

Treatment

Both drugs and psychotherapy have been described as useful for the treatment of patients prone to rage outbursts, although drug treatment seems to be emphasized in the psychiatric literature (Kellner 1982). Lion (1972a, 1972b) has described the basic strategies of treating impulsive aggression and commented on the psychotherapeutic task of teaching these individuals how to recognize the affective state of rage and how to verbalize such anger and give vent to the fantasies surrounding it. He has also reviewed common psychodynamic themes which emerge in therapeutic work with violence-prone patients, such as sexuality and body boundaries. Group psychotherapy (Lion et al. 1977) for patients prone to tempers has also been described in the literature.

A variety of pharmacologic agents have been used to treat episodic aggressiveness (Lion 1976). The benzodiazepines (Lion 1978) have been utilized empirically to treat the explosiveness of those with certain character disorders, such as the paranoid personality that is prone to hypervigilance and outbursts of anger; this class of drugs is less apt to cause the subtle neurologic side effects associated with the use of antipsychotic agents. The central nervous system stimulants such as dextroamphetamine and methylphenidate have long been used (Allen et al. 1975) in the therapy of hyperactive children with attention deficit disorders and have been shown to have a beneficial effect on the temper component of this illness, as well as on other target symptoms. Use of such drugs in adults, however, would be hazardous because of concerns about addiction. Lithium has an antiaggressive effect (Sheard et al. 1976) and in controlled studies has been shown useful in the control of aggressive patients. However, the clinician would be best advised to use this drug in patients felt to have some affective component to their illness. The beta blockers such as propanolol (Yudofsky et al. 1981) and metoprolol (Mattes 1985) appear to be efficacious for impulsive aggression, particularly that associated with organic brain impairment. Mentally retarded patients with organicity have been found to improve on the medication. Reasons for the efficacy of lithium or beta blockers in aggression are still speculative and may be related to effects on noradrenergic systems and norepinephrine metabolism (Eichelman 1988).

Diphenylhydantoin and primidone (Monroe 1974) have previously been found useful for the treatment of aggression in which there exists an epileptoid basis. More recently, carbamazepine (Mattes 1984; Neppe 1982; Tunks and Dermer 1977) has been shown to be effective in the treatment of impulsive aggression presumed to be due to limbic system disturbance. Though the drug has potentially more serious toxicity than other agents, it may be the agent of choice for the violent patient whose aggressiveness is perceived as resulting from an epileptoid disturbance and in whom more conventional anticonvulsant drugs have failed.

Guidelines concerning the choice of pharmacologic agents remain imprecise; the studies listed above (with the exception of the work with lithium) are largely uncontrolled, and the clinician must make a decision about which drug to choose on an individual case basis, bearing in mind underlying etiologies of dysfunction (Eichelman 1988).

Chapter 230

Atypical Impulse Control Disorder

Diagnostic Considerations

The DSM-III (American Psychiatric Association 1980) diagnosis of atypical impulse control disorder was a residual classification applied to those individuals who demonstrate pathologic impulsivity which cannot be defined under more specific categories, that is, persons whose lack of behavioral control is not limited to a specific kind of impulse. These individuals have been referred to as having "character impulse disorders," as opposed to "symptom impulse disorders" (Frosch 1971), having an impulse disturbance that permeates their personality. They are described as infantile, immature, and intolerant of tension and anxiety. Wishes are experienced as urgent needs, and therefore gratification must come immediately. The actions resulting from such impulsivity may take many forms, including violence against others; property crimes (robbery, burglary, vandalism, shoplifting); drug abuse; sexual promiscuity; spending sprees; and a whole host of seemingly hedonistic, potentially self-destructive behaviors. Again, what characterizes such an individual is the extent to which impulsivity dominates many facets of his or her life.

People with various kinds of impulse disorder often use alcohol or drugs to try to control, soothe, and calm themselves.

Atypical impulse control disorder shares certain general characteristics with the other disorders of impulse control. These include failure to resist the impulse; a sense of increasing psychic tension culminating in the impulsive act; and an experience of pleasure or gratification at the time of committing the act. These acts are ego syntonic in that they are an undisguised representation of the immediate conscious wish of the individual. They are, at least initially, pleasurable, although genuine regret or guilt may be experienced shortly thereafter. Such qualities distinguish impulsive acts from the ego dystonic, highly symbolic, often ritualized behaviors which are characteristic of obsessive compulsive disorders.

As a symptom, impulsivity is an aspect of many psychiatric syndromes. The differential diagnosis must include mania; paranoia; psychotic disorders; and a variety of personality disorders that may, as one of their features, show impulsivity (e.g., borderline and histrionic). In mania, paranoia, and psychosis, other symptoms are also prominent, and the impulsivity is apt to be intermittent rather than pervasive. Similar distinctions can be made between the impulsive and other personality disorders. Patients with a history of organic brain injury (e.g., traumatic, vascular, toxic, or metabolic) are appropriately diagnosed as having an organic personality disorder. Recent attempts to associate impulsivity with regional brain dysfunction, specifically temporal lobe epileptiform activity, have generally yielded negative results (Leicester 1982).

History of Treatment

Individuals generally begin to demonstrate signs of an impulse-ridden character in childhood or adolescence. Developmentally speaking, it is traditionally thought that inconsistent deprivations and over-indulgence at very early stages of psychic development result in disturbances of the ability to delay gratification and prevent impulse from becoming action. In essence, impulsivity has been viewed as representative of psychic deficits rather than defense against structured and highly organized fantasies. As such, psychotherapy with these individuals has generally been of a supportive nature, emphasizing reality testing, pragmatic issues, and emotional support. Clarification, confrontation, and interpretation have been considered unproductive and potentially disorganizing to such patients (Frosch 1971).

Clinical Experiences

Severe impulse dyscontrol may result in serious difficulties both at home and at work. This may range from slight disturbance of social or occupational functioning to near total failure to maintain a job or social relations.

As mentioned above, patients with generalized impulsivity usually manifest such disturbances in childhood or adolescence. They may initially be brought to the attention of mental health professionals for discipline problems, school difficulties, or impaired peer relations. Conduct disorders, attention deficit disorder, and learning disabilities must all be considered as possible diagnoses in such cases.

Because of the ego syntonicity of the impulse control disorders, patients often may not seek out psychiatric intervention. Rather, they may come to treatment after altercations with the legal system, frequently under legal mandate, perhaps as a condition of probation or parole.

On the other hand, although impulsive acts are associated with pleasure in the short-term, these feelings are often short-lived. Relief and gratification can quickly be replaced by feelings of emptiness, regret, guilt, and self-depreciation. Fenichel (1945) described the depressive presentation of impulsive characters.

Research

A substantial body of research exists directed toward discovering the neurologic substrate of impulsive behavior (Bach-y-Rita et al. 1971; Leicester 1982; Monroe 1970). However, the vast majority of this work has focused specifically on violent, explosive behavior, not impulsivity as a pervasive trait. As mentioned previously, comprehensive neurologic evaluations can demonstrate abnormalities accounting for generalized impulsivity in only a small minority of cases. This leaves a large group in whom impulsivity seems to be an integral part of their personalities.

Research concerning attention deficit disorders (ADD) has shown that while only a minority of ADD children continue to suffer severe psychopathology, many show a persistence of symptoms as young adults, including impulsive personality traits

(Weiss et al. 1979). It is unclear to what extent generalized impulsiveness in adults can be accounted for as residual childhood ADD. However, impulsive individuals with such a history have been found to benefit from treatment with psychostimulants even as adults (Arnold et al. 1972; Mann and Greenspan 1976; Wender et al. 1981; Wood et al. 1976).

Treatment Modalities

Psychopharmacology

Impulsive acts of the type being discussed herein occur in response to a crescendo of psychic tension, which may build slowly or suddenly. This tension, unlike anxiety, does not motivate or inhibit adaptive behavior, but rather results in disorganization of cognition and disinhibition of behavioral controls. As a result, treatment of patients with generalized impulsivity with benzodiazepines or other anxiolytics should be carefully monitored because these agents may reduce rather than enhance behavioral controls (Frosch 1971). In fact, there have been some reports of paradoxical rage reactions when benzodiazepines have been used.

Certain impulsive patients seem to benefit from treatment with low doses of neuroleptic antipsychotic medications. Those who seem to respond best are those who are acutely aware of pre-impulse tension, and subjectively experience feelings of cognitive distortion and confusion prior to committing an impulsive act (Brinkley et al. 1979). Of course, documentation of a specific and clinically significant beneficial response to antipsychotic medications is crucial if long-term treatment is being considered, due to the potentially adverse consequences of chronic exposure to these agents.

Rifkin et al. (1972) described the beneficial effects of lithium carbonate in some impulse-ridden patients. In addition to generalized impulsivity, the lithium-responsive group was characterized by the presence of subaffective mood swings lasting from several hours to several days.

A substantial amount of clinical research indicates that a significant number of impulsive adults with a history of childhood attention deficit disorders will benefit from treatment with psychostimulants such as methylphenidate and pemoline without developing a tolerance to the beneficial effects.

The usefulness of carbamazepine in the treatment of complex partial (temporal lobe) seizures, which can include violent behaviors, is widely acknowledged. Patients with non-epileptogenic temporal lobe disorders, other localized brain lesions, or diffuse CNS disease processes can often experience non-ictal outbursts of temper and violence, and have benefited from treatment with carbamazepine (Luchins 1983). Recent investigations have shown that patients with episodic temper outbursts related to functional psychiatric disorders may also respond to treatment with carbamazepine (Mattes et al. 1984). This "calming" effect of the drug occurs in patients with episodic explosive disorders as well as those with other primary psychiatric disorders for which episodic violence and/or rage is a feature, including those with associated, generalized impulsivity. However, patients with atypical impulse control disorders do not seem to experience a reduction in their generalized impulsiveness with carbamazepine. In controlling episodic rage and violence, carbamazepine is used in typical anti-convulsant doses, and plasma levels should be monitored to ensure the adequacy of treatment. The usual precautions related to the drug's potential hematologic toxicity need to be observed, including periodic monitoring of the complete blood count.

The mixed beta-1 and beta-2 blocker, propranolol, has been used successfully for the treatment of uncontrolled rage outbursts and violent behavior in patients with both acute (Elliott 1977) and chronic (Yudofsky et al. 1981) organic brain syndromes of both structural and metabolic origins. The control of such behaviors by propranolol in patients with various functional psychiatric disorders has also been demonstrated (Mattes et al. 1984). As is the case with carbamazepine, patients with both episodic outbursts of temper and violence and atypical impulse control disorders show little, if any, improvement in their generalized impulsivity with propranolol. However, their explosiveness may be diminished by such treatment. Typical dosages of propranolol reported for the control of episodic rage/violence of both organic and functional etiology range from 60 to 320 mg/day. The selective beta-1 blocker, metoprolol, has recently been reported to be effective in controlling episodic rage and violence in patients who have not responded to either carbamazepine or propranolol (Mattes 1985).

Psychotherapy

A psychotherapeutic approach similar to that taken with borderline patients has been recommended for those with impulse control disorders (Frosch 1971). Because a defect in the capacity for delay often contributes to severe impairment of reality testing, the therapist can serve periodically to act as a reality tester for the patient, but not until a working relationship and therapeutic alliance have been established. Once this has developed, it becomes possible to point out the consequences of certain types of behavior and impose limits. In imposing limitations, the therapist must be willing to be tolerant when such restrictions are not observed. Later in treatment, it may be possible for the therapist to express displeasure openly at the patient's failure to accept limits. The fear of loss of love may be a powerful inducement to the patient to comply with behavioral restrictions. Above all, the therapist must be available to such patients as they often live from crisis to crisis. The telephone is an important means of maintaining contact. During vacations, the patient should have some means of reaching either the therapist or at least an associate with whom the patient is familiar, if only by name.

As a general rule, hospitalization can be reserved for times when patients experience severe, perhaps psychotic, distortions of reality testing which are persistent; when their impulses pose an imminent threat of danger to themselves or others; or when severe depressive symptoms are present, warranting aggressive somatic treatment.

To summarize, a significant number of individuals demonstrate impulsive behaviors which are often detrimental to themselves and others. Such impulsivity pervades many facets of the person's life, and may result in severe social and occupational dysfunction as well as adverse legal consequences. These individuals are immature, demanding, and intolerant of frustration, and in most cases their symptoms cannot be explained by the existence of a demonstrable organic brain disorder.

Many psychiatric disorders are associated with impulsive behavior. It is therefore important to rule out such illness before proceeding with the treatment of an individual with a presumed atypical impulse control disorder. Various psychotropic agents have been found to be helpful in such patients as determined by such factors as cognitive disorganization, emotional lability, and a history of attention deficit disorders in childhood. Such modalities work best when coupled with a psychotherapeutic approach which combines emotional support, availability for crisis intervention, assistance in reality testing, and behavioral limit setting.

Chapter 231

Trichotillomania

Diagnosis

The term trichotillomania was originally applied by the French physician, Hallopeau (1889), to a condition in which the patient manifested an "irresistible urge" to pull out his hair. Though typically from the scalp, the pulled hair can be from the eyebrows, eyelashes, beard, pubic, or axillary areas. The symptom has been noted to occur in individuals with diagnoses of schizophrenia, borderline personality, obsessive compulsive neurosis (Greenberg and Sarner 1965), retardation (Krishnan et al. 1985), and depression (Krishnan et al. 1984), but it may also occur in isolation or in connection with other compulsive symptoms such as nail biting and eating of the hair (trichophagy).

The incidence of the syndrome of trichotillomania is difficult to establish. There are no estimates of incidence available for hair pulling when considered a symptom of an underlying condition. As a presenting symptom, studies by child psychiatrists have found the incidence on the order of three in 500 and seven in 1,368, respectively, at different clinics (Krishnan et al. 1985; Mannino and Delgado 1969). Dermatologists are said to see a higher number of these patients, and Greenberg and Sarner (1965), who saw patients referred both from a private dermatologist and a dermatology clinic, as well as those referred from an inpatient and outpatient psychiatric service, collected a total of 19 cases in three years.

A summary of 17 studies reported in the U.S. and British literature over the last 30 years (Dalquist and Kalfus 1984; Delgado and Mannino 1969; De Luca and Holborn 1984; Fabbri and Dy 1974; Galski 1981, 1983; Gardner 1978; Greenberg and Sarner 1965; Krishnan et al. 1984, 1985; Lantz et al. 1980; Mannino and Delgado 1969; Oguchi and Miura 1977; Ottens 1981; Rowen 1981; Snyder 1980; Stevens 1984; Sticher et al. 1980) reveals a total of 48 patients, of which the proportion of females to males is nearly four to one. In 94 percent of the cases, the age of onset was under 17, with a slight preponderance in the 11–16 age group (n = 25) over ages 2–10 (n = 17). Of those for whom information is available, nearly half (13 of 27) did not present for treatment until after the age of 17, even though the behavior may have been occurring since childhood. By this time, the hair pulling had generally assumed the status of a habit, insofar as it was no longer necessarily associated with feeling states and experiences known to have precipitated the behavior in the past.

The severity of the symptom can extend from insignificant to very severe, and in some cases the patient may use wigs or scarves to cover the head. Feelings of shame and embarrassment can lead to social withdrawal. Permanent harm can be done to the scalp, limiting the ability of the follicles to regenerate healthy hair. The pattern can be of a linear or circular alopecia with a characteristic "moth-eaten" quality to the hair loss (Sticher et al. 1980). Occasionally, a biopsy is required to differentiate this condition from other medical conditions or in those situations where the patient denies the behavior.

Behavioral therapists approach the syndrome as a habit in the belief that "whatever initially produced compulsive hair-pulling behavior, there is a strong habitual component by the time the person presents for treatment" (De L Horne 1977, p 195).

History of Treatment

The treatment of trichotillomania, based as it is upon etiological hypotheses, has mirrored the history of modern psychiatry. In the 1940s, 1950s, and early 1960s, such papers as were written on the subject were psychodynamic in nature, explaining the symptom in psychoanalytic terms (Greenberg and Sarner 1965; Mannino and Delgado 1969). The behavior was often seen in children as a consequence of a loss or separation, typically from the mother, or when the child felt its relationship with the mother had been threatened. Accordingly, hair pulling, often in combination with trichophagy, was interpreted as representing fixations and regressions at multiple points in the oral, anal, and genital phases (Greenberg and Sarner 1965; Krishnan et al. 1985; Oguchi and Miura 1977; Sorosky and Sticher 1980).

The obvious treatment imperative following from such theory was intensive psychotherapy, which was found to be intermittently successful.

One paper in the late 1950s describes the successful use of chlorpromazine in two chronic schizophrenic individuals with "longstanding trichotillomania" (Childers 1958). However, no reports of the successful use of neuroleptics for trichotillomania as a syndrome rather than a symptom of a major illness appear in the literature.

Since the early 1960s, trends in the treatment of hair pulling have followed three different paths: behavioral, including hypnotic approaches; psychodynamic, including family-based approaches; and medication. In one well-documented case (Galski 1981, 1983), hypnosis was used as an adjunct to ongoing individual psychotherapy, which had reduced but not eliminated the symptom prior to hypnosis.

Specific Treatment Modalities

Medication

Two reports describe effective treatment of trichotillomania with tricyclic and monoamine inhibiting antidepressants, respectively (Krishnan et al. 1985; Snyder 1980). In one of these patients, the hair pulling coexisted with a frank depression and anxiety serious enough to result in hospitalization. Treatment was with appropriate dosages (30 mg/day) of isocarboxazid after the patient showed a dramatic response to this medication during a double-blind medication study. Hair pulling did not recur during the four months of hospitalization with medication. The authors suggest the possibility that hair pulling may at least on some occasions represent a "depressive equivalent."

In the other case (Snyder 1980), an adult female without signs of depression was treated successfully with amitriptyline. The dosage was raised to 150 mg/day over three months with a gradual reduction in symptoms according to a careful monitoring of hairs pulled per day. A three month follow-up revealed no more than five hairs pulled per day, no more than twice weekly. In addition, other symptoms present at the outset including nail biting, tongue chewing, and "compulsive eating binges" disappeared entirely.

The use of amitriptyline here was premised upon the hypothesis that obsessive compulsive behavior, including hair pulling, is associated with relative deficiencies of available brain serotonin. As a blocker of serotonin reuptake, amitriptyline increases available brain serotonin, which theoretically may lead to some relief from the compulsive symptoms. While this author notes the "often-overlapping relationship between obsessive-compulsive phenomena and depression," he hypothesizes that this "direct" effect of amitriptyline upon compulsions best explains the improvement in this case.

Medication of an entirely different sort may be employed in the dermatologic treatment of the affected area of skin. Anti-inflammatory agents and antihistaminics are often used in cases where inflammation and itching have either caused the hair-pulling behavior or resulted from it. At least one reported case of trichotillomania in a child resulted not from any psychiatric cause, but because of itching secondary to an underlying scalp condition.

Psychological treatment

Psychodynamic

Success has been achieved with psychodynamic and psychoanalytic therapies varying from brief and supportive dynamically oriented counseling of parents of child patients to analytically oriented treatment of the individual and intensive dealing with families. In several cases reported by Oguchi and Miura (1977), the onset of hair pulling followed some experience of loss within the relationship with the mother, either through physical separation or because of the competing presence of another child, such as a newborn. When the family was made aware of the connection between these developments and the onset of symptoms, increased attention paid to the patient was successful in every case in eliminating the symptom of hair pulling.

Mannino and Delgado (1969) reviewed the literature on treatment of trichotillomania in children and found only one report of the use of psychoanalysis, which was successful in two cases. Complete or moderate success in treating adolescents and adults has been reported by, among others, Sticher et al. (1980) and Sorosky and Sticher (1980), who supplemented the treatment of both of their patients with family sessions and peer group therapy. Galski (1981, 1983) also noted some improvement in a 26-year-old woman after 10 months of analytically oriented psychotherapy, but it was not until hypnosis was applied as an adjunct that the hair pulling ceased entirely.

The rationale for individual psychotherapy is based upon viewing hair pulling as symbolic behavior. One view is that the hair serves as a transitional object and that pulling it defends against fears of separation. Another is that it represents the penis, so that hair pulling becomes a symbolic castration which can be undone when the hair grows back. Hair pulling may also represent the struggle for control over one's own body when the relationship to authority has not been resolved by the individual.

Many see the underlying issue as the presence of a "symbiotic" relationship between child and parent, making it impossible for the child to negotiate properly the separation and individuation phases of normal development. Rather complete descriptions of the psychotherapy can be found in the reports of Galski (1983) and Sorosky and Sticher (1980).

Behavioral

Numerous cases have appeared in the cognitive and behavioral therapy literature regarding hair pulling. The authors typically define the hair-pulling behavior as a "maladaptive habit" (De Luca and Holborn 1984). One author (Ottens 1981) believes that cognitive distortions play a role in the condition as well and has suggested a "multifaceted" treatment involving both behavioral and cognitive treatments. Elements of both operant and classical conditioning have been employed in dealing with hair-pulling behavior. The rationale for treatment is that maladaptive habits can be extinguished by the application of behavior techniques over time.

The large number of behavioral techniques which have been utilized in this area can be subsumed into five general categories: feedback to provide enhanced awareness; positive and negative reinforcement of non-pulling behavior and pulling behavior, respectively; aversive conditioning; relaxation techniques to achieve general anxiety reduction; and competing response.

Heightened awareness is achieved through various techniques, including instructing the patient to keep track of all hair-pulling incidents and, often, to save and bring in all pulled hairs. In addition, the individual is asked to speak out loud about the behavior while enacting it, calling attention to the earliest part of the pulling behavior ("early warning"), and enlisting family members to alert the patient to the behavior. It is felt that habits often persist below the threshold of awareness, so heightening awareness combats the habitual behavior.

Positive reinforcement may be achieved by praising the patient for successes and training the patient to praise himself. Especially in children, small monetary incentives may be used in conjunction with systematic study of the scalp for signs of hair regrowth (Gardner 1978). Negative reinforcement techniques center around instructing family and friends to ignore hair-pulling behavior.

A variety of aversive techniques are used in connection with hair pulling. De L Horne (1977) used electrical shocks to both hands as his patient viewed videotapes of hair-pulling behavior. Stevens (1984) utilized a rubber band around each wrist that the patient plucked and snapped to punish the pulling hand after each episode of pulling.

Relaxation techniques have been used in conjunction with more specific attacks upon the symptom and appear not to be totally effective in and of themselves (De L Horne 1977; De Luca and Holborn 1984). Hypnosis is an exception to this rule and is discussed in further detail below.

Competing response training has been defined as aimed at getting the patient to practice movements that are topographically incompatible with the problem behavior, such as clenching the fists for several minutes whenever the urge to pull was experienced. Self-administered aversive stimuli can also function as competing responses. In some cases, the use of head coverings, mittens, or tape on the hands during the night are successful in cutting down hair pulling by interposing physical barriers to the act.

Adherents of cognitive approaches have supplemented these behavioral approaches by encouraging awareness of "maladaptive inner speech by which . . . (the patient) would . . . give herself permission to pull" (Ottens 1981, p 78). Patients develop self-dialogues in which they warn themselves of high risk situations and dispute with themselves the "irrational beliefs" felt to be part of the hair-pulling cycle.

Behavioral treatments attempt to isolate the particular behavior and treat it as an entity. The best results appear to have been obtained in those patients in whom this behavior does exist in isolation. In cases where other difficulties complicate the patient's life, the use of other modalities of therapy is necessary in conjunction with these techniques and the results may be less definitive and less permanent (De L Horne 1977).

Hypnosis

Several papers have appeared in the literature regarding the treatment of trichotillomania using hypnosis (Fabbri and Dy 1974; Galski 1981; Gardner 1978; Rowen 1981). As in the case of other behavioral techniques, the symptom is seen as a compulsive behavior or a habit, even in those cases where a dynamic association to existing or prior experiences of anxiety or loss is present. Several authors see the symptom as part of a control struggle, which connects the symptom to roots in the anal stage. They take pains in the hypnotic technique to allow for the patient to make choices, in order to reinforce the patient's sense of control.

The specific approaches include the use of suggestions aimed toward relaxation, habit substitution, and negative conditioning. The latter technique, where the patient was told he would get sick to his stomach and retch upon pulling his hair, was only briefly successful. In the case of a child of 10, the symptom was successfully treated using suggestions that enhanced awareness of the upcoming behavior and counteracted the desire with "a powerful thought from the part of her that wanted pretty hair: 'Stop! Please do not hurt' " (Gardner 1978, p 839). In most cases, self-hypnosis was encouraged as a reinforcement for whenever the patient feels the need.

Hypnosis alone may not be effective in cases where the individual is not motivated to stop the behavior, where considerable secondary gain is achieved from the symptoms, or when the symptom is binding severe anxiety or depression. In such cases, hypnosis may be useful as an adjunct to psychotherapy, as in the case described by Galski (1981). In another case, symptom disappearance was achieved only when the other hypnotic techniques were supplemented by age regression through which the original stimulus to the habit, which had continued for years into adulthood, was revealed (Rowen 1981). Fabbri et al. (1974) supplemented their other techniques of progressive relaxation, decreased need to pull the hair, and substitution of touching the hair for pulling it, with a suggestion facilitating discussion of "personal problems" with the therapist. This led to a "spontaneous abreaction of feelings" from years before when the habit had been established. This experience appears to have been the finally curative one (Fabbri and Dy 1974).

Thus hypnosis, as in other behavioral therapies, relies upon suggestions that promote increased awareness of the habit, increased sensitivity to the discomfort and disfiguring aspects of the hair pulling, substitution of other responses, and an enhanced sense of control by the patient.

Family Approaches

While many dynamic and even behavioral studies of patients with this disorder point to its origins within the family, only one report (Lantz et al. 1980) describes the use of family treatment techniques to deal with it. In the four families treated, the authors found the symptom to be employed by the families as a device to avoid possible disruption from conflict. The symptomatic members in two families were seen as children acting as marital therapists, and the symptomatic child of a third family was seen as gratifying the needs of a symbiotic mother. In another case, serious family problems had led to splitting and scapegoating of the eight-year-old identified patient.

In all cases, the families were seen as "enmeshed" and using the children's symptoms to avoid threatening the equilibrium. Treatment, which was successful in abolishing the symptom in all cases, centered upon manifesting the underlying conflicts between the parents and helping to negotiate them in front of the patient. A decrease in the child's anxiety level regarding family conflict was achieved and led to full remission of the hair pulling without any supplemental treatment. In another case, the strategy was to weaken the dependency of the mother upon the symptomatic daughter by strengthening the ties of each with other family members and with outside persons and activities.

While the hair pulling is conceptualized as playing a role within the family, family meetings may be supplemented by a variety of other techniques, including meetings with subgroups of the whole family or supplementary treatment outside the family altogether. The most effective treatment may be that offered to a family member other than the identified patient or to a subgroup of the family that does not include him or her.

Efficacy, Evaluations, Recommendations

The treatment literature is relatively sparse for the syndrome of trichotillomania, but every technique reported has seen success with at least the reported cases, not unlike the general tendency to report success, and ignore failure.

In those cases where hair pulling appears to be a symptom of a more pervasive underlying disease, it is the underlying disease that should be treated, as recommended elsewhere in this volume. In those where the symptom presents as a syndrome in and of itself, considerable judgment is required of the clinician in his choice of treatments.

Trichotillomania appears to be a symptom or syndrome that arises most commonly in childhood or adolescence as a compulsive but symbolic behavior reflective of a developmental crisis. The clinician is thus well advised to investigate the child's emotional and psychological status within the family for signs of difficulty, especially concentrating on the mother-child relationship. In adolescents, the struggle for separation and individuation may be more difficult because of conflicted and controlling parental figures and lead to symptoms. Here, the treatment of choice ranges from counseling for parents and child to intensive family and individual therapy.

Trichotillomania, though often starting in childhood, may show long remissions with reappearance in young adulthood or later. In such situations, individual psychotherapy may not be the treatment of choice for rapid remission of symptoms. It is often most productive at these points to treat the symptom as a residue of past dynamic conflict, that is, a habit. Here, behavioral techniques including hypnosis have been successful in removing the habit entirely or decreasing the incidence significantly. On the other hand, case reports suggest that when underlying dynamic issues need to be addressed, behavioral techniques alone will be inadequate for lasting relief.

Whether or not hair pulling is associated with frank depression in adults, its status as a compulsive symptom makes a trial with antidepressants feasible, especially if neither psychotherapy nor behavioral techniques lead to success.

Chapter 232

Conclusion

Although the impulse disorders "not elsewhere classified" would appear to be a wastebasket of leftover psychiatric syndromes, fundamentally they represent people who are beset with patterns or discrete episodes of psychological and psychobiologic deficit, people who act rather than think or feel, and people who generally are difficult to treat.

As our knowledge of neurobiology and neurophysiology expands, the promise of psychopharmacology for some of these disorders will be tested. Certainly, regulation, control, and discharge—psychological concepts—are mediated through brain chemistry. We can say a good deal about these impulse-ridden individuals because of the wealth of clinical experience in evaluating and treating them using psychological methods. The psychoanalytic understandings of drive and defense, of fantasy and perversion, of regulation and discharge, of negative transference and traumatic over-stimulation, and of acting out have been supplemented with more recent concepts of progressive neutralization, primitive narcissism, the selfobject, idealization and deidealization, fragmentation and cohesion, empathy and transmuting internalization.

Yet these disorders are similar, too, in the kinds of countertransference responses they provoke: conscious and unconscious feelings; the fear of acting out; but, most significantly, the unconscious fear of the content of our fantasies. The developmental arrest these patients represent confront the therapist with the fear everyone has of regression.

We need to educate the public and ourselves about the need for more adequate assessment and treatment programs and about the recognition that "not elsewhere classified" was coined because these people lack our structure. Because these patients are not readily treatable, we need to teach about these patients, discuss them, and supervise diagnostic and treatment cases, each of which are sometimes difficult to do.

References

Section 241
Impulse Control Disorders Not Elsewhere Classified

Aichhorn A: Wayward Youth (1925). New York, Viking Press, 1935

Aichhorn A: Delinquency and Child Guidance—Selected Papers. New York, International Universities Press, 1964

Alexander F, Staub H: The Criminal, the Judge and the Public: A Psychological Analysis (1931). New York, Collier Books, 1956

Allen RD, Safer D, Covi L: Effects of psychostimulants on aggression. J Nerv Ment Dis 160:138–145, 1975

American Psychiatric Association: Diagnostic and Statistical Manual of Mental Disorders, 1st ed (DSM-I). Washington, DC, American Psychiatric Association, 1952

American Psychiatric Association: Diagnostic and Statistical Manual of Mental Disorders, 2nd ed (DSM-II). Washington, DC, American Psychiatric Association, 1968

American Psychiatric Association: Diagnostic and Statistical Manual of Mental Disorders, 3rd ed (DSM-III). Washington, DC, American Psychiatric Association, 1980

American Psychiatric Association: Diagnostic and Statistical Manual of Mental Disorders, 3rd ed, revised (DSM-III-R). Washington, DC, American Psychiatric Association, 1987

Arieti S: Hallucinations, delusions, and ideas of reference treated with psychotherapy. Am J Psychiatry 16:52–59, 1963

Arnold LE, Strobl D, Weisenberg A: The hyperkinetic adult. JAMA 222:693–694, 1972

Bach-y-Rita G, Lion JR, Climent C, et al: Episodic dyscontrol: a study of 130 violent patients. Am J Psychiatry 127:1473–1478, 1971

Baittle B, Kobrin S: On the relationship of a characterological type of delinquent to the milieu. Psychiatry 27:6–16, 1964

Bergler E: The Psychology of Gambling. New York, International Universities Press, 1985

Bird B: A specific peculiarity of acting out. J Am Psychoanal Assoc 5:630–647, 1957

Bloch DA: The delinquent integration. Psychiatry 15:297–303, 1952

Blos P: The concept of acting out in relation to the adolescent process, in A Developmental Approach to Problems of Acting Out. Edited by Rexford EN. New York, International Universities Press, 1966, pp 118–136

Boyd WH, Bolen DW: The compulsive gambler and spouse in group psychotherapy. Int J Group Psychother 20:77–90, 1970

Brinkley JR, Bertman BD, Friedel RO: Low-dose neuroleptic regimens in the treatment of borderline patients. Arch Gen Psychiatry 36:319–326, 1979

Bumpass ER, Via BM, Forgotson JH, et al: Graphs to facilitate the formation of a therapeutic alliance. Am J Psychother 28:500–516, 1974

Bumpass ER, Fagelman FD, Brix RJ: Intervention with children who set fires. Am J Psychother 37:328–345, 1983

Bumpass ER, Brix RJ, Reichland RE: Triggering events, sequential feelings and fire-setting behavior in children. In Proceedings for Papers and New Research Posters. J Am Acad Child Psychiatry 10:18, 1985a

Bumpass ER, Brix RJ, Preston D: A community based program for juvenile firesetters. Hosp Community Psychiatry 36:529–533, 1985b

Carstens C: Application of a work penalty threat in the treatment of a case of juvenile firesetting. J Behav Ther Exp Psychiatry 13:159–161, 1982

Casper RC, Eckert ED, Halmi KA, et al: Bulimia: its incidence and clinical importance in patients with anorexia nervosa. Arch Gen Psychiatry 37:1030–1035, 1980

Childers RT Jr.: Report of two cases of trichotillomania of long standing duration and their response to chlorpromazine. J Clin Exp Psychopath 19:141–144, 1958

Custer RL: Gambling and addiction, in Drug Dependent Patients, Treatment, and Research. Edited by Craig RJ, Baker SL. Springfield, Ill, Charles C. Thomas Publishers, 1982a

Custer RL: An overview of compulsive gambling, in Addictive Disorders Update: Alcoholism, Drug Abuse, Gambling. Edited by Carone PA, Yolles SF, Kiefer SN, et al. New York, Human Sciences Press, 1982b

Custer RL: Profile of the pathological gambler. J Clin Psychiatry 45:35–38, 1984

Custer RL, Milt H: When Luck Runs Out. New York, Facts on File, 1985

D'Elia A, Fugere R: Women who shoplift share characteristics with women who commit fraud, study shows. Psychiatric News. American Psychiatric Association, Feb 7, 1986, p 12

Dalquist LM, Kalfus GR: A novel approach to assessment in the treatment of childhood trichotillomania. J Behav Ther Exp Psychiatry 15:47–50, 1984

De L Horne D: Behaviour therapy for trichotillomania. Behav Res Ther 15:192–196, 1977

De Luca RV, Holborn SW: A comparison of relaxation training and competing response training to eliminate hair pulling and nail biting. J Behav Ther Exp Psychiatry 15:67–70, 1984

Delgado RA, Mannino FV: Some observations on trichotillomania in children. J Am Acad Child Adolesc Psychiatry 8:229–246, 1969

Eichelman B: Toward a rational pharmacotherapy for aggression. Hosp Community Psychiatry 39:31–39, 1988

Eissler RM: Crisis intervention in the family of a firesetter. Psychother: Theory, Res, Pract 9:76–79, 1972

Elliott FA: Propranolol for the control of belligerent behavior following acute brain damage. Ann Neurol 1:489–191, 1977

Fabbri R Jr, Dy AJ: Hypnotic treatment of trichotillomania: two cases. Int J Clin Exp Hypn 22:210–215, 1974

Fenichel O: The Psychoanalytic Theory of Neurosis. New York, Norton Co, 1945

Fine S, Lourie D: Juvenile firesetters: do the agencies help? Am J Psychiatry 136:433–435, 1979

Fineman KR: Firesetting in childhood and adolescence. Psychiatr Clin North Am 3 (3):483–499, 1980

Fras I: Typical firesetter "unchecked" hyperkinetic teenager. Clin Psychiatry News 11:11, 1979

Freud A: Dissociality, delinquency, criminality, in Normality and Pathology in Childhood: Assessment of Development. New York, International Universities Press, 1965

Freud S: Three essays on the theory of sexuality (1905), in Standard Edition, vol 7. Edited by Strachey J. London, Hogarth Press, 1958

Freud S: The acquisition of power over fire. Int J Psychoanal 13:405–410, 1932

Friedlander K: The Psycho-Analytical Approach to Juvenile Delinquency: Theory, Case Studies, Treatment. New York, International Universities Press, 1960

Frosch J: Technique in regard to some specific ego defects in treatment of borderline patients. Psychiatr Q 45:216–220, 1971

Galski TJ: The adjunctive use of hypnosis in the treatment of trichotillomania: a case report. Am J Clin Hypn 23:198–201, 1981

Galski TJ: Hair pulling (trichotillomania). Psychoanal Rev 70:331–346, 1983

Gamblers Anonymous. Los Angeles, Gamblers Anonymous, 1977

Gammon C: Tales of self-destruction. Sports Illustrated 64:64–72, March 10, 1986

Gardner GG: Hypnotherapy in the management of childhood habit disorders. J Pediatr 92:838–840, 1978

Gauthier J, Pellerin D: Management of compulsive shoplifting through covert sensitization. J Behav Ther Exp Psychiatry 13:73–75, 1982

Glover E: On the desirability of isolating a "functional" (psychosomatic) group of delinquent disorders. Br J Delinquency 1:104–112, 1950

Glover E: The Roots of Crime: Selected Papers on Psychoanalysis, vol 2. New York, International Universities Press, 1960

Glover JH: A case of kleptomania treated by covert sensitization. Br J Clin Psychol 24:213–214, 1985

Greenberg HR, Sarner CA: Trichotillomania: symptom and syndrome. Arch Gen Psychiatry 12:482–489, 1965

Grinstein A: Stages in the development of control of fire. Int J Psychoanal 33:416–420, 1952

Gruber AR, Heck ET, Mintzeer E: Children who set fires: some background and behavioral characteristics. Am J Orthopsychiatry 51:484–488, 1981

Hallopeau X: Alopecia par grottage (trichomania ou trichotillomania). Ann Dermatol Syphilology 10:440, 1889

Heath GA, Gayton WF, Hardesty VA: Childhood firesetting. Can Psychiat Assn J 21:229–237, 1976

Heath GA, Hardesty VA, Goldfine PE: Childhood firesetting: an empirical study. J Am Academy Child Adolesc Psychiatry 22:370–374, 1983

Hellman DS, Blackman N: Enuresis, firesetting, and cruelty to animals: a triad predictive of adult crime. Am J Psychiatry 122:1431–1435, 1966

Herbert W: Dousing the kindlers. Psychol Today 14:28, 1985

Hoffer W: Deceiving the deceiver, in Searchlights on Delinquency. Edited by Eissler KR. New York, International Universities Press, 1949, pp 150–155

Holland CJ: Elimination by the parents of firesetting behavior in a 7-year-old boy. Behav Res Ther 7:135–137, 1969

Hudson JI, Pope HG Jr, Jonas JM, et al.: Phenomenologic relationship of eating disorders to major affective disorder. Psychiatry Res 9:345–354, 1983

Jasper K, Heimweh, Verbrechen H: Gross Archiv fur Kriminal-Anthropologie und Kriminalistik. Leipzig, Saxony, East Germany, 1909

Jayaprakash S, James J, Panitch D: Special report: multifactorial assessment of hospitalized children who set fires. Child Welfare 63:74–78, 1984

Johnson AM, Szurek SA: The genesis of antisocial acting out in children and adults. Psychoanal Q 21:323–343, 1952

Jones FDE: Therapy for firesetters. Am J Psychiatry 138:261–262, 1981

Justice V, Justice R, Kraft L: Early warning signs of violence: is a triad enough? Am J Psychiatry 131:457–459 1974

Kaufman I, Heims LW, Reiser DE: A reevaluation of the psychodynamics of firesetting. Am J Orthopsychiatry 22:63–72, 1961

Kellner R: Disorders of impulse control (not elsewhere classified), in Treatment of

Mental Disorders. Edited by Greist JH, Jefferson JW, Spitzer RL. New York, Oxford University Press, 1982, pp 398–418

Klein M: Psychoanalysis of Children. London, Hogarth Press, 1932

Kohut H: Forms and transformations of narcissism. J Am Psychoanal Assoc 14:243–272, 1966

Kohut H: The psychoanalytic treatment of narcissistic personality disorders. Psychoanal Study Child 23:86–113, 1968

Kohut H: The Analysis of the Self. New York, International Universities Press, 1971

Kohut H: Thoughts on narcissism and narcissistic rage. Psychoanal Study Child 27:360–400, 1972

Kohut H: The Restoration of the Self. New York, International Universities Press, 1977

Kohut H: How Does Analysis Cure? Chicago, University of Chicago Press, 1984

Kolko DJ: Multicomponent parental treatment of firesetting in a six year old boy. J Behav Ther Exp Psychiatry 14:349–353, 1983

Kolko DJ, Kazdin AE, Meyer EC: Aggression and psychopathology in childhood firesetters: parent and child reports. J Consult Clin Psychol 53:377–385 1985

Krishnan KR, Davidson J, Miller R: MAO inhibitor therapy in trichotillomania associated with depression: case report. J Clin Psychiatry 45:267–268, 1984

Krishnan KR, Davidson J, Guajardo C: Trichotillomania—a review. Compr Psychiatry 26:123–128, 1985

Krystal H: Alexithymia and psychotherapy. Am J Psychother 33:17–31, 1979

Kuhnley EF, Hendred R, Quinlan DM: Fire-setting by children. J Am Acad Child Psychiatry 21:560–563, 1982

Lande SD: A combination of orgasmic reconditioning and covert sensitization in the treatment of a fire fetish. J Behav Ther Exp Psychiatry 11:291–296, 1980

Lantz JE, Early JP, Pillow WE: Family aspects of trichotillomania. J Psychiatric Nursing 18:32–37, 1980

Leicester J: Temper tantrums, epilepsy and episodic dyscontrol. Br J Psychiatry 141:262–266, 1982

Lesieur HR: The compulsive gambler's spiral of options and involvement. Psychiatry 42:79–87, 1979

Lesser IM: Review article: a review of the alexithymia concept. Psychosom Med 43:531–543, 1981

Lester D: Firesetting. Corrective and Soc Psychiat and J Applied Behav Technology 21:22–26, 1975

Lewis NDC, Yarnell H: Pathological firesetting (pyromania) (monograph). J Nerv Ment Dis 82:8–26, 1951

Linden RD, Pope HG, Jonas JM: Pathological gambling and major affective disorder: preliminary findings. J Clin Psychiatry (in press)

Lion JR: The role of depression in the treatment of aggressive personality disorders. Am J Psychiatry 129:347–349, 1972a

Lion JR: Evaluation and Management of the Violent Patient. Springfield, Ill, Charles C Thomas Publishers, 1972b

Lion JR: Conceptual issues for the use of drugs in the treatment of aggression in man. J Nerv Ment Dis 160:76–81, 1976

Lion JR: The Art of Medicating Psychiatric Patients. Baltimore, Williams and Wilkins, 1978

Lion JR, Christopher R, Madden DJ: Group psychotherapy with violent outpatients. Int J Group Psychother 27:67–74, 1977

Luchins DJ: Carbamazepine for the violent psychiatric patient. Lancet 1:766, 1983

Mann HB, Greenspan SI: The identification and treatment of adult brain dysfunction. Am J Psychiatry 133:1013–1017, 1976

Mannino FV, Delgado RA: Trichotillomania in children: a review. Am J Psychiatry 126:87–93, 1969

Marc M: Considerations medico-legales su la monomanie et particulierement sur las monomanie incendiare. Ann d'hygiene publique et de medecine legale 10:367, 1833 (Chapter De la monomanie incendiare, p 398. English paraphrase in Esquirol's Mental Maladies, pp 35–62)

Marohn RC: Trauma and the delinquent. Adolesc Psychiatry 3:354–361, 1974

Marohn RC: The "juvenile impostor": some thoughts on narcissism and the delinquent. Adolesc Psychiatry 5:186–212, 1977

Marohn RC: The negative transference in the treatment of juvenile delinquents. Ann Psychoanal 9:21–42, 1981

Marohn RC, Dalle-Molle D, McCarter E, et al: Juvenile Delinquents: Psychodynamic Assessment and Hospital Assessment. New York, Brunner/Mazel, 1980

Marohn RC, Locke EM, Rosenthal R, et al: Juvenile delinquents and violent death. Adolesc Psychiatry 10:147–170, 1982

Mattes JA: Carbamazepine for uncontrolled rage outbursts. Lancet 2:1164–1165, 1984

Mattes JA: Metoprolol for intermittent explosive disorder. Am J Psychiatry 142:1108–1109, 1985

Mattes JA, Rosenberg J, Mays D: Carbamazepine versus propranolol in patients with uncontrolled rage outbursts. Psychopharmacol Bull 20:98–100, 1984

Mavromatis M, Lion JR: A primer on pyromania. Dis Nerv Syst 38:954–955, 1977

McCormick RA, Russo AM, Ramirez LF, et al: Affective disorders among pathological gamblers seeking treatment. Am J Psychiatry 141:215–218, 1984

McGrath P, Marshal PG, Prior K: A comprehensive treatment program for a firesetting child. J Behav Ther Exp Psychiatry 10:69–70, 1979

Meeks JE: Behavioral and antisocial disorders, in Basic Handbook of Child Psychiatry, vol. 2. Edited by Noshpitz JD. New York, Basic Books, Inc, 1979, pp 482–530

Menninger K: The Vital Balance. New York, Viking Press, 1963

Monroe RR: Episodic Behavior Disorders. Cambridge, Harvard University Press, 1970

Michaels JH: Disorders of Character. Springfield, Ill, Charles C Thomas, 1955

Michaels JH, Steinberg A: Persistent enuresis and juvenile delinquency. Br J Delinq 3:114–123, 1952

Minuchen S: Families and Family Therapy. Cambridge, Mass, Harvard University Press, 1974

Molnar G, Keitner L, Harwood B: A comparison of partner and solo arsonists. J Forensic Sci 29:574–583, 1984

Monkmoller X: Zur Psychopathologie des Brandstifters. Arch Kriminol Lubeck, West Germany 48:193–312, 1912

Monopolis S, Lion JR: Problems in the diagnosis of the intermittent explosive disorder. Am J Psychiatry 140:1200–1202, 1983

Monroe RR: Episodic Behavioral Disorders. Cambridge, Mass, Harvard University Press, 1970

Monroe RR: Anticonvulsants in the treatment of aggression. J Nerv Ment Dis 160:119–126, 1974

Morrison G: Therapeutic intervention in a child psychiatric emergency service. J Am Acad Child Adolesc Psychiat 8:542–558, 1969

Moskowitz JA: Lithium and lady luck. NY State J Med 80:785–788, 1980

Nemiah JC: Denial revisited: reflections on psychosomatic theory. Psychother and Psychosom 26:140–147, 1970

Neppe VM: Carbamazepine for the violent psychiatric patient. Lancet 2:334, 1982

Nurcombe B: Children who set fires. Med J Aust 1:579–584, 1969

Offer D, Marohn RC, Ostrov E: The Psychological World of the Juvenile Delinquent. New York, Basic Books, 1979

Oguchi T, Miura S: Trichotillomania: its psychopathological aspect. Compr Psychiatry 18:177–182, 1977

Ornstein A, Gropper C, Bogner JZ: Shoplifting: an expression of revenge and restitution. Annual Psychoanalysis 11:311–331, 1983

Ottens AJ: Multifaceted treatment of compulsive hair pulling. J Behav Ther Exp Psychiatry 12:77–80, 1981

Pfeffer CR: Predictors of assaultiveness in latency age children. Am J Psychiatry 140:31–35, 1983

Psychiatric News: Disorder not defense for tax evasion. American Psychiatric Association, Nov 1, 1985, pp 1, 23

Redl F: When We Deal with Children. New York, Free Press, 1966

Redl F, Wineman D: The Aggressive Child. Glencoe, Ill, Free Press, 1957

Rifkin A, Quitkin F, Carillo C, et al: Lithium carbonate in emotionally unstable character disorder. Arch Gen Psychiatry 27:519–523, 1972

Ritvo E, Shanok S: Firesetting and nonfiresetting delinquents: a comparison of neuropsychiatric, psychoeducational, experiential, and behavioral characteristics. Child Psychiatry Hum Dev 13:259–267, 1983

Robbins E, Robbins L: Arson with special reference to pyromania. NY State J Med 67:795–798, 1967

Rowen R: Hypnotic age regression in the treatment of self-destructive habit: trichotillomania. Am J Clin Hypn 23:195–197, 1981

Royers FL, Flynn WF, Oseadea BS: Case history: aversion therapy for firesetting by a deteriorated schizophrenic. Behav Ther 2:229–232, 1971

Russo AM, Taber JI, McCormick RA, et al: An outcome study of an inpatient treatment program for pathological gamblers. Hosp Community Psychiatry 35:823–826, 1984

Schmid H: Zur Psychologie der Brandstifter. Psychologische Abhandlungen 1:80–179, 1914

Sheard MH, Marini JL, Bridges CI, et al: The effects of lithium on impulsive aggressive behavor in man. Am J Psychiatry 133:1409–1413, 1976

Sifneos PE: A reconsideration of the psychodynamic mechanisms in psychosomatic symptom formation in view of recent clinical observations. Psychother Psychosom 24:151–155, 1974

Simmel E: Incendiarism, in Searchlight on Delinquency. Edited by Eissler KR. New York, International Universities Press, 1949

Snyder S: Trichotillomania treated with amitriptyline: a single case study. J Nerv Ment Dis 168:505–507, 1980

Sorosky AD, Sticher MB: Trichotillomania in adolescence. Adolesc Psychiatry 8:437–454, 1980

Stawar TL: Fable mod: operantly structured fantasies as an adjunct in the modification of firesetting behavior. J Behav Ther Exp Psychiatry 7:285–287, 1976

Stekel W: Peculiarities of Behavior, vol 2. New York, Boni and Liveright, 1924

Stevens MJ: Behavioral treatment of trichotillomania. Psychol Rep 55:987–990, 1984

Stewart MA, Culver KW: Children who set fires: the clinical picture and a follow up. Br J Psychiatry 140:357–363, 1982

Sticher M, Abramovits W, Newcomer VD: Trichotillomania in adults. Cutis 26:90–101, 1980

Stone L: Remarks on certain unique conditions of human aggression: (the hand, speech, and the use of fire). J Am Psychoanal Assoc 27:27–63, 1979

Strachan JG: Conspicuous firesetting in children. Br J Psychiatry 138:25–29, 1981

Tolpin PH: A change in the self: the development and transformation of an idealizing transference. Int J Psychoanal 64:461–483, 1983

Tunks ER, Dermer SW: Carbamazepine in the dyscontrol syndrome associated with limbic system dysfunction. J Nerv Ment Dis 164:56–63, 1977

US Fire Administration/National Fire Academy: Interviewing and Counseling Juvenile Firesetters. Washington, DC, Federal Emergency Management Agency, 1979

US Fire Administration/National Fire Academy: Juvenile Firesetter Handbook, Dealing with Children Ages 7-14. Washington, DC, Federal Emergency Management Agency

Vandersall JA, Wiener JM: Children who set fires. Arch Gen Psychiatry 22:63–71, 1970

Victor RG, Krug CM: "Paradoxical intention" in the treatment of compulsive gambling. Am J Psychiatry 21:808–814, 1967

Vreeland RG, Waller MB: The Psychology of Firesetting: A Review and Appraisal. Chapel Hill, University of North Carolina Press, 1978

Weiss G, Hechtman L, Perlman T, et al: Hyperactives as young adults. Arch Gen Psychiatry 36:675–681, 1979

Welsh RS: The use of stimulus satiation in the elimination of juvenile firesetting behavior, in Behavior Therapy with Children. Edited by Graziano AM. Chicago, Aldine-Atherton, 1974

Wender PH, Reimherr FW, Wood DR: Attention deficit disorder in adults. Arch Gen Psychiatry 38:449–456, 1981

Winnicott DW: The antisocial tendency, in Collected Papers. New York, Basic Books, 1958

Winnicott DW: Delinquency as a sign of hope. Adolesc Psychiatry 2:364–371, 1973

Wood DR, Reimherr FW, Wender PH, et al: Diagnosis and treatment of minimal brain dysfunction in adults. Arch Gen Psychiatry 33:1453–1460, 1976

Wooden WS: The flames of youth. Psychol Today 14:22–28, 1985

Yarnell H: Firesetting in children. Am J Orthopsychiatry 10:272–286, 1940

Yudofsky S, Williams D, Gorman J: Propranolol in the treatment of rage and violent behavior in patients with chronic brain syndromes. Am J Psychiatry 138:218–220, 1981

Adjustment Disorder

Chapter 233

Introduction

For the mental health researcher, the discovery of a temporal relationship between an event and the onset of symptoms can be an exciting event in and of itself. Indeed, when placed in the context of a good personal history, such discoveries seem like the very essence of dynamic psychiatry. Any attempt to write about the treatment of the adjustment disorders, however, confronts one with a number of uncertainties. There is an extensive array of stressors, a wide variation of individual coping response, and a necessarily broad range of treatment modalities.

A given individual would be expected to cope with the loss of a loved one differently than he would with property damage due to flood; or would he? It is likely that certain mechanisms of defense, such as denial, may predominate in both instances; nonetheless, behavioral responses would probably be quite different. This is an interesting issue which has not been carefully studied. Would a rather dependent person who wept bitterly at the loss of his mother also weep as he watched the flood waters rise around his home? Perhaps so. Would he be unable to make the funeral arrangements and tend to his mother's estate in the first instance and, similarly, be unable to save some of his more valuable possessions in the second? No one knows the answer, but it is reasonable to expect that even within a single individual, the tremendous diversity of stressful situations would be likely to mobilize an equally various spectrum of defenses.

On the other hand, the classical study of U.S. Army draftees would, to some extent, indicate otherwise. Based on psychological data alone (conflicts over separation from home), the investigators were able to predict which soldiers would develop peptic ulcer disease as a response to the stress of basic training. There are no other studies, however, that would either confirm or refute the contention that variations among stressors would lead to variations in response within the individual.

A discussion of the adjustment disorders must, therefore, consider the wide variation among stressors, and in responses to them, before focusing on specific treatment modalities.

The diagnostic criteria for assessing persons suspected of having an adjustment disorder, as set forth in DSM-III-R (American Psychiatric Association 1987), are shown in Table 1. Though the criteria are seemingly rather straightforward, the clinician must make many "judgment calls," some of which are fraught with pitfalls. For example: What is a psychosocial stressor? Are the symptoms beyond what one would expect under the circumstances? Is it safe to assume a remission of symptoms will occur within six months of the cessation of the stressor? Can one assume a successful adaptation if the stressor is ongoing?

Table 1.   DSM-III-R Diagnostic Criteria for Adjustment Disorder

A.   A reaction to an identifiable psychosocial stressor (or multiple stressors) that occurs within three months of onset of the stressor(s).

B.   The maladaptive nature of the reaction is indicated by either of the following:
(1) impairment in occupational (including school) functioning or in usual social activities or relationships with others
(2) symptoms that are in excess of a normal and expectable reaction to the stressor(s)

C.   The disturbance is not merely one instance of a pattern of overreaction to stress or an exacerbation of one of the mental disorders previously described.

D.   The maladaptive reaction has persisted for no longer than six months.

E.   The disturbance does not meet the criteria for any specific mental disorder and does not represent Uncomplicated Bereavement.

Psychosocial Stressors

It is beyond the scope of this chapter to review the genesis of the word stressor as opposed to stress since this controversy was so ably put to rest by Mason (1975). Three distinctly different categories of stressors appear in the literature and in clinical practice. First are the major, discrete events which occur throughout the life cycle, such as deaths, divorces, and job losses.

Second, there is a group of chronic stressors such as the disturbed environments in which some children are raised and the chaotic homes so common among the lower socioeconomic classes (Rutter 1983). Such situations certainly contribute to mental as well as to physical illnesses. In DSM-III-R, however, there is a clear implication that the duration of an adjustment disorder should not exceed six months, apparently ruling out chronic situations as "identifiable psychosocial stressors."

Third, at the other end of the spectrum are what we might call micro events. When a parent fails to keep a promise to visit a hospitalized child, the hospital staff who must console the child understand the impact of the event; nonetheless, it is not ordinarily considered a stressor. Some examples are having to wait, being exposed to noise, and struggling with traffic. An adolescent rejected for a role in a class play or an adult unfairly judged by a peer are other examples. The result may be far more detrimental than one would expect. Other events such as the first report of precordial pain in one's 60-year-old spouse, a near accident while driving, and receipt of a disturbing phone call might also be classed as micro events. Although most stressors are discrete events or conditions, the absence of events, such as monotony or lack of change, can also serve as stressors.

Future research may enable us to consider all events from a systems theory perspective. There are national events such as the assassination of John F. Kennedy which, for some individuals, serve as very personal psychosocial stressors (Table 2). More distant events such as the famine in Kenya, natural disasters, and micro events can also be classed as psychosocial stressors. In Table 2 an attempt has been made to enumerate in hierarchical order some of the occurrences which can, with our current worldwide communication capability, affect individual Americans. It would appear that among all of these events, a common denominator is the meaning they have for the individual and the way they are perceived by him.

It is evident from the foregoing that one can take a very broad view of the

Table 2. Classes of Psychosocial Stressors

Class	Examples
Global events	World war Famine in Kenya Taking of hostages
National events	Assassination of John F. Kennedy Assassination of Martin Luther King
Regional events	Earthquake, flood, tornado Farm economic crisis
Large group events	Strikes Closing of a factory Racial discrimination
Small group events	Loss of a hard fought athletic event
Personal macro events	Loss of loved ones Divorce Hospitalization
Personal micro events	Threatened loss of a friend through a disagreement Broken promise by parent or friend

adjustment disorders. One may argue that most nongenetic mental illnesses begin as adjustment disorders and then develop into other, more precisely defined entities. Furthermore, variation in the degree of penetrance of inherited illnesses may also depend on the advent of a psychosocial stressor. It is well established that when adaptation to the stressor fails, the ensuing stress can play an etiologic role in many physical illnesses.

The identification of a psychosocial stressor that occurred not more than three months prior to the onset of symptoms would seem to be a rather straightforward task; however, considerable clinical judgment is often called for. Discrete events which occur on a particular day are easily recalled, but they may have no causative relationship with the ensuing symptomatology. Since they are remembered as preceding the illness, their significance is commonly overestimated by the patient, by the family, and by the clinician in their combined effort to arrive at logical causative linkages. Theoretical formulations regarding the significance of events have been espoused for so long that many people, patients and physicians alike, expect symptoms to appear following a stressor and deem them socially acceptable. In trying to date the onset of an illness, a patient will frequently assert that it began right after his wedding anniversary or after his wife died, or following some other easily remembered date. Perhaps he is using the event merely as a benchmark in his effort to recall the onset, or perhaps he is assigning undue significance to the event. A man may admit to the development of alcoholism and date its onset as occurring after his wife died in an automobile accident while denying that for years prior to the event he had already been drinking too much. The inexperienced clinician too is motivated to accept a history with a discrete onset and a plausible cause-effect relationship.

Thus there is a distinct tendency to overestimate the significance of a psychosocial stressor and to erroneously attribute unrelated symptomatology to this stressor; at the same time, however, underestimation of event significance may also occur. Since it is very common, having trouble with one's boss may seem insignificant to the clinician, but it can be overwhelming to a particularly vulnerable person. Furthermore, the patient may be ashamed to admit to difficulty in coping with a given stressor and deny or suppress its significance. Distant events or micro events are frequently overlooked.

In their empirical study of 3,000 medical records, Holmes and Rahe (1967) discovered that many events, positive as well as negative, had been recorded as occurring in the preceding six months. Coddington (1984) provided anecdotal data supporting the concept that events which would ordinarily be deemed highly desirable sometimes prove quite traumatic. In both cases, the investigators have argued that it is the readjustment in the person's life which is important, rather than the inherent valence of the event as such. As a case in point, one gets the impression from the media that the readjustment necessitated by winning a multimillion dollar lottery is not always easy.

On the other hand, Gersten et al. (1974) and Kellam (1974) question this position and raise the interesting question: Do positive events cancel out the negative? Tennant et al. (1981) have pointed out the beneficial effect of these so-called neutralizing events. For example, a stressful geographic move required by one's employer may be neutralized by a raise in pay sufficient to warrant repeated trips to visit family and old friends. It would seem that the alert clinician should keep an open mind in this regard.

The clinician must also judge the stressfulness of a series of events. The loss of a job may require not only relocation a thousand miles away, but an accompanying loss of friends plus the uneconomic forced sale of a home. These would usually be considered to be cumulative events and together comprise a psychosocial stressor. But if, with the exception of job loss, the same events had occurred during the career of a military man, the series would probably not be considered traumatic since new assignments are expected periodically and are usually anticipated well in advance.

Though seemingly an easy task, the identification of psychosocial stressors which appear relevant to a diagnostic formulation is not as easy as it looks. In our super-industrial society, psychosocial stressors are very common; indeed, when taking a medical or psychiatric history, it is not difficult to identify one or more significant events. Ultimately it is always the meaning of the event that counts. It would therefore seem wise to list, as clearly as possible, all apparently relevant stressors under Axis IV, and then proceed to evaluate the patient's response to each. Cumulative aspects of stresses over periods of two months to two years are also significant. Likewise, it is not clear at what rate a person recovers from psychophysiologic strain following single or multiple stressors.

Factors Influencing Responses to Stressors

The age at which one experiences the event is crucial. Coping skills and psychological defense mechanisms are developed over time. Although young children often seem amazingly resilient or particularly able to repress the meaning of psychological trauma, little is known about the actual effect of various relatively common traumata at different ages or developmental epochs. Garmezy (1983) reviewed the literature in regard to childhood but, for the most part, research has focused on uncommon traumata, such as war, death, and concentration camp incarcerations. The "normal and expectable" reaction of children of various ages to the sudden death of a beloved grandmother might be evident to most child psychiatrists but not so well understood by others. An adjustment disorder should not be diagnosed unless the symptoms exceed such expectable reactions. Many other stressors are also age-dependent. Thus, the loss of a job is quite a different matter for a 25-year-old as compared to a 50-year-old man who feels he is too old to be readily re-employed and too young to retire. A hysterectomy affects a young woman who wants additional children quite differently from the way it impacts on a woman in her 40s, and this premenopausal woman will in turn respond differently than her post-menopausal friend. Thus, age is the first variable the clinician must consider.

Another variable which will, in large measure, determine an individual's reaction to a stressor is his or her previous experience with it and other stressors. Nevertheless, a success or a failure in coping with a given event will undoubtedly affect the manner with which one copes with subsequent occurrences of the same or similar events. The first occurrence may either sensitize the victim or better prepare him for the future. We have all seen children who have lost a significant object and who than appear particularly anxious about subsequent losses, real, threatened, or fantasized. It is hard to conceive of a child at age 10 who, following the death of a parent, becomes better able to cope with the death of the other parent five years later. Yet we know that young physicians who mourn the loss of their first patient eventually become "steeled" to later losses (the use of the word "steeled" is suggested in Garmezy 1983).

The beneficial effect of previous experience is, of course, the basis for many training programs. The Outward Bound program for adolescents is a good example. Military training uses the same principle.

For want of a better term, the cohort effect is chosen to indicate the need to consider the era within which the event occurred. In the Schedule of Recent Experience (Casey et al. 1967), the assumption of a $10,000 mortgage is listed as an event. Today such a sum appears relatively minor and might better be classified as a micro event. Hogan (1984) has, in a most erudite manner, described the importance of considering the birth cohort of the individual. For example, in 1942 the United States was involved in a popular war. Being drafted into the armed services at age 18 at that time was entirely different from being drafted at the same age during the unpopular Vietnam conflict. Times change! Growing up today is dissimilar from growing up in the 1920s or 1950s or in any other era. So the cohort to which the individual belongs must be taken into account when judging the significance of a stressor.

Many influences play a role in determining response to a stressor. Thus, whether events are under the individual's control, whether they had been anticipated, and the amount of social support received from family and friends are all of central importance.

Sociocultural expectations will also influence one's response to a stressor, as will family attitudes and religious practices. The behavior of people at funerals is largely culturally dependent. Behavior that would seem overly dramatic and hysterical in one environment would be viewed as normal in another. There is a tendency for whole tribes or neighborhood groups to respond to floods or other natural disasters by returning to their home sites despite the risk of repeated episodes of the event. This behavior seems to be influenced by tradition or by an unrealistic attachment to the physical location. Victims may be more concerned with folkways and the reaction of their peers than by economic reality or their own safety and that of their families.

The individual's personality structure provides for at least a measure of consistency in one's response. Much has been written in recent years about the individual coping style attributable to a person and about attempts to modify maladaptive styles. Unfortunately, such individual consistency is of little help in our task of writing a treatment manual because of our lack of knowledge about the epidemiology of personality development. There have been two or three studies of personality disorders but none of personality traits. The latter are defined as enduring patterns of perceiving, relating to, and thinking about the environment and oneself. Together, these traits will largely determine coping style.

There are a myriad of possible responses to psychosocial stressors. It has been shown that these are determined by age, previous experience, the cohort effect, and sociocultural and individual personality variables. They will vary from responses which anyone would consider to be normal to those whose deviance is of psychotic proportions. The clinician will perforce have to make many judgments about what is "normal and expectable" in the particular situation.

The Signal to Noise Ratios

Some of the variability in response to a stressor may be viewed in terms of an alternative conceptualization, as a reflection of the signal to noise ratio. When the signal is clear, even though the stressor is tragic or catastrophic, adaptation is facilitated. But when noise (in the form of confusion, conflict, or the presence of multiple minor stressors) predominates, adaptation is more difficult. Following a natural disaster, for example, the healthy goal must be to re-establish one's home, mourn the victims, and get on with life. There may be much activity as community and individual efforts are mobilized, but there should be little emotional confusion over one's goals; under such conditions, the signal to noise ratio is high (a strong signal with little noise). Hence, even under such tragic circumstances, adaptation may prove to be considerably easier than in the face of another, less traumatic but less clear situation. Consider, for example, a family move brought on by the offer of a promotion. The family income is raised along with the wage earner's prestige but at the cost of the loss of friends and a change in life style. The goal, professional advancement, is clear enough, but there are many pros and cons (noise) which make adaptation to it (the signal) more difficult.

It would seem that a soldier facing combat would be better prepared to deal with the associated stress if noise were minimized by clarification regarding the reasons and justness of the cause (as was true in World War II). Noise was maximized in the Vietnam conflict by confusion and controversy at every national level from the Presidency on down. In the latter instance the prevalence of posttraumatic stress disorder is apparently much higher.

Remission of Symptoms

In order to diagnose an adjustment disorder, the clinician must assume that the symptoms will remit within six months of the cessation of the stressor and its consequences. If the symptoms can be explained on the basis of some other condition, or seem to be "merely one instance of a pattern of over-reaction to stress," then an adjustment disorder should not be diagnosed. The assumption that the symptoms of an adjustment disorder will remit spontaneously suggests that no treatment at all is indicated if the clinician feels that the patient can ride out the storm. The intensity of the symptoms will dictate whatever intervention is needed.

One might ask: When does the loss of a loved one cease to be a stressor? It would seem that such a loss ceases to be a stressor when, and only when, the patient has made a reasonable adaptation to the loss. But we are in danger of rather circular reasoning, for if we assume the patient will eventually function without impairment (as we must if we diagnose the condition as an adjustment disorder), we can take the return to health as an indication of the cessation of the stressor. In other words, we think A has caused B and will continue to do so as long as A exists. But we can not measure A directly, only by the continued existence of B; if B ceases, A must have ceased.

It may well be that if one takes a narrow enough cross-section of history, including only the stressor and onset of symptoms, an adjustment disorder can often be diagnosed. In other words, almost anything from alcoholism to zoophobia could begin as an adjustment disorder. But expansion of the anamnesis longitudinally with the emergence of a developmental perspective and inclusion of familial, sociocultural, and religious data will regularly lead to a more precise alternative diagnosis. Often, however, the working diagnosis will, of necessity, be an adjustment disorder.

One further point needs expression here, namely: the distinction which is sometimes drawn between the adjustment disorders and the posttraumatic stress disorders (PTSD) on the basis of the characteristics of the stressor. Indeed, in the DSM-III (American Psychiatric Association 1980), PTSD is said to follow stressors that "would evoke significant symptoms of distress in most people [and are] generally outside the range of such common experiences as simple bereavement, chronic illness. . . ." Natural disasters such as floods and earthquakes are given as examples. On the other hand, the same volume makes no such distinction in the discussion of adjustment disorders and even includes the same example, natural disasters, as an identifiable psychosocial stress. Hence the distinction between the kinds of stressors that lead to these conditions is at best hazy and to some extent arbitrary. The time interval between the event and the appearance of symptoms is quite another matter. If the onset of symptoms occurs within three months of the traumatic experience, either diagnosis may be made; if, however, the onset is delayed, the posttraumatic stress disorder designation would be the correct one. Ultimately, there are other, much more significant evidential points which will emerge in the subsequent clinical picture.

In this chapter, we have chosen to avoid the seemingly artificial classification of stressors for two reasons. First, we recognize the widespread effect of the media which bring rare tragic and catastrophic events into almost every home, allowing the average citizen to feel their impact and to share in their meaning, at least vicariously. Second, most investigators recognize the remarkable variability in response to any stressor studied and for this reason do not classify stressors either by their frequency or by their severity (as generally perceived). Therefore, no such restriction was placed on those who contributed to this chapter.

In the chapters that follow, adjustment disorders as they occur in different age groups are reviewed, followed by discussions of 10 different interventional modes. Suitable citations accompany each supportive and therapeutic approach to allow each reader the opportunity for further exploration.

Chapter 234

Adjustment Disorders in Adulthood and Old Age

Adulthood and old age are no longer seen as static periods in the evolution of a human life. It is clear that adults go through a series of recurrent changes until they die; these are often referred to as stages or periods of transition. Adults and the elderly are vulnerable to different kinds of stressors at different times in their lives. Therefore, the concept of stressors can be understood only in terms of each individual's own vulnerability and symbolic interpretation.

Some elderly are especially vulnerable to stress; others, however, have developed lifelong coping styles that serve them well. Many of the elderly may have fewer material, social, and sometimes intellectual capabilities and must therefore strive to cope with limited resources. One of the characteristics of an aged person is a tendency to react to problems more rigidly (Brink 1978), an adaptive style that may result in maladaptive behavior or affect. Given the vulnerability of the elderly to stressors and the limited repertoire of their responses to them, the probability that an adjustment disorder will develop is likely to increase with advancing years. At the same time, variability in responses increases with age so that it is difficult to generalize. Some events may be perceived as less stressful because they are on time in the life cycle or were expected.

It is sensible to retain the conceptual model of adjustment disorder which allows for an effort to restore function in the elderly without assuming an organic disease or ongoing psychiatric illness (Straker 1982). Thus an 80-year-old man who has moved from his family home to a nursing home, and who then seems to lose interest in his usual activities and who shows distractibility and decreased recent memory, should not first be assumed to be demented. He is very likely reacting to the stressors of the move and his changed role. Therefore, while the diagnosis of adjustment disorder may at times be controversial, the dynamic concept behind it provides an empirically useful approach to psychiatric treatment.

Diagnosis

Adjustment disorders are characterized by a maladaptive response or reaction to an identifiable psychosocial stressor that has occurred within the past three months.

This stressor does not have to be overwhelming, but it is perceived as psychologically painful by the patient. When identifiable symptoms occur, they consist of responses that exceed "normal or expected" reactions. These symptoms include impairment of significant social, interpersonal, or work functions.

The fact that these identifiable symptoms exceed "normal or expected" reactions introduces the complicated issue of "clinical judgment." That is, the symptoms are judged to be excessive by the individual clinician according to his own standards of what is appropriate. It is important to note that this reaction is not part of the pattern with which this patient usually responds to a stressor. This reaction is also not a reappearance of a previous psychiatric disorder. The diagnosis implies that the maladaptive response and symptoms will improve when the stressor is removed. Alternatively, when the patient comes to a point where he or she no longer perceives the stressor as unmanageable, the individual will have reached a "healthier" level of adaptation with an accompanying relief of symptoms. A teacher who has developed symptoms of anxiety under the supervision of a new principal may feel a complete relief of these symptoms when the principal is fired. However, this teacher may also learn to adapt to the new person by becoming more efficient and thus feel an increase in his or her own sense of competence.

An adjustment disorder requires that the clinician conduct a detailed examination of both the patient and the stressors precipitating the symptoms. The stressors may be singular or multiple, and recurrent or chronic. They may occur in a family setting with a good deal of accompanying family turmoil, they may also affect only a single individual, or they may affect an individual as part of a group or community. Certain stressors are associated with specific developmental stages.

It is clear that the severity of a stressor (as perceived by a given individual) is not predictable without knowing that individual's psychological makeup and history. Both the severity and the specificity of the stressor may be noted as Axis IV characteristics. The stressor can be described by its duration, timing, and context in a person's life.

An adjustment disorder may begin at any time within the three months following an encounter with a stressor. If the patient has had a personality disorder or organic mental disorder, it is possible that he will be more vulnerable to seemingly innocuous stressors and therefore be more predisposed to the development of an adjustment disorder.

No information is available as to the sex ratio or familial pattern typical of an adjustment disorder, but the condition is apparently common among both adult and elderly patients. It is likely that when such patients go through difficult developmental stages such as the "mid-life crisis" or retirement, they may be far more vulnerable to stressors.

Adjustment disorders, then, may present with symptoms of depressed mood, anxious mood, a mixture of depressive and anxious symptoms, a disturbance in conduct (which may involve a violation of the rights of others), or a disturbance of behavior mixed with anxiety and depression. It may also take form as an inhibition in work or academic functioning (in a patient who previously had good adaptation to work and to academics); as social withdrawal without significant depression or anxiety; and, finally, with "atypical features" (where the predominant manifestations of interference with social or interpersonal function are not covered by the previously mentioned categories). As noted, all of the symptoms are a reaction to an identifiable stressor; it is this factor in particular which sets this condition apart from other diagnoses.

The DSM-III-R (American Psychiatric Association 1987) diagnosis of adjustment disorder is made only after the examination of several issues. As mentioned, the stressor needs to be evaluated thoroughly, along with the patient's personality development and characteristics. It is important to explore the medical, physiologic, and genetic characteristics of the patient with some care since these all bear on symptom formation. When a patient is considered a potential candidate for a diagnosis of adjustment disorder, the medical evaluation is an important part of the diagnostic efforts.

Differential Diagnosis

In the DSM-II (American Psychiatric Association 1968), the term *transient situational disturbances* was the category which has been replaced in DSM-III-R by *adjustment disorder*. In the former category of transient situational disturbance, one criterion for the appearance of symptoms was the fact that the stressor was "overwhelming." This is no longer required for an adjustment disorder. Among the differential diagnoses to be pondered in the course of making this diagnosis is the appearance of a stress-related posttraumatic stress disorder. This condition is one of the anxiety disorders and is characterized by the existence of a "recognizable stressor that would evoke significant symptoms of distress in almost anyone." The stressors include natural disasters such as hurricanes, fires (Green et al. 1983), and earthquakes, as well as man-made disasters such as flooding due to a collapsed dam, a train wreck, and so on. This also refers to the overwhelming stressor experienced in a wartime setting, either as a civilian or as a soldier.

This is a particularly important concept in differentiating an adjustment disorder from a posttraumatic stress disorder in the elderly. Such a patient may respond to what is a relatively minor stressor for a younger adult as though it were in fact overwhelming; for example, the elderly person may develop severe symptoms after having been robbed or verbally insulted. He may display the full spectrum of post-traumatic stress disorder, that is, he may re-experience the trauma with intrusive recollections and recurrent dreams, and may act or feel as if the traumatic event were reoccurring. In addition, he may show a numbing of responsiveness, reduced involvement with the external world, diminished interest in usual activities, or feelings of detachment or estrangement. This can have a progressively downhill course and the patient may develop increasingly severe symptoms of a posttraumatic stress disorder, including a decision not to leave home, hyperalertness, constricted affect, a sleep disturbance, memory impairment, and difficulty in concentrating. In the elderly patient such symptoms may be misinterpreted as the onset of a delirium or dementia; accordingly, placement in an extended care facility may be considered. When an overwhelming stressor occurs during the life of a younger adult, it is usually obvious and does not present such a differential diagnostic problem.

Adults and the elderly, of course, may suffer from personality disorders. When such individuals are placed in a stressful setting, they may experience symptoms of anxiety, depression, withdrawal, or other manifestations which can be confused with an adjustment disorder. Careful history taking will usually elucidate the maladaptive interpersonal relationships that the patient has had for many years (Lion 1981). The important differential diagnostic clue is whether or not the personality-disordered patient has been stressed within the last three months and, as a result, has developed new and significant symptoms superimposed on his personality disorder. If this is the case, the adjustment disorder and personality disorder diagnoses can both be made. This implies that when the stressor is removed or a better level of adaptation is achieved, the symptoms of the adjustment disorder will abate, whereas the symptoms of a personality disorder will continue. This sort of differential diagnostic process occurs in both adult and elderly patients.

The DSM-III-R (American Psychiatric Association 1980) listing entitled Psychological Factors Affecting a Physical Condition can also be confusing in the differential diagnosis of an adjustment disorder. Where psychological factors affect a physical condition, the process of symptom development is usually the reverse of that seen in adjustment disorder. In an adjustment disorder, stressors produce symptoms within three months. In psychological factors affecting a physical condition, psychologically meaningful environmental stimuli or stressors initiate or exacerbate a previous physical condition such as hypertension or ulcerative colitis. This physical condition clearly involves demonstrable organic pathology or a known pathophysiologic process such as migraine headache or vomiting. The aspect which may be confusing is that a patient who develops medical problems can then go on to develop an adjustment disorder because of the stress of the developing physical problem. The clue to making the diagnosis is in the convergent timing of the stressor and the onset of symptoms.

Bereavement, of course, is a stressor for anyone. The normal process of grief is well understood (Lindemann 1944). Its phenomenology can approach that of the full depressive syndrome, but it is inherently self-limited, a normal reaction to the loss of a loved one. The individual who is suffering from uncomplicated bereavement generally regards the feeling of depressed mood as "normal." This patient may, nonetheless, seek professional help for relief of such associated symptoms as insomnia and anorexia even though he or she regards them as clearly related to the grieving process.

Psychosomatic or psychophysiologic disorders may also occur in older people in response to situations perceived by the patient as sources of chronic or acute distress (Brink et al. 1979; Verwoerdt 1981). Therefore, it is important, in an elderly patient particularly, to rule out conversion disorders, psychogenic pain disorders, and dissociative disorders (including psychogenic amnesia and psychogenic fugue).

Frequently, when older patients become severely depressed they develop a "pseudo-dementia" (Cavenar et al. 1979). When an older patient develops cognitive impairment following a stressor, it becomes important to rule out a major depressive disorder. (In all age groups, it is also vital to distinguish between a major depressive disorder occurring alone or as part of a bipolar affective disorder.)

In the elderly it is particularly important to consider the possible presence of an organic disorder as a cause of anxiety or depression. Thus when a patient presents with cognitive, behavioral, or affective symptoms, it is essential to rule out organic brain pathology. In the elderly patient an organic brain syndrome may give rise to a variety of behavioral or affective symptoms, so that an exploration for central nervous system pathology must be routine.

In the nature of things, some elderly patients in the past will have developed maladaptive character traits or personality disorders (Straker 1982) which the aging process itself may exaggerate. As such troublesome personality traits or disorders increase in severity, interpersonal or social functioning may deteriorate, acting as a stressor, and an adjustment disorder may then occur. It is important to differentiate the exacerbation of an existing personality disorder from the de novo appearance of adjustment disorder.

Course and Prognosis

There is a great deal that we still do not know about the course and prognosis of adjustment disorders. Nonetheless, the few studies which have been completed do indicate that these conditions, particularly in adults, have a good outcome. The symptoms may be acute; alternatively, they may become chronic and continue indefinitely because the stressors have not been altered or adaptation has not improved. Nonetheless, it is assumed that if the stressor is removed or a different level of adaptation is reached, the symptoms will remit.

If the symptoms do not remit when the stressor is removed, it is probable that an alternative diagnosis would be more accurate. It also appears that adult patients so diagnosed improve to a greater extent than do adolescents (Andreasen 1982).

In terms of outcome, special consideration needs to be given to the elderly patient, particularly the frail elderly. Since many elderly patients are more vulnerable to environmental and psychological stress (Eisdorfer and Wilkie 1977), an aggressive approach needs to be taken toward alleviating such stressors.

It is notable that stressors may be re-creations of previous stressful events and are interpreted as stressful only the by patient (Sandler 1967, p. 154). Thus the effects of a previous stressful event can remain largely unresolved only to emerge later in the face of a seemingly innocuous additional stressor. Therefore, in the examination of any person presenting with the symptoms of an adjustment disorder, one needs to attempt to make such links.

In predicting the course and prognosis of an illness in adults, the functioning of the patient throughout childhood and adolescence needs to be considered. The evaluation should include the history of the patient's childhood and adolescence, the difficulties experienced, and the skills acquired in proceeding through these developmental stages. This will help to clarify the more vulnerable areas within the patient's personality structure. When weighing the stressors an individual has borne, several factors need to be pondered. Predisposing factors, precipitating factors, and perpetuating factors form part of the profile of any distressing event (Winer and Pollock 1980). In elderly patients, evaluating their previous level of social, interpersonal, and intrapsychic abilities is an important part of predicting outcome and future response to stressors.

Obviously, the elderly have a particular vulnerability to stressful circumstances. This is in part because of the way they perceive themselves and in part because in reality their resources are limited. Younger adults will probably require less social or environmental intervention than will elderly patients (Straker 1982). In particular, for an elderly patient the family support system becomes exceedingly important.

Toward Treatment

It is clear that a nearly infinite variety of environmental, interpersonal, or intrapsychic phenomena can occur which can act as stressors for any given individual. This has been called "configurational specificity" by Winer and Pollock (1980). Therefore, the potential to develop an adjustment disorder depends upon the perception of the stressor by the individual, the individual's overall intellectual-perceptual levels of brain functioning, the individual's unique psychological background and organization, and the individual's cultural milieu. Treatment recommendations are usually empirical, although based on experience in the treatment of other, more defined psychiatric disorders.

Generally speaking, treatment is oriented toward improving the patient's level of adaptation, using environmental manipulation to remove the stressor, and utilizing psychotherapy both to explore the patient's attitude and, hopefully, to change his perspective. The concepts set forth by Caplan (1961) are useful in developing a treatment approach at the levels of primary, secondary, and tertiary intervention. Primary prevention of the adjustment disorder would revolve around education. It would be helpful to teach adolescents and adults as well as elderly people to recognize the power of stressors to create symptoms. Once the concept is accepted that distress can produce psychiatric disorders, an educational program involving adaptive and "healthy" ways of handling stressful situations could be developed (Alexander and French 1946; Sifneos 1979). This would include the concept that at different ages, different stressors cause symptoms.

Adults can be helped to recognize the evolutionary nature of adult life along with the fact that personality developmental stages continue after adolescence; this opens the way to pointing out stressful times (Erikson 1959; Levinson 1978). Sensitizing elderly patients and their families to a given patient's particular vulnerability would also be helpful (Andrews et al. 1978). If certain types of stressors could then be prevented, this would hopefully reduce the appearance of adjustment disorder symptoms.

Secondary prevention is aimed at minimizing the impact of symptoms which have already appeared (Butler 1975). Patients need help in finding alternative modes of responding to stressors, tactics that would induce a more adaptive response. Hence a variety of interventions may be employed, including individual treatment, family treatment, or alteration of community sources of stressors, to name a few.

The treatment methods are eclectic and draw from the clinician's training and orientation. Individual psychotherapy on a short-term basis, using a model such as that recommended by Horowitz and Kaltreider (1979), may be very effective. They recommend a 12-hour treatment program to help the adjustment-disordered patient understand and respond to his stressors. Where patients are vulnerable to the stresses and strains of everyday life because of either their past developmental difficulties, their present developmental stage, or previous personality disorder, long-term psychotherapy (Lawton 1976) may be indicated. Psychotherapy will help the patient understand the nature of the stressor, put it into a different perspective, and deal with it in a more effective and adaptive way; this will hopefully remove or reduce the cause of the symptoms. Individual and group therapy of various kinds, alone or in combination, can be very effective (Budman 1981). The importance of a careful evaluation period cannot be overemphasized since a structured problem-solving technique can be rationally applied only after the nature of the stressor and the patient's response to it are understood.

Some elderly patients may require a more aggressive (Straker 1982; Verwoerdt 1981) intervention program which includes environmental manipulation. As an example, an elderly patient with reduced vision and hearing who is living alone may need to be encouraged to move in with his or her family or to enter an extended care facility.

Where the environment cannot be changed, the next step may be to reduce the amount of conflict within it. This may involve attempting to get those around the patient to change their behavior or the character of their interaction with the patient. Certainly, individual psychotherapy would seek to alter the patient's attitude toward and perception of his own response to stressors and thereby alleviate the symptoms. Family therapy may be a useful part of the overall treatment program. Other valid treatments to reduce distress and the patient's response to it might include a behavioral treatment program with the use of biofeedback, adjunctive use of relaxation techniques, and referral to support groups oriented toward changing destructive behavior.

It is clear, then, that depending upon the urgency of the symptoms, magnitude of the stressors, and quality of the symptoms, a hierarchy of treatment modalities can be recommended. Initially, crisis intervention may be helpful, to be followed by thorough evaluation. Brief psychotherapy may be appropriate at this point or it may be clear that insight-oriented individual psychotherapy will be required. If long-term psychotherapy becomes the focus of treatment, the diagnosis may need to be re-evaluated every few months. Another major interventional mode is consultation. The goals here are to help the people who deal with the patient understand him better, understand their reactions to him, and learn new methods of dealing with him.

If a patient has symptoms that are incapacitating, or that result in suicidal or self-destructive behavior, or that involve behavior dangerous to others, hospitalization is indicated. This may serve to remove the patient from an environment that is causing the production of symptoms, or to prevent homicidal or suicidal behavior. This protected setting will also help to further define the patient's adaptive mechanisms.

In summary, then, it is apparent that the adjustment disorders present a logical way of looking at the human condition and at a particular array of responses which are at once maladaptive and harmful. Because the disorder is a result of complex systems interacting upon one another, it is easy to oversimplify and reject the appearance of such a condition. Nonetheless, it is clear to the clinician that these disorders do exist, that they cause suffering and impairment, and that after careful evaluation and problem formulation they can be treated.

Generally, this psychiatric disorder has a time-limited course and a good prognosis; its diagnosis offers an effective and logical way of approaching those psychiatric symptoms which result from everyday stressors. There is, however, one area of special concern. The suicide rate rises significantly in each of the later decades; in the elderly certain varieties of adjustment disorder (those accompanied by a strong depressive coloring) may have a fatal outcome. Other than this, the condition tends to have a positive prognosis, and appropriate treatment holds out the opportunity for increasing the adaptive functioning of the affected individual.

Chapter 235

Adjustment Disorders in Childhood and Adolescence

The overall concept of a category of adjustment disorders of childhood and adolescence is theoretically useful and clinically sensible; scientifically, however, it remains poorly validated. The child is sensitive and reactive to both environmental and developmental events. Indeed, every child manifests a combination of real and psychological dependence on the one hand and immature or unformed coping/adaptive capacities on the other. In the face of this, a direct relationship between age and degree of vulnerability to stress during infancy and childhood is by-and-large expectable, at least through adolescence. However, the diagnostic criteria and classification of these reactions, the differentiation of normal from pathologic, and the nature of the indicated treatments or interventions continue to be at once elusive and controversial. Before current thinking on the topic is considered, a brief historical review will be presented.

History

The third edition of Kanner's child psychiatry text (1957) does not include the terms *adjustment* or *reactive* in the index or table of contents. Kanner's discussion of the meaning of symptoms (pp. 175–180), age-related symptoms (p. 45), regression (p. 46), situational therapy (p. 250), and the nature of many behavioral problems implies a recognition and understanding of adjustment and reactive disturbances, but no delineation of these as a separate category.

A major advance in the classification of childhood disorders occurred with the publication of a monograph on this subject in 1966 by the Group for the Advancement of Psychiatry (GAP). This classification offered "healthy responses" and "reactive disorders" as its first two categories.

The first grouping (healthy responses) specified the concepts of stage-appropriate functioning, psychosocial tasks, and developmental crises (as per Erikson), anxiety-related manifestations of separation-individuation (e.g., eight months anxiety, separation fears, and phobic reactions), and "transient situational crises" (p. 224) such as grief reactions "considered to be normal adaptive responses and not disturbed behaviors" (p. 221). This category required a confirmation of intact functioning (by age and stage) in major areas of development, including cognitive, social, emotional, and personal-adaptive. It also accommodated "mild regressive" and symptomatic behaviors specified from a symptom list. Specific descriptively based criteria were not addressed.

The category of reactive disorders in GAP was used for those disorders that were primarily a "reaction to an event, a set of events, or a situation" (p. 222). However, the reaction had to be of "pathological degree" and reflective of a conscious conflict between the child and the environment, that is, not an "unconscious internalized process" (p. 222). In the GAP discussion of this disorder, emphasis was placed on the developmental dynamics in terms of state, stage, and reaction of the child, and not on the nature or severity of the stressor. The disorder itself might take any number of forms: developmental arrest; symptomatic regressions (bedwetting, thumbsucking, nightmares, dependence); phobic conversion, or obsessive symptoms; or various behavioral (conduct) disturbances. The nature of the reaction and its outcome depended on the interaction of the child's endowment with developmental stage, past experiences, established personality resources, family constellation and attitude, and the nature of the intervention. The disorder might remit or progress to a more internalized and/or structured disorder.

DSM-II (American Psychiatric Association 1968) followed shortly after the GAP report and formally introduced the concept of reactive disorders into the official diagnostic nomenclature. At the time, the category was designated "transient situational disturbances." This group included the diagnoses of adjustment reactions of infancy, childhood, and so on, according to developmental stage. This category included "more or less" (p. 48) transient conditions without apparent "underlying mental disorder" (p. 49). As a response to an "overwhelming stress" (p. 49), these conditions could be of any level of severity of reaction (including psychosis). If remission occurred as the stressor diminished, this was considered to confirm the diagnosis. If symptoms persisted after the stressor was removed, this indicated that some other diagnosis must apply. Examples included a grief reaction following loss, sibling rivalry with attention-seeking behaviors (after the birth of a new sibling), and a reactive depression to school failure. These disorders were to be distinguished particularly from the category of "behavior disorders of childhood and adolescence" which were defined as more "stable, internalized and resistant to treatment" (p. 50).

Diagnosis

DSM-III (American Psychiatric Association 1980) replaced the term "transient situational disturbances" with the category of "adjustment disorders," subclassified according to type (with depressed mood, anxious mood, withdrawal, and so on) rather than by developmental stage as in DSM-II. While the concept itself was continued from DSM-II and GAP, the category now contained much more detailed and descriptive criteria for both inclusion and exclusion.

Differential Diagnosis

With the criteria established in DSM-III in mind, one may delineate three major areas of differential diagnosis: other stress-related disorders; other disorders manifesting similar symptoms of greater intensity; and an exacerbation of a pre-existing personality disorder or organic mental disorder. Each of these major categories will be discussed separately.

Under the category of "other stress-related disorders," one may consider the posttraumatic stress disorders; the somatoform disorders (specifically a conversion disorder, and perhaps a psychogenic pain disorder); the dissociative disorders (including psychogenic amnesia, psychogenic fugue, depersonalization disorder, and atypical dissociative disorder); the category of psychological factors affecting physical condition; and the category of conditions not attributable to a mental disorder which are a focus of attention or treatment (so-called code V disorders).

The differentiating symptomatic criteria for a posttraumatic stress disorder include a re-experience of the trauma as evidenced by recurrent and intrusive recollections of the event, recurrent dreams of the event, or acting or feeling as if the traumatic event were re-occurring in the present; a numbing of responsiveness or reduced involvement with the external world, manifested by a markedly diminished interest in activities, feelings of detachment or estrangement, or a constricted affect; and finally by the presence of other symptoms which were not present before the trauma, including hyperalertness, sleep disturbance, survival guilt, memory impairment, difficulty with concentrating, and so on. Clinically, such a response is more severe than an adjustment disorder. The symptoms are more overt and dramatic and cause the patient severe distress.

At the other extreme are those conditions that are coded as not attributable to a mental disorder, including such states as academic problem, occupational problem, uncomplicated bereavement, phase of life problem or other life circumstance problem, marital problem, parent/child problem, and so on. They are identified by relatively mild symptomatology insufficient to warrant diagnosis as an adjustment disorder.

Course and Prognosis

Knowledge about course and prognosis of the adjustment disorders remains uncertain and even confusing (Andreasen and Wasek 1980). Very few studies have been performed validating the concept of the adjustment disorders (Andreasen and Hoenk 1982; Chandler and Lundahl 1983; Looney and Gunderson 1978), and an extensive search of the literature failed to discover a single scientifically controlled study examining the course and prognosis (or treatment) of this disorder. Therefore, in examining the issues of course and prognosis several factors must be taken into consideration, including DSM-III-R (American Psychiatric Association 1987) criteria; the general issue of the individual's response to stress, and, in particular, the response of children and adolescents; the nature of the stressor; the lack of follow-up studies (both short- and long-term) on large numbers of individuals who have undergone a major stress; the contrasting phenomenon of the serendipitous finding of major stressor(s) in symptomatic so-called "normals"; and, finally, nonprofessional assistance in coping as a means of affecting outcome.

To review DSM-III-R briefly, the criteria established define the disturbance associated with an adjustment disorder as beginning within three months of the onset of the stressor. The course of the illness may be acute or chronic. However, again by these criteria, it is assumed that the disturbance will eventually remit.

Related to the above discussion, there may be times when initially psychosocial stressors do in fact precipitate symptoms of sufficient intensity to warrant the diagnosis of adjustment disorder and no other specific DSM-III-R diagnosis, and yet the symptoms do not remit. Since one of the criteria of an adjustment disorder is eventual remission of symptoms, and since in this instance they do not remit, a review and revision of the diagnosis may be necessary.

There is ample literature to validate such occurrences. A study by Looney and Gunderson (1978) reports on the outcome of 2,078 male Navy enlisted personnel who were hospitalized with a diagnosis of transient situational disturbance (the DSM-II designation). Of the group approximately 60 percent were able to return to duty effectively. They required no further psychiatric hospitalizations and completed their military enlistments satisfactorily. Of the remaining approximately 40 percent, 27 percent were rehospitalized for psychiatric reasons, an additional 10 percent were prematurely discharged from the service for administrative reasons (primarily unsuitability), and 4 percent were not recommended for re-enlistment because of substandard performance. A large majority of the patients who were re-admitted to the hospital received diagnoses other than a second transient situational disturbance. Looney and Gunderson concluded that the results generally supported the validity of the diagnostic category; nonetheless, they were aware that of the patients initially so diagnosed, many in fact may be suffering from other more chronic disorders.

Similarly, a study was done by Andreasen and Hoenk (1982) regarding the predictive value of the diagnostic category of adjustment disorders (DSM-III). They concluded that almost 71 percent of adult patients so diagnosed recovered completely and had good psychosocial adjustments at follow-up. However, in the case of adolescents, the situation was somewhat different. Only 44 percent of the adolescents with this diagnosis were found to be completely well at follow-up. Andreasen concluded that such a diagnosis has somewhat limited predictive validity; nonetheless in a sizable percentage of the adolescent and adult patients to whom it is assigned, it is still appropriate.

Finally, Masterson (1966, 1967, 1968) and others have examined the phenomenon of the symptomatic adolescent; they have concluded that such individuals are not demonstrating part of the normal, stage-specific developmental phenomena of adolescence. Although conceding the difficulty of arriving at a definitive diagnosis in such teenagers at the time of initial presentation, Masterson argues that these symptomatic adolescents can be differentiated from reasonably healthy ones. Such adolescents do in fact require treatment to allow for continued normal growth and development.

Any discussion of the course and prognosis of stress-related disorders brings to mind the notion of crisis theory as described by Caplan (1960, 1964). Without describing the theory in detail, an essential hypothesis of Caplan's is that periods of crisis are times of special significance for future mental health. The outcome will be influenced by premorbid functioning and support systems and may be either healthy (i.e., there may be emotional growth and an improved level of functioning) or unhealthy (deterioration with crystallization of emotional dysfunction). Such a hypothesis has obvious implications for the conceptualization of course and prognosis (and according to Caplan's theory should dictate intervention strategies as well). Many authors have supported Caplan's views, including Kaplan and Mason (1960), Chodoff et al. (1964), and Wynne (1975). Other authors, such as Vaillant (1971) and Bartolucci and Drayer (1973), although they do not directly contradict Caplan, nonetheless place more emphasis on the nature of the individual personality structure of the patient (and perhaps especially on the ego adaptive mechanisms) and on the characteristics of the family and social group.

Thus in considering the outcome of an adjustment disorder in a particular child or adolescent, one must take into account the special vulnerabilities of children. These include such factors as immaturity of ego function; literal dependence upon parents and other adults in the community for support, guidance, and sustenance; and finally the apparent frequency of stressors occurring in the form of divorce, sexual and physical abuse, developmental conflicts (Nagera 1966), and so on. Although Boyd (1981) speaks of children's remarkable resistance to disaster, the authors believe that the preponderance of opinion would side with Shapiro (1973), Kessler (1979), and May (1979) in indicating a special vulnerability on the part of children in such situations. Children have relatively immature ego mechanisms of adaptation, and they lack experience, knowledge, and a capacity for abstract reasoning. They are also quite dependent upon their parents and other support figures, especially in times of crisis, as pointed out by Block et al. (1955). After discovering 10 severely frightened children among a group of 25 "normals," Terr (1983b) suggests that traumatic events and their psychological aftermaths may be far more common than is thought.

Clinical reports and laboratory studies with animals (Anderson 1941) indicate that some stressors may be so overwhelming as to cause permanent psychic dysfunction. Examples of clinical reports include the studies of Terr (1979, 1981b, 1983a) which describe the outcome in a group of 26 children who were kidnapped in Chowchilla, California. She found that every child involved in the kidnapping continued to suffer from symptoms as late as four to five years after the incident and that the trauma continued to exert an influence on the everyday life, the personality development, and the future expectations of all these previously normal children. Such children, however, are not described as having adjustment disorders, but instead have been diagnosed as suffering from a posttraumatic stress disorder.

Similarly, in a 20-year follow-up of veterans suffering from "combat fatigue," Archibald and Tuddenham (1965) found that symptoms following sufficiently severe trauma may persist for very long intervals, if indeed they ever do disappear. In addition, studies by Chodoff (1963) and others regarding concentration camp survivors also indicate that these survivors may demonstrate late effects of such an overwhelming stress. Finally, in a paper describing symptomatology and management of acute grief, Lindemann (1944) notes that in place of a picture of the typical grief reaction, distorted pictures of such a process may ensue with longstanding consequences. Whether the effects of an adjustment disorder in childhood may be lifelong as well remains unknown.

Another issue regarding prognosis is the question of outcome in persons who undergo moderate to severe psychosocial stress and who receive no treatment. The numbers of such individuals are apparently high, as indicated, for example, in studies by Lindy et al. (1981). This investigation reviewed the outcome of an outreach program developed to identify survivors of a fire at the Beverly Hills Supper Club in Southgate, Kentucky. The program offered preventive services to such survivors who were felt to be at risk for long-term impairment. It was estimated that there were more than 2,500 patrons in the club at the time of the fire; out of all those, only 125 survivors contacted the team within the first year after the fire. Although a number of hypotheses were formulated regarding the small number of survivors so identified, one factor among those mentioned was a persistent reluctance among the survivors to seek out professional help because of a perceived need to be protected from further external psychic stress even in the form of professional help. Such individuals may or may not come to the attention of psychiatric treatment facilities years after the trauma.

Again there is conflicting evidence in the literature supporting both viewpoints. A study by Futterman and Pumpian-Mindlin (1951) indicated that in 1951 they were "still encountering fresh cases (of persistent stress reaction after combat in World War II) that have never sought treatment until the present time" (p. 401). In contrast to the previously reported study by Chodoff (1963) is a study by Leon (1981) regarding the survivors of the Holocaust and their children. The findings of these investigations clearly indicated that as a group, at the time of the study, concentration camp and other Eastern European Jewish survivors of World War II and their children did not manifest serious psychological impairment. Indeed, the individuals studied had been able to cope with the terrible experiences they lived through, along with residue of these experiences, with no differences in psychological adjustment between the survivors and control groups. Similarly, no differences in psychological adjustment were noted between the survivors' and control group's children.

To return to the previously mentioned study by Terr (1983b) in which she recorded life attitudes, dreams, and psychic trauma in a group of "normal" children, she discovered that psychic trauma had occurred in 10 of her 25 "normals" and that such children were in fact symptomatic. She postulates that psychic trauma is a spectrum of conditions whose manifestations depend upon the type and number of ego functions which are compromised by the shock. She wonders how much severe fright in childhood is never worked through, but rather is swept under the rug in the expectation that eventually it will simply disappear.

A final point to be mentioned regarding course and prognosis involves nonprofessional assistance in coping as a means of affecting outcome. This factor is especially important for children and adolescents since at the time of crisis they are more dependent upon family (and community) support than are adults. Block (1955) states this emphatically: "Parental handling of the disaster experience influenced the ability of the child to deal with it" (p. 416). It appears, however, that after children have experienced a trauma, their parents may be unable, reluctant, or unaware of the need to intervene on their behalf. The experience of Terr (1979, 1981b, 1983a, 1983b) seems to point this out dramatically. The study by Lindy et al. (1981) reaches the same conclusion, as the title of their article suggests, referring to survivors of a disaster as a "reluctant population." They postulate the existence of a "trauma membrane," described as a small network of trusted people who serve to protect and buffer the survivor from perceived further external psychic stress (even in the form of professional help). Such a description is in harmony with the observations of Tyhurst (1951) regarding the "period of recoil" (from trauma). Tyhurst speaks of a transitory period of dependency after which the survivor may be quite unwilling to talk as freely as he had initially, and may be quite unwilling to accept help even though badly needed. Futhermore, there may be professional reluctance or a lack of knowledge about prognosis (see Terr 1981b) which interferes with the readiness of professionals to offer appropriate help to parents and children after a traumatic event.

In predicting a course of illness or prognosis for a particular child, one must take several factors into account. These include the child's premorbid function, the special vulnerability of all children to stressors, the nature of the stressor, the intensity of recommended therapeutic endeavors, and the family's capacity to be supportive and assist in recovery. Nonetheless, much remains to be learned regarding the prognosis of attempts to cope with stress, with psychic trauma in general, and with the outcome of the adjustment disorders in particular.

Treatment

Since, to our knowledge, there are no controlled treatment outcome studies for the adjustment disorders of childhood and adolescence, treatment recommendations remain empirical. We will outline what we consider to be a logical approach to treatment planning for such individuals.

Using terminology borrowed from Caplan (1964) and now incorporated into the public health lexicon, one may divide the treatment of stress-related disorders into primary, secondary, and tertiary prevention. Primary prevention is defined as any program for reducing the incidence of all types of mental disorders in the community. Such programs may be carried out by a child psychiatrist or other mental health specialist in a variety of ways which reflect child advocacy, including consultation, publishing research, and so on. For example, many articles (Kaerscher and Kuczen 1984) and books (Kuczen 1982) appear in the lay press which seek to inform parents how to recognize signs of stress in children and adolescents and how to handle such situations when they do arise.

Clinical studies may be designed with the specific task of discovering ways to reduce the discomfort of situations which nearly uniformly expose children to levels of considerable stress. Such experiments may be reported in the professional literature with the hope that professional planners would then incorporate such innovations into existing and forthcoming programs. An example of such a study is that of Felner et al. (1982) who describe the use of social support and environmental structure as a means of primary prevention during school transitions (to high school). The results of clinical research may also be used to assist professionals in establishing guidelines for parents who desire information on ways to reduce common forms of developmentally·related stress. Such a study was recently published by Rierdan et al. (1983), establishing guidelines for preparing girls for menstruation.

Secondary prevention measures are those invoked to address problems that have already appeared. They are aimed at decreasing the duration and severity of the disorders which do occur (thereby reducing morbidity). Such intervention is usually directed toward the single individual, toward members of a family, or, sometimes, toward a community in need. Tyhurst (1951) delineated three phases of reaction to an acute disaster—the period of impact, the period of recoil, and the posttraumatic period. He suggested that, ideally, secondary prevention should begin during the period of recoil since there is a need then to ventilate and receive concrete reassurance of aid. He reports, in fact, that shortly thereafter the survivors of disasters may become independent in their manner and unwilling to accept help even though it is badly needed. He goes on to state that "the management of responses during this period can have crucial significance for subsequent psychological events" (p. 767). His remarks are echoed by Block et al. (1955) and Boyd (1981). Treatment strategies for secondary prevention are consistant with typical disaster relief programs. Such approaches to intervention include a rapid assessment of needs, the provision of shelter and other physical supports if necessary, emergency medical and mental health intervention, and assistance in the establishment of community network programs. From the perspective of an individual child psychiatrist, when dealing with a specific child or family, there may be a considerable degree of overlap in the techniques of secondary and tertiary prevention. Many of the treatment strategies outlined below for the adjustment disorders may be incorporated into crisis intervention case management. The development of strategies to deal with the mental health aspects of community disasters is, however, a topic beyond the scope of this chapter.

Tertiary prevention is resorted to after a condition has appeared and has caused significant damage. It is defined as any intervention aimed at reducing the impairment which may result from such disorders. Such reactions typically occur during Tyhurst's (1951) "post-traumatic" period. The ensuing patterns of behavior are closer to those phenomena with which psychiatrists are familiar and include the posttraumatic stress disorders and adjustment disorders. Numerous studies have reported on treatment strategies; however, such reports remain experiential or anecdotal (see Archibald and Tuddenham 1965; Feinstein 1980; Horowitz 1974; Schultz 1982; Shapiro 1973; Terr 1979; Winer and Pollock 1980; Wynne 1975). However, with all, certain common themes do tend to be expressed. First and foremost among these is the need for treatment of sufficient intensity and duration instituted as early as possible in the posttraumatic course. Because of a need to individualize treatment, widely divergent treatment modalities are recommended. Finally, most authors conclude that for children and adolescents the aim of treatment is to facilitate removal and/or modification of symptoms, to restore or at least to improve function, and ultimately to resolve conflicts in order to allow for the further unfolding of the normal ongoing developmental processes.

Within the anecdotal reports available in the literature, specific treatment recommendations have ranged from inpatient to outpatient treatment. The methods suggested encompass the most widely used treatment modalities, including individual insight-oriented psychotherapy, behavioral therapy, pharmacotherapy, family therapy, crisis intervention treatment, and psychoanalysis (see Archibald and Tuddenham 1965; Burden 1980; Lindy et al. 1981; Rosenthal 1979; Shapiro 1973; Winer and Pollock 1980; Wynne 1975). It seems to us that any therapist dealing with a child or adolescent undergoing an adjustment disorder needs to be able to approach the patient's problem from an eclectic point of view with an individualized treatment plan. Such a plan may bear the stamp of the specific theoretical framework with which the therapist feels most comfortable, but the disorder should always be addressed with a systematized, stepwise approach of intervention hierarchies in mind.

First, specific attention must be paid to the nature and source of the stressor. In certain instances, environmental manipulations may be possible, reducing the intensity of the stress and thereby decreasing the pressure experienced by the patient.

Under some circumstances, this may be the only intervention strategy necessary. For example, an adjustment disorder may arise when a child with developmental reading disorder is placed in a mainstream reading group alongside children reading normally. Behavioral acting out in the classroom might then occur. Removal of the child from that classroom situation and placement in a special reading group for children with reading disorders might dramatically diminish the behavioral reactions to such a stress. Similarly, a two-year-old child admitted to the hospital may demonstrate great distress if the parents elect or are required to leave, and are therefore unable to provide emotional and physical support. A simple manipulation of the situation, such as providing sleeping-in arrangements for the parents, may remove the source of stress and preclude the need for any other intervention.

However, there may be times when the environment cannot be affected or changed in and of itself, or when such change is insufficient. Such a situation may include a family move, birth of a sibling, or much more stressful situations such as the death of a parent. Again, one may view the situation within the framework of hierarchies of intervention. After environmental manipulation, the next level of intervention would be an array of strategies aimed at decreasing the stress and conflict experienced by the child. Often enough, these could be put in effect through work with the parents or caretakers with no direct intervention with the child. An example would be helping the parents deal with a regression in the toddler's newly gained bowel or bladder control after the birth of a sibling. In such a case, intervention would be directed along two avenues: first, parents would be instructed to provide some specific time to be spent exclusively with the older sibling(s); and second, the parents would also be instructed to forego coercive pressure for toilet training. Similarly, parents could be counseled regarding the psychological impact of separation and divorce on their children. In general, these intervention strategies would be aimed at containing stress-induced symptomatology in the child through intervention with the child's parents.

It is important to keep in mind that such interventions may be neither successful nor sufficient. When that is the case, a more thorough individualized assessment of the child is necessary in order to develop specific treatment recommendations. Again, depending on the symptomatology present, a hierarchy of treatment interventions for a specific child could be established. This would be shaped by the degree of distress, by the child's capacity to handle the stress, and, finally, by the parents' capacity to be supportive of the child. Such a hierarchy implies the simultaneous involvement of a range of modalities and intensities. In its simplest form, treatment would consist of a single mode of brief therapy. In more complex situations or where limited forms of treatment have not succeeded, multiple short-term strategies would be necessary.

Using the example of the death of a parent, one could define an entire spectrum of reactions in a child such as: a normal grief response; an adjustment disorder with depressed mood manifested by protracted crying spells; an adjustment disorder with school inhibition manifested by a child's inability to complete his school work; an adjustment disorder with conduct disturbance in the form of fighting, truancy, minor uncharacteristic stealing, and so on; or finally a major depressive disorder with a suicide attempt. If one thinks about the adjustment disorder diagnoses in such a case, one can construct a graded series of interactions.

The simplest type of intervention which might be appropriate is "release therapy" as described by Levy (1939). The method of release therapy "is in the use of the acting-out principle in play to its highest degree" (p. 716) with interpretations absent or reduced to a minimum. The children treated with this form of therapy were thought to have repressed the traumatic event. Through individually appropriate structured play interactions, Levy helped bring such material into consciousness and fostered a working through of the trauma. A word of caution, however, seems appropriate; indeed, Levy himself addresses the issue of the importance of appropriate case selection.

In her investigation of children suffering from severe stress-related disorders, Terr (1981a) indicates that the posttraumatic play of children (the "forbidden games") provides no relief to the traumatized individual, as this stands for normal play which serves as a coping mechanism that fosters growth and development as well as dissipation of anxiety. In fact, Terr's impression is that the posttraumatic play itself engenders additional anxiety because it almost literally recreates the traumatic event. Therefore, she concludes, the more the play fails, the more anxiety is generated because the child perceives that, even in retrospect, he or she cannot find effective mechanisms to deal with the traumatic event. Terr contends that until it is interpreted therapeutically, the connection between posttraumatic play and the trauma itself remains unconscious.

The next step in the treatment hierarchy might be brief individual insight-oriented psychotherapy with the use of the techniques of clarification, confrontation, and interpretation to help the child understand the conflictual nature of his behavior. Or else, if it seemed more appropriate, one might use a behavior modification strategy, as, for example, a contingency contract for performance of homework and other school behaviors. An appropriate use of pharmacotherapy might also be indicated; for example, the use of a hypnotic in a child who had spent two or three sleepless nights. In any particular case, each specific technique might be sufficient in itself to help a child overcome his or her difficulties. On the other hand, in some cases it might be necessary to combine a few or even many treatment strategies, including environmental manipulation, parent interventions, direct child interventions, and so on.

One treatment issue of special note is that of hospitalization for treatment of children with adjustment disorders. There are instances when such treatment is unequivocally necessary. Examples would include seriously suicidal behavior or other instances when a child's safety cannot be guaranteed in a less restrictive setting. However, alternative treatments should be considered first (halfway house, emergency foster placement, temporary removal of a parent or sibling, and so on) and such treatment should be short term and limited in scope. Lengthy hospital stays intended to achieve "character change" are inconsistent with an adjustment disorder diagnosis.

To reiterate briefly, there are no controlled treatment studies of children and adolescents with adjustment disorders. Outlined here is a common sense hierarchical approach to treatment strategies useful in the treatment of an individual child suffering from this condition. Research is needed in the specific area of treatment with the goal of developing rational, successful intervention strategies for children with adjustment disorders.

Chapter 236

Crisis Intervention: Theory and Technique

For the last several decades in many settings there have been an increasing interest in and appreciation for crisis intervention as a treatment of choice for a variety of mental health problems. Mental health professionals are faced with the same dilemma as are all health care providers today: to supply needed services in a cost-effective way, without jeopardizing the quality of treatment received.

The majority of people who seek professional help for their emotional problems are motivated by discomfort. Often, because of cost, stigma, ignorance, etc., help is not sought until the pain is considerable and the problems have developed to a point where the level of seriousness goes beyond the usual coping mechanisms of the individual. Consequently, many of those who seek professional help do so in a state of emotional crisis. Crisis states usually result from perceptions of loss or threat of loss caused by a stressor. When coping styles are maladaptive, an adjustment disorder can develop. Crisis intervention can then offer an important treatment option.

Crisis intervention offers a sound and effective model for brief therapy, the principal aim of which is immediate and permanent symptom reduction. It is designed with an emphasis on prevention which helps the patient develop new means of coping with future crises (Parad 1965). Used in appropriate situations, crisis intervention offers a treatment strategy that is superior to more traditional forms of psychotherapy.

Stemming from the pioneering work of Erich Lindemann (1944) and Gerald Caplan (1964), current crisis theory represents a synthesis of contributions from several disciplines, including public health, psychiatry, psychology, sociology, and social work. Perhaps in part because of its eclectic nature, the crisis intervention model has broad appeal to mental health practitioners who work in a variety of practice settings dealing with diverse problems and populations.

Crisis intervention is a holistic approach based on the public health model of a "population at risk." This assumes that proper intervention at an opportune moment can prevent more serious problems from developing.

The crisis intervention model assumes that during the normal course of their lives everyone, even well-functioning people in good mental health, can be confronted with emotional stress. Therapeutic emphasis is on the individual's strengths rather than on weaknesses.

Crisis intervention is a proven approach to helping people in the pain of an emotional crisis (Decker and Stubblebine 1972; Flomenhaft and Langsley 1971; Hoffman and Remmel 1975; H. Parad and L. Parad 1968; L. Parad and H. Parad 1968). This chapter is an attempt to bring together concepts from a variety of sources which combine to define crisis intervention in terms of the current state of the art.

General Therapeutic Concepts

Definition

Gerald Caplan (1964) was the first to conceptualize a model of emotional crisis. According to Caplan's model, the individual is constantly working to maintain a state of equilibrium, in effect, to be in a condition of balance with his environment. When an individual is faced with a problem which he defines as important and which he believes he cannot solve, this balance is upset. As tension mounts, the individual becomes increasingly disoriented and disorganized; eventually he enters a state of disequilibrium signifying an emotional crisis. Simply put, a crisis is the upset of a steady state (Parad 1966).

Gleaning the positive aspects of crisis from the developmental theories of Erik Erikson (1950, 1959), Caplan perceived the crisis to be both a danger and an opportunity. It is a danger in the sense that individuals may resolve the crisis by maladaptive means leading to a decreased level of social and psychological functioning; in some cases they may even attempt or commit suicide. However, Caplan also noted that those individuals who succeed in mastering such a critical situation are often strengthened by the experience, and as a result, they are better able to deal with subsequent difficulties even when these go beyond the scope of the original crisis. This concept of crisis as an opportunity for growth has become one of the tenets of crisis intervention.

Crisis Sequence

In his classic study of acute grief reactions following the fire at the Coconut Grove nightclub, Lindemann (1944) observed that survivors experiencing acute grief had common, predictable reactions. Building on this knowledge, many authors (including Caplan 1964; Golan 1969; Klein and Lindemann 1961; Rapoport 1962; Sifneos 1960) have supported the notion that individuals reach emotional crisis by going through predictable stages. Some theorists, among them Smith (1978), Sachs (1968), and Hill (1958), have attempted to illustrate the crisis sequence visually. In an effort to consolidate much of what is common to these theories, we have developed our own model of the crisis sequence (Figure 1).

The sequence begins with the individual in his pre-crisis state of equilibrium. During this time he is able to maintain a steady state with his environment by using his usual repertoire of coping techniques and problem-solving skills. As long as this works, the individual is in no danger of crisis.

However, he may be confronted by a very stressful occurrence. We have named this the "hazardous event" (1) on our figure. This stressor is perceived by the individual as ominous, posing a real threat to life goals and/or self-image. As usual he utilizes his available repertoire of problem-solving skills, but finds them inadequate to the task. He is faced with a problem he cannot solve. At this point there is a beginning sense of disequilibrium. The occurrence of the hazardous event has begun to put the crisis sequence in motion.

As the tension and anxiety mount, the individual finds himself in a "vulnerable state." Now he resorts to emergency efforts to cope with the threat; these efforts indicate an emerging feeling of desperation. Lydia Rapoport (1962) contends that while in a vulnerable state, the individual perceives the situation to be a threat, a loss, or a challenge. If experiencing a threat, the individual will feel a rise in anxiety.

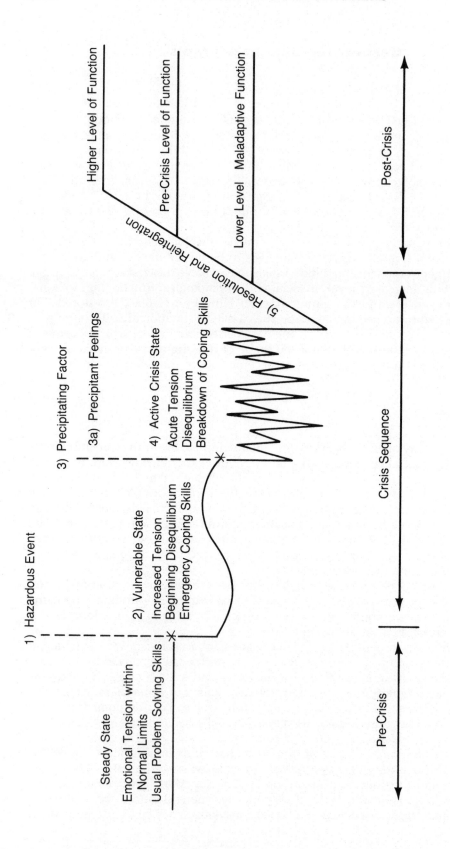

Figure 1. Development of a Crisis

He may become quite hostile, venting his anger indiscriminately. If he experiences loss, he may become depressed, feeling helpless and lost. If, however, he is able to experience the situation as a challenge, he will feel an increase in anxiety coupled with a hope that things can be resolved. On the other hand, if there is no resolution at this time, the tension will continue to mount.

At some point a "precipitating factor" (3) takes place. This is the final stress which plunges the vulnerable individual into an "active crisis state" (4) (Harris et al. 1963). This precipitating factor is usually part of the presenting problem for which the individual ultimately seeks help (Bloom 1963). It can be of catastrophic proportions, or it may be a minor, seemingly insignificant, event that marks the exhaustion of the individual's capacity to maintain the tenuous vulnerable state (Korner 1973). There are instances where the hazardous event is of such explosive magnitude that it simultaneously becomes the precipitating factor and pushes the individual immediately into a state of acute disorientation and disequilibrium. Such a reaction is often seen in victims of rape.

Hoffman and Remmel (1975) identify the "precipitant" (3A) as the repressed feelings aroused by the precipitating factor. This dormant pain has links to past conflicts. These in turn fuel the pain of the precipitant. This link to the past gives rise to the psychodynamic and psychoanalytic dimensions of crisis intervention (Ewing 1978; Glick and Meyerson 1980; Talbott 1980). It provides a partial explanation for the distinct, unique vulnerability which each individual manifests in the face of a crisis. It also offers an opportunity to rework some of the issues from the past, even while keeping the therapeutic focus on the present acute stress situation. Glick and Meyerson suggest that a person in crisis presents the therapist with an opportunity to observe "a cross section of important character patterns" (p. 173) which have contributed to the present distressed responses.

During the state of active crisis, the tension and anxiety increase to an intolerable level, leaving the individual desperate for relief. This active state is accordingly time limited, usually lasting no longer than six to eight weeks. During this time, as a last resource, many individuals will seek professional help. Others, unable to tolerate the high level of tension and anxiety, may experience an emotional breakdown. Still others may attempt to decrease the tension by using maladaptive forms of behavior, such as alcohol or drugs, which in themselves can lead to impaired social functioning. In addition to lowering the acute anxiety, however, this dysfunctional behavior brings secondary gains (a temporary high), so that this troublesome activity is reinforced and maintained.

People in an acute state of active crisis are in the throes of a great deal of pain and are consequently very receptive to help from the therapist. On the other hand, those who have learned to cope in some way, even maladaptively, are often not at all eager to change their behavior; indeed they may cling tenaciously to the tactic they have initiated, and they are, therefore, usually not good candidates for crisis intervention (Rapoport 1967).

The period of reintegration (5) is an extension of the crisis state in which the tension and the anxiety level are lowered, and some form of reorganization takes place. The final level of adjustment, the post-crisis level of functioning, can be lower than, equal to, or higher than the pre-crisis level. Crisis therapists increase the probability that, following professional intervention, the patient will at least regain his pre-crisis level of functioning, and preferably attain a higher level.

In the following case example, this type of crisis sequence is illustrated by the experience of a young divorced woman, Mrs. N., who was held hostage during a robbery at her place of employment, a dry cleaning establishment.

Before the robbery Mrs. N. was a well-functioning individual with no more than the expected amount of problems in her daily life. To her friends and family she was happy and well-adjusted.

One day, during a driving rainstorm, two nice-looking men entered the cleaners where Mrs. N. was working along with two other women employees. The men brandished guns and declared their intention to rob the place. One of the men grabbed Mrs. N. by the arm and put the gun to her head, telling her that he did not want to hurt her but he would if she did not cooperate. (Mrs. N. was understandably very frightened. In other words a very hazardous event had taken place and Mrs. N. was now in a vulnerable state.)

In relating this part of the story Mrs. N. seemed surprised to report that she remembers laughing at this point and trying to make jokes with the robbers, all the while she really feared for her life. It was pointed out in therapy that laughing and joking were emergency measures which she had put into effect in an effort to cope with an extremely stressful situation.

During the course of the robbery, a friend of Mrs. N., an off-duty police officer, stopped in as he frequently did during the week. He could tell something was wrong, so he left quickly and notified the police. He returned, however, in an attempt to help Mrs. N. and her co-workers. The robbers threatened to shoot him if he did not leave immediately. As he tried to leave, the robber holding Mrs. N. panicked and shot the friend several times. It was a bloody scene with the friend on the ground writhing in pain.

This was the precipitating event which pushed Mrs. N. into an active crisis state. She began to scream, and one of the robbers told her to shut up or be shot. The police arrived at this point and called to the robbers to come out. The man holding Mrs. N. pushed her out of the store, all the while hiding behind her with his gun still at her head. All of the police on the scene were in a ready position with guns drawn and aimed at the robber, and consequently at Mrs. N. It took the police several minutes to talk the robber into surrendering, but not before they had shot and wounded his accomplice. Mrs. N. was in a state of hysteria when the ordeal ended.

In the days following the robbery Mrs. N. became extremely frightened and depressed. She suffered from terrible headaches and she had great difficulty sleeping, even with the diazepam prescribed to help "calm her nerves." She resorted to drinking large quantities of alcohol to induce sleep. She became very fearful and afraid to leave her house. She became short-tempered with those around her, especially her nine-year-old daughter. She contemplated suicide by taking all of her pills at once. She felt sure that she was going crazy, and her family members were harboring similar concerns.

She was first interviewed four weeks following the robbery, and it was evident that this heretofore well-adjusted individual was in a fragmented emotional state. The treatment of choice in this case was crisis intervention. For Mrs. N., long-term therapy was not necessary and, indeed, could have been counterproductive. Effective crisis intervention (to be discussed later) allowed Mrs. N. to return to her normal, healthy pre-crisis level of functioning.

Crisis Intervention as a Therapeutic Framework

Bruce Baldwin (1977) agrees that crisis intervention should be considered a "limited framework" (p. 562) for therapeutic intervention. Primarily, it sets parameters within which the crisis therapist is free to use his or her preferred orientation to psychotherapy, whether psychoanalytic, behavioral, cognitive, experiential, etc. Yet there does exist a core of therapeutic concepts basic to crisis intervention theory.

1. Crises are normal life experiences and do not represent illness or pathology. An emotional crisis reflects a realistic struggle in which the individual works to maintain a state of equilibrium between himself and his surroundings (Caplan 1964).
2. The stress which brings on the crisis may be either an internal or an external

event (Erikson 1950). It may occur as a single catastrophic event, or as a series of milder happenings which may have a cumulative effect (Korner 1973).

3. The severity of the crisis is not directly related to the severity of the stressor; it is a function, rather, of the individual's perception of the event (Rapoport 1962).

4. There may be a link between the individual's current situation and past conflicts. This connection is experienced emotionally by the patient (Hoffman and Remmel 1975).

5. Emotional crises are self-limiting events. The period of acute disorganization is usually resolved within four to six weeks, with either adaptive or maladaptive results (Bloom 1977).

6. An individual in a state of crisis has weakened defenses. This increased vulnerability makes him more amenable to help (Schwartz 1971). A minimal effort at this time can have a maximal effect (Rapoport 1962).

7. Adaptive crisis resolution offers a triple opportunity (a) to master the present situation, (b) to rework some past conflicts, and (c) to learn better ways to deal with crises in the future (Caplan 1964).

8. Adaptive crisis resolution is not determined by past experiences or character structure, but by processes occurring in the present (Paul 1966).

9. An inherent component of every emotional crisis is an actual and/or anticipated loss sustained by the individual. Reconciling this loss is part of the crisis resolution process (Hitchcock 1973; Stickler and LaSor 1970).

10. With adaptive crisis resolution, new ego sets emerge as new coping and problem-solving skills are developed which will help the individual in the future (Golan 1978).

Implications for Practice

Model for Crisis Intervention

Crisis intervention differs from more traditional forms of therapy in that there are several limitations on both the time and the scope of the treatment. From the beginning, there are well-defined goals, the achievement of which marks the end of the treatment. Usually these goals deal with relieving the immediate pain of the person in crisis, and with helping him resume normal social functioning at his pre-crisis level (Butcher and Koss 1978; Ewing 1978).

The focus of the therapy is always the resolution of the present crisis. Some connections may be drawn to the patient's past (Glick and Meyerson 1980; Hoffman and Remmel 1975). However, while these links may be used to help the patient understand why he is in the present crisis, treatment remains focused on helping him deal with the current situation (Kardener 1975) with an eye to improving his chances for coping in the future.

To achieve the goals agreed upon, both the patient and the therapist must be willing to take an active role to resolve the crisis (Patterson and O'Sullivan 1974; Porter 1966; Sebolt 1973). The therapist must not be afraid to use his authority (Kaffman 1963; Weinberger 1971) to capitalize on the patient's regressive state in order to develop a working relationship very rapidly, but he must be very careful not to foster dependence in the patient. The patient must be encouraged and permitted to do everything he is capable of doing in order to resolve the crisis himself (Aquilera and Messick 1982).

This means that the therapist must accurately assess the patient's strengths. These strengths are emphasized. The patient comes to treatment in a state of disintegration, with his ego defenses weakened. The therapist wants to avoid further regression in the patient. At the initial contact the patient is usually seeking a magical helper. The therapist must begin immediately to base the crisis in reality (Rapoport 1962). This reality gives the patient hope that the crisis can and will be resolved, but it also indicates that the patient will have to work hard to achieve this resolution. The therapist makes it clear that he is willing to help the patient but that he will not assume responsibility which belongs to the patient in resolving the crisis.

To aid the patient in helping himself, the therapist undertakes an assessment of the patient's social support systems, that is, family, friends, community resources (Schwartz 1971), and works to strengthen these supports. Or, if necessary, the therapist begins to build a support network for the patient (Ewalt 1973; Rapoport 1962). This is a preventive intervention as well, to prepare for the future and the eventual departure of the therapist. Crisis intervention is a very fast paced, positive, growth-oriented intervention. The momentum is always toward the future.

In order to expedite the patient's progress, the therapist takes on the responsibility of confronting any magical thinking on the part of the patient. This can include pointing out maladaptive or unrealistic goals, as well as the negative consequences of current behavior (Butcher and Maudal 1976). Because crisis intervention is firmly based in reality, any negative transference, cognitive distortions, or inappropriate affect is immediately confronted and explored (Schwartz 1971). This removes them as obstacles to the resolution of the crisis and the ensuing emotional growth of the patient.

In the case of Mrs. N. the therapist made several of the interventions listed here. In the first interview Mrs. N. was made aware that she was in a crisis situation. She was informed that her present behavior was "normal" crisis behavior, but that because of its dysfunctional nature it would have to change. The therapist emphasized that this behavior could indeed be changed and that if Mrs. N. was willing to do her part, the therapist was committed to helping her resume her normal life.

A serious assessment of potential suicide was made. Mrs. N. reported that although she had felt desperate before, she felt remarkably better just knowing the therapist was willing and able to help her. She agreed to sign a no-suicide contract and was given information about what to do if she felt like harming herself. This included information about the crisis line, a community resource. Mrs. N. also agreed to sign a no-alcohol contract as well as to throw away all the alcohol in the house. Mrs. N. was told that rather than helping, her drinking was actually contributing to her current problems of depression and anxiety. Initially this patient was scheduled to be seen on a twice-a-week basis so that the therapist could carefully monitor the situation. The patient left the first interview visibly more optimistic with the well-grounded encouragement of the therapist.

Throughout the course of therapy, which took several months, many other interventions were made by the therapist. These included two sessions with members of the patient's family in order to educate them to the situation, and to define their roles in the treatment plan, as well as to put to rest their fears that Mrs. N. was going crazy. This family support is crucial to the success of many crisis cases.

Mrs. N. was taught techniques for relaxation, thought stopping, thought substitution, and self-hypnosis to relieve her headaches. These exercises had the additional effect of putting Mrs. N. back in control of things. This is very important because people in crisis feel out of control.

As Mrs. N. began to feel better, she was encouraged to do more socially. This was difficult for her at first but became easier over time. As she began to feel more like her pre-crisis self, her relationships with her family began to improve. In fact, along with her progress in therapy, all aspects of her life improved.

Mrs. N. became eager to return to work, opting for a job that does not involve the exchange of money. She is now training to be a teacher's assistant at a local elementary school. Therapy will conclude when she is in her new job, returning her to her pre-crisis level of functioning. However, with the new skills Mrs. N. has gained, she will be much stronger emotionally, having resolved this crisis successfully.

Treatment Strategy: Generic versus Individual

Ever since Lindemann (1944) conceptualized states of bereavement, researchers in the field of crisis intervention have sought to predetermine the psychological tasks individuals must master in order to regain their emotional equilibrium following a specific crisis. The generic approach (Jacobson et al. 1968) presumes that for each crisis reaction there are specific tasks which every patient must complete in order to resolve the crisis successfully. The specific character of the crisis determines the treatment plan for every patient seeking help.

This approach has its roots in the concepts of maturational and situational crises as developed by Erikson (1950, 1959). Generic treatment is an attempt to place the tasks a therapist must help the patient master into neat categories. This treatment strategy became important during the community mental health movement, when the front-line service providers of crisis services in the community mental health centers were often lay volunteers and paraprofessionals.

Rosemary Lukton (1982) poses some serious questions about the advisability of accepting this cookbook approach to crisis intervention. Reviewing much of the literature on the treatment of rape victims, Lukton pinpoints major contradictions in the generic approaches to their management (Burgess and Halmstrom 1974; Scherl 1972). She also notes that subsequent research has indicated that a variety of factors help determine the nature and extent of the victim's response to rape.

Lukton warns that with total emphasis on the crisis situation, the individual has been forgotten. While keeping the social situation in mind, crisis therapists cannot forsake the client in order to treat the situation.

Recently more crisis therapists and theorists are recommending the kind of individualized approach that takes into consideration each patient's special needs (Dixon and Sands 1983; Glick and Meyerson 1980; Kennedy 1983; Viederman 1983). These needs vary from patient to patient, and are based on factors such as personality structure, prior life experiences, and presence of social support systems. This move to a more individualized approach may indicate a process of evolution and maturation of crisis intervention as a bona fide form of psychotherapy.

When to Use Crisis Intervention

There exists no universally accepted rule-of-thumb to determine which clients are appropriate for crisis intervention. Bloom (1963) demonstrated that even highly skilled clinicians have difficulty in agreeing upon which features indicate that an individual or family is in crisis. In Bloom's study, the factor most often cited was the presence of a definable precipitating event.

Some clinicians have taken the position that anyone requesting mental health services is ipso facto "in crisis" (Lang 1974; Schwartz 1971; Wolkon 1972). Others disagree with this notion, arguing that crisis intervention is not always the treatment of choice (Kaplan 1968; LaVietes 1974). These authors state that the therapist must exercise keen professional judgment in determining the appropriateness of using the crisis model of intervention with a given patient.

Although we agree with Ewing (1978) that it is impossible to suggest any hard-and-fast rules for selecting suitable patients for crisis intervention, we have compiled a list of selection criteria expanded from Golan (1969) and Porter (1966). Crisis intervention is applicable when there is:

1. Evidence of a specific precipitating event that can be related directly to the patient's present state of disequilibrium.
2. Evidence of an acute rise in anxiety and emotional pain.
3. Evidence of recent breakdown in problem-solving skills.
4. Evidence that the patient has the motivation and potential capacity for change.
5. Evidence that treatment is being sought before the patient has begun to receive secondary gains from maladaptive coping strategies.

Therapeutic Intervention

Intervention with patients in crisis can be divided into four phases. The first phase consists of an assessment of the current situation focusing on the "individual-in-situation." This is followed by an initial formulation of treatment goals. Usually both assessment and formulation phases are completed by the end of the initial interview with the patient. The third phase includes implementation of treatment strategies designed to help the patient develop the skills needed to resolve the crisis. The length of this phase is determined by the patient's ability and readiness to achieve treatment goals. The final phase involves termination of the therapeutic relationship. The last one or two sessions are usually spent dealing with this closure.

Initial Phase: Assessment

The scope of crisis therapy differs from that of the more traditional therapies. The focus is on the current problem which brings the patient in for help. The therapist assesses what is happening, what coping mechanisms the patient is using, and how well these are working. Since all crises involve real or threatened loss, the therapist determines the losses perceived by the patient in view of the presenting problem.

In assessing the presenting problem, the therapist pays special attention to how the patient has been able to cope with the situation thus far. Of particular interest is the existence or the lack of a social support network. This includes family, friends, and community resources. A brief assessment is made of pre-crisis functioning in order to determine how well the patient had been able to function on his own. However, the customary psychosocial history typical of the more traditional intake interview is not taken, for, if essayed, it actually destroys the momentum so vital to successful crisis intervention.

Note.   An alternative view of this point has been stated by one commentator as follows:

> The suggestion that the customary psychosocial history should not be taken because it decreases the momentum of the consultation-therapeutic process is in error, for if well done the opposite is true. An active interviewing stance will effectively elucidate the broad outlines of the critical events of a patient's life in a dynamic way over a brief period of time and will engage the patient at the same time. The activity of the therapist and his efforts to clarify will lead to the revelation of new and pertinent material, and the use of knowledge of the past to demonstrate to the patient the logic of his current predicament, is a powerful tool in such an intervention. History taking is not the [mere] accumulation

of pertinent information useful for interventions . . . [it] . . . serves the [additional] purpose of establishing a connection.

An accurate assessment of whether or not the patient can be helped on an outpatient basis is of crucial importance. This involves a suicide/homicide assessment; because of the acute and intense disorganization of the patient's ego functioning, this can be of real life-and-death importance. This issue must not be minimized by the therapist! All persons assessed to be a serious threat to themselves or others must be referred immediately to a psychiatrist for evaluation and possible hospitalization. This same precaution is necessary if the patient is exhibiting psychotic behavior according to the DSM-III-R (American Psychiatric Association 1987) definition of the term. Such referral is necessary to protect the patient when he is unable to protect himself, and to protect the nonphysician therapist from legal liability in a very dangerous situation. Because of the disruptive effect it has on many people's lives, hospitalization should be considered very carefully and used only when other methods of helping the patient are considered ineffective or dangerous.

Formulation. The therapist needs to take advantage of the patient's willingness to change, a willingness brought on by the pain and confusion arising from his current state of disequilibrium. The therapist takes an active role as an authority figure to educate the patient to the fact that he is in a state of crisis. The therapist conveys that the crisis can be successfully resolved, and that he is willing to do whatever is necessary to help the patient achieve this resolution. At this point the therapist also emphasizes the patient's responsibility to take an active role in carrying out the work necessary for the successful resolution of the crisis. This accomplishes two objectives. First, most patients in crisis seeking professional help are looking for a magical helper. This is, of course, because of their regressed state. By skillful use of his authority and knowledge, the therapist offers the patient hope and fulfills his need for a competent helper. This tends rapidly to establish a positive rapport, a relationship which would take much longer to build if one adopted a more passive approach. Secondly, this action grounds the patient in reality and lessens his magical thinking. The therapist offers his help to work with the patient realistically, and emphasizes the patient's responsibility to join in the effort. The message is, "We can solve this problem, but it is going to take a lot of work. I am willing to do my part. How about you?"

The therapist restates to the patient in an objective way what he perceives the problem to be. The therapist also explains the patient's role in the problem and why he is in a crisis state. This sharpens the patient's focus, offering realistic hope. The patient is then asked to give his report of the situation. This should be a clearer, more organized presentation than originally given. The patient is asked to state what he sees as the biggest need. This begins formulation of treatment goals.

Second Phase: Setting Treatment Goals

These goals are specific and realistic, based on the perceived needs of the patient. These goals address the patient's pain and present dysfunction. The therapist brings up the fact that when these goals are reached, and the patient is able to resume pre-crisis functioning, the treatment will end. This is a good opportunity for the therapist to let the patient know that, because of the new skills he will learn in therapy, his ability to handle problems and his overall functioning may be better after treatment than before. (These original goals may be amended during the course of treatment.)

It is important to the therapeutic relationship that both patient and therapist enter into a contract to work together in therapy. This contract may be in written or oral form. The contract includes mutual understanding and a joint agreement to work toward specific, reachable treatment goals.

Third Phase: Implementation (Number of Sessions Determined by Patient's Need)

The therapist organizes his data and gathers any missing information which he deems important. All information should have some bearing on the crisis situation.

The therapist looks for themes and patterns of behavior and cognition which emerge from the information. Once these are noted, the therapist looks for evidence of these same themes being played out in the therapy sessions. These are brought to the patient's attention.

In crisis therapy confrontation is necessary to keep the patient rooted in reality. Any negative transference or cognitive inattention is explored to remove them as obstacles to the treatment process. The therapist can expect much ventilation during this period of treatment.

Tasks. The therapist assigns tasks for the patient to meet easily achieved short-term goals. These tasks may involve behavior and/or thought. The tasks are determined by the specific situation, taking into consideration the patient's strengths and weaknesses. As short-term goals are met, new ones are set, moving the patient ever closer to successful resolution of the crisis. As the patient masters these tasks he will develop new coping skills. These new skills should be acknowledged, both to mark the patient's progress and to increase his hope for a successful resolution.

Significant others. Because social support systems are so important to proper crisis resolution, it is often necessary to bring the patient's significant other(s) to treatment at least for an education session. This helps give the family added strength and hope, which in turn aids the patient in his efforts to resolve the crisis. This also helps address the threat of triangulation, that is, where those outside the therapeutic relationship undercut the progress made in treatment. If the therapist suspects this might be happening, he is wise to bring the significant others in for a nonconfrontational educational session.

Other resources. A good crisis therapist has a broad knowledge of community resources, or at least the knowledge of how to find out what resources are available to a patient with a particular need. In most communities there exists a wide variety of resources ranging from emergency food and shelter to peer support groups. Opening up the support network can be of great assistance to the patient.

Final (Fourth) Phase: Termination

As treatment progresses the therapist calls attention to the passage of time and the progress being made by the patient. Continued focus on the original goals of therapy, and the patient's progress toward reaching them, means that the decision to terminate is not unexpected, but is mutually agreed to by both therapist and patient. Termination should not be considered unless the patient has reached a state of emotional equilibrium and achieved a level of social functioning equal to that of his pre-crisis state.

In this connection, a word of caution is appropriate. Therapists often want to hold on to patients after the treatment goals have been achieved. Patients also get apprehensive about separating from the therapist, especially if the therapist is sending out unconscious signals of his own insecurities about the termination. A healthy termination can be the most growth-producing aspect of the entire treatment.

As stated, both therapist and patient will have strong feelings about ending the therapeutic relationship. It is important that the therapist be aware of his feelings in order to keep them from intruding on the termination process. The patient must be given the opportunity to acknowledge and express the feelings he has about the loss of therapy and the therapist. On some level, termination of treatment will be experienced by the patient as a loss, one which will stir up feelings of past losses. Remember that the crisis state resulted from the perception of loss (or threat of loss) in the first place. If the therapist can make the patient aware that these feelings are a natural part of the termination process, this can do much to minimize the regressive termination resistance so often described in this phase of treatment.

By reviewing the case with the therapist, the patient can gain better understanding of the process involved in the successful resolution of the crisis. This involves looking back on the work they have done together and identifying areas of change and growth. New problem-solving techniques and additional resources utilized should be emphasized, so that the patient feels that these are now a part of his repertoire of coping skills.

This is a logical follow-up to reviewing the case. The skills used to solve the present crisis are elaborated so that the patient can feel comfortable about facing the future on his own. He is a stronger individual now and this should add to his confidence in handling stressful situations in the future. The therapist's genuine support and enthusiasm are important elements in this phase.

The therapist must assess the patient's need for further treatment. Often in the treatment process old conflicts emerge from the past. Within the scope of crisis intervention treatment, these are not dealt with, except to link them with some of the same feelings the patient is experiencing in the present crisis. Many patients want to pursue further treatment on these same issues. Before a more insight-oriented therapy begins, it is beneficial to the patient that there be a formal termination of the crisis treatment, including transfer to another therapist, if possible. Even if therapy is to continue with the same therapist, it is helpful to effect a real closure of the crisis treatment and to put that issue behind the patient. This helps define the successful crisis resolution as a strength the patient now possesses as he enters into the new treatment, which, of course, will involve a different treatment plan.

When the crisis resolution has been achieved, the patient's case is closed. The patient is then sent on his way with the therapist's sincere encouragement and belief that he will be able to resume life without his previous difficulty. The therapist shuts the door but leaves a crack open. He tells the patient that if he should being to feel overwhelmed in the future, the therapist will be happy to work with him again at that time.

Chapter 237

Stress Management by Behavioral Methods

A behavioral conceptualization of stress and adjustment will be highlighted in this chapter and various behavioral approaches to treatment will be outlined.

A brief, revised version of Dr. R. Suinn's conceptual model is shown in Figure 1. In this model, a stressor impacts on the person, leading to stress responses, and, eventually, either to successful coping and adjustment or to unsuccessful coping and maladjustment. If the outcome is maladjustment, then behavioral treatment must take into account the nature of the stressor, the characteristics of the person, the nature and availability of support systems, the organization of the stress responses, and the character of the ensuing symptoms. Hence, within the proposed conceptualization, behavioral treatment is tied directly to the stressor-reaction-adjustment model.

Behavioral Treatment: Matching to Stress Responses

Critics of both psychotherapy and behavior therapy agree on the need for better matching between patient characteristics and the kinds of treatments which are selected (Akins et al. 1983; Bergin and Suinn 1975; Frank 1979). One way of properly fitting the behavior therapies to the appropriate patients is to consider the stress response system which characterizes the patient's problems (Suinn 1983a). Is the major outcome of the posttraumatic stress disorder a repetition of autonomic responses, such that "the autonomic nervous system continues to prepare for action" (Van der Kolk 1984) with the patient continuing to "live in the emotional, traumatic environment" (Kardiner 1941)? If so, then treatments designed for control of affective-autonomic conditioned responses may be best. On the other hand, if the trauma of object loss or unknown surgery precipitates ruminations or worrisome cognitions, then cognitively oriented therapies might be most appropriate—for example, Borkovec's programs for ruminations, or the surgery videotape and modeling programs of Melamed (Borkovec 1983; Melamed et al. 1983a).

Instead of matching treatment to stress symptoms and responses, an alternative would be to match on the basis of patient coping characteristics. Patients can be identified in terms of their primary coping styles, and these coping styles in turn relate to adjustment outcomes in the face of stressors. We can then rely upon the behavioral treatment that best takes advantage of the patient's own style of coping.

For instance, in the course of working with a person whose autonomic and behavioral systems were immediately responsive to her cognitions, it turned out that cognitive restructuring and problem solving were successful. Akins and his colleagues

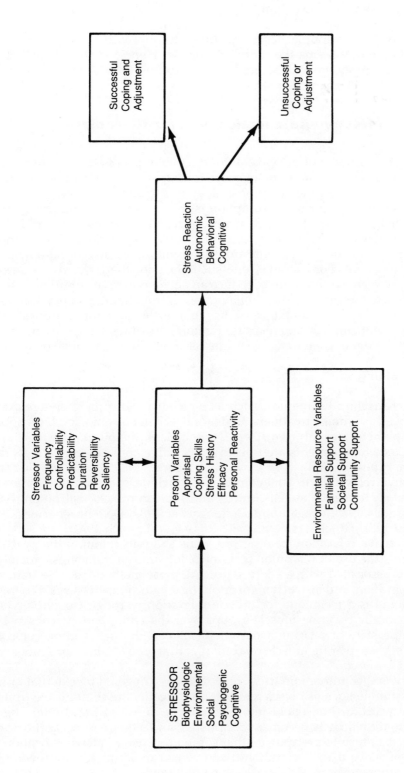

Figure 1. The Stressor-Variable Paradigm

are pursuing this concept of matching by seeking to classify dental patients according to their cognitive information-processing styles (Akins et al. 1982).

However, of the two approaches to matching, the approach based upon symptom characteristics currently seems the more productive. Hence, in this chapter the behavioral treatment programs will be organized according to this dimension of stress responses related to the particular stressor.

Affective-Autonomic Behavior Therapies

The essential characteristic of affective-autonomic therapies is the assumption that the patient suffers from a state of emotional arousal which is of central importance. In some cases it dominates the symptomatology of the disorder, and in other cases it is the disorder itself. A further assumption is that the arousal state (e.g., anxiety, anger) sequentially precedes the other symptom expressions; for instance, it can be antecedent to behavioral disruptions or to ruminative depression. Finally, there is evidence that reduction of the tensional arousal permits access to other problem areas confronting the patient. For example, one such behavior therapy, anxiety management training, was shown not only to reduce anxiety among schizophrenic patients, but also to enhance significantly their ability to profit from traditional psychotherapy.

Examples of three behavioral approaches to affective-autonomic arousal will be presented: treatment emphasizing relaxation training, treatment emphasizing anxiety induction, and treatment combining the elements of relaxation and anxiety induction.

Relaxation Training

There are relaxation techniques, such as biofeedback or progressive relaxation, which can be used as primary treatment modes and lead to physiologic effects opposite to that of sympathetic arousal from stress. Nonetheless, the more productive use of relaxation occurs where patients are trained in its active application to stress, rather than in passive exposure (Agras and Jacob 1979; Denney 1983; Stoyva and Budzynski 1974). The active relaxation treatment programs include cue-controlled relaxation, applied relaxation, relaxation as self-control, and self-control desensitization (Barlow et al. 1984; Cautela 1966; Cragan and Deffenbacher 1984; Deffenbacher and Suinn 1982; Goldfried 1971; Hutchings et al. 1980; Russell and Sipich 1973).

All of the active relaxation training programs share in common the practice of teaching patients the use of relaxation for controlling arousal from stress, mainly the form of arousal associated with anxiety states. All these methods include training in progressive relaxation, and instruction for applying it in the patients' lives. Progressive relaxation training is a technique for muscle relaxation, through isometric-type exercises systematically covering muscle groups over the entire body (Jacobsen 1938). Control over the state of relaxation may be facilitated through adding cue-control conditioning, such as pairing muscle relaxation with words ("calm") or actions (deep breaths).

The theory is that autonomic stress responses are triggered by external or internalized stress stimuli, such as noises reminiscent of battle, the stimulus environment of the surgical ward, or household reminders of the deceased loved one. The conditioned autonomic reactivity becomes precipitated, and either persists as the primary symptom or acts in turn to precipitate other coping/defensive behaviors or thoughts. In the course of active use of relaxation, two events can occur: active prevention or reduction of autonomic arousal, and counterconditioning.

In the first instance, as soon as the patient becomes aware of building autonomic arousal, he or she is able to deal with it through engaging in relaxation activities as a conscious countermeasure—in short, as the anxiety builds, the patient engages in relaxation exercises to reduce the arousal. Alternatively, as a preventive measure, the patient engages in relaxation prior to facing settings known to evoke stress.

In the second instance, the original conditioning can be extinguished through a new pairing of the relaxation response with the stress stimuli; in this way, the conditioned anxiety response is now replaced by a relaxation response. A special format which aims at this latter result is known as systematic desensitization. In this response the patient constructs a listing of situations, all involving anxiety, but each of which precipitates differing levels of anxiety (the anxiety hierarchy). Then, while in a relaxed state, the patient is guided in visualizing these situations, starting with the lowest. Systematic desensitization has been used with veterans for fears associated with war trauma (Kipper 1977), and with rape victims whose anxieties and fears were associated with the violent sexual assault (Turner 1979).

Anxiety Induction

Among the anxiety induction approaches are implosive therapy and flooding (Levis and Boyd, in press; Marks 1972; Stampfl 1966a). Although differing in important ways, the two approaches have major similarities. Historically, implosion was a treatment that involved the induction of anxiety. This was accomplished by presenting the patient with cues that reconstructed not only the reality cues of the environment during initial conditioning, but also a number of psychodynamic cues as well. Flooding, on the other hand, has generally been restricted to anxiety induction associated with the observable cues associated with symptom onset.

In implosion or flooding, the patient is re-exposed to anxiety cues in order to prompt an intense anxiety state. In sessions usually extending beyond 20 to 30 minutes, the patient is exposed to this anxiety activation, either in vivo or symbolically, through guided imagination. For example, Fairbank and Keane (1982) aroused anxiety in a post-traumatic stress disorder (PTSD) Vietnam veteran through intensive imaginal exposure to four events associated with recurrent nightmares and flashbacks. The guided imagery was enhanced by the therapist repeating details associated with the traumatic event, including references to auditory cues (screams of the wounded), visual cues (sight of a decomposed body), olfactory cues (smell of gunpowder), motoric responses (aiming the rifle), cognitive cues (fearful thoughts), and physiologic cues (pounding heart rate). The treatment demands that the salient cues be presented, that these lead to anxiety arousal, that the arousal be at maximum intensity, and that the patient be prevented from escape or avoidance behaviors of any type.

The theoretical rationale for implosion/flooding derives from a two-factor conceptualization of neurosis. The conditioned traumatic response is believed to have become associated not only with the obvious external cues (such as the sounds or sights), but also with other stimuli which may be less obvious or more internal (such as thoughts, appraisals, or emotions). In any conditioning experience, the results may involve primary cues (S1) along with various secondary cues (S2, S3, etc.), all of which are encoded and stored and subject to reactivation. In accord with the two-factor concepts, symptom maintenance is further ensured by avoidance behaviors, perhaps as a function of reinforcement or the principle of conservation of anxiety (Stampfl 1966b), or the process of incubation (Eysenck 1979), or possibly even through shaping of cognitive expectancies (Seligman and Johnston 1973).

In essence, according to two-factor theory, extinction of such learned experiences is best accomplished through re-exposure to the conditioned stimuli, along with prevention of those avoidance behaviors which reduce the anxiety experience. In order to ensure that all primary as well as secondary stimulus patterns have been given the opportunity to extinguish, repeated exposure may be essential. Toward this end, differing events may be used in the guided exposure, such as different battle scenes for PTSD or different themes in the treatment for reactions to rape (Frank and Stewart 1983). Partly because of the intensity of the anxiety induction experience, caution should be applied with the anxiety induction methods (Kilpatrick and Best 1984; Shipley and Boudewyns 1980).

Anxiety Induction and Relaxation Control

An integrated approach, anxiety management training (AMT) (Suinn 1983b; Suinn and Deffenbacher 1988), appears to avoid some of the limitations of both the anxiety induction therapies and the active relaxation training techniques. If an improper format is used, such as inadequate exposure, implosion or flooding can strengthen the conditioning and increase the level of anxiety (Chaplin and Levine 1981; Grey et al. 1981). Further, as a consequence of the treatment, the anxiety induction therapies leave the patient emotionally exhausted, which may in turn lead to increased dropouts (Barlow et al. 1984). On the other hand, the relaxation training methods may not be as suitable for controlling severe autonomic reactivity or the kinds of emotional activation that accompany flashback symptomatology or hypervigilance. Anxiety management training uses anxiety induction, but always to demonstrate the use of anxiety control. Thus, the patient experiences the traumatic cue conditions along with the conditioned autonomic (as well as behavioral and cognitive) responses in order to learn mechanisms of control, namely relaxation skills.

AMT involves a treatment regime which includes anxiety induction followed by anxiety control, graduated homework assignments for transfer of training and for efficacy gains, increased training in self-control, cue-discrimination training utilizing both physiologic and cognitive stimuli for prevention, and emphasis on an active involvement in stress and autonomic management. These are covered in five basic stages of treatment.

In general, a typical treatment session is similar to implosion/flooding in the use of guided imagery to reintegrate the traumatic cues and the anxiety responses. However, the patient is guided in the application of relaxation to reduce and eliminate the arousal state and regain stability and control. As sessions proceed, the patient is given more responsibility not only for the initiation of the anxiety arousal, but also for the establishment of control. In an interim phase, anxiety control is augmented through reliance upon relaxation imagery as a method for eliminating the anxiety imagery. In the last phase, the patient eventually becomes capable of initiating anxiety arousal by means of anxiety imagery, and then, while still in the presence of the anxiety imagery cues, of regaining control via relaxation procedures. In addition, AMT trains the patient in the early identification of signs of anxiety onset, and in how to take preventative steps in order to abort such reactions.

The AMT procedure acknowledges the importance not only of resolving prior learned stress responses, but also of training the patient in the skill of problem-solving itself. Inasmuch as efficacy, perceived control, and coping strategies all impact on vulnerability to and recovery from stress, the broad-spectrum approach of AMT can have multiple contributions.

Since AMT was originally designed for the treatment of generalized anxiety disorder, the underlying theory derives from conceptualizations of anxiety states and their treatment. Although behavioral therapies had been quite successful in designing treatments for tensional states precipitated by specific cue conditions (i.e., phobic disorders), no treatment could handle the more free-floating anxieties which did not appear to be stimulus-bound. On the other hand, laboratory studies of motivational states concluded that anxiety was similar to other drive states in possessing both stimulus and response properties (Brown 1961; Miller 1951). In fact, some of the evidence for the two-factor theory derived from the concept that by means of its cue properties, anxiety stimulated avoidance behaviors.

As a basis for AMT treatment, it was theorized that if anxiety possessed cue properties, and if maladaptive responses could be learned and attached to such anxiety cues, then adaptive responses could also be acquired in the same way. Furthermore, if the adaptive responses were in fact incompatible with the anxiety-autonomic state, then the cueing off of such coping behaviors would automatically eliminate the arousal state.

Currently, the view is that AMT may actually be relevant for any pathologic condition that involves a state of arousal or activation. This would be true in particular where this arousal involves either a generalized feeling of inner pressure or a press for a specific activity, and where the generalized state or the specific activity is considered undesirable. In this sense, AMT may be appropriate not only for generalized anxiety, phobic disorders, and adjustment disorders, but also for anger control and impulse disorders. Some research has been completed on generalized anxiety, phobias, anger, and some other minor impulse control problems (Deffenbacher, Brandon, and Demm, personal communication 1985; Hart 1984; Hazaleus and Deffenbacher 1986; Hsi, personal communication 1982; Suinn 1983b, 1984). In addition, to the degree that the chronic anxiety or uncontrolled stressor also precipitates secondary reactions (such as depression or ruminations), AMT has been found to alleviate these secondary symptoms as well (Butler et al. 1984; Cragan and Deffenbacher 1984; Hutchings et al. 1980; Jannoun et al. 1982).

With the growing recognition that patients benefit from treatments involving self-regulation and self-control training and general coping strategies, AMT has evolved into the form previously described (Kanfer and Hagerman 1981). Steps have been added which are designed to increase both the ability for self-management and the capacity to apply the skills to new problem areas; these have broadened the scope and theoretical foundation of AMT. Such components permit the establishment of improved efficacy, of a sense that the environment (both external and internal) is subject to control, and of an increased capacity to cope with future issues.

Research data have confirmed that with phobic disorders, the self-control approach of the AMT is equivalent, in immediate fear reduction, to desensitization that does not employ self-control training. However, with extensive follow-up, AMT is superior both in the demonstration of further gains, and in the transfer of its effects in the resolution of other problems (Deffenbacher and Shelton 1978). In one study with anxious delinquents, not only was the incidence of misconduct reduced but self-esteem increased (Nally 1975).

In essence, AMT is appropriate not only where there are general levels of activation to stressors, but also where there are ancillary cognitive or behavioral symptoms with some potential for the appearance of adjustment disorders with depressed mood and with disturbance of conduct. Where there is anger associated with the stressor, such as might arise in response to assault, police-engendered stress, or social exclusion, then AMT might also be of value in dealing with the inappropriate levels of this rage.

Somatic-Behavioral Behavior Therapies

The essential characteristic of these approaches is the targeting of behavioral change with the expectation that the arousal state will be resolved. A major assumption is that either the arousal has not yet reached a level which prevents new behavioral learning, or the learning can take place during periods of lowered or absent arousal. Depending upon the formulation of the case through behavioral analysis and assessment, the actual behavioral technique might have the goal of stressor stimulus control, development of coping behaviors, resolution of subsidiary symptoms, or prevention. Illustrations of each type will be presented next.

Stimulus Control

Where one of the major expressions of stress is cognitive, that is, worrying and ruminating, one treatment approach relies upon achieving stimulus control. Initially, the major stress response is acquired through the stage of classical conditioning, followed by avoidance behaviors. One such avoidance behavior which serves to prevent extinction of the trauma is worry (Borkovec et al. 1983; Levey and Martin 1983). However, as Borkovec observes, the initial stimulus control over the worry is weakened, and instead generalizes so widely that stimulus control is actually lost. As Borkovec and his colleagues comment, ". . . although worry is elicited by internal or external fear cues, the uncontrollable nature of this cognitive process results in its occurrence under, and therefore its association with, a wide variety of environmental circumstances, thus creating *poor discriminative control* for the activity" [italics mine] (p. 247).

In this regard, worry, as a maladaptive response, is very similar to habitual smoking. In its earlier stages, a person may smoke as a specific response pattern to specific cues (a social environment, anxiety or work cues, etc.). However, as the smoking habit becomes stronger, it is enacted under highly diverse conditions, and becomes self-stimulating in a maladaptive sense. One treatment therefore has been to reattach smoking responses to a definable stimulus environment, then to take steps eventually to extinguish the response entirely.

Borkovec's (1983, 1984) worry clinic program includes such stimulus control. After completing a daily log, individuals are asked to identify those worries which are unnecessary or unpleasant. A "worry period" is then established, that is, a time and a place during which a half-hour of worry is to occur. If an individual starts to worry at any other time, he or she is to "catch yourself worrying, postpone the worry to the worry period and replace it with attending to present-moment experiences" (p. 248). Finally, worry behaviors are engaged in during the "worry period," along with attention to problem-solving to eliminate the source of such concerns.

Coping Behavior Development

To an extent, the development of an adjustment disorder represents a failure of the available coping skills to deal with the consequences of the traumatic learning. Hence, repeated arousal of anxiety by conditioned stimulus patterns, depressive symptomatology, constricted life space, loss of efficacy and a sense of helplessness, etc. can all be sequelae. Other symptoms may be dependent upon the exact nature of the traumatic stressor; for example, sexual dysfunction may be a consequence of rape. Coping behaviors can be used as part of behavior training in a variety of ways, such as to countercondition anxiety responses, to resolve a major symptom (such as depression) directly, or to restore efficacy.

A few illustrations will demonstrate the diverse and flexible applications of this general approach. Harris and Johnson (1983) and Suinn and Richardson (1971) trained clients in retrieving competency imagery. Clients visualized past experiences in which they had demonstrated competency or proficiency. Harris and Johnson then had their clients visualize themselves in a setting associated with their primary fear (i.e., test anxiety), but with instructions this time to emphasize feelings of competency. In an earlier version of AMT, Suinn and Richardson used the same approach, using the feelings of competency to counteract the anxiety that had been elicited as part of treatment. In both approaches, the expectation was that a type of counterconditioning (Harris and Johnson) or active coping (Suinn and Richardson) would occur, whereby the anxiety would be displaced or controlled. As a result of the positive responses associated with competency imagery, Harris and Johnson also anticipated some reduction of negative cognitions. In both studies, some concerns were raised that such an approach might be inadequate for clients who had never experienced competency/proficiency events, or who had never perceived such events to have been experienced in their lives.

A different approach would be to set up conditions for successful actions as part of therapy. Although depression may be attributable to cognitive misperceptions (Beck 1983), one view is that depression reflects a narrowing of behaviors and a subsequent loss of reinforcement in life (Lewinsohn 1983). According to this viewpoint, treatment should be aimed at gradually increasing the patient's activity levels, particularly those associated with reinforcement and pleasure. Several programs taking this orientation have led to improvements among depressives (Fuchs and Rehm 1977; Zeiss et al. 1979). As treatment for rape survivors, Veronen and Kilpatrick (1983) provide "reentry training." This training is basically the assignment of tasks to open up reinforcements and to eliminate the restriction, the retrenchment, and the narrowing of life activities characteristic of many rape victims.

The aforementioned approaches either retrieve prior accomplishments and competency experiences, or direct a person toward activities which can lead to success and reinforcement. As a byproduct, they may influence efficacy and the recovery of a sense of control. Bandura (1977) and Mahoney (1979) identify several methods for promoting positive efficacy, including guided success experiences, viewing the successes of others, physiologic feedback, imaginal practice, reassurance, and self-statements. Some of the affective-autonomic therapies cited previously build in enactive achievements through in vivo applications, confirming to the patient that new skills have been acquired, and hence strengthening a sense of control and efficacy. Those therapies which rely upon self-control training are even more likely to create gains in self-efficacy, since the reasons given for therapeutic gains are internally directed. Such strategies as self-statements will be taken up in more detail in the discussion of cognitive approaches later in this chapter. Friedman et al. (1984) have used positive life affirmations as part of a multimodal behavioral approach which sought to alter Type A behaviors and thus lower the risk of heart disease. In another area, Suinn (1986) has designed self-statements and imagery rehearsal training programs for promoting peak performance among athletes of U.S. Olympic Teams.

Modeling is another behavioral technique which can influence either the acquisition of coping behaviors, or the reduction of affective-autonomic responses, or the prevention of maladaptive emotional learning. This approach is based upon the premise that learning is possible through observation. In a typical preventive training approach, surgical or dental patients view a film aimed at preparing them to cope with the forthcoming procedures (Klorman et al. 1980; Melamed et al. 1983). Generally, the situations involve the anxiety-related setting, but with a model who not only provides information on how to cope, but also deals with the situation in a nonanxious way. Research has indicated that a "coping model" (one who is initially cautious and anxious, but who then succeeds) has greater influence than a "mastery model" (one who faces the situation with confidence from the very beginning). Further, models similar to the client in age and sex appear to foster identification and are thus more useful.

Although symbolic modeling, that is, through films or videotapes, has been shown to have significant value, the addition of participant modeling appears to strengthen such effects (Klingman et al. 1984). In participant modeling, the patients first observe a model performing the desired adaptive behaviors, and then practice these behaviors themselves. This practice appears to consolidate the learning which derives from the symbolic modeling itself.

Not only can modeling provide direct relief from acquired stress reactions, it can also add other benefits. Bandura et al. (1977) treated phobic disorder subjects and obtained follow-up on other symptoms. The therapists noted that their clients showed "marked or moderate relief from aversive thoughts and recurrent nightmares . . . were no longer preoccupied with frightening ruminations . . . (and showed elimination) of distressing nightmares of long-standing (character)" (p. 135). Given that traumatic stress disorders, such as PTSD, are frequently characterized by recurring flashbacks and nightmares, this type of recovery is especially important.

Prevention and Reduction of Secondary Symptoms

A final application of somatic-behavioral approaches is the prevention of stress responses, or the elimination of secondary symptoms. Although such applications have been mentioned in prior discussions, for instance, regarding depressive symptoms, two additional topics deserve brief mention: coping and prevention, and sexual dysfunction.

In the earlier conceptual model of stress (Figure 1), the role of coping skills was identified as a moderating variable. It can also be stated that either a lack of coping skills specific to the stressor, or inadequate coping skills (coping skill deficit) may contribute to vulnerabilities. In turn, such characteristics may also be associated with a more general sense of poor efficacy or lack of control over the environment.

It is this general sense which deserves more speculation in terms of behavior training and prevention. Rosenbaum and Palmon (1984) divided epileptic patients into two groups: one considered to be "high-resourceful" and the other "low-resourceful," based upon assessment of self-control coping skills. They discovered that where seizures were of medium or low frequency, high-resourceful epileptics coped better with their chronic disability; they were significantly less depressed and less anxious than were the low-resourceful patients. These authors viewed epilepsy not only as an illness deserving attention in and of itself, but also as a "naturalistic model of learned helplessness."

Klee and Meyer (1979) were also interested in ways of protecting persons from the effects of learned helplessness. Before exposing their subjects to conditions precipitating learned helplessness, they provided training in self-control through a physiological self-regulation experience (actually using false biofeedback). This "strong controlling type of experience" (p. 411) appeared successful in "immunizing" the subjects to later helplessness exposure. Such studies suggest the value of coping behaviors not only as a means for the direct management of stressors, but also as a way to mediate self-efficacy. Under conditions of stress, such a state of "acquired resourcefulness" may well have substantial protective or immunization value.

Sexual dysfunction is not a common symptom of the adjustment disorders. However, since it can appear as an adjunct to some stress disorders, some comments should be made. For instance, sexually assaulted women appear to experience sexual dysfunctions involving response-inhibitory interferences (Becker and Skinner 1983; Becker et al. 1982). In addition, veterans diagnosed as PTSD have experienced interpersonal difficulties associated with intimacy with wives or lovers (Blank 1981; Roberts et al. 1982).

There are a variety of behaviorally oriented conceptualizations and treatment approaches toward sexual dysfunction which are now available (Annon 1976; Lo-Piccolo and LoPiccolo 1978; Walker 1982; Wincze 1981; Wolpe 1982). Typically, these approaches begin with a careful behavioral assessment of the target problem area and of any contributing factors (LoPiccolo and Nowinski 1981). Targeted problems may range from low sexual desire, to sexual aversion, to performance deficits, to sexual phobias, to relationship or intimacy conflicts. In general, treatment involves behavioral prescriptions aimed at promoting acquisition of new learning, and subsequent emotional and attitudinal changes.

Cognitive Behavior Therapies

Cognitive approaches to therapy have developed from the belief that not only can cognitions be expressions of stress, but that cognitions may also serve to precipitate or further maintain stress. It is possible to distinguish between two types of learning conditions and hence two types of sensitivities to stress: interoceptive and exteroceptive.

The onset of a traumatic stress experience leads to stress learning, but the individual is not always attentive to or able to encode the fact that conditioning is occurring. This form of acquisition may be called exteroceptive learning of stress. Consider a person who is raised in a high-density environment, or in a setting filled with persistent noise. Such environmental conditions are stressors leading to autonomic responsiveness, which may become attached to other stimulus patterns concurrently present. In effect, even though the individual may not have been aware of its development, a conditioned stress response exists. In the future, the presence of the conditioned stimuli can prompt the reactivity; at this point the individual is likely to be puzzled about his or her feelings. This level of conditioning represents the separation between emotional processing and emotional insight discussed by Rachman (1980).

In the second form of acquisition, on the other hand, the individual cognitively processes the learning. Such interoceptive learning of stress thus includes the step of encoding, as the person is additionally attentive to the learning experience. In fact, the person's past learning history may contribute significantly to the current interoceptive learning process. Specifically, the individual's prior experience may have established a tendency to interpret otherwise neutral events as threats (overinclusiveness), to exaggerate the severity of perceived threat in a stressor (overextensivity), or to be inappropriately overreactive to a perceived stress (overresponsivity). In all cases, what takes place is an appraisal of the current environment, and it is this appraisal which codes the environment as threatening. This, in turn, governs the nature of the response to such threat.

To the degree that such appraisals are incorrect or prompt inappropriate responses, their revision or removal would be therapeutic. Cognitive behavior therapies are aimed at such cognitions. Two approaches to cognitive behavior therapy will be discussed next: cognitive restructuring, and stress inoculation training.

Cognitive Restructuring

This form of behavior therapy aims at altering an incorrect belief system. Among the more prominent methods are rational emotive therapy (RET) (Ellis 1962) and systematic rational restructuring (SRR) (Goldfried et al. 1974). The RET approach gives the rationale but provides few details on steps for promoting cognitive change beyond therapist confrontation of client beliefs. SRR was able to organize RET into more systematic steps and includes a self-control aspect. In these two therapies, the first step requires patients to monitor their thoughts, especially during stress reactions. Thoughts occurring before, during, and after the stress-associated periods are studied in order to determine the context and the sequencing of cognitions.

A major part of the therapy then consists of getting patients to learn how to evaluate their thoughts, specifically to become alert to those that are irrational and inappropriate. It has been discovered that a variety of cognitive distortions are commonly held to be truths. For example, that "there is invariably a right, precise, and perfect solution to human problems and that it is catastrophic if this correct solution is not found" (Ellis 1962, p. 87). Additional characteristics of irrational cognitions are the anticipations of catastrophic consequences, ruminations centering on negative rather than positive features of life (gloom and doom), and reliance upon absolute standards of evaluation. In the analysis of depression, Beck (1983) noted that a distorted negative triad is present: a pessimistic view of the world, a pessimistic self-concept, and a pessimistic view of the future. Based on his theory of learned helplessness, Seligman adds the conception that those persons who are subject to depression tend to attribute negative events to internal, stable, and global factors (Abramson et al. 1978; Abramson et al. 1980). Cognitive treatment is aimed at searching out the validity of such irrational beliefs, assumptions, or attributions. RET achieves this through forceful challenges, while SRR engages in a collaborative testing of reality, authentication of observations, validation of assumptions, and adoption of objectivity and perspective.

As a final step, the cognitive restructuring therapies seek the development of alternate, realistic cognitions. To the extent that negative cognitions precipitate a sequence leading to maladaptive symptoms, then realistic cognitions should prompt adaptive behaviors. In this step of treatment, patients learn to modify their thoughts as they arise, and to work with these thoughts before they add to the existing problems. Rehearsal and modeling may be added to ensure that the patients are capable of improving on their cognitions.

Working in a community mental health center, Lipsky et al. (1980) used cognitive restructuring for outpatients, some of whom were diagnosed as having adjustment disorders. As the patients progressed, they displayed an increase in rational cognitions and a decrease in the endorsement of irrational beliefs. Improvement was noted as well in the realms of anxiety, mood disturbances, and general neuroticism. Where the RET was enhanced by other rehearsal exercises, which were included in order to provide practice in applying the restructuring skills, the gains appeared to be stronger.

Frank and Stewart (1983) used cognitive restructuring to help rape victims who were experiencing depression and anxiety; the investigators found it to be of significant benefit, but equivalent to results obtained with systematic desensitization. In their work with rape victims, Veronen and Kilpatrick (1983) and Veronen and Best (1983) used concepts derived from cognitive therapy. For instance, they aided some clients to view the rape experience as one which can have the "positive" outcome of increase in life appreciation or as a challenge for the future. Also, they argue for the term rape "survivor" instead of rape "victim" as one offering a better perspective. They feel that such usage would acknowledge the strengths of the person, and remove the stigma of blame or unconscious collaboration.

Stress Inoculation Training

Stress inoculation training (SIT) (Meichenbaum 1985) is a good example of an approach which both emphasizes cognitive elements and at the same time includes some of the affective-autonomic strategies, such as relaxation, as well as some behavioral rehearsal. In the first step of SIT, a primary emphasis is given to thoughts as controlling variables, and patients are directed toward perceiving the role of their thoughts in their stress responses. The patients are also instructed that it is necessary to reach several goals, namely: skill in preparing for future stressors, skill in handling such stressors, skill in coping with feelings of being overwhelmed, and skill in self-reinforcement for successful coping. Within any stress sequence, each skill is considered to be associated with a postulated progression of stages.

In the second stage of SIT, the clients are trained in cognitive coping strategies and in certain direct actions. In cognitive coping, the clients are taught how to use thoughts to stimulate coping, to inhibit distorted cognitions, to restructure feelings, and to provide self-praise. These thoughts are introduced at each of the stages of the proposed stress sequence. In terms of direct action, patients are provided information pertinent to the forthcoming stressor (e.g., the expected effects of the anesthetic used for dentistry, or the correct method for approaching an unfamiliar dog), they are given relaxation training, or they are shown how to identify alternative methods for preventing the stressor from appearing.

In the final stage of SIT, the patients test out and rehearse their cognitive and behavioral coping skills. Practice might be achieved through simulated experiences such as stress-inducing films or laboratory-induced stress via shock. Imagery rehearsal might be employed as well. In all instances, the major interest is in encouraging the patients to develop a general learning set or general strategy for coping. As with the self-control approach of anxiety management training, SIT rests on the assumption that therapy sessions can set the stage for the patients to apply their new skills to a variety of diverse situations in their life environments.

Most research has centered around the applicability of SIT to phobic disorders (Suinn 1984) or for the management of laboratory-induced or medically induced pain stimuli (Turk et al. 1983). Such research confirms the value of SIT for the elimination of anxieties and phobias, as well as for the control or reduction of pain. In addition, Kilpatrick et al. (1982) have been studying the use of SIT for stress management by rape victims. They begin by defining the target problems in terms which especially reflect the rape consequences, and then proceed to design cognitive and action coping skills. For instance, in one case, one of the target problems involved fears of being alone at home. In implementing the SIT program, they utilize relaxation, cue-controlled relaxation, role-playing, covert rehearsal, thought stopping, and guided self-talk.

Clinical Issues

A major advantage of a behavioral approach is the ability of the practitioner to determine which are the core elements of the problem and symptom development. Behavioral conceptualizations require that there be a systematic assessment of the patient, a review of the antecedent conditions and contributing factors, an evaluation of possible organic or social variables, and identification of the sequential evolution of the pathology. A treatment plan is then developed in accord with the diagnosis, with an eye toward separating the core issues from secondary symptoms. In planning intervention, it is necessary to coordinate the model of stress, the analyses from the perspectives of interoceptive and exteroceptive stress learning, and the basic principles regarding the acquisition and maintenance of maladaptive behaviors. Where particular symptoms are known to be uniquely responsive to specific behavioral interventions, then prescriptive assignments are made in a manner similar to the way pharmacologic decisions are made by physicians.

The matching of behavior therapy to disorders can be achieved by means of several strategies. As implied by the organization of the previous discussions on therapies, one method for matching is to select the behavioral treatment which has the most impact on the dominant symptom system or domain. Thus, where the dominant symptom is anxiety (as expressed through intense affective-autonomic symptoms), anxiety management training might be the appropriate technique. On the other hand, where worry, distorted sequences of cognitions, and disruptive thoughts are the chief expressions of the stress, then some form of cognitive behavior therapy would be preferable.

As mentioned earlier, it is also possible to match the behavior therapy to the patient's dominant coping style. Cognitively oriented patients who seek answers, and who can alter their emotions and/or behaviors once their thoughts are restructured, may best attack problems through the cognitive therapy strategies. On the other hand, action-oriented or feeling-oriented patients may best develop controls through the skill training programs which involve participant modeling, behavioral prescriptions, applied relaxation, or anxiety management approaches.

Finally, the quality of the stress learning itself may be extremely important as a means of matching treatment to problem. Differing symptom outcomes would be expected in situations where the initial learning is interoceptive as compared with exteroceptive conditioning. Where a stressor is appraised as a threat and perceived as harmful, for example, the reaction should include not only behavioral disruption and autonomical arousal, but also a sense of distress (Figure 2).

On the other hand, where stressors exist but are not necessarily encoded, the stress acquisition which takes place might lead to autonomic arousal but not necessarily to behavioral disruption or subjective distress (Figure 3).

In addition, such an analysis would also predict the type of behavior therapy that would be most appropriate as well as the expected consequences of each type of behavior therapy. In its most complex form (Figure 3), a reality stressor (leading to exteroceptive conditioning of stress) is exacerbated by distorted or irrational appraisals or cognitions (leading to interoceptive learning of stress) and is further affected by behavioral deficits (lack of coping skills or presence of inappropriate coping skills). Depending upon the combination of such variables, differing behavior therapies (affective-autonomic, somatic-behavioral, cognitive) would be expected to have differing therapeutic outcomes (Suinn 1983a, 1984).

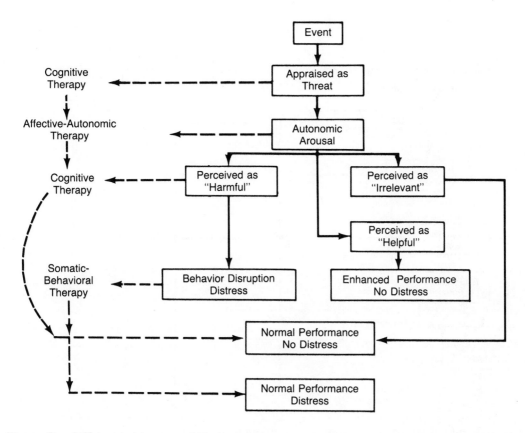

Figure 2. Differential Impact of Therapies

General Treatment Considerations

In terms of selecting among behavioral therapies for stress reactions or adjustment disorders, a variety of recommendations can be advanced:

1. The treatment(s) of choice should seek a matching among the dominant problem areas, client characteristics, and the quality of the learning leading to the maladaptive behaviors.
2. Assessment and diagnosis should include not only identification of the initial conditions of acquisition, but also the factors involved in the maintenance of the maladaptive behaviors. Not only might these be different and hence require differing stages of treatment, but the independence of some of the variables may be important to recognize. Thus, emotional conditioning without encoding or cognitive processing may be puzzling if a patient is struggling to comprehend. However, undue focus on such comprehension might only add to the worry-avoidance component, and may actually be irrelevant to a direct resolution of the initial learning. Knowing when to deal with and when to ignore autonomic, behavioral, or cognitive issues can be important in treatment efficiency.

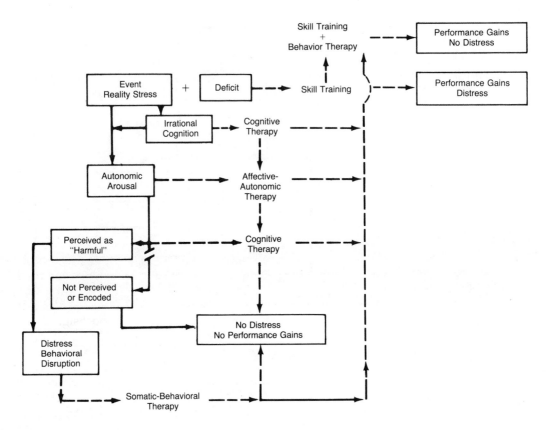

Figure 3.   Interplay of Stress, Therapies, and Outcome

3. Interventions provide conditions for new adaptive learning. Where the intervention program includes opportunities for direct rehearsal and practice of the new coping responses, such learning is strengthened. This is true whether these be cognitive or noncognitive skills. In general, behavioral intervention might best be conceptualized as a form of skill training.

4. The transfer of skill training is best achieved where the behaviors are overlearned, and where they are applied under stimulus conditions comparable to those in which they will ultimately be required. Treatment problems that enhance this kind of transfer include those which have such components as homework assignments, in vivo applications, active practice, and attention to real life stimulus conditions (such as through role playing, imagery rehearsal, and participant modeling).

5. The evidence indicates that many of the therapeutic effects of different behavior therapies produce overlapping results. Thus, an affective-autonomic approach such as anxiety induction therapy cannot only reduce physiologic reactivity but also remove irrational beliefs. Similarly, a cognitive restructuring approach may aim at eliminating distorted assumptions but will also control behavioral disruptions. And behavior changes can both alter pathologic thoughts and influence affect. Part of the reason for the overlap is the interlocking of the stress response sequence, as the various symptoms of stress in one domain can prompt responses in other

domains (autonomic arousal may precipitate behavioral disruption which in turn prompts negative thoughts) (Suinn 1983a). Another reason may be the additional benefits of such therapies—for instance, in favorably altering efficacy and a sense of resourcefulness and self-control (Zeiss 1979). Hence, treatment programs which rely upon the development of self-control and which build esteem and self-efficacy can enhance therapeutic outcomes.

6. Within a general learning set, training in self-regulation strategies for coping, and for understanding and applying the principles of stress management, are likely to aid in recovery throughout follow-up (Kanfer 1985). Further, such learning can help develop resistance to future stress, and decrease vulnerability or sensitivity to threats to adjustment. The therapy model which yields the maximum benefits is one which views the treatment meetings as training sessions where the steps toward recovery are well understood by the patient and where the self-control skills necessary for such recovery are strengthened.

7. In treatment programs where the immediate reality goal is emotional coping rather than problem solving, patients need to be helped to understand the differences. For instance, with clearly immutable external stressors that will disappear only with the passage of time (such as in some forms of chronic illness, or in loss of a loved one through death), nothing can really be done to remove or alter the basic conditions. Instead, managing the emotional responses may be the most significant target. Avoidance-based emotional coping might be used as a temporary palliative; however, there is a risk that the patient would not consider such an approach as a true attempt at solving the problem and would consequently experience lower self-esteem (Folkman and Lazarus 1984). Alternatively, one could aim at making the patient aware that there is a difference between general defensive suppression or avoidance, as opposed to attending systematically to cues of emotional arousal for the purpose of initiating countermeasures. Counter-responses, such as relaxation, are employed to prevent the emotional arousal from spiraling out of control; hence they are more accurately understood as coping rather than as defensive behaviors. Techniques such as AMT or SIT, in fact, provide substantial training in awareness of the signs of oncoming stress, in order for the patient to respond immediately in a positive coping fashion.

8. Programs with training in objective self-monitoring can enhance future problem prevention or problem solving. Those with some sense of self "consciousness" are more likely to anticipate conditions which could precipitate problems, become more conversant with their available coping repertoire, and be less subject to distorted communications or interpretations. Many of the behavioral treatments begin with daily logs; in this way patients obtain data which serve as a baseline, but which can also add diagnostic information. By means of such logs, patients can learn to assess their reactions realistically, to evaluate progress in therapy, and, ultimately, to see the evidence of their recovery directly. In addition, they develop skills in objective evaluation of themselves and of their environment.

9. Termination should be a distinct part of the treatment program, and the initial steps toward termination should be implemented prior to the last session. Prior to termination, one useful assignment is to require that the patient directly test out his or her gains in vivo. This should occur before any discussion about termination, and should be initiated as a step for "checking progress." In the next session, the concrete behavioral evidences of recovery should be reviewed. These signs of improvement can then be matched against the patient's recall of his or her status on initial entry into treatment. Such comparisons not only tend to confirm the effects of treatment, but serve as well to stimulate appropriate feelings

of personal accomplishment. The discussion about termination can then emerge as a natural conclusion which is drawn directly from experience, rather than as a decision based upon the therapist's opinion. Where unique circumstances render such planning infeasible, then a number of checking-in sessions may be scheduled at specific time intervals. These intervals can gradually be lengthened or replaced by telephone contacts or other means of exchange.

Chapter 238

Brief Dynamic Psychotherapy

An adjustment disorder, by definition, is a type of stress response syndrome. It indicates that a change has occurred in the life circumstances of an individual and that efforts to cope with this change have not been sufficiently adaptative. Such a change provides a focus for brief dynamic psychotherapy, aimed at symptom relief by improving adaptation.

Stress Response Syndromes

Stress response syndromes are disorders that occur in the context of adaptation to life changes. These reactions include posttraumatic stress disorder, adjustment disorder, complicated bereavement reactions, and brief reactive psychosis. While posttraumatic stress disorder is currently categorized under the DSM-III-R anxiety disorders section, a future nomenclature may include a separate category of these stress response syndromes. The rationale is that in the nature of these syndromes, many of the symptoms and explanations of symptom formation are quite similar (Horowitz 1986).

The etiology of these disorders lies in the matching of the external events and the inner personal schemata of the meaning according to which these outer events are appraised. Discrepancies between what is, what used to be, and what is wished for lead to emotional reactions. Changed circumstances, whether or not they have the sharp and shocking onset of a psychic trauma or the gradual occurrence of a shift in one's way of life, are part of the external cause; the other part is the internal meaning system which interprets these life changes. These inner organizations articulate the self to the surrounding world in a series of schemata. Where a disorder appears, the individual's schemata may once have been realistic but have now become unrealistic, because changes in external circumstances have since rendered them inappropriate to current realities. In addition, the pre-existing schemata may have been fantasy based and unrealistic for a long time; now, because of life changes, they may have become even more inappropriate and in conflict with reality (Horowitz 1988).

Significant discrepancies between the inner schemata and actual life circumstances can lead to a variety of maladaptive responses. Brief dynamic psychotherapy is often the treatment of choice for these disorders; it is the particular discrepancy between external and internal meaning which is especially suitable for this treatment modality. In such an approach, the therapeutic effort focuses on clarifying the details of the new maladaptive life pattern, on how to attain a life pattern that would, it is hoped, be more adaptive. This approach involves a sequential understanding of the changes that have taken place, placement of the recent events in a personal life story context, and differentiation of reality from fantasy. Based on these appraisals, fantasy and reality are examined as they relate to focal questions about why the life changes occurred, what the changes mean, and what coping strategies are now available.

Brief Dynamic Psychotherapy

Changes of external circumstance necessitate changes in basic psychological schemata; such changes take place slowly because they require the establishment of continuities and associational linkages among mean structures. Recognition of the implications of the changes usually gives rise to emotional states, especially those characterized by fear, sadness, anger, guilt, or shame. Because these affects are unpleasant, in encountering change the person may attempt to avoid recognition of some of its implications. Brief dynamic psychotherapy deals with these avoidances and uses the establishment of a therapeutic alliance to bolster each patient's sense of self-competence.

With such support the patient may be helped to confront the painful implications of the change more directly and realistically. Thus, the interpretation of defenses, clarification of the reasons for needing defenses, and the suggesting—or discovering—of alternative modes of coping are important aspects of such brief therapies. Such an approach involves attention to the person's habitual defensive style as well as to pre-existing personality problems.

The news that a change has occurred is perceived by the person at various levels, both conscious and unconscious. Stressful events lead to the laying down of an active memory trace which tends to repeat itself, sometimes in the form of intrusive images. Each such repeated representation sets in motion a sequence of information processing which may lead to mastery of the change. The intrusive ideas and feelings provide the first clues to warded-off or unbearable aspects of the current need for adjustment.

As mastery is achieved, a new schematic meaning structure is eventually established and the news about revised circumstances becomes a part of long-term memory. At this time the intrusive symptomatology which may occur in such stress response syndromes as the adjustment disorders tends to subside. At the same time, the periods characterized by emotional numbing and ideational avoidance also begin to diminish in favor of more normal conscious reviews and acknowledgments of the circumstances in which the person finds himself. At this time of increasing safety, the repressed, suppressed, disavowed, denied, and dissociated mental contents which were not previously thrusting themselves into consciousness may now appear, perhaps intrusively. They may then be examined in therapy. Such a review occupies the important mid-phase of dynamic psychotherapy for stress response syndromes.

Therapeutic efforts are aimed at providing support through a difficult life passage by means of contemplating "the unthinkable" and facing the emotional themes which have thus been activated. Thoughtful clarifications and tactful interpretations are very supportive; success with such interventions reduces the need for excessive self-regulatory maneuvers. The alterations in circumstances which have led to an adjustment disorder will often have activated in the patient previously dormant concepts of the self as weak, damaged, defective, or bad (Horowitz et al. 1984). These irrational self-views need to be carefully identified in the therapy, with special attention to differentiating reality and fantasy. This will enable the patient's more competent self-concepts to become once again the dominant organizers of his or her mental life.

It is noteworthy that in the brief dynamic therapy of the adjustment disorders, we find an important convergence of symptom formation and symptom treatment with modern trends in cognitive-behavioral theories (Bandura 1982; Beck and Emory 1985; Wilson 1984). All are focusing on the importance of helping patients to maintain or to reestablish a sense of self-competence. It is thus possible to use a multimodal treatment approach which employs the psychodynamic framework to contain other interventions, such as 1) suggesting that the persons seek active exposure to life situations which they have been avoiding, 2) having them keep a journal of current symptoms and adaptive accomplishments, 3) teaching stress reduction techniques, and 4) getting them to join mutual help groups.

Sequence: The Early Phase of Brief Therapy

Brief dynamic psychotherapy for a stress response syndrome will often begin with the person telling the story of the change in his life circumstances, while relating those events to his current problems and symptomatology. The recounting of the story of the changed life circumstances and the responses of the self to the changes offer an important opportunity for the early establishment of both a therapeutic alliance and a focus. The characteristic nonintegration of the sequence of life events means that memories may be presented in a choppy, disorganized fashion. Establishing organization in order to get a clear immediate record is useful to both patient and therapist but is secondary to the formation of a therapeutic alliance. It is important to listen empathically and quietly to the *emotional* experience of the patient instead of hurrying to get the chronological sequencing of the events established.

The earliest phase of treatment includes a clear description of all the symptoms and problems that occur. (An account of brief dynamic psychotherapy along with case examples is described in the following books by the author of this chapter: *Stress Response Syndromes* (1986), *States of Mind* (1979, 1987), and *Personality Styles and Brief Dynamic Psychotherapy* (1984).) In essence, the emphasis falls on placing the problems and symptoms into the context of a series of states of mind which are important current characteristics for the individual.

State Formulation

State formulation procedures have several advantages. One advantage is that the process allows both the person and the treating clinician to understand that the symptoms are not always present. They may occur when the person confronts a situation in a given state of mind, and they may not arise when the person encounters the same situation in some other state of mind. The states-of-mind approach allows one to include in the range of states an understanding of some of the individual's more positive states of mind. This means examining current abilities or inabilities of the person to enter into states of relaxation, sensuous pleasure, creative work, and the like, as well as examining states of anxiety, depression, rage, shame, or guilt (Horowitz 1987, 1988).

Another advantage of the state formulation approach is that it allows the person to pay attention to the current level of excitation and mood. He or she can also begin to use conscious efforts to bend toward more adaptive and well-modulated expressions of affects which have heretofore (as part of the symptom picture) been experienced or expressed in an uncontrolled or impulsive manner. More than that, the state formulation permits a naming and labeling process which allows the patient not only to have a feeling of shared understanding with the clinician, but also to accept a label and to speak of entering into a problematic state of mind that has an agreed-upon meaning to both parties in the psychotherapeutic exploration. This label may be provided by the patient himself or may aptly be named by the therapist.

Once it is clear that certain problematic states of mind exist, these may then be examined in terms of their defensive meaning. For example, even so problematic a state as self-righteous rage or terrifying panic may help the person avoid certain other, still more dreaded states of mind such as suicidal despair and searing guilt.

Self-Concepts and Role Relationship Models

This approach leads to a recognition that for a given individual each specific state of mind tends to be characterized by certain views of self and other. Views can be characterized as role relationship models with a particular self-concept, object concept, intended or feared aim of self toward other, and the expectation of intentions, aims, and responses from the other person. The motivational, successfully defensive, and defensive failure aspects of these various motivated role relationship models can then come to be gradually understood in the interpersonal context of psychotherapy.

This interpersonal context involves all the current transactions between the therapist and the patient, including transference manifestations, the current outside relationship patterns, and the history of past maladaptive interpersonal relationship patterns. Within the therapy the patient may begin to enact the stress events and his reactions to them. He may act out behavior patterns aimed unconsciously at causing within the therapist the same type of emotional upheaval characteristic of the patient's syndrome. By watching how the therapist responds, this role reversal can lead the patient to learn by identification as an aspect of his own working through process.

Clinical Example

A middle-aged executive was passed over for a promotion that had been given to all his peers. He became anxious and depressed and sought psychiatric consultation, with the specific complaints that he found his life dull and unrewarding, and was unable to make decisions. He could not think productively about how to cope with the change in his position within the corporation.

In the first two hours of psychotherapy, feeling accepted by the psychotherapist and interested in examining the purposes and plans for his future career, he entered a state of open and flowing communication.

In the sessions that followed, after he had told the basic story of the situation at work and his more recent psychological responses, he seemed to become more aware of the therapist as a person. Then his state of mind shifted once again, and he was halting, guarded, indecisive, and self-shielding. It appeared that he was expecting to be rejected and scorned by the therapist as he communicated his uncertainty about what to do next within the therapy context itself. This expectation of derision was interpreted as the same role relationship model that he felt confronted with at work; he was inadequate, authorities would scorn him. This interpretation led to a state change and a restoration of a better feeling in his relationship with the therapist.

The restoration of the open, flowing, communicative state then led to yet another transition, this time to a new state in which, in a subtle way, he mocked the therapist. At this point the focus of therapy became diffuse, and the patient sat back as if to watch what the therapist would do about the impasse. A reversal of roles had occurred, the patient was now the observer, while the therapist had moved into the anxiety-provoking (and eventually depression-provoking) position of not knowing what to do.

Recognizing his own emotional discomfort in this position, the therapist analyzed the role relationship model which had led to it. He used this insight within himself gradually to interpret to the patient what was going on, why it was going on, and how this transference and countertransference related to life changes. In the therapy, as in the patient's career, there now had to be a realignment of the focus, a recommitment to personal values as purposes, and a restoration of the sense of self-competence. The fear of rejection and scorn had led to a defensive state of mind of aloof isolation, a stance intended to avoid humiliated dejection. Albeit understandable, this defensive position did not consider all the realistic alternatives, such as working together for the same purposes. Thus the therapy relationship did not recapitulate the one in the past, when the patient's father had ambivalently both supported and undermined him if he was the least bit unsuccessful.

The restabilization of the role relationship model subsuming the therapeutic alliance restored the patient's morale. With this the patient began examining the sadistic relationship patterns at work and his unrealistic expectations of excessive hostility both within himself and in male authority figures. He felt hopeful that he could now differentiate some of the fantasies from the realities of competition and "toughness" in the work place. He felt stronger and moved more boldly in the therapy.

Middle Phases of Brief Therapy

As the therapeutic alliance deepens, the patient often begins to bring up themes which have heretofore been warded off from conscious awareness or from communicative expression to the therapist and others. These themes are associated to the life changes. Such themes often include memories of past traumas which are similar to the current and changed life circumstances, as in the memory of parental rejection in the above case vignette. This allows the therapist to make more interpretations which help differentiate reality from fantasy. These clarifications also serve as linkages which help the patient establish a sense of greater continuity between the current stressor events, his own past life story, and his sense of future possibilities.

All this is helpful, but it should be kept in mind that having received this initial help, some patients then expect more than has been delivered by the therapist. If the therapist is quietly open to such expressions, transference reactions which have a negative emotional tone often occur at this point, as illustrated in the case example. It may then be possible to link these observed negative transference reactions to other aspects of meaning in the changed life circumstances. At this mid-phase of therapy it is often possible for the patient/therapist pair to work at deeper aspects of meaning of the change, relating responses to pre-existing neurotic conflicts.

Later Phases of Brief Therapy

At the midpoint of such therapy, around the sixth hour of a 12-session time-limited course, it is wise for the therapist to bring up the theme of termination. The patient will often be surprised that the time limit which was explicitly specified or implicitly indicated at the beginning of the work will actually be adhered to. This creates an occasion in which the patient can once again be asked to reflect upon his relationship with the therapist; it is important to link these reactions in a meaningful way to the pattern of maladaptive responses evoked by the recent life changes.

In subsequent hours, the issue of termination will tend to come up in both explicit and covert forms. At such times, the therapist can help clarify transference projections and can continue as well to work through central conflicts and issues around the focal theme. In particular, the patient must give up the idea that the therapist will presently restore the life circumstances which have been swept away by the life changes.

It is also wise for the therapist to clarify unfinished issues which might indicate consideration of a longer term or time-unlimited therapy; in addition, the therapist could suggest something for the patient to work upon in his everyday life after the conclusion of the brief therapy. The final task is saying goodbye, which often takes place in the 11th hour of a 12-hour course of therapy. Patients seem to want less emotional turmoil in the last hour so that they can manifest their more effective self-concepts in action and be more nonchalant with their therapist as they leave the intimate situation.

Some of the features characteristic of a 12-session time-limited dynamic psychotherapy are summarized in Table 1.

Dealing with Personality Styles

While the above efforts are fairly straightforward when put into such a general form, they are usually resisted by the patient in terms of habitual styles of warding off unpleasant emotional states of mind. It is usually not the task of a brief therapy to alter these characterological traits; the goal, rather, is to work through and around them in order to change attitudes about the focal theme.

Some specific encounters for defensive maneuvers have been abstracted according to common character typologies. These are illustrated in a summarized manner in Tables 2, 3, and 4.

Table 1.   Sample Outline of a 12-Session Dynamic Therapy

Session	Relationship Issues	Patient Activity	Therapist Activity
1	Initial positive feeling for helper	Patient tells story of event	Preliminary focus is discussed
2	Lull as sense of pressure is reduced	Event is related to previous life	Takes psychiatric history. Gives patient realistic appraisal of syndrome
3	Patient testing therapist for various relationship possibilities	Patient adds associations to indicate expanded meaning of event	Focus is realigned; resistances to contemplating stress-related themes are interpreted
4	Therapeutic alliance deepened	Implications of event in the present are contemplated	Defenses and warded-off contents are interpreted, linking of latter stress-event and responses
5		Themes that have been avoided are worked on	Active confrontation with feared topics and reengagement in feared activities are encouraged
6		The future is contemplated	Time of termination is discussed
7–11	Transference reactions interpreted and linked to other configurations Acknowledgment of pending separation	The work-through of central conflicts and issues of termination, as related to the life event and reactions to it, is continued	Central conflicts, termination, unfinished issues, and recommendations all are clarified and interpreted
12	Saying good-bye	Work to be continued on own and plans for the future are discussed	Real gains and summary of future work for patient to do on own are acknowledged

Note.   Reproduced with permission from Horowitz (1986).

Conclusion

A brief dynamic psychotherapy for adjustment disorders relates the meanings intrinsic to changed life circumstances to the person's pre-existing and current repertoire of self and object concepts, his agendas for life, and his purposes and values. In such treatments, therapists regard the current moment of symptoms as part of a life change toward a developmentally enhanced future. This optimistic stance treats any adjustment disorder, with its inevitable pain and suffering, as an opportunity for emotional growth.

The tables recapitulate these concepts in outline form. Table 1 offers a model for the kinds of activity likely to be engaged in by both the patient and therapist as they build and then terminate their working relationship during the 12 sessions of a typical brief therapeutic course.

Table 2. Histrionic Style and Therapeutic Technique

Function	Style as "Defect"	Therapeutic Counter
Perception	Global or selective inattention	Ask for details
Representation	Impressionistic rather than accurate	"Abreaction" and reconstruction
Translation of images and enactions into words	Limited	Encourage talk Provide verbal labels
Associations	Limited by inhibitions Misinterpretations based on schematic stereotypes, deflected from reality wishes and fears	Encourage production Repetition Clarification
Problem solving	Short circuit to rapid but often erroneous conclusions	Keep subject open Interpretations
	Avoidance of topic when emotions are unbearable	Support

Note. Reproduced with permission from Horowitz (1986).

Table 3. Compulsive Style and Therapeutic Technique

Function	Style as "Defect"	Therapeutic Counter
Perception	Detailed and factual statements about emotional experiences	Ask for overall impressions
Representation	Isolation of ideas from emotions	Link emotional meanings to ideational meanings
Translation of images into words	Misses emotional meaning in a rapid transition to partial word meanings	Focus attention on images and felt reactions to them
Associations	Shifts sets of meanings back and forth	Holding operations Interpretation of defense and of warded-off meanings
Problem solving	Endless rumination without reaching decisions	Interpretation of reasons for warding off clear decisions

Note. Reproduced with permission from Horowitz (1986).

Tables 2, 3, and 4 detail some of the varieties of therapeutic experience in the course of working with adults of different personality types.

Table 2 describes the way the histrionic (or hysteroid) patient handles therapy, and recounts some of the therapeutic maneuvers appropriate for this pattern of engagement.

Table 3 is a summary account of the work with a compulsive personality, the patient's gambits, and the therapist's counters.

Table 4 offers a similar detailing of the relationship style of the narcissistic patient, and lists some of the responses the therapist can offer in return in order to make the work go forward.

Table 4.　Narcissistic Style and Therapeutic Techniques

Function	Style as "Defect"	Therapeutic Counteraction
Perception	Focuses on praise and blame	Avoids being provoked into either praising or blaming but is realistically supportive
	Denies "wounding" information	Uses tactful timing and wording to counteract denials by selective confrontation
Representation	Dislocates bad traits from self to other	Repeatedly reviews in order to clarify who is who in terms of the sequence of acts and intentions in a recall interpersonal transaction
Translation of images into words	Slides meanings	Consistently defines meanings; encourages decisions as to most relevant meanings and how much to weight them
Associations	Overbalances when finding routes to self-enhancement	Holds to other meanings; cautiously deflates grandiose beliefs
Problem solving	Distorts reality to maintain self-esteem	Points out distortion while (tactfully) encouraging and supporting reality fidelity
	Obtains illusory gratifications	Supports patient's self-esteem during period of surrender of illusory gratification (helped by the real interest of the therapist, by identification with the therapist as a noncorrupt person). Finds out about and gradually discourages unrealistic gratifications from therapy
	Forgives self too easily	Helps develop appropriate sense of responsibility

Note.　Reproduced with permission from Horowitz (1986).

Chapter 239

Individual Child Psychotherapy

Management of the child with an adjustment disorder requires a broad, flexible approach. Attention to the child as an individual and to his own unique experience needs to be coupled with a view toward his family and his environment. The ability of both to offer the child protection from potentially traumatic experiences and to mobilize interpersonal supportive and reparative forces on his behalf will be key to his capacity to cope.

The emphasis in this chapter is on the individual psychotherapy of the child and on how to help him with his inner personal experience. However, the relative role of psychotherapy within the overall management of a case will vary from child to child and from situation to situation. With some children the psychotherapy may be relatively unimportant; with others, it may be the central focus of the treatment effort. Whatever the overall plan, the goal of case management is to aim for the child's assimilation or integration of the experience. Whether it be internally or externally induced, whether it be a reaction to developmental or accidental stressors, the difficulty might well color future experiences and the way in which the child structures his world. However, the aim is for the patient to deal with the matter in such a manner that it would not unduly distort either.

Models of Intervention

The overall aim in management of the child with an adjustment disorder is to help him cope with the stressful experience so as to assimilate and integrate it into his psychological functioning. Within that context individual psychotherapy has a singular role to play. It enhances the process through removing hindrances to the child's emotional growth and mobilizing his healthy coping mechanisms. To accomplish this, the psychotherapist is likely to design his approach by drawing on methods from the realms of crisis intervention, brief psychotherapy, and individual psychodynamic psychotherapy.

Crisis Intervention

Crisis intervention is the subject of another chapter in this section; however, it is helpful merely to highlight certain essential elements of that strategy for purposes of comparison and contrast with individual psychotherapy. Caplan (1964) conceptualized crisis as a transitional period which offers both an opportunity for personal growth and the danger of increased vulnerability to mental disorder. That is, the person in crisis can return to his previous level of functioning, rise to a higher level, or sink to a lower one. To some extent the outcome is dependent on the person's way of handling the experience. The aim of intervention must therefore be to help him deal with the crisis and to cope with it in a way that will enable him to master it rather than to regress and end up with a maladaptive pattern.

Caplan's conceptualization bridges models of crisis intervention and short-term psychotherapy. He proposes that in the disequilibrium of the crisis, it is necessary to understand the nature of the reactions as well as the strengths and vulnerabilities of the afflicted person so as to intervene in a manner that might increase the possibility of a healthy outcome.

Short-Term Psychotherapy

Psychotherapy of adjustment disorders in children is likely to be brief, at least in terms of time. Therefore, one should borrow from models of short-term psychotherapy. Marmor's (1979) differentiation between crisis intervention and short-term dynamic psychotherapy is helpful here. Marmor regards crisis intervention as necessary for the individual who is coping poorly and who is in danger of decompensating as a result of internal or external stress. The goal is at once to reduce or to remove the stressful situation, and/or to help the patient deal with it more effectively. In contrast short-term dynamic psychotherapy is designed to work with individuals who are in conflict but not necessarily in crisis (although a crisis situation may indeed be involved). The goal of brief psychotherapy is primarily to modify the patient's coping abilities and only secondarily to relieve stress.

Time frame.   Treatment of adjustment disorder takes on some of the character of short-term psychotherapy in respect to both the time frame and the process. In terms of time, in a review of brief child psychotherapy Dulcan (1984) notes that the number of sessions may be as few as one to four; more commonly such a treatment will consist of 6 to 12 sessions extending over a period of six weeks to six months. Proskauer's time-limited therapy utilized 6 to 20 sessions distributed over a six-month period. While Rockwell et al. (1982) observe that one psychotherapy session may be sufficient when significant affect has been mobilized, a therapist should be cautious about not having a patient return for at least a second session. More often than not in the second session the therapist can help the child deal with the discomfort of "I talked too much" or "I spilled my guts" in the first session. This allows for consolidation of gains rather than their dissipation through personal recriminations from embarrassment and/or guilt.

Process.   As for process, several principles inherent in short-term therapy do lend themselves for consideration in designing a mode of psychotherapy for adjustment disorders. It is helpful to remember, as Dulcan (1984) notes, that short-term therapy models are not simply brief versions of long-term therapy; rather, from the outset the plan is for the treatment to be not only brief but also relatively focused, with a predominant emphasis on the patient. In this way, one may take advantage of the strengths implicit in the focus on goals, with maximum activity and participation invited from child and family in the course of the therapeutic process.

Marmor (1979) maintains that setting a time limit is a unique and important element of the short-term psychotherapies. Rosenthal (1971) has also emphasized setting a time limit in brief psychotherapy of children. In the nature of things, the time limit emphasizes separation and individuation. To the extent that it does so, it reflects a basic respect for and encouragement of the patient's capacity to be autonomous; this comes at the very time the patient is likely to see himself as helpless, inadequate, and in need of dependent support. Hence setting a time limit might well be considered a possibility in the therapy of adjustment disorders.

With the late adolescent, however, Austin and Inderbitzen (1983) see it important to maintain a strict neutrality regarding duration of treatment. It is of note that these investigators draw their conclusion from the treatment of college students who were caught up in the separation-individuation developmental crisis of late adolescence. These patients were unable to be aware of and to assert their own autonomous strivings.

Rather than approach the treatment in terms of time limits, one might prefer to think in terms of attainment of goals, e.g., how to arrive at a point where the child is able to deal more freely with the source of his or her stress so that resolution is likely. Admittedly, such a goal is more nebulous, but it is one which lends itself to ever clearer delineation during the course of psychotherapy. With such an approach the length of treatment is likely to be brief; this comes about because many of the children with adjustment reactions tend to respond favorably with relatively few sessions.

Individual Psychotherapy

To get caught up in the specifics of the different models of psychotherapy may distract from a grasp on its essential nature. Psychotherapy of any duration is a psychological means of helping children primarily through the development of a relationship between the child and his therapist. Any psychotherapeutic encounter ought to engage the child as an active participant in the process of reflecting on himself and his experiences; where therapy is working, the child acts to bring himself naturally and spontaneously into the psychotherapeutic relationship. The ultimate aim is for the child to develop a deeper awareness of himself and others, and to find a path to the reasonable expression of emotions, and to allow the child to seek out less disruptive means for assimilating and integrating painful realities.

In addition to the relationship itself and the ultimate development of awareness, all types of psychotherapy rely as well on a number of therapeutic forces or principles. These include the corrective emotional experience, catharsis or abreaction, suggestion or persuasion, and maturational pull. Central to the efficacy of these forces in any therapy is the mobilization of affect. The experience of affect appears to be especially crucial for the efficacy of therapy with children who have adjustment disorders. Such youngsters cannot tolerate the associated troublesome affects, and consequently have difficulty in the mastery of stressful events. It is the affect against which the child's defenses are generated, but it is the experience and awareness of the affect with its associated fantasy material which allow for integration and assimilation of the traumatic event. Lacking such affective insight, the trauma may well remain a pathologic force within the person's psychological organization.

It is especially important to place a primary emphasis on affect since psychotherapists, eager to effect quick resolutions, may be all too ready to concentrate on symbolism and its interpretation. However, without the mobilization of affect, their efforts are likely to effect nothing but sterile intellectualizations. An example of this occurred in the treatment of a 10-year-old boy who came to the pediatric clinic with a one-week history of chest pain that radiated down his left arm and that was associated with shortness of breath. His symptoms began shortly after he learned that a neighbor had suffered a fatal "heart attack." It soon became obvious that his complaints corresponded to his mother's description of the neighbor's coronary occlusion.

The boy was quick to acknowledge the interpretation. He recognized that his response appeared to reflect his identification with the neighbor who had died, and that he seemed to be "converting" his anxiety into physical symptoms which symbolized his fears. However, his symptoms persisted, and it became ever more evident that such intellectual understanding was not sufficient. Rather, it was only through the subsequent encounter with and awareness of his intense fear that his symptoms did disappear. Indeed, they did so with the help of four therapeutic sessions over the next two weeks.

Fraiberg et al. (1975) have noted the central role of affect in the treatment of mothers who had been abused as children and who now had impaired relationships with their own infants. The investigators concluded that those mothers who manifested pathologic parenting via the mechanism of "identification with the aggressor" were able to remember the events of childhood abuse, tyranny, and desertion, but were unable to recapture the associated affective experience. In the course of therapeutic work these affects were revived, and the mother could re-experience them from her earlier childhood. Only then could she become identified with her child and was no longer as likely to abuse him. Through the re-experiencing of childhood anxiety and suffering, the afflicted parents became the protectors of their children against the repetition of their own conflicted past.

Principles from Brief Psychotherapy

In conducting the treatment of adjustment disorders, the psychotherapist might well heed the following three principles of brief, dynamic psychotherapy (these were derived by Gustafson (1984) from a review of various clinical studies):

1. The principle of focal inquiry, i.e., emphasis on establishing the core issues which generate the disturbance. A diagnosis of adjustment disorder implies that there is a central issue begging for resolution and that it lends itself to persistent focus throughout the therapy. It may be thought of in terms of Marmor's delineation of the "core conflict" or of MacLean and MacIntosh's (1982) establishment of the "focal hypothesis" in the assessment interview for brief therapy.
2. The principle of managing resistance, i.e., getting through to the affect, or in Gustafson's words, "the full recurrence of the disturbance." Lester (1968) further observes that it is important to enter into an affective contact with the child before his resistances are too firmly established. He concludes that the first interview may be all the more important because at that time the child is likely to be most open. The overall importance of mobilization of affect has been noted above.
3. The principle of providing the missing developmental capability, i.e., supplying the bit of psychological functioning which is relatively deficient and which makes the patient vulnerable. Herein lies the value of building the relationship and initiating the empathic overtures which make dealing with painful realities more tolerable.

Interventions in Psychotherapy

A variety of ameliorative sequences appear during psychotherapy; these range from catharsis to the development of awareness. In a similar sense, there is an array of corresponding interventions which range from attempts to obtain a clearer picture of the child and his problems and extend to the practice of advising the child on how to utilize the newly acquired information about himself. Proceeding on from information gathering, there are a number of points on the spectrum of techniques which merit attention. There is clarification by recapitulation and reorganization of the child's productions, followed by confrontation which is a bid to engage the child in an active examination of the material at hand in order to get at the implications of what he says and does. The next step is interpretation which explores meanings and attitudes beyond the patient's conscious awareness (Carek 1972).

Though the types of intervention required will vary, it seems safe to say that in the treatment of the child with an adjustment disorder the therapist is likely to concentrate on clarification and confrontation as the methods most likely to enhance the mobilization of affect. In such an instance the therapist is likely to be more active (as is typical of brief or short-term psychotherapy). However, it behooves the therapist to heed Marmor's admonition that one must still follow essentially the nondirective line of psychoanalytic therapy, with the increased activity consisting primarily of persistent confrontations and interpretations rather than of interventions like counseling and advice giving.

The anticipated need for increased activity may detract from the importance of the traditional (psychoanalytic), relatively passive, reflective stance of the therapist during a psychotherapeutic encounter. The effectiveness of such an approach is illustrated in the treatment of Susan, a 16-year-old girl, who came for psychiatric evaluation because of depression and "feeling confused" for the previous week. She was tense and tearful as she talked of not knowing what was causing her recent state. Initially she had thought she was going through one of her episodic bouts of depression. However, this "down" seemed to be lasting longer and had now become associated with an unaccustomed feeling of confusion. She spontaneously compared these feelings to those she had experienced seven months previously after her father died.

After a digression to some recent pleasant experiences, she returned to talk about her dad. She began to sob uncontrollably and mentioned repeatedly that she just had not realized that something about her dad had been bothering her. Among other things, Susan reported that her dad had committed suicide by means of an overdose of drugs. Though she sobbed, she also sounded annoyed. When confronted with her apparent annoyance, she indicated it was embarrassing to tell people about his suicide, and reluctantly acknowledged her annoyance with him for having caused her such embarrassment. She proceeded to sob convulsively as she talked of how much she missed him. She spoke of how bad she felt when she heard other youngsters saying bad things about their fathers. Still lost in her sobbing, she added, "I do not want any father; I just want my father back!"

Susan remembered having felt depressed after her father died and having talked with her mother about her feelings, only to be given a book from their minister for her to read. Repeatedly thereafter the mother would respond to Susan's expressions of depression by saying that she needed to be strong. Sobbing profusely Susan added, "I'm so tired of being strong!" She then talked of her recent added responsibility at home because her mother spent so much time at a nursing home, tending to her own father who had become seriously ill.

At the end of the session, Susan reflected on how she had really never talked with anybody about her father's death as she had today. She went on to wonder what she could now do about her feelings. Her psychiatrist reflected back on how she had been doing something about them during that session. He further noted that in fact she could not do anything about them directly, but since they now were out in the open, she should be able to cope with them more adequately than when they were tucked away and inaccessible. As the session ended, Susan looked much relieved and readily agreed to another appointment.

In the second session several days later, Susan was more comfortable and reported that she had been feeling better, though at times she was still feeling "confused" and was just not her usual self. She still felt like something was bothering her, though she also recalled that since the previous session she felt much relieved as though rid of a tremendous burden.

In the course of two more sessions over the following two weeks, Susan became progressively more comfortable and asymptomatic; this was corroborated by her mother who marveled at the dramatic change. She had no need for further treatment, and in the last session, her psychiatrist attempted to help her consolidate her gains by having her reflect back on her feelings and thoughts about her father's death. She was now able to consider these in a more open manner.

While catharsis and elements of a corrective emotional experience were the prominent curative forces, mobilization of repressed anger in therapy also removed what had been serving as a prime hindrance to effective mourning. That is, there was the anger she harbored toward her father for what she felt he had done to her. This was anger of which she was not aware, but which she was able to acknowledge after being confronted with the annoyed manner in which she talked about his taking an overdose.

Play Therapy

A similar, relatively passive, reflective stance by the therapist is seen in the unstructured play therapy of eight-year-old Janet. This child had been referred because of almost daily nightmares over the previous two months. With the help of comforting reassurance in combination with sleeping in another room with a light on or having someone sleep with her, she could get through the night, but the frequent nightly awakenings continued. There had been much turmoil in the family. The parents had divorced five years previously and Janet had gone to live with her mother on a Caribbean island where life had many chaotic moments. Three months previously, Janet's oldest sister had found her being taken care of by a neighbor while the mother was "stoned" with barbiturates and dope. Because of this, the sister kidnapped Janet and brought her back to the States to live with their father and his new wife.

As she began therapy, almost immediately Janet became involved with toys in the play cabinet. In the first session she concentrated primarily on drawing a tropical garden scene. In the subsequent two sessions, she became much involved with both animal and human puppets. She proceeded through a number of scenes which consisted of a family being attacked by one of the animals and being saved by the other. Invariably puppet play had a happy ending as the family eventually was saved and reunited. Outside of the puppet play, the only noteworthy content was her report in the latter sessions that she had awakened at night, afraid that somebody was going to break into their house.

There followed three sessions in which talks between her and her psychiatrist centered around a similar pattern of play. The themes involved families in jeopardy, but eventually they were always happily rescued. Over the course of this work, Janet began to sleep through the night, and, overall, she became more settled. The psychiatrist concluded with the parents that Janet had been reacting to the recent upheaval in her life, but that there really did not seem to be anything drastically wrong with her. As the troublesome sleep difficulties subsided, it appeared that her father and stepmother were attuned to helping her through the adjustments necessary to her learning to live with them. Accordingly, no further therapy was deemed necessary.

The next example recounts the treatment of Jim, a 10-year-old boy with a history of recent onset of behavior problems associated with a convulsive disorder. This case further illustrates how the use of play lends itself to getting at the elements of an adjustment disorder. In one of his early sessions, Jim fell from his chair in the course of a convulsive seizure associated with very brief loss of consciousness. In a few minutes, after he became fully conscious, he returned to the play table and initiated a game in which characters fell to their death from the edge of the table. Previously there had been no getting Jim to reflect on possible fears of his illness; now, in addressing Jim's fearfulness, the psychiatrist was able to tie together the convulsive attack and the ensuing play.

A more directive approach with the aid of structured play therapy—which by its nature involves directiveness by the therapist—is illustrated in the therapy of Alex. This three-year-old boy had begun to have fecal retention and secondary soiling two months previously. This began when, shortly after the birth of a sibling, his mother had insisted that he use a training chair. Unsuccessful pediatric interventions to allay the symptom finally led to psychiatric consultation.

During the course of the first session, the therapist arranged a doll family of mother, father, and two brothers and asked Alex to tell him about this family. Presently, Alex had mother giving one of the boys a bath because "he got all dirty from coffee." From there it was an easy transition to talk of Alex's bowel problems and eventually his extreme fear of having bowel movements on the potty chair. Repetition of this structured play in subsequent sessions allowed for further exploration of Alex's idiosyncratic fears.

Activity by Therapist

While there is much to be said for taking a relatively passive, reflective stance, at times the psychotherapist may feel the need to be more active in a rapid, confrontational manner. This is illustrated in the following clinical vignette.

Jeff was an 11-year, 10-month-old boy who had been referred with the suspected diagnosis of schizophrenia. Ever since he had undergone a tonsillectomy the previous month, he had been unable to attend school. His immediate postoperative course had been unremarkable; upon his return home two days after surgery, however, he withdrew to his room where he sang, hummed, and yodeled (especially old songs and commercials). He was in constant motion even when on his bed, and every few hours he arose to eat voraciously.

When Jeff was seen in psychiatric consultation a month after surgery, he looked preoccupied and glassy eyed. He would say some things in a perseverative manner, and he showed increased motor activity. Superficially he was disoriented for time and date and acted as though he could not carry on a rational conversation. However, there was a histrionic element associated with all these areas of disturbance, and, when pressured, he gave indications of being more intact. It seemed that the apparent organic signs and symptoms could be part of an hysterical picture. In one of his more lucid intervals, he even reported that he felt as though he had been under anesthesia the previous week.

For the most part, the early therapy sessions were directed toward keeping Jeff focused on what he was experiencing at the moment, and confronting him with how his behavior reflected feeling states. For example, when Jeff acted confused and groggy and would attempt to lie down on the chairs in the office or to scribble his name illegibly, the therapist would focus on the regressive behaviors and underlying anxiety. These interventions led to behavior more appropriate to his age and to Jeff's acknowledging how frightened he had been.

Presently his behavior became less regressed, but the pattern continued of confronting him and offering superficial interpretations of his behavior when he tried to avoid dealing with feeling states. For example, he swaggered into the seventh session nonchalantly asking how long therapy would continue, as though ending it at that moment would be none too soon. When his psychiatrist suggested the persistence of pent-up feelings, Jeff began to cry as he talked of how he could be home making a fort. Dried tears led to sullen silence. The therapist addressed his behavior and underlying feelings which in turn led to his describing feelings of dizziness.

He continued to vacillate between more open expression of feelings and concerns, and regressed behaviors which defended against affect. At home there were still times when he retired to his room where he hummed, yodeled, and stayed in constant motion, intermittently eating great amounts of food. In therapy sessions he would sit back looking preoccupied, at times talking in an irrational manner. However, when confronted with his anger and, more especially, when he recalled feelings associated with his surgery, there was some intermittent semblance of rationality.

The focus throughout was on confrontation and interpretation about how Jeff seemed to fend off terrifying feelings and fantasies that he must have had at the time of surgery. His psychiatrist repeatedly suggested that it would help if Jeff could face these feelings and deal with them consciously rather than express them through the symptoms he was presenting. Ultimately, on one of the occasions when Jeff defended himself in a session by a retreat into humming and perseverative preoccupation with phrases, he was again confronted with his running away into "goofy" talk in order to get away from scary thoughts and feelings. This time Jeff protested: "If I think about these scary things, they will keep coming back to haunt me." His psychiatrist in turn assured him that one could expect quite the contrary.

Improvement in Jeff's condition was slow but steady. After 15 sessions, he was said to be "looking more himself," that is, he was once again the shy, smiling, quiet, pleasant boy he was said to have been prior to surgery.

Developmental Issues

Treatment of Jeff also illustrates the need to direct primary attention to the child's developmental level rather than to his age. This clinical example also illustrates how at a later age, a child may manifest reactions related to unmastered developmental tasks of an earlier epoch. The therapeutic material pointed specifically to the following three features of his tonsillectomy experience to which he had reacted:

The anesthetic. He talked in detail of how frightening it had been to be "under their power" while he was not able to do anything about their putting him to sleep. While this may have reflected some age-specific needs to be in control, it was also related to his fear of passivity. This was the state to which he ordinarily retreated, but about which he was conflicted.

The surgery itself.   He recalled that prior to surgery he imagined that his tongue was to be cut off. After surgery, he had had three different nightmares. In the first, he dreamed that he had been pushed off of a cliff. In the second he had his four extremities tied to four different horses which galloped off in different directions. In the third, he dreamed that elephants were stomping on him. This material strongly indicates possible sadomasochistic elements and concerns about body integrity from earlier stages of development.

Separation from mother.   He recalled in therapy how after surgery he had looked for his mother in the recovery room and later in his hospital room. Though he could not describe any reaction to her absence, he had dreams which bespoke the crucial quality of the associated feelings. That is, on four different occasions he dreamed that his mother had been killed in an accident on the expressway while on her way to the hospital to visit him.

Overall it appeared that his dissociative status reflected a reliving of the narcosis of the anesthetic, and the associated behavior reflected his attempts to master the multidetermined emotional turmoil precipitated by his surgical experience. His withdrawal and gorging himself with food further appeared to express his wallowing in the passivity into which he had retreated.

After things had settled down, it was apparent that Jeff had adopted a passive stance in order to avoid dealing with unresolved developmental issues which had rendered him vulnerable. Arrangements were accordingly made to engage him in long-term psychotherapy. In fact, he was subsequently seen over the next three years for a total of 120 sessions. Such a course illustrates how the initial psychotherapy for an adjustment disorder may in fact become part of a longer process.

In several of the cases reported here, it is evident that initially children are likely to be referred for psychiatric care without any appreciation that they are actually manifesting an adjustment disorder. Over the course of one year, Carek (1982) found that 17 of 73 patients referred to him (23 percent) merited such a diagnosis; one year later the findings at follow-up supported this view since all had done well, as had been anticipated.

With such children, one is likely to find that some recent stressor, often related to developmental issues, has generated the acute symptoms. This is true even though there may be underlying neurotic or characterological vulnerabilities. The influence of these underlying elements may be to make the clinical picture at the time of crisis appear more serious; later on, once the acute symptoms of anxiety or depression have subsided, the child may look considerably more intact. In many cases the acute symptoms are likely to subside regardless of what is done; if, however, one can address core conflicts or central issues by initiating a psychotherapeutic process, one may be able to effect change through healthful modification of personality functioning rather than through the mere alleviation of anxiety or depression.

Conclusion

Individual psychotherapy has a place in the management of children with adjustment reactions by helping them assimilate and integrate the stressful experience through its singular contributions in the following areas:

1. In the re-experiencing of or a richer experience with the full range of associated

feelings and fantasies so as to delineate more clearly the character of the stress to which the child has been reacting.
2. In the child's recognition of how he has structured the experience through embellishment of the realistic elements and his coming to distinguish his idiosyncratic neurotic elaborations from the realistic events.
3. In having the child appreciate what developmental vulnerabilities he brings to the experience as an unwitting accomplice (akin to the neurotic in search of a traumatic experience).

Chapter 240

Family Therapy

The diagnosis and treatment of stress and its sequelae from a family viewpoint necessarily have a somewhat different focus than does the use of an individual or group approach to this clinical problem. A family viewpoint focuses on the strengths and vulnerabilities of individuals as factors in the pathogenesis of stress-related adjustment disorders. It also brings out the fact that family relationship processes are major factors, not only in the location of symptoms in the family, but also in the intensity of the symptomatic response.

Family theory and therapy as a conceptual and therapeutic framework is a relatively new way of examining stress and its sequelae; nonetheless, many different points of view within the field of family theory and therapy have developed (American Psychiatric Association 1984; Gurman and Kniskern 1981; Beal 1980). However, in spite of the diversity within the family field, there are some principles and points of view about which most family therapists agree. Four major principles include the following:

1. The family is viewed as a system—as the unit of observation and of intervention.
2. Both in the presence and in the absence of stress, there are predictable relationship patterns and behavior which characterize a family.
3. These response patterns are sufficiently predictable that concepts like "the nuclear family emotional system" and "the extended family emotional system" have been developed.
4. One central concept is the differentiation of self; while alluded to by many family clinicians, it is most highly developed within the Bowen Family Systems framework (Bowen 1978).

The Family as a System

To understand the response patterns and adjustments made by families, it is necessary to appreciate how a family functions as an operational system. During the 18th century, it was noted that body temperature remained stable within a limited range even in the face of extreme variations in environmental temperature (Siever and Davis 1985). Since that time, medicine has accepted the importance of systematic homeostatic mechanisms in maintaining the viability of the individual biologic organism. However, it is only within the last several decades that psychiatry has begun to appreciate that the behavior of the family system is best understood as a product of its organizational characteristics. This came about with the advent of general systems theory, with the further refinement of the principles of biologic evolution, and with the kind of thinking that followed from the development of computers.

From a systems viewpoint, individuals within families do not primarily respond to stress just "because" of their individual strengths and weaknesses; rather they respond secondarily to the functional position they occupy in the network of family relationships. This concept has a major impact on the way family therapists think about clinical problems. Instead of assuming that symptoms or behavior is the product of a linear chain of events (the billiard ball concept in which A collides with B collides with C), family members are viewed as functioning interdependently, so that each member is connected to and has his or her action and reaction effect upon every other member. Returning to the billiard ball analogy, rather than having the balls in a straight line, where the effect stops with the last ball struck, the balls or family members are viewed as if arranged in a circle so that the last one one affected in turn exerts an effect on the first one affected. (This concept of linear versus circular causality can be studied in greater detail in the *Family Process* article by Bradford Keeney (1979).)

This radically different way of defining response patterns has shifted the focus away from identifying individual vulnerabilities and pathology and directed attention instead toward the organizational characteristics of the family system. Once one accepts the premise that an individual's response patterns are significantly shaped and determined by the nature of family relationships or by the functional position of that individual within that family, it becomes a compelling reason for turning to family therapy as an intervention technique, especially in the treatment of adjustment disorders.

Reasoning from this assumption, it follows that the symptoms within any individual family member can best be altered by changing the functional and organizational characteristics of the family system. Even if the diagnosis of adjustment disorder continues to be defined in individual terms (a practice which seems most likely to persist), it is nonetheless possible that modification of family relationship patterns may be the most efficacious way of treating the condition. Although the linear and systematic models are distinct, this difference does not necessarily mean that family systems therapy is in conflict with individual therapy. Each model has different concepts, techniques, and loci of intervention, and should be evaluated on its own merits (American Psychiatric Association 1984).

A clinical example can illustrate systems thinking and the family. The introduction of a first-born child into the relationship of a recently married couple requires a considerable measure of adjustment on the part of all three participants. The mother-child relationship must be understood not only in terms of their mutual influence on one another but also in terms of the influence of the father's emotional functioning on the mother-child dyad. Father's functioning may vary from great positive support, to emotional distance, to psychotic withdrawal.

All these responses might fall into the category of some form of adjustment; the specific form of the response patterns, however, should alert the clinician to the differences in the degree of interdependency and organization within the family.

Like the effects of infectious disease, the effects of emotional stress can be understood in terms of the systemic response of the family or organism to the stimulus itself. No one would deny that the tubercle bacillus is important in the onset of tuberculosis or that the inciting allergen is important in the onset of an anaphylactoid reaction. However, it is the response of the body, the growth of a tuberculous granuloma or the overall anaphylactoid response, that creates the significant damage. By analogy, it is often the reactivity of the responding organism or family member that brings about so much of the damage to the system itself.

Predictable Relationship Patterns

The major distinction in thinking about relationship patterns within a linear versus a system framework is the focus on a dyadic relationship as against a triadic. Linear thinking focuses, for example, on the importance of the mother-child dyad and its replication in transference-countertransference phenomena. Systemic thinking states that in an anxious emotional field, a two-person relationship is basically unstable; as a result, the more uncomfortable person will seek to "resolve" the relationship anxiety by engaging a third person. If the more anxious one is successful in engaging that third person, then the less anxious member of the original twosome becomes an outsider to the new dyad. The outsider can be either relieved or distressed by his or her position, depending on the level of anxiety in the emotional field.

For example, a mother may direct her relationship energy more to a child than to a spouse. A husband may respond to this shift with relief at not having to deal with his wife and the emotional issues between them. On the other hand, he may feel rejected at the withdrawal of this wife's emotional interest and respond with depression or angry efforts to become more emotionally, albeit negatively, engaged with her. If the child becomes symptomatic over time secondary to the mother's over-emotional investment, the mother may seek her husband's help in dealing with the child. This process may lead to temporary conflict between the father and the child, leaving the mother for the moment in the more comfortable outside position. This reciprocal emotional process is fostered by verbal and nonverbal cues and often develops into a relatively fixed pattern.

If the tension is mild to moderate, it may be contained in the central family triangle. If the tension remains high and yet continues to be contained within the central triangle, the classic scapegoating pattern may occur, leading to an identified patient—the one member who is most chronically and persistently focused on by the other two. The relative relationship harmony between the comfortable twosome occurs at the expense of the symptomatic identified patient (Minuchin et al. 1978). Multiple examples of this process could be given in which the stress activates the family relationship patterns, leading to a reaction pattern in one member who becomes labeled as the identified patient. In children, it can manifest itself as school phobias, school failures, obesity, drug abuse, psychosomatic problems, and/or runaways. In spouses, the process may result in reactive depression, excessive drug or alcohol use, physical illness, or extramarital affairs and divorces.

These patterns of family interaction described by the concept of the emotional triangle are such that they can be thought of as a homeostatic mechanism. Although medicine first appreciated the importance of systemic homeostatic mechanisms in maintaining biologic stability as long ago as the 18th century, the concept of "family" homeostasis in psychiatry was first introduced by Don Jackson in 1957. This concept refers to the tendency of any set of family relationships to preserve the organizing principles of its existence. The existence, therefore, of an identified patient within a family indicates that these symptoms are the end result of an adjustment response to the increased stress of the family relationship processes. From a systemic viewpoint, the labeling of an individual as sick allows the family to contain the stress within the family and to keep the family intact, albeit at the expense of compromising the functioning of one of its members. However, when the medical profession labels an individual as sick in isolation from his or her family, the effect is to collude with the disturbed family relationship processes and thus to risk the intensification of these processes.

Nuclear Family and Extended Family Emotional Systems

During the past 20 to 30 years, these above-mentioned triangular family patterns have been observed with such frequent regularity in clinical families (those who bring a member for psychiatric attention) that the basic patterns have been elaborated into the concept of the nuclear family emotional process (Bowen 1978). When families exchange information or work at resolving differences, tension is often generated. In general, the greater the differences or the more traumatic or emotionally toxic the information, the greater the potential anxiety elicited.

According to family systems theory, four basic relationship patterns develop within a nuclear family in the management of stress-related interactions: 1) individuals can come into conflict with one another, 2) individuals can emotionally distance themselves from one another, 3) one of the pair can adapt to or compromise his or her own functioning so as to preserve relationship harmony, or 4) the twosome can join together over a common worry. All four of these patterns exist to some degree in all families in the regulation of acute stress. When one pattern is used excessively or repeatedly in response to chronic stress, the process can lead to the problems about which families commonly complain: marital conflict, emotional distance between family members, dysfunction in one spouse, or problems with a child.

Each one of these patterns or mechanisms operates to preserve stability within individuals or to preserve the organizing principles within the family. However, the stability of a system or of one individual may be preserved at the expense of another's functioning. Marital conflict in moderate intensity may preserve the emotional, albeit negative, bond between the spouses but at the expense of their own individual functioning. Compromising one's own functioning is a common way to preserve relationship harmony. It can indeed keep the marriage or family intact but always at the expense of some one individual. Alternatively, a conflict couple uniting together over their concern for a child may thus preserve their marriage, but they will ultimately place undue responsibility on the child for marital preservation.

Marital Conflict

Marital conflict provides a relatively stable solution to the relationship problem of needing, on the one hand, enough emotional closeness to preserve the relationship and, on the other, enough emotional distance to preserve a sense of autonomy.

Conflictual marriages involve intense emotional relationships in which each spouse's emotional reactivity is focused on the other. The multitude of specific issues introduced as causes of the disharmony is not as critical as the emotional intensity of the conflictual process itself. A therapeutic focus on reducing stress or reducing the automatic reactivity of the conflictual process itself will ameliorate the symptoms.

Emotional Distance

This mechanism is used by couples to preserve a sense of autonomy in an intense relationship or to avoid the anxiety or discomfort associated with too much emotional closeness. Emotional distance is based on a pattern of automatic emotional reactivity in which one may avoid speaking to, looking at, being near, or thinking about another individual. This adaptive mechanism can be maintained externally through physical avoidance or internally by denial mechanisms.

Spouse Dysfunction

Stress between marital partners can be reduced by means of one spouse giving in to or adapting to the other. The dominant spouse often feels he or she knows best, and the adaptive spouse may want to avoid the responsibility of decision making. Compromises based on which of the spouses has the best judgment and expertise in a certain area are quite functional. However, compromises that are emotionally determined remain functional for both spouses only so long as the stress in the system remains within manageable limits. If the stress is sustained and/or reaches high levels, the overfunctioning-underfunctioning pattern may gradually impair the ability of one of the spouses to function. The symptomatic or vulnerable spouse is the one whose sense of self is the most compromised by the relationship, either through underfunctioning or through overfunctioning.

The symptoms in the dysfunctional spouse may take the form of socially acting-out behavior, or of mental or physical illness. The functional spouse may then respond to the symptomatic or adaptive spouse by seeking physical or emotional distance, a pattern which could ultimately lead to divorce. For example, the anxious and depressed spouse (although possibly a goal-directed, professionally oriented individual) may be referred to a psychiatrist, allowing the nonsymptomatic spouse to leave the marriage with less guilt because the symptomatic spouse is in "good hands."

Child Focus (Impairment of a Child)

While the above mechanisms refer to the manner in which the immaturity and reactivity of the two spouses are contained within the marital relationship or absorbed by one of pair, emotional reactivity between spouses can be detoured by a parental concentration on one or more children. Child focus is a mechanism by means of which family members deal with stress through focusing their anxiety on one or more children. In general, all the siblings in the family are not equal recipients of parental anxieties or conflict. To the extent that one child becomes the center focus of parental anxieties, he or she becomes a more "relationship-oriented" rather than "task-oriented" child. The child's energy is diverted from the developmental tasks appropriate to his or her age, and invested instead in the parent and the parent's problems.

When parental anxiety is shared with the child, the more that anxiety increases, the more the parent-child relationship is defined around mutual concerns and worries. Emotional energy and stress in the parent are typically matched by an approximately equal amount of emotional energy devoted to worry in the child, and the child is then vulnerable to a number of symptoms, including school failure and physical illness. Children who are the recipients of strong parental emotional investments, that is, who are the targets of a child-focused family, are therefore most likely to be highly relationship-oriented and less task-item oriented, and most likely to have significant difficulty coping with parental stress. Because these children cannot emotionally separate themselves from their parents and their parents' problems, parental anxiety regarding such issues as divorce is added to their own anxiety and fears about their parents' marriage.

This concept of emotional fusion as the process underlying the etiology of childhood mental problems contrasts with the widely held view of maternal deprivation as a major etiologic factor. When parents are confronted with a problem in their child, their automatic emotional reaction is to attempt to repair what has gone awry with the child. This in turn may lead to a level of activity or emotional focus on the vulnerable child which in the long run can add to the youngster's stress and enhance his or her dysfunction. As a professional and as parent, it is always difficult to know how to walk the tightrope of overinvolvement or underinvolvement in obtaining the appropriate degree of professional and personal intervention for an impaired child. Child focus is a concept within family systems theory that underscores the idea that the intensity of the intervention process is itself a significant factor in the outcome of the medical intervention with impaired children.

Differentiation of Self

All family relationships have an emotional balance or equilibrium, but not all families have the same degree of intensity in the emotional balance that exists between their members. The intensity of emotional attachment reflects the integration of two broad processes which are present in all families. One process leads toward individuality and emotional autonomy—that which an individual defines as important for himself or herself. The other process leads toward emotional fusion and dependency between individuals—that which a family defines as important for its members. The balance within an individual of these two processes, individuality versus togetherness, is one measure of the level of differentiation of self.

The concept of differentiation (which can be viewed as a continuum) refers to one important way in which humans differ from one another. Individuals at the higher end of the continuum, where individuality predominates over togetherness, can be effective team players within the family as well as well-defined individuals in their own right. Individuals at the lower end of the continuum, where togetherness predominates over individuality, are often very good team players but are much less effective as individuals in their own right.

Although much more could be elaborated about the concept of differentiation (Bowen 1978), the importance of including it here is in understanding the response of families to stress. Over the years it has been a consistent clinical observation that families with individuals who maintain a higher level of differentiation have a greater repertoire of responses to stress, are in general more adaptive, and are less vulnerable to symptom development. Individuals at the lower end of the continuum have less flexibility in responding to stress, are less adaptive, and are more vulnerable to symptom development.

Each marital relationship falls somewhere on the continuum between emotional autonomy and emotional fusion. The greater the fusion between two people, the more one person's attitudes, beliefs, and behavior are influenced by the other. The degree to which a person is emotionally influenced by others reflects the degree to which that person loses self-direction in life. Where emotional fusion is extreme, the sudden death of one spouse will be followed by total dysfunction in the remaining spouse over the course of a lifetime. An individual whose attachments and marriage are characterized by more emotional autonomy is likely to be able to negotiate sudden and serious losses of important family members with a minimum of stress and with a set of self-defined goals (albeit after a period of some dysfunction).

Stress and the Use of Family Compensatory Mechanisms

Like emotional attachment, stress affects the characteristics of family relationships. The greater the stress, the more intense the relationships; the more intense the relationship, the greater the degree of emotional fusion and, therefore, the more emotional influencing. Whenever individuals are stressed, compensatory mechanisms reestablish the balance of emotional forces in the relationships. Acute stress may produce temporary changes in the character of family relationships; chronic stress may produce more long-lasting changes.

These family compensatory mechanisms are present to some degree in all families; they serve to maintain balance and harmony within the family relationship system by readjusting the frequency and intensity of emotional contact. Families with less emotional attachment and a low level of stress can function well with periodic, moderate use of compensatory mechanisms. Families with more intense emotional attachment or lower levels of differentiation and a higher level of stress will resort to these mechanisms more frequently. Families with the highest degree of emotional attachment or the lowest level of differentiation may find it necessary to employ these mechanisms almost continuously in order to remain intact and functioning. Finally, families with high degrees of emotional attachment under low to moderate stress are likely to have one or more symptomatic dysfunctional members at any given time (Kerr 1979).

Levels of differentiation are not to be equated with psychiatric diagnoses. Individuals or families at one end of the continuum should not be considered normal nor are those at the other end necessarily abnormal. Individuals at either end who experience stress of sufficient intensity and duration will develop symptoms.

From a family systems viewpoint, stress is not just a quantitative issue; it is also a relational issue. From a family's viewpoint, stress can be described as the sum of all the nonspecific changes which arise as a response to function or reactivity or the rate of wear and tear on the family. The response patterns may be a function of the stimulus, a cognitive interpretation of the stimulus, and/or an individual family predisposition. The stimulus is called the stressor by virtue of its cognitive interpretation. The family member reacts to his or her own interpretation of the stimulus; with mild to moderate stimuli, the greatest part of excessive stress may therefore be self-initiated or self-propagated. Nevertheless, severe stress (such as a natural disaster) is most often disabling to everyone, even the family members not directly involved in the disaster (Psychiatric Annals 1985).

How Family Therapy Operates

A family systems viewpoint suggests that important emotional attachments are present within the entire network of the nuclear and extended family. This perspective conceptualizes symptoms as distortions of emotional attachment or as imbalances in the system of family relationships. If symptoms are conceptualized in this manner, then therapy requires working with the family as a unit to modify the management of relationships, attachments, and symptoms.

Family therapists begin their work by asking the questions that will identify relationship patterns and family emotional processes. The therapist's first task is to define the dysfunctions or symptoms in the context of the overall family emotional system. After identifying family patterns of emotional attachment, the therapist attempts to identify the part each individual plays in establishing and maintaining these overall patterns. The focus is on helping each person to change himself or herself, rather than on encouraging family members to try to change one another.

The therapist relates to the family but attempts to remain outside of the family emotional field. In that way he or she can provide feedback to the family on how their interactional patterns lead to or maintain specific dysfunctions or symptoms in each family members. The unique aspect of family therapy is its emphasis on emotional attachment as it is reflected in emotional distance and conflict between individuals, emotional or physical dysfunction within an individual, child focus, and the multigenerational origins of these processes.

The therapist approaches the family by asking questions that define the symptoms, locate the symptoms (in father, mother, or child), and identify the patterns that promote and perpetuate the symptoms. Depending on the location of the symptoms, the therapist may see all the family members together, just the marital couple together, one spouse or parent individually, or either spouse alone, with a focus on the multigenerational origins of the problem. The choice among the goals of containing symptomatic regression, decreasing individual reactivity, and teaching new coping skills is determined in part by who has the symptoms and what family pattern perpetuates the symptoms. Motivation and willingness of individual members to work on the family problem is also a determining factor.

The following three clinical examples will illustrate the diversity and flexibility of this approach. The first example is a child-focused family problem with moderate symptoms present in both parents and child. The second example is one in which physical, social, and emotional problems occur in both members of the marital couple with no symptoms in the child. The third example is one of the development of acute physical symptoms in an important family member, with an account of its impact on the member and the other family members.

A frequent approach in family therapy is to try to shift the intensity of the family emotional focus away from the symptomatic individual to the patterns in the family that perpetuate and sustain the symptoms. This shift is more difficult as the intensity of the family emotional focus increases. When the focus is on the child, it may be especially difficult to shift the parental focus to the marital relationship as such or to each spouse's relationship to his or her own family of origin. In mildly child-focused families, this shift may be relatively easy. In severely child-focused families, however, the problem may be of sufficient intensity that little can be accomplished beyond reducing anxiety and relieving some of the pressures on the child.

The greatest potential for modifying child-focused family problems occurs if there is a shift away from the child focus by both parents. This shift can be accomplished most easily if parents can cease to see the family as an extension of the child, and can instead learn to view the child as an extension of the marital dyad. This therapeutic viewpoint is predicated on the assumption that the more responsibly the parents can act toward the child and the more they can decrease the child-focused process, the greater the chance of symptomatic improvement in the child and the better the child can cope with the family problems that sustain his or her symptoms.

Case A.   The first case is that of a 10-year-old girl from a divorced family who had been experiencing anxiety, depression, declining school performance, and problematic peer relationships of six months' duration. Her mother, Mrs. A., although quite anxious about the daughter's functioning, refused to acknowledge it to her former husband for fear of his criticism of her and a possible ensuing custody fight. Mr. A, the father, had recently remarried, and, motivated by his strong sense of guilt of having left his daughter, was most anxious to be helpful to her. Mr. A. was a highly motivated, upwardly mobile professional with an advanced degree. Initially he had married a woman who was willing to support him through graduate school. Their courtship lasted approximately one year. During the first years of their marriage, it became apparent that the husband made most of the decisions involving the marital pair, and the wife adapted to whatever the husband wanted.

A child was born about three years after the marriage. The father then developed a chronic illness secondary to an infectious process which forced the mother to be primary caregiver to both her husband and their daughter. Once the father recovered, he became progressively more involved in his studies and bored with family life. Because of the frequent conflicts, Mr. A. was often away from home, and Mrs. A. became tearful and depressed. This process continued until Mr. A., in spite of his enormous sense of guilt, decided to leave the family and seek a divorce. Following the divorce itself, Mr. A. kept in fairly regular contact with his daughter. Although the divorce process had been conflictual, the couple had been able to work it out through their respective lawyers.

The father sought therapy when the mother decided to remarry and move to another part of the country with their daughter, who was beginning to do badly in school. After the initial interview, it was apparent that the father was trying to make a continuous re-entry into the emotional life of his daughter, that he was becoming progressively more anxious about the close emotional intensity between his ex-wife and daughter (as well as about the fact that his ex-wife was planning to marry a man much like himself), and that his ex-wife's anxiety about this decision was leading to considerable dysfunction in their daughter. When Mr. A. attempted to talk about this with his ex-wife, she complained that he was interfering with her life.

After the initial consultation, the therapist advised Mr. A. to contact a highly competent lawyer in the area who would evaluate the possibility that Mr. A. could bring suit to prevent the removal of his daughter from the area and would advise as to whether or not he might obtain custody. The therapist surmised that symptomatic regression would increase if the father utilized the litigation system as a means of intervention. From a therapeutic standpoint it was deemed more useful to contain the anxiety within the family itself by clarifying the litigation option. No therapy or mediation seemed appropriate unless Mr. A. clearly understood his chances of resolving the situation through litigation.

After it became clear that little could be resolved through litigation, meetings were held between Mr. A., his ex-wife, and their daughter. Initially, considerable anxiety was generated by this partial resurrection of the shattered marital relationship; it became clear, however, that the lack of resolution of that prior emotional relationship was contributing to the current symptoms. While the wishes of a 10-year-old child in this case were taken into consideration, it was believed that the resolution would be more effective if the process focused on the relationship between Mr. A. and his ex-wife.

Through several sessions spread over a number of months, the former Mrs. A. was able to see the similarity between her new relationship and her previous one with Mr. A. She was also able to see how anxiety about the new relationship was being transmitted to the child. Mr. A. came to be seen as a support rather than as an interference when it was made clear that he would have open and appropriate access to his child following the move. The major emphasis on this process was to clarify the general interactional patterns within the family and the part each individual played. In discussing the practical details of decision making and planning, the family became more aware of the depression and guilt remaining from previously unresolved issues. Together, Mr. A. and his ex-wife were able to make very appropriate plans for contact between their child and both parents subsequent to the move. When it was clear to both parents that each had a significant contribution to make to their daughter's welfare, they were able to stop blaming each other and begin to focus on what each of them could do.

After the marriage and the move, Mr. A. and his new wife visited in the home of Mrs. A. and her new husband; they reported that the social visit went very well. At last report the daughter had become a very good student and had been placed in advanced courses within her school. The early intervention in this case was designed to contain the anxiety within the family, to work on previously unresolved issues, and to keep the unresolved prior marital problems from focusing on the child.

Case B.   The second clinical case illustrates the interrelationship between acute and chronic stress within a family. Stressors are most often conceptualized as events or discrete occurrences which are experienced as challenges or insults to family life. This concept may be accurate when referring to catastrophic or acute events in which all family members appear affected. However, chronic stressors which are less time bound can be viewed as persistently difficult life problems or chronic overuse of certain family coping mechanisms. The second case represents just such a clinical problem in which the acute stressors, the husband's alcoholism, his affair, and his plans to leave his wife, are a function of the chronic stressors—the failing family coping mechanisms.

Mrs. P., an attractive 40-year-old mother of two children, calls a psychiatrist because she is experiencing panic attacks precipitated, she believes, by her husband's recent announcement that he no longer loves his wife, has been having an affair for the past one or two years, and plans to move out of the home within a few weeks. A careful history reveals a woman who is incapacitated by acute anxiety, and who describes a 17-year marriage in which she has dedicated herself to her husband and children, resulting in what she thought was a "perfect" marriage. Mr. P., the oldest son of highly successful parents, was a college graduate doing odd jobs when he met Mrs. P. A brief, highly romantic courtship led to a marriage in which Mr. P. describes receiving much emotional energy from his relationship with Mrs. P. During the early years of the marriage Mr. P. moved from being unemployed to obtaining two postgraduate degrees, subsequently rising rapidly in the corporate world until obtaining his current job as the head of an international consulting group. Mrs. P., on the other hand, felt she was unable to pursue her working career while raising her two children and "taking care of her husband." Mrs. P. feels that she has organized her life so as to avoid upsetting her husband, much as her own mother had related to her father. Mrs. P. had a history of one prior episode of panic attacks which had lasted for several months and which was associated with her children both entering school; this condition had responded to medication and brief supportive psychotherapy. At that time Mr. P. had refused to see the psychiatrist, saying he thought that only his wife had symptoms.

Over the ensuing years Mr. P. met the challenges of corporate life by increasing his alcohol intake and social activity away from home. Although he perceived his wife as very dedicated to him, he became progressively more anxious by her demands for his time and bored by her lack of interest in herself. His distance from his wife eventually led to an extramarital affair. His increasing guilt over being away from home so much, along with his inability to satisfy his wife's demands for his time, led to his decision to leave home.

This case illustrates a chronic family relationship process where initially the wife adapts to the husband in order to enhance his functioning, but presently gets emotionally consumed and loses herself in the process. The husband emotionally distances from the marriage through work, an affair, and alcohol, while the wife's denial allows her to think they have a "perfect" marriage. Her anxiety about problems never allows marital conflicts to surface directly.

The acute stressor is the husband's announcement of his transgressions and his perceived need to leave home. The family approach to this case could involve seeing the wife alone, the husband alone, or the couple together. As it happened, all three interventions occurred.

The initial goals of containing regression and decreasing emotional reactivity involved seeing Mrs. P. in an effort to define the symptoms and outline the basic family relationship patterns which had led to this acute distress. Gradually Mrs. P. came to realize that her insecurity about the other woman and continued emotional reactivity would serve only to drive her husband further away. When it became obvious that she had done all the planning for personal matters throughout the marriage, the therapist suggested that she matter-of-factly inquire about his plans, raise questions, but never offer to help. As her overfunctioning for him and reactivity to him gradually decreased, Mr. P.'s inability to manage his own personal affairs became more obvious. Mrs. P. insisted that the husband discuss his plans with the children once he had finalized them. Mr. P. would set dates for his departure, but then would not be able to find an apartment. Although Mrs. P.'s anxiety about the ambiguity of what would happen increased, she managed to contain her impulse to help Mr. P., knowing that her overfunctioning for him was just designed to contain her own anxiety. Eventually Mr. P. managed to acknowledge his alcoholism, give up his affair, and call his wife's family therapist for help.

This couple was seen briefly together to set a goal of containing regression while avoiding legal intervention, and to help each of them to decrease their own reactivity to one another. A longer term goal of enhancing their coping skills focused on recognizing their obsessive interdependency, defining the part each played in that interdependency, reducing their denial mechanisms, and suggesting more effective ways of relating to one another. As Mrs. P. learned to contain her reactivity, and to communicate her preference for staying married, Mr. P. began experiencing panic attacks (illustrating that a change in how families relate can lead to a shift in symptoms). At last report they were experiencing a no longer "perfect," but a nonetheless rather satisfying marriage.

Case C. The third clinical case illustrates the effects of acute physical illness on family functioning, the part that chronic family coping mechanisms may play in the genesis of acute physical illness, and the family therapy approach to these problems. A 35-year-old married father of four children developed pain in his leg while walking to work. He was a highly responsible, well-functioning high executive who owned his own business and prided himself on meeting all challenges which came his direction. He assumed his pain was a jogging-related muscle spasm and continued on to work. Within the next few days the pain increased and he developed a foot drop.

While attending business meetings, he assumed that if he walked behind people and they didn't notice his foot drop, then he didn't have one.

Finally, unable to endure the pain any longer, he drove himself to a sports medicine clinic, where the examining orthopedic physician explained that he probably had a lumbar disk herniation. As the executive slowly began to realize that the physician was talking about him, he had an anxiety attack and lost consciousness. The patient was admitted to the hospital for bed rest, traction, medication, and further evaluation. Each day during medical rounds the patient produced new medical journal articles describing what he assumed was his condition and asked his physician if the physician was familiar with the new treatment. Sensing the high level of denial and anxiety in the patient, the physician asked for a psychiatric consult.

The psychiatrist accurately evaluated that, notwithstanding the anatomical factors contributing to this man's symptoms, the overfunctioning position he assumed in his life in relation to others might be contributing to the tension and pain in his back and leg. Assuming the patient was still denying the implications of his condition, the psychiatrist referred him for biofeedback training and relaxation exercises which gave the patient concrete techniques and tasks for reducing the intensity of the pain. This referral was consistent with the family therapy principle that patients should be taught how their behavior relates to and affects their symptoms and what part they can plan in controlling the symptoms.

As the patient learned he could reduce his own pain, he gradually realized that he himself may have been a factor in generating it. Simultaneously, the psychiatrist asked to see the family with the patient in order to mobilize sufficient social support to help counteract the depression secondary to the loss of functioning this executive experienced. The potential regression secondary to the enormous anxiety the patient had about "not being able to financially support his family" was curtailed by the calm reassurance of his wife and children that they could support themselves.

Once these chronic patterns of overfunctioning have been identified, the family therapist can work either with the patient alone, with both spouses, or with the entire family. In this case the therapist chose to work primarily with the identified patient, and occasionally with the spouse and/or children. This choice was based in part on the principle that it is often easier to coach an overfunctioning individual to reduce his or her excessive functioning than to get an underfunctioning individual to function better.

The use of biofeedback to help this patient identify how his chronic tension and overfunctioning influenced his symptoms was a powerful motivator. Nevertheless, after discharge from the hospital, his chronic pain and neurologic deficit persisted for weeks. Weekly therapy sessions underscored the necessity to reduce his over-functioning and identify what factors had led to his acute collapse. Within a relatively brief period this patient could identify how his emotional distancing into and excessive investment in his work had led to a more intense involvement between his wife and children. When tension erupted between mother and children, he would "solve" the problem for them, continuing to add to his own overfunctioning.

The existence of a more expanded version of this interaction in his own extended family became apparent when he realized that he was the central figure in the overly helpful resolution of problems for other conflicting extended family members. In conversations with other family members he realized that he was seen as the one successful individual who never had problems. Following the therapist's suggestion, he made attempts to reverse that trend by discussing his current dysfunction and his longer term worries and concerns with important family members. These efforts over time led to a much closer relationship with a variety of important family members and a decision to reduce his excessive involvement in his own business.

After a long asymptomatic period, the patient began to think that although his back pain and tension were originally considered a very unfortunate liability, he could now use the onset of symptoms as a reliable marker for his ensuing overfunctioning within the family relationship and his own work system. This patient experienced a complete recovery from his physical symptomatology, and at last report has been functioning well with occasional reoccurrences.

Chapter 241

Group Therapy

There are numerous environmental circumstances and physical disorders that can produce acute or chronic maladaptive responses in emotionally healthy persons; moreover, in many of these situations, the environmental stressors or physical impairment cannot be altered. Under such conditions, group techniques are used widely in facilitating adjustment, with the psychotherapeutic endeavor aimed at diminishing maladaptive responses. There are a host of external events which bring people to seek group therapy. These include marital stress, academic (collegiate) stress, the onset of serious illness, serious illness in a near relative, loss of someone close (through death, divorce, or abandonment), the experience of rape or assault, and many others.

One of the environmental circumstances commonly addressed by group techniques is "job stress," where methods involving stress management classes, group relaxation, and support groups are used.

Why Groups?

In medical practice there has been a shift away from the traditional doctor-patient model in which the doctor first makes the diagnosis and prescribes the treatment, and the patient then accepts the doctor's formulation and follows the prescription. We have come to realize that in many instances the doctor cannot be fully responsible for the treatment, and that under certain circumstances patients with long experience in dealing with their disease may know more about its practical day-to-day management than do their physicians. This has been coupled with the rise of consumerism and with increasing demands by the public to have a say in their own treatment. Instead of shunning others who are similarly afflicted, patients now recognize their peers as potential allies. In the case of self-help groups, one consequence has been to relegate the physician to an advisory role.

There has also been a shift in attitude toward psychological treatment. It has now become legitimate to suffer from "stress," which in the workplace can lead to "burnout" (Edelwich, 1980). This term in fact designates a group of conditions which probably include adjustment disorders, but which may also refer to a great deal of psychopathology which is more severe. Currently it is not only legitimate, but de rigueur to discuss these topics in workshops sponsored by employers who seek at the same time to reduce employee turnover and to maintain or increase productivity.

There has thus been a shift in medical practice toward dealing with chronically ill patients who want to assume responsibility for themselves, plus changes in attitude in the workplace which make emotional reactions an acceptable part of the job. One consequence of these trends has been that the use of groups has become an immensely popular and useful approach.

There are several reasons for this. Group members do not have to designate themselves as emotionally ill and may view themselves as having legitimate reactions to stressors. Having a particular identified stressor to deal with provides members with a focus outside the group itself. With their symbolic badness or defect projected outside of themselves, group members do not feel nearly so demeaned or criticized in the face of self-management suggestions which are made by peers.

Because everyone's problem is automatically established when they enter the group ("We all have heart disease, colostomies, etc.") each person begins in the group with his or her worst aspect already known. Thus, "We are all working in a stressful environment and doing our best to cope with it," or "We've all got to face the fact that we have heart disease and that we may need to modify certain behaviors." The fact that everyone has the same problem, whether it is job stress or coronary artery disease, means that nobody is uniquely afflicted or defective.

The discovery that one is not alone in dealing with a life situation or an illness enhances a sense of belonging—perhaps to an exclusive club—which gives each individual a feeling of importance and entitles him or her to give constructive criticism. This sense of belonging also facilitates the acceptance of input from others.

Another positive aspect of groups is the opportunity they offer members to try out new behaviors in the group. Here, dealing with the "problem" becomes an avenue for seeking to enhance or preserve the quality of life as others demonstrate that they have done.

What Principles Are Important?

The most important principle to be observed by the patient (or the professional) is to avoid the tendency to hold the group members responsible for causing their own environmental situation or their disease. They are, however, held responsible for dealing with their reactions to the job or the illness. The theme is, "You may not have caused your problem, but you have the ability to modify how you deal with it." In this way, emphasis is placed on dealing constructively with real problems instead of assigning blame.

It is important for the therapist to have a good working knowledge of the stressful environment or medical problem. To head a job-stress group, one must be able to make practical recommendations and to understand which suggestions are impractical. Accordingly, the leader needs first-hand knowledge of the job. With regard to acute or chronic medical conditions or treatments, it may be wise for the leader to team up with a professional (often a nurse) who is knowledgeable about the disease or treatment, and who can deal in concrete terms with questions about dressing changes, side effects of medications, and so forth.

Emphasis on the realities of dealing with the stressful factors is also important, and can be achieved by an educational focus (lessons in relaxation, self-care, exercises) reinforced by demonstration. The best choice for demonstrator is a senior group member or, indeed, any person who is coping positively with the situation, the disease, or the treatment. This offers the hope that others can become equally successful and shifts the responsibility for progress onto the group members and their resources. On the other hand, outside experts can be called upon from time to time to lecture on topics important to group members' well-being.

The group leader needs to be available as a person and not as a neutral therapeutic instrument or a screen on which transferences can be projected. Fostering group interaction in a friendly, positive way stimulates the positive transference needed for the conduct of such groups. The group leader's willingness to share that he too suffers from stress or has experienced medical problems does not hinder the process. It helps instead to reduce group members' alienation and reminds them that every person has burdens to bear. Given these general principles, the leader makes use of certain mechanisms in order to accomplish the group task, that is, to prevent or modify maladaptive patterns of reaction to the identified stressors.

Therapeutic Elements

The following elements, common to all psychotherapeutic endeavors, are most important in groups dealing with adjustment disorders: stimulation of hope, education, reframing, encouragement to face emotional issues, facilitation of catharsis, desensitization, promotion of identification, and attribution of meaning.

Hope and Education

The leader approaches the group in an optimistic way, suggesting that improvement in environmental circumstance or physical condition can occur, or, if not, that these problems can nonetheless be dealt with in some positive manner. The educational element consists of first learning which aspects of the environment (work schedules, staffing ratios) can be altered and which cannot. The next issue is addressed educationally in terms of how to minimize the negative effects of what cannot be changed, and what positive coping techniques can be devised.

In a high-stress environment, part of the answer to alleviating adjustment disorders is periodic rotation of staff to less stressful work areas. In the case of critical care nursing, for example, stress may be lessened by avoiding five-day-a-week contact with any single patient. In the realm of physical disorders and their treatment, information is needed about the usual course of the disorder, the treatment, and expected side effects. This information can be provided by guest lecturers drawn from the medical or nursing staff or by a medical co-leader of the group. The information must be couched in such a way that group members can understand it.

Often, visual aids such as models, drawings, and videotape presentations, or actual demonstrations of self-care techniques are needed. Written material can also be handed out. Pre- and post-group written or oral quizzes are good means to ensure that the material taught has been absorbed.

Reframing

In therapies dealing with adjustment disorders, reframing is a powerful approach, in part because it does not require the development of a therapeutic alliance. Thus, reframing statements can be made early in the therapeutic process. In general, the stressors with which group members are dealing can be reframed as an opportunity to learn new means of coping, better means of communication, and new ways to appreciate what life and other persons have to offer.

Newly diagnosed diabetics, for example, can be told that having diabetes emphasizes what we all need to do in life, but often fail to do. We need to eat health-giving foods, regulate our physical activity, plan ahead, and work together. Having diabetes presents the opportunity to learn how to do these things. In addition to staving off the complications of diabetes, the reward is a better rounded emotional and interpersonal life. Dealing with cancer can be treated in a similar way. It can be reframed as an opportunity to reevaluate what is important in life, to take charge actively of those aspects of living that are most important, and to relinquish what serves mere vanity or social approbation.

Encouragement to Face Emotional Issues

Encouragement to face emotional issues includes the significance of loss of a breast or of a limb to one's self as person, to one's mobility, to one's appearance, and to one's relationship with others. In the case of loss of a breast, women who are dealing with the issue may wish to have their spouses join them in the group for a session. This enables the women to utilize the support of other group members as they express their feelings to their husbands.

In the case of intensive care unit (ICU) nurses, their omnipotent wishes, their identification with certain patients, their anger with God, and their grief over patients who die are all important emotional issues which need to be confronted. Discouragement about childbearing was an issue for a group of pediatric ICU nurses. They asked themselves, "How can we allow ourselves to become pregnant knowing the ills that befall children?"

In the course of dealing with life-threatening illness, with work situations that are life-threatening, or with threats to others' lives, certain transcendent issues arise. A common question among ill persons is, "What have I done to deserve this?" or, "Am I being punished by God?" The encounter with other good people who are leading reasonable lives and who are nonetheless similarly afflicted tends to diminish the self-perception of being singled out or uniquely punished. Members of the clergy can make guest appearances at groups to deal with such issues, or in hospitals for chronic illness they may serve as one of the group leaders.

One must distinguish between factors that the individual can control, such as smoking and diet in coronary artery disease and hypertension, and factors that the individual cannot control, such as the need for medication to lower blood pressure or for insulin to facilitate carbohydrate metabolism in diabetes.

Catharsis

The discharge of tension through expression of feelings is facilitated in groups dealing with adjustment to stressful situations. Catharsis may initially take the form of blaming others, but the group leader or leaders eventually enable group members to express directly the anger, desperation, hopelessness, guilt, or fear that each feels.

Catharsis on the part of one group member also has the effect of helping the others who witness it. They feel good about having helped stimulate the process in one of their numbers, and are helped as well to face feelings of their own which they may have denied, rationalized, or projected.

An undesirable side effect of the cathartic process is the danger that inappropriate action may be stimulated: "I hate my doctor, so I won't take my medicine," or "My supervisor is a bitch, so I won't do what she tells me to do." In these instances a distinction is drawn between feelings, which are always legitimate, and actions, which in many instances cannot be based on feelings but must be adapted to the realities of the situation within which the individual lives. The source of anger with the doctor can be explored and means of renegotiation proposed. The same holds for emotional reactions to supervisors.

Desensitization

Desensitization occurs through repeatedly addressing issues which group members try to avoid. Recurrent exposure lessens the emotional impact of painful thoughts and feelings. If difficult topics are not approached with an eye toward graduated exposure, traumatization can occur instead of desensitization. A nurse support group was paralyzed when its leader asked, during its first session, "What are your feelings about death?" The members responded by leaving the group and seeking a new group leader.

Similarly in a first session with a group of newly diagnosed diabetics, it is not useful to deal at length with blindness or renal failure. Discussing the pathophysiology of the disease and its management comes first. Later on, members become more accepting of themselves as diabetics and more confident of being able to deal with their disease in terms of diet, exercise, and insulin. It is then that they can usefully integrate awareness of the possible complications of the disease.

Identification

The leader(s) should promote the group's self-identification as persons dealing with a particular stressor or set of stressors; this helps ease the burden of feeling uniquely afflicted or of being uniquely impaired. The sense that all the participants are "in the same boat" tends to diminish each person's view of himself or herself as bad, inadequate, or alone.

Through identification, the emotional disturbances discussed in the group come to be accepted as average or normal, and not as symptoms of an underlying emotional disorder. A great deal of reassurance is obtainable through this means as the group members learn that their reactions are ordinary human responses. In time, this reduces the members' sense of alienation; in addition, it enables them to make use of suggestions given by others who are facing the same situation with similar personal and emotional resources.

Attribution of Meaning

Attribution of meaning is the final important element in groups for adjustment disorders. Emotional symptoms or discomfort are ascribed to stress. Thus, members are not regarded as suffering from psychopathology but as having understandable, ordinary emotional reactions to difficult circumstances. They are told that given the circumstances with which they are coping, what they feel is what ordinary people feel. Because there is no significant underlying psychiatric disorder, this reassurance alleviates group members' fear that they are falling apart psychologically.

This stands in contrast to the effects of trying to reassure persons suffering from an anxiety disorder that nothing is really wrong. The person with an anxiety disorder knows his or her reaction is far out of proportion to the existing environmental pressures and becomes even more concerned about not being fully understood.

Formats

Many different formats are useful for treating persons with adjustment disorders. The simplest format is a time-limited class. This might take the form of a class for stress management in high-stress work situations or of in-hospital classes for post-myocardial infarction (MI) patients or for newly diagnosed diabetics. In most conditions, emphasis is placed on learning about one's illness. After learning some elementary physiology and pathology, patients are instructed in self-care. A typical week-long series for cardiac patients (which is repeated as soon as enough patients or students are available) is 1) What is heart disease? 2) Exercise and your heart. 3) Diet and heart disease. 4) Medications for heart disease. 5) Physical and emotional complications of heart disease. 6) Stress management for the heart disease patient.

These sessions are often led by different professionals with a nurse serving as coordinator or moderator. After hospitalization, patients can join clubs that meet monthly. One such club, a cardiac club, is led by a nurse. The club's monthly meetings are held in the hospital cafeteria, where a low-cholesterol meal is served. After the meal, members who have lost weight are recognized and applauded, as are those who have stopped smoking. A speaker deals with some aspect of cardiac disease and a general discussion follows.

In addition to classes and clubs, there are more formal groups which are open-ended or time-limited depending on the wishes of the group members. At times nurse support groups are led by mental health professionals. They meet on the nursing unit for an hour a week. They are often organized on a time-limited basis to deal with crises. Short-term groups have been held for post-coronary patients and their spouses (Adsett and Bruhn 1968; Baker and McCoy 1979; Hackett 1978; Rahe et al. 1979). Long-term groups have been employed with terminally ill persons (Yalom and Greaves 1977). Formats are variable, ranging from one hour several times a week to 90 minutes once a week, depending on the group and its setting. Groups can also be set up in clinics dealing with special populations (such as renal dialysis and transplant patients) as part of the regular clinic visit.

An important factor in long-term groups is the presence of a "senior" patient or a group of senior patients who are doing well. These senior patients serve as models for identification, stimulate hope, and offer practical advice and suggestions from a person who has been there. These persons often have a special relationship with the group leader, who in turn must take care that the relationship is not seen as excluding others in the group.

Termination

Termination is part of the process of each group. It is built into the contract in time-limited groups. Members are reminded during the course of the group that it is time-limited, and the time-limited nature of the group is used both to press for prompt examination of pertinent here-and-now issues and to shut off exploration of other material as too time consuming. The pain and sorrow of group termination is softened by the prospect of continued intermember relationships after the group is over, and indeed, the aim of these groups is to establish strong bonds among members.

In long-term or open-ended groups, members graduate when they are coping adequately with their reality situation. Such graduations are heralded by feelings of optimism or relative satisfaction that one is doing the best one can. These feelings are shored up by the knowledge that the group is still available should further formal support be needed.

Problems

Many technical problems face the leader of groups dealing with problems of adjustment. The primary problem is the therapists' tendency to deal with the members as neurotic patients whose unconscious motivations and contributions to their own illness require exploration. In treating problems of adjustment, the therapeutic work involves identifying external sources of stress, shoring up intrapsychic defenses, and devising means to cope with situations that produce strong affects. The danger of focusing on adjustment is that treatable psychiatric disorders may be overlooked. On the other hand, group members can usually identify persons whose emotional reactions suggest the need for special treatment. Those persons can then be referred for the necessary therapy instead of or in addition to continuing in the group.

In conducting groups for the medically ill, other problems arise which are specific to the leader. These include the stimulation of countertransference feelings. It is easy for the leader to become overwhelmed by the gravity of patients' illnesses. It is also tempting to try to outguess patients' primary physicians. At times, the leaders of groups for medical patients can spot countertransference problems in the primary physician which are best dealt with in face-to-face interactions. At other times, group leaders may fall into the type of splitting characteristic of patients with severe regressive reactions or personality disorders.

In nurse support groups, it is easy to become competitive with the regular medical staff, aligning with the nurses and promoting acting out against "them."

Premature mobilization of affect is another problem. Therapists are often in a hurry to indoctrinate group members into the mystique of expressing feelings. Unless a person is affectively overwhelmed, the expression of feelings requires the lowering of defenses, and that in turn requires some recovery from the shock of illness or disfigurement. Providing cognitive structure is the first requisite of these groups. Emotional display is safe when members become more certain that they are not falling apart physically and emotionally.

It is especially important to make sure that intense negative affects are directed outside the group instead of against the group members. Any expression of anger toward other group members should also await the establishment of firm bonds among group members and with the leader. A problem in turning aggression outside the group is the possibility that within a work environment, such a support group will organize to act out against administration.

The issue of acting out raises an important contextual question having to do with the motivation for planning or requesting a group intervention. A support group should not be offered or undertaken in a work situation where it is clearly a means to avoid realistic issues such as understaffing or inadequate facilities. Nor should such groups be offered as a means to save staff time by deferring all questions to the group instead of dealing with doctor-patient or nurse-patient issues as they arise.

Structure

Nurse support groups may be organized as ongoing or as time-limited discussion groups (Weiner and Caldwell 1981). The structuring of these groups depends both on nurses' perception of their own needs and on what the administrative structure of the hospital unit will allow. Ordinarily, the change between afternoon and evening shifts is a good time for weekly, one-hour meetings. The idea of a group is introduced as a chance to discuss feelings about work-related issues. The stated aim is to facilitate the nurses' work with each other, the medical staff, and their patients.

These groups are initiated by formulating an agenda; often this consists of a list of problems which nurses typically encounter during a work day. The agenda items are discussed one at a time, and the nurses are encouraged to share the means by which they have themselves learned to cope with these stresses. In short-term groups, the discussion is primarily patient-oriented; the topics may deal with the dying patient, the uncooperative patient, the delirious patient, or the patient's family. Longer term groups allow for the discussion of tensions among nurses; this is effective if care is taken to modulate the expression of aggression among group members, whether present or absent.

In medical settings patient groups work best when they are part of the overall treatment regimen (Lonergan 1982). The meetings are introduced to each patient as part of the treatment. Patients are selected for groups solely on the basis of their diagnosis and their willingness to learn and to talk about their illness; those who are delirious or severely demented are best excluded. Groups need to be located near the medical unit on which the treatment takes place, but the group session should ordinarily not be interrupted by other medical treatments.

Groups are started with an agenda that usually consists of conveying information about the patients' disease or its treatment. Then, depending on the stability of individual group members, emotionally charged issues can be raised. The session length depends on the physical capacity of the group members and their ability to concentrate; 45 minutes to an hour is a reasonable length of time. In short-term hospital groups there is no senior member, but recovered patients can be invited to attend group meetings in order to address various issues with which they have coped successfully.

Chapter 242

Pharmacotherapy

Despite the known efficacy of psychopharmacologic agents in a wide variety of conditions, and despite the presumed frequency of stress-related disorders, there have been remarkably few systematic, controlled studies of the effectiveness of medication(s) in the treatment of these syndromes. This is true even of the most common of these syndromes, acute grief. Different theoretical views are prevalent in the field concerning the adaptive value of grief; it has been regarded as normal working through, and it has also been viewed as a stressor in and of itself.

It may well be that it is these different views which fuel the controversy as to the appropriateness of the use of medication (Osterweis et al. 1984). Even a psychopharmacologist such as Hollister has stated, "The final resolution of loss is better accomplished by psychological help than by the use of drugs. Although drugs may be helpful in treating the . . . bereaved, their use is adjunctive, symptomatic, and limited in time" (Hollister 1972). Similar controversies surround some of the other stress-related disorders.

Principles of Pharmacotherapy

When symptoms appear in connection with acute and significant stress, the primary treatment is psychotherapy. This may be supportive or insight-oriented, and it may be addressed to the individual or to the family. Pharmacotherapy should be seen as adjunctive and directed toward the relief of distressing and complicating symptoms, rather than toward the treatment of the stress response itself.

Unfortunately, many physicians prescribe anxiolytics or antidepressants, often in homeopathic doses, without providing the indicated psychotherapy. This is especially true of nonpsychiatrists, who probably see the majority of these patients. The use of "a touch" of a psychotropic medication, "to take the edge off," especially when it substitutes for talking to the patient, should be discouraged.

In treating these patients, the clinician must first decide whether or not to use psychotropic medication, then which medication to choose and what dosage to prescribe, and finally, when to start and when to stop. A first principle guiding these decisions is that pathology is more important than etiology; if a patient shows disabling symptoms of frank depression, the clinician should prescribe antidepressants regardless of whether the depression appears to be endogenous or reactive to stress. Similarly, the decision to use anxiolytic medication depends primarily on how severe and disabling the symptoms are, as well as on other pharmacologic considerations, rather than on the source of the anxiety.

A second principle is that, when used properly, medication will not interfere with either psychotherapy or the mourning process. Clinicians have been reluctant to use medication, especially in patients with acute grief responses, for fear that the drugs will facilitate avoidance of painful affects, "medicalize" a normal process, or prevent proper working-through of the grief response. Such caution is warranted if the grief response is, in fact, a normal one. But if, in the clinician's judgment, the response has become pathologic, medication may indeed be indicated. It is possible for patients to overuse medicines, especially sedatives, in the service of avoiding necessary psychological work, but in appropriately controlled and properly timed doses, sedatives need not interfere with this work and can often facilitate it.

This point leads to the third principle: medications used in these situations should be limited in time and in dosage to the minimum necessary. Because they are not the primary mode of treatment in stress-related disorders, and because of their various side effects and addictive properties, psychotropic drugs should be started only when it is clear that the symptoms will not remit spontaneously. Such medications should be limited to the dose necessary for symptom relief, and discontinued as soon as possible (i.e., after symptoms abate without triggering relapse). As is always true in employing these powerful agents, due concern must be directed toward possible misuse of medications in the direction of self-destruction. Care in the number of pills or capsules prescribed, the alerting of family members and others in contact with the patient, and active monitoring by the physician are always important.

Sedative-Hypnotics and Anxiolytics

Several specific symptoms which develop in patients with stress-related disorders may require treatment with sedative-hypnotics. Insomnia which continues for more than a few nights can interfere with the patient's ability to function during the day and thus trigger a cycle of increasing stress and further insomnia. If the sleep difficulty occurs in the setting of the full syndrome of depression, antidepressant medication may be indicated, but if not, an anxiolytic can interrupt the cycle. The optimal regimen is a moderate dose (one-third to one-half of the recommended daily dose) of a short- or medium-acting benzodiazepine half an hour before bedtime.

Panic disorders and phobias may develop in response to acute trauma or chronic stress. Treatment with sedative-hypnotics is one option, along with a variety of psychological and behavioral measures. The decision as to whether or not to use medication will depend on how severely the symptoms disrupt the patient's life; however, the benefits of easing this disruption must in turn be weighed against the risk of addiction to these drugs. The short-acting, high-potency benzodiazepines, especially alprazolam, have been found particularly effective in panic disorder (Rickels et al. 1983). As a result of research in this area, other medications which were formerly considered exclusively for use in epileptic disorders and depression are evidencing themselves as effective, but are not yet FDA approved.

In patients with an acute stress response, the syndrome described as "affect block" is another specific indication for the use of benzodiazepines. Klein et al. (1980) describe patients who have suffered major losses (e.g., death of a loved one) but who, because of a characterologic reluctance to show weakness, are unable to mourn; instead they become emotionally rigid. In these cases, small doses of anxiolytic drugs can reduce the patient's fear of being overwhelmed by emotion, thus permitting the emergence of the blocked affect and facilitating engagement in psychotherapy.

A similar but more dramatic use of sedative-hypnotic drugs to facilitate psychotherapeutic work is the barbiturate interview (Dysken et al. 1979; Klein et al. 1980). This technique, developed during World War II, involves the intravenous administration of a short-acting barbiturate (usually amobarbital) while the patient is being interviewed. The interviewing technique may vary, but the general goal is to promote the recovery of repressed memories and the catharsis of associated affects by pharmacologically relaxing the patient's defenses. The short-acting barbiturates are used both because they were the agents employed when the technique was originally described, and because their rapid pharmacokinetics permit flexible titration of the patient's level of arousal during the interview. However, if a sufficiently short-acting intravenous benzodiazepine were available, it could presumably be used for the same purpose with less risk of respiratory complications.

Many clinicians prescribe homeopathic doses of sedative-hypnotic drugs for their placebo effect. Patients with pathologic stress responses are highly susceptible to placebo effects, and this practice is not necessarily objectionable. However, the clinician should be aware of this susceptibility and not mistake a placebo effect for a pharmacologic response. Again, the use of medication should not substitute for psychotherapy with these patients, and the placebo effect can be greatly enhanced by a positive transference. Some phobic and dependent patients can obtain placebo benefit without actually taking medication; they find their anxiety relieved simply by having the medication available or even by carrying an unfilled prescription with them.

The sedative-hypnotic class of medications includes the barbiturates, several older nonbarbiturate drugs such as ethclorvinyl and meprobamate, and the benzodiazepines. When given in equi-potential doses, all these groups cause comparable degrees of generalized CNS sedation; they differ from each other in their side effects and pharmacokinetics. The benzodiazepines have major advantages over the other groups: they are less likely than the barbiturates to cause respiratory complications, and they are less extensively fat-stored than the older sedative-hypnotics; they therefore produce smoother and more predictable serum levels.

Rickets et al. (1978) investigated the predictors of response to benzodiazepines, and found that the presence of an identifiable stressor precipitating anxiety symptoms was associated with improvement. Other predictors of favorable response included recent onset of symptoms, previous exposure to few medications but good response to those few, and the physician's comfort in prescribing the drugs. No controlled studies have been conducted on bereaved persons.

Antidepressants

In general, the guidelines for using antidepressants in stress-related disorders are the same as those for many other drugs: the decision to prescribe depends on the nature and severity of the symptoms rather than on the etiology of the disorder. It is often possible for the patient or the clinician to establish a plausible connection between depressive symptoms and life stresses, and the questions about whether and how the stress leads to the depressive symptoms are of considerable diagnostic and theoretical significance. But the clinical decision about whether or not to prescribe antidepressants should not be guided by these issues. Antidepressants should be considered if the symptoms interfere seriously with the patient's functioning, and/or if the symptoms do not remit after a reasonable time.

However, the judgment as to whether a depression is stress-related does affect the clinical decision about when to start antidepressant treatment. Generally, the more purely "reactive" a depression is, the more likely it is to remit spontaneously (assuming that the stress is transient); therefore the longer one should wait before beginning antidepressant treatment.

Thus, for example, let us consider a patient who shows symptoms of depression in clear relationship to a major stressor, but who has no history of previous depression and is not psychotic or actively self-destructive. In such a case one should wait at least two months (Klein et al. 1980) before beginning antidepressants. During this time, either one might offer no treatment beyond regular contact for monitoring or one might initiate psychotherapy, but a period at least this long should be allowed for the stress response to run its own course. On the other hand, if the patient has a history of previous depressions requiring somatic therapy or hospitalization, or if the patient is psychotic, suicidal, or otherwise endangering work or social relationships, one should begin medication sooner.

In addition to these general indications for the use of antidepressants in stress-related depression, certain specific syndromes, which can be stress-related, have been found to respond to specific antidepressants. Hogben and Cornfield (1981) have treated posttraumatic stress symptoms (including nightmares, flashbacks, startle reactions, and aggressive outbursts) in combat veterans refractory to other forms of medication and psychotherapy, and have reported success with phenelzine in doses of 45–75 mg per day. Marshall (1975) reported three cases of night terrors, including recurrent dreams of traumatic incidents, which were relieved by imipramine in doses as low as 75 mg per day. In an uncontrolled study of 17 combat veterans with posttraumatic stress disorder, improvement was reported with a variety of tricyclic antidepressants (Falcon et al. 1985). Imipramine has also been used extensively to prevent the "spontaneous" panic attacks which occur in patients with phobic anxiety (Klein et al. 1980), but the relationship of this syndrome to environmental stress is unclear.

Antipsychotics

DSM-III-R includes the diagnosis of "Brief Reactive Psychosis," characterized by the abrupt onset of psychosis "immediately following a recognizable psycho-social stressor that would evoke significant symptoms of distress in almost anyone" (American Psychiatric Association 1987) and by complete resolution of the symptoms in less than two weeks. This type of psychosis is stress-related by definition, but psychotic episodes in patients with schizophrenia or major affective disorders may also occur in connection with identifiable stressors.

Once again, the use of medication should be determined by the symptom picture rather than by the etiology of the psychosis. Psychotic symptoms will, in general, respond equally well to antipsychotic medications whether the symptoms are secondary to overwhelming stress or arise within the context of a chronic functional disorder. The considerations governing the choice of antipsychotic medication and the dosage employed are the same for brief reactive psychosis as for schizophrenia and the affective psychoses. However, the duration of treatment might be shorter in a patient with brief reactive psychosis. Thus, a person with no previous history of psychosis who becomes psychotic immediately after a major stress should be treated with antipsychotics, and will probably respond quickly and return to his premorbid condition within a few days. In this case, one should then taper the medication over a week or two, and, if there is no relapse, discontinue it.

A common error in the treatment of agitated patients, including those with brief reactive psychosis, is the use of antipsychotic drugs for the primary purpose of sedation. Psychotic patients are often disruptively and uncomfortably agitated, and agitated patients may be so uncooperative that it is difficult to determine whether or not they are psychotic. But the clinician should be able to distinguish, at least conceptually, between agitation and psychosis, and to decide whether the primary treatment goal at a given moment is to calm the patient or to relieve psychosis. The antipsychotic drugs, especially the low-potency agents, all have sedative effects, and they are therefore often used to calm agitated patients; thus the misnomer "major tranquilizers." There are now a wide variety of safe, effective sedative-hypnotic drugs, which are free from many of the serious side effects of the neuroleptics, and which should be used when sedation is desired. Thus, when the primary aim is to sedate the patient, one should use a sedative; when the primary purpose is to relieve psychosis, one should use an antipsychotic.

Beta-Blockers

Beta-adrenergic blocking drugs have been tried in a variety of psychiatric conditions, including some which appear to be stress-related. A number of studies comparing beta-blockers to benzodiazepines and placebo in the treatment of phobias and generalized anxiety have found that the beta-blockers have some anti-anxiety effect but less than that of the benzodiazepines (Cole 1979). But beta-blocking drugs have been found to be especially useful in particular stress situations, especially those in which an anxiety-induced tremor might interfere with performance, as in the treatment of "stage fright" in musicians (James et al. 1977; Liebowitz et al. 1985).

In summary, the absence of scientific evidence makes it difficult to offer firm recommendations for clinical practice. Therefore, clinical judgments should be governed by pharmacologically based principles, properly tempered by caution, and arrived at in the individual instance. Until the necessary and appropriate studies are done, these are the views which must prevail.

Chapter 243

Religion as Ego Support

Life is difficult and the world presents an unpredictable and risky environment. The complexities of modern life make such a statement even more poignant. We live on this fragile, blue-green orb spinning in a solar system and galaxy that have only recently come to be somewhat understood. The natural world presents the human species with an endless variety of calamities, contingent risks, and challenges. Religion, usually including a community of shared beliefs, offers support and structure for coping with these stressful, inevitable events. It may also enhance positive experiences. This chapter reviews those aspects of religion which may be relevant in supporting and promoting ego functioning in the prevention or adjunctive treatment of adjustment disorders.

Erikson suggests that religious sentiment can help restore hope (Erikson 1969). Neubauer et al. observe that in spite of man's attempts to master nature through scientific endeavor, religious feelings and faith have a profound place in man's psyche (Neubauer et al. 1972). Many authors, including O'Donnell, have emphasized the common goals of religion and medicine in promoting the good of mankind (O'Donnell 1970). Dr. M. N. Beck, past President of the Canadian Psychiatric Association, has stated that as a Christian he finds, in Jesus, the peace of knowing a "still point" in a rapidly changing world (Beck 1973). Dr. Walter Barton, former President and Medical

Director of the American Psychiatric Association, has stated, "As a psychiatrist I don't believe that scientific technology has replaced God's truth. Nor do I believe that psychiatric jargon satisfies man's search for meaning in his life" (Barton 1972, p. 17). Both psychiatry and religion affirm the significance of the individual and the meaningfulness of human experience. Both emphasize peace of mind and man's happiness within the context of social demands and realities.

Stressors for Which Religious Support Is Appropriate

Birth and Death

An obvious role for religious involvement centers around the event of birth. We welcome the neonate with a sense of renewal and religious joy. Most religions have created such rituals as baptism, circumcision, and blessings for acknowledging the birth and helping to ensure the health, welfare, and fertility of the new arrival. The infant embodies man's hope for survival.

Confronting death is another major function of religion. Funerals, wakes, and interment are the events for which religious support is commonly sought. Families are comforted and consoled at this time of greatest suffering. All can unite around shared religious symbols and rites to focus on the life of the deceased, to ponder the meaning and purpose of life and death, and to help the bereaved endure the pain of their immense loss. Religious institutions help support the grieving process and the mourner toward psychological closure and readjustment.

Life Passages

Developmental life passages are ritualistically recognized by religion. The transition from childhood to adolescence is honored by the Jewish bar-mitzvah and bas-mitzvah. Christian and non-Christian as well as primitive cultures often give special attention to the arrival of puberty. Underlying concerns about emerging sexuality and aggressive drives may be more comfortably focused and controlled, and a more socially responsible role acknowledged by these events.

Marriage

Marriage has long been seen as the province of religious traditions. Even in an increasingly secular world, couples often turn to the religious symbols of their heritage for wedding plans. Families frequently utilize churches to give credibility and sanction to their children's weddings. A blending of cultural and religious traditions is well exemplified in the wedding ceremony.

Child Rearing

Religion is usually seen as a necessary part of the moral and ethical education of young children. The birth of children often renews parental motivation for religious involvement. New parents feel a need to train their offspring in the ways of their own religious experience. This may lead to marital and family conflict concerning methods, especially if the individuals are from different religious backgrounds. Churches and synagogues become powerful repositories for providing helpful support to young couples rearing families. This can be especially important if an extended family and familiar neighbors are not available, a situation increasingly present in current culture.

Aging

Religious activities can affect adaptation to aging (Ruhback 1977). This was particularly true when middle age was a time of religious activity. The general reduction in religious belief, along with the associated existential crises, often produces uncertainty and anxiety in the elderly. Organized religion represents one of the few forms of community available to our aging population. In an increasingly mobile society, this may be a crucially important resource for providing a sense of family, belonging, and continuity.

Disasters

National disasters predictably mobilize religious support through clergy and lay assistance. Physical intervention and prayers for strength, patience, and forbearance are offered to victims of floods, fires, earthquakes, war, and political terrorism. Both civilian and military populations seek out religious support when these events occur.

Care Centers

Hospitals, nursing homes, and hospices are routinely visited by those with gifts of the religious message. Illness and injuries are often more bearable when one is offered a spiritual promise of hope. Traditionally a primary concern of the churches has been providing hospitals and other medical care. However, these institutions are now being replaced by business-oriented, "for profit" hospitals which do not attempt to invoke any theological message in their activities. This exemplifies the erosion of the sectarian and the growth of the secular in Western culture. Some view this as a failure of religion to sustain humanistic concerns traditionally associated with and provided by religious organizations. Religions view this as an appropriate response to their own fiscal health and cumbersome governmental controls.

Mobile Life Styles

Religious support is often desired by those relocating to unfamiliar situations and geographical areas. This occurs in all groups from the most affluent to the most disadvantaged. Churches and synagogues are identified by newcomers along with schools, hospitals, and libraries. The spire, cross, and star are considered symbols of security and acceptance by a sizable share of "pilgrims" in an unfamiliar community. Networks for support can be quickly established through the active help of religion. Although churches and synagogues may occasionally fail to respond to those in need because of established cliques and indifference, in many instances a new "extended family" is quickly created.

Traditional Ways Religion Offers Ego Support

Religion can offer ego support in a variety of ways. Walter Kaufman, citing Leuba, has described three common features generally present in the religious experience: the intellectual, the affective, and the practical-participatory (Kaufman 1978).

In the intellectual approach the individual is given answers to questions about ultimate meaning. This often comes in the form of theological explanations or quotes from scriptural sources. Confronting the "problem of suffering" has long confounded both the theologian and the psychotherapist (Kaufman 1978). Some prefer a religious explanation while others seek existential answers. The recent bestseller, *When Bad Things Happen to Good People* (Kushner 1981), has been used as a comfort by many who have faced tragedy. Religious explanation can fail, however, leaving a confused sufferer who may then slip into nihilism and despair.

The affective responses mediated by a religious experience can leave the individual comforted. The "peak experiences" described by Maslow are examples of transcendent, ecstatic feelings that become some of the most important inner events captured in the memories of human beings (Maslow 1970).

Powerful symbols and rituals utilized in the practical-participatory mode of religion give continuity, tradition, and ways of binding the intellect and emotions into a workable format. Ego support is thus enhanced as the individual shares these rituals of prayer, fasting, sacraments, and sacrifice with fellow believers.

Religion as a Therapeutic Adjunct

Life Meaning

Many authors, including Fromm, Frankl, and Peck, have emphasized the importance of searching for life meaning. Fromm views all human beings as religious, defining religion as any system of thought and action which gives one a needed frame of orientation and object of devotion. He relates "salvation" by the Christian, "liberation" and "enlightenment" by the Buddhist, and love and union by the nontheistic (Fromm 1973).

Frankl comments on the despair of those living in an "existential vacuum." He believes that frantic efforts to combat boredom and a sense of emptiness through sexual encounters and other means are futile. However, he suggests that these problems can be productively addressed by the psychotherapist. Calling this search for life-meaning and purpose "logotherapy," he proposes supplementing psychotherapy with an emphasis on individual uniqueness, spiritual dimension, and finding one's place in the global order of things (Frankl 1967).

Peck maintains that spiritual growth is a journey from a microcosm of personal experience to an ever greater macrocosm. The macrocosm is a "world view" which reflects a higher, more meaningful level of reality and awareness. As with Fromm, Peck believes that everyone has a religion. . .a world view primarily determined by experience within the nuclear family. Attitudes toward other people, authority, and reality are components of this world view. He comments on resisting change in order to avoid the death of cherished notions, and the need to see things as one desires them to be rather than as they are. Peck sees psychiatrists as obliged to acknowledge and understand religion for the welfare of patients, and cautions against overcommitment to scientific principles of measurement and natural law, perhaps cloaking a therapist's personal bias (Peck 1978).

Longing for Relatedness

A major survey asked Americans what they most desired in life. Of the many choices including "sincerity and love between myself and others," "salvation through faith," "a good job worth doing," "money and position," "freedom from restrictions," and so forth, the most desired condition was overwhelmingly "sincerity and love between myself and others." Nationally, 66 percent chose this condition while none of the others was the choice of more than 10 percent (Gallup 1975). Longing for relatedness, the need to avoid separation and abandonment, is a basic human need.

Change in Emphasis of Religion in the United States

Most major religions in the United States are descreasing or minimizing fear and guilt as guides to behavior. Most are increasing their emphasis on love of mankind and humanistic concerns. There is greater emphasis on everyday-life issues, responsible behavior, healthy self-image, and increased self-understanding and self-worth, with diminished emphasis on dogma and the superiority of the given faith to the teachings of other religions (Whitehead 1979).

Religion as a Deterrent to Suicide

The lower incidence of suicide among Roman Catholics and Jews compared to Protestants suggests that religious beliefs are significant in determining reactions to stress (Durkheim 1957). Durkheim pointed to society's impact on the individual, noting that individuals commit suicide because the meaning and stability provided by the social order have been modified, weakened, or erased. He suggests that suicide is reduced through involvement in social groups . . . religious, family, occupational, etc. Although Durkheim's study of suicide is almost 40 years old, his observations on anomie have been further validated by a study of 9,189 suicides in the Netherlands between 1961–1970 (Jasperse 1976).

Religion as Ego Disruptive

Misuse and Misapplication

While the central theme of both the Old and the New Testament is love of God and fellow man, this message may be obscured by misuse and misapplication. Examples are holy wars, persecution, brutality, inquisitions, bigotry, book burning, witch burning, hypocrisy, superstition, fear, and rigidity. Religion can build fences rather than bridges and can generate morbid guilt and fear. The basic spirit of religious endeavors may be lost by overemphasizing the "letter of the law," misusing content, or focusing on dogma that ignores new information and realities. The support individuals expected from religion can turn sour, and the desired solace and security can be experienced as rejection and isolation.

Religion and Family

Religion is often used as a substitute for the "extended family," and the same risks associated with the familial group are transferred to the church. The vulnerable individual can quickly become disillusioned when expectations are frustrated or violated. Religion can be a fertile field for cultivating guilt, feelings of unworthiness, and self-contempt. The potential for polarized experiences exists in both religious groups and families. Psychopathology can infiltrate either institution with disastrous results. At times, the line between the desired ego support and flawed ego sabotage seems to be a thin one.

Healthy and Hazardous Religion

Kepler defines a "healthy religion" as one that promotes understanding of the world, gives meaning to the mystery of life, adds relevance to the daily world, increases the realization of one's dignity and worth, instills feelings of security not dependent on bigotry and prejudice, and expands the ability to receive new truths. He views an "unhealthy religion" as one causing frustration, tension, debasement of the self, and a sense of hopelessness (Kepler 1970).

Chesen describes the hazards of religion, arguing that theology should be viewed as "a kind of consumer good that is without question potentially harmful to the user's mental health" (Chesen 1972, p. 1). As a statement of balance, he adds ". . . (religion) is very often a supportive and even enriching force that can facilitate mental well-being and general happiness" (p. 92).

In William James' *Varieties of Religious Experience,* "healthy-mindedness" religion is contrasted to the "sick soul" type. The healthy-minded view life optimistically, while the sick soul focuses on the darker corners of human experience and maximizes evil (James 1902). Faith is not a blind leap into nothing but a thoughtful walk in the light we have (Trueblood 1957).

Harris, Fromm, and Kaufman, among other writers, have examined the ego constructive aspects of religion in the lives of human beings. Each has emphasized the need for healthy interpretation and practice of the religious life. Surrendering one's personal dignity to a religious despot or dogmatist can scuttle any change in the direction of growth and self-determination. There exists a constant danger of perversion and cultism through substituting for healthy religious activity the charismatic promises of an unscrupulous, exploitative theology.

Conclusion

Religion is significant in the lives of most people and can be supportive of mental health. Many observers, including Freud, Fromm, Harris, and Peck, have emphasized self-awareness and responsibility as cornerstones of mental health. In times of stress, religion may provide culturally meaningful ego support to the individual that will "bolster adaptive coping." Society generally is, and has been, admirably served by our religious institutions. Opportunities remain abundant and growing for such service to mankind. Psychiatry should actively support and encourage meaning, comfort, and a sense of belonging. Religion offers an important adjunct to successful psychotherapy for adjustment disorder and a means for promoting mental health.

Chapter 244

Self-Help and Mutual Aid Groups for Adults

Since the establishment of Alcoholics Anonymous and Recovery, Incorporated some 50 years ago, the self-help and mutual aid group movement has grown to address a great variety of conditions and afflictions. It appears now that self-help groups may be found for all of the 17 disease categories recognized by the World Health Organization. Numerous self-help groups are springing up in cities throughout the United States and Canada. The directories which list them indicate that over a very short period of time the number of groups formed for various kinds of conditions has doubled and redoubled. For example, in the Chicago area alone from 1980 to 1984 the number of groups identified more than doubled; the directory published by the Self-Help Center in Evanston identified over 1,100 groups for nearly 300 conditions. (See *Directory of Self-Help/Mutual Aid Groups, Chicago Metropolitan Area, 1983–84*, published by the Self-Help Center.)

Increasingly one finds self-help support groups formed for the several types of stressors. Specifically, these include object loss, illness, birth-related reactions, developmental issues, major disasters, bodily trauma, social trauma, moving to a new environment, loss of ideals, and economic trauma.

Moreover, since the 1960s research findings indicate that these groups represent a growing and effective resource for helping vast segments of our society. A number of policy papers and commission reports have attested to this; in particular, the President's Commission on Mental Health in 1978 noted that "Self-help groups have long played a role in helping people cope with their problems. Similar groups composed of individuals with mental and emotional problems are in existence and being formed all over America. These largely untapped community resources contain a great potential for innovation and creative commitments in maintaining health and providing human services. In spite of the recognized importance of community supports, even those that are working well are too often ignored by human service agencies. Moreover, many professionals are not aware of, or comfortable with, certain elements of community support systems. The nation can ill afford to waste such valuable resources. The Commission believes that this is one of the most significant factors in mental health at all levels of care."

Thus, it seems important that self-help and mutual aid groups for adults be considered in helping to alleviate problems arising from adjustment disorders. The plan in this chapter is to consider the nature of self-help groups and their relations to professionals, and to identify some of the important research findings that have emerged about their functioning. Moreover, an effort will be made to specify some of the key helping mechanisms which make for the effectiveness of self-help groups. In addition, consideration will be given to the ways in which self-help groups are helping to redefine pathologic states, and the increasing role that such groups are playing in the field of prevention. The groups are thus designed both to reduce human stress and to maintain wellness and health. Finally, we will consider some implications of the development of self-help centers as "new social instruments," sites of exchange which provide new interfaces between professionals and self-help groups. At the same time, they help to increase the number and utilization of such groups in communities across the country.

General Characteristics of Self-Help Groups

One might think that self-help and mutual aid groups were a new phenomenon, something rather current and fashionable in our society. While they are growing considerably among those who face a wide range of afflictions, they represent a kind of informal social organization that has been present in one form or another in all societies and on all continents. As common interest groups and voluntary associations, they are found at most points in the history of human society; they are present in complex societies as well as in slowly developing preindustrial nations during times of rapid change. Consider the number of mutual aid fraternal organizations which sprang up among all migrant ethnic groups which resettled in the United States (Borman 1984). Studies of tribal and peasant societies worldwide reveal the elaborate formation of common interest groups coalescing among youth, soldiers, widows, bachelors, and indeed almost every recognizable segment of society.

This suggests that modern-day self-help and mutual aid groups have a long history as a collective social form which has existed in practically every known society; certainly they do not represent a development unique to our Western society. They often exist side by side with other forms of organizations or they may indeed take over the functions of an eroded family, a displaced tribe, or an inefficient professional agency. One brief characterization of self-help and mutual aid groups is the following:

> Their membership consists of those who share a common condition, situation, heritage, symptom, or experience. They are largely self-governing and self-regulating, emphasizing peer solidarity rather than hierarchical governance. As such they prefer controls built upon consensus rather than coercion. They tend to disregard in their own organization the usual institutional distinctions between consumers, professionals, and boards of directors, coming and exchanging such functions among each other. They advocate self-reliance and require equally intense commitment and responsibility to other members, actual or potential. They often provide an identifiable code of precepts, beliefs, and practices that include rules for conducting group meetings, entrance requirements for new members, and techniques for dealing with backsliders. They minimize referrals to professionals or agencies since in most cases no appropriate help exists. Where it does, they tend to cooperate with professionals. They generally offer a face-to-face or phone-to-phone fellowship network, usually available and accessible without charge. Groups tend to be self-supporting, occur mostly outside the aegis of institutions or agencies, and thrive largely on donations from members or friends rather than government or foundation grants or fees from the public. (Borman 1975, p. vi)

Relations to Professionals

These self-help groups have assisted in providing new approaches and resources in dealing with a wide range of conditions. Nor has the importance of these self-help groups been ignored by professionals. Indeed, in a recent review of 10 major self-help groups, it turned out that in six of the groups a seasoned professional had played a key role in founding or co-founding the organization. These include Recovery, Incorporated (Dr. Abraham Low), Integrity Groups (Dr. O. Hobart Mowrer), GROW (Father Con Keogh), Compassionate Friends (Reverend Simon Stephens), Parents Anonymous (Mr. Leonard Lieber), and epilepsy self-help groups (Dr. Lawrence Schlesinger). In a great variety of others as well, professionals have played instrumental roles at various stages of the organization's development. Our studies of heart surgery groups, epilepsy groups, consciousness-raising groups, widows, cancer groups, and others indicate not only a close involvement with professionals, but that the participants in these groups utilize professional services to a very considerable extent and report general satisfaction with these services. (See Lieberman and Borman 1979; Borman 1983.)

How can we characterize those professionals who became actively involved in founding, supporting, or in other ways participating in the development and encouragement of self-help groups? Clearly they did not adhere rigidly to the conventional theories or practices within their own disciplines. In the analysis of their roles in the groups listed above, we have found at least nine ways in which these professionals have gone beyond such conventional restraints, leading them to participate actively in the development of self-help groups. They can be characterized as follows:

1. Some professionals clearly took issue with the theories which dominated their field. Both Abraham Low and O. Hobart Mowrer were avowedly disenchanted with prevailing theories of psychotherapy, especially psychoanalysis. For Low, the fundamental contrast between the theory underlying psychoanalysis and his own development of Recovery was his recognition that "Adult life is not driven by instincts but guided by will" (Low 1950, p. 12). In developing Integrity Groups, Mowrer saw this as a "reconceptualization of the causes and treatment of the so-called neuroses." He suggested that "the hypotheses of Freud and Wolpe, relating such disorders of personality, respectively, to an overstrict conscience or false fear are replaced by an alternative view. We have found that a remedy for such persons is to enter a group of six to ten persons similarly struggling to recover their integrity and enhance their sense of identity." (Mowrer and Vattano 1976, pp. 419–420).

    Both Harry Tiebout and Carl Jung, psychiatrists who treated original founders or members of Alcoholics Anonymous, found theoretical justification for the principles being developed by AA. In an early paper published by Tiebout, he noted, "It is presumed that, as the blocking emotions are uncovered and freed through analysis, positive, synthetic ones will appear instead. It is just as logical though, to change emotions and then after the change has been brought about, to bring the mind and intellect into play to anchor the new set of emotions into the structure of the personality. In a sense, this is just what occurs in Alcoholics Anonymous; religion plays upon the narcissism and neutralizes it to produce a feeling of synthesis" (Tiebout in *Alcoholics Anonymous* 1967, p. 318).

2. The second way professionals contributed to the formation of self-help groups was by recognizing a broader defintion of afflictions. Dr. William Silkworth, one of the physicians who treated Bill Wilson, a founder of AA, did not accept the prevailing view that alcoholism was due to a character defect, that it was a form of moral weakness, and that it was not to be regarded as a medical problem. Dr. Silkworth saw the problems of alcoholics as being due to a combination of mental obsession and physical allergy. The founders of AA, moreover, adopted this view as one of the basic tenets of their organization. In his development of Recovery, Dr. Low observed that the essential definitions of mental illness which needed to be ad-

dressed were the disgracing, stigmatizing views held by the community (1938, p. 4).

3. A third dimension characteristic of these professionals was their effort to recognize a broader repertoire of skills and techniques than that which was conventionally utilized in their fields. Among other innovations, Daniel Casriel saw the value of "attack therapy." Initially this had been employed at Synanon, and then developed more fully at Daytop Village for the treatment of drug addicts (Casriel 1963). Leonard Lieber, co-founder of Parents Anonymous for child abusers, was convinced that Jolly K. could help other abusive parents and described their early efforts this way:

> Jolly saw a voluntary coming together of abusers, a sort of Mothers Anonymous group where venting of inner and outer horrors could be shared together under the watchful eye of an agency that directly or indirectly ran the show. We did not knowingly use an already established treatment model with which to formulate ideas. Rather our respective backgrounds converged on a mutual goal—to reach the abuser and stop, or reduce child abuse. (Lieber 1971; also Borman and Lieber 1984)

Harry Tiebout identified in AA what has come to be known as the helper therapy principle when he noted:

> Helping others is a two-way situation since it not only assists the beginner in his first efforts but also aids the helper, who derives from his efforts something which is essential for his continued sobriety. (Tiebout in *Alcoholics Anonymous* 1957, p. 309)

Mowrer viewed AA's central recognition of the fellow as stemming from the early Jewish and Christian communities where exomologesis was practiced. This involved complete openness about one's life in the presence of a small, meaningful group or congregation. This was adopted as a basic technique in the development of Integrity Groups (Mowrer 1975).

4. A fourth dimension which characterized these professionals was their focus on neglected stages of conditions. Following treatment for acute conditions, the problem of rehabilitation and aftercare was a major focus for many of these professionals and for the self-help group with which they were identified. Silkworth and Tiebout were intensely concerned with the problem of relapse in the treatment of alcoholics influenced by AA, and Keogh was originally concerned with the quality of aftercare for patients leaving mental hospitals in Australia. Eventually, however, he began to shift his focus to prevention as well. Elizabeth Kubler-Ross was one of the few psychiatrists to focus early on terminal illness, including the psychological problems faced by surviving relatives.

5. A fifth dimension is the concern for populations normally neglected by conventional professional service delivery. Lieber noted that,

> I was involved with hundreds of young victims whose destiny was always cloudy, but more often than not, they were legally removed from their parents' custody because the home situation was found unfit for a variety of reasons. Some form of psychiatric treatment was usually available to the children. But even if strongly advised by the authorities, treatment for the parent has been consistently hard to come by (1971, p. 3; also see Borman 1985).

6. A sixth dimension involved an altered view of the professional role to a collaborative or cooperative one. Simon Stephens, who launched Compassionate Friends, recommended that professionals stay in the background.

> Originally when we started self-help groups, we invited a psychiatrist who felt that before the beginning of each group he should talk, and he talked for about one hour and a half about psychoanalysis. This is no good. The parents feel that the only person who can help them is somebody who is watching their own child die, who has buried their own child and who has come through it. The psychiatrist had to take a back seat and the same with the clergy. In all our groups we do our very best to match all the parents up—parents whose children die in road accidents can only best be helped by parents who have been through that situation. (1972)

Even in the case of Dr. Low, whose books and tapes continue to be used in Recovery meetings throughout the world, leadership of the organization is vested in the volunteer leaders and members, and professionals are excluded from group leadership positions (see Toseland and Hacker 1982).

7. A seventh way in which professionals have gone beyond conventional boundaries is in the development of new auspices under which self-help groups can form. Not bound by hospitals, clinics, or churches, they have formed in homes, libraries, or any settings which would allow small groups to gather. Integrity Groups were formed for graduate students in social work and psychology on the campus of the University of Illinois in Urbana. Frequently there was little concern with legal liability, professional prerogatives, or accountability and reporting requirements.

8. Professionals involved in the development of self-help groups encouraged the recruitment of members informally through word of mouth or through media publicity. Parents Anonymous used newspaper ads, Compassionate Friends contacted mortuaries and coroners' offices, the media provided a major boost for AA and other groups.

9. Finally, professionals and the groups they helped form were rarely concerned with fees. Most of the professionals who have participated in the development of self-help groups have done so without concern for remuneration for themselves. In addition to their time, they have frequently invested their own funds in the early and continuing efforts. Some groups, of course, such as AA and Recovery, have refused government grants and sought to be self-supporting through contributions from members and the eventual sale of literature and material.

Some Research Findings

Until recently, there has been little substantive knowledge about the effectiveness of self-help groups. One of the reasons that such outcome studies are rare is the fact that the self-help researcher has less control of the intervention system he studies than is ordinarily experienced by the investigators of outcome or evaluation who address the traditional, professional helping systems. In addition, many participants of self-help groups may cycle their participation, moving freely from active involvement to inactive status and back. Thus, they might withdraw for a time, but when the trauma or condition recurs they would once again re-enter the group. Such patterns of usage add to the problem of studying the impact of the group on an individual participant.

Nevertheless, there have been some impressive findings. The studies which Mort Lieberman and Leonard Borman have published report significant findings with women's consciousness-raising groups, members of Mended Hearts, participants in Theos (a self-help group for widows and widowers), and participants in Compassionate Friends (for parents who have lost children). In utilizing a variety of measures which focus around mental health, personal values, marital relationships, and attitudes and orientation, there appeared to be a highly specific set of effects such groups had on their participants. With women's groups, significant increments were found in self-esteem, self-concept, and alterations in life style. With Mended Hearts, significant effects were found for those individuals who were forced to retire because of their health. Those who were members of Mended Hearts complained of fewer somatic symptoms, endured fewer physical symptoms, and experienced higher levels of self-esteem and coping mastery.

Using a variety of mental health indices (such as depression, anxiety, somatic symptoms, utilization of psychotropic drugs, self-esteem, coping mastery, and well-being), a study of widows and widowers in Theos indicated significant effects of activity participation in groups compared to similar measures among those who did not participate. The highest benefit seemed to accrue to widows who became linked to an active, ongoing resource exchange social network which grew out of the relationships they had established in the self-help group. Likewise the study of Compassionate Friends found a significant effect of group participation on the strategies participants used to cope with the death of a child (see Lieberman and Borman 1979, 1981; Borman 1982).

It appears generally true that interest and involvement in self-help and support groups are greater among the more educated, higher income, upper middle socio-economic level families. This was found to be true in our studies of Mended Hearts and Compassionate Friends, as well as in studies of Parents Anonymous (Wheat and Lieber 1979). Families of this type may be more highly motivated or knowledgeable about these resources or more capable of organizing such support networks.

From his studies Katz notes that at more advanced stages of an organization's development there was a lesser degree of participation by parents. He suggested too that, among the organizations he studied, if at some point a professional staff was acquired there was a subsequent reduction of parent effort in the work activities. With two of the groups surveyed, the Muscular Dystrophy Association and the League for Emotionally Disturbed Children, parent involvement and participation were actually deemphasized and discouraged, and were not regarded as important in the realization of the groups' purposes. It was also reported that with a parent-controlled organization, such as the New York Association for Help to Retarded Children, a strain existed in its relations to the wider community. "Its relative isolation from coordinating groups, its failure to win the support of other community agencies for its legislative program, the overt hostility expressed toward it by some agency professionals—all would seem to derive primarily from the intense degree and quality of parent participation" (Katz 1961, p. 68).

When confronted with crises in their lives, why do some individuals utilize self-help groups rather than other societal resources? Indeed, help seeking is the rule rather than the exception. When faced with high levels of distress, most adults do seek out others for aid. More often than not, participants in self-help groups are multiple users not only employing their informal social networks but, more frequently than our contrast samples (individuals with the same affliction who had equal access but chose not to participate in self-help), seeking out professional helping systems as well. Thus, whatever the motivation for turning to self-help groups, it cannot be explained by the lack of other available resources in our society, or by the simple hypothesis of disappointment in previous aid. Our findings point in the direction of the specification of service hypothesis, that is, a match between the individual's particular motivational structure, what the person seeks, and the unique characteristics of self-help groups.

Some of the factors which account for who joins such groups and who does not are based upon organizational characteristics. Methods of recruitment are important. They carry with them built-in biases regarding social class as well as the basis of self-help groups' legitimization for providing help. A group that meets in a suburban middle class home or church may signal which "appropriate" participants are welcome. Attendance at a meeting of Mended Hearts or Compassionate Friends may reveal a more educated or professional or articulate population, making others who may drop in (minority members or less educated individuals) feel uncomfortable.

Perceptions of legitimization are not randomly distributed across society. The level of predictability for who will join a self-help group is based upon demographic characteristics; however, although statistically significant, it is not large. For example, in the medical self-help groups, Mended Hearts, or the level of general volunteer activities, the class bias has not been sufficient to explain with any precision who would migrate toward the self-help groups. In NAIM, a large widow organization, the furtherance of the person's informal social network rather than professional helping systems had the most influence on self-help utilization.

In short, most of the hypotheses regarding pathways to self-help systems which have been portrayed in the field proved to be overly simple. A general finding is that it is the form of service rather than the lack of alternative services which is most likely to provide the closest answer to the question of why individuals utilize self-help groups. Obviously participants are influenced by professionals, the media (Ann Landers), national organizations that publicize local groups, as well as family and friends.

Helping Mechanisms

One of the most significant findings emerging in studies of self-help and mutual aid groups has been the identification of the "helping mechanisms" at work in these groups. These derive largely from their natural helping network characteristics. They do not lend themselves easily to control and supervision by the usual highly structured human service agencies.

Moreover, they present a striking contrast to the psychodynamic mechanisms utilized by most psychotherapists. There is little emphasis on catharsis, feedback, or the expression of affect; and, somewhat surprisingly, not many of these groups focus on self-disclosure. While many studies of group therapy (e.g., Irvin Yalom 1975) reveal a great variety of "curative factors" or "helping mechanisms," most psychotherapists utilize a very small range of such processes. Most of the approaches used are those that can be controlled by the therapist, such as developing insight and understanding, providing opportunities for the expression of affect and self-disclosure, and the use of feedback from the therapist during the course of a session.

Self-help groups, on the other hand, focus on the simple transmission of information, or offer belief systems about the source, cause, and care of an affliction. Members of a group are exposed to each other's experiences, and the cognitive restructuring they may undergo occurs in settings where they join with others who share common dilemmas. Or participants may be influenced through group newsletters or telephone networks.

Studies (see Lieberman and Borman 1979) reveal that most self-help groups do not have consistent leadership patterns, at least in the sense of a professional who conducts the meeting. In lieu of these, most groups have developed an articulated belief system which provides a pathway offered by a professional therapist in group therapy. The role of ideologies and procedures in self-help groups then becomes very important. The following will identify some of these mechanisms more fully:

1. One might be called "instant identity." Being part of a group of others who share your condition and understand what you are experiencing seems to be central to the self-help group experience. The participant is not isolated, unique, and alone, but has a sense of cohesion, involvement, and belonging. Leon Levy reports on an analysis of 28 help-giving activities in self-help groups and concludes that "on the whole, self-help groups focus the major portions of their efforts on fostering communication between their members, providing them with social support, and responding to their needs on both cognitive and emotional levels. Taken as a group, moreover, these activities appear to be noncoercive, non threatening and likely to foster group cohesiveness" (Levy 1979, pp. 234–235). Ben Gottlieb's study of 18 self-help groups in Canada found that the therapeutic mechanisms rated the highest by most group members were "sharing commonalities" and "meeting others with similar problems/conditions" (Gottlieb 1982).

2. The mechanism of altruism, or what has been termed the helper therapy principle, recognizes the impact of the act of helping on the person who gives the help rather than on the one who receives it. This is the 12th step of Alcoholics Anonymous; it is the motto of Mended Hearts for helping surgery patients which suggested, "It is great to be alive and to help others." This finds expression in both groups and, for that matter, in most other self-help groups as they make themselves available to help others dealing with the same or similar afflictions.

3. A third mechanism found to be extremely effective is the teaching of the belief system or group ideology. Essentially this consists of the wisdom which each group imparts to its participants, be they alcoholics, ex-mental patients, persons with cancer, or drug addicts. Such ideologies have been termed "cognitive antidotes." A belief system can change a person's view of pain or of a difficult family situation; it can alter prevailing views on death or dying; it can create a new attitude for dealing with people outside the immediate social network. As Isenberg found, these mechanisms can counter the isolation, bitterness, and fears which individuals with cancer and their families often confront (Isenberg 1981). As such, self-help groups can be viewed as relatively fixed communities of belief.

4. Another key mechanism, both remarkable and effective, is the development of a network of peers. As a quasi-extended family, it often becomes the heart of the self-help network. This means that the helpful activities do not necessarily occur within a group meeting, or in a one-to-one relationship, but through contacts with peers at any time. The use of the phone is extensive and requires no appointments. Newsletters are circulated widely. Distance is overcome, and most groups meet at conventions, at self-help fairs, and informally on other occasions, all of which allow the peer network to develop and expand. Accordingly, socialization occurs, there are increased communications along with a sharing of information, and, of course, support.

5. An important mechanism of equal participation prevents leadership elites, and emphasizes the importance of member participation in what gets done. Self-help and mutual aid groups are clearly labor intensive. The oldtimers and founders abound in self-help groups, and newcomers quickly become the helpers.

6. In focusing on a positive, inspiring philosophy, most groups manifest an important element of hope which gives people facing a difficult problem or chronic condition some prospect of a better life. Many groups focus on taking life "one day at a time" or "making today count," or recognizing that "this is the only moment there

is." While hope can be related to the group's ideology, it is also part of the larger existential reality which comes to be addressed.

7. Some of the most helpful mechanisms found in groups involve the specific sharing of information, derived both from science and from personal experience. Bibliographies of helpful reading material are made available through newsletters, at regular meetings, and at annual and regional conventions. Groups focusing on specific conditions such as Alzheimer's, miscarriage, trauma, or bereavement provide some of the best sources of up-to-date information about problems associated with these conditions. They become important sources of information not only for the group members and families, but for professionals as well.

Redefining Pathologic States

Self-help groups often become advocates for new ways to think about afflictions. Their viewpoint, of course, does not represent the disinterest or objectivity often attributed to the scientist; they have a special vantage point. They represent the self-interest of those for whom the findings become a matter of life or death. Often the viewpoints they represent or espouse become widely accepted among both the professionals and the public. For example, the activities of the National Gay Alliance succeeded in helping to eliminate homosexuality as a pathologic condition in the APA Diagnostic Manual. For many gay groups, homosexuality is considered a chosen life style, distinct from any problems of sexual dysfunction which may require professional help.

In the 1930s, alcoholism was viewed as a personal and moral weakness, and the views held by Alcoholics Anonymous represented a minority position. Nonetheless, AA's efforts to define alcoholism as a disease eventually led to their views becoming widespread and accepted by both scientists and the public.

As mentioned earlier, a number of self-help groups in the mental health field have sought to clarify the positions of those they represent. Recovery's effort to focus on brains and muscles and willpower continues to clash with the more commonly accepted professional approaches based on instincts or psychosexual development. GROW, found by a Jesuit priest in Australia, has already developed 60 groups in Illinois. It follows an adapted version of the 12 steps of Alcoholics Anonymous, placing responsibility on the individual in the context of group support.

The position of Integrity Groups has already been mentioned; it focuses on the individual recovery, integrity, and identity in the presence of a small group of others with similar objectives and intrapsychic conflicts. As with GROW, Integrity places primary emphasis on interpersonal relations. In addition, GROW and Recovery have emphasized the stigmatizing conditions mental patients face on returning to their homes and communities. From this vantage point, psychopathology needed to be understood in terms of mental patients' relationships to others and to society in general.

Many of the consciousness-raising groups founded by women to overcome sexism and to strengthen feminism have had an important influence on redefining women's health issues. While the health-related goals of the women's movement have focused on infusing women's experience into health care systems, they have been equally concerned with encouraging women's knowledge of and responsibility for their own bodies.

Schizophrenics Anonymous, and some chapters of the Alliance for the Mentally Ill, have focused on orthomolecular theories of mental illness, which attribute much of pathology to nutritional deficiencies and allergic reactions. Many of these groups have been encouraged by the Huxley Institute which conducts research and disseminates information on the use of nutritional means for reducing the incidence of chronic mental illness, retardation, learning disabilities, and related disorders. Many of these groups have supported special professional facilities where schizophrenics and others who have not responded to conventional treatments can be presented with these alternative options which promise to reduce dependence upon medication.

Studies of epilepsy self-help groups reveal the critical importance of the nonmedical aspects of this malady. A person who develops seizures faces an increasing atrophy of social ties, along with frequent fear and rejection by the public and mounting psychological stress. These social and personal relations can contribute to a vicious cycle in which seizure activity and its consequences grow worse. The findings about the nature of this affliction which emerge from epilepsy self-help groups seem quite consonant with the results of recent epidemiologic studies. These suggest that, "A whole new understanding of epilepsy must be generated—one that is consistent with the evidence that epilepsy is a societal disease, a disease generated by many of the facets of our modern technological society, a disease that afflicts the poor of our society in disproportionate numbers" (see Whitman et al. 1980, p. 268; see Borman et al. 1980).

Many self-help groups have formed around conditions which have been ignored both by modern medicine and by human service agencies. These would include groups formed for persons who have faced life-threatening illness (including cancer), senile dementia, and sudden traumas. Many of their efforts are directed not so much at attempts to change existing practice and theories as they are at methods which would draw attention to the several conditions. Accordingly, groups such as the Alzheimer's Association raise funds for basic research on crippling dementias and provide support for families dealing with patients so afflicted. Groups formed around cancer seek to interest professionals in paying more attention to the psychological and social conditions which terminal patients face. These groups find that many of the stages of the affliction, including the ways in which treatments are administered, can be affected in important ways by both the therapist's and the patient's outlook, the support provided by family and friends, and the belief systems fostered by specific self-help groups (see Borman 1983).

Self-Help Groups and Prevention

Self-help groups have an important part to play in promoting and maintaining competence, reinforcing positive mental health, and lowering the incidence and prevalence of disease and disorder. Let us consider the role self-help has played in formulating five criteria for developing new strategies of prevention. These were identified by the President's Commission on Mental Health.

1. A shift in conventional human service paradigms. Self-help groups aid this shift through their focus on peer support and education, and the changed nature of their dependence upon professionals and professional services. They rely more heavily on experiential learning rather than on formal training. They utilize a network approach to an identified population for which information, support, and other help are provided. They are not preoccupied with individual one-on-one case-by-case relationships. They involve family members, friends, and asso-

TREATMENTS OF PSYCHIATRIC DISORDERS

ciates. They place a heavy emphasis on psychological, emotional, existential, social, and spiritual dimensions of the affliction. They rely on a "dispersed community" which has little relationship to the usual client roles, catchment areas, or intake procedures found in most human service delivery systems.

2. A proactive approach to strengthening adaptive capacity. Self-help groups become proactive in their voluntary activity which reaches out to others with the same affliction. Recruiting is continuous as there is strong motivation to maintain and expand group participation. Self-help groups do not wait for funds to arrive in order to assist in developing services, nor is there a dependence on these funds for offering service.

3. A concentration on a total population. While each individual self-help group may focus on a special affliction, their combined efforts are broad indeed. To be sure, a case-by-case approach is not the general pattern; on the other hand, neither are they bounded geographically by catchment areas or neighborhoods. Chapters and networks can develop wherever there is interest. Many groups may work with specific organizations such as the Epilepsy Foundation, the American Cancer Society, the Arthritis Foundation, and the mental health societies. Often these self-help groups may spearhead the educational campaigns conducted by the organization, with highlights on diet, exercise, the problems of smoking, the problems of life style, etc.

4. Articulation with existing service delivery systems. While self-help groups can be initiated by, developed by, and articulated with existing professional systems, the potentials of this articulation have hardly been tapped. To be sure, many self-help groups have been founded by or developed in close collaboration with professionals; nonetheless, the development of linkages with existing services is still in a formative stage. Clearly professional support, credibility, energy, and referral can aid the spread of self-help networks immeasurably.

5. Increasing the knowledge base. At present, research in self-help activities is still in an embryonic stage. However, the potential for understanding the role of groups in the field of prevention is indeed considerable. We need to expand knowledge about group process, the emergence of particular groups, the pathways by which individuals find their way into given groups, the impact of the groups on the individual adherents, and the various roles of professionals and agencies.

Self-Help Centers: New Social Instruments

A number of self-help centers and clearinghouses are being established, both in the United States and abroad, which are serving to bridge the gap between traditional, conventional forms of service and the emerging self-help group movement. The Self-Help Center in Evanston, established in 1974, was the first such center in the country. There are now nearly two dozen centers of this kind, including three statewide clearinghouses. In some cases, these clearinghouses are part of mental health centers, or they may be part of hospitals, universities, or independent not-for-profit organizations.

Such centers produce directories of groups in their region and often maintain a telephone line to offer information on the whereabouts of groups both to professionals and to the public. Many centers facilitate the development of new self-help groups in their local communities, bringing them together in local workshops, and providing technical assistance in their formation. These centers also assist established groups in their efforts to recruit potential members, reach professional audiences for educational programs, and extend their chapters to reach new regions and populations. Frequently these centers provide the groups with important two-way linkages to agencies and professionals, as well as to the public at large.

All these organizations seem to engage in media campaigns on television, radio, and with the local press, informing the public as to the nature and whereabouts of self-help groups. They also conduct formal workshops, conferences, and training sessions around a variety of issues where self-help group representatives can meet with one another and review common interests and objectives. Some centers are actively involved in research on the nature and emergence of groups. Accordingly, they provide valuable internship opportunities for graduate students. They all publish materials; in addition, they are increasingly involved in the development of curricula for the training of human service professionals, and, wherever possible, for the training of self-help group leaders.

As with the Self-Help Center in Evanston, these clearinghouses may demonstrate the way in which society can develop a "mixed strategy" of professional support and self-help group leadership, and thus offer important new helping resources to countless persons who may benefit from such groups (see Borck and Aronowitz 1982).

Chapter 245

Self-Help, Mutual-Help, and Peer-Helping Services for Youth

The last two decades have seen a remarkable rise in the availability of, and interest in, self-help and mutual-help resources; these are now providing assistance in the areas of both prevention and treatment and are particularly relevant to the discussion of adjustment disorders. Currently, there are estimated to be some 750,000 self-help and mutual-help groups in the United States with 15,000,000 members. There are also at least two major Self-Help Clearing Houses listing hundreds of different varieties of self-help and mutual-help activities for physical, emotional and social problems.

The origins of the self-help and mutual-help movement may be traced to three historical forces:

1. The rising consumer movement with its belief that professionals and service organizations have not adequately served the public (the question remains as to whether the professional organizations can meet the expectations which arise among

so many people in distress, and whether peer help is indeed the best means to meet certain needs).

2. A search for new sources of family and community supports, many of which have broken down over the last few decades (with the great geographical distances and the high divorce rate, family and community supports have been difficult to maintain).

3. Efforts to rebuild and restructure communities in new ways in order to respond to the very rapid pace of a modern technological society (in some ways, this can be seen as one of the goals of the community mental health movement).

Definitions and Roles

However, despite the great rise in self-help and mutual-help activities, their definitions, functions, and roles have not been clearly articulated. The very terms, *self-help*, *mutual-help*, and *peer-help*, have often been used interchangeably or in a very confusing fashion. Since each of these approaches differs in respect to how they can and do function within the health care system, it is important that their differences be defined. For the purposes of this chapter, self-help, mutual-help, and peer-help groups are defined as follows.

Self-Help. This term applies where a person tries to bring about psychological and behavioral change through self-improvement activities and approaches. This is the social and psychological equivalent of self-care, a type of activity which has been increasing in frequency. Such activities include exercise programs, autohypnosis, biofeedback, self-improvement audio tapes, relaxation techniques, information from books or recorded messages, and, more recently, self-help computer software. Although the activities may be recommended by another person, the individual alone is totally responsible for carrying them out for his or her own benefit. This area differs from the others in not containing social support elements. Among adolescents, activities such as body building, dieting, jogging, relaxation exercises, and transcendental meditation are common examples of self-help.

Mutual-Help. Although often confused with self-help, in mutual-help individuals who have a problem, or who have family members with problems, join others with similar problems in assisting one another in supporting, eliminating, or controlling the difficulty. The focus is on developing interpersonal supports from the sharing of a common experience. When groups are established, they are totally autonomous. Professionals are used primarily as guests, consultants, or for referral. The oldest and probably best known example of a mutual-help group is Alcoholics Anonymous.

Peer-Helping Services. Peer-helping services are distinguished from the other two by the fact that nonprofessional peers are systematically trained to help bring about behavioral changes in individuals their own age. These peer helpers usually have not had a similar experience to those they are helping. The services are founded on the assumption that similarities in age, race, ethnic background, or social class may facilitate accepting help and thus bring about more rapid change.

The characteristics common to all three of the above helping services are that they build on natural helping networks and offer assistance in dealing with adjustment problems in nontraditional and nonprofessional ways. There is great reliance on one's own or a peer member's effort, skill, knowledge, and concern. Professionals may be used as consultants, guides, supervisors, or sources of information, but they do not deliver the service. Primary contact, control, operation, and implementation are in the hands of the indigenous peers, with efforts made to encourage peer interaction, the sharing of common status, and the development of mutual supports. Gartner and Riessman (1977) have stated the effects of these activities as follows:

> The power of self-help mutual aid groups derives from the fact that they combine a number of very important properties: These include the helper-therapy principle, the aprofessional dimension, consumer intensivity, the use of indigenous or peer support, and the implicit demand that the individual can do something for him or herself. Self-help groups show that people need not be passive, that they have power—particularly in a group that, while permitting dependence, demands autonomy and independence; a group that demands that its members do something for each other; a group that, while giving support, demands action and work; a group that is not leader or professional centered, but peer centered. In essence, one of the most significant characteristics of mutual aid groups is the fact that they are 'empowering' and thus potentially dealienating. They enable their members to feel and use their own strengths and their own power and to have control over their own lives. This empowering dimension is extremely important for health and mental health. In addition, many self-help groups combine these features with an ideological, antisystem bias that to some extent limits their bureaucratization and limits some of the negative consequences of institutionalization. (pp. 98–99)

Initially, these peer- and self-help systems of care were established as a substitute for the professional-helping systems, and were sometimes adversarial and competitive with the professional community. Currently, however, they are increasingly likely to be working with, complementing, or supplementing professional intervention. Indeed, in the second volume of *Psychiatric Therapies*, in the chapter on self-help (Gottlieb et al. 1984) it is recognized how such self-help and peer-support groups are working alongside professionals and playing an increasing role in the mental health care system. Such recognition was affirmed by the special report on self-help written for the President's Commission on Mental Health in 1978.

Despite the rise of self-help, mutual-help, and peer-help as an aspect of the total system of mental health care in the community, it is not yet clear what role this system should play at the level of national policy. For example, with a general reduction of concerns about quality of care, some politicians have urged that self-help, mutual-help, and peer-help activities substitute for professional mental health personnel as a major way of reducing health costs.

In addition to the political issues, other questions also need to be addressed. Can self-help or mutual-help activities be harmful rather than helpful? What, if any, standards need to be set? What are the best models of self-, mutual-, and peer-help? How do these activities work either successfully or unsuccessfully with professionals?

Self-help, mutual-help, and peer-helping activities have been organized for adults significantly more commonly than for adolescents. Those which have developed for pre-adult individuals tend to be more informal than those developed for adults. One reason may be the general resistance in our society to empowering youth, a resistance considerably greater than that encountered when adults are being empowered.

Adolescence is a time of major change in social relationships, with the peer group becoming more and more important. Nevertheless, the number of planned self-help, mutual-help, and peer-helping activities for psychological problems of a formal nature remain few. For example, a bibliography on self-help lists some 334 articles published between 1970 and 1982, but includes only five references on adolescent self-help groups (Todres 1982). Research has shown that, when asked, adolescents list their families as their greatest source of emotional support, indicating that they share their problems mostly with their parents (Mannino and Shore 1976). However, observations indicate that peers play a very considerable role in adolescent decision-making. McCubbin et al. (1985) point to the natural tendency of adolescents to turn to friends and peers for social support, particularly when faced with family problems and strains. However, the research demonstrated as well that peers may not only influence each other in positive ways by offering advice, emotional support, and opportunities to discuss problems and conflicts, but may also influence each other negatively by such means as manipulation and coercion.

The potential of peer-support groups to serve as effective means of preventing mental health problems lies in the fact that they can be oriented to dealing with stress and the building of coping skills. Nevertheless, despite the importance of different peer groups in adolescence, and their observed role in psychological support and help, they have not been adequately or systematically studied.

There are a number of ways of categorizing various self-help, mutual-help, and peer-helping activities:

1. *By problem.* Most mutual-help activities are defined by problem area. Thus, we have groups for drug addicts, various physical diseases, alcoholism, etc.
2. *By setting.* Different helping roles have arisen in different settings. Some schools have developed peer-counseling programs. Hospitals have used mutual-help groups to assist children and adolescents in becoming oriented to the medical setting or to offer aid in recovery from illness.
3. *By type of service.* Some mutual-help groups have a great deal of independence and autonomy, while others are limited to short contacts or telephone conversations. Some are face-to-face individual services, whereas others are drop-in. Still others are formally structured.
4. *By degree of disturbance.* Peer counseling in schools often assists young people with normal adjustment and transitional problems. Some mutual-help groups aid in crises. Some peer groups assist in stress reduction. Others help people who are already showing symptoms. In addition, some are involved in tertiary prevention activities, working with formerly institutionalized clients.
5. *By purpose.* Peer-help and self-help may vary in purpose. Some may focus on support, some on information; some try to be psychotherapeutic. One of the major new roles these groups have been playing is advocacy, that is, actively seeking services for those who see themselves as discriminated against (former mental patients, gays, women, etc.). Each type is describe below, with a focus on the adolescent.

Self-Help

In this chapter, we have stressed the necessity of separating self-help from mutual-help activities, and from other peer-helping services. This distinction is important because the strategies in the self-help area differ widely from those one would use in mutual- or peer-helping groups.

Parents have noted the significant increase in adolescents' concerns about themselves. One of the features of adolescents, in general, is how these young people attempt on their own to change their behaviors in a variety of different ways; indeed, as part of the developmental process, at different times they are likely to play a number of different roles. These changes can result from introspection and from reading, as well as self-development actions such as body building and dieting. Unfortunately, we do not have data on the extent and nature of these self-help phenomena. We do know that one major area of concern among adolescents is nutrition. Indeed, in its pathologic form, dieting can lead to anorexia nervosa, a disease which occurs most frequently in adolescent young women.

New areas of computer software are developing self-help health programs for teenagers. One computerized self-test has been developed on alcohol use and abuse (Berger and Colm 1980); it is designed to help adolescents understand the social and psychological forces which influence their decisions in situations when they are drinking and driving. Another computerized program identifies health risks and makes suggestions to the teenager for behavioral change (Centers for Disease Control 1983).

A third program, the BARNY (Body Awareness Resource Network), is being tested at the University of Wisconsin to help adolescents in a number of areas— smoking, alcohol and drug abuse, nutrition and exercise, human sexuality, stress management, and family communication. This program tailors interactions with adolescents to specific characteristics of their problem and can help these youngsters find out who is available for help and how to interact with the helping network. It can even stimulate a dialogue on health-related topics when more than one person (e.g., parent, peer) view the program together. Hence, this self-help program provides a linkage to the social support element and perhaps to other helping services. It is located in schools, clinics, family planning agencies, and 4-H Clubs, and may be used alone or as part of a larger program (American Family, 1983).

We must keep in mind that the role of computers in the mental health field is still quite new, and not without certain potential dangers. For example, mention has been made of a widespread belief in the authority of the computer and, therefore, a conclusion that anything the computers say must be true. Thus, in the absence of professional guidance, individuals might make wrong decisions which could cause damage or aggravate mental health problems. Another danger is the potential of the computer to isolate individuals and families in their homes or at computer terminals (American Family, 1983).

Mutual-Help

In mutual-help, individuals or families of individuals with similar problems, symptoms, or syndromes assist each other. The model for many of these groups is the oldest of mutual-help groups—Alcoholics Anonymous—a program for adult alcoholics which has been described in Emrick et al. (1977). Using the work of Dean and Hurvitz, Killilea (1976) has listed criteria for mutual-help psychotherapy which distinguishes it from more traditional techniques (Table 1). Four types of mutual-help groups have been described by Levy (1976):

1. Groups that have as their objective some form of conduct reorganization or behavioral control (such as Alcoholics Anonymous, Synanon, Parents Anonymous).
2. Groups that share a common status or predicament which entails some degree of stress. The aim is to ameliorate the stress through mutual support and the sharing of coping strategies and advice. No attempt is made to change the status, which is regarded as given, and the problem for members is how to carry on despite that state of affairs (Parents Without Partners, Recovery Inc.).
3. Groups seen as survival-oriented, composed of people whom society has labeled deviant or who have been discriminated against because of lifestyles or values, or

Table 1. Criteria for Mutual-Help Psychotherapy

Orthodox Psychotherapy	Self-Help Group Therapy
1. Professional, authoritative	Nonprofessional leaders, group parity
2. Fee	Free
3. Appointments and records	None
4. Therapy-oriented milieu (psychiatrist's office, clinic, etc.)	Nontherapy-oriented milieu (church rooms, community centers, etc.)
5. Therapist is presumed to be normal, does not identify with patient	Peers are similarly affected, identify with each other
6. Therapist is not a role model, does not set personal examples	Peers are role models, serve as examples for each other
7. Therapist is noncritical, nonjudgmental, neutral, listens	Peers are active, judgmental, supportive, critical, talk
8. Patients unilaterally divulge to therapist, disclosures are secret	Peers divulge to each other, disclosures are shared
9. Patients expect only to receive support	Patients must also give support
10. Concerned about symptom substitution if underlying causes are not removed	Urges appropriate behavior, not concerned about symptom substitution
11. Emphasis on etiology, insight	Emphasis on faith, will power
12. Therapist-patient relationship has little direct community impact	Peers' intersocial involvement has considerable community impact
13. Everyday problems subordinated to long-range cure	Primary emphasis on day-to-day victories; another day without liquor or drugs, another day without panic, etc.
14. Lower cumulative dropout percentage	Higher drop-out percentage
15. Patient cannot achieve parity with psychiatrist	Members may themselves become active therapists

Note. Reproduced with permission from Killilea (1976).

on the basis of other grounds (such as sex, socioeconomic class, or race). The group interaction helps members enhance their self-esteem through mutual support and consciousness-raising activities, as well as through political activities (gay groups, black power groups, Gray Panthers).

4. Groups that share a common goal of personal growth, self-actualization, and enhanced effectiveness in living and loving. No core problem is present, but there is a shared desire to help each other live better lives and a particular belief in how this can best be accomplished (Gestalt Therapy groups).

Although there are a large number of such mutual-help groups in existence for adults, as noted, very few have been reported for adolescents. One such group is Dropouts Anonymous, organized for school and societal "dropouts." Others include

Prison Children Anonymous, for children of prisoners; Speakeasy International, organized for stutterers; Teenagers Anonymous and Youth Anonymous, for delinquents (Eglash 1958); and Daughters and Sons United for victims of sex abuse. In addition, there are adolescent rape survivor groups, and, for those with chronic illness, there is Young Fighters. The most common and well-known group is that for teenage alcoholics and teenage children of alcoholics (Al-ateen). Founded in 1957 and based on the Alcoholics Anonymous model, by 1984 it had 3,300 chapters worldwide with an estimated 50,000 members. It is built on 12 steps and 12 traditions overlaid by spiritual beliefs in the manner of Alcoholics Anonymous.

As part of their overall therapeutic plan, drug rehabilitation programs have developed another mutual-help activity. In their attempt to effect change, these settings use peer pressure in order to arouse anxiety in their drug addict clients. Also, a number of teenage mutual-help groups have been reported in hospital settings; these groups were developed around specific illnesses (hemophilia, cerebral palsy, and diabetes), but have not as yet been documented in the literature.

Kutchins and Kutchins (1982) vividly describe the natural course of an urban gang (which can be seen perhaps as one type of mutual-help group), which transformed itself into a socialized self-help group, only to be subverted over time by political forces and the traditional power structure. The conflicts between the cultures of the urban black youth and the white power structure are emphasized.

A recent development in prevention is the array of peer groups which have been set up to reduce drunk driving among teenagers; a spinoff from Mothers Against Drunk Driving (MADD) is called Students Against Drunk Driving (SADD). Young people have organized themselves to educate and influence their peers around the hazards of drunk driving, and to develop services to help young people not drive when they are under the influence of alcohol (O'Gorman 1981).

Very little research has been done in the teenage mutual-help area. One study by Hughes (1977) on Al-ateen found that members of this group had significantly better mood states, higher self-esteem, fewer problems in school, and less involvement with law enforcement officials than did the members of a control group. Although assignment to groups was not random, the author concluded that children who are members of Al-ateens are better off emotionally than those who are not.

However, in a review of self-help groups, Emrick et al. (1977) present findings from studies that are not as positive. For example, in a self-help drug program with adolescents, Biase found a high dropout rate, with the dropouts showing significantly higher depression scores than the nondropouts. This suggests that the more disturbed adolescents may be those who drop out of self-help groups. Another study, by Lieberman, Yalom, and Miles, reported on a group of college students in an experience at Synanon, a peer self-help group that developed directly out of Alcoholics Anonymous in 1958. The college students were not accepted, but instead were isolated and attacked within the group.

Emrick and associates' evaluation of these findings (along with other studies involving adults) suggested that peers may not lead each other to positive results. Instead, they may foster dysocial groups, that is, groups that are so immersed and isolated in their own values and norms that they are not compatible with the larger society in which they exist. In addition, they point to the possibility of group members overidentifying with sociopathic peer leaders, resulting in beliefs that are not representative of the larger culture. These studies lend support to the findings by McCubbin et al., mentioned earlier, that peers may influence each other in negative ways, as well as in positive directions.

Peer-Helping Services

Peer-helping services are those where youth are trained and supervised to help their age-mates, and where the trainees usually do not have the same problems as those they are helping. These services have increased greatly in number over the last decade. A major characteristic of peer-helping services is that they are developed in natural settings, such as schools and the community, and/or that they use natural (and often anonymous) communication resources, such as the telephone. Thus they weave quite easily into the helping networks described by Collins and Pancoast (1976), which are seen as important mental health resources in the community.

Drawing on material from McCubbin et al. (1985), we have identified four types of peer-helping groups:

1. Positive peer-influence programs designed to channel peer pressure in positive directions; they can also help to develop and enhance adolescent self-esteem and problem-solving skills.
2. Peer-teaching programs designed to provide useful information and skills, as well as to provide participating youth with meaningful roles and real-world responsibilities.
3. Peer-counseling-facilitating-helping programs designed to assist young adults in solving problems and coping with some of the challenges with which they are inevitably confronted in modern society.
4. Peer-participation programs designed to offer a link between the peer world and the adult world by providing peers with real-world tasks and responsibilities, along with adult guidance in accomplishing them.

As compared with mutual-help groups, peer-helping services tend to be less ideological, less structured, and less autonomous, and more frequently associated with professional or trained individuals who supervise and may oversee them.

One peer-helping service which has been in existence for many years is tutoring. A review of the research on children (Devin-Sheehan et al. 1976) has concluded that peer-tutoring services tend to be haphazard and unsystematic. Nevertheless, there is evidence that tutoring programs can effectively improve the academic performance of those being tutored and, in some cases, of the tutors as well. However, in evaluating attitudinal and self-concept changes consequent on improved academic achievement, the results were inconclusive.

A very popular peer-helping service in secondary schools and colleges is peer counseling. Although a great deal has been written in educational and guidance journals about peer counseling—the training of the peer counselors, their effectiveness (McGee et al. 1977), and the ethical problems to which they give rise (Duncan 1976)—only one article on peer counseling could be found in a psychiatric journal (Hamburg and Varenhorst 1972).

In addition to peer counseling in school settings, there have been attempts to train youth to assist peers who have been the victims of abuse (Garbarino and Jacobson 1978). These authors believe such attempts are important interventions for teenagers in introducing them to social problems.

While most peer counseling has limited itself to prevention, crisis intervention, or relatively minor problems (with referral to professionals encouraged when the problems are severe), there have also been some recent efforts to train children systematically to function as therapeutic-change agents for their peers (McGee et al.

1977). Organized primarily within a behavior modification framework, these attempts claim to have been successful.

Alternative services, where volunteers and salaried youth (usually a meager salary) assist their peers (Shore 1987), is another category of peer-helping services. Alternative services include telephone hot-lines, rap centers, crisis centers, runaway centers, etc. The major characteristics of these alternative—compared to more traditional—services are increased accessibility, comprehensiveness, flexibility, and advocacy. Because of their availability, these services encounter a wide range of problems, including the severely mentally disturbed youth who, for many reasons, may not have made contact with professional services. Youth running these alternative programs often go through an intensive training period, sometimes organized by professionals who are associated with the ideology on which these services are founded.

As can be seen from the above, peer counseling can be used by any number of types of organizations to deal with a wide variety of problems. Regardless of the setting, however, certain preliminary steps should be implemented to ensure that a program achieves its maximum potential. These have been outlined by Varenhorst (1980) as follows:

1. *Identify the purpose or goal.* The purpose should determine the type, content, and length of training, the procedure for recruiting, and the kind of youth recruited.
2. *Enlist adult support.* The organizational base of a program will determine those groups from which support must be enlisted. For example, in a school system, contact should be made with the superintendents, principals, counselors, psychologists, and the PTAs.
3. *Identify personnel.* A project coordinator must take responsibility for initiating a program and administering it. Students must be recruited and trained, and those to be counseled must be identified.
4. *Develop training curriculum.* Choosing an appropriate curriculum requires careful analysis of the needs of the target population to be served and the skills required to reach that population.
5. *Evaluate.* Before beginning a program, methods and kinds of evaluations should be determined. These include evaluations of training and evaluations of the success of those counseled by peer counselors.

A major issue is the establishment of criteria for selection of peer counselors or leaders in these peer-helping services. As noted, in most of these settings the counselors are carefully selected and intensely trained. However, it has been found that if they are closely supervised, even disturbed youth can effectively deliver academic and human services (Duggan 1978). In fact, what has been found is that those who are delivering the service may change dramatically, even when the clients themselves do not (Oster 1983). Gershon and Biller (1977) note that student paraprofessionals gain: 1) an increased sense of competence; 2) opportunities to explore career options; 3) a chance to acquire experience relevant to their education; 4) an increased confidence in their own self-worth; 5) job satisfaction; 6) an increased range of personal contacts; and 7) the tangible benefits, of course—credit or monetary remuneration.

Recent reviews of research in the area of peer-helping services indicate that peer-mediated interventions can be effective in changing social behavior (Odom and Strain 1984). Research specific to telephone crisis interventions shows that these nonprofessionals can function as helping persons, but that their effectiveness as referral agents and behavior changers is questionable (France 1975). Evaluation of peer-counseling programs at a large university in Washington, D.C. by way of client feedback indicated a high degree of success on both goal attainment scales and satisfaction ratings (Leventhal 1976).

Although we could find no research related to potential harm in peer-counselor-counselee relationships, some of the points raised by Emrick et al. (1977) with regard to the sponsor-sponsoree relationship in Alcoholics Anonymous programs seem relevant. These include the potential for overinvolvement and overidentification, particularly when both parties have or have had a common problem, such as drug abuse; the counselor preferring clients who are dependent, compliant, and grateful, and rejecting those who are less dependent; using the maladjustment of others to maintain the peer counselor's own adjustment; and being insensitive to the client's needs when the counselor's own needs are threatened. It is because of the potential of such problems developing that the selection, training, experience, and supervision are so very important in peer-counseling programs.

References

Section 25
Adjustment Disorder

Abramson L, Seligman M, Teasdale J: Learned helplessness in humans: critique and reformulation. J Abnorm Psychol 87:102–109, 1978

Abramson L, Garber J, Seligman M: Learned helplessness in humans: an attributional analysis, in Human Helplessness. Edited by Garber J, Seligman M. New York, Academic Press, 1980

Adsett CA, Bruhn JG: Short-term group psychotherapy for postmyocardial infarction patients and their wives. Can Med Assoc J 99:577–584, 1968

Agras W, Jacob R: Hypertension, in Behavioral Medicine: Theory and Practice. Edited by Pomerleau O, Brady J. Baltimore, Williams and Wilkins, 1979

Akins T, Hollandsworth J, O'Connell S: Visual and verbal modes of information processing and their relation to the effectiveness of cognitively-based, anxiety-reduction techniques. Behav Res Ther 20:261–268, 1982

Akins T, Hollandsworth J, Alcorn J: Visual and verbal modes of information processing and cognitively-based coping strategies: an extension and replicaton. Behav Res Ther 21:69–74, 1983

Alexander F, French T: Psychoanalytic Therapy: Principles and Applications. New York, Ronald Press, 1946

American Psychiatric Association: Diagnostic and Statistical Manual of Mental Disorders, 2nd ed. Washington, DC, American Psychiatric Association, 1968

American Psychiatric Association: Diagnostic and Statistical Manual of Mental Disorders, 3rd ed. Washington, DC, American Psychiatric Association, 1980

American Psychiatric Association: Diagnostic and Statistical Manual of Mental Disorders, 3rd ed, revised. Washington, DC, American Psychiatric Association, 1987

American Psychiatric Association: Family Therapy and Psychiatry: A Report of the Task Force on Family Therapy and Psychiatry. Washington, DC, American Psychiatric Association, 1984

Anderson V, Parmenter K: Long Term Study of Experimental Neurosis in Sheep and Dog, with Nine Case Histories. Med monogr 2, III, IV. Washington, DC, 1941

Andreasen NC, Hoenk PR: The predictive value of adjustment disorders: a follow-up study. Am J Psychiatry 139(5): 584–590, 1982

Andreasen NC, Wasek P: Adjustment disorders in adolescents and adults. Arch Gen Psychiatry 37:1166–1170, 1980

Andrews G, Tennant C, Hewson DM et al: Life event stress, social support, coping style, and risk of psychological impairment. J Nerv Ment Dis 166:307–316, 1978

Annon J: Behaviorial Treatment of Sexual Problems: Brief Therapy. Hagerstown, Md, Harper and Row, 1976

Aquilera D, Messick J: Crisis Intervention: Theory and Methodology, 4th ed. St. Louis, CV Mosby, 1982

Archibald H, Tuddenham R: Persistent stress reaction after combat—a 20 year follow up. Arch Gen Psychiatry 12:475–481, 1965

Austin L, Inderbitzen LB: Brief psychotherapy in late adolescence: psychodynamic and developmental approach. Am J Psychother 37:202–209, 1983

Baker KG, McCoy PL: Group sessions as a method of reducing anxiety in patients with coronary artery disease. Heart Lung 8:525–529, 1979

Baldwin B: Crisis intervention in professional practice: implications for clinical training. Am J Orthopsychiatry 47:659–670, 1977

Bandura A: Self-efficacy: toward a unifying theory of behavioral change. Psychol Rev 84:191–215, 1977

Bandura A: The self and mechanisms of agency, in Psychological Perspectives on the Self. Edited by Guis J. Hillsdale, NJ, Erlbaum, 1982

Bandura A, Adams N, Beyer J: Cognitive processes mediating behavioral change. J Pers Soc Psychol 35:125–139, 1977

Barlow DH, O'Brien GT, Last G: Couples treatment of agoraphobia. Behav Ther 15:41–58, 1984

Bartolucci G, Drayer C: Overview of crisis intervention in the emergency rooms of general hospitals. Am J Psychiatry 130:953–960, 1973

Barton W: Healer of the Mind. Edited by Johnson P. Nashville, Tenn, Abingdon Press, 1972

Beal EW: Teaching family therapy. Psychiatric Annals 10:744, 1980

Beck A: Negative cognitions, in Depression: Concepts, Controversies, and Some New Facts, 2nd ed. Edited by Levitt E, Lubin B, Brooks J. Hillsdale , NJ, Erlbaum, 1983

Beck AT, Emery G: Anxiety Disorders and Phobias: A Cognitive Perspective. New York, Basic Books, 1985

Beck M: Presidential Address: Christ and Psychiatry. Can Psychiatr J 18:355–370, 1973

Becker J, Skinner L: Assessment and treatment of rape-related sexual dysfunctions. J Clin Psychol 36:102–104, 1983

Becker J, Skinner L, Abel G, et al: Incidence and types of sexual dysfunctions in rape and incest victims. J Sex Marital Ther 8:65–74, 1982

Berger R, Colm NJ: Final Report of the Teen-Age Self-Test: Drinking and Driving. McLean, Va, Automated Services, 1980

Bergin A, Suinn R: Individual psychotherapy and behavior therapy. Ann Rev Psychol 26:509–556, 1975

Block D, Silber E, Perry S: Some factors in the emotional reaction of children to disaster. Am J Psychiatry 113:416–422, 1955

Bloom B: Definitional aspects of the crisis concept. J Consult Clin Psychol 27:498–502, 1963

Bloom B: Community Mental Health: A General Introduction. Monterey, Brooks/Cole, 1977

Borck LE, Aronowitz E: The role of the self-help clearinghouse, in Helping People to Help Themselves. Edited by Borman LD. New York, Hayworth, 1982

Borkovec T: Worry: physiological and cognitive processes. Paper presented at the 14th Meeting of European Association for Behavior Therapy, Brussels, Belgium, 1984

Borkovec T, Wilkinson L, Folensbee R, et al: Stimulus control applications to the treatment of worry. Behav Res Ther 21:247–252, 1983

Borman LD (Ed.): Explorations in Self-Help and Mutual Aid. Evanston, Ill, Center for Urban Affairs, Northwestern University, 1975

Borman LD: Self-help groups, professionals, and the redefinition of pathologic states, in Clinical Anthropology: A New Approach to American Health Problems. Edited by Shimkin DB, Golde P. Lanham, Md, University Press of America, 1983

Borman, LD: Self-help/mutual aid in changing communities. Social Thought, 49–62. Summer 1984

Borman LD: Self-help/mutual aid groups in Issues in the Care of Children with Chronic Illness: A Source Book on Problems, Services and Policies. Edited by Hobbs N, Perrin JM. San Francisco, Jossey-Bass, 1985

Borman LD, Lieber LL: Self-Help and the Treatment of Child Abuse, National Committee for Prevention of Child Abuse, 1984

Borman LD, Davies J, Droge D: Self-help groups for persons with epilepsy, in A Multidisciplinary Handbook of Epilepsy. Edited by Hermann BP. Springfield, Ill. Charles C Thomas Publishing Company, 1980

Bowen M: Family Therapy in Clinical Practice. New York, Jason Aronson, 1978

Boyd S: Psychological reactions of disaster victims. S Afr Med J 60:744–748, 1981

Brink T: Geriatric rigidity—psychotherapeutic implicatons. J Geriatrics 26:274, 1978

Brink T, Capri D, DeNeeve V, et al: Hypochondriasis and paranoia. J Nerv Ment Dis 167:224, 1979

Brown J: The Motivation of Behavior. New York, McGraw Hill, 1961

Budman SH: Looking toward the future, in Forms of Brief Therapy. Edited by Budman H. New York, Guilford Press, 1981, pp 461–467

Burden R: Measuring the effects of stress on the mothers of handicapped infants: must depression always follow? Child Care Health Dev 6:111–125, 1980

Burgess AW, Holmstrom LL: Rape: Victims of Crisis. Bowie, Md, Robert J Brady Co, 1974

Butcher J, Koss M: Research on brief and crisis-oriented therapies, in Handbook of Psychotherapy and Behavior Change. Edited by Garfield S, Bergin A. New York, John Wiley and Sons, 1978

Butcher J, Maudal G: Crisis intervention, in Clinical Methods in Psychology. Edited by Weiner I. New York, John Wiley and Sons, 1976

Butler G, Cullington A, Munby M, et al: Exposure and anxiety management in the treatment of social phobia. J Consult Clin Psychol 52:642–650, 1984

Butler RN: Why Survive? Being Old in America. New York, Harper and Row, 1975

Caplan G: Patterns of parental response to the crisis of premature birth. Psychiatry 23:365–374, 1960

Caplan G: Principles of Preventative Psychiatry. New York, Basic Books, 1961

Caplan G: Principles of Preventative Psychiatry. New York, Basic Books, 1964

Carek DJ: Principles of Child Psychotherapy. Springfield, Ill, Charles C Thomas Publishing Co, 1972

Carek DJ: A study of a child psychiatrist's interventions. J Am Acad Child Psychiatry 21:492–495, 1982

Casey RL, Masuda M, Holmes TH: Quantitative study of recall of life events. J Psychosom Res 11:239–247, 1967

Casriel D: So Fair a House: The Story of Synanon. Englewood Cliffs, NJ, Prentice-Hall, 1963

Cavenar JO, Maltbie AA, Austin L: Depression simulating organic brain disease. Am J Psychiatry, 136:521–523, 1979

Centers for Disease Control: Teen Health Risk Appraisal. Atlanta, Center for Disease Control, 1983

Chandler L, Lundahl W: Empirical classification of emotional adjustment reactions. Am J Orthopsychiatry 53:460–467, 1983

Chaplin E, Levine B: The effects of total exposure duration and interrupted versus continuous exposure in flooding therapy. Behav Res Ther 12:360–368, 1981

Chesen ES: Religion May Be Hazardous to Your Health. New York, Collier Books, 1973

Chodoff P: Late effects of the concentration camp syndrome. Arch Gen Psychiatry 8:323–333, 1963

Chodoff P, Friedman S, Hamburg D: Stress, defenses, and coping behavior: observations in parents of children with malignant disease. Am J Psychiatry 120:743–749, 1964

Coddington RD: Measuring the stressfulness of a child's environment, in Stress in Childhood. Edited by Humphrey JH. New York, AMS Press, 1984

Cole J: Beta-blocker drives in psychiatry. McLean Hospital Journal 4:48, 1979

Collins AH, Pancoast DL: Helping networks: a strategy for prevention. Silver Spring, Md, National Association of Social Workers, 1976

Cragan M, Deffenbacher J: Anxiety management training and relaxation as self-control in the treatment of generalized anxiety in medical outpatients. Journal Counseling Psychology 31:123–131, 1984

Decker J, Stubblebine J: Crisis intervention and prevention of psychiatric disability: a follow-up study. Am J Psychiatry 129:725–729, 1972

Deffenbacher J, Shelton J: A comparison of anxiety management training and desensitization in reducing test and other anxieties. J Counsel Psychol 25:277–282, 1978

Deffenbacher J, Suinn R: The self-control of anxiety, in The Psychology of Self-Management: From Theory to Practice. Edited by Karoly P, Kanfer F. Elmsford, NY, Pergamon Press, 1982

Denney D: Relaxation and stress management training, in Handbook of Clinical Psychology. Edited by Walker C. Homewood, Ill, Dow Jones-Irwin, 1983

Devin-Sheehan L, Feldman RS, Allen VL: Research on on children tutoring children: a cultural review. Review of Educational Research 46:355–385, 1976

Directory of Self-Help/Mutual Aid Groups, Chicago Metropolitan Area, 1983-84. Edited by Pasquale FL. Evanston, Ill, Self-Help Center, 1983

Dixon S, Sands R: Identity and the experience of crisis. Social Casework 64:223–230, 1983

Duggan HA: A Second Chance. Lexington, Mass, DC Heath, 1978

Dulcan MK: Brief psychotherapy with children and their families: the state of the art. J Am Acad Child Psychiatry 23:544–551, 1984

Duncan JA: Ethical considerations in peer-group work. Elementary School Guidance and Counseling 11:59–61, 1976

Durkheim E: Suicide: A Study in Sociology. Glencoe, Ill, Free Press, 1957

Dysken MW, Chang SS, Casper RC, et al: Barbiturate-facilitated interviewing. Biol Psych 14:421–432, 1979

Edelwich JL: Burn-out: Stages of Disillusionment in the Helping Professions. New York: Human Sciences Press, 1980

Eglash A: Youth anonymous. Federal Probation 22:47–49, 1958

Eisdorfer C, Wilkie F: Stress, disease, aging and behavior, chapter 12 in Handbook of the Psychology of Aging. Edited by Birren JE, Schaie KW. New York, van Nostrand Reinhold Company, 1977, pp 251–275

Ellis A: Reason and Emotion in Psychotherapy. New York, Lyle Stuart, 1962

Emrick CD, Lassen CL, Edwards MT: Nonprofessional peers as therapeutic agents, in Effective Psychotherapy. Edited by Gurman AS, Razin AM. Pergamon Press, 1977

Erikson EH: Childhood and Society. New York, Norton, 1950

Erikson EH: Identity and the life cycle. Psychol Issues, Monograph 1, 1959

Erikson EH: Identity and the Life Cycle. New York, WW Norton, International Universities Press, 1959

Erikson EH: Insight and Responsibility. New York, Norton and Company, 1964

Erikson EH. Identity, Youth, and Crisis. New York, WW Norton, 1968

Ewalt P: The crisis treatment approach in a child guidance clinic. Social Casework 54:406–411, 1973

Ewing C: Crisis Intervention as Psychotherapy. New York, Oxford University Press, 1978

Eysenck H: The conditioning model of neurosis. Behav Brain Sci 2:155–199, 1979

Fairbank JA, Keane TM: Flooding for combat-related stress disorders: assessment of anxiety reduction across traumatic memories. Behav Ther 13:499–510, 1982

Falcon S, Ryan C, Chamberlain K, et al: Tricyclics: possible treatment for posttraumatic stress disorder. J Clin Psychiatry 46:385–389, 1985

Families and Telematics. American Family VI:8–9, June 1983

Farberow N, Shneidman E (eds): The Cry for Help. New York, McGraw Hill, 1961

Feinstein S: Identity and adjustment disorders of adolescence, in Comprehensive Textbook of Psychiatry, 3rd ed. Edited by Freedman A, Kaplan H, Sadock B. Baltimore, Williams and Wilkins, 1980

Felner R, Guiter M, Primavera J: Primary prevention during school transitions: social support and environmental structure. Am J Community Psychol 10:277–290, 1982

Fielding RA: A note on behavioral treatment in the rehabilitation of myocardial infarction patients. Br J Soc Clin Psychol 19:158–161, 1980

Flomenhaft K, Langsley D: After the crisis. Mental Hygiene 55:473–477, 1971

Folkman S, Lazarus R: Intra- and interindividual analysis of coping: different questions, different answers. Paper presented at meeting of the American Psychological Association, Toronto, August 1984

Fox SS, Scherl DJ: Crisis intervention with victims of rape. Social Work 17:37–42, 1972

Fraiberg S, Adelson E, Shapiro V: Ghosts in the nursery. J Am Acad Child Psychiatry 14:387–421, 1975

France K: Evaluation of lay volunteer crisis telephone workers. Am J Community Psychol 3:197–200, 1975

Frank E, Stewart B: Treating depression in victims of rape. J Clin Psychol 36:95–98, 1983

Frank J: The present status of outcome studies. J Consult Clin Psychol 47:310–316, 1979

Frankl V: The Doctor and the Soul: From Psychotherapy to Logotherapy. New York, Bantam Books, 1967

Freud S: Totem and Taboo, in the Standard Edition, vol 13. Edited by Strachey J. London Hogarth Press, 1955, p 61

Freud S: The Future of an Illusion, in the Standard Edition, vol 21. Edited by Strachey J. London, Hogarth Press, 1961

Friedman M, Thoresen C, Gill J, et al: Alteration of Type A behavior and reduction in cardiac recurrences in postmyocardial infarction patients. Am Heart J 109:237–248, 1984

Fromm E: Psychoanalysis and Religion. New York, Bantam Books, 1967

Fromm E: The Anatomy of Human Destructiveness. New York, Holt, Rinehart and Winston, 1973

Fuchs C, Rehm L: A self-control behavior therapy program for depression. J Consult Clin Psychol 45:206–215, 1977

Futterman S, Pumpian-Mindlin E: Traumatic war neuroses five years later. Am J Psychiatry 108:401–408, 1985

Gallup G: Religion in America. Princeton, The Gallup Opinion Index, Report No 114, 1975

Garbarino J, Jacobson N: Youth helping youth in cases of maltreatment of adolescents. Child Welfare 57:505–510, 1978

Garmezy N: Stressors of childhood, in Stress, Coping and Development in Children. Edited by Garmezy N, Rutter M. New York, McGraw Hill, 1983

Gartner A, Riessman F: Self-Help in Human Services. San Francisco, Jossey-Bass, 1977

Gershon M, Biller HB: The Other Helpers. Lexington, DC Heath, 1977

Gersten JC, Langner TS, Eisenberg JG, et al: Child behavior and life events: undesirable or change per se?, in Stressful Life Events: Their Nature and Effects. Edited by Dohrenwend BS, Dohrenwend BP. New York, John Wiley and Sons, 1974

Glick R, Meyerson A: The use of psychoanalytic concepts in crisis intervention. Int J Psychoanalytic Psychotherapy 8:171–188, 1980-1981

Golan N: When is a client in crisis? Social Casework 50:389–394, 1969

Golan N: Treatment in Crisis Situations. New York, Free Press, 1978

Goldfried MR: Systematic desensitization as training in self-control. J Consult Clin Psychol 37:228–234, 1971

Goldfried MR, Decenteceo ET, Weinberg L: Systematic rational restructuring as a self-control technique. Behav Ther 5:247–254, 1974

Gottlieb BH: Mutual help groups: members' views of their benefits and roles for professionals, in Helping People to Help Themselves. Edited by Borman LD. New York, Hayworth, 1982

Gottlieb F, Kirkpatrick M, Marmor J, et al: Self-help groups, in Psychiatric Therapies, II: Psychological Therapies. Edited by Karasu T. Washington, DC, American Psychiatric Association, 1984

Green BL, Grace MC, Lindy JD, et al: Levels of functional impairment following a civilian disaster: the Beverly Hills Supper Club fire. J Consult Clin Psychol 51(4): 573–580, 1983

Grey S, Rachman S, Sartory G: Return of fear: the role of inhibition. Behav Res Ther 19:135–144, 1981

Group for the Advancement of Psychiatry Reports and Symposiums #62: Psychopathological Disorders in Childhood: Theoretical Considerations and a Proposed Classification, Committee on Child Psychiatry, vol 6, June 1966, pp 173–343

Gulledge AD: The psychological aftermath of myocardial infarction, in Gentry WD, Williams RB, Jr. Psychological Aspects of Myocardial Infarction and Coronary Care. Edited by Gentry WD, Williams RB Jr. St. Louis, CV Mosby, 1975, pp 107–123

Gurman AS, Kniskern DP (eds): Handbook of Family Therapy. New York, Brunner-Mazel, 1981

Gustafson JP: An integration of brief dynamic psychotherapy. Am J Psychiatry 141:935–944, 1984

Hackett TP: The use of groups in the rehabilitation of the postcoronary patient. Adv Cardiol 24:127–135, 1978

Hamburg BA, Varenhorst BB: Peer counseling in the secondary schools: a community mental health project for youth. Am J Orthopsychiatry 42:566–581, 1972

Harris GM, Johnson SB: Coping imagery and relaxation instructions in a covert modeling treatment for test anxiety. Behav Ther 14:144–157, 1983

Harris M, Kalis B, Freeman E: Precipitating stress: an approach to brief therapy. Am J Psychother 17:465–471, 1963

Hart K: The treatment of Type A behaviors and anger by anxiety management training. J Behav Ther Exp Psychiatry 15:133–140, 1984

Hazaleus S, Deffenbacher J: Relaxation and cognitive treatments of anger. J Consult Clin Psychol 54:222–226, 1986

Hill R: Generic features of families under stress. Social Casework 39:139–150, 1958

Hitchcock J: Crisis intervention: the pebble in the pool. Am J Nurs 73:1388–1390, 1973

Hoffman D, Remmel M: Uncovering the precipitant in crisis intervention. Social Casework 56:259–267, 1975

Hogan DP: Cohort comparisons in the timing of life events. Developmental Review 4:289–310, 1984

Hogben GL, Cornfield RB: Treatment of traumatic war neurosis with phenelzine. Arch Gen Psychiatry 38:440–445, 1981

Hollister L: Psychotherapeutic drugs in the dying and bereaved. Journal of Thanatology 2:623–629, 1972

Holmes TH, Rahe RH: The social readjustment rating scale. J Psychosom Res 11:213–318, 1967

Horowitz M: Stress response syndromes—character style and dynamic psychotherapy. Arch Gen Psychiatry 31:768–781, 1974

Horowitz MJ: Stress Response Syndrome, 2nd ed. NJ, Jason Aronson, 1986

Horowitz MJ: States of Mind, 2nd ed. New York, Plenum Press, 1987

Horowitz MJ: Introduction to Psychodynamics. New York, Basic Books, 1988.

Horowitz MJ, Kaltreider NB: Brief therapy of the stress response syndrome. Psychiatr Clin North Am 2:365–377, 1979

Horowitz MJ, Marmar C, Krupnick J, et al: Personality Styles and Brief Psychotherapy. New York, Basic Books, 1984

Hughes JM: Adolescent children of alcoholic parents and the relationship of Ala-teen to their children. J Consult Clin Psychol 45:946–947, 1977

Hutchings D, Denney D, Basgall J, et al: Anxiety management and applied relaxation in reducing general anxiety. Behav Res Ther 18:181–190, 1980

Isenberg DH: Coping with Cancer: The Role of Belief Systems and Support in Cancer Self-Help Groups. Doctoral dissertation. Evanston, Ill, Department of Counseling Psychology, Northwestern University, 1981

Jackson DD: The question of family homeostasis. Psychiatr (Suppl) 31:79–90, 1957

Jacobsen E: Progressive Relaxation. Chicago, University of Chicago Press, 1938

Jacobson G, Strickler M, Morley W: Generic and individual approaches to crisis intervention. Am J Public Health 58:338–343, 1968

James IM, Griffith DNW, Pearson RM, et al: Effect of oxprenolol on stage-fright in musicians. Lancet 2:952–954, 1977

James W: Varieties of Religious Experience. New York, Longmans, Green, 1902

Jannoun L, Oppenheimer C, Gelder M: A self-help treatment program for anxiety state patients. Behav Ther 13:103–111, 1982

Jasperse C: Self-destruction and religion. Mental Health Society 3:154–158, 1976

Kaerscher D, Kuczen B: How you can help your child cope with stress. Better Homes and Gardens 62:114, 1984

Kaffman M: Short-term family therapy, in Family Process 2: 1963. Reprinted in Crisis Intervention: Selected Readings. Edited by Parad H. New York, Family Service Association of America, 1965

Kanfer F: The limitations of animal models in understanding human anxiety, in Anxiety and the Anxiety Disorders. Edited by Tuma A, Maser J. Hillsdale, NJ, Erlbaum, 1985

Kanfer F, Hagerman S: The role of self-regulation, in Behavioral Therapy for Depression: Present Status and Future Direction. Edited by Rehm L. New York, Academic Press, 1981

Kanner L: Child Psychiatry. Springfield, Ill, Charles Thomas Publishing, 1957

Kaplan D: Observations on crisis theory and practice. Social Casework 49:151–155, 1968

Kaplan D, Mason E: Maternal reactions to premature birth viewed as an acute emotional disorder. Am J Orthopsychiatry 30:539–547, 1960

Kardener SH: A methodologic approach to crisis therapy. Am J Psychother 29:4–13, 1975

Kardiner A: The Traumatic Neuroses of War. New York, Hoeber, 1941

Katz AH: Parents of the Handicapped. Springfield, Ill, Charles C. Thomas Publishing, 1961

Kaufman W: Critique of Religion and Philosophy. Princeton, 1978a

Kaufmann W: The Faith of a Heretic. New York, Meridian Books, 1978b

Keeney BP: Ecosystem epistemology: an alternative paradigm for diagnosis. Fam Process 18:117–129, 1979

Kellam SG: Stressful life events and illness: a research area in need of conceptual development, in Stressful Life Events: Their Nature and Effects. Edited by Dohrenwend BS, Dohrenwend BP. New York, John Wiley and Sons, 1974

Kennedy D: Implications of the victimization syndrome for clinical intervention with crime victims. Personnel and Guidance Journal 62:219–222, 1983

Kepler M: The religious factor in pediatric care. Clin Pediatr (Phila) 9:128–130, 1970

Kerr M: Emotional factors in the onset and course of cancer, in Georgetown Family Symposia, vol 4. Edited by Sagar RR. Georgetown Univ, Dept of Psychiatry, Family Section Medical Center, Washington, DC, 1979

Kessler E: Reactive disorders, in Basic Handbook of Child Psychiatry, vol 2: Disturbances of Development. Edited by Noshpitz J. New York, Basic Books, 1979

Killilea M: Mutual-help organizations: interpretations in the literature, in Support Systems and Mutual-Help: Multidisciplinary Explorations. Edited by Caplan G, Killilea M. New York, Grune & Stratton, 1976

Kilpatrick D, Best C: Some cautionary remarks on treating sexual assault victims with implosion. Behav Res Ther 15:421–423, 1984

Kipper D: Behavior therapy for fears brought on by war experiences. J Consult Clin Psychol 45:216–221, 1977

Klee S, Meyer R: Prevention of learned helplessness in humans. J Consult Clin Psychol 47:411–412, 1979

Klein DF, Lindemann E: Preventive intervention in individual and family crisis situations, in Prevention of Mental Disorders in Children. Edited by Caplan G. New York, Basic Books, 1961

Klein DF, Gittleman R, Quitkin F, et al: Diagnosis and Drug Treatment of Psychiatric Disorder: Adults and Children, 2nd ed. Baltimore, Williams and Wilkins, pp 443, 544–545, 1980

Klingman A, Melamed B, Cuthbert M, et al: Effects of participant modeling on information acquisition and skill utilization. J Consult Clin Psychol 52:414–422, 1984

Klorman R, Hilpert P, Michael R, et al: Effects of coping and mastery modeling on experienced and inexperienced pedodontic patients' disruptiveness. Behav Res Ther 11:156–168, 1980

Korner I: Crisis reduction and the psychological consultant, in Crisis Intervention. Edited by Spector G, Claiborn W. New York, Behavioral Publications, 1973

Kuczen B: Childhood Stress: Don't Let Your Child Be a Victim. New York, Delacourte, 1982

Kushner HS: When Bad Things Happen to Good People. New York, Schochen, 1981

Kutchins H, Kutchins S: A self-help organization of black teen-age gang members, in Beliefs and Self-Help: Cross-Cultural Perspectives and Approaches. Edited by Weber GH, Cohen LM. New York, Human Sciences Press, 1982

Lang J: Planned short-term treatment in a family agency. Social Casework 55: 369–374, 1974

LaVietes R: Crisis intervention for ghetto children: contraindications and alternative considerations. Am J Orthopsychiatry 44:720–727, 1974

Lawton MP: Geropsychological knowledge as a background for psychotherapy with older people. J Geriatr Psychiatry, 9:221–233, 1976

Leon G: Survivors of the Holocaust and their children: current status and adjustment. J Pers Soc Psychol 41:503–516, 1981

Lester EP: Brief psychotherapies in child psychiatry. Canad Psychiatr Assoc J 13:301–309, 1968

Leventhal A: The PEACE Program at the American University: Final Report. Washington, DC, The American University Counseling Center, 1976

Levey A, Martin I: Cognitions, evaluations, and conditioning: rules of sequences and rules of consequence. Adv Behav Res Ther 4:181–195, 1983

Levinson DJ: Seasons of a Man's Life. New York, Ballantine Books, 1978

Levis D, Boyd T: The CS exposure approach of implosive (flooding) therapy: a review of the theoretical model and treatment literature, in Evolutionary Behavior Therapy. Edited by Ascher M, Latimer P, Turner S. New York, Springer (in press)

Levy D: Release therapy. Am J Orthopsychiatry 9:713–736, 1939

Levy LH: Self-help groups: types and psychological processes. J Appl Behav Sci 12:310–322, 1976

Levy LH: Processes and activities, in Self-Help Groups for Coping with Crises. Edited by Lieberman MA, Borman LD. San Francisco, Jossey-Bass, 1979

Lewinsohn P: Defective social skills, in Depression: Concepts, Controversies, and Some New Facts, 2nd ed. Edited by Levitt E, Lubin B, Brooks J. Hillsdale, NJ, Erlbaum, 1983

Lieber LL: Mothers Anonymous: A New Direction Against Child Abuse. Paper presented at First Biennial Conference of Society for Clinical Social Work. San Francisco, 1971

Lieberman MA, Borman LD: Self-Help Groups for Coping with Crisis. San Francisco, Jossey-Bass, 1979

Lieberman MA, Borman LD: The impact of self-help groups on widows' mental health. National Reporter 4, 1981

Liebowitz MR, Gorman JM, Fyer AJ, et al: Social phobia. Arch Gen Psychiatry 42:729–736, 1985

Lindemann E: Symptomatology and management of acute grief. Am J Psychiatry 101:141–148, 1944

Lindy J, Grace M, Green B: Survivors: outreach to a reluctant population. Am J Orthopsychiatry 51:468–478, 1981

Lion JR: Personality Disorders Diagnosis and Management, 2nd ed. Baltimore, Williams and Wilkins, 1981, pp 10–31

Lipsky M, Kassinove H, Miller N: Effects of rational-emotive imagery on the emotional adjustment of community mental health center patients. J Consult Clin Psychol 48:366–374, 1980

Lonergan EC: Group Intervention: How to Begin and Maintain Groups in Medical and Psychiatric Settings. New York, Jason Aronson, 1982

Looney J, Gunderson E: Transient situational disturbances: course and outcome. Am J Psychiatry 135:660–663, 1978

LoPiccolo J, LoPiccolo L: Handbook of Sex Therapy. New York, Plenum Press, 1978

LoPiccolo L, Nowinski J: Sex therapy principles and practice, in Techniques in Behavioral Medicine. Edited by Golden C, Alcaparras S, Strider F, et al. New York, Grune & Stratton, 1981

Low AA: Lost and Found (bulletin). The Association of Former Patients of the Psychiatric Institute of the University of Illinois and the State Department of Public Welfare. Chicago, Recovery, Inc, 1938

Low AA: Mental Health Through Will Training. Boston, Christopher, 1950

Lukton R: Myths and realities of crisis intervention. Social Casework 63:276–285, 1982

MacLean G, MacIntosh BA: A clinical approach to brief dynamic psychotherapies in child psychiatry. Can J Psychiatry 27:113–118, 1982

Mahoney M: Cognitive skills and athletic performance, in Cognitive-Behavioral Interventions: Theory, Research, and Procedures. Edited by Kendall P, Hollon S. New York, Academic Press, 1979

Mannino FV, Shore MF: Perceptions of social supports by Spanish-speaking youth with implications for program development. J Sch Health 45: 471–474, 1976

Marks I: Flooding (implosion) and allied treatments, in Behavior Modification. Edited by Agras W. New York, Little, Brown and Company, 1972

Marmor J: Short-term dynamic psychotherapy. Am J Psychiatry 136:145–149, 1979

Marshall JR: The treatment of night terrors associated with the posttraumatic syndrome. Am J Psychiatry 132:293–295, 1975

Maslow AH: Religions, Values, and Peak—Experiences. New York, Viking Press, 1970

Mason JW: A historical view of the stress field, I. J Human Stress 1:6–12, 1975

Masterson J: The symptomatic adolescent five years later: he didn't grow out of it. Am J Psychiatry 123:1338–1345, 1967

Masterson J: The psychiatric significance of adolescent turmoil. Am J Psychiatry 124:1549–1554, 1968

Masterson J, Washburne A: The symptomatic adolescent: psychiatric illness or adolescent turmoil? Am J Psychiatry 122:1240–1247, 1966

May J: Nosology and diagnosis, in Basic Handbook of Child Psychiatry, vol 2: Disturbances of Development. Edited by Noshpitz J. New York, Basic Books, 1979

McCubbin H, Needle R, Wilson M: Adolescent health risk-behaviors: family stress and adolescent coping as critical factors. Family Relations 34:51–62, 1985

McGee CS, Kauffman JM, Nussen JL: Children as therapeutic change agents: reinforcement intervention paradigms. Review of Educ Research 47:451–477, 1977

Meichenbaum D: Stress Inoculation Training. New York, Pergamon Press, 1985

Melamed B, Dearborn M, Hermecz D: Necessary considerations for surgery preparation: age and previous experience. Psychosom Med 45:517–525, 1983a

Melamed B, Jerrell R, Klingman A: Use of modeling techniques to reduce anxiety and enhance cooperative behaviors in children, in The President's Conference on the Dentist-Patient Relationship and the Management of Fear, Anxiety and Pain. Edited by Moretti R, Ayers W. Chicago, American Dental Association, 1983b

Miller N: Learnable drives and rewards, in Handbook of Experimental Psychology. Edited by Stevens S. New York, John Wiley and Sons, 1951

Minuchin S, et al: Psychosomatic Families. Cambridge, Mass, Harvard University Press, 1978

Mowrer OH: Small groups in historical perspective, in Explorations in Self-Help and Mutual Aid. Edited by Borman LD. Evanston, Ill, Center for Urban Affairs, Northwestern University, 1975

Mowrer OH, Vattano AJ: Integrity groups: a context for growth in honesty, responsibility and involvement. Journal of Applied Behavioral Science 12:419–431, 1976.

Nagera H: Early child disturbance: the infantile neurosis and the adult disturbances. Monograph 2, Monograph Series of the Psychoanalytic Study of the Child, New York, International Universities Press, 1966

Nally M: AMT: A Treatment for Delinquents. Doctoral dissertation. Fort Collins, Colo, Colorado State University, 1975

Neubauer, P, Ostow M, Blumenthal M, et al: The jewishness of Jewish young people: a symposium. Am J Psychiatry 129:553–562, 1972

Odom SI, Strain PS: Peer-mediated approaches to promoting children's social interactions: a review. Am J Orthopsychiatry 54:544–557, 1984

O'Donnell T: Medicine and religion. JAMA 211:815–816, 1970

O'Gorman P: Prevention issues involving children of alcoholics, in Services for Children of Alcoholics (DHHS Publication No. ADM 81-1007). Edited by Matlins S, Walker W, Warte B. Rockville, Md, National Institute on Alcohol Abuse and Alcoholism, 1981

Oster RA: Peer counseling: drug and alcohol abuse prevention. J of Primary Prevention 3:188–199, 1983

Osterweis M, Solomon F, Green M (eds): Bereavement: Reactions, Consequences, and Care. Washington, DC, National Academy Press, 1984

Parad H (ed): Crisis Intervention: Selected Readings. New York, Family Service Association of America, 1965

Parad H: The use of time-limited crisis intervention in community mental health programming. Social Service Review 40:275–282, 1966

Parad H, Parad L: A study of crisis-oriented planned short-term treatment: I. Social Casework 49:346–355, 1968a

Parad L, Parad H: A study of crisis-oriented planned short-term treatment: II. Social Casework 49:418–426, 1968b

Patterson V, O'Sullivan M: Three perspectives on brief psychotherapy. Am J Psychother 28:265–277, 1974

Paul L: Crisis intervention. Mental Hygiene 50:141–145, 1966

Peck S: The Road Less Traveled. New York, Simon and Schuster, 1978

Porter R: Crisis intervention and social work models. Community Ment Health J 2:13–21, 1966

President's Commission on Mental Health: Commission Report, vol 1. Washington, DC, US Government Printing Office, 1978a

President's Commission on Mental Health: Task Panel on Community Supports, vol 2. Washington, DC, US Government Printing Office, 1978b

Psychiatric Annals: The psychological consequences of disasters. Psychiatric Annals 15, 1985

Rachman S: Emotional processing. Behav Res Ther 18:51–60, 1980

Rahe R, Ward J, Hayes V: Brief therapy in myocardial infarction rehabilitation: three- to four-years follow-up of a controlled trial. Psychosom Med 47:229–242, 1979

Rapoport L: The state of crisis: some theoretical considerations. Social Service Review 36:211–217, 1962

Rapoport L: Crisis-oriented short-term casework. Social Service Review 41:31–42, 1967

Rapoport L: Crisis intervention as a mode of treatment, in Theories of Social Casework. Edited by Roberts R, Nee R. Chicago, University of Chicago Press, 1970

Resick PA, Veronen LJ, Calhoun KS, et al: Assessment of fear reactions in sexual assault victims: a factor analytic study of the Veronen-Kilpatrick modified fear survey. Behavioral Assessment 8:271–283, 1986

Rickels K, et al: Anti-anxiety drugs: clinical use in psychiatry, in Handbook of Psychopharmacology. Edited by Iversen LL, Iverson SD, Snyder SH, et al. New York, Plenum Press, 1978

Rickels K, Csanalosi I, Greisman P, et al: Controlled clinical trial of alprazolam for the treatment of anxiety. Am J Psychiatry 140:82–84, 1983

Rierdan J, Koff E, Flaherty J: Guidelines for preparing girls for menstruation. J Am Acad Child Adolesc Psychiatry 22:480–486, 1983

Roberts W, Penk W, Gearing M, et al: Interpersonal problems of Vietnam combat veterans with symptoms of posttraumatic stress disorder. J Abnorm Psychol 91:444–450, 1982

Rockwell WJ, Pinkerton RS: Single-session psychotherapy. Am J Psychother 36:32–40, 1982

Rosenbaum M, Palmon N: Helplessness and resourcefulness in coping with epilepsy. J Consult Clin Psychol 52:244–254, 1984

Rosenthal AJ: Brief psychotherapy with children: process of therapy. Am J Psychiatry 128:141–146, 1971

Rosenthal A: Brief focused psychotherapy, in Basic Handbook of Child Psychiatry, vol 3: Therapeutic Interventions. Edited by Noshpitz J. New York, Basic Books, 1979

Rubach G: Zeitschrift fur Geronotologie. Jan-Feb, 10:10–14, 1977

Russell R, Sipich J: Cue-controlled relaxation in the treatment of test anxiety. J Behav Ther Exp Psychiatry 4:47–49, 1973

Rutter M, Garmezy N (eds): Stress, Coping, and Development in Children. New York, McGraw Hill, 1983

Sachs V: Crisis intervention. Public Welfare 26:112–117, 1968

Sandler J: Trauma, strain, and development, in Psychic Trauma. Edited by Furst SS. New York, Basic Books, 1967

Schultz S: Common psychiatric causes of school absenteeism in diabetic children. J Psych Treatment Evaluation 4:125–128, 1982

Schwartz S: A review of crisis intervention programs. Psychiatr Q 45:498–508, 1971

Sebolt N: Crisis intervention and its demands on the crisis therapist, in Crisis Intervention. Edited by Spector G, Claiborn W. New York, Behavioral Publications, 1973

Seligman M, Johnston J: A cognitive theory of avoidance learning, in Contemporary Perspectives in Learning and Conditioning. Edited by McGuigan F, Lumsden D. Washington, DC, Scripta Press, 1973

Shapiro S: Preventive analysis following a trauma: a 4½-year-old girl witnesses a stillbirth. Psychoanal Study Child 28:249–285, 1973

Shipley R, Boudewyns P: Flooding and implosive therapy: are they harmful? Behav Ther 11:503–508, 1980

Shore MF: Alternative services for youth, in Basic Handbook of Child Psychiatry, vol 5. Edited by Noshpitz J. New York, Basic Books, 1987, pp 526–533

Siever LJ, Davis KL: Overview: toward a dysregulation hypothesis of depression. Am J Psychiatry 142:1017–1031, 1985

Sifneos P: A concept of emotional crisis. Mental Hygiene 44:169–179, 1960

Sifneos PE: Short-Term Dynamic Psychotherapy: Evaluation and Technique. New York, Plenum Press, 1979

Smith L: A review of crisis intervention theory. Social Casework 59:396–405, 1978

Stampfl T: Implosive therapy, I: the theory, in Behavioral Modification Techniques in the Treatment of Emotional Disorders. Edited by Armitage A. Battle Creek, Mich, Veterans Administration Publications, 1966a

Stampfl T (cited by Levis D): Effects of serial CS presentation and other characteristics of the CS on the conditioned avoidance response. Psychol Rep 18:755–766, 1966b

Stephens S: Death Comes Home. New York, Morehouse-Barlow, 1972

Stickler M, LaSor B: The concept of loss in crisis intervention. Mental Hygiene 54:301–305, 1970

Stoyva J, Budzynski T: Cultivated low arousal—an anti-stress response?, in Recent Advances in Limbic and Autonomic Nervous Systems Research. Edited by DiCara L. New York, Plenum Press, 1974

Straker M: Adjustment disorders and personality disorders in the aged. Psychiatr Clin North Am 5:121–129, April 1982

Suinn R: Matching behavior therapy to stress theory: why the mismatch? Academic Bulletin 5:417–434, 1983a

Suinn R: Anxiety Management Training. Fort Collins, Colo, Rocky Mountain Behavioral Sciences Institute, 1983b

Suinn R: Generalized anxiety disorder, in Behavioral Theories and Treatment of Anxiety. Edited by Turner S. New York, Plenum Press, 1984

Suinn R: Seven Steps to Peak Performance. Toronto, Ontario, Hans Huber Publishers, 1986

Suinn R, Deffenbacher J: Anxiety management training. Counsel Psychol 16:31–49, 1988

Suinn R, Richardson F: Anxiety management training: a nonspecific behavior therapy program for anxiety control. Behav Ther 2:298–510, 1971

Talbott JA: Crisis intervention and psychoanalysis: compatible or antagonistic? in International Journal of Psychoanalytic Psychotherapy, vol 8. Edited by Langs R. New York, Jason Aronson, 1980

Tennant C, Bebbington P, Hurry J: The short-term outcome of neurotic disorders in the community: the relation of remission to clinical factors and to "neutralizing life events." Br J Psychiatry 139:213–330, 1981

Terr L: Children of Chowchilla—a study of psychic trauma. Psychoanal Study Child 34:552–623, 1979

Terr L: Forbidden games—posttraumatic child's play. J Am Acad Child Adolesc Psychiatry 20:741–760, 1981a

Terr L: Psychic trauma in children: observations following the Chowchilla school bus kidnapping. Am J Psychiatry 138:14–19, 1981b

Terr L: Chowchilla revisited: the effects of psychic trauma four years after a school bus kidnapping. Am J Psychiatry 140:1543–1550, 1983a

Terr L: Life attitudes, dreams, and psychic trauma in a group of "normal" children. J Am Acad Child Adolesc Psychiatry 22:221–230, 1983b

Tiebout HM: Therapeutic mechanisms of AA, in Alcoholics Anonymous Comes of Age. New York, Alcoholics Anonymous World Series, 1957

Todres R: Self-Help Groups: An Annotated Bibliography, 1970–1982. New York, National Self-Help Clearing House, 1982

Toseland RW, Hacker L: Self-help groups and professional involvement. Soc Work 27:341–347, 1982

Trueblood E: Philosophy of Religion. New York, Harper and Row, 1957

Turk D, Meichenbaum D, Genest M: Pain and Behavioral Medicine. New York, Guilford Press, 1983

Turner S: Systematic desensitization of fears and anxiety in rape victims. Paper presented at meeting of the Association for the Advancement of Behavior Therapy, San Francisco, December 1979

Tyhurst J: Individual reactions to community disaster. Am J Psychiatry 107:764–769, 1951

Vaillant G: Theoretical hierarchy of adaptive ego mechanisms. Arch Gen Psychiatry 24:107–118, 1971

Van der Kolk B: Posttraumatic stress disorder. Harvard Medical School Health News 1:4–6, 1984

Varenhorst B: Innovations 7:26–29, 1980

Veronen L, Kilpatrick D: Rape: a precursor of change, in Life-Span Developmental Psychology: Nonnormative Life Events. Edited by Callahan E, McCluskey K. New York, Academic Press, 1983

Verwoerdt A: Clinical Geropsychiatry, 2nd ed. Baltimore, Williams and Wilkins, 1981

Viederman M: The psychodynamic life narrative: a psychotherapeutic intervention useful in crisis situations. Psychiatry 46:236–246, 1983

Wakefield RA, Mooney J (eds): Experts say role of mental health professionals to change dramatically with use of home computers. American Family: The National Newsletter on Family Policy and Programs Since 1977, vol 8:1–4, Sept 1983

Walker C: Sexual disorders, in Behavioral Medicine. Edited by Doleys D, Meredith R, Ciminero A. New York, Plenum Press, 1982

Weinberger G: Brief therapy with children and their parents, in Brief Therapies. Edited by Barten H. New York, Behavioral Publications, 1971

Weiner MF: Practical Psychotherapy. New York, Brunner/Mazel, 1986

Weiner MF, Caldwell T: Stresses and coping in ICU nursing, II: nurse support groups on intensive care units. Gen Hosp Psychiatry 3:129–134, 1981

Wheat P, Lieber LL: Hope for the Children—A Personal History of Parents Anonymous. Minneapolis, Winston, 1979

Whitehead P: Changes in religious doctrines and practices, in Basic Handbook of Child Psychiatry, vol 4. Edited by Noshpitz JD, Berlin IN, Stone LA. New York, Basic Books, 1979

Whitman S, Coleman T, Berg B, et al: Epidemiological insights into socioeconomic correlates of epilepsy, in A Multidisciplinary Handbook of Epilepsy. Edited by Hermann BP. Springfield, Ill, Charles C Thomas Publishing Company, 1980

Wincze J: Sexual dysfunction, in Handbook of Clinical Behavior Therapy. Edited by Turner S, Calhoun K, Adams H. New York, John Wiley and Sons, 1981

Winer J, Pollock G: Adjustment disorders, in Comprehensive Textbook of Psychiatry, 3rd ed. Edited by Freedman AM, Kaplan HI, Sadock BJ. Baltimore, Williams and Wilkins, 1980

Wolkon G: Crisis theory, the appreciation for treatment and dependency. Compr Psychiatry 13:459–464, 1972

Wolpe J: The Practice of Behavior Therapy. New York, Pergamon Press, 1982

Wynne L: Adjustment reaction of adult life, in Comprehensive Textbook of Psychiatry, 2nd ed. Edited by Freedman A, Kaplan H, Sadock B. Baltimore, Williams and Wilkins, 1975

Yalom ID: The Theory and Practice of Group Psychotherapy. New York, Basic Books, 1975

Yalom ID, Greaves C: Group therapy with the terminally ill. Am J Psychiatry 134:396–400, 1977

Zeiss A, Lewinsohn P, Munoz R: Nonspecific improvement effects in depression using interpersonal skills training, pleasant activity schedules, or cognitive training. J Consult Clin Psychol 47:427–439, 1979

Personality Disorders

Chapter 246

Introduction

Overview

The purpose of this section is to provide a comprehensive and balanced review of the treatments currently advocated for patients with personality disorders. A conscious effort has been made throughout the text to provide a summary of different treatment perspectives and to highlight contributions that could help clinicians manage the problems presented by their patients.

This task has been undertaken with full recognition that by no means can the existing diagnostic categories be considered well established. Therefore, two approaches are used in organizing this section. Treatment modality, without reference to specific diagnostic categories, is the first approach. The first seven chapters of this section review psychoanalysis and dynamic psychotherapies, behavioral therapy, family and couple therapy, group therapy, somatic therapy, and residential treatment.

The second approach complements the first by reflecting the fact that personality disorders include heterogeneous forms of psychopathology and present a broad range of clinical problems. To do justice to this diversity the 11 Axis II categories provide the organization for the second half of the text. Despite the questions about the durability and validity of Axis II categories, this second approach is based on the recognition that important differences exist between types of personality disorders and these differences require different clinical strategies.

In this introductory chapter, I will attempt to provide a historical background showing the evolution of attitudes and approaches toward the treatment of personality disorders and then summarize some common themes that are found across chapters.

Establishing a Conceptual Base

The task and the possibility of changing personality remains one of the most interesting and controversial frontiers for psychiatry. Through the introduction of psychoanalysis, Freud provided a method of treatment offering hope that deep, unconsciously determined aspects of a person's functioning could be altered through corrective psychological interventions. Although the treatment methods derived from Freud's work are frequently very helpful in individual cases, it eventually became apparent to analysts that the illumination of unconscious motives, which psychoanalytic methods allowed, did not always lead to alterations in the ongoing problems in loving or working nor even in the symptoms for which patients sought help.

In a penetrating historical essay, Auchincloss and Michaels (1983) have described Freud's primary interest in the psychogenic sources and resolution of symptoms and how progress in the history of psychoanalytic thinking regarding character is actually a retreat from Freud's initial strikingly "anticharacterological position." It was left for a later generation of psychoanalysts, still using Freud's methods, to elaborate and emphasize how psychological conflict is reflected in personality structure. In the process, these contributors reformulated the nature of the psychopathology that Freud considered neurotic into problems and disorders of personality.

In the first model of personality after Freud, theorists such as Abraham (1949), Anna Freud (1937), and Waelder (1930) continued to consider personality as the generally stable compromises (defenses) formed out of early childhood conflicts between, for example, aggression and fear or other impulses and their consequences. It remained tied to innate drives and personality was left as an exclusively intrapsychic resolution. Later psychoanalytic theorists paid more attention to early social experiences, in particular, the relationship between the child and his or her parents. Such diverse observers as Sullivan (1950), Erikson (1950), and Fairbairn (1952) shifted the psychoanalytic theory of character toward a consideration of the complementary adaptation to the more or less stable aspects of one's environment. They defined personality as the person's characteristic pattern of participation in activities with the world.

These developments in theory led to shifts in therapeutic technique. Whereas early ideas about treatment rested on the concept of the uncovering and resolution of unconscious conflicts, later thinking shifted the emphasis toward defense analysis. Reich (1949) in particular presented a theory of therapy advocating persistent and uncompromising, repetitious interpretations of characterologic defenses. With the advent of psychosocial theories, it was thought that personality was adaptive and to some extent dependent on the social and interpersonal milieu in which the person lived. Within this model, Sullivan (1950) and Maxwell Jones (1953) provided models of interpersonal and social therapies that reportedly could change personality. In its broader implications, this model encouraged the idea that the social expressions of personality could be modified directly by shaping the person's intervention with the environment—leading to the behavioral therapies that began to appear in the 1950s. Despite these shifts in what were thought to be the critical therapeutic processes, and despite the occasional enthusiasm shown by pioneers such as Reich and Jones, the prevailing wisdom was that although "character neuroses" were treatable, more severe personality disorders were at best manageable.

The earliest nosology for personality disorders, found in DSM-I (American Psychiatric Association 1952), divided disorders of personality into four categories: 1) disturbances of pattern; 2) disturbances of traits; 3) disturbances of drive, control, and relationships; and 4) sociopathic disturbances. These categories reflected a close relationship between diagnosis and psychoanalytic concepts. In DSM-I and subsequently in DSM-II (American Psychiatric Association 1968), personality diagnoses were generally used only when patients did not fit comfortably into neurotic or psychotic disorders. To a large extent, this practice reflected the perhaps exaggerated optimism of dynamically trained clinicians regarding treatment of disorders of the latter two types, as opposed to the conceptual ambiguities and therapeutic pessimism associated with the former. Even by the time of DSM-II in 1968, it was unclear whether personality diagnoses should legitimately be employed for stable but socially deviant patterns; and there remained little enthusiasm for the treatment potential of anyone whose personality disturbances were severe. Hence, by 1968, in terms of practical therapeutics, symptomatic disturbances remained the central concern and personality features were secondary background considerations. Yet, in psychoanalytic theory, symptomatic disturbances were viewed as embedded in and secondary outgrowths of a primary predisposing personality pattern, condition, or disorder.

Recent Developments

Three major developments since 1968 have helped establish new interest in the treatment of personality disorders. One of these has to do with therapeutic enthusiasm among those involved in psychosocial therapies; a second derives from the advance of biologic psychiatry; and the third has to do with diagnosis itself.

Psychosocial Initiatives

The interest of people working in residential treatment centers was stirred by reports that psychopathic patients (Kiger 1967; Sturup 1968) and primitive impulse-ridden adolescents (Masterson 1972; Rinsley 1967) could be rehabilitated by long-term residential placements that employed the socializing, impulse-controlling, and responsibility-enhancing features of therapeutic communities.

Therapeutic enthusiasm within individual psychoanalytic psychotherapy was also given impetus by Kernberg (1968; Kernberg et al. 1972) and a growing list of other analysts (e.g., Balint 1968; Chessick 1977; Giovacchini 1973; Masterson 1976) who began to endorse intensive, long-term exploratory psychotherapy with such patients. These authors departed from their psychoanalytic predecessors by arguing that a psychoanalytically oriented psychotherapy was indicated and potentially curative for patients with severe character problems. Reports of these leaders and others within the dynamic psychiatry tradition captured widespread attention and mobilized more ambitious and enthusiastic efforts to treat such patients within both residential settings and office practice.

Biologic Psychiatry

A similar impetus for interest in the treatment of personality disorders has arrived by quite another avenue, namely, the conceptual and therapeutic inroads derived from biologic psychiatry. These developments have revived interest in the biogenetic substrates of character pathology. It is ironic that stabler forms of psychopathology traditionally had been seen as largely determined by an ever-changing environment, whereas symptomatic disturbances, which are usually time limited, are often assumed to be largely determined by stable biogenetic factors (Gunderson and Pollock 1985). In any event, the growth of biologic psychiatry has directed attention to issues of heritability and temperament in the pathogenesis of personality disorders and has helpfully encouraged exploration of biologic therapies. There is currently a growing number of efforts to test the possible utility of pharmacotherapies for personality-disordered patients—tests that would have been considered fruitless, a priori, a decade ago. A more nonspecific effect on treatment from the biogenetic advance will probably be felt in years ahead. It is likely to set the stage for more methodologically rigorous treatment evaluations.

Diagnostic Shifts

The third major development that has renewed and invigorated the interest in treating personality disorders derives from advances in diagnosis. The advent of DSM-III (American Psychiatric Association 1980) reflected a major shift in the foundations for psychiatric diagnosis from expert clinical observation (usually based in psychodynamic principles) to controlled, standardized, and systematic research observations. Some DSM-III categories of personality disorders have been criticized for departures from psychodynamic concepts, arbitrariness in the absence of any empirical base, and highly overlapping criteria (Frances and Cooper 1981; Gunderson 1983; Kernberg 1984). Other categories (e.g., antisocial and borderline) have been praised. Despite fears that the arbitrariness or overlapping of nonscientifically based criteria would lead to premature rigidification and closure, DSM-III has actually stimulated further research on the existing categories and already is leading to revisions. The nature of the DSM-III definition of personality disorder has also reserved these diagnoses for clearly socially maladapted and subjectively disturbed persons who place the heaviest demands on public health attention—and dollars.

The fact that DSM-III asks clinicians to make personality diagnoses on patients, regardless of the presence or absence of symptomatic conditions, has profoundly influenced therapeutic interest. Clinicians are paying much more attention to the characterologic traits or disorders that accompany all major forms of psychopathology. These personality traits or disorders are being found to influence the prognosis and treatment responsivity of symptomatic problems (e.g., Akiskal 1981; Gaviria et al. 1982; Pope et al. 1983).

Common Themes

The quality and amount of the literature about each of the modalities of treatment for the DSM-III Axis II disorders are extremely variable. There are, however, several themes that run across most of the chapters in this section. Three of these reflect recurrent issues in integrating existing literature.

1. Almost all of the contributing authors found themselves handicapped by the difficulties of relating the available literature to the present DSM-III definitions. Sometimes the literature for a putative category is extremely limited (e.g., avoidant and dependent) or, even if extensive, has little to say about treatment (e.g., schizotypal and paranoid). In these instances, the authors have had to depend on their own experience and have had to worry about the breadth and credibility of their views. Often the literature is tied to definitions that are at variance with those currently employed by DSM-III (e.g., borderline with borderline personality organization, antisocial with criminality, compulsive with obsessive-compulsive, avoidant with phobic character, and histrionic with hysterical). In these instances, the authors have had to worry about whether the literature they selected is applicable to the DSM-III definitions.

   A more serious and even less resolvable issue is that few categories found in DSM-III have established validity. Many academic psychologists and psychoanalysts have serious doubts about the use of a categorized approach for personality classification. Indeed, in 25 years, the diagnostic system may be unrecognizable by today's standards.

2. A second problem concerns the credibility of the predominant and central role individual psychotherapy is given in the treatment for virtually all of these disorders. This prevailing wisdom must be considered, at least in part, a product of the fact that a majority of mental health professionals have been trained to do individual psychotherapy. In most instances, behavioral therapy, pharmacotherapy, family therapies, or residential therapies are used adjunctively or concurrently with individual therapy. Yet these other approaches all require either specialized training or special resources beyond those commonly available in office practice. Even less often are professionals involved in and able to evaluate the benefits of support groups and self-help programs. Hence, although the central role given to individual psychotherapy throughout this monograph is strongly supported by the changes observed and reported by its practitioners, there is often a more limited observational base from which the authors could evaluate the claims for other treatments.

3. A third problem is the striking absence of eventitative research on treatment of personality disorders. Virtually all of the literature is based on detailed observations of experienced clinicians. The eventitative research that does exist is largely limited to the modalities of behavioral therapy and pharmacotherapy. Even in these areas, the studies have limited application because the outcome is generally measured on what might be considered symptomatic exacerbations or outgrowths of the personality disturbance rather than the personality itself. With the other modalities, which are directed at altering the internal organization or interpersonal style of personality-disordered patients, there is very limited quantitative research—none of which has yet been directed at DSM-III categories and little of which is relevant to long-term strategies.

Beyond the problems of limited knowledge, another common theme concerns the overall difficulty of treating personality disorders. Virtually every author speaks to the multiple and complex treatment resistances that are encountered with personality-disordered patients. Some of these problems cut across enough categories and modalities that they can be presented here as general principles—or warnings—for would-be therapists to appreciate.

One source of trouble is that therapists often are attempting to alter aspects of the person that are experienced as syntonic and perhaps even considered adaptive by the patient. There is frequently a difference between what therapists define as psychopathology and what patients observe about themselves as needing change. A major issue in the treatment of many personality-disordered patients is to make aspects of themselves with which they are comfortable dystonic and thus generate motivation for change. This problem is dramatically illustrated by a recent study in which patients with borderline personality disorder differed from their families, their therapists, and their nursing staffs in how they viewed changes in themselves. When the patients felt themselves to be improved, family, therapists, and nursing staff thought they were worse, and when the patients felt themselves to be worse, the others thought they were improved (Cowdry and Gardner 1988).

A second major problem in the treatment of patients with personality disorders concerns the chronicity and duration of the problems. Even when the patient shares the therapist's view of what is maladaptive and in need of change, the process of bringing about that change is usually slow, gradual, and marked by much repetition. This takes a toll on the motivation and enthusiasm of both therapist and patient. Moreover, the changes that can be expected are not only gradual but partial. Unlike earlier models of change, which involved symptom remission or conflict resolution, shifts in the configuration of a personality are always resisted by the force of habits, by reinforcing factors within the patient's ongoing social and interpersonal context, and by the adaptive limitations and capabilities imposed by temperament. In addition to the restrained motivation resulting from the duration of treatment and the partial nature of changes, neither patients nor therapists can enter into treatment for a personality disorder with much foreknowledge of the likely effects. The conviction and commitment to such therapies must be based on extensive personal experience and do not have a reservoir of controlled scientific evidence from which to replenish themselves.

The amount of literature the contributors have been able to identify and synthesize for the purpose of this text is impressive. Clinicians in all of the mental health disciplines will find new information that can help them in planning and executing treatment for the very common, but very difficult, personality-disordered patients in their practice. I hope this section will also serve two other important purposes. First, it may foster the recognition that the patient's personality is of primary importance in treatment planning and intervention. Second, by presenting the "best" of what can be and has been learned from the collective experience of expert clinical observers, these chapters may provide the background needed for a different type of observational base. Future books on this subject should record naturalistic or controlled but, in any event, quantitative and systematic research of the treatments recommended here. The results will inevitably reinforce some aspects of current practice while altering others.

Treatment Modalities

Chapter 247

Psychoanalysis and Dynamic Psychotherapy

Although acknowledged broadly as an advance, DSM-III's (American Psychiatric Association 1980) section on personality disorders remains troubled by diagnostic imprecision (Charney et al. 1981; Gunderson 1983; Mellsop et al. 1982; Pfohl et al. 1983). Causes are the poor demarcation between normal and disordered and between various disorders as well as the difficulties of distinguishing between state or role and trait (Frances 1980). Psychoanalysts and dynamically oriented therapists are less troubled by this fact because they largely believe personality disorders are on a continuum with the normal rather than discrete illnesses. Such a view goes back to the work of Sigmund Freud and his contributions to the understanding of character. Some psychoanalysts have gone so far as to take the position that character nosologies may in the long run impede scientific progress (Kohut and Wolfe 1978).

Historical Development

Psychoanalytic theory has always held the position that character is the product of the complex interaction of the biology of homo sapiens, the constitution of the individual, and human and nonhuman environmental influences, particularly of the early years. Emphasis on biologic drives characterized the first period of psychoanalysis. More attention was given to adaptation to the environment in the middle period. In recent years the influence of interpersonal relationships on the establishment of mental representations of self and others has received most attention (Dorpat 1979). Modifications in therapeutic technique have consequently been advocated. In general, however, theoretical shifts have far outrun the therapeutic.

Freud (1959b) began the psychoanalytic study of personality when he described the regular combination of three characteristics—being orderly, being parsimonious, and being obstinate—as interrelated character traits. He claimed that this triad was to be found in persons whose childhoods were typified by an exceptionally strong erotogenicity of the anal zone. The three adult character traits result from a compromise between expression of and defense against anal eroticism—orderliness and cleanliness are a reaction formation opposing involvement with feces; parsimony and obstinacy relate to the gratification of stool retention and the anal-sadistic struggle with the mother. Freud's enormous conceptual breakthrough was that character traits of adulthood are derivatives of infantile drives or defenses against them. He actually wrote little about the mechanism of character formation (Baudry 1983; Strachey in Freud 1959, p. 175). Freud's brilliant associate Karl Abraham (1927a, 1927b, 1927c) elaborated his teacher's libido theory into a nosology intimately related to the stages of psychosexual development. Abraham further delineated oral, anal, and genital character types derived from the associated libidinal phases. Abraham's treatment technique remained centered on interpretation aimed at making the unconscious drive derivatives conscious.

Freud believed that describing a character trait was arbitrarily isolating only one aspect of an enormously complex mental and behavioral field. In fact, Freud was using his conceptualization about character as a "protostructural model of the mind" that would account for both stability and change (Boesky 1983, p. 229). Freud grew more cautious about the role of the instincts with the years, claiming that anal eroticism was only a powerful contributor to the triad in 1917. In 1923 Freud stated, "The character of the ego is a precipitate of abandoned object-cathexes and it contains the history of those object-choices" (p. 29), thereby adding an interpersonal and object relations matrix to character development. This advance was accompanied by a shift from an "id psychological" treatment technique aimed at making unconscious wishes conscious to a treatment aimed at understanding the patient's mental life more broadly.

By the early 1930s, Reich (1949) saw character as the chief source of resistance to treatment, analogizing it to armor. He advocated that the analyst mobilize these frozen conflicts by vigorous confrontation so that character neurosis (in DSM-III terminology, personality disorder) would be changed into symptom neurosis (in DSM-III, an Axis I disorder).

Fenichel (1945) claimed that the study of character neuroses was the youngest branch of psychoanalysis because psychoanalysis had originated in the study of ego alien phenomena (symptoms), that is, phenomena that did not fit into the patients' customary views of themselves or of their standards and modes of behavior. To Fenichel, character was constituted by "the ego's habitual modes of adjustment to the external world, the id, and the superego, and the characteristic types of combining these modes with one another" (p. 467). Fenichel extensively reviewed and synthesized the work of psychoanalysts up to and including his own time with respect to conditions of tolerance or defense against instinctual impulses. He elaborated upon oral, anal, urethral, and phallic character types, with the genital character being the ideal, fully developed type. He went on to discuss other pathologic character problems that had at their centers guilt, absence of feeling, success, pseudosexuality, and social anxiety. With respect to treatment he warned that character analysis is a much lengthier procedure than symptom analysis.

Alexander and French (1946) proposed shorter approaches to the analytic psychotherapy of character neuroses, approaches that included less frequent sessions and the combination of analytic therapy with drugs and other modalities. A host of short-term dynamic approaches have since been developed. Most of these have the patient sitting up, set a time limit, persistently focus on an agreed-upon problem (the focal conflict), and demand considerable activity on the part of the therapist, consisting of confrontations and interpretations meant to promote insight and discourage regression (Marmor 1979). Although successful short-term work with personality disorders has been reported (Malan 1976; Piper et al. 1986), most psychoanalytic therapists choose longer term individual psychotherapy or analysis because short-term methods can treat current problems but not lifelong maldevelopment. This is particularly so when previous short-term efforts have failed, or when the clinician detects evidence that the patient may not be immediately capable of a basically positive transference and a good therapeutic alliance (Zetzel 1956) or working alliance (Greenson 1967).

Regardless of the method of treatment selected, most modern analysts would agree that character is more than a stable collection of compromises between impulse, defense, internal standards, and the demands of reality. Analysts who remain close to this earlier point of view claim that psychoanalysis has less to say about those stable personality configurations that are outside the realm of intrapsychic conflict than those based upon it (Boesky 1983). Others have attempted to research the interplay of innate behavioral tendencies (temperament) with the products of experience from a psychoanalytic point of view regarding character (Rainer 1979; Stone 1979). Schafer (1979) has established a fresh perspective by abandoning much of traditional metapsychology and describing character as the actions people "typically perform in the problematic situations they typically define for themselves. It thus refers to what they regularly do when they experience danger or when they must choose between or accommodate courses of action that they view as desirable though incompatible" (p. 875). Schafer claims character refers to the typical ways people organize what they do and how they act within more or less stable contexts of meaning. To Schafer, the most important part of all these actions goes on unconsciously. It is therefore the therapist's task to help the patient with a personality disorder to learn the meanings of his or her actions.

Before concluding the discussion of psychoanalytically based treatment of personality disorders, it is necessary to mention the distinction between dystonic and syntonic traits and its importance both theoretically and clinically. Analysts have used the term ego-syntonic to describe instincts or ideas that are "acceptable to the ego" (Laplanche and Pontalis 1973, p. 151), or, as Jones (1948) put it, "consonant, compatible, or consistent with the standards of the self" (p. 497). Traditionally, personality traits that are inflexible and maladaptive yet ego-syntonic have been viewed by psychoanalysts as highly defended frozen residues of old intrapsychic conflicts. Although these character patterns are rigid and inflexible and are often offensive to others, the patient may be unaware of them or consciously agree with them (Fenichel 1945, p. 465). The patient pays a high price for this steady state because the energy necessary for defense against instinctual wishes is not available for other investment. Whenever the frozen conflict is touched upon, alternative modes of perceiving, relating to, and experiencing self and others are impossible.

In classic terminology, symptom neuroses are based on ego-dystonic experience—what had been warded off is breaking through and causing psychic pain. Clinically, ego-syntonic personality traits require technical stances that often make patients feel worse after treatment begins. Ego-syntonic traits become dystonic or are broken down to release dystonic elements. The personality traits become accessible to this change when they appear as resistances within the therapeutic relationship. The advent or increase in temporary suffering may, however, cause the patient with little motivation to leave treatment. Nevertheless, the unique technical contribution of psychoanalytic theory for the treatment of personality disorders rests on the belief that exploration of the relationship between therapist and patient is essential to change in personality structure. Both the patient and the therapist must be prepared for an arduous process.

When personality disorder is the outcome of development, special emphasis in the treatment is placed on the degree and nature of effects of psychopathology found in the parents. Loss of a parent through death, divorce, abandonment, or premature separation can be a crucial therapeutic issue. The individual's reactions to specific traumatic events such as serious physical illness and actual seduction are also of special significance (Anthony and Pollock 1985).

Nature and Quality of Available Evidence

No outcome studies attempting to demonstrate the effectiveness of psychoanalysis or dynamic psychotherapy specifically on personality disorders as described in DSM-III and DSM-III-R (American Psychiatric Association 1987) in the aggregate or individually have been reported. The Menninger Psychotherapy Project (Kernberg et al. 1972; Wallerstein 1985) comes closest to evaluating these modalities with severely disturbed personality-disordered patients. The researchers in this study, like Luborsky and Spence (1978), concluded that patients with better ego strength, or better functioning patients, respond better than poorer functioning patients, certainly no surprise to any experienced clinician. Schlessinger and Robbins (1983) reported on follow-up of psychoanalytic treatment. Although DSM-III criteria were not utilized, the subjects were personality-disordered patients. Schlessinger and Robbins were most impressed not with the resolution of psychic conflicts but with the development of an "identification with the analyzing function of the analyst, as a learned mode of coping with conflicts" (p. 8). The components of this "self analytic function" were enhanced self-observation, better reality processing, and greater tolerance of frustration, anxiety, and depression.

DSM-III and DSM-III-R group the personality disorders into three clusters: the "odd" or eccentric (paranoid, schizoid, and schizotypal); the dramatic, emotional, or erratic (histrionic, narcissistic, antisocial, and borderline); and the anxious or fearful (avoidant, dependent, obsessive-compulsive, and passive-aggressive). Clinical tradition holds that results of psychoanalysis and psychodynamic psychotherapy are best with the third group. The work of Kernberg (1975, 1984), Kohut (1971, 1977, 1984), and others has created a modicum of therapeutic optimism toward members of the second group, and this optimism probably affects outcome positively, although such an effect has yet to be documented carefully. No such advances have occurred with respect to the "odd" or eccentric personality disorders.

Duration and Frequency of Visits and Length of Treatment

Duration and Frequency

Generally, Freud saw his patients six times a week, but mild cases and those well advanced in treatment only three times (Freud 1913). He did "marathon" sessions, such as his four-hour single session with Gustav Mahler (Jones 1957), and brief treatment as well. He usually saw patients for most of a clock hour—the traditional "50-minute hour." Regardless of the exact length of the session, clinicians practicing psychoanalysis or dynamic psychotherapy generally favor starting and stopping at preset times so that earliness and tardiness as well as the patient's saving crucial material for the end of the session can be examined for dynamic significance.

With personality-disordered patients, at least two 45-minute sessions per week for dynamic psychotherapy and four for analysis are recommended. The rationale for nearly daily sessions in classical analysis is to promote a regressive transference neurosis, that is, the reemergence of childhood conflicts with the analyst in the here-

and-now experienced as if the analyst were one or another significant figure from the there-and-then (usually a parent) so that the conflicts may be resolved by interpretation.

With "sicker" patients, including most of those who have DSM-III personality disorders, analysts and therapists are experienced almost immediately as if they were significant past figures, and some clinicians argue that further regression is to be avoided. Therefore, they consider only one or two sessions per week optimal. Others argue that the regression is present anyway and infrequent sessions serve only to protect the therapist from its countertransference effects. They reason that the sicker the patient is, the more frequent the sessions should be in order to allow for vigorous interaction with the therapist as well as the support of his or her presence. These sicker patients frequently have fragile or brittle defenses, those habitual, unconscious patterns of coping with a variety of adaptive problems, including unpleasant feelings such as fear of loss of love, guilt, and shame. These defenses operate with only marginal effectiveness and tend to give way under objectively minimal stress. They are usually seen in association with significant disturbances in self-esteem, along with low tolerance for anxiety, frustration, or other tension. When these defenses give way, the patients experience overwhelming anxiety and feelings of helplessness, often leading to cognitive disorganization or impulsive, perhaps self-destructive, behavior or both. The subsequent restitutional processes may involve primitive mechanisms such as paranoid projection. Effective therapeutic work with such fragile or brittle defenses may require that interpretation occur in the context of continuous support such as is available in the psychoanalytic situation.

Similarly, these patients may have rigid character structures, (i.e., habitual patterns of coping with guilt, shame, and fear of loss of love) that tend to operate inflexibly and totally, regardless of the objective degree of stress. These patterns are tightly organized into a well-integrated hierarchy. For example, a well-compensated compulsive character disorder may use rationalizations that, when challenged, give way to intellectualization and finally to sullen withdrawal or self-righteous anger. Such ways of coping have usually been relatively successful in dealing with certain fears (often fears about loss of control), although at the cost of impaired flexibility of adaptive responses. The methods of coping also become a secondary source of gratification in providing a pleasurable sense of mastery for persons who are intolerant of ambiguity. These defensive patterns are tenaciously maintained in the face of most therapeutic interventions and, therefore, may require the consistent confronting interpretive approach and the therapeutically adaptive regression, possible only in regular psychoanalysis.

Offenkrantz and Tobin (1974) explained that the duration of the sessions is not so important as the patient's sense that the sessions are regular and predictable and that during each the patient will have the therapist's full attention. This regularity and predictability is often under the personality-disordered patient's close scrutiny, so that the slightest variation becomes a stimulus for reaction. Too often, such data are neglected by therapists and analysts because sessions are not frequent enough.

Length of Treatment

Analyses and dynamic therapies have gotten longer over the years for reasons that are uncertain but certainly multifactorial. Gedo (1979a), in a retrospective report on the 36 patients he treated with psychoanalysis in the 1960s and 1970s, claimed that successful analysis required 600 to 1,000 sessions, taking three to seven years. As with Schlessinger and Robbins's patients, DSM-III categories were not applied, but it is safe to say that most of Gedo's patients would have carried an Axis II diagnosis. McGlashan and Miller (1982), agreeing with Gedo, suggested that longer treatments have evolved not because of differences in patients' psychopathology but because of the accrual of extensive and varied treatment goals. The psychoanalyst purportedly attempts to realize more of the goals than the dynamic psychotherapist. Gedo (1979a) felt that the length of treatment in his series was not directly related to the severity of psychopathology but more to how rapidly he was able to develop a meaningful way of communicating with each analysand. In either analysis or psychotherapy, failure to attend to the effects of early developmental problems has been noted to contribute to extended treatment, stalemates, endless tasks, and reanalysis (Gedo 1979a; Kohut 1979; Schlessinger and Robbins 1983).

Personality-disordered patients often produce powerful countertransference. Liking or disliking the patient intensely may lead, in either case, to a pre- or post-mature termination of therapy. The therapist's integrity is necessary to prevent retaining a patient to fulfill the therapist's need for income, satisfy training goals, or enhance self-esteem because a patient is obviously doing well (Offenkrantz and Tobin 1974).

Goals of Treatment

Older views of personality disorders minimized the role of the patient's own distress. The view that conflict was frozen by character in an ego-syntonic fashion was accompanied by the belief that the patient with a personality disorder was a source of distress to others but not to himself or herself. Goals of treatment centered around better interpersonal relationships and better adaptation to family, job, and society. DSM-III recognizes that a variety of painful affects are regularly found in many patients with personality disorders, and relief of psychic distress has taken on enhanced importance as a goal of treatment. In Schafer's (1979) view, the psychoanalytic concept of character helps the clinician define how and why each person unconsciously yet systematically makes the life that he or she does. It follows easily that psychoanalytic and dynamic treatment of a personality disorder has an important goal: making the patient aware of unconscious beliefs, attitudes, and fantasies that make his or her personality style seem the safest means of being and interacting with others despite the pain.

Contemporary dynamic psychotherapy with personality disorders involves interpersonal concepts as well as intrapsychic ones. Psychoanalytic theorists over the past couple of decades have increasingly viewed personality disorders as the product of pre-oedipal developmental vicissitudes of the mother-child relationship, resulting in alterations in object relations and ego and superego development, and in persistent states of conflict between id, ego, and superego. As Winer et al. (1984) have noted, Freud's structural theory of the mind assumes a well developed psychic apparatus, that there has been "an average expectable environment" (Hartmann 1939), "good enough mothering" (Winnicott 1953), sufficient parental empathy (Kohut 1971), and maternal support of the child's separation and individuation (Mahler et al. 1975). The structural theory with its tripartite model of the mind (id, ego, and superego) has interpretation as its primary therapeutic intervention (Gedo and Goldberg 1973).

Personality-disordered patients often need more supportive measures and respond poorly to interpretation alone. Gedo and Goldberg have established a hierarchy of therapeutic interventions ranging from the most infantile to the most advanced pre-oedipal need. Starting with the most primitive, pacification treats an overstimulated traumatic state (analogous to that of the helpless infant) via frequent, regular sessions, or with more radical measures such as medication, provision of protective environments, or even isolation. Unification is appropriate when the difficulty is at a somewhat higher level of personality development and fragmentation of the established but fragile self is the problem. At this level, the provision of an uninterrupted relationship with a real person or a reliable setting is sufficient, for the therapist serves more as a transitional object. At the next higher level of organization, the personality-disordered patient must relinquish infantile grandiosity, and the therapeutic aim is optimal disillusionment. Unattainable ambitions, shame propensity, and problems of idealization are central therapeutic issues. Only after considerable psychic growth is the patient with a serious personality disorder ready for interpretation as the central therapeutic intervention.

Five additional elements that elucidate how psychoanalytically based therapy with personality disorders works are cited here: First, there is the element of identification with the therapist (Loewald 1960; Miller et al. 1968; Schlessinger and Robbins 1983). Even in the simplest form of therapy, the personality-disordered patient begins to address his or her problems and the world in new ways—those of the therapist. The therapist provides a model of empathy for others, searching for causes rather than blame, and of more adaptive responses to stress, conflict, or frustration. Second, the therapist provides emotional support—the patient does not feel alone in a sea of troubles. With these patients, interpretation of unconscious conflict is usually not as important as the accepting relationship with the therapist. Third, the therapist provides insight into ways in which the past is influencing the present and into the ways unconscious processes are at work. Personality-disordered patients frequently believe that the source of their troubles lies outside themselves completely. They tend to disavow their own motives. Insight makes them more comfortable about accepting themselves as they really are. Fourth, an element of conditioning takes place. Positive reinforcement of more adaptive behaviors occurs in even the most analytically neutral situations. Finally, interventions with a spouse, parents, or children do occur, particularly in psychotherapy, and provide opportunity for psychological growth to resume by interrupting pathologic vicious cycles.

McGlashan and Miller (1982) have identified 34 clusters of aims of psychoanalysis and psychoanalytic psychotherapy and assembled them into categories. The following discussion is based largely on their work, but with particular application to goals in the treatment of personality disorders. It should be stated, however, that these goals might more aptly be termed desirable outcomes because they are not usually made explicit at the outset of treatment.

Developmental Level

In the psychoanalytic view, the experience of the present is based on previously acquired attitudes. A favorable treatment outcome in the personality-disordered patient would depend on the appearance of qualities less typical of an immature period of life. Departing from the exclusive focus on childhood and adolescence, about 10 years ago, psychoanalysts began to study the normal developmental stages of adult life (Colarusso and Nemiroff 1981; Pollock 1980; Vaillant 1977), enriching the usefulness of development as a goal.

A goal that is particularly important with the eccentric or "odd" cluster (i.e., schizoid, schizotypal, and paranoid personality disorders) and with the avoidant personality is the establishment of the capacity to trust. With the borderline and narcissistic personality disorders, the completion of separation/individuation (Mahler et al. 1975) is often a central goal. Separation/individuation includes the capacity to differentiate self from others consistently, the ability to remain attached to others (or any aspect of the outer world) regardless of their immediate availability or despite their failure to gratify, the tolerance of aloneness, and the development of autonomy and a feeling that one can provide for oneself. This process also requires the resolution of the tendency for splitting, that is, learning in an affective way, by repetitious confrontation from the therapist, that the patient's exalted and depreciated experiences of the therapist are two aspects of the same person, as are the exalted and the depreciated experiences of the self.

Development includes the establishment of a superego that although capable of experiencing and bearing guilt, does so without excessive and disabling pain. This is especially relevant to the antisocial personality disorder at one extreme and the obsessive-compulsive personality disorder at the other. The developmental goal of healthy assertiveness is of special importance to the passive-aggressive, avoidant, and dependent personality disorders.

Aspects of the Self

Goals in this area have most to do with the dramatic, emotional, and erratic personality disorders (histrionic, narcissistic, antisocial, and borderline). These goals include the patient's accepting greater responsibility for his or her own actions and less responsibility for experiences realistically outside his or her control. A solid, cohesive self-sense, independent of external sources of confirmation, includes a sense of personal continuity over time regardless of place or mood. Successful treatment should also enable these personality-disordered patients to experience painful affects but retain core self-esteem.

Object Relations

Achieving more satisfactory contact with others and decreased withdrawal and preoccupation with unrealistic and private wishes and fantasies is often a goal of treatment of personality disorders, particularly so with schizoid, schizotypal, avoidant, paranoid, and narcissistic patients. Another goal is for the patient to develop a more realistic notion about his or her parents, with decreased but more appropriate intimacy. The ability to establish and keep extrafamilial friendships is an important goal to many therapists who work with personality-disordered patients. This often involves establishing or augmenting empathy and the capacity for intimacy.

Reality Acceptance

Optimal treatment means the attainment of a significant capacity to see one's life as it really is—with attenuated omnipotence and recognition of one's limitations in the case of narcissistic patients especially. This goal includes relinquishing demands for compensation for past suffering and establishing a capacity for gratitude, both very difficult for paranoid personality-disordered patients. A capacity to mourn is an essential ingredient of reality acceptance (Pollock 1961), as is the acceptance of the inevitability of frustration of drives and displeasure.

Fullness of Experience

This is a category of goals most applicable to the anxious or fearful personality disorders. Goals in this area are the ability to be in touch with one's feelings, the presence of energy and vitality, the ability for appropriate relaxation, and the capacity for pleasure and play. Energy put into maintaining rigid character defenses can be freed up for creative living with others, as well as one's self. For the gifted, scientific, and esthetic, creativity may become possible.

Coping Mechanisms

After successful therapy, defenses become less automatic and more flexible, adaptive, and varied. More mature defenses are employed, for example, sublimation and humor rather than projection or splitting (in the case of paranoid and borderline personality disorders). Successful treatment often results in the patient making adaptive changes in his or her environment.

Integrative Capacity

Goals particularly relevant to personality disorders are the ability to explore new sources of emotional enrichment, the tolerance of change (leading to a greater freedom to experience), and greater choice of responses and behaviors within a stable character structure.

Indications and Contraindications

When evaluation has indicated the presence of personality disorder, plans to proceed with psychoanalysis or dynamic psychotherapy should begin with a trial of treatment. Freud (1958) felt that only a trial of analysis could establish analyzability. Only relatively recently has dynamic psychotherapy for the aged (Nemiroff and Colarusso 1985; Pollock 1981) and the underprivileged (Lerner 1972) begun to be considered appropriate. Even repeated failures in previous attempts can yield to the therapist who combines a belief in his or her own capacity to effect change with a sense of positive regard for the patient. The technical recommendations of Kernberg and Kohut have made cases that seemed treatable by only the virtuoso a decade or two ago often within the range of the average well-trained therapist.

Certain contraindications remain clear, however. Therapists should not attempt to treat friends or relatives or other persons with whom they are in close professional or social proximity. An intense dislike of the patient by the potential therapist or of the therapist by the patient should be taken as a sign to avoid beginning treatment. Absence of motivation to change remains a very poor sign, as does motivation based solely on the attempt to meet the demand of a third party. A patient's total unwillingness to make any sacrifice (of money, time, or travel) on behalf of the treatment can also be considered a contraindication.

A modicum of "psychological-mindedness" is necessary for any form of psychoanalytically based therapy. Psychological-mindedness includes a capacity for introspection, a curiosity about one's own role in producing one's experience, an interest in how the past influences the present, and a belief that unconscious motives exist.

Which form of treatment to use for the personality-disordered patient—ranging from psychoanalysis to extended or brief psychoanalytic psychotherapy to supportive therapy based on psychoanalytic understanding—is always a difficult question. Psychoanalysis was thought to be a treatment for only "healthy neurotics" when it was characterized by a neutral analyst dedicated to interpretation of the patient's resistances without the use of any supportive measures. Those who see such a technical stance as unduly depriving and indeed noxious to many patients with personality disorders have suggested modifications that allow a treatment that closely resembles a classical approach (Kernberg 1984; Kohut 1971, 1977, 1984; Modell 1981). Often, despite new techniques, the lack of availability of time, money, or a trained analyst makes analysis impossible. Certainly, many patients with personality disorders are unsuitable for psychoanalysis proper because they cannot bear the affects generated. More often, treatment for these patients involves psychoanalytic psychotherapy in which some supportive measures are inculcated and solving of current problems is a conspicuous activity. The therapist is more active in eliciting material, in focusing on specific issues, and in providing soothing interventions.

Major Controversies

Support Versus Confrontation and Interpretation

Clinical tradition since Reich's work in the early 1930s (Reich 1949) has stressed the need to confront a personality-disordered patient with his or her behavior. The influence of Winnicott (1965) and Kohut (1971, 1977, 1984) has led to dynamic approaches that aim at repairing pre-oedipal developmental deficit rather than resolving conflict. Kernberg (1975) stands more on the side of confrontation—not so much with the aim of drive-defense conflict resolution, but rather to assist in the integration of split self and object representations and the abandonment of other primitive defenses. Differences stand out most sharply in the patient for whom Winnicott would provide a "holding environment" and whose idealization of the therapist Kohut would not interfere with initially. Kernberg might interpret the idealization as a defense against an underlying rage that must be acknowledged.

Combined Therapies

Once controversial, psychoanalytically oriented therapy combined with other therapy is more widely advocated by dynamic clinicians today. Pharmacotherapy or marital, group, or family therapy—particularly in the case of personality disorders—can be profitably combined with insight-oriented individual sessions, often in a synergistic fashion. Patients with personality disorders often necessitate combined or collaborative therapy with family members to ensure the protection of the individual therapy. Such combined approaches must be weighed carefully for possible enhancement of resistance. Combined therapy is sometimes best carried out by a collaboration of therapists rather than one clinician serving in both modalities.

Chapter 248

Behavior Therapy

Overview

Individuals with personality disorders are noted for unusual or maladaptive behaviors that adversely affect others. Although these individuals experience emotional pain at times, many aspects of their psychopathology are ego-syntonic and are viewed as the only possible response to an unforgiving world. Behavior therapy may be useful in modifying some maladaptive responses, including behaviors (e.g., aggressiveness and disturbances in complex social role functioning), cognitive beliefs, and affects (including anger). Because learning theory forms the basis for behavior therapy, this approach may be especially useful for individuals with histories of learning difficulties or deficits in social skills due to poor social role models.

The roots of behavior therapy can be traced back many centuries. For example, Pliny the Elder devised an aversive treatment for alcoholism in the first century B.C. (quoted in Franks 1963). However, most of the developments in behavior therapy have occurred since the term was first coined (Skinner and Lindsley 1954) and Wolpe (1958) popularized systematic desensitization. Recently, clinical behavior therapy has advanced the treatment of mental retardation, social skills deficits in patients with chronic psychoses, conduct disorders, impulse disorders, phobias, other anxiety disorders, and depression. In addition, there has been a laudable emphasis on the development of treatment techniques and assessment methods. Although there has been extensive work in these areas, however, the literature on the treatment of adult personality disorders is not extensive. A relevant exception is the rich literature on the behavioral treatment of juvenile delinquency (Burchard and Lane 1982).

Specialized terms and techniques that are frequently cited in this review are briefly defined in this section. A more complete description of behavior therapy is available in the basic behavioral textbooks (Ayllon et al. 1968; Bandura 1969; Wolpe 1979).

Assertiveness training involves teaching persons the skills to express ideas and both positive and negative feelings toward other people in a way that is socially acceptable and does not invite punishment. It involves some specific procedures such as modeling, cuing, prompting, and behavioral rehearsal. Attention is also paid to nonverbal aspects of communication. The efficacy of the individual's behavior is then shaped and reinforced by immediate feedback.

Behavioral analysis is a process of assessing the stimulus-response relationships in a maladaptive behavior pattern. Emphasis is placed on identifying both specific antecedent conditions to the patient's symptoms or maladaptive responses and the ensuing consequences. Treatment techniques are selected to modify the identified stimulus-response pattern. Behavioral analysis is an ongoing process, and treatment may be modified as new information becomes available, including the patient's response to treatment.

Extinction involves removing the reinforcing consequences of a maladaptive behavior in order to decrease its occurrence.

Operant techniques are based on the assumption that behavior is influenced by its consequences. Sometimes the environment rewards or punishes an individual's behavior and other times the environment ignores it (i.e., extinction). Operant techniques modify the consequences after a behavior occurs. These techniques may involve shaping new responses by successive approximation and reinforcement until the desired response is established. Contingency contracting may be employed to reinforce new or infrequent responses by specifying a relationship between the patient's desired responses and consequent rewards and penalties. Contingency contracting may be used in inpatient settings (e.g., a contract to modify disruptive or self-destructive behavior) or in family or residential settings.

Punishment is the presentation of an aversive stimulus that decreases the probability of an undesirable response occurring. The stimulus must be carefully chosen, generally with the patient's agreement, and utilized in line with ethical considerations. Punishment is never the sole method employed in behavior therapy, because the patient must also be taught more adaptive ways to cope.

Relaxation training involves the use of deep muscle relaxation to induce a physiologic state that lowers anxiety and tension. Such training may be supplemented by imaginal techniques (such as the recall of pleasant scenes) to prolong the period of relaxation. Relaxation training is often used in the initial treatment of anxiety-related disorders.

Social skills training refers to techniques of teaching patients basic coping skills. It is an operant procedure in which adaptive behavior patterns are shaped and then reinforced after they occur. Activities of daily living skills, vocational interaction, and interpersonal communication (both verbal and nonverbal) may all be influenced through one-to-one or group approaches that utilize discussion, modeling, behavioral rehearsal, role playing, feedback, and reinforcement. An extensive behavioral literature on these techniques is available (L'Abate and Milan 1985).

Systematic desensitization is a procedure to decrease a stimulus configuration's aversive properties resulting from past learning. The procedure pairs an incompatible physiologic response (relaxation) with the previously learned response (anxiety). Desensitization to phobic and anxiety-producing situations is attained by constructing a hierarchy of pertinent scenes graded from least to most anxiety-provoking. After learning deep muscle relaxation, the patient is presented with the least anxiety-provoking scene or stimulus situation while in the relaxed state. This procedure is systematically repeated for increasingly anxiety-provoking stimuli until the patient reports no anxiety in response to any of the scenes or situations in the hierarchy. The procedure can be done using visual imagery (i.e., imaginal) or real-life situations (i.e., in vivo).

Nature and Quality of the Available Evidence

Reports of several studies indicate that behavioral techniques can be successful with personality disorders. A well-controlled study (Sloan and Staples 1975) established that short-term behavior therapy is as effective as dynamic therapy and more effective than no treatment for outpatients with neurotic or personality disorders. Highly experienced therapists administered both treatments. Patients with Minnesota Multiphasic Personality Inventory (MMPI) profiles suggesting tendencies to act out did less well in dynamic psychotherapy, and patients for whom the MMPI suggested more severe psychopathology or more behavioral acting out problems did better with behavior therapy. In an uncontrolled study, Dahl and Merskey (1981) reported that behavior therapy may be successful in enabling recently discharged inpatients with personality disorders to live independently in the community for at least three months.

There are a number of reasons for the dearth of efficacy studies of behavior therapy for personality disorders. First, personality-disordered patients are hard to treat and study. They are not usually motivated to change and often resent being asked to consider it, often fail to comply with treatment or follow-up, and subvert behavioral contracts by refusing to practice newly learned skills, to complete homework, and to attend sessions. Their lives are filled with intervening crises, whether self-caused or fateful, that necessitate attention and interrupt treatment. These problems may be exacerbated when clinicians overlook Axis I syndromes that are amenable to pharmacologic treatment but interfere with learning new behavior when untreated. Finally, patients with personality disorders tend to drop out of treatment after crises resolve, whatever the type of treatment.

Second, psychopathology of personality disorders is seldom focal and discrete, but rather is usually complex, multifocal, and interwoven into multiple aspects of the patient's life. This makes it difficult to isolate maladaptive behaviors and attitudes, much less design contingencies to alter them. Unassertive behavior, for example, can be due to poor learning, a wish to remain passive, a wish to force others to act on one's behalf, a reaction to the expectation of punishment for asserting oneself, a wish not to change, or opposition to the therapist's wish for results. All of these factors may operate, especially in the passive-aggressive or masochistic patient, making behavioral analysis complicated and treatment difficult (Perry and Flannery 1982).

Third, behavior therapists have shown more interest in target behaviors and symptoms than in psychiatric diagnosis although it would be most advantageous to use both. This tendency makes it difficult to generalize from studies in the behavioral literature to the treatment of personality disorders.

Finally, with exceptions (Hersen 1979), behavior therapists have not—until recently—studied patients' resistance in treatment to the same degree as have dynamically oriented therapists (Wachtel 1982). This is a major area for potential development as behavioral therapists attempt to elucidate what maintains resistance and as techniques are modified and tested for the treatment of personality disorders.

Usual Duration and Frequency of Visits

The duration of behavior therapy is variable. For focal anxiety problems, treatments may average between three and nine months of weekly outpatient visits. However, it is likely that personality disorders would require longer treatment, because they involve complex, multifocal problems. Most therapists schedule weekly sessions, but then decrease the frequency of visits as termination nears. This practice also diminishes the patient's dependency on the therapist's reinforcing qualities while the patient develops other sources of reinforcement. Final sessions involve a review of the treatment goals, interventions, and outcome. Emphasis is placed on helping the patient understand how newly acquired skills might continue to generalize to other life problems.

Inpatient behavior therapy usually involves programs, such as token economies or contingency contracts, that are in effect 24 hours daily for the duration of hospitalization. Also, individual and group treatment sessions usually occur two to five times weekly, focusing on specific problems. Each patient's individual treatment program is administered on a daily basis and modified weekly or sooner, as needed. Hospitalization may continue several weeks or months, depending on the problem and hospital setting.

Target Behaviors, Treatment Techniques, and Outcome

The treatment studies reviewed here were chosen for their probable applicability to personality disorders because psychiatric diagnoses were frequently unspecified. Both controlled and uncontrolled studies and case reports are included.

The techniques in the treatments reviewed here are those commonly used in behavior therapy, that is, relaxation training (Wolpe 1979), imagery techniques (Cautela 1979), modeling (Bandura 1969), token economies and contingency contracting (Allyon and Azrin 1968), and assertiveness training (Wolpe 1979). Cognitive-behavioral approaches (Meichenbaum 1977) have largely not been studied in this population.

Antisocial and Delinquent Behaviors

Antisocial, delinquent, impulsive, and undersocialized individuals have received extensive attention. These studies typically involve incarcerated, juvenile males, rather than subjects who are noninstitutionalized, adult, or female. This may limit generalizability.

In extensive reviews of controlled trials, Shamsie (1981) and Burchard and Lane (1982) concluded that conventional case work, individual psychotherapy, group counseling, and family therapy have less than promising results in the treatment of delinquent behaviors (e.g., truancy, stealing, aggressiveness, crimes against persons). In contrast, behavior modification techniques, such as contingency contracting, may modify specific target behaviors, such as academic behaviors and cooperative task behaviors. These techniques render juveniles with conduct disorders easier to handle in both institutional and home settings. Unfortunately, the evidence does not suggest that these improvements generalize to preventing recidivism for legal offenses.

Outpatient behavioral interventions with intact families of young first offenders show promise when communication and negotiation skills are emphasized along with contingency contracting. This suggests the importance of working in the "normal" environment rather than in group settings that may socialize patients into further antisocial behaviors. In contrast, older adolescent offenders do better with shorter term, contingency contracting programs, initiated at times of crises or arrests, that focus on employment-related behaviors (Burchard and Lane 1982).

Henderson (1981) treated stealing in motivated children and adolescents. He employed self-control procedures (relaxation and practice imagining not stealing) and external contingency controls with individualized reinforcers administered by parents. Although not controlled, the treatment was highly successful on two-year follow-up (20 percent relapse).

Ollendick et al. (1980) found that incarcerated juvenile offenders scoring high on external locus of control responded less well to token economies and flexible behavioral contracting, perhaps because they attributed contingencies such as stealing and getting apprehended to luck rather than to something for which they could accept personal responsibility. This finding suggests that behavioral techniques for specific problems may sometimes need to be adapted depending on certain characteristics of the patients. It also implies a role for techniques such as cognitive restructuring to deal with problems in self-attribution of success and failure.

Marshall (1973) treated problematic sexual behaviors in adult sexual offenders using a combination of techniques. He employed aversion therapy by pairing electrical shocks with slides presenting relevant aspects of the offending behaviors (fetishes, rape, pedophilia) to decrease the aberrant sexual fantasies. He then had subjects use orgasmic reconditioning (i.e., viewing appropriate sexual stimuli while masturbating) to enable them to develop heterosexual fantasies. A 75 percent rate of complete cessation of deviant behavior was maintained on short-term follow-up. Hayes et al. (1978) employed self-administered covert sensitization with an antisocial adult with sadistic and exhibitionistic sexual problems. After imagining one of the deviant scenes, the subject would immediately imagine an aversive scene as a consequence. Treatment reportedly led to rapid and sustained reduction in both physiologic and self-reported levels of arousal to the deviant fantasies. Heterosexual functioning remained intact.

Self-Destructive Impulsive Behavior

Rosen and Thomas (1984) devised a substitute behavior for chronic wrist cutting and taught it to three women with borderline personality disorder. The authors began with the assumption that the pain induced by wrist cutting has some negatively reinforcing properties in these patients (i.e., the physical pain causes something more aversive, such as emotional suffering, to diminish) and had the patients exercise beyond the point of inducing ischemic muscle pain (e.g, by squeezing a rubber ball) whenever they felt like cutting themselves. On follow-up, all three remained free of wrist cutting. If the results are replicated, such an innovative approach should prove very helpful for this difficult problem.

Liberman and Eckman (1981) compared behavior therapy and dynamic therapy for the inpatient treatment of repeated suicide attempters. The behavior therapy consisted of an intensive eight-day combination of individual and group approaches to social skills training, anxiety management (relaxation and imagery), and contingency contracting with family members to improve family relationships. On 36-week follow-up, both treatment groups remained less depressed and suicidal than prior to hospitalization. There was a trend for the behavior therapy patients to show more improvement than the other group on most measures, including having full-time employment.

Linehan (1987) developed a manualized treatment for suicidal and parasuicidal patients, most commonly diagnosed with borderline personality disorder. The treatment, called dialectical behavior therapy, requires both individual and group treatment formats. The group is psychoeducational and teaches interpersonal, distress tolerance, and self-management skills. The individual sessions focus on target behaviors, with behaviors earlier in the hierarchy taking precedence over later ones, whenever they recur. These include 1) suicidal behaviors, 2) behaviors interfering with the conduct of therapy, 3) escape behaviors interfering with a reasonable life (e.g., impulsive drinking), 4) behavioral skill acquisition (emotion regulation, interpersonal effectiveness, distress tolerance, self-management), and 5) other goals the patient wishes to focus on. The results of a controlled treatment trial are pending as of this writing.

Basic Social Skills

There is extensive literature on social skills training reviewed elsewhere (Brady 1984; L'Abate and Milan 1985), although a limited number of studies directly apply to personality disorders. Marzillier et al. (1976) compared systematic desensitization and social skills training in socially anxious outpatients who had personality disorders or neuroses. Social skills training, which employed role playing and feedback, was the only treatment that had a beneficial effect on the range and frequency of patients' social contacts at the termination of treatment. Gains were generally maintained at six-month follow-up. Neither treatment reduced social anxiety, however.

To treat adolescent offenders, Spence and Marzillier (1979) employed a social skills training package, which included instructions, modeling, role playing, video-taped feedback, and social reinforcement. They were generally effective in helping subjects increase eye contact and decrease fidgeting during conversation, but somewhat less successful in increasing conversational aids such as acknowledgments, head movements, and questioning. In a subsequent study, Spence and Marzillier (1981) found similar results but concluded that there was little positive effect on more complex social skills, social problems, friendliness, social anxiety, or employability. The authors suggested that this technique is best used in conjunction with other treatments for adolescent offenders.

Franco et al. (1983) reported on an adolescent with severe social impairment and friendlessness because of extreme shyness. They used social skills training that targeted four components of social conversations: asking questions, reinforcing and acknowledging the partner's comments, making good eye contact, and expressing affect and warmth. A multiple baseline assessment of each component demonstrated success over 15 weeks of twice weekly sessions. Follow-up at 16 months revealed much improvement in peer relationships and friendships.

Complex Social Skills

Jones et al. (1977) worked with psychiatric inpatients in the military diagnosed as having behavior or character disorders. In a randomized design, half were discharged back to active service (standard procedure) and half were treated in a special open ward program for 16 weeks. The program involved contingency contracting that targeted specific behaviors, such as managing cooperative work tasks. Inappropriate behaviors, such as argumentativeness, were extinguished or punished. Reinforcers included increased privileges and recreation. At 11-month follow-up, positive outcomes were significantly more common in the treated group than in the control group (80 percent versus 52 percent). Control patients were more likely to have deserted or to have been incarcerated or discharged for undesirable reasons.

Smith et al. (1979) used a behavioral program targeted to improve skills in interpersonal relations, money management, and leisure time activities for inmates on work release from a penitentiary. All procedures were carried out in group settings. Smith et al. presented didactic material (which included practical advice and guidelines) covering each area and then asked subjects to discuss individual examples. Also, for one group, project staff gave the subjects' significant others from the community advice on how to help the subjects with the targeted skills. Treated persons improved more on target behaviors than nontreated control subjects, but no advantage was gained by including significant others as an adjunct to treatment. There was no community follow-up after release.

In a psychodynamically oriented inpatient setting for nonaggressive antisocial adults, Gralnick (1976) employed a system of task groups requiring progressively sophisticated interpersonal skills. By working with other patients and staff, the subjects were progressively socialized into useful behavior, cooperativeness, and the value system of the ward. Progression through the task groups led to increases in privileges and greater freedom, and reversion to antisocial behavior resulted in loss of privileges. The treatment was not systematically evaluated. This article demonstrates that applying social learning principles to help antisocial adults learn complex prosocial behaviors is compatible with a psychodynamically oriented inpatient setting.

Dahl and Merskey (1981) employed an operant behavioral program with involuntarily committed inpatients with personality disorders. Patient and therapist set specific personal, vocational, and educational goals; frequent feedback was given, and successful performance resulted in more rewards and progression through successive stages of the program. Breaking rules was punished by return to a lower stage. Some aspects of the plan (especially performance feedback) were continued after discharge into the community. Seventy-five percent of the patients were living independently at three-month follow-up.

Turkat and Carlson (1984) demonstrated the importance of a data-based case formulation in the behavioral treatment of an outpatient with dependent personality. Pervious behavioral treatment that was directed solely at the presenting symptoms had failed. Formulating that the patient's central problem was due to anxiety over independent decision making led to constructing a relevant hierarchy of behavioral rehearsals and assignments to improve independence skills. The authors' data-based behavioral analysis is compatible with a dynamic formulation, although the former also has specific implications for social learning.

Managing Affects and Expressing Oneself

As noted by Fehrenbach and Thelen (1982), three studies have demonstrated improvement in aggressive outbursts among nonpsychotic aggressive adults (Foy et al. 1975; Frederiksen et al. 1976) and college students (Fehrenbach and Thelen 1981). Combinations of focused directions, assertiveness training, modeling appropriate responses, behavioral rehearsal, and role playing were used. Treatment resulted in a decrease in aggressive behavior and an increase in more adaptive assertive responses. Rahim et al. (1980) decreased aggressiveness in an adult by showing videotaped examples of modeled, appropriate assertive responses, in addition to employing instructions, relaxation exercises, behavioral rehearsal, and feedback.

Novaco (1979) devised a stress inoculation approach focusing on the cognitive components and concomitant physiologic arousal that precede aggression. As a first step, subjects are encouraged to determine (i.e., learn to discriminate) whether circumstances have aroused justified or unnecessary anger. Second, modeling and rehearsal of appropriate expressive skills are used. These skills are then practiced by imaginal rehearsal (i.e., imagining the appropriate response) and interactive role playing. The author referred to unpublished studies upholding the efficacy of this approach for adolescents and adults with problems controlling anger.

Conclusions Based on the Literature

Based on the literature and our clinical experience, we offer the following tentative ideas regarding the efficacy of behavior therapy techniques for the treatment of personality disorders.

1. Some behaviors in personality disorders can be modified with lasting results.
2. Sometimes behavior changes as a result of treatment without a corresponding change in attitudes or beliefs.
3. A given treatment may not be effective for different target behaviors, or for the same target behavior in different individuals.
4. The best results are obtained when a treatment program is individually tailored and patient and therapist agree on a specific contract (Barlow 1980; Hersen 1979)— not when the same treatment package is used with all patients having a given diagnosis.
5. Some techniques found effective with chronic patients and the mentally retarded have proven efficacious with personality-disordered patients. These techniques include using instructions, modeling, rehearsal, feedback, and contingency contracting.
6. Techniques that employ imagery (e.g., systematic desensitization) are not well studied in this diagnostic group. Comparative data suggest the superiority of operant techniques (Marzillier et al. 1976). It may be that personality-disordered individuals have short attention spans (e.g., Andrulonis et al. 1981) and learn better from actions than from imagery.
7. Most of the research derives from institutional settings where external controls and rewards are easily administered. Institutionalized patients or inmates may also have additional incentives to cooperate with treatment programs. There is less evidence demonstrating the efficacy of behavior therapy with outpatients.
8. Inadequate attention has been paid to the problem of generalizing treatment effects to naturalistic settings, and to treatment modifications that might facilitate this. More follow-up evaluations of treatment effects are necessary.
9. Most researchers report some nonresponders who appear unmotivated to change. The issue of treatment resistance is especially important in the treatment of personality disorders.

Treatment Recommendations for Personality Disorders

The following specific techniques and considerations may be employed in the behavioral treatment of an individual with a personality disorder.

1. A thorough diagnostic evaluation should be conducted initially to identify major psychiatric syndromes or medical conditions (e.g., hyperthyroidism and hypoglycemia) requiring separate treatment. Failure to address other conditions may impede behavioral treatment. Untreated anxiety disorder, for example, disrupts learning in the treatment of passive-aggressive personality disorder (Perry and Flannery 1982). Furthermore, certain personality disorders are often associated with major Axis I syndromes, for example, antisocial personality disorder with alcoholism (Lewis et al. 1983) and borderline personality disorder with depression (Gunderson and Elliott 1985; Perry 1985).
2. The therapist should use behavioral analysis to identify specific behaviors targeted for treatment rather than more general personality traits.
3. Whenever possible, the therapist should gather data and treat clinical cases employing an ABA design (Barlow 1980): efficacy is best determined when there are measures of the frequency of target behaviors at baseline (A), during the active treatment phase (B), and at follow-up (A).

4. The therapist should give instructions for socially adaptive responses that are consistent with the patient's ethics and culture (Flannery and Marlow 1978). It is best to work on tangible operants (new behaviors and situations) rather than to employ imagery techniques (such as systematic desensitization) alone.

5. The therapist should break the tasks into manageable components and shape the patient's responses by successive approximations until the final goal behavior is attained. Then the therapist should emphasize gradual change and match the task to the patient's motivational level.

6. Relaxation training or hard exercise should be employed for a patient with high levels of affective arousal (e.g., chronic anxiety or impulsive anger states) that disrupt learning self-control. Stress management programs are an additional effective way to address this problem (Flannery 1986).

7. Modeling, behavioral rehearsal, and role playing should be used to shape socially adaptive behaviors. Assertiveness training is usually too complex for the neophyte patient but can be added later on.

8. Disruptive or socially maladaptive behaviors (e.g., stealing) should be dealt with through contingency contracting that employs extinction of maladaptive responses and differential reinforcement of new or existing adaptive behaviors. When concrete rewards are not available, reinforcement can be given following the Premack principle. New, infrequent behavior can be reinforced by letting the patient engage in more familiar and frequent behavior following the new behavior. When extinction procedures fail, punishment of maladaptive behaviors may be employed. The type of punishment should be chosen following ethical and practical guidelines, generally with the patient's overall approval.

9. Homework between sessions, especially in vivo practice, facilitates learning and generalization to the patient's natural environment.

10. Liberal feedback on performance should be used to shape and reinforce new learning.

11. The therapist should continually evaluate the patient's attitudinal changes, including resistance. It is important to facilitate cognitive change as the therapy proceeds, because adaptive changes in attitude may help maintain newly learned behaviors.

12. The frequency of sessions should be determined by the requirements of the case. If disruptive behavior is severe, as with a behaviorally regressed borderline, histrionic, or antisocial inpatient, daily attention to administering and modifying treatment contingencies may be required. As self-control and disruptive behaviors (e.g, wrist cutting or temper tantrums) improve, the frequency of sessions can be decreased. In general, enough time should lapse between sessions to allow adequate opportunity for homework and for practicing new behaviors.

Special Problems and Controversies

Patient Resistance

In behavior therapies as in psychodynamically oriented treatments, progress may halt because of the development of patient resistance (i.e., the patient either stops cooperating or actively obstructs treatment). Resistance can occur without evidence of an inadequate or faulty behavioral analysis or treatment intervention. This may result in premature termination and poorer outcomes (Chamberlain et al. 1984).

Treatment resistance is of central importance in personality disorders. Maladaptive beliefs (e.g., powerlessness) and a sense of that others and not oneself should change are common and lead to negative (transference) feelings toward the therapist and resistance to progress. These issues may be exacerbated if the therapist has not initially negotiated a realistic behavioral contract with the patient (Hersen 1979).

Resistance may also occur when a patient's target symptom is exerting a protective effect in some area of life (Hafner 1981). Less common but more problematic sources of resistance are covert or overt wishes to subvert the treatment, especially common in patients with many areas of resentment, such as patients with passive-aggressive personality disorder (Perry and Flannery 1982). In such cases, the therapist will need to deal with the resistance for the treatment to survive. Certain authors have begun integrating psychodynamic and behavioral approaches in addressing this problem (Papajohn 1982; Wachtel 1977, 1980).

The following is a list of suggestions for managing resistance:

1. As part of the behavioral analysis or contract, the therapist should inquire about fears of change or pessimism about the effects of change. The patient may, for example, feel overburdened by current problems and experience attempts to change as adding to this burden. Numerous real-life problems may intervene (e.g., new debts, job change, or family illness), requiring attention while temporarily suspending the treatment plan. There may be factors preventing the patient from changing, such as a punishing spouse or boss (Perry and Flannery 1982). Finally, the patient may not be motivated to carry out the treatment program. Termination would then be appropriate.

2. Employing stress management techniques (e.g., the removal of excessive stimulants and depressants, relaxation training) early in treatment may alleviate dysphoric levels of physiologic and emotional arousal that heighten the development of resistance (Flannery 1986). Early success in helping the patient feel better strengthens the working alliance. The therapist may then continue the treatment, although switching to less interpersonally complex tasks than were initially negotiated.

3. The therapist should explore any active resistance. Whenever fear of change, growth, or giving up dependent behaviors is operative, discussion of the positive results of change may help. Sometimes it is important to confront or interpret resistance in the same manner as in psychodynamically oriented therapy. This requires that the therapist identify the meaning and associated affect of the resistance and discuss it with the patient.

4. Whenever maladaptive beliefs are a salient part of the resistance, a switch to a cognitive-behavioral approach may help.

5. If the patient is invested in continuing despite resistance, the therapist may consider adding therapeutic manipulations such as using the patient's wish for a therapeutic relationship as an incentive or reward. An example is cutting the length of sessions during periods of noncompliance with homework, but then restoring the original length when compliance improves. Therapeutic manipulation, however, should be carried out only with exquisite attention to its potential negative effects on the patient.

6. When resistance is severe, especially if accompanied by self-destructive behavior, the therapist should consider an inpatient admission allowing greater external control over contingencies. This is especially true with behaviorally regressed patients with borderline personality disorder.

7. Finally, if resistance continues, the therapist may use an option to terminate as an

incentive or as an ultimate limit. Either the patient begins to cooperate in a treatment plan or the therapist terminates.

Choice of Treatment

There is little evidence at present to help the clinician determine whether behavior therapy is the treatment of choice for a given type of personality disorder. Patients who are impulsive, action oriented, and easily overwhelmed by their emotional responses may do well initially in behavior therapy. This evidence, however, is limited to short-term treatment (Sloan et al. 1975). Until there are more studies of the differential efficacy of behavior and other therapies, the clinician must be guided by other factors. These include the patient's previous response to treatment and preference for treatment modality and the clinician's expertise with both the type of patient and the treatment modality.

Experienced behavior therapists would certainly maintain that behavior therapy is a comprehensive and sufficient treatment approach for many personality disorders. However, people are complex, behavior has multiple determinants, and there is no reason to view behavior therapy as exclusive of other approaches. Rather, the clinician should decide whether the addition of another approach (e.g., medications or dynamic therapy) would be of added benefit to the patient.

Ethics of Punishment

The use of punishment procedures in behavior therapy has some controversial aspects. Most of the ethical questions about punishment occur in involuntary settings like prison or locked wards, but few problems arise in the treatment of outpatients.

The use of punishment should follow general behavioral and ethical guidelines. Punishment should be used only to eliminate undesirable behaviors when other procedures, such as extinction, do not work. The negative consequences of allowing the target behavior to continue should outweigh the negative aspects of using punishment. The patient should agree to the overall treatment plan, if informed consent is possible. If informed consent is not possible, there should be some safeguard of the patient's interest, like monitoring of the overall treatment by a third party (e.g., parent or patient advocate). Finally, punishment should only be continued if it proves effective.

Conclusion

Behavior therapy has not been utilized in the treatment of personality disorders as much as its potential warrants. The basic behavioral treatments outlined here, including special attention to the problem of resistance, may facilitate better treatment outcomes. Persons thoroughly trained in behavioral analysis and therapy techniques and fully versed in psychodynamic approaches are perhaps best qualified to meet the unique needs of patients with personality disorders.

Chapter 249

Family and Couples Therapy

Personality traits are the individual's characteristic ways of being in his or her interpersonal world. Family theorists and therapists are concerned with the degree to which these traits become disorders within interpersonal contexts. From this perspective, interpersonal aspects of personality disorders are considered as they contribute to, sustain, or interfere with the expression of the individual's personality (Voth and Orth 1973).

In this chapter, we will provide some background and then review the interpersonal approaches that are available in contemporary psychiatric practice to respond to the needs of patients with personality disorders. This task is made more complicated because much of the clinical literature of systems theory does not use the language of individual diagnosis, so the relevance to individual diagnosis must be inferred. Systems thinkers who do use individual diagnostic terms have focused on schizophrenia or more specific symptom pictures like asthma or anorexia. It is only relatively recently that these concepts have been applied to the various personality disorders.

Background

Early exploration of the family context of personality disorder came through the investigations of Johnson and Szurek (Johnson 1948; Johnson and Szurek 1952). Using the modality of collaborative treatment of parent and child in cases of antisocial personality, these investigators described the manner in which unconscious conflict within parents leads to unwitting sanctioning of antisocial behavior in their children. Johnson and Szurek avoided the larger context of family relationships as well as the reasons for the child's collaboration with unconscious parental pressures, emphasizing the power of the parents over the relatively helpless child. Nonetheless, these dyadic formulations led to an increasingly coherent view of the unconscious interactive pressures that contribute to symptomatic behavior.

Dicks (1967), in his studies of marital interaction, and Ackerman (1966), in his family studies, began to unravel the detailed dynamics of interpersonal conflict and the ways in which intrapsychic conflict is stabilized in relationships. These investigations, as well as those of Lidz et al. (1965) and Wynne et al. (1958), marked the beginning of the psychoanalytic study of family interaction and led the way to much subsequent investigation.

In his early work at National Institute of Mental Health, Bowen (1978) described the manner in which marital partners of relatively equivalent degrees of immaturity and self-differentiation tend to be attracted to each other. He suggested that partners tend to choose people with opposite or complementary patterns of defensive organization, in particular, what he called "overadequacy" and "underadequacy." This idea has been elaborated to suggest that marital partners choose an object who will complement and reinforce certain unconscious assumptions and fantasies.

The central questions in this process are: What mechanisms do individuals use to involve each other in complementary behaviors? How does internal conflict get externalized in relationships? What is the link between the intrapsychic and the interpersonal? To understand this dynamic, therapists have relied on the concept of projective identification, initially described by Klein (1946) as an intrapsychic phenomenon, but now used to define an "interpersonal defense," created in a relationship between people.

Projective identification involves the dissociation of uncomfortable aspects of the personality (elements of impulse, self-image, or superego) and the projection of them onto another person, resulting in an identification with the other person because of having attributed qualities of the self to him or her. Included in this intrapsychic and interpersonal mechanism is the unconscious attempt to evoke in the other person feelings or behaviors that conform with the projection. Also, the recipient of the projection must be willing (consciously or not) to accept these attributes as part of himself or herself. The person using this defense is selectively inattentive to the real aspects of the other that may contradict or invalidate the projection. In addition, the other (now seen as possessing the disavowed characteristics) is consciously identified as unlike the self, while an unconscious relationship in which the projected attributes can be vicariously experienced is sustained. This defense differs from projection in that the individual maintains some contact with that which is projected. The projections are not simply placed onto another; an unconscious attempt is made to develop a relationship with the other and to involve him or her as a collusive partner in conforming to the way in which he or she is perceived (E. Shapiro 1978a; Zinner and R. Shapiro 1972).

This notion of a collusive partner begins to address the manner in which this defense is mutual and not unidirectional. Each participant in an intimate relationship in which projective identification is used is involved in a system of complementarity. Willi (1982) suggested that collusion takes place when partners with similar unconscious conflicts unwittingly work out a system in which one partner regressively acts out the conflict and the other uses reaction formation or other forms of denial and "adult facade" formation. He described four pathologic patterns: narcissistic (grandiosity and devaluation versus inferiority and idealization), oral (being nurturing and critical versus being nurtured and ungrateful), anal (autonomous and tyrannical versus passive and negligent), and phallic (assertive and impotent versus confirming and contemptuous). Though Willi regularly saw these four patterns in his outpatient couples, there are many other subtle forms of complementary projective identification that serve to stabilize and destabilize various types of personality functioning.

To the extent that these patterns represent relatively fixed aspects of behavior, they are perceived as personality traits or disorders in an individual. However, these patterns may be relationship specific in that the individual may demonstrate a more varied and healthier personality style in other relationships. Treatment is indicated for troubled relationships in which complementarity leads to stereotyping, lack of flexibility and depth, and a general impoverishment of emotional life.

For example, in the case described by Zinner (1976), Mr. and Mrs. A come for an evaluation because of Mr. A's complaint that his wife is too passive and Mrs. A's complaint that her husband is unnecessarily aggressive. This stereotyped relationship is manifest in their marriage conflict, but other relationships appear to be more flexible for each of them. On individual evaluation, Mr. A is found to have passive as well as aggressive and assertive aspects to his personality. His major conflict, however, involves his anxiety about passive longings. Mrs. A is found to have both aggressive and passive aspects to her personality, but her major conflict is in relation to her guilt about her aggressive strivings. This couple manages intrapsychic conflicts through a shared and complementary use of projective identification. Mr. A projects his passivity into his wife, hates her for it, and behaves in such a way as to evoke it in her. Thus, he rids himself of conscious awareness of an area of conflict within himself and, through an unconscious identification with his wife's behavior, maintains contact with this conflicted area of his own personality. Similarly, Mrs. A projects and provokes aggressivity in her husband, maintaining an unconscious contact with her own denied and conflicted aggression. Though each partner is individually complex, within the relationship each appears one-sided in relation to conflicted issues. One consequence of such a complementary, defensive marital system is that although individual treatment might lead to improvement in one of the partners, it might result in increased symptomatology in the other. If, for example, Mrs. A were treated for her guilt about her aggression, she might become more assertive in the couple's sexual relationship. Such a change would put Mr. A in the passive role, possibly leading to anxiety and impotence.

Such mobilization and stabilization of intrapsychic conflicts in an intimate relationship over time can lead to the marital conflicts that lend themselves to conjoint treatment. Such issues can become even more complexly structured when children are added to the family group.

R. Shapiro and his collaborators have suggested that in families of adolescents with character pathology, the family as a group develops shared, unconscious assumptions about developmental issues and that these assumptions contribute to an environment in which openness, collaboration, change, and flexibility are unacceptable (E. Shapiro 1982a, 1982b; R. Shapiro 1978; R. Shapiro and Zinner 1971). For example, there is clinical evidence that in families with antisocial adolescents, the family group develops shared assumptions about the meaning of impulse and restraint. Through the use of projective identification, the adolescent may come to represent impulsivity (with his or her own capacity for judgment repudiated and projected), and the parents may be experienced (and experience themselves) as only judgmental, denying their own impulsive wishes (Zinner and R. Shapiro 1974). In such a family, antisocial behavior can be understood as a product of family interaction, and family intervention is required to interrupt the behavior because, the family group acts as if integration of impulse and restraint within each member (i.e., intrapsychically) is impossible.

Families with borderline adolescents are said to demonstrate group phenomena in which aggression is unintegrated and projected. These families develop shared fantasies in which autonomous moves are experienced as hateful repudiations of the family and dependent wishes are experienced as draining demands (E. Shapiro et al. 1975). These projections result in an atmosphere in which the separating adolescent cannot obtain support for autonomous or dependent behaviors and, in an aggressively charged family atmosphere, cannot easily proceed with his or her affective development. In these families, the splitting characteristically observed in the borderline individual may be utilized as a shared family defense and inhibit the possibility of a more flexible integration of conflicting perceptions (Levy and Brown 1981; Schwoeri and Schwoeri 1980; Zinner and E. Shapiro 1975).

In families with narcissistic adolescents, the adolescent separation may be presented by the child and experienced by the parents as a narcissistic injury and threat to self-esteem (Berkowitz et al. 1974a, 1974b). In such an environment, family members attempt to restore narcissistic equilibrium by projecting disowned, negative valuations of themselves. An unsteady peace may be sustained in the family at the price of an intense dependency on each other and an inability on the part of individuals to integrate aspects of narcissistic grandeur and helpless, dependent inferiority into a cohesive sense of self.

Such narcissistic projections can create an atmosphere of "pathological certainty" in the family (E. Shapiro 1982b), meaning that family members are unquestioning about their interpretations of each other. In such an environment, an adolescent may sustain a more schizoid withdrawal in order to protect his or her inner core of identity.

Therapy

The literature on family and couples therapy for personality disorder is limited. In part, this limitation is due to the fact that many who write about these therapies do not accept or utilize standard diagnostic categories (see Skynner 1976). Even among authors who do combine a family focus with individual diagnosis, most present single case studies or clinical vignettes to illustrate concepts or techniques (Fine 1973; Framo 1970; Levy and Brown 1980; Schwoeri and Schwoeri 1981; E. Shapiro 1982a; E. Shapiro et al. 1977; Zinner 1978). Such selected case material has the obvious drawbacks of small sample size and clinician bias.

The literature on the effectiveness of family and couples therapy is even more limited. Minuchin and his collaborators (1978) made impressive claims for the family treatment of anorexia, and there are anecdotal illustrations of the process of change in the family treatment of borderline adolescents and of symptomatic obsessive children (Dalton 1983; E. Shapiro 1978a, 1982a). Systematic controlled studies of outcome in family or couples therapy for personality disorder have not yet been conducted.

In a review of outcome studies for couples and family therapy for all disorders, Gurman and Kniskern (1981) drew the following conclusions relevant to personality disorders:

1. The existing evidence from controlled studies of nonbehavioral marital and family therapies suggests that such treatments are often effective beyond chance. Summarizing all studies of couples and family therapy producing such information (including behavioral interventions), Gurman and Kniskern found an improvement rate of roughly two-thirds during treatment.
2. Behavioral family therapy shows positive results, but appears of limited use when severe marital difficulties coexist with deviant child behavior. Behavioral marital therapy appears useful for minor difficulties, but appears less useful for severe disturbances.
3. Among nonbehavioral marital therapies, conjoint treatment is the most effective.
4. Increased communication skills are "the 'sine qua non' of effective marital therapy" (p. 749).

Types of Family and Couples Therapy

In general, the types of family interventions include the behavioral, the manipulative, the educative, and the interpretive. Behavioral interventions (O'Leary and Turkewitz 1978) stress problem definition and problem solving, reinforcement (including contracts), desensitization (particularly for sexual dysfunction), and communication techniques (including cognitive therapy). Specific interventions may include teaching communications skills (listening without interrupting, minimizing critical statements, etc.), encouragement, relabeling, listing desirable behaviors and reinforcing their appearance, and stimulus control strategies (e.g., limiting the time and settings for particular discussions).

Manipulative interventions utilize the authority of the therapist and the dependency of the family to interfere with fixed family structures. The notion is that interventions containing directions or injunctions to which the family must attend will lead to new experiences so dramatic that fixed patterns will be altered. Such techniques include paradoxical interventions (e.g., telling the family of a runaway child to take him to the bus terminal), "structural" interventions (e.g., moving the seat of the "momma's boy" in the family therapy so that the father sits between him and the mother), and various types of role playing (e.g., enacting how other family members are experienced and playing out fantasies in staged scenes).

Educative interventions are of particular use when conflict is not a central aspect of the symptomatology and when the patient lacks specific information. Child guidance, educative sexual therapies, and giving information about the course, etiology, and prognosis of various illnesses fit into this category. Therapists who utilize these techniques rely on family members' motivation and a relatively unconflicted capacity to learn.

Treatment based on systems theory addresses symptomatic behavior as a clue to how the family system is regulated. For example, Steinglass et al. (1976) suggested that alcoholism can become an organizing principle for interactional life within certain families, serving to stabilize rather than to disrupt interactional behavior. In this view, elimination of the symptom without addressing the systematic need for it would lead to unnecessary disruption in family life. The therapist uses these insights both educatively and interpretively to prescribe clearer problem definition and new problem-solving techniques that replace the use of alcohol.

In psychoanalytically oriented family therapy, interpretation of unconscious content is a primary modality, though behavioral and affective management in hospitalized cases is essential. The content of family interpretation differs according to the nature of the projected material. For example, if aspects of impulse life are projected and the recipients of these projections are treated with anxiety and hostility, interpretations might usefully center around the need to defend against the anxiety and guilt associated with acknowledging the forbidden impulse(s) (Tourkow 1975).

In such a family, for instance, a child might be acting out sexually, while the parents react in stereotyped horror (Zinner and Shapiro 1974). Alternatively, the roles might shift, with the child becoming the voice of conscience as the parents' impulsivity is displayed. Both the exaggerated hostility and the experience of a family member as "alien" are evidence of the conscious disconnection from and aversion to a projected element of impulse life. An interpretation such as the following might allow for a different perspective: "This family acts as though sexuality is something only adolescents know anything about; perhaps it serves a purpose for parents to take this role of horrified innocence."

In families with intolerable depression, interpretations about the anxiety and helplessness of unbearable sadness can be helpful (E. Shapiro 1978b). Members of such families react to manifestations of depression with anxious attempts to cheer the person up, to change the subject, or otherwise to flee from the situation. To help focus attention on the flight from affect and lead to a more adaptive exploration of shared sadness and shared resources for managing it, a useful interpretation might be "In this family, there is a notion that sadness is something to hide. Someone is always in the role of cheering people up."

If family members project devalued aspects of the self-image, interpretations might well deal with the need to defend against the mortification and narcissistic pain that would result from acknowledging these aspects of the self (Berkowitz et al. 1974b). For example, in one family, parents told their son not to inform his siblings of a low grade on a report card lest they tease him "unmercifully." The interpretation "There is a sense in this family that only perfection is acceptable" could draw attention to irrational standards for maintaining self-esteem (in this case, projected into the siblings) and lead to an exploration of the sources in the parents' past of anxieties about their own "imperfect" performances.

These interpretations call family members' attention to their own conflicts and illuminate the manner in which they distance themselves from each other through projection. The resultant discovery of affective links between family members can serve as a means for deepening their relationships without alienation and increasing their flexibility.

Duration and Frequency

There is no agreement on duration and frequency of visits or length of treatment for couples and family therapy, though behavioral interventions tend to be shorter (Alexander and Parsons 1973; Dalton 1983; Fine 1973) than psychoanalytically oriented ones (Levy and Brown 1980; E. Shapiro et al. 1975). The usual length of dynamically oriented family treatment sessions ranges from 60 to 90 minutes. Some clinicians (Skynner 1976) suggest that less frequent sessions might be useful, though Skynner (1976) warned that infrequent sessions could be undesirable if there is a history of deprivation or depression against which family members are successfully defending themselves.

In general, the length of treatment appears to relate to the goals of treatment. For young patients in crisis situations, short-term behavioral interventions in which family responses are modified to reduce constraints on the child appear to be adequate (Alexander and Parsons 1973; Dalton 1983; Fine 1973). For these interventions, the focus of the work is to define problematic behaviors in the symptomatic family member and to discern family reinforcement patterns that can be modified.

For intensive psychodynamically oriented family therapy with severely disturbed, hospitalized adolescents, weekly family and couples therapy of an hour or longer, in combination with intensive (two or three hours per week) individual treatment of a year or more, seems necessary. The tasks of this more intensive treatment include making a treatment alliance with otherwise unengageable adolescents (E. Shapiro et al. 1977; Zinner 1978) and finding a way to make unbearable feelings that are acted out in family interaction more manageable. Then thinking and feeling can be integrated and individuals more clearly perceived (E. Shapiro 1978a, 1982a). This kind of intensive and extensive treatment is necessary for the disengagement of adolescents from the pulls of the family projections so that development can proceed without conflicts of loyalty (Boszormenyi-Nagy 1972).

Indications and Contraindications

Any personality-disordered patient who requests individual treatment alone should be given the opportunity to be treated with the requested modality. For many patients, however, particularly for those with the more unstructured disorders (borderline, narcissistic, antisocial, and schizoid), discomfort may be experienced primarily by persons in the patient's interpersonal environment. In such circumstances, a family or marital evaluation and treatment are indicated. This is particularly true for the personality disorders of adolescence, which are often manifest by drug use, delinquency, or other problems of adolescent autonomy and separation. In these cases, the family invariably is involved intensely in the process and can be a major asset to the work (E. Shapiro 1982a; R. Shapiro 1978).

In families with separation and divorce, it is often helpful to bring in the separated family members, particularly during the adolescence of the children, so that the facts and meanings of the separation can be addressed in the children's presence and they can realistically determine what supports are available to them. In such cases, family members may develop the fantasy that the family work is designed to reconstitute the family. This fantasy must be explored actively, because the therapeutic task in such cases is often to facilitate a less chaotic separation. This task involves a shared mourning of what was irretrievably lost in the breakup.

If the clinician has sufficient training and experience and is comfortable managing the often chaotic affects involved in this type of treatment, there are few contra-indications to an evaluation (E. Shapiro 1982a). If the members of the family can stay in the same room without violence or such psychotic disorganization that communication cannot be sustained, an evaluation will yield useful information for treatment planning.

Summary

In the past three decades, intensive clinical investigation of the dynamics of patients with personality disorder has begun to reveal the degree to which these illnesses are sustained and supported within intimate relationships. In more severe personality disorders (borderline, narcissistic, antisocial, and schizoid), clinical evidence suggests that family and marital interaction in combination with the individual's specific ego deficits may inhibit the possibility of alternative developmental outcomes.

The subtle, complementary, and unconscious interpersonal manipulations involved in projective identification require careful investigation to unravel, particularly when they occur in passionately heated family environments where individuals are caught up in pathologic certainty and blaming. For patients embroiled in such fixed interlocking systems, family and marital therapy may be the treatment of choice, with a goal of moving from the externalization of conflict to its internalization, and with individuals taking more responsibility for their own difficulties.

A variety of treatment interventions may help with this process. These include behavioral, educative, manipulative, and interpretive approaches, each of which has specific indications. Evaluation of the interpersonal meaning of these illnesses can help the clinician to decide amongst a range of individual and environmental interventions.

Chapter 250

Group Therapy

Central to the therapeutic considerations of group psychotherapy is the characteristic exploration of the interpersonal interactions and relationships within the therapeutically created microcosm of the group (Yalom 1985). The interface between disorder and therapy has contributed to the elaboration of theoretical models and clinical recommendations that will be reviewed in this chapter. It is noteworthy that much of the literature describing group therapy of individuals with personality disorders is clinically determined. Diagnoses have generally been based on either psychodynamic considerations or a general diagnosis of personality disturbance. Notwithstanding the lack of empirical research in this area, certain treatment rationales have developed.

Historical Developments

The pioneering work of Maxwell Jones (1953) in the treatment of character-disordered, antisocial men and women in therapeutic communities focused attention on the effectiveness of group approaches with this difficult population. Living and working together within the therapeutic community exposed individuals both to peer confrontation of maladaptive interpersonal behavior and to peer support and encouragement of more responsible, adaptive ways of relating. The patients acquired a sensitivity to social influence. In early clinical reports about ambulatory settings, authors described the therapeutic effect of adding group therapy to the individual psychotherapy of highly resistant oral, hostile, and withdrawn patients (Fried 1954; Jackson and Grotjahn 1958). The specific advantages of group therapy cited included the group's potency in 1) confronting resistant, ego-syntonic character traits (Durkin 1951); 2) fostering the integration of strong positive and negative affects kept separate by the resistant patient in response to fears of being overwhelmed by these emotions or of overwhelming and destroying the individual therapy (Fried 1954); 3) providing in vivo demonstration of maladaptive behaviors and a chance to experiment with new and adaptive ones, adding behavioral action to insight; and 4) reducing the intensity of difficult transference reactions that might occur in individualized treatment (Fried 1961). The model of group psychotherapy focused primarily on the individual within the group.

At the same time, Bion's work (Rioch 1970) was drawing attention to the nature of regression in groups and the emergence of primitive anxieties and concerns that could be studied by viewing the group as a whole. British object relations theory and, more recently, Kernberg (1975) and Kohut (1977) have greatly influenced the practice of group psychotherapy by deepening the understanding of the intrapsychic aspects of manifest interpersonal relationships of characterologically disturbed patients (Kosseff 1975).

Separate developments have arisen from behavioral approaches based on the view that the primary psychological disturbance of personality-disordered persons is a failure in social learning that can be addressed best by acquiring and learning new social skills.

Evidence for Effectiveness

With the exception of the antisocial personality disorder, research into the efficacy of group psychotherapy with the personality disorders is quite limited, although clinical and theoretical reports abound (Parloff and Dies 1977). A variety of significant defects in research design impair the evaluation of effectiveness. In the literature, authors often describe patients as personality disordered without detailing specific personality diagnoses. Furthermore, personality-disordered patients are often mixed with broader samples of outpatients, and have rarely been studied as a homogeneous population in terms of group therapy. The failure of integration between clinicians and researchers is being addressed (Dies 1983), however, and with greater stability, clarity, and relevance in diagnostic criteria, better research should follow.

In one well-designed study, patients treated with psychodynamic group therapy by experienced clinicians and followed up for 18 months achieved significant and enduring improvement of their long-standing interpersonal problems (Pilkonis et al. 1984). Luborsky et al. (1975) in a review of the effectiveness of psychotherapy, found group therapy and individual therapy equally efficacious. The review by Malan et al. (1976) was less encouraging. Studying the outcomes of a mixed sample of neurotic and personality-disordered ambulatory patients treated by group-as-a-whole approaches, they found few patients showed marked improvement and, overall, patients who stayed in therapy for more than two years fared no better than early dropouts. These results led Malan and his associates to recommend modifications that would deemphasize the group-as-a-whole approach in group therapists' technique.

In one study, character-disordered patients valued group therapy highly during acute hospitalization (Gould and Glick 1976). In another study, patients with borderline personality disorders valued a dynamic interactional group therapy very highly, often ranking it as the single most important treatment experience during their acute hospitalization (Leszcz et al. 1985). In contrast, schizophrenic patients preferred a less structured, less intensely interactive group focused on supportive discussion of external problems and problems of daily life. This distinction mirrors the general differences between the aims of group therapy for schizophrenic patients and for personality-disordered patients (Leszcz 1986).

Behavioral group treatment focused on improving interpersonal skills through role playing and behavioral reinforcement has also been effective (Argyle et al. 1974). Ten weekly group sessions of social skills training (SST) for patients diagnosed as inadequate personalities resulted in a significant and stable improvement in target symptomatology, work adjustment, and general adjustment (Falloon et al. 1977). Similar findings were reported for patients who were diagnosed as having avoidant personality disorder and treated with SST weekly for 12 weeks (Stravynski et al. 1982). Treated patients showed a significant reduction in isolation, depression, irrational social beliefs, and target behaviors as measured by patients' self-reports, questionnaires, and assessors blind to the treatment received.

Frequency and Duration of Treatment

Dynamic group psychotherapy traditionally consists of a once weekly session, 90 minutes long. Yalom (1985) stated that more positive outcomes are obtained with treatment lasting at least one year. Similarly, Carney (1972) endorsed one year as a minimum period of treatment for antisocial patients under mandate. In samples that include, but are not limited to, personality-disordered patients, 35 to 50 percent of patients stay in treatment for longer than two years (Stone and Rutan 1984). Ten to 35 percent of patients drop out, usually within the first three months of therapy (Yalom 1966). Interpersonal difficulties with intimacy and engagement increase the risk for premature dropout from group therapy. Such difficulties are common to many personality-disordered patients; hence, therapists should be cognizant of this risk. Prior or concurrent individual therapy tends to increase an individual's tenure in group treatment (Stone and Rutan 1984) and promotes a positive outcome in group therapy (Malan et al. 1976; Stone and Rutan 1984). It is unclear whether this tendency is a reflection of individual therapists supporting patients to remain with the group, or if it is a nonspecific sign of high patient motivation and amenability to change.

Behavioral group therapy approaches aimed at modifying patients' social skills deficits or other specific target symptoms are generally brief in duration, often consisting of six to 12 sessions lasting one to two hours each.

Effects, Goals, and Outcome of Group Therapy

The aims and process of group therapy for patients with personality disorders can be examined both by way of a general overview and by a more specific focus on the various personality disorders. A common feature of personality-disordered patients is the presence of maladaptive ego-syntonic character traits, often associated with diminished tolerance for frustration, affect, and anxiety. Tension is rapidly discharged into the external environment, resulting in diminished motivation for internal change. Defenses are rigid and often brittle, and the risk of serious regression, self-destructiveness, transient psychotic episodes, and acting out is present. Acting out can function to discharge tensions, induce wished-for responses from the environment, reestablish a sense of self, and regulate the degree of interpersonal intimacy and distance. Primitive defenses such as splitting, projective identification, and denial are prominent, representing a fundamental failure in the integration of a stable, constant view of oneself and of the important people in one's world.

Bellack (1980) found group therapy more effective than dyadic therapy for patients with these difficulties. Treatment blind spots and factual distortions are greatly reduced by virtue of the patient recreating his or her characteristic difficulties in the group, in vivo, here and now, in words and behavior. Aims of treatment include confrontation and clarification of maladaptive ego-syntonic personality traits, increasing the sphere of the observing ego, increasing the capacity to tolerate and integrate one's affect, and learning about the impact of one's behavior on others—interpersonal learning. The patient becomes subject to the group's reality orientation and group pressure to work things through, rather than use avoidance or denial. The scrutiny and feedback of multiple observers make it hard to refute the group's feedback about one's behavior; feedback from peers cannot be dismissed readily as a professional ploy. In addition, the presence of multiple supporters who can empathize with the patient's struggle can make confrontation more tolerable for the patient. In contrast, in individual psychotherapy, the patient may not be able to feel simultaneously supported and confronted by the therapist. The provision of a stable, nondeviant, and affirming group with real and positive relationships, coupled with the presence of an accurately empathic therapist, promotes a period of ego strengthening (Scheidlinger and Holden 1966). This may set the stage for reconstructive work and for new ways of perceiving the self and others.

Patients often experience the group therapy setting as less intense and less regressive than individual therapy. Each individual's view of the therapist is influenced by his or her knowledge of how other group members see the therapist, hence reducing the risk of serious transference distortions. This asset of group therapy is most prominent when the group fosters and values peer relationships and is not centered around a passive, abstinent therapist.

Many of these therapeutic advantages require a heterogeneous group, ideally composed of no more than one or two borderline or narcissistic patients and four to six less disturbed patients. A homogeneous group of severely character disordered patients may exacerbate regression because of the patients' impaired ego boundary maintenance and primitive competitiveness and the lack of alternative and less pathologic viewpoints that can clarify distortions and challenge projections. Furthermore, the primitive demanding nature of such a group can place enormous demands on the therapist, producing intense countertransferential reactions (Roth 1980).

An alternative perspective to the psychodynamic approach is a behavioral, or SST model (Bellack and Hersen 1979). In this model, group therapy is conceptualized as a laboratory in which specific maladaptive target behaviors are identified. Clear alternative behaviors are prescribed, without a focus on causal explanations. The aim of treatment is to break the vicious circle of poor interpersonal and social skills leading to negative feedback from the environment, which causes more psychological distress, and further impairs social functioning (Brady 1984).

Social skills training has expanded beyond traditional assertiveness training focused on achieving more effective and relaxed expression of negative and positive affects. Target behaviors and situations are identified for each individual. A process of instruction and therapist modeling of more adaptive strategies is followed by in-group behavioral rehearsal. Group feedback and coaching further enhance the practice of the newly acquired skill, and homework assignments help promote generalization of the new behavior into the rest of the patient's world. Typical social skills addressed include making eye contact, initiating and maintaining conversation, improving reading of social cues, dealing effectively with confrontation, and disagreeing and expressing positive regard. Social behavior shows demonstrable changes after SST, but gains made are often not translated to more intimate situations (Stravynski and Shahar 1983).

Paranoid Personality Disorder

Classically, the diagnosis of paranoid personality has been a contraindication for group psychotherapy, because of the patient's fundamental mistrust, rigidity, and refusal to scrutinize his or her interpersonal distortions (Yalom 1985). Such patients generally avoid groups and other forms of psychiatric care. Patients who do maintain a degree of self-awareness, and who are able to sustain a therapeutic alliance in the face of group confrontation over their paranoid distortions, may derive substantial benefit from the supportive reality base of the group members, however. This can lead to improvement in reality testing and a reduction of projection. A mature and cohesive group is able to work with the impact of such distortions more effectively than a newly formed group that might withdraw or aggressively confront the paranoid patient. Hence, it is best to defer addition of such a patient until the group has reached sufficient cohesion and tolerance for divergent opinions from its members.

Schizoid Personality Disorder

The schizoid person's fundamental defect in the capacity to form and enjoy social relationships, and the resultant isolation, often result in a request for treatment. In contrast to the avoidant person, who retains an intact capacity for object relations, but who is inhibited by fears of rejection, the schizoid's intense fear of catastrophe resulting from engagement poses special challenges. Cohesion-breeding remarks will be valued by the avoidant patient but feared by the schizoid patient, who may be frightened by too much intimacy or self-exposure. Yalom (1985) cautioned that a slow, steady engagement, encouraging differentiation of affects and relationships, rather than a potentially overwhelming and cathartic breakthrough, is the advised treatment approach. The patient's individual pace needs to be respected by both the therapist and the group. A developmental approach in which the patient first forms a stable dyadic relationship with the therapist and then proceeds to group therapy with the same therapist offers an opportunity for reworking the failed negotiation of a highly special and intense primary relationship and its later loss, which has resulted in feelings of rage, envy, and abandonment (Wolff and Solomon 1973). Kosseff (1975), using an object relations perspective, suggested that the group may offer the schizoid patient an opportunity for closeness to others, but in less overwhelmingly intense fashion than individual therapy.

Schizotypal Personality Disorder

In addition to the interpersonal difficulties of the schizoid patient, the schizotypal patient presents the typical ambulatory group with an uncomfortable eccentricity and characteristic bizarreness. This poses a significant risk in both dropout and extrusion rates. Clinical reports of group psychotherapy with this patient population have not yet appeared. However, these patients may make good use of supportive groups offered in clinics that aim for improvement of adaptive function in day-to-day living, without dynamic exploration and with diminished demand for intimacy and disclosure.

Histrionic Personality Disorder

The characteristic interpersonal style of the histrionic personality with its lability, dramatism, egocentricism, and manipulativeness is clearly demonstrated within the psychotherapy group. Bar-Levav (1981) viewed the group as the ideal setting for working through the histrionic patient's wish for the group therapist's exclusive attention, which now must be undeniably shared. Because of the greater reality orientation of the group and the therapist's obvious involvement with other patients, the histrionic patient is more likely to view the group therapist as real and three-dimensional than the individual therapist. The group is also unlikely to allow a compliant, appproval-seeking posture to go unchallenged. Accordingly, the risk of an eroticized transference developing is reduced.

Cass et al. (1972) reported on an inpatient behavioral group treatment that significantly modified specific histrionic behaviors in a small patient sample. Characteristic ego-syntonic but maladaptive behaviors, such as inappropriate passivity, manipulativeness, and acting out, were identified for each patient. A system of specific rewards and contingencies detailed for each patient was enforced and supported by the peer group, thereby reinforcing the expression of effective, assertive interpersonal behavior. Significant reduction in target behaviors was achieved within four to six weeks and maintained at 18-month follow-up.

Narcissistic Personality Disorder

The treatment of narcissistic problems in group psychotherapy has been of long-standing interest (Glatzer 1965) and still remains an area of intense clinical and theoretical interest.

The patient with a narcissistic personality disorder usually seeks psychiatric treatment following loss of a sustaining relationship or a narcissistic injury that threatens a fragile sense of self-worth. In the group, however, what usually draws the most attention is not the narcissistic vulnerability and feelings of helplessness and emptiness. Rather, it is the narcissistic defenses, such as devaluation of others and self-aggrandizement, that become the focus of the group's reactions. Excessive and premature focus on the narcissistic defenses often leads to therapeutic failure as the patient feels assaulted and misunderstood. This problem, coupled with the patient's enormous demanding nature and nonreciprocative entitlement, has led some authors to view this diagnosis as a relative contraindication to group psychotherapy (Horner 1975). However, combining confrontation of the maladaptive, narcissistic defenses with maintenance of an empathic connection to the patient's need to be special, or to idealize the group or therapist, can make treatment viable and useful (Schwartzman 1984; Stone and Gustafson 1982).

Several factors contribute to the effectiveness of group psychotherapy with the narcissistic person. Glatzer (1962) noted the following: the group therapist is more likely than the individual therapist to be viewed as a three-dimensional person, rather than in a one-dimensional transferential fashion; peer feedback is more acceptable than the therapist's feedback, which may be viewed with devaluing envy; conversely, peer support may make the therapist's confrontation more tolerable. Working through intense and divergent affects is more possible because of the patient's positive attachments within the group, and the greater scrutiny by the peer group of the patient's disavowed affects. Belonging to a group can provide the narcissistic patient with three of his or her psychological essentials—mirroring of the patient's sense of worth and specialness, objects for idealization to bolster the patient's sense of security and comfort, and opportunities for peer relationships (Grotjahn 1984). The patient can see clearly the impact of his or her abrasive behavior and often modulates this behavior in response. The patient's capacity to empathize with others may be enhanced, also. In this way, the group becomes a vehicle for exploring and addressing the patient's failure in maintaining a clear and stable sense of self and the interpersonal consequences of defensive efforts to reestablish a sense of self.

Fluctuating idealization and devaluation of self and others requires the group therapist to be attuned to how the patient is experiencing the group. Devaluation of self or of the treatment may be related to the patient's experiencing a failure in being understood, valued, or appreciated. This reflects how fragile the narcissistic patient's sense of self-worth is, and how much it depends on external regulation. At times, other group members may have strong negative reactions to the patient's inability to experience them as autonomous and valuable in their own right. Successfully working through these issues can lead the narcissistic patient to attaining greater clarity and stability in his or her sense of self.

Attention to the unique needs of the patient may warrant a deemphasis of group-as-a-whole interpretations and a focus on individual contributions and needs. This is particularly the case at moments when one patient's needs or capacities are different from those of the group's (Stone and Whitman 1980). Concurrent individual therapy is valuable in this instance much as in the case of the borderline patient and will be discussed below.

Borderline Personality Disorder

Pronounced interpersonal difficulties reflect the ego impairment and fundamental instability in regulation of affect, impulses, and sense of self found in the borderline patient. Poorly integrated, part-object relationships predominate over whole-object relations. Intense fears of abandonment and engulfment alternate, and psychotherapy can be difficult because of the emergence of intense affects and pathologic regressions and distortions.

The chief aim of intensive psychotherapy is the integration of the patient's fundamental split of the self and object representations into powerful and antithetical good and bad parts. Many clinicians believe that group psychotherapy provides a unique benefit, what Horwitz (1980) referred to as a dilution of intense transferences. This results from the presence of multiple transferential objects, rather than a single all-encompassing therapist. Demanding socially appropriate and realistic responses, groups modulate aggression and offer alternative models for its expression. Distortions are more readily challenged by the contrasting perspective of other group members, and unrealistic fears of engulfment by the therapist are decreased by the presence of peers. Both the patient and the therapist can deintensify their own reactions by "pulling back" within the group, without stopping treatment. The realistic demand to coexist with others can decrease abrasive and self-serving behavior and increase the patient's capacity to empathize with others, instead of seeing them only as either gratifiers or frustrators. Intense wishes for relatedness can be met more safely by virtue of the interpersonal relationships within the group and the group therapist's more active and transparent posture (Grobman 1980). In short, the group provides many opportunities for clarification, confrontation, and working through of the patient's tendency to experience his or her interpersonal world in all-or-nothing, black-or-white fashion.

The borderline patient in a group may require individual treatment for support through group-engendered stress and to help integrate the experience and affect the group evokes (Horwitz 1980; Spotnitz 1975; Wong 1980). The individual psychotherapy may be coequal or supportive to the group therapy, and more intensive individual psychotherapy may follow. Failing to add individual therapy when necessary commonly leads to premature termination of the individual's group therapy (Horwitz 1980). Pines (1975) viewed concurrent individual psychotherapy as unnecessary, however. He saw group therapy as a sufficiently powerful agent by itself, able to contain the patient's primitive rage over perceptions of repeated abandonments and engulfments, without the group withdrawing or punishing the patient.

Supportive group approaches with borderline patients have also been employed. For short-term inpatient units, Kibel (1978, 1981) advocated a group approach as part of a treatment aimed at returning patients to their precrisis function. This approach supports the patient's splitting, protecting the positive, libidinal part-object relations emerging within the group from contamination with the patient's more aggressive affects and part-object relations. Encouragement is given to the verbalization of anger, but it is deflected outside the group. Interpretations are at the level of the group as a whole to foster cohesion and decrease the individual's risk of being overwhelmed by a confrontation. Patients' reactions to events within the larger ward milieu are also explored in the group, thereby reducing tension on the ward.

Antisocial Personality Disorder

The length of time this diagnostic group has been studied, the stability of treatment because of its frequent occurrence by mandate, and the presence of a clear outcome variable, recidivism, have resulted in more scientific study of this personality disorder than others. The connection of the antisocial adult to the delinquent adolescent also warrants reference to the group therapy of the latter population, although overviews of such therapy are not very encouraging (Julian and Kilman 1979; Parloff and Dies 1977). Yet specific reports offer hope, and although outpatient group therapy is probably contraindicated for the unreliable and resistive antisocial personality (Yalom 1985), treatment in homogeneous groups within institutions and therapeutic communities can lead to positive outcomes (Carney 1972; Jones 1953; Reid 1981). In particular, behavioral and modeling approaches addressing particular antisocial behaviors appear to be more effective than traditional psychoanalytic groups (Julian and Kilman 1979).

Recurrent themes in treatment include the concept that the antisocial person is ill and not just bad, that he or she is ego-impaired as well as superego-impaired. This caveat reflects the potential for antitherapeutic countertransference reactions to arise in the treatment of antisocial patients. They are intolerant of intense affect, use primitive defenses, and act out impulsively and aggressively in response to threats to self-esteem and feelings of impotence and worthlessness (Carney 1972; Maas 1966). Benefits of group psychotherapy derive from the esteem-sustaining effect of membership in a stable group that operates within responsible and clear norms, and with a clear, predictable therapist (Kiger 1967).

The development of a cohesive group in an institutional setting is aided by the enforced attendance, the honesty demanded, and the group's genuine responsibility for itself. An opportunity for therapeutic action, such as role playing and behavioral rehearsal, coupled with group pressure to express reactions to insults and frustration verbally, can reduce the amount of aggressive acting out. Positive results have been reported in both institutional (Jew et al. 1972) and certain ambulatory settings (Borriello 1979; Lion and Bach y Rita 1970).

Avoidant Personality Disorder

This new diagnosis differentiates patients whose marked isolation results from an intense fear of rejection and humiliation, but whose capacity for relatedness is intact, from schizoid patients, who have a fundamental defect in their capacity for relatedness. Because patients with avoidant personality disorder yearn for affection and acceptance (American Psychiatric Association, 1980, p. 323), psychotherapy groups that offer multiple opportunities for intimate relatedness without premature or excessive hostility may be an ideal treatment. The therapist's role in pacing the avoidant patient's disclosure and engagement within the group can be very important (Cramer Azima 1983). Alternatively, a briefer course of therapy centered on social skills training can be highly effective in ameliorating social skills deficits that exacerbate anxiety about social relatedness (Stravynski et al. 1982).

Dependent Personality Disorder

The central feature in this diagnosis is passive dependence on others, to the total exclusion of self-reliance. The therapist must consider whether the aim of treatment is to support this characterological stance through the provision of reliable objects of dependency or to attempt to modify the dependency and promote growth and independence. If the dependent traits reflect severe personality impairment, a clinic-based, ongoing, supportive, problem-solving group may be appropriate. Social skills training may have a role as well. If potential and motivation for growth exists, a more interactional psychotherapy group is an excellent arena in which to explore the inappropriateness of dependency-seeking behavior and to experiment with greater assertiveness.

Montgomery (1971) reported on the effective utilization of group therapy for difficult clinic patients previously seen individually on a monthly basis. The patients were very clingy and dependent and demanded medication and magical cures, frequently disrupting the clinic's routine with their urgent demands. Engagement within the group provided the patients with a chance to redirect their attention-seeking behavior from regressive aims to socially adaptive ones. Group norms encouraged verbalization and mature problem solving. A marked decrease in the use of psychotropic medication and crisis visits resulted.

Compulsive Personality Disorder

A major problem area for the compulsive personality is the inability to share spontaneously or tenderly with others. A wish for less interpersonal isolation, often at the urging of a spouse, can precipitate a request for therapy. The patient may find the affective atmosphere of an active psychotherapy group overwhelming at first, resulting in either further isolation or a detached, intellectual approach to the group. The core issues of fear and loss of control, beneath the controlling and distancing defensive style, require careful attention. The group leader may need to intervene and clarify these issues in order to avoid unnecessary power struggles arising between the patient and other group members. If this is achieved, the compulsive patient has the opportunity to enjoy vicariously others' emotional expressiveness in the group, and ultimately to experiment with his or her own increasing range of feeling.

Passive-Aggressive Personality Disorder

The passive-aggressive patient's unwillingness to comply and unwillingness to protest directly, even when both options are available, lies at the heart of this disorder (Malinow 1981). The paralysis that follows from the poorly resolved conflict over dependency and aggressiveness often stands out clearly in a group situation. Group members may readily detect the patient's contradictions and hidden affects. By the simultaneous confrontation of denied emotion and support for its expression, the group mitigates against the patient's disavowal of his or her feared affects (Glatzer 1965). In particular, the indirect obstructiveness of the passive-aggressive person can be challenged effectively. Accordingly, the group may be the first safe interpersonal forum in which the patient can feel that he or she has real influence and can in fact protest safely.

Indications and Contraindications

Three main indications for dynamic group psychotherapy are maladaptive interpersonal relationships, the tendency to act on feelings immediately, and the development of a transference that impedes individual therapy (Grunebaum and Kates 1977). These criteria subsume many personality-disordered patients. A mixed, dynamic outpatient group is contraindicated for patients with seriously paranoid and exploitative antisocial personality disorders, however (Yalom 1985). Furthermore, patients in acute crises related to suicidality or substance abuse require more active management than can be readily provided upon entering a new group.

The personality disorders are a diverse group, and a single diagnosis may encompass a spectrum of pathology. Therefore, a phenomenologic diagnosis alone may be an inadequate criterion for recommending treatment. Silver (1983) recommended a detailed assessment of the patient's history of interpersonal relationships, psychological-mindedness, distancing and engaging maneuvers, capacity to empathize and to be empathized with, capacity to self-soothe, and other ego functions prior to making a recommendation for any psychotherapy. Extreme difficulties in these areas may pose insurmountable challenges to therapy and forewarn the therapist of potential problem areas. Kibel (1980) advised an evaluation of how a particular patient will fit into the group in terms of the group's composition and developmental stage. A stable, mature group would be better able to work therapeutically with a difficult, projecting patient than would a poorly cohesive group of ego-impaired patients. The role of concurrent individual therapy should be ascertained as well. Will it be required to maintain the patient in the group? If it is necessary, will the therapies have compatible goals? (See Major Controversies.)

More focused behavioral group therapy, such as SST, is indicated when specific interpersonal defects are evident, the patient is not seriously disturbed, and the patient and the therapist agree on the target behaviors (Stravynski et al. 1982).

Special Training and Qualifications of the Therapists

Treating difficult patients in a dynamic psychotherapy places substantial demands on the therapist. In addition to an understanding of individual psychology, the group therapist should have an in-depth knowledge of group process and dynamics. This is best obtained through a multimodal training that includes didactic, observational, and experiential components, as well as supervision (Dies 1980). The therapist must be able to deal with the inevitable countertransferential reactions that arise as a result of working closely with difficult, sometimes defeating, patients. The patients' primitive defenses, intense affects, self-destructive actions, and feelings of entitlement can arouse powerful feelings within therapists (Adler 1972; Groves 1978; Maltsberger and Buie 1974; Roth 1980).

The capacity to understand and empathize may be temporarily overwhelmed in the face of a patient's violent or self-destructive behavior. It is therefore important for therapists to utilize peer consultation and supervision, and to be professionally and personally secure.

Major Controversies

Two controversial issues in group psychotherapy of the personality disorders are 1) whether the group therapist should direct interventions primarily to the group as a whole or to the individual interacting within the group process and 2) what the role of concurrent individual therapy should be. In its strictest practice, the group-centered approach offers more insight into the dynamics of the group process. It may aid in the dilution of transferences, because no single patient is the therapist's sole focus, and all co-members share in the therapist's intervention. Each member is always involved, and sharing of time is less contentious. Failure to distinguish individual needs from group ones, however, may exacerbate pathologic regression by increasing anxiety about ego boundary diffusion and may also be experienced by narcissistic patients as unempathic and out of tune with their personal experience of the group (Stone and Gustafson 1982). The abstinent posture of the therapist and the leader-centered dependency may be unnecessarily frustrating, especially to disturbed patients who require more real engagement and therapist activity (Malan et al. 1976). Another key drawback is that a relative deemphasis of peer relationships emerges when these relationships are viewed essentially as only a treatment resistance originating in the central transference to the leader. This can undermine the importance of interpersonal learning, a key therapeutic factor (Yalom 1985).

Therefore, Kibel and Stein (1981) recommended an active therapeutic posture, more inductive than deductive, that involves exploring peer transferences as reflections of genuine and important object relations. After the peer transferences are clarified, group-centered interventions, focused on the primary transference to the therapist, are appropriate. A model of group therapy that emphasizes peer interaction while also attending to the group process, as described by Yalom (1985), takes full advantage of the unique attributes of group approaches in providing opportunities for increased self-awareness, interpersonal learning, and behavioral practice.

The issue of concurrent group and individual psychotherapy has involved two levels of controversy. Is concurrent individual therapy necessary, and should it be with the same therapist (combined) or with separate therapists (conjoint)? Many clinicians now advocate such therapy as either necessary with certain difficult patients or facilitative in general.

Regarding the second issue, combined therapy facilitates integration and decreases distortions because the therapist is present in both settings and is aware firsthand of what the patient recounts. There may be some practical limitations, however. Having only certain patients in one-to-one psychotherapy with the group leader may produce iatrogenic issues of specialness and envy. Conjoint therapy offers the advantage of tailoring the group and one-to-one therapy to each patient's needs. The second treatment modality is beneficial because it adds multiple transferential reactions, observers, settings, interpreters, and maturational agents (Ormont and Strean 1978). It is essential to avoid exacerbating the patient's inherent failure in integration. To avoid confusion and ensure that the right hand knows what the left hand is doing, the two therapists involved in conjoint therapy must communicate frequently, agree fully with the aims of treatment, trust each others' competence, and be able to deal effectively with their own competitive feelings. This is necessary to reduce the chance that the patient's devaluing and idealizing projections will find fertile ground in which to grow. These issues are more thoroughly reviewed elsewhere (Porter 1980; Rutan and Alonso 1982).

Conclusion

A chief benefit of group psychotherapy is its ability to clarify, elaborate, and confront ego-syntonic personality traits in a less regressive atmosphere than dyadic therapy. In addition, group therapy provides the personality-disordered patient with an opportunity to acquire and practice new methods of relating and interacting. Empirical research is now required to substantiate current clinical models.

Chapter 251

Somatic Therapy

At present personality disorders can be considered one of the frontiers of psychiatric research. Systematic data on prevalence, pathophysiology, transmission, treatment, and natural history are sparse. Even more fundamental, there is no consensus concerning the nature and validity of the construct of personality disorder per se.

The biologic approach to personality disorders has a lengthy history. The modern era began with Kraepelin (1921), who observed affective temperaments in the premorbid history of many manic-depressives and in their non-ill biologic relatives. Later investigators such as Kretschmer (1936) and Schneider (1959) described constitutional factors thought to underlie both normal and deviant personality types. The major thrust of these studies was the notion that diluted versions of major schizophrenic, affective, and organic disorders could express themselves as chronic maladaptive patterns of experiencing and functioning in the world (i.e., as personality disorders). With the modern tools of psychopharmacology, psychobiology, and family and clinical studies, these theories can now be better tested.

In this chapter, I draw on both biologic and psychoanalytic traditions to discuss biologic therapies of personality disorders. The roles of biologic (for the most part, psychopharmacologic) therapy are to decrease vulnerability to affective or cognitive decompensation, enhance capacity for pleasure, and normalize activation and dysregulation. These changes render patients more able to function normally and more able to benefit from psychotherapy, if indicated. The fact that biologic therapies can be helpful suggests that at least some people with personality disorders are chronically coping with neurochemically based pathologic vulnerabilities to affective or cognitive instability, or both.

The available evidence for the effectiveness of somatic treatments for the DSM-III (American Psychiatric Association 1980) personality disorders is meager. One reason for this is that the DSM-III personality disorder classification is quite new, and a number of categories did not appear in previous taxonomies of personality disorder. Also, when an organic etiology is suspected or a somatic treatment for a personality disorder is elucidated, the disorder is often removed from the personality disorder classification. This was the case with cyclothymia, present in DSM-II (American Psychiatric Association 1968) as a personality disorder but reclassified in DSM-III as an affective disorder. Similarly, the old concept of depressive personality has been reformulated into dysthymia, a DSM-III affective disorder.

The literature on biologic therapies of personality disorder is confined to psychopharmacologic trials, which take one of three forms:

1. Trials of specific drugs in patients labeled as having "personality disorder" without regard to subtype.
2. Either open (clinical reports or uncontrolled series) or controlled (placebo and comparative drug) trials in patients meeting criteria for a specific DSM-III Axis II personality disorder.
3. Drug trials in patients with syndromes commonly thought of as personality disorders (e.g., pseudoneurotic schizophrenia), but not so listed in DSM-III, or involving psychopathologic constellations (e.g., explosive violence) normally thought of as manifestations of, or contributing toward, deviant personality.

Pharmacotherapy Trials in Mixed Personality-Disordered Samples

Barnes (1977) compared the effects of mesoridazine, a low-potency neuroleptic structurally similar to thioridizine, and placebo in 30 adolescents (ages 13 to 18) diagnosed as having some form of personality disorder. Included in the group were patients with passive-aggressive, antisocial, schizoid, explosive, hysterical, paranoid, and inadequate personalities. The study lasted six weeks, and the mean daily mesoridazine dose for the last week was 44.7 mg. There was a significantly greater dropout rate in the placebo group than in the group receiving mesoridazine. Statistical analyses revealed superiority for mesoridazine on a variety of measures relevant to personality-disordered patients, such as tendency to blame others, outbursts of rage or verbal aggressiveness, low tolerance for frustration, and conflict with authority, as well as anxiety, hostility, and depression.

This study should be kept in mind when neuroleptic trials in borderline patients are discussed later. One disadvantage of the study is that the patients in the sample had a variety of personality disorders, and Barnes did not elucidate whether treatment was helpful for any specific personality disorder. A second potential problem is difficulty in maintaining the double-blind with a drug like mesoridazine; however, the investigators reported a low incidence of side effects in both treatment groups. Also, statistical comparisons included some of the dropouts; because there were more placebo dropouts, this may have made mesoridazine look better than if dropouts had been excluded.

In a second study, Reyntjens (1972) examined the effects of the antipsychotic drug pimozide in 120 outpatients with a variety of personality disorders, including schizoid, paranoid, obsessive-compulsive, hysterical, borderline, inadequate, and sexually deviant. This open clinical trial lacked a fixed dosage schedule, and pimozide was administered according to clinical condition. The optimal mean daily dose was found to be 3 mg, with a range of 1 to 8 mg. Patients were treated for two months. Global improvement was rated as excellent in 30 patients (25 percent), good in 53 (44 percent), moderate in 27 (23 percent), and poor in 10 (3.5 percent). Separate analyses of subgroups showed a trend toward a better response in the two largest subgroups, schizoid and paranoid personality, but the superiority was not statistically significant. A strength of this trial was the attempt to analyze treatment effects in specific subtypes. A weakness was that it was an open clinical trial in which 36 psychiatrists collaborated with no apparent standardization of diagnostic or outcome criteria.

Although both these studies produced promising leads, future studies should focus on particular categories of personality disorder. If an investigator is comparing more than one (which has advantages), then patients in each type should be separately randomized and included in sufficient numbers to allow meaningful analyses within each type of personality disorder.

Pharmacotherapy Trials of Specific DSM-III Axis II Personality Disorders

One or more studies are available for patients with borderline, antisocial, and schizotypal personality disorders. Treatment studies of Axis II personality-disordered patients can clarify the overall drug responsivity of a given disorder, highlight drug-responsive features of the disorder, identify possible synergism with other treatments such as psychotherapy, and suggest the existence of discrete subtypes responsive to particular classes of medication.

Borderline Personality Disorder

Several reviews of pharmacotherapy of borderline patients are available (Cole and Sunderland 1982; Klein 1975; Liebowitz 1983; Soloff 1981; Synder 1984). Despite the current interest in the overlap of borderline and affective disorders, the majority of the drug trials in borderline patients have involved neuroleptics.

Neuroleptic Trials in Borderline Patients

Open trials.   Brinkley et al. (1979) reported on a number of borderline patients who were substantially helped by low dosages of high-potency neuroleptics. The most important predictor of success, which makes sense clinically, was "the recurrence of history of regressive psychotic symptoms, frequently of a paranoid quality, and including some looseness of associations, thought blocking, impairment of reality testing and disturbed states of consciousness, all of which are stress-related, reversible, transient, ego alien and unsystematized" (p. 322). Brinkley et al. did not advocate using neuroleptics for borderline patients who have not had such brief psychotic experiences; even in patients with such symptoms, they viewed the medication as adjunctive to psychotherapy.

Comparative drug trials.   Leone (1982) reported on 80 borderline patients randomly assigned to six weeks of treatment with a neuroleptic, either loxapine or chlorpromazine, in a double-blind outpatient study. Both groups showed significant global improvement over baseline, with a nonsignificant trend favoring loxapine. Loxapine was reported rapidly effective in controlling anxiety, hostility, suspiciousness, and depressed mood. A major problem with this study was the lack of a placebo group, rendering it impossible to determine whether either drug was truly effective.

Serban and Siegel (1984) reported findings from a controlled, double-blind comparison of treatment with thiothixene (mean dose = 9.4 mg) and haloperidol (mean dose = 3.0 mg) in 52 patients meeting criteria for borderline personality disorder, schizotypal personality disorder, or both. Prior to admission, each patient had experienced a mild transient psychotic episode. Eighty-four percent of the sample showed marked to moderate improvement, with greater reductions in general symptoms, depression, and paranoia (ideas of reference) in patients receiving thiothixene. Interestingly, thiothixene's superiority over haloperidol for general symptoms and paranoia was mainly in the schizotypal group. Again, however, it is difficult to document efficacy in the absence of a placebo group.

Placebo-controlled trials. Goldberg et al. (1985) studied 50 outpatients who met DSM-III criteria for borderline personality, schizotypal personality, or both and had at least one psychotic symptom. Subjects were randomly allocated to thiothixene or placebo and treated for 12 weeks. The mean dose of thiothixene at the end of the study was 8.7 mg per day. There were no differences between groups for global improvement or total borderline or schizotypal scores. Interviewer-rated scores on illusions and ideas of reference and self-rated scores on psychoticism, obsessive-compulsive symptoms, and phobic anxiety, however, showed greater improvement with the active drug. The placebo had large effects on self-rated anger-hostility and interpersonal sensitivity and on observer-rated suspiciousness and overall borderline and schizotypal scores. These results show why a placebo control is so important for drug treatment studies of borderline and schizotypal patients.

Soloff et al. (1986) are currently completing a five-week study comparing haloperidol (mean dose at end of study = 7.2 mg), amitriptyline (mean dose at end of study = 147.6 mg), and placebo in borderline and schizotypal patients. In the 64 patients studied thus far, haloperidol was found superior to placebo on the hostility, paranoia, and total scores of the Inpatient, Multidimensional Psychiatric Rating Scale (IMPS), on all 10 SCL-90 factors, and on the Beck Depression Inventory. Amitriptyline was superior to placebo on the Beck Depression Inventory and IMPS excitement scores, but was associated with worsening of impulsivity as measured by a ward behavior scale. Haloperidol was superior to amitriptyline on the hostility, paranoia, anxiety, and interpersonal sensitivity factors of the SCL-90, on a schizotypal symptom inventory, and on the ward behavior scale. Haloperidol resulted in greater decrement in overall severity than did amitriptyline or placebo (which did not differ). Patients with prominent affective or cognitive symptom profiles, or both, benefited from haloperidol. Borderline patients with major depression were no more likely to benefit from amitriptyline than those without major depression.

Taken together, these results suggest modest but distinct and diverse benefits from low-dose neuroleptics in borderline, as well as schizotypal, patients. However, further studies are needed.

Other Drug Trials in Borderline Patients

Neuroendocrine (Baxter et al. 1984; Carroll et al. 1981; Garbutt et al. 1983), sleep electroencephalogram (EEG) (Akiskal 1981; McNamara et al. 1984), family (Akiskal

1981; Stone 1979), and clinical (Akiskal 1981; Klein 1975; Liebowitz 1979) data all suggest an overlap between borderline personality as defined in DSM-III and affective disorder. As noted, Soloff et al. (1986) found moderate doses of amitriptyline were less effective than haloperidol, but other trials of tricyclic antidepressants and mono-amine oxidase inhibitors (MAOIs) in borderline patients are particularly needed. There is one positive report of three borderline children (ages 7 to 9) who failed to benefit from intensive hospital treatment until imipramine (5 mg per kg) was added to the treatment regimen (Petti and Unis 1981). In one child, the beneficial results disappeared during double-blind substitution of placebo and returned when imipramine was reinstated.

With regard to benzodiazepines, Faltus (1984) described three extensively treated patients who benefited from the new triazolobenzodiazepine, alprazolam. However, alprazolam has also been reported to occasionally cause dangerous emotional and behavioral disinhibition (Rosenbaum et al. 1984), and so must be given to borderline patients with caution.

Cowdry and Gardner (1988) and Gardner and Crowdry (1986) are conducting placebo-controlled trials of a variety of drugs in borderline patients with prominent behavioral dyscontrol (overdoses, angry outbursts, wrist cutting) and rejection sensitivity. Alprazolam (up to 6 mg per day) and the anticonvulsant carbamazepine (up to 1,200 mg per day) were compared with placebo in random-order crossover trials; the phenothiazine trifluoperazine (up to 12 mg per day) and the MAOI tranylcypromine (up to 60 mg per day) were compared in the same patients in a second study. Patients found tranylcypromine the most consistently helpful. Therapists gave highest ratings to carbamazepine and to tranylcypromine, both of which helped dyscontrol, as well as having antidepressant, antianxiety, and antianger effects. Carbamazepine helped dyscontrol most, although patients did not particularly like the drug. Tranylcypromine had primarily antidepressant effects, with antidyscontrol features as a secondary benefit. Several instances of serious behavioral disinhibition with alprazolam were noted (Gardner and Cowdry 1985).

There have been no systematic trials of other benzodiazepines in borderline patients (Schatzberg and Cole 1981).

Other Personality Disorders

No other DSM-III personality disorder has been subject to extensive trials of drug therapy. Antisocial behavior occurring in the context of other disorders has shown some drug responsivity. Stringer and Josef (1983) reported that two hospitalized patients with antisocial personality disorders and histories of childhood attention deficit disorder became less aggressive during trials of methylphenidate. For a patient with episodes of psychosis and sociopathic behavior, lithium, used in a double-blind, crossover design, diminished the antisocial activity (Liebowitz et al. 1976). Features that suggested possible lithium responsivity in this patient were a family history of lithium-responsive illness; recurrent depression; and aggressiveness, impulsivity, and hyperactivity between psychotic episodes.

Schizotypal, schizoid, and paranoid personality disorders phenomenologically lie closer to the "schizophrenic pole" than other personality disorders and might, therefore, be expected to show neuroleptic responsiveness. In one study, 14 outpatients and six inpatients satisfying DSM-III criteria for schizotypal personality disorder were treated with low doses of haloperidol (up to 14 mg per day) for a period of six weeks after two weeks of placebo. Hymowitz et al. (1984), in a preliminary report of this open trial, noted improvement in schizotypal features, social isolation, and ideas of reference. However, only 50 percent of the patients were able to complete the full medication trial because of side effects such as akathesia and drowsiness.

These findings are difficult to compare with the findings of the placebo-controlled trials involving schizotypal patients. Goldberg et al. (1986) did not find thiothixene had an effect on schizotypal features in a mixed schizotypal-borderline sample. They did find improvement, however, in illusions, ideas of reference, psychoticism, phobic anxiety, and obsessive-compulsivity in the sample as a whole (without distinguishing between diagnostic types). Soloff et al. (1986) found antipsychotic drugs effective in a mixed borderline-schizotypal sample, but did not report results for the schizotypal patients separately.

Drug Treatment of Non-DSM-III Personality Disorder Constellations

The Affective Spectrum

Yerevanian and Akiskal (1979) applied neuroendocrine, sleep EEG, family, follow-up, and pharmacologic challenge strategies to distinguish "characterological" depressions from chronic, subsyndromal affective disorder. One study sample was characterized by depressive onset before age 25, illness duration of at least five years, prominent depressive symptoms most days of the year, and symptoms falling short of DSM-III criteria for major depression. In all cases the clinical presentation made it difficult to decide whether the patient suffered an affective or character disorder. Twenty of 65 patients showed a good response to tricyclic antidepressants, suggesting subsyndromal affective disorder. An even higher percentage might have responded had systematic trials of MAOIs and lithium also been carried out.

Studies have shown MAOI responsivity of the depressive subtype called hysteroid dysphoria (Klein and Davis 1969; Liebowitz and Klein 1979, 1981; Liebowitz et al. 1984). These patients are highly sensitive to rejection and vulnerable to severe depressive crashes in the face of romantic or other disappointments. They also crave attention and admiration, often choosing inappropriate romantic partners or being so demanding that appropriate partners are driven away.

A preliminary drug and psychotherapy study involved 16 young women who met criteria for hysteroid dysphoria. Seventy-five percent of the sample also met DSM-III criteria for borderline personality disorder in terms of usual behavior during the two years prior to treatment (Liebowitz and Klein 1981). Patients were all treated with twice-weekly dynamic psychotherapy for six months. They also received the MAOI phenelzine for the first three months. After this, they were randomized double-blind to continue on active phenelzine or switch to placebo. The group as a whole showed significant reductions in mean number of borderline symptoms and in the number of patients who still met criteria for borderline personality disorder after three months of combined MAOI and psychotherapy. Four of six patients who were switched to placebo after three months of phenelzine showed at least temporary relapses, despite continuation of psychotherapy. Exaggeration of previously well controlled borderline symptoms, including feelings of chronic emptiness and boredom, problems being alone, impulsivity, unstable close relationships, and physically self-damaging acts, were noted in three of the four cases.

Recently, the clinical profile of atypical depressives specifically responsive to MAOIs has become clearer. A placebo-controlled comparison of the MAOI phenelzine and the tricyclic imipramine was conducted in patients who met Research Diagnostic Criteria for major, minor, or intermittent depression, who could still be cheered up at least temporarily while depressed, and who showed two or more of the following symptoms: overeating while depressed, oversleeping while depressed, extreme fatigue when depressed, and chronic rejection sensitivity. The group as a whole did better on phenelzine than imipramine or placebo (Liebowitz et al. 1984). However, patients meeting criteria for hysteroid dysphoria (extreme sensitivity to rejection and extreme demand for attention) in addition to exhibiting features of atypical depression, or atypical depressives with any history of panic attacks, may constitute specifically MAOI-responsive subgroups within this larger atypical depressive spectrum.

Subtle manifestations of bipolar disorder may also be the basis of some of the psychopathology labeled as personality disorder. Akiskal et al. (1979) found that patients with cyclothymic disorder manifested irritable-angry-explosive outbursts that alienated loved ones, episodic promiscuity, and repeated conjugal or romantic failure. These patients also had frequent shifts in line of work, study, interest, or plans; frequently resorted to alcohol and drug abuse as a means for self-treatment or augmenting excitement; and occasionally were financially extravagant. These features, which at least in cyclothymics may be lithium responsive, are seen in many patients with other forms of personality disorder.

One controlled study has demonstrated the utility of lithium in characterologically disturbed patients who also have frequent unprovoked mood shifts (emotionally unstable character disorder). Rifkin et al. (1972) studied patients with chronic, maladaptive character traits such as difficulty with authority, truancy, job instability, and manipulativeness. These patients also had apparently unprecipitated depressive and hypomanic mood swings that lasted from hours to days and benefited from lithium. In a placebo-controlled study, lithium significantly diminished the mean daily range in mood, reducing both hypomanic and depressive swings. In addition, these patients became more responsive to nonpharmacologic treatment when their mood dysregulation was diminished.

A number of studies have demonstrated antidepressant responsivity of pseudoneurotic schizophrenia, a nosological forerunner of borderline personality disorder. In one trial (Klein 1967, 1968), placebo, chlorpromazine, and imipramine were administered in a randomized, double-blind fashion to 311 hospitalized patients, including 32 pseudoneurotic schizophrenics. For the pseudoneurotic group, a significant difference from placebo was found for imipramine but not chlorpromazine with regard to global improvement.

Similarly, Hedberg et al. (1971) compared the MAOI and antidepressant tranylcypromine with the neuroleptic trifluoperazine and a combination of both. The study was a double-blind crossover trial in a schizophrenic population that included 28 pseudoneurotic patients. In contrast to the group as a whole, significantly more of the pseudoneurotic patients responded to tranylcypromine than to the other drug regimens. More recently, amoxapine was found useful in five of seven pseudoneurotic patients in an open clinical trial (Aono et al. 1981).

MAOI or tricyclic responsivity, however, can no longer automatically be equated with affective disorder, given the findings of effectiveness for these drug classes in patients with anxiety disorders. These findings are pertinent also to bulimics, who characteristically report both anxiety and depressive symptoms. In recent open trials, bulimic patients appeared to benefit from both tricyclics (Pope et al. 1983) and MAOIs (Stewart et al. 1984; Walsh et al. 1982).

The Anxiety Spectrum

Some borderline, narcissistic, and histrionic personality disorders may be part of an affective spectrum. Other DSM-III personality disorders, such as compulsive, dependent, passive-aggressive, and avoidant types, phenomenologically appear to lie closer to the anxiety disorders. The progress in psychopharmacologic therapies for anxiety disorders may, therefore, have relevance for treatment of certain DSM-III personality disorders.

Both tricyclic antidepressants (Klein 1964, 1967) and MAOIs (Kelly et al. 1970; Sheehan et al. 1980) have been shown effective in blocking panic attacks. These are sudden, unprovoked episodes of extreme anxiety accompanied by palpitations, tachycardia, sweating, trembling, shortness of breath, and feelings that one is about to die, lose control, or go crazy. Panic attacks are the core psychopathologic feature of panic disorder and of almost all cases of agoraphobia. Most patients with panic attacks and agoraphobia show unusual interpersonal dependency as adults. Many have histories of childhood separation anxiety as well. Therefore, tricyclics and MAOIs should be kept in mind for patients demonstrating unusual separation anxiety, pathologic dependency, panic attacks, or widespread phobic avoidance.

Social phobia may be characterized as an exaggerated anxiety response to situations in which an individual feels, or anticipates, evaluation or scrutiny by others (Liebowitz et al. 1985). In some cases it is limited to a fear of public speaking or auditioning. Other patients are so frightened by almost any interpersonal exchange that they avoid all but the most superficial interactions with anyone outside their nuclear family. These latter patients are also hypersensitive to criticism and usually meet criteria for avoidant personality disorder. Yet they appear responsive to MAOIs (Liebowitz et al. 1986). At times one sees dramatic reversal of long-standing social anxiety and avoidance. Based on studies of atypical depressives (Liebowitz et al. 1984), nonendogenous depressives (Nies et al. 1982), social phobics (Liebowitz et al. 1986), and hysteroid dsyphorics (Liebowitz and Klein 1979, 1981), a prime indication for responsivity to MAOIs may be hypersensitivity to interpersonal disapproval or criticism, a cardinal feature of many personality disorders. Physicians should be thoroughly familiar with the risks of MAOIs, however, before employing them.

Studies have also demonstrated the responsivity of obessive-compulsive disorder to pharmacotherapy with the tricyclic clomipramine (Insel and Murphy 1984; Thoren et al. 1980). Although these findings have not yet been extended to compulsive personality disorder, they bear investigation. Similarly, the finding of imipramine (Burstein 1984) and phenelzine (Hogben and Cornfield 1981) responsivity for traumatic stress disorder in open clinical trials may be relevant to personality-disordered patients.

The Organic Spectrum

Subtle neurologic dysfunction may also underlie some syndromes thought to be personality disorders. In patients with emotionally unstable character disorder, Quitkin et al. (1976) found a higher than expected incidence of neurologic soft signs. Wood et al. (1976) claimed efficacy for methylphenidate in the treatment of adult, minimal brain dysfunction (MBD) (now called attention deficit disorder, residual type, or

ADD-R). They assembled a sample of 15 adults identified on the basis of current MBD-like complaints, self-description of MBD characteristics in childhood, and parental rating of a standardized form for hyperactivity in childhood. Hypothesized ADD-R characteristics include history of long-standing impulsiveness, inattentiveness, restlessness, short temper, and emotional lability. Eight of 11 patients given a double-blind, placebo-controlled, crossover trial of methylphenidate showed a significant response to the active drug, with no tendency to abuse the drug. The maximum dose of active drug varied from 20 to 60 mg a day in the four-week trial (two weeks on the active drug, two weeks on placebo). Interestingly, drug improvement seemed to occur on dimensions of calmness, concentration, and temper, rather than the dimension of happiness. This suggests that the drug was not acting as a simple euphoriant.

In a second study, Wender et al. (1981) examined the efficacy of the psychostimulant pemoline for adult MBD. A drug-placebo difference was not found for the study group as a whole. A subgroup of patients whose parents had rated their childhood behavior as evidencing hyperactivity, however, did show a significant effect of pemoline on motor hyperactivity, attentional difficulties, hot temper, impulsivity, and stress intolerance.

Turnquist et al. (1983) reported a case of a 25-year-old man with a diagnosis of attention deficit disorder and alcoholism. Treatment with pemoline substantially improved the patient's response to alcoholism treatment and aftercare.

Examining 91 hospitalized, psychiatric patients meeting DSM-III criteria for borderline syndrome, Andrulonis et al. (1980b) found that 27 percent of the total sample had a positive history of childhood minimal brain dysfunction or learning disability (including 53 percent of the 32 males in the sample). In the same sample, 27 of the male patients and 32 of the female patients met criteria for episodic dyscontrol syndrome. There was substantial overlap between this group and those with a history of minimal brain dysfunction.

People who are intermittently, impulsively violent can be classified in DSM-III as having intermittent explosive disorder. Many such patients would probably meet criteria for borderline personality disorder (Andrulonis et al. 1980b). These patients have explosive episodes that are provoked by little or no stress, are repetitive, are short in duration, and result in efficient, coordinated, and even purposeful violent behavior. This loss of control is followed by partial amnesia and relief of tension (Andrulonis et al. 1980; Bach-y-Rita et al. 1971). In addition, these patients are characterized by drug or alcohol abuse, traffic violations, arrests, job or school failures, suicide attempts, and resistance to conventional psychiatric interventions. There is often a history of head trauma, hyperactivity, and learning disability in childhood. Family history of alcoholism, sociopathy, and violence; certain characteristic EEG abnormalities; and positive findings for soft neurologic signs are also common. Andrulonis et al. (1980a) suggested that the acts of violence in these patients are triggered by ictal events resulting from recurrent discharges from the temporal lobes to the limbic system. They presented preliminary data supporting the efficacy of the anticonvulsant ethosuximide for these patients.

Pharmacotherapy for pathologic aggression has been investigated. In both uncontrolled (Tupin et al. 1973) and controlled (Sheard et al. 1976) studies, lithium has been found useful in treating aggressive prisoners. Propranolol (Elliot 1977; Ratey et al. 1983; Yudofsky et al. 1981) has been found helpful in uncontrolled studies of both provoked and unprovoked episodes of rage in individuals with organic brain damage. On the basis of an open clinical series, Mattes (1984) reported carbamazepine useful for adult patients with uncontrolled rage outbursts of diverse etiologies.

Summary of the Evidence

Studies to date suggest that drug therapies may be of use to some patients who meet criteria for DSM-III personality disorders. Future studies are needed to clarify which personality disorders, and which subsets of patients specifically, benefit from neuroleptics, tricyclics, MAOIs, lithium, benzodiazepines, psychostimulants, anticonvulsants, and beta adrenergic blockers.

Practicalities of Treatment

The initial visit for assessing suitability for somatic therapy for a personality-disordered patient should be scheduled to last at least 90 minutes. During this consultation, the mental health professional must take a very active role in obtaining history of the present illness, past psychiatric history, medical history, family history, and personal history. A mental status exam is also necessary. Detailed questioning is needed to learn about possible affective episodes and fluctuations. The therapist must specifically question about unprecipitated mood shifts (either highs or lows), excessive mood reactivity (into dysphoric and hypomanic states), vegetative symptoms when depressed, and chronic hypersensitivity to criticism or rejection. It is also important to ask about spontaneous panic attacks, transient psychotic symptoms, or a childhood history of MBD. A significant other in the patient's life should be interviewed, with the patient out of the room, to obtain another perspective. The biologic work-up should always include T3, T4, and TSH to rule out occult thyroid disease, and an EEG with nasopharyngeal leads may be indicated to rule out temporal lobe epilepsy.

If a possible indication for drug therapy is present, the patient should be started on appropriate medication and the dosage raised systematically. It is important that any medication be given a thorough trial before being abandoned. Although neuroleptic dosages for personality-disordered patients remain to be established, phenelzine should be increased to six pills per day (90 mg per day, or its equivalent) and imipramine to 300 mg per day. Patients not responding to imipramine in this dose range should have their blood level checked; if the combined imipramine-desipramine level is below 150 to 200 mg per ml, dosage can be raised further after checking the EKG to rule out significant cardiac conduction impairment. Lithium and carbamazepine administration should involve monitoring to ensure that blood levels are in therapeutic ranges (0.6 to 1.2 meq per L for lithium, 8 to 12 μg per ml for carbamazepine). Drug trials to relieve symptoms should last at least six weeks for a given drug, with at least two weeks at top dose. Prophylactic trials, of course, require more time.

A reasonable plan is to see patients on a weekly to biweekly basis, depending on their stability, and to monitor progress and adjust dosage between visits by phone. Medication trials usually last six months to a year if improvement is noted before gradual tapering is attempted. Many patients relapse when drug therapy is discontinued. Excluding possible tolerance, however, long-term use of the various classes of psychotropic drugs does not appear to present additional risk beyond that incurred by short-term use, with the exception of neuroleptics and perhaps lithium.

Although the goals for somatic therapy vary according to the patients' particular problems, it is important in all cases to specify treatment targets prospectively. These may include reducing transient psychotic episodes or relieving agitation with a neuroleptic, achieving greater affective stabilization or blockade of pain attacks with a tricyclic, reducing autonomous mood shifts with lithium, or obtaining relief from depression, social phobia, panic attacks, or hypersensitivity to rejection with a MAOI. Again, discussion with a family member or close friends (with the patient's permission) from time to time during the course of treatment is useful for monitoring progress. For some personality-disordered patients, a goal of medication is to render them more able to participate in psychotherapy. For others, effective medication helps them leave psychotherapy.

Specific indications for drug therapy in personality-disordered patients can be gleaned from the foregoing discussions. Given the current state of knowledge, drug treatment for any given patient should be thought of as a mini-experiment in which therapist and patient participate. A medication is tried, and the results examined over time. Therapeutic gains support a hypothesis that a drug-treatable condition existed, although in the absence of placebo controls, contribution of other treatment factors, such as the therapeutic relationship, cannot be discounted.

Contraindications to a specific drug therapy include previous failures with a vigorous trial of that medication. Active drug or alcohol abuse, prominent suicidal ideation or behavior, or inability to otherwise comply with certain commonsense requirements (such as following a low-tyramine diet on MAOIs) may suggest that drug trials be conducted on an inpatient basis. The hope is that once stabilized, the patient can safely be transferred to outpatient status. Chronic neuroleptic therapy should be undertaken with great reluctance, given the risk of tardive dyskinesia.

Treating personality-disordered patients with drug therapy is both similar to and different from applying the same treatments to patients with other psychiatric disorders. The similarity is the requirement of basic knowledge of the indications, dose ranges, dosage schedules, and potential adverse effects of the different drug classes. A difference is that personality-disordered patients experience interpersonal difficulties in a variety of encounters, including those with psychopharmacologists. Thus, establishing rapport and setting limits may require more attention with personality-disordered patients than with other patients. Medication may reinforce already hypertrophied tendencies to externalize blame and responsibility. Histrionic types may experience an abundance of unusual side effects (or overreact to standard ones); obsessionals may view medication as a loss of control and need extra educational efforts; and patients with borderline personality disorder may act out with their medication (including overdosing), split between psychopharmacologist and psychotherapist, and attach unrealistic expectations to pharmacotherapy. Gunderson (1984) described a series of issues that should be addressed when considering adding medication to the treatment of a personality-disordered patient already in psychotherapy. In addition to practical matters, transference and countertransference distortions often come to the fore when pharmacotherapy is introduced for borderline patients in intensive psychotherapy.

Pharmacotherapist-psychotherapist interactions can take one of several forms for patients meeting Axis II personality disorder criteria. At times the patient is in what both patient and therapist consider a productive psychotherapy when sent to the pharmacotherapist. In this case the role of pharmacotherapy is adjunctive—to see what can be added to the treatment. Patients often see a pharmacotherapist because anxiety surges or affective swings are not under satisfactory control even though they are making gains in other ways. Proper diagnosis and somatic therapy can often be quite helpful.

In other cases the patient is in psychotherapy that is not proceeding satisfactorily. If the patient has a drug-treatable disorder or there is a drug-treatable aspect to the disorder, pharmacotherapy may facilitate the psychotherapy by alleviating distress that hindered its progress. Alternatively, pharmacotherapy may hasten the conclusion of the psychotherapy by rendering it unnecessary or allowing the patient to end an unsatisfactory dependency. Whether the patient ultimately requires additional psychotherapy (dynamic or behavioral) beyond the supportive therapy inherent in a good psychopharmacologist-patient relationship can often be better determined after attempting pharmacologic stabilization.

Chapter 252

Residential Treatment

Historically, residential treatment meant asylum. With the advent of the moral treatment principles of "kindness and firmness," however, the mental hospital evolved beyond its custodial niche. The concept of institutional care as treatment germinated in residential centers for children and, aided by the proliferation of psychoanalytically catalyzed psychosocial treatments, quickly spread to adult asylums as well. The therapeutic "milieu" and "community" developed as a mutative alternative to everyday society. Advances in many areas of psychiatry, biological and psychological, have rendered feasible brief and partial hospitalization, thus challenging many old distinctions between inpatient and outpatient and demanding construction of milieus within the fabric of society.

Today, residential treatment comprises many innovative and complex modes of therapy from short-term hospital layovers to long-term sheltered community networks. In between these extremes diversity reigns. Nevertheless, closer inspection reveals that most programs are built on common foundations. Differences depend on the nature of individual patients and therapeutic goals. In this chapter I will discuss both general and specific features of residential treatment.

Most developments in residential treatment stemmed from the care of psychotic patients, but many of the principles proved applicable to patients with borderline personality disorder. Treatment of the latter patients will be reviewed at some depth, not because the borderline personality is prototypic of all personality disorders, but because, with few exceptions (Kemp 1981), little has been written about the residential treatment of patients with any other personality disorder (except antisocial) as currently defined in DSM-III (American Psychiatric Association 1980).

I will cover the following topics in this chapter: 1) personality-disordered patients and the nature of their problems, 2) indications for treatment and goals, 3) common elements, principles, and strategies of residential treatment, 4) special milieus, 5) recent process developments, 6) specialized short- and long-term programs and their indications, and 7) issues and controversies.

The overall focus will be on residential care for therapeutic purposes; residential care for custodial purposes, although important, will not be addressed. Specific treatment modalities like psychopharmacology or individual, group, or family psychotherapy are described in other chapters. These modalities are crucial elements in most residential treatment programs, but the focus here is on what the milieu can offer in addition to and in coordination with these modalities. Finally, the residential treatment of antisocial personalities refers to treating and rehabilitating criminals incarcerated in society's penal systems. Such programs are sufficiently unique to require separate review and will be dealt with elsewhere (see Chapter 258).

The Personality-Disordered Patient

The identifying defensive characteristics of patients with character problems are rigid, repetitive, and persistently inappropriate (American Psychiatric Association 1980; Kernberg 1975). Maladaptive behaviors of these patients usually occur in an interpersonal context, invariably alienate others, and result in serious disabilities in working and loving (Vaillant and Perry 1980). Personality disorders are usually chronic, are often multiple, and may exist concommitantly with other psychiatric syndromes.

Patients sufficiently impaired to require residential treatment are particularly difficult to treat. As the Frosches (1964, 1983b) noted, the traits that define personality disorders also subvert the aims of traditional therapy. Such patients do not want treatment and view their problems as external. Usually their maladaptive behaviors are more disturbing to others than to themselves. They cannot bear dysphoric internal states such as anxiety, guilt, depression, anger, or ambivalence, and readily use impulsive action or primitive defenses (splitting, projective identification) to eradicate or expel discomfort. Except for some patients with borderline personality disorder, most of the "symptoms" in personality disorders are ego-syntonic, thus rendering their removal a formidable undertaking.

In contrast to psychotic patients requiring residential treatment, patients with personality disorders generally possess intact reality testing and remain interpersonally related under stress. They may regress in the hospital, but this is not a process of disintegration or fragmentation as in psychosis. Rather, they become more passive, immobilized, and helpless or destructively active and impulsive.

The unattractiveness of these patients has frequently led to the rationalization that they can manage without treatment, especially residential. The recent proliferation of chronic, young adult patients wandering homeless, however, clearly refutes such an assertion. Most descriptions of this growing population identify these people as primarily personality disordered or, if psychotic, riddled with major character problems (Bachrach 1982). They are clearly a group in need of energetic and structured treatment.

Good prognostic features have been identified for patients with borderline personality disorder (Adler 1980; McGlashan 1985). To some extent these may apply to other personality disorders. Such patients have relationships capable of providing support and structure, are interpersonally oriented rather than schizoid, possess good reality testing, and use primitive defenses like projection and projective identification sparingly. Their superegos are not overly attenuated or primitive, and they possess some capacity for delay under stress. They are bright, affectively even (rather than unstable and fluctuating), and not chronic by history.

Indications and Goals

When weighing indications for residential treatment, it is important to remain flexible and remember that few hard and fast criteria exist. In addition to diagnosis and goals (to be elaborated), other dimensions merit consideration: 1) factors about the patient, such as response to prior treatment, motivation for help, impulsivity, tolerance for anxiety, reality testing, honesty and integrity, value system, capacity for concern, previous adjustment, and sublimatory capacity; 2) psychopathologic factors, such as the acuteness and severity of the disorder; and 3) environmental factors, such as financial resources, family support, and adequacy of alternative treatment facilities in the community (Hartocollis 1980).

Hospitalization is often precipitated acutely by external necessity when the patient requires protection from society or society from the patient. Situations in this category include life crises, dangerous acting out of suicidal or assaultive behavior, acute mini-psychotic breakdowns, and chaotic life situations that preclude less structured diagnostic evaluation and treatment. Hospitalization is indicated also when chronic and severe psychopathology interferes significantly with adaptation outside a protected setting—especially if the patient has tried one or more treatments without response. In short, acute or chronic inability to cope in the community, even with help, should lead to a recommendation for residential treatment.

Once a personality-disordered patient has been identified as needing structured treatment, the next task involves defining the goals of that effort. Although the goals of residential treatment are at issue, these can seldom be segregated from overall treatment considerations. Accordingly, the larger perspective must be considered. A whole range of goals may apply, from crisis intervention to completing emotional growth and development. Whichever ones are indicated or chosen, it is vital for subsequent treatment that they be clearly defined and well understood by everyone involved. For heuristic purposes, treatment goals can be dichotomized as focused or extensive.

Focused treatment goals are also identified in the literature as short-term, adaptational, supportive, and symptomatic. They include 1) relief from immediate, especially life-threatening crises, 2) control of destructive and self-destructive acting out, 3) direct reduction of acute symptoms of disequilibrium, 4) decrease of maladaptive behaviors to precrisis levels, 5) reestablishment of emotional homeostasis through a strengthening of defenses, 6) sealing over of dysphoric states and erupted unconscious conflicts, 7) "social recovery" without personality change, 8) circumscribed fostering of pragmatic adaptations, and 9) mobilization of a healthy ego to enable functioning despite a continuing defect (Gordon and Beresin 1983; McGlashan 1982).

Extensive treatment goals are also referred to as long-term in the literature, the aim being "characterological" or "structural" change and fostering (or resuming) emotional growth. These goals include helping the patient achieve at least some of the following: 1) a capacity for attachment and trust or object constancy; 2) mastery of separation-individuation or the capacity for autonomy and self-object differentiation; 3) a cohesive sense of self-identity; 4) a solid and realistic self-esteem; 5) a sense of responsibility as the agent of one's behavior; 6) effective social relatedness; 7) a capacity for durable intimacy and comfort with dependency; 8) a capacity for productive work; 9) the ability to tolerate frustration, helplessness, conflict, and dysphoric affective states; 10) utilization of more mature, adaptive, and flexible mechanisms of defense; 11) the integration of ambivalence with mastery of all-or-none attitudes;

and 12) a capacity for self-observation and insight (Gordon and Beresin 1983; Mc-Glashan 1982; McGlashan and Miller 1982; Rinsley 1981).

Extensive goals often reflect more about the profession's definition of normality and less about what can be expected in the treatment of every patient. Nevertheless, although these goals may be realized with only some of the patients some of the time, they constitute the implicit working guidelines among many practitioners who treat patients with personality disorders. Finally, for many patients with severe personality disorders, the sheer magnitude of their psychopathology demands extensive treatment effort even when the changes desired may be quite limited. Thus, although extensive treatment goals undoubtedly require extensive treatment efforts, the latter may be called for even if the formulated treatment goals are modest.

General Treatment Considerations

Hospital Structure and Staff

Residential treatment teams or units are organized in a variety of ways ranging between the strict medical model on the one hand and the pure therapeutic community on the other. In the former, trained staff possess authority and responsibility for all decisions under the guidance of one professional who stands accountable for the patients' welfare. In the latter, patients assume active responsibility for treatment in the residential community and decisions are usually made by democratic vote.

The most common administrative structure, however, combines elements of both extremes and has been described by Edelson (1970a, 1970b) and Kernberg (1973, 1981). Hierarchical power and lines of authority are preserved. Top administration delegates authority clearly and nonambiguously to unit staff. The unit milieu consists of an organized social structure centered around meetings of staff and patients. Responsibility may also rest with patients when delegated by staff. The authority of the unit milieu may be substantial, but never equals or exceeds that of the hospital's administrative head, who is ultimately accountable for each patient. Decision making is not democratic but "functional," that is, in the hands of whoever possesses the greatest skill, expertise, and information for making the decision in question.

In the literature, comments about staffing are quite consistent. Above all, staff should be highly trained and adequate in number to implement treatment goals. As individuals, the best staff are accepting, flexible, and humble, but able to draw boundaries and set limits. Interpersonally, they are energetic, highly verbal, and warm. Staff's excitement about and belief in what they are doing—as a group—also bear strongly on results (Gossett et al. 1983; Noshpitz 1983; Tucker 1983).

Working Attitudes and Principles

The overall working principle of any residential treatment milieu should be to create a lively and balanced dialectic between programmatic consistency on the one hand and flexible accommodation of the individual patient on the other.

Programmatic consistency means achieving consensus within the milieu regarding theoretical orientation and operational goals. It involves the explicit articulation of organizing concepts such as the nature of psychopathology, philosophy of treatment, and criteria of healthy behavior. The specifics are secondary; more important is the staff's commitment to and predictable application of the concepts and their ramifications. Frank and Gunderson (1984), for example, demonstrated that therapists whose treatment orientation conflicted with that of the milieu had significantly more trouble engaging and maintaining patients in therapy than therapists whose treatment orientation matched that of the milieu. They suggested that therapists should either avoid working in milieus with different treatment philosophies or keep their differences to themselves. Likewise, Gordon and Beresin (1983) admonished striving for "goodness of fit" between treatment model and milieu.

Because no single program can serve all patients, however, the need for consistency cannot justify rigidity. Efforts must be made to design and tailor the milieu to the individual patient within the limits of reason and pragmatism (Gunderson 1983b, 1984). If a workable match cannot be realized, the patient should be referred to an alternate program offering a better match.

Functions of the Hospital and Technical Strategies

Generally applicable program functions and strategies are elaborated here and organized according to the following components of any standard milieu treatment plan: 1) protection, 2) evaluation, 3) alliance with patient and family, 4) structured milieu interventions, 5) activities and rehabilitation, and 6) discharge planning and aftercare.

Protection.   Residential programs and facilities are often chosen over alternatives because of a need for the patient's protection from danger to self or others, from a noxious environment, from a psychopathologic family, or from any of a host of other stresses. This function is also called containment when it involves structuring the environment to prevent or minimize overwhelming stress. It is also known as holding when it involves providing the patient a haven or moratorium for development advance (Modell 1976).

The type and amount of protection needed determine the setting required (i.e., 24-hour facility with or without locked units or some form of partial facility like a day hospital or half-way house). Virtually all other hospital functions (evaluation, activities, etc.) can be provided in any setting, but not so the protective function. Safety needs largely determine the choice of physical facility.

Evaluation.   The following strategies are essential at the time of and shortly after admission: 1) rapid evaluation of the need for protection with immediate institution of any necessary structure (e.g., a locked unit); 2) intensive, thorough 24-hour observation and evaluation of the patient, both "informal" (e.g., milieu) and "formal" (e.g., mental status examination and psychological testing), to ascertain primary diagnosis; 3) elaboration of a thorough differential diagnosis, including a complete physical examination to rule out contributing medical-organic problems, paying special attention to any concomitant Axis I disorders (especially depression, because this is one of the few indications for medication in personality disorders) (McGlashan 1983b); 4) estimation of baseline severity and prognosis for treatment planning and for judging progress; and 5) formulation of an initial treatment plan articulating goals and appropriate treatments (Adler 1977).

Alliance.   With personality-disordered patients, a classical treatment alliance, if present at all, is likely to be tenuous and constitutes a goal of treatment rather than the foundation of treatment. Some therapists insist on evidence of a wish for treatment, such as voluntary admission (Erlich 1983). Most, however, assert that motivation cannot be expected as a given. It germinates in the emerging transferences to the staff and therapists. Accordingly, it is technically important to establish an initial positive rapport and to utilize the positive transference in maintaining a relationship. An active, friendly, nonorthodox style serves this aim best. The T-A (therapist-administrator) split may significantly aid attachments. It helps the therapist or primary treating person avoid early negative transference and struggles for control around administrative decisions. This is especially useful with delinquent and antisocial patients.

An alliance with the family is usually easier to establish than an alliance with the patient because family members are often in more distress than the patient at admission. Nevertheless, certain attitudes and strategies can secure a solid and less crisis-oriented relationship. Staff should provide 1) support and education; 2) an accepting, nonvillainizing attitude; 3) information about the patient's problems, prognosis, and treatment needs in clear, nonjargon terms; 4) immediate knowledge about with whom in the unit milieu the family relates; and 5) information about who makes what decisions and when regarding the patient's treatment plan. Once established, this alliance should be maintained through repeated contact with the patient's therapist.

Structured milieu interventions.   The most effective residential treatment units are small and have high staff-to-patient ratios; high levels of staff-patient interaction; a minority of low-functioning or chronic patients; a cultural base compatible with the community in which the patients live; active and structured lines of communication with opportunities for observation, confrontation, and discussion; a task-oriented group structure that is not open-ended; and a routine daily schedule of activities to which everyone is expected to adhere. Effective milieus possess an overall gestalt of interest, patience, tolerance, and flexibility tempered with objectivity, consistency, and the natural formality of professional roles (Ellsworth 1983; Gralnick 1979; Liberman 1983; Wishnie 1975).

The patient spends most of his or her time in the hospital talking with people. Verbal interactions with staff, therefore, constitute a central aspect of residential treatment. They are basically ego-building and geared toward the development of mastery. A sampling follows: 1) focus on behavior and not explanations of behavior; 2) confront rather than interpret in a setting where support (especially of peers) is available; 3) call attention to patterns—especially those that defeat adaptation; 4) educate the patient to identify signs of signal anxiety; 5) introduce reality factors and reinforce reality testing; 6) promote delay in action and support sublimation; and 7) encourage thinking versus doing—especially the capacity to think through the consequences of one's behavior.

Frequently these strategies prove ineffective, their failure being signaled by persistent or emergent symptomatic behavior. Verbal structuring must then be supplemented by limit setting, especially when the patient's defensiveness takes the form of dangerous acting out. The opportunity and capacity to set limits is the unique contribution that residential treatment has to offer any treatment plan. It is also one of the most powerful technical strategies available to the professional and should be handled with care. Limits should be set firmly but not punitively. If applied too rigidly, they impede the unfolding of psychopathology. If applied too sluggishly or inconsistently, they encourage regression and acting out. A balanced, evenhanded application is best, recognizing that one cannot ultimately control the patient's behavior. Furthermore, the unit as a whole must define its ultimate limits, that is, the level of symptomatic behavior it is willing to tolerate before deciding to discharge or transfer the patient.

Activities and rehabilitation. Specific adjunctive therapies (recreational therapy, occupational therapy, etc.) structure the patient's time with concrete, directed tasks that provide needed diversion and sublimation. Their regular scheduling also establishes an organizing and calming routine. They are particularly useful for the fragmented psychotic patient. For the average personality-disordered patient, however, these programs become "busy work" rather quickly, and rehabilitation moves into center stage as the most relevant "activity" in the residential treatment.

Through structured, task-oriented, and often didactic activities, rehabilitation teaches the patients more adaptive and practical ways of coping. According to Lamb (1977), because no clear relationship exists between instrumental capacity and degree of emotional recovery, rehabilitation efforts should be introduced on a trial basis as soon as possible. Goals should be clearly defined and geared to ambitious but not unrealistic levels. Rehabilitation counseling should focus on reality issues while meeting the patient's dependency needs within the milieu. Rehabilitation programs located primarily in the community provide more useful in vivo experience and enhance the retention of gains over time.

Discharge planning and aftercare. Reintegration into the community is one of the most important but neglected functions of residential treatment. Hospitalization seldom cures, and improvements must be generalized and maintained on the outside by continued treatment, rehabilitation, and supportive aftercare services. Such efforts, however, are best initiated and coordinated while the patient is still hospitalized.

When a patient meets the criteria for discharge, an intensive reevaluation should commence to ascertain the degree to which he or she needs, wants, and can utilize further help and what programs are available to provide the requisite services. This is not easy, for once the dust of crisis has settled, personality-disordered patients often appear relatively intact. They seldom present as wanting further treatment, although many borderline patients are an exception. Personality-disordered patients often vanish from the scene once the need for protection has abated, thus avoiding an opportunity to have enduring deficits and their appropriate treatment assessed.

Several areas of the patient's functioning should be assessed prior to discharge: 1) dangerousness to self or others, 2) living arrangements, 3) finances, 4) family, 5) social (peer) network, 6) employment, and 7) intimate relationships. Obviously, no patient should be released until the situation is safe. Assurance, of resources for adequate food, clothing, and shelter is the first and most powerful prophylaxis against recidivism. This often involves establishing liaisons with key community agencies, welfare offices, and legal services. Proper family and peer contact can be crucial for supporting more social and adaptive coping strategies. Deficits in this area can be remedied with a variety of outpatient treatments (family therapy, group psychotherapy, social skills training, Alcoholics Anonymous, social clubs, etc.). Employment, especially if self-sustaining, can often represent the turning point between being a "patient" and being a "citizen." Difficulties in this area can be addressed with various types of vocational rehabilitation, education, and training. The capacity for intimacy perhaps eludes these patients the most; it is certainly their most enduring deficit over time (McGlashan 1986). Treatment for this requires long-term psychotherapy. Such efforts may not be necessary to prevent recidivism, but may be desired to enrich the quality of life.

Special Milieus

Two special kinds of milieus, behavior modification and the therapeutic community, although not the predominant forms of treatment in today's residential facilities, have contributed important operating principles and techniques to the field.

Behavior Modification

Most of the literature on behavior modification addresses the application of these techniques to the chronically psychotic patient. Dahl and Merskey (1981), however, described a behavioral program for personality-disordered patients including staged privileges and transfers to less restrictive wards contingent upon specific responsible behavior. This program sounds strikingly similar to the garden variety systems of limits and privileges operative in most residential treatment facilities, attesting to how thoroughly behavior modification principles have been integrated into the fabric of today's average milieu.

Therapeutic Communities

Therapeutic communities are programs that encourage patients to be active therapeutic agents for themselves via communication, confrontation, and feedback in a variety of open group meetings and collective (democratic) decision-making processes regarding treatment issues. The assumption is made that the patient is capable of a responsible role in the milieu and in understanding his or her own behavior. This kind of milieu requires appropriate selection of patients; a therapeutic community of regressed psychotic patients is not possible.

Optimal populations appear to be those for whom the techniques were originally developed: personality-disordered patients who are substance abusers, or sociopathic, or both (Jones 1983). Therapeutic community organizations are popular, for example, in drug self-help groups and programs aimed at rehabilitating delinquent adolescents and antisocial adults. For these populations, therapeutic communities offer several advantages over the medical model: 1) avoidance of the passive-helpless role or identity, 2) peer authority, which is more acceptable than hierarchical authority, 3) protection of self-esteem by accepting help from others who have similar problems, and 4) enhancement of self-esteem by helping others who have problems.

The pure therapeutic community is seldom used in residential treatment facilities. Time is required for meaningful relationships (i.e., a community) to develop, and without meaningful relationships there can be no effective peer pressure. Most hospital units have programs that are simply too short, and long-term residential treatment programs serving more chronic and less functional populations require hierarchical, medical model organizations, which are incompatible with therapeutic communities. Finally, most residential treatment units admit diagnostically heterogeneous patient groups, including psychotic patients who are chronically and severely disabled. As noted, these patients cannot fulfill the basic assumption of therapeutic communities.

Many of the principles and practices of the therapeutic community, however, have become integrated into almost every existing residential treatment program. Community group meetings and the ideals of honesty and open communication, for example, are absolutely standard. So, too, are such principles as allowing patients to help others, encouraging group support, and delegating responsibilities to patients whenever feasible. Even if lines of authority remain hierarchical and treatment decisions "functional" rather than democratic, most residential facilities still expect everyone, including patients, to provide relevant information and opinion as the vital basis for these decisions.

Process Developments

Much of the literature on the residential treatment of personality disorders (especially borderline) deals with process developments, that is, phenomena emerging from the patient's interaction with the milieu. Two are especially common, if not inevitable: resistance and regression. Their elaboration and management are often crucial to the success of inpatient treatment, hence their special consideration here.

Resistance

Personality-disordered persons usually become patients because of maladaptive behavior. Predictably, this behavior soon emerges in relationships within the milieu—an important development that elaborates maladaptive strategies for mutative review and drives the therapeutic process. These strategies take the form of exaggerated "character resistances" consistent with the patients' descriptive, diagnostic labels (Kemp 1981). The passive-aggressive personality, for example, becomes obstructionistic; the paranoid personality, suspicious and argumentative; the schizoid personality, withdrawn and aloof; the avoidant personality, shy but anxious; the dependent personality, helpless and clinging; the histrionic personality, flamboyant and demanding; the compulsive personality, exacting and controlling; the narcissistic personality, arrogant and devaluing; the antisocial personality, manipulative and indifferent; and the borderline personality, fluctuating and unpredictable.

These character resistances are similar to any symptomatic resistance. In personality-disorderd patients, however, resistances form quickly and are more stereotyped, rigid, and ego-syntonic. Their development inevitably creates trouble between the patient and the milieu. This should be anticipated, if not welcomed as an opportunity for meaningful therapeutic interactions. These patterns, after all, are the problems for which the patient needs help. Treatment generally consists of identifying individually characteristic patterns of resistance, demonstrating their defensive and self-defeating nature, and encouraging the development of more adaptive coping strategies.

Regression

Regression is an especially dramatic and troublesome form of resistance frequently encountered in the residential treatment of personality-disordered patients—especially borderline patients. It has been the subject of much consideration, concern, and debate in the literature (Adler 1974). Broadly defined, regression refers to the ascendance of impulsive resistance or acting-out defenses against dysphoric states that cannot be contained intrapsychically by one's usual psychological coping strategies.

The process of regression is typically catalyzed on the ward by an interpersonal relationship that mobilizes an intense idealizing transference. The patient's high expectations regarding the staff's omnipotence and capacity to care are inevitably disappointed by reality, leading to reactive guilt, disappointment, and rage. Regressive behavior is then elaborated to deal with these intolerable affects and may take many forms, such as lack of change, negative therapeutic reactions, devaluation of the idealized other, and numerous forms of acting out (e.g., suicide, self-mutilation, substance abuse, promiscuity, running away, and assaultiveness toward people or property). The patient often preserves an idealized other by "staff splitting," associating the negative side of his or her ambivalence with different people in the milieu.

Inevitably, regression mobilizes strong feelings or countertransferences in staff. Those who are idealized feel special, nurturing, and powerful. Those who are devalued feel depleted, helpless, guilty, and vengeful. To the former, the patient appears troubled, misunderstood, and needing of attention. To the latter, the patient is bad, willful, and in need of limits. If such a division is ignored, pathologic regression of the entire milieu ensues; the symptoms of such regression are an overemphasis on controlling behavior, reactive treatment planning, loss of flexibility, role diffusion among staff, and fragmentation of the team.

The proper strategy for regression is as much a matter of attitude as of technique. Staff must be realistic with themselves and the patient concerning what they can and cannot provide. They must be flexible and serve as models for compromise in the resolution of differences. Overall, they must traverse the thin line between tolerance of the patient's pathology and setting limits empathically and nonpunitively. Splitting can be anticipated through staff education and supervision and minimized by frequent staff meetings under adequate leadership to tease out polarized opinions but firmly protect communication lines.

In the event of a "malignant regression," that is, one that is unremitting and unresponsive to structuring efforts, it may prove necessary to discharge or transfer the patient to another facility (Gunderson 1984; Scharff 1969). This can be risky if it is a rationalization of disavowed staff anger but useful if it is an acknowledgment of the milieu's realistic limits or unworkable countertransferences.

Specialized Programs

In actual practice, programs often specialize in different types of patients, goals, treatment philosophies, and operational strategies. Three types of programs are particularly frequent and will be described. They are 1) short-term hospitalization with focused goals, 2) short-term hospitalization in the context of extensive goals, and 3) long-term residential treatment. All adhere to most of the general functions and strategies of residential treatment heretofore elaborated; their differences lie more in emphasis and degree. Accordingly, this discussion will highlight only the differences.

Short-Term Hospitalization with Focused Goals

The need for immediate hospitalization may be precipitated by any of the acute situations already mentioned. Once the patient is under a residential umbrella, however, there are several indications for keeping treatment goals focused and hospitalization short. One indication is that the patient is basically healthy and the acute crisis appears largely secondary to external factors or to clearly identifiable and time-limited stress, such as a grief reaction. Such patients are likely never to have been hospitalized before and to have histories of good premorbid functioning. For patients who have been hospitalized before, the same considerations apply if there is a clear history of rapid reconstitution in the hospital with subsequent satisfactory functioning in the community.

The second indication for brief hospitalization with focused goals is psychopathology not likely to be affected by residential treatment. Many patients at risk for not responding are chronically dependent and treatment addicted, with extensive histories of prior residential efforts without sustained improvement. Such patients require consideration for custodial placement if unable to cope without structure. Other patients at risk for not responding are those likely to profit financially or legally from hospitalization.

A third indication for brief hospitalization with focused goals is a risk for developing a severe, negative response to residential treatment. The past history of response to hospitalization is key. A clear history of severe, regressive episodes, especially frequent in primitive borderline patients, signals the need for caution. The same is true for repeated life-threatening or treatment-destroying therapeutic reactions, especially common in masochistic, narcissistic, and oppositional personality disorders (Frances and Clarkin 1981).

Brief hospitalization is also indicated for patients with continuing disability if less structured but viable alternate modes of treatment, such as outpatient psychotherapy, vocational rehabilitation, or family therapy, can be established relatively soon after admission and evaluation. Finally, brief hospitalization must be accepted, even if not recommended, with patients who are not dangerous but who eschew therapeutic engagement.

Operationally, the goals of such hospitalizations are circumscribed and, as outlined earlier, consist basically of reconstitution to premorbid levels of functioning and return to the mainstream as soon as possible. Lengths of stay are measured in days, and are certainly no longer than two or three months. Most units that provide programs of this type are medical in orientation and hierarchical in administrative structure, without T-A splits. They serve populations acutely disturbed and generally refer subacute and chronic cases elsewhere.

At admission, modest and realistically obtainable aims and expectations are clearly outlined to the patient and family, as are the rules of acceptable conduct. The milieu staff clarify their limited role in the patient's life, avoid treatment aimed at providing a "good relationship," and stress "real" relationships. Such milieus have fewer open group meetings than other milieus and focus on concretely structured program activities.

Staff avoid dealing with transference and unconscious conflict. They narrow the investigative focus to here-and-now issues, such as the reasons for hospitalization and problems of immediate importance. Existing defenses are supported if adaptive. Controlled behavior is expected, and regressions are actively prevented or reversed with the early use of firm limits.

Discharge planning begins from the moment of admission. It aims at providing the minimally supportive environment necessary to maintain the patient at premorbid levels of functioning. More than this may be available but is considered the patient's responsibility to pursue.

Short-Term Hospitalization in the Context of Extensive Goals

There may be indications for brief hospitalization of a patient already engaged in outpatient treatment—usually some form of psychotherapy with goals that are more or less extensive. This is a special but not uncommon situation. The residential treatment goals are focused and serve the primary purpose of reconstituting and fostering the long-term outpatient treatment.

In this context, brief hospitalization may be indicated under the following circumstances: 1) for transference regressions, especially with transference psychosis involving unmanageable, destructive, and self-destructive acting out; 2) for countertransference regressions, especially if the therapist requests consultation; 3) for temporary supporting psychotherapy in which overwhelming affects are mobilized as the relationship deepens; 4) for a troublesome psychotherapy with difficulties forming or sustaining a therapeutic alliance; and 5) for a confusing outpatient therapeutic situation that requires a thorough reevaluation (Bernstein 1980; Marcus 1981).

The goal of such hospitalization, beyond the immediate issue of safety, is to protect the viability of the outpatient treatment framework. The primary therapeutic alliance remains between the patient and the outpatient therapist, who usually continues to see the patient during the residential period. Nevertheless, while the patient is hospitalized, the extended treatment setup can undergo a thorough evaluation and overhaul, with the hospital serving as consultant. The result may be either a strengthening of the ongoing effort or its dissolution and replacement with something new.

Patient populations run the gamut from acutely to chronically disturbed. Lengths of stay are usually measured in weeks. The T-A split is commonly employed, with the hospital taking the administrative role. It is important for the outpatient therapist and the milieu to share similar treatment philosophies or at least to be willing to compromise on differences; otherwise antitherapeutic divisiveness is likely to occur, especially with borderline patients.

The milieu's goals are circumscribed. Accordingly, interactional strategies correspond to those already described for short-term hospitalization and include a rather stringent approach to regression. Discharge planning is abbreviated and focused on returning the patient to the extended treatment framework.

Long-Term Residential Treatment

The recommendation for long-term residential treatment appears to be determined mostly by the severity and chronicity of the patient's disability. Almost by default, long-term hospitalization is indicated if the patient cannot function outside a structured situation, especially if prior treatment efforts, including briefer hospitalizations, have proven ineffective. The following characteristics are frequently regarded as indications for long-term hospitalization: antisocial traits, schizoid traits, persistent poor judgment, lack of tolerance for anxiety, poor impulse control, lack of concern for others, attenuated insight or self-observation, low motivation, absent or fragile object relations, chronic and severe acting out against self or others, repeated negative therapeutic reactions, and chronic recidivism (Hartocollis 1980; Kernberg 1973).

Contrary to popular belief, especially among professionals, crippling and chronic mental illness is not limited to psychosis (Green and Koprowski 1981). As noted, patients with personality disorders constitute a significant proportion of today's most troubled and troublesome population—the homeless, young adult, chronic patients. They, more than any other single group, desperately need residential facilities that can provide long-term care and treatment.

These programs are long term not because ambitious treatment efforts are guaranteed to succeed, but because modest treatment efforts are guaranteed to fail. Treatment goals may be focused (e.g., rendering the patient capable of functioning extrainstitutionally) or extensive (e.g, structural change and emotional maturation). Whatever the goals, however, treatments tend to derive from some variation of the intensive psychotherapeutic model originally developed for the long-term residential treatment of schizophrenia (McGlashan 1983a).

Lengths of stay are seldom less than six months and usually extend into one or more years. Administrative structure varies. The lengths of stay and the slow turnover of the resident population make these milieus less volatile and more predictable than other milieus. Such familiarity often encourages experimentation. Some programs, therefore, follow a standard hierarchical medical model administratively; other introduce variations like T-A splits; still others are organized around the therapeutic community model.

In long-term residential treatment programs, a significant proportion of the treatment comes from being in residence, that is, from living for an extended period of time with new people in an accepting and structured, or "holding," environment. The milieu is designed to encourage the development of long-term and meaningful relationships. Such relationships are regarded as the foundation of treatment, especially with patients for whom more technical and manipulative ego-oriented strategies have failed. The hope is for a resumption of emotional growth and development via new attachments that, through observation and insight, are rendered more resistant to destruction by old distortions and disillusions (Masterson 1972; Rinsley 1971).

The strategies by which relationships are used for therapeutic gain have been described repeatedly in the literature on schizophrenia; experience suggests validity for personality-disordered patients as well. These strategies, although relevant at any point in the treatment process, are often clustered sequentially: 1) establishing a relationship with the patient, 2) elucidating the patient's experience in the here and now, 3) tolerating the mobilized transferences and countertransferences, 4) integrating the patient's experience into an expanded perspective of the self, and 5) working through (McGlashan 1983a).

Long-term milieus are generally organized around a primary individual psychotherapeutic relationship. Unlike short-term hospitals serving extensive goals, however, primary therapists are intramural, thus preventing frequent mismatches in the treatment philosophies of the therapist and the milieu. Milieu staff support the primary relationship and echo it in their frequent individual and group interactions with the patient. The patient's defenses are confronted, not supported; the patient's transferences and unconscious conflicts are addressed, not ignored. Observations are feeling oriented, not behavior oriented, in the service of helping the patient "acknowledge, bear and put into perspective" his or her painful affects and life experiences (Rako and Mazer 1980, p. 30).

Responsible behavior is expected of the patient, but regression is not viewed as a major cause for alarm. It is regarded as informative and as a potentially adaptive precursor to more flexible coping strategies. In short, regression is to be understood, as well as managed with appropriate limits. When set, limits tend to be restrictive (e.g., transfer to a locked unit or seclusion within the hospital) rather than extrusive (e.g, transfer to another facility).

Because functional deficits are very common in chronic patients, social and vocational rehabilitative strategies are vital aspects of long-term programs. So, too, is adequate aftercare. Long-term residential treatment, despite its length, is only a beginning for chronic patients. Institutionalization and continuing disability demand continuity of care beyond discharge if the gains of hospitalization are to be consolidated and extended.

Issues and Controversies

Among the many issues concerning residential treatment, three seem particularly important. The first involves some time-honored ethical issues that will always be relevant; the second involves the best way to handle regression; and the last, cost-effectiveness, is by far the most popular current issue about residential treatment.

Ethical Considerations

Ethical issues relevant to residential treatment have to do with involuntary commitment, confidentiality in an institution, and informed consent.

A large number of personality-disordered patients enter residential treatment against their will, either through direct legal commitment or under the threat of such action. They are citizens deprived, however briefly, of some of their freedoms—an important fact that should not be taken lightly but acknowledged openly with patients at the outset. Involuntary commitment poses a dilemma for therapists and treatment programs. Are they serving patients or society? The answer usually lies in a compromise. That is, a program serves the patient except in circumscribed and specifiable situations, usually involving dangerous behavior. This dilemma and the hospital's limits, beyond which it will become society's servant, should be communicated directly to the patient either at or shortly after admission.

In peaceful (i.e., nondangerous) outpatient treatment, what transpires between patient and therapist is none of society's business. In peaceful residential treatment, the same is true. What transpires between an inpatient and one part of the milieu, however, can never justifiably be kept confidential from another part of the milieu. In residential settings, the team is the treatment. In order to function, it must have access to all information. Secrets within a milieu are highly destructive and invariably represent a symptomatic, antitherapeutic response to the patient—a response that requires confrontation, lysis, and analysis. This attitude and working principle should be spelled out clearly to the patient.

Patients are citizens and consumers; they should be informed and provide consent. The information presented to each patient varies, however, depending on what the patient is capable of assimilating. The subjects about which, ideally, every patient should be apprised include the reasons for hospitalization, legal status and rights, diagnostic impression, likely course of illness (with short- and long-term prognostic estimates), goals of treatment, recommended interventions (including their benefits and risks), the minimal and ideal criteria for discharge, financial costs, policies about dangerousness and confidentiality, and any rules regarding expected behaviors in the milieu.

Regression and Theories of Therapy

The psychiatric community has been split for at least a generation about how to handle regressive behavior in personality-disordered patients, especially borderline patients. The divergent attitudes prevail concerning short- and long-term residential treatments. To oversimplify, the "empathizers" are on one side of this split and the "limit setters" are on the other.

Empathizers pursue extensive, long-term goals and try to understand regression. They regard it as an opportunity and vehicle for the resumption of developmental progression, individuation, and integration. They consider abbreviated therapy and excessive limits as stifling this process by driving the patient's psychopathology "underground," where it cannot be seen, dealt with, or changed.

Empathizers adhere to theories of therapy highlighting the relationship between the therapist and milieu and the patient. The patient undergoes a mutative emotional experience via transactional learning and identification with the helping other(s). The therapist and milieu present to the patient a transitional object available for attachment, soothing, and holding but also absorb the patient's rage and distress without retaliation—all of which is regarded as a necessary precursor to the natural development of autonomy (Adler 1973; Crafoord 1977; Schulz 1984).

Limit setters pursue focused, short-term goals and try to control regressions. They see many more dangers than opportunities in such states, among them iatrogenic dependency and institutionalization, adoption of the passive-sick role, loss of observing ego, and the entitled abrogation of responsibility. Controlling regression minimizes these risks and restores the patient to status quo ante before the siren call of pathologic gratification becomes too compelling (Friedman 1969, 1975; Wishnie 1975).

Limit setters espouse theories of therapy that highlight supporting and developing the most mature and healthy aspects of the patient. The infantile, needy side of the patient is ordered to keep quiet, or ignored. Crippled ego defenses are revitalized with the splint of hospital support. This tips the balance back in favor of the effective sealing over of conflict, which further clears the slate for learning new and more effective coping strategies. This, too, is a learning model, but one that emphasizes assimilation via cognitive-didactic processes rather than emotional-identificatory ones.

Because the human being has both a mind and a heart, neither the empathizers nor the limit setters appear to have a corner on the realities of regression. In fact, both viewpoints are valid, and continued polarization of the issue is self-defeating and may represent an identification with the patients in question. It is clear that regression can reap rewards; it is also clear that it holds considerable risks.

The answer lies in a balanced integration of both viewpoints and their associated strategies and a careful assessment of the benefit-to-risk ratio for regression with each patient in any given program. The best estimate of this ratio is an accurate history of the patient's behavior in prior residential treatment settings. For some patients, placement on even minimally permissive wards can prove too tempting and lead to iatrogenic disorganization (Quitkin and Klein 1967). Such patients, however, leave a trail that can be traced. For patients with no prior history, it is wise to proceed as an "empathic limit setter" and see what happens. Program realities must also be taken into account. Nurturing strategies cannot be applied liberally in a hospital requiring a 48-hour patient turnover. More than can be delivered should not be promised— whatever the ideal.

Cost-Effectiveness

The old struggle between the needs of the mental patient and those of society has found a new battlefield on the accountant's balance sheet under the label of cost-effectiveness. As an idea, cost-effectiveness (the most efficacious treatment for the least price), is unassailable. Current enthusiasm for the idea, however, may have outstripped the capacity to come up with unbiased and objective ledgers.

Estimating the cost of treatment services is difficult enough, but is easier than calculating effectiveness because everyone more or less agrees on the value of the dollar. How does one evaluate clinical effectiveness, however, in the absence of consensus about what constitutes reasonable outcome? In several studies, for example, researchers have found an association between shorter hospitalization and reduced utilization of treatment resources after hospitalization. The "natural" conclusion that shorter programs are more cost-effective, however, may be seriously misleading—for who is to say that less utilization of treatment resources is a good outcome? As noted by Kellam (1983), one of the best services a residential treatment program can provide is linking the patient to adequate long-term aftercare services. A good outcome is attachment to a network providing continuity of care, not disconnected brownian movement from one crisis center and city to another. In terms of countable dollars, adequate continuity of care is more expensive than homeless wandering, but what about the hidden cost of chronic disability?

Even with the current armamentarium of organic and psychological therapies, most personality-disordered patients who require residential treatment, however briefly, have chronic difficulties that can benefit from prolonged attention. Furthermore, therapists offer not only techniques for limited and rapid reconstitution, but also techniques for extended growth experiences and emotional realignment. The latter, especially, take time and resources, and cost-effectiveness may be impossible to estimate.

Treatment of Specific Disorders

Chapter 253

Paranoid Personality Disorder

General Comments

The paranoid personality disorder is an enduring pattern of maladaptive behavior and thinking that shows pervasive personality traits that can be exhibited in a wide range of social and personal situations. Such conditions are not psychotic, but some evidence suggests a weak genetic link to schizophrenic spectrum disorders. The characteristic personality traits may be already established by adolescence, and may have been present in some modified or precursory form even in childhood.

Diagnosis

According to the DSM-III-R (American Psychiatric Association 1987), the paranoid personality is marked by a pervasive and long-standing suspiciousness and general mistrust of others (see Table 1 for DSM-III-R diagnostic criteria for paranoid personality disorder). Such individuals are hypersensitive and easily slighted. Their habitual style

---

Table 1.   DSM-III-R Diagnostic Criteria for Paranoid Personality Disorder

A. A pervasive and unwarranted tendency, beginning by early adulthood and present in a variety of contexts, to interpret the actions of people as deliberately demeaning or threatening, as indicated by at least *four* of the following:
  (1) expects, without sufficient basis, to be exploited or harmed by others
  (2) questions, without justification, the loyalty or trustworthiness of friends or associates
  (3) reads hidden demeaning or threatening meanings into benign remarks or events, e.g., suspects that a neighbor put out trash early to annoy him or her
  (4) bears grudges or is unforgiving of insults or slights
  (5) is reluctant to confide in others because of unwarranted fear that the information will be used against him or her
  (6) is easily slighted and quick to react with anger or to counterattack
  (7) questions, without justification, the fidelity of the spouse or sexual partner

B. Occurrence not exclusively during the course of schizophrenia or a delusional disorder.

of relating to the world is marked by a vigilant scanning of the environment for any clues or suggestions that will serve to validate their prejudicial ideas or biases. Their attitudes are marked by guardedness and suspiciousness, and their emotional lives are usually quite constricted. The incapacity for meaningful emotional involvement and the general pattern of isolated withdrawal often lend a quality of schizoid isolation to their life experience.

Often the hypervigilance, hypersensitivity, suspiciousness, and guardedness are quite muted, so that their role in the patient's difficulties is not immediately apparent. Ideas of reference may be present, but lack the delusional conviction found in psychotic paranoids. Characteristically, paranoid personalities are unwilling to accept responsibility for themselves, their lives, and the consequences of their behavior. They are ready to blame others, or even fate, for their disadvantage or unhappiness. This constant blaming is a typical paranoid posture. As part of their general guardedness, such patients often keep their ideas to themselves and are reluctant to communicate them even under the best of circumstances. Consequently, the external impairment of these patients tends to be minimal, although difficulties characteristically arise in more intimate contexts, for example, marital relationships and work situations (particularly in relation to authority figures).

Difficulties

Although the paranoid personality has a long and well-established identity in the catalogue of personality disorders, the clinical literature on its specific treatment is rather sparse, as is the amount of research reported in the literature. Most discussions of the treatment of paranoid disorders focus more or less exclusively on the psychotic forms of paranoid pathology. The lack of careful study of this not uncommon personality disorder is striking, but may be due to a series of factors: 1) in many paranoid personalities, the defensive organization is ego-syntonic and does not give rise to symptoms or impairment—if there is impairment it is more often interpersonal than intrapsychic, more disturbing or disruptive to those around the patients than to the patients themselves; 2) even when such individuals come to psychiatric attention, they often keep their emotional or interpersonal difficulties hidden because of their guardedness and mistrust; 3) for similar reasons, such patients are unlikely to lend themselves to systematic investigation; 4) paranoid personalities tend to maintain a level of reasonably good functioning, coming to psychiatric attention only when the usual defenses have crumbled and the patient experiences a regressive episode that may place him or her in some other, more severe, diagnostic category; 5) often enough, the paranoid characteristics are mingled with other pathologic personality features that allow the patient to be classified as narcissistic, borderline, schizoid, or even depressed.

The diagnosis of paranoid personality is both easy and difficult. When the paranoid characteristics can be identified, the diagnosis can be made readily. The problem is that these traits often cannot be so easily recognized. Even when recognition is not complicated, mixed personality configurations and the potential overlap between paranoid personality characteristics and those of other personality disorders are persistent problems.

Paranoid Traits

The presence of paranoid traits may be muted and subtle. These "soft signs" of paranoia are continuous with a more normal range of personality characteristics and functioning, and often are difficult to evaluate for this reason. Such paranoid traits include the following:

1. *Centrality*, that is, the notion that the patient is somehow in the center of other people's interest or attention. This can reflect the patient's sense of being the passive recipient of external influences over which he may feel he has little or no control. This pattern is classically seen in paranoid disorders, in which malignant and often powerful external forces or influences are seen as directed against the patient, or in ideas of reference.
2. A facade of *self-sufficiency*, which may represent the patient's attempt to defend against an underlying sense of vulnerability. The self-sufficiency may involve a certain grandiosity and isolation similar to that seen in schizoid conditions.
3. A *concern over autonomy*, which is fragile and easily threatened in the paranoid patient.
4. A tendency to *blaming*.
5. *Feelings of inadequacy* or deficiency, which may take the form of concerns about being different or being an outsider, or often a more diffuse concern with having values or beliefs different from those of associates.
6. *Concerns over power and powerlessness.* Paranoid individuals typically have difficulty in relating to authority figures, taking orders, assuming appropriate responsibility, and generally fitting into preexisting social structures (Swanson et al. 1970).

Psychotherapies

From the perspective of the paranoid process (Meissner 1978), the patient's symptoms can be seen as expressing attitudes and feelings that derive from the patient's pathologic sense of self. Consequently, the emphasis in therapy falls on the inner attitudes and feelings toward the self rather than on the projective system. This internal focus serves as the basis for certain principles that can serve to set priorities and provide a sense of direction for the therapeutic work.

Therapeutic Alliance

The first principle has to do with establishing and maintaining a meaningful therapeutic alliance. The therapeutic alliance is a major part of any meaningful therapy and provides the more or less realistic basis on which the therapeutic work proceeds, but in paranoid patients it is of major importance and looms as the most critical area of therapeutic work. The therapeutic alliance obviously requires that the patient have a certain degree of trust in the therapist, and it is precisely this aspect of the relationship that gives rise to the greatest difficulties for the paranoid patient. The inherent suspiciousness and guardedness that are such a major part of this pathology run counter to any capacity for a trusting relationship.

The basic issues center on questions of trust and autonomy. The alliance is stabilized to the degree that the patient can develop a meaningful trust in the therapist and to the extent that he or she is also increasingly able to sustain a sense of autonomy within the therapeutic relationship. Important contributions on the therapist's part have to do with empathic responsiveness to the idiosyncratic needs (largely narcissistic), anxieties, and inner tensions felt by the patient, so that the therapist responds to the patient in terms of the latter's own individuality rather than in terms of the therapist's needs or in terms of some preexisting therapeutic or theoretical stereotype.

Conversion of Paranoia to Depression

A second principle is that the effort of the therapy is directed to converting the paranoid manifestation into depression. As the projective and externalizing defenses are gradually eroded, the patient comes more directly and immediately into contact with the form and content of the inner sense of self that is connected with feelings of vulnerability, weakness, inferiority, and inadequacy. This brings the patient to experience more immediately those hidden elements of himself or herself against which the paranoid system has served as an elaborate defense. Previously, the patient's defensive effort has been directed to avoiding taking responsibility for these elements, and shifting the blame for these shortcomings elsewhere.

If the patient becomes depressed, he or she must come to terms with, understand, work through, and resolve the depressive elements that are contained in his or her pathologic sense of self as victim. The therapeutic effort is directed toward focusing, understanding, and resolving the elements of weakness, vulnerability, and impotence that are embedded in the sense of victimhood, along with the feelings of worthlessness, inferiority, and shamefulness that reflect the underlying narcissistically inferior aspect of the patient's sense of self.

Techniques

Working with projective defenses calls for special techniques. Confrontation, or challenge, or even reality testing of projection creates a situation of opposition and runs the risk of making the therapist an enemy. More progress can be made through empathically eliciting the patient's projective system, focusing along the way the patient's feelings, particularly the feelings of doubt, insecurity, vulnerability, weakness, inadequacy, or inferiority that lie behind the paranoid facade. An added technique is so-called counterprojection: this involves acknowledging and accepting the patient's feelings and perceptions, without disputing or reinforcing them. Temporarily accepting the patient's perceptions avoids confrontation and allows access to real underlying feelings.

Autonomy

A third principle in the treatment of paranoid patients involves respect for the patient's autonomy and the effort to build and reinforce it in the therapeutic relationship. The patient's fragile and threatened sense of autonomy, and the issues related to establishing and maintaining it, permeate all aspects of the therapy. The therapist's effort is in the direction of fostering and maintaining autonomy at all points possible within the therapeutic work. Complete openness, honesty, and confidentiality are essential in all dealings with the patient. Any decisions that need to be made must be explored with the patient, and insofar as possible, the ultimate choice should be left in the patient's hands—even decisions about taking drugs, if and when their use seems indicated.

Countertransference

An area of special concern in therapy with the paranoid patient is the countertransference that reflects the therapist's unconsciously derived and motivated reactions to the patient. This kind of patient can often be difficult, resistant, provocative, and contentious. Not only are the paranoid defenses usually rigid and unyielding, but the patient may resort to argumentative or contemptuously demeaning attacks. The patient, reacting to an inner sense of vulnerability and powerlessness, will often see the therapist as hostile, attacking, sadistic, and persecuting. Behind the defensive attitudes of self-sufficiency and arrogance, there may be exquisite narcissistic vulnerability and passive longings for dependence. Such dependency needs are associated with a sense of shameful vulnerability and fears of humiliation. The paranoid patient often tries to counter these anxieties by turning the tables and making the therapist feel helpless, vulnerable, and humiliated in turn.

For each of these projective dimensions, the therapist is subjected to an emotional pull to respond in terms that satisfy the projective demand and reinforce the patient's victimized and embattled position. The therapist may react with annoyance or impatience. In the face of the patient's unyielding argumentativeness, the therapist may come to play the aggressor to the patient's victim, becoming more forceful, argumentative, or confrontative. Or the therapist may become frustrated and discouraged, feeling inadequate, helpless, and worthless, thus playing out the role of victim. These reactions must be carefully monitored and their impact on and implications for the therapy analyzed. The therapist's task in such circumstances is to bring the therapeutic interaction back to some more effective therapeutic balance in which real therapeutic work takes precedence over the acting out of transference and countertransference.

Litigiousness

An added matter of concern is the threat of legal action by the litigious patient. Given the hostile, defended, suspicious, and overly sensitive disposition of paranoid patients, legal threats against the psychiatrist are not uncommon. A litigious stance can generally be avoided by careful attention to the therapeutic alliance and the arrangements for dealing with matters of privacy and confidentiality. When threats of legal action arise, they must be regarded as reflecting a disruption of the alliance and should be worked with accordingly. If restitution of the alliance fails and the patient moves toward legal action, the therapy should probably be terminated. Appropriate arrangements should be made for referral of the patient to other treatment resources, if indicated, and the therapist should take steps to protect his or her legal interest. This is a course of last resort, implemented only when efforts to deal therapeutically with the patient's threatening attitude have failed. Psychotherapy cannot be conducted under conditions of threat.

Adjunctive Therapies

The primary and preferred approach to the treatment of the paranoid personality is long-term, relatively intensive (two or more sessions weekly) individual psychotherapy. The patient's pathology is embedded in his or her character structure and yields to therapeutic influence only gradually over an extended period of time. However, in specific cases, adjunctive therapeutic interventions may prove useful and productive. Paranoid patients do not usually willingly or easily involve themselves in the therapeutic process, but at certain points they may experience a failure of characterological defenses, and as their paranoid defensive systems weaken, they may begin to experience acute anxiety of depression. At such points they may find themselves forced into short-term therapeutic work, which can serve to sustain them through the crisis, and may open the way to more extensive therapeutic endeavor.

Short-term Psychotherapy

Some therapists have undertaken short-term psychotherapy with paranoid patients. Balint et al. (1972) described the treatment of a patient who had acute paranoid difficulties, but would not qualify as a paranoid personality. Similarly, Malan (1976) described patients with acute paranoid reactions and said they could be helped by brief psychotherapy, but only if their personalities manifest a strong healthy part struggling against paranoid feelings. Usually the pathology in paranoid personalities is more deeply embedded and enduring than reactive, so that paranoid personalities do not have good prospects for brief psychotherapy.

Family or Group Therapy

In the long-term treatment of the paranoid personality, there may be opportunity for combining individual psychotherapy with other therapeutic modalities, such as family therapy or group therapy. Family therapy may be indicated particularly for an adolescent patient whose family has dynamics and patterns of interaction that may be interfering with or contributing to the patient's difficulties. Also, the resources of a group situation may enable a relatively healthy paranoid patient to sort out and resolve difficulties in socialization, and may thereby facilitate the course of therapeutic improvement. Such approaches should remain adjunctive to the primary psychotherapeutic approach, however. Paranoid patients generally do not do well in group settings of any kind, usually because of their hypersensitivity, suspiciousness, and tendency to misinterpret comments or contributions from other group members. If group approaches are employed, the therapist must be alert to possible paranoid reactions, particularly in relation to involvement of the family. A paranoid adolescent, for example, may see the therapist as joining forces with the family against him or her.

Behavioral therapy

Behavioral therapies have no demonstrable role in the treatment of paranoid personality, although at times secondary symptoms (e.g., phobic anxiety) may be modified by behavioral techniques. Usually the patient's suspiciousness, guardedness, distrust, and easily threatened autonomy contraindicate a behavioral approach.

Biologic Therapies

The only biologic intervention pertinent to the treatment of the paranoid personality is the use of drugs. Although the psychotic process in a delusional paranoid may be effectively treated by antipsychotic medication, such is not the case in the paranoid personality. Attempts to treat these patients with a combination of phenothiazines and lithium have proved unrewarding (Klein et al. 1980). Slight improvement has been noted in some cases with low-dose neuroleptics, but for all practical purposes, the role of drugs with such patients is more or less limited to helping specific target symptoms that may occur because of the failure of characterological defenses. Thus, at certain times in the course of the treatment, limited use of minor tranquilizers for the treatment of anxiety or of tricyclic antidepressants or MAO inhibitors for the treatment of phobic anxieties or depression would be indicated.

One of the difficulties in the overall management of such patients is that they are often extremely resistant to taking medications of any kind, frequently seeing them in terms of issues of control, powerlessness, and loss of autonomy. The clinician must often make a difficult decision whether the potential advantages of the chemotherapy outweigh the consequences of insisting on the medication (i.e., possibly harming the therapeutic relationship and process). Because of the nature of the symptomatology, chemotherapy is not often effective, so the gains from insisting on the patient's taking the medication can be minor, whereas the negative implications for the patient's overall therapy may prove to be major.

Residential Therapies

Residential therapies do not have a big role in the treatment of paranoid personalities as such. When paranoid personalities deteriorate and undergo psychotic decompensation, however, hospitalization and associated residential therapies may be called into play. These therapies pertain, then, to the treatment of the psychoses rather than the personality disorder.

Conclusion

It is important to emphasize that patients with paranoid personalities are treatable. Often, such patients lead reasonably adaptive and productive lives, but get into difficulties in circumstances of loss or under specific forms of life stress. Their treatment, however, is not easy, but requires patience, empathy, and great sensitivity to the vulnerability and sensitivity that are inexorably part of the pathology. The therapist must be willing to work slowly toward minimal, long-term goals with the patient, foregoing any illusion of quick or easy resolution of the patient's difficulties and aiming for a more enduring and fundamental change in the patient's personality structure.

The essential therapeutic progression in such patients runs through the gradual undermining of paranoid defenses and attitudes to the corresponding emergence of an underlying depression in terms of which the patient's inner sense of weakness, defectiveness, vulnerability, and powerlessness gradually comes into focus. In working through this depressive core, the therapist helps the patient to gradually undermine and resolve the core elements of the pathology and the fundamental motivation underlying the paranoid symptoms.

Chapter 254

Schizoid Personality Disorder

Schizoid: The Term in Psychiatric Parlance

Despite the widespread use of the term schizoid in psychiatric, especially in psychoanalytic, parlance, the psychotherapy of schizoid personality has not received much attention in the literature. Treatment of the subject becomes all the more unsatisfying if one takes into account the ambiguity surrounding earlier definitions and usages of this label.

The tendency on the part of the psychiatric community, particularly among those concerned with detecting attenuated forms of the heredofamilial psychoses, has been to reserve "schizoid" for persons exhibiting personality attributes reminiscent of schizophrenia. This usage could be broad or narrow, depending whether one viewed the schizoid on a continuum with the schizophrenic, as did Kretschmer (1921), or whether one agreed with the more restrictive use of Schneider (1923), who objected to the notion "that a destructive psychosis like schizophrenia could be only an extreme form of normal properties" (cf. Essen-Moller 1946, p. 261). Bleuler (1922) considered schizoid traits part of everyone's basic constitution—ingredients, in effect, that varied only in the strength or weakness of their development and outward expression. In contrast, psychogeneticists often speak rather uncertainly of schizoid personality as the mildest manifestation of the genetically controlled tendency to schizophrenia, of which the intermediate phenotype is borderline schizophrenia (roughly equivalent to the schizotypal personality of DSM-III) (American Psychiatric Association 1980).

The schizoid persons who are the focus of this chapter display characteristics similar to those described in the earlier literature (Kasanin and Rosen 1933; Rado 1956) and, more recently, in the DSM-III: emotional coolness or aloofness (absence of warm, tender feelings for others), indifference to praise or criticism or to the feelings of others, and the absence (or near absence) of close friendships. Anhedonia was stressed in the older literature, as were shyness, distrust, and a conviction of unlovability (Meehl 1962).

The psychoanalytic community tended toward a broad definition of schizoid. Fairbairn (1952) referred to what is now called schizoid personality as the "schizoid character," which was similar to Jung's "introvert" (cf. Kirsch 1979). He described the schizoid within the framework of unconscious conflict and defense mechanisms, stating that "some measure of splitting of the ego is invariably present at the deepest mental level," that is, "the basic position in the psyche is invariably schizoid" (p. 8). These opinions are echoed in the writings of Guntrip (1962). It is this analogy between *splitting* (of the ego) and its Greek parent-word *schizoid* that conduces to the imprecise use of the latter. Balint (1968), in fact, sought to minimize this confusion by creating another name for the schizoid's tendency to be preoccupied with thinking as opposed to interaction. He used the term "philobat" (as opposed to the "ocnophile," who, like the depressive, loves to cling). The succinct criteria for schizoid personality in

DSM-III-R (see Table 1) (American Psychiatric Association 1987) should reduce confusion. It should be noted, however, that strict attention to these criteria will leave relatively few patients of pure types. An admixture of paranoid and compulsive features is, for example, common in this group. The label schizoid personality should be limited to persons who exhibit *only* the criteria mentioned in DSM-III-R or who exhibit *chiefly* these criteria.

Individual Psychotherapy

Schizoid patients are generally uncomfortable with the intimacy inherent in the psychotherapeutic encounter. Many, despite their loneliness and their dissatisfaction with the emotional impoverishment of their lives, avoid contact with the mental health profession. If they do come for help (as often as not, only at the urging of a family member), they discontinue of their own accord after a short time.

The frequency of visits should in most cases be once or twice weekly. More intensive schedules might engender inordinate anxiety and thus prove counterproductive (Rosenfeld 1969). Schizoid patients often react, for example, as though the "basic rule" of sharing with the therapist their every thought is unendurable (Markowitz 1968): they worry about losing their sense of separateness and identity or (if paranoid features are somewhat prominent) about coming under the control of the therapist. They are hesitant about involving themselves in the world of people and still more hesitant about forming close, especially sexual, ties (Kasanin and Rosen 1933). There is little forward movement in therapy. Several years may go by without any appreciable rise in scores on mental health scales (cf. the Global Assessment Scale of Endicott et al. 1976; Stone 1983a) or in any other measure of outcome. This sluggishness in treatment response is in large part a reflection of the schizoid's discomfort in the social sphere; when improvement becomes discernible, it is more likely to be within the realm of work or avocation.

In general, patients who experience serious difficulties in forming harmonious, close relationships can change only in two ways: they may succeed in resolving interpersonal conflicts and achieve stability and comfort with a close relationship (Abel 1960), or they may eventually give up on further efforts in this direction in

---

Table 1.   DSM-III-R Diagnostic Criteria for Schizoid Personality Disorder

A. A pervasive pattern of indifference to social relationships and a restricted range of emotional experience and expression, beginning by early adulthood and present in a variety of contexts, as indicated by at least *four* of the following:
   (1) neither desires nor enjoys close relationships, including being part of a family
   (2) almost always chooses solitary activities
   (3) rarely, if ever, claims or appears to experience strong emotions, such as anger and joy
   (4) indicates little if any desire to have sexual experiences with another person (age being taken into account)
   (5) is indifferent to the praise and criticism of others
   (6) has no close friends or confidants (or only one) other than first-degree relatives
   (7) displays constricted affect, e.g., is aloof, cold, rarely reciprocates gestures or facial expressions, such as smiles or nods

B. Occurrence not exclusively during the course of schizophrenia or a delusional disorder.

favor of developing a greater capacity to endure, and to make the best of, aloneness. Affectively ill patients, because of their greater dependence on others and capacity to get along with others, are inclined to bend their efforts in the direction of forming stable bonds. Schizoid patients, apart from those who already show some capacity for harmonious coexistence (usually with a rather undemanding and emotionally cool partner), often go in the other direction—toward a solitary life that is more bearable and gratifying than the solitary life they led prior to therapy (cf. Battegay 1981).

Despite these cautionary remarks, dynamic psychotherapy is indicated in selected schizoid patients. A few years ago, Kernberg (1982) and Grinberg and Rodriguez-Perez (1982) reported good outcomes in dynamic psychotherapy of individual cases. Grinberg and Rodriguez-Perez mentioned the schizoid's preoccupation with compensatory, omnipotent fantasies (that develop around a sense of futility and strangeness) and singled out splitting and projective identification as important mechanisms of defense. Writing about the technical aspects of dynamic therapy with schizoids, Liberman (1957) advocated the use of interpretations aimed at linking together the various feelings isolated at different moments of the session ("schizoid isolation of feelings").

In connection with dynamic (analytically oriented) psychotherapy, it is important to remember that the large number of patients who exhibit the prominent schizoid defenses (viz., splitting) and psychodynamics (viz., anxieties concerning the mother-child symbiosis, accompanied by mistrust and avoidance of the maternal and other close relationships) depicted in the analytic literature are not all schizoid by DSM-III criteria. Khan (1960) referred to the outwardly normal but excessively "plastic" persons Deutsch (1942) labeled "as-if" personalities, whose social facades have a staged quality. Khan mentioned the propensity of these patients to make, via projective identification, their analysts feel their anger, neediness, love, and despair—countertransference feelings (in the broad sense of the term) that, once recognized by the analyst, can often be interpreted back to the patient in such a way that he or she begins to recognize and take responsibility for these hitherto warded-off emotions.

The ability of the therapist to resonate empathically with the schizoid patient and to crystallize an accurate rating of the patient's moment-to-moment feeling state into an "affective experience" (Khan 1960, p. 436) is necessary for schizoid as well as for the less well integrated schizotypal patients. It will be necessary for the therapist, whether analytically oriented or not, to "say the first word" more often in sessions with the schizoid than with less aloof and inhibited patients. The therapist may make an opening remark about the patient's probable feeling state ("you seem particularly uncomfortable today") or volunteer an interpretation when the patient seems unable to go on or too embarrassed to initiate some painful topic. Schizoid patients tend to be secretive (Fairbairn 1952), and are especially prone to conceal feelings of utter unworthiness—but also of superiority.

One such patient, a schizoid woman whose marriage was under strain because of her inability to share her deeper feelings with her husband, grew silent when recounting certain aspects of her early history. Her therapist, thinking out loud, told her, "Your silence suggests to me one of three things, because there are few topics one avoids so strenuously: sexual abuse, being brutalized physically, or being abandoned by someone you loved." At this point she broke down in tears and revealed for the first time that her mother had beaten her throughout her childhood. She was so ashamed that she had never told her husband; therefore, he had not been able to understand her reluctance to visit her family.

Many schizoid patients have endured similar humiliation as children, and have, out of loyalty to the offending caretaker(s), developed a cripplingly low self-esteem (rather than the sense of outrage one would anticipate), as though the abuse were somehow deserved. In instances of this kind, psychotherapy, whether supportive or exploratory, can often bring about a more realistic view of the past and can effect at least some elevation of self-esteem.

Some schizoid patients have such a poor grasp either of other people's feelings or of the customary ways in which people deal with various social situations as to need considerable educative measures (Eidelberg 1957) alongside the supportive and exploratory interventions that might suffice for patients more comfortable in social situations. Other schizoids, however, are exquisitely tuned in to the feelings of others, but are nevertheless ill at ease with people because of their unassertiveness and lack of confidence in their own opinions. Psychotherapy aims at helping such patients develop a more realistic attitude toward their skills and judgment, so that they can mingle with others less self-consciously (Stone 1983a).

During the opening phases of therapy, inanimate objects, including artistic productions, often play a compensating role in the lives of schizoid patients—taking the place of relationships, but ultimately serving as bridges to the world of other people (Abel 1960). Some schizoid patients, out of their characteristic shyness and oversensitivity, will rely on inanimate objects in the therapist's office as springboards for broaching, on a symbolic plane, the personal (especially, transference) feelings they would be too uncomfortable to speak of openly. A schizoid sculptress, for example, communicated feelings about herself and her mother through the medium of small sculptures she brought to her sessions. At first she could say almost nothing about them. The therapist placed them upon his shelves, one after the other, until the office was nearly converted into her personal museum. After a year, she was finally emboldened (perhaps because she began to sense how important she had become to her therapist) to speak about her longing for—and her destructive feelings toward—her mother. Eventually, and with no prodding from the therapist, she was able to relate her transference feelings without the need for the symbolic intermediaries.

Schizoid patients are often unable to suppress painful thoughts (Meehl 1962). These ideas, in turn, may serve as defenses against the emergence of even more painful ones. A schizoid patient may, for example, begin a session complaining about the unhealthy effects of the city air on his lungs, only to reveal much later how hurt he felt by a parent's insulting remark during a recent visit home. It is a measure of the therapist's skill to be able to detect these mechanisms and then to get behind them through adroit and empathic remarks.

The proper pace and depth of one-to-one therapy with schizoids are controversial issues. Although some therapists advocate modulating the tempo and intensity in order to avoid precipitating overwhelming anxiety (or even psychosis), others caution against backing away from energetic therapy, lest the patient feel discouraged by, or contemptuous of, the therapist's reluctance to confront anxiety-laden topics. Bonime (1959) argued for maintaining the pace and depth customary with intensive therapy, so as to avoid this vote of no confidence, underlining the schizoid's cynicism, which regularly takes the form of distorting perceptions of others by way of "refuting the existence of decent human relationships" (p. 239). One of Bonime's patients made sure relationships failed by outrageously mistreating people she loved. Eventually she felt terrified of her own cruelty, which Bonime turned to nice advantage in the therapy, by pointing out that the basis of this terror was the emergence of her own genuine humanity. Negative therapeutic reactions are common in such patients, who at the outset distrust the therapist's friendliness and decency.

The majority of authors argue against rapid and probing therapy with schizoid patients. One must respect the emotional distance from the therapist that schizoid persons generally require. Many such patients are intensely lonely and are correspondingly grateful for the opportunity of having in their therapist a reliable audience and temporary companion. Yet to reveal this gratitude or to talk of the loneliness out loud may engender humiliation in the schizoid, who will avoid these topics for a long time—in some cases, throughout the therapy. The therapist must be careful not to misconstrue his or her growing awareness of these hidden emotions as carte blanche to insist the patient talk about them. Many embarrassing topics will remain under wraps for a long time or even forever (especially if unusual or grotesque sexual and aggressive fantasies dominate the patient's inner life). In this respect, the word "patient" applies chiefly to the therapist—who must wait patiently until the schizoid feels emboldened to reveal this kind of information. The Roman shibboleth "festina lente" (make haste slowly) is good advice. The overeager therapist will succeed only in frightening, and ultimately in alienating, the schizoid patient.

Some schizoid patients tend to experience inordinate guilt over masturbation, which Jackson (1958) understood as subserving a curiously integrative function, mediating between the patient's urge toward autonomy and apprehension about extricating himself or herself from parental control. The mother of the schizoid, in Jackson's view, fears loss of control of her child. Guilt, in this context, is the sop that is thrown to mother and reinstates her authority, and the sexual pleasure itself constitutes the forbidden leave-taking from her dominion. Guilt atones for the defiance. In a like vein, the schizoid's fear of going crazy may represent the outwardly uncomfortable-appearing compromise between the wish for the gratification of every whim (going crazy) and the desire for the parents to exert maximal control (via hospitalization).

Unusual psychodynamics of this sort do seem to operate in a number of schizoid patients. Searles (1965) offered abundant clues about the secret meanings of various thoughts and behavior patterns of schizoids, though his papers were inspired mostly by sicker (schizotypal and frankly schizophrenic) patients.

To summarize, individual psychotherapy for patients with schizoid personality is indicated in the majority of cases. Whether one should pursue a more active, confrontative mode of interaction, as Bonime (1959) advocated, or a more restrained technique depends on the psychological-mindedness of the patient and, more important, on his or her apparent resilience (stress tolerance). Patients who seem vulnerable to micropsychotic episodes, despite a normal facade, require a less confrontative approach. Less brittle schizoids may do well with the more frequent meetings and greater depth of exploration necessary to an insight-oriented therapy.

Other Treatment Modalities

Family Therapy

Therapists who work with young schizoid patients still living at home often confront tense family situations, with marked discrepancies between the expectations of the parents and the all too often rather meager capabilities of the patient. The family of a seemingly talented or intellectually precocious but schizoid child often has trouble grasping that the emotional disorder is as chronic as it actually is and is likely to force on the child a lower ceiling of potential (whether in work or in forming friendships) than the family has estimated. Family therapy may help alleviate the impatience and intolerance of the other family members (Anderson 1983). Improvement may begin to occur, in ways that seem paradoxical to the family, when the other members begin to tolerate the patient and to intrude less on his or her privacy.

Schizoid patients, to the extent that they are less prone to marry or to become self-supporting than are their affectively ill counterparts, may remain dependent on and reside with their families until well into their 20s, or beyond. This enhances the likelihood of the emergence of a vicious circle in which slow progress leads to interference and bitterness on the part of the family, followed by lowered self-esteem in the patient and a still greater reluctance to leave home.

Behavior Therapy

Therapy directed at the modification of maladaptive behavior patterns may be useful in the many schizoids who show overlap with compulsive personality. Behavior therapy may lead to constructive changes in patterns that are not too noticeable socially (e.g., compulsive handwashing or interminable locking and unlocking of one's door) or are alienating (e.g., picking at oneself or always interrupting others). Liberman (1972) reviewed behavior modification methods applicable to chronic, hospitalized schizophrenics; some of these methods can be extended to schizoid patients in clinic settings.

More difficult to correct are certain speech patterns noticeable in a minority of schizoid patients, such as a flatness of tone that gives the voice a robotlike quality. This lack of normal lilt and inflection makes such persons seem crisp and standoffish, even at times when they are hungering for affection from others. Speech therapy, with heavy reliance on audio-playback devices (permitting the patient to hear his or her flatness) may be of some benefit though high motivation and prodigious amounts of time would be necessary (Albert 1983).

Group Therapy

Little has been written about the use of group therapy for persons with schizoid personality per se. At the clinical level, schizoid patients present many difficulties that should be amenable to group therapy in one form or another. For example, shy patients might be induced, under the impact of the group, to "come out of" themselves. There would be an inevitable tendency within the group both to set schizoid patients at ease via the group's general attitude of acceptance and to urge them to reveal themselves. Self-revelation and candor within the context of an accepting milieu can lead to a lessening of the shame and sense of "otherness" with which schizoids are characteristically burdened.

Many of Spotnitz's (1957) remarks concerning borderline schizophrenics in group therapy are pertinent to schizoid patients. He argued in favor of a group homogeneous with respect to level of psychopathology, economic status, and social and educational background. There should be divergence of personality type, though, to ensure diversity of reactions and attitudes (i.e., there should be some obsessive and histrionic patients among the schizoid patients). Heavy reliance on analytic interpretation is probably contraindicated for the schizotypal patient, as Spotnitz suggested, but may not be for the schizoid. Anything approaching the emotional aridity of encounter groups, inspired by Bion's (1961) work, might heighten anxiety in the schizoid, just as much as analytic interpretation might foster disintegration in the schizotypal. The group should provide emotional connectedness and serve as a vehicle for appropriate release of uncomfortable accumulations of angry, lusty , and other emotions. Schizoids are often sensitive to slights; some are narcissistic and secretly grandiose enough to experience the group as having come together for their unique benefit. They tend to polarize feelings and regard their sexual wishes, however ordinary, as incestuous.

Conversely, mild anger may be equated with a volcanic rage that needs to be capped at all times. These constitute some of the typical issues that come up, and are capable of adequate resolution, with schizoids in a group. Some, but not all, schizoid persons will benefit from the built-in system of social contacts that the group represents. A few will remain aloof despite group efforts to reach out to them. Group therapy and dyadic therapy should be seen as complementary, rather than as competing thera-peutic systems.

Pharmacotherapy

Schizoid patients seldom show the target symptoms (e.g., anxiety and depres-sion) for which the common psychoactive medications are indicated. Their funda-mental temperamental traits of aloofness, oversensitivity, and uncommunicativeness are likewise resistive to these drugs—which, therefore, have little place in the treat-ment of schizoid personality. See Chapter 251 on Somatic Therapy for more infor-mation.

Inpatient Care

Residential treatment is rarely indicated for schizoid patients. Even day-hospital treatment, widely utilized with schizotypal and schizophrenic patients, is seldom required for schizoid patients.

Outcome

In assessing long-range results of therapy in schizoid patients, one must rely more on sporadic, anecdotal reports than on methodological research. Millon (1982, p. 296) described the prognosis with regard to psychotherapy as owing to the schizoid's diminished capacity for affective expression. The lack of motivation in this population makes it improbable, in his opinion, that many such patients would seek or remain in treatment of any sort. If the deficits are mild, however, and the life circumstances favorable, vocational and social adjustment may be good. Millon emphasized the need to counter schizoids' tendency to withdraw and to isolate themselves. Although this recommendation is valid at the outset, however, therapists should be prepared in less favorable instances to relinquish their efforts to push schizoids toward the world of people. Some will, as becomes clear after a year or two of treatment, remain incapable of all but the most superficial kinds of relatedness. These patients should be accepted as they are and should be encouraged to improve strategies for extracting some satisfaction from solitary life (saving up for trips, collecting art objects or mem-orabilia in which they can develop a specific interest, etc.). Some schizoid patients can learn in this way to live by themselves without too keen a sense of loneliness.

Chapter 255

Schizotypal Personality Disorder

Schizotypal personality is a term, added by DSM-III (American Psychiatric Association 1980) to the psychiatric nomenclature, depicting an abnormal pattern of personality with features resembling schizophrenia. Derived from clinical descriptions by Kety et al. (1968) of "borderline schizophrenia," noted among certain close relatives of schizophrenics, the description of schizotypal personality includes such qualities as odd communication, suspiciousness, and social isolation. DSM-III enumerated eight characteristics, at least four of which are necessary for the diagnosis. Ideally, such clarification should increase uniformity in recommendations about therapy. Because of the newness of the term and the absence of a prior literature devoted specifically to this condition, however, it remains unclear whether this ideal will be realized. Furthermore, proposing recommendations for the treatment of personality disorders is always complicated by the fact that amenability to the various therapeutic interventions is dependent not only on the particular mix of diagnostic traits presented by any one patient, but also on key nondiagnostic attributes, such as psychological-mindedness and motivation. Patients seldom conform to the pure types sketched in DSM-III-R (see Table 1) (American Psychiatric Association 1987) showing instead a mix of features from more than one personality disorder. These factors affect therapy. A schizotypal patient free of antisocial features would, for example, be easier to treat and have a better outcome than one in whom such characteristics were prominent. Schizotypal personality may be diagnosed correctly (because only five items are needed) in a patient showing only suspiciousness, aloofness, ideas of reference, and magical thinking, as well as in a patient showing only odd communication, illusions, isolation, and social anxiety. The latter may respond favorably to medication, whereas the former may experience no such benefit.

Individual Psychotherapy

The psychotherapy of patients with schizotypal personality shares many features with the therapy appropriate to other severe personality disorders; for example, employment of an "active" or confrontative approach is often advisable, and attention to countertransference is particularly important. But there are some modifications and shifts in emphasis that are peculiar to the schizotypal patient.

Sense of Discontinuity

Some schizotypal patients, particularly those prone to "cognitive slippage" (and to other manifestations of thought disorder resembling those seen in schizophrenia), experience a disturbing sense of discontinuity with respect to time and person. Clarifying remarks addressed to this problem may help diminish it. Even more helpful

---

Table 1.   DSM-III-R Diagnostic Criteria for Schizotypal Personality Disorder

A. A pervasive pattern of deficits in interpersonal relatedness and peculiarities of ideation, appearance, and behavior, beginning by early adulthood and present in a variety of contexts, as indicated by at least five of the following:

  (1) ideas of reference (excluding delusions of reference)

  (2) excessive social anxiety, e.g., extreme discomfort in social situations involving unfamiliar people

  (3) odd beliefs or magical thinking, influencing behavior and inconsistent with subcultural norms, e.g., superstitiousness or belief in clairvoyance, telepathy, or "sixth sense," "others can feel my feelings" (in children and adolescents, bizarre fantasies or preoccupations)

  (4) unusual perceptual experiences, e.g., illusions, sensing the presence of a force or person not actually present (e.g., "I felt as if my dead mother were in the room with me")

  (5) odd or eccentric behavior or appearance, e.g., unkempt, unusual mannerisms, talks to self

  (6) no close friends or confidants (or only one) other than first-degree relatives

  (7) odd speech (without loosening of associations or incoherence), e.g., speech that is impoverished, digressive, vague, or inappropriately abstract

  (8) inappropriate or constricted affect, e.g., silly, aloof, rarely reciprocates gestures or facial expressions, such as smiles or nods

  (9) suspiciousness or paranoid ideation

B. Occurrence not exclusively during the course of schizophrenia or a Pervasive Developmental Disorder.

---

is the punctuality and consistency of the therapist—over long stretches of time. These qualities help patients develop an integrated and stable image of the therapist, and by extension, of themselves and of other people.

Anhedonia

The chronic and pervasive anhedonia to which schizotypes are prone may well be, in large part, a neurophysiologic sequela of the schizophrenic genotype. This tendency plays an important role in the social isolation of these patients. Human relationships are ambivalent and seldom gratifying in an uninterrupted way from beginning to end. The joys make the sorrows and the annoyances endurable. Not so for schizotypes, who, oftentimes impervious to the joys, are exquisitely sensitive to conflict and unpleasantness. Close relationships, associated as they are only with pain, are therefore to be avoided. Schizotypal patients, though less likely to resort to suicidal acts than affectively ill patients, often complain about a sense of inescapable grayness to life that robs them of enthusiasm and motivation. Sometimes, at critical junctures in the treatment, therapists have to place before schizotypal patients two unpleasant alternatives: to continue languishing in this marginal and unvaried existence or to engage more fully in life. Although these patients may not feel keen pleasure in either choice, with proper preparation, they can begin to grasp that a full, variegated, and joyless life is superior to a secluded, barren, and joyless life. Such patients may expand participation in travel, hobbies, cultural events, and the like, but will still find intimacy too threatening.

Tendency to Misinterpret

Therapy with schizotypal patients is generally a slower and more painstaking process even than with other types of personality-disordered patients. Put simply, the mood-disordered patient sees the world more or less as it is, but either overreacts or underreacts. A minor, but real, annoyance provokes a rage outburst, for example. The schizotypal patient, in contrast, may react less violently, but seems *not* to see the world as it is. Faulty cognitive machinery does not permit him or her to evaluate situations (especially if people are involved) with sufficient accuracy; the patient reacts to symbols, to possible meanings, rather than to facts. In short, the schizotype misinterprets. For example, one schizotypal patient tried to kill his wife when he saw some cigarettes lying about the house. He said the cigarettes meant she no longer loved him—because three years before he had told her he hated for her to smoke. He could not understand that, for reasons unrelated to any change in her feelings toward him, she had felt unusually tense and had yearned, momentarily, for a cigarette.

To compound the difficulty of misinterpretation the schizotype is often poor at generalizing from one situation to another analogous one. Lessons, as from a therapist, must be repeated endlessly; each nuance and variation on a theme has to be dealt with as though a brand-new experience.

Concreteness

Concreteness and humorlessness are particularly common among schizotypal patients. The humorlessness is at times related to the concreteness: the schizotype often responds only to the literal and not to the figurative meanings of what people say. Humorlessness may also be a reflection of the schizotype's joyless life.

These characteristics often give a leaden and sterile quality to therapy sessions, particularly because the schizotypal patient is usually less comfortable than are affectively ill patients to discuss personal, let alone transference, feelings. The therapist feels bored on many occasions and has to find ways of using this boredom constructively. Sometimes it proves beneficial to use the boredom as an index of what the patient is suffering in his or her own life or of what the patient is uncomfortable to talk about. It may help the patient to move onto more feelingful ground—if the therapist makes a gentle comment alluding to this boredom: "You seem particularly on guard today, revealing what is mildly interesting, but holding back what is really upsetting you"; "The atmosphere here seems particularly barren today. Is what I'm sensing a reflection of what you've been up against?"

Ego-boundary Problems

Ego-boundary problems are intense in schizotypals, though less dramatic than those displayed by schizophrenics. Both schizotypal and borderline patients may exhibit "ego-diffusion" (Erikson 1951), but merging phenomena and other severe distortions of the sense of self tend to be the preserve of the schizotype. These distortions resemble, though in exaggerated form, the phenomena addressed with special attention by Kohut and his colleagues: mirroring, narcissistic disturbances, and faulty sense of identity, among others.

Therapeutic measures that may prove helpful in dealing with ego-boundary problems in the schizotype include setting appropriate limits, being strictly punctual about time and duration of sessions, and being decisive and firm bordered when dealing with the patient (the boundary between a vague, wishy-washy therapist and a schizotypal patient will be intolerably indistinct for the latter). In addition, the therapist should phrase many interventions so as to convey the notion "you seem to be seeing me as . . .," implying that the therapist understands how the patient is experiencing him or her but cannot entirely agree with this view. Remarks of this sort, besides being aimed at clearing up transference distortion, also help establish more precisely the psychological space where, in effect, the patient leaves off and the therapist begins.

Need for Education

As a corollary to schizotypal patients' propensity toward misinterpretation, they need more advice, education, and clarification than might be necessary in the treatment of other types of personality disorder. In many phases of the work, interpretive remarks, exploration of dreams, and the like play a much less important role than educative remarks, in which the therapist serves as a "reality-organ" for the patient. Schizotypal patients may be unusually handicapped at sensing what other people are all about or else at knowing how best to respond when their perceptions of interpersonal situations happen to be accurate. For example, therapy with one schizotypal woman became stalemated because frequent and seemingly endless telephone calls from her mother and sister had unnerving effects on her. Their criticisms and demands had a disruptive effect on her efforts to pursue her artistic career because she felt incapable of refusing or of terminating the conversations. Interpretive work and reassurances about her entitlements to her own "space" were unavailing. What helped was the direct advice that she install a second, unlisted phone, so she would have a phone for "safe" calls from people she was comfortable with, alongside the old "unsafe" phone her relatives used. Ignoring the latter until she had finished her painting, she was finally able to get her work done, to bolster her self-esteem through her work, and, eventually, to summon the courage to deal more firmly with her relatives. Another schizotypal patient was able to share some of his sexual fears and fantasies only after he had begun to work (impediments to which constituted the major focus during the first year of therapy). At that point he felt enough of a man to admit his fears of not having been enough of a man.

Need for Human Relatedness

As Rado (1956) pointed out, a schizotype may function on any of the customary levels of function: The "well-compensated" schizotype he described corresponds closely to what in DSM-III is designated as a schizoid personality. Patients showing his "decompensated schizoadaptation" would be called schizotypal personalities now, and those showing disintegration and chronic psychosis are the schizophrenics of DSM-III. Thus, in the center of this continuum are the schizotypals, themselves arranged along a narrower continuum—with individuals prone to brief psychotic episodes at one end and, at the other, those who, although chronically withdrawn and socially insecure, are seldom vulnerable to such episodes. The latter, their lives less in torment and less buffeted by ego-alien symptoms, are less prone to seek psychotherapy. Some are pushed into treatment by family members, who see them, for example, as "not living up to their potential" or "not getting the most out of life." As patients, these schizotypals are not very motivated and often drop out of psychotherapy after some "decent" interval (i.e., long enough to convince their families that they tried). Some of the less symptomatic schizotypals do seek therapy, motivated not so much by a desire to conquer particular problems as by the desire to ease an extreme loneliness. Committed to professionalism and to the goal of improving the lives of patients, the therapist talks about this or that dream symbol, this or that interpersonal conflict, but this talk becomes, if anything, merely the legitimate currency of exchange between therapist and patient. The patient is basking in the human relatedness with the therapist, whose interpretations, qua interpretation, go in one ear and out the other. Because the lives of certain schizotypals (both at work and at home) go much better, thanks to the security of this relationship, than would be the case without it, the therapeutic relationship—despite the therapist's embarrassment that "nothing is happening"—is a crucial and positive factor.

Hypochondriasis

Schizotypal patients tend to exhibit hypochondriacal symptoms. Hypochondriasis was noteworthy in about a third of the schizotypal patients. Vanggaard (1979) pointed out that in these patients the hypochondriasis often takes on bizarre qualities, focusing on "mute organs . . . from which normally no conscious sensations are experienced, as the blood, the bones, the connective tissue, etc." (p. 144). Sometimes there are several bodily complaints at once, and one symptom relates to an actual ailment, though in an exaggerated form ("This cough I'm sure will never go away and probably means I have TB."), but the other has no discernible physiologic counterpart ("And I have this pain that starts in my maxilla and goes down into my sternum.").

There appears to be an inverse relationship between the level of comfort with other people and the tendency to hypochondriasis: as the former increases, the latter recedes, and vice versa. At times of particular stress, including the stress posed by the therapist's temporary absence, hypochondriacal symptoms may suddenly intensify. One schizotypal patient had certain bronchitic symptoms before each separation, and (because he was rarely comfortable to talk about transference feelings) these symptoms provided the only clue that the therapist's absence made any impact on him at all. The dynamic involved may be reminiscent—in the reverse—of Freud's (1914) comment on hypochondriasis: "a person who is tormented by pain and discomfort gives up his interest in the things of the external world" (p. 82). The schizotypal patient experiencing setbacks in the external world often becomes "tormented by pain and discomfort" and may, especially as the years advance, present a clinical picture, simultaneously, of chronic indifference to the world of other people and of chronic hypochondriasis.

Hypochrondriacal symptoms in schizotypal patients are quite challenging from a therapeutic standpoint. They are often more ego-syntonic than they appear, compensating for the barrenness of the patient's interpersonal life. It does little good for the therapist to make a frontal assault on such symptoms (i.e., question their validity): the patient has at first too much need for them. At the same time, the therapist does not want a patient to undergo medical testing for every imaginary ache and may simply encourage the patient to share some uncertainty as to the diagnosis of the physical complaint and may temporize about expensive tests ("Let's see what happens over the next few weeks; sometimes these pains diminish as mysteriously as they appear."). More important, the therapist must realize that the hypochondriasis is an integral element in the schizotypal patient's shaky and object-poor adaptation. One cannot budge the hypochondriasis or fix it unless improvement has been fostered somewhere else in the patient's psychological space. If, for example, the therapist enables the schizotypal patient, over time, to establish a friendship or, failing that, to live a richer and more varied life, still without other people (e.g., to travel more or to pursue a craft or musical hobby), then there will be, because the real life is less lonely and painful, less need for hypochondriacal substitutes. Under such favorable circumstances, the latter will gradually wane, even in the absence of much interpretive work on the "meaning" of the symptoms.

Frequency of Visits and Duration of Therapy

The optimal frequency of sessions in dyadic therapy with a schizotypal patient depends in part on preexisting state, the patient's goals, and the balance between vulnerability and resiliency to the stresses of an exploratory therapy. An office patient who has been out of work and is particularly prone to feelings of humiliation over this lack of accomplishment and self-sufficiency may find the probing of certain hidden fears (especially ones centering on the theme of homosexuality) too threatening (cf. Frosch 1983). In such an instance, the therapist must direct efforts first, through chiefly supportive techniques, toward the patient's rehabilitation and autonomy. To the extent these can be fostered, the patient may become more comfortable exploring hitherto tabu areas. This may be a lengthy process involving not months but years. The more noticeable are the paranoid trends, the more caution must be exercised regarding frequency of visits, especially with a patient the same sex as the therapist, lest homosexual fears be mobilized prematurely via multiple visits per week.

Goals of Therapy

Some schizotypal patients are highly motivated for exploratory psychotherapy and make dramatic gains over a period of several years (coming for twice- or thrice-weekly sessions throughout most of the treatment period), after which only an occasional meeting or phone call is necessary, usually following some life stress.

Long-term therapy of a more supportive type is indicated for the majority of schizotypal patients, especially for those exhibiting odd communication and poor ability to resonate empathically with others. In the latter situation, the therapist may need to serve as a reality-organ ("auxiliary ego") for many years, or even for life.

Short-term therapy is relevant to crisis intervention and situational difficulties (in personal life or at work) and may serve as a "refresher course" after a halt in a previous course of long-term treatment. In general, the ego deficits and personal eccentricities of many schizotypals make some form of long-term contact advisable.

Other Forms of Therapy

Behavior Modification

The reeducative approach necessary to work with schizotypal patients may at times have to be reinforced after the manner of behavior modification therapy. Schizotypal persons who have marked peculiarities of speech, dress, and habit, but who aspire to "fit in" better with other people, will need special help in these areas. For example, help may take the form of elocution lessons, a Dale Carnegie course, accompanying the patient at a clothing shop to aid in selecting a suit or dress appropriate to a job interview, encouraging the keeping of a diary detailing the nature of conflicts with other people, or using videotape to point out awkwardness of gait or gesture (cf. Albert 1983). Other guidelines relevant to behavior modification techniques with this patient population may be gleaned from the article by Liberman (1972). Paul (1980) discussed methods for the careful assessment of maladaptive behavior.

Group and Marital Therapy

There is as yet no literature devoted specifically to group or marital therapy with schizotypal patients. Some of the remarks of Spotnitz (1957), Roth (1982), and Mosher and Gunderson (1979) are pertinent, though based on patients with somewhat different diagnostic labels and clinical pictures. Many schizotypal patients are inordinately shy and prone to paranoid thoughts concerning other people disliking them or looking down on them. Provided their anxiety in the presence of others is not too extreme, such patients may benefit from group therapy. The therapy should be oriented toward practical goals because an insight-oriented group focusing on dreams and other "deep" material might prove too threatening.

A practical goal relevant to shy schizotypes is developing awareness that other people may harbor fantasies and self-criticisms similar to their own and may find them likable despite their conviction of unlikability. Positive experiences of this sort may diminish social anxiety and widen opportunities for friendship. With schizotypal patients who have irritating personalities or other socially alienating tendencies, group therapy may be able, via the impact of the other patients in the group, to correct some of these tendencies. If they are too pronounced, however, the group members may reject the patient. The key is the perceived degree of deviation from the average of the other group members. In general, there will be levels of shyness, eccentricity, peculiarity of speech, standoffishness, and other traits that the group can comfortably deal with, but at levels beyond the limits of tolerability, the traits so affect either the patient or the other group members as to nullify the utility of remaining in the group. The clinical judgment of the group leader should be refined enough to permit approximately correct selection of which schizotypals could benefit from being in the group and which could not.

Schizotypal patients appear to remain single more often than the statistical averages would predict. Some of these patients are very tuned in to the feelings of others, but are exquisitely sensitive to criticism, and avoid intimacy for this reason. Others, as mentioned, are so out of tune with people's feelings as to be rejected repeatedly. Thus, schizotypals who do marry may have problems stemming either from insensitivity to the feelings of the spouse or from oversensitivity to the spouse's behavior. The first task of the marital therapist is to assess the degree of and the balance between these two tendencies. As a rule, it is easier to help an oversensitive marital partner react more appropriately than to make an insensitive spouse more empathic.

Pharmacotherapy

Schizotypals subject to transient psychotic experiences are, for this very reason, more motivated than other schizotypals to seek help spontaneously, especially as they begin to realize how susceptible they are to decompensation under certain recurring life stresses. It is with this group of schizotypals that a brief course of treatment with anxiolytic medications may be distinctly beneficial during times of crisis, particularly with patients of keen intelligence.

Favorable response to small doses of anxiolytics has been reported for schizotypal patients who present with a fair degree of anxiety and other distressing symptoms (Akiskal 1981; Serban and Siegel 1984). Only a minority of schizotypals are symptomatic to this degree, and usually only during the early months of therapy. Therefore, medication may not be an integral part of treatment for most schizotypal patients.

The particular clinical features that are most apt to prove drug responsive include, as outlined in a recent article by Goldberg et al. (1986), illusions, ideas of reference, "psychoticism," phobic anxiety, and obsessive-compulsive symptoms. Goldberg et al. found that thiothixene proved beneficial in schizotypal patients with these features, and the patients responded to doses lower than those customarily prescribed for outpatient schizophrenics. Because not all the relevant symptoms are mentioned in the DSM-III definition, these authors recommended that a trial of thiothixene or a related drug might be useful if the clinician is able to make a subdiagnosis (when confronted with a patient presenting schizotypal features) that embodies the above-mentioned symptoms. The effectiveness of haloperidol in borderline patients with schizotypal traits has, in a similar fashion, been described by Soloff et al. (1986). Gunderson (1986) has ably discussed and summarized indications and contraindications for pharmacotherapy in this domain.

Residential Therapies

Schizotypal patients rarely show violence toward themselves or others. Therefore, they are admitted less often to inpatient facilities. By virtue of their social handicaps, in contrast, they do make up a significant proportion of patients in day-hospitals and halfway houses. In these settings, especially in day-hospitals, the focus is often on stimulating the patient to make more social contacts within the community. Schizotypals who are able to work incline toward jobs that call for little interaction with people. Vocational rehabilitation, geared to these types of employment, is often necessary during the early stages of residential therapy in schizotypal patients who are as yet unable to work. The residential facilities foster better ability to socialize even though they contain other patients whose presence makes the schizotypal person feel less strange and alone. Some day-hospitals are also equipped to carry out behavior modification techniques, which may be applied to alleviate compulsive handwashing and other abnormal habits of schizotypal patients.

Occasional schizotypal patients do have strong suicidal tendencies. It is difficult to generalize about this group except to note that some actually do complete suicide. Other suicidal schizotypals can appear quite well at long-term follow-up. Probably for certain suicidal schizotypals, long-term, intensive inpatient psychotherapy is life-saving and is the treatment of choice.

Summary

Although schizotypal personality is generally a stable configuration of traits, occurring in persons who usually do not become schizophrenic, it is a disorder associated with considerable social disability. Proneness to brief psychotic episodes, often paranoid in nature, is also characteristic.

Persons with this disorder seek help most often because of an inability to "connect" meaningfully and pleasurefully with other people. Intense loneliness is common. Their lives tend to be marginal; they gravitate toward jobs that either seem below their capacity or demand little interaction with others. Proportionally, more are treated in offices, clinics, and day-hospitals, and relatively few in acute inpatient facilities. Suicidal gestures are less common than in persons with borderline personality disorder, but some will make definitive attempts. As a group, patients with schizotypal personality make only modest gains in therapy, though a few make impressive gains.

Chapter 256

Histrionic Personality Disorder

General Comments

In DSM-III (American Psychiatric Association 1980) the histrionic personality disorder (formerly and still widely known as the hysterical personality disorder)* is defined in behavioral terms by the presence of overly dramatic, reactive, and intensely expressed behavior and certain characteristic disturbances in interpersonal relationships (see Table 1 for DSM-III-R diagnostic criteria for histrionic personality disorder) (American Psychiatric Association 1987). To be designated as a disorder, in DSM-III, the symptoms must be responsible for significant, subjective distress or maladaptive social

Table 1. Diagnostic Criteria for Histrionic Personality Disorder
A pervasive pattern of excessive emotionality and attention-seeking, beginning by early adulthood and present in a variety of contexts, as indicated by at least *four* of the following:
(1) constantly seeks or demands reassurance, approval, or praise
(2) is inappropriately sexually seductive in appearance or behavior
(3) is overly concerned with physical attractiveness
(4) expresses emotion with inappropriate exaggeration, e.g., embraces casual acquaintances with excessive ardor, sobs uncontrollably on minor sentimental occasions, has temper tantrums
(5) is uncomfortable in situations in which he or she is not the center of attention
(6) displays rapidly shifting and shallow expression of emotions
(7) is self-centered, actions being directed toward obtaining immediate satisfaction; has no tolerance for the frustration of delayed gratification
(8) has a style of speech that is excessively impressionistic and lacking in detail, e.g., when asked to describe mother, can be no more specific than, "She was a beautiful person."

*In this chapter, the two terms will be used interchangeably and will also be referred to as the HPD.

or occupational functioning. It is wise to keep these limiting criteria in mind in view of the pejorative implications of the term "hysterical" in popular usage.

To serve as a basis for later psychotherapeutic suggestions, we will elaborate on the DSM-III criteria (Chodoff and Lyons 1958). HPD patients manifest a high degree of overt emotionality, often both strident and superficial and at times taking the form of emotional storms. They constantly seek to call attention to themselves. Sexually seductive behavior is a hallmark characteristic, although like the emotionality, it has a superficial quality and may not be accompanied by appropriate, intense erotic response. Above all, and consistent with the DSM-III name change, hysterics are histrionic. They are always on stage and in performance, sometimes to such a degree that they have difficulty distinguishing fantasy from reality. In the absence or weakness of a "central core," the histrionic personality seems to consist simply of a number of different exteriors (Jaspers 1963)—almost like a kind of chameleon in which the uncovering of each layer serves only to reveal another layer with a different emotional coloration in compliance with the perceived requirements of the interpersonal environment. A characteristic submissiveness and eagerness to please found in some of these patients may be the other side of a kind of ruthless willfulness that can be very disconcerting, especially in psychotherapeutic relationships. Although some features of hysterical cognition were described by Shapiro (1965), their importance is now becoming better recognized. These patients display a cognitive style characterized by imprecision and exaggeration. They have difficulty in focusing their attention and rely on a mode of perception and information processing that is global and diffuse rather than detailed and consecutive. Horowitz (1977) pointed out that their usual answer to a question of fact is "I don't know." The inordinate and demanding dependency displayed by many of these patients plays so important a role in hysterical psychopathology as to constitute a kind of organizing principle for many of the other features, which can be seen as distorted efforts to gratify dependency or as defensive reactions to its presence.

Although the HPD can and does occur in men (Luisada et al. 1974), it is a diagnosis predominantly applied to women (Chodoff 1982). This may be related to the historical subordination of women to men, a factor that must be taken into account in any psychotherapeutic approach. Women have had to come to terms with a world in which the dominant values have always been set by men. When combined with certain more specific genetic and psychodynamic determinants, this cultural tradition and the attitudes that result lead to the caricature of femininity called the HPD (Chodoff and Lyons 1958).

Individuals with the diagnosis vary over a wide clinical continuum (Chodoff 1974) ranging from the disturbed and unstable oral and hysteroid, the "so-called good" hysterics (Zetzel 1968), to the relatively healthy phallic variety. It is clear that the DSM-III description of the HPD applies much more to the former than to the latter group. This has implications for the choice of psychotherapeutic methods.

In view of this wide variation within the diagnostic category, it is clear that no one set of genotypes could be responsible for the widely varying phenotype called the HPD. However, Hollender (1971) described a particular family constellation that may play an important role in distorting personality development toward this form of psychopathology: A serious interference in the patient's early relationship with her mother turns the little girl to her father for fulfillment of her needs for nurture. When an erotic element is introduced into the relationship, the child learns that the way to be cared for by men is through sexual display. Consequently, she tends to go through life attempting to seduce men into serving as substitute mothers by presenting herself in a sexual mode. She enters on a career of pseudosexuality in the service of dependency (Chodoff 1982).

Psychotherapies

Individual Dynamic Psychotherapy and Psychoanalysis

At the outset, it needs to be stated emphatically that there is no standard mode of psychotherapy that can be guaranteed to produce beneficial change in patients with HPD, or any other diagnosis. Each psychotherapist's approach is shaped by three factors: 1) the psychopathology, that is, the symptoms with which the patient presents, and the therapist's assessment of the patient's personality strengths and weaknesses; 2) the particular theoretical approach guiding the psychotherapist and the therapeutic goals he or she sets; and 3) the kind of person the psychotherapist is, the mixture of qualities and experiences of which his or her method of therapy is a reflection.

A central dynamic (Fromm-Reichmann 1950) in the psychopathology of these patients is their excessive, unresolved, and sometimes angry dependency, their desperate and doomed efforts to have all of their needs met by someone else, often through a sexual involvement with a man. This dynamic is not in conscious awareness, so the major therapeutic thrust must be directed toward bringing it into the open, in the interest of helping the patient experience and change the various ways in which she attempts to secure total satisfaction from someone else. The patient needs to examine the origins of this pattern and explore the methods, like sexual seductiveness, little-girl cuteness, temper tantrums, or alogical cognition, she has employed to try to fulfill her needs. She must learn that her goal cannot be achieved or is attainable only at the cost of abasement and loss of self-respect. But recognition and awareness are not enough. The patient must also be helped to find more independent ways of living and of achieving satisfactions on her own, as opposed to always needing to suck sustenance from a man.

In view of this central dynamic, it is almost inevitable that transactions between the patient and the therapist, from the beginning, assume a very important role in the psychotherapeutic relationship.

Transferential processes can be expected to be strong and unmistakable. The therapist, especially if male, is likely to be invested with the role of the patient's fantasy father. This has been termed a "maternal transference" (Kohon 1984) in accordance with the formulation that the patient is seeking nurturance, not sexual gratification. In her endeavor to manipulate the therapist to meet all her needs, the patient will express very positive feelings toward him as she admires his powers and ability. But it is very important to keep in mind that these are pseudopositive rather than truly loving feelings. Considering their origin in an essentially exploitative early relationship, it is inevitable that they will be shot through with ambivalence. Rather than being the object of a truly human regard, the therapist is being set up by the patient in the service of her voracious demands.

The story of hysteria and psychoanalysis is one of infinite interest. Hysteria was Freud's "Galapagos" (Erikson 1979). Most of Freud's early formulations were derived from patients so labeled, although many would not receive this designation today (Reichard 1956). Frequently Freud's hysterics failed to justify their high (phallic) placement in the psychosexual hierarchy, however, and at a certain point in his career,

Freud (1959c) expressed frustration with his understanding of hysteria. Afterwards, he devoted little attention to it. Later psychoanalytic theorists tried to reconcile the obvious dependent (oral) characteristic of many of these patients with their putative oedipal and phallic fixation point. The resulting compromise is the phallic-oral spectrum of hysteria in current psychoanalytic thinking.

The classical psychoanalytic method, with its emphasis on abstinence and neutrality and its requirement that the patient have enough ego strength to regress in a controlled manner, is applicable and appropriate for the relatively healthy, "good" patient. For such cases, the model of transference development in an atmosphere of abstinence and neutrality, to be followed by mutative transference interpretations, offers promise of a thoroughgoing and durable personality change.

But these phallic patients, although in a broad sense they may be considered hysterical, are not likely to be the kind of exigent and fragile individuals who satisfy DSM-III criteria for the diagnosis of the HPD. This conclusion is attested to by the fading of the early enthusiasm for the results of standard psychoanalytic treatment with a mixed bag of "hysterics." The legacy of this disillusionment has been a lessening both of interest in this area (Chodoff 1954) and of therapeutic optimism about these patients (Khan 1975a). When dealing with hysterics diagnosed using DSM-III criteria, departures from the classical psychoanalytic method are usually required.

Employing the abstinent-neutral stance with a histrionic patient having serious ego weakness may actually be counterproductive. The therapist's refusal as a matter of principle to answer the patient's questions, give advice, or express an opinion may very well have a paradoxical effect. Fantasies about the therapist's omnipotence may be stimulated as the patient concludes that the therapist fails to respond directly not because he or she lacks the power to solve all problems, but because of a decision not to exercise such power. The urgent and importunate pressure from the patient to extract guidance, and the sometimes desperate efforts of the therapist to avoid gratifying the patient, can have a distinctly disruptive effect on the therapeutic relationship. It can be responsible for an uneasy atmosphere of unresolved tension within which it is difficult to do any useful therapeutic work. Therapist and patient may find themselves in a double-bind situation in which the therapist ostensibly maintains an abstinent position, while in fact responding to the tension in the relationship by covert attempts to meet the patient's needs. Of course, the therapist should not move to the opposite extreme and attempt to respond to and gratify all the patient's desires. In the face of the apparent seductiveness of hysterical patients, such attempts may result in overt sexual acting out. This is not only absolutely disruptive to treatment but probably occasion for legal action.

Rather than consistent denial of direct gratification or attempts to reduce all frustrations, a flexible approach is advisable. Thus, a sympathetic and interested but noncommittal attitude toward the patient's questions and requests for guidance may be all that is required to turn the transaction from importunate demand to fruitful inquiry. There are instances, however, when such an approach simply does not suffice. In such cases the therapist must give at least a little—and at times a good deal. The therapeutic skill lies in being able to titrate the appropriate degree of give. By maintaining a tension between responding and withholding while at the same time focusing the spotlight on such patient-therapist transactions, the therapist can help the patient become aware of the difference between what she reasonably can expect from other people and what is simply unattainable (or is attainable only at a prohibitive cost in terms of humiliation and lower self-esteem). To the extent the patient learns to understand this difference and to incorporate and integrate it, therapy has a chance to be successful.

Resolving transference distortions principally by interpretive means must be undertaken with great caution with the more disturbed and unstable HPD patients in view of the importunate nature of their demands and their tendency to enmesh therapists in sticky and intractable relationships. Although useful at times, overreliance on this method in inappropriate cases may be one of the factors leading to psychoanalytic disenchantment with the treatment of hysterics and even to signs of frustration such as Khan's (1975b) recommendation that the erotic transference not be interpreted in these cases. Because of the potentially regressive and irreducible quality of transferences, it may be wise not to allow them to develop too firmly. This can be accomplished by the use of so-called counterprojective techniques. Firmly identified with the work of Sullivan (1954) and also strongly advocated by Rado (1956), these have more recently been reemphasized by Havens (1976).

Counterprojective techniques are direct or subtle responses, usually but not always verbal, which convey to the patient that the therapist is not a transference figure of her childhood. The effect, as Havens (1976) put it, is to take the patient-therapist relationship out of the psychotherapeutic medium itself and place it in the screen between the two participants, where it can be scrutinized in a cooler and more productive fashion. In a clinical vignette Chodoff described how he responded to a patient who was wistfully recalling that her daddy would always tell her what to do. Chodoff said to her, in a mildly sarcastic tone, "Yes, and he always had all the answers, didn't he?" By doing this, Chodoff sharply differentiated himself from her father instead of allowing this misperception to ripen, and fostered discussion of the nature of their patient-therapist relationship. His intention was also to make the patient feel that he was on her side, thus strengthening the therapeutic alliance that must underlie all successful psychotherapy and that is often difficult to establish with HPD patients. Of course, the use of sarcasm must be undertaken with caution and only after scrutinizing oneself for the presence of unresolved countertransference elements (Paul Chodoff, personal communication).

Despite the need for a participatory and dialogic approach with histrionic patients, it is very important for the therapist to be nonintrusive and to pay attention to the attitude that he or she is projecting. It is especially important to pay sober and respectful attention. The kind of playful banter that is sometimes therapeutically useful can have the effect of encouraging seductive behavior in the histrionic patient. The respectful therapeutic stance is consciously intended to differ significantly from the pathogenic attitudes of the patient's parents and provides the patient with a corrective emotional experience. It also strengthens the therapeutic alliance.

Throughout their lives, many hysterics seem to have learned little more than how to present and display themselves, how to be noticed and taken care of. It is extraordinarily difficult for them to learn anything else, thus the difficulty with their acquisition and integration of self-knowledge through therapeutic insights. Their "insights" are often not genuine. The triumphal acquisition of blockbuster pseudoinsights followed by quick erasures is so characteristic as to be emblematic of these patients.

What are the factors contributing to the phenomenon of pseudoinsight? One is the peculiar, vague, and forgetful cognitive style of the hysteric. Another is the eagerness of the hysteric to inflate the ego of her therapist (in this case, by responding positively to an interpretation) so as to flatter him or her in hopes of having dependent needs filled. The willfulness of some histrionic patients can also play a role. Farber (1966) described how this willfulness can usurp the domain of the imagination and the intellect, thus producing roadblocks to the capacity to be reflective and reasonably critical. Still another determinant of pseudoinsight is the peculiar time sense of these patients. As the paranoid lives in the past, brooding over old wrongs, and as the obsessional worries about the future consequences of any commitment or decision, so the hysteric is trapped in the present, mourning and raging over the frustration of her efforts to extract what she wants from those around her—right now! It is these qualities—an eagerness to please in order to win immediate gratification, a nonreflective willfulness, and the immersion in the present—that are responsible for the hysterical patient's immediate obeisance to an interpretive remark. They also contribute to inevitable disappointments with the supposed insights, so that even if the insights are not forgotten, they are recalled with a leaden and accusatory lack of interest that gives rise in the therapist to irritation, anger, exasperation, and feelings of inadequacy. The therapist needs to be aware of the false quality of many of these apparent revelatory responses and to realize that it is possible to be seduced not only sexually but also intellectually. Understanding these motivations will arm the therapist with the tolerance necessary to avoid disruptive feelings of disappointment. In view of the role of interpretive remarks in precipitating pseudoinsights, it is well to be cautious about enthusiastic responses to interpretations, particularly "deep" ones.

The distorted cognitive style of histrionic patients also presents difficulties for dynamic psychotherapy. In a sense it is necessary to teach these patients to think, just as it is necessary to teach obsessional patients to feel. Horowitz (1977) described his attempts to repair the cognitive defect of histrionics, using the microanalysis of events to encourage them to pay attention to details, rather than to vague and global perceptions, and to attend carefully to their own nonverbal communications as well as to the context of interpersonal relations in which they occur. Another thrust of therapy is to bring to the patients' attention their tendencies to draw premature conclusions dominated by internalized fantasies and their limited role repertoires. The goal is for them to learn to perceive closely, to gather and evaluate clues, and to consider their own motives and those of others so as to put cause and effect into their proper relationship. It is also important in this repair effort to pay close and respectful attention to what the patient is saying, asking for enlightenment when confused and concentrating on the verbal exchange to convey to the patient that she is being taken seriously. Of course, these efforts, which have a didactic element, can be effective only in the context of a durable therapeutic alliance. They must be supplemented by interpretation of the defensive reasons underlying the inability to perceive and notice.

Even more direct ways of dealing with the histrionic's memory lapses, cognitive style, and inappropriate behavior may be considered. Orne (personal communication) has suggested the use of audio playback for this purpose. Returning after sessions to review the tapes allows hysterical patients to become aware of what their actions look like and how their preoccupation with the way others respond to them can compromise awareness of what they themselves are doing. Under certain circumstances, the use of videotape playback may be even more illuminating (Chodoff 1972).

It would be incomplete in a discussion of the HPD to ignore the quality that has become the hallmark of histrionic patients, their ticket to popular ill fame and the principal reason for their bad reputation. I refer to the incontinent and excessive nature of hysterical emotional life. Hysterical rages, tears, exultations, and depressions seem to be too much—unbridled and apparently meretricious reactions to whatever has precipitated the patients' moods. Observers doubt the genuineness and authenticity of such pyrotechnical emotional displays, which give the impression of serving a defensive function in denying rather than expressing true emotions. What are the roots of such behavior? It can rest upon a misjudgment of what is appealing—a temper tantrum ensuing when the pose of the little girl does not result in special treatment or a regressive flight into childishness when the strain of adulthood proves too arduous—or it can be a protest stemming from the patient's realization that she has traded independence and integrity to become a pampered slave. As with any other kind of complex behavior, no one reason fully accounts for these emotional storms. Motivation is always multiple, and the skill of the psychotherapist lies in his or her ability to decipher and disentangle the various strands. There is no single technique or method that can be counted on reliably to bring about a better balance between emotions and thoughts.

Positive and durable changes can occur in hysterical patients with regard not only to their emotionality but also to other aspects of their maladaptive behavior. Such personality maturation is the fruit of a relationship in which the therapist consistently offers a model of fairness and honesty to the patient. Certainly the therapist has to demonstrate that he or she will not subscribe to the patient's exploitative maneuvers. It is necessary to establish a line, or at least a zone of demarcation, between what the patient can hope realistically to obtain from other people and what is not available or can be obtained only at prohibitive personal cost (e.g., having a demeaning temper tantrum). But, as noted, the therapist's resistance to excessive demands must be coupled with genuine respect for the patient. It is difficult, especially for super-logical therapists with excessively orderly minds, to conceal a negative bias toward hysterical patients. Offenkrantz and Tobin (1974) pointed out that psychotherapists, usually more obsessional than hysterical, are made uneasy, perhaps annoyed, by the extravagant emotional displays of hysterics. A regular occasion for such mutual frustration is any discussion of termination of treatment. A therapist's ambivalent attitudes can well convert what was intended to be a firm but understanding refusal to be maneuvered into a rejection, thus generating an emotional storm. A therapist's lack of respect for or actual dislike of the patient will be recognized regardless of efforts at concealment and inevitably will result in a deepening of the basic feelings of desperation and inauthenticity that may lie at the roots of the apparent insatiability and demandingness of this character disorder. The ultimate therapeutic goal in working psychotherapeutically with the HPD patient is to provide a kind of interpersonal ambience within which a caricature of femininity may progress toward humanness.

Other Psychotherapies

Although it is generally acknowledged that individual, dynamic psychotherapy must be the centerpiece of psychotherapeutic efforts for HPD patients, other psychotherapeutic approaches may be mentioned. It should be noted, however, that brief, group, and family therapists do not discuss their work primarily in terms of the diagnostic categories contained in DSM-III. One reason for this may be the relatively recent introduction of the diagnostic manual. More fundamentally, however, therapists using these other approaches generally conceptualize their theories and methods in very different terms. Thus, a few years ago, Frances et al. (1984) acknowledged the lack of relevance of DSM-III categories to family therapy. For this reason, only some rather general remarks can be made about the indications and goals of these forms of psychotherapy for the HPD.

Time-limited Psychotherapy

The brief psychotherapies comprise a group of related methods that employ the active application of psychodynamically oriented procedures over a limited period of time. Sifneos (1984a) listed the criteria for one of these methods—short-term anxiety-provoking psychotherapy (STAPP). These criteria, which are generally similar to those enunciated by Malan (1976), have to do with patients' characteristics, such as a circumscribed chief complaint and previous history of good interpersonal relationships, the ability to interact with the therapist, psychological-mindedness, above-average intelligence, and, especially, motivation for change. It seems unlikely that these criteria would be satisfied by most of the patients bearing the DSM-III diagnosis of the HPD, but some less severely disturbed "hysterics" might benefit from STAPP. Attempts are being made to offer STAPP for sicker individuals also (Sifneos 1984b).

In the criteria for another variant of brief therapy called time-limited psychotherapy, Mann (1984) emphasized a "capacity for engaging quickly and disengaging quickly without suffering unduly." This requirement seems to pose difficulties for HPD patients, who characteristically involve themselves in intense and sticky transference relationships with their therapists. Rush (1985) noted a specific hindrance to success in brief psychotherapy for patients with "hysterical" style. Mostly interested in pleasing the therapist in face-to-face encounters, they may balk at the "picky" details of prescribed homework tasks. As for cognitive therapy, a method that recently has received a good deal of attention with regard to depressed patients, its indications (Rush 1984) include only Axis I conditions, although the indications and contraindications are under study and may be widened.

Group Therapy

This term encompasses so varied a group of psychotherapeutic and educational methods that it is difficult to make general statements about its applicability to particular conditions. Interactional, psychodynamic, or psychoanalytically oriented groups that attempt to bring about personality change could include certain HPD patients. There are some warnings in the older psychoanalytic group literature (Slavson 1939) about the dangers of including "hysterics" for theoretical reasons, but also because the changeableness and unpredictability of some of these patients may cause stress and anxiety in other group members. More recently, Halleck (1978) noted that many group therapists may exclude from their groups patients who cannot identify with the group or participate in group processes without monopolizing or disrupting them. In this category he included hysterical patients. In a review article on group therapy, Fuchs (1984) did not specifically mention the HPD category in the section on indications and limitations. However, it can be inferred that within the spectrum of such patients, some would be acceptable whereas the demanding behavior of others would be disruptive. Factors other than the diagnosis per se seem to determine acceptability for group therapy. Sheidlinger and Porter (1980) suggested that concurrent therapy (a combination of individual and group treatment) may be the treatment of choice in patients with characterological disorders, especially those with primitive, pre-oedipal transferences and rigid character structures—a description that includes a number of HPD patients.

Family Therapy

All forms of family therapy depend on an underlying conception of the family as a system with interacting components. Accordingly, when therapeutic interests are focused on family dynamics, diagnostic consideration applied to individuals in the family is not the predominant factor influencing the choice of family over individual psychotherapy. Grunebaum and Glick (1983) made this point explicit and referred to ongoing research on the value of family therapy for various symptoms.

However, there is one mode of family therapy that is clearly relevant for certain HPD patients. The fact that there are characteristic difficulties in the course of marriages between obsessional males and hysterical females is common knowledge among therapists. For such disharmonious unions, couples therapy is a relevant therapeutic possibility, whether alone or in combination with individual therapy for either of the participants.

Referring to this kind of marriage, Berman (1983) described a marital style in which the husband appears overbearing, distant, overorganized, and paternal and the wife comes across as childlike and "hysterical." The husband tends to assume more and more responsibility as the wife becomes increasingly helpless. The goal of the therapist is to provide conditions that allow each partner to change this pattern. This is done by revealing the hidden complementarity or reversal of functions underneath what is apparent—the frightened, undernurtured feelings of the "competent" husband and the rage of the passive wife. It is essential in such cases not to see the wife as the only patient, and both marital partners should enter into couples therapy.

Behavioral Therapy

Andrews (1984) reviewed the subject of behavioral therapy for "hysteria," contrasting this method with psychoanalytic approaches. In fact, his review dealt mainly with behavioral treatment of hysterical symptoms, not primarily of the HPD, although he remarked on the agreement among behavioral therapists that a compliant eagerness to please is characteristic of hysterics. Thus, to the extent that hysterical symptoms (aphonia, paralysis of the leg, etc.) are associated with hysterical character (by no means always the case) (Chodoff 1974), behavioral therapy may be instrumental in modifying the personality characteristics as well as the symptoms. Behavioral therapists accomplish this goal by attempting to harness the patient's need to please in a reinforcement schedule that rewards abatement of symptoms. If this effort is supplemented by providing "patients with tools for getting their needs met in assertive ways and expressing their feelings in conflict with others instead of withdrawing to the sick role," it may have the effect of modifying "precisely those life strategies central to the hysterical style [and of] dealing with change goals that are far more fundamental than the removal of an isolated habit" (Andrews 1984, p. 224).

Difficulties with this behavioral approach include the possibility of symptom substitution, often mentioned but seldom documented. More seriously, with DSM-III HPDs, behavioral therapists must deal with the same dilemma that confronts psychodynamic therapists—the patient may "change" to please the therapist even if, paradoxically, to generate this approval the patient acts as if she no longer needs approval.

Biologic Therapies

When severe depression is the presenting symptom of an HPD patient or appears in the course of treatment, antidepressive medication may be indicated. This can occur as part of a supportive program primarily aimed at relieving the depression but may be an ongoing aspect of a long-range psychotherapeutic effort. The question of a specific "hysterical" depression will be discussed in the next section. However, it has been reported that the presence of hysterical traits in a cluster of other symptoms in depressed patients was predictive of a greater response to phenelzine than amitriptyline (Robinson et al. 1983). The condition called hysteroid (or rejection-prone) dysphoria, occupying a position at the boundary between the borderline personality disorder and the HPD, has been responsive also to MAOI drugs (Liebowitz and Klein 1979) (see Chapter 251 on Somatic Therapy). Complaints about somatic side effects are likely to be prominent with HPD patients receiving drugs.

Residential Therapies

The principal indication for hospitalization of patients bearing the diagnosis of the HPD is the presence of depression. When depression is manifested primarily by suicidal ideation or suicidal gestures, the therapist may be confronted with a difficult decision. Is the suicidal behavior serious enough to warrant protective measures? Is it a device intended to provoke the therapist's concern or to express anger at him or her for failing to pay attention? The patient may also wish to be hospitalized as a form of dependency gratification. Hospitalization may be avoided and the therapeutic work forwarded in the presence of a strong therapeutic alliance and if the factors leading to the suicidal behavior can be dealt with consensually.

However, when hospitalization is required, there is some reason to believe that some so-called hysterical depressions are likely to present differently than depressions in individuals with other personality structures. For instance, depressed hysterics are more likely to display open hostility than depressed obsessionals. It has also been noted that depressed HPD patients are likely to be more hypochondriacal and to have less intense feelings of depression, hopelessness, and worthlessness (Gershon et al. 1968; Lazare and Klerman 1968).

What about hysterical psychosis? The idea that an untoward environmental event may precipitate a brief psychotic episode in individuals with hysterical personality features has had a certain amount of currency, especially since the publication of the article by Hollender and Hirsch (1964). Gift et al. (1985), however, found no cases satisfying Hollender and Hirsch's criteria in a sample of 217 first-admission patients with functional psychiatric disorder. Among other reasons for the absence of such cases, they may have been included in the DSM-III diagnosis of brief reactive psychosis even though this condition differs from hysterical psychosis by not requiring the absence of significant psychopathology before the onset of psychotic symptoms.

Chapter 257

Narcissistic Personality Disorder

The literature about the treatment of patients with narcissistic personality disorder has been growing over the past 15 years. Although important issues related to narcissism and narcissistic vulnerability were described earlier, the contributions of Kernberg (1975, 1976) and Kohut (1971, 1977), who specifically discussed patients with narcissistic personality disorder and their treatment, stimulated this recent literature. The complexity of the subject is due in part to the fact that often narcissism, narcissistic features in other disorders, and narcissistic vulnerability are linked to or confused with narcissistic personality disorder. In addition, the DSM-III-R (American Psychiatric Association 1987) description does not address the complex and often contradictory psychoanalytic formulations of major contributors, who sometimes include in this disorder patients who go beyond the narrower confines of DSM-III-R. Finally, authors often link descriptions and discussions of narcissistic personality disorders with borderline personality disorders, inadequately distinguishing between the two. An aspect of the confusion relates to the varying ways that different contributors view the relationship between the two kinds of disorders. For example, Kernberg described both narcissistic and borderline personality disorders within the broader category of borderline personality organization. Kohut, in contrast, placed borderline personality disorder closer to psychosis, distinctly separate from narcissistic personality disorder. He also added a category of narcissistic behavior disorder for patients more pathologic and impulse ridden than those with narcissistic personality disorder. My belief (Adler 1985) is that borderline and narcissistic personality disorder are on a continuum, which can be utilized to monitor therapeutic progress as patients close to the borderline end of the spectrum move toward a higher level of integration. See Table 1 for the DSM-III-R diagnostic criteria for narcissistic personality disorder.

Psychotherapies

Individual Psychotherapies

Individual psychotherapy, alone or in conjunction with group or family therapy, is viewed as the basic form of treatment for patients with narcissistic personality disorder. However, a major area of controversy in the literature relates to the choice between individual psychotherapy and psychoanalysis.

Table 1.   DSM-III-R Diagnostic Criteria for Narcissistic Personality Disorder
A pervasive pattern of grandiosity (in fantasy or behavior), lack of empathy, and hypersensitivity to the evaluation of others, beginning by early adulthood and present in a variety of contexts, as indicated by at least *five* of the following: (1) reacts to criticism with feelings of rage, shame, or humiliation (even if not expressed)   (2) is interpersonally exploitative: takes advantage of others to achieve his or her own ends   (3) has a grandiose sense of self-importance, e.g., exaggerates achievements and talents, expects to be noticed as "special" without appropriate achievement   (4) believes that his or her problems are unique and can be understood only by other special people   (5) is preoccupied with fantasies of unlimited success, power, brilliance, beauty, or ideal love   (6) has a sense of entitlement: unreasonable expectation of especially favorable treatment, e.g., assumes that he or she does not have to wait in line when others must do so   (7) requires constant attention and admiration, e.g., keeps fishing for compliments   (8) lacks empathy: unable to recognize and experience how others feel, e.g., is annoyed and surprised when a friend who is seriously ill cancels a date   (9) is preoccupied with feelings of envy

There is agreement that patients with narcissistic personality disorder are much more stable than borderline personalities, having greater ego capacities to tolerate frustration and delay and a vulnerable self-structure that is less prone to disorganization. Kernberg viewed patients with narcissistic personality disorder as more likely to benefit from psychoanalysis than any other patients with diagnoses in the category of borderline personality organization, with the exception of patients functioning on an overt borderline level, that is, with severe problems of impulsivity and inability to tolerate delay. Kohut, whose clinical experience was largely psychoanalytic, and who seemed to have worked mostly with better functioning narcissistic personality disorders, discussed the psychoanalytic treatment of these patients. Both Masterson (1981) and Rinsley (1982) focused their attention on a form of treatment similar to Kernberg's expressive psychotherapy, which Kernberg also recommended for better functioning narcissistic personality disorders when psychoanalysis is not available.

Psychoanalysis

Although Kernberg and Kohut agreed that psychoanalysis can be the treatment of choice for many patients with narcissistic personality disorder, their formulations of the disorder led to differing clinical approaches. Because Kernberg viewed issues of anger and envy, and the patient's need to be self-sufficient, as being at the core of the disorder, he emphasized active interpretation and confrontation of the patient's defenses against acknowledging these affects and this need. The approach includes confronting the patient's idealization, which Kernberg formulated largely as a defense. In addition, the narcissistic personality disorder's pathologic self-structure, which Kernberg defined as an amalgam of ideal self, ideal object, and real self, supports a position of self-sufficiency and requires this active, confrontational approach.

In contrast, Kohut defined the core of the disorder as the stunted development of the patient's grandiose self, based on parental failures to mirror and allow idealization in phase-appropriate ways from early childhood through latency and adolescence. He described the formation of selfobject transferences (both mirroring and idealizing) that recreate the situation with parents that was partially unsuccessful in childhood. Kohut emphasized that the establishment of one or the other of these transferences is necessary before the diagnosis of narcissistic personality disorder can be made. However, it is sometimes not easy for the psychoanalyst to know early in treatment whether a selfobject transference has actually occurred, until the fragmentation of the cohesive sense of self takes place, that is, after there has been an emphatic break or a literal absence of the analyst. This may be followed by 1) archaic grandiosity (manifested, e.g., by imperious behavior, affected speech, or unrealistic grandiose fantasies), 2) archaic idealization (manifested, e.g., by religious feelings such as a merging experience with God or some other, vaguely experienced outside power), or 3) autoerotic tension states (manifested, e.g., by hypochondria or perverse fantasies and activities). In a selfobject transference, the analyst functions for the patient in ways that fill in the missing self-structure. The everyday empathic failures that are inevitable in treatment often become the basis for work in the transference, which is also related to parental failures through the use of interpretation. Kohut noted that when a correct empathic interpretation is made, the patient reintegrates quickly, via the reestablishment of the selfobject transference and the disappearance of the fragmentation phenomena. This is associated with the return of the patient's ability to function. In contrast to Kernberg's view, idealization in Kohut's framework is a manifestation of the idealizing self-object transference. Confrontation of the idealization would be an empathic failure, repeating the parental failures of childhood.

Modell (1976) described a framework that utilizes elements from the work of Winnicott, Kernberg, and Kohut. For Modell, in the early phase of treatment, the analyst provides a holding environment. At the same time the patient contains himself or herself within a protective cocoon of illusionary self-sufficiency. The analyst's sense of being bored or sleepy is a common countertransference response induced by the patient's nonrelatedness. The illusion of self-sufficiency is often paradoxically combined with a deep dependency on the analyst and a denial of separateness. These conflicts and paradoxical needs enter into the transference and lead to necessary confrontations by the analyst. At this point Modell's approach becomes similar to Kernberg's, involving confrontation of the patient's need to retain the illusion of self-sufficiency (Modell 1975).

The goals of psychoanalysis are 1) to effect a significant personality change so that envy and rage do not overwhelm the patient and lead to a protective need to withdraw to a self-sufficient position (Kernberg) or 2) to heal the patient's incomplete self-structure, including low self-esteem, through transmuting internalization, that is, the taking in of missing functions from the self-object analyst (Kohut). However, no studies available demonstrate that a psychoanalytic approach is more effective than psychotherapy that utilizes many of the principles described for psychoanalysis. Both forms of treatment are expected to take several years or more, because significant personality change is the goal.

Psychoanalytic Psychotherapy

Kernberg defined a modified psychoanalytic treatment he called expressive psychotherapy, recommending this form of psychotherapy for patients with a narcissistic personality disorder who are not in psychoanalysis, with the exception of patients who are functioning relatively primitively and require supportive psychotherapy. In this approach, the psychotherapeutic work focuses on the negative transference, in which early manifestations of anger toward the therapist are explored. This is combined with an emphasis on examining the defenses of splitting, projection, and projective identification, described by Kernberg as major defenses for borderline personality organization. Both Masterson (1981) and Rinsley (1982) emphasized the importance of this approach in developing a therapeutic alliance with the patient. However, in my view, a therapeutic alliance exists only toward the end of the treatment with these patients, although the therapist may utilize the alliance concept to deal with his or her own experience of not being perceived as a separate person by narcissistic patients or of feeling unrelated to these patients when they behave as if they were self-sufficient. Masterson also described the exquisite sensitivity of patients with narcissistic personality disorder to the therapist's empathic failures and the importance of exploring this vulnerability in the psychotherapy.

Kohut did not describe the psychotherapeutic treatment of narcissistic personality disorders within his framework. Goldberg (1973), Chessick (1985), and others have demonstrated, however, that self-object transferences do become established in psychotherapy and can be interpreted in ways similar to that described by Kohut.

Therapists who treat narcissistic personality disorders usually utilize one to three sessions a week. More frequent schedules are recommended when patients retreat to a position of self-sufficiency. However, there is only case report evidence at present to support increased frequency of sessions or psychoanalysis as leading to more profound or rapid personality changes, even though the formulation for the need for more frequent sessions addresses a basic defense of these patients.

Supportive Psychotherapy

Kernberg's description of supportive psychotherapy for patients with narcissistic personality disorders emphasizes an avoidance of working with the negative transference and a focus on supporting the patient to develop new ego skills and capacities. Kernberg stated that these patients may make the most rapid symptomatic improvement, even though their personality difficulties are not modified.

Short-Term and Time-Limited Psychotherapy

Although there is evidence for permanent personality change using short-term (10 to 20 sessions) psychotherapy for a variety of disorders (Malan 1976), the small amount of literature currently available on the treatment of narcissistic personality disorder leaves the issue of such change unanswered for this group of patients. Kernberg described short-term crisis intervention to help these patients with the immediate situation, while awaiting the patients' increased motivation and readiness for long-term treatment. Binder (1979) and Lazarus (1982), utilizing a short-term treatment model, demonstrated increases in the patients' self-esteem and self-cohesion, but questioned long-term change. However, such treatment can be a preparation for long-term psychotherapy. Questions to be answered include what are the dangers, as well as utility, of work within the transference and to what degree issues of envy and anger should be interpreted and confronted. It is clear that selfobject transferences do form in short-term treatment and tend to be transiently disrupted at termination. Further studies are needed to demonstrate how much of these therapeutic experiences is internalized.

Family Therapy

The family therapy literature stresses the treatment of adolescents in families with severe narcissistic disturbances (e.g., Berkowitz et al. 1974; Shapiro 1982). Such families utilize the adolescent to maintain their self-esteem, and project onto him or her their own devalued view of themselves. When the adolescent tries to separate, the parents' rage and projections intensify. Family treatment in conjunction with individual and couples therapy appears to be a useful approach to the exploration and resolution of these issues.

The most frequently described model consists of conjoint weekly sessions of approximately one and one-half hours with the entire family. Two therapists (e.g., the adolescent's individual therapist and the couple's therapist) function as co-therapists and lead these sessions. The goals of the treatment are to help individual family members acknowledge and bear their own feelings and conflicts without projecting them or acting them out within or outside the family and, of course, to help the adolescent separate when ready.

Utilizing Kohut's model of narcissistic vulnerability and selfobject needs, an understanding of projection and projective identification, and methods defined in family treatment, Berkowitz (1985) described the treatment of marital disharmony in patients with narcissistic vulnerability and narcissistic personality disorder. The goals of the weekly sessions are also the "owning" of projected aspects of each member of the couple, as well as the internalization of needed selfobject functions as a result of the treatment.

Family as well as couples treatment is usually described as long-term work of at least one year's duration; however, the treatment model is also applicable to short-term therapy or crisis intervention.

Group Therapy

Although patients with narcissistic personality disorder have been treated in groups for many years, there are few publications on this work that are about these patients only and do not include borderline patients. There is agreement that patients with narcissistic personality disorder initially form relatively stable selfobject transferences and exhibit in groups the behavior described by Kernberg, Kohut, and others in individual treatment. Because these patients respond with rage or withdrawal to the inevitable empathic failures of the group leader or other group members as the group progresses, much of the literature describes group treatment of these patients as difficult and relatively unsuccessful.

Wong (1979) defined an approach that is based on Kohut's and Kernberg's theoretical and clinical work and utilizes both group and individual therapy with the same therapist. Before the patient enters the group, there is a period of preparation through work in individual therapy. In the group setting, the therapist allows the selfobject transferences to develop before systematically examining defenses and transferences in the ways that Kernberg described.

Biologic Therapies

At present there is little literature defining the use of psychopharmacologic agents in the treatment of narcissistic personality disorder. Abramson (1983) described the successful use of lorazepam in conjunction with individual psychotherapy for the treatment of narcissistic rage in three patients who appeared to have narcissistic personality disorders. Klein's (1975) discussions of the use of monoamine oxidase inhibitors in hysteroid dysphoria could possibility relate to narcissistic personality disorders, because he emphasized his patients' sensitivity to rejection as well as chronic emptiness and boredom.

Because some patients with narcissistic personality disorder at times manifest difficulties similar to those of borderline patients, the discussion of the psychopharmacology of borderline patients may be relevant (see also Chapter 259 on Borderline).

Residential Therapies

There is no literature on residential therapies that clearly separates narcissistic from borderline personality disorders. However, as already discussed, patients with narcissistic personality disorder can present with many of the issues that are relevant to borderline patients. These have been described in detail in Chapter 259 on Borderline Personality Disorder. Among patients with narcissistic personality disorder those that are functioning at a relatively primitive level can require full or partial hospitalization for suicidal concerns as well as chronic impasses in their lives and psychotherapy. A short-term setting can be useful in carrying out the careful evaluation of a treatment that does not appear to be progressing. Such an evaluation would include involvement of the therapist and family in order to arrive at an understanding of the impasse. The brief hospitalization can also be used to apply the new understanding to work with the patient (and family, when appropriate).

Summary

The literature on the treatment of narcissistic personality disorder is so new that empirical studies do not exist to support the efficacy of any treatment approach, even though there are many contributions that define apparently useful clinical work. In addition, there are treatment areas in which little or no literature exists. However, there is sufficient information available to support the sense that individual long-term treatment by psychotherapy or psychoanalysis is useful. Family work also seems to yield good results.

Chapter 258

Antisocial Personality Disorder

The treatment of antisocial personality, and of related antisocial syndromes, is an unpopular topic in psychiatry. Regardless of choice of terms—psychopath, sociopath, or antisocial personality—authors have almost traditionally been pessimistic about treatment of characterologic antisocial syndromes. Different clinicians draw the line between antisocial and mentally ill in different places, but most see psychopathy as quite apart from such disorders as schizophrenia or major depression. In this chapter, in the tradition of Cleckley (1941) and Sturup (1968), I view psychopathy as mental illness, a true emotional deficiency, and specifically separable from other disorders, culturally based syndromes, or simple antisocial behavior.

Medicine has never relied on complete cure as its end-all of treatment. Symptom relief is a noble aim when more definitive approaches are not available. Many of the treatments for psychopathy address only the behaviors other people find troublesome. Other treatments are attempts to change the entire person.

The strength of psychiatry's and society's interest in treatment of antisocial personality rests largely on the willingness to devote resources to the betterment of people who hurt other people and make them angry. This philosophical point must not be forgotten during the following technical discussion of treatment methods. The patient with antisocial personality is treatable, sometimes changeable, and (arguably) occasionally curable. The question is, are the clinician and the treatment system willing to invest time, money, and other resources to treat this patient, knowing that the process will be frustrating, perhaps fruitless, and possibly dangerous?

Description

The primary consideration in the treatment of any disorder is diagnosis. Strict reliance on DSM-III-R criteria for antisocial personality (American Psychiatric Association 1987), and especially the ruling out of more easily treatable disorders, is crucial. Except where specifically noted, this chapter refers solely to antisocial personality disorder. The patients are adults who have had childhood onset of the signs and symptoms noted in DSM-III-R, as well as persistent antisocial behavior in multiple spheres of adult functioning. See Table 1 for diagnostic criteria for antisocial personality disorder.

It is important to note that most of the literature concerning antisocial personality or behavior does not relate to the DSM-III-R definition at all. Therefore, much of what has been written regarding treatment has an unknown relationship to the population identified by DSM-III-R.

Psychodynamic issues related to antisocial personality have been sources of considerable controversy. The common notion that disturbed families are at the root of psychopathic development must be seen in the context of the many such families that do not give rise to such persons. It is useful to consider very primitive defenses against loss, at the level of basic trust, expressed through the hostility of grievance (Glover 1960) and the protecting of oneself from abuse or leaving by others (Greenwald 1967). The weaknesses of the antisocial personality are of both superego and ego-ideal, at the near-id level, where externalization and avoidance of consciousness of one's inner life lead to ego splits reminiscent of narcissistic or borderline personality, but "riddled with rage and sadism" (Person 1986).

There is a particular emptiness, even a sadness, at the core of the psychopath's personality (Karpman 1941; Reid 1978). Such patients do not suffer merely a behavioral problem, but a deep emotional, perhaps physical, deficit.

Criminals and Cons

Although antisocial personality is overrepresented in the criminal population, it is far from ubiquitous there. Among incarcerated felons, Guze (1978) found a prevalence of 52 percent for males and roughly 65 percent for females. The recent Epidemiologic Catchment Area (ECA) study (Robins et al. 1984) reported a lifetime prevalence of antisocial personality in the general population ranging from 2.1 percent to 3.3 percent. The peak was in the 24- to 44-year-old group (3.1 percent to 5.2 percent), with an abrupt drop in the 45- to 64-year-old group (1.1 percent to 1.9 percent) at three ECA study sites. The "disappearance" of cases has been attributed to spontaneous improvement (Robins 1978). This "burnout," an age-related effect, must be considered in treatment studies. Guze (1978) suggested that one approach to incarceration would be to keep recidivists in prison until they reach middle age.

The treatment approaches described herein often focus on criminal patients, and therapeutic success is often expressed in terms of changes in illegal behavior. Focus on this population may lead to bias because, as Robins has noted, subjects studied tend to be severely antisocial. There are few agencies to recognize or monitor less seriously disordered adults.

In addition, the relationship between treatment and outcome in the short run may be impossible to assess because the patient can fake conformity to treatment expectations. This effect may be most marked if outcome measures relate to release

Table 1. DSM-III-R Diagnostic Criteria for Antisocial Personality Disorder

A. Current age at least 18.

B. Evidence of conduct disorder with onset before age 15, as indicated by a history of *three* or more of the following:

   (1) was often truant
   (2) ran away from home overnight at least twice while living in parental or parental surrogate home (or once without returning)
   (3) often initiated physical fights
   (4) used a weapon in more than one fight
   (5) forced someone into sexual activity with him or her
   (6) was physically cruel to animals
   (7) was physically cruel to other people
   (8) deliberately destroyed others' property (other than by fire-setting)
   (9) deliberately engaged in fire-setting
  (10) often lied (other than to avoid physical or sexual abuse)
  (11) stole without confrontation of a victim on more than one occasion (including forgery)
  (12) stole with confrontation of a victim (e.g., mugging, purse-snatching, extortion, armed robbery)

C. A pattern of irresponsible and antisocial behavior since the age of 15, as indicated by at least *four* of the following:

   (1) is unable to sustain consistent work behavior, as indicated by any of the following (including similar behavior in academic settings if the person is a student):

     (a) significant unemployment for six months or more within five years when expected to work and work was available
     (b) repeated absences from work unexplained by illness in self or family
     (c) abandonment of several jobs without realistic plans for others

   (2) fails to conform to social norms with respect to lawful behavior, as indicated by repeatedly performing antisocial acts that are grounds for arrest (whether arrested or not), e.g., destroying property, harassing others, stealing, pursuing an illegal occupation

   (3) is irritable and aggressive, as indicated by repeated physical fights or assaults (not required by one's job or to defend someone or oneself), including spouse- or child-beating

   (4) repeatedly fails to honor financial obligations, as indicated by defaulting on debts or failing to provide child support or support for other dependents on a regular basis

   (5) fails to plan ahead, or is impulsive, as indicated by one or both of the following:

     (a) traveling from place to place without a prearranged job or clear goal for the period of travel or clear idea about when the travel will terminate
     (b) lack of a fixed address for a month or more

   (6) has no regard for the truth, as indicated by repeated lying, use of aliases, or "conning" others for personal profit or pleasure

   (7) is reckless regarding his or her own or others' personal safety, as indicated by driving while intoxicated or recurrent speeding

   (8) if a parent or guardian, lacks ability to function as a responsible parent, as indicated by one or more of the following:

     (a) malnutrition of a child
     (b) child's illness resulting from lack of minimal hygiene
     (c) failure to obtain medical care for a seriously ill child
     (d) child's dependence on neighbors or nonresident relative for food or shelter

Table 1. DSM-III-R Diagnostic Criteria for Antisocial Personality Disorder (continued)
(e) failure to arrange for a caretaker for a young child when parent is away from home
(f) repeated squandering, on personal items, of money required for household necessities
(9) has never sustained a totally monogamous relationship for more than one year
(10) lacks remorse (feels justified in having hurt, mistreated, or stolen from another)
D. Occurrence of antisocial behavior not exclusively during the course of schizophrenia or manic episodes.

from a controlled setting. Thus, paradoxically, the better the con, the better the apparent outcome. Long-term follow-up is necessary.

Psychotherapies

Psychodynamic Therapies

There is little literature describing the successful application of traditional dynamic psychotherapy to patients with antisocial personality disorder. There is virtually no note of optimism for treating sociopaths in outpatient settings without external controls over their behavior. This is generally felt to be due to the poor tolerance such patients have for intimacy and the strong countertransference they produce in the therapist (Vaillant and Perry 1985). Many observers think that even where external controls exist, such as parole, prison, or hospital, individual psychotherapeutic relationships rarely change sociopaths' behavior (Vaillant 1975; Vaillant and Perry 1985, pp 958–986).

Once external controls limit the ability to flee, the psychopath's apparent inability to experience depression and anxiety often vanishes. Apparent lack of motivation to change can likewise be overcome by treatment within a group of peers (Vaillant 1975; Vaillant and Perry 1985). This process makes the sociopath's defenses recognizable and enables the therapist to confront them and help the patient develop more mature, adaptive ones.

Lion (1972) argued that outpatient treatment with "aggressive personality disorders" can be undertaken successfully if patients are taught to handle the frustrations of daily living. He suggested that encouraging fantasy about consequences of behavior might be helpful in teaching sociopaths to avoid acting out. The appearance of strong affect, usually depression, after a period of intensive psychotherapy is a positive sign. Patients are universally anxious about the "new" experience of true feeling; they must be encouraged to continue the painful work.

Leaff (1978), Person (1986), and others have written about the narcissistic aspects of antisocial patients. Person, in particular, discussed noncriminal sociopathic patients and the exploration of primitive narcissistic vulnerability. She noted these individuals' need for defensive maneuverability and their propensity for decompensation when defensive options are severely restricted. This speaks to the fragility of the psychopath, whom many see, conversely, as strong and resilient.

Behavioral Therapy

Programs that depend heavily on operant conditioning or learning theory paradigms have not been shown to be of lasting benefit for these patients. Although certain specific antisocial symptoms have been said to respond to specific techniques, for example, aversive conditioning, these methods have not been useful for more general syndromes, nor have many limited successes generalized or persisted very long beyond the treatment setting. Moss and Rick (1981), in an overview of operant technology in behaviorally disordered adolescents, documented the minimal impact these methods have had in psychiatric treatment, noting that this may be due not to a lack of efficacy, but to lack of interest by treating professionals.

This lack of success may also have to do with two principles, one inherent in the method, the other in psychopaths. First, the success of behavioral programs depends on, among other things, a highly consistent conditioning environment. Second, psychopaths may have severe difficulty in learning from experience.

Family Treatment

Family treatment refers in this context to treatment for the family, not to family therapy to alleviate psychopathy. The psychopath's relatives are in significant, chronic discomfort. They deserve support, including alleviation of misplaced guilt for the behavior of their antisocial relative. They should also be helped to see the ways in which the antisocial person manipulates them into behavior destructive for both him or her and the family. Parsons and Alexander (1973) and Harbin (1979), from outpatient and inpatient perspectives, respectively, described family treatment strategies that may have utility in the treatment of sociopaths and their families. Parsons and Alexander demonstrated that changes in destructive communication patterns of delinquent families could be achieved systematically on a short-term basis. There are no data available on predominantly family therapy methods and long-term outcome; however, these methods have often been included as part of treatment, particularly in residential programs.

Biologic Therapies

Kellner (1978, 1981) found few controlled studies of drug treatments for antisocial personality. The findings from studies of minor tranquilizers are "inconsistent and their effects complex." The data on neuroleptic use are inconclusive. Anticonvulsants may be of benefit in some patients with impulsive or explosive behavior. In this section, I will discuss the use of stimulants and lithium.

The potential relationship between antisocial personality disorder and disorders such as attention deficit disorder (ADD), residual type, also called adult attention deficit disorder, has stimulated both interest and controversy. The residual subtype, not acknowledged in DSM-III-R, is described as persistence of attentional deficits and impulsivity without signs of hyperactivity, resulting in impairment in social and occupational functioning (Amado and Lustman 1982).

Cantwell (1978) found a strong association between the hyperactive child syndrome and the development of delinquent, antisocial behavior in childhood and later life. He hypothesized that a subgroup of hyperkinetic children with low central nervous system arousal (Satterfield et al. 1974) might be related to a population of adult sociopaths (Satterfield and Cantwell 1975), and therefore that some antisocial patients might respond to central nervous system stimulants.

The relationship of ADD (or, in DSM-III-R, ADHD) to antisocial personality has also been approached from the perspective of adult ADD. Workers have reported that approximately one-quarter (Wood et al. 1976) to one-third (Wender et al. 1981) of their adult patients with ADD meet criteria for sociopathy. Treating these subjects with stimulants has been effective in certain cases (Stringer and Josef 1983; Wender et al. 1981; Wood et al. 1976), but there is to date no systematic, well-controlled study of this treatment, and little recent evidence to support its use.

Lithium salts appeared some years ago to hold some therapeutic promise. Several studies suggested that lithium exerts an antiaggressive effect (Shader et al. 1974; Sheard 1975; Tupin et al. 1973). Although the utility of the drug remains to be completely determined, it appears the primary antiaggressive effect is not on the personality disorder per se, but in prevention of recurrent impulsive, violent behavior (Tupin 1981).

Cloninger (1983) described a complex classification system for antisocial personality based on four target symptoms of treatment: aggression, deficits in social learning, deficits in attention and impulse control, and electrocerebral abnormalities. Using these symptoms and their neurophysiologic correlates, Cloninger described seven antisocial subtypes, with potentially useful drug therapies for each, and proposed clinical trials to stimulate a more comprehensive approach to clinical assessment and to differentiate medication-responsive subtypes of psychopathy. As Cloninger noted, however, because the syndromes are so developmentally complex, drugs must be only an adjunct to more comprehensive treatment programs. (See also Chapter 251 on Somatic Therapy.)

Residential Therapies

Community Residential Therapies

Treatment in a variety of residential settings, such as hospitals, prisons, and farms, tends to make use of a therapeutic community (Abruzzi 1979; Jones 1953, 1954; Kiger 1967) in a closed, structured environment. Success in eliminating antisocial behavior has been reported for a few programs that provide a hierarchical, somewhat confrontive experience within unlocked residential facilities (Reid and Solomon 1981; Tyce et al. 1980). These are not halfway houses, but offer active treatment programs, usually for criminal offenders, within nonmedical, counseling models.

The programs focus on several issues, using experienced staff and other offenders to recognize both progress and lack thereof. Responsibility to others is stressed, including honesty with peers, willingness to "inform" when a peer breaks a rule, restitution to victims, and financial responsibility for one's stay in the program. The offender contracts with the program to go through four or five levels of increasing freedom and responsibility, over a minimum of four to six months. Progress is based solely on the measurable results of the offender's efforts and concrete interpretations of his or her behavior. Excuses are not accepted.

Many offenders find it difficult to tolerate these social and emotional restrictions, despite the relative freedom compared with incarceration, and opt to return to jail or prison. For those who stay and complete such programs, recidivism rates are considerably lower than rates for simple incarceration, probation, or traditional psychotherapy programs.

Special Institutions

There are a few hospitals that specialize in treatment of severe antisocial syndromes in a secure (i.e., locked) setting. Some accept criminal offenders with antisocial character disorders. Patuxent Institution in the United States and Herstedvester (no longer a hospital of this type) in Denmark are among the most recognized of these facilities.

The Patuxent "experiment" in intensive correctional treatment of mentally abnormal criminal offenders began in 1955. Its administrative parameters changed in 1977, when indeterminate sentencing for criminals was repealed by the Maryland legislature. Under the pre-1977 system, "defective delinquents" were treated in individual, group, and milieu therapy, with emphasis on a trained custodial staff and functioning therapeutic community (Lejins 1977). Another feature was a progressive tier system that patients could gradually climb to gain parole.

The treatment programs have retained much of their character since 1977. Patuxent is its own paroling authority. There is a prerelease center several miles away in Baltimore. Educational, psychological, vocational, and recreational needs of the inmates are well met.

Such institutions are not as prominent today as several decades ago. Even successful programs (such as that at Herstedvester) have been significantly weakened, probably because of public and cultural priorities and concern about the rights of offenders (e.g., the suitability of indeterminate sentences), among other reasons (Hoffman 1977; Lejins 1977). As numerous evaluations of Patuxent Institution and of Herstedvester revealed, the issues of treatment and cost-effectiveness are extraordinarily complex (Gordon 1977; Shear 1977; Sturup 1978), but the decline of the best institutions seems to be related more to social and political issues than to program failings.

Sturup (1968) and Carney (1978) described in detail the principles of the character restructuring that is attempted in such programs. The first principle is to regard the offender as a human being who has feelings and the potential for change. The second is to provide an extremely consistent setting in which it is very difficult to con other people and in which the patient must traverse a hierarchy of levels over several years in order to gain privileges and eventual release. Within this system, issues of the patient's emotional deficits with respect to feeling affect, experiencing fantasy, learning from experience, and trusting self and others are continuously addressed. Clinical staff and custodial personnel are highly competent and experienced and realize the importance of countertransference and related issues.

Aftercare is of extraordinary importance to the success of long-term institutional programs, not only to continue treatment after a smooth transition to mandated outpatient care, but also to provide monitoring of potentially dangerous patients and a continuing, slowly decreasing, connection with the hospital for patients who have become attached to it during extended treatment. Patients use this connection to alleviate anxiety that arises in their new lives and often contact the hospital to stem impulses that might otherwise result in criminal activity.

Yochelson and Samenow's (1977) approach to residential treatment has received much publicity. This approach focuses on the voluntariness of antisocial thought and behavior, and eschews issues of the patient's fragility (Samenow 1980). The method relies on the patient's responsibility for his or her actions and on rapid and consistent environmental consequences of inappropriate thoughts or actions.

Wilderness Programs

For several years, physically and mentally demanding treatment approaches called wilderness programs have been available in many parts of the country (Reid and Matthews 1980). These programs are superficially similar to Outward Bound expeditions but differ in that they focus on the social and interpersonal inadequacies of antisocial persons. Several Outward Bound schools, notably Pacific Crest, offer Youth-At-Risk programs for antisocial adolescents (Pacific Crest Outward Bound School 1985).

Successful wilderness programs have several components in common. The difficult group task requires both individual and group commitment. There is an element of perceived danger in the task or experience, which carries with it the prospect of survival or passage upon completion. Finally, nature is present as an unconnable participant: no excuse will obviate rapid and unforgiving consequences of inappropriate behavior.

Wilderness programs are usually structured hierarchically, beginning with an introduction to camping, mountaineering, or whatever the requisite skills will be. Then a seven- to 12-day expedition is carried out. Some programs follow this with a solo expedition in which the group (or sometimes an individual) strikes out alone toward some difficult objective.

Results are often good for strenuous, truly challenging programs, but not for those that are merely camping exercises. Not only is criminal recidivism decreased, but social and interpersonal skills are usually improved. Psychological testing frequently shows lasting increases in self-confidence and self-esteem (Kimball 1979).

Chapter 259

Borderline Personality Disorder

Because the term borderline has been used so variably in the literature, it is difficult to limit this chapter to accounts that reflect the DSM-III-R definition (American Psychiatric Association 1987) of this disorder. In the psychoanalytic literature, for instance, the term borderline generally reflects an infrastructure of personality encompassing other Axis II disorders, whereas behaviorists and some psychopharmacologists tend to ignore personality categories by focusing on symptomatic behaviors. Despite efforts to limit this chapter to the DSM-III-R definition of borderline personality, if anything, it is too inclusive rather than too specific. See Table 1 for DSM-III-R diagnostic criteria for borderline personality disorder.

Table 1. DSM-III-R Diagnostic Criteria for Borderline Personality Disorder

A pervasive pattern of instability of mood, interpersonal relationships, and self-image, beginning by early adulthood and present in a variety of contexts, as indicated by at least *five* of the following:

  (1) a pattern of unstable and intense interpersonal relationships characterized by alternating between extremes of overidealization and devaluation

  (2) impulsiveness in at least two areas that are potentially self-damaging, e.g., spending, sex, substance use, shoplifting, reckless driving, binge eating (Do not include suicidal or self-mutilating behavior covered in [5].)

  (3) affective instability: marked shifts from baseline mood to depression, irritability, or anxiety, usually lasting a few hours and only rarely more than a few days

  (4) inappropriate, intense anger or lack of control of anger, e.g., frequent displays of temper, constant anger, recurrent physical fights

  (5) recurrent suicidal threats, gestures, or behavior or self-mutilating behavior

  (6) marked and persistent identity disturbance manifested by uncertainty about at least two of the following: self-image, sexual orientation, long-term goals or career choice, type of friends desired, preferred values

  (7) chronic feelings of emptiness or boredom

  (8) frantic efforts to avoid real or imagined abandonment (Do not include suicidal or self-mutilating behavior covered in [5].)

Psychotherapies

Individual Psychotherapies

Individual psychotherapy remains the cornerstone of most treatments for patients with borderline personality disorder. Since Knight's (1953) early descriptions, it has generally been accepted that strict classical psychoanalysis is a form of psychotherapy that is contraindicated for most borderline patients. Some case reports of psychoanalysis have been published (Abend et al. 1983), but these patients would not be considered borderline by current criteria. The reason for this relative contraindication is the proclivity for psychotic transferences and uncontrolled acting out in treatment as unstructured as classical analysis. For the occasional exception to this rule, careful consideration and expert consultation should be prerequisite.

In the vast literature on vis-à-vis psychotherapies with borderline patients, there are a number of controversies, but also areas of agreement. In his summary of this literature, Waldinger (1986) identified the following areas of agreement:

1. A stable treatment framework. The capacity to regress into psychotic perceptions and the proclivity to both self-destructive and aggressive actions make the stability in terms of roles, schedule, payment of fees, and other boundary issues critically important.

2. Activity of the therapist. The therapist must remain alert and verbally active in identifying, confronting, and directing the patient's behaviors during sessions. Activity by itself diminishes the likelihood of transference distortions and provides supportive reassurance of the therapist's presence and interest.

3. Establishing a connection between the patient's actions and feelings in the present. The borderline patient needs to be able to identify feelings and motives behind his or her actions. This examination often calls for the therapist to set limits on behaviors that threaten the safety of the patient, the therapist, or the continuation

of the therapy. For example, silences during sessions or phone calls out of sessions are actions that serve to deflect an awareness and communication of feelings.

4. Making self-destructive behaviors ungratifying. The therapist must consistently and repeatedly draw the patient's attention to the adverse consequences of behaviors such as drug abuse, promiscuity, manipulative behavior, and inappropriate rage by focusing on the maladaptive or undesirable results.

5. Careful attention to countertransference feelings. A good portion of the literature concerns the capacity of borderline patients to evoke intense feelings of rage and helplessness (e.g., Adler 1972) or to evoke more sustained patterns of distortion within a psychotherapeutic relationship involving countertransference needs to be omnipotent, idealized, needed, or submissive (Masterson 1976; Searles 1979). Clearly, the dangers of such severe countertransference problems, combined with the life-and-death problems presented by borderline patients, mandate considerable prior experience in dealing with such patients, ongoing supervision, or both. Even experienced therapists often undertake work with such patients only if they have institutional and collegial support.

Psychoanalytic Psychotherapy

Within the domain of psychoanalytic psychotherapy, controversy exists about the role of early interpretation and the management of negative transference. Kernberg (1968, 1975) was most articulate in identifying the need for early confrontation and interpretations of primitive transferences in the here-and-now situations. Kernberg, Masterson (1976), and Gunderson (1984) all emphasized the need to identify the aggressive motives that exist in the here and now so as to make their inappropriateness visible and dystonic. At times, this involves drawing patients' attention to the sadistic and controlling motives behind their manipulative behaviors. Because interpretations are often transformed or experienced as attacks, linking statements that anticipate such reactions are often needed.

In contrast, Buie and Adler (1982) and Chessick (1982) argued that interpretations of aggressive themes are at best ineffectual and at worst harmfully disruptive in the early phase of treatment. Consistent with the self-psychology school of Kohut (1971), Buie and Adler emphasized the need to validate the real role of bad parenting in the patient's past as a motivating force for the patient's aggression and reserved transference interpretation to developing aloneness themes. Borderline patients who present particularly negativistic and devaluative attitudes toward therapy may need more confrontation to engage in therapy. For patients who have more optimistic and idealized attitudes, confrontation may be contraindicated and validating techniques become central.

Despite the theoretical differences among those who have written about psychoanalytic psychotherapy with borderline patients, there is agreement that basic personality change is a legitimate goal. There is also agreement that this type of treatment is preferably scheduled three or more times a week and conducted by people with psychoanalytic training. Therapy can be expected to last a minimum of four years, and usually considerably longer. The results of such treatment are not well documented. Recently, however, a detailed examination of five successfully completed therapies has validated the potential for basic changes (Waldinger and Gunderson 1987). A diminution of impulsive behaviors or other regressive maladaptive reactions to stress and an improved stability in relationships were observed. The personality transformation enabled the borderline patients to function normally or on a neurotic level. In some instances, though, basic underlying psychological liabilities in identity formation and self-esteem persist alongside these successful outcomes.

Supportive Psychotherapy

Despite the enormous literature about psychoanalytic psychotherapy with borderline patients, this kind of therapy constitutes a small fraction of the treatment actually given to borderline patients. Most borderline patients are seen in once-weekly individual psychotherapy in which the primary focus is on the reality problems of daily life and there is relatively little opportunity to examine and work through primitive transferences. Nevertheless, within this less intensive and more supportive form of psychotherapy, the same demands for saving interventions and the same accusations of cruel withholding are predictable strains on the therapists. Again, psychotherapy is expected to last for a long time, generally tapering off into an as-needed schedule after three to five years. The goals of this psychotherapy are not explicitly directed at changing personality, but at improving the patients' adaptation to their life circumstances and diminishing the likelihood of self-destructive responses to expectable interpersonal frustrations.

A recent report from the Menninger Outcome Study has cast the role of supportive psychotherapy in a new light for borderline patients (Wallerstein 1986). This work shows that even when analysts start with intensive interpretive strategies, they shift toward a more supportive strategy and that, despite this shift, supportive treatments are able to bring about basic changes in personality—changes of the types that have generally been expected to result only from more intensive, exploratory, transference-based treatment.

Short-Term or Time-Limited Psychotherapy

Early advocates for the use of short-term psychotherapy specifically excluded borderline patients as suitable for such treatment (Mann 1973; Sifneos 1972). The intense and chaotic personality issues of such patients cannot be expected to change over the course of the 10 to 20 sessions usually offered in short-term therapy. Despite the prevailing consensus, however, clinics with training functions are often forced to adopt time-limited (six months or one year) strategies for borderline patients to conform with the rotation of trainees. These time-limited psychotherapies are focused on specific situational or interactional problems, and the likelihood that a regressive transference will develop is diminished. Because of the time-limited transference-gratifications inherent in such treatment, many borderline patients drop out. Those who remain can profit, however, and may subsequently return for further "doses" of similarly circumscribed treatment. This sort of strategy (i.e., with specific time limits and focused subjects) may be particularly well suited for borderline patients who have a history of dropping out of more ambitious treatments and for those who present with concerns about being engulfed, being overwhelmed, or becoming too dependent. Some patients move from short-term treatment into a long-term therapy for which they were initially unmotivated.

As such clinical experiences have accumulated, the initial pessimism about the role for short-term psychotherapy with borderline patients has given way, and the approach is gaining advocates (Krupnick and Horowitz 1985; Leibovich 1981, 1983).

Family Therapy

Although borderline psychopathology can arise from many different types of family background, there are two patterns of family involvement that can help clinicians plan family interventions (Gunderson et al. 1980). One pattern is characterized by overinvolvement. Borderline offspring of such families are often actively struggling with dependency issues by denial or by anger at their parents. Whether denied or reviled, these needs for dependency are often being actively gratified by the family (Shapiro et al. 1975). Such a family requires active, ongoing family participation in treatment. To exclude the family from involvement in the index borderline person's treatment leads the parents to withhold support and, moreover, causes the patient to feel as if participation in therapy is disloyal to the parents and will lead to abandonment.

Borderline patients also come from families characterized by abuse (violent or incestuous) or neglect. In this pattern, the parents are likely to be angry at their offspring for having either solicited or been sent for treatment. These parents will be overtly resentful of treatment efforts that require their involvement in an examination of the family interactions. Meetings with the parents alone may be required in order to solicit their support for the borderline person's treatment. In such meetings, it is useful to be formally educative about the nature of the offspring's illness and to attempt to reassure the parents that the treatment is directed toward helping the patient develop more independence and, specifically, that it is not directed at blaming them.

These guidelines for using either the family therapy approach per se or a more supportive educational approach directed toward the parents independently apply to both inpatient and outpatient psychotherapy. Regardless of the family pattern, family treatment and interventions may be necessary to maintain an outpatient psychotherapy as long as the borderline patient remains emotionally or financially dependent on his or her parents. At present, there is no reason to believe that family treatment by itself, however, can be sufficient.

Conjoint family therapy is usually conducted in hour-and-a-half sessions once weekly, but may be more frequent. The educative, supportive interventions for parents alone usually involve sessions lasting an hour or less. Sessions may be conducted either by the patient's therapist or by someone who works collaboratively but independently of the therapist. Such meetings are likely to take place on an as-needed basis for an indefinite period until the patient has achieved sufficient autonomy from the parents for the other parts of the patient's treatment plan to be safely stable.

Group Therapy

It is widely accepted that group therapy is useful for borderline patients. However, most clinicians find that it is difficult for borderline patients to enter and remain in such treatment. The chances of entering and remaining in group therapy are enhanced if participation is made a contingency from the beginning of an individual therapy.

The presence of peers in a group therapy has a number of benefits not available in individual therapy. Peers are more able than a therapist to confront maladaptive and impulsive patterns without being written off as trying to control the patient. Groups are also very effective in identifying dependent or manipulative gratifications and making them more dystonic. At the same time, the group provides a set of peers with whom communication of feelings and personal problems can be experienced without harmful repercussions; groups provide a very supportive function that may extend to the development of new and better relationships outside of as well as within the therapy.

A controversy exists about the relative advantages of having multiple borderline patients within the same group (Stone and Weissman 1984; Wong 1980). Clearly, it is important to recognize that such patients present major strains on a group's functioning, and most people agree that concurrent individual therapy is required.

Behavioral Therapy

Despite the fact that borderline patients present a number of management problems requiring systematic positive and negative reinforcers in individual therapy or inpatient settings, the explicit use of behavioral techniques with such patients has not been widely written about. Rather, the behavioral literature generally focuses on problems common to borderline patients without discussing personality types. In this context (and as already described by Perry earlier in this chapter), impulsivity, self-destructiveness, and expression of aggression are all targets for which promising behavioral techniques have been developed. Likewise, as will be described later, inpatient settings and other residential placements invariably set limits on behavior so as to extinguish destructive acts toward self and others and to increase the tolerance of dysphoric affects in borderline patients. These settings clearly borrow a behavioral paradigm in practice if not in theory.

Linehan has developed a manual-guided behavioral strategy for the treatment of self-destructiveness in a largely borderline cohort (Linehan 1987b). This approach combines weekly individual counseling sessions employing directive techniques and a practical, sympathetic approach along with twice-weekly group sessions. Group sessions use didactic, skill-training, and rehearsal techniques directed at interpersonal (especially dependency) patterns and at improving affect tolerance. A rotating staff is available by telephone around the clock. Although the efficacy of this approach, like other treatment approaches to borderline personality, has yet to be demonstrated by research evaluation, this is the first monodynamic effort to modify a basic problem (i.e., self-destructiveness) in the borderline patient.

Biologic Therapies

Pharmacotherapy is a commonly employed form of treatment for borderline personality disorder. On the basis of clinical experience, psychiatrists have advocated the use of tricyclic antidepressants, monoamine oxidase (MAO) inhibitors, low doses of phenothiazines, lithium, and carbamazepine. Only recently have controlled clinical trials been used to sort out the proliferating and conflicting series of claims for these types of pharmacotherapy.

The existing evidence most strongly supports the use of low-dose neuroleptics for borderline patients (Goldberg et al. 1986; Leone 1982; Serban and Sieg 1983; Soloff et al. 1986). The evidence suggests that neuroleptics cause reductions in depression, anxiety, hostility, and psychoticlike symptoms. The latter include depersonalization, derealization, illusions, and ideas of reference. Borderline patients who have the most enduring symptoms of these types are those for whom the greatest response can be expected. For borderline patients who are not particularly affected in these areas, neuroleptics cannot be expected to have much effect.

The role of either MAO inhibitors or tricyclic antidepressants is less well established in borderline patients. Liebowitz and Klein (1981) have suggested that such core borderline features as chronic emptiness, boredom, discomfort in being alone, and impulsivity might be responsive to MAO inhibitors. More discouraging has been the report that response to tricyclic antidepressants does not appear to be particularly closely linked to initial levels of depressive disturbance and that these drugs may increase agitation for some patients (Soloff et al. 1986).

Carbamazepine (Tegratol) has shown promise of effectiveness in borderline patients—especially in the area of control over discharge of angry impulses (Gardner and Cowdry 1986). The improved control over such impulses appears to be independent of neurologic referents. In contrast, minor tranquilizers such as alprazolam (Zanax) or chlordiazepoxide (Librium) should be used with special caution in this patient group insofar as they may liberate untoward destructive actions.

A recent rush of enthusiastic reports about the apparent value of various pharmacologic treatments for borderline patients should not diminish the clinician's concerns about the potential complications or liabilities in providing pharmacotherapy. One of these complications is a possible paradoxical relationship between subjective response and therapeutic effectiveness. Patients who feel better with a given treatment agent may seem no better—or even worse—to their therapists and others. Patients who report they feel worse may seem better from the perspective of others. This apparent paradox may be caused if the patient expects symptomatic improvement to bring undesirable social consequences (e.g., abandonment or loss of dependent gratifications) or if inhibitions of impulse discharge increase dysphoria.

Another complication of pharmacotherapy with borderline patients concerns the common misuse of drugs or noncompliance with prescribed regimens. Noncompliance may, of course, come from side effects or, as noted, from the secondary gains associated with illness. A form of noncompliance that is specifically related to borderline psychopathology involves the frequent mismanagement of prescriptive regimens because of angry transference reactions toward the prescriber or the predilection to use overdoses as a means of manipulating caregivers. Given the ongoing risks of suicide attempts, if alternative drugs are available, the one with the least lethality should be used. Some clinicians feel the benefits from drugs are not commensurate with the risks. Others believe that drugs should be prescribed only under protective circumstances, such as a residential setting, or by someone more neutral than the therapist.

Residential Therapies

Overview: Role, Indications, Types

Borderline patients constitute between 8 and 25 percent of inpatient admissions. Borderline personality disorder is easily the most common form of personality disorder found in psychiatric hospitals.

The overall role of the hospital in the treatment of borderline patients usually involves management of regressions or crises and seldom involves long-term inpatient care—as long as the patient has an ongoing outpatient psychotherapy. For a patient not in psychotherapy, one of the major functions of the hospital is to complete an evaluation and to initiate and consolidate some form of outpatient therapy program. For a patient hospitalized in the context of an already ongoing psychotherapy, the hospital serves to diminish transference distortions, intervene in response to self-destructive or antisocial acting out, prevent foreseeable harmful reactions to a therapist's absence, or allow needed diagnostic, pharmacotherapeutic, or family consultations to occur.

Even though utilization of a hospital may not be necessary for all borderline patients, access to a hospital and the readiness to employ it are essential before undertaking outpatient treatment. The mere presence of a hospital helps diminish the countertransference feelings of helplessness or anger.

Halfway Houses

Often, borderline patients who are in outpatient psychotherapy can be managed better in a halfway house than in a hospital. Halfway houses offer distance from toxic family or other social situations. They also offer social relationships with peers without the potential for regressive functioning common in inpatient settings.

Day Care

Where individual psychotherapy is not available, day care often provides stabilizing and life-sustaining functions for borderline patients. Like halfway houses, day care programs offer therapeutic supports and structures along with the opportunity for corrective relationships with staff and peers. The regressive potential in a day care setting is greater than in a halfway house, but still less than in a hospital. Day care programs have an added advantage over halfway houses because they can offer active rehabilitation programs that are of value to many borderline patients who have histories of academic or vocational failures.

General Principles of Residential Therapies

From the still expanding literature on hospital treatment of borderline patients, a number of areas of consensus, as well as persistent areas of disagreement, are identifiable (Gunderson 1984). Most writers agree that hospitalization contains the danger of nontherapeutic regressions, that is, the emergence of patterns of behavior more infantile or maladaptive than those that existed outside the hospital. Common expressions of regressive behavior are angry, negativistic behaviors vis-à-vis the controls imposed by the hospital and the development of a childlike or even psychotic demand for dependent gratification. Disagreement exists about the causes for these regressions. Almost certainly they derive from a combination of factors. One is the stimulus offered by the supportive and nurturant functions inherent in hospitals. This is compounded by the inevitable disruptions in relationships during hospitalization. In addition, residential settings can stimulate and maintain regressions by being either overly controlling or overly supportive.

A second consensus regards the need for early, consistent imposition of limits on regressive behaviors. Limits do not necessarily mean restrictions, which often signify being "held." Rather, limiting access to a facility or staff in response to behaviors judged to be controllable but destructive is usually more effective. Limits are used to enforce the expectation that patients will collaborate to the best of their abilities, which means they must accept the realistic limitations of the staff's availability.

Another area of agreement involves the ubiquitous staff conflicts ("splits") that complicate the hospital experience for borderline patients. There is general agreement about the content of these conflicts, namely, the contrast between viewing borderline patients as helpless waifs in need of nurturance or as angry manipulators in need of limits. Beyond this, though, clinicians disagree about causes. Some emphasize the importance of the patient's projections as a cause for disagreements; others offer varying forms of countertransference reaction among different staff as an explanation. A third cause is that members of a hospital team may have had different prior training or clinical exposures.

Most clinicians concur that effective milieu programs emphasize interpersonal issues, identifying maladaptive interpersonal patterns and providing new strategies for managing the frustrations inherent in interpersonal involvement. Most hospital programs utilize groups in which the leaders and other patients repeatedly confront— often bluntly—the usual manipulative and devaluative patterns of borderline patients. Groups and one-to-one talks are both used to help these patients see the angry and controlling motives that lie behind such interpersonal patterns.

Long- Versus Short-Term Strategies

There are important differences in the utilization, design, and goals of optimal short-term and long-term residential treatment. The decision about length of treatment depends less on the severity of psychopathology than on the degree to which a given borderline patient has ongoing social structures and supports. Hence, the most common reason to depart from the usual reliance on short-term hospitalization is the presence of unpredictable or abusive social contexts, such as a household that patently stimulates an adolescent's destructive actions toward self or others. There are other rationales for long-term treatment, but they rest largely on having an established track record of failure with less ambitious and restrictive treatment strategies, including short-term hospitalizations.

Differences between effective long-term and short-term hospital programs are outlined in Table 2. Short-term hospital units should set a tone of high behavioral expectation. Patients are expected to act as collaborators in their own treatment, and failure to do so is often used as a reason for "therapeutic discharge." That is, patients who insistently regress within the hospital are informed of the program's failure to be helpful and discharged on this account, with the stipulation that they can return when they feel motivated to work toward common goals with the treatment staff.

Effective short-term units maintain clear role definition among staff and a highly structured schedule of activities. Groups are oriented toward practical issues and focus on adaptation to life in the community. As noted earlier, groups within inpatient units serve the valuable functions of confronting maladaptive interpersonal behaviors so as to make them more dystonic, identifying the angry motives behind such behaviors, and illustrating the untoward consequences (i.e., being found undesirable) that result.

In contrast, effective long-term units invoke and encourage a strong sense of community in which patients are expected to use their strengths to guide decisions about their own programs and those of other patients as well. Groups in this setting serve the additional function of being a vehicle by which common problems in relationships can be identified and discussed. The value of open and honest communication of feelings and problems is underscored by the fact that privileges and restrictions are awarded in accord with the degree to which the community feels that an individual patient has adequately communicated with everyone that an informed consensus can be reached.

There is some controversy over the relative merits of having a long period of initial containment, as described by Rinsley (1971) and Masterson (1972), or of fol-

Table 2. Characteristics of Short-Term Versus Long-Term Hospitalization

Short-Term Units	Long-Term Units
Indications	
• Crises (rage, overdoses)	• Inadequate social supports (incest, assaults, abandonments)
• Consultations, evaluations	
• Therapist anxiety (preventive admission)	• Malignant self-destructiveness
• Psychotic transference	• Sustained depersonalization
Milieu Characteristics	
• Support	• Containment
• Structure (limits, tasks)	• Structure (limits, tasks)
• Groups (problem oriented, focused)	• Groups (community expressive meetings)
• Clear leadership (by professionals)	• Shared decision making
	• One-to-one meetings
Objectives	
• Prevent self-destructive action	• Modify manipulative patterns
• Decrease anxiety	• Internalize capacity for delay and decrease impulsiveness
• Support strengths	
• Perform triage to aftercare	• Develop social and verbal communication skills
• Modify prior therapies	
	• Increase trust in and dependency on people
	• Participate in vocational training

lowing the more traditional therapeutic community approach in which patients, from the beginning of their hospitalization, are encouraged to participate flexibly in the administration of privileges and restrictions for each other. An initial, lengthy period of containment supports the hospital's in loco parentis functions and facilitates a strong, early emphasis on the separation issue. The therapeutic community approach is more ego directed insofar as it gives more attention to decision making, judgment, and consequences of impulsive actions (Edelson 1970).

The overall usefulness of long-term treatment for borderline patients is a subject of controversy. Some clinicians believe that long-term residential stays for borderline patients encourage and support regressive tendencies by validating a sense of prior injustice and supporting claims for dependent gratifications. Other clinicians, however, feel that long-term hospitalization offers many borderline patients opportunities not otherwise available for corrective growth experiences through the internalization of impulse control, identification with positive role models, and exposure to educational and rehabilitation programs. Follow-up studies by Masterson and Costello (1980), McGlashan (1986), and Stone et al. (1987) indicate that a significant number of patients who complete extensive residential treatment are leading relatively stable, treatment-free lives in the community even many years later.

Summary

The major areas of agreement about treatment outlined here are meant to be specific for DSM-III-R borderline personality disorder, but it should be noted in closing, as it was at the beginning, that the literature often requires interpretive screening as to the kind of patient being discussed.

The literature indicates that, regardless of modality, treatment is difficult, severe countertransference problems are common, and the results are uneven. Individual psychotherapy remains the backbone of most treatment strategies for borderline patients. The potential use of behavioral and psychopharmacologic modalities is being evaluated and offers hope for more diverse and effective treatment in the future. The role of family and group therapies can be critical but is quite variable. Likewise, the need for hospitalization is variable, but hospitalization is always a resource that should be available in the overall treatment program.

Chapter 260

Avoidant Personality Disorder

Avoidant personality disorder (APD) is one of the more common presenting complaints in private practice. The criteria for APD in DSM-III (American Psychiatric Association 1980) are hypersensitivity to rejection, unwillingness to enter relationships without strong guarantees of uncritical acceptance, and lack of self-confidence. This initial formulation was criticized for being narrowly interpersonal (i.e., it did not include an unwillingness to take chances in other areas of life) and failing to represent adequately features of the phobic character construct in the psychoanalytic literature (Fenichel 1945; MacKinnon and Michaels 1971; Rado 1969). DSM-III-R (American Psychiatric Association 1987) broadened the definition in response to these criticisms. See Table 1 for the DSM-III-R diagnostic criteria for avoidant personality disorder.

The avoidant personality disorder has many historical antecedents: the psychoanalytic "phobic character" (Fenichel 1945; MacKinnon and Michaels 1971), Kretschmer's (1925) "hyperaesthetic," Schneider's "aesthenic," and the 'introverted" personality (Eysenck 1981; Leary 1957; Pilkonis 1984; Wilson 1978). It also seems plausible that APD is an Axis II personality spectrum presentation closely related to the Axis I anxiety disorders.

The avoidant personality disorder was included in the nomenclature for the first time in DSM-III; there is no systematic research concerning its optimum treatment. The recommendations in this chapter are based on clinical experience, reports in the literature, and the application to APD of the much better established treatments already developed for anxiety disorders, particularly social anxiety and phobias.

Psychotherapies

Regardless of the type of psychotherapy provided, APD patients tend to evoke two types of countertransference that may in different ways confirm the patient's expectations and reinforce pathologic behavior. The patient's timidity invites a therapeutic

Table 1. DSM-III-R Diagnostic Criteria for Avoidant Personality Disorder
A pervasive pattern of social discomfort, fear of negative evaluation, and timidity, beginning by early adulthood and present in a variety of contexts, as indicated by at least *four* of the following: (1) is easily hurt by criticism or disapproval   (2) has no close friends or confidants (or only one) other than first-degree relatives   (3) is unwilling to get involved with people unless certain of being liked   (4) avoids social or occupational activities that involve significant interpersonal contact, e.g., refuses a promotion that will increase social demands   (5) is reticent in social situations because of a fear of saying something inappropriate or foolish, or of being unable to answer a question   (6) fears being embarrassed by blushing, crying, or showing signs of anxiety in front of people   (7) exaggerates the potential difficulties, physical dangers, or risks involved in doing something ordinary but outside his or her usual routine, e.g., may cancel social plans because he or she anticipates being exhausted by the effort of getting there

protectiveness that may reaffirm the patient's belief that he or she is an insecure weakling (Young and Beier 1982). Alternatively, the therapist may err in the opposite direction and become excessively ambitious. The patient may be forced to face new situations prematurely and with inadequate preparation, and then be criticized for not being braver.

Individual Psychotherapies

Psychodynamic Therapy

Interpretive techniques are often useful either as the primary intervention or as an adjunct to a behavioral approach. The uncovering approach consists of the interpretation of unconscious fantasies related to the patient's fear that his or her impulses will fly out of control and cause danger, guilt, or embarrassment. The avoidant behavior typically helps to maintain a denial of an unconscious wish or impulse (MacKinnon and Michaels 1971). APD patients are also likely to have harsh superegos, to project their own unrealistic expectations of themselves onto others, and to evade expected criticism and embarrassment by avoiding interpersonal relationships. A complete interpretation identifies the unconscious impulse (sexual, aggressive, or dependent) and the fear and guilt it evokes, and traces the ensuing avoidant defensive pattern in the transference, in outside relationships, and in early life experience (Fenichel 1945). Patients with avoidant personalities are often excellent candidates for all types of psychodynamic treatment (focal, long-term, psychoanalytic), and the choice of one of these or a behavioral approach usually depends on the patient's goals, preferences, and psychological-mindedness (Frances and Clarkin 1981).

Interpersonal Therapy

In this approach, the healing interpersonal or corrective emotional experience of the therapeutic relationship cuts across the particular format and technique chosen for the treatment. Patients who initially fear interpersonal rejection learn to take additional chances outside the treatment as they discover that they are acceptable to the therapist and succeed in the chances they take within the treatment. Interactional psychotherapy is a treatment in which the patient's maladaptive behavior is dealt with directly in the context of the therapist-patient relationship (Cashdan 1982). In treating avoidant personality disorder, the therapist might at first complement the patient's timidity and avoidance through sympathetic reassurance and protection. After establishing the patient's sence of security in the treatment relationship, the therapist acts in a manner that is complementary to more self-confident and extroverted behavior, for example, by directly encouraging assertive behavior (McLemore and Benjamin 1979), refusing to support avoidance, withholding sympathy and protection (Cashdan 1982), or bringing in significant others with whom the patient can actively try out new behaviors (McLemore and Hart 1982).

Strategic Approaches

Strategic, paradoxical approaches may help to reduce fear of rejection as a motivator in the APD patient. The therapist prescribes that the patient seek rejection in a way that is predictable and under control. For example, an unmarried, 35-year-old man who was afraid to date and had never experienced sexual intercourse helped to develop a treatment assignment that required he be rejected for dates by two women during the next week. If one of the women he approached accepted his offer, he could go out with her, but only on the condition that he had asked out an additional woman who rejected him. This intervention took the mortification out of the rejections that inevitably occur in social intercourse. Being rejected became a goal of the treatment, and the patient's failure to expose himself to rejection in social experiences would have placed him at risk of rejection by the therapist for not trying. With severely oppositional avoidant patients, avoidance may paradoxically be extolled and prescribed in order to capitalize on the patient's need to defeat the therapist by doing the opposite of everything he or she suggests (Haley 1978; Weeks and L'Abate 1982).

Behavioral and Cognitive Techniques

The extensive literature in behavior therapy for shyness and social anxiety may be pertinent to the treatment of avoidant personality disorder (Hersen and Bellack 1976; Pilkonis 1984). Assertiveness and social skills training through role playing, direct instruction, or modeling have been shown to be helpful in developing effective and confident social behavior (Curran 1977; Gambrill 1977; Hersen and Bellack 1976; Marzillier 1978). Graded exposure, flooding, and systematic desensitization are likely to be useful in extinguishing the avoidant behavior and anxiety intolerance of APD, just as these techniques are effective with similar symptoms in Axis I anxiety disorders (Marks 1982; Shaw 1979; Wilson 1982). Cognitive and rational emotive techniques, originally developed to focus on the pathologic assumptions, attributions, and self-statements associated with Axis I social anxiety (Alden and Safran 1978; Meichenbaum and Cameron 1982), may work equally well when such beliefs are part of the presentation of APD. The low self-confidence of these patients usually improves with the removal of symptoms and increasing social facility, but can also be addressed directly with cognitive and behavioral techniques (Beck et al. 1979).

Group Therapy

It is not surprising that APD patients typically fear group treatments in the same way that they fear other new and socially demanding situations. It is for this very reason that group therapy may be specifically and especially effective for avoidant patients who can be cajoled and role induced to undertake the exposure (Yalom 1975). The value of a group treatment as a corrective emotional experience in reducing social embarrassment and increasing social skills cuts across the particular orientation or techniques used in the group (i.e., psychodynamic, behavioral, or social systems).

Family Treatment

Not uncommonly, the avoidant behavior of the APD patient is reinforced by the family context in a manner that is analogous to the workings of the phobic partnerships formed by Axis I agoraphobic patients. Family members may become overprotective with the intent of being helpful, but in fact help to maintain the patient's unwillingness to take chances (Carson 1982; Kiesler 1982). Couple and family treatments may be indicated in order to establish a family structure that allows more room for interpersonal exploration outside the tightly closed family circle (Gurman and Kniskern 1981).

Biologic Therapies

Most APD patients fear medication and its side effects just as they do any other new experience. Some few avoidant patients, however, may be especially prone to substance abuse in an effort to treat their anxiety (Marks 1982). For most patients, medication is not necessary; it should be used only adjunctively or after psychotherapeutic efforts have been unsuccessful. Anxiolytics are sometimes useful during periods when the patient is trying new and previously avoided behavior (except if the patient is also participating in behavioral treatment that requires exposure to anxiety). The mere possession of the pills, or even of the prescription, often provides sufficient reassurance that the patient finds it unnecessary to make use of them. Tricyclic or MAO antidepressants may be useful if the patient develops a superimposed panic disorder (Liebowitz 1983; Marks 1982).

Chapter 261

Dependent Personality Disorder

Clinical Overview

Clinical interest in dependent personality disorder has existed since Abraham (1924) first described the oral character. As a disorder, the personality type first appeared in a War Department Technical Bulletin in 1945 (Nomenclature and Method of Recording Diagnoses 1945); in DSM-I (American Psychiatric Association 1952) it appeared as a subtype of passive-aggressive personality disorder. Since then, a surprising number of studies have upheld the descriptive validity of dependent personality traits viewed as submissiveness (Presley and Walton 1973), oral character traits (Gottheil and Stone 1968; Kline and Storey 1977), oral dependence (Lazare et al. 1966, 1970; van den Berg and Helstone 1975), or passive dependence (Tyrer and Alexander 1979). DSM-III (American Psychiatric Association 1980) emphasized three characteristics of the dependent personality disorder: passivity in allowing others to assume responsibility for major areas of life because of an inability to function independently, subordinating one's own needs to those of a person on whom one depends, and a lack of self-confidence. This description overlaps that of the asthenic personality disorder in ICD-9 (Mental Disorders: Glossary 1978), which emphasizes compliance and a weak response to the demands of daily life. Table 1 lists the DSM-III-R diagnostic criteria for dependent personality disorder (American Psychiatric Association 1987).

The treatment literature is limited largely to case descriptions and uncontrolled studies apart from one report of a large series of treated patients (Whitman et al. 1954) and one controlled trial of medications (Klein et al. 1973). Nonetheless, there is an apparent consensus in the clinical literature that the treatment of dependent personality disorder is often successful. This is indirectly supported by the relative lack of publications reporting failures or focusing on difficulties in treatment, in contrast to the plethora of such reports for antisocial, borderline, passive-aggressive, and other personality disorders.

Although dependency is a universal personality trait, this chapter is limited to reports that are relevant specifically to the treatment of the personality disorder. Dependent personality is common in the general population—the Midtown Manhattan Study found it in 2.5 percent of the entire sample (Langer and Michael 1963)—but passive-dependent and passive-aggressive personality features often occur together, and treatment may require using techniques that are applicable to both disorders. Patients with coexisting histrionic or borderline personality disorder may also require modifications in the treatment of their dependent personality traits or disorder. (See the chapters on passive-aggressive, histrionic, and borderline personality disorders.) This chapter does not include a discussion dealing with the dependency that

Table 1. DSM-III-R Diagnostic Criteria for Dependent Personality Disorder

A pervasive pattern of dependent and submissive behavior, beginning by early adulthood and present in a variety of contexts, as indicated by at least *five* of the following:

  (1) is unable to make everyday decisions without an excessive amount of advice or reassurance from others
  (2) allows others to make most of his or her important decisions, e.g., where to live, what job to take
  (3) agrees with people even when he or she believes they are wrong, because of fear of being rejected
  (4) has difficulty initiating projects or doing things on his or her own
  (5) volunteers to do things that are unpleasant or demeaning in order to get other people to like him or her
  (6) feels uncomfortable or helpless when alone, or goes to great lengths to avoid being alone
  (7) feels devastated or helpless when close relationships end
  (8) is frequently preoccupied with fears of being abandoned
  (9) is easily hurt by criticism or disapproval

often accompanies major psychiatric syndromes, such as chronic schizophrenia or major depression.

Presenting Complaints

In a study of 400 consecutive outpatients, Whitman et al. (1954) noted that 23 percent had a passive-dependent personality, the most prevalent personality type. Presenting complaints in these patients included depression (36 percent), anxiety (29 percent), somatic symptoms (11 percent), phobias (7 percent), and situational reactions (7 percent). Agoraphobia, with or without panic attacks, also seems to be a common presenting complaint. Common psychosocial precipitants for seeking treatment are disturbances in or loss of valued attachments, as well as situational or occupational changes that require increased assertive and independent behavior (Vaillant and Perry 1985).

Behaviors

Hirshfeld et al. (1977), in a factor analytic study, suggested that dependency is best characterized by three related dimensions. The first dimension encompasses close attachments and strong emotional reliance on others. Persons with this trait are prone to separation anxiety and will remain in relationships, even with those who mistreat them, to avoid the resurgence of feeling alone and helpless. In order to entice others to like them or to secure succorance, they often act in ingratiating or demeaning ways. When hospitalized, they often transfer their attachment needs to the hospital, which may cause a recurrence of their presenting symptoms as separation anxiety increases prior to discharge, and may necessitate a prolongation of hospitalization (Sarwer-Foner and Kealey 1981). This is less likely to occur if the patient has a good, close relationship with someone outside the hospital.

A second dimension of dependency involves a lack of self-confidence in social situations, often accompanied by submissive behavior. Individuals with this trait have difficulty asserting themselves and often outwardly agree with others regardless of what they truly believe. They fear self-expression whether it involves anger, criticism, or their own wishes and needs, and they are often passive when events call for an active response. However, they may be able to confront anxiety-provoking situations in order to take care of others dependent on them.

The desire for (or avoidance of) autonomy is the third dimension that characterizes dependency. Those who avoid autonomy want others to make decisions for them; otherwise they are indecisive and have difficulty initiating or completing activities on their own. They often seek guidance and direction, and thereby subordinate their freedom of choice to the will of others.

Cognitions

Dependent individuals doubt themselves and view themselves as incompetent and less worthy or deserving than others. This results in a pessimistic view of their chances for social and occupational success, although this view may be masked by an external attitude of optimism (Kline and Storey 1977). They may constantly ruminate over their fearful attitudes and phobic anxieties about self-assertion, social activities, independence, and abandonment.

Psychodynamics and the Functional Maintenance of Dependent Behaviors

What causes excessive dependency to develop and continue into adulthood? Kagan and Moss (1960) found passive and dependent behaviors at six to 10 years of age had high correlations with such behaviors in young adulthood. For women there were correlations across a broad array of dependent behaviors, but for men the only correlation was between dependent behavior around childhood tasks and a dependent vocational choice in adulthood. The authors suggested that these sex differences were cultural because American society punishes dependent behavior in males but rewards it in females.

Whitman et al. (1954) suggested that when dependent needs are stimulated, passivity results because the individual finds these needs unacceptable. This response may be due either to an internal sense of guilt or to external frustration. The individual may become demanding in minor ways as a secondary effect of the frustration. Millon (1981) suggested that dependent individuals have had their independence stifled by oversolicitous and controlling parents but have had a relatively good relationship with at least one parent, so the anxiety experienced in situations that require independent action is counterbalanced by the expectation that someone will step in to help. Independence is further stifled by the expectation that someone will criticize them for making independent decisions or taking action. Because they do not channel hostile feelings into assertive behavior, dependent individuals often smooth over troubles by acting in an especially friendly, helpful, and concerned manner.

Alexander and Dibb (1977) compared control subjects with addicts who were still living with their families of origin. Both the addicts and their parents perceived the addicts as passive, dependent, and incapable of autonomy and success. Neither the addicts nor the overindulgent parents encouraged self-reliance.

Vaillant and Perry (1985) noted that dependent individuals often act in a submissive, compliant way in order to earn others' gratitude. In fantasy, this ingratiating behavior entitles them to maintain their important attachments and protects them from abandonment and separation anxiety.

Epstein (1980) compared the social consequences of assertive, aggressive, passive-aggressive, and submissive behaviors. Submissive behavior—such as making a request accompanied by an indication that one will capitulate easily—elicited consistently high intentions to comply, low anger, and high sympathy from observers, generally equal to the levels obtained by assertive behavior. Thus, submissive behavior may have positive social consequences, depending on the characteristics of those with whom the submissive person interacts.

In a study of passive adolescents, Rosenheim and Gaoni (1977) postulated that the failure to make decisions, enter into personal commitments, and take independent action is due to a fear of having to mourn childhood fantasies about the future. The refusal to take an active stance in working toward any plan is a way to avoid having to set aside cherished, if overvalued or unrealistic, hopes for the future and to avoid the sadness of mourning.

Andrews et al. (1978) suggested a biologic hypothesis for dependency based on finding high levels of anxiety-proneness and emotionality and easy fatiguability in individuals with asthenic personality. A constitutional predisposition to develop high anxiety levels under stress may underlie the inability to cope.

Psychotherapies

The literature on the treatment of dependent personality disorder is limited. There is still a need for both individual case studies and series to generate hypotheses about the response of dependent psychopathology to specific treatment techniques. The following is a summary of the treatment literature to date.

Problems Arising in Psychotherapy

Four types of transference and countertransference problems often arise in the treatment of individuals with dependent personality disorder. First, the patient entering therapy may make many unrealistic demands or requests of the therapist for advice, succorance, or concrete help. One study showed that such patients often dropped out of treatment early and with unsuccessful outcomes (Alexander and Fibeles 1968). Such individuals need special attention to help modulate their demands early in treatment in order to prevent overwhelming disappointment and dropping out. They also invite a countertransference reaction of withdrawing from the patient, which then reinforces the guilt they experience over their needs.

Second, the patient may consistently make attempts to have the therapist both take responsibility for all decisions and tell the patient how to run his or her life (Hill 1970; Saul and Warner 1975). To the extent that the therapist assumes this directing countertransference role, he or she may become an external substitute for the patient's own will. A therapist may do this out of exasperation at the patient's protestations of helplessness or in response to an enticing request to assume an eminent role as wise and all-knowing. This countertransference reinforces the patient's emotional reliance on the therapist without helping the patient learn more independent ways of coping. Such directive therapies may have a useful, if limited, role during crisis interventions, but even behavior therapies, such as assertiveness training, require that the therapist foster the patient's independent decision making.

Third, the patient may stay in therapy in order to maintain the emotional attachment to the therapist but avoid making real changes (Leeman and Mulvery 1975). The patient's compliant attitude toward the therapist may be mistaken for cooperation with the goals of therapy. Such a patient has tacitly refused to accept responsibility for making changes and may have his or her passivity reinforced if the therapist does not recognize and deal openly with this problem.

Fourth, the therapist may challenge the patient to leave or to assert himself or herself in an unsatisfying and punitive relationship (Perry and Flannery 1982; Vaillant and Perry 1985). This may be very anxiety provoking because of the strength of the emotional attachment or because of the realistic threat of a punitive response from the patient's partner. Such a challenge may result in panic or early termination of treatment. These reactions are especially prominent in patients with masochistic relationships (Chapter 263).

Individual Dynamic Psychotherapy

There is a consensus in the psychotherapy literature about two central elements in the therapy of dependent personality disorder. The first involves allowing the emergence of a dependent transference toward the therapist, which is then dealt with in a way to promote emotional growth. The second element is the use of the therapist's expectations and direct support to promote self-expression, assertiveness, decision making, and independence. If both elements are not included, treatment may be incomplete (Hill 1970; Malinow 1981a; Saul and Warner 1975).

At the outset of therapy, it is important to aid the development of a trusting relationship and allow the patient to begin to transfer dependent wishes onto the therapist. Hill (1970) suggested that the therapist tell the patient that extra sessions may be allowed early in therapy, especially during episodes of panic. This assurance of readily available support helps the patient develop trust. As therapy progresses, the therapist may help the patient find substitute ways of dealing with panic feelings and limit extra sessions.

Studying short-term therapies, Alexander and Abels (1968) found that dependency on the therapist increased from the beginning of therapy to the middle and then remained fairly high until termination. The failure of dependency on the therapist to diminish necessitated working through transference up until termination. By contrast, the patients' dependency on outside relationships began to diminish from the middle of treatment until termination. Alexander and Abeles attributed this to a real effect of treatment on the resolution of dependency conflicts.

The hardest work of therapy occurs when the patient begins to experience increased dependency on the therapist and simultaneously has setbacks in his or her outside life. Offering sympathy for the patient's misery is not helpful by itself (Hill 1970). The therapist should encourage the patient to express real feelings and wishes and to bear the anxiety of making decisions, accepting pleasurable experiences, and dealing with episodes of anxiety. When the patient experiences frustration over the wish to have the therapist take a more directive role in his or her life, the therapist should clarify and interpret the transference elements in addition to supporting the patient in finding more self-reliant ways to cope (Hill 1970; Malinow 1981; Saul and Warner 1975). Only Leeman and Mulvey (1975) advocated limiting attention to transference issues in favor of focusing on relationships outside therapy.

At this stage, it is most important for the therapist to avoid taking a directing role in the patient's life, which might lead to a transference-countertransference fixation (Leeman and Mulvey 1975; Saul and Warner 1975). The patient expects professional and authoritative individuals to make decisions for him or her and will try to manipulate the therapist into doing so. The therapist must actively resist these attempts.

Saul and Warner (1975) described the optimal circumstances under which the therapist may give direct suggestions and encourage various activities or solutions to problems. First, the treatment should have progressed long enough for the therapist to have a good understanding of the patient's dynamics. Second, the therapist should be aware of the state of the patient's transference and his or her own reaction to it. Third, the patient should be at some impasse in treatment, so that direct intervention can mobilize the patient and prevent a repetition of feeling powerless and helpless. Given these circumstances, the therapist should help the patient conceptualize his or her own goals. If the goals are healthy, the therapist should discuss and support them. If there are conflicting goals, then it is helpful to discuss the consequences of each goal and encourage the patient to bear the anxiety of making choices. This cognitive approach also makes use of previous insights about the patient's motivations. The therapist may urge the patient to commit to actions that are within his or her reach (e.g., to take a job) or encourage perseverance despite the urge to give up (e.g., to continue in school rather than drop out). In active intervention, the therapist must use his or her influence in accordance with the patient's own values, not the therapist's.

Covert dependency on the therapist, in which the patient experiences the therapist as a benign, powerful parent figure (Goldman 1956), can facilitate therapeutic change. It is important not to underestimate the effect that the sincere interest, attention, and reliable presence of the therapist has on increasing the patient's belief in the benevolent power of the therapist. This affects the patient's self-esteem in several ways. First, the patient tends to identify with the therapist and wishes to be like him or her (Offenkrantz and Tobin 1974). This process of identification leads to a temporary rise in self-esteem. Second, when the patient remembers or experiences hitherto unacceptable feelings for the first time, the therapist's response is important. Whenever the therapist is comprehending and accepting, the patient's self-esteem is enhanced, because the patient can identify with the benevolent attitudes and responses of the therapist as an authority figure, rather than react according to his or her old prohibitions and ideals. This rise in self-esteem is only temporary as long as it relies on the reassuring presence of the therapist. However, if the patient can use this increased feeling of self-esteem to risk trying new behaviors outside the office, he or she may experience other rewards, including approval from others. It is important for the therapist both to communicate genuine pleasure when these outside efforts succeed and to accept failures, which occur inevitably. This helps cause a shift in the patient's self-perception from dependency toward social self-confidence.

During the final stage of therapy, the therapist gradually increases the level of expectations for autonomous decision making and action and for socially effective responses (Leeman and Mulvey 1975). The therapist reinforces the patient's increasing ability to handle crises without extra sessions and to manage panic episodes by soothing himself or herself (Hill 1970). This requires helping the patient to resolve transference wishes to be dependent and instead to accept a more self-reliant position in relationships.

The consensus in the literature is that psychotherapy is usually helpful for the patient with dependent personality disorder. Hill (1970) noted that only two of 50 patients she treated showed no observable improvement. Treatment required at least several months and, in some cases, lasted more than two years. Leeman and Mulvey (1975) noted that short-term (three to seven months' duration), focused psychotherapy was successful in five of six cases, although one patient required a second course of treatment.

The efficacy of short-term versus long-term treatment has not been adequately addressed. In general, short-term treatment psychotherapies are most likely to succeed when a circumscribed, dynamic conflict or focus is present, the patient can form a therapeutic or working alliance rapidly, and the patient's tendency to regress to severe dependency or acting out is limited (Davanloo 1978; Horowitz et al. 1984; Luborsky 1984; Malan 1976; Strupp and Binder 1984). Short-term dynamic therapies usually require once-weekly sessions over three to nine months. Many patients with dependent personality disorder do not meet the criteria for short-term treatment, however. Patients who are likely to do better in longer term, dynamic psychotherapies or psychoanalysis include those who have failed to improve in short-term treatments or have multifocal conflicts. Long-term treatments generally require two to four sessions per week over several years to work through the dependent transference.

Behavior Therapy

Turkat and Carlson (1984) reported two behavioral treatments of a patient with dependent personality disorder. The patient had initially been treated with behavioral techniques for anxiety-related complaints but had relapsed immediately following termination. The authors then reformulated the case, focusing on the dependency constructs of excessive reliance on others and deficient autonomous behavior, which resulted from long-standing anxiety over independent decision making. The therapist and patient constructed a hierarchy of situations in which the patient was required to make independent decisions but had little experience. The therapist emphasized anxiety management skills, which had been taught previously. Treatment proceeded every other week over a two-month period. The patient showed decreasing levels of self-rated anxiety over these situations as treatment progressed, and these gains were maintained over a one-year follow-up interval. Avoidance of situations requiring independent decisions also diminished. Although involving only one patient, this report is striking in that treatment was based on a formulation of a common mechanism for a wide variety of the patient's dependent features. The behavioral formulation is also compatible with a psychodynamic view. Further study of the efficacy of behavior therapy for dependent personality disorder may be fruitful.

Group Psychotherapy

Several authors have reported results suggesting that group psychotherapy can be successful for the treatment of dependent personality disorder. Montgomery (1971) used group therapy for dependent patients who used medications for chronic complaints such as insomnia and nervousness. All but three of 30 patients eventually discontinued medications and began to confront their anger at being dependent on the therapist.

Sadoff and Collins (1968) employed weekly group psychotherapy for 22 stutterers, most of whom had passive-dependent traits. Although the drop-out rate was high, and authors found that the interpretation of the patients' passive-dependent behavior and attitudes (e.g., asking for help and believing that others are responsible for helping them) as a defense against recognizing the expressing anger proved helpful. Stuttering and passive dependency both improved in two patients who became angry and were able to confront their anger.

Torgersen (1980) studied college students who attended a weekend-long encounter group. On follow-up several weeks later, students who initially scored high on dependent traits had mixed responses. They found the group experience frightening; it left them feeling disturbed and anxious. However, they also reported becoming more accepting of their own feelings and opinions. No other changes were found.

In summary, these studies suggest the usefulness of group psychotherapy in the treatment of dependent personality disorder. For this kind of treatment, most clinicians employ weekly session lasting one to one and one-half hours. Treatment generally lasts several years.

Biologic Therapies

The two studies of using medications in the treatment of dependent patients have limitations that prevent firm conclusions about efficacy.

Klein et al. (1973) compared placebo with imipramine and chlorpromazine in hospitalized patients diagnosed as having passive-aggressive and passive-dependent personality disorders according to DSM-I criteria. None of the patients showed a positive drug response.

Lauer (1976) gave tricyclic antidepressants to patients who had passive-dependent traits in addition to their primary diagnoses. On follow-up questionnaires, patients who have received active drugs reported less anxiety and increases in available energy, assertiveness, and outgoing behavior in day-to-day life. The results suggest that some patients with dependent personality disorder do respond to antidepressants in the presence of an Axis I disorder, but, in any event, the benefits are not striking.

Residential Therapies

Although hospitalization is sometimes necessary for the treatment of an Axis I disorder in individuals with dependent personality disorder, residential treatments are generally not indicated, unless other more severe personality disorders, such as borderline, are also present.

Conclusion

For all of the treatment modalities reviewed, there are reports of successful treatment of some individuals with dependent personality disorder. Although large case series and controlled treatment trials are largely absent, the literature does suggest that a positive response to psychological treatments is common. Treatment is generally shorter and less difficult than for other personality disorders, such as borderline, antisocial, or passive-aggressive. At present there is no clear indication whether the different therapies have differential treatment effects. The treatment literature would benefit from further case studies and controlled trials in which specific treatment hypotheses and interventions are tested, measuring short-term and long-term (follow-up) outcome.

Chapter 262

Compulsive Personality Disorder

The present treatment of compulsive personality disorder encompasses a range of psychological, pharmacologic, and behavior modification approaches, as well as a few surgical and experimental approaches. The most encouraging developments are in the pharmacologic and behavior modification areas, although psychotherapy remains the underpinning to these modalities.

Compulsive personality disorders are maladaptive and extreme manifestations of compulsive personality traits, which cause varying degrees of anxiety and impairments in functioning in social and occupational areas. The term compulsive is related to the obsessive-compulsive phenomena, which are manifested by thoughts, feelings, ideas, and behavioral impulses that a person cannot alter or dispel despite an intense wish to do so. The compelling, unwillful nature of the activity, whether in thought (obsession) or behavior (compulsion), is the central issue. An obsession is a persistent, ritualized thought pattern—thoughts, images, words, or presumed wishes that intrude into awareness against the person's will and choice, and beyond his or her conscious capacity to terminate them. Doubting, procrastination, and indecision are generally present, and the person is incapable of closure in the consideration of an issue or train of thought. See Table 1 for the DSM-III-R diagnostic criteria for obsessive-compulsive personality disorder (American Psychiatric Association 1987).

The earliest theories about these disorders involved the notion of possession by outside agents or evil forces that required a ritual of exorcism by witch doctors, mystics, or religious leaders. This practice continued until the first dynamic hypotheses were developed by Freud and Janet. Although others had recognized that such behavior had important symbolic meaning, Freud and Janet conceptualized compulsive symptomatology in terms of the unconscious, tracing the development of the symptoms from psychic tension and psychosexual roots in the libido theory. Freud viewed compulsions as defenses against unconscious, hostile or sexual impulses derived from the pre-oedipal, anal, sadistic era of psychosexual development. Later theorists such as Rado (1956) emphasized other elements, for example, repressed rage and the idea of the control of unacceptable hostile or sexual impulses. Because the disorder involves behavior and thinking beyond one's conscious or willful choice, the concept of an unconscious was uniquely applicable to the understanding of these irrational and incomprehensible behaviors. Psychoanalytic treatment designed to clarify hidden motivating forces seemed appropriate.

Freud described compulsive personality structures as orderly, stubborn, and parsimonious; others have described them as obstinate, perfectionistic, punctual, meticulous, frugal, and inclined to intellectualism. Janet described compulsive personalities as rigid, inflexible, lacking in adaptability, overly conscientious, and persistent even in the face of undue obstacles. Compulsive persons generally appreciate order and discipline, are dependable and reliable, and have high standards and ethical values. They are practical, precise, and scrupulous in their moral requirements, but have great impatience and intolerance of anxiety. Magical thinking or the omnipotent

Table 1.   DSM-III-R Diagnostic Criteria for Obsessive-Compulsive Personality Disorder
A pervasive pattern of perfectionism and inflexibility, beginning by early adulthood and present in a variety of contexts, as indicated by at least *five* of the following: (1) perfectionism that interferes with task completion, e.g., inability to complete a project because own overly strict standards are not met (2) preoccupation with details, rules, lists, order, organization, or schedules to the extent that the major point of the activity is lost (3) unreasonable insistence that others submit to exactly his or her way of doing things, **or** unreasonable reluctance to allow others to do things because of the conviction that they will not do them correctly (4) excessive devotion to work and productivity to the exclusion of leisure activities and friendships (not accounted for by obvious economic necessity) (5) indecisiveness: decision making is either avoided, postponed, or protracted, e.g., the person cannot get assignments done on time because of ruminating about priorities (do not include if indecisiveness is due to excessive need for advice or reassurance from others) (6) overconscientiousness, scrupulousness, and inflexibility about matters of morality, ethics, or values (not accounted for by cultural or religious identification) (7) restricted expression of affection (8) lack of generosity in giving time, money, or gifts when no personal gain is likely to result (9) inability to discard worn-out or worthless objects even when they have no sentimental value

expectation of magical capacity to control or influence others by thinking is a regular feature. Under conditions of stress or extreme demands, these personality characteristics may congeal into symptomatic behavior that becomes ritualized. Fortunately, all of the symptoms are rarely present in one patient.

A compulsion is a persistent, ritualized behavior pattern—sometimes bizarre, irrational, and beyond choice or decision to terminate. Although bizarre behaviors are very noticeable, lesser compulsive rituals involving meticulous, rigid, organized, and well-controlled activities are almost always present. The compulsive person exerts severe control over his or her emotions, producing a pseudoplacid, unaffected, flattened emotional state. The behavior is inflexible, unspontaneous, obstinate, stubborn, routinized, and ritualized beyond necessity. A need for certainty, guarantees, and absolute perfection is a fixed feature in this behavior.

In recent years the adaptive value of compulsive behavior has come to be recognized more clearly; the insistent, preoccupying, obsessive thoughts or compulsive actions so fill attention that it is scarcely possible for any other thought processes to take place. In this way the behavior serves the purpose of directing attention away from more significant and distressing thoughts. This process is easy to understand when the obsessive thought is a pointless rumination or the compulsive behavior is totally irrelevant. The distracting or controlling function of such behavior is more difficult to recognize, however, when the behavior itself is alien and highly upsetting. Screaming obscene words, for example, may seem to suggest that the person wants to become the focus of public attention—a contradiction of the belief that such behavior is designed to shelter the person from public notice and crucial concerns. However, regardless of how extreme or revolting the behavior might be, it is still much less distressing than the idea it is covering up. This process is called displacement, which is a paramount defense in this disorder.

Recently, the concept of compulsions has been altered by behavioral conditioning theorists, who visualize such phenomena as conditioned avoidance responses intended to minimize anxiety. Compulsive behavior traits, however, may be constructive and adaptive, whereas in compulsive disorders the behavior is maladaptive.

Although there is no single issue involved in the ultimate development of compulsive personalities, several theories have been advanced. They may be divided roughly into two categories: biogenetic and psychodynamic. Recent studies suggest the possibility of genetic factors in compulsive disorders. Psychodynamic theories basically center around two issues: 1) the control of unacceptable aggressive impulses and 2) the battle for autonomy between the growing child and the mother. In both ego and instinct theories, behavior is viewed as intrapsychic and interpersonal. Thus, both theories involve anality but postulate an environmental situation imposing undue interference with the normally occurring anal phase.

Freud abandoned his earliest theory emphasizing a psychosexual genesis when he altered his views on the role of sexual trauma. According to this theory, compulsions were caused by an active genital experience in which the child both participated and found pleasure. By 1913 the concepts of anality and sadism had evolved, and obsessive-compulsive disorders were thought to involve hostile impulses against the parents. These impulses were consequently dealt with, in theory, by the ego defenses. The notion of hatred and sadism remain key issues in psychoanalytic conceptualizations (Jones 1923).

The second theme of psychodynamic theory goes beyond libidinal concepts of anality and refers to the more generalized acculturating process of the person. In this theory it is not anality but enraged defiance that alternates with guilty fear. The focus is on the interrelationship of the child with the nurturing and acculturating agent (i.e., mother), who demands restraints and expects performances that may or may not be within the capacity of the child (Monroe 1948).

Later theorists such as Sullivan (1953), Horney (1950), and Salzman (1980) postulated that the child's need for acceptance and recognition is what leads to a compulsive personality. The focus moved away from rage and defiance to the extreme need for acceptance and being loved.

Psychotherapies

Individual Dynamic Psychotherapy

General Principles

Individual psychodynamic psychotherapy or classical analysis is the backbone of treatment for most patients with compulsive personality disorders (Nemiah 1980). Even though there has been no systematic, quantitative evaluation of the efficacy of psychotherapy, the theoretical conceptualization of the underlying unconscious etiology requires this approach. In fact, the prevailing wisdom, based on clinical tradition rather than outcome studies, still justifies the emphasis on psychotherapy with the ancillary support of drugs and behavior modification approaches. Although such treatment may be long, lasting two or three years with hourly sessions once or twice a week, the reduction of symptoms and distress is notable. When the patient's and therapist's goals are reasonable, psychotherapy can be effective. Although psychotherapeutic treatment is difficult, tedious, and at times painful for patient and therapist, it is still the most effective means of dealing with this disorder (Hussain and Ahad 1970).

The problems implicit in the therapy of compulsive personality disorder derive from the characteristic defenses, which in most cases are antithetical to the therapeutic task. Various modalities, such as dynamic psychotherapy, cognitive therapy, hypnosis, and behavioral therapy, are all handicapped by the patient's rigidities, avoidance of risk taking, and lack of commitment. Excessive zeal, which often looks like active cooperation, may, by its very intensity, complicate or undermine the therapeutic program. These issues must be confronted whatever the therapeutic program might be.

Psychotherapy requires basic agreements with the patient concerning issues such as the regularity of sessions and the willingness to express feelings and relate thoughts without censure. Many of these requirements are inimical to the compulsive defensive structure and tend to make the process of therapy difficult and tedious. However, because of the intricacies and variety of tactics played out in this disorder, the therapist will have a fascinating and rewarding encounter if he or she can be free, flexible, and open enough to deal effectively with the patient's maneuvers.

The essential task in the therapy of the compulsive personality disorder is to convey insight and initiate learning and change without getting caught in a tug-of-war, the compulsive patient's way of maintaining a rigid style of functioning that avoids novelty and change. The work lies in identifying, clarifying, and altering the defensive patterns that maintain the neurosis. Although the problems that brought about these defenses are comparatively easy to uncover, the defensive structure is most difficult to unravel. For example, a patient with a ritualistic avoidance of knives may be aware that he has some uneasiness about losing control of his hostile impulses. The identification of the problem is simple enough. However, it is soon evident that the patient has an uneasiness and uncertainty about the possibility of losing control in general or of being unable to control himself at all times. The fear of loss of control is the central conflict. In fact, tenderness is often a more significant feeling than hostility and also needs to be controlled, because the feeling of tenderness may leave the person feeling exposed.

It is paradoxical that in the attempts to clarify a compulsive patient's life the issues become more complicated and confused. Ordinarily, increasing one's knowledge about a particular problem helps to focus on the relevant components. This is not so with the compulsive patient, who appears to be deliberately confusing the situation by introducing new issues when there is a real danger of clarifying something. By bringing in more details and qualifications, the patient is trying to be precise and to avoid making errors. Before accepting responsibility in some matter, the patient tries to involve every possibility outside himself or herself, and these new factors often lead the investigation into a cul-de-sac from which no fruitful return is possible.

In the service of maintaining control over inner and outer functioning, compulsive mechanisms such as intellectualizing, emotional flatness, perfectionism, doubting, procrastinating, indecisiveness, and unwillingness to make commitments prevent the person from functioning in uncertain, novel, and risky areas, thereby guaranteeing safety and security. These mechanisms are all devices to eliminate risks by rigid, ritualized patterns of behavior. These behavioral patterns are so distinct and predominating that they demand special focus and concern.

Both knowledge of the personality structure and awareness of the overpowering need to maintain it intact are crucial in the treatment of the compulsive person. Clinical intervention must take into account the extraordinary capacity of the compulsive patient to evade, distract, obfuscate, and displace in order to avoid feelings and change. Tactics that reinforce these defenses must be avoided by the therapist, who may have obsessional characteristics also.

Rigidity and the use of strict rules in pursuing dynamic individual therapy can undermine therapeutic progress. Although free association can be effective, a rigid tendency to say everything that comes to mind may occupy a great deal of time with trivia and irrelevant material. Consequently, the therapist must be active and intervene when the communication is overwhelmed with too many unrelated details. He or she must interrupt and focus on the relevant data. The notion that everything is relevant can lead to interminable inquiries that reinforce the search for certainties. However, the therapist must be careful not to discourage significant and illuminating details, using clinical judgment based on the initial focus and knowledge of what experiences are related to the development and maintenance of the neurosis.

Activity on the part of the therapist is essential from the beginning of therapy to the end. However, the therapist's activities must never be so intense as to overwhelm the patient or make the therapist feel he or she is controlling the therapy.

The Past Versus the Here and Now

The search for the ultimate causes in the form of early traumatic experiences is mostly unrewarding, excessively time-consuming, and unlikely to influence significantly the course of therapy except to prolong it. Moreover, the search encourages greater obsessionalism. The most effective approach in the therapy of the compulsive patient lies in the examination of recent events, especially those that occur in the ongoing relationship with the therapist. The transference and countertransference phenomena play unique roles in advancing the therapeutic process. In addition, therapy must unravel the detailed and widespread defensive techniques that underlie compulsive behaviors. Such therapeutic maneuvers do not imply a deemphasis of development and the role of early interpersonal patterning, which must ultimately be incorporated into the treatment, but simply a realistic awareness of the technical problems in treating compulsive disorders.

To help a compulsive patient see and understand how he or she actually reacts and deals with anxiety requires the clarity of a recent event. For compulsive patients, past events are fertile ground to use all their powers of verbal manipulation and distortion, aided by the hazy atmosphere of uncertainty. Compulsive patients, left to their own inclinations, tend to discuss the frustrations, disappointments, and despair of previous years. Present hostilities and frustrations, especially as they involve ongoing relationships, are much more difficult to admit and examine.

Control and the Tug-of-War

The compulsive person generally becomes involved in a tug-of-war when he or she attempts to "one-up" others. Because the person's security rests on the need to be right, each exchange, even the most trivial, becomes a duel in which the best person wins. Winning may mean something as simple as having the last word. At other times the patient may make a direct statement about the therapist's deficiency in an attempt to put the therapist in the inferior role of having to explain his or her actions to another person who sits in judgment. This is a pervasive technique in all personality configurations and is especially common in the compulsive's relationships.

The therapist cannot enter the tug-of-war or compete in this one-upmanship; rather, the therapist needs to demonstrate to the patient how the patient's insistent need to win or to be on top interferes with learning and relating to people. To win in an immediate sense may often mean gaining control, but the control can prove useless and ineffective. When the tug-of-war occurs in therapy, it provides an opportunity for the compulsive patient to see in miniature how he or she functions in the world at large. Winning, which may override all other values, can be more costly than its real worth. Consequently, the tug-of-war can become a most effective therapeutic tool. The therapist should not avoid the challenge on the assumption that the patient may convert it into a battle. Intelligent confrontation and involvement in which the therapist stands firm but yields at opportune moments can provide great enlightenment to the patient.

One-upmanship is frequently accompanied by veiled or direct feelings of contempt toward the therapist, who may occasionally feel depreciated. This is true even if the therapist does not have a problem with competitive strivings, because many therapists do not enjoy having their best offerings being devalued by their patients.

Effective treatment requires therapists to wait until they have their own feelings under control before trying to help patients understand what they are doing. Many compulsive patients are aware that they are unsuccessful in their relations with other people, because they perceive they are disliked. However, they have no clear sense of why. Clarifying the tendency to depreciate others may help these patients see what they do to many different people.

Familiar in this tug-of-war are the alternating attitudes of defiance and submission and the compulsive patient's experience of feeling depreciated by the therapist's observations.

Hostility and Other Feelings

Hostile and aggressive feelings are responsible for many of the compulsive patient's difficulties. However, the patient's major concern is the need to maintain control over the environment. If this control is endangered, as in a therapeutic situation in which the patient is being forced to recognize his or her fallibility, the patient may well react with anger and irritation and attack the therapist. The basis for the attack can be understood clearly in terms of a need to control rather than some underlying hostile core.

Despite the prevalence of hostile feelings, the compulsive patient has more difficulty dealing with tender impulses. The patient experiences tenderness as weakness, dependency, and giving up, and therefore feels tenderness means vulnerability to being taken advantage of.

The compulsive patient sees himself or herself as a superior being who has high moral standards and is devoted to duty, very knowledgeable to and disinclined to settle for imperfections. Secretly, the patient feels superior to and contemptuous of the therapist. The patient catalogues all the therapist's deficiencies, storing them up to use at a proper time, thus maintaining a secret ammunition dump and an advantage over the therapist. This issue must be confronted for therapy to proceed.

Risks

The compulsive patient views the process of change as a potential source of danger that leaves him or her more vulnerable and uncertain. Therefore, the patient refuses to take risks in and out of therapy, even if attracted to some of the insights gained. Why risk the possibility of being more anxious or of discovering that one is only mediocre? This is the kind of question that interferes with the patient's attempts to try new solutions in living.

The only possible position that the therapist can take is to convey the notion that there are no guarantees in living and every new experience contains some risks and may turn out badly. This point may be reemphasized constantly, even while the therapist encourages new adventures by focusing on the possible rewards and positive results of new behavior. The therapist should actively encourage facing risks, not take the nondirective approach favored by most psychoanalysts.

If the patient is definitely negativistic, the traditional psychoanalytic approach might be more effective. Familiarity with the patient's major defense strategies should enable the attentive therapist to modulate his or her pressures for activity on the part of the patient.

Doubting and Rituals

Any attempt to explore the origins of compulsive doubting in order to eliminate it is fruitless because the doubting does not arise as a result of any single event or group of events in the past. The search would be obstructed by the very doubting itself and would involve the patient's perfectionistic tendencies, thus minimizing any conviction about the discoveries. Because the doubting is a device to guarantee certainty and avoid decision in the face of uncertainty, it will remain in the picture until the patient feels sufficiently secure to be willing to take some risks, which are implicit in every choice.

The search for the origins of compulsive rituals is also largely a waste of time. What might be learned about the origins will only demonstrate areas or occasions of marked anxiety, which can be explored better in other contexts. Like doubting, rituals cannot be addressed directly with the hope of altering their manifestations. Diminution of rituals depends entirely on the person's capacity to abandon the absolute need to control his or her own feelings through magical performances. Intellectual clarification and statements about the patient's wasting time, energy, and skill in these rituals are of no avail. Generally, the patient is fully aware of all these facts. However, in some instances the rituals may be so incapacitating that the patient may pressure the therapist to cure him or her by direct intervention. Such demands must be dealt with; otherwise the therapist, too, will become preoccupied with the rituals, impeding the ultimate therapeutic goal of altering the compulsive personality traits.

Psychoanalysis

Orthodox psychoanalytic therapy that utilizes the couch requires three or more sessions per week by a qualified psychoanalyst. It requires adherence to the techniques that involve free association and the development of a transference neurosis. The goals of psychoanalysis are the full development, understanding, and resolution of the transference neurosis. Traditional psychoanalysis was the earliest psychodynamic approach to the treatment of the compulsive personality disorder. Attention is directed to the underlying unconscious factors and genetic origins of the disorder and toward profound understanding of the defensive structure (Nagera 1983). Analysis usually includes the issues of anger, hostility, and anal characterological traits.

Extensive review of patients' psychosexual development can allow them to develop convictions about their relationships with their parents and can illuminate the origins of the compulsive defenses and foster the resolve to abandon them. The traditional psychoanalytic techniques are often very effective for patients with severe and tenacious compulsive disorders, but often require the occasional use of parameters. Psychoanalytic therapy requires an extensive relationship that usually takes years to develop and resolve. Some psychoanalysts feel that this relationship by itself will effect deep and lasting change in a compulsive personality.

Short-Term Therapy

Compulsive personality disorders may be responsive to short-term psychotherapy because of the requirements of a focused, active, and time-limited procedure. The suggestions detailed in this chapter (focus on the here and now, use of confrontation, an active role for the therapist) are all directed at abbreviating the therapeutic program. Agreement on a limited goal with a clear focus on essential issues can advance the treatment noticeably. The brief therapies of various innovators are applicable to this disorder.

All short-term therapies that derive from a dynamic view of the psychotherapeutic process require a focused, interpretive goal of exposing the displaced, screened, or denied elements that produce the compulsive symptoms. Because the patient tends to rely heavily on the defenses of intellectualization and isolation of feelings and the tactic of control through various means, including rituals, the therapist must mobilize the resources of the transference by displaying an empathic, nonauthoritarian attitude. This enhances the patient's readiness to remove some of the defenses and start to recognize his or her feelings, a step that is essential to the ultimate ability to feel safe and secure enough to abandon the compulsive symptoms.

In Alexander's corrective therapy, the patient's current difficulties are viewed in relation to their genetic development (Alexander and French 1946). Alexander encouraged a planned attack involving manipulating the frequency of visits, interrupting the therapy, and stressing terminating the regressive tendencies of the patient. Alexander's views were echoed by Mann (1973), who attempted to overcome the residual effects of disturbed childhood relationships. Mann emphasized the role of empathy in encouraging greater self-esteem, needed to overcome dependency and passivity. His views press toward early termination by focusing on the separation and individuation that are precipitated by a definite termination agreement. Sifneos (1972) and Malan (1963) focused on specific unconscious, pre-oedipal problems, using interpretations that illuminate these conflicts and aggressively setting termination dates early on. Other short-term approaches, like Beck's (1976) cognitive therapy, focus on the patient's cognition of self, which is distorted and fragmented and requires rebuilding.

In short-term therapy the patient sits up and faces the therapist. This position is intended to stimulate active interaction between therapist and patient and the setting of a time limit. The time limit should be set only after several introductory interviews and an evaluation of the intensity and rigidity of the patient's defenses. As many as 30 to 60 once-a-week sessions can be agreed upon. A new agreement can be made later if, for example, twice-a-week sessions seem to be required. The main point is to avoid an open-ended agreement at the outset, so that the therapy proceeds with a continued focus on the issue, allowing for a few digressions and avoidance tactics. This approach is difficult for the compulsive patient because he or she is rigid and resists change, viewing it as giving up control. The therapist must focus on the issue of control and ask the patient to put aside feelings of uncertainty and doubt, to risk new insights and approaches to living. Support, encouragement, and approval, despite inevitable setbacks, can move the therapy toward reasonable insight and change.

Family Therapy

Although there is considerable evidence that compulsive personality disorder is directly related to the patient's relationship with his or her parents and siblings, there are many difficulties in family therapy. The family approach must be carefully reviewed for its appropriateness in each case. Some family therapists have found that particularly anxious compulsive patients cannot participate in family network sessions until their anxiety has been reduced in individual sessions. The compulsive patient is often a tyrant in family sessions and immobilizes the family members so that the sessions may aggravate the problems. Although it may be difficult to develop a therapeutic atmosphere in which to do family therapy, the termination of ritualistic behavior or other compulsive symptoms may have a major impact in reducing distress within the family. Family therapists such as Minuchin (1974), Haley and Hoffman (1967), and Zwerling et al. (1967) have cited good results with compulsive patients, especially those with prominent eating disorders. Constellations that involve contamination and touching rituals may be less responsive to the family approach.

Group Therapy

The use of group therapy in the treatment of compulsive personality disorder has certain complications. Whether the group is composed exclusively of patients with compulsive disorders or of persons with various diagnoses, the tendency toward competitiveness and demands for control of the situation disrupts the development of a collaborating group with common goals. Compulsive patients have great difficulty in participating in the group process because of their need to be in control and to preoccupy the group with their dominating problems. They cannot learn from the experience of others because they generally consider others unworthy and unlike themselves. They will quickly feel contempt for the others.

Behavioral Therapy

Learning theories have been extensively applied to various clinical psychopathologies, including the compulsive disorders (Walton 1960). Behavioral therapy can be used independently or as an ancillary to dynamic psychotherapy whether by separate therapists or by the unusual therapist who is proficient in both areas. A trial program of behavioral modification approaches may be attempted before dynamic psychotherapy is initiated, or the two modalities may be combined in a joint program. Compulsive behavior can often be modified with notable alleviation of serious impediments in a patient's life (Wolpe 1964).

Behavioral modification approaches are indicated particularly when the compulsive behavior is the single most distressing symptom or the major impediment in the individual's functioning. They are useful in treating many phobic avoidance behaviors, ritualistic behavior, and, at times, simple phobias without incapacitating characterological impediments. Behavioral therapy is also indicated when the compulsions prevent occupational pursuits. Although obsessional symptoms do not respond as readily to behavioral modification, they should be included in the treatment program if psychotherapy is not making adequate progress.

There is general agreement that learning can be defined as the modification of a behavioral tendency by such experiences as exposure or conditioning. According to learning theory, if a person voluntarily performs and maintains a certain act, that behavior becomes self-selecting. For learning to take place, reinforcement (defined as any event that is contingent on the response of the organism and alters the future likelihood of that response) must occur. Learning theory indicates that compulsive behavior produces anxiety because the behavior is paired with an unconditioned, anxiety-producing stimulus. A compulsion is established when the person discovers that the compulsive act reduces the anxiety attendant to an obsessional thought. Eventually, the reduction in anxiety serves to reinforce the compulsive act.

Behavioral modification treatment proceeds only after a detailed analysis of the patient's behavior has been completed. Thereafter, multiple techniques are used to alter the patient's responses to the presumed stimuli, especially fear-evoked behavior (Beech and Vaughan 1978; Foa and Steketee 1979; Marks 1981; Rachman et al. 1971). Briefly, the theory behind many behavioral treatments is that the anxiety experienced by the compulsive patient is a response to stimuli in the environment; rituals reduce the experienced anxiety and thus serve as an avoidance response. Whatever the patient consciously assigns his or her anxiety to is accepted as the cause, and treatment is aimed at desensitizing the patient to that anxiety. The aim of desensitization is to eliminate the anxiety by exposing the patient to distressing situations until he or she adapts to them. Rituals are not dealt with directly; the idea is that when the patient's anxiety is reduced, the rituals will no longer be necessary. The essentials of treatment are 1) to establish a hierarchy of anxiety-provoking stimuli, 2) to train the patient in relaxation techniques, and 3) to present the hierarchy in the presence of the incompatible relaxed state (reciprocal inhibition), which is induced by drugs or imagery.

A variety of behavioral techniques have been used in treating this disorder. The technique of exposure can be viewed as a spectrum, ranging from flooding (sudden confrontation with the provocative stimulus, designed to elicit the greatest emotional reaction over a prolonged period) to desensitization (a slow, brief exposure to the provocative stimulus until minimal tension is attained). The theoretical justification for these procedures is that the patients perform rituals to undo their thoughts or rid themselves of contamination. Other aversive techniques utilized include modeling, response prevention, satiation training, and thought stopping.

No theoretical base adequately explains the beneficial effects of these behavioral techniques on compulsive persons. Some techniques have obviously helped, but definitive treatment remains elusive. Behavioral modification seems to be an effective technique for treatment when well-circumscribed or ritualistic compulsions are present.

Somatic Therapies

Pharmacology

Pharmacologic approaches to the treatment of compulsive disorders have included anxiolytic, antiobsessive, and antidepressant agents (Insel and Murphy 1981). Anxiolytics can relieve anxiety that coexists with compulsive disorders, and antidepressants may relieve the secondary depression. In addition, there are some indications that anticonvulsants may have antiobsessive effects.

Chlorimipramine appears to have some specific effect on compulsive behavior over and above its antidepressant effect (Thoren et al. 1980). Bromazepam has also been reported to be useful in compulsive, phobic, and related states (Burrel and Culpan 1974).

More definitive studies are needed before positive recommendations can be made for the use of drugs. (See Chapter 251 on somatic therapy.)

Surgery

Surgery involves the cutting of tracts from the cortex to the thalamus on the presumption that intractable compulsions are caused by reverberating circuits that need to be interrupted (Tan et al. 1971). The operation is performed with a thin probe by undercutting the frontal lobes, especially the orbital surface and various limbic structures. The original surgical approach was leucotomy (bilateral prefrontal lobotomy), but as time went on, smaller and smaller operations were performed because of disabling personality changes. With stereotactic surgery there is less tissue damage between cortex and lesion. Surgery should not be recommended until all other approaches have failed and extensive consultations have been obtained. Although surgical procedures may relieve the anxiety, the compulsive behavior may remain.

Residential Therapies

Hospitalization may be indicated in severe cases when the compulsive disorder prevents the patient from functioning at work or at home. The behavior may be so severe that it disorganizes the household and prevents the patient from pursuing the daily demands of living. In addition, some behavioral therapies require the kind of supervision and constant intervention possible only in a hospital setting. However, hospitalization should be viewed as a last resort; whenever possible, dynamic psychotherapy or drug therapy is best pursued as the patient participates in his or her "normal" activities. Although hospitalization may provide temporary relief from anxiety, the return to the prior setting may renew the compulsive symptoms; therefore, the discharge planning must include inpatient or outpatient care.

Conclusion

Compulsive disorders require a combined approach involving the following factors:

1. Reduction of anxiety to allow relaxation of defenses in order to attempt new patterns of behavior. This can often be done more rapidly through drugs and desensitization used alone or in combination with psychotherapy.
2. Elaboration of the dynamic function of the symptoms and their origins, which will enable the patient to attempt some reorganization of his or her behavioral patterns in abandoning the compulsive symptoms.
3. Achievement of a secure and enhanced self-esteem to permit risk taking and abandonment of phobic and other distracting activities. A psychodynamic approach to this step is best, but behavior modification tactics can help.
4. In pursuing these steps, the therapist must take into account the possibility of genetic or constitutional factors yet to be clarified.

The goals and treatment plan for the compulsive disorders may be summarized as follows:

1. To discover and elucidate the basis for the excessive feelings of insecurity, which require absolute guarantees before action is pursued.
2. To demonstrate by repeated interpretation and encouragement that absolute guarantees are not necessary and only interfere with living. The therapist must actively assist in stimulating new adventures for the patient.
3. To help the patient acknowledge that anxiety is universal and omnipresent and cannot be permanently eliminated from life. This means abandoning attempts at perfection and superhuman performance and accepting one's humanness with its

limitations. It does not mean being mediocre, average, or without ambition; rather, this attitude allows one to utilize all of one's assets and potentialities.

Goals such as these are achieved through trust and intimacy that grow out of a relationship in which one person is trying sincerely to be useful to another. The therapeutic goals must be limited. A favorable outcome may involve the relief of anxiety, symptom amelioration, increase of productivity, behavioral change, or attitudinal change. These limited goals do not necessarily involve more superficial alteration, than psychoanalysts attempt to accomplish in psychoanalysis. The ambitiousness of therapeutic goals does not necessarily correspond with effectiveness. In recent years behavioral therapy has placed increased emphasis on cognitive factors while psychodynamic theory has become less restrained in adopting behavioral tactics. However, the goals may still differ despite the tendency in each modality to compromise long-term goals for short-term gains and vice versa.

Experience indicates that the various therapeutic models are supplementary and not mutually exclusive. A rational approach is to utilize various modalities because they reinforce the potential for change. The reduction of anxiety through drugs may enhance the psychotherapeutic potentialities, and the reduction of focus on rituals through behavior modification may allow clarification of the underlying psychodynamics. In less extreme cases, some compulsive rituals may be treated solely with behavior modification approaches, especially if phobic problems are present. In contrast, the more general compulsive characteristics such as perfectionism, doubting, procrastination, and indecisiveness are best reached by a psychotherapeutic approach. Lobotomy may be considered only if the patient's functioning is so totally disorganized that he or she does not have a moment's repose and only after a reasonable test in an inpatient setting with maximum utilization of behavior modification, drugs, and psychotherapy.

Patients need to know the limits of their therapists' capacities and understanding. False promises leading to false hopes, however sincere, can only result in dramatic failure and lead to the pursuit of metaphysical and magical therapies, which are themselves part of the disease process. Understanding of the compulsive disorder potentially requires an integration of psychodynamic, pharmacologic, and behavior therapies, because the resolution of the disabling disorder demands cognitive clarity plus behavioral and physiologic alterations. Each modality alone deals with only a piece of the puzzle. A therapist who can combine all these approaches will be the most effective.

Chapter 263

Passive-Aggressive Personality Disorder

Clinical Overview

Interest in the treatment of passive-aggressive personality disorder has always been greatest in settings where hierarchical relationships to authority are commonplace. It is no accident that this diagnosis was first described by military psychiatrists and then incorporated in the psychiatric nosology used by the Veterans Administration Hospitals following World War II (Whitman et al. 1954). This history highlights the context in which the central feature of the passive-aggressive disorder (i.e., resistance to demands for adequate performance) becomes most evident. More so than persons with many other disorders, passive-aggressive persons involve those around them in their distress and the effects of their occupational and social impairment. See Table 1 for the DSM-III-R diagnostic criteria for passive-aggressive personality disorder (American Psychiatric Association 1987).

The basic features of the diagnosis have remained similar throughout the three editions of the Diagnostic and Statistical Manual (American Psychiatric Association 1952, 1968, 1980). Therefore, it is possible to compare earlier and later treatment studies of the disorder. Unfortunately, clinical researchers have not made the most of this opportunity. There are two follow-up studies of treated patients (Small et al.

Table 1. DSM-III-R Diagnostic Criteria for Passive-Aggressive Personality Disorder

A pervasive pattern of passive resistance to demands for adequate social and occupational performance, beginning by early adulthood and present in a variety of contexts, as indicated by at least *five* of the following:

    (1) procrastinates, i.e., puts off things that need to be done so that deadlines are not met
    (2) becomes sulky, irritable, or argumentative when asked to do something he or she does not want to do
    (3) seems to work deliberately slowly or to do a bad job on tasks that he or she really does not want to do
    (4) protests, without justification, that others make unreasonable demands on him or her
    (5) avoids obligations by claiming to have "forgotten"
    (6) believes that he or she is doing a much better job than others think
    (7) resents useful suggestions from others concerning how he or she could be more productive
    (8) obstructs the efforts of others by failing to do his or her share of the work
    (9) unreasonably criticizes or scorns people in positions of authority

1970; Whitman et al. 1954), one controlled drug treatment study (Klein 1968; Klein et al. 1973), one case series report (Perry and Flannery 1982), and a series of anecdotal reviews of various treatment modalities (Burns and Epstein 1983; Malinow 1981b; Millon 1981; Prout and Platt 1983; Reich 1949; Stricker 1983; Vaillant and Perry 1985). There are no adequate controlled trials of specific treatments.

In this chapter, I will distill what these reports say about the presenting problems, associated disorders, treatment, and basic psychopathology of passive-aggressive personality disorder. I will also summarize current hypotheses regarding treatment. There is still a need for greater understanding of the factors that produce and maintain passive-aggressive personality, as well as for fresh ideas for its successful treatment. Systematic, controlled treatment studies can then proceed from a richer clinical base.

Presenting Complaints

In a study of 400 consecutive outpatients, Whitman et al. (1954) noted that the presenting symptoms in 62 patients with passive-aggressive personality were anxiety (41 percent), depression (25 percent), or psychophysiologic symptoms (11 percent). The initial visit was most often precipitated by a problem in the work setting involving some ambiguously defined duties that led the patient to have difficulties in the authority hierarchy. In a study of 100 hospitalized patients with passive-aggressive personality, Small et al. (1970) noted that 30 percent were experiencing depressive episodes and 18 percent were alcoholics. All patients had multiple somatic complaints.

Behaviors

The most salient aspect of the passive-aggressive patient's psychopathology is maladaptive behavior displayed in both work and interpersonal relationships. The patient develops covertly hostile but dependent relationships and commonly lacks adaptive, assertive social skills, especially in relationship to authority figures (Perry and Flannery 1982; Prout and Platt 1983). The problems may be complicated by the existence of a punishing relationship that the person is unable to leave (e.g., an abusive spouse or boss). Such a relationship inhibits the development of normal assertiveness, and to the degree that the patient's inability to seek less punishing relationships is emotionally based, he or she is considered masochistic (Millon 1981; Perry and Flannery 1982; Reich 1949). There is also a tendency to prolong periods of passive support although more active employment would be more remunerative (Stricker 1983). In these circumstances the patient's dependency and passivity are rewarded by unemployment or disability insurance, welfare, or parental support.

In the hospital setting, Small et al. (1970) noted that many passive-aggressive patients had frequent outbursts of anger and periods of tearfulness. On long-term follow-up, the patients Small et al. studied had become increasingly socially isolated, but there was only one suicide. In a study of 40 adolescents who attempted suicide, Crumley (1979) found only one individual with passive-aggressive personality but 22 with borderline personality. When passive-aggressive individuals do attempt suicide, however, the potential for lethal outcome is high, because they often make these attempts in isolated settings, use irreversible means, and make no subsequent effort to obtain help (Kiev 1976).

Cognitions

Certain cognitions or attitudes appear to serve an organizing role and are activated when the individual experiences needs, demands, or frustrations vis-à-vis others. The passive-aggressive person wishes to be passive and dependent (and believes he or she is entitled to be), letting others take care of his or her needs. The patient also wishes to avoid making decisions yet feels entitled to complain about the decisions of others. Furthermore, the patient believes that his or her own passive-aggressive behaviors are natural and reasonable. This perception of maladaptive behavior as ego-syntonic makes it difficult for the patient to accept the need to change.

A second set of beliefs surrounds self-expression, resentment, and the wish for revenge. The individual believes that direct self-expression will not result in a beneficial outcome and instead expects others to ignore, disappoint, or even punish him or her. Each failure reinforces an attitude of resentment. In the extreme, the individual construes the worst motives in others and sets up failures in order to confirm the belief that he or she is always victimized or treated unfairly. Given a resentful attitude, the person finds it difficult to believe that trying anything new could possibly be of benefit. Seeking to thwart others or to get revenge then serves as a substitute for seeking success. This results in the belief that it is important to resist others.

Affects, Psychodynamics, and the Functional Maintenance of Passive-Aggressive Behaviors

Reich (1949) hypothesized that the passive-aggressive individual (whom he termed masochistic) has experienced a deep disappointment in the parent (either an actual disappointment or a failure to satisfy the individual's need for love sufficiently). This results in an attitude of defiance and provocation toward the parent and significant others, including the therapist. The provocative behavior is intended to cause the other person to behave badly and be put in the wrong. Satisfaction results whenever the individual feels confirmed that the other person has wronged him or her.

According to Whitman et al. (1954), passive behavior results when the expression of aggression is inhibited by internal guilt or fear of external retaliation. Passive behavior may also result from an inability to act in ambiguously defined roles, such as at work. Although not noted by Whitman et al., the passive-aggressive individual often exploits role ambiguities to explain his or her failure to act. Hostility arises when the individual experiences dependent wishes or the external frustration of these wishes, because normal assertiveness is blocked. A sense of shame derived from cultural attitudes toward passivity further reinforces the individual's hostility.

Malinow (1981) suggested that the passive-aggressive individual externalizes an internal conflict over hostility and dependency and therefore sees others as frustrating his or her dependent needs. The person then reacts with superficial compliance but covertly hostile behavior. Depression and anxiety arise whenever the individual becomes aware of his or her own role in bringing about frustrations and failures. Because of an inability to tolerate and modulate these affects, the passive-aggressive person prefers to keep them out of awareness.

Several authors have noted that pessimism and expectation of failure are reinforced by the consequences of the passive-aggressive individual's behavior. Retaliation by others and failures in self-assertion and autonomy are experienced as self-fulfilling prophecies. Taking this as a source of bitter satisfaction, the person reinforces his or her own otherwise maladaptive behavior (Millon 1981; Perry and Flannery 1982; Prout and Platt 1983; Reich 1949). Further reinforcement is obtained by the pleasure taken from making others uncomfortable or from obtaining outright revenge, while covertly eluding being held directly responsible (Perry and Flannery 1982; Stricker 1983). This manner of indirectly expressing anger and disagreement may have been modeled for the patient in the early learning environment (Prout and Platt 1983). Passive and dependent behaviors may also continue because of lack of training or effective modeling in assertiveness skills (Burns and Epstein 1983; Perry and Flannery 1982; Prout and Platt 1983).

Psychotherapeutic Treatments

Problems Arising in Psychotherapy

The central problem arising in the psychotherapy of passive-aggressive personality is the negative transference to the therapist and the resistance to the requirements of the therapy. The negative transference is experienced as a desire to struggle to avoid giving in to the therapist's demands (i.e., the requirements of treatment) (Burns and Epstein 1983; Perry and Flannery 1982; Stricker 1983). Resistance is displayed by the following kinds of actions:

1. Being tardy
2. Missing sessions with or without excuses
3. Not paying the bill
4. Being silent for prolonged periods during sessions
5. Failing to complete agreed-upon therapeutic homework
6. Rationalizing failures to comply with treatment requirements
7. Responding to confrontation increasingly with feelings of shame, humiliation, resentment, and blame
8. Increasing passive resistance to the therapy and to change, including becoming oppositional and purposefully failing or becoming more symptomatic (negative therapeutic reaction)
9. Increasing the amount of help-rejecting complaining and anger over the therapist's failure to help
10. Talking about other types of treatments or scheduling consultations with other therapists without prior discussion

Helping the patient overcome his or her resistance to change and to the therapy is a prerequisite to making adaptive changes in the outside.

Because of these difficulties, the prognosis for treatment is poor and moderate, with a high dropout rate, especially in the early phase of treatment (Perry and Flannery 1982; Stricker 1983; Whitman et al. 1954). Nonetheless, Small et al. (1970) noted that on follow-up, patients who had supportive psychotherapy appeared to have good outcomes.

Psychodynamic Psychotherapy

Reich's (1949) recommended treatment included a therapeutic confrontation in response to the patient's interminable whining and complaining. Reich literally mimicked the patient's behavior and used the patient's reaction to this (laughter and embarrassment) in an alliance-building way to get beyond the patient's resistance to more productive exploration.

Malinow (1981) offered several suggestions for treatment. First, because resistance is present almost from the start of treatment, it may help to set guidelines initially to contain it, for example, by discussing prematurely dropping out and the possibility of returning to treatment after periods of cessation. Second, it is important to interpret resistance and negative transference from the start "as angry acts directed at the therapist in order to provoke a punishing response and ultimately defeat therapist and therapy" (Malinow 1981, p. 129). (See also Perry and Flannery 1982; Reich 1949; Stricker 1983.) Third, it is important to help the patient learn to tolerate and modulate hidden anxiety and depression, to verbalize these affects rather than let them remain vague. The deleterious effects of these affects can be bound up and mitigated at times through the use of symbols, for instance, by discussing fantasy and dreams. Also, the judicious use of minor tranquilizers and antidepressant medication may mitigate the patient's reaction to painful affects when an Axis I disorder supervenes.

Stricker (1983) noted that the passive-aggressive patient asks the therapist many questions. He suggested that the therapist try to return the responsibility to the patient by such replies as "What do you think?" and "What are your options?" This helps develop an attitude of self-examination and self-reliance while refusing to accept passivity. Stricker also suggested that as therapy progresses, the therapist should clarify the good feelings that go along with being dependent on others as well as the anger. In addition, both early relationships and the transference should be explored to discover how the patient's anger is blocked and then expressed in passive-aggressive behavior whenever dependent wishes are frustrated.

Behavior Therapy

Perry and Flannery (1982) selected assertiveness training as a behavioral treatment because passive-aggressive patients cover their lack of adaptive self-expression by using indirect, often hostile, self-expression. The form of the treatment is modified if the patient falls into one of the following categories. The first type of patient has a co-existing Axis I syndrome (such as dysthymia or an anxiety disorder) that may inhibit new learning. Adequate attention to this syndrome through relaxation training or psychotropic medication may facilitate the patient's ability to tolerate psychotherapy and to engage in learning that seemed too difficult or anxiety-provoking before.

The second type of patient (often called masochistic) has a punishing partner, commonly a spouse or boss, who inhibits the patient from trying more positive and assertive forms of self-expression. Attempting to induce the patient to leave the punishing relationship often heightens anxiety and leads to premature termination. Instead, the therapist should teach ways to increase physical and emotional safety and work on assertiveness issues that are not central to the punishing relationship. This helps build skills and increases self-confidence without provoking the partner to punish the patient for displaying new behavior. With increasing self-confidence and lessening fear of abandonment, the patient may eventually be able to leave the punishing relationship.

The third type of patient is resentful and vindictive. This patient offers the strongest resistance to any therapy technique and tries to thwart the therapist. It is helpful initially to focus the therapy on minor but solvable problems in self-expression, while limiting digressions and averting struggles over the patient's perceptions of events that happen to him or her. When discussing ways of expressing oneself (e.g., as part of role playing), the therapist should point out the ultimate aversive consequences of the patient's hostile or indirect expressions. If the patient does not cooperate with homework, part of the session could be devoted to homework or the length of the session could be decreased. It is important to discuss two dynamics with the patient: 1) the increasing resentment that occurs if the patient does not express himself or herself when the occasion arises and 2) how the patient views the therapist in the same way as the patient experienced his or her parent(s), so that agreeing to try a new behavior feels tantamount to "giving in." The therapist will need to clarify the patient's feelings and interpret this second dynamic repeatedly, as well as point out that the patient may choose a more constructive alternative to this repetition. Finally, if the patient brings the therapy to a stalemate, the therapist should suggest a therapeutic vacation or termination. This provides an incentive if the patient wishes to stay in treatment and avoids reinforcing the passive-aggressive pattern.

The fourth type of passive-aggressive patient has made an existential choice to remain in a difficult situation that may inhibit growth. An example is the individual who cares for a cantankerous, aging parent at home. Once the therapist has clarified the patient's options and determined that a fully informed, free choice has been made, therapy may proceed to help the person deal better with problems without challenging the basic choice.

Prout and Platt (1983) emphasized the value of role-playing techniques augmented by videotaping, feedback, and coaching to improve both the verbal and nonverbal (eye contact, tone of voice, etc.) components of assertive requests and replies. In lieu of struggling over the choice of the way to behave, they suggested that the patient add up what each particular response would cost emotionally and then compare the prices of new, adaptive responses and familiar passive-aggressive responses. This approach aids the patient's ability to solve problems.

Emphasizing a cognitive-behavioral approach, Burns and Epstein (1983) suggested that the therapist focus on discovering the patient's automatic thoughts and the habitual ways in which the patient sees the worst in everything and thereby reinforces his or her hostile reactions. The patient keeps a daily record of thoughts in response to problematic situations. Patient and therapist examine the thoughts for common errors that lead to negative outcomes (e.g., always forecasting disaster, disqualifying positive statements) and then discuss more rational responses. This is a helpful prelude to assertiveness training. Whenever resistance arises, the therapist should elicit negative feelings about the therapy and emphasize whenever possible by agreeing with something. In addition, uncovering negative, automatic thoughts should be followed by the above examination technique.

Group Psychotherapy

Anecdotal evidence suggests that passive-aggressive patients are likely to terminate group psychotherapy prematurely with the claim that it is not helpful. They do not ask for attention, help, or understanding in ways that generally elicit positive responses. The group leader must actively confront the group's tendencies to ignore these patients, blame them for their troubles, or collude with their passive, complaining stance. The likelihood of a positive outcome with group psychotherapy is not known.

Pharmacotherapy

Although several authors have suggested that Axis I syndromes which occur along with passive-aggressive personality disorder should at times be treated pharmacologically (Malinow 1981; Perry and Flannery 1982), only one study has examined the pharmacologic treatment of the personality disorder per se. Klein and associates (Klein 1968; Klein et al. 1973) compared the differential effects of chlorpromazine, imipramine, and placebo for various diagnostic groups, including patients with DSM-I passive-aggressive personality disorder. Although only 10 such patients were involved, they showed no placebo or active drug effects. This result suggests that current biologic treatments are unlikely to have any direct effect on distress or impairment that is attributable to the personality disorder, in the absence of an Axis I syndrome.

The clinician needs to keep in mind that individuals with passive-aggressive personality disorder are more likely than many patients to present difficulties concerning medication, including noncompliance, misuse, and, most serious, overdosing (Kiev 1976; Vaillant and Perry 1985). The clinician needs to weigh the advantages of medication against the likelihood of these problems and monitor the patient's condition and medication use closely whenever a medication is prescribed.

Conclusion

The prognosis for treatment of the patient with passive-aggressive personality disorder is guarded. Nonetheless, case reports and reviews suggest that both psychodynamic and behavioral psychotherapy can be successful in some cases. Although premature termination is common, there are some treatment techniques that can be used to improve social skills while dealing with the deeply ingrained resistance and desire to provoke the therapist that usually characterize this disorder. Further work describing actual treatments and generating clinical hypotheses for novel treatment would be useful prior to the design and execution of treatment trials.

References

Section 26
Personality Disorders

Abel TM: Shift in intermediary object-gradient during the course of psychotherapy. Am J Psychother 14:691–704, 1960

Abend S, Porder M, Willick: Borderline Patients, Psychoanalytic Perspectives. New York, International University Press, 1983

Abraham K: The influence of oral eroticism on character formation. Int J Psychoanal 6:247–258, 1924

Abraham K: Character-formation of the genital level of the libido, in Selected Papers of Karl Abraham. New York, Basic Books, 1927a

Abraham K: Contributions to the theory of the anal character, in Selected Papers of Karl Abraham. New York, Basic Books, 1927b

Abraham K: Selected Papers on Psychoanalysis (1921–25). London, Hogarth Press, 1949, pp 370–417

Abramson R: Lorazepam for narcissistic rage. J Operational Psychiatry 14:52–55, 1983

Abruzzi W: Blue Heaven Farms. Int J Addict 14(6):779–784, 1979

Ackerman N: Treating the Troubled Family. New York, Basic Books, 1966

Adler G: Helplessness in the helpers. Br J Med Psychol 45:315–326, 1972

Adler G: Hospital treatment of borderline patients. Am J Psychiatry 130:32–36, 1973

Adler G: Regression in psychotherapy: disruptive or therapeutic? Int J Psychoanal 3:252–264, 1974

Adler G: Hospital management of borderline patients and its relation to psychotherapy, in Borderline Personality Disorders: The Concept, the Syndrome, the Patient. Edited by Hartocollis P. New York, International Universities Press, 1977

Adler G: A treatment framework for adult patients with borderline and narcissistic personality disorders. Bull Menninger Clin 44:171–180, 1980

Adler G: Borderline Psychopathology and Its Treatment. New York, Jason Aronson, 1985

Akiskal HS: Subaffective disorders: dysthymic, cyclothymic and bipolar, II: disorders in the "borderline" realm. Psychiatr Clin North Am 4:26–46, 1981

Akiskal HS, Khani MK, Scott-Straus A: Cyclothymic temperamental disorders. Psychiatr Clin North Am 2:527–554, 1979

Albert H: Special aids to therapy with schizophrenics, in Treating Schizophrenic Patients. Edited by Stone MH. New York, McGraw Hill, 1983

Alden L, Safran J: Irrational beliefs and nonassertive behavior. Cognitive Therapy and Research 2:357–364, 1978

Alexander BK, Dibb GS: Interpersonal perceptions in addict families. Fam Process 16:17–28, 1977

Alexander JF, Abeles N: Dependency changes in psychotherapy as related to interpersonal relationships. J Consult Clin Psychol 32:685–689, 1968

Alexander JF, French TM: Psychoanalytic Therapy: Principles and Application. New York, Ronald Press, 1946

Alexander JF, Parsons B: Short-term behavioral intervention with delinquent families: impact on family process and recidivism. J Abnorm Psychol 8:219–225, 1973

Allyon T, Azrin N: The Token Economy. New York, Appleton, Century Crofts, 1968

Amado H, Lustman PJ: Attention deficit disorders persisting in adulthood: a review. Compr Psychiatry 23:300–314, 1982

American Psychiatric Association: Diagnostic and Statistical Manual of Mental Disorders, 1st ed. Washington, DC, American Psychiatric Association, 1952

American Psychiatric Association: Diagnostic and Statistical Manual of Mental Disorders, 2nd ed. Washington, DC, American Psychiatric Association, 1968

American Psychiatric Association: Diagnostic and Statistical Manual of Mental Disorders, 3rd ed. Washington, DC, American Psychiatric Association, 1980

American Psychiatric Association: Diagnostic and Statistical Manual of Mental Disorders, 3rd ed, revised. Washington, DC, American Psychiatric Association, 1987

Anderson CM: A psychoeducational program for families of patients with schizophrenia, in Family Therapy in Schizophrenia. Edited by McFarlane WR. New York, Guilford Press, 1983

Andrews G, Kiloh LG, Keho L: Asthenic personality, myth or reality? Aust N Z J Psychiatry 12:95–98, 1978

Andrews JDW: Psychotherapy with the hysterical personality: an interpersonal approach. Psychiatry 47:211–232, 1984

Andrulonis PA, Donnelly J, Glueck BC, et al: Preliminary data on ethosuximide and the episodic dyscontrol syndrome. Am J Psychiatry 137:1455–1456, 1980a

Andrulonis PA, Glueck BC, Stroebel CF, et al: Organic brain dysfunction and the borderline syndrome. Psychiatr Clin North Am 4:47–66, 1980b

Anthony EJ, Pollock GH: Parental Influences: In Health and Disease. Boston, Little, Brown, 1985

Aono T, Kaneko M, Numata Y, et al: Effects of amoxapine, a new antidepressant, on pseudoneurotic schizophrenia. Folia Psychiat Neurol Jap 35:115–121, 1981

Argyle M, Trower P, Bryant B: Explorations in the treatment of personality disorders and neuroses, by social skills training. Br J Med Psychol 47:63–72, 1974

Auchincloss E, Michaels R: Psychoanalytic theory of character, in Personality Disorders. Edited by Frosch J. Washington, DC, American Psychiatric Press, 1983

Bachrach LL: Young adult chronic patients: an analytical review of the literature. Hosp Community Psychiatry 33:189–197, 1982

Bach-y-Rita G, Lion JR, Climent CE, et al: Episodic dyscontrol: a study of 130 violent patients. Am J Psychiatry 127:1473–1478, 1971

Balint M: The Basic Fault: Therapeutic Aspects of Regression. London, Tavistock, 1968

Balint M, Ornstein PH, Balint E: Focal Psychotherapy. London, Tavistock, 1972

Bandura A: Principles of Behavior Modification. New York, Holt, Rinehart and Winston, 1969

Bar-Levav R: The psychotherapy of the hysterical character in a group, in Group and Family Therapy. Edited by Wolberg LR, Aronson ML. New York, Brunner/Mazel, 1981

Barlow DH: Behavior therapy: the next decade. Behav Therapy 11:315–328, 1980

Barnes RJ: Mesoridazine (Serentil) in personality disorders—a controlled trial in adolescent patients. Dis Nerv Syst, April 1977, pp 258–264

Battegay R: Grenzsituationen. Bern, Huber, 1981

Baudry F: The evolution of the concept of character in Freud's writings. J Am Psychoanal Assoc 31:3–31, 1983

Baxter L, Edell W, Gerner R, et al: Dexamethasone suppression test and Axis I diagnoses of inpatients with DSM-III borderline personality disorders. J Clin Psychiatry 45:150–153, 1984

Beck AT: Cognitive Therapy and Emotional Disorders. New York, International University Press, 1976

Beck AT, Rusch A, Shaw B, et al: Cognitive Therapy of Depression. New York, Guilford Press, 1979

Beech HR, Vaughan M: Behavioral Treatment of Obsessional States. New York, John Wiley and Sons, 1978

Bellack AS, Hersen M: Research and Practice in Social Skills Training. New York, Plenum Press, 1979

Bellack L: On some limitations of dyadic psychotherapy and the role of group modalities. Int J Group Psychother 30:7–21, 1980

Berkowitz DA: Selfobject needs and marital dysharmony. Psychoanal Rev 72:229–237, 1985

Berkowitz DA, Shapiro RL, Zinner J, et al: Family contributions to narcissistic disturbances in adolescents. 1:353–362, 1974a

Berkowitz DA, Shapiro RL, Zinner J, et al: Concurrent family treatment of narcissistic disorders in adolescence. Int J Psychoanal 3:371–396, 1974b

Berman E: The treatment of troubled couples, in Psychiatric Update, vol 2. Edited by Grinspoon L. Washington, DC, American Psychiatric Press, 1983, pp 215–227

Bernstein SB: Psychotherapy consultation in an inpatient setting. Hosp Community Psychiatry 31:829–834, 1980

Binder JL: Treatment of narcissistic problems in time-limited psychotherapy. Psychiatr Q 51:257–270, 1979

Bion W: Experience in Groups. New York, Basic Books, 1961

Bleuler E: Das Problem der Schizoidie und der Syntonie. Zietschr für die gesamte. Neur U Psych 78:373–399, 1922

Boesky D: Resistance and character theory: a reconsideration of the concept of character resistance. J Am Psychoanal Assoc 31(suppl):227–246, 1983

Bonime W: The pursuit of anxiety-laden areas in therapy of the schizoid patient. Psychiatry 22:239–244, 1959

Borriello JF: Group psychotherapy with acting-out patients: specific problems and techniques. Am J Psychother 33:521–530, 1979

Boszormenyi-Nagy I: Loyalty implications of the transference model in psychotherapy. Arch Gen Psychiatry 27:374–380, 1971

Bowen M: Family Therapy in Clinical Practice. New York, Jason Aronson, 1978

Brady JP: Social skills training for psychiatric patients, I. Am J Psychiatry 141:333–341, 1984

Brinkley JR, Beitman BD, Friedel RO: Low-dose neuroleptic regimens in the treatment of borderline patients. Arch Gen Psychiatry 36:319–326, 1979

Buie D, Adler G: The definitive treatment of the borderline personality. Int J Psychoanal 9:51–87, 1982

Burchard JD, Lane TW: Crime and delinquency, in International Handbook of Behavior Modification and Therapy. Edited by Bellack AS, Hersen M, Kazdin AE. New York, Plenum Press, 1982

Burns DD, Epstein N: Passive-aggressiveness: a cognitive-behavioral approach, in Passive-Aggressiveness Theory and Practice. New York, Brunner/Mazel, 1983

Burrel RH, Culpan RH: Use of bromazepam in obsessional phobic and related states. Curr Med Res Opin 2:430–436, 1974

Burstein A: Treatment of posttraumatic stress disorder with imipramine. Psychosomatics 25:681–687, 1984

Cantwell DP: Hyperactivity and antisocial behavior. J Child Psychol Psychiatry 17(1):252–262, 1978

Carney FL: Some recurring therapeutic issues in group psychotherapy with criminal patients. Am J Psychother 26:34–41, 1972

Carney FL: Inpatient treatment programs, in The Psychopath: A Comprehensive Study of Antisocial Disorders and Behaviors. Edited by Reid WH. New York, Brunner/Mazel, 1978

Carroll BJ, Greden JF, Feinberg M, et al: Neuroendocrine evaluation of depression in borderline patients. Psychiatr Clin North Am 4:89–98, 1981

Carson R: Self-fulfilling prophecy, maladaptive behavior, and psychotherapy, in Handbook of Interpersonal Psychotherapy. Edited by Anchin J, Kiesler D. New York, Pergamon Press, 1982, pp 64–77

Cashdan S: Interactional psychotherapy: using the relationship, in Handbook of Interpersonal Psychotherapy. Edited by Anchin J, Kiesler D. New York, Pergamon Press, 1982

Cass, DJ, Silvers FM, Abrams GM: Behavioral group treatment of hysterics. Arch Gen Psychiatry 26:42–50, 1972

Cautela JR: Covert Conditioning. New York, Pergamon Press, 1979

Chamberlain P, Patterson G, Reid J, et al: Observation of client resistance. Behav Therapy 15:144–155, 1984

Charney DS, Nelson C, Quinlan DM: Personality traits and disorder in depression. Am J Psychiatry 138:1601–1604, 1981

Chessick R: Intensive Psychotherapy of the Borderline Patient. New York, Jason Aronson, 1977

Chessick R: Intensive psychotherapy of a borderline patient. Arch Gen Psychiatry 39:413–419, 1982

Chessick R: Psychology of the Self and the Treatment of Narcissism. New York, Jason Aronson, 1985

Chodoff P: A re-examination of some aspects of conversion hysteria. Psychiatry 17:75–81, 1954

Chodoff P: Supervision of psychotherapy with videotape: pros and cons. Am J Psychiatry 128:7, 1972

Chodoff P: The diagnosis of hysteria: an overview. Am J Psychiatry 131:1073–1078, 1974

Chodoff P: Hysteria and women. Am J Psychiatry 139:545–551, 1982

Chodoff P, Lyons H: Hysteria: the hysterical personality and "hysterical" conversion. Am J Psychiatry 114:734–740, 1958

Cleckley HM: The Mask of Sanity, 1st ed. St. Louis, CV Mosby, 1941

Cloninger CR: Drug treatment of antisocial behavior, in Psychopharmacology, vol 1. Edited by Grahame-Smith DG, Hippius H, Winokur G. Amsterdam, Excerpta Medica, 1983

Colarusso CA, Nemiroff FA: Adult Development: A New Dimension in Psychodynamic Theory and Practice. New York, Plenum Press, 1981

Cole JO, Sunderland P: The drug treatment of borderline patients, in Psychiatry 1982, V, 1982, pp 456–470

Cowdry R, Gardner D: Pharmacotherapy of borderline personality disorder. Arch Gen Psychiatry 45:111–119, 1988

Crafoord C: Day hospital treatment for borderline patients: the institution as transitional object, in Borderline Personality Disorders: The Concept, the Syndrome, the Patient. Edited by Hartocollis P. New York, International Universities Press, 1977

Cramer Azima F: Group psychotherapy with personality disorders, in Comprehensive

Group Psychotherapy, 2nd ed. Edited by Kaplan HI, Sadock BJ. Baltimore, Williams and Wilkins, 1983

Crumley FE: Adolescent suicide attempts. JAMA 241:2404–2407, 1979

Curran J: Skills training as an approach to the treatment of heterosexual-social anxiety. Psychol Bull 84:140–157, 1977

Dahl G, Merskey DM: Clinical patterns in a behavior modification unit. Can J Psychiatry 26:460–463, 1981

Dalton P: Family treatment of an obsessive compulsive child. Fam Process 22:99–108, 1983

Davanloo H: Basic Principles and Techniques in Short-term Dynamic Psychotherapy. New York, Spectrum, 1978

Deutsch H: Some forms of emotional disturbance and their relationships to schizophrenia. Psychoanal Q 11:301–321, 1942

Dicks H: Marital Tensions. New York, Basic Books, 1967

Dies RR: Current practice in the training of group psychotherapists. Int J Group Psychother 30:169–185, 1980

Dies RR: Bridging the gap between research and practice in group psychotherapy, in Advances in Group Psychotherapy Monograph Series No. I. Edited by Dies RR, MacKenzie R. American Group Psychotherapy Association, 1983

Dorpat TL: A developmental perspective on character pathology. Compr Psychiatry 20:548–559, 1979

Durkin H: Analysis of character traits in group psychotherapy. Int J Group Psychother 1:133–143, 1951

Edelson M: Sociotherapy and Psychotherapy. Chicago, University of Chicago Press, 1970a

Edelson M: The Practice of Sociotherapy. New Haven, Conn, Yale University Press, 1970b

Eidelberg L: A schizoid patient. J Am Psychoanal Assoc 26:298–300, 1957

Elliot FA: Propranolol for the control of belligerent behavior following acute brain damage. Ann Neurol 1:489–491, 1977

Ellsworth RB: Characteristics of effective treatment milieus, in Principles and Practice of Milieu Therapy. Edited by Gunderson JG, Will OA, Mosher LR. New York, Jason Aronson, 1983

Endicott J, Spitzer RL, Fleiss JL, et al: The global assessment scale. Arch Gen Psychiatry 33:766–771, 1976

Epstein N: Social consequences of assertion, aggression, passive-aggression, and submission: situational and dispositional determinants. Behav Res Therapy 11:662–669, 1980

Erikson E: Childhood and Society. New York, W.W. Norton, 1950

Erikson EH: Growth and crises of the healthy personality, in Symposium on the Healthy Personality. Edited by Senn M. New York, Josiah Macy, Jr., Foundation, 1951

Erikson E: Freud, Biologist of the Mind: Beyond the Psychoanalytic Legend (quoted in Sulloway FJ). New York, Basic Books, 1979

Erlich HS: Growth opportunities in the hospital: intensive inpatient treatment of adolescents, in Psychiatric Treatment of Adolescents. Edited by Esman AH. New York, International Universities Press, 1983

Essen-Moller E: The concept of schizoidia. Monatschr für Psychiatrie und Neurologie 112:258–271, 1946

Eysenck H: A Model for Personality. Berlin, Springer-Verlag, 1981

Fairbairn WRD: An Object-Relations Theory of the Personality. New York, Basic Books, 1952, pp 3–27

Falloon FRH, Lindley P, MacDonald R, et al: Social skills training of outpatient groups. Br J Psychiatry 131:599–609, 1977

Faltus FJ: The positive effect of alprazolam in the treatment of three patients with borderline personality disorder. Am J Psychiatry 141:802–803, 1984

Farber L: The Ways of the Will. New York, Basic Books, 1966

Fehrenbach PA, Thelen MH: Assertive-skills training for inappropriately aggressive college males: effects on assertive and aggressive behaviors. J Behav Ther Exp Psychiatry 12:213–217, 1981

Fehrenbach PA, Thelen MH: Behavioral approaches to the treatment of aggressive disorders. Behav Modif 6:465–487, 1982

Fenichel O: The Psychoanalytical Theory of the Neurosis. New York, Norton and Company, 1945

Fine S: Family therapy and a behavioral approach to childhood obsessive-compulsive disorder. Arch Gen Psychiatry 28:695–697, 1973

Flannery RB Jr: Towards stress resistant persons: a stress management approach in the treatment of anxiety. Am J Prevent Med, 1986

Flannery RB Jr, Marlow N: Ethnicity in the behavioral treatment of a socially isolated adult. Psychother Theory Res Prac 15:237–240, 1978

Foa ER, Steketee G: Obsessive-compulsives: conceptual issues and treatment interventions, in Progress in Behavior Modification. Edited by Eisler RM, Herson M, Miller PM. Boston, Little, Brown and Company, 1979

Foy DW, Eisler RM, Pinkston S: Modeled assertion in a case of explosive rages. J Behav Ther Exp Psychiatry 67:135–137, 1975

Framo JL: Symptoms from a transactional point of view, in Family Therapy in Transition. Edited by Ackerman, Lieb, Pierce. Boston, Little, Brown and Company, 1970

Frances A: The DSM-III personality disorders section: a commentary. Am J Psychiatry 137:1050–1054, 1980

Frances A, Clarkin JF: No treatment as the prescription of choice. Arch Gen Psychiatry 38:542–545, 1981a

Frances A, Clarkin JF: Differential therapeutics: a guide to treatment selection. Hosp Community Psychiatry 32:537–546, 1981b

Frances A, Cooper A: Descriptive and dynamic psychiatry: a perspective on DSM-III. Am J Psychiatry 138:1198–1202, 1981

Frances A, Clarkin JF, Perry S: DSM-III and family therapy. Am J Psychoatry 141:406–409, 1984

Franco DP, Christoff KA, Crimmins DB, et al: Social skills training for an extremely shy young adolescent: an empirical case study. Behav Ther 14:568–575, 1983

Frank AF, Gunderson JG: Matching therapists and milieus: effects on engagement and continuance in psychotherapy. Psychiatry 47:201–211, 1984

Franks CM: Behavior therapy, the principles of conditioning, and the treatment of the alcoholic. Quart J Stud Alcohol 24:511–529, 1963

Frederiksen LW, Jenkins JO, Foy DW, et al: Social-skills training to modify abusive verbal outbursts in adults. J Appl Behav Anal 9:117–126, 1976

Freud S: On narcissism: an introduction (1914). Complete Psychological Works, Standard Edition, vol 14. London, Hogarth, 1976, pp 69–102

Freud S: General Introduction to Psychoanalysis. New York, Liveright, 1935

Freud S: The Ego and the Mechanisms of Defense. London, Hogarth, 1937

Freud S: On transformations of instinct as exemplified in anal eroticism, in Complete Psychological Works, Standard Edition, vol 17. London, Hogarth Press, 1955a

Freud S: Notes upon a case of obsessional neurosis, in Complete Psychological Works, Standard Edition, vol 10. London, Hogarth Press, 1955b

Freud S: On beginning the treatment: further recommendations on the technique of psychoanalysis (1913), in Complete Psychological Works, Standard Edition, vol 12. London, Hogarth Press, 1958

Freud S: Predisposition to obsessional neurosis, in Collected Papers, vol 2. New York, Basic Books, 1959a

Freud S: Character and anal eroticism (1908), in Complete Psychological Works, Standard Edition, vol 9. London, Hogarth Press, 1959b

Freud S: Inhibitions, Symptoms and Anxiety (1926), in Complete Psychological Works, Standard Edition. London, Hogarth Press, 1959c

Freud S: The ego and the id, in Complete Psychological Works, Standard Edition, vol 19. London, Hogarth Press, 1961

Fried E: The effects of combined therapy on the productivity of patients. Int J Group Psychother 4:42–55, 1954

Fried E: Techniques of group psychotherapy going beyond insight. Int J Group Psychother 11:297–304, 1961

Friedman HJ: Some problems of inpatient management with borderline patients. Am J Psychiatry 126:47–52, 1969

Friedman HJ: Psychotherapy of borderline patients: the influence of theory on technique. Am J Psychiatry 132:1048–1052, 1975

Fromm-Reichmann F: Principles of Intensive Psychotherapy. Chicago, University of Chicago Press, 1950

Frosch J: The psychotic character: clinical psychiatric considerations. Psychiatr Q 38:81–96, 1964

Frosch J: The Psychotic Process. New York, International University Press, 1983a

Frosch J: The psychosocial treatment of personality disorders, in Current Perspectives on Personality Disorders. Edited by Frosch J. Washington, DC, American Psychiatric Press, 1983b

Fuchs RM: Group therapy, in The Psychiatric Therapies. Edited by Karasu T. Washington, DC, American Psychiatric Association, 1984

Gambrill E: Development of effective social skills, in Behavior Modification. Edited by Gambrill E. San Francisco, Jossey-Bass, 1977

Garbutt JC, Loosen PT, Tipermas A, et al: The TRH test in patients with borderline personality disorder. Psychiatry Res 9:107–113, 1983

Gardner DL, Cowdry RW: Alprazolam-induced dyscontrol in borderline personality disorder. Am J Psychiatry 142:98–100, 1985

Gardner DL, Cowdry RW: Positive effects of carbamazepine on behavioral dyscontrol in borderline personality disorder. Am J Psychiatry 143:519–522, 1986

Gaviria M, Flaherty J, Val E: A comparison of bipolar patients with and without a borderline personality disorder. Psychiatr J Univ Ottawa 7:190–195, 1982

Gedo JE: A psychoanalyst reports at mid-career. Am J Psychiatry 136:646–649, 1979a

Gedo JE: Beyond Interpretation: Toward a Revised Theory for Psychoanalysis. New York, International Universities Press, 1979b

Gedo JE, Goldberg A: Models of the Mind. Chicago, University of Chicago Press, 1973

Gershon ES, Cromer M, Klerman GL: Hostility and depression. Psychiatry 31:224–235, 1968

Gift TF, Strauss JE, Young Y: Hysterical psychosis: an empirical approach. Am J Psychiatry 124:3, 1985

Giovacchini P: Character disorders: with special reference in the borderline state. Int J Psychoanal Psychotherapy 2:7–36, 1973

Glatzer HT: Aspects of transference in group psychotherapy. Int J Group Psychother 12:448–455, 1962

Glatzer HT: Handling narcissistic problems in group psychotherapy. Int J Group Psychother 15:167–176, 1965

Glover E: The Roots of Crime. New York, International Universities Press, 1960

Goldberg AJ: Psychotherapy of narcissistic injuries. Arch Gen Psychiatry 28:722–726, 1973

Goldberg S, Schulz S, Schulz P, et al: Borderline and schizotypal personality disorders treated with low-dose thiothixene versus placebo. Arch Gen Psychiatry 43:680–690, 1986

Goldman A: Reparative psychotherapy, in Changing Concepts of Psychoanalytic Medicine. Edited by Rado S, Daniels G. New York, Grune & Stratton, 1956

Gordon C, Beresin E: Conflicting treatment models for the inpatient management of borderline patients. Am J Psychiatry 140: 979–983, 1983

Gordon RA: A critique of the evaluation of Patuxent Institution, with particular attention to the issues of dangerousness and recidivism. Bull Am Acad Psychiatry Law 5:210–255, 1977

Gossett JT, Lewis JM, Barnhardt FD: To Find a Way: The Outcome of Hospital Treatment of Disturbed Adolescents. New York, Brunner/Mazel, 1983, pp 15–31; 135–158

Gottheil E, Stone GC: Factor analytic study of orality and anality. J Nerv Ment Dis 146:1–17, 1968

Gould E, Glick ID: Patient-staff judgments of treatment program helpfulness on a psychiatric ward. Br J Med Psychol 49:23–33, 1976

Gralnick A: Management of character disorders in a hospital setting. Am J Psychother 33:54–66, 1979

Green RS, Koprowski PF: The chronic patient with a nonpsychotic diagnosis. Hosp Community Psychiatry 32:479–481, 1981

Greenson RR: The Technique and Practice of Psychoanalysis, vol 1. New York, International Universities Press, 1967

Greenwald H: Treatment of the psychopath. Voices, Spring, 1967

Grinberg L, Rodriguez-Perez JF: The borderline patient and acting out, in Technical Factors in the Treatment of the Severely Disturbed Patient. Edited by Giovacchini PL, Bryce Boyer L. New York, Jason Aronson, 1982

Grobman J: The borderline patient in group psychotherapy: a case report. Int J Group Psychother 30:299–318, 1980

Grotjahn M: The narcissistic person in analytic group psychotherapy. Int J Group Psychother 34:243–257, 1984

Groves JE: Taking care of the hateful patient. N Engl J Med 298:883–887, 1978

Gruman A, Kniskern D (eds): Handbook of Family Therapy. New York, Brunner/Mazel, 1981

Grunebaum H, Glick ID: The basics of family treatment, in Psychiatry Update, vol 2. Edited by Grinspoon L. Washington, DC, American Psychiatric Association, 1983, pp 185–202

Grunebaum H, Kates W: Whom to refer to group psychotherapy. Am J Psychiatry 134:130–133, 1977

Gunderson, JG: DSM-III diagnoses of personality disorders, in Current Perspectives on Personality Disorders. Edited by Frosch JP. Washington, DC, American Psychiatric Association, 1983a

Gunderson JG: An overview of modern milieu therapy, in Principles and Practice of Milieu Therapy. Edited by Gunderson JG, Will OA, Mosher LR. New York, Jason Aronson, 1983b

Gunderson JG: Borderline Personality Disorder. Washington, DC, American Psychiatric Association, 1984

Gunderson JG: Pharmacotherapy for patients with borderline personality disorder. Arch Gen Psychiatry 43:698–700, 1986

Gunderson JG, Elliott GR: The interface between borderline personality disorder and affective disorder. Am J Psychiatry 142:277–288

Gunderson J, Pollock W: Conceptual risks of the Axis I-Axis II division, in Biological Response Styles: Psychological Implications. Edited by Klar H. Washington, DC, American Psychiatric Association, 1985

Gunderson J, Kerr J, Englund D: The families of borderlines: a comparative study. Arch Gen Psychiatry 37:27–33, 1980

Guntrip H: The manic-depressive problem in the light of the schizoid process. Int J Psychoanal 43:98–112, 1962

Gurman AS, Kniskern DP: Family therapy outcome research: knowns and unknowns, in Handbook of Family Therapy. Edited by Gurman AS, Kniskern DP. New York, Brunner/Mazel, 1981

Guze SB: Criminality and Psychiatric Disorders. New York, Oxford University Press, 1978

Hafner RJ: Behavior therapy for the neuroses: some conceptual and practical problems. Aust N Z J Psychiatry 15:287–300, 1981

Haley J: Problem Solving Therapy. San Francisco, Jossey-Bass, 1978

Haley J, Hoffman L: Techniques of Family Therapy. New York, Basic Books, 1967

Halleck SL: The Treatment of Emotional Disorders. New York, Jason Aronson, 1978

Harbin HT: A family-oriented psychiatric inpatient unit. Fam Process 18:281–291, 1979

Hartmann H: Ego Psychology and the Problem of Adaptation. New York, International Universities Press, 1939

Hartocollis P: Long-term hospital treatment for adult patients with borderline and narcissistic disorders. Bull Menninger Clin 44:212–226, 1980

Havens LL: Discussion: how long the Tower of Babel? Proc Am Psychopathol Assoc 64:62–73, 1976

Hayes SC, Brownell KD, Barlow DH: The use of self administered covert sensitization in the treatment of exhibitionism and sadism. Behav Ther 9:283–289, 1978

Hedberg DL, Houck JH, Glueck BC: Tranylcypromine-trifluoperazine combination in the treatment of schizophrenia. Am J Psychiatry 127:1141–1146, 1971

Henderson JQ: A behavioural approach to stealing. J Behav Ther Exp Psychiatry 12:231–236, 1981

Hersen M: Limitations and problems in the clinical applications of behavioral techniques in psychiatric settings. Behav Ther 10:65–80, 1979

Hersen M, Bellack A: Social skills training for chronic psychiatric patients: rationale, research findings, and future directions. Compr Psychiatry 17:559–580, 1976

Hill DEC: Outpatient management of passive-dependent women. Hosp Community Psychiatry 21:402–405, 1970

Hirschfeld RMA, Klerman GL, Gough HG, et al: A measure of interpersonal dependency. J Pers Assess 41:610–618, 1977

Hoffman PB: Patuxent Institution from a psychiatric perspective, circa 1977. Bull Am Acad Psychiatry Law 5:171–199, 1977

Hogben GL, Cornfield RB: Treatment of traumatic war neurosis with phenelzine. Arch Gen Psychiatry 38:440–445, 1981

Hollender MH: The hysterical personality. Contemporary Psychiatry 1:17–24, 1971

Hollender MH, Hirsch SJ: Hysterical psychosis. Am J Psychiatry 120:1066–1074, 1964

Horner JA: A characterological contraindication for group psychotherapy. J Am Acad Psychoanal 3:301–305, 1975

Horney K: Neurosis and Human Growth. New York, Norton and Company, 1950

Horowitz M: Structure and the processes of change, in Hysterical Personality. Edited by Horowitz MJ. New York, Jason Aronson, 1977, pp 329–399

Horowitz M, Marmar C, Krupnick J, et al: Personality Styles and Brief Psychotherapy. New York, Basic Books, 1984

Horwitz L: Group psychotherapy for borderline and narcissistic disorders. Bull Menninger Clin 44:181–200, 1980

Hussain MZ, Ahad A: Treatment of obsessive-compulsive neurosis. Can Med Assoc J 103:648–650, 1970

Hymowitz P, Frances AJ, Hoyt R, et al: Neuroleptic treatment of schizotypal personalities. Presented at 137th Annual Meeting of the American Psychiatric Association, 1984

Insel TR, Murphy DL: The psychopharmacological treatment of obsessive-compulsive disorder: a review. J Clin Psychopharmacol 1:304–311, 1984

Jackson DD: Guilt and the control of pleasure in schizoid personalities. Br J Med Psychol 31:124–130, 1958

Jackson J, Grotjahn M: The treatment of oral defenses by combined individual and group psychotherapy. Int J Group Psychother 8:373–381, 1958

Jaspers K: General Psychopathology. Translated by Hoenig J, Hamilton MW. Chicago, Chicago University Press, 1963

Jew CC, Clanon TL, Mattock AL: The effectiveness of group psychotherapy in a correctional institute. Am J Psychiatry 129:602–605, 1972

Johnson AM: Sanctions for superego lacunae of adolescents, in Searchlights on Delinquency. Edited by Eissler K. New York, International Universities Press, 1948

Johnson AM, Szurek SA: The genesis of antisocial acting out in children and adolescents. Psychoanal Q 21:323–343, 1952

Jones E: Hate and anal eroticism in the obsessional neurosis, in Papers of Psychoanalysis. Baltimore, Wood, 1923

Jones E: Papers on Psychoanalysis, 5th ed. London, Bailliere, Tindall, and Cox, 1948

Jones E: The Life and Work of Sigmund Freud, vol 2. New York, Basic Books, 1957

Jones FD, Stayer SJ, Wichlacz CR, et al: Contingency management of hospital diagnosed character and behavior disordered soldiers. J Behav Ther Exp Psychiatry 8:333, 1977

Jones MS: The Therapeutic Community—A New Treatment in Psychiatry. New York, Basic Books, 1953

Jones MS: The treatment of psychopathic personalities in a therapeutic community. Proc R Soc Lond 47:636–638, 1954

Jones MS: Therapeutic community as a system for change, in Principles and Practice of Milieu Therapy. Edited by Gunderson JG, Will OA, Mosher LR. New York, Jason Aronson, 1983

Julian A III, Kilman PR: Group therapy of juvenile delinquents: a review of the outcome literature. Int J Group Psychother 29:3–37, 1979

Kagan J, Moss H: The stability of passive and dependent behavior from childhood through adulthood. Child Dev 31:577–591, 1960

Karpman G: On the need for separating psychopathy into two distinct types: the symptomatic and the idiopathic. J Criminal Psychopathology 3:112, 1941

Kasanin J, Rosen ZA: Clinical variables in schizoid personalities. Archives on Neurology and Psychiatry 30:538–566, 1933

Kellam SG: Ward atmosphere, continuity of treatment, and the mental health system, in Principles and Practice of Milieu Therapy. Edited by Gunderson JG, Will OA, Mosher LR. New York, Jason Aronson, 1983

Kellner R: Drug treatment of personality disorders and delinquents, in The Psychopath: A Comprehensive Study of Antisocial Disorders and Behaviors. Edited by Reid WH. New York, Brunner/Mazel, 1978

Kellner R: Drug treatment of personality disorders, in The Treatment of Antisocial Syndromes. Edited by Reid WH. New York, Van Nostrand Reinhold, 1981

Kelly D, Guirguis W, Frommer E, et al: Treatment of phobic states with antidepressants. Br J Psychiatry 116: 387–398, 1970

Kemp KV: Hospitalization for personality disorders, in Personality Disorders Diagnosis and Management (revised for DSM-III), 2nd ed. Edited by Lion JR. Baltimore, Williams and Wilkins, 1981

Kernberg OF: The treatment of patients with borderline personality organization. Int J Psychoanal 49:600–619, 1968

Kernberg OF: Psychoanalytic object-relations theory, group processes and administration: toward an integrative theory of hospital treatment. The Annual of Psychoanalysis, vol 1, pp 363–388, 1973

Kernberg OF: Borderline Conditions and Pathological Narcissism. New York, Jason Aronson, 1975

Kernberg OF: Object-Relations Theory and Clinical Psychoanalysis. New York, Jason Aronson, 1976

Kernberg OF: The therapeutic community: a re-evaluation. NAPPH Journal 12:46–55, 1981

Kernberg OF: The theory of psychoanalytic psychotherapy, in Curative Factors in Dynamic Psychotherapy. Edited by Slip S. New York, McGraw Hill, 1982, pp 21–43

Kernberg OF: Problems in the classification of personality disorders, in Severe Personality Disorders. New Haven, Conn, Yale University Press, 1984a, pp 77–94

Kernberg OF: Severe Personality Disorders: Psychotherapeutic Strategies. New Haven, Conn, Yale University Press, 1984b

Kernberg OF, Burstein E, Coyne L, et al: Final report of the Menninger Foundation's Psychotherapy Research Project: psychotherapy and psychoanalysis. Bull Menninger Clin 34:1–2, 1972

Kety SS, Rosenthal D, Wender PH, et al: Mental illness in the biological and adoptive families of adopted schizophrenics, in Transmission of Schizophrenia. Edited by Rosenthal D, Kety SS. Oxford, Pergamon Press, 1968

Khan MMR: Clinical aspects of the schizoid personality, affects and technique. Int J Psychoanal 41:430–437, 1960

Khan MMR: Grudge and the hysteric. Int J Psychoan Psychother 4:349–357, 1975a

Khan MMR: Seminars on the "Psychoanalytic Models of the Mind." London, Institute of Psychoanalysis, 1975b

Kibel HD: The rationale for the use of group psychotherapy for borderline patients in a short-term unit. Int J Group Psychother 28:339–358, 1978

Kibel HD: The importance of the comprehensive clinical diagnosis for group psychotherapy of borderline and narcissistic patients. Int J Group Psychother 30:427–444, 1980

Kibel HD: A conceptual model for short-term model in patient group psychotherapy. Am J Psychiatry 138:74–80, 1981

Kibel HD, Stein A: The group-as-a-whole approach: an appraisal. Int J Group Psychother 31:409–429, 1981

Kiesler D: Interpersonal theory for personality and psychotherapy, in Handbook of Interpersonal Psychotherapy. Edited by Anchin J, Kiesler D. New York, Pergamon Press, 1982

Kiev A: Cluster analysis profiles of suicide attempters. Am J Psychiatry 133:150–153, 1976

Kiger R: Treating the psychopathic patient in a therapeutic community. Hosp Community Psychiatry 18:191–196, 1967

Kimball RO: Wilderness Experience Program: Final Evaluation Report. Santa Fe, NM, Health and Environment Department, 1979

Kirsch TB: Reflections on introversion and/or schizoid personality. J Anal Psychol 24:145–152, 1979

Klein DF: Delineation of two drug-responsive anxiety syndromes. Psychopharmacolog 5:397–408, 1964

Klein DF: Importance of psychiatric diagnosis in the prediction of clinical drug effects. Arch Gen Psychiatry 16:118–126, 1967

Klein DF: Psychiatric diagnosis and a typology of clinical drug effects. Psychopharmacology (Berlin) 13:359–386, 1968

Klein DF: Psychopharmacology and the borderline patient, in Borderline States in Psychiatry. Edited by Mack J. New York, Grune & Stratton, 1975, pp 75–92

Klein DF, Davis J: Drug Treatment and Psychodiagnosis. Baltimore, Williams and Wilkins, 1969

Klein DF, Honigfeld G, Feldman S: Prediction of drug effects in personality disorders. J Nerv Ment Dis 156:183–197, 1973

Klein DF, Gittelman R, Quitkin F, et al: Diagnosis and Drug Therapy of Psychiatric Disorders: Adults and Children, 20th ed. Baltimore, Williams and Wilkins, 1980

Klein M: Notes on some schizoid mechanisms. Int J Psychoanal 27:99–110, 1946

Kline P, Storey R: A factor analytic study of the oral character. Br J Soc Psychol 16:317–328, 1977

Knight R: Borderline states. Bull Menninger Clin 17:1–12, 1953

Kohon G: Reflections on Dora: the case of hysteria. Int J Psychoanal 651:73–84, 1984

Kohut H: The Analysis of the Self. New York, International Universities Press, 1971

Kohut H: The Restoration of the Self. New York, International Universities Press, 1977

Kohut H: The two analyses of Mr. Z. Int J Psychoanal 60:3–27, 1979

Kohut H: How Does Analysis Cure? Edited by Goldberg A, Stepansky PE. Chicago, University of Chicago Press, 1984

Kohut H, Wolfe E: The disorders of the self and their treatment. Int J Psychoanal 59:414–425, 1978

Kosseff J: The leader using object relations theory, in The Leader in the Group. Edited by Liff ZA. New York, Jason Aronson, 1975

Kraepelin E: Manic Depressive Insanity and Paranoia. Edinburgh, E & S Livingstone, 1921

Kretschmer E: Korperbau and Charackter. Berlin, J. Springer, 1921

Kretschmer E: Physique and character. New York, Harcourt, Brace, 1925

Kretschmer E: Physique and Character, 2nd ed. London, Routledge, 1936

Krupnick J, Horowitz M: Brief psychotherapy with vulnerable patients: an outcome assessment. Psychiatry 48:223–233, 1985

L'Abate L, Milan MA: Handbook of Social Skills Training and Research. Somerset, NJ, John Wiley and Sons, 1985

Lamb HR: Rehabilitation in community mental health. Community Mental Health Review 2:1–8, 1977

Langer TS, Michael ST: Life Stress and Mental Health. New York, Free Press of Glencoe, 1963

Laplanche J, Pontalis J: The Language of Psychoanalysis. New York, W.W. Norton and Company, 1973

Lauer J: The effect of tricyclic antidepressant compounds on patients with passive-dependent personality traits. Curr Ther Res 19:495–505, 1976

Lazare A, Klerman GL: Hysteria and depression: the frequency and significance of hysterical personality features in hospitalized depressed women. Am J Psychiatry 124:48–56, 1968

Lazare A, Klerman GL, Armor D: Oral, obsessive, and hysterical personality patterns:

an investigation of psychoanalytic concepts by means of factor analysis. Arch Gen Psychiatry 14:624–643, 1966

Lazare A, Klerman GL, Armor D: Oral, obsessive, and hysterical personality patterns: a replication of factor analysis in an independent sample. J Psychiatry Res 7:275–290, 1970

Lazarus LW: Brief psychotherapy of narcissistic disturbances. Psychotherapy: Theory, Research and Practice 19:228–236, 1982

Leaff LA: The antisocial personality: psychodynamic implications, in The Psychopath: A Comprehensive Study of Antisocial Disorders and Behaviors. Edited by Reid WH. New York, Brunner/Mazel, 1978

Leary T: Interpersonal Diagnosis of Personality. New York, Ronald Press, 1957

Leeman CP, Mulvey CH: Brief psychotherapy of the dependent personality: specific techniques. Psychother Psychosom 25:36–42, 1975

Leibovich M: Short-term psychotherapy for the borderline personality disorder. Psychother Psychosom 35:257–264, 1981

Leibovich M: Why short-term psychotherapy for borderlines? Psychother Psychosom 39:1–9, 1983

Lejins PB: The Patuxent experiment. Bull Am Acad Psychiatry Law 5:116–133, 1977

Leone N: Response of borderline patients to loxapine and clorpromazine. J Clin Psychiatry 43:148–150, 1982

Lerner B: Therapy in the Ghetto. Baltimore, Johns Hopkins University Press, 1972

Leszcz M: Inpatient groups, in American Psychiatric Association Update, V. Washington, DC, American Psychiatic Association, 1986

Leszcz M, Yalom ID, Norden M: In-patient group psychotherapy: patients' perspective. Int J Group Psychother 35:411–433, 1985

Levy J, Brown RD: The uncovering of projective identification in the treatment of the borderline adolescent. Int J Psychoanal 8:137–149, 1980

Lewis CE, Rice J, Helzer JE: Diagnostic interactions: alcoholism and antisocial personality. J Nerv Ment Dis 171:105–113, 1983

Liberman D: Interpretacion correlativa entre relato y repeticion: su applicacion en una paciente con personalidad esquizoido. Rev de Psicoan 14:55–62, 1957

Liberman RP: Behavior modification of schizophrenia. Schizophr Bull 1:37–48, 1972

Liberman RP: Research on the psychiatric milieu, in Principles and Practice of Milieu Therapy. Edited by Gunderson JG, Will OA, Mosher LR. New York, Jason Aronson, 1983

Liberman RP, Eckman T: Behavior therapy versus insight-oriented therapy for repeated suicide attempters. Arch Gen Psychiatry 38:1126–1130

Lidz T, Fleck S: Schizophrenia and the Family. New York, International Universities Press, 1965

Liebowitz JH, Rudy V, Gershon ES, et al: A pharmacogenetic case report: lithium-responsive postpsychotic antisocial behavior. Compr Psychiatry 17:655–660, 1976

Liebowitz MR: Is borderline a distinct entity? Schizophr Bull 5:23–38, 1979

Liebowitz MR: Psychopharmacological intervention in personality disorders, in Current Perspectives on Personality Disorders. Edited by Fosch JP. Washington, DC, American Psychiatric Association, 1983

Liebowitz MR, Klein DF: Hysteroid dysphoria. Psychiatr Clin North Am 2(3):555–575, 1979

Liebowitz MR, Klein DF: Interrelationship of hysteroid dysphoria and borderline personality disorder. Psychiatr Clin North Am 4:67–87, 1981

Liebowitz MR, Quitkin FM, Stewart JW, et al: Phenelzine versus imipramine in atypical depression: a preliminary report. Arch Gen Psychiatry 41:669–677, 1984

Liebowitz MR, Gorman JM, Fyer AJ, et al: Social phobia: review of a neglected anxiety disorder. Arch Gen Psychiatry 42:729–736, 1985

Liebowitz MR, Fyer AJ, Gorman JM, et al: Phenelzine in social phobia. J Clin Psychopharmacol 6:93–98, 1986

Linehan M: Dialectical behavior therapy: a cognitive behavioral approach to parasuicide. Journal of Personality Disorders 1:328–333, 1987a

Linehan M: Dialectical behavior therapy for borderline personality disorder: theory and method. Bull Menninger Clin 51:261–276, 1987b

Lion JR: The role of depression in the treatment of aggressive personality disorders. Am J Psychiatry 129:347–349, 1972

Lion JR, Bach y Rita G: Group psychotherapy with violent outpatients. Int J Group Psychother 20:185–191, 1970

Loewald H: On the therapeutic action of psychoanalysis. Int J Psychoanal 41:16–33, 1960

Luborsky L: Principles of Psychoanalytic Psychotherapy: A Manual for Supportive Expressive Treatment. New York, Basic Books, 1984

Luborsky L, Spence DP: Quantitative research on psychoanalytic psychotherapy, in Handbook of Psychotherapy and Behavior Change: An Empirical Analysis. Edited by Garfield SL, Bergin AE. New York, John Wiley and Sons, 1978

Luborsky L, Singer B, Luborsky L: Comparative studies of psychotherapies: is it true that "everyone has won and all must have prizes?" Arch Gen Psychiatry 32:995–1008, 1975

Luisada PV, Peele R, Pittard EA: The hysterical personality in men. Am J Psychiatry 131:518–521, 1974

Maas J: The use of actional procedures in group psychotherapy with sociopathic women. Int J Psychother 16:190–197, 1966

MacKinnon R, Michaels R: The Psychiatric Interview in Clinical Practice. Philadelphia, WB Saunders Company, 1971

Mahler MS, Pine F, Bergman A: The Psychological Birth of the Human Infant. New York, Basic Books, 1975

Malan DH: A Study of Brief Psychotherapy. New York, Plenum Press, 1963

Malan DH: The Frontier of Brief Psychotherapy: An Example of the Convergence of Research and Clinical Practice. New York, Plenum Press, 1976

Malan DH, Balfour FHG, Hood VG, et al: Group psychotherapy: a long-term follow-up study. Arch Gen Psychiatry 33:1303–1315, 1976

Malinow KL: Dependent personality, in Personality Disorders: Diagnosis and Management, 2nd ed. Edited by Lion JR. Baltimore, Williams and Wilkins, 1981a

Malinow KL: Passive-aggressive personality, in Personality Disorders: Diagnosis and Management, 2nd ed. Edited by Lion JR. Baltimore, Williams and Wilkins, 1981b

Maltsberger JT, Buie TH: Countertransference hate in the treatment of suicidal patients. Arch Gen Psychiatry 30:625–633, 1974

Mann J: Time-limited Psychotherapy. Cambridge, Mass, Harvard University Press, 1973

Mann J: Time limited psychotherapy, in Psychiatry Update, vol 3. Edited by Grinspoon L. Washington, DC, American Psychiatric Association, 1984

Marcus E: Use of the acute hospital unit in the early phase of long-term treatment of borderline psychotic patients. Psychiatr Clin North Am 4:133–144, 1981

Markowitz I: Respect, disrespect and the schizoid individual. Psychiatr Q 42:452–478, 1968

Marks IM: Review of behavioral psychotherapy, I: obsessive-compulsive disorders. Am J Psychiatry 138:5, 1981

Marks IM: Anxiety Disorders, in Treatment of Mental Disorders. Edited by Greist J, Jefferson J, Spitzer R. New York, Oxford University Press, 1982

Marmor J: Short-term dynamic psychotherapy. Am J Psychiatry 136:149–155, 1979

Marshall W: Modifications of sexual fantasies: combined treatment approach. Behav Res Ther 11:557–564, 1973

Marzillier JS: Outcome studies of skills training: a review, in Social Skills and Mental Health. Edited by Trower P, Bryant B, Argyle M. Pittsburgh, University of Pittsburgh Press, 1978

Marzillier JS, Lambert C, Kellett J: A controlled evaluation of systematic desensitization and social skills training for socially inadequate psychiatric patients. Behav Res Ther 14:225–238, 1976

Masterson J: Treatment of the Borderline Adolescent: A Developmental Approach. New York, John Wiley and Sons, 1972

Masterson J: Psychotherapy of the Borderline Adult. New York, Brunner/Mazel, 1976

Masterson J: The Narcissistic and Borderline Disorders. New York, Brunner/Mazel, 1981

Masterson J, Costello J: From Borderline Adolescent to Functioning Adult: The Test of Time. New York, Brunner/Mazel, 1980

Mattes JA: Carbamazepine for uncontrolled rage outbursts. Lancet 2:1164–1165, 1984

McGlashan TH: DSM-III schizophrenia and individual psychotherapy. J Nerv Ment Dis 170:752–757, 1982

McGlashan TH: Intensive individual psychotherapy of schizophrenia: a review of techniques. Arch Gen Psychiatry 40:909–920, 1983a

McGlashan TH: The borderline syndrome, II: is it a variant of schizophrenia or affective disorder? Arch Gen Psychiatry 40:1319–1323, 1983b

McGlashan TH: The prediction of outcome in borderline personality disorder: the Chestnut Lodge follow-up study, V, in The Borderline: Current Empirical Research. Edited by McGlashan TH. Washington, DC, American Psychiatric Association, 1985

McGlashan T: The Chestnut Lodge follow-up study, III: long-term outcome of borderline personalities. Arch Gen Psychiatry 43:20–30, 1986

McGlashan TH, Miller GH: The goals of psychoanalysis and psychoanalytic psychotherapy. Arch Gen Psychiatry 39:377–388, 1982

McLemore C, Benjamin L: Whatever happened to interpersonal diagnosis? a psychosocial alternative to DSM-III. Am Psychol 34:17–34, 1979

McLemore C, Hart P: Relational psychotherapy: the clinical facilitation of intimacy, in Handbook of Interpersonal Psychotherapy. Edited by Anchin J, Kiesler D. New York, Pergamon Press, 1982

McNamara E, Reynolds CF, Soloff PH, et al: EEG sleep evaluation of depression in borderline patients. Am J Psychiatry 141:182–186, 1984

Meehl PE: Schizotaxia, schizotypy, schizophrenia. Am Psychologist 17:827–838, 1962

Meichenbaum D: Cognitive-behavior Modification: An Integrative Approach. New York, Plenum Press, 1977

Meichenbaum D, Cameron R: Cognitive behavior therapy, in Contemporary Behavior Therapy. Edited by Wilson G, Franks C. New York, Guilford Press, 1982

Meissner WW: The Paranoid Process. New York, Jason Aronson, 1978

Mellsop G, Varghese F, Joshua S, et al: The reliability of Axis II of DSM-III. Am J Psychiatry 139:1360–1361, 1982

Miller AA, Pollock GH, Bernstein H, et al: An approach to the concept of identification. Bull Menninger Clin 32:239–252, 1968

Millon T (ed): Disorders of Personality: DSM-III Axis II. New York, John Wiley and Sons, 1981a

Millon T: Dependent personality disorder, in Disorders of Personality: DSM-III Axis II. Edited by Millon T. New York, John Wiley and Sons, 1981b

Millon T: Disorders of Personality. New York, John Wiley and Sons, 1982

Minuchin S: Families and Family Therapy. Cambridge, Mass, Harvard University Press, 1974

Minuchin S, et al: Psychosomatic Families. Cambridge, Mass, Harvard University Press, 1978

Modell AH: A narcissistic defense against affects and the illusion of self-sufficiency. Int J Psychoanal 56:275–282, 1975

Modell AH: The holding environment and the therapeutic action of psychoanalysis. J Am Psychoanal Assoc 24:285–308, 1976

Modell AH: The narcissistic character and disturbances in the "holding environment," in The Course of Life: Psychoanalytic Contributions toward Understanding Personality Development, vol 3: Adulthood and the Aging Process. Edited by Greenspan SI, Pollock GH. Washington, DC, US Government Printing Office, 1981

Monroe RR: The compulsive in phenomenology of will and action, in Nervous and Mental Diseases. Edited by Strauss EW, Griffith RM. New York, 1948

Montgomery J: Treatment management of passive-dependent behavior. Int J Soc Psychiatry 17:311–319, 1971

Mosher LR, Gunderson JG: Group, family milieu and community-support-systems treatment for schizophrenia, in Disorders of the Schizophrenic Syndrome. Edited by Bellak L. New York, Basic Books, 1979

Moss GR, Rick GR: Overview: applications of operant technology to behavioral disorders of adolescents. Am J Psychiatry 138:1161–1169, 1981

Nagera H: Obsessional Neurosis: Developmental Psychopathology. New York, Jason Aronson, 1983

Nemiah JC: Obsessive-compulsive neurosis, in A Comprehensive Textbook of Psychiatry. Edited by Freedman AM, Kaplan H, Sadock B. Baltimore, Williams and Wilkins, 1980

Nemiroff RA, Colarusso CA: The Race Against Time: Psychotherapy and Psychoanalysis in the Second Half of Life. New York, Plenum Press, 1985

Nies A, Howard D, Robinson DS: Antianxiety effects of MAO inhibitors, in The Biology of Anxiety. Edited by Mathew RJ. New York, Brunner/Mazel, 1982

Noshpitz JD: Notes on the theory of residential treatment, in The Psychiatric Treatment of Adolescents. Edited by Esman AH. New York, International Universities Press, 1983

Novaco RW: The cognitive regulation of anger and stress, in Cognitive-behavioral Interventions: Theory, Research, and Procedures. Edited by Kendall PC, Hollons SD. New York, Academic Press, 1979

Offenkrantz W, Tobin A: Psychoanalytic psychotherapy. Arch Gen Psychiatry 30:593–606, 1974

O'Leary KD, Turkewitz H: Marital therapy from a behavioral perspective, in Marriage and Marital Therapy. Edited by Paolino TJ, McCrady BS. New York, Brunner/Mazel, 1978

Ollendick TH, Elliott W, Matson JL: Locus of control as related to effectiveness in a behavior modification program for juvenile delinquents. J Behav Ther Exp Psychiatry 11:259–262, 1980

Ormont L, Strean H: The Practice of Conjoint Therapy. New York, Human Sciences Press, 1978

Pacific Crest Outward Bound School: Informational materials available from 0110 S.W. Bancroft Street, Portland, OR 97201. Spring-Summer, 1985

Papajohn JC: Intensive Behavior Therapy. New York, Pergamon Press, 1982

Parloff MB, Dies RR: Group psychotherapy outcome research, 1966–1975. Int J Group Psychother 27:281–319, 1977

Parsons BV, Alexander JF: Short-term family intervention: a therapy outcome study. J Consult Clin Psychol 41:195–201, 1973

Paul GL: Comprehensive psychosocial treatment, in The Psychotherapy of Schizophrenia. Edited by Strauss JS, Bowers M, et al. New York, Plenum Medical Press, 1980, pp 167–179

Perry JC: Depression in borderline personality disorder: lifetime prevalence at interview and longitudinal course of symptoms. Am J Psychiatry 142:15–21, 1985

Perry JC, Flannery RB: Passive-aggressive personality disorder: treatment implications of a clinical typology. J Nerv Ment Dis 170:164–173, 1982

Person E: Psychoanalytic treatment of antisocial personality, in Unmasking the Psychopath. Edited by Reid WH, Dorr D, Walker J, et al. New York, WW Norton, 1986

Petti TA, Unis A: Imipramine treatment of borderline children: case reports with a controlled study. Am J Psychiatry 138:515–518, 1981

Pfohl B, Stangl D, Zimmerman M: Increasing Axis II reliability. Am J Psychiatry 140:270–271, 1983

Pilkonis P: Avoidant and schizoid personality disorders, in Comprehensive Handbook of Psychopathology. Edited by Adams H, Sutker P. New York, Plenum Press, 1984

Pilkonis PA, Imber SD, Lewis P, et al: A comparative outcome study of individual, group and conjoint psychotherapy. Arch Gen Psychiatry 41:431–437, 1984

Pines M: Group therapy with difficult patients, in Group Therapy 1975, An Overview. Edited by Wolberg LR, Aronson ML. New York, Stratton Intercontinental Medical Book Company, 1975

Piper WE, Debbane EG, Bienvenu J, et al: Relationship between the object focus of therapist interpretations and outcome in short-term individual psychotherapy. Br J Med Psychol 59:1–11, 1986

Pollock GH: Mourning and adaptation. Int J Psychoanal 42:341–361, 1961

Pollock GH: Aging or aged: development or pathology, in The Course of Life: Psychoanalytic Contributions Toward Understanding Personality Development, vol 3: Adulthood and the Aging Process. Edited by Greenspan SI, Pollock GH. Washington, DC, US Government Printing Office, 1980

Pollock GH: Reminiscences and insight. Psychoanal Study Child 36:279–287, 1981

Pope HG, Hudson JI, Jonas JM, et al: Bulimic treated with imipramine: a placebo controlled, double blind study. Am J Psychiatry 140:554–558, 1983a

Pope HG, Jonas J, Hudson J, et al: The validity of DSM-III borderline personality disorder. Arch Gen Psychiatry 40:23–30, 1983b

Porter K: Combined individual and group psychotherapy: a review of the literature 1965–1978. Int J Group Psychother 30:107–114, 1980

Presley AS, Walton HJ: Dimensions of abnormal personality. Br J Psychiatry 122:269–276, 1973

Prout MF, Platt JJ: The development and maintenance of passive-aggressiveness: the behavioral approach, in Passive-Aggressiveness Theory and Practice. Edited by Parsons RD, Wicks RJ. New York, Brunner/Mazel, 1983

Quitkin FM, Klein DF: Follow-up of treatment failure: psychosis and character disorder. Am J Psychiatry 124:499–505, 1967

Quitkin FM, Rifkin A, Klein DF: Neurologic soft signs in schizophrenia and character disorders: organicity in schizophrenia with premorbid asociality and emotionally unstable character disorders. Arch Gen Psychiatry 33:845–853, 1976

Rachman S, Hodgson R, Marks IM: Treatment of chronic obsessive-compulsive neurosis. Behav Res Ther 9:237–247, 1971

Rado S: The Psychoanalysis of Behavior. New York, Grune & Stratton, 1956

Rado S: Adaptational Psychodynamics. New York, Science House, 1969

Rahim S, LeFebvre C, Jenkins JO: The effects of social skills training on behavioral and cognitive components of anger management. J Behav Ther Exp Psychiatry 11:3–8, 1980

Rainer D: Heredity and character disorders. Am J Psychother 33:6–16, 1979

Rako S, Mazer H (eds): Semrad: The Heart of a Therapist. New York, Jason Aronson, 1980

Ratey JJ, Morrill R, Oxenkrug G: Use of propranolol for provoked and unprovoked episodes of rage. Am J Psychiatry 140:1356–1357, 1983

Reich W: Character Analysis, 3rd ed. New York, Farrar, Strauss, Giroux, 1949

Reichard S: A re-examination of studies in hysteria. Psychoanal Q 25:155–177, 1956

Reid WH: The sadness of the psychopath. Am J Psychother 32:496–509, 1978

Reid WH: The anti-social personality and related symptoms, in Personality Disorders, Diagnosis and Management, 2nd ed. Edited by Lion JR. Baltimore, Williams and Wilkins, 1981

Reid WH, Matthews: A wilderness experience treatment program for antisocial offenders. Int J Offender Therapy and Comparative Criminology 24:171–178, 1980

Reid WH, Solomon GF: Community-based offender programs, in The Treatment of Antisocial Syndromes. Edited by Reid WH. New York, Van Nostrand Reinhold, 1981

Reyntjens AM: A series of multicentric pilot trials with pimozide in psychiatric practice, I: pimozide in the treatment of personality disorders. Acta Psychiatr Belg 72:653–661, 1972

Rifkin A, Quitkin F, Carrillo C, et al: Lithium carbonate in emotionally unstable character disorder. Arch Gen Psychiatry 27:519–523, 1972

Rinsley D: Intensive residential treatment of the adolescent. Psychiatr Q 41:134–143, 1967

Rinsley D: Theory and practice of intensive residential treatment of adolescents. Adolesc Psychiatry 1:479–509, 1971

Rinsley D: Borderline and Other Self Disorders. New York, Jason Aronson, 1982

Rioch MJ: The work of Wilfred Bion on groups. Psychiatry 33:56–66, 1970

Robins LN: Sturdy childhood predictors of adult antisocial behavior: replications from longitudinal studies. Psychol Med 8:611–622, 1978

Robins LN, Helzer JE, Weissman MM, et al: Lifetime prevalence of specific psychiatric disorders in three sites. Arch Gen Psychiatry 41:949–958, 1984

Robinson DS, Kayser A, Corrella J, et al: Hyperphagia, hypersomnia, panic attacks, hysterical traits, and somatic anxiety predict phenelzine response in depressed outpatients. Presented at the annual meeting of the American College of Neuropharmacology, San Juan, Puerto Rico, Dec 13, 1983

Rosen LW, Thomas MA: Treatment technique for chronic wrist cutters. J Behav Ther Exp Psychiatry 15:33–36, 1984

Rosenbaum JF, Woods SW, Groves JE, et al: Emergence of hostility during alprazolam treatment. Am J Psychiatry 141:792–793, 1984

Rosenfeld H: On the treatment of psychotic states by psychoanalysis. Int J Psychoanal 50:615–631, 1969

Rosenheim E, Gaoni B: Defensive passivity in adolescence. Adolescence 12:449–459, 1977

Roth BE: Understanding the development of a homogeneous, identity impaired group through countertransference phenomena. Int J Group Psychother 30:405–426, 1980

Roth BF: Six types of borderline and narcissistic patients: an initial typology. Int J Group Psychother 32:9–27, 1982

Rush AJ: Cognitive therapy, in Psychiatry Update, vol 3. Edited by Grinspoon L. Washington, DC, American Psychiatric Press, 1984, pp 44–55

Rush AJ: The therapeutic alliance in short term directive therapies, in American

Psychiatric Association Annual Review, vol 4. Edited by Hales RE, Frances AJ. Washington, DC, American Psychiatric Press, 1985

Rutan JS, Alonso A: Group therapy, individual or both? Int J Group Psychother 32:267–283, 1982

Sadoff RL, Collins DJ: Passive dependency in stutterers. Am J Psychiatry 124:1126–1127, 1968

Salzman L: Treatment of the Obsessive Personality. New York, Jason Aronson, 1980

Samenow SE: Treating the antisocial: confrontation or provocation. Transactional Analysis Journal 10:247–251, 1980

Sarwer-Foner GJ, Kealey LS: Reactions to hospitalization: passive dependency factors—recurrence of original symptoms and attempts to prolong hospitalization on the announcement of discharge. Compr Psychiatry 22:103–113, 1981

Satterfield JH, Cantwell DP: Psychopharmacology in the prevention of antisocial and delinquent behavior. Int J of Mental Health 4:227–337, 1975

Satterfield JH, Cantwell DP, Satterfield BT: The pathophysiology of the hyperkinetic syndrome. Arch Gen Psychiatry 31:839–844, 1974

Saul LJ, Warner SL: Mobilizing ego strengths. Int J Psychoanalysis 4:358–386, 1975

Schafer R: Character, ego syntonicity and character change. J Am Psychoanal Assoc 27:867–892, 1979

Scharff DE: The inpatient treatment of a borderline personality disorder. Psychiatric Opinion 6:37–43, 1969

Schatzberg AF, Cole JO: Benzodiazepines in the treatment of depressive, borderline personality and schizophrenic disorders. Br J Clin Pharmacol 11:17S–22S, 1981

Scheidlinger S, Holden MA: Group therapy of women with severe character disorders. Int J Group Psychother 16:173–189, 1966

Schlessinger N, Robbins FP: A Developmental View of the Psychoanalytic Process: Follow-up Studies and Their Consequences. New York, International Universities Press, 1983

Schneider K: Die psychopathischen Personlichkeiten, in Aschaffenburg's Hanbuch. Leipzig, 1923

Schneider K: Clinical Psychopathology. New York, Grune & Stratton, 1959

Schulz CG: Chestnut Lodge symposium: the struggle toward ambivalence. Psychiatry 47:28–36, 1984

Schwartzman G: The use of the group as self-object. Int J Group Psychother 34:229–242, 1984

Schwoeri L, Schwoeri F: Family therapy of borderline patients: diagnostic and treatment issues. Int J Fam Psychiatry 2:237–250, 1981

Searles HF: Collected Papers on Schizophrenia and Related Subjects. New York, International Universities Press, 1965

Searles HF: Countertransference and Related Subjects of Selected Papers. New York, International Universities Press, 1979

Serban G, Siegel S: Response of borderline and schizotypal patients to small doses of thiothixene and haloperidol. Am J Psychiatry 141:1455–1458, 1984

Shader RI, Jackson AH, Dodes LM: The antiaggressive effects of lithium in man. Psychopharmacology 40:17–24, 1974

Shamsie SJ: Antisocial adolescents: our treatments do not work—where do we go from here? Can J Psychiatry 26:357–364, 1981

Shapiro D: Neurotic Styles. New York, Basic Books, 1965

Shapiro ER: Research on family dynamics: clinical implications for the family of the borderline adolescent. Adolesc Psychiatry 6:360–376, 1978a

Shapiro ER: The psychodynamics and developmental psychology of the borderline patient: a review of the literature. Am J Psychiatry 135:1305–1315, 1978b

Shapiro ER: The holding environment and family therapy for acting out adolescents. Int J Psychoanal 9:209–226, 1982a

Shapiro ER: On curiosity: intrapsychic and interpersonal boundary formation in family life. Int J Family Psychiatry 3:69–89, 1982b

Shapiro ER, Zinner J, Shapiro R, et al: The influence of family experience on borderline personality development. Int Review of Psychoanalysis 2:399–411, 1975

Shapiro ER, Shapiro RL, Zinner J, et al: The borderline ego and the working alliance: indications for family and individual treatment in adolescence. Int J Psychoanal 58:77–87, 1977

Shapiro RL: Adolescence and the psychology of the ego. Psychiatry 26:77–87, 1963

Shapiro RL: Action and family interaction in adolescence, in Science and Psychoanalysis. Edited by Marmor J. New York, Grune & Stratton, 1968

Shapiro RL: The adolescent, the therapist and the family: the management of external resistances to psychoanalytic therapy of adolescents. J Adolesc 1:3–10, 1978

Shapiro RL, Zinner J: Family organization and adolescent development, in Task and Organization. Edited by Miller E. London, Tavistock Publications, 1971

Shaw P: A comparison of three behavior therapies in the treatment of social phobia. Br J Psychiatry 134:620–623, 1979

Shear HB: An overview of the Contract Research Corporation evaluation of Patuxent Institution. Bull Acad Psychiatry Law 5:134–143, 1977

Sheard MH: Lithium in the treatment of aggression. J Nerv Ment Dis 16:108–118, 1975

Sheard MH, Marini JL, Bridges CI, et al: The effect of lithium on impulsive aggressive behavior in man. Am J Psychiatry 133:1409–1413, 1976

Sheehan DV, Ballenger J, Jacobsen G: Treatment of endogenous anxiety with phobic, hysterical, and hypochrondriacal symptoms. Arch Gen Psychiatry 37:51–59, 1980

Sheidlinger S, Porter K: Group therapy combined with individual psychotherapy, in Special Techniques in Individual Psychotherapy. Edited by Karasu T, Bellah L. New York, Brunner/Mazel, 1980

Sifneos PE: Short-Term Psychotherapy and Emotional Crisis. Cambridge, Mass, Harvard University Press, 1972

Sifneos PE: Short-term anxiety producing psychotherapy, in Psychiatry Update, vol 3. Edited by Grinspoon, L. Washington, DC, American Psychiatric Association, 1984a, pp 24–33

Sifneos PE: The current status of short-term dynamic psychotherapy and its future: an overview. Am J Psychother 38:472–487, 1984b

Silver D: Psychotherapy of the characterologically difficult patient. Can J Psychiatry 28:513–521, 1983

Skinner BF, Lindsley OR: Studies in behavior therapy, status reports II and III. Office of Naval Research Contract N5 ori-7762, 1954

Skynner ACR: Systems of Family and Marital Psychotherapy. New York, Brunner/Mazel, 1976

Slavson SR: Dynamics of Group Psychotherapy. New York, Jason Aronson, 1939

Sloan RB, Staples FR, Cristol AH, et al: Psychotherapy Versus Behavior Therapy. Cambridge, Mass, Harvard University Press, 1975

Small IF, Small JG, Alig VB, et al: Passive-aggressive personality disorder: a search for a syndrome. Am J Psychiatry 126:973–983, 1970

Smith RR, Jenkins WO, Petko CM, et al: An experimental application and evaluation of rational behavior therapy in a work release setting. J Counseling Psychology 26:519–525, 1979

Soloff PH: Pharmacotherapy of borderline disorders: Compr Psychiatry 22:535–543, 1981

Soloff PH, George A, Nathan RS, et al: Progress in pharmacotherapy of borderline disorders. Arch Gen Psychiatry 43:691–697, 1986

Spence SH, Marzillier JS: Social skills training with adolescent male offenders, I: short-term effects. Behav Res Therapy 17:7–16, 1979

Spence SH, Marzillier JS: Social skills training with adolescent offenders, II: short-term, long-term, and generalized effects. Behav Res Therapy 19: 349–368, 1981

Spotnitz H: The borderline schizophrenic in group psychotherapy. Int J Group Psychother 7:155–174, 1975

Steinglass P, Davis DI, Berenson D: Observations of conjointly hospitalized "alcoholic couples" during sobriety and intoxication: implications for theory and therapy. Fam Process 16:1–16, 1976

Stewart JW, Walsh BT, Wright L, et al: An open trial of MAO inhibitors in bulimia. J Clin Psychiatry 45:217–219, 1984

Stone MH: A psychoanalytic approach to abnormalities of temperament. Am J Psychother 33:263–280, 1979a

Stone MH: Contemporary shift of the borderline concept from a subschizophrenic disorder to a subaffective disorder. Psychiatr Clin North Am 2:577–594, 1979b

Stone MH: Psychotherapy with borderline schizophrenic patients. J Am Acad Psychoanal 11:87–111, 1983a

Stone MH: Treating Schizophrenic Patients. New York, McGraw Hill, 1983b

Stone MH, Weissman R: Group therapy with borderline patients, in Contemporary Perspectives in Group Psychotherapy. Edited by Slavinska-Holy N. London, Routledge and Kegan Paul, 1984

Stone M, Hurt S, Stone D: The PI 500: Long-term follow-up of borderline inpatients meeting DSM III criteria, I: global outcome. J. Personality Dis 1:291–298, 1987

Stone WN, Gustafson JP: Technique and group psychotherapy of narcissistic and borderline patients. Int J Group Psychother 32:29–42, 1982

Stone WN, Rutan JS: Duration of treatment in group psychotherapy. Int J Group Psychother 34:93–111, 1984

Stone WN, Whitman RM: Observation and empathy in group psychotherapy, in Group and Family Therapy, 1980. Edited by Wolberg LR, Aronson ML. New York, Brunner/Mazel, 1980

Stravynski A, Shahar A: The treatment of social dysfunction in nonpsychotic outpatients: a review. J Nerv Ment Dis 171:721–728, 1983

Stravynski A, Marks IM, Yule W: Social skills problem in neurotic outpatients. Arch Gen Psychiatry 39:1378–1383, 1982

Stricker G: Passive-aggressiveness: a condition especially suited to the psychodynamic approach, in Passive-Aggressive Theory and Practice. Edited by Parsons RD, Wicks RJ. New York, Brunner/Mazel, 1983

Stringer AY, Josef NC: Methylphenidate in the treatment of aggression in two patients with antisocial personality disorder. Am J Psychiatry 140:1365–1366, 1983

Strupp HH, Binder JL: Psychotherapy in a New Key: A Guide to Time-limited Dynamic Psychotherapy. New York, Basic Books, 1984

Sturup GK: Treating the "Untreatable": Chronic Criminals at Herstedvester. Baltimore, Johns Hopkins University Press, 1968

Sturup GK: Changing patterns of treatment in Herstedvester: forensic psychiatric considerations in retrospect and prospect. Bull Am Acad Psychiatry Law 6:176–194, 1978

Sullivan HS: The illusion of personal individuality. Psychiatry 13:317–332, 1950

Sullivan HS: Interpersonal Theory of Psychiatry. New York, Norton and Company, 1953

Sullivan HS: Psychiatric Interview. New York, Norton, 1954

Swanson DW, Bohnert PJ, Smith JA: The Paranoid. Boston, Little, Brown, and Company, 1970

Synder S: The interaction of psychopharmacology and psychoanalysis in the borderline patient. Psychiatr Q 52:240–250, 1984

Tan E, Marks I, Marset P: Bimedial leucotomy in obsessive compulsive neurosis: a controlled serial enquiry. Am J Psychiatry 118:156–164, 1971

Thoren P, Asberg M, Cronholm B, et al: Clomipramine treatment of obsessive-compulsive disorder. Arch Gen Psychiatry 37:1281–1285, 1980

Torgersen S: Personality and experience in an encounter-group. Scand J Psychol 21:139–141, 1980

Tourkow P: A discussion of "The family group as a single psychic entity" by Zinner and Shapiro. Int Rev Psychoanal 2:247–249, 1975

Tucker GJ: Therapeutic communities, in Principles and Practice of Milieu Therapy. Edited by Gunderson JG, Will OA, Mosher LR. New York, Jason Aronson, 1983

Tupin JP: Treatment of impulsive aggression, in The Treatment of Antisocial Syndromes. Edited by Reid WH. New York, Van Nostrand Reinhold, 1981

Tupin JP, Smith DB, Clanon TL, et al: The long-term use of lithium in aggressive prisoners. Compr Psychiatry 14:311–317, 1973

Turkat ID, Carlson CR: Data-based versus symptomatic formulation of treatment: the case of a dependent personality. J Behav Ther Exp Psychiatry 15:153–160, 1984

Turnquist K, Frances R, Rosenfeld W, et al: Pemoline in attention deficit disorder and alcoholism: a case study. Am J Psychiatry 140:622–624, 1983

Tyce FA, Olson RO, Amdahl R: PORT of Olmsted County, Minnesota, in Current Psychiatric Therapies. Edited by Masserman J. New York, Grune & Stratton, 1980

Tyrer P, Alexander J: Classification of personality disorder. Br J Psychiatry 135:163–167, 1979

US War Department: Nomenclature and Method of Recording Diagnoses, War Department Technical Bulletin: Med 203, October 1945

Vaillant GE: Sociopathy as a human process: a viewpoint. Arch Gen Psychiatry 32:178–183, 1975

Vaillant GE: Adaptation to Life. Boston, Little, Brown, and Company, 1977

Vaillant GE, Perry JC: Personality disorders, in Comprehensive Textbook of Psychiatry/III, 3rd ed, vol 2. Edited by Kaplan HI, Freedman AM, Sadock BJ. Baltimore, Williams and Wilkins, 1980

Vaillant GE, Perry JC: Personality disorders, in Comprehensive Textbook of Psychiatry, 4th ed. Edited by Kaplan HI, Sadock BJ. Baltimore, Williams and Wilkins, 1985

van den Berg PJ, Helstone FS: Oral, obsessive, and hysterical personality patterns: a Dutch replication. J Psychiatr Res 12:319–327, 1975

Vanggaard T: Borderlands of Sanity. Copenhagen, Munksgaard, 1979

Voth HM, Orth MH: Psychotherapy and the Role of the Environment. New York, Behavioral Publications, 1973.

Wachtel P: Psychoanalysis and Behavior Therapy: Toward an Integration. New York, Basic Books, 1977

Wachtel P (ed): Resistance: Psychodynamic and Behavioral Approaches. New York, Plenum Press, 1982

Waelder R: The principle of multiple function: observations on overdetermination. Psychoanal Q 5:45–62, 1936

Waldinger R: Intensive psychodynamic psychotherapy with borderline patients: an overview. Am J Psychiatry, 144:267–274, 1986

Waldinger R, Gunderson J: Effective Psychotherapy with Borderline Patients. New York, MacMillan Publishing, 1987

Wallerstein R: Forty-Two Lives in Treatment: A Study of Psychoanalysis and Psychotherapy. New York, Guilford Press, 1986

Walsh BT, Stewart JW, Wright L, et al: Treatment of bulimia with monoamine oxidase inhibitors. Am J Psychiatry 139:1629–1630, 1982

Walton D: The relevance of learning theory to the treatment of an obsessive-compulsive state, in Behavior Therapy and the Neuroses. Edited by Eysenck HJ. Oxford, Pergamon Press, 1960

Weeks G, L'Abate L: Paradoxical Psychotherapy: Theory and Practice with Individuals, Couples, and Families. New York, Brunner/Mazel, 1982

Wender PH, Reimherr FW, Wood DR: Attention deficit disorder ("minimal brain dysfunction") in adults. Arch Gen Psychiatry 38:449–456, 1981

Whitman R, Trosman H, Koenig R: Clinical assessment of passive-aggressive personality. Arch Neurol Psychiatry 72:540–549, 1954

Willi J: Couples in Collusion. New York, Jason Aronson, 1982

Wilson G: Introversion/extroversion, in Dimensions of Personality. Edited by London H, Exner J. New York, John Wiley and Sons, 1978

Wilson G: Adult disorders, in Contemporary Behavior Therapy. Edited by Wilson & Franks C. New York, Guilford Press, 1982

Winer JA, Jobe T, Ferrono C: Toward a psychoanalytic theory of the charismatic relationship. Annual of Psychoanalysis 12–13:155–175, 1984–1985

Winnicott DW: Transitional objects and transitional phenomena. Int J Psychoanal 34:89–97, 1953

Winnicott DW: The Maturational Processes and the Facilitating Environment. New York, International Universities Press, 1965

Wishnie HA: Inpatient therapy with borderline patients, in Borderline States in Psychiatry. Edited by Mack JE. New York, Grune & Stratton, 1975

Wolff HH, Solomon EB: Individual and group psychotherapy: complementary growth experiences. Int J Group Psychother 23:171–184, 1973

Wolpe J: Psychotherapy by Reciprocal Inhibition. Stanford, Calif, Stanford University Press, 1958

Wolpe J: Behavior therapy in complex neurotic states. Beh J Psychiatry 110:28–34, 1964

Wolpe J: The Practice of Behavior Therapy, 3rd ed. New York, Pergamon Press, 1979

Wong J: Combined group and individual treatment of borderline and narcissistic patients: heterogeneous versus homogeneous groups. Int J Group Psychotherapy 30:389–404, 1980

Wong N: Clinical considerations in group treatment of narcissistic disorders. Int J Group Psychother 29:325–345, 1979

Wong N: Combined group and individual treatment of the borderline and narcissistic patients, heterogeneous versus homogeneous groups. Int J Group Psychother 30:389–404, 1980

Wood DR, Reimherr FW, Wender PH, et al: Diagnosis and treatment of minimal brain dysfunction in adults: a preliminary report. Arch Gen Psychiatry 33:1453–1460, 1976

World Health Organization: Mental Disorders: Glossary and Guide to Their Classification in Accordance with the Ninth Revision of the International Classification of Diseases. Geneva, World Health Organization, 1978

Wynne LC: Some indications and contraindications for exploratory family therapy, in Intensive Family Therapy. Edited by Boszormenyi-Nagy I, Framo JC. New York, Hoeber, 1965

Wynne LC, Ryckoff IM, Day J, et al: Pseudomutuality in the family relations of schizophrenics. Psychiatry 21:205–220, 1958

Yalom ID: A study of group therapy dropouts. Arch Gen Psychiatry 14:393–414, 1966

Yalom ID: The Theory and Practice of Group Psychotherapy. New York, Basic Books, 1985

Yerevanian BI, Akiskal HS: "Neurotic," characterological, and dysthymic depressions. Psychiatr Clin North Am 2:595–617, 1979

Yochelson S, Samenow SE: The Criminal Personality, vol 1 and 2. New York, Jason Aronson, 1977

Young D, Beier E: Being asocial in social places: giving the client a new experience, in Handbook of Interpersonal Psychotherapy. Edited by Anchin J, Kiesler D. New York, Pergamon Press, 1982

Yudofsky S, William D, Gorman J: Propranolol in treatment of rage and violent behavior in patients with chronic brain syndrome. Am J Psychiatry 138:218–220, 1981

Zetzel ER: Current concepts of transference. Int J Psychoanal 37:369–376, 1956

Zetzel ER: The so-called good hysteric. Int J Psychoanal 49:256–260, 1968

Zinner J: The implications of projective identification for marital interaction, in Contemporary Marriage: Structure, Dynamics and Therapy. Edited by Grunebaum H, Christ J. Boston, Little, Brown and Company, 1976

Zinner J: Combined individual and family therapy of borderline adolescents: rationale and management of the early phase. Adolesc Psychiatry 6:420–427, 1978

Zinner J, Shapiro RL: Projective identification as a mode of perception and behavior in families of adolescents. Int J Psychoanal 53:523–530, 1972

Zinner J, Shapiro RL: The family as a single psychic entity: implications for acting out in adolescence. Int Rev Psychoanal 1:179–186, 1974

Zinner J, Shapiro ER: Splitting in families of borderline adolescents, in Borderline States in Psychiatry. Edited by Mack J. New York, Grune & Stratton, 1975

Zwerling I, Scheflen A, Jackson D, et al: Expanding Theory and Practice in Family Therapy. New York, Family Service Association, 1967